Biological Psychology

Biological Psychology

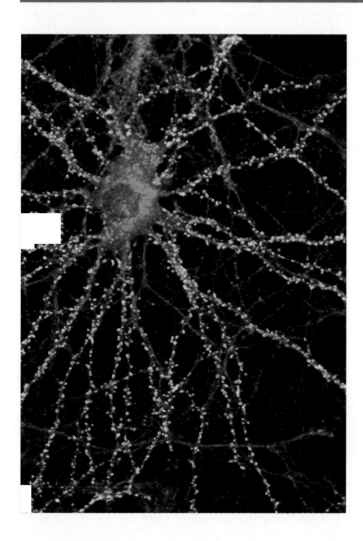

Mark R. Rosenzweig

Arnold L. Leiman

S. Marc Breedlove

University of California, Berkeley

Sinauer Associates, Inc. • Publishers • Sunderland, Massachusetts

About the cover

The image on the cover shows a hippocampal neuron in dissociated cell culture, with green staining for a postsynaptic density protein, PSD-95, and red staining for a presynaptic protein, synapsin 1. Yellow areas show overlapping staining for both proteins. The image was taken by Mary B. Kennedy and Leslie T. Schenker at the California Institute of Technology with a Zeiss laser-scanning confocal microscope.

Biological Psychology

 For information or to order, address: Sinauer Associates, Inc., P.O. Box 407, Sunderland, Massachusetts, 01375–0407 U.S.A. FAX: 413-549-1118. Internet: publish@sinauer.com

Library of Congress Cataloging-in-Publication Data

Rosenzweig, Mark R.
Biological psychology / Mark R. Rosenzweig, Arnold L. Leiman, S. Marc Breedlove.
p. cm.
Includes bibliographical references and index.
ISBN 0-87893-775-7
Psychobiology. I. Leiman, Arnold L. II. Breedlove, S. Marc.
QP360.R658 1996 95-26775
612.8–dc20 CIP

Manufactured in the United States of America

10 9 8 7 6 5 4 3 2 1

We dedicate this book affectionately to our wives, children, and grandchildren.
We appreciate their support and patience over the years of this project.

M.R.R.	A.L.L.	S.M.B.
Janine	*Lannon*	*Cindy*

M.R.R.

Janine

Anne *Suzanne* *Philip*
Jim *Kent* *Laura*

Lauren *Thomas*
David
Gregory
Elise

A.L.L.

Lannon

Jessica *Timothy*

S.M.B.

Cindy

Ben *Nick* *Tessa* *Kit*

Brief Contents

Contents

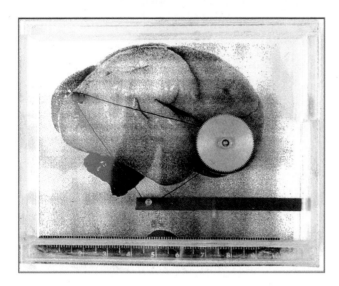

Part 1

Bodily Systems Basic to Behavior 31

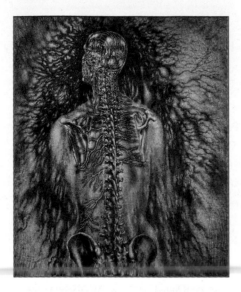

CHAPTER 2

Neuroanatomical Bases of Behavior 33

CHAPTER 3

Comparative and Evolutionary Perspectives on the Nervous System and Behavior 71

CHAPTER 4

Development of the Nervous System over the Life Span 99

Part 2

Communication and Information Processing in the Body 137

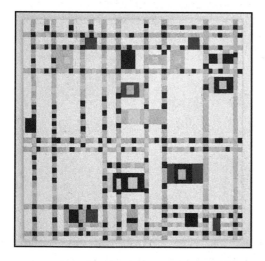

CHAPTER 5

Neural Conduction, Synaptic Transmission, and Neural Circuits 139

CHAPTER 6

Psychopharmacology   *175*

CHAPTER 7

Hormones: A Chemical System for Communication and Regulation 209

Part 3

Information Processing in Perceptual and Motor Systems   243

CHAPTER 8

Principles of Sensory Processing and Experience: Touch and Pain   245

Sensory Processing   246

- **An Overview of the Plan of Sensory Systems 246**

- **Optimal Sensory Systems Must Meet Five Criteria 246**

  A Sensory System Requires Different Receptors to Discriminate among Forms of Energy 246

  A Sensory System Should Discriminate among Different Intensities of Stimulation 247

  A Sensory System Should Respond Reliably 248

  A Sensory System Should Respond Rapidly 248

  A Sensory System Should Suppress Extraneous Information 248

- **Different Species Detect Different Aspects of the World 249**

  Sensory Systems of Particular Animals Have a Restricted Range of Responsiveness 249

  Receptor Cells Are Responsible for the Initial Stage of Sensory Processing 250

- **Change in Electrical Potential in Receptors Is the Initial Stage of Sensory Processing 250**

CHAPTER 9

Hearing, Vestibular Perception, Taste, and Smell 285

CHAPTER 10

Vision: From Retinal Processes to Perception 325

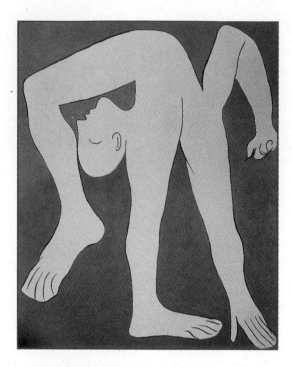

CHAPTER 11

Movements and Actions 369

Part 4:

Control of Behavioral States: Motivation   409

CHAPTER 12

Sex   411

CHAPTER 13

Regulation of Internal States   **449**

CHAPTER 14

Biological Rhythms and Sleep   487

Part 5

Emotions and Mental Disorders 527

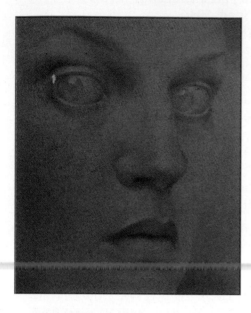

CHAPTER 15

Psychobiology of Emotions 529

CHAPTER 16

Psychobiology of Mental Disorders 565

Part 6

Learning, Memory, and Cognition 609

CHAPTER 17

Learning and Memory: Biological Perspectives 611

CHAPTER 18

Neural Mechanisms of Learning and Memory 645

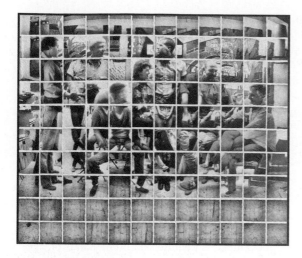

CHAPTER 19

Language and Cognition   691

CHAPTER 20

A Final Word   735

Preface

As we write, the day's newspaper announces the discovery of a gene that accounts for a significant fraction of the personality trait of novelty-seeking. The previous week's news magazine featured a story on a diet pill that may eliminate obesity. Other recent news articles have dealt with the following questions:

- Can experience increase the capacity of the brain?
- Is sexual orientation inherited?
- How much sleep do we really need?

These are important questions, but the basic problems and the research on them cannot be reduced to sound bites. A meaningful approach to each of these problems requires a background of knowledge about the behavioral and bodily systems involved. Our aim in this book is to provide the necessary background and to discuss these and other important problems in the proper context.

Biological Psychology explores the bodily bases of our experience and behavior—the ways in which bodily states and processes produce and control behavior and cognition, and the ways in which behavior and cognition influence bodily systems. Many scientific disciplines contribute to this theme, so we draw upon the research of psychologists, anatomists, biochemists, endocrinologists, engineers, geneticists, immunologists, neurologists, physiologists, and zoologists. In order to gain a panoramic view of the field, we try to rise above the limits of any single specialty.

We have tried to make this material accessible to students with a variety of interests and from a variety of backgrounds. Both the behavioral and biological foundations are provided for each main topic. Some students can skip or skim some of this, but those who need the background information should study it carefully before proceeding.

We realize that some instructors may prefer a different order of topics or may want to omit some areas of study, so we have written each chapter as a relatively self-contained unit. Recognizing that courses also vary in length from a single quarter or semester to two semesters, we should point out that most of this text can be covered in a single quarter; in that case the instructor may decide to omit a few chapters depending upon his or her emphasis. On the other hand, the text provides the basic material for a two-quarter or even a two-semester course. Among us, we have taught the course in each of these formats. For a two-semester course the instructor can assign some supplementary reading to fill out particular areas. Specific suggestions for courses with various orientations are made in the Instructor's Manual. Many features of the text are designed to enhance students' mastery of the material:

- Throughout, the text uses a five-fold approach to biological psychology—description; comparative and evolutionary aspects; developmental aspects; biological mechanisms; and applied or clinical issues.

- In considering neuroscience research, the book emphasizes the viewpoints of psychologists and others who are concerned with behavior. This approach highlights neural plasticity (the continual changes of the nervous system), and a final chapter drives home the major contribution this viewpoint offers.

- We have put together what we feel is the finest full-color illustration program in a biological psychology text available today. The hundreds of illustrations are carefully designed to clarify important concepts. Graphs and data from many sources have been reorganized and redrawn to ensure student comprehension.

- To further aid student understanding, each chapter (1) is preceded by an outline that provides an organizational framework for the chapter; (2) contains an "orientation" that lays the groundwork for the discussion; (3) concludes with summary points to highlight and review important concepts; and (4) lists recommended readings.

- Key terms are printed in clear boldface and defined at their first main use; they are also included in the glossary.

- Brief boxed articles feature contemporary applications and historical information, providing relevant examples from real life and a broad perspective on specific topics.

- Icons in the margins call attention to four main themes in the text: competing hypotheses, methods, animal models, and "unsolved mysteries" of neuroscience:

 Science advances by testing competing hypotheses to account for an observation. Sometimes further research indicates which of the hypotheses is correct; sometimes both are rejected for a new, more adequate hypothesis.

 Often the invention of new methods of research makes it possible to solve previously intractable problems. This icon highlights new or important research methods.

 Animal models often enable investigators to make progress on a question that is important for human behavior.

 There are still many gaps and mysteries in present knowledge of biological psychology. The unsolved mysteries icon points to some of these, which can also be thought of as opportunities for future investigators.

A study guide offers a complete chapter outline, a review of general concepts, a list of study objectives, illustrations from the text with study questions, chapter tests, self-evaluation exercises, concept application questions, and answers to questions and exercises.

Some of the most satisfying experiences in writing this book have been the lively and creative discussions among the three authors. Each of us has a different area of research and each of us covers certain fields more fully than the others. Pooling our information and discussing the relevance of findings in one area to other aspects of biological psychology has been an enriching experience, and we believe that this integration of knowledge from different fields enriches the book.

Despite all our efforts, we know that no book is perfect, so we welcome comments and suggestions from students, instructors, and colleagues. You may send e-mail to us at biopsych@violet.berkeley.edu or write a letter to us care of the Department of Psychology, 3210 Tolman Hall, University of California, Berkeley, CA 94720-1650.

Acknowledgments

In preparing this book, we benefitted from the help of many people. These include foremost members of the staff of Sinauer Associates: our conscientious and tireless editor Peter Farley, our ever-patient and cheerful project editors Kathaleen Emerson and Kerry Falvey, and production manager Christopher Small. The J/B Woolsey Studio artistically and skillfully transformed our rough sketches into the handsome and dynamic art program of this text. Molly Lojo word processed and organized our disparate materials with skill and humor. We also want to thank our past undergraduate and graduate students ranging back to the 1950s for their helpful responses to our instruction. Many of our fellow researchers and scientists generously provided their photos for our use; they are acknowledged in the figure legends or in the Illustration Credits. We are grateful to many colleagues who provided information and critical comments about our manuscript, including Brian Derrick, Karen De Valois, Russell De Valois, Jack Gallant, Ervin Hafter, Richard Ivry, Lucia Jacobs, Raymond E. Kesner, Joe L. Martinez, Jr., James L. McGaugh, Frederick Seil, Arthur P. Shimamura, and Irving Zucker.

The following reviewers provided insightful suggestions for refining the manuscript, and we are thankful for their assistance:

Duane Albrecht *University of Texas, Austin*
Catherine P. Cramer *Dartmouth College*
Loretta M. Flanagan-Cato *University of Pennsylvania*
James Gross *Stanford University*
Wendy Heller *University of Illinois*
Janice Juraska *University of Illinois*
Joseph E. LeDoux *New York University*
Michael A. Leon *University of California, Irvine*
Randy J. Nelson *Johns Hopkins University*
James Pfaus *Concordia University*
Jeffrey D. Schall *Vanderbilt University*
Dale Sengelaub *Indiana University*
Matthew Shapiro *McGill University*
Cheryl L. Sisk *Michigan State University*
Franco J. Vaccarino *University of Toronto*
Cyma Van Petten *University of Arizona*
Charles J. Vierck *University of Florida*
Walter Wilczynski *University of Texas, Austin*

Finally, we would like to thank all our colleagues who contribute research in biological psychology and related fields.

Mark R. Rosenzweig
Arnold L. Leiman
S. Marc Breedlove

DON JUAN: . . . Will you not agree with me
. . . that it is inconceivable that Life,
having once produced [birds],
should, if love and beauty were her
object, start off on another line
and labor at the clumsy elephant
and hideous ape, whose grandchildren
we are?

THE DEVIL: You conclude then, that Life
was driving at clumsiness and
ugliness?

DON JUAN: No, perverse devil that you
are, a thousand times no. Life was
driving at brains—at its darling
object: an organ by which it can
attain not only self-consciousness
but self-understanding.

George Bernard Shaw
Man and Superman, Act III

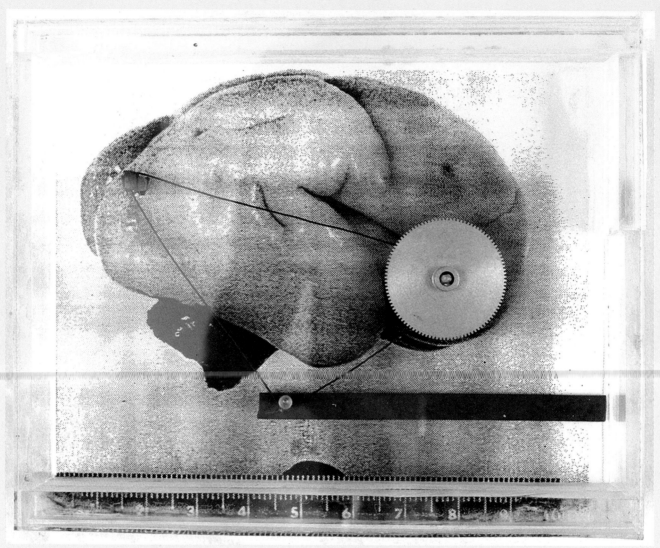

Nadia Coen, *Brain and Cogwheel*, 1989

CHAPTER Biological Psychology

1

Orientation

A legend from India (retold by Thomas Mann in *The Transposed Heads*) provides a colorful introduction to the main theme of this book. In this story the beautiful Sita marries a slender, intellectual merchant, but she is also attracted to his best friend, a spirited, strong, brawny blacksmith. One day each young man beheads himself in a temple of the goddess Kali. Sita enters the temple, looking for them, and finds them lying in pools of blood in front of the statue of Kali. Horrified, Sita prays to Kali, begging the goddess to restore the men to life. Kali grants the wish and instructs Sita to place the heads carefully on the bodies. Sita undertakes the task with feverish energy and soon sees the men come back to life. Only then does she realize that she has placed each head on the wrong body! Now the three young people are faced with a baffling problem: Which young man is Sita's spouse? The one with the intellectual's head and the muscular body? Or the blacksmith's head on the intellectual's body? While the legend explores the complexities of this puzzle, it also considers how each head affects the body that it now controls and how each body influences the head.

This old Hindu legend emphasizes that individual identity, personality, and talents are mainly functions of the brain. Who we are—our thoughts, dreams, memories, beliefs, desires, fears—are all the workings of the brain. In this book we explore the many ways in which the structure and actions of the brain produce mind and behavior. But that is only half our task. Like the author of the legend of Sita, we are also interested in the ways that behavior in turn modifies the structures and actions of the brain. One of the most important lessons we hope to convey is that interactions between brain and behavior are reciprocal.

1.1 Biological Psychology in the News
Many newspaper and magazine articles feature topics in biological psychology.

What Is Biological Psychology?

The themes of this book have great scope and breadth. The neuroscience revolution of the past twenty-five years spans many scientific disciplines. Psychologists, anatomists, chemists, endocrinologists, engineers, geneticists, neurologists, physiologists, and zoologists have all contributed to solving the mysteries of the brain. Our aim in this book is to weave a story through the many achievements of the rapidly developing field of biological psychology that rises above the limits of any single view or academic specialty. Our range will extend from the scrutiny of the fine details of brain organization and function to the broader scopes of evolution and behavior. The frequent coverage in the press of topics in biological psy-

chology reflects popular interest in this field. Articles illustrate the rapid pace of research and indicate the relevance of brain research to pressing human problems. Newspapers and magazines herald new findings that improve our understanding of why we do what we do, and why we are what we are. Figure 1.1 shows some recent newspaper articles and magazine covers on topics in biological psychology.

Biological Psychology Has Many Names and Uses

Over the years the field that relates behavior to bodily processes has acquired a variety of names and an increasing number of applications.

What's in a Name?

We had some difficulty deciding on the title of this book. We chose the title *Biological Psychology*, because the term "biology" is the broadest category of the life sciences, encompassing physiology, anatomy, endocrinology, and many other realms of interest to us in understanding behavior. But we considered many alternatives to this title. Some instructors use terms like "physiology of behavior" or "behavioral neuroscience" to describe their courses. Other names emphasize relations of biological psychology to clinical neurology; such terms include "neuropsychology" and "behavioral neurology." This text could be used in courses that go by each of these names, as well as others. If the scope of the field is made clear, the exact title is not important. A map of the relations of biological psychology to other disciplines is shown in Figure 1.2.

Applications of Biological Psychology

The United States Congress has declared the 1990s to be the "Decade of the Brain," and there are many different participants in this story, for the umbrella of neuroscience is very wide. The main goal of biological psychologists is to understand behavior and experience in terms of their biological mechanisms. The main subject fields that draw upon biological psychology are general psychology, behavioral sciences, neuroscience, and health sciences. Almost every textbook in introductory psychology has a section devoted to biological psychology, and fuller knowledge of biological psychology is important for deeper understanding of psychology in general.

Workers in the health sciences increasingly recognize the reciprocal interactions between behavior and bodily structure and function. For example, one new area is psychoneuroimmunology, which includes studies of connections between illness, the immune system, the brain, and psychological factors (Ader and Cohen, 1993). The American Psychological Association, in evaluating graduate programs in professional psychology (including clinical, guidance, and school psychology), requires that each student demonstrate competence in four substantive areas. The first area listed is "biological bases of behavior (e.g., biological psychology, comparative psychology, neuropsychology, sensation, psychopharmacology)" (American Psychological Association, 1980). Neuropsychology, a professional specialty that focuses on impairments related to brain dysfunction, draws largely upon biological psychology (Kolb and Whishaw, 1990).

Investigators who conduct research and who teach neuroscience find a home in many departments and disciplines. Some are in psychology departments, and many others in departments such as physiology, neuroscience, and pharmacology. There is clearly a need for people trained in both behavioral and biological sciences. Furthermore, biological psychology, like other sciences, is dedicated to improving the human condition. As Einstein once said in an address to students, concern for humanity and its fate must always form the chief interest of all scientific endeavor ". . . in order that the creations of our minds shall be a blessing and not a curse."

Many readers of this book will take only a single course in biological psychology; others will go on to careers in this or related fields. Whatever your own case, this book is meant to help you gain a fuller understanding of behavior and its biological bases. Our goal is to provide an interesting and coherent account of the main ideas and research in biological psychology. Because there are so many pieces to tie together, we try to introduce a given piece of information when it makes a difference to the understanding of a subject rather than withholding it until we arrive at the precise pigeonhole in which it belongs. Most important, we seek to communicate our own interest and excitement about the mysteries of mind and body.

Some Examples of Current Research

The accelerated pace of advances in biological psychology, neuroscience, and related fields has provided answers to some fundamental questions and offers prospects of new productive approaches (for example, *Scientific American,* 1992; Gerstein et al., 1988). Here are some examples of current research that will be considered in this book.

> **Problem:** *How does the brain grow, maintain, and repair itself over the life span, and how are these capacities related to the growth and development of the mind and behavior from the womb to the tomb?*
>
> By six months after conception, the developing human is equipped with a brain that contains billions of nerve cells organized in precise arrays with specific interconnections. The plan for development of the human brain resembles in many ways those of other mammals, and even those of all other vertebrates, but with important species-specific features. Each species has to be prepared to carry out many behaviors at birth and to acquire others soon after birth. The

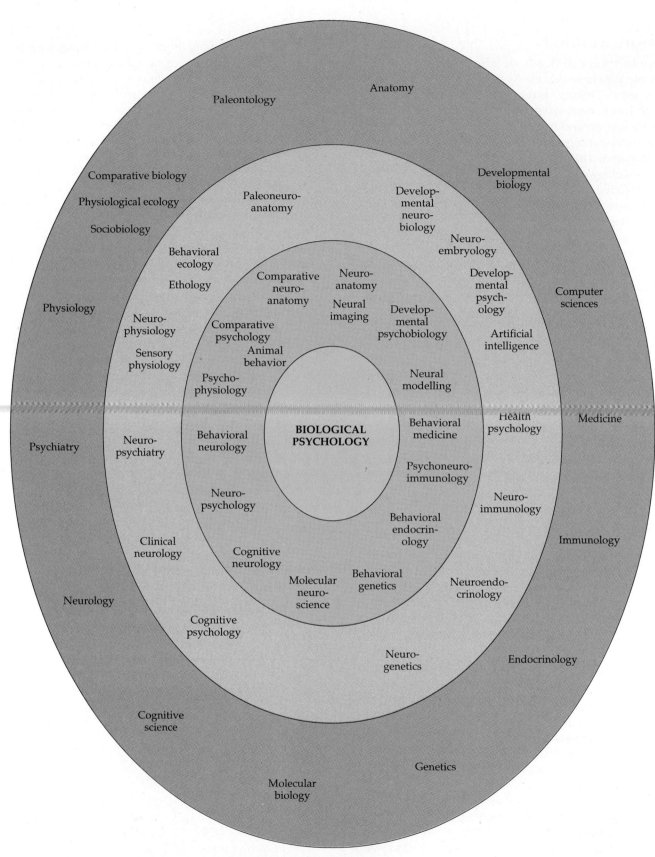

1.2   The Relations of Biological Psychology to Other Fields of Study
In this graphical representation of the relationships among biological psychology and other scientific disciplines, fields toward the center of the map are
closest to biological psychology in their history, outlook, aims, or methods.

developmental blueprint not only specifies the arrangement of most nerve cells long before birth, but it also provides for and depends upon environmental influences to help shape neural development after birth.

Current Research: *Brain transplants can repair damaged brains.*

A short while ago brain transplants were unreal, the stuff of science fiction. Can a piece of the brain be replaced by cells derived from other animals? Can the transplanted cells be incorporated into neural circuits much as one might replace transistors in your radio? The prospect for this kind of intervention is especially important for many human neurological disorders characterized by nerve cell degeneration produced by disease or **stroke**. (Strokes are disorders of blood vessels—either a block or a rupture of a vessel—that destroy or cripple particular brain regions, disabling many elderly people.) During the 1980s, basic research showed the feasibility of brain transplants in experimental animals (Figure 1.3). A crucial finding from these studies was that cells from *fetal* animals are far more likely to provide successful transplants than are cells from adults. Donor tissue derived from an embryonic or fetal animal is placed on the surface of a damaged region or broken up into cells and injected into the brain. Brain-damaged animals can show functional recovery after such injections of brain transplants (Ralph and Lehman, 1991; Ridley and Baker, 1991). The success of these demonstrations led to efforts to use transplants to remedy Parkinson's disease in afflicted humans. Parkinson's disease is characterized by many changes in movements, including tremors and slowness of actions (see Chapter 11). Injections of fetal cells or other donor tissue into some brain regions has alleviated the symptoms of Parkinson's disease in some humans (Madrazo et al., 1990).

Problem: *How does the nervous system capture, process, and represent information about the environment?*

The world around is abuzz with many energies packaged in varied ways. Only some of these become sights, sounds, touches, and smells that

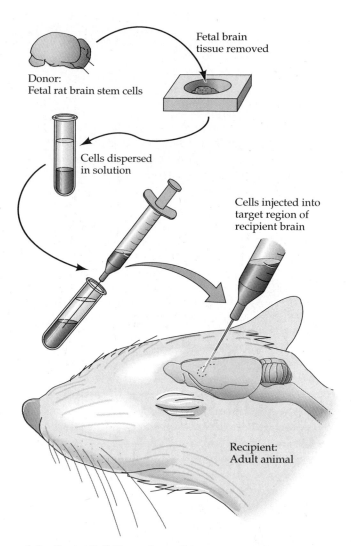

1.3 Brain-Cell Transplantation
A brain-cell transplantation procedure that has been employed in both humans with brain diseases and in research studies with animals.

we can recognize and respond to. What are the computational activities of the brain that underlie our sensory abilities? Investigators have learned much about how our world is represented in circuits and activities of the brain. Sensory stimuli—from simple touches to complex sounds and elaborate displays of color and form—are processed by many specialized brain regions. The brain's information about our world is often modified by processes such as attention. A matter of considerable interest to researchers is understanding how complex perceptual categories such as distinctive visual patterns or the sounds of language are organized in the brain.

Current Research: *Some nerve cells prefer faces.*

Recognition of faces is very important to the social life of primates, including humans. For example, facial expression is important for the communication of emotions (see Chapter 15). Individual identity is intimately tied to distinctive facial features. Neurologists studying the effects of brain changes from stroke have described an intriguing syndrome that suggests that the brain's visual system has distinct sets of nerve cells involved with particular perceptual categories. Some patients lose the ability to recognize human faces after strokes that involve specific regions of cerebral cortex. A striking finding is the observation that some nerve cells are particularly excited by faces as opposed to other stimuli that might involve the same amount of light and visual complexity. One such finding from research by Robert Desimone (1990) is shown in Figure 1.4, which shows that some cells in monkeys' brains are especially excited by frontal views of the monkey face, whereas others are maximally excited by lateral views of a face. The face as a perceptual category seems organized in a distinctive way; we will discuss more about this aspect of visual information processing in Chapter 10.

are activated or inhibited by chemical messages. For example, investigators are now studying both similarities in and differences between the sexes in details of brain structure and chemistry as clues to understanding commonalities and differences in behavior.

Current Research: *Depression can be seen in the brain.*

All of us from time to time feel a little low and listless, but for millions of people across the world depression is a major psychiatric disorder that is life-threatening. The lethality of depression is increasingly prominent in younger patients—in the form of suicide (see Chapter 16). Many different causes of depression have been suggested, including psychosocial factors, stress, and brain states. The advent of new ways of looking at the living brain has given us novel insights into the biology of this disorder. Brain scans derived from comparing normal subjects and depressed patients show striking increases in the activity of frontal cortex and a decrease in blood flow in a deeper portion of the patients' brains.

Problem: *What are the brain sites and activities that underlie feelings and emotional expression?*

The organization of many regions of the nervous system is influenced by neurochemicals, including hormones, and many neural circuits

Problem: *How does the brain store information?*

The ability to recollect and use the past is critical for the survival of any animal, from the most simple to the most complex. Learning and memory are among the most extraordinary abilities of human beings. Breakthrough re-

1.4   A Preference for Profiles

Responses of a single monkey brain cell to different pictures of monkey heads. This nerve cell fired vigorously when the monkey was shown a lateral view of a monkey head (80° and 100°), but weakly when a frontal (0°) or near-frontal (30°) view was presented. Other cells in monkey brains respond best to full-face views. The responses outside the periods of stimulation (shown as black bars) are due to ongoing neural activity. After Desimone et al., 1984.

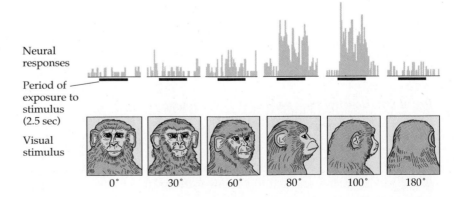

Neural responses

Period of exposure to stimulus (2.5 sec)

Visual stimulus

0°   30°   60°   80°   100°   180°

search in this area is exploring how the brain accomplishes these feats (see Chapter 18).

Current Research: *Memory can be established in a dish.*

Is memory a property of the whole brain or are there different kinds of memory devices in many different parts of the brain? One approach to this issue involves an unusual phenomenon, discovered more than twenty years ago, that still fascinates researchers. This phenomenon has a fancy name—long-term potentiation—and was initially detected in a brain region involved in learning and memory, the hippocampus. Researchers showed that a brief period of electrical stimulation of this area could enhance nerve cell electrical activity for minutes or hours—a kind of memory device since the cells seemed to "remember" that they had been stimulated. Figure 1.5 shows a more dramatic example. A small piece of tissue from this region can remain alive when bathed with nutrients in a small dish. Such a tissue slice will also show long-term potentiation when it is electrically stimulated. Thus, a simple neural memory device can be studied in a dish.

Problem: *What are the neurobiological bases of language in humans?*

Of all our attributes, none is more distinctively human than speech and language. Within the past ten years considerable new information has been obtained about structures in the brain essential for language and the activities of the brain during language tasks.

Current Research: *Language lights up the brain.*

For years, the complexity of language and the limited tools for exploring brain activity in humans prevented detailed studies of brain activities during language performance. Biological study of language was largely restricted to examining impairments following brain injury and disease. Brain scans provide a more dynamic portrait of cortical organization and functioning during language tasks in normal subjects. Figure 1.6 shows an example of scans during different types of language performance, such as listening to, seeing, and speaking words.

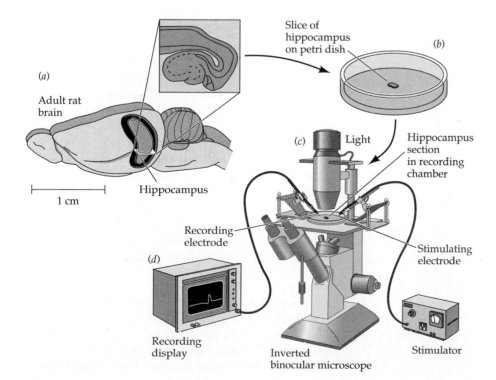

(a) Adult rat brain

1 cm

Hippocampus

Slice of hippocampus on petri dish

(b)

(c) Light

Hippocampus section in recording chamber

Recording electrode

(d)

Stimulating electrode

Recording display

Inverted binocular microscope

Stimulator

1.5   Memory in a Dish
In a research preparation that has become important in the study of the neural bases of memory, a small slice of tissue from an area of the brain called the hippocampus, which is believed to be important for memory, is removed from the brain (*a*) and placed in a dish (*b*). (*c*) A brief, intense train of stimulation is applied to the tissue with an electrode. Electrical recordings from the slice (*d*) show that the amount of electrical activity produced by subsequent stimuli is changed for a period of hours as a result of the brief train of intense stimulation. That the cells in the slice "remember" the initial stimulation in this way has led researchers to use this preparation as a model of memory formation and storage.

1.6 The Brain Activated by Language

These images show which brain regions were most active when subjects performed four tasks involving language. The techniques used to generate such images are described in Chapter 2. Courtesy of Marcus Raichle.

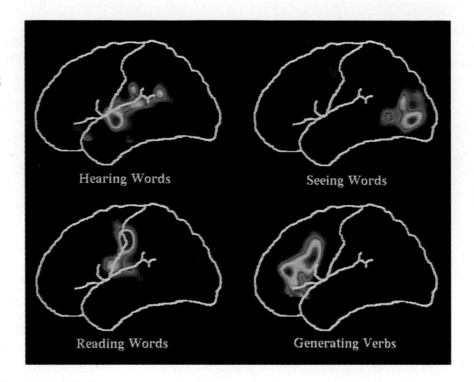

Hearing Words

Seeing Words

Reading Words

Generating Verbs

Problem: *How does sexual orientation develop?*

For the vast majority of us, a point comes in our lives, usually during adolescence, when we begin forming romantic attachments to and consider having sexual relations with certain types of people. For most of us, that "type" is someone of the opposite sex, but some of us are attracted to people of the same sex. Whether homosexual or heterosexual, this orientation, once formed, is rather stable, especially for males. How does this orientation come about, and what factors affect which orientation we develop?

Current Research: *There are brain correlates of sexual orientation.*

In every human culture, some individuals display a homosexual orientation. Cultures differ widely in their reaction to and treatment of homosexuals and have various traditional theories about why some people develop this sexual orientation. Modern research also wrestles with this problem.

The report by LeVay (1991) that the brains of heterosexual and homosexual men are slightly different in the region known as the hypothala-mus has fueled the debate about whether some people are "born gay." Several other brain regions were subsequently reported to be different in gay and straight men, but despite the almost universal reaction to these studies in the media, these findings tell us nothing about whether child-rearing practices, genes, or a combination of the two are responsible for these structural and behavioral differences. These reports are part of a long-standing series of studies investigating how the brains of male and female animals (including humans) come to be different, a process in which hormones play a crucial role. In Chapter 12 we'll use those studies to help us understand the limits and opportunities for studying biological correlates of sexual orientation in humans.

Each of the foregoing questions will be taken up in later chapters. Some of the examples we will consider may seem almost as fantastic as the legend of the transposed heads but these findings have led to cures for psychoses, the relief of pain, the restoration of partial sight to some blind people, and stimulation of the growth of the brain, which thereby improves the capacity to learn. These and other achievements that are now becoming familiar to us would have seemed unbelievable a few decades ago. As science fiction writer Arthur C. Clarke stated, "The science of one generation was the magic of the preceding one."

The Human Brain Can Break Down

Like any complex mechanism, the brain is subject to a variety of malfunctions and breakdowns. People afflicted by disorders of the brain are not an exotic few. At least one person in five around the world cur-

rently suffers from neurological and/or psychiatric disorders that vary in severity from complete disability and incapacity to significant changes in quality of life. Figure 1.7*a* shows the estimated numbers of U.S. residents afflicted by some of the main neurological disorders. Figure 1.7*b* gives estimates of the numbers of U.S. adults who suffer from certain major psychiatric disorders in a six-month period. The division of disorders between Figure 1.7*a* and *b* reflects the traditional distinctions between neurology and psychiatry, but much of psychiatry is becoming oriented more toward neuroscience.

The toll of these disorders is enormous, both in terms of individual suffering and in social costs. A recent presentation of the National Foundation for Brain Research estimated that direct and indirect costs of behavioral and brain disorders amount to $400 billion a year in the United States. For example, $160 billion a year is spent for treating alcohol and substance abuse, and the cost for treatment of dementia exceeds those for cancer and heart disease (*Science*, 1992). This high cost has impelled researchers to try to understand the mechanisms involved in these disorders and in some cases to alleviate or even to prevent them. Here are some examples of research that is providing relief from some of these grave disorders—examples that will be discussed in later chapters:

1. The introduction of antipsychotic and anti-anxiety drugs in the 1950s has enabled many patients to lead fuller lives less haunted by the crippling con-

(*a*) Prevalence of psychiatric disorders

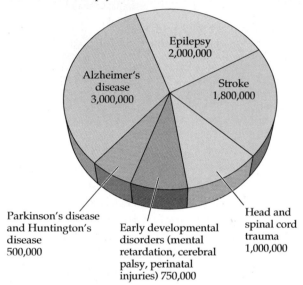

(*b*) Incidence of neurological disorders

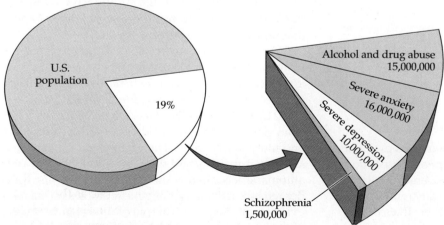

1.7 The Toll of Brain Disorders
The prevalence of psychiatric disorders (*a*) and the incidence of neurological disorders (*b*) in the United States. As brain research progresses, many disorders previously characterized as psychiatric are thought of as neurological in origin.

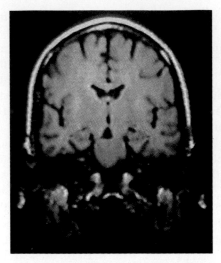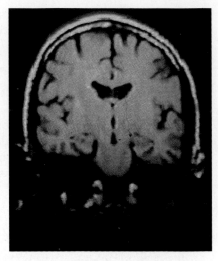

1.8   Identical Twins but Nonidentical Brains and Behavior
In these images of the brains of identical twins, the fluid-filled cerebral ventricles are prominent as dark "butterfly" shapes. The twin whose brain is seen on the right is schizophrenic, and has the enlarged cerebral ventricles that some researchers believe are characteristic of this disorder. His twin is not schizophrenic, and his brain clearly has smaller ventricles (left). From Weinberger et al., 1991. Courtesy of Daniel Weinberger.

sequences of intense symptoms. Studies of the effects of these drugs have also produced profound insights into the nature of some psychiatric disorders.

2. Discoveries that reveal the modes of action of habit-forming drugs and their effects on the nervous system give hope of effective cures for people addicted to drugs and of preventing lasting damage to infants born to mothers who take drugs.

3. The fastest growing affliction in industrialized societies is Alzheimer's disease, a profound loss of cognitive abilities that especially strikes people over 65. Current research is exploring some of the causes and brain mechanisms of this devastating condition.

Visualization of Psychiatric Disorders

Some humans spend the bulk of their lives plagued by hallucinations, unwarranted fears of persecution and other delusions, and blunted emotional responses. They frequently appear socially withdrawn, and many such individuals spend their lives on the margins of society. Many of these people seem unresponsive to all forms of intervention including modern drug treatments. The term **schizophrenia** is the diagnostic category for this disorder, which investigators have long sought to understand as some kind

of brain disease. Contemporary brain imaging techniques have revealed some structural abnormalities in the brain that characterize this disorder from its earliest stages, commonly during late adolescence. Figure 1.8 shows changes deep within the brains of these patients that can be visualized using imaging techniques such as computerized tomography (CT) scans and magnetic resonance imaging (MRI) scans of living patients. Both techniques produce cross-sectional pictures of the living brain (see Chapter 2). These data may help to pinpoint circuitry changes that underlie this disorder.

The ability to visualize brain structures in living patients has also offered insights into an odd and tragic disorder that appears early in life—infantile autism. Unlike the usual cuddly infants, autistic children avoid eye contact with parents when held, push away from close contact, and, as they get older, seem more and more inaccessible. Their language acquisition is severely impaired, and they begin to exhibit strange automatic acts, such as incessant rocking. This disorder remains a mystery, but genetic studies reveal clear evidence of the powerful role of inheritance. Images of the brains of some of these patients reveal a reduction in the size of the corpus callosum (Figure 1.9), and of regions within the cerebellum, a large structure in the brain associated with motor control mechanisms and with some kinds of learning.

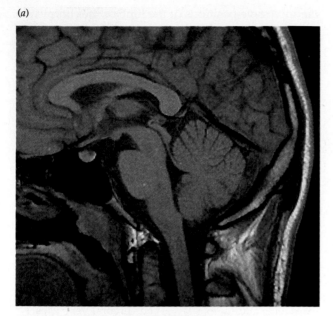

(a)

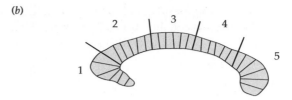

(b)

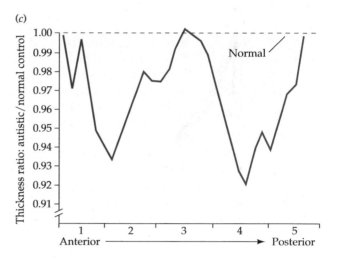

(c)

1.9 Brain Differences in Autism
A difference in the size of some brain structures in autistic patients and normal control subjects has been found using magnetic resonance imaging. (*a*) In this image, a structure known as the corpus callosum is clearly seen as a large white region. A recent study showed that when the thickness of this structure was measured at many positions (*b*), autistic patients showed significant thinning, especially in the posterior regions (*c*). After Egaas, Courchesne, and Saitoh 1995; *a* courtesy of Eric Courchesne.

Laboratory and Clinical Approaches Complement One Another

Basic research and clinical practice influence each other. Basic research provides concepts and techniques that clinicians use to understand and help people with malfunctioning brains. At the same time, clinical observation of these patients provides data and stimulates the development of theories about brain mechanisms. This exchange is mutually beneficial, and the boundaries between the laboratory and clinic are disappearing. Research on the functions of the two cerebral hemispheres, discussed in the next section, illustrates the productive interplay between laboratory and clinic.

Two Brains in One Head

Suppose that each time a right-handed person buttoned a shirt, the person's left hand sought to unbutton it! Two separate controllers would seem to be involved, but is this possible? Most of us are saved from such frustration because information from the right and left sides of the body is integrated by pathways that connect the two sides of the brain. But what happens when these connections are severed? Can we then observe two different types of consciousness? Although the *structures* of the left and right sides of the brain seem very much alike, *functional* differences between the cerebral hemispheres of human brains become evident after brain damage such as that resulting from a stroke. For instance, injury to certain parts of the left cerebral hemisphere can produce striking changes in speech and language, whereas injury to the right hemisphere rarely affects speech. This situation used to be described as "cerebral dominance," implying that a talkative left cerebral hemisphere dominated a mute right hemisphere.

New information about hemispheric specialization of function has come from studies of patients in whom the connections between the right and left cerebral hemispheres have been cut, who are referred to as **split-brain individuals**. Early work with such patients in the 1930s did not reveal clear differences between the functions of the two hemispheres, because of a lack of appropriate methods of behavioral assessment.

Coming from a background of animal research, Roger Sperry (1974) and his collaborators (Gazzaniga, 1992)

Roger Sperry (1913–1995)

understood how to test separately the functioning of the two hemispheres, and they found remarkable differences. These results prompted Sperry to speak of separate forms of consciousness in the two hemispheres of the brain. The patients seemed literally to be of two minds. Indeed, one of Sperry's patients was seen to button a shirt with one hand and try to unbutton it with the other. For his research with split-brain subjects and other contributions, Sperry was awarded the Nobel Prize in 1981.

Tests have indicated similar but much more subtle differences in cognitive style of the two hemispheres even in normal humans. The left is said to be analytic and verbal, whereas the right has been characterized as spatial and holistic. The differences in the ways the cerebral hemispheres process information have prompted some researchers to suggest that the educational needs and capabilities of the cerebral hemispheres differ. However, most researchers emphasize the integrative functioning of the hemispheres in human cognitive activities.

We Will Use Five Viewpoints to Examine the Biology of Behavior

Our aim is to understand the biological bases of behavior, and in this pursuit we use several different perspectives. Since each one yields different information, the combination of perspectives is especially powerful. The five major perspectives are: (1) *describing* the behavior, (2) studying the *evolution* of the behavior, (3) observing the *development* of behavior and its biological characteristics over the life span, (4) studying the biological *mechanisms* of behavior, and (5) studying *applications* of biological psychology—for example, to dysfunctions of human behavior.

First, Behavior Must Be Described Adequately

Until we describe what we want to study, we cannot get far. Depending on the goals of our investigation, we may describe behavior in terms of detailed acts or processes or in terms of results or functions. An analytic description of arm movements might record the successive positions of the limb or the contraction of different muscles. A functional behavioral description, on the other hand, would state whether the limb was being used in walking, running, hopping, swimming, or shooting dice. To be useful for scientific study, a description must be precise and reveal the essential features of the behavior, using accurately defined terms and units.

By Comparing Species We Can Study the Evolution of Brain and Behavior

Darwin's theory of evolution through natural selection, as updated and elaborated by ongoing research, is central to all modern biology and psychology. Because this perspective provides rich insights into many kinds of behavior and behavioral mechanisms, we will use it in most of the chapters to come. From this perspective emerge two rather different emphases: (1) the *continuity* of behavior and biological processes among species and (2) the *species-specific* behaviors and biology that have evolved in adaption to different environments. Our evolution has resulted many features that are common to all animals, but each species has features that are unique, too. At some points in this book we will concentrate on continuity—that is, features of behavior and its biological mechanisms that are common to many species. At other points, we will look at species-specific behaviors.

Continuity of behaviors and mechanisms. Nature is conservative. Bodily or behavioral inventions, once evolved, may be maintained for millions of years and may be seen in animals that otherwise appear to be very different. For example, the nerve impulse (see Chapter 5) is essentially the same in a jellyfish, a cockroach, and a human being. Some of the chemical compounds that transmit messages through the bloodstream (hormones) are also the same in diverse animals (although the same hormone may do different things in different species). Some of the sex hormones occur in all mammalian species.

But similarity of a feature between species does not guarantee that it came from a common ancestor. Similar solutions to a problem may have evolved independently in different classes of animals. For example, color vision has emerged independently in insects, fish, reptiles, birds, and mammals, and each group hit upon a slightly different way of distinguishing colors. Much current research on neural mechanisms of learning and memory is being done with relatively simple invertebrates. The assumption is that there is an evolutionary continuity of mechanisms among a very wide range of species. Some findings suggest, however, that more complex invertebrate and vertebrate animals may have evolved additional mechanisms of learning beyond those that they share with simpler organisms.

Species-specific behaviors. Different species have evolved some specific ways of dealing with their environments. An earthworm's sensory endowments, for example, are quite different from those of a robin. Certain species of bat rely almost exclusively on hearing to navigate and find their prey; vision in these species has degenerated until it has become almost unusable. Other species of bat, however, are visually oriented, depending on their eyes to find their way around and to secure their food. Human beings use both vision and audition (hearing). However, we ignore electrical fields in the environment, whereas certain kinds of fish are highly sensitive to them. These fish emit electrical pulses and use the resulting electrical fields to guide their locomotion.

Communicative behavior also differs greatly among species. Some species rely chiefly on visual signals, some on auditory signals, and some on olfactory (smell) signals. In many species the production of signals does not require learning but simply follows an inherited species-specific pattern. In other species, the young must learn behavior from adults. For example, some songbirds must learn their song from their parents, and even though there are many varieties of bird song, each individual's song conforms fairly closely to the pattern of its species.

Human beings can produce a wide variety of vocal sounds, but any single language uses only a fraction of them. Moreover, the functional significance of sounds is rather arbitrary in human languages; the same sequence of sounds may have different meanings in different languages.

The Body and Behavior Develop over the Life-Span

Ontogeny is the process by which an individual changes in the course of its lifetime—grows up and grows old. Observing the way a particular behavior changes during ontogeny may give us clues to its functions and mechanisms. For example, we know from observation that learning ability in monkeys increases over several years of development. Therefore we can speculate that prolonged maturation of neural circuits is required for complex learning tasks. In rodents the ability to form long-term memories lags somewhat behind the maturation of learning ability. Young rodents learn well but forget more quickly than older ones, suggesting that learning and memory in-

volve different neural processes. Studying the development of reproductive capacity and of differences in behavior between the sexes, along with changes in bodily structures and processes, enables us to throw light on bodily mechanisms of sex behaviors.

Biological Mechanisms Underlie All Behavior

The history of a species tells us the evolutionary determinants of its behavior, and the history of an individual tells us the developmental determinants. To learn about the *mechanisms* of an individual's behavior, we study his or her *present* bodily endowments and states. To understand the underlying "mechanisms" of behavior, we must regard the organism (with all due respect) as a "machine." We must ask, How is this thing constructed to be able to do that? Our major aim in biological psychology is to examine bodily mechanisms that make particular behaviors possible. For example, in the case of learning and memory, we would like to know the sequence of electrophysiological and biochemical processes that must occur between the initial capture of an item of information and its eventual retrieval from memory. We would also like to know what parts of the nervous system are particularly involved in learning and memory. In the case of reproductive behavior, we would like to know the developmental processes in the body that produce the capacity for sexual behavior. We also want to understand the neuronal and hormonal processes that underlie reproductive behavior.

Research Can Be Applied to Human Problems

A major goal of biological psychology is to use research findings to improve the health and well-being of humans and other animals. Earlier we noted the large number of human diseases that involve malfunctioning of the brain. Many of these are already being alleviated as the result of research in the neurosciences and the prospects for continuing advances in this area are good. Attempts to apply knowledge also feed back to benefit basic research. For example, the study of memory disorders in humans has pushed investigators to extend knowledge of the brain regions involved in different kinds of memory (see Chapter 17).

We have defined five ways of looking at behavior, and Table 1.1 shows how each of them can be applied to three kinds of behavior. We will take up each of the entries in the table in later chapters. In fact, we will use these five perspectives to examine all the categories of behavior that we consider in the later parts of this book: sensation, perception, and motor coordination (Part Three); motivation (Part

Four); emotion (Part Five); and cognition: learning, memory, and language (Part Six).

Biological Psychologists Use Several Levels of Analysis

Finding explanations for behavior often involves dealing with several levels of biological analysis. The units of each level of analysis are simpler in structure and organization than those of the level above. Figure 1.10 shows how we can analyze the brain into successively less complex units until we get down to single nerve cells and their even simpler, molecular constituents.

Scientific explanations usually involve analyzing something on a simpler or more basic level of organization than that of the structure or function to be explained. This approach is known as **reductionism.**

1.10 Levels of Analysis in Biological Psychology ▶
The scope of biological psychology ranges from the individual behaving organism to the molecular level. Depending on the question at hand, investigators use different techniques to focus on these many levels, but always with an eye toward how their findings apply to behavior.

In principle it is possible to reduce each explanatory series down to the molecular or atomic level, though for practical reasons this is rarely done. For example, the organic chemist and the neurochemist usually deal with large complex molecules and the laws that govern them; seldom do they seek explanations in terms of atoms.

Naturally, in all fields different problems are carried to different levels of analysis, and fruitful work

Table 1.1

Five Research Perspectives Applied to Three Kinds of Behavior

	KINDS OF BEHAVIOR		
RESEARCH PERSPECTIVES	**SEXUAL BEHAVIOR**	**LEARNING AND MEMORY**	**LANGUAGE AND COMMUNICATION**
1. Description			
Structural description	What are the main patterns of reproductive behavior and sex differences in behavior?	In what main ways does behavior change as a consequence of experience, for example, conditioning?	How are the sounds of speech patterned?
Functional description	How do specialized patterns of behavior contribute to mating and to care of young?	How do certain behaviors lead to rewards or avoidance of punishment?	What behavior is involved in making statements or asking questions?
2. Comparative/ Evolutionary	How does mating depend on hormones in different species?	How do different species compare in kinds and speed of learning?	How did the human speech apparatus evolve?
3. Development	How do reproductive and secondary sex characteristics develop over the life span?	How do learning and memory change over the life span?	How do language and communication develop over the life span?
4. Mechanisms	What neural circuits and what hormones are involved in reproductive behavior?	What anatomical and chemical changes in the brain hold memories?	What brain regions are particularly involved in language?
5. Applications	What kind of hormonal treatments can treat sexual inadequacy?	What are the prospects for a "smart pill," one that will improve abilities to learn and remember?	What kinds of treatments can aid recovery of language following stroke?

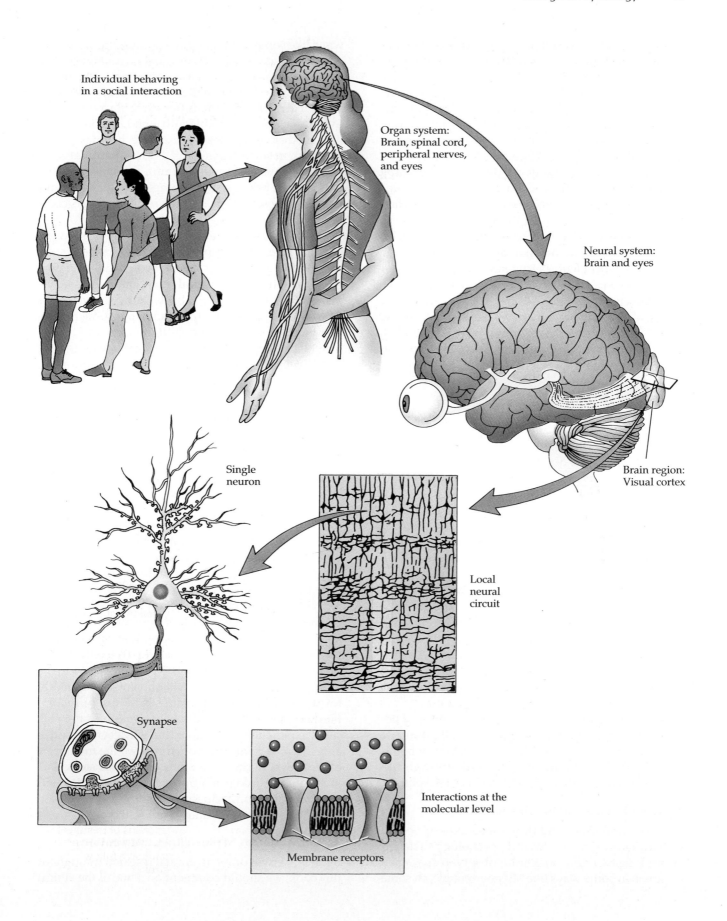

Individual behaving in a social interaction

Organ system: Brain, spinal cord, peripheral nerves, and eyes

Neural system: Brain and eyes

Brain region: Visual cortex

Single neuron

Local neural circuit

Synapse

Interactions at the molecular level

Membrane receptors

is often being done simultaneously by different workers at several levels. Thus, in their research on visual perception, behavioral psychologists advance analytical descriptions of behavior. They try to determine how the eyes move while looking at a visual pattern, or how the contrast among parts of the pattern determines its visibility. Meanwhile, other psychologists and biologists study the differences in visual endowments among species and try to determine the adaptive significance of these differences. For example, how is the presence (or absence) of color vision related to the life of a species? At the same time, other investigators trace out brain structures and networks involved in different kinds of visual discrimination. Still other neuroscientists try to ascertain the electrical and chemical events that occur at synapses in the brain during vision.

Useful applications can be found at many levels of analysis of a system. For a given problem, one level of analysis is often more appropriate than another. For example, common problems of visual acuity are caused by variations in the shape of the eyeball. These problems can be solved by prescribing corrective lenses without having to analyze the brain processes involved in pattern vision. On the other hand, a partial loss of sight in certain parts of the visual field suggests pressure on the two optic nerves where they run together. This symptom may be an early sign of a tumor whose removal restores full vision.

Other restrictions of the visual field are caused by localized damage to the visual area of the cerebral cortex. Recent research shows that training can help recover some vision in some of these cases. If a person's epileptic attacks are regularly preceded by a peculiar visual image, that person may have a scar or an injury to the visual cortex. Understanding how color vision works has been advanced by studying how information from different kinds of retinal cells converges on nerve cells and how the nerve cells process this information. Investigators are also studying the way visual patterns are analyzed by the brain at the level of nerve cells and their connections.

As we consider explanations of many kinds of behavior in terms of bodily events, we will point out the main levels of analysis that are currently being used to study each problem. We will also indicate some of the applications of each level of research.

We Are All Alike and We Are All Different

How do similarities and differences among people and animals fit into biological psychology? The anthropologist Clyde Kluckhohn observed that each person is in some ways like all other people, in some

ways like some other people, and in some ways like no other person (Kluckhohn, 1949). As Figure 1.11 shows, we can extend this observation to the much broader range of animal life. In some ways each person is like all other animals (for example, we all need to ingest complex organic nutrients), in some ways like all other vertebrates (for example, having a spinal column), in some ways like all other mammals (for example, having a spinal column), and in some ways like all other primates (for example, in having a hand with an opposable thumb and a relatively large, complex brain).

Whether knowledge gained about a process in another species will apply to humans depends on whether we are like that species in regard to that process. Thus, the fundamental research on the mechanisms of inheritance in the bacterium *Escherichia coli* proved to be so widely applicable that some molecular biologists proclaimed, "What is true of *E. coli* is true of the elephant." To a remarkable extent, that statement is true, but there are also some important differences in the genetic mechanisms of *E. coli* and mammals. With respect to each biological property, researchers must determine where animals are identical and where differences arise. When we seek model animal systems with which to study human behavior or biological processes, we must ask, Does the proposed model really share the same sphere of identity with human beings with respect to what is being studied? We will see many cases in which it does.

Even within the same species, however, individuals differ from one another: cat from cat, blue jay from blue jay, and person from person (see Figure 1.11). Biological psychology seeks to understand individual differences as well as similarities. This interest in the individual is one of the most important differences between psychology and other approaches to behavior. The lottery of heredity ensures that each individual draws a unique genetic makeup (the only exception being identical twins). The way the individual's unique genetic composition is translated into bodily form and behavioral capacities is part of our story. Furthermore, each individual has a unique set of personal experiences. Therefore, the way each person is able to process information and store the memories of these experiences is another part of our story. Our focus on physiological approaches to behavior will not ignore the individuality of people but will help show how this individuality comes about.

Animal Research Makes Vital Contributions

Because we will draw on animal research throughout this book, we should comment on some of the ethical

Each person has some characteristics shared by . . .

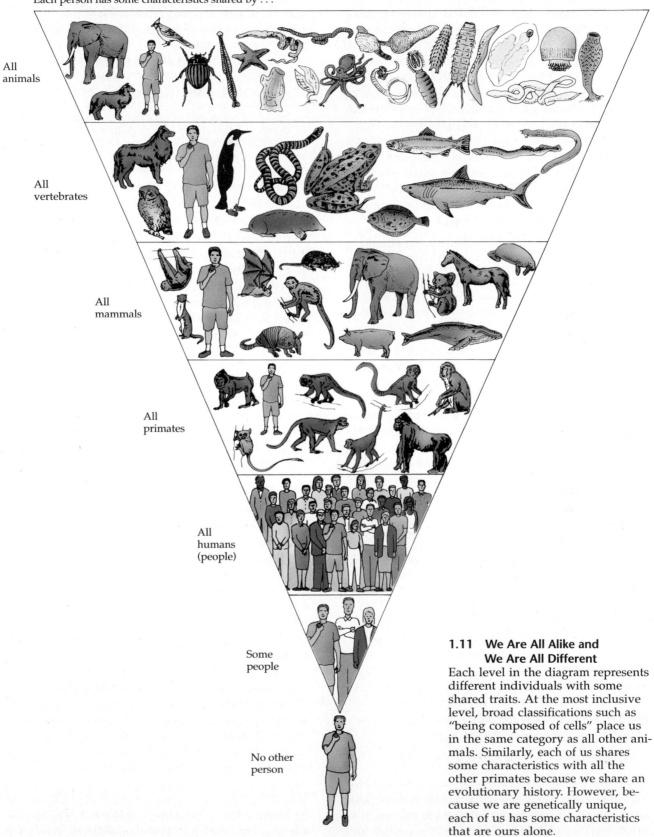

All animals

All vertebrates

All mammals

All primates

All humans (people)

Some people

No other person

1.11 We Are All Alike and We Are All Different

Each level in the diagram represents different individuals with some shared traits. At the most inclusive level, broad classifications such as "being composed of cells" place us in the same category as all other animals. Similarly, each of us shares some characteristics with all the other primates because we share an evolutionary history. However, because we are genetically unique, each of us has some characteristics that are ours alone.

issues of experimentation on animals. Human beings' involvement and concern with other species predates recorded history. Early humans had to study animal behavior and physiology in order to escape some species and hunt others. To study biological bases of behavior inevitably requires research on animals of other species as well as on human beings. Because of the importance of animal research for both human and animal health and well-being, the National Academy of Sciences (1988, 1991) undertook a study on the many uses of animals in research. The study notes that 93% of the mammals used in research are laboratory-reared rodents. It also reports that most Americans agree that animal research should continue and that this conclusion is well-founded:

> It makes no sense to sacrifice future human health and well-being by not using animals in research today. We owe our good health to past investigators and the animals they studied. As we decide on the future of animal research we should keep in mind the generations who will look back at us and ask if we acted wisely.

Further improvements in human health and well-being and reduction of the disorders listed in Figure 1.7 depend upon ongoing research, much of which requires animal subjects.

Students of psychology usually underestimate the contributions of animal research to all the main fields of psychology because, as a recent study found (Domjan and Purdy, 1995:501), the most widely used introductory textbooks obscure the contributions of animal research:

> In a study of eight leading introductory psychology textbooks, we found that with the exception of chapters on conditioning and learning, the contributions of animal research often were not acknowledged explicitly. In addition, major findings from animal research were presented as if they had been obtained with human participants. These errors of omission and commission obscure the role of animal research in psychology and promote the misimpression that major advances in knowledge concerning the biological bases of behavior can be obtained without animal experimentation.

Biological Psychologists Use Many Different Methods But Share Certain Basic Principles

Biological psychology is one of many areas in biological science. There are some issues that it shares with any scientific pursuit and others that are distinctive to its approaches. Our initial aim in this section is to present some comments that relate to the general scientific perspective; we will then focus directly on scientific approaches distinctive to research in biological psychology.

An appropriate benediction to this section is provided by the biologist Peter Medawar in his book, *The Art of the Soluble* (1967:132):

> Scientists are people of very dissimilar temperaments doing different things in very different ways. Among scientists are collectors, classifiers and compulsive tidiers-up; many are detectives by temperament and many are explorers; some are artists and others artisans. There are poet-scientists and philosopher-scientists and even a few mystics.

Despite the cookbook claims of some textbooks, these varied scientists do not follow a single scientific method but rather use a body of methods particular to their work. Some of these methods are shared by the entire scientific community; others evolve over time and vary from one scientific discipline to another. Scientific methods include not only making observations, whether experimental or normative, but also making inferences. The inferences are then tested by making further observations to test whether they are supported or not. Scientists try to set up tests that are as rigorous as possible to see whether they can disprove a hypothesis. The more tests a hypothesis can withstand, the more widely it becomes accepted. Like any human activity, this process is not error-free.

Scientific Research Involves Recognizing and Correcting Errors

Scientists work very hard to be accurate when they make observations and draw inferences, but they are not immune to error. Fortunately science has built-in provisions for correcting errors that may occur. One such provision is that no finding or hypothesis is considered part of a science until it is published and open to the scrutiny of other scientists. Another is that all fields of science have many scientists working independently in different institutions and in different countries. Therefore, once a finding or hypothesis is published, other scientists examine it carefully. If the finding or hypothesis appears to be interesting and/or important, they often try to repeat the same procedures to see if they can replicate the finding, or they devise new tests of the hypothesis. Thus, any scientist who publishes findings knows that his or her work will be scrutinized carefully, which is certainly a strong incentive to put forth only accurate data and carefully reasoned conclusions. Occasionally a scientist has manipulated or even fabricated data in order to win some temporary advantage of fame, advancement, or monetary gain. But such ill-considered activities are usually uncovered quickly in the scrutiny and open debate that characterize science.

In some cases governments have tried to control the free give-and-take of science to promote the views of an official scientist or a national "school" of scientific thinking. Examples are the Nazis' attacks on Einstein's theory of relativity and Stalin's backing for the incorrect theory of the Soviet geneticist Lysenko. But such governmental interference with science backfires because it inhibits growth and advance of science within that country and causes it to fall behind other countries that allow science to progress freely.

Occasionally a loss of objectivity by investigators—with no component of fraud—has led to errors that have been called "pathological science." A recent article (Rousseau, 1992) examined three pathological examples coming from natural sciences:

1. *Polywater.* Polywater, an alleged polymerized form of water, attracted much attention in the 1960s and 1970s. It was probably the basis for Kurt Vonnegut's novel *Cat's Cradle* (1969) in which all the water in the world eventually changes into a viscous material. But the "discoverers" of polywater could produce it only in very small amounts, and its unusual properties were finally shown to be caused by contamination by perspiration.

2. *Infinite dilution.* It was reported in 1988 that biological effects of substances persisted even after so many dilutions had been performed that not even a single molecule of the substance could be detected in most samples; this was proposed as a basis for the old school of medicine called homeopathy that is still popular in many countries. The results did not hold up in replication experiments with proper controls.

3. *Cold fusion.* In 1988 it was reported that "cold fusion" had been accomplished by two experimental groups. Fusion of nuclei of two elements with release of energy had been thought to be possible only at extremely high temperatures, but the two groups reported fusion in a simple apparatus at room temperature. These results attracted wide coverage in the press because they promised inexhaustible and inexpensive production of energy, but other laboratories were unable to repeat the observations and other scientists pointed to errors in the observations and reasoning.

In analyzing these cases of pathological science, Rousseau (1992) points out three main sources of error: (1) The result is not very clear, that is, the effect being studied is at the limits of objective measurement and the results are of low statistical significance. (2) The investigators are quite willing to disregard prevailing ideas and theories. Of course, existing ideas have to change when new data compel it, but scientists should take special care to test very carefully results or hypotheses that fly in the face of existing knowledge. (3) The investigators who announce the novel findings avoid conducting critical experiments that could bring down their whole house of cards.

Biological psychology and related fields have not been immune to occasional cases of pathological science. A revealing example is the alleged transfer of memory from one animal to another by extracts of neural tissue. That is, when animals received extracts prepared from tissue of animals that had been trained, the recipients were reported to show evidence of the training given to the donors; this was in comparison to control animals that received injections prepared from non-trained donors. Reports of such results appeared from the 1950s into the 1970s but then trailed off. The early research on this topic used as subjects the flatworm *Planaria*, and then some investigators claimed to find similar effects in laboratory rats. It was suggested that this research could provide a use for the brains of retired professors (although from the authors' points of view, this is hardly funny).

In accordance with Rousseau's analysis above, three main kinds of difficulties appeared in the initial positive reports of memory transfer: (1) Although measures of learning and memory can be obtained in objective ways, some of the investigators used subjective indices of memory, and the results were often rather weak. (2) The proponents ignored the widely accepted concepts that memory storage involves changes in the synaptic connections between neurons; instead they proposed that memory is encoded chemically. (3) A number of experimenters concentrated on a peptide that had been isolated from animals trained to avoid the dark side of an apparatus, but they did not undertake experiments to find what effects this compound might have in other apparatuses or situations. Thus, no clearly convincing decisive results were obtained, and the work gradually faded out.

We will try in this book to give mainly results and hypotheses that have been tested critically and that appear to have withstood careful scrutiny and decisive tests. Occasionally we will present some challenging new research that has not yet been thoroughly tested but that is stimulating to consider; we will label such examples carefully so that you will realize that they should be considered with special caution. As you read accounts of research in other sources, ask yourself whether the findings and conclusions have passed the strict tests that allow you to place your trust in them, even provisionally.

Three Approaches Are Used to Relate Brain and Behavior

Biological psychologists use three approaches to relate brain and behavior. Experiments and theories in many disciplines have contributed to our understanding of the working of the body in relation to behavior. Since the different disciplines vary in focus, they provide insights that complement each other. The anatomist portrays the structure of nervous systems, the components and pathways of the brain. The physiologist examines how these components work, often studying the electrical signals of the nervous system. The chemist identifies the chemicals found in the brain and charts the metabolic pathways that generate different substances. The engineer seeks to determine whether quantitative concepts derived from inanimate systems can be applied to brain functions. Biological psychologists are a bit more eclectic, but generally start with an interest in the mechanisms of behavior. Their investigations include observing and measuring (1) behavior and (2) bodily structures and processes.

Biological psychologists use three approaches to relate brain and behavior: somatic intervention, behavioral intervention, and correlation. In the most commonly employed approach, **somatic intervention** (Figure 1.12*a*), the investigator alters a structure or function of the brain or body to see how this change alters behavior. In this approach, somatic intervention is the independent variable, and the behavioral effect is the dependent variable. That is, the resulting behavior presumably *depends on* how the brain has been altered. In later chapters we will describe many kinds of somatic intervention with both humans and other animals, such as:

1. A hormone is administered to some animals but not to others. Various behaviors of the two groups are later compared.

2. A part of the brain is stimulated electrically, and behavioral effects are observed.

3. A connection between two parts of the nervous system is cut, and changes in behavior are measured.

The opposite approach is **behavioral intervention**

(Figure 1.12*b*). In this approach, the scientist intervenes in the behavior of an organism and looks for resultant changes in bodily structure or function. Here behavior is the independent variable, and change in the body is the dependent variable. Among the examples that we will consider in later chapters are the following:

1. Putting two adults of opposite sex together may lead to increased secretion of certain hormones.

2. Exposing a person or animal to a visual stimulus provokes changes in electrical activity and blood flow in parts of the brain.

3. Training animals in a maze is accompanied by electrophysiological, biochemical, and anatomical changes in parts of their brains.

The third approach to brain–behavior relations, **correlation** (Figure 1.12*c*), consists of finding the extent to which a given bodily measure *varies with* a given behavioral measure. Some questions we will examine later are:

1. Is there a significant correlation between brain size and intelligence? (Box 1.1.)

2. Are individual differences in sexual behavior correlated with levels of certain hormones in the individuals?

3. Is the severity of schizophrenia correlated with the magnitude of changes in brain structure?

Such correlations should not be taken as proof of causal relationship. For one thing, even if a causal relation exists, the correlation does not reveal its direction—that is, which variable is independent and which is dependent. For another, two terms might be correlated only because a third factor determines the values of the two factors measured. What the existence of a correlation does indicate is that there is some link—direct or indirect—between the two variables. Such a correlation often stimulates investigators to formulate hypotheses and to test them by somatic or behavioral intervention.

Combining these three approaches yields the circle diagram of Figure 1.12*d*. This diagram incorporates the basic approaches to studying relationships between bodily processes and behavior. It also emphasizes the theme (brought out in the myth of the transposed heads) that the relations between brain and body are reciprocal; each affects the other in an ongoing cycle of bodily and behavioral interactions. We will see examples of this reciprocal relationship throughout the book.

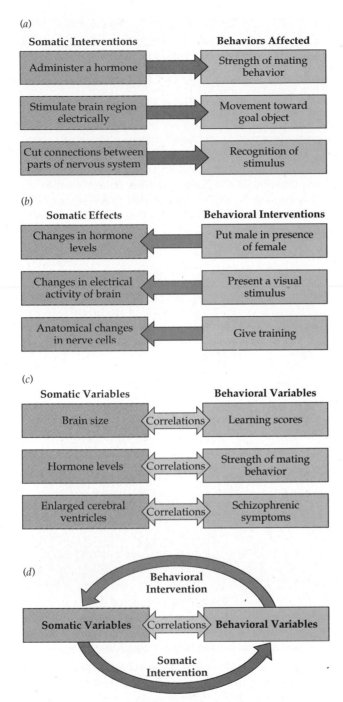

1.12   Three Main Approaches to Studying the Physiology of Behavior

(*a*) In a somatic intervention, investigators make some change in an animal's body structure or chemistry and observe and measure any resulting behavioral effects. (*b*) Conversely, researchers may change an animal's behavior or its environment and try to ascertain whether the change results in physiological or anatomical changes. (*c*) Measurements of both kinds of variables allow researchers to arrive at correlations between somatic changes and behavioral changes; (*d*) each approach enriches and informs the others.

The History of Research on Brain and Behavior

Although the brain has long been studied, only recently have scientists recognized the central role of the brain in controlling behavior. In this section we will note some of the ways in which the brain has been viewed throughout history.

The knowledge that the brain mediates and controls behavior emerged rather recently in human history. When Tutankhamen was mummified (around 3300 years ago), four important organs were preserved in alabaster jars in his tomb: liver, lungs, stomach, and intestines. The heart was preserved in its place within the body. All these organs were considered necessary to ensure the pharaoh's continued existence in the afterlife. The brain, however, was removed from the skull and discarded. Although the Egyptian version of the afterlife entailed considerable struggle, the brain was not considered an asset.

Neither the Old Testament (written from the twelfth to the second century B.C.) nor the New Testament mentions the brain. However, the Old Testament mentions the heart hundreds of times and makes several references each to the liver, the stomach, and the bowels as the seats of passion, courage, and pity. "Get thee a heart of wisdom," said the prophet.

The heart is where Aristotle (around 350 B.C.), the most prominent scientist of ancient Greece, located mental capacities. He considered the brain to be only a cooling unit to lower the temperature of the hot blood from the heart. Other Greek thinkers, however, did consider the brain to be the seat of intellect and the organ that controls behavior. Thus around 400 B.C., Hippocrates, the great physician of Greek antiquity, wrote:

> Not only our pleasure, our joy and our laughter but also our sorrow, pain, grief, and tears rise from the brain, and the brain alone. With it we think and understand, see and hear, and we discriminate between the ugly and the beautiful, between what is pleasant and what is unpleasant and between good and evil.

The dispute between those who located intellect in the heart and those who located it in the brain still raged 2000 years later, in Shakespeare's time: "Tell me, where is fancy bred, / Or in the heart or in the head?" (Merchant of Venice, Act III, Scene 2). We still reflect this ancient notion when we call people kind-hearted, open-hearted, hard-hearted, faint-hearted, or heartless, and when we speak of learning "by heart."

Around 350 B.C. the Greek physician Herophilus (called the Father of Anatomy) advanced the knowledge of the nervous system by dissecting bodies of

Box 1.1

Is Bigger Better? The Case of the Brain and Intelligence

Does a bigger brain indicate greater intelligence? This question has been the subject of lively controversy for at least two centuries. Sir Francis Galton (1822–1911), the scientist who invented the correlation coefficient, stated that the greatest disappointment in his life was his failure to find a significant relationship between head size and intelligence. But Galton didn't have the proper tools to conduct this investigation. He had to use head size when he really wanted to measure brain size (Figure A). Also, at the time he undertook this study, there were no good measures of intelligence. Galton had to rely on teachers' estimates of their students' intelligence, and every student knows that teachers can be quite wrong. Other investigators in the nineteenth century measured the volumes of skulls of various groups and made estimates of intelligence based on occupations or other doubtful criteria.

The development and standardization of intelligence tests in the twentieth century provided invaluable help for one side of the question, but until recently measures of head size still had to be used to estimate brain size for any sample of living subjects. Such studies usually showed positive but small correlations between brain size and intelligence. In one review of several such studies, the correlations ranged from +0.08 to +0.22 (Van Valen, 1974). The reviewer estimated that, allowing for errors in estimation of brain size and in measurement of intelligence, the true correlation between brain size and intelligence might be as high as +0.30.

The invention of noninvasive techniques to visualize and measure the brains of living subjects has made possible a direct approach to the question of relations between brain size and intelligence. Recently a team of psychologists and other neuroscientists (Willerman et al., 1991) undertook a direct study in which they selected college students with no history of neurological problems and whose intelligence test scores were either high (IQ >130) or average (IQ <103). By excluding students

(A) *A nineteenth-century apparatus for head measurement*

both people and animals. Among other investigations he traced spinal nerves from muscles and skin into the spinal cord. He also noted that each region of the body was connected to separate nerves. A second-century Greco-Roman physician, Galen (frequently described as the Father of Medicine), treated the injuries of gladiators and dissected some animals. He advanced the idea that animal spirits—a mysterious fluid—passed along nerves to all regions of the body. Although this concept did not advance the understanding of the nervous system, Galen provided interesting drawings of the organization of the brain. His assessment of the behavioral changes produced by injuries to the heads of gladiators also drew attention to the nervous system as the controller of behavior.

Renaissance Scientists Began to Understand Brain Anatomy and Physiology

The eminent Renaissance painter and scientist Leonardo da Vinci studied the workings of the hu-

(B) *Images from a modern brain-measurement study*

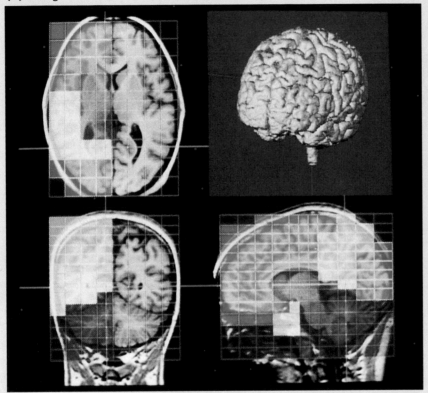

study, 67 normal adult subjects were recruited through newspaper advertising and screened for neurological or psychiatric disorders, then given IQ tests. MRI scans such as those shown in Figure B were used for accurate measurement of the size of different brain regions. After correction for body size, the correlation between brain size and IQ scores was 0.38. Thus, on the basis of modern techniques, it appears that the long-standing controversy has been settled in favor of a significant correlation between brain size and intelligence. Note, however, that the modest size of the correlation, while highly significant, still allows for many additional important factors as determinants of intelligence. We should also mention that historically scientists have often misused information about brain size in racially or ethnically prejudicial ways (Gould, 1981). In fact, all racial groups show overlapping and widely varying brain size.

In later chapters we will refer to other aspects of the study of Andreasen et al. (1993), because these investigators measured not only total brain size but sizes of different regions and components of the brain. They found that some of these structures were clearly related to intelligence but others were not, as we will see. (Figure A from the Bettmann Archive; Figure B courtesy of Nancy Andreasen.)

with a middle range of IQ scores, the investigators wanted to increase the possibility of finding a relationship between IQ and brain size. Brain size was measured for each student from magnetic resonance imaging (MRI). Any influence of body size on brain size was removed statistically so it could not affect the final results. The overall result was a highly significant correlation coefficient, 0.51, with no significant difference between values for men and women. Since this correlation was probably increased by the selection for high or average IQ, the investigators applied a statistical correction and estimated that the correlation would be about 0.35 for a more representative sample. Another independent study with normal adult subjects has borne this conclusion out (Andreasen et al., 1993). In this second

man body and laid the foundations of anatomical drawing. He especially pioneered in providing views from different angles and cross-sectional representations. His artistic renditions of the body included portraits of the nerves in the arm and the ventricles of the brain (Figure 1.13). Descriptions of the brain by Renaissance anatomists emphasized the shape and appearance of the external surfaces of the brain, since these were the parts that were easiest to see when the skull was removed. It was immediately apparent to anyone who looked that the brain has an extraordinarily strange shape. The complexity of its visible form led to the use of an elaborate, precise vocabulary to label different regions.

In 1633 René Descartes (1596–1650) wrote an influential book, in which he tried to explain how the behavior of animals, and to some extent of humans, could be like the workings of a machine. Among other topics, Descartes proposed the concept of spinal reflexes and a neural pathway for them (Figure 1.14).

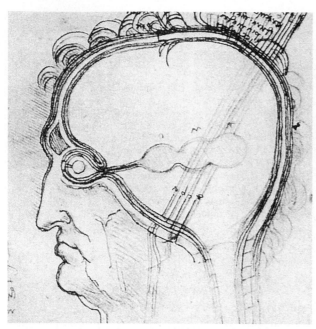

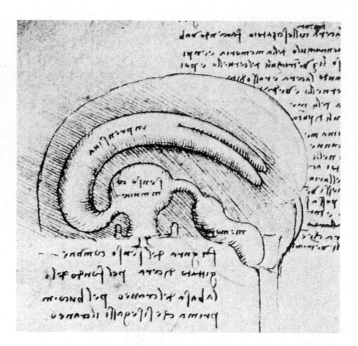

1.13 Leonardo da Vinci's Changing View of the Brain
In an early representation (left), da Vinci (1472–1519) simply copied old schematic drawings that represented the cerebral ventricles as a linear series of chambers. Later, he made a drawing based on direct observation (right); da Vinci made a cast of the ventricles of an ox brain by pouring melted wax into the brain, letting it set, and then cutting away the tissue to reveal the ventricles' true shape.

Attempting to relate the mind to the body, he suggested that the contact between the two takes place in the pineal gland, located within the brain. His reasons for suggesting the pineal gland were these: (1) Whereas most brain structures are double, located symmetrically in the two hemispheres, the pineal gland is single, like consciousness. (2) Descartes believed, erroneously, that the pineal gland exists only in humans and not in animals. Although this aspect of his reasoning did not hold up, Descartes did pose clearly problems of relations between mind and brain that later thinkers and investigators have continued to wrestle with. As Descartes was preparing to publish his book, he was informed by a friend that the Vatican had forced Galileo to renounce his teaching that Earth revolves around the sun, threatening to execute him if he did not recant. Fearful that his own speculations about mind and body could also incur the wrath of the church, Descartes withheld the book from publication, and it did not appear until 1662, after his death. Descartes believed that if people were nothing more than intricate machines, they could

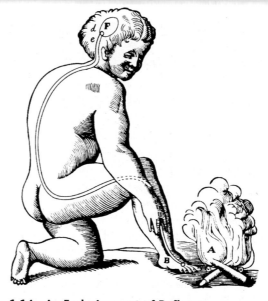

1.14 An Early Account of Reflexes
In this depiction of an explanation by René Descartes (1596–1650), when a person's toe touches fire, the heat causes nervous activity to flow up the nerve to the brain. There, the nervous activity is "reflected" back down to the leg muscles, which contract, pulling the foot away from the fire; the idea of activity being reflected back is what gave rise to the word "reflex." In Descartes's time, the difference between sensory and motor nerves had not yet been discovered, nor was it known that nerve fibers normally conduct in only one direction. Nevertheless, Descartes promoted thinking about bodily processes in scientific terms, and this focus led to steadily more accurate knowledge and concepts.

have about as much free will as a pocket watch and no opportunity to make the moral choices that were so important to the church. He asserted that humans, at least, had a nonmaterial soul as well as a material body. This notion of "dualism" spread widely and left other philosophers with the task of determining how a nonmaterial soul could exert influence over a material body and brain.

The Concept of Localization of Function Arose in the Nineteenth Century

Only in the nineteenth and twentieth centuries did educated people in the Western world finally accept the brain as the mechanism that coordinates and controls behavior. A popular notion of the nineteenth century, called **phrenology**, held that the cerebral cortex consisted of separate functional areas, or "organs," and that each organ was responsible for a behavioral faculty; faculties were qualities such as love of family, perception of color, or curiosity (Figure 1.15). The assignment of functions to brain regions was made by observing the behavior of individuals and noting, from the shape of the skull, which underlying regions of the brain were more or less developed. The assignment of faculties to regions of the brain was rather arbitrary, but most opponents of the idea rejected the entire concept of localization of brain function; they insisted that the brain, like the mind, functions as a whole. Thus, one camp proclaimed the localization of function, whereas the opposing camp supported the unity of brain function; neither side had very strong evidence in the first half of the nineteenth century. In fact, debates on this question continued into the twentieth century.*

In the 1860s the French surgeon Paul Broca engaged in heated discussions about the relation between language and the brain. He argued against formidable critics that language ability was not a property of the entire brain but rather was localized in a restricted brain region. The theme that psychological functions could be localized in specific brain regions was strongly advanced when Broca presented a postmortem analysis of a patient who had been unable to talk for many years. The findings of the autopsy of the brain conducted by Broca revealed destruction of a region within the frontal portions of the brain on the left side—a region now known as "Broca's area." The study of additional patients further convinced Broca that language expression was mediated by a specific brain region rather than being a reflection of the activities of the entire brain. These nine-

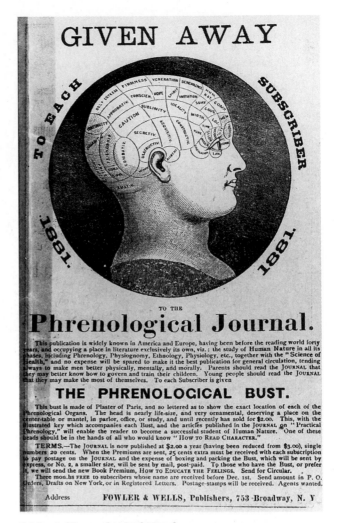

1.15 A Phrenological Head

In the early nineteenth century, it was believed that certain "faculties," such as skill at mathematics or a tendency toward aggression, could be directly associated with particular brain regions. Phrenologists used diagrams like this one to measure bumps on the skull, which they took as an indication of how fully developed each brain region was in an individual, and hence how fully that person should display particular qualities. Courtesy of the Bettmann Archive.

teenth-century observations form the background for a continuing theme of research in biological psychology, notably the search for distinguishing differences among brain regions based on their structural attributes and the effort to relate different features of behavior to different brain regions. A major part of research in biological psychology is directed toward uncovering the behavioral specializations of different brain regions. An additional theme emerging from

---

* The icons that appear in the margins throughout the book are explained in the Preface.

1.16 A Nineteenth-Century Anatomist's Look at Nerve Cells

These drawings of brain cells, still cited today, were made by the great Spanish anatomist Santiago Ramón y Cajal (1852–1934) based on his careful observations with the microscope.

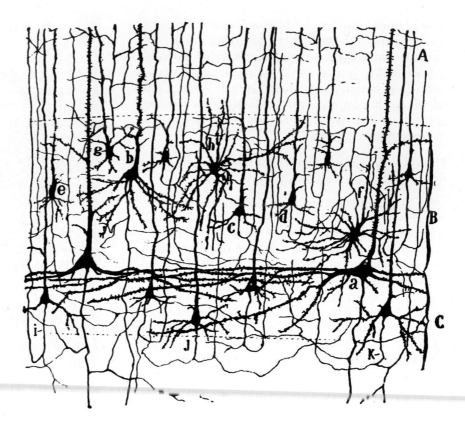

these studies is the relation of brain size to ability (see Box 1.1). Nineteenth century anatomy included microscopic studies of sections of the brain. These studies revealed for the first time the shapes, sizes, and identity of nerve cells of the brain (Figure 1.16).

In 1890, *Principles of Psychology*, by William James, signaled the beginnings of a modern biological psychology. The strength of the ideas described in this book is evident by the continuing frequent citation of this work, especially by contemporary cognitive neuroscientists. In James's work, psychological ideas such as consciousness and other aspects of human experience came to be seen as properties of the nervous system, and a more complete understanding of psychological phenomena was to be achieved by the study of the nervous system. A true biological psychology began to emerge from this approach.

The Twentieth Century Saw the Dawn of Modern Biological Psychology

The end of the nineteenth century and the start of the twentieth brought many important developments for biological psychology. German psychologist Hermann Ebbinghaus had shown in 1885 how to measure learning and memory in humans. In 1898, American psychologist Robert L. Thorndike showed in his doctor-

al thesis how to measure learning and memory in animal subjects. Early in the twentieth century, Russian physiologist Ivan P. Pavlov announced research in his laboratory on the conditioned reflex in animals. American psychologist Shepard I. Franz (1902) sought the site of learning and memory in the brain, combining Thorndike's training procedures with localized brain lesions in animal subjects. This work started a search for the traces of experience in the brain—a quest that Karl S. Lashley (1890–1958) referred to as the "search for the engram." Lashley studied with Franz and took over the problem of investigating the locations and mechanisms of memory functions in the brain. His

Karl S. Lashley (1890–1958)

approach was primarily anatomical, and he focused on assessing the behavioral effects of brain lesions. In a long career, Lashley contributed many important findings and trained many students to study the biological mechanisms not only of learning and memory, but also of perception and motivation (Thompson, 1992).

Current biological psychology bears the strong imprint of Canadian psychologist Donald O. Hebb (1904–1985), a student of Lashley. By the 1940s, electrophysiological studies of the nervous system began to offer tantalizing pictures of an incessantly active brain. In his book *The Organization of Behavior* (1949), Hebb showed in principle how complex cognitive behavior could be accomplished by networks of active neurons. He suggested how initially more or less random connections between brain cells could become organized by sensory input and stimulation into strongly interconnected groups that he called cell assemblies. His hypothesis about how neurons strengthen their connections through use became known as the "Hebbian synapse," a topic much studied by current neuroscientists. We will refer to Hebb's work in later chapters. Brief accounts of Hebb's career and contributions have been written by Peter Milner (1992, 1993).

An Explosion of Data: National Databanks and the Mapping of the Brain

Within a relatively short period of time neuroscientists throughout the world have amassed an enormous amount of data about how nervous systems work. This data explosion extends from the level of molecular details to the complexity of behaviors such as memory and emotions. New techniques, such as those that help identify genetic mechanisms and nervous system functioning, promise to add many more important pieces in the puzzle of the brain. Recently, committees of neuroscientists (Pechura and Martin, 1991) have advocated the establishment of a major national project that would enable all these pieces discovered by individual researchers to be assembled in national computerized databases that would become a comprehensive blueprint of the brain. A direct quote summarizes the goals of this project (Pechura and Martin, 1991):

> The committee recommends that the Brain Mapping Initiative be established with the long-term objective of developing three-dimensional computerized maps and models of the structure, functions, connectivity, pharmacology, and molecular biology of human, rat, and monkey brains across developmental stages and reflecting both normal and disease states.

These databases, now being formed, include the ability to relate integrated maps of the anatomy of the brain with maps of physiological activity and maps that relate to behavioral processes.

Recommended Reading

Ackerman, S. 1992. *Discovering the Brain*. National Academy Press, Washington, D.C.

Finger, S. 1994. *Origins of Neuroscience*. Oxford University Press, New York.

Harrington, A. 1987. *Medicine, Mind, and the Double Brain*. Princeton University Press, Princeton, NJ.

Pechura, C. M. and Martin, J. B. (eds.) 1991. *Mapping the Brain*. National Academy Press, Washington, D.C.

To keep in touch with progress in this field, you can find reviews and evaluations of research in the following publications:

Annual Review of Neuroscience. Annual Reviews, Palo Alto, CA. (Founded in 1978)

Annual Review of Psychology. Annual Reviews, Palo Alto, CA. (Founded in 1950)

Trends in Neurosciences. Elsevier, Amsterdam. (Founded in 1978)

PART 1

Bodily Systems Basic to Behavior

Within your head is an information processing system, the brain, that contains at least 100 billion nerve cells. These cells are connected to one another in extremely varied and elaborate patterns. A single cell may receive connections from thousands of others! The essence of our identity is locked up in the character of these brain connections. An extensive web of nerve fibers connects the brain to every part of the body, monitoring, regulating, and modulating the functions of every bodily structure and system. The workings of this vast assembly make possible our perceptions, thoughts, movements, motives, and feelings.

Our first objective in this section is to describe the basic structures of the adult human brain (Chapter 2). In Chapter 3 we consider nervous systems from the perspectives of comparisons among species and the evolution of the nervous system over long epochs of time. Another significant time frame is the life history of the individual. Chapter 4 describes some of the many changes that occur in the nervous system during the life span of the individual and the interplay of developmental controls such as genes and experience.

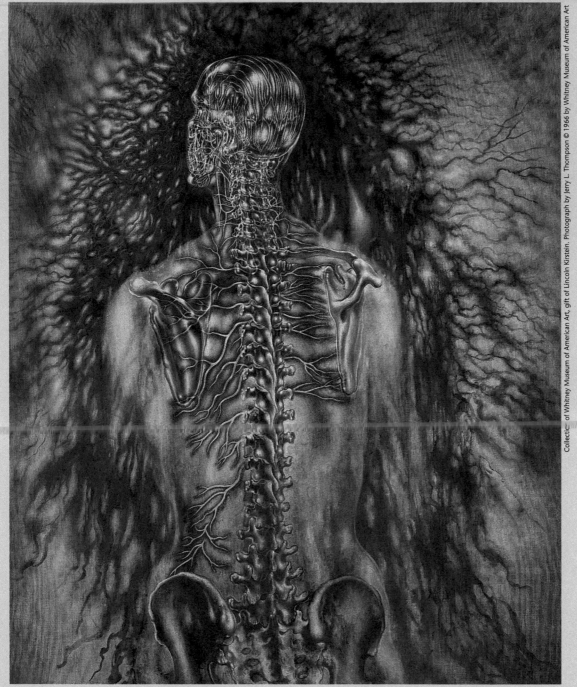

Pavel Tchelitchew, *Anatomical Painting*, 1946

- *A Small-Scale View of the Nervous System: Cells*

- *Nerve Cells*

- *Glial Cells*

- *A Large-Scale View of the Nervous System: Regions*

- *The Peripheral Nervous System Consists of Three Components*

- *Some Functional Descriptions of Brain Structures*

- *The Brain Is Well Protected and Has an Abundant Blood Supply*

- *Neural Systems: Functional Aggregates of Widespread Neurons*

- *Today We Can Look into the Living Human Brain*

CHAPTER

2

Neuroanatomical Bases of Behavior

Orientation

Thoughts, feelings, perceptions, and acts—all are products of the workings of the human brain. These accomplishments depend on the architecture of the brain and the way it works. In this chapter we will discuss the structural character of the brain. The basic ways in which those structures work will be taken up in Chapters 5 and 6.

To understand the structure of the brain we have to consider its components and the extensive network of linkages among them. These paths and circuits form the anatomical basis for information processing. This structure is a highly precise arrangement of parts; our efforts to achieve a biological understanding of behavior must start with an appreciation of basic units, their connections, and their arrangements into networks that process information. We will try to relate the details of the architecture of the nervous system that are especially important for subsequent chapters.

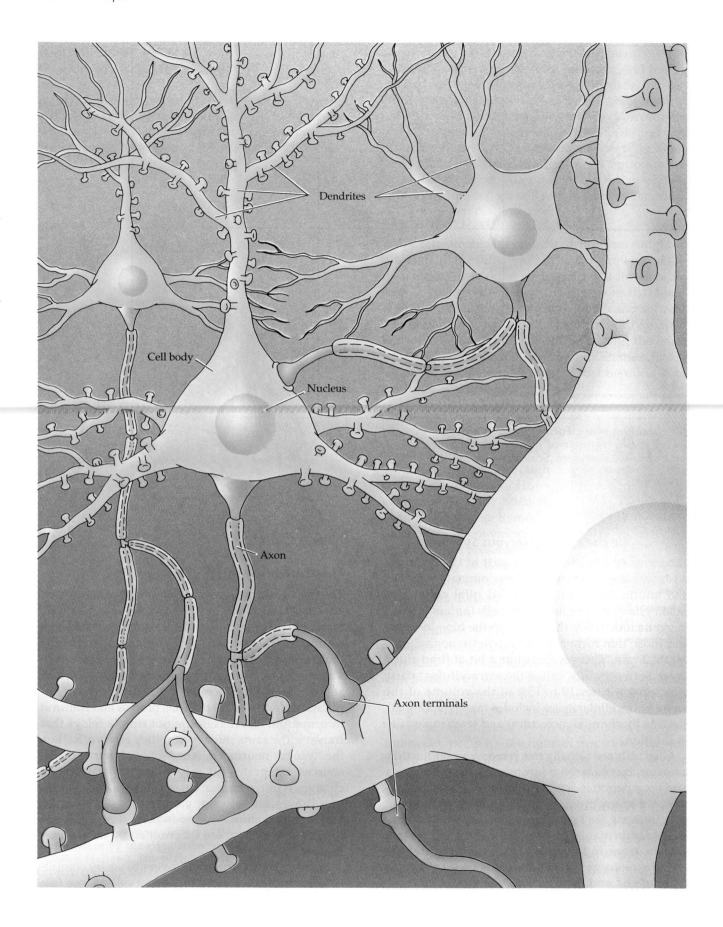

Dendrites

Cell body

Nucleus

Axon

Axon terminals

◀ **2.3   Typical Nerve Cells with Their Major
Components**
Many axon terminals contact dendritic spines; others
contact dendrites directly. Note that the many dendritic
spines shown here would probably be occupied by an
axon terminal; they have been left empty for clarity.

tures are common to all nerve cells. Most neurons
have three distinct structural zones, or parts, that are
directly related to the functional properties of the
cell. These are (1) a **cell body** region, which is defined by the presence of the nucleus, (2) extensions
of the cell body called **dendrites** (from the Greek
dendron, "tree"), which vastly increase the receptive
surface of the neuron, and (3) a single extension of
another type, the **axon**. These three zones are illustrated in Figure 2.3. In many neurons the axon is
only a few micrometers long, but in spinal sensory
and motor neurons, it can reach more than a meter.[*]
For example, the giraffe has axons that are several
meters long! In order for you to wiggle your toes,
individual axons must carry the instructions from
the spinal cord to muscles in your foot. Long fibers
of sensory neurons then carry messages back to the
spinal cord.

The ability to see and measure nerve cells and
trace their connections is vital to solving many problems in biological psychology and neuroscience. A
few of these problems are: How do neurons grow
and make connections during individual development? In what ways do the nervous systems of men
and women differ? What differences in nerve cells
and their connections characterize Alzheimer's disease? What changes occur in nerve cells as a consequence of learning? What changes in neurons and
their connections permit recovery of function after
damage to the nervous system?

But neurons are difficult to examine and measure
for several reasons. First, they are small, and their
extensions (dendrites and axons) are even smaller (1
to 3 μm). Furthermore, if you cut a thin slice of brain
tissue and look at it under a microscope, it is hard to
see any brain cells because they don't contrast with
surrounding areas such as extracellular space. The
ability to see details of cells requires special chemical
agents to make cells or parts of cells stand out from
the background. The study of tissue structure is
known as **histology**. We describe some histological

techniques for visualizing neurons, as well as some
methods used to trace pathways in the nervous system in Box 2.1.

Neurons Can Be Classified in Three Ways

Shape.   Anatomists use the shapes of cell bodies,
dendrites, and axons to classify the many varieties
of nerve cells into three principal types: multipolar,
bipolar, and monopolar neurons. These different
types of neurons are specialized for particular kinds
of interactions. **Multipolar neurons** are nerve cells
with many dendrites and a single axon (Figure 2.4*a*).
Most of the neurons of the vertebrate brain are multipolar. **Bipolar neurons** are nerve cells with a single dendrite at one end of the cell and a single axon
at the other end (Figure 2.4*b*). This type of nerve cell
is found in some sensory systems, including the retina and the olfactory (smell) system. **Monopolar
neurons** have a single branch (usually thought of as
an axon) which, after leaving the cell body, extends
in two directions (Figure 2.4*c*). One end is the receptive pole, the other the output zone.

Size.   Another common way of classifying nerve
cells is by size. Examples of small nerve cells are the
types called granule ("grains"), spindle, and stellate
("star-shaped"). Large cells include the types called
pyramidal, Golgi type I, and Purkinje. Each region
of the brain is a collection of both large and small
neurons. Vertebrate nerve cell bodies range from as
small as 10 μm to as large as 100 μm in diameter.

Function.   A third simple classification of neurons
is by function. Some neurons send their axon to a
muscle or gland, and the job of these neurons is to
make the muscle contract or to change the activity
of the gland. Such neurons are called **motoneurons**
(or motor neurons). Other neurons are directly
affected by changes in the environment; they
respond to light, a particular odor, or touch. These
cells are **sensory neurons**. The remaining neurons,
which constitute the vast majority, receive input
from and send their output to other neurons. Thus
they are called **interneurons**.

The Neuronal Cell Body and Dendrites
Receive Information Across Synapses

The diversity of neuronal shapes arises especially
from the variation in the form and shape of dendrites,

---

[*] The meter (m), the unit of length in the metric system,
equals 39.37 inches. A centimeter (cm) is one-hundredth of
a meter (10^{-2} m); a millimeter (mm) is one-thousandth of
a meter (10^{-3} m); a micrometer, or micron (μm), is one-mil-
lionth of a meter (10^{-6} m); and a nanometer (nm) is one-bil-
lionth of a meter (10^{-9} m).

2.1

Neuroanatomical Methods Provide Ways to See Small Things in the Brain

In the middle of the nineteenth century, dyes used to color fabrics provided a breakthrough in anatomical analysis. Dead, preserved nerve cells treated with these dyes, known in histology as stains, suddenly become vivid, and hidden parts become evident. Different dyes have special affinities for different parts of the cell, such as membranes, the cell body, or the sheaths surrounding axons.

The **Golgi** method outlines the full cell, including details like dendritic spines (Figure A). Golgi staining is often used to characterize the variety of cell types in a region. For reasons that remain a mystery, this technique stains only a small number of cells, each of which stands out in dramatic contrast to adjacent unstained cells.

Nissl stains outline all cell bodies because the dyes are attracted to RNA, which encircles the nucleus. Nissl stains allow one to measure cell body size and the density of cells in particular regions (Figure B).

Other stains are absorbed by myelin, the fatty sheaths that surround some axons (see the sections of spinal cord shown in Figure 2.12). Exposing slices of brain tissue to particular chemicals can transform some neurotransmitters into fluorescent chemicals. Nerve cells treated in this way light up when exposed to ultraviolet light. Injecting fluorescent molecules directly into a neuron provides a Golgi-like view of its dendrites (Figure C).

Some histological techniques can reveal aspects of the dynamic neurochemistry of nerve cells, particularly the cell's metabolic processes. Cells can be manipulated into tak-

ing their own photograph—a method called **autoradiography**. For example, you might inject a living animal with radioactively labeled **2-deoxyglucose** (**2-DG**). 2-DG resembles glucose enough that active cells take it up more readily than inactive cells do. But once the 2-DG is inside, it cannot be broken down, so it just sits inside even the most active neurons. To create an autoradiogram, the experimenter presents the animal with a stimulus condition that results in neural activity while the 2-DG is injected. The neurons that are active during that stimulus will take up more of the radioactive 2-DG than will the inactive neurons. The experimenters then sacrifice the animal, cut thin sections of brain tissue, and place them on slides, which they cover with photographic emulsion. Radioactivity emitted by the 2-DG in the cells causes silver to be deposited—the same effect that light has on film. The silver deposition produces fine dark grains immediately above the active neurons that took up the radioactive substance (see Figure 14.3).

Improved microscopes have also broadened our understanding of the fine structure of cells. Observations with routine forms of light microscopy provide detailed resolution down to about 1 to 2μm. Smaller objects fail to deflect light particles (photons), so they cannot be detected with light. But because electrons are even smaller than photons, electron microscopy extends a hundredfold the range of structures that can be visualized, making it possible to see some of the smallest details within cells (see Figures 2.5, 2.7c, and 2.8).

Scanning electron microscopy adds a dimension of depth, and structures take on a startlingly intimate appearance (Figure 4.11). All these forms of microscopic study are now being coupled with computers to provide rapid, automatic, quantitative assessment of aspects of nerve cells, such as dendrite length. These techniques will increasingly supplement the heretofore intuitive judgments of anatomists.

Another approach to the marking of cells of the brain comes from the application of immunological techniques. These techniques allow neuroanatomists to mark groups of cells that have an attribute in common such as particular membrane components, or particular proteins within a cell. This technique, known as **immunocytochemistry** because it uses immune system molecules (antibodies) to detect cells (the Greek *cyto*, means "cells"), is described in detail in the Appendix.

Tracing Pathways in the Brain

The cells of the brain are interconnected through a complex web of pathways. Understanding the circuits formed by these cells and their extensions required the development of techniques that clearly outlined the terminals of particular cell groups or showed the cells of origin of particular axon tracts. Tracing pathways in the nervous system is difficult for several reasons: (1) axons have an even smaller diameter than cell bodies (see Table 2.1); (2) axons from different sources look alike; and (3) fibers with different destinations often travel together over parts of their routes, making it

(A) *Golgi stain*

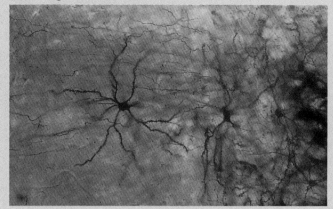

(B) *Nissl stain*

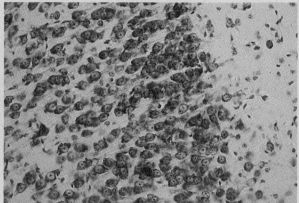

(C) *Neuron injected with fluorescent dye*

(D) *HRP-filled motoneuron*

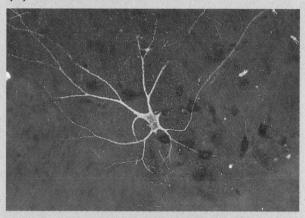

hard to disentangle one set from the rest. Although at first glance this task of tracing neural pathways seems insurmountable—remember, our brain contains billions of neurons—anatomists were not daunted.

Classical anatomical techniques for tracing pathways rely on visualizing the products of degenerating axons. First, the cell bodies of origin are surgically damaged. Within a few days the axons of the cells begin to degenerate, and during this phase they are especially likely to accumulate silver salts. When the dying axons are exposed to silver compounds, they acquire a dark brown-black color. Examining a series of sections for the presence of such marked axons makes it possible to trace a pathway over some distance. Newer procedures accomplish the same goal by the injection of radioactively labeled amino acids into a collection of cell bodies. These radioactive molecules are taken up by the cell, incorporated into proteins, and transported to the tips of the axons. Brain sections are then coated with a sensitive emulsion as a film would be. After some time (which ranges from hours to weeks), the slides are developed and stained. If the pathway originates in the area of the injected cells, developed silver grains will be located in axons and their terminals, making the whole pathway visible.

A more recent, powerful technique to determine the cells of origin of a particular set of axons employs **horseradish peroxidase** (**HRP**), an enzyme found in the roots of horseradish and many other plants (Figure D). HRP catalyzes certain chemical reactions that leave a visible reaction product of dark granules. HRP acts as a tracer of pathways because it is taken up into the axon at the terminals and transported back to the cell body. After HRP is injected into one part of the nervous system, any neurons that have axon terminals there will transport the HRP back to the cell body, which can be made visible with chemical reactions. All along the way stainable reaction products are formed—akin to footprints along a pathway. (Figure A courtesy of Timothy DeVoogd; Figure C courtesy of Carla Shatz.)

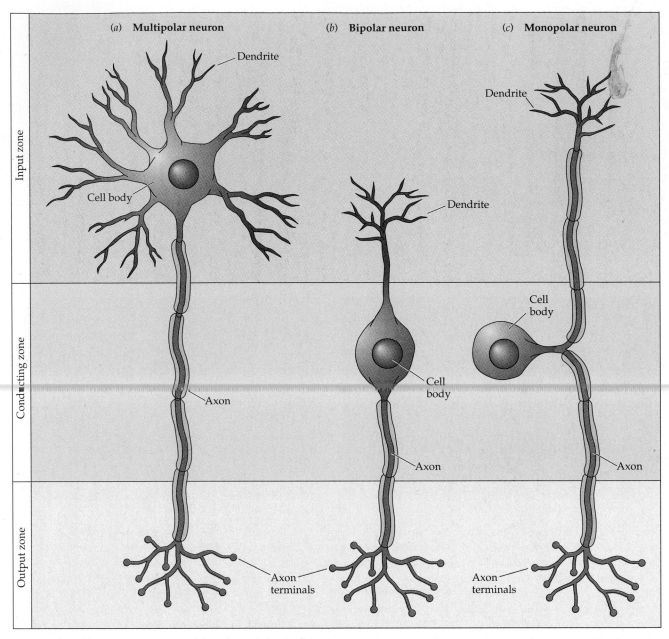

(a) **Multipolar neuron**   (b) **Bipolar neuron**   (c) **Monopolar neuron**

Input zone

Conducting zone

Output zone

Dendrite

Cell body

Axon

Axon terminals

Dendrite

Cell body

Axon

Axon terminals

Dendrite

Cell body

Axon

Axon terminals

2.4   A Classification of Neurons into Three Principal Types
(*a*) Multipolar neurons have many dendrites extending from the cell body, and a single axon. (*b*) Bipolar neurons have a single dendrite extending from the cell body, and a single axon. (*c*) Monopolar neurons have a single branch that emerges from the cell body and extends in two directions.

the extensions that arise from the nerve cell body and branch out in highly complex ways (see Figure 2.2). The shape of the dendritic tree—the full arrangement of a single cell's dendrites—provides clues about a particular cell's information processing. All along the surface of the dendrite are many contacts, the synapses. It is through the synapses that information is transmitted from one neuron to the next. A synapse,

or synaptic region, has three principal components (Figure 2.5):

1. the presynaptic specialization, in many instances a swelling of the axon terminal called the **synaptic bouton** ("button");

2. a specialized **postsynaptic membrane** in the surface of the dendrite or cell body;

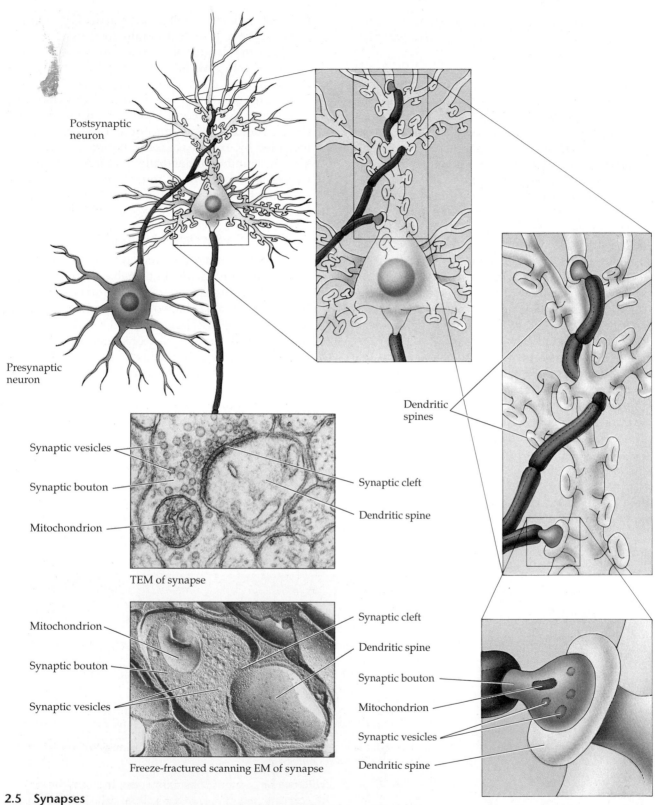

Postsynaptic
neuron

Presynaptic
neuron

Dendritic
spines

Synaptic vesicles

Synaptic bouton

Mitochondrion

Synaptic cleft

Dendritic spine

TEM of synapse

Mitochondrion

Synaptic bouton

Synaptic vesicles

Synaptic cleft

Dendritic spine

Synaptic bouton

Mitochondrion

Synaptic vesicles

Dendritic spine

Freeze-fractured scanning EM of synapse

2.5 Synapses

Axons may form a synapse upon the cell body or dendrites of a neuron. On dendrites, synapses may form upon dendritic spines or upon the shaft of a dendrite. Electron micrographs (*insets*) reveal the fine structure of synapses. Micrographs from Peters, Palay, and Webster, 1991

3. a **synaptic cleft**, that is, a space between the presynaptic and postsynaptic elements. This gap measures about 20 to 40 nm.

Detailed electron microscopic examination of the presynaptic terminal reveals many small spheres called **synaptic vesicles.** They range in size from 30 to 140 nm. There is strong evidence that these vesicles contain a chemical substance that can be released into the synaptic cleft. This release is triggered by electrical activity in the axon. The released chemical, called a **synaptic transmitter**, or **neurotransmitter**, flows across the cleft and produces changes in the postsynaptic membrane. Many different transmitters have been identified in the brain, including acetylcholine, dopamine, and glutamate, but many more remain to be discovered. The electrical changes in the postsynaptic membrane are the basis of the transmission of excitation or inhibition from one cell to another. The synaptic cleft is filled with a dense material that is different from other extracellular regions. Similarly, the surface of the postsynaptic membrane is different from adjacent regions of the membrane. It contains special **receptor molecules** (often referred to simply as receptors) that capture and react to molecules of the transmitter agent. Numerous synapses cover the surfaces of dendrites and of the cell body. This number is possible because the size of a single synaptic junction is very small—less than 1 square micrometer (Shepherd, 1990). Some individual cells of the brain have as many as 100,000 synapses, although the more common number for larger cells is around 5,000 to 10,000. Synaptic contacts are particularly numerous in nerve cells with elaborate dendrites.

Along the dendrites on many nerve cells of the brain are outgrowths called **dendritic spines** or thorns (Figure 2.5*b*). These spines give some dendrites a rough or corrugated surface. They have become the focus of considerable attention, because their structural appearance and function may be modified by experience (see Chapter 17). Both the size and number of dendritic spines are affected by various treatments of an animal, such as training or exposure to sensory stimuli. Table 2.1 compares the main structural features of axons and dendrites.

The Axon Is a Specialized Output Zone

A typical axon has several regions that are structurally and functionally distinguishable (Figure 2.5*c*). In multipolar neurons the axon originates out of the cell body from a cone-shaped region called the **axon hillock**. The electrical impulse that carries each neuron's message to other neurons begins in the axon hillock and travels down the axon (see Chapter 5). The axon beyond the hillock is tubular, with a diameter ranging from 0.5 μm to 20 μm in mammals and as large as 500 μm in the "giant" axons of some invertebrates. With very few exceptions, nerve cells have only one axon. But axons often divide into many branches called **axon collaterals**. Because of this extensive branching, a single nerve cell can exert influence over a wide array of other cells. Toward its ending, an axon or collateral typically divides into numerous branches of fine diameter. At the end of the branches (the **axon**

Table 2.1	
Distinctions between Axons and Dendrites	
AXONS	DENDRITES
Usually one per neuron, with many terminal branches	Usually many per neuron
Uniform diameter until start of terminal branching	Diameter progressively tapers toward its ending
Join cell body at a distinct region called the axon hillock	No hillock-like region
Usually covered with myelin	No myelin covering
Lengths from practically non-existent to several meters	Usually much shorter than axons
Along length, branches tend to be perpendicular	Along dendrites, branches occur over wide range of acute angles

terminals), specialized structures form the synapse, the connection to the next nerve cell. By synapsing upon this target nerve cell, the axon terminals are said to **innervate** (or provide innervation to) the cell.

A pair of terms are used to describe axons, always in relation to a particular brain region or structure under discussion. Axons carrying information *into* the region are said to be **afferents**. Axons carrying information *away* from the brain region are called **efferents**. So every axon can be described as either an *efferent from* the region containing its cell body, or an *afferent to* the target it innervates. Most often the structure under discussion is the brain, so if you read "af-

ferents" without any qualification, you may assume that these are axons bringing information into the brain. Similarly, unless the context provides some other structure as a reference point, "efferents" are axons carrying commands from the brain out to the body.

The cell body manufactures proteins under the guidance of DNA in the cell nucleus (see Appendix A). Therefore proteins needed for growth and function must be transported from the cell body to distant regions in the axon. The movement of materials within the axon is referred to as **axonal transport** (Figure 2.6). Some molecules are transported along axons at a "slow" rate (1 to 3 mm/day), while others

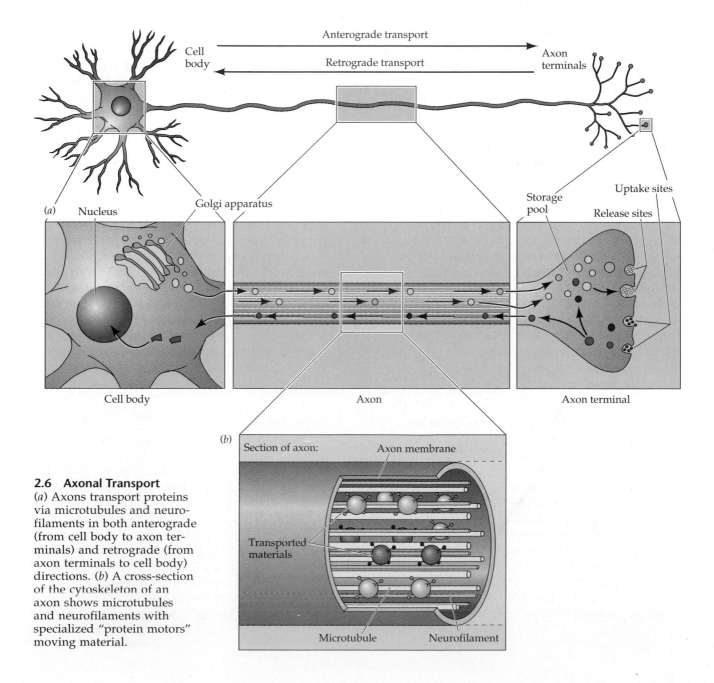

2.6 Axonal Transport
(*a*) Axons transport proteins via microtubules and neurofilaments in both anterograde (from cell body to axon terminals) and retrograde (from axon terminals to cell body) directions. (*b*) A cross-section of the cytoskeleton of an axon shows microtubules and neurofilaments with specialized "protein motors" moving material.

are transported by a "fast" system (400 mm/day). How does anything move in these structures? This question has been studied mainly in axons whose length and uniformity facilitate such investigation. Investigators have observed structures in axons referred to as **microtubules** (20 to 26 nm in diameter) that look like hollow cylinders (Figure 2.6*b*). There are also systems of smaller rods (10 nm in diameter) called **neurofilaments** (found only in neurons). Smaller yet are **microfilaments** (7 nm in diameter), which are found in all cells. These three molecules determine the shape of a cell, but evidence suggests that they are also involved in axonal transport. The deciphering of the molecular machinery of axonal transport has been quite dramatic over the past ten years (Vallee and Bloom, 1991). At least three types of proteins have been identified that are part of the "motor" mechanism that moves substances in conjunction with microtubules.

Glial Cells

Glial Cells Support Neural Activity

Glial cells are named after the original conception of their function—that they serve as something like glue (from the Greek *glia*, "glue"). Clearly, structural support—or some aspects of it—is one biological role of glial cells. Glial cells may also serve a nutritive role, providing a pathway from the vascular system to the nerve cells, for delivering raw materials that neurons use to synthesize complex compounds. Unlike nerve cells, glia are produced throughout our lifetime. Although many aspects of the functional roles of neuroglia remain a puzzle, we do know some things—and there are many interesting ideas—about their function.

There are four classes of glial cells. One type, called an **astrocyte** (from the Greek *astra*, "star"), is a star-shaped cell with numerous extensions (or processes) in all directions (Figure 2.7). Some astrocytes form end feet on the blood vessels of the brain. These end feet look as though they are attached to the vessels by suckerlike extensions. Extensions of astrocytes form the tough sheets that wrap around the outer surface of the brain, the dura mater. Bundles of astrocyte extensions interweave among nerve fibers, as though giving a structural support.

Contemporary research has suggested that astrocytes also play a more active role in the functions of the brain (Kimmelberg and Norenberg, 1989). Astrocytes may contribute to the metabolism of synaptic transmitters and may regulate the balance of ions. Astrocytes also release growth factors, proteins that are important in the growth and repair of nerve cells.

A second type of glial cell is **microglia**. As the name suggests, these cells are very small. Microglia migrate in large numbers to sites of injury or disease in the nervous system, apparently to remove debris from injured or dead cells.

Some Glial Cells Wrap Around Axons, Forming Myelin Sheaths

The third and fourth types of glial cells—oligodendrocytes and Schwann cells—perform a vital function for nerve cells. Wrapped around most axons are sheaths formed by glial cells that lie close to the axon. For many axons, mainly those with large diameters, these accessory cells come close to the axon and form a regular wrapping called **myelin** (Figure 2.7*b*). The process of the formation of this wrapping is called **myelination**. This sheathing affects the speed of conduction of neural impulses. Anything that interferes with the myelin sheath can have catastrophic consequences for the individual, as is evident in various demyelinating diseases, such as multiple sclerosis, which is caused by the loss of myelin on the axons of the brain.

Within the brain and spinal cord, the myelin sheath is formed by a type of glial cell called an **oligodendrocyte** (see Figure 2.7). This cell is much smaller than an astrocyte and has fewer extensions (the Greek *oligo* means "few"). The myelination provided by oligodendrocytes continues over extended periods of time in human beings—in some brain regions up to 10 to 15 years after birth. Oligodendrocytes are also commonly associated with nerve cell bodies, especially the bodies of larger neurons. Because of this association, they are frequently regarded as satellite cells of neurons.

For axons *outside* the brain and spinal cord, myelin is provided by another type of glia—the **Schwann cell**. A single Schwann cell produces the myelin coat for a very limited length of the axon, seldom extending for more than 200 µm. Hence, numerous Schwann cells are needed to myelinate the length of a single axon. Between the Schwann cells are small gaps in the coating. Such a gap, where the axon membrane is exposed, is called a **node of Ranvier**. The regularity of the wrapping is nicely illustrated in cross sections of the axon (see Figure 2.7). Myelination by Schwann cells differs from myelination by oligodendrocytes. Whereas a single oligodendrocyte may myelinate several segments of the same axon or several different

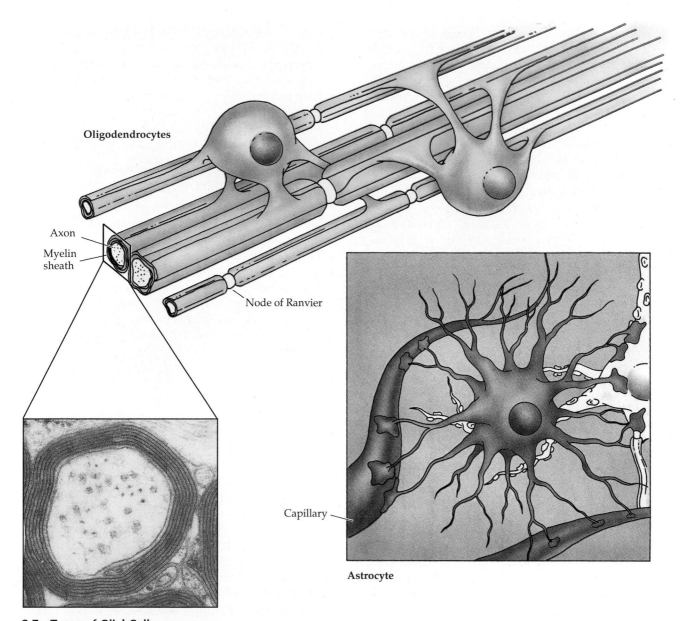

Oligodendrocytes

Axon

Myelin
sheath

Node of Ranvier

Capillary

Astrocyte

2.7   Types of Glial Cells
(*Top*) Extensions or arms of oligodendrocytes form myelin wrapping (blue)
on axons (yellow); four axons are shown in this view. (*Inset*) Electron micrograph of a myeliated axon shows the many layers of the myelin sheath.
(*Bottom right*) A type of astrocyte—the protoplasmic astrocyte—contacts
capillaries and is adjacent to nerve cell membranes. Micrograph from Peters,
Palay, and Webster, 1991.

axons, each Schwann cell myelinates only a single
segment of one cell.

Many very thin diameter axons have no close
wrapping of myelin; they are commonly referred to
as unmyelinated fibers or axons. Although these
fibers do not have an elaborate coating, they still have
a relationship with an accessory cell. Several axons
become embedded in troughs of the Schwann cell but
without elaborate wrapping (Figure 2.8). The manner
in which these glial cells surround neurons, especially the synaptic surfaces of neurons, suggests that one
of their roles is to isolate receptive surfaces to prevent
interactions among synapses by keeping various inputs segregated.

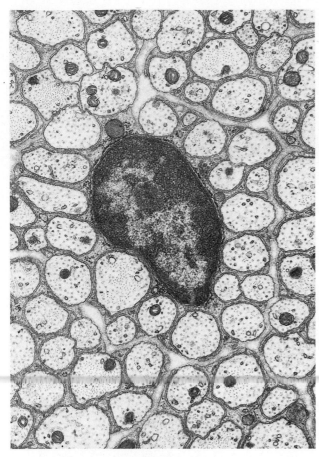

2.8   Unmyelinated Axons Viewed by Electron Microscopy

Unmyelinated axons do not show the regular wrapping shown in Figure 2.7. Instead they are embedded in the troughs of glial cells, and are seen here in cross-section as the light-colored circular shapes. From Peters, Palay, and Webster, 1991.

Glial cells are of clinical interest because they form the principal tumors of the brain and spinal cord. Furthermore, some classes of glia, especially astrocytes, respond to brain injury by changing in size, that is, by swelling. This **edema** damages neurons and is responsible for many symptoms of brain injuries.

A Large-Scale View of the Nervous System: Regions

To this point, we have described the basic building blocks of the nervous system—neurons and their synapses, and glia. Structural analysis in neuroscience research involves many different levels extending from these basic building blocks to features

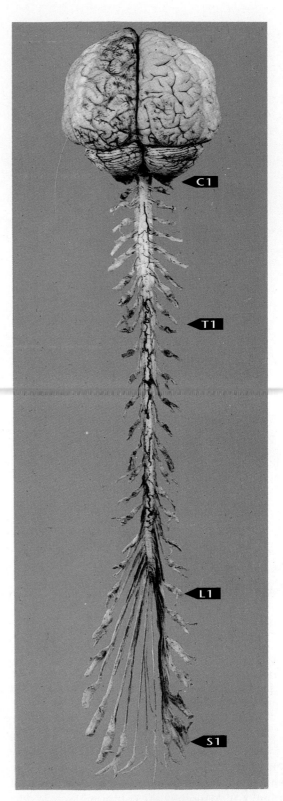

2.9   The Central Nervous System

The brain and spinal cord form the central nervous system. Spinal nerves are abbreviated as follows: C1 is the first cervical nerve; T1 is the first thoracic nerve; L1 is the first lumbar nerve; and S1 is the first sacral nerve.

of an entire brain. These levels are analogous to the different views of a scene that a zoom lens can provide, ranging from close-up, intimate views of fine detail to a much broader view of interactions of different brain regions or the properties of the whole brain (see Figure 1.10).

In this section we will describe the human nervous system on a much larger scale, viewing the brain with the unaided eye. For this discussion you will need to understand the conventions that anatomists use for describing various viewpoints of the body and the brain. These are described in Box 2.2.

The Nervous System Consists of a Central and a Peripheral Division

A view of the entire human nervous system is presented in Figure 2.1. Examining the nervous system from this viewpoint reveals a natural subdivision into a **central nervous system** (**CNS**), consisting of the brain and spinal cord (Figure 2.9), and a **peripheral nervous system** (all nervous system parts that are outside the bony skull and spinal column). Figure 2.10 shows the complete breakdown of these two major parts and their subcomponents. After discussing the peripheral nervous system, we will turn our attention to the control center of the entire nervous system, the brain.

The Peripheral Nervous System Consists of Three Components

The peripheral nervous system consists of **nerves**—collections of axons bundled together—that extend throughout the body. These nerves transmit information to muscles (motor pathways) or arise from sensory surfaces (sensory pathways). The peripheral nervous system also includes pathways that transmit information in both directions (using separate axons) between the CNS and various internal organs, such as the heart. Three components make up the peripheral nervous system: (1) the cranial nerves, which are connected di-

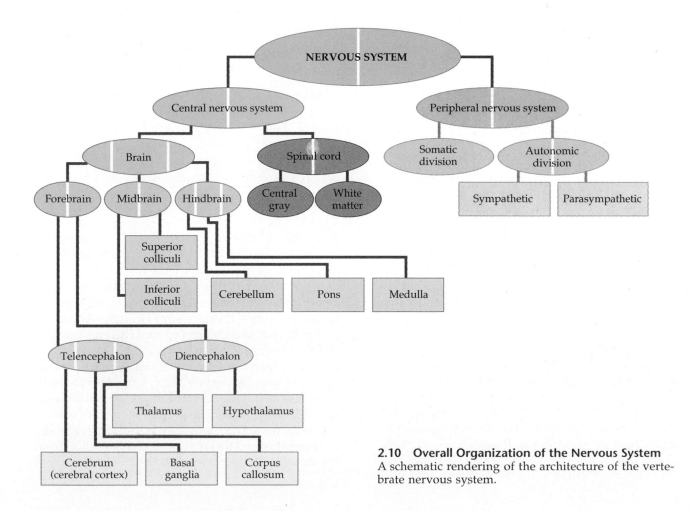

2.10 Overall Organization of the Nervous System
A schematic rendering of the architecture of the vertebrate nervous system.

Box 2.2

Three Customary Orientations for Viewing the Brain and Body

Because the nervous system is a three-dimensional structure, two-dimensional illustrations and diagrams cannot represent it completely.

The brain is usually cut in one of three main planes in order to get a two-dimensional section from this three-dimensional object. Thus it is useful to know the terminology and conventions that apply to these sections, which are shown in the figure.

The plane that bisects the body into right and left halves is called the sagittal plane (from the Latin *sagitta*, "arrow"). The plane that divides the body into a front (anterior) and back (posterior) part is called by several names: **coronal** (from the Latin *corona*, "crown"), frontal, or transverse. By convention such a section is usually viewed from behind so that the right side of the figure represents the right side of the brain. The

third main plane, which divides the brain into upper and lower parts, is called the **horizontal plane** and is usually viewed from above. These three planes are used to describe the whole body.

In addition, several directional terms are used. **Medial** means toward the middle and is contrasted with **lateral**, toward the side. The head end is referred to by any of several terms: anterior, cephalic (from the Greek for "head"), or **rostral** (from the Latin *rostrum*, prow of a ship). The tail end is called posterior or **caudal** (from the Latin for "tail"). **Proximal** (from the Latin *proximus*, nearest) means near the trunk or center, and **distal** means toward the periphery or toward the end of a limb (distant from the origin or point of attachment).

Dorsal means toward or at the back, and **ventral** means toward or at the belly or front. In four-

legged animals, such as the cat or the rat, "dorsal" refers to both the back of the body and the top of the head and brain. For consistency in comparing brains among species, this term is also used to refer to the top of the brain of a human or of a chimpanzee, even though in such two-legged animals the top of the brain is not at the back of the body. Similarly "ventral" is understood to designate the bottom of the brain of a two-legged as well as of a four-legged animal.

Although these terms seem strange at first, they provide a means of describing anatomy without ambiguity. If you want to become adept with these terms, get together with a friend and quiz each other about anatomical relations. "Where's the navel? In a medial position on the ventral surface, caudal to the ribcage and rostral to the pelvis." (Photographs courtesy of Arthur Toga.)

---

rectly to the brain; (2) the spinal nerves, which are connected at regular intervals to the spinal cord; and (3) the autonomic nervous system, which originates from both the brain and spinal cord. All three components inform the CNS about events in the environment and transmit commands from the CNS to the body.

The Cranial Nerves

The 12 pairs of cranial nerves in the human brain are concerned mainly with sensory and motor systems associated with the head (Figure 2.11). These nerves pass through small openings in the skull to enter or leave the brain. The cranial nerves are known both by name and by Roman numeral. Some cranial nerves are exclusively sensory pathways to

the brain: the olfactory (I), optic (II), and auditory (or vestibulocochlear; VIII) nerves. Others are exclusively motor pathways from the brain: the oculomotor (III), trochlear (IV), and abducens (VI) nerves innervate (that is, form synapses on) muscles to move the eye, the accessory (XI) nerves control neck muscles, and the hypoglossal (XII) nerves control the tongue. The remaining cranial nerves have both sensory and motor functions. The trigeminal (V), for example, serves facial sensation through some axons, but also controls chewing movements through other axons. The facial (VII) nerves control face muscles and receive taste sensation, while the glossopharyngeal (IX) nerves receive sensation from the throat and control muscles there. The vagus (X)

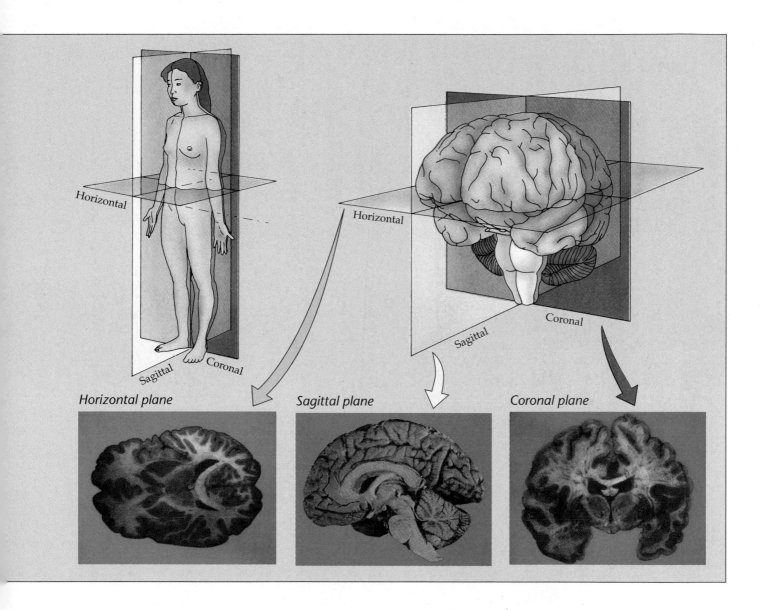

Horizontal plane   Sagittal plane   Coronal plane

nerve extends far from the head, running to the heart, liver, and intestines. Its long, convoluted route is the reason for its name, which is Latin for "wandering." The vagus and some other cranial nerves are also part of the parasympathetic nervous system, which we'll describe shortly.

The Spinal Nerves

Along the length of the spinal cord are 31 pairs of **spinal nerves**, with one member of each pair for each side of the body (Figure 2.12). These nerves join the spinal cord at regularly spaced intervals through openings in the bony structures of the spinal column. Each spinal nerve consists of the fusion of two distinct branches, called roots. These are functionally dif-

ferent. The **dorsal** (back) **root** of each spinal nerve consists of sensory pathways from the body to the spinal cord. The **ventral** (front) **root** consists of motor pathways from the spinal cord to the muscles.

The name of a spinal nerve is the same as the segment of spinal cord to which it is connected: **cervical** (neck), **thoracic** (trunk), **lumbar** (small of the back), or **sacral** (bottom of the spinal column). Thus, the T12 spinal nerve is the spinal nerve that is connected to the twelfth segment of the thoracic portion of the spinal cord (see Figure 2.9). Fibers from different spinal nerves join to form peripheral nerves, usually at some distance from the spinal cord. An example of spinal nerves that supply the sensory surface of the arm is shown in Figure 2.13.

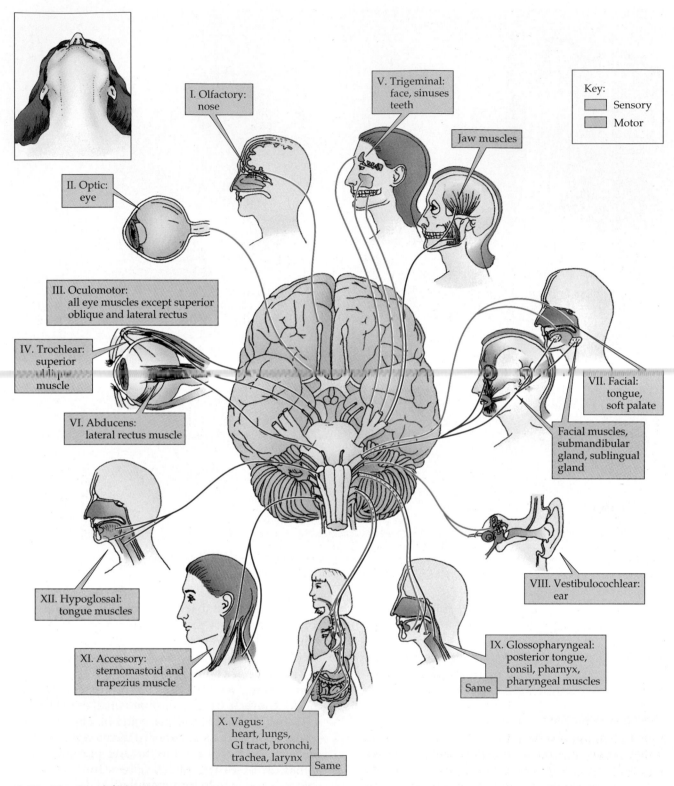

Key:

Sensory

Motor

I. Olfactory: nose

II. Optic: eye

III. Oculomotor: all eye muscles except superior oblique and lateral rectus

IV. Trochlear: superior oblique muscle

VI. Abducens: lateral rectus muscle

V. Trigeminal: face, sinuses teeth

Jaw muscles

VII. Facial: tongue, soft palate

Facial muscles, submandibular gland, sublingual gland

VIII. Vestibulocochlear: ear

IX. Glossopharyngeal: posterior tongue, tonsil, pharnyx, pharyngeal muscles

Same

XII. Hypoglossal: tongue muscles

XI. Accessory: sternomastoid and trapezius muscle

X. Vagus: heart, lungs, GI tract, bronchi, trachea, larynx

Same

Same

2.11 The Cranial Nerves

Cell bodies within the brain send axons out to form the 12 pairs of cranial nerves, which are conventionally referred to with the roman numerals I through XII. This basal view of the brain (see inset for orientation) shows the cranial nerves and their primary functions.

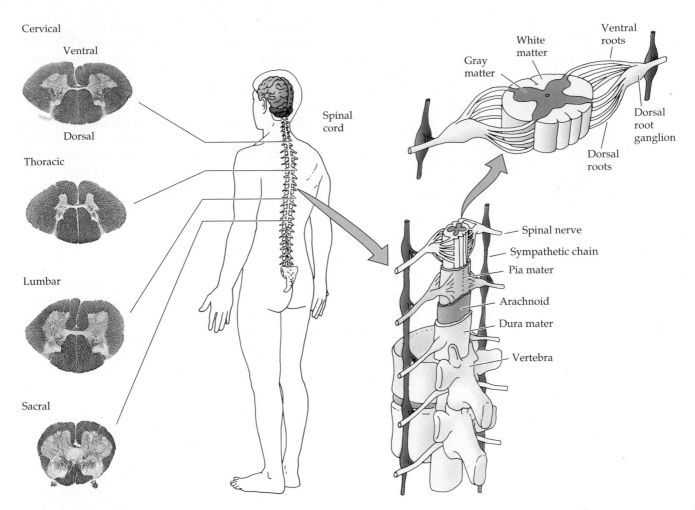

Cervical
Ventral
Dorsal

Thoracic

Lumbar

Sacral

Spinal cord

Gray matter
White matter
Ventral roots
Dorsal root ganglion
Dorsal roots

Spinal nerve
Sympathetic chain
Pia mater
Arachnoid
Dura mater
Vertebra

2.12   The Spinal Cord and Spinal Nerves
(*Middle*) The spinal column runs from the base of the brain to the sacrum; a pair of nerves emerges from each level (see Figure 2.9). (*Bottom right*) The spinal cord is surrounded by bony vertebrae and is enclosed in a membrane called the dura mater. Each vertebra has an opening on each side through which the spinal nerves pass. (*Top right*) Location of spinal cord gray matter and the white matter that surrounds it. In the gray matter are interneurons and the motoneurons that send axons to the muscles. The white matter consists of myelinated axons that run up and down the spinal column. (*Left*) Stained cross-sections of the spinal cord at the cervical, thoracic, lumbar, and sacral levels. The stain turns the fatty myelin sheaths of the axons dark, so the white matter looks dark in this presentation. Photographs from DeArmond, Fusco, and Dewey, 1989.

The Autonomic Nervous System

Ancient anatomists found collections of neurons outside the CNS, which we call **ganglia** (singular: ganglion). Because they were outside the CNS, these neuron aggregates were named **autonomic** ("independent") **ganglia**. Today we know that the autonomic ganglia are controlled by neurons in the CNS; the autonomic nervous system actually spans both the central and peripheral nervous systems.

Autonomic neurons within the brain and spinal cord send their axons out to innervate neurons in the ganglia. These neurons, which have their cell bodies within the ganglia, in turn send their axons out to innervate all the major organs. The central neurons innervating the ganglia are known as **preganglionic** autonomic cells; the ganglionic neurons innervating the body are **postganglionic** autonomic cells.

are found exclusively in the spinal cord, specifically in the thoracic and lumbar regions. These cells send their axons a short distance to innervate a chain of ganglia running along each side of the spinal column, called the **sympathetic chain** (Figure 2.14). Cells of the sympathetic chain innervate smooth muscles in organs and in the walls of blood vessels. A convenient, if somewhat oversimplified, summary of the effects of sympathetic activation is that it prepares the body for action—blood pressure is increased, the pupils of the eyes widen, and the heart quickens.

The parasympathetic nervous system gets its name (*para*, "around") because its preganglionic neurons are found above and below those of the sympathetic system—in the brain and the sacral spinal cord (see Figure 2.14). These preganglionic cells also innervate ganglia, but parasympathetic ganglia are not collected in a chain, as are sympathetic ganglia. Rather, parasympathetic ganglia are dispersed throughout the body, usually near the organ affected. For many bodily functions, the sympathetic and parasympathetic divisions act in opposite directions, and the result is very accurate control. For example, the rate of heartbeat is quickened by the activity of sympathetic nerves during exercise, but heartbeat is slowed by the vagus nerve (part of the parasympathetic system) during rest. Sympathetic activation constricts blood vessels, raising blood pressure, while parasympathetic activation relaxes vessel walls. The functions of the autonomic nervous system are "independent" in another sense—we cannot voluntarily control the activity of this system the way we can control our movements.

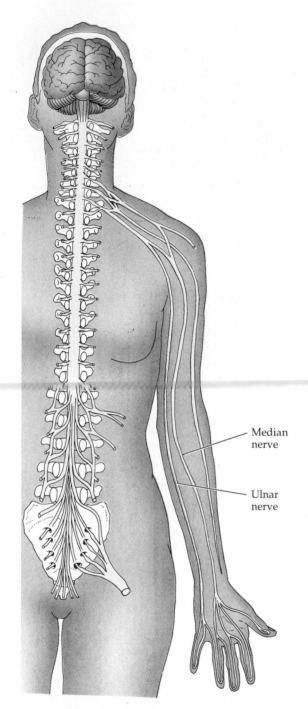

Median nerve

Ulnar nerve

2.13   Spinal Nerves to the Arm and Hand
The spinal nerves that innervate the sensory surfaces of the arm and hand emanate from the cervical region of the spinal cord.

The autonomic nervous system is divided into two components: the **sympathetic nervous system** and the **parasympathetic nervous system**. The preganglionic cells of the sympathetic nervous system

2.14   The Autonomic Nervous System   ▶
The sympathetic division of the autonomic nervous system, depicted on the left, consists of the sympathetic chains and the nerve fibers that flow from them. The parasympathetic division arises from both the cranial and sacral parts of the spinal cord. Preganglionic axons all release acetylcholine as a neurotransmitter, as do postganglionic cells in the parasympathetic division. Sympathetic postganglionic cells use noradrenaline (norepinephrine) as a neurotransmitter. The two different postganglionic transmitters allow the autonomic nervous system to have two opposing effects upon target organs.

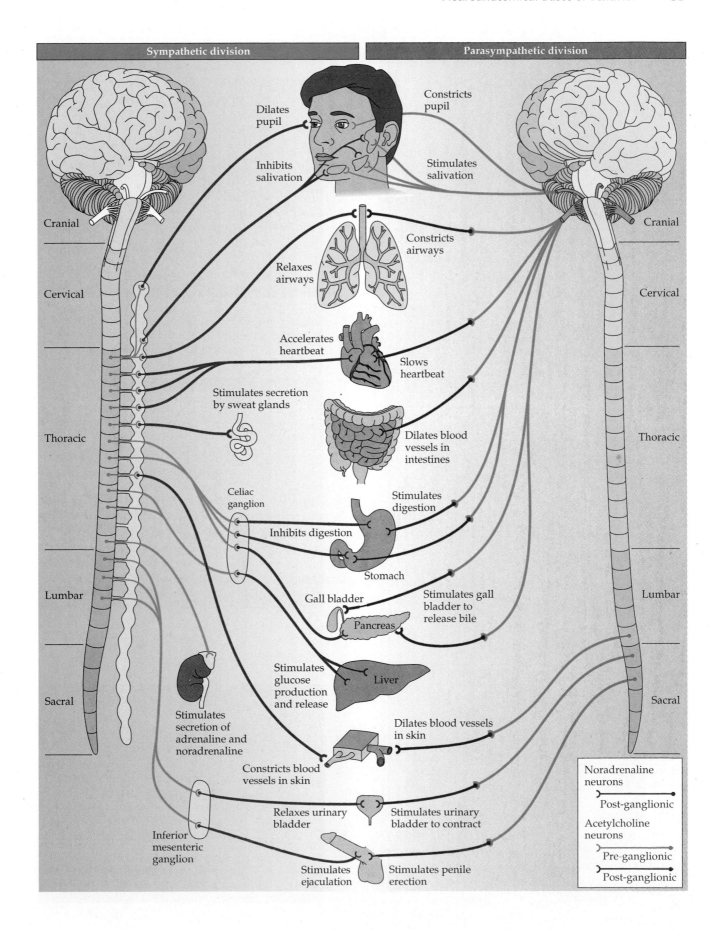

Sympathetic division

Parasympathetic division

Dilates pupil

Constricts pupil

Inhibits salivation

Stimulates salivation

Cranial

Cranial

Constricts airways

Relaxes airways

Cervical

Cervical

Accelerates heartbeat

Slows heartbeat

Stimulates secretion by sweat glands

Thoracic

Dilates blood vessels in intestines

Thoracic

Celiac ganglion

Stimulates digestion

Inhibits digestion

Lumbar

Stomach

Lumbar

Gall bladder

Stimulates gall bladder to release bile

Pancreas

Stimulates glucose production and release

Liver

Sacral

Stimulates secretion of adrenaline and noradrenaline

Dilates blood vessels in skin

Sacral

Constricts blood vessels in skin

Inferior mesenteric ganglion

Relaxes urinary bladder

Stimulates urinary bladder to contract

Noradrenaline neurons

Post-ganglionic

Acetylcholine neurons

Pre-ganglionic

Post-ganglionic

Stimulates ejaculation

Stimulates penile erection

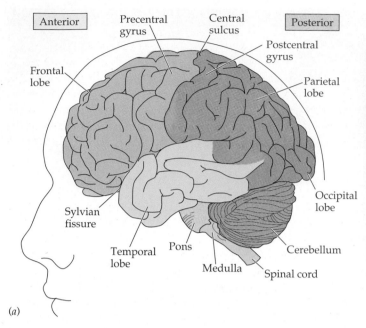

Anterior | Posterior

Precentral gyrus
Central sulcus
Postcentral gyrus
Frontal lobe
Parietal lobe
Sylvian fissure
Occipital lobe
Temporal lobe
Pons
Medulla
Cerebellum
Spinal cord

(a)

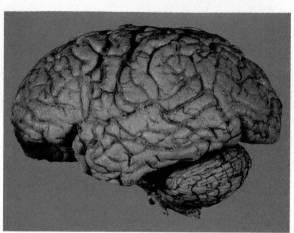

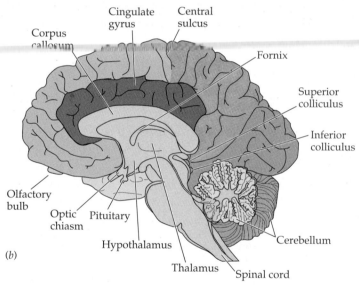

Cingulate gyrus
Central sulcus
Corpus callosum
Fornix
Superior colliculus
Inferior colliculus
Olfactory bulb
Optic chiasm
Pituitary
Hypothalamus
Thalamus
Spinal cord
Cerebellum

(b)

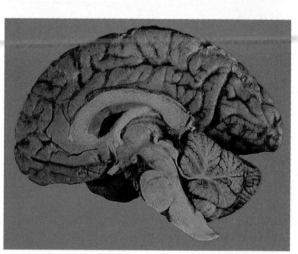

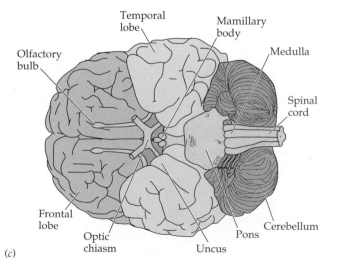

Temporal lobe
Mamillary body
Olfactory bulb
Medulla
Spinal cord
Frontal lobe
Optic chiasm
Uncus
Pons
Cerebellum

(c)

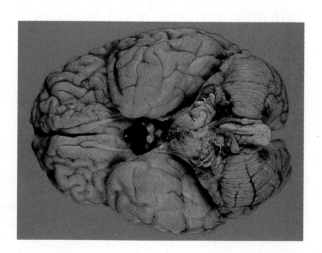

◀ **2.15   The Human Brain from Three Viewpoints**
The brain (*a*) seen from the side (lateral view); (*b*) a
midline view (midsagittal view); (*c*) viewed from below (basal view). On the right in each panel are actual
postmortem brain specimens seen from each view.
Photographs courtesy of Michael Mega.

The Central Nervous System Consists of the Brain and Spinal Cord

From our point of view the spinal cord is a conduit that
funnels sensory information from the body up to the
brain, and directs brain motor commands out to the
body. Thus we will discuss the spinal cord in later
chapters concerning sensation (Chapter 8) and movement (Chapter 11). The remainder of this chapter will
deal with the executive portion of the CNS: the brain.

Many Features of the Brain Can Be Seen by the Naked Eye

Given the importance of the adult human brain, it is
surprising that it weighs a mere 1400 grams, 2% of the
average body weight. However, even gross inspection
reveals that what the brain lacks in weight it makes
up for in intricacy. Figure 2.15 offers three views of the
human brain in standard orientations. These views
will be helpful in our future discussions. Viewed from
the side (Figure 2.15*a*) or from the top, the human
brain is dominated by the **cerebral hemispheres** (telencephalon), which sit atop and surround the brain
stem, which is continuous with the spinal cord.

The shape of the paired cerebral hemispheres is
the result of elaborate folding together of tissue. The
resulting ridges of tissue, called **gyri** (singular: gyrus),
are separated from each other by furrows called **sulci** (singular: sulcus). Such folding enormously increases the cerebral surface area; about two-thirds of
the cerebral surface is hidden in the depths of these
folds. Because the pattern of folding has many features that are common to all humans, the major divisions of the cerebral hemispheres can be labeled. The
major sectors of the cerebral hemispheres are the
frontal, **parietal**, **temporal**, and **occipital** regions, or
lobes. Some of the boundaries defined by folds are
clearly marked (for example, the lateral sulcus, or **Sylvian sulcus**, which demarcates the temporal lobe, and
the **central sulcus**, which divides frontal from parietal lobes, are quite prominent); others (those dividing parietal from occipital and occipital from temporal lobes) are less well defined. The outer shell of the
hemispheres is the **cerebral cortex** (the word "cortex" refers to the outermost layers of a structure),
sometimes referred to as simply the cortex.

Whereas the cerebral hemispheres seem to serve
"higher," more abstract functions—damage to the
cerebrum may deprive us of speech or sight—"lower" parts of the brain regulate respiration, heart rate,
and other basic functions. Occipital cortex receives information from the eyes and analyzes that information to give us sight. Most sound information reaches the temporal lobe, and damage there can impair
hearing. Touch information is integrated in a strip of
parietal cortex just behind the central sulcus (the
postcentral gyrus of the parietal lobe), while in front
of the central sulcus, the **precentral gyrus** of the
frontal lobe seems to be crucial for motor control. A
view from a midline position (Figure 2.16*b*) shows a
large bundle of axons called the **corpus callosum**,
which connects corresponding points of the right and
left cerebral hemispheres.

No matter what plane is used to section the brain
(see Box 2.2), two distinct shades of color are evident
(Figure 2.16). The whitish areas contain tracts that appear relatively white because of the lipid (fat) content
of myelin covering the axons. Darker gray areas are
dominated more by cell bodies, which are devoid of
myelin. Thus, the term **white matter** refers to bundles of nerve fibers, and the term **gray matter** refers
to areas that are rich in nerve cell bodies. The importance of this distinction between gray and white matter is clear in the study by Andreasen et al. (1993) noted in Box 1.1. In that study, the correlation between
intelligence and the volume of gray matter in the
cerebral hemispheres is much higher than that between intelligence and the volume of white matter.
By sectioning the brain, we can now begin to examine the internal portions of the nervous system.

The Brain Can Be Subdivided on the Basis of Its Development

The complex form of the adult human brain makes it
hard to understand why anatomists use terms the
way they do. For example, the part of your brain closest to the back of your head is labeled as part of the
forebrain. How can we make sense of this terminology? The clue to how the brain is subdivided lies in
the way it develops early in life. In Chapter 4 we will
consider brain development as a subject in its own
right. For now we will discuss brain development in
the context of categorizing brain structures.

In a very young embryo of any vertebrate, the
CNS looks like a tube. The walls of this neural tube
are made of cells, and the interior is filled with fluid.
A few weeks after conception, the human neural tube
begins to show three separate swellings at the head
end (Figure 2.17*a*): the **forebrain** (or prosencephalon),
the **midbrain** (or **mesencephalon**), and the **hind-**

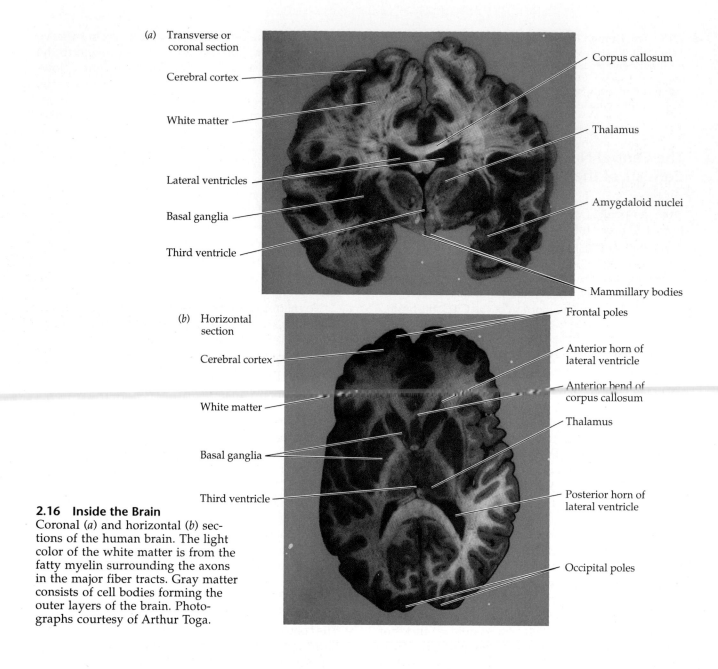

(a) Transverse or coronal section

Cerebral cortex

White matter

Lateral ventricles

Basal ganglia

Third ventricle

Corpus callosum

Thalamus

Amygdaloid nuclei

Mammillary bodies

(b) Horizontal section

Cerebral cortex

White matter

Basal ganglia

Third ventricle

Frontal poles

Anterior horn of lateral ventricle

Anterior bend of corpus callosum

Thalamus

Posterior horn of lateral ventricle

Occipital poles

2.16   Inside the Brain
Coronal (*a*) and horizontal (*b*) sections of the human brain. The light color of the white matter is from the fatty myelin surrounding the axons in the major fiber tracts. Gray matter consists of cell bodies forming the outer layers of the brain. Photographs courtesy of Arthur Toga.

brain (or rhombencephalon). (The term *encephalon*, meaning brain, comes from the Greek roots *en*, "in," and *kephalon*, "head.") Six weeks after conception, the forebrain and hindbrain have already developed clear subdivisions. At the very front of the developing brain is the **telencephalon**, which will become the cerebral hemispheres. The other part of the forebrain is the **diencephalon** (or "between brain"), which will include regions called the thalamus and hypothalamus. The midbrain comes next. Behind it the hindbrain has two divisions: the **metencephalon**, which will develop into the **cerebellum** ("little brain")

and the **pons** ("bridge"); and the **myelencephalon**, or **medulla.** The term **brain stem** usually refers to the midbrain, pons, and medulla combined. Figure 2.17*b* shows the positions of these main structures and their relative sizes in the human brain. Even when the brain achieves its adult form, it is still a fluid-filled tube, but one of very complicated shape.

Each of these five main sections (telencephalon, diencephalon, mesencephalon, metencephalon, and myelencephalon) can be subdivided in turn (Figure 2.17*c*). We can work our way from the largest, most general divisions at the left of the figure to more spe-

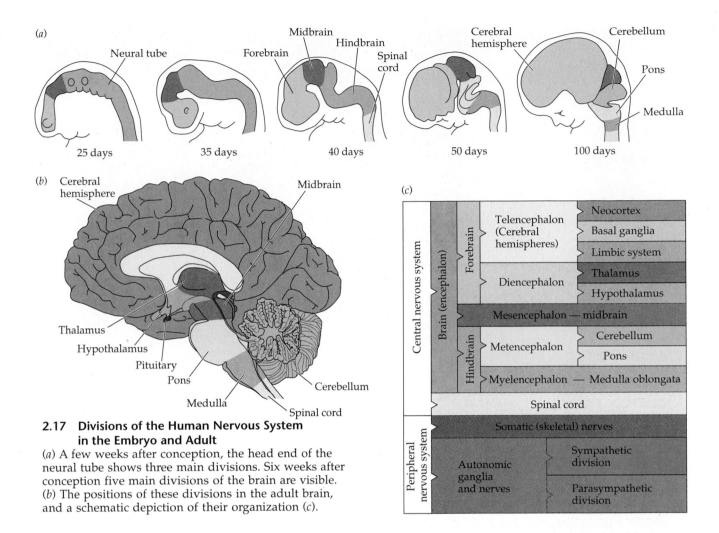

2.17 Divisions of the Human Nervous System in the Embryo and Adult
(a) A few weeks after conception, the head end of the neural tube shows three main divisions. Six weeks after conception five main divisions of the brain are visible. (b) The positions of these divisions in the adult brain, and a schematic depiction of their organization (c).

cific ones at the right. Within each region are aggregations of neurons called **nuclei** (singular: nucleus) and bundles of axons called **tracts.** (Recall that in the periphery, aggregations of neurons are called *ganglia,* and bundles of axons are called *nerves.*) Because these nuclei and tracts are recognizable from individual to individual, and often from species to species, they have names, too. You are probably more interested in the functions of all these parts of the brain than in their names, but each region serves more than one function, most functions are spread out through several structures, and ideas about function are constantly being revised by new data. Thus, having oriented you to the general organization of the brain, we will embark on a *brief* look at the functions of specific parts, leaving the detailed discussion for later chapters.

Now that you've seen both small- and large-scale views of the nervous system, you can refer to Table 2.2 to compare the actual sizes of some important neural structures.

Some Functional Descriptions of Brain Structures

Although we list simple, capsule statements about functions here, later chapters take them up more fully, so concentrate on understanding the physical layout of the parts rather than their functions. We'll look at each of the five basic parts of the brain in turn. Although there are some single structures around the midline, such as the corpus callosum, pineal gland, and pituitary gland (see Figure 2.15b), each of the structures we'll describe next is found in both the right and left sides of the brain.

Within the Cerebral Hemispheres Are the Basal Ganglia and the Limbic System

The **basal ganglia** include the **caudate nucleus,** **putamen,** and **globus pallidus** deep within the telencephalon, under the cerebral cortex (Figure 2.18a). The **amygdala** (Latin for "almond," which it resem-

Table 2.2

Some Neural Structures and the Units of Measurement and Magnifications Used to Study Them

	Structure	Sizes of some structures	Unit of measurement
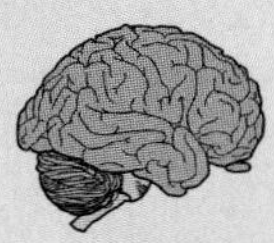	Whole brain	Adult human brain measures about 15 cm from front to back	1 centimeter (cm) = 10^{-2} meter (m)
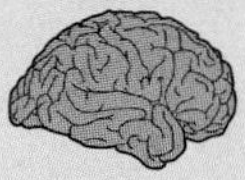	Cerebral cortex	Cortex of human brain is about 3 mm thick	1 millimeter (mm) = 10^{-3} m
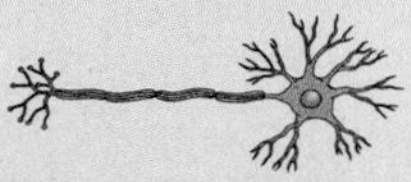	Nerve cells	Large neuron cell bodies are about 100 micrometers (μm) in diameter (0.1 mm)	0.1 mm = 10^{-4} m = 100 micrometers (μm, microns)
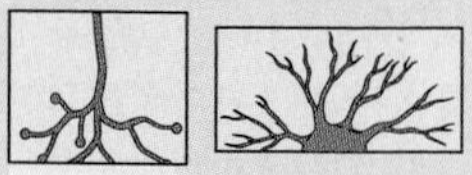	Parts of neurons	Large axons and dendrites are about 10 μm in diameter (0.01 mm)	0.01 mm = 10^{-5} m = 10 μm
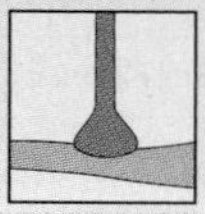	Synapse	An end bouton is about 1 μm in diameter	1 micrometer (μm) = 10^{-6} m
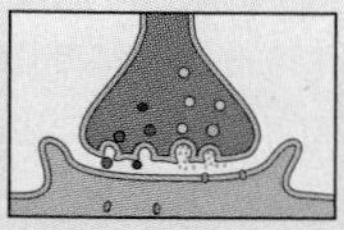	Synaptic cleft	The gap or cleft between neurons at a synapse is about 20 nanometers (nm) across	0.1 μm = 100 nanometer (nm) = 10^{-7} m
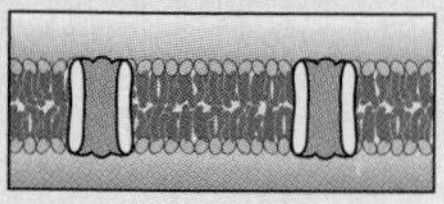	Neuronal membrane	A neuronal membrane is about 5 nm thick	10 nm = 10^{-8} m
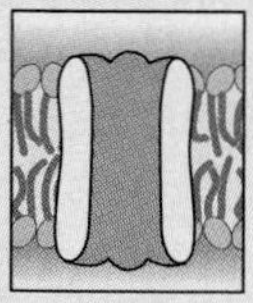	Ion channel	The diameter of an ion channel is about 0.5 nm	1 nm = 10^{-9} m

bles in shape) is embedded in the temporal lobe. These four nuclei (not really ganglia, despite the unfortunate name "basal ganglia") send axons back and forth to innervate one another, forming a neural system. The basal ganglia are very important in motor control, as we will see in Chapter 11.

The term **limbic system** is a rather loosely defined designation for a widespread group of brain nuclei (Figure 2.18*b*) that innervate each other to form a network intimately involved in mechanisms of emotion and learning. The **hippocampus** (Latin for "seahorse," which it resembles in shape) and **fornix** form two arcs under the surface of the hemispheres. Oth-er components of the limbic system include a strip of cortex called the **cingulate gyrus**, the amygdala (also a part of the basal ganglia), and the **olfactory bulb**. The rest of the limbic system is found in the diencephalon (which we discuss next), including the hypothalamus and the breast-shaped **mammillary bodies** (see Figure 2.15*c*).

The Diencephalon Is Divided into the Thalamus and Hypothalamus

The topmost portion of the diencephalon is the **thalamus**, a complex swirl of nuclei that act as go-betweens for the cerebral cortex. Almost all sensory in-

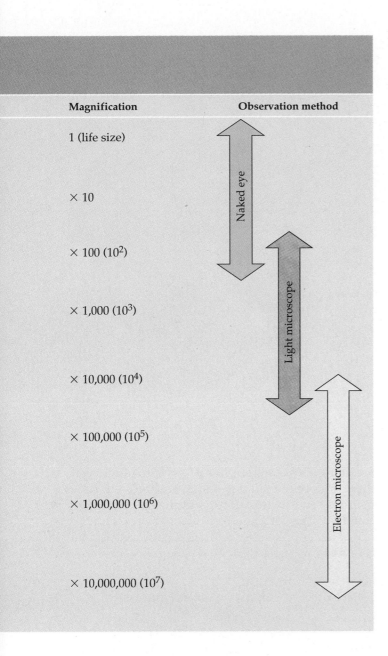

Magnification	Observation method
1 (life size)	
$\times$ 10	Naked eye
$\times$ 100 (10^2)	
$\times$ 1,000 (10^3)	Light microscope
$\times$ 10,000 (10^4)	
$\times$ 100,000 (10^5)	Electron microscope
$\times$ 1,000,000 (10^6)	
$\times$ 10,000,000 (10^7)	

The Midbrain Forms the Top of the Brain Stem

Within the midbrain are groups of neuronal cell bodies which send their axons out to form cranial nerves. For example, the cell bodies of motoneurons that send their axons to form the oculomotor nerve (III, controlling many eye movements) are clustered together in the midbrain, forming the oculomotor nucleus. Other such cranial nerve nuclei are found throughout the brain stem. Two pairs of bumps are visible on the dorsal surface of the midbrain—the more rostral pair are the **superior colliculi** (singular: superior colliculus), and the caudal pair are the **inferior colliculi**. The superior colliculi receive visual information; the inferior colliculi receive information about sound. Also found in the midbrain is a distributed network of neurons which are collectively referred to as the **reticular** ("net-like") **formation**. The reticular formation stretches from the midbrain down to the medulla. Many varied functions have been attributed to different parts of this loose aggregation of neurons, including sleep and arousal, temperature regulation, and motor control.

The Cerebellum Is Attached to the Pons

The lateral, midline, and basal views in Figure 2.15 show the cerebellum. Like the cerebral hemispheres, the cerebellum includes an elaborately folded surface sheet; in this case the folds are very close together. The arrangement of cells within the sheet is much simpler than in the cerebral cortex (Figure 2.19). A middle layer is composed of a single row of very large, multipolar neurons called **Purkinje cells**, after the anatomist who first described their elaborate fan-shaped dendritic patterns. All along the surface of these dendrites are numerous dendritic spines. An outer, "molecular" layer is composed of an orderly array of axons that runs parallel to the surface; hence they are called **parallel fibers**. In the depths beneath the Purkinje cells is a huge collection of very small **granule cells**, whose axons form the parallel fibers of the surface. The cerebellum plays a role in motor coordination and some types of learning.

Immediately below (ventral to) the cerebellum, contributing to the brain stem, is the **pons** (see Figure 2.15). The pons includes regions involved in motor control and sensory analysis, including several cranial nerve nuclei. Information from the ear first enters the brain in the pons. The pons also contains several groups of neurons which send their axons down to affect the spinal cord, primarily to regulate movement.

The Medulla Maintains Vital Body Functions

The medulla forms the bottom of the brain stem and marks the transition from brain stem to spinal cord.

formation enters the thalamus, where neurons send that information to the overlying cortex. The cortical cells in turn innervate the thalamus, perhaps to control which sensory information is passed through. Because it is under the thalamus, the second part of the diencephalon is known as the **hypothalamus**. The hypothalamus is relatively small but is packed with many distinct nuclei with vital functions. The hypothalamus has been implicated in hunger, thirst, temperature regulation, reproductive behaviors and much more. The hypothalamus also controls the pituitary gland, which in turn controls almost all hormone secretion, as we'll learn in Chapter 7.

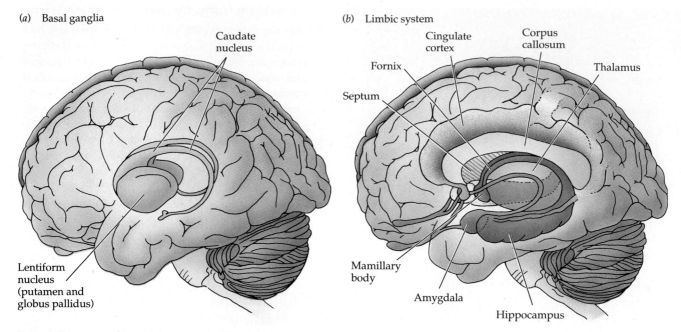

(a) Basal ganglia

Caudate nucleus

Lentiform nucleus (putamen and globus pallidus)

(b) Limbic system

Cingulate cortex

Corpus callosum

Fornix

Thalamus

Septum

Mamillary body

Amygdala

Hippocampus

2.18 Two Important Brain Systems
(a) The basal ganglia, which consist of caudate, putamen, and globus pallidus, are important in movement. (b) The limbic system—the hippocampus, thalamus, cingulate cortex, fornix, olfactory bulb, amygdala, and mammillary bodies—is important for emotion, learning, and memory.

Within the medulla are the XI and XII cranial nerve nuclei—cell bodies of neurons controlling the neck and tongue muscles, respectively. The reticular formation, which we first saw in the midbrain, stretches through the pons and ends in the medulla. The medulla also seems to contribute to the regulation of breathing and heart rate, so **lesions** (tissue damage) there are often fatal. Several groups of medullary neurons send their axons down the spinal cord to communicate with neurons there. Axons from the rest of the brain that reach down to affect the spinal cord must also pass through the medulla.

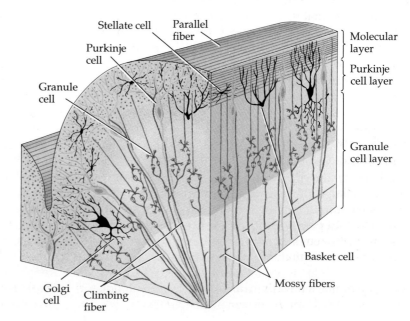

Stellate cell

Parallel fiber

Purkinje cell

Molecular layer

Purkinje cell layer

Granule cell

Granule cell layer

Basket cell

Golgi cell

Climbing fiber

Mossy fibers

2.19 Arrangement of Cells Within the Cerebellum
Large Purkinje cells dominate the cerebellum. Innervation between the various types forms a very consistent pattern. Cells depicted in black serve to inhibit the actions of other cells.

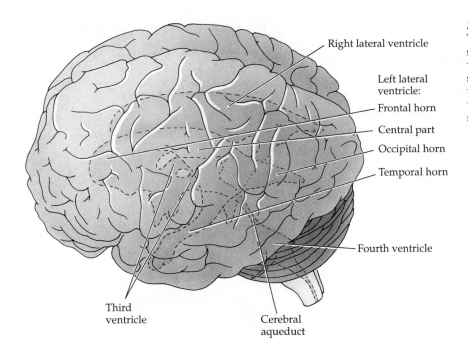

Right lateral ventricle

Left lateral ventricle:

Frontal horn

Central part

Occipital horn

Temporal horn

Fourth ventricle

Third ventricle

Cerebral aqueduct

2.20 The Cerebral Ventricles
This view of an adult human brain shows the position of the cerebral ventricles within the brain. Cerebrospinal fluid is made in the lateral ventricles, and exits from the fourth ventricle to surround the brain and spinal cord.

The Brain Is Well Protected and Has an Abundant Blood Supply

Within the bony skull and vertebrae, the brain and spinal cord are surrounded by three protective sheets of tissue called **meninges**. The outermost sheet is a tough envelope called the **dura mater** (from the Latin for "hard mother"). The innermost layer, called the **pia mater** (Latin for "tender mother"), adheres tightly to the surface of the brain and follows all its contours. (The term mater, "mother," reflects the medieval belief that these tissues gave birth to the brain.) The delicate, weblike membrane between the dura mater and pia mater is called the **arachnoid** ("spiderweblike"). Space within the arachnoid is filled with **cerebrospinal fluid (CSF)**, which is a clear, colorless liquid that supports and cushions the brain.

The Cerebral Ventricles Are Chambers Filled with Fluid

Inside the brain is a series of chambers filled with CSF (Figure 2.20). These cavities are known as the **ventricular system**. A highly vascular (full of blood vessels) portion of the lining of the ventricles, called the **choroid plexus**, secretes cerebrospinal fluid, essentially by removing blood cells from plasma. CSF has at least two main functions:

1. It acts mechanically as a shock absorber for the brain. The brain floats in CSF as the head moves.

Thus, movements of the head do not result in forceful shifting of the brain inside the skull cavity.

2. It also mediates between blood vessels and brain tissue in the exchange of materials, including nutrients.

Each hemisphere of the brain contains a **lateral ventricle** that has a complex shape. CSF is formed in the lateral ventricles and flows from them into the **third ventricle** which is located in the midline and down a narrow passage, to the **fourth ventricle**, which lies anterior to the cerebellum. Just below the cerebellum is a small aperture, through which CSF leaves the ventricular system to circulate over the outer surface of the brain and spinal cord. CSF is absorbed back into the circulatory system through large veins beneath the top of the skull.

The Brain Has an Elaborate Vascular System

Because the brain works intensely, it has a strong metabolic demand for its fuels: oxygen and glucose. Since the brain has very little reserve of either fuel, it depends critically on its blood supply to supply them. Blood is delivered to the brain via two main channels, the carotid arteries and the vertebral arteries.

The common **carotid arteries** ascend the left and right sides of the neck. The internal carotid artery enters the skull and branches into anterior and middle cerebral arteries (Figure 2.21), which supply blood to large regions of the cerebral hemispheres. The **vertebral arteries** ascend along the bony vertebrae and enter the base of the skull. They join together to form

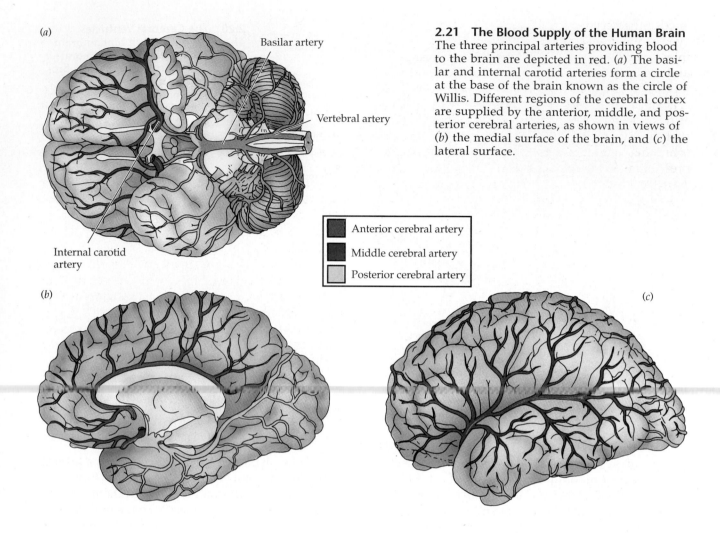

(a)

Basilar artery

Vertebral artery

Internal carotid artery

2.21 The Blood Supply of the Human Brain
The three principal arteries providing blood to the brain are depicted in red. (*a*) The basilar and internal carotid arteries form a circle at the base of the brain known as the circle of Willis. Different regions of the cerebral cortex are supplied by the anterior, middle, and posterior cerebral arteries, as shown in views of (*b*) the medial surface of the brain, and (*c*) the lateral surface.

Anterior cerebral artery

Middle cerebral artery

Posterior cerebral artery

(b)

(c)

the **basilar artery**, which runs along the ventral surface of the brain stem. Branches of the basilar artery supply blood to the brain stem and to posterior portions of the cerebral hemispheres. At the base of the brain, the carotid and basilar arteries join to form a structure called the circle of Willis. This joining of vascular paths may provide some needed "backup" if any of the main arteries to the brain should be damaged or blocked by disease. The common term "stroke" refers to changes in the flow of blood in the brain produced by blockage or rupture of blood vessels, or by reduced flow due to heart impairment. Stroke is among the most common life-threatening disorders of humans.

The site of the delivery of nutrients and other substances to brain cells and the removal of waste products from them is the very fine capillaries that branch off from small arteries. This exchange in the brain is quite different from exchanges between blood vessels

and cells in other body organs. In the brain, capillaries offer much greater resistance to the passage of large molecules than do capillaries elsewhere. The brain is thus protected from exposure to some substances found in the blood. We refer to this protective mechanism as the **blood–brain barrier**. This barrier occurs because the cells that make up the walls of capillaries (endothelial cells) fit together very tightly in the brain, so they do not readily let large molecules through. The blood–brain barrier may have evolved to protect the brain from substances that other organs can tolerate.

Neural Systems: Functional Aggregates of Widespread Neurons

In our look at the structures of the brain we began with a small-scale view at the level of cells and then moved to a much larger scale—the overall appearance of the nervous system as seen by the unaided eye. We noted several neuron groups that seemed to interact with one another, sending their axons back and forth to exchange information. This approach represents an intermediate anatomical view—the level at which aggregates of cell groups can be described as neural systems. We have described briefly several such systems; the organization of the cerebral cortex is another neural system that we must consider in preparation for future chapters.

The Cerebral Cortex Is an Example of a Neural System

Neuroscientists have long argued that understanding human cognition depends on unraveling the structure and fundamental functions of the cerebral cortex. In fact, by accepting electrical silence of the cortex as a criterion for defining death, many governments now define human life in terms of the workings of the cerebral cortex. Within this folded sheet of cells, there are about 50 to 100 billion neurons—the majority of the neurons in the human brain. If the cerebral cortex were unfolded, it would occupy an area of about 2000 cm^2 (315 square inches) or a square about 45 cm (18 inches) on a side (Hubel and Wiesel, 1979). How are these cells arranged? How do the arrangements allow for particular feats of human information processing?

The neurons of the cerebral cortex are arranged in distinct layers—a laminar form of organization. Cell body and axon stains, such as those illustrated in Figure 2.22a, show six distinct layers in most of the cerebral cortex. (In the next chapter we'll discuss the three types of cerebral cortex.) Each **cortical layer** is distinct because it consists either of groups of cells of particular sizes, or of patterns of dendrites or axons. For example, the outermost layer, layer 1, is distinct because it has few cell bodies, while layer 3 stands

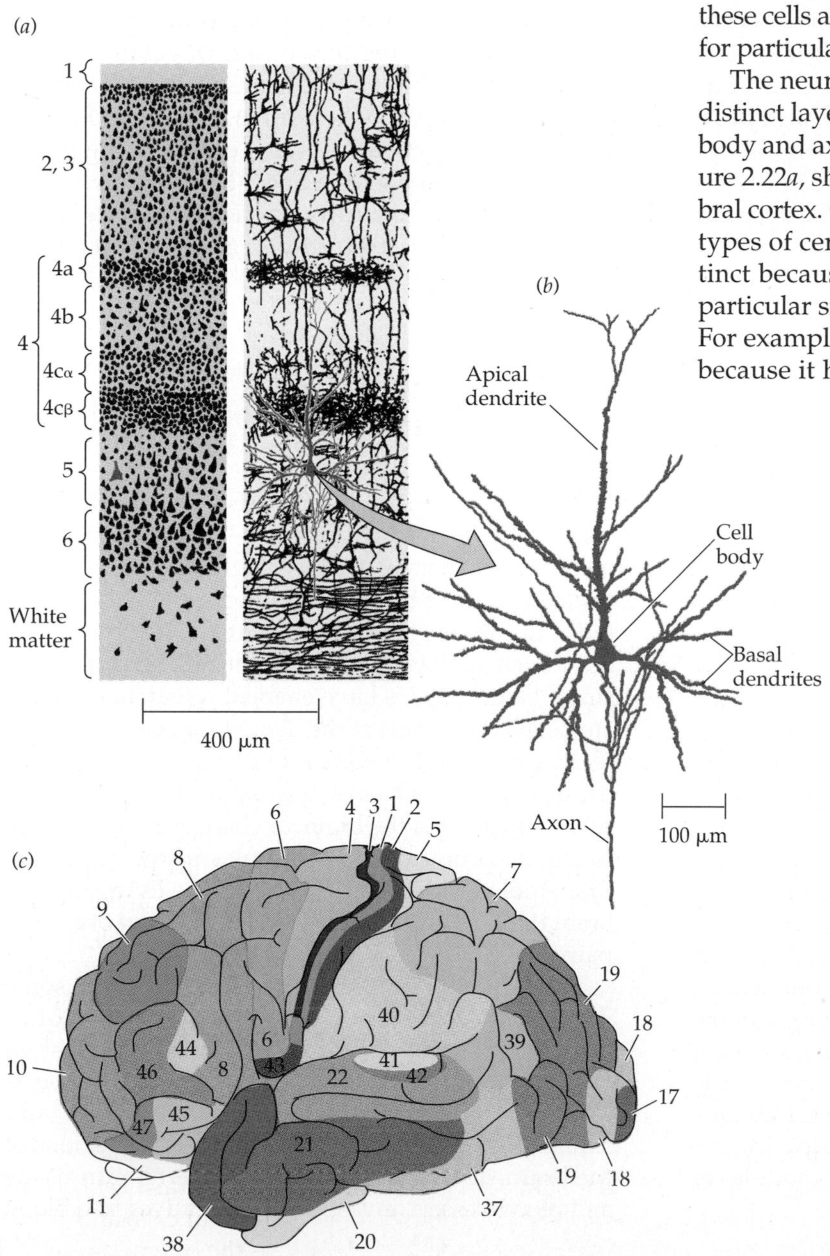

2.22 Layers of the Cerebral Cortex (*a*) The six layers of cortex can be distinguished with stains that reveal all cell bodies (left), or with stains that reveal a few neurons in their entirety. (*b*) A single pyramidal cell enlarged about 200 times. (*c*) Regions of the cortex as delineated in a classical cytoarchitectonic map. *c* after Brodmann, 1909.

out because of the many neurons with large cell bodies. The relative thickness of the layers varies across the cerebral cortex, suggesting a division of the cortex into subregions defined in terms of small differences in the aggregation of nerve cells. Researchers have developed maps of these subregions of the cerebral cortex based on differences in cell density, sizes and shapes of cortical neurons and intracortical connection patterns. Figure 2.22*c* is a map based on these criteria. Divisions based on these structural criteria also seem to define functional zones such as sensory and motor zones.

The most prominent kind of neuron in the cerebral cortex—the **pyramidal cell**—usually has its cell bodies in layers 3 to 5 (Figure 2.22*b*). One dendrite of each pyramidal cell (called the **apical dendrite**) usually extends to the outermost surface of the cortex. The pyramidal cell also has several dendrites (called **basal dendrites**) that spread out horizontally from the cell body. Frequently neurons of the cortex appear to be arranged in columns perpendicular to the layers, as we'll see in the next section.

The variation in thickness of the different layers of cerebral cortex is related to differences in their functions. Incoming sensory fibers from the thalamus terminate especially in layer 4, so this layer is particularly prominent in regions that represent sensory functions. In fact, in part of the visual cortex in the occipital lobe, layer 4 is so prominent that it appears to the naked eye as a stripe in sections cut through this area. This is why this part of the visual cortex is known as striate ("striped") cortex. Fibers that leave the cerebral cortex arise especially from layer 3, which is particularly prominent in the main motor regions of the cortex. Layer 3 is also characterized by especially large pyramidal cells.

Cortical columns.   Some brain regions have distinctive geometrical arrangements of cells that can function as information processing units. Visible in the cortex are columns of nerve cells that extend through the entire thickness of the cortex, from the white matter to the surface. In humans these columns are about 3 mm deep and about 400 to 1000 µm in diameter. Within such a column, the functional connections among cells (synaptic connections) are mainly in the vertical direction, but there are also some horizontal connections. Mountcastle (1979) calls these units **macrocolumns** and estimates that there are about a million of them in the human cerebral cortex. Macrocolumns are thought to be the functional modules of cortical operations.

The macrocolumns in turn are composed of what Mountcastle calls **minicolumns**. On the average, such columns are about 30 µm in diameter in the human cortex, and there are an estimated half billion of them. Rockel, Hiorns, and Powell (1974) have counted the number of cells per minicolumn in five species, from mouse to human, and in several cortical regions. These authors assert that, regardless of species and of cortical region, a minicolumn contains about 100 to 120 neurons. Swindale (1990) suggests that there is much greater variation in the appearance of columns than this model proposes.

Connections among cortical regions are mainly tracts of axons (Figure 2.23). Some of these connections are short pathways that loop beneath the cortex to nearby cortical regions; others travel longer distances through the cerebral hemispheres. The largest of these pathways is the corpus callosum, through which run connections between corresponding points on the two hemispheres. Longer links between cortical regions involve multisynaptic chains of neurons that loop through subcortical regions such as thalamus and basal ganglia.

Today We Can Look into the Living Human Brain

Most of the material that anatomists work with is preserved slices and whole brains—postmortem specimens. Researchers have long sought ways to peer into the *living* human brain to see structures and how they work in different behavioral states. This dream has now been realized. Major technical developments since the mid-1970s have enabled researchers to create detailed portraits of the living human brain. These techniques involve elaborate computer analysis of measures such as X rays, the distribution of radioactive substances in the brain, or changes in the electromagnetic properties of molecules in the brain. All these tools yield intimate views of the living human brain that greatly aid clinical assessment of brain impairments and contribute to basic research.

Let's review some earlier techniques to gain some perspective on these newer developments. An ordinary X-ray of the head reveals an outline of the skull with little or no definition of brain tissue. Since the X-ray density of virtually all parts of the brain is very similar, there is very little contrast between regions of the brain. To provide contrast between brain tissue and blood vessels, investigators inject dyes into blood

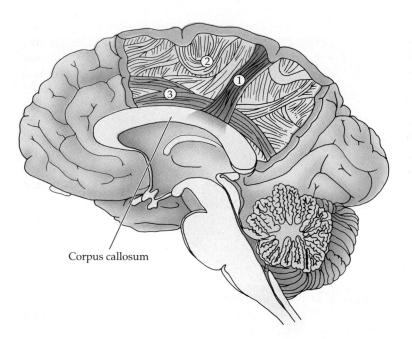

2.23 Cortical Tract Connections among Cortical Regions
Long projection fibers run to and from the cerebral cortex. (1) Some go through the corpus callosum connecting homologous regions of the two hemispheres. (2) Short tracts arch between nearby areas of the cortex. (3) Several long tracts run in an anterior–posterior direction.

Corpus callosum

vessels. The resultant X-ray pictures—called **angiograms**—provide an outline of the vascular paths of the brain and are useful in describing vascular disease, such as stroke.

Newer Imaging Techniques

Developments in computers and computer programs have enabled us to integrate many different X-ray views into a portrait of the brain that resembles a cross section of the brain. These portraits are referred to as tomograms (from the Greek *tomos*, "crosscut" or "section," and *gramma*, "record" or "picture"). **Computerized axial tomograms (CAT)** or **CT** (computerized tomography) **scans** involve moving an X-ray source in an arc around the head. The picture is obtained by placing the patient on a table and inserting his head into the middle of a doughnut-shaped ring (Figure 2.24). An X-ray source is moved in a circular path around the head; at each position it delivers a small amount of X-radiation, which passes through the head. How much of this radiation is absorbed within the head depends on the density of the tissue. A ring of detectors opposite the X-ray source analyzes the amount of X-radiation that has passed through the head. The X-ray tube and detectors are then moved to a new position, and the process is repeated until a composite picture can be constructed by a computer on the basis of the many X-ray views from different angles around the head. This procedure allows the very small differences in X-ray density of the different regions of the brain to be greatly

accentuated. Figure 2.24*a* shows a typical CT scan of one level of the brain. Each picture element (or pixel) in the final portrait is the result of a complex mathematical analysis of this small brain region viewed from many different angles. The spatial resolution of this technique has now been improved to the point where relatively small changes, such as shrinkage of a gyrus, can be visualized. Figure 2.24*a* illustrates the use of CT in the study of the behavioral effects of stroke. This technique has enabled observation of cerebral cortical changes in Alzheimer's disease, schizophrenia, dyslexia, and many other disorders.

CT has been a most valuable tool, although a newer approach, **magnetic resonance imaging (MRI)**, has become a robust competitor. MRI generates pictures that reveal some structural details in the living brain without exposure to X rays (Andreasen, 1989). MRI involves the use of radio waves and other magnetic energy. The patient lies within a large magnet (Figure 2.24*b*), and the molecular effect of applied magnetic fields is registered by a coil detector whose successive outputs are analyzed by computer. The resultant image (Figure 2.24*b*) can display extremely small changes in the brain, such as the loss of myelin around groups of axons, a symptom characteristic of demyelinating diseases. Using this technique, structural abnormalities have been studied intensively in humans of all ages and conditions.

Images of the physiological *functioning* of the brain were first provided by a technique called

(*a*)   Computerized tomography (CT)   Normal   Stroke victim

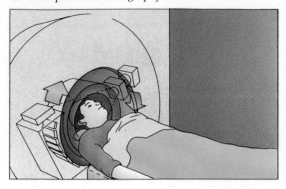 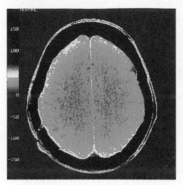 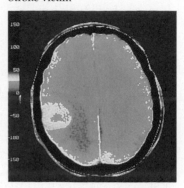

(*b*)   Magnetic resonance imaging (MRI)   Horizontal view   Coronal view

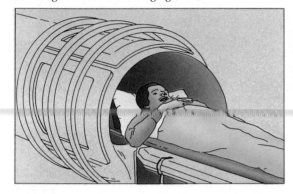 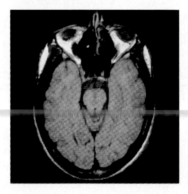 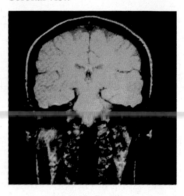

(*c*)   Positron emission tomography (PET) Normal   Alzheimer's patient

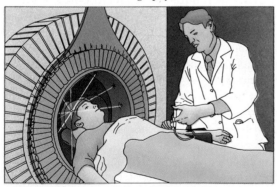 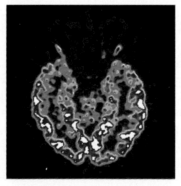 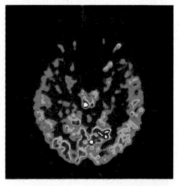

2.24   Visualizing the Living Human Brain
The procedures (*left*) and images obtained (*middle and right*) from three important brain imaging techniques. (*a*) CT scans can be used in studying brain organization and language. The CT scans shown here are from a normal patient and from a stroke patient; the stroke lesion is visible as a large yellow area. (*b*) MRI images are notable for their great detail, as seen in these horizontal and coronal sections of a normal human brain. Note the clarity in the definition of gyri of the cerebral cortex. (*c*) PET scans show levels of metabolic activity in the brain, as in these images from a normal human and an Alzheimer's patient; note the greater level of activity in the normal brain.

positron emission tomography (PET). To obtain images of the functional state of the brain, radioactive chemicals are injected into the blood vessels. These radioisotopes travel to the brain, and their emission can be assessed by detectors outside the body (Figure 2.24c). Computerized analysis of these data reveals the differential uptake and use of the chemicals in various brain regions. The most commonly used substance is a type of radioactive glucose that is taken up into different brain regions according to their levels of metabolic activity (Figure 2.24c). A color transform of this information yields a striking picture that highlights areas of intense metabolic response (Holcomb et al., 1989). Using this technique, we can generate metabolic maps of

the brain during states such as attention, movements, responses to sensory stimuli, and decision making. Special techniques can identify brain regions that are activated by specific stimuli or tasks (Box 2.3). In addition, we can identify regions that are abnormal in metabolic responses even if they are structurally intact.

Each technique that we have described here has limitations: It is too slow (has poor temporal resolution), or not sharp enough (has poor spatial resolution), or too costly. But improved techniques are rapidly overcoming these problems. The progress of brain imaging is reminiscent of the progress of photography. When the first photographs were taken in about the 1850s, they required exposures of several

Box 2.3
Isolating Specific Brain Activity

Many illustrations in this and later chapters show positron emission tomography (PET) scans of brain activity specifically related to brain disorders or cognitive processes. Usually most of the brain is active, so isolating specific activity requires special procedures.

The PET scan at the upper left (labeled Visual Stimulation) was made while a person looked at a fixation point surrounded by a flickering checkerboard ring; the scan next to it (Control) was made while a person looked at a fixation point alone. Comparing the two, it is hard to see differences, but subtracting the control values from the stimulation values yields a difference figure such as that shown at the upper right (Difference); in this scan, it is easy to see that the main difference in activity is in the posterior part of the brain (the visual cortex).

The middle row of PET scans are difference images for five individuals who performed the same two Stimulation and Control tasks. Averaging these five scans results in the mean differ-

ence image for all five subjects shown at the bottom. Such images yield more reliable results than individual images, but lacks some of the specificity seen in the individual images.

All the PET images shown in this book are difference images, usually made from scans of a sin-

gle individual's brain. When you see brain function images in this book or in the popular press, note whether they are direct scans or difference images; if the latter, note whether they show values for an individual or for the mean of a group. (PET scans courtesy of Marcus Raichle.)

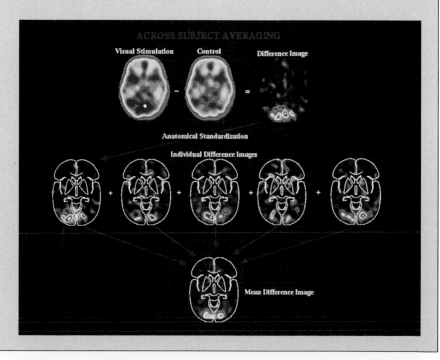

minutes (their temporal resolution was poor), the images were grainy (they had poor spatial resolution), and the pictures showed no color. Gradually photographic film became faster, so that now it can freeze a hummingbird's wing or a bullet in flight; the grain became finer, permitting sharp, detailed pictures; and full-color pictures are possible.

Poor temporal resolution has been a particular problem for CT, MRI, and PET scans. A recent development, however, a computer-enhanced form of CT, known as ultrafast CT (or electron beam tomography), allows a complete image to be made in 50 milliseconds. In the case of MRI, much greater speed has now been achieved using a technique called **functional MRI (fMRI)** or fast MRI. This technique is based on the use of high-powered, rapidly oscillating magnetic field gradients and improved, powerful computation. A refinement of fMRI technique now allows scientists to detect oxygen consumption by active brain regions, providing an fMRI portrait of activity. PET and fMRI scans have become critical tools in deciphering information processing in human brains. We will see many examples of their use in later chapters.

Summary

1. The nervous system is extensive, monitoring, regulating, and modulating the activities of all parts and organs of the body.

2. Nerve cells, or neurons, are the basic units of the nervous system. The typical neuron of most vertebrate species has three main parts: (1) the cell body, which contains the nucleus; (2) dendrites, which receive information; and (3) an axon, which carries impulses from the neuron. Because of the varieties of functions they serve, neurons are extremely varied in size, shape, and chemical activity.

3. Neurons make functional contacts with other neurons, or with muscles or glands, at specialized junctions called synapses. At most synapses a chemical transmitter liberated by the presynaptic terminal diffuses across the synaptic cleft and binds to special receptor molecules in the postsynaptic membrane.

4. The axon is the specialized output zone of the nerve cell and is generally tubular, branching at the end into many collaterals. Axonal transport refers to the movement of materials within the axon.

5. Glial cells serve many functions, including metabolism of transmitters, production of myelin sheaths around axons, exchange of nutrients and other materials with neurons, and removal of cellular debris.

6. The nervous system of vertebrates is divided into a central and a peripheral nervous system.

7. The central nervous system (CNS) consists of the brain and spinal cord. The main divisions of the brain can be seen most clearly in the embryo. These divisions are the forebrain (telencephalon and diencephalon); the midbrain, or mesencephalon; and the hindbrain (metencephalon and myelencephalon).

8. The peripheral nervous system includes cranial nerves, spinal nerves, and autonomic ganglia. The autonomic nervous system consists of the sympathetic nervous system, which tends to activate the body for action, and the parasympathetic nervous system, which tends to have an effect opposite to that of the sympathetic system.

9. The human brain is dominated by the cerebral hemispheres, which include the cerebral cortex, an extensive sheet of folded tissue. The cerebral cortex is responsible for higher order functions such as vision, language, and memory. Other neural systems include the basal ganglia, which regulate movement; the limbic system, which controls emotional behaviors; and the cerebellum, which aids coordination and some kinds of learning.

10. The brain and spinal cord are protected by a covering of tissue called meninges and by cerebrospinal fluid (CSF), which surrounds and infiltrates (via cerebral ventricles) the brain to act as a shock absorber.

11. The blood system of the brain is an elaborate array of blood vessels that deliver nutrients and other substances to the brain. The blood vessels of the brain provide a barrier to the flow of large, potentially harmful molecules into the brain.

12. New techniques make it possible to visualize the anatomy of the living human brain and regional metabolic differences using external monitoring devices. These techniques include computerized axial tomography (CT scans), positron emission tomography (PET scans), and magnetic resonance imaging (MRI).

Recommended Reading

Bolam, J. P. 1993. *Experimental Neuroanatomy: A Practical Approach.* Oxford University Press, New York.

Brodal, P. 1992. *The Central Nervous System: Structure and Function.* Oxford University Press, New York.

Martin, J. H. 1989. *Neuroanatomy: Text and Atlas.* Elsevier, Amsterdam.

Paxinos, G. (ed.) 1990. *The Human Nervous System.* Academic Press, San Diego, CA.

Porter, R. (ed.) 1991. *Exploring Brain Functional Anatomy with Positron Tomography.* Ciba Foundation Symposium 163. Wiley-Liss, New York.

Posner, M. I. and Raichle, M. E. 1994. *Images of Mind.* Scientific American Library, New York.

Shepherd, G. 1991. *Foundations of the Neuron Doctrine.* Oxford University Press, New York.

Stewart, M. G. 1992. *Quantitative methods in neuroanatomy.* Wiley-Liss, New York.

Alexis Rockman, *The Bounty*, 1991

- *Why Study Other Species?*

- *How Can We Find Out How Closely Related Two Species Are?*

- *Comparative Methods Help in Studying the Biological Mechanisms of Behavior*

- *Nervous Systems Differ Widely in Structure*

- *Relating the Evolution of Vertebrate Brains to Changes in Behavior*

- *Applications of Comparative Research*

Comparative and Evolutionary Perspectives on the Nervous System and Behavior

CHAPTER

3

Orientation

In this chapter we consider the intriguing story of how brains have evolved in relation to behavior. Research on this topic involves the study of many species of animals, both extant and extinct. Since we share many biological and behavioral features with all other animals, it is not surprising that the search for understanding ourselves leads us to study apes, monkeys, carnivores, rodents, birds, and amphibians. The brains of all these vertebrates reveal the same basic plan as ours, although in some ways theirs are simpler and in some ways theirs differ distinctively. The quest to understand the nervous system has also led to the study of animals that are quite different from us—invertebrates, and even single-celled animals. But it would be a tall order to describe the nervous systems of all the different kinds of animals in this world. By some estimates the insects alone—buzzing, crawling, and flying about us—account for as many as 30 million species. Describing, cataloging, and understanding the relationships between the nervous system and behavior in even a small fraction of Earth's inhabitants would be an awesome (and dull) task unless we had some rationale beyond mere completeness. But as we'll see, studying and comparing well-chosen species throws much light on the principles of organization of nervous systems.

Why Study Other Species?

One old-fashioned reason for comparing species was human-centered, based on the question, Why does the human being end up on top of the animal order? This human-centered perspective was properly criticized because it implicitly pictured other animals as "little humans," a view that no modern scientists see as a valid basis for comparison. Contemporary studies of human lineage consider comparative studies as part of a story of evolutionary history—the **phylogeny** of humans. A phylogeny (from the Greek *phylo*, "tribe, kind," and *gen-*, "to produce or bear") is the evolutionary history of a particular group of organisms; it is often represented as a "family tree" that shows which species may have given rise to others. Comparisons among extant animals, coupled with fragmentary but illuminating data from fossil remains, yield information and stimulate concepts about the history of the human body and brain and the forces that shaped them. Figure 3.1 shows a recent attempt to reconstruct the family tree of apes and humans. This tree shows humans and chimpanzees as being closer to each other than either is to the gorilla. Not all investigators agree about the actual branching pattern, but all agree that these species are closely related. We will say more about phylogenetic trees a little later in the chapter.

No animal is simply sitting around providing researchers with the details of human biological history; rather, each species is busily engaged in satisfying its needs for survival, which must include an active interchange with its environment. Species with varying biological histories show different solutions to the dilemmas of survival and reproduction. In many cases, adaptations to particular ecological niches can be related to differences in brain structure. Understanding the neural structures and mechanisms mediating specific behaviors in various other animals can provide a new perspective and intriguing clues about the neural bases of human behavior. For example, some relatively simple animals show changes in behavior that arise from experience. Understanding the changes in the nervous system of these simpler animals that permit memory formation and storage is providing insights into the workings of more complex animals, including human beings, as we will see in Chapter 18.

How Can We Find Out How Closely Related Two Species Are?

The attempt to construct the "family trees" of animals raises the question, How can we find out how

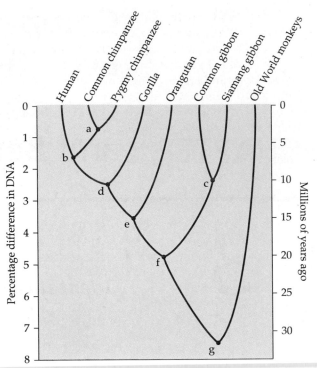

3.1 Family Tree of Apes and Humans

This tree was derived from measurements of differences between pairs of species in samples of their genetic material—molecules of deoxyribonucleic acid (DNA). To see how different two species are in their genetic endowments, trace the lines from the two members of the pair to the point that connects them, and match the point with the scale to the left. For example, the line from humans and the line from the chimpanzees converge at point b, so the DNA of humans and of chimpanzees differs by only about 1.6%. The DNA of humans and of chimpanzees, in turn, differs from that of the gorilla (point d) by about 2.3%. The scale to the right gives the estimated number of millions of years ago since any pair of species shared a common ancestor. Thus, humans and the chimpanzees diverged from a common ancestor about 7 million years ago. After Sibley and Ahlquist, 1987; Sibley, Comstock, and Ahlquist, 1990; Goodman et al., 1990; Horai et al., 1995.

closely related two species are? Some basic knowledge of this topic is important for the examples that we will consider later in this chapter and in other chapters.

Early Views of Classification and Evolution

Probably people have always classified the animals they saw around them and realized that some forms resemble each other more closely than others. The heightened contact between Europe and the Americas beginning late in the fifteenth century brought many new kinds of animals to the attention of scholars and led to questions about how best to classify them. In the mid-eighteenth century the Swedish biologist Carolus Linnaeus proposed the basic system we use today. In Linnaeus's system each species is assigned two names, the first name identifying the genus and the second name indicating the species. Both names are always italicized, and the genus name is capitalized. Thus, the modern human species is *Homo sapiens;* Table 3.1 shows the classifications of some other species. The different levels of classification in Table 3.1 are illustrated and defined in Figure 3.2. Each successively broader category above the species level takes in more and more animals, so the members of the higher categories show increasingly greater variety. Linnaeus and his immediate successors classified animals mainly on the basis of gross anatomical similarities and differences; classification of animals did not at the start imply anything about evolution or common ancestry.

Until about 200 years ago, it was generally believed that each species had been created separately. Then, about the time of Linnaeus, some naturalists, students of animal life and structure, began to have doubts. For example, in the 1760s the French naturalist Georges Louis Leclerc de Buffon wrote his *Nat-*

ural History of Animals, which contained a clear statement of the possibility of evolution:

> As [Buffon] studied animals, he observed that the limb bones of all mammals, no matter what their way of life, are remarkably similar in many details. If they had been specifically created for different ways of locomotion, Buffon reasoned, they should have been built upon different plans rather than all being modifications of a single plan. He also noticed that the legs of certain animals, such as pigs, have toes that never touch the ground and appear to be of no use. Buffon found it difficult to explain the presence of these seemingly useless small toes by special creation. Both of these troubling facts could be explained if mammals had not been specially created in their present forms but had been modified from a common ancestor. Buffon therefore suggested that pigs have two functionless toes because they inherited them from ancestors in which the toes were fully formed and functional (Purves, Orians, and Heller, 1995:12–13).

The idea of evolution slowly became more acceptable as other naturalists adopted it and as geologists showed in the first half of the nineteenth century that the Earth had been undergoing changes for millions of years. The fossils discovered early in the nineteenth century and their inclusion in the Linnaean system were additional evidence for evolution. But a

Table 3.1

Classification of Some Species of Animals

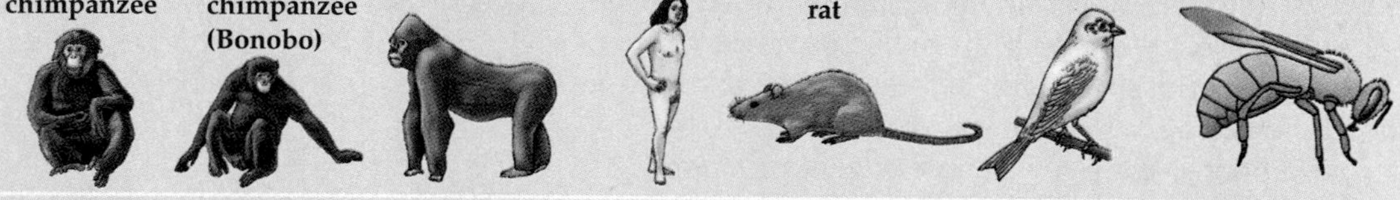

TAXONOMIC CATEGORY	Common chimpanzee	Pygmy chimpanzee (Bonobo)	Gorilla	Human	Common rat	Canary	Honeybee
Kingdom	Animalia	Animalia	Animalia	Animalia	Animalia	Animalia	Animalia
Phylum	Chordata	Chordata	Chordata	Chordata	Chordata	Chordata	Arthropoda
Class	Mammalia	Mammalia	Mammalia	Mammalia	Mammalia	Aves	Insecta
Order	Primates	Primates	Primates	Primates	Rodentia	Passeriformes	Hymenoptera
Family	Pongidae	Pongidae	Pongidae	Hominidae	Muridae	Fringillidae	Apidae
Genus	Pan	Pan	Gorilla	Homo	Rattus	Serinus	Apis
Species	*Pan troglodytes*	*Pan paniscus*	*Gorilla gorilla*	*Homo sapiens*	*Rattus norvegicus*	*Serinus canaria*	*Apis mellifera*

plausible *mechanism* for evolution was lacking. Early in the nineteenth century the French naturalist Jean-Baptiste de Lamarck promoted the idea of evolution and proposed that evolution occurred through the gradual accumulation of characteristics acquired by individual animals throughout life as they exercised and stretched their bodies. But this idea would prove to be incompatible with later discoveries about genetic inheritance. Half a century after Lamarck, in 1859, Charles Darwin and Alfred Russel Wallace announced the hypothesis of **evolution by natural selection.** Darwin and Wallace each had hit upon the idea independently, and had furnished much evidence to support it. The hypothesis was based on three main observations and one important inference. The facts were these: (1) individuals of a given species are not identical; (2) some of this variation is heritable (that is, can be inherited); and (3) not all offspring survive. The inference was that the variations among individuals affect the probabilities that they will survive and reproduce.

Charles Darwin
(1809–1882)

Alfred Russell Wallace
(1823–1913)

Darwin knew about variability from his studies of many species of plants and animals. As a pigeon fancier, he saw close parallels between artificial selection by breeders, which can produce differences in a few generations, and selection in nature, which may be less sharply defined but which can work over many generations. The concept of evolution by natural selection has become one of the major organizing principles in all the life sciences, directing the study of behavior and its mechanisms as well as the study of morphology (form and structure).

Newer Methods Aid in Classifying Animals and Inferring Evolution

The field of **taxonomy,** (from the Greek *taxis,* "arrange, classify") or classification, of animals, is a continuing endeavor. Taxonomists are challenged as previously unknown animals are discovered, as new

KINGDOM. All living beings can be divided into five kingdoms: **animals**, plants, fungi, bacteria, and protists.

    Animalia. Approximately 1 million species of animals are known. The full total has been estimated to be as high as 30 million.

PHYLUM (plural: phyla). The main—and most inclusive—subdivision of a kingdom; a group of similar, related classes. Some phyla are **Chordata**, Mollusca, and Arthropoda. Chordata differ from the other phyla by having an internal skeleton.

    Chordata. Approximately 40,000 species

CLASS. The main subdivision of a phylum; a group of similar, related orders. Some classes within the phylum Chordata are **Mammalia**, Aves (birds), and Reptilia. Mammals are characterized by production of milk by the female mammary glands and by hair for body covering.

    Mammalia. Approximately 4300 species

ORDER. The main subdivision of a class; a group of similar, related families. Some orders of the class Mammalia are **Carnivora** (meat eaters such as dogs, cats, bears, weasels, etc.) and the Primates (humans, monkeys, and apes).

    Carnivora. Approximately 235 species

FAMILY. The main subdivision of an order; a group of similar, related genera. Some families in the order Carnivora are **Canidae** (dogs, foxes, and related genera) and Felidae (domestic cats, lions, panthers, and related genera). Family names always end in -idae.

    Canidae. Approximately 35 species

GENUS. The main subdivision of a family; a group of similar, related species. Some genera in the family Canidae are *Canis* (dogs, coyotes, two species of wolves, four species of jackals) and *Vulpes* (ten species of foxes).

    Canis. 8 species

SPECIES. The basic (most specific) unit of taxonomic classification, consisting of a population or set of populations of closely related and similar organisms capable of interbreeding. The domestic dog is the species *Canis familiaris.* There are about 400 breeds of dogs, all considered to belong to one species.

    Canis familiaris

3.2 Linnaean Classification of the Domestic Dog

techniques become available, and as new concepts arise. There are disagreements about how some species are classified and about the best overall methods of classification. For example, some of the relationships among the apes and humans are being debated. You may have noticed that Figure 3.1 and Table 3.1 differ in their placement of human beings. Figure 3.1, based on differences between samples of DNA, shows the chimpanzees closer to humans than to gorillas in their genetic endowment; Table 3.1, based on bodily measurements, puts both the chimpanzees and gorillas in the family Pongidae (the great apes), whereas humans are placed in their own family, the Hominidae. The difference between these two classifications of primates remains to be resolved.

In addition to the patterns in gross anatomy that Linnaeus used, more recent developments help us classify animals and make inferences about their evolution. One is the recognition of fossils as evidence to trace the families of many living species into the remote past and to clarify some classifications. This fossil record has been invaluable, but it is still very incomplete; important fossils are being discovered every year. The fossil record also reveals many extinct species. For example, it is estimated that since birds first evolved about 150 million years ago, a total of about 150,000 species of birds have existed, but today there are only about 9,000 living species (Sibley and Ahlquist, 1990).

A much more recent development in classification is molecular techniques that allow us to study genetic material and to measure genetic variation with precision. Analysis of genetic material—fragments of molecules of deoxyribonucleic acid (DNA)—from many species has confirmed many classifications and improved others. Furthermore, quantification of the amount of difference between base pairs in DNA samples from two species allows investigators to estimate the genealogical distance between them. (The method used in this quantification—nucleic acid hybridization—is described briefly in the Appendix.) Thus, DNA analyses and comparisons help in constructing phylogenetic trees, such as the one in Figure 3.1. Also, DNA appears to change at a relatively steady average rate in all lineages of a given order of animals (Hillis, Moritz, and Mable, 1996). This means that the proportion of differences between DNA samples from two species can be used as a "molecular clock" to estimate how long ago they diverged from a common ancestor. The absolute times on the right-hand scale in Figure 3.1 should be considered with caution, however, because there is disagreement about the calibration of the "molecular clocks." This debate does not lessen the value of the *relative* times; that is, the overall picture appears to be accurate even if future research expands or contracts the time scale. Recently, samples of DNA have been obtained from insects fossilized in amber as long as 40 million years ago, helping us to discriminate among possible lines of descent of some modern insects and to test further the "clock" of changes in DNA over time (De Salle et al., 1992; Poinar, 1994). A fictionalized version of this technique helped to make millions of dollars for the writer and producer of *Jurassic Park*.

At present, investigators use both morphological and molecular analyses to determine the evolutionary relationships among animals. Classification is difficult for animals that resemble each other strongly in some characteristics but differ strongly in others. Instances in which responses to similar ecological features bring about similarities in behavior or structure among animals that are only distantly related (differ in genetic heritage), are referred to as **convergent evolution.** For example, the body forms of a tuna and a dolphin resemble each other because they evolved for efficient swimming, even though the tuna is a fish and the dolphin is a mammal descended from terrestrial ancestors. A resemblance that is due to such convergence rather than to common ancestry is called an **analogy.** By contrast, a **homology** is a resemblance based on common ancestry, such as the similarities in forelimb structures of mammals as noted by Buffon (Figure 3.3).

Comparative Methods Help in Studying the Biological Mechanisms of Behavior

Comparisons of behavior and of neural mechanisms across different kinds of animals and across different ecological niches are common in biological psychology and related disciplines. We will use such comparisons in every chapter of this book. Some of this research is done under natural, or field conditions, some under controlled laboratory conditions. Although studying only one species may yield important information, comparing two or more carefully chosen species or a large representative sample of species puts observations in a perspective that can lead to a much deeper understanding of the phenomena being observed. Let's look at a few examples.

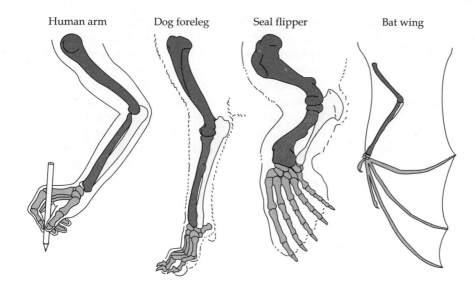

Human arm Dog foreleg Seal flipper Bat wing

3.3 Homology
Bones of the same sort are shown in the same color in all species. The sizes and shapes of the bones have evolved so that they are adapted to widely different functions: skilled manipulation in humans; locomotion in dogs; swimming in seals; flying in bats. The similarities among the sets of bones reflect descent from a common ancestor.

Some Ways of Obtaining Food Require Bigger Brains Than Others

Most species of animals spend much of their time and energy in the pursuit of food, often using elaborate strategies. Researchers have found that the strategies that different species employ to obtain food influence brain size and structure. For example, mammals that eat food distributed in clusters that are difficult to find tend to have brains that are larger than those of related species whose food is rather uniformly distributed and easy to find. Within several families of mammals, species that eat leaves or grass have brains that are relatively smaller than those of species that feed on fruit or insects that are distributed less densely and less uniformly. This relationship has been found among families of rodents, insectivores (such as shrews and moles), lagomorphs (such as rabbits and pica; Clutton-Brock and Harvey, 1980), and primates (Mace, Harvey, and Clutton-Brock, 1981).

Within the order of bats, which includes several hundred species, relatively large brains appear to have evolved independently in several instances. When body size is held constant, species of bats that eat mainly fruit or nectar or live mainly on blood have brain weights that are about 70% greater than those of species that live mainly on insects captured in flight. Finding fruit and assessing its quality requires integrating information from several senses, whereas capturing insects in flight requires only acute hearing. As Eisenberg and Wilson (1978:750) put it, larger brains are found among bat species whose techniques of locating food—their foraging strategies—are "based on locating relatively large packets of energy-rich food that are unpredictable in temporal and spatial distribution."

Some behavioral adaptations have been related to differences in relative sizes of certain structures within the brain. For example, some species of bat find their way and locate prey by audition; others rely almost entirely on vision. In the midbrain, the auditory center (the inferior colliculus) is much larger in bats that depend on hearing, whereas bats that depend on sight have a larger visual center (the superior colliculus). Families of birds that store bits of food for later use (for example, the acorn woodpecker, nutcracker, or black-capped chickadee) have a larger hippocampus relative to the forebrain and to body weight than do families that do not store food (Sherry, 1992). This difference has been found among both North American species (Figure 3.4) and European species. We will see in Chapters 17 and 18 that the hippocampus is important for memory formation, and in some species especially for spatial memory, which is needed to recover stored food. The families of birds that store food are no more closely related to each other than they are to other, non-food-storing families and subfamilies of birds. Thus, food storers are not all descendants of an ancestral species that stored food and that also happened to possess a large hippocampus. Rather, the evidence suggests that a large hippocampus is necessary for successful storage and recovery of food, and that several families of birds show convergent evolution for these attributes (Sherry, 1992).

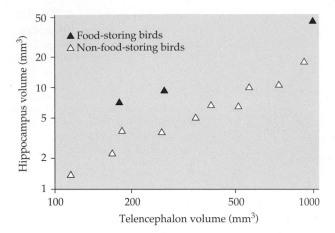

3.4   Food-Storing in Birds and Hippocampal Size
Food-storing species of birds have twice as large a hippocampus in relation to their forebrain as do species that do not store food. Note that both axes are logarithmic. After Sherry et al., 1989.

Box 3.1 provides other examples of how different species show different solutions to the dilemmas of adaptation. As a general rule, the relative size of a brain region is a good guide to the importance of the function of that region for the adaptations of the species. In this sense "more is better," but even small brain size is compatible with some complex behavior, as we will see in many instances in this book. Our understanding of how these differences in size and structure of the brain promote behavioral specializations should help us understand the neural basis of human behavior. For example, the size of some regions in the human temporal lobes seems to be related to language function (Chapter 19).

Ecological Factors and Body Build Help Determine the Length of Sleep

Some mammals spend more than half their lives sleeping (for example, monkeys, rats, and cats); others sleep much less (for example, cows, rabbits, and humans). In Chapter 14 we'll see how different kinds of sleep occur in different species, but for now let's

Box 3.1

Differences in Lifestyles of Mammals Are Reflected in Differences in Their Brain Maps

Differences in organization of the cerebral cortex are related to differences in behavioral function among mammals, as the example in the figure shows.

The North American raccoon and its Central and South American relative, the coati, are similar in appearance, and both belong to the family Procyonidae. Whereas the coati uses olfaction (smell) as much as touch, the raccoon uses touch much more than smell. The brains of the two animals reflect these differences. The raccoon cortex contains a large area representing the forepaw but only a tiny olfactory area; in contrast, the coati cortex has as large an area for olfaction as for touch.

Related research shows the differential sizes of cortical repre-

sentations in animals that use especially vision (with a large visual cortex), or audition (with a large auditory cortex), or touch, (with a large somatosensory cortex). Note also that in the midbrain the superior colliculus (SC), the midbrain visual center, is largest in the visual animal; in contrast, the inferior colliculus (IC), the midbrain auditory center, is largest in the animal that relies on hearing. Such a difference is observed in species of bats that use mainly vision versus species of bats that use mainly audition.

Differential expansion of parts of the tactile area has been found depending on whether an animal feels chiefly with its mouth and snout, its hands, or its tail.

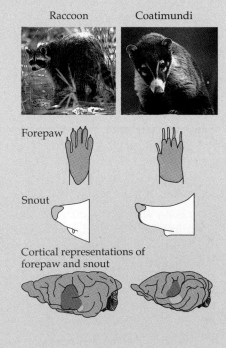

consider briefly how the ecology and body build of a species affect its overall sleep time. This relationship provides clues to the mysteries of why we sleep at all.

Allison and Cicchetti (1975) studied sleep data and ecological and constitutional factors in 39 species distributed over 13 mammalian orders. Two ecological factors stood out: First, predators (such as cats) tend to sleep for long periods and sleep readily in a laboratory, whereas species subject to heavy predation (such as rabbits) are poor sleepers. Second, animals that sleep in relatively secure places (such as bats) tend to sleep more than animals that sleep in exposed places (such as sheep). Body build is also a major factor, with large animals tending to sleep less than small animals; brain weight is an even better predictor than body weight. On the basis of these factors, the human sleep pattern fits in well with the patterns of other mammals.

Relating Bird Song to Brain Structure

In recent years songbirds that learn their songs (rather than inheriting them) have become the model for studies of vocal learning. Of the 23 orders of birds, only three learn their songs: the perching birds (Passeriformes), such as canaries, mockingbirds, and crows; the hummingbirds (Trochiliformes); and the parrots (Psittaciformes). The other birds that sing or call develop their species-specific vocalizations even if they are raised in isolation and do not hear another bird. Normally only males learn songs, although females of these species can learn songs if they are given special hormonal treatment, showing that they have the neural and vocal equipment for this behavior. Vocal learning may be advantageous in many ways, such as for attracting mates and defending territory. Perhaps because of these advantages, the three orders of birds that learn their songs include more species than all the 20 other orders together.

A phylogenetic tree of the 9000 species of living birds has been constructed by comparing the DNA of many different species of birds (Sibley and Ahlquist, 1990). This family tree, part of which is given in Figure 3.5, shows that the three orders that exhibit vocal learning are not closely related and have not shared a common ancestor for tens of millions of years. In fact, each of the orders with vocal learning is more closely related to some orders that do not learn their song than to the other orders that do learn their songs. This relationship suggests that innate development of vocalization is the primitive condition and that song learning is an example of convergent evolution in the three orders—perching birds, hummingbirds, and parrots (Brenowitz, 1991b).

In the 1970s investigators began to study the brains of canaries to determine which structures govern their singing (Nottebohm, Stokes, and Leonard, 1976). This and subsequent research (which we will take up in some detail in Chapter 19) revealed a special network of interconnected forebrain nuclei that control song. These nuclei contain receptors for gonadal sex hormones, and the hormones modulate the development and activity of this song-control system in the brain. By now, this hormone-sensitive system of forebrain nuclei has been found in at least 47 species of songbirds, including the five (out of six) main families of songbirds that have been studied in this way (Brenowitz, 1991b). Furthermore, comparisons of closely related species of songbirds reveal

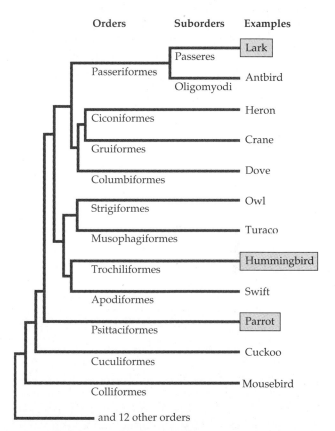

3.5   A Partial Family Tree of Birds
This tree emphasizes the orders of birds that learn songs. Only a few orders include species that learn their vocalizations; these are designated in color. The phylogenetic relationships have been deduced from measurements of the similarity of DNA from different species. In the Passeriformes order, species in one suborder—the Passeres—learn their songs. This suborder includes the largest number of species of any order or suborder; among them are larks, sparrows, wrens, swallows, mockingbirds, thrushes, crows, and magpies. After Sibley, Ahlquist, and Monroe, 1988.

that those that are capable of learning larger numbers of songs have larger song-control centers in the forebrain nuclei than do species that cannot acquire as many songs (Brenowitz and Arnold, 1986). Only a few orders of birds with innate development of vocalization have been inspected for the presence of this forebrain system, and none have shown it. But there is more than one way to achieve bird song, because the parrot forebrain song system differs from that of the songbirds.

Thus, by investigating the brain structures of a relatively small number of species carefully chosen for their phylogenetic relationships and their song ability, researchers are making important progress toward understanding the evolution of bird song. If investigators had studied an equal number of species chosen at random among the 9000 current species of birds, the results would have been much less informative and less able to yield general conclusions.

Box 3.2 gives further answers to the question, Why study a particular species? Recent examinations of the comparative enterprise in psychology are provided by Shettleworth (1993*b*), Timberlake (1993), and Kamil (1994).

Nervous Systems Differ Widely in Structure

Having compared aspects of the nervous systems of a few species, let's look more broadly at the variety of nervous systems of a few phyla of animals. Figure 3.6 shows the gross anatomy of the nervous system of some representative animals.

Invertebrates Show Enormous Diversity

Most of the animals on Earth are invertebrates, animals without backbones. (In fact, the order Coleoptera [the beetles] contains far more animal species than any other, so it's been said that, to a first approximation, every animal is a beetle!) The invertebrates far exceed vertebrates in many ways, including number, diversity of appearance, and variety of habitat. Whereas invertebrates make up 17 phyla the vertebrates are only a part of the phylum chordata (the chordates). The abundance of invertebrates is clearly demonstrated by the following estimate: for each person on earth, there are at least one billion insects, which are just one type of invertebrate. Neuroscientists focus on certain invertebrates because of the relative simplicity of their nervous systems and the great varieties of behavioral adap-

tation they display. Simplicity of structure has not ruled out some forms of behavior, such as some types of learning and memory, that are also seen in more complex organisms. Furthermore, invertebrates possess elaborate sensory systems that permit detection of some stimuli with exquisite sensitivity. Every conceivable niche on land, sea, or air has been successfully exploited by one or more invertebrate species.

A leading researcher in comparative neurosciences, Theodore H. Bullock, asserts that "we cannot expect truly to comprehend either ourselves or how the nervous system works until we gain insight into this range of nervous systems, from nerve nets and simple ganglia in sea anemones and flatworms to the optic lobes of dragon flies, octopuses, and lizards to the cerebral cortex in primates" (1984:473). Bullock's message has been well heeded by investigators of the neural mechanisms of behavior. Faced with the enormous complexity of the vertebrate brain with its billions of nerve cells, researchers have turned instead to the nervous systems of some invertebrates that have only hundreds or thousands of neurons. An exhaustive description of the "wiring diagram" of the nervous system and how it relates to behavior may be possible with these invertebrates. Complex aspects of behavior, such as memory and species-typical eating or aggressive behaviors, have been explored in an exciting manner in several invertebrates that have become laboratory favorites.

Theodore H. Bullock

With all the diversity of invertebrate nervous systems, we cannot select a few as "representative," but we will describe some features of the nervous systems of molluscs and insects in preparation for our treatment of research with these animals in later chapters.

The mollusc Aplysia.   Slugs, snails, clams, and octopuses are a few of the almost 100,000 species of molluscs. These soft-bodied animals display an enormous range of both bodily and behavioral complexity. Some molluscs, such as the octopus, show excellent problem-solving capabilities; other molluscs exist in a near parasitic form. The head end of a mollusc usually consists of a mouth, tentacles, and eyes. The typical

Box 3.2
Why Study Particular Species?

With all the species available, why choose certain ones for study? Investigators usually follow several criteria in selection of species for study. Here are several reasons for choosing a species:

1. **Outstanding features.** Some species are "champions" at various behaviors and abilities, such as sensory discrimination (for example, the owl has acute auditory localization, and the eagle has extremely fine visual acuity) and controlling movement (for example, some insects display remarkable escape behavior). These abilities are often linked to highly specialized neuronal structures. Such structures incorporate and optimize particular neuronal designs that may be less conspicuous in organisms that lack these superior capacities (Bullock, 1984, 1986). Study of such species may yield general principles that apply to other species.

2. **Convenience.** Some species, such as the laboratory rat, are particularly convenient for study because they breed well in the laboratory, are relatively inexpensive to maintain, are not rare or endangered, have relatively short life spans, and have been studied extensively already, so there is a good base of knowledge about them to begin with. In addition, they may serve as good models because their morphology and behavior

show clear relationships to other species. Other species are convenient because they offer advantages for certain methods of study. For example, some molluscs have relatively simple nervous systems that aid in tracing neural circuits, and the fruit fly *Drosophila* is excellent for genetic studies because it has a relatively simple genome and a short time period between generations.

3. **Uniqueness.** Species that exhibit unusual behavior and/or morphology help illuminate issues. For example, the female of the spotted hyena appears to have a penis and is dominant over the smaller male. This sex "reversal" has been found to be caused by unusual hormonal adaptations (see Chapter 12).

4. **Comparison.** Close relationships between species that behave very differently enable the testing of hypotheses. For example, whereas in some closely related species of rodents the home ranges of males and females differ in size, in others they do not. Comparison of these species tests whether differences in maze-solving ability are associated with the size of the home range and with the size of the hippocampus (see Chapter 17).

5. **Preservation.** Studies of rare and/or endangered species can help preserve these ani-

mals. Because of their predicament these species are seldom used for laboratory research, but they may be investigated in field studies or in zoos.

6. **Economic importance.** Species that are economically important include agricultural animals (for example, sheep), animals that furnish valuable products (for example, fish), predators upon agricultural animals (for example, wolves), or destroyers of crops (for example, elephants). Studying these animals can provide information that helps to increase production and/or decrease losses.

7. **Treatment of disease.** Some species are subject to the same diseases as other species and therefore are valuable models for investigation (here we focus on diseases of the nervous system and endocrine [hormonal] system). Examples include: certain kinds of mice, which provide a model for the behavior and the anatomy of Down syndrome (see Chapter 4); baboons, which are prone to epilepsy (see Chapter 5); several breeds of dogs that are afflicted by narcolepsy (see Chapter 15); some strains of rodents that provide models for depression (see Chapter 16); and monkeys, which are susceptible to a drug that can cause Parkinson's disease in humans (see Chapter 11; McKinney, 1988).

structure also includes a footlike appendage and a visceral section that is frequently covered by a protective envelope called the mantle. A rather simple marine mollusc, *Aplysia,* has gained considerable notoriety

because of its extensive use in cellular studies of learning and memory (see Chapter 18). Here we review briefly the principal structures of the nervous system of *Aplysia.*

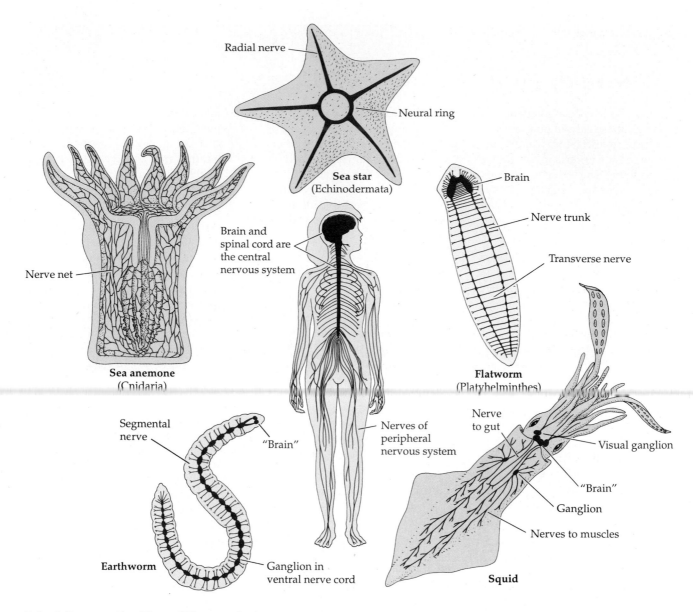

3.6   A Comparative View of Nervous Systems
Gross anatomy of the nervous system in representative animals from six phyla.

The nervous system of *Aplysia* consists of four paired ganglia at the head end that form a ring around the esophagus (Figure 3.7*a*). Below these ganglia is a single abdominal ganglion. The ganglia are interconnected by tracts. One head ganglion innervates the eyes and the tentacles; a second head ganglion innervates the mouth muscles. The other two paired ganglia innervate the foot. The abdominal ganglion controls such major visceral functions as circulation, respiration, and reproduction. Comprehensive research by Eric R. Kandel and his collaborators over the past 20 years has led to detailed maps of **identifiable neurons** in these ganglia, especially the ab-dominal ganglion. (These cells are called identifiable because they are large and similar from one *Aplysia* to the next, so investigators can recognize them and give them code names.) Since the nervous system of *Aplysia* includes many identifiable cells (Figure 3.7*b* and *c*), it has become possible to trace the circuits mediating various behaviors in this animal (Kandel, 1976). Work with *Aplysia* has also provided much detailed understanding of the molecular basis of learning (Kandel et al., 1986; Krasne and Glanzman, 1995), supporting the view that simpler invertebrate nervous systems can provide useful models for examining complex features of nervous system operations.

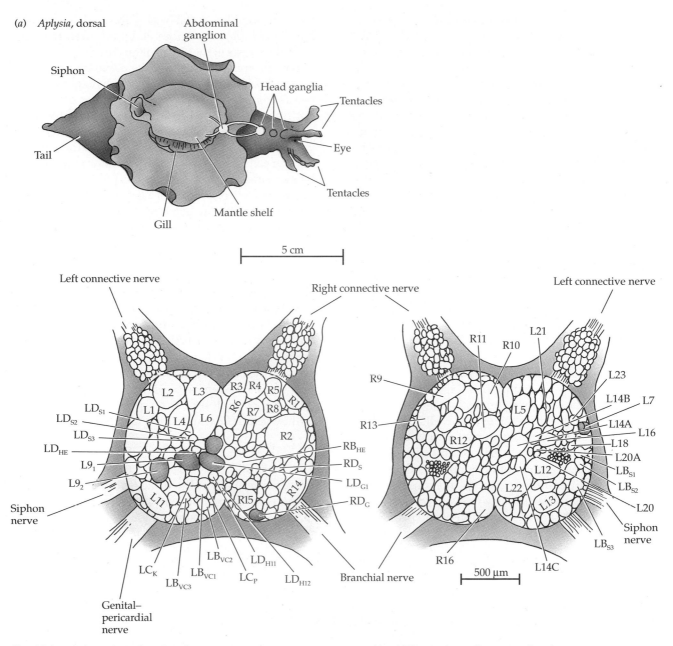

(a) *Aplysia*, dorsal

Abdominal ganglion

Siphon

Head ganglia

Tentacles

Eye

Tail

Tentacles

Mantle shelf

Gill

5 cm

(b) Abdominal ganglion, dorsal surface

(c) Abdominal ganglion, ventral surface

3.7   The Nervous System of *Aplysia*

The sea snail *Aplysia* has a relatively simple nervous system with large identifiable neurons, which has made it a popular species in research on the neural basis of learning and memory. (a) Dorsal view. The neural ganglia and connecting nerve cords are shown in yellow. (b) Dorsal view of an abdominal ganglion with several identified neurons labeled. Neurons that are in the circuit involved in habituation are shown in pink. (c) Ventral view of an abdominal ganglion with several identified neurons labeled. *a* after Kandel, 1976; *b* and *c* from Frazier et al., 1967, and Koester and Kandel, unpublished.

Insect nervous systems.   Insects, with more than 1 million living species, have no rival in the animal kingdom for color, architecture, and variety of habitats. The life cycle of many insects includes striking morphological changes (for example, from caterpillar to butterfly) that not only affect the external form of the animal but also involve a resculpturing of the nervous system. The sense organs of insects display great variety and sensitivity. Success in the battle for survival has affected this group of animals in many distinctive ways, and it is easy to appreciate why neuroscientists have focused much research on the neural mechanisms of the behavior of insects. In spite of the diversity of insect body form, the central nervous systems of insects are remarkably similar: they vary "astonishingly little from the most primitive to the most advanced" (Edwards and Palka, 1991:391).

The gross outline of the adult insect nervous system consists of a brain in the head end and ganglia in each body segment behind the head (Figure 3.8). Bundles of axons connect ganglia to the brain. The number of ganglia varies; in some insects all the ganglia of the chest and abdomen fuse into one major collection of cells. In other insects there are as many as eight ganglia in a chain. The brain itself contains three major compartments: the protocerebrum, deutocerebrum, and tritocerebrum. The most complex part of the insect brain is the protocerebrum, which consists of a right and left lobe, each continuous with a large optic lobe, an extension of the compound eye. Within the optic lobe there are distinct masses of cells that receive input from the eye as well as from the brain. Electrical stimulation of sites within the protocerebrum of various insects elicits complex behaviors. The relative sizes of different components of the protocerebrum differ among insects, and some of these variations may be particularly relevant to behavioral variations. For example, a portion of the protocerebrum called the corpus pedunculatum is especially well developed in social insects; the behavior of these animals tends to be more elaborate than that displayed by insects that live solitary lives.

One prominent feature of the nerve cord of insects is **giant axons**—fibers that are much bigger in diameter than most fibers are. The properties of these giant fibers have been explored in some interesting studies, using many different orders of insects (Edwards and Palka, 1991). In these insects there are receptive cells (the cerci) in the tail that can be excited by movement of the air; these receptors connect with giant interneurons with very large axons that ascend the nerve cord to the head. Along the way they excite some motor neurons. This system originated to allow insects to escape from predation by making rapid movements. In many insects (for example, cockroaches) this system still functions as an escape system; in other insects the cerci and the connections of the giant interneurons have been modified so that they also play a role in reproductive behavior (in crickets) or help to regulate flight maneuvers (in grasshoppers). Whatever its function in a particular species, the basic organization and cellular composition of this system appears to have remained the same for a very long period, perhaps as long as 400 million years (Edwards and Palka, 1991).

All Vertebrate Nervous Systems Share Certain Main Features

After a brief look at the basic features of vertebrate nervous systems, we will compare some of their main features with those of molluscan and insect nervous systems. The following are main features of the

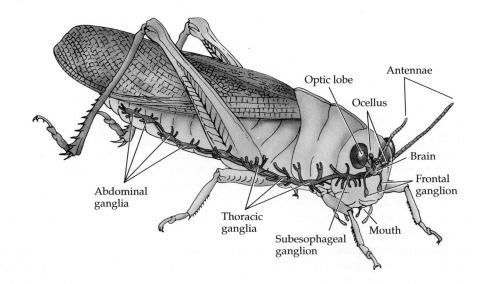

3.8   The Nervous System of a Typical Insect
In insects, the brain with its subdivisions is linked via bundles of axons (connectives) to a group of ganglia in the thorax and abdomen. The brain, connectives, and ganglia are shown in purple.

Optic lobe

Antennae

Ocellus

Brain

Frontal ganglion

Mouth

Subesophageal ganglion

Thoracic ganglia

Abdominal ganglia

vertebrate nervous system, some of which are illustrated in Figure 3.6:

1. *Development* from a hollow dorsal neural tube (see Chapters 2 and 4).

2. *Bilateral symmetry.* (The human cerebral hemispheres are not *quite* identical anatomically or functionally, as we'll see in Chapters 9, 18, and 19; see Box 19.3 for a discussion of this and other exceptions.)

3. *Segmentation.* Pairs of spinal nerves extend from each level of the spinal cord.

4. *Hierarchical control.* The cerebral hemispheres control or modulate the activity of the spinal cord.

5. *Separate systems.* The CNS (brain and spinal cord) is clearly separate from the periperal nervous system.

6. *Localization of function.* Certain functions are controlled by certain locations in the CNS.

Presumably vertebrates have all of these features in common because they descended from a common ancestor.

Anatomists have examined the brains of many classes of the 10,000 to 20,000 vertebrate species, and it is apparent that vertebrates with larger bodies tend to possess larger brains. No matter what the size, however, all vertebrate brains have the same major subdivisions. The main differences among vertebrates are the absolute and the relative sizes of different regions.

A comparison of human and rat brains illustrates basic similarities and differences (Figure 3.9). Each of the main structures in the human brain has a counterpart in the rat brain. This comparison could be extended to much greater detail, down to nuclei, fiber tracts, and types of cells. Even small structures in the brains of one species are found to have exact correspondences in the brains of other species. All mammals also have similar types of neurons and similar organization of the cerebellar cortex and the cerebral cortex.

The differences between the brains of humans and the brains of other mammals are mainly quantitative; that is, they concern both actual and relative sizes of the whole brain, brain regions, and brain cells. Whereas the brain of an adult human being weighs about 1400 grams (g), that of an adult rat weighs a little less than 2 g. In each case the brain represents about 2% of total body weight. The cerebral hemispheres occupy a much greater proportion of the brain in the human than in the rat, and the surface of the human brain shows prominent gyri and fissures, whereas the rat cerebral cortex is smooth and unfissured. The rat has, relatively, much larger olfactory bulbs than the human. This difference is probably related to the rat's much greater use of the sense of smell. The size of neurons also differs significantly between human and rat; in general, human neurons are much larger than rat neurons. In addition, there are great differences in the extent of dendritic trees. Figure 3.10 gives some examples of size differences among neurons of different species.

How Vertebrate Nervous Systems Differ from Those of Molluscs and Insects

To summarize some of the features of the vertebrate nervous system that we have described up to now, let's compare them with features of invertebrate nervous systems, focusing specifically on molluscs and insects.

1. *Basic plan.* All vertebrates and most invertebrates have a basic plan that consists of a central nervous system and a peripheral nervous system.

2. *Brain.* All vertebrates and many invertebrates, including molluscs and insects, have brains. The general evolutionary trend in both vertebrates and invertebrates is toward increasing brain control over ganglia at lower levels of the body.

3. *Number of neurons.* Vertebrate brains usually have many neurons devoted to information processing, whereas invertebrate brains usually have fewer, but larger and more complicated neurons that manage key integrative processes.

4. *Identifiable neurons.* Some of the large invertebrate neurons are identifiable. In contrast, there are only a few cases of identifiable neurons in vertebrates.

5. *Ganglion structure.* Vertebrate ganglia have the cell bodies on the inside and the dendrites and axons on the outside. Ganglia in invertebrate nervous systems have a characteristic structure: an outer rind that consists of monopolar cell bodies and an inner core that consists of the extensions of the cell bodies forming a dense neuropil (a network of axons and dendrites).

6. *Axons and neural conduction.* Many axons of mammalian neurons are surrounded by myelin, which helps them conduct impulses faster than the unmyelinated invertebrate axons (see Chapter 2). Many invertebrates have a few giant axons to convey messages rapidly in escape systems; vertebrates, with their generally rather rapid neural conduction, do not have such giant axons.

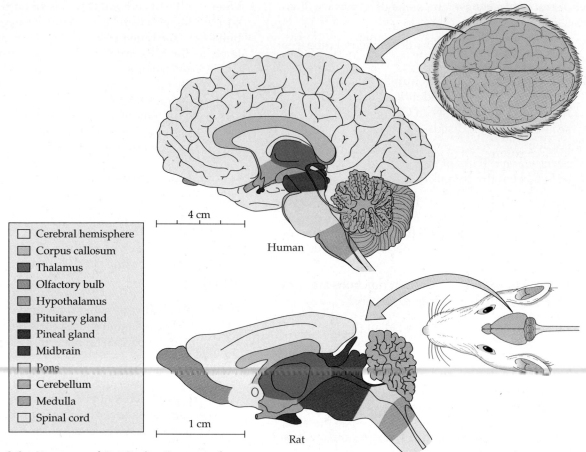

Cerebral hemisphere
Corpus callosum
Thalamus
Olfactory bulb
Hypothalamus
Pituitary gland
Pineal gland
Midbrain
Pons
Cerebellum
Medulla
Spinal cord

4 cm

Human

1 cm

Rat

3.9 Human and Rat Brains Compared
Mid-sagittal views of the right hemisphere of human and rat brains; the rat brain has been enlarged about six times in linear dimensions in relation to the human brain. In both brains, the main structures are the same and they have the same topological relations to each other. Note that the cerebral hemispheres are relatively much larger in the human brain, whereas the rat has a relatively larger midbrain and olfactory bulb.

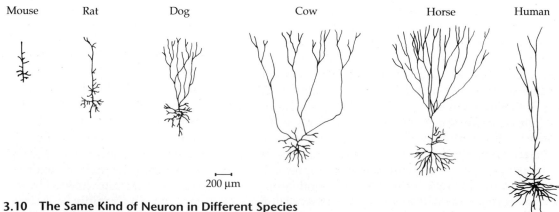

Mouse   Rat   Dog   Cow   Horse   Human

200 μm

3.10 The Same Kind of Neuron in Different Species
These pyramidal neurons from the motor cortices of different mammals are all drawn to the same scale. After Barasa, 1960.

7. *Structural changes.* Large-scale changes in the structures of the nervous system occur among some invertebrates during metamorphosis. Vertebrates show important changes in neural structure during development, but these are not as dramatic as the changes during invertebrate metamorphoses.

8. *Location in the body.* In vertebrates, the central nervous system is encased in the bony skull and spinal column. In many invertebrates the nervous system is built around the digestive tract.

9. *Constancy.* The basic structure and connections of the insect nervous system have remained similar throughout hundreds of millions of years, even though bodily forms have varied greatly. The vertebrate nervous system has also maintained the same basic structure for hundreds of millions of years of evolution. Although differences in body form are less extreme among the vertebrates than among the insects, nevertheless many evolutionary changes have taken place in vertebrate brains.

Relating the Evolution of Vertebrate Brains to Changes in Behavior

During the course of evolution, the characteristics of the nervous system changed progressively. One especially prominent feature during the last 100 million years has been a general tendency for the brain size of vertebrates to increase, and the brains of our human ancestors have shown a particularly striking increase in size over the last 2 million years. How, then, has the evolution of the brain been related to changes in behavioral capacity?

We could learn more about the evolution of the brain by studying the brains of fossil animals. But brains themselves do not fossilize—at least, not literally. Two methods of analysis have proved helpful. One is to use the cranial cavity of a fossil skull to make a cast of the brain that once occupied that space. These casts (called **endocasts**) give a good indication of the size and shape of the brain.

The other method is to study present-day animals, choosing species that show various degrees of similarity to (or difference from) ancestral forms. Although no modern animal is an ancestor of any other living form, some present species resemble ancestral forms more closely than others do. For example, present-day frogs are much more similar to vertebrates of 300 million years ago than are any mammals (Figure 3.11). Among the mammals, some

species, such as the opossum, resemble fossil mammals of 50 million years ago more than do other species, such as the dog. Thus, a species such as the opossum is said to retain primitive or ancestral states of particular anatomical features. Anatomists who study the brains of living species can obtain far more detailed information from them than from endocasts, because they can investigate the internal structure of the brain: its nuclei, fiber tracts, and the circuitry formed by connections of its neurons.

We must be careful not to interpret the evolutionary record as if it were a linear sequence. The main classes of vertebrates in Figure 3.12, for example, represent different lines or radiations of evolution that have been proceeding separately for at least 100 million years. Thus a particular evolutionary development may not have been available to mammals even if it occurred before the first mammals appeared. For example, among the sharks, some complex forms long ago evolved much larger brains than primitive sharks had, but the evolution of large brains in sharks cannot account for the large brains of mammals. The line of descent that eventually led to mammals had separated from that of the sharks before the large-brained sharks evolved. Let's consider some examples of changes in the size and organization of vertebrate brains.

Through Evolution, Vertebrate Brains Have Changed in Both Size and Organization

Recent research shows that even the most primitive living vertebrate, the lamprey (a kind of jawless fish), has a more complex brain than it used to be given credit for. The lamprey has not only the basic neural chassis of spinal cord, hindbrain, and midbrain, but also a diencephalon and telencephalon. Its telencephalon has cerebral hemispheres and other subdivisions that are also found in the mammalian brain. All vertebrate brains appear to have these regions. One difference in basic brain structure between the lamprey and other vertebrates is that the cerebellum in the lamprey is very small and may consist of only some brain stem nuclei. The evolution of large cerebellar hemispheres in birds and mammals appears to be a case of parallel evolution from the small cerebellum in their common reptilian ancestor; the increased size of the cerebellum may be related to increased complexity of sensory processing and increased motor agility (Figure 3.12).

The differences among the brains of vertebrate species, then, lie not in the existence of basic subdivisions but in their relative size and elaboration. At what stages of vertebrate evolution do various re-

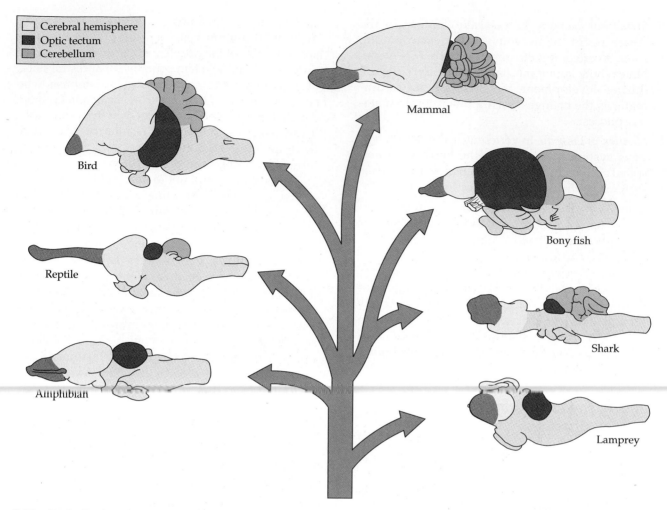

| □ Cerebral hemisphere |
| ■ Optic tectum |
| ▨ Cerebellum |

3.11   Brain Regions in Six Classes of Vertebrates

Representative brains from six major vertebrate classes are shown on a phylogenetic tree; early evolutionary branches appear lower, and more recent
branches toward the top of the tree. In each brain, the cerebral hemispheres
are shown in blue, the cerebellum in green, and the optic tectum in purple.
Note the relatively large sizes of the cerebral hemispheres and the cerebellum in the bird and mammal brains. After Northcutt, 1981.

gions of the brain first become important? Large
paired optic lobes in its midbrain probably represent
the lamprey's highest level of visual integration. In
bony fish, amphibians, and reptiles, the relatively
large optic tectum in the midbrain is the main center
for vision in the brain (see Figure 3.11). In birds and
mammals, however, complex visual perception requires an enlarged telencephalon.

Reptiles were the first vertebrates to exhibit relatively large cerebral hemispheres. Reptiles were also
the first vertebrates to have a cerebral cortex, but their
cortex has only three layers, unlike the six-layered
neocortex of mammals. Part of the cortex in reptiles

appears to be homologous to the hippocampus in
mammals. The hippocampus in mammals has three
layers and is called **archicortex** (from the Greek *archi*,
"ancient") because this cortex is extremely old in an
evolutionary sense.

Some mammals that have primitive traits, such as
the opossum, have a relatively large **paleocortex**
(from the Greek *paleo*, "old," but not as old as *archi*);
this and related structures are grouped under the
name **limbic system**. (This system was introduced in
Chapter 2. We will take up the limbic system in
Chapter 15 in connection with emotion and motivation, and in Chapters 17 and 18 in connection with

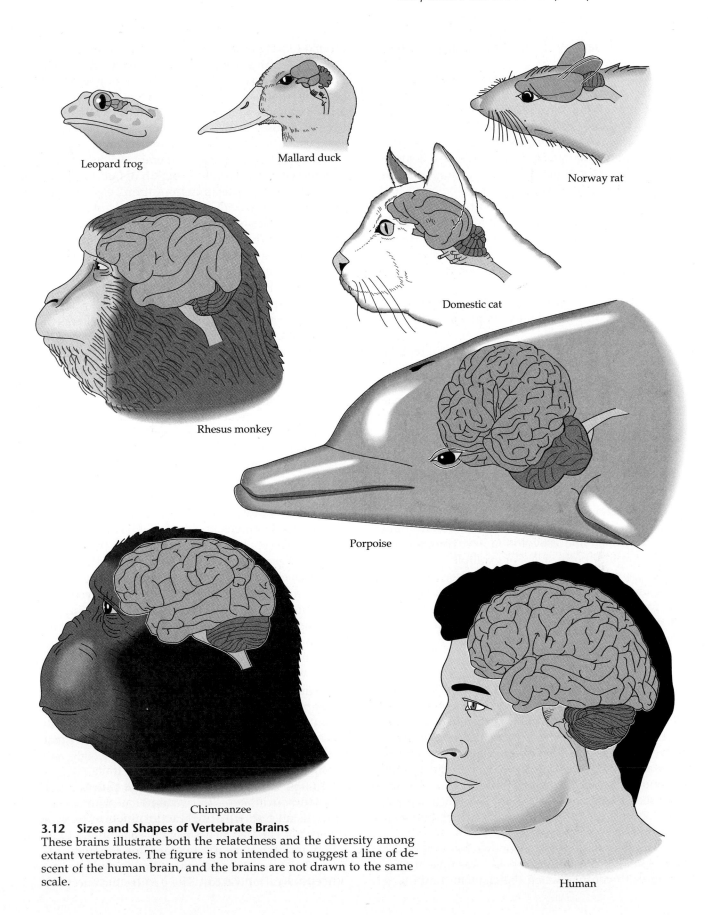

3.12 Sizes and Shapes of Vertebrate Brains
These brains illustrate both the relatedness and the diversity among extant vertebrates. The figure is not intended to suggest a line of descent of the human brain, and the brains are not drawn to the same scale.

learning and memory.) In humans, the olfactory bulb is part of paleocortex.

All mammals have a six-layered **neocortex.** In more advanced mammals the neocortex accounts for more than half the volume of the brain. In many of the larger mammals the neocortex is deeply fissured, so that a large cortical surface covers the brain. In the more advanced mammals, the cortex is what is mainly responsible for many complex functions, such as the perception of objects. Regions of the brain that were responsible for perceptual functions in less encephalized animals—such as the midbrain optic lobes (in the lamprey) or the midbrain optic center (in the frog)—have in present-day mammals become visual reflex centers or way stations in the projection pathway to the cortex. (We will take up the neocortex in several chapters in connection with not only perception but also complex cognitive functions.)

Evolution of brain size.   It is sometimes said that the brain increased in size with the appearance of each succeeding vertebrate class shown in Figure 3.11, but that statement is wrong in several respects. For one thing, there are exceptions among the present-day representatives of the various classes—birds appeared later than mammals but do not have larger brains. For another, the generalization arose from the old way of viewing vertebrate evolution, as one linear series of increasing complexity rather than as a series of successive radiations.

Actually there is considerable variation in brain size within each line of evolution if we compare animals of similar body size. For example, within the ancient class of jawless fish, the hagfish, which are considered the advanced members of that class, possess forebrains four times as large as those of lampreys of comparable body size. The increase of brain size in relation to behavioral capacity has been studied most thoroughly in the mammals.

Brain size, body size, and encephalization.   The study of brain size is complicated by the wide range of body sizes. You would not expect animals that differed in body size to have the same brain size. But exactly what relation holds between the size of the body and that of the brain? A general relationship was found first for present-day species and then applied successfully to fossil species. This function turns out to be useful in finding relationships between brain and behavioral capacities.

We humans long believed our own brains to be the largest of all brains, but this belief was upset in the seventeenth century when the elephant brain was found to weigh three times as much as our own. Later, whale brains were found to be even larger. These findings puzzled scholars who took it for granted that human beings are the most intelligent of animals and therefore must have the largest brains. To address the problem posed by the discovery that elephant brains and whale brains are larger than the brains of humans, they proposed that brain weight should be expressed as a fraction of body weight. On this basis humans outrank elephants, whales, and all other animals of large or moderate body size. But a mouse has about the same ratio of brain weight to body weight as a human, and the tiny shrew outranks a human on this measure. Without trying to prove that one species or another is "brainiest," we would like to know much brain is needed to control and serve a body of a given size. From a comparative point of view, what is the general relation between brain size and body size?

When we plot brain weights and body weights for a large sample of mammals, we see some generality (Figure 3.13*a*). All the plot points fall within a narrow polygon. Since both scales are logarithmic, the graph encompasses a great variety of animal sizes, and departures from the general rule tend to be minimized. The diagonal area of the graph has a slope of about 0.69 (Harvey and Krebs, 1990).

Let's test the generality of this rule by examining the relation between brain weight and body weight for six vertebrate classes (Figure 3.13*b*). In each class except the mammals, the data yield a diagonal area with a slope of about three-quarters, so the relationship between brain weight and body weight is similar for all classes of vertebrates. But notice that the diagonal areas are displaced from each other vertically in Figure 3.13*b*, with the mammals highest, bony fish and reptiles clearly lower, and cyclostomes (for example, the lamprey) the lowest. This configuration reflects the fact that these classes have successively less brain weight for a body of the same size. Thus, a mammal or a bird that weighs about 100 grams (for example, a rat or a blue jay) has a brain that weighs about 1 g, but a fish or a reptile of the same body weight has a brain that weighs only a little more than 0.1 g; a 100-g cyclostome has a brain that weighs only about 0.03 g.

To take into account the variation both between classes and within classes, we need a measure of vertical distance above or below the diagonal lines on the graph. This distance is usually called k and is different for each class and for each species. Because k indicates the relative amount of brain, it is called the **encephalization factor.** The greater the encephal-

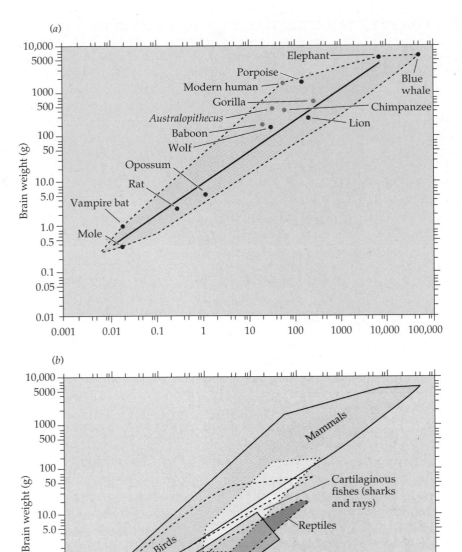

(a)

3.13 Brain Weight–Body Weight Relations

(a) Brain weight in several mammal species related to body weight. A polygon has been drawn to connect the extreme cases and include the whole sample. The diagonal line shows the basic relationship, with brain weight related to the 0.69 power of body weight. (b) Brain weight plotted against body weight for various species in six classes of vertebrates. Each class is represented by a polygon that includes a large sample of species in that class. The other classes of animals fall below the mammals, reflecting the fact that the constant that relates brain weight to body weight is smaller in those classes; they are less "brainy" than the mammals. *a* after Stephan, Frahm, and Baron, 1981; *b* after Jerison, 1985, 1991.

ization factor for a species, the higher its value is above the diagonal line for its class. In Figure 3.13*a* the point for humans is farther above the diagonal than the point for any other species. In terms of the encephalization factor, human beings rate higher than any other species. Values of the encephalization factor for several mammalian species are given in Figure 3.14.

Brain size has been studied in many species of mammal, both living and fossil. These studies have

yielded clues about some selection pressures that have led to larger brains. For example, you may have heard the statement that dinosaurs became extinct because of the inadequacy of their small ("walnut-sized") brains (see Figure 3.15). Is this true? Examination of endocasts of dinosaur brains and use of the equation that relates brain weight (which can be estimated from brain volume) to body weight show that dinosaur brain weights fit the relationship for reptiles shown in Figure 3.13*b*. For example, the brain of

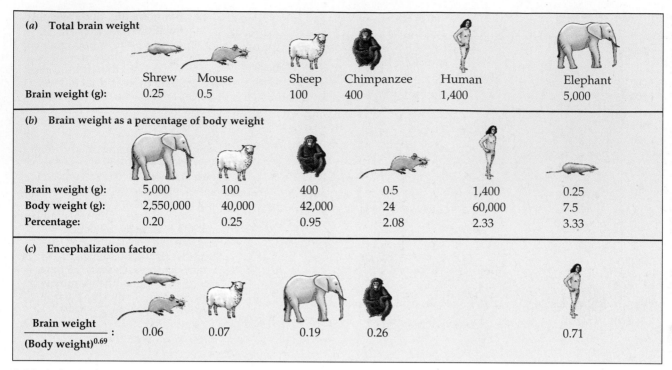

3.14 Who Is the Brainiest?
For this sample of large to small mammals, the answer depends on what measure is used: total brain weight (*top*), brain weight as a percentage of body weight (*middle*), or the encephalization factor (*bottom*).

Tyrannosaurus rex probably weighed about 700 grams—only half the size of the human brain, but much heavier than a walnut and appropriate for a reptile of its size—so it seems unlikely that dinosaurs perished because of a lack of brains (Jerison, 1991).

Brain size evolved as a whole. As the brain has evolved, it has shown adaptive size changes both in specific regions and overall; this illustrates both the specificity and the continuity among species that we mentioned in Chapter 1. Certain capabilities, such as those for foraging for food and for bird song, have been linked to sizes of particular brain regions, as we saw earlier in this chapter. In contrast, some other capabilities are related to overall neocortical volume rather than to the volume of any particular region of cortex; this suggests that the amount of cortex devoted to some capabilities could increase only as the result of an increase in total cortical volume, although that seems like an inefficient and expensive way to increase the tissue related to a specific function. The conclusion that changes occur in the overall size of the brain rather than in specific brain regions is consistent with the concept that overall developmental factors

and programs (which we will consider in Chapter 4) severely constrain the magnitude of local adaptations. Supporting this conclusion is the recent finding that, if you know the weight of the brain of any mammalian species, you can predict the weight of each part (Finlay and Darlington, 1995). In this study the investigators compiled published data on sizes of the main parts of the brain in 131 species of mammals—insectivores, bats, prosimians, and simians (including *Homo sapiens*). Their data set had the advantages for comparative study of including a large number of species, a wide range of ecological niches (including terrestrial, arboreal, burrowing, amphibious, and flying), a wide range of body weights (2 to 105,000 g) and brain sizes (60 to 1,252,000 mm^3), and the fact that the 11 brain divisions measured constitute the entire brain. Because of the wide range of sizes, the logarithms of the sizes were used in the analyses.

On logarithmic scales, the size of each brain structure, except for the olfactory bulb, showed a highly linear relation to brain weight; Figure 3.16*a* shows examples for a few structures. The size of each structure, except the olfactory bulb, correlated 0.96 or higher with total brain size; for the olfactory bulb the

"The picture's pretty bleak gentlemen . . . The world's climates are changing, the mammals are taking over, and we all have a brain about the size of a walnut."

3.15 Was the Dinosaur Being Too Modest?

correlation was only 0.70. Thus, for all parts of the brain except the olfactory bulb, a simple rule relates the size of the particular structure to total brain size.

Although the different parts of the brain increase regularly in size as total brain size increases, each part increases at a different rate from the others; this is seen in the different slopes of the lines in Figure 3.16a

and more dramatically when the same data are plotted on linear axes in Figure 3.16b. Thus, in a series of mammalian brains from small to large, the medulla increases relatively little, the cerebellum considerably more, and the neocortex grows most of all the parts. So the *proportion* of brain devoted to each part differs importantly from small to large brains.

The fact that the brain shows overall developmental constraints does not contradict the existence of some specific size adaptations of brain structures. For one thing, the brain divisions analyzed by Finlay and Darlington are relatively large, and most of them contain subdivisions that may vary in their development. Thus, for example, one of the brain divisions in their study is the metencephalon, which includes both the inferior colliculus and the superior colliculus; as we have mentioned, the inferior colliculus is larger in animals that depend mainly on audition, whereas the superior colliculus is larger in animals that rely on vision. So, although general constraints on development are strong, specific adaptations of brain regions can also occur.

Hominid brains evolved relatively rapidly. Valuable information about evolutionary relationships between brain and behavior comes from the study of **hominids,** that is, primates of the family Hominidae, of which humans (*Homo sapiens*) are the only living species. This approach is intriguing for the light it sheds on our distant ancestors, and it helps us understand how the body adapts to the environment through natural selection.

The structural and behavioral features that we consider characteristic of humans did not develop simultaneously (Falk, 1993). Our large brain is a relatively late development. According to one estimate the trunk and arms of hominids reached their present

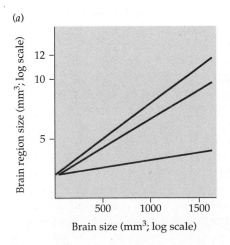

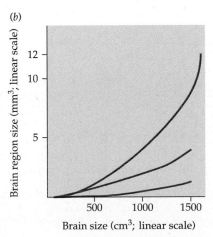

3.16 The Evolution of Brain Size
(*a*) A logarithmic scale for the size of the neocortex, cerebellum, and medulla in 131 mammalian species; the values for humans are at the far right of each plot. (*b*) On a linear scale, neocortex is seen to increase in size at a greater weight than the cerebellum or medulla as a proportion of brain size. After Finlay and Darlington, 1995.

form about 10 million years ago. (Note that the time span of human evolution and the dates of fossils have been altered by recent methods of dating. All authorities do not agree on these dates; they should be considered only approximate.) Hominids began walking on two feet more than 3.5 million years ago, and the oldest stone tools date back to about 2.6 million years ago (Figure 3.17). The early tool users were bipedal hominids called Australopithecines. Endocasts of their skulls show a brain volume of about 350 to 400 cubic centimeters (cm^3), about the size of the modern chimpanzee brain. Chimpanzees do not make tools from stone, although they collect stones to use as tools. But the Australopithecines made and used crude stone tools in hunting and in breaking animal bones to eat. With use of tools, there was less selection pressure to maintain large jaws and teeth, and hominid jaws and teeth became steadily smaller than the ape's and more like those of modern human beings. Even though the brain did not grow much among the Australopithecines, never becoming larger than 600 cm^3, they were successful animals, lasting—relatively unchanged—until about 1.5 to 2 million years ago. Examination of ancient campsites suggests that these early hominids lived in small nomadic groups of 20 to 50 individuals. They hunted and gathered plant foods. This life of hunting and gathering was a new lifestyle that was continued by later hominids.

About 1.5 to 2 million years ago, when the Australopithecines died out, *Homo erectus* appeared. This early representative of the genus *Homo* started with a cranial capacity of about 700 cm^3 and a smaller face than the Australopithecine. As *Homo erectus* developed, the brain became steadily larger, reaching the present-day volume of about 1400 cm^3, and the face continued to become smaller. *Homo erectus* made elaborate stone tools, used fire, and killed large animals. Fossils and tools of *Homo erectus* are found throughout three continents, whereas those of the Australopithecines are found only in Africa. *Homo erectus* may have represented a level of capacity and of cultural adaptation that allowed the hominids to expand into new environmental niches and to overcome barriers that kept earlier hominids in a narrower range. Evolution of the brain and increased behavioral capacity advanced rapidly during the time of *Homo erectus* (see Figure 3.17). By the time *Homo sapiens* appeared, about 200,000 years ago, brain volume had reached the modern level. Thus, after remaining virtually unchanged in size during about 2 million years of tool use by the Australopithecines,

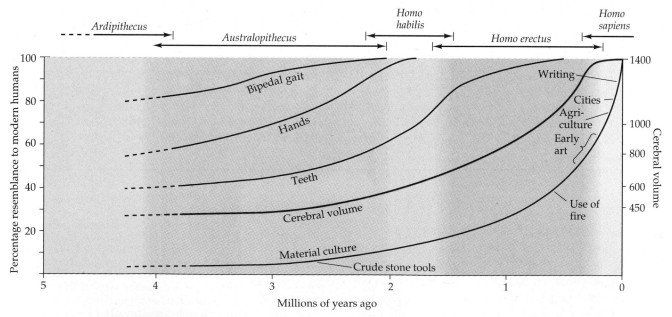

3.17   Aspects of Hominid Evolution
Note that bipedal (two-footed) gait was similar to those of modern humans even in *Australopithecus,* whereas cerebral volume reached its current size only in *Homo sapiens.* High culture (art, agriculture, cities, writing) emerged only relatively recently and was not associated with any further change in brain size. After Tobias, 1980; updated with the assistance of T. White.

the hominid brain almost tripled in volume during the next 1.5 million years.

The size of the human brain now appears to be at a plateau. The recent changes in human lifestyle shown in Figure 3.17—such as the appearance of language, the introduction of agriculture and animal husbandry (about 10,000 years ago), and urban living (the last few thousand years)—have all been accomplished and assimilated by a brain that does not seem to have altered in size since *Homo sapiens* appeared.

A change in any organ during evolution suggests that the change confers advantages with respect to the survival of the individuals in that environment. A rapid change, as in the size of the hominid brain, implies strong advantages for survival. Can we then determine in what ways the evolution of the human brain accompanied and made possible certain changes in human behavior?

Unfortunately, we cannot directly examine the brains of Australopithecines. All we have is the information about size and external shape that endocasts afford. Chimpanzees have brains of about the same size and shape as Australopithecine brains, but chimpanzees have never been seen to fashion a stone tool, even crudely. They catch small game, but not in the frequent manner that is suggested by the collections of bones of prey found in association with Australopithecine tools and fossils. Thus, behavioral evidence suggests that the Australopithecine was our closer relative, further advanced toward human culture than is the chimpanzee. Keeping in mind that the brain organization of the Australopithecine probably also differed somewhat from that of the chimpanzee, let's see how the modern human brain differs from that of the chimpanzee to give us some clues about the evolution of the hominid brain. Prominent differences between the organization of the brain of *Homo sapiens* and that of the chimpanzee include the following:

1. The human brain has larger motor and sensory cortical areas devoted to the hands.

2. Both the human brain and the chimpanzee brain have parts of the limbic system involved in vocalization. However, the human brain shows, in addition, large neocortical regions devoted to the production and perception of speech. Nonhuman primates have relatively smaller neocortical regions controlling vocalization.

3. For speech, manual dexterity, and other functions, the human brain shows striking hemispheric specialization of functions. In the chimpanzee the two hemispheres are more equivalent in function.

4. The primary sensory regions of the cortex are somewhat greater in the human than in the chimpanzee. But the main expansion in the human cortex lies outside these sensory regions; that is, in the human a larger proportion of the brain is devoted to more varied and more elaborate processing of information.

In trying to account for the evolution of the human brain and for the special capabilities of *Homo sapiens*, different theorists have emphasized different behavioral traits: "Dexterity and tool use, language, group hunting, various aspects of social structure, and the ability to plan for the future have all been proposed as primary in the cascade of changes leading to the constellation of traits we now possess" (Finlay and Darlington, 1995:1583). From their analysis of evolution of the mammalian brain, Finlay and Darlington suggest that the multiple facets and rapid rate of human evolution may be explained by the fact that large primates are on the part of the curve relating neocortex weight to brain weight where small increases in brain weight are associated with large increases in neocortex weight. Selection for any one cognitive ability might therefore cause, in parallel, greater processing capacity for all the other abilities. Finlay and Darlington suggest that the neocortex, as a general purpose processor, may allow "the organism to take advantage of the extra brain structure in ways not directly selected for during evolution" (1995:1583). Charles Darwin (1888:169) made almost the same point in the last century:

> In many cases, the continued development of a part, for instance the beak of a bird or the teeth of a mammal, would not aid the species in gaining its food, or for any other object; but with man we can see no definite limit to the continual development of the brain and mental faculties, as far as advantage is concerned.

The survival advantage of larger brains does not hold only for human beings, or primates, or mammalian predators and prey. It would even be too limited to maintain, as Shaw's Don Juan does in the epigraph at the beginning of this book, that large brains are the specialty of the mammalian line. Within each line of vertebrate evolution relative brain size varies, with the more recently evolved species usually having the larger encephalization factors. Furthermore, in each vertebrate line it is the dorsal part of the telencephalon that has expanded and differentiated in the species with more advanced capabilities. We will discuss the expansion in size of the prefrontal cortex in Chapter 19 (see Figure 19.21). As we find more such common responses to selection pressures, they may reveal the "rules" of how nervous systems adapt and evolve.

A large brain is expensive. Having large brains entails costs as well as benefits for human beings and other large-brained animals. Growth of a large brain requires a long gestation period, which is a burden on the mother, and childbirth is difficult because of the large size of the baby's head. Much of the growth of the brain continues during the years after birth, which means prolonged dependence of the infant and prolonged parental care. Although the brain makes up only about 2% of our total adult body weight, it accounts for about 15% of our cardiac output and metabolic budget when we are at rest. These percentages decrease when the body is active, because muscles increase their demands, but even then the brain's energy requirements remain high. The genetic specifications of the brain require more than half of the human genome, because there are so many kinds of brain cells and connections. These complex genetic messages are vulnerable to accidents; many of the known disorders of behavior are related to mutations of single genes. The evolution of large brains is especially remarkable when viewed in the context of these costs.

Chemical Messengers Have Evolved

We have discussed brain evolution in anatomical terms, but the growing understanding of brain chemistry and its importance for behavior makes it appropriate to say a little here about the evolution of chemical messengers. It is probable that long before nerve cells evolved, organisms were regulating and coordinating their functions and activities by using chemical molecules as messengers. The advent of neural signaling did not replace these chemical messengers but instead extended the possibilities of chemical communication. (Chemical stimulation at one end of a neuron leads to the output of chemical messenger molecules at distant terminals of the neuron, as we will see in Chapter 5.) Furthermore, purely chemical signaling still exists in organisms with complex nervous systems; they have endocrine systems whose hormonal messengers are closely coordinated with neural signals (see Chapter 7).

Although we cannot directly measure chemical messengers in fossils of early organisms, simple present-day organisms that resemble early forms of life employ many chemical messengers, some of which are similar to those of complex organisms. For example, yeast cells manufacture steroid molecules that closely resemble mammalian sex hormones. The hypothesis that chemical messengers are very old in evolution is supported by the fact that they are so widespread. For example,

some molecules that mammals use as neurotransmitters are also found not only in unicellular animals, such as protozoans, yeasts, and amoebas, but even in plants (Le Roith, Shiloach, and Roth, 1982). The well-known synaptic transmitter acetylcholine has been found throughout the animal kingdom, as well as in many plants. But acetylcholine may have had earlier nontransmitter functions, so the presence of acetylcholine is no guarantee that it is acting as a chemical messenger (Arbas, Meinertzhagen, and Shaw, 1991). A substance has to satisfy a number of criteria before we can conclude that it acts as a synaptic transmitter in a particular location in the body (see Chapter 5).

Because human beings and other vertebrates employ many of the same chemical messengers as do invertebrates, many studies of invertebrate neurochemistry and behavior are relevant to the understanding of vertebrate nervous systems.

Applications of Comparative Research

As is true of other areas of biological psychology, comparative and evolutionary studies of behavior and of bodily mechanisms have a variety of applications. Some examples were given in Box 3.2; here are a few others.

Revealing studies of parental care have been done in several species of monkeys; in some of these (for example, some tamarins) the father shares in parental care (Snowdon, 1990). This comparative research tries to define the conditions that lead to fathers' participation in parental care in some species of monkeys but not in others. A monogamous mating system has been found to promote, but not to guarantee, direct paternal care. When a monogamous female monkey can rear the young by herself, she allows little or no male involvement in their care. But where the demands on the mother are great—in the case of the tamarins, to nurse and carry twins—help from the father is necessary. Two applications have come from this research: (1) helping to save endangered species of tamarins, under both natural conditions and in zoos; (2) suggestions for further understanding of parental care and fathering in other species, including humans.

Another application of comparative studies is the use of model animal systems to throw light on biological mechanisms in other species, including humans. For example, many drugs have similar effects on learning and memory over a wide range of species, indicating particular neurochemical mechanisms may be involved in learning and memory (see Chapter 18).

Summary

1. Studies of classification and taxonomy of animals help determine how closely different species are related. Knowing this relationship, in turn, helps us interpret similarities and differences in behavior and structure of different species.

2. Comparative studies of the nervous system help us understand the evolution of the nervous system, including the human brain. They also provide a perspective for understanding species-typical behavioral adaptations.

3. The nervous systems of invertebrate animals range in complexity from a simple nerve net to the complex structures of the octopus. The nervous systems of certain invertebrates may provide a simplified model for understanding some aspects of vertebrate nervous systems.

4. Some of the distinctive features of invertebrate nervous systems include large, identifiable monopolar neurons and large axons that are frequently components of circuits mediating rapid escape behaviors.

5. The main divisions of the brain are the same in all vertebrates. Differences among these animals are largely quantitative, as reflected in differences in the relative sizes of nerve cells and brain regions.

6. Size differences in brain regions among various mammals are frequently related to distinctive forms of behavioral adaptation.

7. Evolutionary changes in brain size are apparent when one compares fossils and contemporary animals.

8. The brain size of a species must be interpreted in terms of body size. The overall rule for vertebrates is that brain weight is proportional to the three-quarters power of body weight.

9. Some animals have larger brains and some have smaller brains than predicted by the general relation between brain and body weights; that is, they differ in encephalization factors. Humans, in particular, have larger brains than would be predicted from their body size.

10. Within each of the lines of vertebrate evolution, relative brain size varies, with the more recently evolved species usually having the larger encephalization factors.

11. The human brain, as compared to brains of nonhuman primates, has larger motor and sensory cortical areas devoted to the hands, larger cortical regions devoted to the production and perception of speech, a larger proportion of the brain devoted to varied and elaborate processing of information, and striking hemispheric specializations of function.

12. Chemical molecules were probably used as messengers before the advent of the nervous system. Such chemicals are evident in many forms of life and continue as an important part of the signals of nervous systems.

13. Research that compares the behavior and structure of species, in relation to their phylogeny, is being applied in many ways to understanding biological bases of behavior and to improving health and well-being.

Recommended Reading

Alcock, J. A. 1993. *Animal Behavior.* 5th ed. Sinauer Associates, Sunderland, MA.

Dewsbury, D. A. (ed.) 1990. *Contemporary Issues in Comparative Psychology.* Sinauer Associates, Sunderland, MA.

Li, W. and Graur, D. 1991. *Fundamentals of Molecular Evolution.* Sinauer Associates, Sunderland, MA.

Mayr, E. and Ashlock, P. D. 1991. *Principles of Systematic Zoology.* 2nd ed. McGraw-Hill, New York.

McKinney, W. T. 1988. *Models of Mental Disorder: A New Comparative Psychiatry.* Plenum, New York.

Betty LaDuke, *Tomorrow*, 1986

Development of the Nervous System over the Life Span

CHAPTER

4

Orientation

Age puts its stamp on the behavior of all animals. Although the pace, progression, and orderliness of changes are especially prominent early in life, change is a feature of the entire span of life. Shakespeare put it well in "As You Like It" when he said

> . . . from hour to hour, we ripe and ripe,
> And then, from hour to hour, we rot and rot . . .

In this chapter we will describe the features of adult brains that we introduced in Chapters 2 and 3 in terms of their progress through life from the womb to the tomb. The fertilization of an egg leads to a body with a brain that contains billions of neurons with an incredible number of connections. The pace of this process is extraordinary: during the height of prenatal growth of the human brain, 250,000 neurons are added per minute. Our discussion of this developmental process will range wide; we will describe the emergence of nerve cells, and the formation of their connections, as well as the roles of genes and of experience in shaping the emerging nervous system.

In the Beginning: A Large-Scale View

The journey from fertilized egg to mature organism is exceedingly complicated. Picture, if you can, the number of neurons in the mature human brain. Recent estimates suggest that there are about 100 billion neurons and at least as many glial cells. Neurons include many cell types, and they form a vast array of connections. The number of synapses on a single large neuron ranges in the thousands, and the overall number of connections in the brain is about 100 trillion (Ackerman, 1992). These numbers alone suggest that the growth and development of the brain is massively complex. In addition to their sheer numbers, these elements are arranged into distinct, ordered species-typical patterns.

Brain Weight and Volume Change from Birth to Old Age

One measure of brain development is the weight of the brain at different stages of life. Weight can be considered a summary of many developmental processes. A study by Dekaban and Sadowsky (1978) gives a definitive portrait of the weight of the human brain over the life span. They measured the brains of 5826 people, selected from more than 25,000 cases from several cities. Figure 4.1 shows the changes with age in the weights of brains in males and females. Note the rapid increase during the first five years. Brain weight is at its peak from about age 18 to about age 30, after which there is a gradual decline. Another type of summary statement of brain development is available from MRI scans, which also reveal regional developmental changes (Jernigan et al., 1991). With MRI, brain development in living persons can be observed repeatedly. MRI also enables a finer scrutiny of developmental periods than do postmortem stud-

ies. For example, Jernigan and colleagues found that increases in brain volume during adolescence are especially evident in frontal and parietal regions. Let's see how the brain starts its developmental journey.

The Brain Emerges from the Neural Tube

A new human being begins when a sperm about 60 micrometers (μm) long penetrates the wall of an egg cell 100 to 150 μm in diameter, producing a **zygote** with 46 chromosomes. Together, these chromosomes contain the complete genetic blueprint for the development of a new individual. (A summary of the life cycle of cells, including a discussion of the basic genetic materials and how they direct cell activities, is provided in the Appendix. More complete details about cell activities and heredity are provided in comprehensive biology texts such as Purves, Orians, and Heller, 1995).

Rapid cell division begins the developmental program. Within 12 hours after conception the single cell has divided into two cells, and after three days these have become a small mass of homogeneous cells, like a cluster of grapes, about 200 μm in diameter.

Within a week the emerging human embryo shows three distinct cell layers (Figure 4.2*a*). These layers are the beginnings of all the tissues of the embryo. The nervous system will develop from the outer layer, called the **ectoderm** (from the Greek for "outer" and "skin"). As the cell layers thicken, they grow into a flat oval plate. In the ectodermal level of this plate, uneven cell division forms a groove—the primitive streak—which will form the midline. At the head end of the groove, a thickened collection of cells forms two weeks after fertilization. Ridges of ectoderm continue to bulge on both sides of the middle position, forming the **neural folds**. These neural folds will give rise to the entire nervous system. The

4.1 Human Brain Weight as a Function of Age
Note that the age scale has been expanded for the first five years in order to show data more clearly during this period of rapid growth. After Dekaban and Sadowsky, 1978.

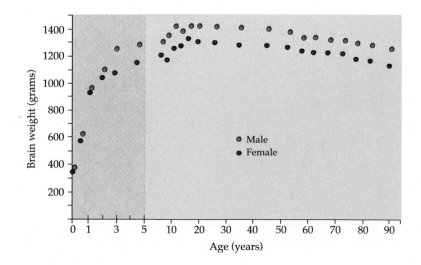

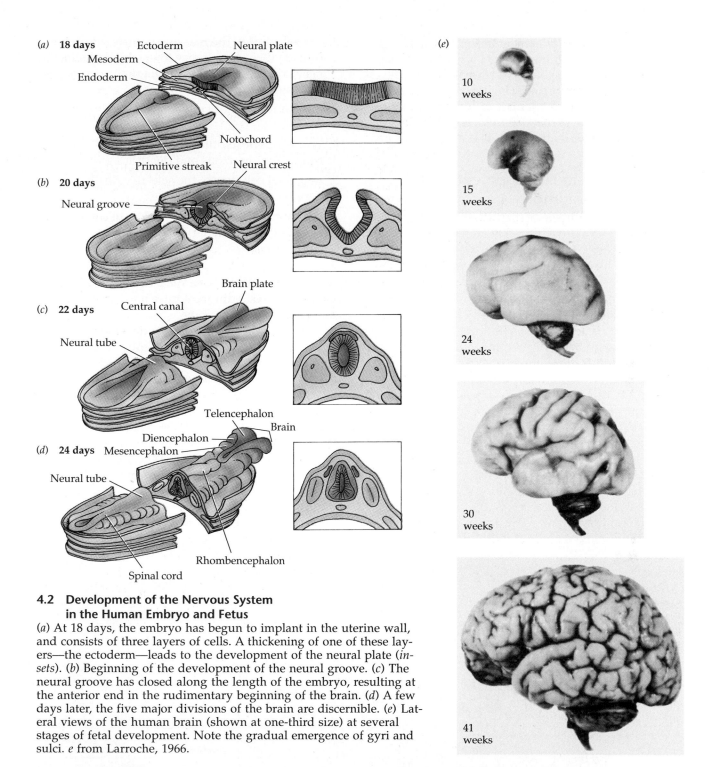

**4.2 Development of the Nervous System
in the Human Embryo and Fetus**
(*a*) At 18 days, the embryo has begun to implant in the uterine wall, and consists of three layers of cells. A thickening of one of these layers—the ectoderm—leads to the development of the neural plate (*insets*). (*b*) Beginning of the development of the neural groove. (*c*) The neural groove has closed along the length of the embryo, resulting at the anterior end in the rudimentary beginning of the brain. (*d*) A few days later, the five major divisions of the brain are discernible. (*e*) Lateral views of the human brain (shown at one-third size) at several stages of fetal development. Note the gradual emergence of gyri and sulci. *e* from Larroche, 1966.

groove between them is now called the **neural groove** (Figure 4.2*b*).

The pace of events now becomes faster. The neural folds come together to form the **neural tube** (Figure 4.2*c*). At the anterior part of the neural tube, three subdivisions become apparent. These subdivisions correspond to the future **forebrain** (prosencephalon),

midbrain (mesencephalon), and **hindbrain** (rhombencephalon) discussed in Chapter 2 (Figure 4.2*d*). The interior of the neural tube becomes the cerebral ventricles of the brain, the central canal of the spinal cord, and the passages that connect them.

By the end of the eighth week, the human embryo shows the rudimentary beginnings of most body organs. The rapid development of the brain is reflected in the fact that by this time the head is one-half the total size of the embryo. (Note that the developing human is called an **embryo** during the first ten weeks after fertilization; thereafter it is called a **fetus**.) Figure 4.2e shows the prenatal development of the human brain from weeks 10 through 41.

Nervous System Development Can Be Divided into Six Distinct Stages of Cellular Activity

From a cellular viewpoint it is useful to consider brain development as a sequence of distinct stages, most of which occur during prenatal life. These are:

1. **neurogenesis**, the mitotic division of nonneuronal cells to produce neurons;

2. **cell migration**, the massive movements of nerve cells or their precursors to establish distinctive nerve cell populations (nuclei in the central nervous system, ganglia elsewhere);

3. **differentiation** of cells into distinctive types of neurons;

4. **synaptogenesis**, the establishment of synaptic connections as axons and dendrites grow;

5. **neuronal cell death**, the selective death of many nerve cells;

6. **synapse rearrangement**, the loss of some synapses and development of others, to refine synaptic connections.

This sequence is portrayed in Figure 4.3. These stages proceed at different rates and times in different parts of the neural tube.

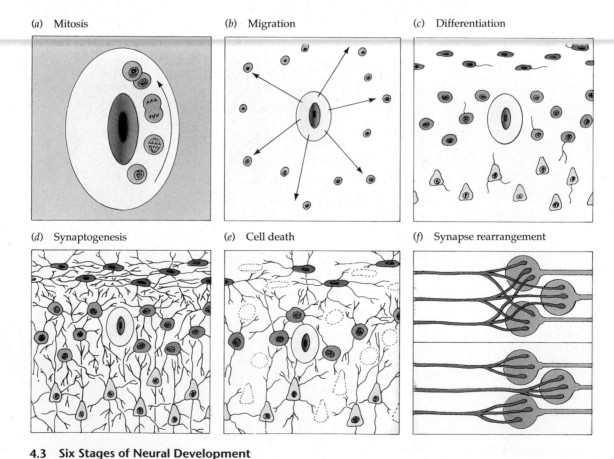

(a) Mitosis   *(b)* Migration   *(c)* Differentiation

(d) Synaptogenesis   *(e)* Cell death   *(f)* Synapse rearrangement

4.3   Six Stages of Neural Development
(a) Cells of the neural tube divide to provide cells. (b) The cells produced migrate to their appropriate region. (c) The cells differentiate to become either a neuron or a glial cell. (d) Neurons extend their axons and dendrites to form many synapses with one another. (e) Many neurons normally die early in development. (f) Many of the synapses initially formed will later be retracted, while other, later-appearing synapses form.

Cell Proliferation Produces Cells
That Will Become Neurons or Glial Cells

In this section we will focus on the developmental stages of cells as they relate specifically to neurons. Glial cells follow the same sequence. The production of nerve cells is called neurogenesis. Nerve cells themselves do not divide, but the cells that will give rise to neurons begin as a single layer of cells along the inner surface of the neural tube. These cells divide (in a process called **mitosis**; see the Appendix) and gradually form a closely packed layer, the **ventricular layer** of cells (Figure 4.4). These cells continue to divide, giving rise to "daughter" cells, which also divide. All neurons and glial cells are derived from cells that originate from such ventricular mitosis. Eventually some daughter cells leave the ventricular layer and begin expressing genes that transform the cell into either a neuron or a glial cell. Some cells of the ventricular layer give rise to glial cells and others to neurons (Levitt, Cooper, and Rakic, 1981). The separation between these two types of cells takes place early in the ventricular layer. In most mammals the formation of neural cells in the ventricular layer continues until birth; very few are added after birth (Jacobson, 1991), although some nerve cells are added to some brain regions after birth. For example, in the human cerebellum cells are added for months after birth, and olfactory receptor neurons are replaced throughout life.

There is a species-characteristic "birth date" for each part of an animal's brain. That is, there is an orderly chronological program for brain development, and it is possible to state the approximate days during development on which particular cell groups stop dividing. Of course, given the complexity of vertebrate brains, it is difficult to trace individual cell development from the initial small population of ventricular cells. Descendants disappear in the crowd. However, in some simpler invertebrate nervous systems with very few neurons, mitotic lineages can be traced more easily and completely. A favorite animal of researchers who study the lineage of nerve cells is the nematode *Caenorhabditis elegans*, a tiny worm with only 302 nerve cells. Because *C. elegans* has a virtually transparent body (Figure 4.5a), researchers have mapped the origins of each nerve cell, and have identified several of the genes controlling the paths of neural development (Wolinsky and Way, 1990). By observing the successive cell divisions of a *C. elegans* zygote, you can predict exactly what each cell will become in the adult—a sensory neuron, muscle cell, skin cell, and so on—based on its mitotic "ancestors."

Whereas cell fate in *C. elegans* is a highly determined and stereotypical result of mitotic lineage (Figure 4.5b), in vertebrates the paths from cell origins to

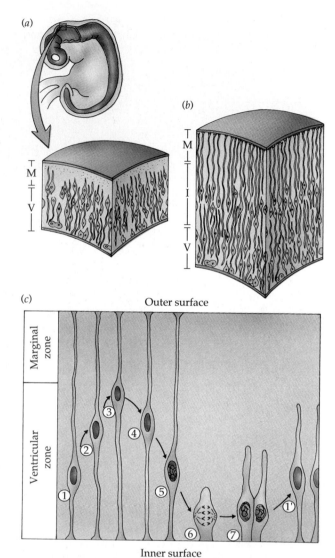

4.4 Proliferation of Cellular Precursors of Neurons and Glial Cells

(a) A small section of the wall of the neural tube at an early stage of embryonic development. Only ventricular (V) and marginal (M) layers are seen. (b) Later an intermediate (I) layer develops as the wall thickens. (c) Nuclei (within their cells) migrate from the ventricular layer to the outer layers. Some cells, however, return to the ventricular layer and undergo division, and the resulting daughter cells migrate to the outer layers, repeating the cycle.

the completed nervous system are more complex. New techniques, such as the injection of substances acting as markers or the use of induced mutations, have shown that in vertebrates the paths of development include more complex regulatory mechanisms. The hallmark of vertebrate development is that cell fate is affected by **cell–cell interactions** as cells sort themselves out and take on the fate that is appropri-

(*a*)

(*b*)

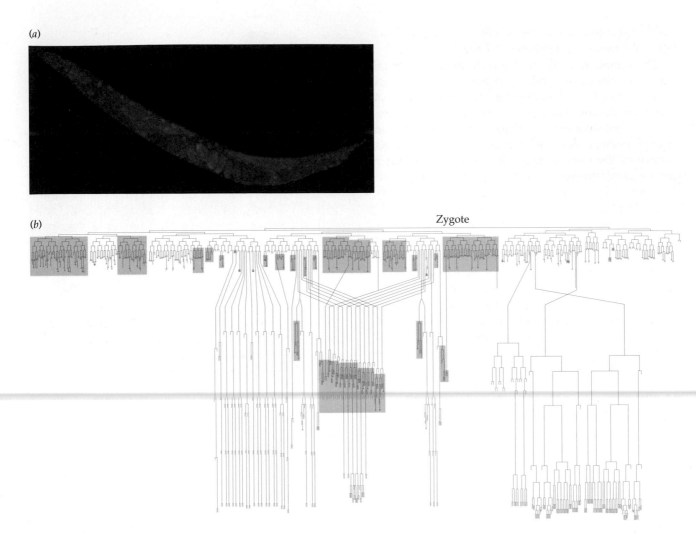

Zygote

4.5 Cell Fate in a Simple Organism

(*a*) The transparent body of *C. elegans*. (*b*) The mitotic lineage of cells that give rise to its body and nervous system; nervous system cells are highlighted in blue. The structure and function of every cell can be predicted from its mitotic lineage. Such mitotic determination of cell differentiation does not seem important to the development of vertebrates. *a* courtesy of Mark Blaxter; *b* after Pines, 1992.

ate in the context of what neighboring cells are doing. Thus, vertebrate development is less determined—that is, more subject to environmental signals and, as we'll see, experience.

Traditionally, investigators of nervous system development believed that most mammals have at birth all the nerve cells they will ever have (with some exceptions, which we have noted already). Researchers have usually attributed the postnatal growth of human brain weight to growth in the size of neurons, the branching of dendrites, the elaboration of synapses, the increase in myelin, and the addition of nonneural (glial) cells. Within recent years, this belief has

been modified, primarily because it now appears that small neurons are added for some period following birth.

All the large neurons the brain will ever contain are indeed present at birth, but in regions around the brain ventricles, the ventricular zone, mitotic division continues after birth. Several regions of the rat brain, including the olfactory bulb and the hippocampus, appear to add small neurons derived from the ventricular zone. In fact, it is now well established that nerve cells of the olfactory end organ are normally replaced throughout life. This process involves a set of cells adjacent to olfactory receptor cells that become neurons, perhaps in response to the ongoing death of olfactory nerve cells (Jacobson, 1991).

The dogma that no new neurons are added to the adult nervous system is strongly challenged by exciting research on the neural basis of bird song (discussed in Chapters 12 and 19). Briefly, bird song velopment in males of some species is under hormonal control, dependent on the hormone testosterone. In earlier research, Nottebohm (1980) determined the parts of the bird brain responsible for song learning and performance. During the course of this work, he noted that at least one part of the relevant brain circuit for bird song is large in spring and shrinks to half that size in the fall. This seasonal change in the size of the brain region is related to male hormone levels and singing behavior (Nottebohm, 1991). Some of this seasonal variation in the size of the brain region is accounted for by seasonal variations in dendritic length and branching. However, Nottebohm has also presented evidence that new neurons are added throughout life. New cells are formed in the ventricular zone, migrate to the nearby vocal control brain region and there differentiate into neurons. These observations suggest the need to reexamine the belief that the adult brain does not add new neurons. At the very least such renewed research could offer a better understanding of the conditions that lead to the usual cessation of neuron addition in adulthood.

New Nerve Cells Migrate to Their Final Location

Neurons of the developing nervous system are always on the move. At some stage the cells that form in the ventricular layer through mitotic division move away, in a process known as cell migration. The cells acquire short extensions at the "head" and "tail" ends. Some descriptions of migrating cells compare them to a trail of active ants (Figure 4.6). In primates the migration of presumptive nerve cells is virtually complete by birth, but in rats, cells that will become neurons continue to migrate in some regions for several weeks following birth.

Cells do not move in an aimless, haphazard manner. Clues to the guidance of cell migration come from studies using radioactive substances that become incorporated into the cell before migration. These substances "tag" the cell so that it can be followed and its migratory paths clearly outlined. Many elegant studies by Rakic (reviewed in Rakic, 1985) show that some cells in the developing brain move along the surface of a particular type of glial cell that ap-

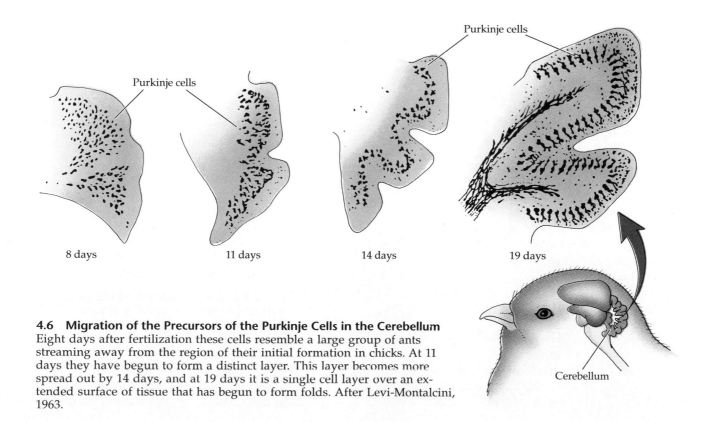

4.6 Migration of the Precursors of the Purkinje Cells in the Cerebellum
Eight days after fertilization these cells resemble a large group of ants streaming away from the region of their initial formation in chicks. At 11 days they have begun to form a distinct layer. This layer becomes more spread out by 14 days, and at 19 days it is a single cell layer over an extended surface of tissue that has begun to form folds. After Levi-Montalcini, 1963.

pears early. Like spokes (radii) of a wheel, these **radial glia** extend from the inner to outer surfaces of the emerging nervous system (Figure 4.7). The radial glia act as a series of guide wires, and the newly formed cells creep along them. A recent article about this process is subtitled "Riding the Glial Monorail" (Hatten, 1991). Some cells that form later migrate in a different manner, attracted to the surfaces of neurons. Rakic (1985) has described examples of this migratory mechanism in the cerebellum, in which newly formed cells migrate along the axons of earlier formed nerve cells. Some cells creep laterally along

horizontal axons and then follow glia downward into the cerebellar cortex. A striking image of this process observed **in vitro** (in a laboratory dish) is shown in Figure 4.8.

Failures in the mechanism of cell migration result in either a vastly reduced population of neurons or a disorderly arrangement and, not surprisingly, behavioral disorders. The migration of cells and the outgrowth of nerve cell extensions (dendrites and axons) involve various chemicals. Molecules that promote the adhesion of developing elements of the nervous system and thereby guide migrating cells and grow-

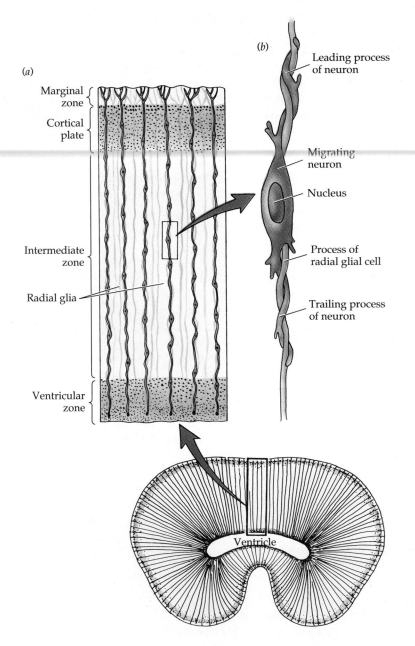

4.7 Glial Spokes Guide Migrating Cells
Early in development radial glial cells span the width of the emerging cerebral hemispheres (bottom). Enlargement (*a*) shows how radial glia act as guide wires for the migration of neurons. Further enlargement (*b*) shows a single neuron migrating out along a radial glial fiber. After Cowan, 1979; based on Rakic, 1971.

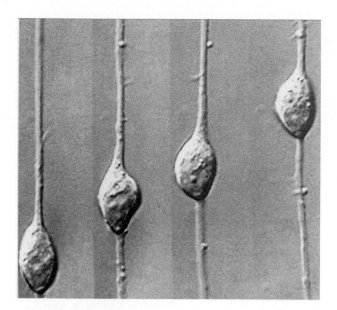

4.8   Cell Migration in a Dish
Time-lapse video shows that, even when placed in tissue culture dishes, cerebellar granule cell neurons will migrate along elongated cell bodies of glia (the long processes extending vertically. The glial cells do not elongate unless granule cells are present, and the granule cells must be able to adhere to the glial cells in order to migrate along them. From Hatten, 1990.

ing axons, are called **cell adhesion molecules (CAMs)**. Knowledge about CAMs and other components of the extracellular matrix surrounding developing cells is important for understanding the major steps in neural development (Reichardt and Tomeselli, 1991). CAMs may also guide axons to regenerate when they are cut in adulthood (Box 4.1).

The single-file appearance of nerve cell precursors during cell migration (see Figure 4.6) is followed by the aggregation, or grouping, of cells in a manner that foreshadows the nuclei of the adult brain that we discussed in Chapter 2. For example, cells of the cerebral cortex and cerebellar cortex become arranged in layers during fetal development. These groupings are the beginnings of the defined regions of the brain.

Cells in Newly Formed Brain Regions Differentiate into Neurons

The newly arrived cells bear no more resemblance to mature nerve cells than they do to the cells of other organs. Once they reach their destinations, however, the cells begin to use ("express") particular genes to make the particular proteins a neuron needs. This process of cell differentiation allows the cell to ac-

quire the distinctive appearance of neurons characteristic of their particular region. Figure 4.9 shows the progressive unfolding of Purkinje cells of the cerebellar cortex. Outgrowths from their dendrites appear soon after their alignment into a single row. Slowly more and more branches form, progressively expanding the receptive surface of the Purkinje cell.

What controls differentiation is not completely understood, but two classes of influence are known. First, intrinsic self-organization is certainly an important factor; both granule cells and Purkinje cells in tissue culture grow in a typical manner, although they are deprived of some normal connections (Seil, Kelley, and Leiman, 1974). When a cell shows characteristics that are independent of neighboring cells, we say it is acting in a **cell-autonomous** manner. In cell-autonomous differentiation, presumably only the genes within that cell are directing events. Some examples exist in the nervous system. It has been shown repeatedly, however, that the neural environment also greatly influences nerve-cell differentiation. In other words, neighboring cells are a second major influence on the differentiation of neurons. In the vertebrates (unlike the case of the nematode *C. elegans*) young neural cells seem to have the capacity to become many varieties of neurons, and the particular type of neuron that a cell becomes depends on where it happens to be and what its neighboring cells are.

For example, consider spinal motoneurons—cells in the spinal cord that send their axons out to control muscles. Motoneurons are large, multipolar cells found on the left and right sides of the spinal cord in the ventral horn of gray matter. Motoneurons are among the first recognizable neurons in the spinal cord and send their axons out early in fetal development. How do these cells "know" they should express motoneuron-specific genes and grow into motoneurons? Experiments that examine the late divisions giving rise to motoneurons make it clear that the cells are not attending to mitotic lineage (Leber, Breedlove, and Sanes, 1990). Instead, other cells lying just ventral to the developing spinal cord—in a structure called the notochord—direct spinal cells to become motoneurons. If we insert a new length of notochord above the spinal cord, cells begin differentiating into motoneurons on each side of the spinal cord adjacent to the notochord (Roelink et al., 1992; Figure 4.10). Presumably the notochord releases a chemical messenger that diffuses to the spinal cord and directs some (but not all) cells to become motoneurons.

The influence of one set of cells on the fate of neighboring cells is called **induction**—the notochord

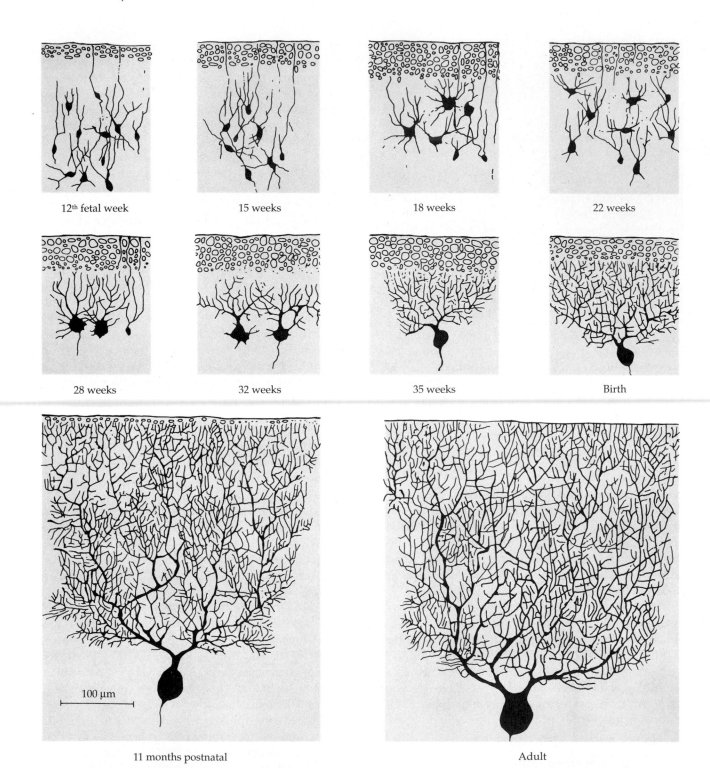

12th fetal week   15 weeks   18 weeks   22 weeks

28 weeks   32 weeks   35 weeks   Birth

100 μm

11 months postnatal   Adult

4.9 Development of Purkinje Cells in the Human Cerebellum
After Zecevic and Rakic, 1976.

induces some spinal cord cells to differentiate into motoneurons. Induction of this sort has been demonstrated many times in the developing vertebrate body and, more recently, brain. Another way to describe the situation is that there is extensive cell–cell inter-

action, with each cell taking cues from its neighbors. The idea of cells influencing each other's differentiation may make the entire affair seem very complex, as indeed it is. But one consequence of this system is that cells differentiate

Box 4.1

Degeneration and Regeneration of Nervous Tissue

When a mature nerve cell is injured, several forms of regrowth can occur. Complete replacement of injured nerve cells is rare in mammals, but the figure illustrates several characteristic forms of degeneration and regeneration in the mammalian peripheral and CNS. Injury close to the cell body of a neuron produces a series of changes that result in the eventual destruction of the cell. This process is called **retrograde degeneration** (2 and 3). If the injured neuron dies, the target cells formerly innervated by that neuron may also show signs of transneuronal atrophy (4).

Cutting through the axon also produces loss of the distal part of the axon (the part separated from the cell body). This process is called Wallerian, or **anterograde**, degeneration (5 and 6). The part of the axon that remains connected to the cell body may regrow. Severed axons in the peripheral nervous system regrow readily. Sprouts emerge from the part of the axon that is still connected to the nerve cell body and advance slowly toward the periphery (7). Cell adhesion molecules (CAMs) help guide the regenerating axons. Some animals have an enviable advantage. After an injury to

the brain, several fish and amphibians appear to be able to regenerate large parts of the brain itself.

From an experimental point of view, our interest in regeneration of the nervous system lies principally in the fact that regeneration involves processes that seem similar to original development. Studying regeneration may thus increase our understanding of the original processes of growth of the nervous system. From a therapeutic viewpoint, these studies may help scientists learn how to induce repair and regrowth of damaged neural tissue in humans.

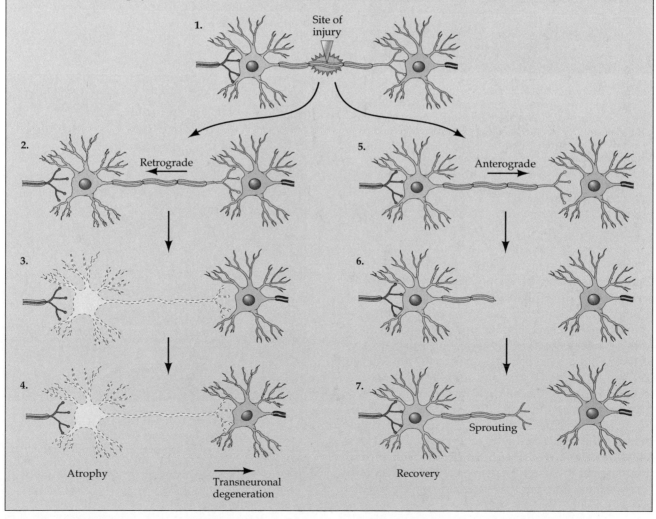

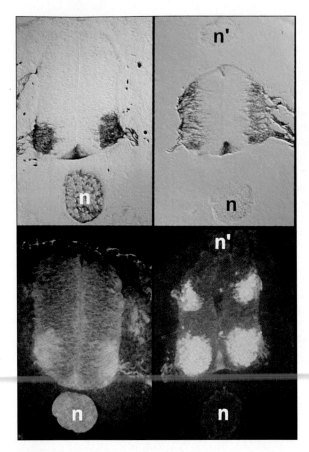

4.10 The Induction of Spinal Motoneurons
(*Left*) Spinal motoneurons in normal chickens, where the motoneurons cluster in the ventral region on either side. The notochord (n) lies just beneath the spinal cord. (*Right*) A spinal cord in which a segment of notochord was placed along the dorsal surface (n'). Some of the spinal cord cells on either side were induced to differentiate as motoneurons, presumably by a chemical signal from the notochord. Courtesy of Thomas Jessell.

into the type of neuron that is appropriate for that brain region; thus cell–cell interaction coordinates development—directing differentiation to provide the right type of neuron for each part of the brain. Another consequence of development relying upon cell–cell interactions such as induction is that, if a few cells are injured or lost, other cells will "answer the call" of inducing factors and fill in for the missing cells. This phenomenon can be observed in any vertebrate and many invertebrate embryos from which some cells have been removed. For example, if you remove the cells from a developing limb bud in a chick embryo early enough, other cells pitch in, and by the time the chick hatches, the limb looks normal—without any parts missing. Embryologists refer

to such adaptive responses to early injury as **regulation**—the developing animal compensates for missing or injured cells.

The Axons and Dendrites of Young Neurons Grow Extensively and Form Synapses

The biggest changes in brain cells from birth to maturity take place in the branches and connections among neurons. There are huge increases in the length of dendrites, which seem to involve processes akin to those involved in the growth of axons. At the tips of both axons and dendrites are **growth cones**, swollen ends from which extensions emerge (Figure 4.11). From the cones extend very fine outgrowths, called **filopodia**, which are spikelike and extend and retract. The filopodia seem to adhere to the extracellular environment, and then contract to pull the growth cone (trailing the growing axon behind it) in a particular direction. The fact that dendrite growth cones have been found in adult animals suggests that elongation and changes of dendrites may continue throughout life in response to functional demands.

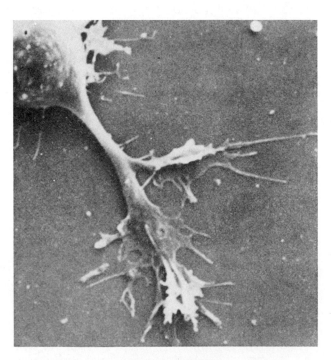

4.11 Growth Cones Form at the Tip of Growing Axons and Dendrites
The fine, threadlike extensions are filopodia, which find adhesive surfaces and pull the growth cone, and therefore the growing axon, in the appropriate direction. Courtesy of Steven R. Rothman.

(a)

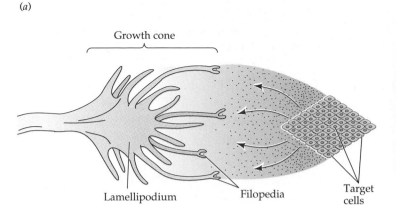

Growth cone

Lamellipodium   Filopedia   Target cells

(b)

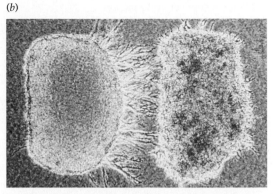

(c)

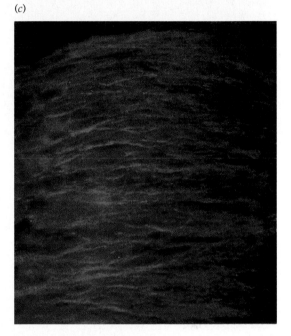

4.12 The Effects of Chemotropic Factors on Target Cells

(*a*) Target cells release a chemical that creates a gradient around them. Growth cones orient to and follow the gradient to the cells. (*b*) Extensions growing out of a sensory ganglion (*left*) toward their normal target tissue. (*c*) Extensions of dorsal spinal cord cells (*left*) growing toward a piece of ventral spinal cord. After Tessier-Lavigne et al., 1988; *b* and *c* courtesy of Marc Terrier-Lavigne.

What guides axons along the paths they take? A long-standing notion is that axons are guided by the attractive force of chemicals released or secreted by the target nerve cells or other tissues such as muscles (Tessier-Lavigne and Placzek, 1991). The axon growth cone responds to the concentration gradient of this chemical that provides directional guidance. This view, formally labeled the "chemotropic guidance of axons," is illustrated in Figure 4.12, which shows the ability of a chemical to act as an attractant for growing sensory neurons. A large body of work examining the way axons from the eye regenerate and find their original brain targets in amphibians also implicates chemotropic guidance of axons. Other chemical signals seem to guide axons by repulsing the growth cones of some cells but not others (Keynes and Cook, 1995). Dendritic growth is also affected by both intrinsic factors and cell–cell interactions, especially the approach of axons from other cells (Brown et al., 1992).

The molecular biology of axonal and dendritic growth has been studied in detail, and many different substances have been implicated in this process. Early in development the growing axon and dendrite contain different proteins, suggesting that the nerve cell acquires a basic polarity—the axonal end and the dendritic end—at the earliest stages of development. How the cell body directs the appropriate molecules to each end is an area of intensive study.

The formation of synapses increases at a rapid rate, particularly on dendrites (Figure 4.13). In many nerve cells, synapses are formed at dendritic spines. The spines themselves proliferate rapidly after birth. These connections can be affected by postnatal experience, as we will see in Chapter 17. To support the metabolic needs of the expanded dendritic tree, the nerve cell body greatly increases in volume. Why is a synapse created at any single site on a neuron or other targets such as muscle? Undoubtedly some type of chemical recognition bonds a presynaptic ending to a particular postsynaptic site; the molecular features of this recognition mechanism are slowly unfolding.

The Death of Many Neurons Is a Normal Part of Development

As strange as it may seem, cell death is a crucial phase of brain development, especially during em-

(*a*)   Rat superior cervical ganglion

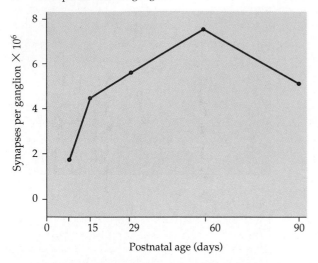

(*b*)   Rat visual cortex

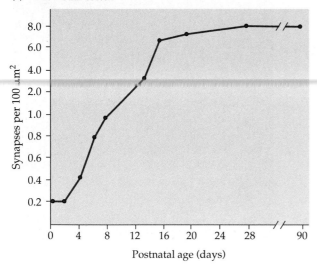

(*c*)   Human visual cortex

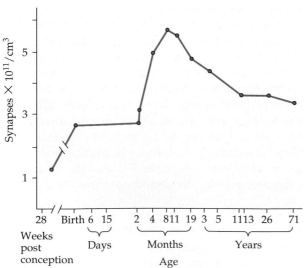

4.13   Postnatal Development of Synapses
(*a*) Rat superior cervical ganglion. (*b*) Rat visual cortex. (*c*) In human visual cortex, note the decline in the density of synapses after the first year of life. *a* after Smolen, 1981; *b* from Blue and Parnavelas, 1983; *c* from Huttenlocher et al., 1982.

bryonic stages. This developmental stage is not unique to the nervous system. Naturally occurring cell death, also called **apoptosis,** (from the Greek *ptosis,* "a dropping," and *apo,* "away"), is evident as a kind of sculpturing process in the emergence of other tissues in both animals and plants (Oppenheim, 1991). In the nervous system, however, the number of cells that die during early development is quite large. In some regions of the brain and spinal cord, almost all the nerve cells die during prenatal development! The magnitude of this developmental phenomenon is shown in Figure 4.14. The proportion of nerve cells that die varies from region to region and ranges from 20 to 80% of the cells. Naturally occurring neuronal death was first described by Viktor Hamburger (1958) in chicks, in which about half the originally produced spinal motoneurons die before the chicks hatch.

Viktor Hamburger

Several factors influence this massive cell death in the nervous system. Regulation of the extent of cell death is controlled in part by factors associated with the synaptic targets of cells. Reduction of the size of the synaptic target invariably reduces the number of surviving nerve cells. For example, if the leg of a tadpole is removed early in development, many more developing spinal motoneurons die than if the leg had remained in position. Conversely, grafting on an extra leg—a technique possible with chicken embryos and amphibians—appreciably reduces the usual loss of cells; in this instance, the mature spinal cord has more than the usual number of neurons. These observations suggest that the target of a developing population of nerve cells influences the survival of these neurons and that the neurons are competing for something in order to survive. These results also suggest that some of the cells that would have died in the absence of the leg were capable of performing the job of motoneurons, so we can conclude that they did not die because of a fatal defect. In fact, there is evidence

(a) Spinal motor neurons (chick)

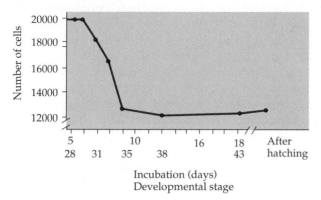

(b) Ciliary ganglion (chick)

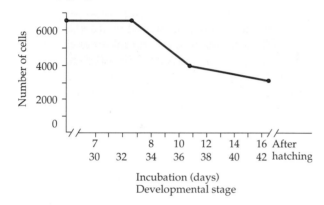

(c) Spinal motor neurons (human)

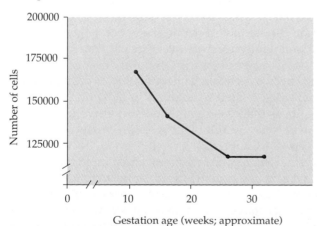

Gestation age (weeks; approximate)

**4.14 Many Neurons Normally Die
During Early Development**
(*a*) Spinal motoneurons in the chick. (*b*) Ciliary ganglion of chick. (*c*) Human spinal motoneurons.
a from Hamburger, 1975; *b* from Landmesser and Pilar, 1974; *c* from Forger and Breedlove, 1987.

that all cells carry **death genes**—genes that are expressed only when a cell "decides" to die (Schwartz, 1992; Johnson and Deckwerth, 1993). The genes seem to encode for enzymes that cut up DNA and proteins, presumably so that the constituents can be recycled.

What are the neurons competing for? Some researchers have suggested that they compete for connections to target structures (other nerve cells or end organs, such as muscle). According to this view, cells that make adequate synapses remain; those without a place to form synaptic connections die. Another view is that the cells compete not for synaptic sites, but for a chemical that the target makes and releases. Neurons that receive enough of the chemical survive, and those that do not die. Such target-derived chemicals are called **neurotrophic factors** (or simply "trophic factors") because they act as if they "feed" the neurons to help them survive. No one has yet found the neurotrophic factor that keeps spinal motoneurons alive, but later in this chapter we'll describe a neurotrophic factor (nerve growth factor) that keeps developing sympathetic neurons alive. It is widely assumed that there are many neurotrophic factors, each specifically maintaining a particular population of neurons during a period of neuronal cell death.

Nerve cell death seems to effect a numerical matching between developing cell populations. For example, consider a hypothetical case in which neuronal population A contains 100 cells. Its axons extend toward nerve cell population B, which consists of 50 cells. The large number in population A assures plenty of connections to neurons in B, but there will probably be a group of cells that will not be needed after effective links are forged. The result is that some cells in population A die.

Afferents (axons providing synaptic input to a neuron) also influence whether that neuron dies during development. A reduction in afferent input produces a significant increase in neuronal death in various developing nervous system regions. Some of this effect may be mediated by the neural activity of the afferents (Oppenheim, 1991).

Sometimes hormones in general circulation affect cell death. This type of nerve cell death is evident in insect metamorphosis. Nerve cell death in moth nervous systems is triggered by the same hormones that produce the transformation from caterpillar to moth (Truman, 1983; Weeks and Levine, 1990). The Mauthner cell (a specialized cell in the metencephalon) of some amphibians changes as a result of the secretion of thyroid hormones. The cell degenerates as the animal's lifestyle changes from aquatic to terrestrial. In Chapter 12 we will note the importance of certain sex hormones in controlling cell death in the spinal cord of mammals.

Synaptic Connections Are Refined by Synapse Rearrangement

Just as not all the neurons produced by the developing individual are kept into adulthood, so too some of the synapses formed early in development are later retracted. Originally this process was described as synapse elimination, but later studies found that although some original synapses are lost, new synapses are also formed. Thus a more accurate term is synapse rearrangement or synaptic remodeling. In most cases synapse rearrangement takes place after the period of cell death, so the two processes are not directly related. For example, we learned that about half of the spinal motoneurons that are made later die (see Figure 4.3e). By the end of the cell death period, each surviving motoneuron innervates many muscle fibers and every muscle fiber is innervated by several motoneurons. But later the surviving motoneurons retract many of their axon collaterals, until each muscle fiber comes to be innervated by only one motoneuron. Then each motoneuron enlarges the remaining synapse (see Figure 4.3f). (In Chapter 11 we'll discuss the significance for motor control of each muscle fiber receiving only one input.) Similar events have been documented in several neural regions including the cerebellum (Mariani and Changeux, 1981); brain stem (Jackson and Parks, 1982); visual cortex (Hubel, Wiesel, and LeVay, 1977); and several autonomic ganglia (Lichtman and Purves, 1980). Each ganglion cell originally receives a few synapses from each of several axons. Then some synapses are retracted while others are formed, until each ganglion cell receives many synapses from only a single source.

There is a large net loss of synapses in the cerebral cortex of developing monkeys (Rakic et al., 1986). After reaching a peak about three months after birth, by three years of age the number of synapses declines to approximately two-thirds of the maximal number. The magnitude of synapse loss seems the same throughout the four cerebral lobes. Whether there is a net loss of synapses in human cerebral cortex during development has not been addressed.

What determines which synapses are kept and which are lost? Although we don't know all the factors, one important influence is neural activity (Box 4.2). Later in this chapter we'll see cases in which active synapses are maintained and inactive synapses are retracted in the mammalian visual system. In Chapter 11 we'll review evidence that synapse rearrangement in the cerebral cortex can continue throughout life. Those studies show that active use of a particular finger leads to an expansion of the cerebral cortical regions responding to that finger. This expansion could be due to the retraction of some synapses and the formation of others.

Glial Cells Are Produced throughout Life

As noted above, glial cells develop from the same populations of immature cells as do neurons. The factors that determine whether a cell differentiates into a neuron or a glial cell remain unknown. Unlike neurons, glial cells continue to be added to the nervous system throughout life. (Sometimes the process becomes aberrant, resulting in glial tumors, or gliomas, of the brain.) The production of glia continues for a longer period than the production of neurons and peaks later in the developmental process. In fact, the most intense phase of glial proliferation in many animals occurs after birth, when glial cells are added from immature cells located in the ventricular zones.

Glial Cells Myelinate Axons after Birth

The development of sheaths around axons—the process of myelination—(Figure 4.15) greatly changes the rate at which axons conduct messages. Myelination should have a strong impact on behavior, since it profoundly affects the velocity of the nerve impulse and thereby affects the temporal order of events in the nervous system. Unfortunately, myelination has yet to be related to changes in behavior. What we know is that disorders that disrupt myelin in adulthood (such as multiple sclerosis) have devastating effects (see Chapter 2).

In humans, the earliest myelination in the peripheral nervous system is evident in cranial and spinal nerves about 24 weeks after conception. But the most intense phase of myelination occurs shortly after birth. Furthermore, some investigators believe that myelin can be added to axons throughout life. The first nerve tracts in the human nervous system to become myelinated are in the spinal cord. Myelination then spreads successively into the hindbrain, midbrain, and forebrain. Within the cerebral cortex, sensory zones are myelinated before motor zones; correspondingly, sensory functions mature before motor functions.

Schwann cell

1. Axon

Nucleus

2.

3.

4.

4.15   Myelin Formation
The repeated wrapping of a Schwann cell cytoplasm around an axon results in a many-layered sheath that electrically insulates the axon, speeding the conduction of electrical signals along its length.

Neocortical Layers Are Formed by Successive Waves of New Neurons

Each brain region is characterized by a distinctive arrangement of nerve cells and their processes. The developmental assembly of each region of the brain follows a precise timetable; many parts of the schedule appear to rely on mutual interactions of cells in the developing region. To show how regions may acquire characteristic orderly forms, let's take the cerebral cortex as an example. The 50 billion neurons of the human cerebral cortex are arranged in six layers, and the cells of each layer differ in form and size. The arrangement of layers depends on where they are in the brain. These variations have been used to define the borders of different cortical regions (see Figure 2.22). Here we will look at the way the cerebral neocortex grows and achieves this distinctive layered organization.

Examination of the closed neural tube of a human embryo at the end of the third week after fertilization reveals a zone of dividing cells all around the inner surfaces—the ventricular zone we mentioned earlier. This early proliferation of cells at the rostral (head) end results in the formation of the **cortical plate**, the beginnings of the cerebral cortex (Allendoerfer and Shatz, 1994). Intense cell division continues to produce cells that will in time become the neurons of the cerebral cortex. This rapid proliferation continues until the sixth month of fetal life, by which time the

cerebral cortex has its full complement of neurons.

The formation of cell layers in the cerebral cortex follows a regular process. Cells that are formed along the ventricular zone migrate away from it. Each new cell migrates beyond those born earlier. Thus, the inner layer (layer 6) has the "oldest" neurons, and the youngest neurons are in the outermost layer (1). Cells within each layer that will become the large neurons are born first; smaller cells are born slightly later. Migration time—the interval between cell birth and arrival of the cell at its final position—becomes progressively longer, taking about five days for the last group of new cortical cells. The most intense phase of dendritic growth and synapse formation in the cerebral cortex occurs after birth. The extent of human postnatal cortical development is illustrated in Figure 4.16.

Brain Growth and Development Reflects the Interaction of Intrinsic and Extrinsic Factors

Many factors influence the emergence of the form, arrangements, and connections of the developing brain. One influence is genes, which direct the production of every protein the cell can make. In *C. elegans*, genes are almost the only factors affecting development; the cells somehow keep track of their mitotic lin-

Box 4.2

The Frog Retinotectal System Demonstrates Intrinsic and Extrinsic Factors in Neural Development

In the 1940s, Roger Sperry began a series of experiments that seemed to emphasize the importance of intrinsic factors such as genes for determining the pattern of connections in the brain. If the optic nerve connecting an eye to the brain is cut in an adult mammal, the animal is blinded in that eye and never recovers. In fish and amphibians such as frogs, however, the animal is only temporarily blinded; in a few months the axons from the eye (specifically, from the so-called ganglion cells of the retina) reinnervate the brain (specifically, the dorsal portion of the midbrain, called the **tectum**) and the animal recovers its eyesight. When food is presented on the left or right, above or below, the animal flicks its tongue accurately to retrieve it. Thus, either (1) the retina reestablishes the same pattern of connections to the tectum that was there before surgery and the brain interprets visual information as before, or (2) the retina reinnervates the tectum at random, but the brain learns how to interpret the information presented in this new pattern.

Several lines of evidence have established that the first hypothesis is correct. One is that sometimes

the first arriving retinal axons pass over uninnervated tectum to reach their original position. The classic case occurred when the optic nerve was cut and the eye was rotated 180 degrees. When the animal recovered eyesight, it behaved as if the visual image had been rotated 180 degrees; it moved to the left when trying to get food presented on the right, flicked its tongue up when food was presented below.

The only explanation for this behavior is that the retinal axons grew back to their *original* positions on the tectum, ignoring the rotation of the eye. Furthermore, once the original connections were reestablished, the brain interpreted the information as if the eye were in its original position. Even years later, the animals never learned to make sense of information from the rotated eye.

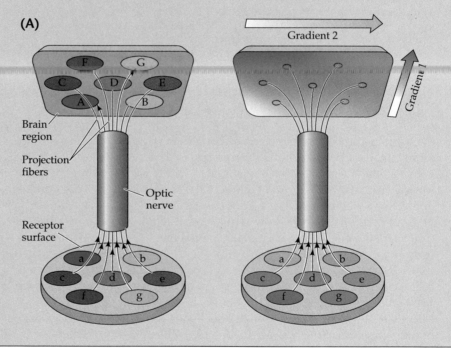

(A)

Brain region

Projection fibers

Optic nerve

Receptor surface

Gradient 2

Gradient 1

eage and then simply express the genes appropriate for the cell fate that their lineage directs. Genes are a major influence on all development, including that of the vertebrate brain. An animal that has inherited an altered gene will make an altered protein, which will affect any cell structure that includes that protein. Thus, every neuronal structure, and therefore every behavior, can be altered by changes in the appropriate gene(s). It is useful to think of genes as intrinsic factors—that is, factors that originate within the developing brain itself. All

other influences we can consider as extrinsic—that is, originating outside of the developing cell.

What are the extrinsic factors? For mammals, which depend on nutrients supplied from the mother during development, an important extrinsic factor is whether the fetus is provided with the nutrients needed to carry out the genetic instructions. As we'll see, the lack of nutrients or the presence of chemicals that interfere with the delivery of nutrients can have a profound effect on brain development. Another im-

(B)

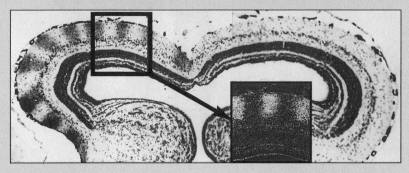

Sperry proposed the **chemoaffinity hypothesis** to explain how retinal axons knew which part of the tectum to innervate. Suppose each retinal cell and each tectal cell had a specific chemical identity—an address of sorts. Then each retinal cell need only seek out the proper address in the tectum and the entire pattern would be reestablished; there may be many chemical cues involved (Figure A, *left*), or only a few (Figure A, *right*). Several preparations indicated that there were limits to how accurately retinal cells could find their original target, but there is one dramatic demonstration.

When retinal cells are placed in culture dishes, their axons grow and show preferences! The axons of ganglion cells from lateral retina prefer to grow over cell membranes from rostral tectum (their normal target) rather than membranes from caudal tectum (Bonhoeffer and Huf, 1985). Axons from medial retina, however, show no preference. Thus there is evidence that chemical cues get the retinal axons to the *roughly* appropriate region of tectum.

The most recent evidence indicates that, having arrived at the roughly appropriate region of tectum, retinal connections are fine-tuned by extrinsic factors, specifically by experience. Normally each retina innervates only the tectum on the opposite side. When two retinas are *forced* to innervate a single tectum by implanting a third eye (Figure B, *top*), they each do so in the same rough pattern, but they segregate; axons from one retina predominate in one area and axons from the other retina predominate in neighboring tectum, so that there are alternating stripes of innervation from the two eyes (Figure B, *bottom*). This segregation is activity-dependent (Constantine-Paton, Cline, and Debski, 1990). If you silence neural activity in one eye (by injecting it with drugs), it loses its connections to the tectum and the other eye takes over, innervating the entire tectum. If you silence both eyes (by keeping the animal in the dark), neither eye predominates, their axons fail to segregate in the tectum, and the detailed pattern of innervation fails to appear. Thus, the retinotectal system appears to use two steps to reestablish the original pattern of innervation: (1) Chemical cues bring retinal axons to the approximately correct region of tectum. (2) The neural activity of the retinal cells, normally driven by patterned visual stimulation, directs these axons to innervate or maintain innervation of the precise tectal region. (Figure B courtesy of Martha Constantine-Paton.)

portant class of extrinsic factors for all vertebrates is cell–cell interactions: whether a cell expresses a particular gene, takes a particular shape, or performs a particular task may depend upon whether neighboring cells exert an inductive influence. The recognition that cell–cell interactions are very important for brain development led to the discovery of another extrinsic factor—neural activity. As we'll see, sometimes the electrical activity of a neuron can affect the fate of other cells (whether they live or die) and can determine whether or not synapses are maintained. Finally, the ability of neural activity to direct brain development identifies another influence—experience. Events in the environment (sounds, lights, odors, and so on) affect the activity of sensory neurons; in several cases the activity of the sensory neurons determines which synapses are maintained and which are lost. In this way experience can alter the connections of the developing brain, thereby effecting an individual's behavior in adulthood. Table 4.1 lists these

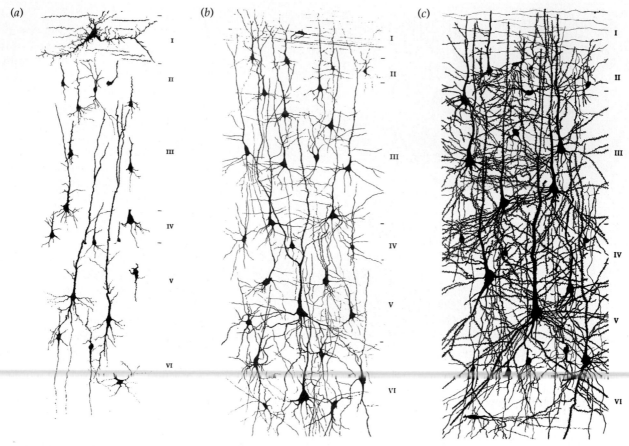

4.16 Cerebral Cortex Tissue in Early Development of Humans
(*a*) In a newborn. (*b*) Three months after birth. (*c*) Two years old. Numerals refer to the six cortical layers. From Conel, 1939, 1941, 1959.

intrinsic and extrinsic factors and some of the examples we'll use to illustrate each.

Genes Are the Intrinsic Factors That Influence Brain Development

Psychologists have shown the importance of genetic factors in a variety of behaviors in many species (Hall and Greenspan, 1979; Wimer and Wimer, 1985), including humans (Loehlin, Willerman, and Horn, 1988; Rende and Plomin, 1995). Of course, genes do not work in isolation. Development should be viewed as the interaction of genetic instructions with the other, extrinsic influences we mentioned in the previous section.

Farmers and pet breeders have used selective breeding to produce distinctive animals. Researchers in behavioral genetics have also used these techniques, charting changes of behavior through generations. The use of these techniques with simpler animals has begun to connect genetic effects on the nervous system with effects on behavior. Bentley (1976) found that the calling songs of crickets have intricate patterns that can be manipulated by selective breeding. These song patterns change in distinctive ways as genes of a particular type are favored by controlled mating through several generations. Recordings 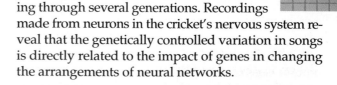 made from neurons in the cricket's nervous system reveal that the genetically controlled variation in songs is directly related to the impact of genes in changing the arrangements of neural networks.

Identical genes, different nervous systems. One breeding technique produces genetically identical animals, called **clones**, which used to be known mainly in science fiction and horror films. But life imitates fiction. Researchers develop clones by means of asexual reproduction; all offspring have the same genes. Using grasshoppers clones, Goodman (1979) compared the uniformity and variability in the growth and devel-

Table 4.1

Intrinsic and Extrinsic Factors That Affect Neural Development

FACTORS	EXAMPLES OF EFFECTS
Intrinsic factors (genes)	
Chromosomal aberrations	Down's syndrome, fragile X syndrome
Single gene effects	PKU, various *Drosophila* mutants
Extrinsic factors	
Nutrients	Malnutrition
Drugs, toxins	Fetal alcohol syndrome
Cell–cell interactions	
Induction directs differentiation	Notochord induces motoneuron differentation
Trophic factors direct cell death or synapse loss	NGF spares developing sympathetic neurons from death
Neural activity affects synapse maintenance and loss	
Non-sensory-driven	Eye segregation in layer 4 cortex before birth in monkeys
Sensory-driven (experience)	Ocular dominance outside layer 4 after birth in monkeys
Birth process in mammals	Hypoxia-induced mental retardation

opment of different neurons. Although the basic shape of larger cells showed considerable uniformity, many neurons of cloned grasshoppers showed differences in neural connections between supposedly identical individuals.

Similar results were derived from a tiny crustacean, the daphnia, well known to aquarium owners (Macagno, Lopresti, and Levinthal, 1973). Female daphnias can reproduce without fertilization by males, and lines of genetically identical female offspring are the result. The daphnia eye contains exactly 176 sensory neurons, which make synaptic contacts with exactly 110 neurons of the optic ganglion. Furthermore, a particular sensory neuron makes contact with only a few specific neurons in the ganglion. But the exact number of synapses established between a particular sensory neuron and a specific neuron in the ganglion can vary by more than threefold between individual daphnia clones. Even between the right and left sides of the eye of an individual, where there are symmetrically placed "twin" neurons, one twin neuron may form more synapses than the other. Thus, both within and between individual daphnias, neurons with exactly the same genes differ in the number of their synaptic connections. Pre-

sumably, the variations are due to variation in extrinsic factors.

Among vertebrates, identical neurons for comparing synaptic connections among twins are harder to find. But there are identifiable neurons in fish—Mauthner cells—and some of these fish reproduce like daphnia does; that is, females produce daughters that are genetically identical to each other and to their mother. Each fish has a single giant Mauthner cell on each side of the brain. Although the pattern of dendritic branching of the Mauthner cells is similar from individual to individual among a clone, there are individual differences in the detail of branching and of synapses. Thus, the finding in daphnias can be extended at least to the Mauthner cells in the fish brain (Levinthal, Macagno, and Levinthal, 1976).

Although mammals have no identifiable neurons, the differences in the nervous systems of mammalian twins seem great. In highly inbred strains of mice, for example, where all individuals of the same sex are essentially identical genetically, a specific region of the brain (such as a part of the hippocampus) shows a small-percentage difference in the number of neurons among individuals (Wimer et al., 1976).

No direct observations of this sort have been made

for humans, but identical human twins often differ in size at birth, and presumably their brains differ at least as much as do those of inbred mice. Some indirect evidence indicates that for human identical twins the branching pattern of nerve endings in the skin must differ. For example, even identical twins show some differences in their fingerprints, although their prints are more similar than are those of fraternal twins. Since the skin of the fingertips is richly innervated, differences in the pattern of the ridges of the skin must mean differences in the distribution of nerve endings. Furthermore, the differences in the ridges must mean differences in the locations of the nerve endings that run to the sweat glands along each ridge. This example indicates that among human beings, as among other animals, identical heredity does not mean that every detail of the nervous system is identical. (We should note that the pattern of fingerprints forms during the fourth month of pregnancy, so these individual differences are **congenital**—present by the time of birth.) Further differences between the nervous systems of identical twins may be caused by responses to differential experiences, as we will see in Chapters 17 and 18 when we consider the effects of experience and learning on the anatomy of the nervous system. Indeed, in several places in this book we'll find that human identical twins do not always share such traits as schizophrenia (see Figure 1.8), sexual orientation, or depression, and these differences between twins cannot be attributed to the genome.

Now we can consider several terms that aid the discussion of intrinsic and extrinsic factors. The sum of all the intrinsic, genetic information an individual has is its **genotype** or **genome**. The sum of all the physical characteristics that make up an individual is its **phenotype**. Your genotype was determined at the moment of fertilization and remains the same throughout your life. But your phenotype changes constantly, as you grow up and grow old and even, in a tiny way, with each breath. Your phenotype is determined by the interaction of your genotype and extrinsic factors, including experience. Thus twins with identical genotypes do not have identical phenotypes because they have not received identical extrinsic influences. Because their nervous system phenotypes are somewhat different, twins do not behave exactly the same.

Effects of mutations.   Sometimes nature produces unusual animals that show a sudden change in genetic structure, a **mutation**, that is related to marked

anatomical or physiological change. Researchers can increase the frequency of mutations by exposing animals to chemicals or radiation that produce changes in genes.

Mutants—animals that display these changes—are interesting to study because their suddenly changed genetic characteristics may be quite specific and striking. For example, Greenspan and Quinn (1984) described mutants of the fruitfly *Drosophila* that seemed normal in every way except that they had memory problems. These mutants—affectionately labeled *dunce, amnesiac,* and *turnip*—either failed to learn or could learn but forgot rapidly. Biochemical deficits in these mutants (due to mutations that render specific genes and therefore specific proteins ineffective) may account for the failures of memory (Dudai, 1988); we will discuss studies on this question in Chapter 18 when we take up neural mechanisms of learning and memory. The strength of research on *Drosophila* mutants derives from the wealth of specific mutations, each one involving a distinct defect in some part of the fly's nervous system (Hall and Greenspan, 1979). For example, a lethal *Drosophila* mutant, *Notch,* has an enlarged nervous system because too many precursor cells are produced. Studies of this mutant may enable researchers to attain a better understanding of processes that control the number of neurons produced during early embryological development.

More than 150 mutations in mice involve the nervous system (Sidman, Green, and Appel, 1965; Hatten and Heintz, 1995). In these animals special defects appear during the development of the nervous system. Some mice fail to produce particular brain regions. Others show specific anatomical derangements, such as a failure to myelinate or to arrange cells in their characteristic alignments. One group of mutants especially intriguing to researchers all have single gene mutations that affect the postnatal development of the cerebellum. The names of these animals—*reeler, staggerer,* and *weaver*—reflect the locomotor impairment that characterizes them. The impact of these genes on the size and arrangement of the cerebellum is illustrated in Figure 4.17. The cerebellum of *reeler* shows an abnormal positioning of cells. There are no characteristic layers in the cerebellum, hippocampus, and cerebral cortex. Strangely, although cells of these regions are in abnormal positions, many connections among these cells are appropriate (Caviness, 1980). The cerebellum of *weaver* has far fewer granule cells than a normal cerebellum, which arises from a failure of granule cells to migrate properly. The granule cells from *weaver* mice fail to make the CAM that would allow them to at-

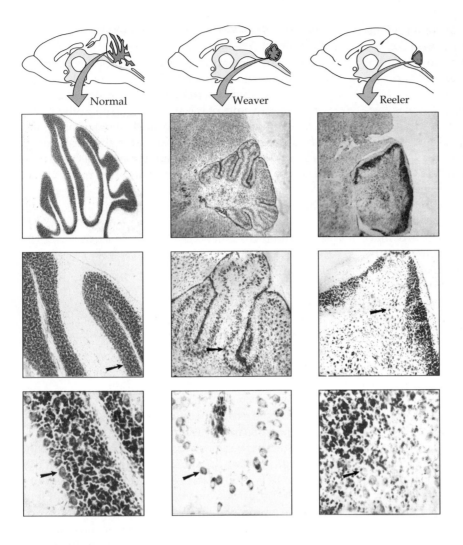

Normal Weaver Reeler

4.17 Cerebellar Mutants among Mice

The left column shows sections of the cerebellum in a normal mouse at three levels of magnification (25x, 66x, and 250x). The middle column shows comparable views in the mutant *weaver*. Note the almost complete absence of granule cells, while the alignment of Purkinje cells (arrows) is normal. The right column shows sections from the cerebellar mutant *reeler*. Marked derangement of the customary layering of cells is evident. Both mutants show overall shrinkage of the cerebellum. From A. L. Leiman, unpublished observations.

tach to and migrate along glia; therefore they fail to reach their appropriate levels and the cerebellum fails to develop the normal laminar (layered) organization.

Atrophy of the cerebellum is also evident in *staggerer* (Sotelo, 1980); this animal fails to form synaptic connections between granule cells and Purkinje cells. The axon of the granule cell—the parallel fiber—comes close to the dendritic surface of the Purkinje cell, but postsynaptic specializations do not develop. Each of these mouse mutants shows impairment due to a single gene, related to the development of a specific kind of cell. Studies of these animals are improving our understanding of the processes of neural development and their behavioral consequences. Later in this chapter we'll consider some genetic disorders in the development of the human nervous system.

Brain Development Requires Proper Nutrition

The good fortune of adequate nutrition is not uniformly shared by people throughout the world. Pe-

riodic starvation confronts many, and this problem grows more urgent as population growth threatens to overwhelm food resources. A recent report suggested that at least 150 million children under the age of five throughout the world suffer protein malnutrition (Udani, 1992). The adult human brain is much less affected by dieting or overeating than are most other organs, but malnutrition is quite detrimental, sometimes irreversibly, to the developing brain (Winick, 1976; Sigman, 1995). Relating these cerebral changes to behavior is complicated. It is hard to disentangle the effects of social disadvantage from the effects of dietary deficiencies, since most of these studies involve mothers and infants living in impoverished circumstances, and massive social dysfunction.

We have learned something about the effects of early malnutrition from comparisons of undernourished children with matched controls who had no early nutritional deficiency. Early malnourishment reduces later performance on many tests of mental capacity (Galler et al., 1990; Udani, 1992). Maternal nutritional deprivation seems to have increased the risk for schizophrenia among the offspring of Dutch women who experienced severe famine during a Nazi wartime blockade of food from 1944 to 1945 (Susser and Lin, 1992). This lack of nutrition was a severe stress for prenatal development, as shown by very low birth weights and mortality of infants who experienced famine effects during the first trimester of pregnancy. Several such studies indicate that children have a greater chance of behavioral recovery if the malnutrition occurred later rather than earlier in life.

It has been shown that effects of severe early malnutrition can be counteracted to some extent by nutritional and behavioral rehabilitation (Nguyen, Meyer, and Winick, 1977; Winick, Meyer, and Harris, 1975). This research was done with Korean orphans who were adopted by middle-class U.S. families. The malnourished orphans developed well in their adoptive families, and they all came to exceed Korean norms of height and weight, although not reaching American norms. In IQ (intelligence quotient) tests and school achievement tests, the means for all three groups that had been adopted by the age of two or older exceeded American means. This study demonstrates that the effects of severe early malnutrition can largely be overcome if rehabilitation starts early and is kept up. An MRI study of brain shrinkage following severe protein deficiency has also shown that these neuroanatomical effects of malnutrition can be reversed in children (Gunston et al., 1992). In this study 12 children of ages 6 months to 37 months were monitored during nutritional rehabilitation. On admission to the hospital they all showed brain shrinkage revealed by MRI. After 90 days of hospitalization, these brain changes had reversed in most of the children.

The brain is most vulnerable to malnutrition during the period of rapid brain growth (Dobbing, 1976; Seidler, Bell, and Slotkin, 1990). This period varies depending on the animal. In humans the period of fastest brain growth and maximum vulnerability to malnutrition occurs in late pregnancy and the first months of postnatal life. Similar malnutrition in the adult produces negligible effects. For example, the size of the cerebellum in rats is especially sensitive to postnatal malnutrition, since this structure forms mainly just after birth in the rat. Abnormal neurochemical functioning was found in the brain in adulthood after rats were exposed to mild neonatal malnutrition, and the effect persisted long after nutritional rehabilitation (Seidler, Bell, and Slotkin, 1990).

Neurotrophic Factors Allow Neurons to Survive and Grow

More than 20 years ago, investigators discovered a substance—**nerve growth factor (NGF)**—that markedly affects the growth of neurons in spinal ganglia and in the ganglia of the sympathetic nervous system (Levi-Montalcini, 1982; Bothwell, 1995). If NGF was administered to a fetus, it resulted in the formation of sympathetic ganglia with many more cells than usual. These cells were also larger and had many extensive processes (Figure 4.18).

Rita Levi-Montalcini

The discovery of NGF earned Rita Levi-Montalcini and Stanley Cohen a Nobel Prize in 1986. Originally, NGF was found in a variety of unusual places, including the salivary glands of mice, certain skin tumors, and the venom of a snake. Later, precise biochemical techniques revealed that NGF is normally produced by various target organs during development. The NGF is taken up by the axons of sympathetic neurons innervating the organs and transported back to the cell body, and it prevents some of the sympathetic neurons from dying. There is a rough correlation between the amount of NGF produced by targets during development and the amount of sympathetic innervation the targets receive in adulthood. This relationship suggests that differing degrees of cell death, controlled by access to NGF, match the sympathetic innervation to each target. NGF was the first identified neurotrophic factor.

Part of the interest in NGF arose from the possibility that there might be more neurotrophic factors, each one affecting survival of a particular cell type at a specific developmental period. Investigators began searching for other neurotrophic factors. One, purified from the brains of many animals, was named **brain-derived neurotrophic factor (BDNF)**. The gene for BDNF turned out to be very similar to the gene for NGF. Investigators used molecular techniques to search for other NGF-related molecules and found several more. The family of NGF-like molecules was named the neurotrophin family. Neurotrophic factors that are unrelated to NGF have also been found, including ciliary neurotrophic factor (named after its ability to keep neurons from ciliary ganglia alive in vitro). The exact role of these various factors (and other neurotrophic factors yet to be discovered) in keeping neurons alive is under intense scientific scrutiny.

Maldevelopment of the Human Brain Results in Behavioral Impairment

Because the processes that guide the development of the human brain are so multiple, intricate, and complex, there are many ways in which they can go wrong. Children that experience complicated deliveries at birth, when a transient lack of oxygen (**hypoxia**) may affect the brain, are at slightly greater risk for mental retardation than children of problem-free births. The many factors that control brain development—those that govern cell proliferation, migration, differentiation, and the formation of synapses—are subject to failures that can have catastrophic consequences for adaptive behavior. The magnitude of this problem is reflected in the incidence of disorders that produce marked cognitive impairment. In the United States approximately 3.6 children per 1000 between the ages of 5 and 17 have IQ levels below 50. In this section we discuss some examples of behavioral impairment related to genetically controlled states and prenatal maternal conditions.

Some Genetic Disorders Have Widespread Effects on the Nervous System

Examples of genetically controlled states that cause developmental disorders focus on the actions of mutant genes and chromosomal abnormalities. Many metabolic disorders profoundly affect the developing brain, and some appear very early in life. In this category are 100 to 200 different disorders involving disturbances in the metabolism of proteins, carbohydrates, or lipids. Characteristically, the genetic defect is the absence of a particular enzyme that controls a critical biochemical step in the synthesis or breakdown of a vital body product. Two main results of enzymatic deficits can affect the brain either: (1) certain compounds build up to toxic levels, or (2) compounds needed for either function or structure fail to be synthesized.

An example of the first kind is **phenylketonuria** (**PKU**), a recessive hereditary disorder of protein metabolism that at one time resulted in many mentally retarded people. One out of 50 persons is a carrier; one in 10,000 births is an affected victim. The basic defect is the absence of an enzyme necessary to metabolize phenylalanine, an amino acid present in many foods. The brain damage caused by phenylketonuria is probably due to an enormous buildup of phenylalanine.

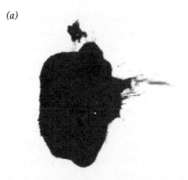

(a)

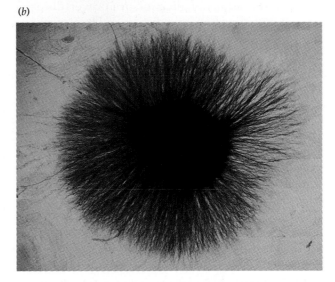

(b)

4.18 Effects of Nerve Growth Factor
(*a*) A spinal ganglion grown in isolation outside the body (in vitro) without the presence of NGF. (*b*) A spinal ganglion grown under similar circumstances but with NGF added to the bathing solution. This figure shows marked proliferation of axonal processes radiating in all directions. From Levi-Montalcini, 1964.

The discovery of PKU marked the first time that an inborn error of metabolism was associated with mental retardation. Nowadays there are screening methods, required by law throughout the United States and in many other countries, that assess the level of phenylalanine in children a few days after birth. Early detection is important because brain impairment can be prevented by administering a diet low in phenylalanine. Recent evidence suggests that such dietary control of phenylketonuria is critical during early years, especially before age two, and that the diet can be relaxed during adulthood. However, behaviorally normal mothers with PKU have a high percentage of mentally retarded offspring. This result may be related to the mother's phenylalanine levels, but dietary treatment during pregnancy does not seem to reduce the fetal effects (Kolodny and Cable, 1981). The mechanism leading to mental retardation may thus be more complex than the original hypothesis of phenylalanine excess suggested (Thompson and Halliday, 1990).

Success in treating phenylketonuria kindled enthusiasm for research on the analysis and possible treatment of many other forms of mental retardation controlled by genes that influence metabolic processes. Chromosomal analysis, biochemical techniques, and forms of fetal visualization are powerful tools that are providing better prediction and treatment for this class of disorders. In addition, genetic therapy that includes introducing healthy genes into the body is now becoming more feasible (Verma, 1990).

New syndromes that probably involve inherited metabolic disorders are constantly being discovered. Recently, researchers have become interested in a disorder called **Williams syndrome**. Patients with this disorder have largely intact linguistic functioning, large vocabularies, and very fluent speech. Yet they also show clear mental retardation on standard IQ tests—they have great difficulty in copying a pattern of blocks or assembling a picture from its parts. MRI studies reveal a selective effect on brain development. Williams syndrome patients show reduced cerebral size but normal cerebellar and subcortical sites (Jernigan and Bellugi, 1990).

One in every 200 live births exhibits some kind of chromosomal abnormality: either an abnormal number of chromosomes (usually 45 or 47 instead of 46) or modifications in the structure of a chromosome. Generally, disorders involving nonsex chromosomes have a more profound impact on behavior than those involving sex chromosomes.

The most common form of cognitive disorder due to a chromosomal abnormality is **Down's syndrome**. The disorder associated with 95% of these cases is an extra chromosome number 21 (for a total of three) This disorder is strikingly related to the age of the mother at the time of conception (Table 4.2). The behavioral dysfunctions are quite varied. Most cases of Down's syndrome have very low IQs, but some rare individuals attain an IQ of 80. Brain abnormalities in Down's syndrome also vary. Biopsies of the cerebral

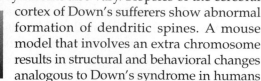

cortex of Down's sufferers show abnormal formation of dendritic spines. A mouse model that involves an extra chromosome results in structural and behavioral changes analogous to Down's syndrome in humans (Epstein, 1986). Investigation of this model is providing valuable insights into how the extra chromo-

Table 4.2	
Risk of Babies with Down's Syndrome Related to Maternal Age	
MOTHER'S AGE AT BIRTH OF CHILD	RISK OF DOWN'S SYNDROME
Under 30	1:1500
30–34	1:1000
35–39	1:300
40–44	1:100
45 and over	1:40

Source: Karp (1976)

some causes the structural and behavioral abnormalities.

Very likely, the most frequent cause of inherited mental retardation is the condition **fragile X syndrome**, which is produced by a fragile site on the X chromosome. At the end of the long arm of the X chromosome is a site that seems prone to breaking because the DNA there is unstable (Yu et al., 1991). Persons with this abnormality have a modified facial appearance, including elongation of the face, large prominent ears, and a prominent chin. A wide range of cognitive impairments—from mild to severe retardation— is associated with this syndrome (Baumgardner, Green, and Reiss, 1994). The disorder is more common in males than in females. The molecular basis of fragile X syndrome provided a surprise for geneticists because it demonstrated that we don't always pass on a faithful copy of our DNA to our offspring. The fragile site in the DNA consists of the same three nucleotides (CGG—see the Appendix if you don't remember what nucleotides are) repeated over and over. Most people have only 6 to 50 of these **trinucleotide repeats** at this site (Laxova, 1994). But during the production of sperm or eggs, the number of repeats sometimes changes, so a father who had only 50 trinucleotide repeats may provide 100 repeats to his daughter. People who have between 51 and 200 of the CGG repeats are themselves unaffected, but if their children receive more than 200 repeats, they will display the fragile X syndrome. No one knows why the number of repeats changes from one generation to the next or what determines whether more or fewer repeats will appear. Trinucleotide repeats are also at the heart of another genetically based behavioral disorder—Huntington's disease (see Chapter 11).

Exposure to Drugs during Pregnancy Can Impair Neural Development

Even in the protected environment of the womb, the embryo and fetus are not immune to what is taking place in the mother's body. Maternal conditions such as viral infection, exposure to drugs, and malnutrition are especially likely to result in developmental disorders in the unborn child. Concern with the maternal environment as a determinant of brain development has spawned a new field: **behavioral teratology**. (Teratology—from the Greek *teras*, "monster"—is the study of malformations.) Those who work in this field are especially concerned with the pathological behavioral effects of drugs ingested during pregnancy.

Although researchers have only recently proven alcohol's potential to affect fetal growth and development, there is a long history of concern about alcohol and pregnancy, dating back to classical Greek and Roman times. Aristotle warned that "foolish, drunken . . . women . . . bring forth children like unto themselves, morose and languid" (cited in Abel, 1982). By now, the wisdom of this observation (if not the misogyny) is well supported by abundant research. Children born to alcoholic mothers show a distinctive profile of anatomical, physiological, and behavioral impairments that is now known as **fetal alcohol syndrome** (Abel, 1984; Colangelo and Jones, 1982). Prominent anatomical effects of fetal exposure to alcohol include distinctive changes in facial features (for example, a sunken nasal bridge, and altered shape of the nose and eyelids). Children born to alcoholic mothers are deficient in both height and weight at birth. Few of these children catch up in the years following birth (Colangelo and Jones, 1982). The most common problem associated with fetal alcohol syndrome is mental retardation, which varies in severity. No alcohol threshold has yet been established for this

 syndrome, but it is clear that it can occur with relatively moderate intake during the course of pregnancy. In addition to mental retardation, children with fetal alcohol syndrome show other neurological abnormalities. Hyperactivity, irritability, tremulousness, and other signs of motor instability are common symptoms. Researchers have yet to establish whether these effects are mediated mainly by alcohol, its toxic metabolites, or the effects of alcohol on the metabolic health and nutrition of the mother. Alcohol may also affect the circulatory links between mother and child. This syndrome may not be distinctive to alcohol; heavy use of marijuana seems to exert a similar effect on fetal growth and development (Hingson et al., 1982).

Experience Is an Important Influence on Brain Development

The young of many species are born in a highly immature state, both anatomically and behaviorally. For example, in humans the weight of the brain at birth is only one-fourth of its adult weight. The infants of such species are totally dependent on the parents. In these species developments in brain and in behavior seem to vary together. The successes and failures of early experience can affect the growth and development of brain circuits.

Varying experience during an individual's early development has been found to alter many aspects of behavior, brain anatomy, and brain chemistry (Bennett et al., 1964; Gottlieb, 1976; Rosenzweig and Bennett, 1977, 1978). The altered behavior itself indicates that the early experience affected brain development. We know that some experimental treatments—for example, the early administration of sex hormones—can determine whether the organism develops into the male or the female body type (see Chapter 12). Can experience have an equally striking role? In one experiment, for example, male mallard ducklings were raised for their first eight to ten weeks with other duck species. As mature drakes, they were given the choice of mating with mallard ducks or with ducks of the species with which they had been raised. Whereas all mallards reared with mallards choose mallards as mates, about two-thirds of the experimental animals chose the other species (Schutz, 1965). The animals seem to have imprinted upon their (foster) parents as the appropriate type of sexual target. Normally such **sexual imprinting** would result in a sexual partner of the same species.

Experience can have negative or positive effects on development. For instance, prenatal exposure to certain sounds can hasten or delay hatching time in quail embryos (Gottlieb, 1976). Early recognition of species and parental vocalizations depend upon the embryo being exposed to specific kinds of auditory stimulation before hatching (Hall and Oppenheim, 1987).

Visual Deprivation Can Lead to Blindness

Some people do not see forms clearly with one eye, even though it is intact and a sharp image is focused on the retina. Such impairments of vision are known as **amblyopia** (from the Greek for "dull, blunt" and "vision"). Some people with this disorder have a "lazy eye," one that is turned inward (cross-eyed) or outward. Some children are born with such a misalignment. They see a double image rather than a single fused image. If the deviated eye is not surgically realigned during childhood, vision becomes impaired. By the time an untreated person reaches adulthood, pattern vision in the deviated eye is almost completely suppressed. Realignment of the eyes in adulthood does not restore acute vision to the turned eye. The inability in these cases to correct the problem in adulthood is quite striking, since throughout the person's development light enters this eye in a normal manner and the nerve cells of the eye continue to be excited. Similar misalignment of the eyes, when it appears for the first time in adulthood, produces double vision, a condition that shows no change with further aging. These clinical observations of humans suggest that unusual positioning of the eyes during early development changes neural connections in the brain. (However, the connections may undergo further changes even in adults if the weak eye is exercised sufficiently [Romero-Apis et al., 1982].)

Understanding the cause of amblyopia in people has been greatly advanced by visual-deprivation experiments with animals. These experiments revealed startling changes related to disuse of the visual system during early critical periods. Depriving animals of light to both eyes (**binocular deprivation**) produces structural changes in visual cortical neurons—a loss of dendritic spines and a reduction in synaptic density. Cragg (1975) emphasized that these effects occur most extensively during the early period of synaptic development in the visual cortex (Figure 4.19). If deprivation is maintained for several weeks during development, when the animals' eyes are opened, they will be blind. Although light enters their eyes and the cells of the eyes send messages to the brain, the brain seems to ignore the messages, and the animals are unable to detect visual stimuli. If the deprivation lasts long enough, the animals are never able to recover eyesight. Thus, early visual experience is crucial for the proper development of vision.

Even subtle manipulations of visual experience have profound effects on the developing visual system. Pioneering work by Hubel and Wiesel, who shared a Nobel Prize in 1981, showed that depriving only one eye of light (**monocular deprivation**) produces profound structural and functional changes in the visual cortex. Monocular deprivation in an infant cat or monkey leads to an absence of response to the deprived eye when the animal reaches adulthood. The effect of visual deprivation can be illustrated graphically by an **ocular-dominance histogram**, which portrays the strength of a brain neuron's response to stimuli presented to either the left or the right eye. Normally, most cortical neurons (except those in layer 4) are excited equally by light presented to either eye (Figure 4.20a). Few neurons are activated solely by inputs to one eye. Monocular deprivation early in development results in a striking shift in this graph—most cortical neurons respond only to input from the nondeprived eye (Figure 4.20b). In cats the susceptible period for this effect is the first four months of life. In nonhuman primates the sensitive period extends to age six months. After these ages visual deprivation has little effect.

The mechanisms proposed for this phenomenon bring us to a possible understanding of the forms of amblyopia we have described. During early development synapses are rearranged in visual cortex, and axons representing input from each eye "compete" for synaptic places. Active, used synapses become effective connections and predominate over inactive, disused synapses. Thus, if one eye is "silenced,"

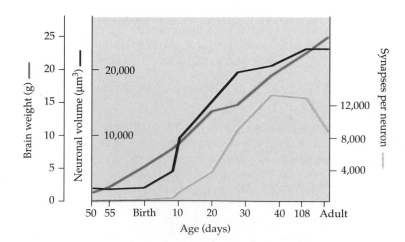

4.19 Brain Development in the Visual Cortex of the Cat Synaptic development occurs most intensely from 8 to 37 days after birth, a period during which visual experience can have profound influence. Note that brain weight and cell volume rise in a parallel fashion and precede synaptic development. Note also the decline in synapse numbers after 108 days of age, evidence of synapse rearrangement. After Cragg, 1975.

(*a*) **Normal**

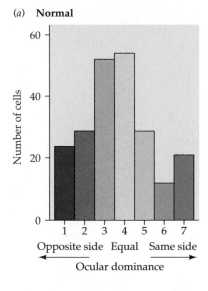

(*b*) **Monocular deprivation**

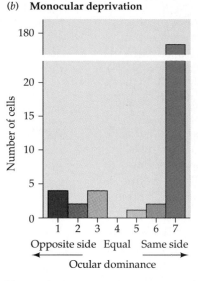

(*c*) **One eye deviated**

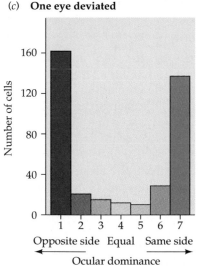

(*d*) **Binocular deprivation**

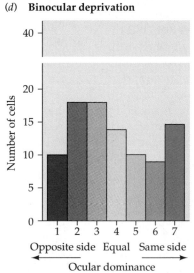

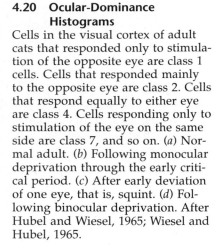

4.20 Ocular-Dominance Histograms

Cells in the visual cortex of adult cats that responded only to stimulation of the opposite eye are class 1 cells. Cells that responded mainly to the opposite eye are class 2. Cells that respond equally to either eye are class 4. Cells responding only to stimulation of the eye on the same side are class 7, and so on. (*a*) Normal adult. (*b*) Following monocular deprivation through the early critical period. (*c*) After early deviation of one eye, that is, squint. (*d*) Following binocular deprivation. After Hubel and Wiesel, 1965; Wiesel and Hubel, 1965.

synapses carrying information from that eye are retracted while synapses derived from the other eye are maintained.

Researchers offer a similar explanation for amblyopia produced by misalignment of the eyes. An animal replica of this human condition was produced by cutting muscles on one side of the eye in young cats (Hubel and Wiesel, 1965). The ocular-dominance histogram of these animals reveals that the normal binocular sensitivity of visual cortical cells is greatly reduced (see Figure 4.20*c*). A much larger proportion are excited by stimulation of either the right or the left eye than in control animals. This effect occurs because after surgery the cells of the visual cortex do not receive simultaneous input from both eyes.

The competitive interaction between the eyes results in a paradox—brief deprivation of both eyes can have a lesser effect on neuronal connections than an equal period of deprivation to only one eye (compare panels *a*, *b*, and *d* in Figure 4.20). Presumably the binocular deprivation keeps both eyes on an equal footing for driving cells into the visual cortex so the predominantly binocular input to the cortical cells is retained.

Early Exposure to Visual Patterns Helps Fine-Tune Connections in the Visual System

At birth the visual cortex is quite immature, and most synapses have yet to form. Evidence cited in the previous sections shows that profound disuse results in changes in both structure and response of visual pathways. The modifiability of the developing brain is also evidenced when animals are exposed to certain visual patterns during early development.

Experiments in which visual patterns are manipulated early in an animal's life have used patterns such as horizontal or vertical lines (Blakemore, 1976), a field of such stripes seen through goggles (Hirsch and Spinelli, 1971), or small spots of light (Pettigrew and Freeman, 1973). In each case, experimenters try to ensure that the animals are exposed to visual stimuli of only one particular type. Then the animals' behavioral responses and/or their brain responses to the visual stimuli are recorded. The question is whether the animals can see stimuli they were exposed to during a sensitive developmental period better than they see novel stimuli. Although controversial (Movshon and van Sluyters, 1981), the results suggest that visual experiences during the critical early periods of life can modify the responses of nerve cells in the visual cortex. The effects are more subtle than those seen with complete deprivation, but the ability of animals to detect visual stimuli of a particular, general pattern (for example, horizontal lines versus vertical lines), depends on their exposure to such visual patterns during development. These experience-dependent effects are probably mediated by synapse rearrangement within the visual cortex. The sensitive period for these effects is roughly the same as for monocular deprivation.

Nonvisual Experiences Also Affect Neural Development

Development of the brain can also be affected by early manipulation of nonvisual sensory inputs—a mouse's whiskers, for example. Thomas Woolsey and collaborators (Woolsey and Wann, 1976; Woolsey et al., 1981) found a unique clustering of nerve cells in a region of the cerebral cortex of the mouse that receives input from the whiskers. The arrangement of these hairs on the skin is distinctive. The hairs are aligned similarly for all animals of the same species. The region of the cortex in which the whiskers are represented contain clusters of cells, called **whisker barrels** because the way they are arrayed makes them look like barrels squeezed together in the cortex. The layout of these cortical barrels corresponds to the map of the whiskers (Figure 4.21). If a whisker is cut a few days after birth, sensory information from that whisker is silenced (because the shortened whisker doesn't brush against anything) and its cortical barrel does not develop. Furthermore, the whisker barrels that represent adjacent, intact whiskers tend to be enlarged, as if expanding at the expense of their neighboring whisker (Figure 4.21*c* and *d*).

We have given only a few examples of the many experiments showing that sensory stimuli influence the development of the brain with respect to both structure and function. The effects differ depending on variables such as age of the subject, duration of the experience, and type of stimulation.

The Brain Continues to Change As We Grow Older

The passage of time brings us an accumulation of joys and sorrows—perhaps riches and fame—and a progressive decline in many of our abilities. Changes with age seem to be inevitable in biological systems. After surveying some of the characteristics of normal aging, we will look at some of the pathological (disease-caused) exaggerations of aging, most notably Alzheimer's disease.

Normal Aging Varies by Brain Regions and by Person

Many aspects of brain structure and function change through the span of a human life. Although slower responses seem inevitable with aging, many of our cognitive abilities show little change during the adult years, until we reach an advanced age. What happens to brain structure from adolescence to that day when we all become a little forgetful and walk more hesitantly? Does the structure of the brain change continuously throughout the life span of any animal?

Changes in the structure of the brain with aging can be viewed at different levels, from subcellular structures to overall brain morphology. Brain weight declines with age, but some have questioned the relevance of aging to these weight changes, since it is hard to distinguish changes due to aging from changes that arise from disease states shortly before death. An excellent study that eliminated such confounding factors (see Figure 4.1) showed that changes are very small up to the age of 45, after which time the weight of the brain begins to decline significantly. The brain weight of elderly humans is 7 to 8% less than that of the peak of adult weight (Creasy and Rapaport, 1985). The course of these changes is the same for men and women, even though women generally live seven to ten years longer than men. Data also emphasize that aging is a variable state. Declines are evident in many people, and exaggerated in some. To some investigators this variablity emphasizes the genetic contribution to aging and reinforces the idea that if you want to live long, choose parents and grandparents who have lived long.

Another measure used in studies of brain aging is the number of neural and glial cells in particular vol-

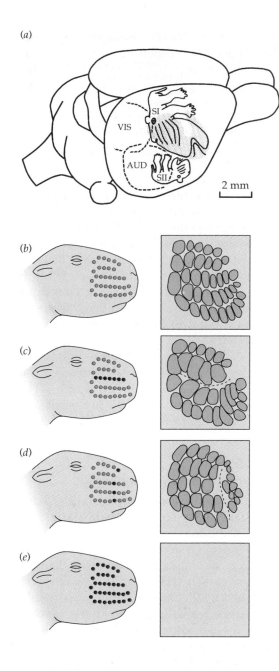

(a)

VIS

SI

AUD

SII

2 mm

(b)

(c)

(d)

(e)

4.21 Cortical Barrels in Mice

(*a*) Representation of the body surface in mouse somatosensory cortex showing the location of barrels. (*b*) Each barrel (*insets*) receives its input from a single whisker on the opposite side of the mouse's snout. (*c, d*) If one row of whiskers is destroyed shortly after birth (as indicated by the red dots), the corresponding row of barrels in the cerebral cortex later will be found to be missing and the adjoining barrels to be enlarged. (*e*) If all whiskers are destroyed, the entire group of barrels will have disappeared. *a* courtesy of Thomas Woolsey; *b–e* after Cowan, 1979.

umes of tissue. Investigators map specific regions and count the number of cells in various areas, using tissue taken from people who have died at different ages. These studies suggest that cell changes begin as early as the third decade of life and are specific to particular regions. Even more noticeable than the decrease in the number of cells is the loss of synaptic connections, which is especially prominent in the frontal cortical regions. However, growth cones can be found in the dendritic terminals of cortical cells of old people, suggesting that some forms of synaptic plasticity continue throughout life.

Memory decline and hippocampal shrinkage. In a recent study of healthy and cognitively normal people, aged 55 to 87, investigators asked whether mild impairment in memory is specifically related to reduction in size of the hippocampal formation (HF) or better explained by generalized shrinkage of brain tissue (Golomb et al., 1994). (In Chapter 18 we'll see that the HF has been implicated in memory formation.) Loss of HF tissue has been reported in cases of mild Alzheimer's disease and in elderly individuals with cognitive impairment (Convit et al., 1993; de Leon et al., 1993; Killiany et al., 1993), but it is unclear to what extent atrophy of the HF can account for milder declines in memory that many neurologically healthy older people experience.

In one study, volunteers took a series of memory tests and were scored for both immediate recall and delayed recall. A series of ten coronal MRI images for each subject was measured for three variables (Figure 4.22): (1) volume of the HF; (2) volume of the supratemporal gyrus, a region that is close to the HF and is known to shrink with age but has not been implicated in memory; and (3) volume of the subarachnoid cerebrospinal fluid (that is, the fluid-filled space between the meninges that line the interior of the skull and the surface of the brain), which yields a measure of overall shrinkage of the brain. Immediate memory showed very little decline with age, but delayed memory did decline. When effects of sex, age, IQ, and overall brain atrophy were eliminated statistically, HF volume was the only brain measure that correlated significantly with the delayed memory score. Of course, brain regions not included in this study may also correlate with memory, so other areas of the brain should be included in future measurements. Also, the techniques of this experiment did not allow the researchers to measure small regions, such as the entorhinal cortex, that animal experiments show are also important for memory.

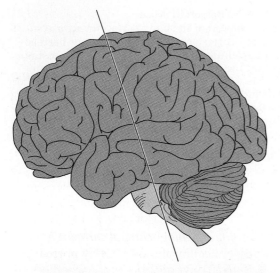

4.22   Some Brain Variables Correlate with Memory Decline in Aging
(*Top*) Plane of MRI images illustrating the variables tested for correlation with memory decline in normal aged people. (*a*) Hippocampal formation. (*b*) Supratemporal gyrus. (*c*) Space between brain and skull. Only shrinkage of the hippocampal formation correlated with memory decline. From Golomb et al., 1994.

(a)

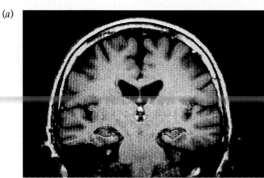

(b)

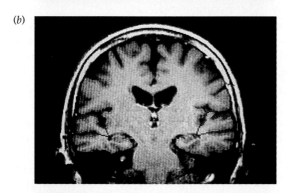

(c)

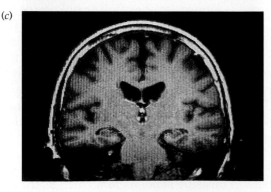

Two regions of the motor system show how different effects of aging can be. In the motor cortex a type of large neuron—the Betz cell—starts to decline in number by about age 50, and by the time a person reaches age 80, many of these cells have shriveled away (Scheibel, Tomiyasu, and Scheibel, 1977). In contrast, other cells involved in motor circuitry—those in an area of the brain stem called the inferior olive—remain about the same in number through at least eight decades of life.

PET scans of elderly people add a new perspective to aging changes. Studies of normal cases reveal that cerebral metabolism remains almost constant. This stability is in marked contrast to the decline of cerebral metabolism in Alzheimer's disease, which we consider next.

Alzheimer's Disease Is a Pathological Exaggeration of Aging

Since 1900, the population of people over the age of 65 in the United States has increased eightfold. By 2000, at least 30 million Americans will be in this age group. Most people reaching this age lead happy, productive lives, although at a slower pace than that of their earlier years. In a growing number of elderly people, however, age has brought a particular agony—the disorder called **Alzheimer's disease**, named after the neurologist who first described a type of **dementia** (drastic failure of cognitive ability, including memory failure and loss of orientation) appearing before the age of 65. Almost 2 million Americans suffer from Alzheimer's disease, and the progressive aging of our population means that these ranks will swell in the next 20 to 40 years. This disorder is found worldwide (with virtually no geographic differences), and its frequency increases exponentially with aging (Rocca et al., 1991).

Alzheimer's disease is characterized by a progressive decline in intellectual functioning. It begins as a loss of memory of recent events. Eventually this memory impairment becomes all-encompassing, so extensive that Alzheimer's patients cannot maintain any form of conversation, because both the context and prior information are rapidly lost. They cannot answer simple questions such as, What year is it?, Who is the president of the United States?, or Where are you now? Cognitive decline is progressive and relentless. In time, patients become disoriented and easily lose themselves in familiar surroundings. Very commonly, this drastic loss of cognitive functioning takes place without any other readily apparent mark of debility, such as motor incoordination.

Observations of the whole brain of Alzheimer's patients reveal striking cortical atrophy, especially in frontal, temporal, and parietal areas. Studies on brain metabolism of these patients are especially revealing. PET scans following the administration of a radioactive form of glucose show marked reduction of metabolism in posterior parietal cortex and some portions of the temporal lobe (Figure 4.23). A substantial

decline in glucose utilization seems to precede the emergence of more severe cognitive impairments (Foster et al., 1984).

Microscopic studies of the brains of Alzheimer's patients reveal characteristic cellular changes. Some cells show abnormalities of neurofilaments called **neurofibrillary tangles**, which are abnormal whorls of filaments that form a tangled array in the cell. Studies of tissue also show strange patches of degenerating axon terminals and dendrites, termed **senile plaques** (Figure 4.24). Contained within each plaque is a substance called β-**amyloid**, an unusual protein that arises from the cleavage of a much larger protein (Selkoe, 1991). The number of senile plaques is directly related to the magnitude of cognitive impairment. Plaques of amyloid deposits are found in Alzheimer's patients in frontal and temporoparietal

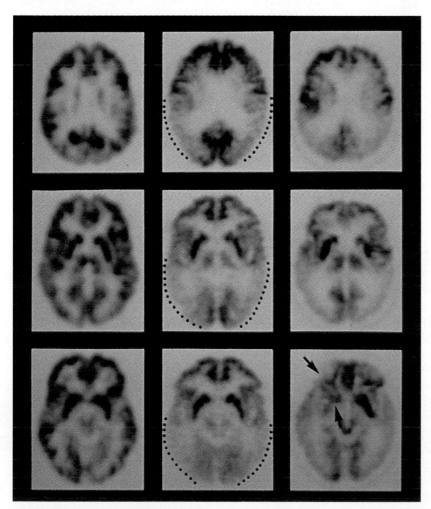

4.23 PET Scans of Elderly People
Those who are suffering from Alzheimer's disease (*middle and right panels*) show less widespread brain activation than normal elderly people.

(a)

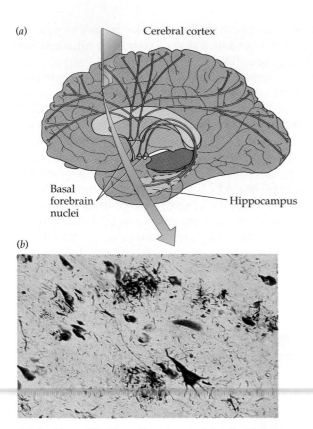

Cerebral cortex

Basal
forebrain
nuclei

Hippocampus

(b)

4.24 Neurofibrillary Tangles and Senile Plaques
(a) Location of basal forebrain nuclei in the brain and
distribution of their axons, which use acetylcholine as
a neurotransmitter. These cells seem to disappear in
Alzheimer's patients. (b) Neurofibrillary tangles (flame-
shaped objects) and senile plaques (darkly stained clusters) in the cerebral cortex of an aged patient. Micrograph courtesy of Elliott Mufson.

cortex, the hippocampus, and associated limbic system sites. Investigators have found both of these cellular changes, typical of Alzheimer's disease, in the
brains of Down's patients as well.

The role of the β-amyloid protein has become a focus of some debate (summarized by Marx, 1992).
Some researchers believe that β-amyloid is toxic to
nerve cells and is the principal cause of the neural degeneration that is characteristic of Alzheimer's disease. However, a recent issue of the journal *Neurobiology of Aging* (1992) presents a number of research
papers that take strong exception to this hypothesis.

Researchers have especially focused on changes in
a group of forebrain cells that may hold a key to the
fundamental understanding of Alzheimer's disease. A
striking loss of neurons occurs in a subcortical region
of the basal forebrain called **Meynert's nucleus** (Figure 4.24a). The axons of these cells extend to many cortical regions, and the cells contain acetylcholine, a sub-

stance used for transmitting neural activity to other
cells (see Chapter 5). Deficiencies of the acetylcholine
system are characteristic of the brains of Alzheimer's
patients, and other chemical neurotransmitters may
also be involved. Cases reported by Coyle, Price, and
Delong (1983) showed a consistent and marked decline in the number of cells in this region, but not in
immediately adjacent brain areas. This is not simply
an exaggeration of change that occurs routinely with
aging, since normal individuals show little loss of neurons in this area as they grow older (Chui et al., 1984).

Intensive research during the last decade has described many neuropathological and neurochemical alterations found in Alzheimer's patients. According to
Terry and coworkers (1991), the progressive decline in
cognitive abilities correlates most strongly with neocortical synapse loss, especially in the frontal and parietal regions. The degeneration of synapses produces a
continuing process of circuitry failure and thus changes
the entire capacity for complex neural interactions.

The causes of Alzheimer's disease remain shrouded
in mystery. Heredity is evident as a factor in some patients, especially those who show an early onset of dementia (starting between 40 and 60 years of age). One
report documented the pattern of inheritance of
Alzheimer's disease in 52 members of a family charted
for several generations (Nee et al., 1983). However,
hereditary factors are not so evident in most cases. Individuals with a family history of Alzheimer's disease
have a faster course of the disorder, and some researchers believe that the familial form may have a different set of neuropathological features (Luchins et al.,
1992).

Some investigators—basing their hypotheses on
the role of unusual viruses in other degenerative brain
diseases, such as one called kuru—have focused on
the possibility that Alzheimer's disease involves a
transmissible agent, such as a virus or subviral particle (Price, Whitehouse, and Struble, 1985). Alterna-
tively, since the salts of aluminum placed directly on
the cerebral cortex produce neurofibrillary tangles in
experimental animals, some investigators have suggested that toxic amounts of aluminum are
responsible for Alzheimer's disease. A focus
on aluminum is also spurred on by the discovery of relatively large amounts of aluminum in the brains of Alzheimer's pa-
tients. However, rather than causing the disorder, this
change might arise as a consequence of it.

Another hypothesis about the origin of Alzheimer's disease emphasizes autoimmune phenomena. According to this view, the patient's body may
produce antibodies that selectively attack acetyl-

choline-containing neurons. An exciting suggestion is that deficiencies in NGF, which is essential for the survival of many cells containing acetylcholine, are the primary cause of Alzheimer's disease (Hefti and Weiner, 1986). This hypothesis has led to the suggestion that administration of NGF might prevent further degeneration of acetylcholine-containing neurons in Alzheimer's patients. Support for this hypothesis comes from studies on primates that show that NGF can prevent the degeneration of acetylcholine-containing cells after injury to their axons (Koliatsos, Crawford, and Price, 1991).

Intensive research is now focused on the causes and treatment of Alzheimer's disease. The aging of our population suggests there is not much time left before we face an enormous public health problem. The replacement of lost brain cells by transplant has been suggested as a treatment for this and other degenerative brain diseases (Box 4.3).

Two Calendars for Brain Development

Let's try to bring together views of brain development from the two vastly different time scales: the weeks, months, and years of growth of an individual discussed in this chapter and the millions of years of evolution discussed in the previous chapter. We might use the analogy of the different but equally essential contributions of an architect and a carpenter in building a house. The architect brings to the construction of houses the same sort of perspective that evolution has brought to the construction of animals. The information in the architect's plan is analogous to the information contained in the genome. In preparing his plans, the architect calls on a long history of human knowledge about structures that meet basic human needs. These plans have incorporated hard-won information gathered over the centuries. But the carpenter's perspective is more like that of a developing individual. He must use these plans to construct a particular house here and now—translating the two-dimensional information given on the blueprints into a three-dimensional structure. During the building process the carpenter's judgment and interpretation are necessary, so two houses built by different carpenters from the same blueprints will not be identical. Another reason for differences in houses is that the materials available for their construction may not be the same. The architect tries to foresee some of the problems of construction and to build safety factors into the plans, so that small deviations or errors will not seriously impair the safety or utility of the completed

building. We are not the first to use such an analogy. An anonymous wit pointed out that a baby is the most complicated object to be made by unskilled labor, and psychologist J. C. R. Licklider characterized God as a great architect but a sloppy workman.

Natural selection has provided plans for construction of the brain with certain characteristics that we should note:

1. *New plans are never started from scratch.* Older plans are reused and modified to adjust to specific situations. The reuse and successive modification of genetic plans mean that the early embryological stages of development of all vertebrates are similar. The early neural tubes look very much the same in the embryos of a frog, a rat, or a person. Furthermore, the basic divisions of the brain are the same in all these forms. However, the whole structure has been scaled up in mammals, and especially in primates, and some parts have been enlarged relative to others.

2. *Not every detail is specified.* Part of the program is implicit in the list of materials and methods of construction. The plans would be hopelessly complex and voluminous if every detail had to be specified. Thus, even individuals with the same genes/blueprints, such as identical twins, wind up with slightly different connections in their brains.

3. *Allowances are made for interaction between the materials and the environment.* An architect knows how certain shingles will weather in a given climate to produce a desired appearance and how landscape planting will stabilize the soil and beautify the home's setting. So, too, the genetic plans for the brain take advantage of information provided by the environment. These plans allow for interaction between the developing organism and its environment.

The genetic code does not seem to have room for all the information necessary to specify the complete wiring diagram for each part of the nervous system. It achieves some economy by using the same information to apply to many different parts of the structure. Thus, the same gene may specify aspects of neural circuitry in different areas of the brain. Any mutation of the gene may therefore cause an abnormal arrangement of neurons in both the cerebellar and cerebral cortex, as in the mutant mice we discussed earlier. Certain hormones stimulate the growth of neural connections throughout the nervous system, as we will see in Chapters 7 and 12. And some fine details of the wiring do not seem to be specified but are worked out locally by cell–cell interactions.

Box 4.3
Brain Transplants or Grafts: Help for the Future?

Research on surgery of the nervous system sometimes makes the present look like the future. We have grown accustomed to heart transplants, kidney exchanges, corneal gifts, and so forth. But what about brain transplants? Journalists once asked Christiaan Barnard, the first surgeon to transplant a human heart (in 1967), what he thought about a brain transplant. He noted all the awesome technical difficulties: connecting axons, blood vessels, nerves, and so on. Then he seemed to recoil from the very idea, noting that such surgery should really be called a body transplant.

Not long ago brain or body transplants were unreal, the stuff of science fiction. The boundaries of the real were extended a bit further, however, with the successful isolation of the entire brain of a chimpanzee by White (1976). He was able to maintain an isolated brain for a few days by connecting it to machines that supplied oxygen and nutrients in the circulation. More

immediate, less quixotic hopes for humans come from work on a less grand scale—transplanting small *portions* of the brain as grafts. Can a piece of the brain be removed from one animal and donated to a second? This prospect is particularly important for possible compensation in brain disorders that involve deficiencies of specific chemicals made in certain brain regions.

Experimental work of the 1980s showed that brain transplants are feasible and that added tissue does become part of the host's brain circuitry (Sladek and Gash, 1984). In fact, we are close to systematic efforts to replace degenerated brain areas of humans using brain grafting techniques, as some examples from the current animal research literature illustrate. These studies show not only that new cells become part of the "wiring diagram" of the host's brain, but that some brain transplants can also correct impaired function caused by brain lesions. In some ways brain tissue is easier to transplant than many

other body tissues because brain tissue is less likely to be rejected by the immune system.

Most brain transplant studies involve the insertion of a small piece of tissue into a brain cavity, such as the ventricle, or on the surface of the brain. Donor tissue is derived from embryonic or fetal animal brains. Some transplant techniques include the injection of dissociated embryonic nerve cells into deeper brain regions. This injection technique involves a suspension of cells floating in a solution after their connections have been disrupted by either mechanical or chemical means (see figure). Eventually it may be possible to "engineer" donor cells by providing them with the required genes, rather than gather such cells from fetal tissue.

Functional recovery produced by brain transplants has been seen in a number of remarkable experiments. One such experiment with rats examined the impact of a brain transplant on performance of a task

---

Both economy of genetic instructions and adaptation to individual circumstances are achieved by depending on the environment to furnish certain information necessary for development. Each species has evolved in relation to a particular ecological niche, and its program of development exploits the environment as a source of information and stimulation. Thus, for example, most vertebrates are exposed to patterned visual stimulation soon after birth. By the time of exposure, the basic plan of the visual system has been laid down, but the formation of detailed connections and maintenance of the visual circuitry require input from the environment. Precise coordination of input from both eyes requires fine-tuning of the system. There are so many variables in the structure of the eyes that it would be extraordinarily costly for genetic specifica-

tion to bring about perfect alignment of the two retinal images. Thus, certain adjustments are required after the individual goes into operation, so to speak. Small misalignments of the two retinal images can be compensated for by minor "rewiring" of the central visual connections. If the misalignment between the two eyes is too great, however, as when the eyes are crossed, the input of one eye is usually suppressed to avoid double vision. This ability to learn from our surroundings and experience enables us to adjust to particular environments and lifestyles.

The short-range and long-range calendars provide complementary perspectives on the development of the nervous system and behavior. We will call on both perspectives to illuminate relations between the brain and behavior in many areas of biological psychology.

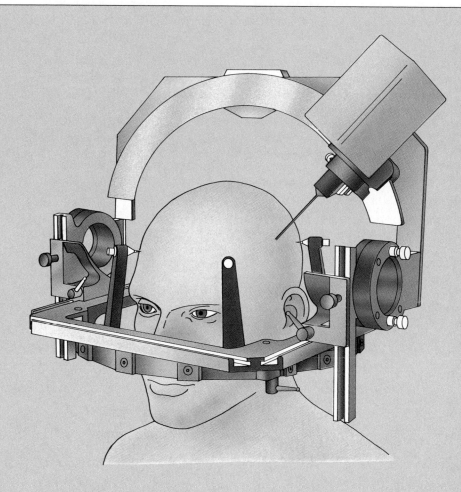

stored when frontal cortical tissue from fetal animals is transplanted to the frontal region (Labbe et al., 1983). Compensation for motor deficits has been a common type of test used to assess the functional advantages of brain transplants. Some of these tests attempt to model Parkinson's disease, a disabling brain disorder that involves destruction of cells in a brain stem area (the substantia nigra).

In Chapter 14 we'll discuss remarkably successful brain transplants affecting daily rhythms in the activity of hamsters. In Chapter 18 we'll see that in some animal experiments, nerve cell transplants are much more effective in restoring problem-solving ability if the animals are housed in complex environments or receive training after the transplant (Kelche, Dalrymple-Alford, and Will, 1988; Kelche et al., 1995). As we've seen already, brain transplants might be useful in treating some of the brain degeneration associated with Alzheimer's disease. Thus, a new window has been opened on the treatment of some of the most anguishing of human afflictions—those that arise from the death of brain cells.

that involved spatial alternation (choose the left arm of a maze this time, right next, then left again, and so on). After frontal cortical brain lesions, rats do poorly on this task. However, their performance is re-

---

Summary

1. Early embryological events in the formation of the nervous system include a sequence of six cellular processes: (1) the production of nerve cells (cell proliferation); (2) the movement of cells away from regions of mitotic division (cell migration); (3) the acquisition, by these cells, of distinctive neuronal forms (cell differentiation); (4) the establishment of synaptic connections; (5) the selective loss of some cells (cell death); and (6) the selective rearrangement of previously formed synapses.

2. Fetal and postnatal changes in the brain include the myelination of axons by glial cells and development of dendrites and synapses by neurons. Although in humans most neurons are present at birth, most synapses develop after birth and may continue developing into adulthood.

3. In simple animals such as the nematode *Caenorhabditis elegans*, the formation of neural pathways and synapses follows an innate, genetic plan that specifies the precise relations between growing axons and particular target cells. However, in more complicated animals, including all vertebrates, genes do not exert such rigid control on specific neural connections.

4. Among many determinants of brain development are (1) genetic information; (2) neurotrophic factors, such as nerve growth factors; and (3) nutrition.

5. Experience also affects the growth and development of the nervous system. Two possible explanations for this influence are that experience (1) induces and modulates the formation of synapses and (2) maintains synapses that are already formed.

6. The brain continues to change throughout life. Old age brings loss of neurons and synaptic connections in some regions of the brain. In some people the changes are more severe than in others, and pathological changes occur in the condition known as Alzheimer's disease, or senile dementia.

7. Maldevelopment of the brain can occur as a result of genetically controlled disorders. Some are metabolic disorders, such as phenylketonuria; others, such as Down's syndrome, are related to disorders of chromosomes.

8. Impairments of fetal development that lead to mental retardation can be caused by the use of drugs, such as alcohol or marijuana, during pregnancy.

Recommended Readings

Brown, M. C., Hopkins, W. G., and Keynes, R. J. 1991. *Essentials of Neural Development*. Cambridge University Press, Cambridge.

Jacobson, M. 1991. *Developmental Neurobiology*. Plenum, New York.

Purves, D. and Lichtman, J. W. 1985. *Principles of Neural Development*. Sinauer Associates, Sunderland, MA.

PART 2

Communication and Information Processing in the Body

Underlying all behavior—seeing, mating, eating, learning—is the processing of information. The sources of information include sensory receptors, ongoing neural activity, and other internal physiological events. The integrated behavior of an individual depends on the signals that communicate information within the nervous system and from the nervous system to the rest of the body. In the following chapters we take up basic questions about the nature of information processing in the body. In Chapter 5 we discuss how an individual neuron receives and integrates information and passes that information along through electrical and chemical signaling. Chapter 6 considers the effects of various drugs on that signaling system and on behavior. Then we discuss an important medium of communication between the nervous system and the rest of the body—hormones—in Chapter 7.

These chapters not only sketch the basic processes of communication and information processing in the body, but they also relate these mechanisms to daily life and to some major problems in human behavior. Thus they take up aspects of cognition and personality, and deal with clinical issues such as epilepsy, drug addiction, and pyschosocial dwarfism.

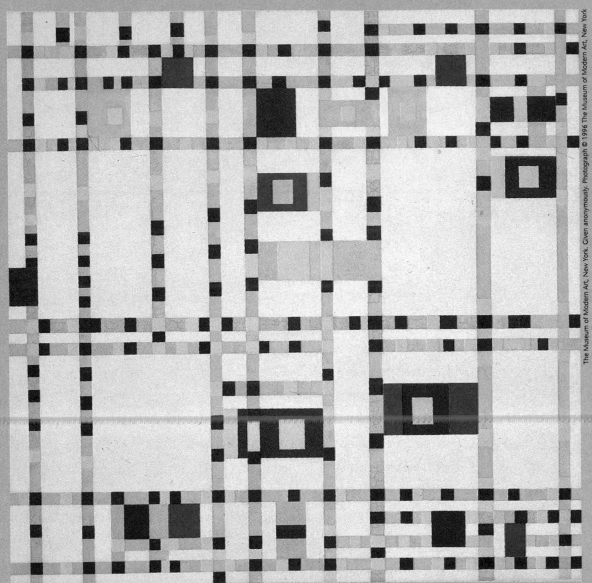

Piet Mondrian, *Broadway Boogie Woogie*, 1942–43

Neural Conduction, Synaptic Transmission, and Neural Circuits

CHAPTER 5

Orientation

As you read this page, light stimulates your eye and starts a barrage of signals that race along nerve cells to your brain. Circuits of neurons in specific regions of the brain process the incoming stream of information. What are the elementary signals of nerve cells? How do these signals speed along axons and jump across the synaptic gaps between neurons? How can neural circuits process information? In this chapter, we will describe the basic electrical signals of nervous systems and discuss the physicochemical basis of these electrical events. Understanding how nerve cells conduct signals prepares us to consider the second main topic of this chapter: how information is transmitted from one neuron to another. Rapid advances in our knowledge of these processes are helping us understand many aspects of experience and behavior, both normal and abnormal. We will use this information in Chapter 6, on psychopharmacology, and in many later chapters. In the last section of this chapter, we will look at some basic kinds of circuits formed from neurons and synaptic connections.

Electrical Signals Are the Vocabulary of the Nervous System

One of the most powerful innovations in animal evolution was the electrical signaling of neurons. This innovation appears in animals as diverse as human beings, insects, and jellyfish—in fact, in almost all multicellular animals. These neural signals underlie the whole range of thought and action, from composing a symphony or solving a mathematical problem to feeling an irritation on the skin and swatting a mosquito.

To understand how the nervous system works, investigators measure three different kinds of electrical events in studying the activity of single neurons:

1. Neurons show a **resting potential**, or **membrane potential**, when they are inactive. This small electrical imbalance between the inner and outer surfaces of the membrane results from the separation of electrically charged particles called **ions**. (An ion is an atom or molecule that has acquired an electrical charge by gaining or losing one or more electrons.) Many other kinds of cells, such as muscle cells and blood corpuscles, also have membrane potentials. Nerve cells are unique because changes in their resting potential are signals that can be transmitted to other cells and integrated in complex ways.

2. **Nerve impulses**, or **action potentials**, are brief propagated changes that travel rapidly along the axon in many kinds of neurons. These changes are conducted in chain-reaction fashion, maintaining a uniform size as they advance, and they enable axons to serve as channels for rapid communication.

3. **Local potentials**, or **graded potentials**, are initiated at postsynaptic sites and vary in size and duration. They are not propagated, but spread passively, so the amplitude of such a potential decreases progressively as it moves farther from its site of origin. These are also called **postsynaptic potentials**. Interaction among graded postsynaptic potentials is a basic mechanism by which the nervous system processes information.

Let's consider the characteristic states of the neuron at rest and during activity with each of these potentials. These potentials can be thought of as the basic vocabulary of the nervous system. Knowing the vocabulary, we can understand much about how information is communicated and processed in the nervous system. As we will see later in this chapter, neuro-physiologists have pushed the analysis of these potentials to a deeper level by investigating the ionic mechanisms of neural activity.

The Neuron Generates a Resting Membrane Potential

A few simple experiments reveal the characteristics of electrical potentials in nerve cells. The initial experimental setup is shown in Figure 5.1. It includes an axon placed in a bathing fluid that resembles extracellular fluids, a pair of electrodes—the one with a very fine tip is called a microelectrode—and devices to amplify, record, and display electrical potentials. As we advance the microelectrode toward the axon, as long as the microelectrode remains outside the axon, there is zero potential difference between the microelectrode tip and a large electrode placed at some distance from the axon in the bath. (There are no potential differences between any two electrodes placed in the extracellular medium, because the distribution of ions in the extracellular fluid is uniform or homogeneous.)

When the electrode penetrates the membrane of the axon (point *d* in Figure 5.1), we note a sudden drop in potential to a level of –70 to –80 millivolts (mV; see Figure 5.1*b*). That is, the inside of the axon is electrically negative with respect to the outside. This difference, called the membrane potential, demonstrates that the axonal membrane separates charges. The composition of the fluid environment of the intracellular compartment differs from that of the extracellular fluid. We will see how that difference is created when we discuss ionic mechanisms later in this chapter.

Our hypothetical experiment would be hard to perform with just any axon. Most axons of mammals are less than 20 micrometers (μm) in diameter and quite difficult to pierce with an electrode. But nature has provided neurophysiologists with an extraordinary solution to this problem: the giant axons of invertebrates, especially those of the squid. Squid axons can attain a diameter of 1 millimeter (mm), so fat and apparent to the unaided eye that observers originally thought that these axons must be part of the circulatory or urinary system. Electrodes in the form of capillary tubes 0.2 mm in diameter can be inserted into a giant axon without altering its properties or activity. The membrane seems to seal around the inserted electrode tip. Experiments with giant axons have led to fundamental advances in understanding neural membrane structure and function.

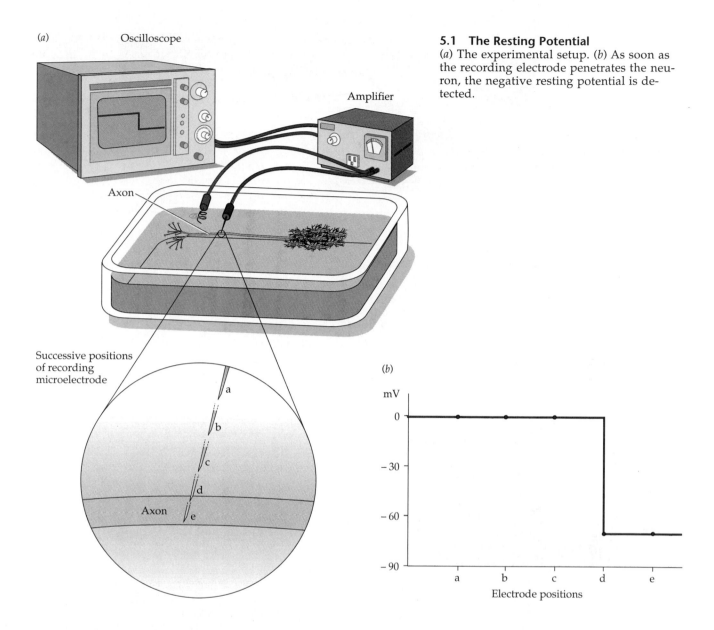

(a) Oscilloscope

Amplifier

Axon

Successive positions
of recording
microelectrode

a
b
c
d
Axon
e

(b)

mV

0

−30

−60

−90

a   b   c   d   e

Electrode positions

5.1 The Resting Potential
(*a*) The experimental setup. (*b*) As soon as
the recording electrode penetrates the neuron, the negative resting potential is detected.

A Threshold Amount of Depolarization Triggers an Action Potential

The next experiments require a source of electrical
stimulation. We must also add two terms to our vocabulary: **hyperpolarization** refers to increases in
membrane potential (greater negativity inside the
membrane in comparison with the outside); **depolarization** refers to reductions of the membrane potential (decreased negativity inside the neuron). The
stimulator will provide hyperpolarizing or depolarizing electrical pulses to the surface of the axon, and
we will see the effects such stimuli have on the membrane potential.

Figure 5.2 displays the changes in membrane potential that occur in response to successively stronger

stimulus pulses. The application of hyperpolarizing
stimuli to the axonal membrane results in responses
that almost mirror the "shape" of the stimulus pulse
(Figure 5.2, left panels). These responses passively reflect the stimulus, with distortions at the leading and
trailing edges resulting from an electrical property of
the membrane: its capacitance, or the ability to store
electrical charges. If we placed several fine electrodes
at successive positions along the axon, and applied a
hyperpolarizing pulse, we would see another important attribute of biological potentials in a conducting
medium: the responses are progressively smaller responses at greater and greater distances from the stimulus site. A simple law describes this relationship: In
a conducting medium, the size of a potential decays

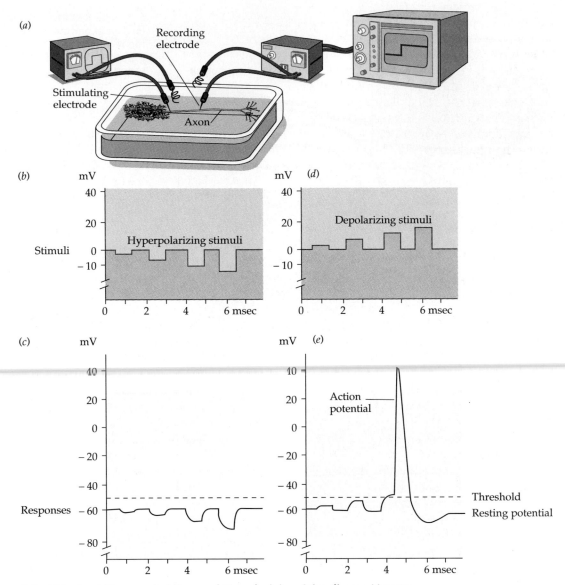

5.2 Effects of Hyperpolarizing and Depolarizing Stimuli on a Neuron
(*a*) The experimental setup. Increasing the strength of hyperpolarizing stimuli
(*b*) leads to greater hyperpolarization of the neuron (*c*). (*d*) Increasing the
strength of depolarizing stimuli leads to increasing depolarization of the neuron until the threshold is reached and an action potential is generated (*e*).

as a function of the square of the distance. Since the
amplitudes of these responses decline with distance,
they are examples of local or graded potentials.

If we apply a series of depolarizing pulses (Figure
5.2, right panels), the membrane response to the initial few stimuli is a series of depolarizing changes—
decreases in the resting potential—with some distortions. These again are local, graded responses.
However, things change suddenly when the depolarizing stimulus reaches a level of 10 to 15 mV. At

this level a rapid, brief (0.5 to 2.0 msec) response is
provoked: the action potential or nerve impulse. This
response is a brief transmembrane change in potential that momentarily makes the inside of the membrane positive with respect to the outside. Our experiment has now illustrated the notion of the
threshold of the nerve impulse, that is, the stimulus
intensity just sufficient to elicit a nerve impulse.

What happens when we increase the level of depolarizing stimuli in successive pulses until they are

well above threshold? This experiment displays a significant property of axonal membranes: with further increases in depolarizing stimulation, the amplitude of the nerve impulse does not change. The size of the nerve impulse is thus independent of stimulus magnitude. This characteristic is referred to as the **all-or-none** property of the nerve impulse. However, increases in stimulus strength are represented in the axon by changes in the *frequency* of nerve impulses rather than the amplitude. Thus, with stronger stimuli, the interval between successive nerve impulses becomes shorter, but the size of the impulses remains the same.

If we continue our experiment on this axon by applying either very strong stimuli or stimulating pulses that are closely spaced in time, we observe another important property of axonal membranes. As we offer our beleaguered axon more and more intense stimuli, we note that there seems to be an upper limit to the frequency for nerve impulse activity—about 1200 impulses per second. (Many neurons have even slower maximum rates of response.) The same underlying property is also shown in experiments in which we compare the effects of varying the interval between two successive stimuli; that is, we space our stimuli closer and closer together until, at some brief interval, only the initial pulse elicits a nerve impulse. In this case the axon membrane is said to be **refractory** to the second stimulus. There is a period following the initiation of a nerve impulse in which the membrane is totally insensitive to applied stimuli. This is called the **absolute refractory phase** and is followed by a period of reduced sensitivity, the **relative refractory phase**.

A closer look at the form of the nerve impulse shows that the return to baseline is not simple. Rather, many axons show oscillations of potential following the nerve impulse. These changes are called **afterpotentials**, and they are related to changes in excitability following an impulse.

Nerve Impulses Are Propagated in All-or-None Fashion

Now that we have explored the characteristics of a nerve impulse at a single location on the axon, we can ask how the axon communicates nerve impulses along its entire length. To examine this process, we place recording electrodes at several points along the axon (Figure 5.3). The nerve impulse is initiated at one end of the axon, and recordings are made with electrodes placed along the length of the axon.

These recordings show that the nerve impulse appears with increasing delays at the successive positions along the length of the axon. The nerve impulse initiated at one location on the axon spreads in a sort of chain reaction along the length, traveling at speeds that range from less than 1 meter per second (m/s) in some fibers to more than 100 m/s in others.

How does the nerve impulse travel? The nerve impulse is a change in membrane potential that is regenerated at successive axon locations. It spreads from one region to another because the flow of current associated with this small and rapid potential change depolarizes and thus stimulates adjacent axon segments. That is, the nerve impulse regenerates itself at successive points along the axon like a fire burning along a fuse.

The axon normally conducts impulses in only one direction because the action potential starts at the axon hillock, the place where the axon emerges from the cell body. As the action potential progresses along the axon, it leaves in its wake a stretch of refractory membrane. Propagated activity does not spread from the hillock back over the cell body and dendrites because the membrane of the cell body and of most dendrites does not produce a regenerated impulse, for a reason that will become clear later in the chapter.

If we record the conduction speed of impulses in axons that differ in diameter, we see that the rate of conduction varies with the diameter of the axon. Relatively large, heavily myelinated fibers are found in mammalian sensory and motor nerves. In these neurons conduction speed ranges from about 5 m/s in axons 2 mm in diameter to 120 m/s in axons 20 mm in diameter. Although once thought to be as great as the speed of light, the highest speed of neural conduction is "only" about one-third the speed of sound in air. This relatively high rate of conduction aids the speed of sensory and motor processes. Small unmyelinated mammalian nerves have diameters of 1 mm or less, and their conduction speeds are 2 m/s or less.

The myelin sheathing on the larger mammalian nerve fibers speeds conduction. The myelin is interrupted by the nodes of Ranvier, small gaps spaced about every millimeter along the axon (see Figure 2.7). Since the myelin insulation offers considerable resistance to the flow of ionic currents, the impulse jumps from node to node. This process is called **saltatory conduction** (from the Latin *saltus,* a leap or jump; the familiar word *somersault* comes from the Latin *supra* meaning "over" and *saltus*). The evolution of rapid saltatory conduction in vertebrates has given them a major behavioral advantage over invertebrates, whose axons are unmyelinated and

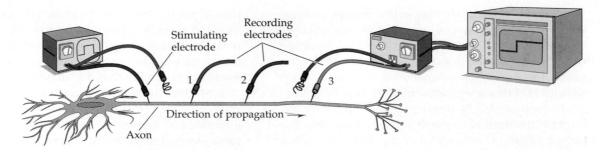

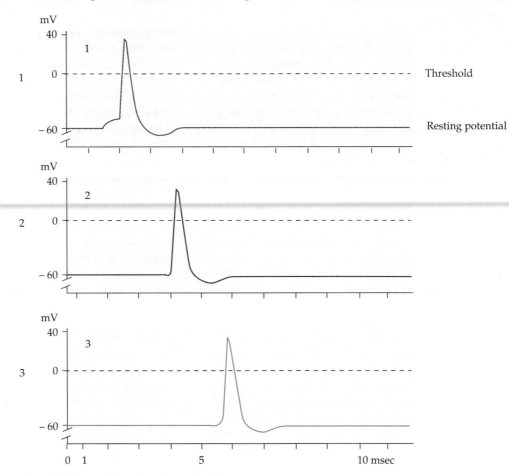

Recordings at different eletrodes following the same stimulus.

5.3 Propagation of a Nerve Impulse along the Axon
The farther the recording electrode is from the site of stimulation, the later
the action potential reaches it. However, the size of the action potential is the
same at each point along the axon.

mostly small in diameter, and thus slow in conduction. One exception to this rule is that many invertebrates have a few giant axons, which mediate critical motor responses, such as escape movements. In
the invertebrate as in the vertebrate, the speed of
conduction increases with axon diameter. The giant
axon of the squid has an unusually high rate of con-

duction for an invertebrate, but the rate still is only
about 20 m/s, about the rate of small myelinated
neurons with diameters of only 5 mm. To conduct
impulses as fast as a myelinated vertebrate axon
does, an unmyelinated invertebrate axon has to
have 10 times the diameter and thus 100 times the
volume. It has been estimated that at least 10% of

the volume of the human brain is occupied by myelinated axons. To maintain the conduction velocity of our cerebral neurons without the help of myelin, our brains would have to be ten times larger than they are.

The importance of myelin sheathing in promoting rapid conduction of neural impulses helps explain why myelination is an important index of maturation of the nervous system (see Chapter 4). It also helps explain the gravity of diseases that attack myelin, such as multiple sclerosis.

Activity of Presynaptic Axon Terminals Can Elicit Postsynaptic Potentials

At a synaptic junction, the presynaptic neuron can affect the postsynaptic neuron by evoking electrical potentials across the membrane of the postsynaptic cell. These postsynaptic potentials vary in amplitude and can be either positive or negative. Interaction between these potentials, in the form of summation and subtraction, is the basis of information processing in the neuron. Although commonplace today, observations of these electrochemical changes is a relatively recent scientific breakthrough. Until the early 1950s, vigorous dispute continued whether

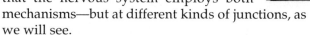

the nature of communication across synapses in the central nervous system was electrical or chemical. As early as the mid-nineteenth century, the German physiologist Emil Du Bois-Reymond proposed two possible mechanisms by which one neuron could excite another or could excite a muscle fiber: either the electrical nerve impulse stimulates the adjacent cell directly, or the neuron secretes a substance that excites the adjacent cell. Attempts to prove various forms of the electrical or the chemical hypothesis provoked lively controversies for a century. Eventually it was found that the nervous system employs both mechanisms—but at different kinds of junctions, as we will see.

Postsynaptic potentials are studied using a setup like that in Figure 5.4*a*. When a microelectrode is inserted delicately into the cell body of a neuron, the membrane seals around the electrode, and the neuron continues to function normally. During the 1950s and 1960s, experiments on synaptic transmission in mammals involved spinal motor neurons because they are large and many characteristics of their inputs were known. The receptive surface of each spinal motor neuron has many synaptic connections,

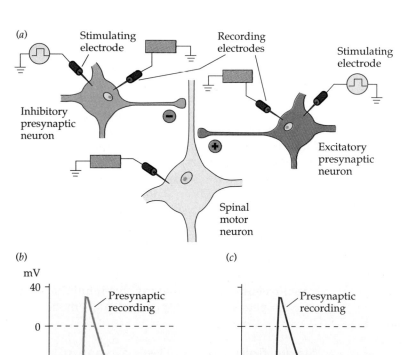

5.4 Recording Postsynaptic Potentials
(*a, left*) When an inhibitory presynaptic neuron is stimulated, its activity causes hyperpolarization of the postsynaptic neuron (*b*). Conversely, stimulating an excitatory presynaptic neuron (*a, right*) causes depolarization of the postsynaptic neuron (*c*). If the postsynaptic potential reaches threshold, an action potential will be generated. The size of the recorded subthreshold postsynaptic potentials will be smaller when the recording electrode is farther from the synapse.

some of which were known on the basis of their behavioral effects to be excitatory and some to be inhibitory. By selecting the presynaptic cell to stimulate, investigators can see how the motor neuron responds to signals from either excitatory or inhibitory connections. The responses of the presynaptic and postsynaptic cells are shown on the same graphs in Figure 5.4*b* for easy comparison of their time relations.

Stimulation of an excitatory presynaptic neuron leads to an all-or-none action potential in the presynaptic cell (Figure 5.4*c*). In the postsynaptic cell, after a brief synaptic delay a small local depolarization is seen. Generally it takes the combined effect of many excitatory synapses to elicit an all-or-none potential in a postsynaptic neuron. If **excitatory postsynaptic potentials (EPSPs)** are elicited almost simultaneously by many neurons that converge on the motor cell, these potentials can summate and produce a depolarization that reaches the threshold and triggers an action potential. Note that there is a delay: In the fastest cases, the postsynaptic depolarization begins about half a millisecond after the presynaptic impulses. This delay was important evidence that the postsynaptic effect was not just a weakened reflection of the presynaptic action current, because a purely electrical response would have essentially no delay.

Further evidence that the synapse makes a special contribution came from analysis of the results of presynaptic inhibitory stimulation (Figure 5.4*b*). The action potential of an inhibitory presynaptic neuron looks exactly like that of the excitatory presynaptic fiber; neurons have only one kind of propagated signal. But the postsynaptic local potentials show opposite polarities. When the inhibitory neuron is stimulated, the postsynaptic signal is an *increase* of the resting potential. This hyperpolarization is inhibitory for the motor neuron—it decreases the probability that the neuron will fire an impulse—so it is called an **inhibitory postsynaptic potential (IPSP)**.

Electrical Synapses Work with No Time Delay

Although most synapses require a chemical substance to mediate synaptic transmission, all species that have been investigated in this regard also have purely electrical synapses. At electrical synapses the presynaptic membrane comes even closer to the postsynaptic membrane than it does at chemical synapses; the cleft measures only 2 to 4 nanometers (nm; Figure 5.5). In contrast, the gap is 20 to 30 nm at chemical synapses. Furthermore, the facing membranes of the two cells have relatively large channels

that allow ions to flow from one neuron to the other. As a consequence, the flow of electrical current that is associated with nerve impulses in the presynaptic axon terminal can travel across the presynaptic and the postsynaptic membranes. Transmission at these synapses closely resembles conduction along the axon. Electrical synapses therefore work with practically no time delay, in contrast to chemical synapses, where the delay is on the order of a millisecond—slow in terms of neurons. Because of their rapidity, electrical synapses are frequently found in neural circuits that mediate escape behaviors in invertebrates. They are also found where many fibers must be activated synchronously, as in the vertebrate oculomotor system.

Inhibition Plays a Vital Role in Neural Processing

Although we have been paying more attention to excitation, inhibition also plays a vital role in neural processing of information. Just as driving a car requires brakes as well as an accelerator, neural switches must be turned off as well as on. The nervous system treads a narrow path between overexcitation, leading to seizures, and underexcitation, leading to coma and death. (Box 5.1 describes physiological and psychological aspects of seizure disorders.)

Whether a neuron fires off an action potential at any given moment is decided by the relation between the number of excitatory and the number of inhibitory signals it is receiving, and it receives many of both at all times. Some neurons and some synaptic transmitter chemicals are specialized to send inhibitory messages. For example, the entire output of the cerebellar cortex consists of messages from the large Purkinje cells that we saw in Figure 2.2. The Purkinje cell axons send only inhibitory messages to the output nuclei deep in the cerebellum, so the cerebellar cortex exercises all its effects on the rest of the brain through inhibition. The terminals of the Purkinje cell axons use the synaptic transmitter gamma-aminobutyric acid (GABA), as do many other cells. A measure of the importance of inhibition is the estimate that GABA is present at about 40% of the synapses in the brain. In later chapters we will see specific neural circuits that involve inhibition—circuits for perception, motor control, and emotion.

Nerve Cells Vary in Their Signaling

The picture of nerve cell signals we have presented to this point is a portrait of a typical cell operating under baseline conditions. Additional information pro-

(a)

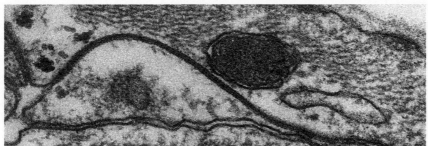

(b)

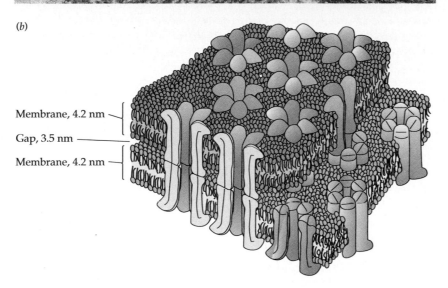

Membrane, 4.2 nm

Gap, 3.5 nm

Membrane, 4.2 nm

5.5 An Electrical Synapse
(a) An electromicroscopic image of an electrical synapse showing the narrow cleft between the two neurons. (b) A diagram of a electrical synapse showing the membranes of the two neurons and ion channels in each membrane facing those in the other and bridging the synaptic cleft. Such synapses do not rely on the release of neurotransmitter, but directly transmit a change in electrical potential from one cell to the other.

cessing flexibility in the nervous system comes from exceptions to these usual properties. To provide a sense of the diversity of neuron "lifestyles," we will briefly mention a few of many such exceptions:

- Some nerve cells have very short axons or no axons at all. In these cells communication with other cells involves only local electrical potentials and not nerve impulses.

- Nerve cells differ in impulse threshold, the amount of depolarization necessary for initiating a nerve impulse.

- Nerve cells vary in the relationship between magnitude of depolarization and rate of nerve impulse firing. For some neurons small increments in depolarization produce large changes in nerve impulse firing; for others the slope of the relation is shallower.

- The form of the action potential (for example, the rate of rise and the duration) differs among neurons.

- Neurons differ in responses of synapses to successive nerve impulses. At some synapses facilitating effects are seen, which means that the size of successive synaptic potentials grows. In contrast, at other synapses the successive responses become smaller and smaller. Both these effects show that the history of recent use affects what happens at a synapse. This memorylike device of the synapse may be related to broader behavioral states such as learning and memory.

- Neurons differ in pacemakerlike activity. Some cells are autorhythmic, regularly generating nerve impulses independent of synaptic inputs. These cells may be especially important in controlling rhythmic behaviors.

- Temperature affects the rate of firing of some neurons, allowing them to act as internal temperature sensors.

- Neurons are influenced by hormones and neuromodulators (called modulators because by themselves they do not produce significant neural effects) that circulate in the brain.

Box 5.1

Seizure Disorders

Epilepsy (from the Greek for "seize" or "attack") has provoked wonder and worry since the dawn of civilization. The seizures that accompany this disease have spawned, through the ages, much speculation about the cause—from demons to gods. Consequently, those afflicted with this disease have sometimes been shunned, sometimes exalted. Epidemiological studies indicate that 30 million people worldwide suffer from epilepsy. Since epilepsy affects so many people, the origin and possible cures of this disease are an important focus of research.

Why do seizures occur? The electrical character of nervous system signals offers the special biological advantages of rapid communication and the ability to generate, receive, and integrate a wide array of messages. However, this fundamental property also comes at a price. In addition to the high metabolic demands of nerve cells, there is also the potential cost of seizures. Because of the extensive connections among its nerve cells, the brain can generate massive waves of intense nerve cell activity that seem to involve virtually the entire brain. A seizure is the synchronized excitation of large groups of nerve cells. These unusual electrical events in the brain have a wide array of possible causes, including trauma or injury to the brain, and chemical changes derived from metabolic faults or exposure to toxins.

Types of Seizure Disorder

Several types of seizure disorders can be distinguished both behaviorally and neurophysiologically. **Generalized seizures** involve loss of consciousness and symmetrical involvement of body musculature. **Grand mal** and **petit mal** are two common types of generalized seizure and account for the largest number of patients. Grand mal seizures involve an EEG pattern evident at many places in the brain (Figure A). The behavior connected with this state is dramatic. The person loses consciousness, and the muscles of the entire body suddenly contract, producing stiff limbs and body. This **tonic phase** of the seizure is followed one to two minutes later by a **clonic phase** consisting of sudden alternating jerks and relaxation of the body. Minutes or hours of confusion and sleep follow. When nonprofessionals refer to epilepsy, they generally mean grand mal seizures.

Petit mal epilepsy is a more subtle variant of generalized seizures. It is revealed by a distinctive electrical pattern in EEG recordings, called the spike-and-wave pattern, that lasts from 5 to 15 seconds (Figure B). Periods of such unusual electrical activity can occur many times a day. During these periods the person is unaware of the environment and later cannot recall events that occurred during the petit mal episode. Behaviorally, the person does not show unusual muscle activity, except for a cessation of ongoing activity and sustained staring.

Both grand mal and petit mal are called generalized seizures because they arise from pathology at brain sites that project to widespread regions of the brain. In contrast, **partial seizures** arise from a local pathological focus. Some partial seizures involve no impairment of consciousness. For example, focal motor seizures involve repetitive motor spasms that frequently start in the periphery of a limb and move to adjacent muscles. Partial seizures that originate in the temporal lobe may involve strange sensory impressions, especially olfactory sensations, sudden feelings of anxiety, and elaborate acts performed automatically, such as complicated gestures.

The Mechanisms of Seizure

The prime ingredients needed for the development and maintenance of a seizure are these:

1. The capacity of membranes in some "pacemaker" neurons to develop intense activity either in response to synaptic input or spontaneously. A pacemaker for seizure activity might emerge from membrane damage that results in exaggerated ion conductances for calcium, sodium, or potassium. Giant excitatory synaptic potentials may also cause intense cell activities that lead to seizures.

2. In many types of seizures there appears to be a selective loss of inhibitory processes. Drugs that reduce the effectiveness of GABA, the most common inhibitory transmitter, are potent seizure producers.

3. Excitatory circuits that propagate excessive neuronal discharges to other regions.

The Consequences of Seizures on Brain and Behavior

Researchers have argued about whether nerve cell changes are the cause or effect of seizures. Recent research suggests both. Seizure-induced death of neurons seems to arise as a consequence of the excessive activation of some types of glutamate receptors (Choi, 1992),

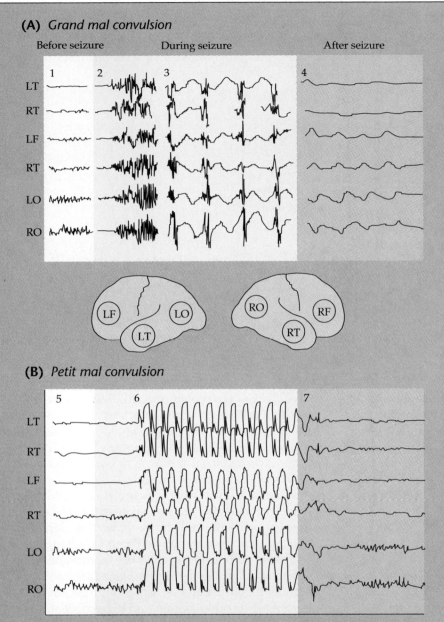

(A) *Grand mal convulsion*

Before seizure   During seizure   After seizure

(B) *Petit mal convulsion*

ral lobe structures involved in some forms of seizure disorder. Temporal lobe epilepsy is also associated with various psychopathological states in both children and adults (Trimble, 1991). Striking varieties of aggressive behavior occur in some patients with temporal lobe seizures. Hindler (1989) described a person in whom strong aggression was elicited by the laughing of an infant, which appeared to trigger odd olfactory sensations and other features of temporal lobe seizure activity. Tonkonogy (1991) reports patients who display violent behavior along with tissue loss in anterior temporal lobe structures and a history of temporal lobe seizure activity.

Animal Models Help Us Study Mechanisms of Seizure

Seizures can occur in the brains of many nonhuman creatures. Spontaneous seizures characterize some animals—for example, some breeds of dog, especially beagles.

One interesting model of seizure disorders uses repeated direct electrical stimulation of brain regions to provoke epileptic seizures. This process of establishing seizures is referred to a **kindling** (McNamara, 1984). To establish seizure activity in this model, an electrical stimulus too weak to cause a seizure on its own is delivered didrectly through implanted electrodes to a particular brain site in the animal. Over a period of days, this brief stimulus comes to produce both behavioral and electrophysiological signs of seizure activity in a progressive manner. Eventually siezures appear spontaneously. The phenomenon of kindling may be relevant to the finding that some human patients develop multiple foci for the initiation of seizures as a result of a history of seizure activity (Morrell, 1991).

but seizures also seem to result in the formation of new synaptic connections that may facilitate seizure activity (Seil, Drake-Baumann, and Johnson, 1994).

Frequent storms of electrical activity that invade the brains of epileptics may leave many marks, including some psychological and behavioral changes. For years, clinical neurologists have suggested a connection between one type of seizure disorder—temporal lobe epilepsy—and certain personality attributes (Trimble, 1991). Some researchers argue that emotional changes observed in these disorders are a direct result of frequent activation by seizures of emotional circuits in the temporal lobe. Others believe that emotional changes arise as a result of psychological responses to the social trauma of having a life with unpredictable seizures. Animal studies demonstrate changes in emotionality that occur with brain damage in tempo-

Table 5.1

Characteristics of Electrical Signals of Nerve Cells

TYPE OF SIGNAL	SIGNALING ROLE	TYPICAL DURATION (msec)	AMPLITUDE	CHARACTER	MODE OF PROPAGATION
Action potential	Conduction along a neuron	1–2	About 100 mV overshooting	All-or-nothing, digital	Actively propagated, regenerative
Excitatory post-synaptic potential (EPSP)	Transmission between neurons	10–100	Depolarizing, from less than 1 to more than 20 mv	Graded, analog	Local, passive spread
Inhibitory post-synaptic potential (IPSP)	Transmission between neurons	10–100	Hyperpolarizing, from less than 1 to about 15 mV	Graded, analog	Local, passive spread

Some properties of the electrical activity of large groups of neurons are discussed in Box 5.2. Table 5.1 gives the principal similarities and differences of the three kinds of neural potentials, emphasizing the distinctive characteristics of each kind of signal.

We have described the main features of the electrical activity of neurons. For a brief review of this material—which we recommend before you continue reading—refer to points 1 through 9 of the Summary at the end of the chapter.

Ionic Mechanisms Underlie Neural Excitation and Conduction

Now that we have seen some of the main characteristics and functions of electrical signals in neurons, let's examine the mechanisms that produce these potentials. This section will provide a nontechnical explanation; more complete accounts can be found in many other sources (for example, Hall, 1992; Nicholls, Martin, and Wallace, 1992).

Ionic Mechanisms Maintain the Resting Potential

Consider the distribution of ions on both sides of the simplified and idealized neural membrane in Figure 5.6. Inside the cell there is a high concentration of potassium ions (K^+), each of which has a positive electrical charge. There is also a high internal concentration of large protein ions, each with a negative charge. The internal concentrations of sodium (Na^+) and chloride (Cl^-) ions are low. Because of their negative charges, the protein and chloride ions are called **anions**. Positively charged ions, such as K^+ and Na^+, are called **cations**. The cell membrane contains many specialized small pores or **channels** through which the potassium ions can flow in or out relatively easily but which are not permeable to the other ions.

What happens when the neuron is placed in a solution that contains the same concentrations of ions as exist inside the cell? Some potassium ions may flow in or out, but there will be no net change, and no charge will develop across the membrane. What happens when the neuron is placed in a solution, such as blood plasma or seawater, that has a low concentration of potassium and high concentrations of sodium and chloride, as in Figure 5.6 (the concentrations of ions inside and outside the squid axon are shown in Table 5.2)? Certain laws of physical chemistry govern the movements of ions in solutions. For example, substances in solution move from regions of high concentration to regions of low concentration, unless there is a barrier, such as a membrane. In the absence of other forces, potassium ions tend to move out of the cell, because their concentration is 20 times greater inside than outside. This movement creates a potential difference across the membrane, as positive charges (K^+) leave the inside and accumulate outside. If the membrane were permeable to negative ions, one anion would accompany each cation out and no potential difference would

ION CHANNEL OPENING	CHANNEL SENSITIVE TO:
First Na$^+$ then K$^+$, in different channels	Voltage (depolarization)
Na$^+$/K$^+$	Chemical (neurotransmitter)
K$^+$ or C$^-$ or K$^+$/Cl$^-$	Chemical (neurotransmitter)

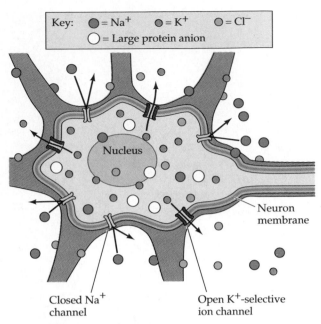

Key: ● = Na$^+$ ● = K$^+$ ○ = Cl$^-$
○ = Large protein anion

Nucleus

Neuron membrane

Closed Na$^+$ channel

Open K$^+$-selective ion channel

5.6   Distribution of Ions inside and outside a Neuron

Most potassium ions (K$^+$) are found inside the neuron; most sodium (Na$^+$) and chloride (Cl$^-$) ions are in the extracellular space. These ions are exchanged through specialized channels in the cell membrane. The large, negatively charged protein molecules stay inside the neuron and account for much of the negative resting potential.

occur, but the membrane of the axon is impermeable to large anions. When the potential difference across the membrane becomes large enough, the net outflow of positive ions stops, because the positive ions outside repel each other but are attracted to the negative ions inside.

At this point in the process, the tendency of the ions to flow from the regions of high concentration is exactly balanced by the opposing potential difference across the membrane. This potential is called the **potassium equilibrium potential** and is so predictable according to the laws of physical chemistry that it can be calculated using an equation, called the Nernst equation. The Nernst equation represents the voltage that develops when a semipermeable membrane separates different concentrations of ions. It predicts that the potential across the squid axon

membrane will be about –75 mV, inside to outside. The actual value is about –70 mV.

The predicted value differs from the observed value because the membrane is not absolutely impermeable to sodium ions. Small numbers leak in gradually through channels for sodium ions that open spontaneously and briefly, and this inward movement of Na$^+$ tends to reduce the membrane potential. The reduced potential, in turn, causes more potassi-

Table 5.2

Concentrations of Ions inside and outside Squid Axons (millimoles)

ION	INSIDE NEURON	OUTSIDE NEURON	
		IN BLOOD	IN SEAWATER
Potassium (K$^+$)	400	20	10
Sodium (Na$^+$)	50	440	460
Chloride (Cl$^-$)	40–150	560	540

Box 5.2
Electrical Activity of the Human Brain

The brain is a large collection of separate elements, and the electrical activity of thousands of cells working together adds up to potentials that can be recorded at the surface of the skull. Recordings of brain electrical activity with large electrodes can present useful glimpses of the simultaneous workings of populations of neurons. Investigators divide brain potentials into two principal classes: those that appear spontaneously without specific stimulation and those that are evoked by particular stimuli.

The Electroencephalogram

A recording of spontaneous brain potentials is called an **electroencephalogram (EEG)**, or more informally, "brain waves" (Figure A). As we will see in Chapter 14, EEG recordings of a sleeping person allow investigators to distinguish different kinds and stages of sleep. Brain potentials also provide significant diagnostic data—for example, in distinguishing forms of seizure disorders (see Box 5.1). They also provide prognostic data—for example, predictions of the functional effects of brain injury. In most states of the United States, brain potential data are used in the legal definition of death.

New developments in computer technology yield detailed quantitative analyses of brain potentials, buoying hopes for even greater clinical applications, especially in psychiatry. One such system of analysis and display of brain potentials is called BEAM (Brain Electrical Activity Mapping; Duffy, Burchfiel, and Lombroso, 1979; Duffy, 1992). An example of a BEAM display is shown in Figure B.

Event-Related Potentials

Gross potential changes provoked by discrete stimuli—usually sensory stimuli, such as light flashes or clicks—are called **event-related potentials (ERPs)** (Figure C). In the usual experiment to study this phenomenon, a series of ERPs is averaged to obtain a reliable estimate of stimulus-elicited brain activity. Sensory-evoked potentials have distinctive characteristics of wave shape and latency that reflect the type of stimulus, the state of the subject, and the site of recording. Subtler psychological processes, such as expectancy, appear to influence some characteristics of evoked potentials.

Computer techniques enable researchers to record brain potentials at some distance from the sites at which they are generated. This is akin to the ability of a sensitive heat detector to pick up minute sources of heat that are located at a distance. An example that has attracted considerable research and clinical attention is known as "auditory-evoked brain stem potentials." The neural generators of these waves are located far from the site of recording—in the auditory nerve and successive levels of the auditory brain stem pathways. These responses provide a way to assess the neural responsiveness of the brain stem and especially its auditory pathways. For example, reduction in amplitude of certain waves or increases in their latency have been valuable in detecting hearing impairments in very young children and noncommunicative persons. Hidden hearing deficits in children initially diagnosed as autistic have been revealed in this manner. Another use of these brain stem-evoked potentials is in the assessment of brain stem injury or damage, such as that produced by tumors or stroke.

Long-latency components of scalp-recorded ERPs tend to reflect the impact of information-processing variables, such as attention, decision making, and other complex psychological dimensions. Another way of contrasting these events with early latency events, such as the brain stem potentials, is to compare the sorts of factors that affect them. The later potentials are influenced more by endogenous factors, such as attention. In contrast early latency responses are more determined by exogenous factors; they are more stimulus-determined so that dimensions like stimulus in-

---

um ions to move out. Eventually the leakage would cause the concentrations inside and outside the cell to become the same, and the membrane potential would disappear. The neuron prevents this by pumping sodium out of the cell and potassium into the cell just rapidly enough to counter the leakage. Thus, maintaining the membrane potential, which is necessary for the neuron to be ready to conduct impulses, demands metabolic work by the cell. In fact, most of the energy expended by the brain—whether waking or sleeping—is thought to be used to maintain the ionic gradients across neuronal membranes.

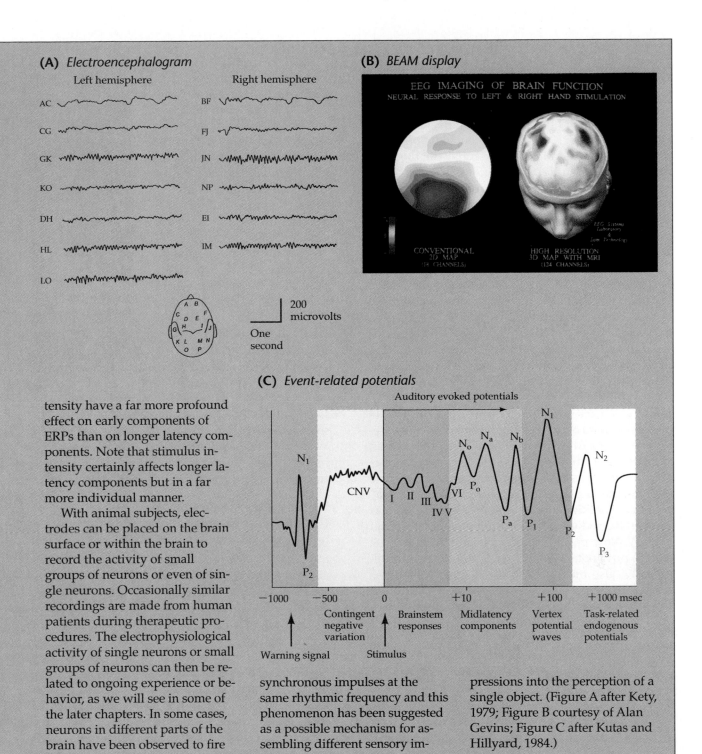

(A) *Electroencephalogram*

Left hemisphere   Right hemisphere

(B) *BEAM display*

(C) *Event-related potentials*

(Figure A after Kety, 1979; Figure B courtesy of Alan Gevins; Figure C after Kutas and Hillyard, 1984.)

tensity have a far more profound effect on early components of ERPs than on longer latency components. Note that stimulus intensity certainly affects longer latency components but in a far more individual manner.

With animal subjects, electrodes can be placed on the brain surface or within the brain to record the activity of small groups of neurons or even of single neurons. Occasionally similar recordings are made from human patients during therapeutic procedures. The electrophysiological activity of single neurons or small groups of neurons can then be related to ongoing experience or behavior, as we will see in some of the later chapters. In some cases, neurons in different parts of the brain have been observed to fire synchronous impulses at the same rhythmic frequency and this phenomenon has been suggested as a possible mechanism for assembling different sensory impressions into the perception of a single object.

Ionic Mechanisms Underlie the Action Potential

It used to be thought that the action potential resulted from a momentary increase in membrane permeability to all ions that caused the membrane potential to drop to zero. But research with the squid axon revealed that the action potential is larger than the resting potential. An "overshoot" briefly makes the inside of the neuron positive with respect to the outside (see Figure 5.2). The amplitude of this overshoot is determined by the concentration of sodium ions (Hodgkin and Katz, 1949), even though sodium does not affect the resting potential. At the peak of the nerve impulse, the potential across the membrane approaches that predicted by the Nernst equation with respect to the concentration of sodium ions: about +40 mV.

In its resting state the neural membrane can be thought of as a "potassium membrane," since it is permeable only to K^+ and the potential is about that of the potassium equilibrium potential. But the *active* membrane is a "sodium membrane," since it is permeable mainly to Na^+ and the membrane potential tends toward the sodium equilibrium potential. Thus the action current occurs during a sudden shift in membrane properties, which revert quickly to the resting state.

What causes the changes from K^+ permeability to Na^+ permeability and back again? A reduction in the resting potential of the membrane (depolarization) increases Na^+ permeability. This depolarization can be thought of as "opening gates" in some pores, or ion channels, that pass from the inside to the outside of the membrane. Some gates and channels admit Na^+ but no other ions. As some sodium ions enter the neuron, the resting potential is further reduced, causing still more Na^+ channels to open. Thus the process accelerates until all barriers to the entry of Na^+ are removed, and sodium ions rush in. This process is an example of positive feedback. The increased permeability to Na^+ lasts less than a millisecond in some neurons; then a process of inactivation blocks the Na^+ channels. By this time the membrane potential has reached the sodium equilibrium potential of around +40 mV. Now positive charges inside the nerve cell tend to push potassium ions out, and the permeability to K^+ also increases, so the resting potential is soon restored.

Earlier in this chapter we stated that the sequence of electrical events observed during conduction of a nerve impulse could be explained in terms of ionic mechanisms. Now we see that they can be accounted for in detail by the sequence of Na^+ and K^+ currents. The basic experiments and interpretation that illuminated these mechanisms were presented in a landmark series of papers in 1952 by English neurophysiologists Alan Hodgkin and Andrew Huxley. In their experiments, Hodgkin and Huxley recorded the electrical activity of the squid axon as they

Alan Hodgkin

varied ionic concentrations in the extracellular fluid. To make these measurements they used the then-new voltage-clamp technique: using a negative feedback circuit to hold the membrane potential at a desired level, they measured the flow of current needed to maintain the potential. For their contributions, Hodgkin and Huxley were awarded the Nobel Prize in Physiology or Medicine in 1963.

Andrew Huxley

The absolute and relative refractory phases also can be related to these changes in membrane permeability to ions. When the Na^+ channels have opened completely during the rise of the nerve impulse, further stimulation does not affect the course of events. And, during inactivation of the Na^+ channels, when stimulation cannot reopen them, the action current falls off. Thus, during the rising and falling phases of an action potential, the neuron is *absolutely* refractory to elicitation of a second impulse. While K^+ ions are flowing out and the resting potential is being restored, the neuron is *relatively* refractory.

Ion Channels Are Gated (Opened and Closed) Rapidly

Because changes in the permeability of the nerve membrane to Na^+ and K^+ during the nerve impulse are so important, many investigators are studying the mechanisms that control these events. One problem is finding the molecular bases of the voltage sensors that indicate when the changes are initiated; another is locating the "gates" in the ionic channels. Gating is thought to involve rearrangements in the shape or positions of charged molecules that line the channel. Making such changes requires the expenditure of energy. Several research groups have reported the measurement of tiny electrical currents that seem to be related to molecular rearrangements that open or shut gates in ion channels; these have been called **gating currents**. As we will see, some ion channels are gated mainly by changes in the electrical potential across the neuronal membrane and are thus referred to as **voltage-gated channels**; other ion channels are gated chiefly by chemical substances that bind to their outer surfaces.

The fact that the cell body and most dendrites do not conduct action potentials, as we mentioned earlier, can be explained in terms of the kinds of membrane channels they contain. Although the cell body and dendrites have ion channels that are gated by certain chemicals, and they can therefore be stimulated chemically, they have few voltage-gated channels. For this reason, a change in electrical potential cannot regenerate itself over the surface of the cell body by affecting voltage-gated channels in the adjacent stretch of cell membrane. The same is true for most dendrites.

How Can We Study Ion Channels?

Let us look briefly at present concepts of the structure of ion channels and then consider how investigators have been able to determine these structures. Figure 5.7 presents a diagram of the neuronal membrane studded with specialized molecular structures. The membrane is a double-layer structure of lipids whose fatty nature tends to repel water. Because ions in water or body fluids are usually surrounded by clusters of water molecules, they cannot easily pass through neuron membranes. Instead, they penetrate the cell through special channels whose inner surfaces do not repel water.

The ion channels in neuron membranes are too tiny to be seen in detail even with the electron microscope. How then can investigators determine their structures and modes of operation? Three main techniques have been used, providing steadily more complete knowledge about ion channels. After briefly outlining these three techniques, we will examine them in more detail:

1. A useful technique, introduced in the 1960s, is to employ pharmacological substances that are selective for one or another aspect of channel functions. Some drugs, especially poisons secreted by glands of certain species, act on specific channels. Important clues have emerged from knowing the sizes and shapes of such molecules and determining whether they are effective at only one or the other side of the neural membrane.

2. The use of very narrow pipette microelectrodes, clamped by suction onto tiny patches of the neural membrane, has made it possible to record the electrical activity of a single square micrometer of membrane. This **patch-clamp technique**, introduced in the late 1970s, enables investigators to study the activity of single membrane channels.

3. Beginning in the 1980s, techniques of molecular biology have made it possible to determine the exact structure of an ion channel. Investigators can now isolate ion channels, characterize their structures, and determine the DNA sequence for each of the subunits of the structure. Based on the amino acid sequences, they can propose and test detailed models of the channel structures. Thus, investigators can now do what was only on the horizon of speculation a decade or two ago.

Increasing knowledge of ion channels, and of the molecular receptors associated with some of them, has led to major advances in understanding the mechanisms of many processes of interest in biological psychology and neuroscience. We will see many examples in later chapters as we deal with psychopharmacology, hormones and behavior, sense organs, motor activity, and motivated behavior. Because of the importance of this topic, let's look a little more closely at the three techniques just described.

Pharmacological techniques.   Certain toxins of animal origin block specific ion channels, some affecting the activation gate near the outer end of the channel, and others inhibiting the inactivation gate at the inner end of the channel (Figure 5.8). Two animal toxins are known to block sodium channels when applied to the outer surface of the membrane; they do not affect other kinds of channels. These toxins are tetrodotoxin (TTX) and saxitoxin (STX). The size and structures of TTX and STX, together with those of other molecules that do or do not alter Na^+ perme-

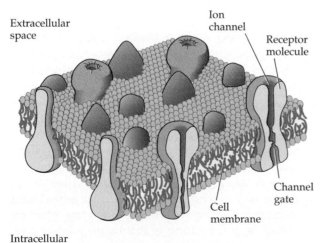

5.7   Neuronal Membranes Are Studded with Receptors and Channels

These receptors and channels consist of several large protein molecules linked together, floating in the fatty layers of the membrane.

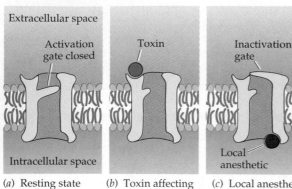

(a) Resting state

(b) Toxin affecting activation gate

(c) Local anesthetic inhibiting the inactivation gate

5.8 Ion Channel with an Activation Gate and an Inactivation Gate

ability, indicate the dimensions of the sodium channel. Tetrodotoxin is found in the ovaries of the pufferfish, which is esteemed as a delicacy in Japan. Fish markets in Japan display dried pufferfish, blown up like globes. If the pufferfish ovaries are not removed properly and if the fish is not cleaned with great care, people who eat it may be poisoned because TTX prevents their neurons from functioning. People die from this cause each year, and now neuroscientists know why.

In contrast to toxins that act at a site near the outer surface of the membrane, certain local anesthetics act at a different site that is accessible only from inside the membrane. Whereas the action of local anesthetics is temporary and wears off, a permanent change is caused if the enzyme pronase is introduced within the axon. Pronase destroys the inactivation gate that normally shuts the Na⁺ channel. Two kinds of scorpions have evolved venoms that block processes basic to neural conduction. The venom of the *Leiurus* scorpion impairs the inactivation gate, but the venom of the *Centruroides* scorpion specifically impairs the activation gate. Thus, it is clear that different molecular processes control the two kinds of gating of the sodium channel.

The patch-clamp technique. In the patch-clamp technique, a small patch of membrane is sealed by suction to the end of a micropipette, enabling investigators to record currents through single membrane channels (Figure 5.9a). Such recordings have been made not only in nerve cells but also in glial cells and muscle cells. The recordings show that the channels open abruptly and remain open only briefly (Figure 5.9b). Opening of some channels is made more likely

by changes in voltage, so these are called voltage-gated channels. An example is the voltage-activated sodium channel responsible for the neural depolarization that underlies the rising phase of the nerve impulse. This type of channel responds extremely rapidly. The other main family of channels respond to chemical substances applied to the surface of the cell; their responses are slower than those of the voltage-gated channels. Examples of chemically gated channels are those that respond to stimulation by the transmitter substance **acetylcholine (ACh)**. Substances like acetylcholine, that bind to receptor molecules at the surface of the cell are called **ligands** (from the Latin *ligare*, "to bind"). Channels that respond to such chemical stimuli are called ligand-activated channels.

Erwin Neher and Bert Sakmann of Germany devised the patch-clamp technique in 1976 so that they could study activity in single membrane channels. The technique has proved so productive that Neher and Sakmann were awarded the Nobel Prize in Physiology or Medicine in 1991, and much research using this technique continues today. In a recent article, Neher and Sakmann (1992) describe how they discovered the patch-clamp technique and what it has revealed about cellular signaling.

Erwin Neher (*left*)
Bert Sakmann (*right*)

Molecular biology and genetics. The first kind of channel to be studied in detail by molecular genetic techniques was the nicotinic ACh receptor (nAChR). This receptor is called **nicotinic** because it can also be activated by the compound nicotine; it is quite different from ACh receptors that are called *muscarinic* because they can be activated by the substance muscarine. We will consider the differences between nicotinic and muscarinic ACh receptors a little later.

Ligand-activated channels are often called receptors because they respond to the substances that bind to them and because research on them has relied on the binding of activating or inactivating molecules. The nicotinic ACh receptor is found in many sites, including the neuromuscular junctions of vertebrates (the junctions between motor neurons and muscles), the ganglia of many vertebrates and invertebrates, and the electric organs of many electric fish. One of these species, a marine ray (*Torpedo marmorata*), has

(*a*)   Preparing a patch clamp recording

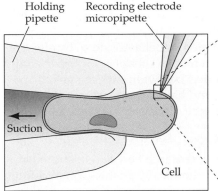
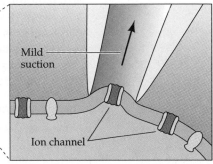
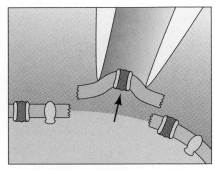

The tip of an electrode is brought into contact with the cell at an ion channel.

Gentle suction in the electrode improves the seal between cell and electrode. Electrical signals can then be recorded from the patch of membrane attached to the electrode.

Gently pulling the electrode removes the patch of membrane attached to the electrode from the cell, enabling recording from the isolated patch of membrane.

(*b*)   Recording made from a patch clamp

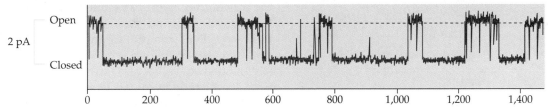

5.9   Patch-Clamp Recording from a Single Ion Channel
(*a*) Preparing to record the activity of a single membrane ion channel by the patch-clamp technique. (*b*) A record of tiny surges of electrical current caused by openings of a single ion channel. The unit of current here is a picoampere (pA), a trillionth of an ampere. A single opening may last less than a millisecond (msec), but a channel often opens several times in quick succession.

been a prime subject for studying the acetylcholine system since the 1930s and recently has been used to study the detailed structure of the nicotinic ACh receptor. This species has a specialized electric organ that it uses both to generate signals for navigation and to generate large shocks with which it stuns prey. The electric organ is composed of stacks of flattened cells, each of which generates a small electrical potential when stimulated by a motor neuron that uses ACh as the transmitter. The potentials of the cells in the stack add up and produce a large electrical discharge.

Because many nicotinic ACh receptors are found in the electric organ of *Torpedo,* it was possible to isolate the messenger RNA for the nAChR from the electric organ. Large amounts of the corresponding DNA could then be cloned, and the sequence of nucleotides that convey the information of the DNA could be determined. From this sequence, the amino

acid structure of the nAChR could be deduced, enabling the construction of models of the three-dimensional structure of the receptor (Figure 5.10; Stroud and Finer-Moore, 1985). The receptor resembles a lopsided dumbbell with a tube running down its central axis. The handle of the dumbbell spans the cell membrane (which is about 6 nm thick); the larger sphere extends about 5 nm above the surface of the membrane into the extracellular space, and the smaller sphere extends about 2 nm inside the cell. The sides of the ion channel (the tube that runs through the handle) consist of five subunits arranged like staves in a barrel. Two units are alike; the other three are different. The genes for each of the four types of subunits have been isolated (Mishina et al., 1984), and neuroscientists have been able to assemble complete or incomplete receptors to study how they work.

After the structure of the nAChR had been determined, similar analyses were carried out for other lig-

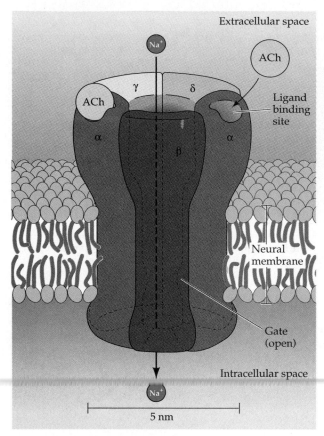

Extracellular space

Na⁺

ACh

γ   δ

ACh

Ligand binding site

α   α

β

Neural membrane

Gate (open)

Intracellular space

Na⁺

5 nm

5.10   A Nicotinic ACh Receptor
Each receptor consists of five subunits. The two sub-units have ligand binding sites which normally bind ACh molecules but also bind nicotine and other "nicotinic" drugs. The ACh molecule and Na⁺ ions are enlarged for diagrammatic purposes.

and-activated receptors. These include receptors for some of the synaptic transmitter molecules that we will be considering later, such as GABA, glycine, and glutamate. Several of these receptors resemble each other, suggesting that they all belong to the same family and have a common genetic origin.

The molecular genetic techniques that were successful in characterizing the structure and behavior of nAChR have been applied with equal success to the voltage-activated sodium channel. Again, the initial source of material was an electric fish—this time the electric eel, *Electrophorus electricus*—because in this animal the electric organ contains voltage-activated sodium channels rather than ligand-activated sodium channels. The voltage-activated sodium channel was found to consist of a single large protein molecule. Other voltage-activated channels have been found to have structures that are rather similar structures to the structures of the channels in the electric eel.

Synaptic Transmission

The principal focus of the second main part of this chapter is on chemical transmission at synapses. Many drugs that modify behavior do so by affecting synaptic events. In the next chapter we will examine substances that affect behavior, such as synaptic poisons, stimulants, and hallucinogens. Drug abuse and addiction will also be discussed in that chapter.

Transmission at Most Synapses Is Chemical

By the early 1950s, research had demonstrated that a combination of chemical transmission and ionic mechanisms offered a complete account of transmission at most synapses. The finding that a chemical step is *required* in synaptic transmission provided explanations for a number of phenomena. For instance, it explained the delay of 0.5 milliseconds or more in synaptic transmission. Time is required for the transmitter agent to be released, diffuse across the synaptic gap, and react with receptor molecules in the postsynaptic membrane. The chemical hypothesis also explained why the synapse acts as a sort of one-way valve; that is, transmission proceeds from presynaptic terminals to postsynaptic cells but not in the reverse direction. When we stimulate the axon of the postsynaptic cell, we see no changes in the presynaptic terminals. The reason is that the presynaptic terminal can liberate a chemical transmitter, but the synaptic membrane of the postsynaptic cell cannot.

There Are Two Main Kinds of Chemical Synapses

Chemical synapses differ according to whether the receptor molecules in the postsynaptic membrane carry out two main functions or only the first of these. The two main functions of postsynaptic cells are:

1. A *receptor* function. The cell has to recognize a specific transmitter molecule coming from the presynaptic cell.

2. An *effector* function. The biochemical state of the postsynaptic cell has to change as a consequence of receiving the message that the synaptic transmitter molecule has arrived at its surface.

The words "receptor" and "effector" are used in different contexts in biological psychology to refer to units that range from individual molecules to complete organs. "Receptor" was first used to designate such organs as the eye (the visual receptor) and the ear (the auditory receptor), because they receive and respond to signals from the environment. We will use "receptor" in that sense in Chapters 9 and 10. Only recently has the word "receptor" (or "receptor protein" or "receptor molecule") been used to designate a molecule that responds specifically to another molecule that binds to it. The word "effector" is often used to refer to organs, such as glands or muscles, that carry out a function such as secretion or contraction, and we will use "effector" in that sense in Chapters 7 and 11. The term "effector cell" is used to refer to a kind of cell in the immune system (see Chapter 15). And in the present chapter, an "effector molecule" is one that carries out a function such as opening a membrane channel. In using these terms, the context should always make clear the level of organization that is meant.

In one main kind of synaptic transmission, the receptor and effector functions occur in the same molecule. When the synaptic transmitter ACh acts at a vertebrate neuromuscular junction or at certain other sites, it binds to a specific kind of molecule at the surface of the postsynaptic membrane: the nicotinic ACh receptor (nAChR) mentioned earlier. The large nAChR molecule has a pore that can open and allow sodium ions to rush into the neuron, so the effector

function is accomplished by the same molecule. This kind of synapse is sometimes called a ligand-activated synapse. Because action at such synapses tends to be rapid and brief, they are sometimes called **fast synapses** (Table 5.3).

In the other main kind of chemical synaptic transmission, the receptor and effector functions are carried out by different molecules. In this type of synapse, the arrival of the transmitter at its receptor molecule has an indirect effect on ionic channels; it starts a cascade of events that operate through other chemicals, which are called **second messengers**. (The synaptic transmitter is considered to be the first messenger in this case.) The activity at these synapses tends to be slower and to last longer than at the directly ligand-activated channels, so these are sometimes called **slow synapses** (see Table 5.3). An example of this kind of synapse is the muscarinic ACh synapse (Figure 5.11). Peptide synaptic transmitters also act through synapses that utilize second messengers, and many of these synapses are rather slow and have prolonged activity.

The speed of synaptic transmission has important functional implications. In Chapter 2 and earlier in

---

Table 5.3

Characteristics of and Names for the Two Main Kinds of Chemical Synapses

	I	II
Characteristics		
Coupling of receptor to ion channel	Direct	Indirect; often uses G protein and/or second messenger
Speed of transmission	Fast	Slow[a]
Duration of response	Brief	Longer[a]
Examples of transmitters	ACh (at nicotinic receptor)	ACh (at muscarinic receptor)
	Glycine	Norepinephrine
	Glutamate	Dopamine
	GABA	Neuropeptides, including vasopressin, substance P, opioids, corticotrophin-releasing factor
Names	Directly coupled	Indirectly coupled
	Fast	Slow
	Ligand-activated	G protein-coupled, or second messenger-coupled
	Ionotropic (directed toward ion flow)	Metabotropic (directed toward chemical events within the neuron)

[a]Especially for neuropeptide transmitters

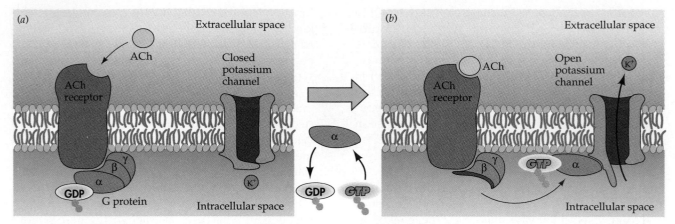

5.11 Modulation of Channel Function by G Proteins
(*a*) A G protein coupled to a muscarinic ACh receptor. (*b*) The binding of a transmitter molecule to the receptor starts a sequence of events. Activation of the G protein leads to separation of its α subunit and conversion of guanine diphosphate (GDP) to guanine triphosphate (GTP). The α subunit then causes a potassium channel to open.

this chapter we mentioned the advantages of large-diameter axons and myelination to promote the speed of neural conduction. Speed in synaptic transmission is also important for rapid neural processes, especially in complex neural circuits that have many synapses. Throughout evolutionary history, animals with slower nervous systems have tended to become meals for animals with faster nervous systems.

The Sequence of Transmission Processes at Chemical Synapses

The sequence of events during chemical synaptic transmission includes the following main steps:

1. The nerve impulse propagates into the presynaptic axon terminal.

2. A set of processes triggered by the impulse aligns some synaptic vesicles onto the presynaptic membrane.

3. Some vesicles release their transmitter molecules into the synaptic cleft.

4. Some transmitter molecules bind onto special receptor molecules in the postsynaptic membrane.

5. Binding of the transmitter molecules to receptor molecules leads—directly or indirectly—to opening of ion channels in the postsynaptic membrane; the resulting flow of ions alters the polarization of the postsynaptic neuron. If there is sufficient depolarization to reach the threshold of the postsynaptic neuron, it will fire an action potential.

6. The transmitter chemical is inactivated or removed rapidly from the synaptic cleft, so the transmission is brief and accurately follows the presynaptic input signal.

Figure 5.12 shows the main structures involved in chemical synaptic transmission: synaptic vesicles, the synaptic cleft, and the postsynaptic membrane, in which the receptors and ion channels are located. We will note some of the main characteristics of these structures and then take up the main processes of chemical transmission.

As we noted in Chapter 2, synaptic vesicles are located within the axon terminal of the presynaptic neuron. These vesicles are small globules that, in a given synapse, are usually the same size and show the same staining properties but vary in size and appearance. The size ranges from 30 to 140 nm. From the time that they were discovered in electron micrographs in the 1950s, synaptic vesicles were linked with chemical transmission, and they have since been demonstrated to store packets of the chemical transmitter used at the synapse. As is true of chocolates in a box, the size and shape of the vesicles provide clues to the identities of the transmitters they contain. Researchers used to believe that any given neuron uses only a single transmitter, but many end boutons (see Chapter 2) have been found to contain two or more kinds of vesicles and transmitters.

The synaptic cleft is the space between the presynaptic and postsynaptic neurons. Only about 20 to 40 nm separate the facing membranes of the two neurons. This is not an empty space; it contains complex

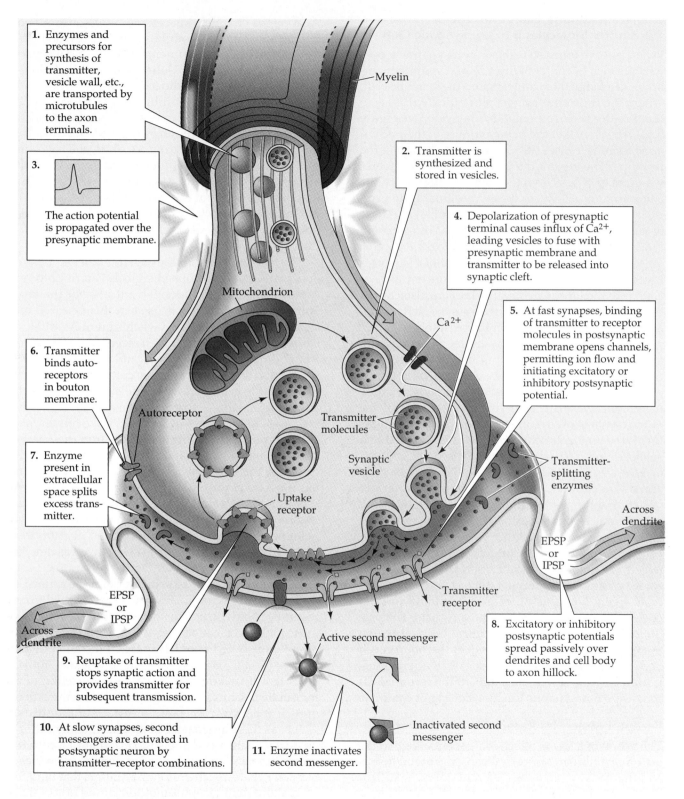

1. Enzymes and precursors for synthesis of transmitter, vesicle wall, etc., are transported by microtubules to the axon terminals.

3. The action potential is propagated over the presynaptic membrane.

2. Transmitter is synthesized and stored in vesicles.

4. Depolarization of presynaptic terminal causes influx of Ca^{2+}, leading vesicles to fuse with presynaptic membrane and transmitter to be released into synaptic cleft.

5. At fast synapses, binding of transmitter to receptor molecules in postsynaptic membrane opens channels, permitting ion flow and initiating excitatory or inhibitory postsynaptic potential.

6. Transmitter binds auto-receptors in bouton membrane.

7. Enzyme present in extracellular space splits excess trans-mitter.

8. Excitatory or inhibitory postsynaptic potentials spread passively over dendrites and cell body to axon hillock.

9. Reuptake of transmitter stops synaptic action and provides transmitter for subsequent transmission.

10. At slow synapses, second messengers are activated in postsynaptic neuron by transmitter–receptor combinations.

11. Enzyme inactivates second messenger.

Myelin

Mitochondrion

Ca^{2+}

Autoreceptor

Transmitter molecules

Synaptic vesicle

Transmitter-splitting enzymes

Uptake receptor

Across dendrite

EPSP or IPSP

Transmitter receptor

Across dendrite

EPSP or IPSP

Active second messenger

Inactivated second messenger

5.12 Steps in Chemical Synaptic Transmission

molecules organized in distinctive patterns that may guide transmitters to their postsynaptic sites.

Receptor molecules are clustered thickly on the postsynaptic side of the cleft (see Figure 5.7). The receptor membrane has different staining properties from the rest of the membrane.

The Nerve Impulse Causes Release of Transmitter Molecules into the Synaptic Cleft

When a nerve impulse reaches a presynaptic terminal, vesicles in contact with the presynaptic membrane discharge their contents into the synaptic cleft, where the transmitter molecules quickly diffuse to the receptor molecules on the other side (see Figure 5.12). The arrival of the nerve impulse at the presynaptic terminal causes calcium ions (Ca^{2+}) to enter the terminal. The greater the influx of Ca^{2+}, the greater the number of vesicles released by the impulse. If the concentration of Ca^{2+} in the extracellular fluid is reduced, fewer Ca^{2+} ions enter the terminal and fewer vesicles are released. (Calcium is also important in the liberation of hormones from endocrine glands; see Chapter 7.) Most synaptic delay at fast synapses is caused by the processes related to the entrance of Ca^{2+} into the terminal. Small delays are also caused by diffusion of the transmitter across the cleft and reaction of the transmitter with the receptor.

The vesicles for a given transmitter in a synapse all appear to contain the same number of molecules of transmitter chemical. The release of each vesicle causes the same change in potential in the postsynaptic membrane. Normally a nerve impulse causes release of the contents of several hundred vesicles at a time. But if the concentration of calcium is lowered at a synapse, only a few vesicles are released per impulse, and the size of unit depolarizations can then be measured. The number of molecules of transmitter per vesicle is probably in the tens of thousands. The presynaptic terminal normally produces and stores enough transmitter substance to ensure that the neuron is ready for activity. Intense stimulation of the neuron reduces the number of vesicles, but soon more vesicles are produced to replace those that were discharged. Neurons differ in their ability to keep pace with a rapid rate of incoming signals. The production of the transmitter chemical is governed by enzymes that are manufactured in the neuron cell body close to the nucleus. These enzymes are transported actively down the axons to the terminals. If they were not, synaptic function could not continue.

Receptor Molecules Recognize Transmitters

The action of a key in a lock is a good analogy to the action of a transmitter on a receptor protein. Just as a particular key can open different doors, a particular chemical transmitter can lead to the opening of different channels in the neural membrane. At excitatory synapses where it is the transmitter, ACh fits into "recognition sites" in receptor molecules located in the postsynaptic membrane. This binding of ACh opens channels successively for sodium and potassium ions, as Hodgkin and Huxley had deduced from their experiments in 1952, and as Jenkinson and Nicholls (1961) demonstrated by following the movement of radioactive sodium (Na^+) and potassium (K^+) ions. At inhibitory synapses, ACh opens a different door. It opens channels for chloride ions (Cl^-), thereby increasing the potential across the membrane (hyperpolarizing it). Thus, the receptor protein itself must be different at different kinds of synapses. Not only must ACh react with proteins that provide different channels for Na^+, K^+, and Cl^-, but other transmitter chemicals (such as norepinephrine, glycine, GABA) must fit like keys into their specific locks.

The lock-and-key analogy is strengthened by the observation that various chemicals can fit onto receptor proteins and block the entrance of the key. Some of the preparations used in this research resemble the ingredients of a witch's brew. As we saw earlier, large quantities of ACh receptor are obtained from the electric organs of eels and rays. Two blocking agents for ACh are poisons: curare and bungarotoxin. Curare is the arrowhead poison used by South American Indians. Extracted from a plant, it greatly increases the efficiency of hunting: if the hunter hits any part of they prey, the arrow's poison soon paralyzes the animal. Bungarotoxin is a lethal poison produced by the bungarus snake of Taiwan. This toxin has proved very useful in studying acetylcholine receptors because a radioactive label can be attached to it without altering its action. With such labeling, it is possible to investigate the number and distribution of receptor molecules at synapses, as well as details of transmitter/receptor binding.

Another poison, muscarine, mimics the action of ACh at some synapses. This poison is extracted from the mushroom *Amanita muscaria*. Molecules such as muscarine and nicotine that act like a transmitter at a receptor are called **agonists** of that transmitter (from the Greek *agon*, "contest, struggle"). Similarly, molecules that interfere with or prevent the action of a transmitter, as curare or bungarotoxin block the action of ACh at nicotinic receptors, are called **antagonists**.

Just as there are master keys that fit many different locks, there are submaster keys that fit a certain group of locks, and keys that fit only a single lock. Similarly, there are chemical transmitters that bind to several different receptor molecules, and others that bind to only one. ACh acts on at least four kinds of receptors. Nicotinic and muscarinic are the two main kinds of cholinergic receptors (all ACh receptors are referred to as "cholinergic.") Nicotine mimics chiefly the excitatory activities of ACh, and muscarine mimics chiefly the inhibitory actions. Nicotinic cholinergic receptors are found at neuromuscular synapses on skeletal muscles and in autonomic ganglia. Muscarinic cholinergic receptors are found on organs innervated by the parasympathetic division of the autonomic system (for example, the heart muscle, the intestines, and the salivary gland; see Figure 2.14). Most ACh receptors in the brain are muscarinic. Researchers used to think they were exclusively so, but small numbers of nicotinic receptors have been found in the brain, and some brain cells show the curious property of responding to both nicotine and muscarine. Most nicotinic sites are excitatory, but there are also inhibitory nicotinic synapses, and there are both excitatory and inhibitory muscarinic synapses, making four kinds of acetylcholine receptors. The existence of many types of receptor for each transmitter agent appears to be a device to produce specificity of action in the nervous system.

The number of receptors for a given transmitter in a region of the brain varies widely. Quantifying changes in the number of receptors has provided valuable insights, showing, for example, when various transmitter systems become active in fetal life and how the number of receptors changes over the life span. The number of receptors remains plastic in adults: not only are there seasonal variations, but many kinds of receptor show a regular daily variation of 50% or more in number, as we will see when we take up daily rhythms in Chapter 14. The numbers of some receptors have been found to vary with the use of antidepressants and other psychoactive drugs (see Chapter 16). Chapter 18 describes how the numbers of some receptors increase with behavioral training.

Recognition of Transmitters by Receptors Gates Ion Channels

The recognition of transmitter molecules by receptor molecules leads to gating of ion channels in two different ways, depending on whether the recognition and effector (ion channel) functions are combined in the same receptor molecules or are carried out by different molecules. Receptor molecules that combine the two functions are a specialty of the nervous system. These receptors achieve a rapidity of response not found in other systems. The receptor molecule changes its shape as soon as the transmitter molecule binds to it; that is, the receptor opens an ion channel contained within itself (Figure 5.13*a*).

At the second type of chemical synapse found in the nervous system, transmission resembles communication in many other bodily systems, including endocrine cells (see Chapter 7), blood cells, immune-system cells, and liver cells. In this type of chemical synapse, receptor molecules recognize the synaptic transmitter, but other molecules, in one or more additional steps, change the state of the postsynaptic cell. If we think of the transmitter as the first signal or messenger at the synapse, then in this type of synapse another substance within the cell is a second messenger. The second messenger amplifies the effect of the first and can initiate processes that lead to changes in electrical potential at the membrane. In many cases second messengers also lead to biochemical changes within the neuron.

How does binding of the synaptic transmitter with the receptor molecule lead to release of the second messenger? Research beginning in the 1970s, mainly with receptors for the synaptic transmitter norepinephrine (NE), showed that at many kinds of synapses the receptor is coupled to what is called a **G protein**. ("G protein" is a convenient designation for proteins that bind the compounds guanosine diphosphate [GDP] and guanosine triphosphate [GTP].) Since about 80% of the known neurotransmitters and hormones activate cellular signal mechanisms through receptors coupled to G proteins, this device is obviously very important (Birnbaumer, Abramowitz, and Brown, 1990). The G protein is located on the inner side of the neural membrane. When a transmitter molecule binds to a receptor that is coupled to a G protein, parts of the G protein complex dissociate—that is, separate from each other. One part, called the alpha subunit, migrates away within the cell and modulates the activity of its target molecules. Depending on the type of cell and receptor, the target may be a second-messenger system, or an enzyme that works on an ion channel, an ion pump. This sequence of events is diagrammed in Figure 5.13*b*. Many combinations of different receptors with different G proteins have already been identified, and more are being discovered at a rapid pace (Kobilka, 1992; Linder and Gilman, 1992).

The different receptor–G protein systems allow various transmitters to convey specific messages. For example, the transmitter dopamine, which has been implicated in depression and schizophrenia, acts on at least five kinds of receptors (called D receptors). The ability of drugs to aid people who suffer from depression or schizophrenia is correlated with the ability of the drugs to bind to some of these D receptors, as we will see in Chapter 16.

One special kind of receptor requires a combination of voltage change and chemical stimulation to activate

(*a*)   Fast, direct synapse (ionotropic)

(*b*)   Slow, indirect synapse (metabotropic)

5.13   Two Types of Chemical Synapses
(*a*) The main structures involved in directly activated (ligand-activated) synaptic transmission. (*b*) The main structures and processes involved in G protein-coupled synaptic transmission.

it. This is the so-called NMDA receptor, described in Box 5.3 along with some of its special functions.

The Action of Synaptic Transmitters Is Stopped Rapidly

When a chemical transmitter such as ACh is released into the synaptic cleft, its postsynaptic action is not only prompt, but usually very brief as well. This brevity ensures that, in many places in the nervous system, postsynaptic neural signals closely resemble presynaptic signals in their timing; that is, the message is repeated faithfully. Such accuracy of timing is necessary in many neural systems—for example, to

ensure rapid changes of contraction and relaxation of muscles in coordinated behavior. The prompt cessation of transmitter effects is achieved in one of two ways: (1) some transmitters, such as ACh, are rapidly broken down and thus inactivated by a special enzyme; (2) other transmitters are rapidly cleared from the synaptic cleft by re-entering into the presynaptic terminal. This not only cuts off the synaptic activity promptly, but also allows the terminal to recycle some materials in manufacturing the transmitter.

In an example of the first instance, the enzyme that inactivates ACh is **acetylcholinesterase (AChE)**. It hydrolyzes (breaks down) ACh very rapidly into

Box 5.3

A Star among Receptor Molecules

Because of its special role in many kinds of information processing, the NMDA receptor is getting star treatment; it is the subject of thousands of recent research articles, more than one hundred review articles in the past few years (for example, Daw, Stein, and Fox, 1993), and a symposium volume (Watkins and Collingridge, 1989). The NMDA receptor is one of the two main kinds of receptors activated by glutamate, which is a major excitatory synaptic transmitter found in all parts of the nervous system. The name NMDA receptor reflects the fact that this receptor is especially sensitive to the glutamate agonist *N-m*ethyl-D-*a*spartate. The other main kind of glutamate receptor is the AMPA receptor, which is particularly sensitive to the glutamate agonist *a*lpha-amino-3-hydroxy-5-*m*ethyl-4-isoxazole-*p*ropionic *a*cid.

The NMDA receptor acts differently from most receptor molecules because it is both ligand-gated and voltage-sensitive. When the NMDA receptor is activated, Ca^{2+} ions flow through its central channel into the neuron. But only very small amounts of Ca^{2+} flow through the NMDA receptor at the resting potential of -75 mV or at any membrane potential between -75 and -35 mV. The reason for the low Ca^{2+} conductance at these membrane potentials is that magnesium ions (Mg^{2+}) block the NMDA channel, as the left panel of the figure illustrates. Sufficient activation of AMPA receptors or other excitatory receptors in the same neuronal membrane can partially de-

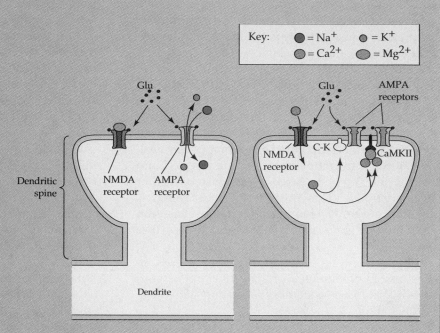

polarize the membrane to less than -35 mV. This depolarization removes the Mg^{2+} block (right panel of the figure); the NMDA receptor now responds actively to glutamate and admits large amounts of Ca^{2+} through the channel. Thus, the NMDA receptor is fully active only when it is gated by a combination of voltage and its ligand. Patch-clamp studies show that activation of NMDA receptors usually has a relatively slow onset and a prolonged effect (up to 500 msec), whereas non-NMDA receptors at the same synapse act rapidly and their channels remain open only a few milliseconds at a time.

The contributions of NMDA receptors can be studied by seeing what functions are impaired or abolished by an NMDA antag-

onist. Such an agent is APV (*a*mino*p*hosphono*v*alerate) which antagonizes the binding of glutamate to the NMDA receptor. Experiments with APV demonstrate that NMDA receptors are not needed for the normal flow of synaptic messages. But when the activity of other receptors reaches a relatively high level and partially depolarizes the membrane, NMDA receptors amplify and prolong the synaptic activity.

Because of these special properties, NMDA receptors play a wide variety of important roles. In later chapters we will see examples of how the NMDA receptor is involved in visual, auditory, and pain perception; in regulating motor and circulatory functions; and in fostering memory formation.

choline and acetic acid, and these products are recycled (at least in part) to make more ACh in the end bouton. AChE is found especially at synapses, but also elsewhere in the nervous system. Thus, if any ACh escapes from a synapse where it is released, it is unlikely to survive and reach other synapses, where it could start false messages.

Norepinephrine and dopamine are examples of transmitters whose activity is terminated by the second mechanism outlined above. In these cases, special receptors for the transmitter are located on the *presynaptic* axon terminal. These receptors take up the transmitter molecules and return them into the interior of the axon terminal, thus preventing them from making further contact with the *postsynaptic* receptors. Once taken up into the presynaptic terminal, some of the transmitter molecules are inserted into vesicles and can be released in response to further nerve impulses. This presynaptic mechanism is called **reuptake**. The reuptake mechanism has been implicated in some kinds of mental illness (see Chapter 16).

Although a cycle of synaptic activity is brief, in some cases it can initiate a prolonged neurochemical cascade that leads to memory formation, as we will see in Chapter 18.

We recommend referring to Figure 5.12 to review the stages in the transmission of nerve impulses at chemical synapses. This illustration emphasizes sources of variability in synaptic activity, since each step is subject to variation in the amounts of necessary substances and the rates of reactions. This review will set the stage for our discussion in Chapter 6 of the vulnerability of synaptic events to chemical agents and drugs that can either facilitate or impair synaptic transmission. In addition, review Table 5.3, a summary comparison of the two main kinds of chemical synapses.

The Search for Chemical Transmitters Continues

To identify the different synaptic transmitter agents and understand how they act is a continuing quest. Some of the amine transmitters—including acetylcholine, norepinephrine, and epinephrine (adrenaline)—were recognized as transmitters in the 1940s. Beginning in the 1950s, investigators discovered that some of the amino acids, the building blocks of proteins, act as transmitters at some synapses; these amino acid transmitters include glutamate, glycine, and GABA, among others. In the 1970s investigators

recognized that many peptides—short strings of amino acids—could be synaptic transmitters; some examples are the endogenous opioids and the neuroactive peptide hormones, such as oxytocin, substance P, and vasopressin. As the search continued, the number of probable synaptic transmitters grew from a few to several dozen during the 1980s, and new discoveries continue to bring surprises.

Among the most startling of these discoveries was the evidence obtained in 1991 that the simple gas nitric oxide (NO) appears to serve as a messenger between neurons, although not in the usual synaptic sense (Ignarro, 1991; Moncada, Palmer, and Higgs, 1991). As small gas molecules, NO can pass from one neuron to another without the aid of receptor molecules in the cell membrane. Since other neural transmitters occur in "families" of similar agents, some neuroscientists reasoned that other simple gases might also be neural messengers. They tested carbon monoxide (CO) for possible messenger properties and obtained positive results. CO can act on enzymes that are found in neurons in some parts of the brain and can thus change neural activity. CO and NO are not stored in vesicles, but they can be released from axon terminals when action potentials arrive. Other small gas molecules are sure to be tested soon, as the story continues.

What does it take to place a substance on the select list of proved transmitters? The criteria come from the anatomical and functional characteristics that we have discussed. To prove that a particular substance is the chemical transmitter at a particular synapse, we must demonstrate the following:

1. The chemical exists in the presynaptic terminals.
2. The enzymes for synthesizing the transmitter exist in the presynaptic terminals, or, in the case of the peptides, in the cell body.
3. The transmitter is released when nerve impulses reach the terminals, and in sufficient quantities to produce normal changes in postsynaptic potentials.
4. Experimental application of appropriate amounts of the chemical at the synapse produces changes in postsynaptic potentials.
5. Blocking the release of the substance prevents presynaptic nerve impulses from altering the activity of the postsynaptic cell.

For many proposed transmitter substances, the evidence about their functioning as transmitters and about their physiological roles is still rudimentary.

Substances that satisfy the criteria for transmitters (see below) include acetylcholine (ACh), **norepinephrine (NE)**, **dopamine (DA)**, **serotonin (5-HT)**, **gamma-aminobutyric acid (GABA)**, **glutamate**, and others listed in Table 5.4. There is considerable positive evidence for several other substances, but most investigators want to see even more evidence before they are convinced. Even if a substance is known to be a transmitter in one location, it may be hard to prove that it acts as a transmitter at another location where it is found. For example, acetylcholine was long accepted as the transmitter agent at vertebrate neuromuscular junctions, but it was harder to prove that it serves as a transmitter in the CNS as well. Investigators are still finding important information about the distribution and roles of ACh in the CNS. For example, the role of ACh in Alzheimer's disease is the subject of much current work (see Chapter 4). The number of suspected peptide transmitters is increasing especially rapidly. About 30 small peptides have been identified within sensory and autonomic neurons and in several CNS pathways. Considering the rate at which these substances are being discovered and characterized, it would not be surprising if there turned out to be several hundred different peptides conveying information at synapses in different subsets of neurons.

Investigators have been able to study the transmitters acetylcholine and norepinephrine more thoroughly than other transmitters because each of the two occurs alone at certain peripheral sites in the nervous system. As noted above, ACh is the transmitter at skeletal neuromuscular junctions in vertebrates, and in the ganglia of the autonomic nervous system.

Table 5.4

Some Synaptic Transmitters and Families of Transmitters

FAMILY	SUBFAMILY	TRANSMITTERS AND TRANSMITTER CANDIDATES
Amines	Quaternary amines	Acetylcholine (ACh)
	Monoamines	Norepinephrine (NE)
		Epinephrine (adrenaline)
		Dopamine (DA)
	Indoleamines	Serotonin (5-hydroxytryptamine; 5-HT)
		Melatonin
Amino acids		Gamma-aminobutyric acid (GABA)
		Glutamate
		Glycine
		Histamine
Neuropeptides	Opioid peptides	*Enkephalins*
		[Met]enkephalin
		[Leu]enkephalin
		Endorphins
		Beta-endorphin
		Dynorphins
		Dynorphin A
	Peptide hormones	Oxytocin
		Substance P
		Cholecystokinin (CCK)
		Vasopressin
		Hypothalamic releasing hormones

NE is the transmitter from neurons of the sympathetic division of the autonomic nervous system to most of the visceral effector organs, such as the heart and the stomach. For example, release of NE in the heart causes the heartbeat to accelerate. Within the CNS it was difficult until recently to trace noradrenergic fibers because they intertwine in a complex way with nerve fibers from other systems. ("Noradrenergic" means "having to do with norepinephrine.") Now, however, techniques of histofluorescence and immunohistochemistry have made it possible to map the distribution of noradrenergic pathways in the brain.

Evolution of Ion Channels, Synapses, and Transmitters

Many investigators are interested in comparative aspects and the evolution of ion channels, synapses, and transmitters (Arbas, Meinertzhagen, and Shaw, 1991; see also Hille, 1992). For example, certain voltage-gated ion channels for K^+ and Ca^{2+} are found in plants and in unicellular animals as well as in multicellular animals; these channels obviously evolved before the appearance of multicellular animals with nervous systems. Na^+ channels seem not to have evolved before the appearance of multicellular animals, and their structures suggest that they evolved from Ca^{2+} channels. The increased variety of ion channels may have been an important factor in promoting flexibility of neural circuits.

Electrical synapses are found in plants as well as animals and appear to be very ancient in an evolutionary sense. The appearance of chemical synapses added new flexibility: transmission could be modulated by a variety of messages from adjoining cells. Some of the simpler compounds that function in multicellular animals as synaptic transmitters—such as ACh, GABA, glycine, and glutamate—are also present in plants and in unicellular animals, but it is doubtful that they act as transmitters there. The transmitter functions of these substances that are evident in multicellular animals probably evolved from and superseded the functions in plants and unicellular animals. The inhibitory ligand-gated receptors (for GABA and glycine) appear to have evolved from the excitatory nicotinic ACh receptor. The neuropeptide transmitters appear to have arisen first in multicellular animals. Thus, in communication of information in the body, as for other functions, evolution has proceeded by conserving and "tinkering with" the available raw material.

Neurons and Synapses Combine to Make Circuits

Now that we have discussed the basic properties of neurons and synapses, it is time for an initial look at how they can be connected together into circuits to perform important functions such as conveying messages and processing information. The use of the term **circuit** for an assemblage of neurons and their synaptic interconnections is an analogy to electrical or electronic circuits, in which an arrangement of components (such as resistors, capacitors, transistors, and their connecting wires) accomplishes some function such as amplification, oscillation, or filtering. Electrical or electronic circuits can represent signals in either analog or digital ways—that is, in terms of continuously varying values or in terms of integers. Neurons also have both analog signals (graded potentials) and digital signals (all-or-none action potentials). Neuroscientists have shown that different kinds of neurons and synapses can perform many kinds of logical operations and computations (Poggio and Koch, 1987). Some investigators are even devising electronic circuits based on neural models to try to obtain some of the advantages of neural networks (Tank and Hopfield, 1987).

The nervous system comprises many different types of neural circuits that accomplish basic functions in cognition, emotion, and action—all the categories of behavior and experience. For now we will take up just three basic types of neural circuit: (1) the **neural chain**, (2) the **feedback circuit**, and (3) the **oscillator circuit**. As we describe each, we will note a few applications; other applications will come up in later chapters.

The Simplest Neural Circuit Is the Neural Chain

The first neural circuit that investigators thought of was the linking of neurons together in a chain. From the seventeenth century until well into the twentieth century, most attempts to understand behavior in neural terms were based on chains of neurons, and this circuit does account for some behaviors. For example, the basic circuit for the stretch reflex, such as the knee-jerk reflex, consists of a sensory neuron, a motor neuron, and a single synapse where the sensory neuron joins the motor neuron. Hundreds or thousands of such circuits work in parallel to enable the stretch reflex. Figure 5.14 shows the sequence and timing of events in the knee-jerk reflex. Note that this reflex is extremely rapid: only about 40 milliseconds elapse between the stimulus and the initiation of the response. Several factors account for this rapidity:

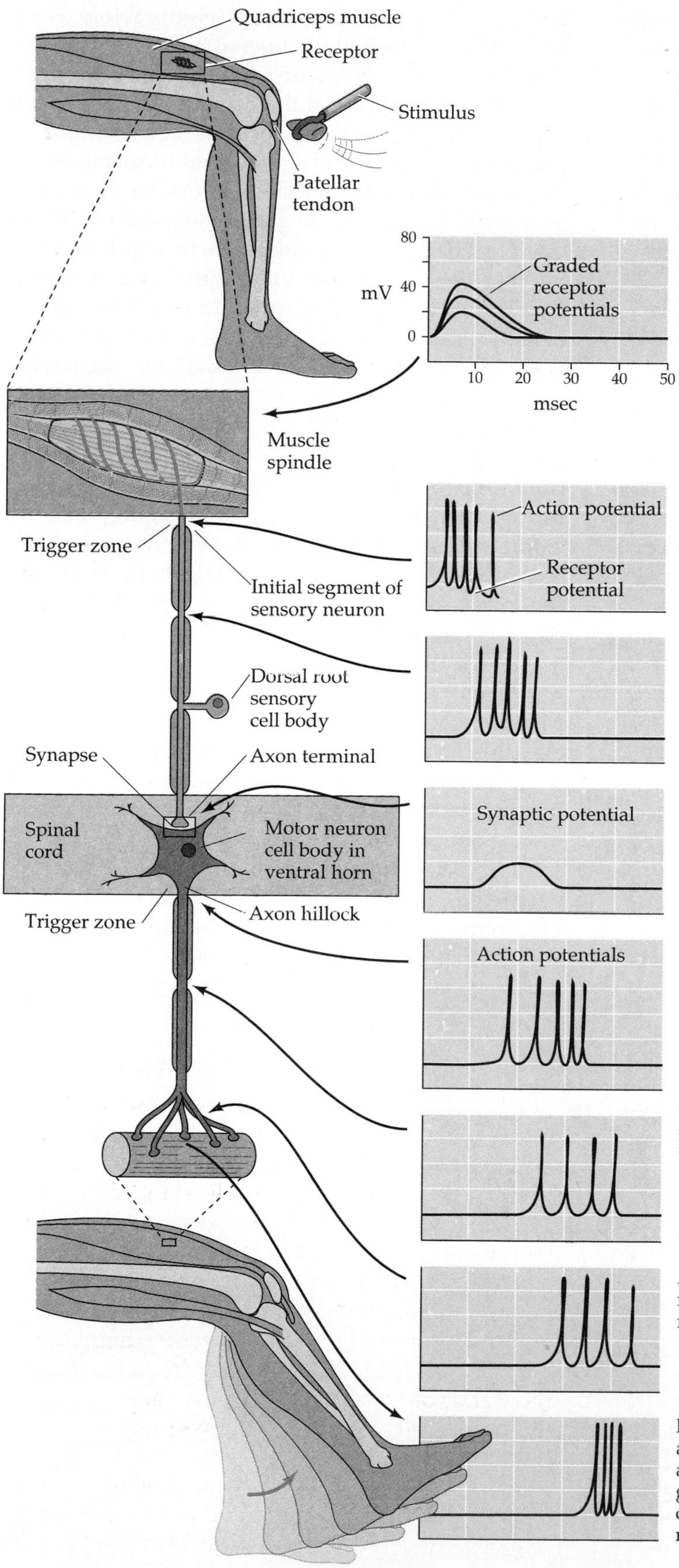
Quadriceps muscle
Receptor
Stimulus
Patellar tendon
80
mV 40
0
Graded receptor potentials
10
20
30
40
50
msec
Muscle spindle
Action potential
Receptor potential
Trigger zone
Initial segment of sensory neuron
Dorsal root sensory cell body
Synapse
Axon terminal
Spinal cord
Motor neuron cell body in ventral horn
Synaptic potential
Trigger zone
Axon hillock
Action potentials

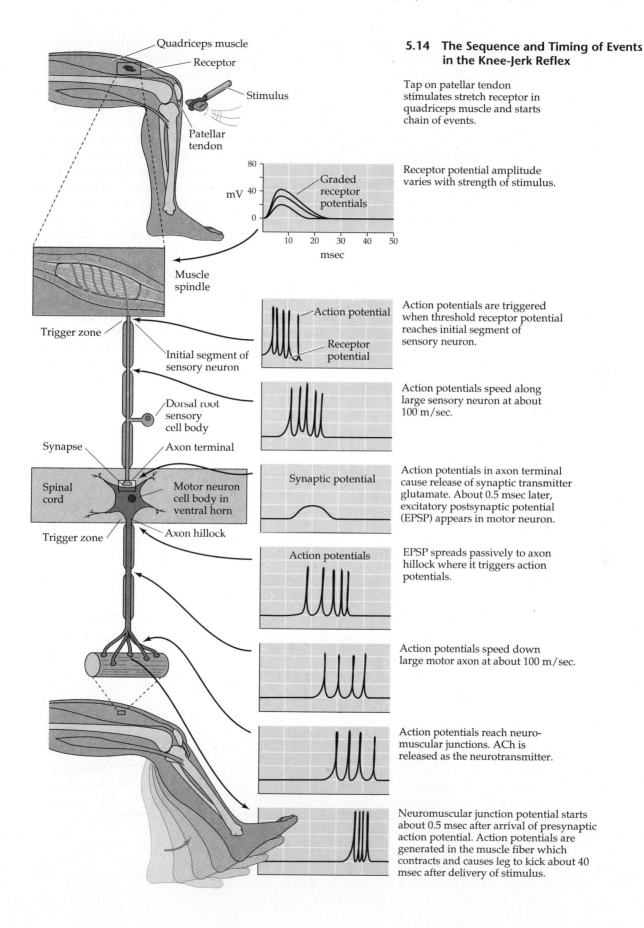

5.14 The Sequence and Timing of Events in the Knee-Jerk Reflex

Tap on patellar tendon stimulates stretch receptor in quadriceps muscle and starts chain of events.

Receptor potential amplitude varies with strength of stimulus.

Action potentials are triggered when threshold receptor potential reaches initial segment of sensory neuron.

Action potentials speed along large sensory neuron at about 100 m/sec.

Action potentials in axon terminal cause release of synaptic transmitter glutamate. About 0.5 msec later, excitatory postsynaptic potential (EPSP) appears in motor neuron.

EPSP spreads passively to axon hillock where it triggers action potentials.

Action potentials speed down large motor axon at about 100 m/sec.

Action potentials reach neuromuscular junctions. ACh is released as the neurotransmitter.

Neuromuscular junction potential starts about 0.5 msec after arrival of presynaptic action potential. Action potentials are generated in the muscle fiber which contracts and causes leg to kick about 40 msec after delivery of stimulus.

(1) both the sensory and the motor axons involved are of large diameter and thus conduct rapidly; (2) there is only one central synapse, and (3) both the central synapse and the neuromuscular junction are fast synapses.

For some purposes, the afferent, or input, parts of the visual system can be represented as a neural chain (Figure 5.15*a*). In reality, the retina contains many kinds of neural circuits, which we will discuss in Chapter 10. A more accurate schematic diagram of the visual system (Figure 5.15*b*) brings out two other features of many neural circuits: **convergence** and **divergence**. In many parts of the nervous system, the axons from large numbers of neurons converge on certain cells. In the human eye, about 130 million receptor cells concentrate their information down on about 1 million ganglion cells; these ganglion cells convey the information from the eye to the brain. Higher in the visual system there is much divergence. The one million axons of the optic nerve speak to hundreds of millions of neurons in several different specialized regions of the cerebral cortex.

The Feedback Circuit Is a Regulator

In a feedback circuit part of the output is fed back to the input. There are two types of feedback circuits: positive and negative. In **positive feedback** circuits, the effect of the output is to sustain or increase the activity of the initial input; in **negative feedback** circuits, the output inhibits the activity of the initial input. In some feedback circuits, a branch of the axon of a neuron loops back and contacts the same neuron (Figure 5.16*a*). In others, one or more intermediate

neurons form the feedback loop (Figure 5.16*b*). Feedback circuits were first discovered in the nervous system in the 1940s, and neuropsychologist Donald O. Hebb (1949) pointed out their relevance for psychological and neuroscience theory. For example, a positive feedback circuit can be used to sustain neural activity, which can contribute to maintaining a motivational state or to forming the cellular basis of memory. Negative feedback circuits help regulate many bodily functions by maintaining relatively constant conditions. A thermostat is an example of an artificial negative feedback device; many neural circuits in the body function in the same basic manner. The stretch reflex, mentioned in the previous section, serves as part of a negative feedback system in maintaining posture as you stand. Swaying a little to the front causes muscles in the back of the leg to stretch; the leg muscles respond by contracting, bringing the body again to the vertical. Similarly, swaying to the back stretches muscles in the front, and again the stretch reflex brings about the necessary compensation.

The Oscillator Circuit Controls Rhythmic Behavior

Many kinds of behavior are rhythmic, and their cycles differ in duration from short to long—from heartbeat, breathing, walking, sleeping and waking, to annual migration or hibernation. Some neurons, mostly in invertebrates, show inherent spontaneous rhythmicity of activity: the frequency of neural impulses of such a "pacemaker" cell waxes and wanes in a regular alternation. Rhythmic wing beating in some insects is controlled by such oscillation.

5.15   The Neural Chain
(*a*) Simple representation of the input part of the visual system. (*b*) A more complex representation, illustrating convergence and divergence.

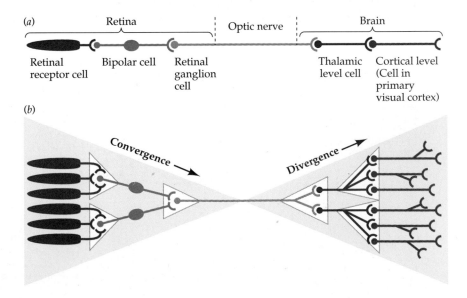

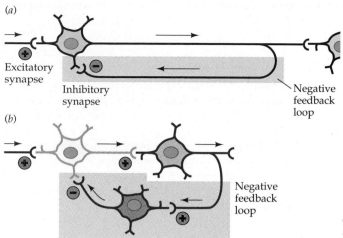

(a)

Excitatory synapse

Inhibitory synapse

Negative feedback loop

(b)

Negative feedback loop

5.16 Negative Feedback Circuits
(a) Within a single cell. (b) Including interneurons.

In both invertebrates and vertebrates, however, oscillatory activity usually depends on *circuits* of neurons. Figure 5.17 shows a simple oscillatory circuit that appears to control the alternation of inspiration (breathing in) and expiration (breathing out) in a freshwater snail, *Lymnaea stagnalis* (Syed, Bulloch, and Lukowiak, 1990). This species of snail has lungs and periodically goes to the surface, where it breathes several times before resubmerging. Several kinds of experiments, made possible by special properties of the invertebrate nervous system, indicate that a circuit of identified neurons is adequate to sustain rhythmic breathing behavior. Electrical recording from the intact nervous system shows alternating bursts of activity in two large, identifiable neurons. Stimulation of one of these causes expiration, and stimulation of the other causes inspiration. Furthermore, each of these interneurons inhibits the activity

of the other. The rhythmic alternation of activity of these two interneurons is initiated in the intact nervous system by a third identifiable interneuron, a giant dopamine cell. Removal of one of the three interneurons from the intact system abolishes respiratory behavior. Transplantation of this kind of neuron back into the system restores respiration after about 24 hours when the transplanted cell has become physiologically connected with the host nervous system (Syed et al., 1992). This miniature circuit can also be established in tissue culture. If the three kinds of neurons are placed in the culture, they grow appropriate connections to each other within 24 hours. Stimulation of the giant dopamine cell then evokes regular alternating activity of the two interneurons, similar to the rhythmic activity seen in the intact preparation. In cultures of only a single type of cell, or only two of the three, rhythmic activity is not observed.

Similar circuits enable the alternation of flexion and extension of a leg during walking. Thus, many other kinds of rhythmic behavior can also be understood in terms of oscillatory circuits of neurons.

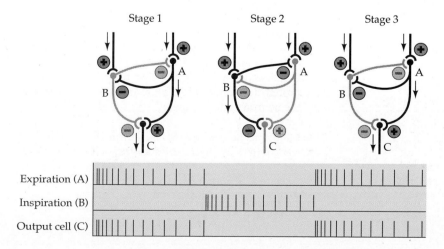

Stage 1   Stage 2   Stage 3

Expiration (A)

Inspiration (B)

Output cell (C)

5.17 A Simple Oscillatory Circuit
This circuit sustains the rhythmic alternation between expiration and inspiration in the snail Lymnaea. In Stage 1, cell A is active; it stimulates cell C which causes expiration, and it inhibits cell B. The rate of activity of A gradually decreases to the level where it no longer inhibits B. Therefore in Stage 2, cell B becomes active and inhibits both A and C, stopping expiration and causing inspiration. The activity of B gradually decreases to the level where it no longer inhibits A. A then springs into activity, and Stage 3 is identical to Stage 1. After Syed, Bulloch, and Lukowiak, 1990.

Summary

Electrical Activity of Neurons

1. Nerve cells are specialized for receiving, processing, and transmitting signals.

2. Neural signals are changes in the resting potential, which is the normal small difference in voltage between the inside and outside of the cell membrane.

3. A propagated impulse (also called an action potential) travels down the length of the axon without diminishing in amplitude; the impulse is regenerated by the successive segments of the axon.

4. Postsynaptic potentials are not propagated. They diminish in amplitude as they spread passively along dendrites and the cell body.

5. Excitatory postsynaptic potentials (EPSPs) are depolarizing (they decrease the resting potential) and make it easier for the neuron to generate an action potential. Inhibitory postsynaptic potentials (IPSPs) are hyperpolarizing (they increase the resting potential) and make it harder for the neuron to fire.

6. Cell bodies process information by integrating (adding algebraically) postsynaptic potentials across their surfaces.

7. A propagated impulse is initiated at the initial segment of the axon when the excess of EPSPs over IPSPs reaches the threshold.

8. During the action potential, the neuron cannot be excited by a second stimulus; it is absolutely refractory.

9. Some synapses use electrical transmission and do not require a chemical transmitter. At these electrical synapses, the cleft between presynaptic and postsynaptic cells is extremely narrow.

The Ionic Mechanisms of Neural Excitation and Conduction

1. The different concentrations of ions inside and outside the neuron—and especially of potassium ions (K^+)—account for the resting potential, with the inside of the neuron about –70 mV compared to the outside. The resting membrane is mainly permeable to potassium ions and is thus a "potassium membrane."

2. Reduction of the resting potential (depolarization of the membrane) makes the membrane more permeable to sodium ions (Na^+); that is, channels open that admit mainly Na^+. If this depolarization reaches a threshold value, the membrane becomes briefly a "sodium membrane," and the neuron becomes briefly more positive inside than outside. Depolarization of a stretch of membrane stimulates the adjacent stretch, so the action potential sweeps along the axon.

3. Knowledge of ion channels has increased through a succession of techniques: (1) study of pharmacological substances that affect one or another aspect of channel function; (2) the patch-clamp technique, which allows electrical recording from a very small region of neuronal membrane that may contain only a single ion channel; and (3) techniques of molecular biology and genetics that have made it possible to characterize the molecular structure of ion channels.

Synaptic Transmission

1. At most synapses the transmission of information from one neuron to another requires a chemical transmitter that diffuses across the synaptic cleft and binds to receptor molecules in the postsynaptic membrane. Because the transmitter binds to the receptor, it is called a ligand.

2. At some synapses, the receptor molecule responds to recognition of a transmitter by opening an ion channel within its own structure.

3. At other synapses, the binding of a transmitter molecule to a receptor molecule leads to opening of channels through the activity of second messengers. The initial second-messenger step usually involves a G protein adjacent to the receptor at the inner surface of the neuronal membrane.

4. Many substances have been confirmed as synaptic transmitters by rigorous tests; others are being tested.

5. Evidence for evolution of ion channels, synapses, and transmitters has been obtained from comparative studies. For example, certain ion channels and electrical synapses are found in plants as well as animals, but Na^+ channels and neuropeptide transmitters appear to have arisen first in multicellular animals.

Neural Circuits

1. Neurons and synapses can be assembled into circuits that process information. Three basic kinds of neural circuit are the neural chain, the feedback circuit, and the oscillator circuit.

Recommended Readings

Hall, Z. W. (ed.) 1992. *An Introduction to Molecular Neurobiology.* Sinauer Associates, Sunderland, MA.

Kandel, E. R., Schwartz, J. H., and Jessell, T. M. 1991. *Principles of Neural Science.* 3rd ed. Elsevier, New York.

Linder, M. E. and Gilman, A. G. 1992. G proteins. *Scientific American,* 267(1):56–65.

Neher, E., and Sakmann, B. 1992. The patch clamp technique. *Scientific American,* 266(3):44–51.

Nicholls, J. G., Martin, A. R., and Wallace, B. G. 1992. *From Neuron to Brain.* 3rd ed. Sinauer Associates, Sunderland, MA.

Shepherd, G. M. Ed. 1990. *The Synaptic Organization of the Brain.* 3rd ed. Oxford, New York.

Ben Shahn, *Man with Wildflowers*, 1956

- *Research on Drugs Ranges from Molecular Processes to Effects on Behavior*

- *Drugs Affect Each Stage of Neural Conduction and Synaptic Transmission*

- *Plant and Animal Poisons Help Reveal Nervous System Function*

- *Behavioral Toxicology Is a New Field*

- *Stimulants Promote Excitatory Synaptic Processes or Block Inhibitory Synaptic Processes*

- *Some Drugs Produce Hallucinations*

- *Drug Abuse Is the Most Common Psychiatric Problem*

- *Drugs Alleviate Psychiatric and Neurological Disorders*

- *The "Same" Drug Can Have Different Effects*

CHAPTER **Psychopharmacology**

6

Orientation

As far back as we can trace human lifestyles, people have tasted, sipped, chewed, or swallowed all kinds of substances—animal, vegetable, and mineral. From these experiences, people have learned to consume some substances and shun others. Social customs and dietary codes evolved to protect people from consuming harmful substances. This long history of seeking, testing, and using different substances came not only from the need for nourishment but also from the need for relief from pain, control of anxiety, and the pursuit of pleasure. Various drugs can fulfill these needs, but many may also cause dependency or even induce panic or psychotic states. Human consumption of drugs is so pervasive that one investigator characterizes human beings as "drug-taking animals" (Leonard, 1992:xi). But we are not alone in this activity; another authority stresses that "almost every species of animal has engaged in the natural pursuit of intoxicants" (R. Siegel, 1989:viii).

In this chapter we will consider how drugs affect the nervous system and behavior, as well as related research on how certain toxins affect the brain. We will also consider the concepts of dependency and addiction, and how biological psychologists are helping to solve the immense social problems associated with substance abuse.

Research on Drugs Ranges from Molecular Processes to Effects on Behavior

The subject of psychopharmacology—how drugs affect the nervous system and behavior—is vast and is changing at a rapid pace. We'll consider a variety of drugs in this and later chapters, but our coverage of psychopharmacology will necessarily be brief and incomplete. Readers who wish to pursue this topic further can consult references cited in the chapter, as well as the Recommended Reading list at the end of the chapter.

The range and complexity of psychopharmacology is suggested by the different meanings of the Greek word *pharmacon* which is the root of "pharmacology." *Pharmacon* has three principal meanings: (1) a charm—that is, an object thought to have a magical effect; (2) a poison; and (3) a remedy or medicine. We also use the term "drug" in different ways. One common meaning is a medicine used in the treatment of a disease (for example, a "prescription drug," or an "over-the-counter drug"). Quite a different meaning of "drug," but also a common one, is a psychoactive agent, especially an addictive one—that is, a drug of abuse. The shared meaning of these usages is a substance that, taken in relatively small amounts, has clear effects on experience, mood, emotion, activity, and/or health. Table 6.1 lists several classes of drugs and the chapters where each is considered.

To understand how drugs work, we must use many levels of analysis—from molecules to behavior and experience. Recall that figure 1.10 depicted several levels of analysis employed by biological psychologists. Because drugs exert their effects at the molecular level, but have profound effects on behavior, we will encounter these levels of of analysis in this chapter.

We start with a few basic questions and ideas about how drug molecules affect bodily processes: (1) Many drugs have been found to act on receptor molecules. What are the natural compounds—the keys—that fit into the receptor locks? (2) Usually a drug acts on more than one kind of receptor molecule. How does the ability of a drug to bind to different receptors help account for different effects of the same drug? (3) How do drug effects vary with dosage? (4) Many drugs are effective because they alter neural conduction or synaptic transmission. What are prominent examples of such effects? (5) Repeated use of a drug can make a given dose either less effective or more effective. What accounts for these changes with repeated use?

Table 6.1

Drugs and Drug Classes, and the Chapters Where They Are Discussed

DRUG OR DRUG CLASS	CHAPTER(S)
Alcohol	4, 6
Analgesics	6, 8
Morphine and other narcotics	6
Antidepressants	6, 16
Antipsychotic (neuroleptic) drugs (drugs for treating schizophrenia)	16
Anxiolytics (anti-anxiety drugs)	6, 16
Cannabis (*see* Hallucinogenic drugs)	
Casually used drugs Caffeine and nicotine	6
Depressants	15
Drugs of abuse (cocaine, heroin, marijuana, etc.)	6
Hallucinogenic drugs	6, 16
Anticholinergic hallucinogenics (atropine, scopolamine)	
Noradrenergic hallucinogenics (mescaline, etc.)	
Serotonergic hallucinogenics (LSD, psilocybin, etc.)	
Tetrahydrocannabinol drugs (marijuana, hashish, cannabis)	
Marijuana (*see* Hallucinogenic drugs)	
Medications for some neurological disorders	
Anti-epileptic drugs	5
Antiparkinsonian drugs	11
Nonnarcotic analgesics	8
Mood stabilizers Lithium	16
Narcotics Morphine and its analogs	6
Poisons that affect the nervous system	
Poisons with direct effects on ion channels	5, 6
Poisons that affect other aspects of synaptic transmission	6
Sleeping pills	14
Stimulants Amphetamines and cocaine	6, 16
Tranquilizers (see Anxiolytics)	

Drugs Fit Like Keys into Molecular Locks

To change the functioning of a cell, molecules of a drug must reach and interact with one or more constituents of the cell. The first component the drug encounters is the cell membrane. Some drugs are effective because they interact with lipid molecules in the membrane, but most drugs of interest to biological psychology react with specialized receptor molecules. Receptor molecules are proteins that may be situated either in the cell membrane—as are the receptor molecules in the postsynaptic membrane that we considered in Chapter 5—or they may be inside the membrane—as are the receptors for certain hormones that we will consider in Chapter 7.

Drug molecules do not seek out particular receptor molecules; rather, drug molecules spread widely throughout the body, and when they come into contact with receptor molecules with the specific shape that fits the drug molecule, the two molecules bind together briefly and begin a chain of events. The lock-and-key analogy is often used for this binding action, as we mentioned in the previous chapter. But now we have to think of keys (drug molecules) trying to insert themselves in all the locks (receptor molecules) in the neighborhood; each key unlocks only one (or very few) doors. Where a drug appears to bind to receptor molecules, investigators try to find the *endogenous* substance that is the natural ligand for that receptor. ("Endogenous" means occurring naturally within the body. Drugs are *exogenous* substances, that is, they are introduced from outside the body.) In some cases, such as the opioids, the key was identified before the structure of the lock was determined. In other cases, such as the receptor for the active ingredient of marijuana, the lock was identified before the endogenous key was found.

Opiates. Opium has a long history of human use that stretches back to the Stone Age, as we will see later in this chapter. It is a mixture of many substances. Morphine, the major active substance in opium, was extracted in pure form at the start of the nineteenth century. Morphine continues to be used medically as a very effective analgesic (painkiller), but it also has a strong potential for addiction. Many people have become addicted to morphine and to an artificially modified form of morphine—heroin (diacetylmorphine).

In 1973, the pharmacologists Candace Pert and Solomon Snyder found that opiate drugs such as morphine bind to receptor molecules concentrated in cer-

tain regions of the brain (Pert and Snyder, 1973). Other investigators published similar findings in the same year. As Figure 6.1 shows, opiate receptors are found especially in the limbic and hypothalamic areas of the brain, and they are particularly rich in the amygdala and in the gray matter that surrounds the aqueduct in the brain stem (the periaqueductal gray). Injection of morphine directly into the periaqueductal gray causes analgesia, indicating that this is a region where morphine acts to reduce pain perception. Refined analyses showed that the opiate receptors are located in postsynaptic membranes, but investigators

Candace Pert

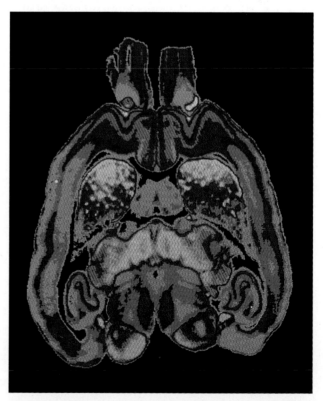

6.1 Distribution of Opiate Receptors in the Rat Brain These receptors are widely distributed in the brain but are concentrated in the medial thalamus and in some brain stem areas—the locus coeruleus, the periaqueductal gray, and the raphe nucleus. Courtesy of Miles Herkenham, NIMH.

still did not know either the structure of the opiate receptors or the identity of their endogenous ligand(s).

Solomon Snyder

They began an intensive search for natural substances in the body that would normally bind to the opiate receptors. In other words, they were looking for the natural keys that fit the lock of the opiate receptors.

In 1975 pharmacologists John Hughes and Hans Kosterlitz announced that they had isolated from pig brain two similar peptides that bind to the opiate receptor. They called these substances enkephalins (from the Greek *en,* "within," and *kephalon,* "head"). Soon afterward the same enkephalins were found in the brains of other mammals. Research with animal subjects demonstrated that the enkephalins relieve pain and that they are addictive. Only a small part of the enkephalin molecule is the same as the morphine molecule; it is this common part that binds to the opioid receptor. In Chapter 8 we'll consider the enkephalins in regard to pain perception. Further research has uncovered whole families of what are called endogenous opioids. One of these families is called the **endorphins**, a contraction of "endogenous morphine"— that is, the brain's own morphine.

On the other side of the transmitter–receptor story, investigators have sought to find the structure of each kind of opioid receptor molecule—that is, the structure of the lock that is opened by the opioids and opiates. Three main kinds of opioid receptor were hypothesized, because different drugs bind most strongly each type; they are called the delta, kappa, and mu opioid receptors. In 1992 the detailed structure of the delta opioid receptor was first announced (Evans et al., 1992), and this was soon followed by discovery of the structures of the kappa (Yasuda et al., 1993) and mu (Wang et al., 1993) receptors. The structures of all three opioid receptors resemble those of other G protein–coupled receptors, such as some of the synaptic receptor molecules we saw in Chapter 5 (see Figure 5.13*b*).

Marijuana. Surveys show that more people in the United States use marijuana than any other illegal drug (U.S. Department of Health and Human Services, 1991). Many investigators have studied marijuana and its effects. Marijuana is obtained from a plant, *Cannabis sativa,* which also furnishes other

preparations, such as hashish. The main active ingredient in marijuana and hashish is the compound tetrahydrocannabinol (THC), which was extracted and identified in 1964 (Gaoni and Mechoulam, 1964). THC, marijuana, hashish, and related preparations are called cannabinoids. Their effects on experience are highly variable among individuals, from stimulating and causing hallucinations to inducing relaxation, or sometimes initially causing almost no effect at all. Continued use of marijuana often causes addiction, although many people start using it without being aware of this potential. Smoking marijuana can also contribute to respiratory diseases, similar to the effects of smoking cigarettes.

In the case of marijuana, investigators deciphered the structure of the receptor molecule before they discovered the endogenous ligand—the body's own marijuana. For a period after THC was discovered, its mode of action was not known. Some researchers thought it might pass through the neural membrane and affect intracellular metabolism. Investigators tried to locate THC receptors by placing THC, tagged with a radioactive tracer, onto slices of brain and observing where THC accumulated. But THC turned out to be a "sticky" molecule that binds nonspecifically to surfaces all through the brain. This case is an example of one molecule binding to another without activating it. In subsequent experiments, scientists used a synthetic THC-like compound that has a more specific affinity for THC receptors. With this ligand they found that the receptor molecules for THC are indeed located in neuronal membranes (Devane et al., 1988). The radioactive tracer marked the brain regions where these receptors are concentrated (Figure 6.2). High concentrations occur in the substantia nigra, the hippocampus, the cerebellar cortex, and the cerebral cortex; other regions, such as the brain stem, show few of these receptors. Soon after these experiments, other investigators found the sequence of amino acids in the receptor molecule by cloning the gene of rats (Matsuda et al., 1990) and of humans (Gerard et al., 1991), enabling them to infer that the receptor molecule is a G protein–coupled receptor. But they still did not know what natural substance in the body might normally bind to this receptor.

In 1992 investigators isolated an endogenous compound in brain tissue that binds to the THC receptor and that has at least some of the properties of THC (Devane et al., 1992). In the hope that they had found an endogenous equivalent to marijuana, the discoverers named this compound anandamide (from the Sanskrit *ananda,* "bliss"). Further research showed

(a)

(b)

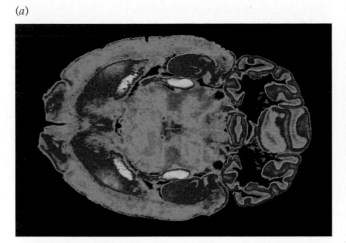

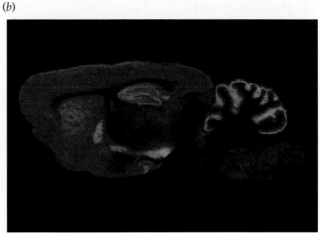

6.2   Distribution of Receptors for the Cannabinoids in the Rat Brain
(*a*) Horizontal section of the brain. (*b*) Sagittal section. High concentrations occur in the amygdala, hippocampus, cerebellar cortex, and especially in the substantia nigra. The cerebral cortex has low concentrations of cannabinoid receptors, and virtually none are found in the brain stem. Courtesy of Miles Herkenham, NIMH.

that anandamide and THC produce several of the same effects—reducing sensitivity to pain, hypothermia, hypomotility, and catalepsy—and these effects vary with dosage and route of administration (Smith et al., 1994). If this substance really is the endogenous equivalent of THC, the discovery will allow researchers to identify the neurons that produce the substance and to study their functions in the nervous system; up to now, the mechanism(s) of the action of marijuana have not been clear. Identification of the ligand will also aid in the search for other drugs that have the clinical effects of marijuana (painkilling, lowering blood pressure, combatting nausea, and lowering eye pressure in glaucoma) without causing an emotional "high" and will help reveal the neural circuits and processes involved in producing the psychological effects of marijuana.

Drug–Receptor Relations Vary in Specificity

The tuning of receptor molecules is not absolutely specific. That is, a particular drug molecule may bind strongly with one kind of receptor molecule, more weakly with some others, and not at all with many others. A drug molecule that has more than one kind of action in the body may do so because it affects more than one kind of receptor molecule. For example, we saw Chapter 5 that the transmitter acetylcholine (ACh) acts at both nicotinic and muscarinic synaptic receptor molecules. As we will see later in

this chapter, some drugs combat anxiety at low doses without producing sedation (relaxation, drowsiness), but at higher doses they cause sedation, probably because at those doses they activate another type of receptor molecule.

We should also note that the binding of a ligand with a receptor molecule does not necessarily mean that the ligand activates the receptor. In some cases a particular ligand (call it ligand *A*) merely occupies the receptor site and prevents another kind of ligand (ligand *B*) from activating the receptor; in this case, substance *A* is the antagonist of substance *B*. If substance *C* works like *B* on the same receptor molecules, *C* is an agonist of *B*. As we learned in Chapter 5, agonists act in the same way, while antagonists act in opposite ways.

Drug Effects Vary with Dosage

Investigators determine dose–response curves for particular drugs in order to quantify the drug–receptor relationship and to find the appropriate dosage to obtain a particular effect. Figure 6.3*a* is an example; it shows the dose–response relationship between the concentration of amphetamine in the blood and the amount of spontaneous activity shown by an experimental animal subject: the higher the concentration of amphetamine, the greater the level of spontaneous activity.

We can use dose–response relationships to compare drugs according to several useful criteria:

(a) Drugs differ in potency

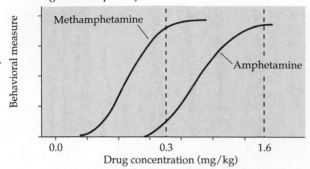

(b) How safe is the drug?

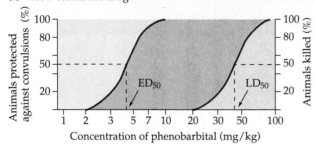

(c) Different drugs have different slopes

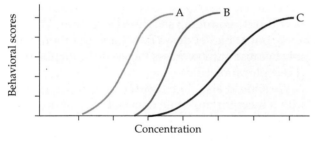

(d) Drugs differ in maximum effects

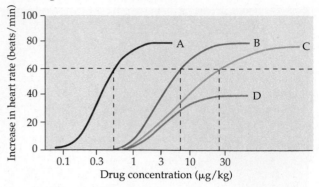

(e) Inverted U-shaped curve

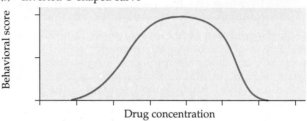

6.3 Dose–Response Relationships and Criteria for Drugs

(a) Dose–response relationships for amphetamine and for methamphetamine show that methamphetamine is more potent; a smaller concentration of methamphetamine produces the same effect. (b) The separation between the effective dose of a drug and its lethal dose is a measure of its *safety*. (c) A more gradual slope in the dose–response curves (*C* in this graph) may indicate a safer drug. (d) Drugs differ in their maximum effects, or efficacy. Here curve *D* has a lower maximum than curves *A*, *B*, or *C*. (e) A dose–response relationship in which one type of receptor is activated at low doses of a drug and a receptor with opposite effects is activated at higher doses may explain this inverted U-shaped curve.

1. *Potency.* The smaller the dose needed to produce a given effect, the more potent the drug is. Thus, in Figure 6.3*a*, the drug methamphetamine is about five times more potent than the related compound amphetamine; that is, only about one-fifth as much methamphetamine is required to produce the same effect as a given amount of amphetamine.

2. *Different potencies for different effects.* The same drug will show different dose–response functions in producing different effects. For example, as already noted, the drug dose that alleviates anxiety is different from that which causes sedation.

3. *Safety.* A drug should be as free as possible of toxic or lethal effects. The separation between the effective dose of a drug and its lethal dose is one

measure of its safety (Figure 6.3*b*). The effective dose is that required to produce a desired effect—often quantified as the dose that produces the desired effect in 50 percent of the subjects, or the **effective dose 50,** (abbreviated **ED$_{50}$**). Similarly, the dose that would be lethal for 50 percent of subjects is called the **lethal dose 50** (or **LD$_{50}$**). The greater the separation between the effective dose of a drug and the lethal dose, the greater the **therapeutic index** of the drug and the lower the chance that the ED$_{50}$ will be lethal for any subject.

4. *The slope of the drug–response relationship.* In Figure 6.3*c*, the dose–response curves for drugs *A* and *B* have the same slope, but drug *C* has a more gradual slope; that is, as the dosage increases, the effect

changes more slowly with drug *C* than with *A* or *B*. A drug with a gradual slope may be safer to give because the effect can be graded more carefully.

5. *The maximum effect, or efficacy.* In Figure 6.3*d*, drugs *A*, *B*, and *C* have the same maximum effectiveness, but drug *D* cannot produce as large an effect, even if its dosage is raised considerably. Aspirin, for example, cannot achieve as much analgesic effect as morphine, so aspirin is a less effective painkiller than morphine. (You might have inferred from this difference that aspirin and morphine achieve their analgesic effects by different mechanisms; Chapter 8 will confirm your guess.) However, aspirin is also much safer than morphine (it has a greater therapeutic index) because its effective dose is far lower than its toxic dose, while for morphine the effective dose is closer to the toxic dose.

You might expect that, as the dose or concentration of a drug increases, more and more receptors are affected and the response increases steadily. Many dose–response functions do show such a regularly increasing, S-shaped curve, like the schematic curves shown in Figures 6.3*c* and *d*, but other dose–response functions resemble an inverted U-shaped curve (Figure 6.3*e*). Different interpretations have been offered for such inverted U-shaped relations. A frequent explanation is that a substance activates one kind of receptor molecule at relatively low concentrations but

activates an additional receptor type with opposing consequences at higher concentrations.

Some dose–response curves are bipolar; that is, part of the curve shows a positive or beneficial effect, whereas another part of the curve shows a negative effect. Examples of substances that are beneficial or even essential at low doses but impair health at higher doses include minerals such as calcium, copper, iron, magnesium, selenium, and zinc; they are sometimes called "trace" minerals because they are needed only in tiny amounts. The curve in Figure 6.4*a* is an example of a bipolar dose–response curve: At moderate doses the drug clonidine improves the memory performance of aged monkeys, but at higher doses this beneficial effect is countered by the effect of sedation and even sleep. In attempts to aid human patients, the usefulness of clonidine for improving memory was impaired by its sedative effects. In addition, the effect of lowered blood pressure (clonidine is used clinically to treat high blood pressure) makes this drug unsuitable for some patients. The search for related drugs that could improve memory without the side effects of sedation or lowered blood pressure led investigators to guanfacine. Guanfacine effectively improves memory in aged monkeys without sedating them or lowering their blood pressure (Figure 6.4*b*). The differences in the effects of these two drugs appear to be related to their affinities for at least two different kinds of noradren-

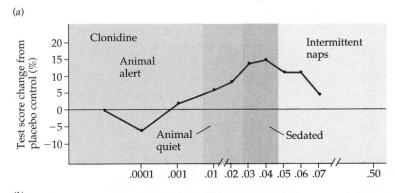

(*a*)

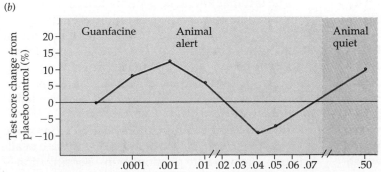

(*b*)

6.4 Some Drugs Have Complex Dose–Response Functions and Side Effects
(*a*) Clonidine improves performance but only at higher doses that are also sedating. (*b*) A related drug, guanfacine, improves performance at lower doses without sedating. Both drugs show bipolar dose–response relationships. After Arnsten, Cai, Goldman-Rakic, 1988.

ergic receptors (Arnsten, Cai, and Goldman-Rakic, 1988). (Noradrenergic receptors are activated by the hormone norepinephrine; see Chapter 7.) Furthermore, drugs like guanfacine protect older animals against distractors while they perform a memory task (Arnsten and Contant, 1992).

Repeated Use of a Drug Can Produce Either Tolerance or Sensitization

With some drugs, as a person or animal takes the drug on successive occasions, a steadily larger dose is required to achieve a particular effect. In such cases, the body is said to build up **tolerance** for larger doses. Barbiturates (used to combat anxiety or to induce sleep) and opiates (such as morphine) are drugs for which tolerance builds up with repeated use. But tolerance increases more rapidly for the intoxicating effects of these drugs than for the lethal dose, so the intoxicating dose gets steadily closer to the lethal dose as the person continues to use the drug. In other words, the therapeutic index decreases as tolerance develops. On the other hand, with some drugs the body experiences **sensitization** with repeated use; that is, a smaller dose achieves the same effect that initially required a larger dose. Cocaine is an example of a drug that can become more effective with repeated use.

Several mechanisms for tolerance have been found, and more than one mechanism is at work for some drugs. The repeated use of alcohol, for example, results in increased synthesis of the liver enzymes that break down and inactivate it. Some mechanisms involve the receptor molecules to which the drug binds. Use of a drug may evoke an increase in the number of receptor molecules, so more drug is required to occupy them. In addition, the responsiveness of the molecules to a drug may decrease. Tolerance to morphine appears to be less a result of the induction of drug-metabolizing enzymes in the liver than of the adaptation of neurons to the drug (Julien, 1992:199; Nestler and Duman, 1995). A large tolerance develops for some effects of morphine (respiratory depression, analgesia, euphoria, and sedation) but not for others (constriction of the pupils and constipation), indicating that morphine has different effects on different neural systems. Development of tolerance for morphine is accompanied by **cross-tolerance** for similar drugs, such as heroin, but not for other drugs, such as nicotine.

Learning can play an important role in tolerance and withdrawal. For example, the effects of drugs can be conditioned to the environmental or behavioral circumstances in which the drug is administered. Pavlov (1927:35–37) discussed experiments in which hypodermic injection of morphine into a dog induced a series of effects, including profuse saliva secretion. Following five or six daily injections, the mere preparation for an injection produced the same series of effects—they had become conditioned to previously neutral stimuli. Such results explain why rituals and procedures of drug procurement and use may come to elicit rewarding effects similar to the drug itself. An example of this phenomenon is the "needle freak," who by the act of injection alone or by the injection of inert substances obtains results resembling the effects of the drug. Such reports by drug users are supported by results of an animal experiment: Rats were put on a schedule in which on alternating days either they ran down an alley to a compartment where they received an injection of amphetamine, or they received a "free" injection in another compartment without having to run for it. When the rats were subsequently given their choice of compartments, they consistently chose the one to which they had run for injection (LaCerra and Ettenberg, 1984). Thus the stimuli associated with active drug seeking had become rewarding.

Conditioned effects are complex because they are accompanied by counteradaptations. For example, morphine causes body temperature to rise. The body temperature of a rat that has been injected with morphine once a day for several days in a particular room will rise if the animal is simply placed in that room. Following this initial response, in a reaction against the conditioned effect of raised body temperature, the rat's body will mobilize heat-dissipating responses to return temperature to normal.

In fact, conditioning of both hyperthermic and hypothermic responses occurs, but the conditioning takes place to different stimuli: Hyperthermia becomes associated with environmental stimuli, such as visual or auditory stimuli, but it does not become conditioned to the time of day at which the drug is administered. In contrast, the countereffect of hypothermia becomes conditioned to temporal cues but not to environmental cues (Eikelboom and Stewart, 1981).

The fact that tolerance is partly learned may help explain some cases of drug overdoses: Tolerance develops in the environment in which an individual frequently takes the drug, and high doses are taken, but if the drug is then taken in a different environment or without the usual rituals, the usual high dose may not be tolerated, and a serious, even lethal reaction may occur.

Although some investigators once considered the development of tolerance to be a necessary sign of addiction, the opposite phenomenon—sensitization—

has attracted much research attention in recent years. In fact, morphine has been found to cause sensitization on some measures, such as locomotor activity, even though it induces tolerance for other effects. Detailed studies of the mechanisms of sensitization to cocaine indicate changes in the response of at least two

kinds of synaptic receptor molecules—the dopaminergic D_1 receptors (Kalivas, Sorg, and Hooks, 1993) and certain serotonin receptors (Cunningham, Paris, and Goeders, 1992), but a definitive account of the mechanisms of sensitization to cocaine is not yet available (Johanson and Schuster, 1995). Further work showed that, while tolerance and sensitization are important phenomena of drug addiction (studying these phenomena reveals a great deal about the plasticity of the nervous system), neither is a requirement for diagnosis of the presence of drug addiction (Pickens and Thompson, 1968; Schuster, 1970).

Drugs Affect Each Stage of Neural Conduction and Synaptic Transmission

Almost all the behavioral effects that we discuss in this chapter are caused by the activities of drugs on synaptic events and processes and on neural conduction. Table 6.2 explains how certain drugs affect the major steps in neural conduction and synaptic transmission (see Figure 5.12). In this section we'll comment on some of these agents and their effects, as well as on related effects of other agents.

Many Drugs Affect Presynaptic Events

If axonal transport is inhibited by a drug (for example, colchicine), enzymes that are manufactured in the cell body are not replaced in the presynaptic terminals. Since enzymes are needed to direct the manufacture of transmitter chemicals and vesicle walls, such drugs prevent the replenishment of the transmitter agent as it is used up and cause synaptic transmission to fail. Although the tranquilizing drug reserpine does not interfere with the synthesis of transmitters, it does inhibit the storage of catecholamine transmitters (dopamine, epinephrine, and norepinephrine) in vesicles. Even if a presynaptic terminal has an adequate supply of transmitter stored in vesicles, various agents or conditions can prevent the release of transmitter when a nerve impulse reaches the terminal. Low concentration of calcium (Ca^{2+}) in the extracellular fluid is such a condition: under these circumstances, only by causing an influx of Ca^{2+} can the impulse lead to the release of transmitter.

Specific **toxins** prevent the release of specific kinds of transmitter (de Paiva et al., 1993; see Table 6.2 for examples). For instance, botulinum toxin, which is formed by bacteria that multiply in improperly canned food, poisons many people each year by blocking the release of acetylcholine. The botulinum toxin binds to specialized receptors in nicotinic cholinergic (that is, activated by acetylcholine) neural membranes and is transported into the cell, where it blocks Ca^{2+}-dependent transmitter release (McMahon et al., 1992). A related bacterial product, tetanus toxin, acts similarly, blocking activity at inhibitory synapses and causing strong involuntary contractions of muscles (McMahon et al., 1992). Tetanus is an acute, often fatal disease characterized by strong contractions of muscles, especially those of the neck and jaw; this condition is also called lockjaw.

Other agents stimulate or facilitate the release of certain transmitters. For example, the venom of the black widow spider exaggerates the release of acetylcholine. The stimulant drug amphetamine facilitates the release of catecholamine transmitters, as well as inhibiting their reuptake, which further increases their synaptic action. Caffeine has an excitatory effect because it competes with the neuromodulator adenosine—a substance that inhibits the release of excitatory catecholamine transmitters—at its presynaptic re- ceptors. (We'll take up neuromodulators in Chapter 7.)

Some Drugs Affect Postsynaptic Events

Postsynaptic receptor molecules can be blocked by various drugs. For example, curare blocks nicotinic ACh receptors. Since the synapses between nerves and skeletal muscles are nicotinic, curare paralyzes all skeletal muscles, including those used in breathing. Behavior can be disrupted not only by blocking but also by prolonging transmitter–receptor action. Agents that inhibit the enzyme acetylcholinesterase (AChE) allow ACh to remain active at the synapse and alter the timing of synaptic transmission. Effects can range from mild to severe, depending on the anti-AChE agent and its dosage. The drug physostigmine has temporary and reversible anti-AChE effects. Mild doses of it are used in certain medical conditions when ACh action at neuromuscular junctions is weak and inadequate. On the other hand, some organic phosphorus compounds, such as DFP (diisopropyl flurophosphate), are potent and persistent inhibitors of AChE. DFP is the active ingredient in certain insecticides, which must be used with caution because they are also highly toxic to human beings.

Table 6.2

How Certain Neural Processes Are Affected by Drugs

NEURAL PROCESS	DRUG EFFECTS
Axonal processes	
Transport of proteins between cell body and axon terminals	Colchicine impairs formation and maintenance of microtubules.
Conduction of action potentials	Tetrodotoxin and saxitoxin block ion channels and prevent conduction.
Synthesis and storage of synaptic transmitters	
Transport of transmitter precursors into nerve terminal	Hemicholinium blocks uptake of choline, a precursor of ACh.
Synthesis of transmitters catalyzed by enzymes	Alpha-methyl-para-tyrosine inhibits tyrosine hydroxylase, thus preventing synthesis of the catecholamine transmitters.
Uptake of transmitters into vesicles	Reserpine inhibits uptake of transmitter into vesicles.
Release of synaptic transmitters	
Release of transmitter from vesicles by calcium-dependent mechanisms	Calcium channel blockers (e.g., verapamil) inhibit release of transmitter.
Release of transmitter by calcium-independent mechanisms	Amphetamines stimulate release of catecholamine transmitters and enhance the release caused by action potentials.
	Black widow spider venom causes overrelease, and thus depletion, of ACh.
Modulation of the release of some transmitters by presynaptic receptors	Adenosine blocks release of catecholamine transmitters; caffeine competes with adenosine for presynaptic receptors, thus preventing its inhibitory effects.
	Binding of opioids to presynaptic receptors decreases release of ACh, norepinephrine, and dopamine.
Activity of transmitters in the synaptic cleft	
Inactivation of ACh by the enzyme acetylcholinesterase (AChE)	Drugs such as physostigmine inhibit AChE and prolong the activity of ACh at the synapse.
Inactivation of catecholamine transmitters by reuptake into the presynaptic terminal	Cocaine and amphetamine inhibit reuptake mechanism, thus prolonging synaptic activity.
Events in postsynaptic neurons	
Alteration of the number of receptor molecules	Alcohol increases number of receptors for inhibitory transmitter GABA.
	Tricyclic antidepressants reduce number of catecholamine receptors.
Activation of receptor molecules	Antipsychotic drugs block some dopamine receptors.
	LSD is an agonist at some serotonin receptors.
	Curare blocks nicotinic ACh receptors.
Activity of second messengers	Lithium inhibits the second messenger cyclic AMP (see Chapter 7).

Plant and Animal Poisons Help Reveal Nervous System Function

As we have noted, many poisons exert their effects by altering or interfering with functions of the nervous system. Learning how these poisons work can help us understand the nervous system. Within the last two decades, many investigators have joined a productive new field of research—**neurotoxicology**, the study of effects of toxins and poisons on the nervous system (Stone, 1994). A related field is behavioral toxicology, which includes both the use of behavioral techniques to detect toxins and the study of how toxins affect behavior (Russell, Flattau, and Pope, 1990; Weiss, 1992). We will discuss behavioral toxicology later in this chapter when we look at how lead affects behavior.

The term "poison" is hard to define. Given in an amount large enough, any substance will impair health and could even be fatal. The sixteenth-century alchemist Paracelsus declared, "The dose makes the poison"; this statement has become the title of a book on toxicology (Ottoboni, 1991). As we learned earlier, some minerals are beneficial or even essential at low doses but impair health at higher doses. Usually the term poison implies a substance that causes injury, illness, or death, even at low doses. The word is derived from the Latin *potio* which meant "a liquid dose, as of medicine or poison."

We often think of poisons as promptly causing illness or death. But many poisons work slowly and insidiously, and there is growing concern about poisons that significantly impair health even if the effects are not dramatic in most individuals. Some poisons have especially harmful effects on the developing nervous system. In Chapter 4 we saw the intricate processes required for normal development of the nervous system; some of these can be disturbed by poisons, as we will see shortly.

Different poisons affect the nervous system in different ways. Some poisons inhibit the activity of the nervous system; examples are curare and morphine. Other poisons overexcite the nervous system; examples are strychnine and amphetamine. Poisons that overexcite neurons so much that they kill them are called **excitotoxins**. Subtle metabolic changes can turn some amino acid synaptic transmitters—such as glutamate and aspartate—into excitotoxins.

Plants Protect Themselves by Producing Poisons

Toxins that inhibit neural activity and toxins that excite nerve cells extend far back into plant and animal history. There is evidence that by the beginning of the Mesozoic Era, about 250 million years ago, flowering plants were producing two kinds of defensive chemicals. One is the tannins, which inhibit growth of fungi and taste bitter. The bitter taste undoubtedly deterred some animals from eating tannin-producing plants, but plants evolved an even more effective chemical defense against animal predators: **alkaloid compounds**, which include many psychoactive agents, such as curare, the opium alkaloids (morphine and codeine), and lysergic acid (to which LSD is related). Other, nonalkaloid psychoactive plant substances also evolved. Animals evolved both de-

fensive and offensive chemical weapons in turn, as we will see in the next section.

One plant that protects itself against predators by producing neurotoxic alkaloids is the locoweed of the western plains (see Box 6.1). This plant received its common name because if sheep or cattle eat it, they seem to "go crazy," or "loco." Another neurotoxic plant alkaloid is curare, which, as we noted earlier, paralyzes animals by blocking ACh receptors. The common potato produces alkaloids that inhibit the enzyme acetylcholinesterase, which inactivates ACh after its release; inhibiting the enzyme impairs synaptic functioning. When potatoes are diseased, bruised, or exposed to light, these and other alkaloids increase to levels that can be lethal to humans (Ames, 1983). These alkaloids help potatoes resist insects and diseases. In trying to improve resistance to insects and decrease the need for pesticides, plant breeders have increased the levels of these alkaloids; one cultivated variety of potato had to be withdrawn from the market because of its toxicity to humans.

Opium (from the Greek *opion,* "vegetable juice") is an extract of the juice of the seedpod of the opium poppy, *Papaver somniferum* (Figure 6.5). Opium may protect the seeds of this plant from insects; most insects avoid the seeds, although they eat other parts of the plant. Humans have used opium as a drug for millenia:

> The archeological evidence suggests that opium poppies were cultivated and used by Stone Age lake-dwellers in areas of Central Europe and present-day Switzerland. From there they were deliberately spread and traded to the eastern Mediterranean in the late Bronze Age. Masses of well-preserved poppy seeds have been found among the remains of Neolithic lakeshore settlements. (R. Siegel, 1989: 127–128).

6.5 The Source of Opium and Morphine
The opium poppy flower and pod.

Box 6.1
People Have Used Drugs throughout History

Observation of the effects of substances on animals goes far back into human history. The first human use of many substances is said to have been prompted by seeing their effects on animals (R. Siegel, 1989). For example, an Ethiopian tradition claims that the human use of coffee originated around the ninth century when a herder noticed that his goats became unusually frisky after eating the small bright red fruits of the wild coffee tree (Figure A). Different groups of Native Americans in Mexico attribute the use of tobacco to observations of insects or birds that ate tobacco leaves or flowers (Figure B). Some groups are said to have noticed that several

species of insects ate tobacco leaves with a speed that suggested the presence of stimulants. More poetic is the tradition of the Huichol Indians of Mexico: their ancestors noticed that certain birds favored tobacco flowers and that consuming tobacco enabled these birds to fly high and strong and to see great visions. Thus, the Indians consumed tobacco in an attempt to communicate with the gods and to see visions. The human use of coca leaves is said to have started when pack animals in Peru, short of food, ate coca leaves (Figure C) and were surprisingly willing to continue their work.

The common names of many plants reflect observations of ei-

ther harmful or beneficial effects on particular species. Names that reflect disturbed behavior or toxicity include locoweed (Figure D), henbane, sheep's bane, and fleabane. The attraction of some animals to certain plant species has inspired names such as catnip (Figure E), hare's lettuce, dog grass, swine grass, and pigeon candy.

Some native groups used plant substances medicinally because of their effects on animals. For example, after observing that birds fell down after flying in and around certain trees, people in tropical Asia discovered the *Rauwolfia serpentina* tree (the source of the drug reserpine) and its use in folk medicine. Reserpine inhibits the storage of catecholamine transmitters in synaptic vesicles. It was used extensively in the West in the 1950s to treat mania, excited schizophrenic states, and high blood pressure. Although reserpine is no longer used for these purposes, it was important in the development of hypotheses about the synaptic bases of depression. Investigations of many such folk remedies throughout the world are giving rise to a field called ethnopharmacology.

(A) *Coffee*

(B) *Tobacco*

(C) *Coca*

(D) *Locoweed*

(E) *Catnip*

Opium was used as a medicine, for example against diarrhea, in ancient Egypt, Greece, and Rome. Later, its sleep-inducing effects were noted by writers in classical Greece and Rome, such as Homer, Virgil, and Ovid. Several nineteenth-century English writers century praised opium for soothing the body and stimulating the imagination. When morphine, one of the active alkaloids in opium, was isolated from opium in the early nineteenth century, it was named after Morpheus, the Roman god of dreams.

Caffeine may have evolved to protect plants against insect predators (Nathanson, 1984). It stimulates and causes uncoordinated behavior in insects and inhibits their growth and reproduction. Caffeine acts through different mechanisms on the nervous system and on some other organs. As noted above, the direct action of caffeine on neurons is to compete with adenosine for its presynaptic receptor sites (Figure 6.6). Adenosine is an endogenous neuromodulator that produces behavioral sedation by inhibiting the release of catecholamine transmitters; it also has anticonvulsant effects. By reducing the action of adenosine, caffeine increases neural activity, producing a syndrome of effects that include nervousness, irritability, increased heart rate, and hyperactivity of muscles. In patients who are subject to attacks of panic, caffeine can cause the attacks. Caffeine occurs in both coffee and tea, and it is added to other beverages, such as Coca-Cola. Tea also contains a related compound, theophylline, which, like caffeine, blocks the receptors for adenosine. Caffeine and theophylline belong to a class of compounds called the methylxanthines. Chocolate contains caffeine and various other methylxanthines.

Caffeine acts directly on other organs (for example, the heart, muscles, kidneys) by regulating the influx of Ca^{2+} through caffeine-sensitive membrane channels; this action helps produce some of the effects noted above (Petersen, 1992). Thus caffeine, which can be considered a stimulant at lower doses, is a poison at higher doses. The insecticidal power of caffeine may not seem so surprising when we note that nicotine is also a natural insecticide. Interestingly, the very substances for which people cultivate the coffee bush and the tobacco plant evolved as means of protecting these plants against predators.

Animals Use Poisons Both Defensively and Offensively

Many animals have evolved poisons for defensive or offensive purposes; examples include molluscs, jellyfish, spiders, scorpions, snakes, frogs, fish, and stingrays. Even a few mammalian species (for example, the shrew and the echidna) have poison glands, but mammalian poisons have not yet been studied extensively (Ellenhorn and Barceloux, 1988). Many animal poisons act by altering the neural conduction or synaptic transmission of predators or prey. The poison of the puffer fish (tetrodotoxin) and the venoms of certain scorpions affect ion channels in the neuron. The venom of the bungarus snake (bungarotoxin) is lethal because it binds irreversibly to the ACh receptor in the postsynaptic membrane and does not allow ACh to act, thus causing paralysis. As we mentioned earlier, the venom of the black widow spider attacks the synapse in another way: It stimulates cholinergic axon terminals strongly, causing a high rate of release of ACh. The result is a burst of uncoordinated activity followed by depletion of the transmitter, and in the end, because no further impulses can be transmitted, paralysis.

Some animals have evolved special effector organs to deliver their poison. For example, rattlesnakes and some other snakes secrete venom in glands in the mouth and deliver the venom through fangs. The fangs are sharp hollow teeth through which the poison can be expelled into the flesh of the victim. When not in use, the fangs lie flat against the roof of the mouth. The venoms of rattlesnakes contain mixtures of toxic substances, and in some species they contain neurotoxins that impair the function of nerve cells.

A tiny but effective animal weapon to deliver poison is the **nematocyst** (from the Greek *nemat*, "thread," and *cyst*, "cell"; Figure 6.7). Some jellyfish and some other animals of the same phylum (sea anemones, corals, and hydroids) are armed with thousands to millions of nematocysts. When an animal brushes against the "trigger" of the nematocyst,

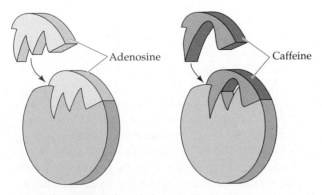

6.6 How Caffeine Stimulates
Caffeine stimulates neurons by competing with adenosine for presynaptic sites.

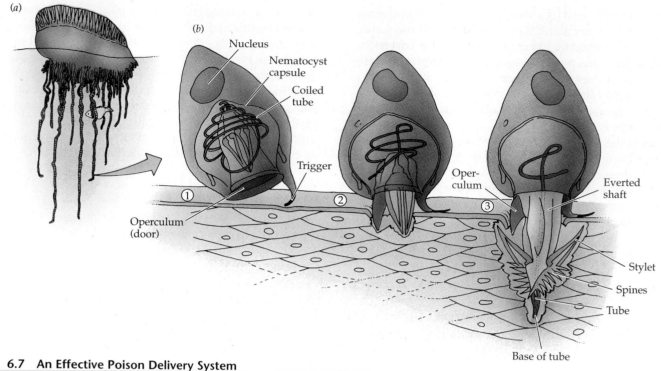

6.7   An Effective Poison Delivery System
(*a*) The Portuguese man-of-war has tens of millions of nematocysts (stinging cells). (*b*) The nematocyst is triggered by contact (1), pierces the skin (2), and is held in place by the stylet while poison is delivered (3).

the door flies open and the barb penetrates the skin and anchors itself there. A long threadlike tube extends into the wound, and the toxin is pumped in through it.   A large jellyfish, such as the Portuguese man-of-war, has more than 500 nematocysts per centimeter of length of its tentacles, which can extend as much as 30 meters, and its poison includes neurotoxins. The man-of-war can kill large fish by stinging them with its thousands of nematocysts.

Behavioral Toxicology Is a New Field

The heavy metal lead is the longest known and best understood of all the neurotoxins. In 1991 the Secretary of the U.S. Department of Health and Human Services declared lead poisoning to be the most serious environmental disease of North American children. Research on the behavioral effects of exposure to lead provides good examples of work in the field of behavioral toxicology. Several trends of the last few decades led to the development of this field (Weiss, 1992) and to the increasing involvement of psychologists in this area:

1. The introduction in the 1950s of drugs to combat psychoses and other behavioral disorders (see Chapter 16) encouraged the development of the field of behavioral pharmacology—the study of the effects of drugs on behavior. Behavioral pharmacology was the precursor for behavioral toxicology, and some investigators moved from the former field to the latter.

2. The need to regulate exposure to toxic substances in the workplace led to an increasing body of legal regulations, usually based on specific studies. By 1970, limits for short-term exposures to many toxic substances were based on behavioral observations and measures.

3. Lawsuits for damages alleged to have resulted from exposure to toxic substances often revolve around complaints of such symptoms as chronic fatigue, depression, and nervousness, in the absence of demonstrable physical damage. These lawsuits have raised questions about the validity of behavioral measures and have led to efforts to improve them.

Lead Is a Toxin That People Have Spread through the Environment

Workers in lead smelters or in factories that work with lead rarely develop clear cases of lead poisoning, but more subtle effects were noted relatively early. These included general feelings of ill health, moderate fatigue, and mental sluggishness that caused increased numbers and severity of accidents (Rieke, 1969). Lead poisoning of children through ingestion of paint chips finally brought about the banning of lead-based paint in the United States in 1978, but this paint remains a hazard in many buildings where it still exists. The use of tetraethyl lead as a gasoline additive, beginning in the 1920s, greatly increased the amount of lead emitted into the environment, and it caused some health professionals to issue grave warnings about the potential effects on general health; some of this history is recounted by Rice (1990). Some workers exposed to tetraethyl lead during its manufacture showed severe neurological and psychiatric symptoms, necessitating special precautions to reduce exposure. A committee convened by the U.S. Surgeon General urged in 1926 that a full investigation be undertaken before tetraethyl lead was allowed to be used in gasoline, but

the automotive and petroleum industries opposed any restriction, and no further data on the subject were collected for many years. Reports continued to accumulate showing that lead from lead-based paints impaired the intelligence of children even when overt signs of lead poisoning did not appear. Some investigators then began to try to measure how behavioral performance varies with levels of lead exposure.

An important, controversial study was published in 1979 by a group of physicians and psychologists (Needleman et al., 1979). Because lead accumulates in the teeth and bones, the investigators collected deciduous ("baby") teeth from children in two Boston suburbs and analyzed their lead concentrations to obtain cumulative measures of lead exposure. They then selected the children in the highest and lowest 10% of lead concentrations, gave them extensive psychological tests of intelligence and ability, and obtained teachers' ratings of them. None of the children showed evidence of lead poisoning and none had been exposed to lead from paint, but those in the lowest 10% of lead accumulation had significantly higher intelligence scores than those in the top 10% (Figure 6.8a). Furthermore, the teachers' ratings of

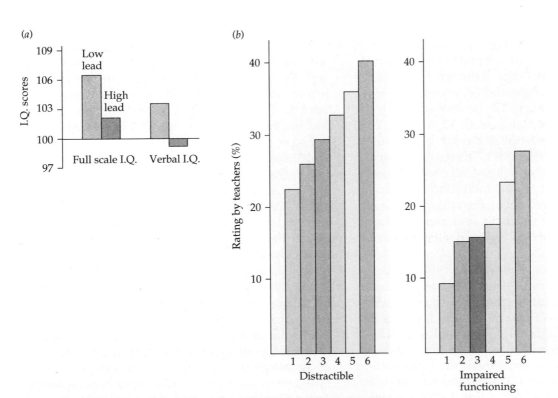

6.8 The Deleterious Effects of Lead on Behavior and Intelligence
Compared to children with low levels of lead, children with high levels fare poorly on intelligence tests (*a*) and in teachers' rating of their behavior (*b*). After Needleman et al., 1979.

behaviors, such as inability to concentrate, indicated more problems in the children with the higher levels of lead (Figure 6.8*b*). As you might expect, these findings aroused a storm of criticism from industry, from governmental agencies, and from some academic sources. There were allegations that the investigators had not controlled or compensated fully for important social, economic, or educational variables, even though the statistical analyses had included many such variables. Despite the criticisms, this study alerted investigators and governmental groups in several countries to the possibility that "normal" exposure to lead was affecting children's abilities.

A subsequent study asked whether *prenatal* exposure to lead might affect children's development (Bellinger et al., 1987). During pregnancy lead passes from the mother through the blood and placenta into the fetus. The investigators collected blood from the umbilical cord at birth from more than 250 mothers and children whom they had recruited to participate in a longitudinal study (a study designed to follow their development over several years). All came from an upper middle-class population and intact families, so there could be no question that unfavorable socioeconomic status of some subjects might bias the results. The children were divided into three groups according to the umbilical lead concentrations: low (1.8 micrograms per deciliter [µg/dl]), medium (6.5 µg/dl), and high (14.5 µg/dl); all of these values were well below the value of 25 µg/dl that the U. S Public Health Service considered until 1991 to be the threshold for clinical intervention. The development of the children was measured at ages 6, 12, 18, and 24 months, using the standardized Bayley Scales of Infant Development (Bayley, 1969). The results showed that the children with the highest lead concentration at birth lagged significantly behind the other groups, although all three scored above the national means. The amount of the difference between the high lead group and the other groups was equivalent to about 8 points on an IQ scale.

A follow-up study on these children showed that those with the higher lead levels at 24 months continued to have lower intellectual and academic performance at 10 years of age; a 10 µg/dl increase in blood level at 24 months was associated with a decline in IQ of 5.8 points at 10 years (Bellinger, Stiles, and Needleman, 1992). Similar results have come from other studies in the United States and abroad (Smith, Grant, and Sors, 1989; Angle, 1993). A recent meta-analysis combining results of many studies reports a highly significant relation between exposure to lead and deficits in children's IQ scores; an increase

from 10 to 20 µg/dl lead is associated with a decrease of 2.6 IQ points (Schwartz, 1994). But another recent meta-analysis found such an increase in lead associated with a decrease of 1 to 2 IQ points and questioned how much priority should be given to detecting and reducing moderate increases in children's blood lead (Popock, Smith, and Baghurst, 1994).

As Weiss (1992) notes, experiments with animals are not subject to the criticisms about socioeconomic or other epidemiological factors that have been leveled at the research with children. Such animal experiments—with rats (Cory-Slechta, Weiss, and Cox, 1985) and with monkeys (Rice and Karpinski, 1988)—have also revealed significant behavioral differences between control animals and those exposed to lead at levels sufficient to raise blood levels to about 15 µg/dl. The lowest levels of exposure that cause developmental neurobehavioral effects are similar in children and in laboratory animals—10 to 15 µg/dl in children, less than 15 µg/dl in primates, and less than 20 µg/dl in rodents (Davis et al., 1990). The Environmental Protection Agency now lists a lead concentration of 10 to 15 µg/dl as an "area of concern."

Some critics dismiss reduction of intelligence by "a few IQ points" through exposure to lead as unimportant, but Weiss (1988) urges us to consider the implications of such a shift in terms of the population. IQ scores are distributed according to the normal curve, with a mean of 100 and a standard deviation of 15, as is true of Stanford-Binet intelligence test scores (Figure 6.9*a*). In a population of 100 million, about 2.3 million individuals score above 130 and the same number score below 70, as the colored areas show. Now what happens if the mean is shifted down by five IQ points, (Figure 6.9*b*) ? If the calibration of the test is not changed, then the number with high IQ scores (above 130) drops to about 990,000, less than half the number with high scores before. And the number scoring below 70, therefore considered to require remedial education, rises to about 3.6 million, many more than before. Such a shift, Weiss states, can be considered a "societal disaster." In addition, as we've seen already, behavioral problems are also associated with exposure to lead (see Figure 6.8*b*).

High levels of lead in the body produce clear evidence of toxicity, including demyelination, inhibition of cholinergic function, impairment of dopamine uptake, and impairment of sodium/potassium-dependent ATPase, which is needed to maintain the normal resting potential (Klaassen, Amdur, and Doull, 1986:600). But much lower levels of lead impair behavior without producing measurable effects in the

(a)

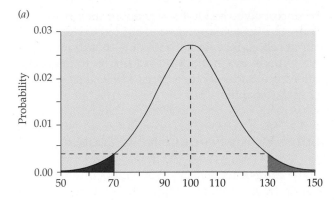

(b)

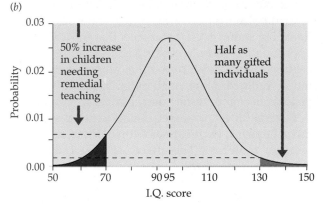

I.Q. score

6.9 Effects of Lead on the Distribution of Intelligence Scores
(*a*) The normal distribution of intelligence scores. The part of the population with IQ scores above 130 is shown by the blue area; the part of the population with scores below 70 is shown by the red area.
(*b*) Here the mean of the distribution has been shifted to 95. Notice the large decrease in the part of the population scoring above 130 (blue) and the large increase of those scoring below 70 (red). After Weiss, 1988.

brain. These results indicate that behavioral tests are more sensitive than are present neurochemical or neuroanatomical measures of lead toxicity, possibly because the behavioral tests integrate many small pathological changes in the nervous system.

Recent evidence suggests some specific ways in which lead affects neural functioning and neural development. Lead ions (Pb^{2+}) can mimic calcium ions (Ca^{2+}) in entering cells through calcium channels and in persistently stimulating processes that are usually stimulated by calcium (Clarkson, 1993). Lead accumulates especially in synaptic regions. It has been suggested that lead continues to stimulate an enzyme important in many neural functions (protein kinase C) and that in the fetus this stimulation is a cause of abnormal development of the nervous system (Gold-

stein, 1990). Of course, even when it is possible to detect the small neural changes that cause the behavioral impairment, observing behavior remains an important way of measuring and diagnosing the effects of lead. The long-range consequences of exposure to lead must be considered, even though lead is no longer being used in gasoline additives or in paint in the United States and lead additives are being discontinued or reduced in other countries (Rice, 1990). Lead still remains in the bones of women of childbearing age, and it is taken up by the fetus and by the nursing infant. Therefore it will require still another generation before the burden of lead in people returns to the level of 1920. Some experts worry that the increasing use of battery-powered ("zero-emission") automobiles, although helping to reduce some kinds of pollution, will increase the spread of lead, as more is mined and manufactured into batteries. Lead is not the only poison whose levels in the environment have risen sharply in recent times; mercury and various pesticides also impair the nervous system and behavior. Their increased concentrations in the environment are also matters for grave concern.

Stimulants Promote Excitatory Synaptic Processes or Block Inhibitory Synaptic Processes

The degree of activity of the nervous system is determined by competing excitatory and inhibitory influences. Stimulants are drugs that tip the balance toward the excitatory side, and they therefore have an alerting, activating effect. Many naturally occurring and artificial stimulants are widely used. Some stimulants act directly by increasing excitatory synaptic potentials. Others act by blocking normal inhibitory processes; one example we've seen already is the blocking of adenosine by caffeine.

Nicotine and Amphetamine Promote Excitatory Synaptic Processes

The stimulant **nicotine** activates one class of ACh receptors, which, as we have already learned, are called nicotinic receptors. Most nicotinic receptors are found at neuromuscular junctions and in neurons of the autonomic ganglia, but many are also present in the central nervous system. When nicotine is absorbed through the action of smoking or chewing tobacco, it increases the heart rate, both directly, by stimulating sympathetic ganglia, and indirectly, by stimulating the adrenal gland to release the hormone epinephrine. Nicotine also increases blood pressure, secretion of hydrochloric acid in the stomach, and motor activity of the bowel. These neural effects, quite apart from the effects of tobacco tar on the lungs, contribute to the unhealthful consequences of heavy and prolonged use of tobacco products.

A molecule of the artificial substance **amphetamine** resembles the structure of the catecholamine synaptic transmitters (norepinephrine, epinephrine, and dopamine). Amphetamine causes the release of these transmitters from the presynaptic terminals even when no nerve impulse arrives at the terminals, and it also potentiates the effects of nerve impulses in causing the release of transmitters. After catecholamine transmitter molecules reach the synaptic cleft, amphetamine enhances their activity in two ways: (1) by blocking the reuptake of catecholamines into the presynaptic terminal, and (2) by competing with the catecholamines for the enzyme that inactivates them (monoamine oxidase). These effects of amphetamine prolong the presence of the catecholamine transmitters in the synaptic cleft, thus increasing their effectiveness. The stimulant cocaine is similar to amphetamine in blocking the reuptake of catecholamines, but it does not have the other synaptic effects of amphetamine. Amphetamine was synthesized in the mid-1930s as a drug to combat asthma by dilating the bronchial tree and increasing the heart rate, but it was already being abused as an addictive drug by the late 1930s.

Because amphetamine stimulates and enhances the activity of the catecholamine transmitters, it has a variety of behavioral effects. On a short-term basis, it produces heightened alertness and even euphoria, and wards off boredom. Its short-term use can promote sustained effort without rest or sleep and with lowered fatigue. Although a person may be able to accomplish more work and feel more confident by using amphetamine, most studies show that the quality of work is not improved by the drug; it appears to increase motivation but not cognitive ability. There may also be annoying side effects caused by the activity of amphetamine at synapses of the autonomic nervous system, including high blood pressure, tremor, dizziness, sweating, rapid breathing, and nausea.

Prolonged use of amphetamine causes tolerance. Continued intake at higher doses often leads to sleeplessness, severe weight loss, and general deterioration of mental and physical condition. It may lead to symptoms that are virtually identical to those of paranoid schizophrenia: compulsive, agitated behavior and irrational suspiciousness. In fact, some users of amphetamine have been diagnosed as schizophrenic

by doctors who did not know about their use of the drug. Study of this syndrome has led to hypotheses about schizophrenia and possible therapy for it, as we will see in Chapter 16. Addiction to amphetamine, nicotine, and other drugs will be discussed later in this chapter.

Some Drugs Produce Hallucinations

Some drugs alter sensory perception, often in striking or dramatic ways, and produce peculiar experiences and even psychotic behavior. These drugs are termed **hallucinogens**—agents that cause hallucinations. But some investigators feel that the term is not appropriate because whereas a hallucination is a perception that takes place without any sensory stimulation, hallucinogens such as LSD, mescaline, and psilocybin *alter* or *distort* perceptions.

Several different classes of hallucinogens are listed in Table 6.1; each class acts on a different kind of receptor molecule. The effects of LSD and related substances are reported to be predominantly visual and interesting, although they can become frightening. Users often see fantastic pictures with intense colors, and are often aware that these strangely altered perceptions are not real events.

Hallucinogenic agents are chemically diverse; several have been found to affect one or another of the amine synaptic transmitter systems. For example, mescaline, the drug extracted from the peyote plant, affects the norepinephrine system. LSD and psilocybin act on one kind of serotonin receptor. Other hallucinogens affect the acetylcholine system. For example, the drug muscarine, one of several psychoactive agents found in certain mushrooms, acts on muscarinic cholinergic synapses.

LSD (lysergic acid diethylamide) was synthesized in 1938 by Albert Hofmann, a Swiss pharmacologist, who was looking for new therapeutic agents. Because tests with animals did not appear to show effects, the compound was put aside. Then one day in 1943, Dr. Hofmann experienced a peculiar dreamlike, almost drunken state. When he closed his eyes, fantastic pictures of intense color and extraordinary plasticity seemed to surge toward him. The state lasted about two hours. Correctly suspecting that he had accidentally ingested a small amount of LSD, Hofmann began to investigate the compound again. LSD proved to be amazingly potent; a fraction of a milligram was enough to induce hallucinations. In the 1950s many investigators worked on LSD, hoping it would provide a useful model of psychosis that would suggest clues about the biochemical processes in mental illnesses. The structure of LSD resembles that of serotonin, and LSD was soon found to act on serotonin receptors, but the mechanism by which it evokes hallucinations is still unknown. Many users of LSD have reported flashbacks—that is, experiences as if a dose of drug had been taken, even though the person is drug-free. These episodes can follow even brief use of LSD, but it is not yet clear whether they reflect permanent neural changes or a special form of memory.

Phencyclidine (commonly known as PCP or "angel dust") was developed in 1956 as a potent analgesic and anesthetic agent. It was soon dropped from use in anesthesia because patients reported such effects such as agitation, excitement, delirium, hostility, and disorganization of perceptions. PCP is often sold illegally as a hallucinogen. Toxic reactions include the "four C's": At lower doses (1) combativeness and (2) catatonia (a condition that may include stupor, stereotyped behavior, mania, and either rigidity or extreme flexibility of the limbs). Overdoses of PCP result in (3) convulsions or coma that may last for days and (4) confusion that may last for weeks. As with amphetamine, users sometimes develop a psychotic condition that resembles schizophrenia, which may provide a useful chemical model of schizophrenia (see Chapter 16). PCP is common in emergency room overdose cases and in psychiatric admissions (Julien, 1992). PCP acts on the NMDA receptor, perhaps at a special binding site, and it also stimulates the release of the transmitter dopamine (Gorelick and Balster, 1995). Research continues to attempt to find the brain circuits specifically affected by PCP.

Drug Abuse Is the Most Common Psychiatric Problem

Substance abuse and addiction have become a social problem that afflicts millions of individuals and disrupts the lives of their families, friends, and associates. The whole community is affected because many people who use tobacco, alcohol, and other drugs die prematurely; substance abusers commit crimes and cause traffic accidents, fires, and other social disorders; the costs of helping addicts control their dependence and abuse and of controlling drug trafficking are high; and many babies whose mothers used psychoactive substances (including alcohol and nicotine) during pregnancy are born with brain impairments. For some perspective on the relative importance of dependence on different substances as causes

of death, consider these figures: Smoking is estimated to cause about 432,000 deaths annually in the United States—20% of all U.S. deaths; more than 100,000 of these deaths are from lung cancer. About 125,000 deaths annually in the United States are associated with the use of alcohol, many of them in traffic accidents caused by drinking. Illegal drugs are estimated to cause about 20,000 deaths annually in the United States, and about 8000 more are attributed to drug-associated AIDS (Institute for Health Policy, Brandeis University, 1993:32–37; Mathias, 1994; Figure 6.10). Even if the number of deaths caused by illegal drugs has been underestimated, it is clear that the legal drugs—nicotine and alcohol—exact a far larger social cost than do the illegal drugs.

The differences in mortality caused by these substances are related to the frequency of use. About half of all Americans use alcohol in a given month, according to a 1991 nationwide household survey by the U.S. Department of Health and Human Services (Table 6.3). Some authorities consider about 10% of the total population to be alcoholic (Helzer, 1987). About 27% smoke cigarettes in a given month, and about 15% report smoking a pack or more a day. Only about 7% report using any illegal drug in a month. Marijuana is the most widely used illegal drug; about 5% report use in a month, and about 1% report daily use. About 0.9% use cocaine (including crack) in a given month.

In addition to frequency of use, the differences in mortality are related to the risks associated with the particular type of substance being used (U.S. Congress Joint Economic Committee, 1988). Among each million persons who smoke, about 3000 are expected to die annually as a consequence of smoking; among each million who consume alcohol, only about 540 are expected to die annually from drinking (illegal drugs were not included in this series of estimates). Thus, although more people use alcohol in a given month than smoke cigarettes, exposure to active smoking is a much greater risk factor than is drinking alcohol. (U.S. Department of Health and Human Services, 1991).

The boldface numerals in Table 6.3 emphasize that those in the 18–34 age group are the primary users of psychoactive substances. Use of alcohol and cigarettes is broadly distributed across adult ages, but use of marijuana and cocaine is confined mainly to the 18–34 age group. Almost as many females as males use alcohol and cigarettes, but only half as many females as males use marijuana or cocaine. Most people who have ever used cigarettes, marijuana, or cocaine have not used these substances in the last year.

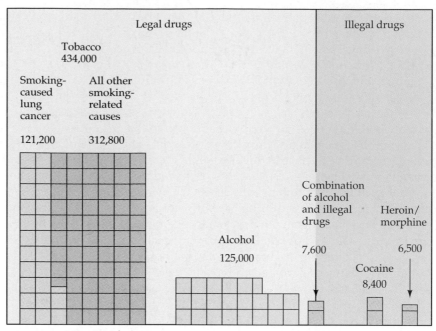

(Each square represents 5000 deaths)

6.10   Deaths Caused by Drugs
The number of deaths caused annually in the United States by the legal drugs tobacco and alcohol far exceeds the number caused by illegal drugs. On the other hand, the illegal drugs tend to kill people at a younger age. After Mathas, 1994.

For more than a century, scientists have been investigating substance dependence. Although much has been learned, many mysteries remain, and fully effective means to combat dependence and abuse have yet to be discovered. Physiological, behavioral, and environmental mechanisms for substance dependence have been proposed and investigated; some investigators put more emphasis on one or the other kind of mechanism (Glantz and Pickens, 1992). We will consider different kinds of mechanisms, taking examples mainly from dependence and abuse related to cocaine, the opiate drugs (such as morphine and heroin), nicotine, and alcohol, because these have been studied the most thoroughly. Scientists and clinicians engaged in this field have developed specific terminology that does not always coincide completely with the way the public uses terms related to substance dependence, substance abuse, and addiction (Box 6.2).

A well-known physician who was a drug user was Sigmund Freud. In 1884 Freud advocated the use of cocaine, which had been isolated in 1859, to treat depression and to alleviate chronic fatigue. While using cocaine to relieve his own depression, he described the drug as inducing "exhilaration and lasting euphoria, which in no way differs from the euphoria of

the healthy person" (Freud, 1974:366). By 1891, other physicians had reported many cases of cocaine intoxication and some deaths, and Freud gave up advocating cocaine. His addiction to smoking, however, lasted all his adult life, and eventually caused cancer of his mouth and throat. He suffered a series of operations and had to wear a painful prosthesis during his last years.

Although our main concern is with substance abuse by humans, many cases have been reported in which animals in the wild administer addictive substances to themselves and even become dependent on them (R. Siegel, 1989). For example, elephants have been observed becoming repeatedly intoxicated on fermented fruits. When confined to game preserves, elephants accept alcohol, and when their space is restricted, which presumably is stressful, they increase their drinking. Baboons have been observed to consume tobacco in the wild, and intoxicating mushrooms are eaten by cattle, reindeer, and rabbits. These observations suggest that the propensity for drug use and possibly even addiction is widespread among animals. In fact, numerous laboratory investigations with animal subjects have revealed important facts about the bases of substance dependence.

Table 6.3

Percentages of Different Age Groups That Used Psychoactive Substances in the United States in 1991

AGE GROUP	EVER USED	USED IN PAST YEAR	USED IN PAST MONTH
Alcohol			
12–17	46	40	20
18–25	90	83	**64**
26–34	92	81	**62**
35–	88	65	50
Total	85	68	51
Male	89	73	58
Female	81	64	44
Cigarettes			
12–17	40	20	11
18–25	71	41	**32**
26–34	76	38	**33**
35–	78	30	27
Total	73	32	27
Male	77	35	29
Female	68	30	26
Marijuana			
12–17	13	10	4
18–25	50	25	**13**
26–34	60	14	7
35–	24	4	2
Total	33	10	5
Male	38	12	6
Female	29	8	3
Cocaine			
12–17	2.4	1.5	0.4
18–25	17.9	7.7	**2.0**
26–34	25.8	5.1	**1.8**
35–	7.0	1.6	0.5
Total	11.7	3.1	0.9
Male	14.4	4.2	1.3
Female	9.2	2.2	0.6

Source: National Institute on Drug Research, National Household Survey (1992)

Because addictive substances are no exception to the general rule that drugs produce multiple effects, it is difficult to determine which mechanisms are most important in producing dependence. For example, cocaine has these major characteristics: (1) it is a local anesthetic; (2) its administration promptly leads to pleasurable feelings so that it is a rewarding agent; and (3) it is a psychomotor stimulant, enhancing activity at synapses that use catecholamine transmitters, speeding the heart rate and evoking other circulatory responses, which sometimes prove fatal. Opiate drugs, such as morphine, also have a variety of effects, including but not limited to the following: (1) they lead to predominance of parasympathetic activity and depression of the activity of the heart and respiratory system; (2) they quickly have a pleasurable and rewarding effect; (3) their use leads to development of tolerance, so dosages must be increased to maintain effects; and (4) they lead to development of strong physical dependence—that is, after repeated use, abstinence from the drug causes a severe withdrawal syndrome. The withdrawal syndrome is so striking that some investigators have proposed that development of dependence is the basic characteristic of addiction. Others insist that the only property that is shared by all habit-forming drugs is the strong reward (Wise, 1984). Still others argue that addiction is an attempt to adapt to chronic distress of any sort (Alexander and Hadaway, 1982). The cause

of addiction is an area of current controversy and we cannot survey it thoroughly here, let alone present a simple conclusion, but we will indicate some of the main findings and positions.

There Are Several Competing Approaches to Understanding Drug Abuse

Attempts to explain drug abuse and addiction have changed widely over the last two centuries. The different explanations have different implications for understanding behavior and for treatment of addiction, and some are better suited to one or another phase of drug abuse, as we'll see. Each explanation continues to be used by some people.

Box 6.2
The Terminology of Substance-Related Disorders

For definitions of mental disorders, psychiatrists, psychologists, and neuroscientists rely on the *Diagnostic and Statistical Manual of Mental Disorders* (4th ed.) often called *DSM-IV* (American Psychiatric Association, 1994; all page numbers cited in this box refer to this manual). What the public usually calls "addiction," the *DSM-IV* calls "substance-related disorders." Within this category, "dependence" is a more severe disorder than "abuse."

The essential feature of **dependence** on psychoactive substances (such as alcohol, tobacco, cocaine, and marijuana) is "a cluster of cognitive, behavioral, and physiological symptoms indicating that the individual continues use of the substance despite significant substance-related problems" (p. 176). To be diagnosed as dependent, a person must meet at least three of seven criteria, four of the which are:

1. The substance is often taken in larger amounts or over a longer period than intended.

2. The persistent desire or efforts to cut down or control substance use are unsuccessful.

3. Much time is devoted to activities necessary to procure the substance (for example, visiting multiple doctors or driving long distances), use the substance (for example, chain smoking), or recover from its effects.

4. Important social, occupational, or recreational activities are abandoned or reduced because of substance use.

We list these criteria only to give you an indication of the symptoms of substance-related dependence. Diagnosis should be left to qualified experts.

The severity of dependence varies from mild, to moderate, to severe. A person exhibiting mild dependence has few, if any, symptoms beyond the three required to make the diagnosis, and the symptoms result in only mild impairment in work or in usual social activities or relationships with others. Severe dependence is

evidenced by many symptoms, which markedly interfere with work or with usual social activities or relationships.

When the criteria for dependence have not been met, but there is evidence of maladaptive patterns of substance use that have persisted at least one month or have occurred repeatedly, the diagnosis is substance **abuse**. Some examples of situations in which a diagnosis of abuse is appropriate are (p. 182):

1. A student has substance-related absences, suspensions, or expulsion from school.

2. A person is repeatedly intoxicated with alcohol in situations that are hazardous—for example, when driving a car, operating machinery, or engaging in risky recreations such as swimming or rock climbing.

3. A person has recurrent substance related legal problems—for example, arrests for disorderly conduct, assault and battery, driving under the influence.

The moral model: "Just say no." The earliest approach was to blame the drug user for lack of moral character or self-control. Explanations of this sort often have a religious character and hold that only divine help will free a person from addiction. Applications based on the moral model have been effective. For example, the temperance movement in the United States, beginning around the 1830s, is estimated to have cut per capita consumption of alcohol to about one-third its level in the period from 1800 to 1820 (Rorabaugh, 1976).

The disease model. The disease model for addiction arose in the latter part of the nineteenth century, partly from concern with abuse of drugs such as opium and morphine that were prescribed by physicians and included in many popular remedies. In this view, the person who abuses drugs requires medical treatment rather than moral exhortation or punishment. This view also justifies spending money on research on drug abuse in the same way that money is spent on other diseases. It is still not clear, however, what kind of a disease addiction is or how a disease causes people to take psychoactive drugs.

Usually the term "disease" is reserved for a state in which we can identify an abnormal physical or biochemical condition; examples include the presence of an infectious agent, such as the syphilis bacterium, damage to brain tissue such as that found in Parkinson's disease, or under- or overproduction of various hormones (see Chapter 7). Investigators have not been able to find such an abnormal physical or biochemical condition in the case of drug addiction. Nevertheless, this approach continues to appeal to many. In 1995, celebrating the 25th anniversary of the U.S. National Institute on Alcohol Abuse and Alcoholism, Director Enoch Gordis stated that ultimately scientific research will lead to "better treatment, better diagnosis, better prevention, and the putting to rest of the notion that alcoholism isn't a disease" (Azar, 1995).

The physical dependence model. The physical dependence model is based on the unpleasant withdrawal symptoms that often occur when a person stops taking a drug that he or she has used frequently, especially at high doses. The specific withdrawal symptoms depend on the drug. For example, the withdrawal symptoms of morphine include irritability, tremor, loss of appetite, and elevated heart rate and blood pressure. Waves of goosebumps occur, and the skin resembles that of a plucked turkey, which is why abrupt withdrawal without any treatment is called "cold turkey." It appears that some of the user's physiological functions have adapted to the actions of the drug and that withdrawing the drug, or even reducing its dosage, disturbs these aspects of functioning. Withdrawal symptoms can be suppressed quickly (within 15 to 20 minutes in the case of morphine) by administering the substance to which the person is addicted. This model provides an explanation of why addicts work compulsively to get drugs—to avoid or overcome withdrawal effects.

The physical dependence model seems to work well for *maintenance* of dependence on alcohol and opiate drugs, and it has become widely accepted. However, it does not explain why abusers acquire the drug habit in the first place. Also, some investigators questioned its generality when they found that powerful addictions could be formed to drugs such as cocaine that do not cause physical symptoms upon withdrawal. Rather than abandon the dependence model, some investigators then proposed that there is psychological dependence on drugs as well as physical dependence. But whereas physiological withdrawal symptoms provide evidence for physical dependence on drugs, the so-called psychological dependence is defined by the *absence* of physiological symptoms! Clearly a better explanation is needed.

The cellular approach. The existence of addiction to nicotine, alcohol, cocaine, heroin, and other drugs indicates that reward centers of the brain can be activated by chemicals with highly selective effects; it also suggests that other chemical agents can be found or synthesized to reverse aspects of addiction (Korenman and Barchas, 1993). In fact, research has already yielded many agonists, antagonists, and modulators of some drugs of abuse. A recent symposium and publication summarize much of the progress in understanding molecular sites of drug action, localizing drug effects in the brain, and attempting to relate the molecular and cellular changes to drug abuse (Korenman and Barchas, 1993).

The positive reward model. The positive reward model of addictive behavior arose from animal research that started in the 1950s (McKim, 1991), and it has been tested in humans. Before the 1950s, researchers believed that animals could not become addicted to drugs. Most of them did not know of observations that wild animals consume psychoactive substances in nature, and they thought (incorrectly) that animals were not capable of learning an association that spanned the 15 to 20 minutes between an injection and relief from withdrawal symptoms. Then a few simple technological and procedural breakthroughs made it possible for laboratory animals to perform tasks that led to self-administration of a drug through a fine flexible tube implanted into a vein (Figure 6.11).

The first investigators to use this technique believed that physical dependence was necessary if animals were to administer drugs to themselves. Therefore they first made rats or monkeys dependent on morphine by giving them repeated injections over a period of days before giving them the opportunity to press a lever that caused delivery of morphine through the implanted tube. The animals quickly learned to respond, and it appeared that the drug infusion was acting as a typical experimental reward, such as food or water (Thompson and Schuster, 1964).

Subsequent experiments by psychopharmacologist Charles R. Schuster demonstrated that animals that had not been made dependent *would* self-administer doses of morphine so low that no physical dependence ever developed (Schuster, 1970). Colleagues in the same laboratory also showed that monkeys would press a lever to self-administer cocaine and other stimulants that do not produce marked withdrawal symptoms (Pickens and Thompson, 1968). Drug self-administration by animals has become a frequently used research method and has many advantages as well as some disadvantages (Koob, 1995).

These and other studies clearly contradicted the assumptions of both the disease model and the physical dependence model of drug addiction. As McKim (1991) notes, although physical dependence may be an important factor in consumption of some drugs, it is not necessary for self-administration and cannot serve as the sole explanation for drug taking. Furthermore, these studies indicated that acquisition of drug self-administration can be interpreted according to principles that govern behavior controlled by positive rewards (operant conditioning theory), thus precluding the need to consider drug self-administration a disease. Many investigators conclude that this model accounts much better for drug addiction than does the model of physical plus psychological dependence. Knowledge of the brain mechanisms of reward and brain reward circuits has also advanced greatly since the 1950s.

Science and Technology Have Furnished More Addictive Drugs

As we consider the importance of the rewarding properties of drugs, it is worth noting that science and technology have contributed to increasing the addictive potential of many drugs and to providing new psychoactive agents. If a drug has the potential for addiction, the stronger the drug and the more rapidly it affects the brain, the more addictive it is likely to be. For the past two centuries, science and technology have continued to furnish drugs that are stronger and that affect the brain more rapidly than previously known drugs. We will discuss a few of the many examples here.

Opium contains a mixture of many addictive substances, the most important of which is morphine. Morphine was extracted from opium in 1803, the first pure drug to be isolated. The invention of the hypodermic syringe in 1853 made it possible to inject morphine into the body. Given by injection, morphine is far more powerful and takes effect much more quickly than when taken by mouth. The world's first morphine addict is said to be the wife of the man who invented the hypodermic syringe (Weil and Rosen, 1993:83). During the Civil War, many soldiers injected themselves with morphine and other opiates, and opiate addiction became known as "the soldiers' disease" (Julien, 1992:186). At that time, opium and morphine were freely available and were included in many popular remedies. Not until the first quarter of the twentieth century did a medical prescription became necessary in most Western countries to obtain opium, morphine, and similar drugs. In the late nineteenth century, chemists began to make variations on the molecules of morphine and other compounds in opium. One of the drugs they produced was heroin (diacetylmorphine), which became available in 1898.

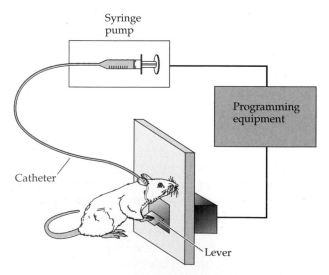

6.11 Experimental Set-Up for Self-Administration of a Drug by an Animal

More potent than morphine, heroin is a frequent drug of abuse.

Cocaine is an alkaloid that comes from the leaves of the coca shrub indigenous to Bolivia, Colombia, and Peru (see Box 6.1). The people in these countries chew coca leaves or drink a tea brewed from the leaves to increase endurance, alleviate hunger, and promote a sense of well-being. This use of coca leaves does not seem to cause problems. However, the indigenous material has been transformed by scientific and technological modifications into addictive forms such as cocaine powder and crack cocaine crystals (Figure 6.12). Cocaine was isolated in 1859 and came into use in the 1890s as a local anesthetic and to relieve depression, until it was found to be addictive. It was used as a psychostimulant in the 1920s but then gave way to amphetamine, a synthetic drug first manufactured in the early 1900s that acts much like cocaine but costs less. When legal restrictions on amphetamine raised its price in the 1960s, cocaine use rose again. Many users inhale cocaine powder, which enters the bloodstream and takes effect rapidly by this route. Crack cocaine is a smokable form of cocaine that appeared in the mid-1980s. Cocaine in this form enters the blood and the brain even more rapidly than through the nasal passages, and crack cocaine is even more addictive than cocaine powder.

Tobacco is also native to the Americas, where European explorers first encountered smoking. When they introduced smoking tobacco to England, King James banned it, but he was unable to prevent its growing use. Widespread use of tobacco did not occur until about 1880, when a technological innovation in curing tobacco made it seem mild so it could be inhaled readily in cigarettes (Bennett, 1983). Exposed to the large surface of the lungs, the nicotine from cigarettes enters the blood and brain much more rapidly than from pipe tobacco or cigars or from chewing tobacco or snuff (Figure 6.13). Taking nicotine in this way is strongly rewarding and is much more addictive than smoking tobacco in cigars or pipes. The consumption of cigarettes soared in the last part of the nineteenth century and has remained high ever since.

Most of the drugs we have mentioned in this section on scientific and technological innovations are derived from natural sources. With the advances of chemistry, however, it has become possible to synthesize new drugs such as amphetamine and to make and test all kinds of variants on existing drugs. A steady stream of new compounds is pouring forth from both pharmaceutical companies and illegal laboratories, so it is hard to predict what this "sorcerer's apprentice" will produce next.

People Differ in Their Vulnerability to Drug Abuse

The positive reinforcement model of addiction does not try to account for the fact that most people who try addictive drugs do not become addicted. Under some circumstances even prolonged use is not accompanied by addiction. For example, medical patients who have been given regular doses of opiates to relieve pain during treatment show very low rates of use or abuse after release from the hospital. Of Vietnam veterans who had become addicted to heroin overseas, only 12% relapsed to dependence within three years after their return. Many investigators have tried to determine which factors in individuals and in their environments may account for vulnerability to developing drug abuse. A recent conference, sponsored by the National Institute on Drug Abuse and the American Psychological Association (Glantz and Pickens, 1992), presented new findings and reviewed and synthesized much of the literature on both vulnerability to drug abuse and factors that protect against such abuse.

The subject is complicated, because different factors appear to operate for transitions between different conditions—from nonusers to moderate users to abusers to former abusers to relapse. Also, factors appear to differ among different drugs of abuse. Some of the most revealing investigations of this subject are longitudinal studies, which follow individuals from infancy on, giving psychological tests and interviews at regular intervals. Some of these longitudinal studies have related personality variables and life experiences to drug use and abuse. Unfortunately, such longitudinal studies are rare because they are expensive to conduct and yield information only slowly. Factors

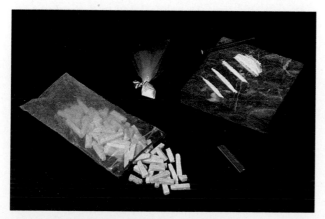

6.12   Cocaine Powder and Crack Crystals

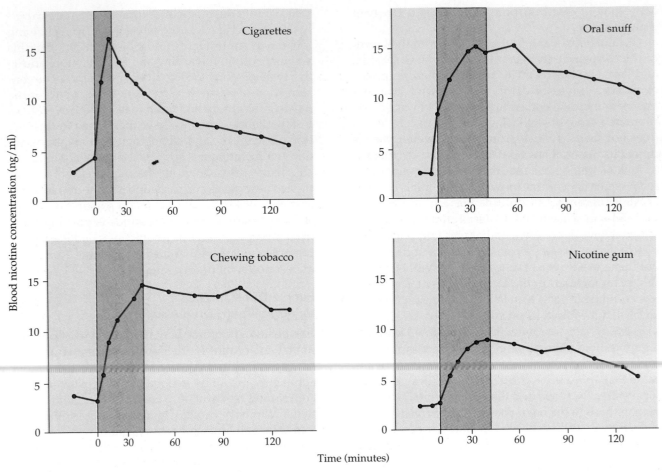

6.13   Rise of Nicotine Concentrations Varies with the Method of Use
The curves show concentrations during the first two hours after taking tobacco in various forms. Note how much more rapidly the concentration rises
after smoking a cigarette than after other methods of consumption. After
Bennett, 1983.

that have been demonstrated to be significant, at least
for some drugs, fall into several categories:

1. *Biological.* Sex is such a variable; males are more
   likely to abuse drugs than are females. There is
   also evidence for genetic predisposition: having an
   alcoholic biological parent makes drug abuse more
   likely, even in the case of children adopted away
   soon after birth (Cadoret et al., 1986).

2. *Personal characteristics.* Characteristics related to
   drug abuse include aggressiveness and the tendency to act out emotional states. Characteristics
   that appear to discourage drug abuse include
   good school achievement, high educational goals,
   and religiousness. Age and maturity are important
   factors; youthful drug use often terminates in the

mid-twenties, when individuals assume adult
roles of employment and marriage.

3. *Family situation.* Factors related to drug abuse include divorce of parents and having an antisocial
   sibling. Strong ties to parents protect against drug
   abuse.

4. *Social and community factors.* A high prevalence of
   drug use in the community, especially by the peer
   group, predisposes an individual toward drug
   abuse.

The greater the number of risk factors that apply,
the more likely an individual will be to abuse alcohol
or marijuana (Brook et al., 1992). Furthermore, these
risk factors do not necessarily operate independently;
in some cases they interact. For example, individuals

with high childhood ratings of aggression show a fairly strong tendency to move from moderate to heavy use of marijuana; the degree of social deviance of their peers has only a moderate effect, as the upper curve in Figure 6.14 shows. Those with low ratings of aggression are much more likely to be influenced in marijuana abuse by the social deviance of their peers, as the lower curve in Figure 6.14 demonstrates. Although in this study only 2% of individuals with low aggression moved to heavy marijuana use if their peers were low in deviancy, those whose peers were high in deviancy had a 25% chance of moving to heavy use (Brook et al., 1992). The multiplicity of factors, the interactions among some of them, and the changing social conditions and attitudes toward drugs all complicate research. A recent review of etiology (causes) and treatment of addictive behaviors calls attention to attempts to integrate biological, psychological, and sociological approaches in a biopsychosocial model of drug use and abuse (Marlatt, 1992). Another model that includes individual differences in vulnerability to drugs is the developmental psychopathology model (Glantz, 1992). So severe are the personal and social problems related to substance abuse and drug addiction that this is a pressing area of research.

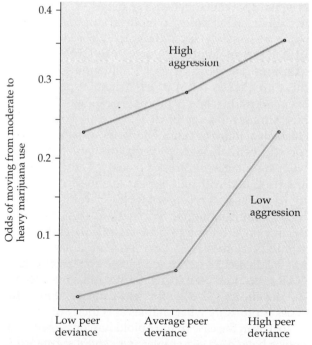

6.14　Social and Personality Factors in Marijuana Use
Individuals who rate low in aggression are not likely to use marijuana if they do not associate with socially deviant peers but are much more likely if their peers are socially deviant. After Brook et al., 1992.

Prevention and Treatment of Drug Use, Abuse, and Dependence

Because drug use, abuse, and dependence cause many personal and social problems, health professionals and investigators have worked to develop a variety of ways to prevent or treat these conditions. Several of these methods are related to the various models used to explain drug use. For example, in keeping with the moral model, which employs exhortations such as "Just Say No," many people do abstain, and many others do not go beyond initial trials of cigarettes, alcohol, or illicit drugs. Even among those who become addicted, many overcome their problems without outside help (Peele and Brodsky, 1991): Investigators report that over 90% of ex-smokers (Cohen et al., 1989) and about half of former problem drinkers (Institute of Medicine, 1990a) appear to have quit on their own.

The positive reward model attributes abuse and dependence to the extremely rewarding properties of drugs for many people, so investigators have attempted either to reduce or abolish the reward provided by a drug or to disconnect the reward from some of the noxious side effects of the drug. Here are a few examples: For alcohol abuse, some therapists prescribe the drug disulfiram (Antabuse). A person who takes this medication suffers unpleasant physiological reactions if he or she drinks alcohol; thus the effects of drinking are negative rather than rewarding. Smokers who fear the withdrawal symptoms if they quit smoking "cold turkey" can use nicotine chewing gum or nicotine skin patches while they attempt to quit smoking. The nicotine still has harmful effects on the body, but at least the lungs escape from tobacco smoke. Also, nicotine delivered through gum or skin patches is less addictive than cigarette smoke, because these methods do not deliver pulses of nicotine as rapidly to the brain as does smoking. Anti-anxiety drugs can also be used to reduce withdrawal symptoms.

The drug methadone is used as a less toxic alternative to opiate drugs: it produces a feeling of satisfaction like that caused by heroin, but it is easier to withdraw patients from methadone than from heroin. The opposite strategy is to use an antagonist to the drug. For example, the drug naltrexone can outcompete heroin in binding to opioid receptors, so administration of naltrexone deprives heroin of its rewarding effect. When therapeutic drugs are prescribed, however, drug users often fail to take them regularly or switch to another addictive drug. In many cases, therefore, pharmacological and behavioral treatments are integrated into a therapeutic program (Stitzer and Higgins, 1995).

The psychiatric/psychological models and the biopsychosocial models of substance abuse have inspired a variety of psychological and behavioral therapies. Many of these types of treatment appear to help at least some substance abusers, but no one approach appears to be uniformly effective (Institute of Medicine, 1990). Rates of relapse remain high, and many studies show that a majority of clients in abstinence programs return to using the psychoactive substance within a year after completing a course of treatment. Research breakthroughs are therefore badly needed to overcome the painful and costly problems of drug abuse and dependence.

Could people be immunized against drug abuse? In 1973 Charles Schuster and his colleagues found that they could immunize a monkey against continuing to self-administer heroin (Bonese et al., 1974). The monkey had been trained to self-administer low doses of heroin and cocaine on alternate sessions; when normal saline solution was substituted for either drug, the monkey stopped working to obtain the infusion. Then the monkey was immunized by injecting morphine bound to a protein. (Recall that heroin is a form of morphine.) In later sessions, the monkey continued to self-administer cocaine but soon no longer took heroin. Apparently the antibody that had been produced in response to immunization reduced the concentration of the drug to a level where it was no longer addictive. With much higher doses of heroin, however, the monkey resumed self-administration; the higher doses probably used up the available antibodies. Further research using this approach was abandoned for two decades.

Recently investigators have developed catalytic antibodies that do not remain bound to their target. Such a catalytic enzyme has been prepared to break down the cocaine molecule (Landry et al., 1993). Another step will be to prepare a vaccine that will incite the body to produce the antibody. Experts hope that this approach will help patients stay drug-free for 6 to 12 months while they undergo psychological and social rehabilitation that may keep them permanently drug-free (Morrell, 1993).

Drugs Alleviate Psychiatric and Neurological Disorders

Many of the serious psychiatric and neurological disorders that we mentioned in Chapter 1 (see Figure 1.7) can now be alleviated and controlled by drugs. Some of these we will discuss in detail in later chapters (for example, Parkinson's disease in Chapter 11, and psychiatric disorders such as anxiety, schizophrenia, depression, and mania in Chapter 16). Here we will give an example of this research, because work on psychotherapeutic drugs is an important part of psychopharmacology.

Most of us suffer at times from feelings of vague dissatisfaction or apprehension that we call anxiety, but here we will be concerned with disabling emotional distress that resembles abject fear and terror. Severe anxiety that prevents people from carrying on normal daily activities is estimated to afflict about 8% of adult Americans. These clinical states of anxiety include phobias—such as the fear of taking an airplane or even of leaving the house—and frank attacks of panic. We will take up anxiety and its mechanisms more fully in Chapter 16, but here we will consider briefly some drugs used to combat anxiety and ways of measuring their effects.

Many substances have been used to combat anxiety. Such substances are called **anxiolytics** (from "anxiety" and the Greek term *luein* "to loosen or dissolve"). One substance that has long been used as an anxiolytic in many cultures is alcohol. Alcohol decreases anxiety in some people, but it also has many harmful effects, some of which will be discussed later in this chapter. Opiates and barbiturates have also been used to relieve anxiety, but they seem to be sedatives or, in higher doses, to produce stupor rather than being true anxiolytics. In the early 1960s, an effective new family of anxiolytics was found, the **benzodiazepines.** The benzodiazepines include some of the most frequently prescribed drugs, especially diazepam (trade name, Valium). The benzodiazepines bind strongly to receptors that appear to be found exclusively within the central nervous system. Agonists for the benzodiazepam receptors are anxiolytic, whereas antagonists arouse anxiety. These receptors are associated with and appear to enhance the activity of a subset of receptors for the inhibitory transmitter gamma-aminobutyric acid (GABA), thus producing larger inhibitory postsynaptic potentials than would be caused by GABA working alone. In fact, several different receptor complexes appear to include GABA receptors, some facilitating and some inhibiting the effect of GABA; this multiplicity of receptor types is probably what enables specificity of action.

Just as in the case of the opioid narcotics, neuroscientists have been searching for a *natural* substance in the nervous system that binds to the so-called benzodiazepine receptor—an endogenous ligand for the receptor—but the quest continues and already has taken a great deal longer than the search for the enkephalins and endorphins. Some investigators have suggested that the endogenous ligand is the neurohormone allopregnanolone, which is derived from the hormone progesterone. This neurohormone is induced and released as a consequence of stress; it has a calming effect. Allopregnanolone binds to GABA/ chloride receptors and increases the activity of the inhibitory neurotransmitter GABA. In turn, GABA inhibits the release of corticotropin-releasing hormone, which triggers stress responses. Thus, allopregnanolone may be an endogenous anxiolytic substance whose actions can be mimicked by the benzodiazepine drugs. Meanwhile, other endogenous ligands have also been proposed for the complex benzodiazepine receptor, and the search continues (Alho, Varga, and Krueger, 1994; Purdy et al., 1992).

Because the anti-anxiety drugs discovered up to now have some potential for addiction, investigators continue to try to develop anxiolytic agents that may have little or no capacity for addicting their users. To screen drugs for possible improved anxiolytic effectiveness, investigators need animal models of anxi- ety. The problem of finding valid animal models for human states and conditions has engendered much thought and discussion on the part of academics, clinicians, and industrial practitioners (Geyer and Markou, 1995; Willner, 1991). We cannot delve deep into this topic here, but we will look at an animal model for anxiety, and later we will consider animal models for other conditions.

Investigators have proposed several behavioral tests as animal models of anxiety (Curran, Schifano, and Lader, 1991; Green, 1991). One popular experimental model for anxiety is based on the observations that conflicting stimulation suppresses response and that some drugs can prevent this suppression (Geller, Backman, and Seifter, 1963). Rats are trained to press a bar to obtain food pellets while a light is illuminated, and they develop a stable rate of response. Then another light comes on for a few minutes, and while it is on, each press of the bar is accompanied by a mild shock as well as by food. The rate of bar pressing is lower during this conflict situation (Figure 6.15*a*). Drugs such as the benzodiazepine chlordiazepoxide reduce the suppression caused by the conflicting shock stimuli. The closer the rate of bar pressing returns to the nonconflict rate, the greater the presumed anxiolytic effect of the drug. Investigators use this method to determine a dose–response function for an anxiolytic drug; for chlordiazepoxide the function is bipolar, the drug helping at lower doses but harming at higher ones (Figure 6.15*b*). Determining the dose–response relationship requires testing animals at different doses in different experimental sessions.

Does the so-called Geller–Seifter procedure really test for suppression of anxiety? For example, may a drug only appear to suppress the conflict by reducing the painfulness of the shocks? Probably not, because analgesic drugs such as morphine do not reduce the suppression of bar pressing in this situation. Or may a drug increase the rate by increasing the animal's motivation for food? In that case the rate would increase throughout, not just during the conflict period. Such control tests show that the Geller–Seifter conflict situation provides a useful animal model of anxiety. It is, however, a rather expensive test because it requires pretraining the animals to press the bar, so other tests are also used. The subject of anxiety and anxiolytic drugs will be taken up more fully in Chapter 16.

The "Same" Drug Can Have Different Effects

What might appear to be the same drug treatment may have widely different effects, depending on a variety of factors. Let's examine some of the reasons for such differences.

Species differences are major factors that account for differences in drug effects. Some species are more susceptible than others to a particular substance. Thus, for example, substances chosen for insecticides are lethal to insects but relatively harmless to people and to domestic and farm animals. However, an agent that works on one species is likely to have some effect on other species (several pesticides are dangerous for people) so every agent of this kind must be tested carefully for possible toxic effects on people and other organisms.

Within a species, subgroups and individuals differ in susceptibility. Among humans, some ethnic differences are known. For example, many Asians lack one of the enzymes that metabolize alcohol; for such people, consuming alcohol promptly produces unpleasant symptoms, including nausea, dizziness, blurred vision, and confusion. The systematic exploration of ethnic differences in responses to drugs is only in its infancy but is getting increased attention (e.g., Lin, Poland, and Nakasaki, 1993). Among individuals, much of the variation in responses to medicines are the result of inherited variations (Weinshilboum, 1984). For this reason a person may find that a substance or an amount is habit-forming or toxic even if his or her friends appear to handle it without difficulty.

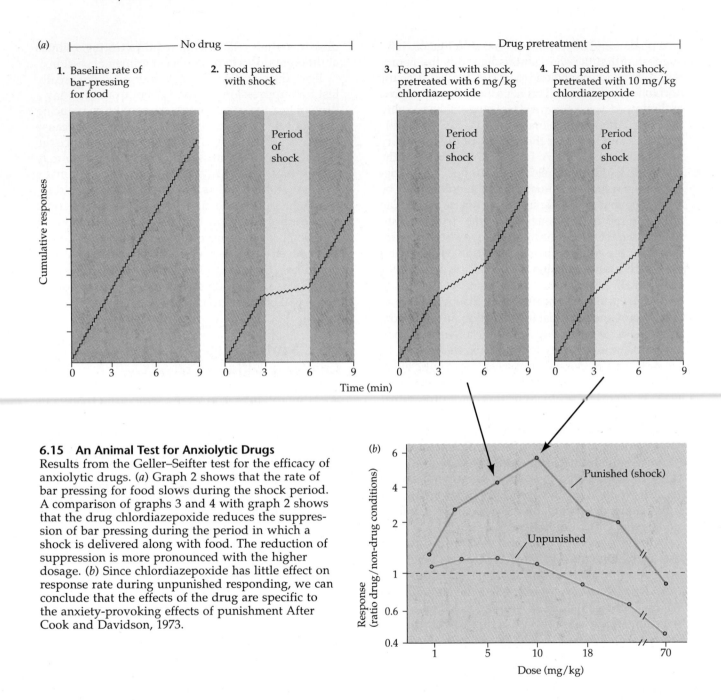

(a) |———— No drug ————| |———— Drug pretreatment ————|

1. Baseline rate of bar-pressing for food

2. Food paired with shock

3. Food paired with shock, pretreated with 6 mg/kg chlordiazepoxide

4. Food paired with shock, pretreated with 10 mg/kg chlordiazepoxide

Cumulative responses

Period of shock

Time (min)

(b) Response (ratio drug/non-drug conditions)

Punished (shock)

Unpunished

Dose (mg/kg)

6.15 An Animal Test for Anxiolytic Drugs
Results from the Geller–Seifter test for the efficacy of anxiolytic drugs. (*a*) Graph 2 shows that the rate of bar pressing for food slows during the shock period. A comparison of graphs 3 and 4 with graph 2 shows that the drug chlordiazepoxide reduces the suppression of bar pressing during the period in which a shock is delivered along with food. The reduction of suppression is more pronounced with the higher dosage. (*b*) Since chlordiazepoxide has little effect on response rate during unpunished responding, we can conclude that the effects of the drug are specific to the anxiety-provoking effects of punishment After Cook and Davidson, 1973.

In the same individual, a drug may vary in effectiveness depending on the time of day it is taken (Scheving, Vedral, and Pauly, 1968). This variation occurs because there are daily rhythms in many aspects of physiology, including body temperature, metabolic rate, synthesis of enzymes, and secretion of hormones. (Circadian rhythms will be discussed in Chapter 14.)

The dosage of many substances can change markedly the kind of effect obtained. As we noted earlier, "the dose makes the poison." Many substances that have favorable or innocuous effects if taken occasionally and in low amounts become habit-forming and/or toxic if taken frequently or in high doses: These include substances such as caffeine, alcohol, anti-anxiety drugs, and many others.

The same dosage of a drug given to the same individual may vary in effectiveness depending on how often the individual has taken the drug previously. For some drugs tolerance develops readily; that is, the dosage must be increased rapidly in order to maintain the same effect. Repeated use of other drugs induces sensitization, so the same dosage causes a larger effect than it did originally. Toxicity and addiction can also build up over time. Many cocaine users who come for medical treatment have been inhaling the drug for four to five years before being overwhelmed by their addiction, but people who smoke crack cocaine become addicted much more rapidly.

Drugs May Interact to Increase or Decrease Their Effects

The effectiveness of some drugs varies according to what other drugs are taken at the same time. Some drugs taken in combination potentiate, or synergize (that is, augment), each other's effectiveness. For example, doses of alcohol and of barbiturates that a person could withstand separately may prove lethal if consumed together. On the other hand, some drugs are antagonists; for example, naloxone, which opposes many of the effects of morphine, is used as an antidote for overdoses of morphine.

Some combinations of substances produce an effect that neither one alone causes. For example, the drug Antabuse is used in the treatment of alcoholism; taken by itself, Antabuse has no effect, but it blocks an enzyme needed for one stage in the metabolism of alcohol. If a person who has taken Antabuse ingests alcohol at any time during the next few days, a toxic product of alcohol builds up in the blood, producing disagreeable symptoms, including nausea, dizziness, blurred vision, and confusion.

Because drugs taken in combination may either synergize or counteract each other's effects, a person should exercise precaution whenever taking more than one drug at the same time:

1. When considering the use of a medication, take into account all medications and substances currently being taken—including over-the-counter drugs, coffee, tea, tobacco, alcohol, stimulants, depressants, and other psychoactive agents.

2. When taking any psychoactive agent—including but not limited to alcohol, stimulants, depressants, or anxiolytics—be aware of the possibility of synergisms with other agents.

The effects of combinations may differ greatly depending on dosages. An example is the interaction between caffeine and alcohol. Many people believe that caffeine can counteract the effects of alcohol, but such a benefit is possible only when the consumption of alcohol has been small to moderate. Studies in both England and the United States found that volunteers who drank alcohol to the point of intoxication were further impaired by drinking coffee! Those who drank two cups of coffee committed nearly twice as many errors in tests of coordination as the drunk volunteers who did not drink the coffee (Goulart, 1984).

The effects of drugs vary markedly over time after administration. For example, alcohol continues to impair performance even after it has completely disappeared from the blood and after drinkers believe they are no longer affected. Automobile drivers made significantly more errors 8 and 11 hours after drinking, and pilots performed significantly worse 14 hours after their blood alcohol had declined to a "safe" level. (For a review of the effects of alcohol on driving and other performance, see Starmer, 1994.)

Two batches of the "same" drug may not actually be the same, especially if they are obtained from an illegal source. Many illegal drugs are adulterated or are entirely different from what they are claimed to be. Some "designer drugs," synthesized to resemble heroin, have proved lethal, and others have crippled users, as we will discuss in Chapter 11. For example, a contaminant in synthesized heroin has caused symptoms of Parkinson's disease in young people and provided new clues to the cause of this disease—at great personal expense to the users.

The examples in this section demonstrate that to predict the effects of a particular drug treatment, you need information about the drug, the individual who takes it, the time of administration, previous usage, and many of the surrounding circumstances.

Summary

1. Because many drugs work by acting on receptor molecules, investigators search for the structure of the receptor molecules and for the endogenous substances that work on the receptors.

2. The tuning of receptor molecules is not absolutely specific. A particular drug molecule may act strongly with one kind of receptor molecule and more weakly with others.

3. Knowing the relationships between the dose of a drug and the responses it induces permits investigators to characterize drugs according to several criteria: potency, safety, slope of the dose–response relationship, and the maximum effect of the drug.

4. Dose–response relationships vary from simple to complex, and include inverted U-shaped functions and bipolar functions.

5. Repeated use of some drugs produces tolerance; that is, an increasingly larger dose is need to achieve a particular effect. Repeated use of other drugs produces sensitization; that is, repeated use causes increasingly larger effects with the same dosage.

6. "The dose makes the poison." Many substances that are innocuous or beneficial at low doses are harmful or even lethal at higher doses.

7. Many plants and animals engage in "chemical warfare" to protect themselves from predators. Poisons from plants include opium and its derivative, morphine, as well as caffeine and nicotine.

8. Lead poisoning has serious effects on the nervous system and on other bodily systems. Even low doses of lead that do not cause obvious poisoning may cause significant impairment of behavior.

9. Some stimulants, such as nicotine, imitate an excitatory synaptic transmitter. Others, such as amphetamine, cause the release of excitatory synaptic transmitters and block the reuptake of transmitters. Still others, such as caffeine, block the activity of an inhibitory neuromodulator.

10. Substances, such as the benzodiazepines, that are used to combat anxiety are called anxiolytic drugs. The benzodiazepines synergize the activity of the inhibitory transmitter GABA at some of its receptors. Animal models are used to screen drugs for anxiolytic properties.

11. Some drugs are called hallucinogens because they alter sensory perception and produce peculiar experiences. Different hallucinogens act on different kinds of synaptic receptors, and it is not yet clear what causes the hallucinogenic effects.

12. Drug abuse and addiction are being studied intensively, and several models have been proposed: the moral model, the disease model, the physical dependence model, the cellular mechanisms model, and the positive reward model.

13. The "same" drug treatment may have widely different effects, depending on a number of factors, including species and individual differences, time of day, dosage, previous usage, and combinations with other drugs.

14. The study of psychopharmacology with animal subjects is useful because many species of animals consume psychoactive substances in nature, and their responses to many substances are similar to those of human beings. Research with animal subjects helps us understand addictive behavior and develop medicines for conditions such as anxiety, depression, and schizophrenia.

15. Applications of research in psychopharmacology occur in many ways, including: (a) identification and removal of poisons from the environment; (b) providing medicines for many psychological and psychiatric illnesses such as anxiety, depression, and schizophrenia; (c) identification of both beneficial and harmful interactions of psychoactive agents; and (d) helping to prevent and cure drug abuse and drug dependence.

Recommended Reading

Bloom, F. E. and Kupfer, D. (eds.) 1995. *Psychopharmacology: The Fourth Generation of Progress.* Raven, New York.

Cooper, J. R., Bloom, F. E., and Roth, R.H. 1991. *The Biochemical Basis of Neuropharmacology.* (6th ed.) Oxford University Press, New York.

Glantz, M. and Pickens, R. 1992. *Vulnerability to Drug Abuse.* American Psychological Association, Washington, D.C.

Julien, R. J. 1992. *A Primer of Drug Action.* (6th ed.) Freeman, New York.

Leonard, B. E. 1992. *Fundamentals of Psychopharmacology.* Wiley, New York.

McKim, W. A. 1991. *Drugs and Behavior: An Introduction to Behavioral Pharmacology.* (2nd ed.) Prentice-Hall, NJ.

Snyder, S. H. 1986. *Drugs and the Brain.* Freeman, New York.

Terry Winters, "k," 1987. Gouache on paper. 11¼ × 14½ in.

- *Hormones and How They Were Discovered*

- *There Are Several Types of Chemical Communication within and between Organisms*

- *Hormones Act According to Ten General Principles*

- *Neural and Hormonal Communication Have Similarities and Differences*

- *Hormones Can Be Classified by Their Chemical Structures*

- *Hormones Act on a Wide Variety of Cellular Mechanisms*

- *Main Endocrine Glands and Their Hormones*

- *Hormones Have Many Different Effects on Behavior*

- *Hormonal and Neural Systems Interact to Produce Integrated Responses*

CHAPTER 7

Hormones: A Chemical System for Communication and Regulation

Orientation

Communication between and among the cells of the body involves chemicals, of which one of the major classes is hormones. Without regular supplies of some hormones, our capacity to behave would be seriously impaired; without others, we would soon die. Deficiency or excess of some hormones can result in striking changes in the cognitive and emotional behavior of humans. Tiny amounts of some hormones can markedly modify our moods and our actions, our inclination to eat or drink, our aggressiveness or submissiveness, and our reproductive and parental behavior. Furthermore, hormones do more than influence adult behavior; early in life they help to determine the development of body form. Later in life the changing outputs of some endocrine glands and the body's changing sensitivity to some hormones are essential aspects of aging.

In this chapter we consider the mechanisms by which hormones accomplish their functions, the main endocrine glands and their hormones, and examples of hormonal influences on physiology and on behavior. After presenting a brief history of discoveries relevant to hormones and their actions, we will compare the ways in which the endocrine and nervous systems communicate and coordinate function. Other chapters will also include detailed behavioral aspects of hormone activities.

Hormones and How They Were Discovered

In general, **hormones** (from the Greek *horman*, "to excite or stir into action") are chemicals secreted into the bloodstream by specialized cells and carried to other parts of the body where they act on specific target tissues to produce specific physiological effects. Specialized organs that manufacture and secrete most hormones are known as **endocrine glands** (from the Greek *endo*, "within," and *krinein*, "to se-

crete"). **Exocrine glands** (the Greek *exo* means "out") such as the tear glands, the salivary glands, and the sweat glands, secrete their products through ducts to sites of action outside the body. Whereas exocrine glands are also called duct glands, endocrine glands are ductless. Endocrine glands come in a variety of sizes and shapes, and they are located in many parts of the body (Figure 7.1).

Hormones are found throughout the animal kingdom and even in plants. Only the vertebrates have specialized endocrine glands to secrete and store hor-

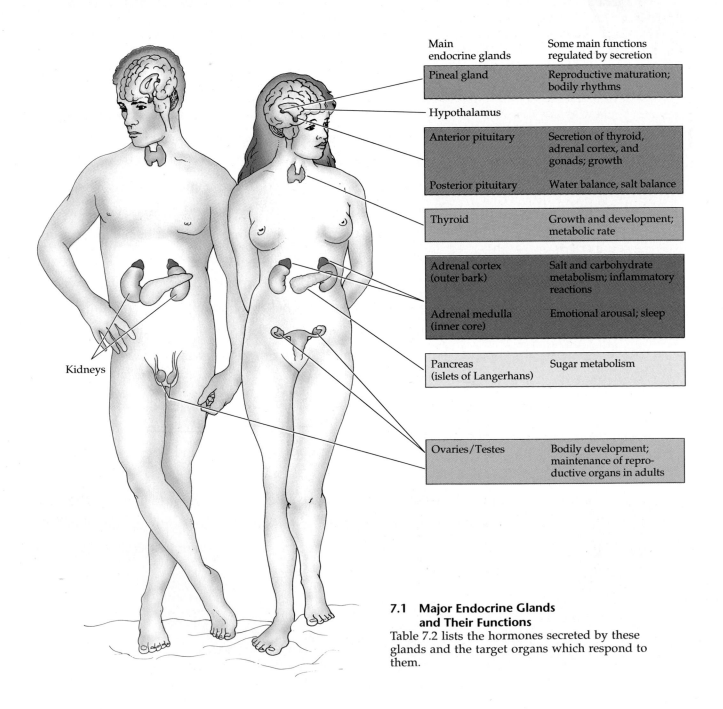

Main endocrine glands	Some main functions regulated by secretion
Pineal gland	Reproductive maturation; bodily rhythms
Hypothalamus	
Anterior pituitary	Secretion of thyroid, adrenal cortex, and gonads; growth
Posterior pituitary	Water balance, salt balance
Thyroid	Growth and development; metabolic rate
Adrenal cortex (outer bark)	Salt and carbohydrate metabolism; inflammatory reactions
Adrenal medulla (inner core)	Emotional arousal; sleep
Pancreas (islets of Langerhans)	Sugar metabolism
Ovaries/Testes	Bodily development; maintenance of reproductive organs in adults

Kidneys

7.1 Major Endocrine Glands and Their Functions
Table 7.2 lists the hormones secreted by these glands and the target organs which respond to them.

mones, but hormonal functions evolved long before endocrine glands. In fact, some human hormones do not come from endocrine glands but are secreted from sources such as neurons in the hypothalamus or cells in the lining of the digestive tract. Recently the heart has been found to produce a hormone that helps regulate blood pressure and sodium balance in the body. In many cases the chemical structure of a hormone is the same or very similar over a wide variety of animal species. The function of a given hormone, however, may change in the course of evolution.

Communication within the body and the integration of behavior were considered the exclusive province of the nervous system until the beginning of this century, when investigators became aware that the endocrine system is also important for these functions. However, the role of such bodily fluids was anticipated in several ancient civilizations in which endocrine glands were eaten to modify health or be-

havior. Ancient societies also noted some of the behavioral and physiological changes from obvious endocrine pathology, such as the disfiguring enlargement of the thyroid called goiter.

In the fourth century B.C., Aristotle accurately described the effects of castration (removing the testes) in birds, and he compared the behavioral and bodily effects with those seen in castrated men. Although he did not know what mechanism was involved, it was clear that the testes were important for the reproductive capacity and sexual characteristics of the male. This observation was consistent with the ancient Greek emphasis on body humors, or fluids, as an explanation of temperament and emotions. It was believed that these fluids—phlegm, blood, yellow bile (also known as choler), and black bile—all interacted to produce health or disease (Figure 7.2). The notion of bodily fluids as the basis of human temperament lingered into the nineteenth century,

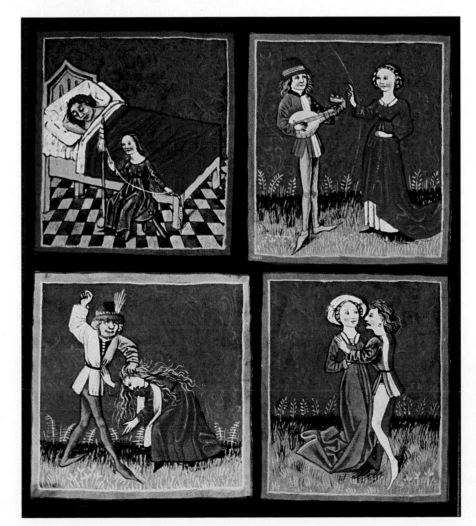

7.2 The Four Humors
A medieval representation of the ancient view that four basic bodily fluids, or humors, flowed through the body and that excess amounts of these fluids resulted in particular temperaments. (*Clockwise from top left*) An excess of black bile was said to cause melancholia; phlegm, sluggishness; blood, a highly changeable temperament; choler or yellow bile, irascibility and anxiousness. Similar concepts found their way into nineteenth-century phrenological texts. Courtesty of the Granger Collection, New York.

when terms such as "phlegmatic" (sluggish), "bilious" (irritable), and "choleric" (hot-tempered) were used to describe people.

The first major endocrine experiment was carried out in 1849 by A. A. Berthold, a professor in Göttingen, Germany. When Berthold castrated young roosters, they showed declines in both reproductive behavior and secondary sexual characteristics, such as the rooster's comb (Figure 7.3). Berthold observed that replacement of one testis into the body cavity restored both the normal behavior of these roosters and their combs. They began crowing and showed usual sexual behaviors. Because the nerve supply to the testis had not been reestablished, Berthold concluded that the testes release a chemical into the blood that affects both male behavior and male body structures. Today we know that the testes make and release the hormone testosterone, which exerts these effects. Berthold's study is important because it was the first experiment in behavioral endocrinology.

Vincent du Vigneaud
(1901–1978)

Frederick Sanger

The French physiologist Claude Bernard helped set the stage in the nineteenth century for the emergence of endocrinology as a science. Bernard stressed the importance of the internal environment (or "internal milieu") in which cells exist and emphasized that this environment must be carefully regulated. As he put it, a constant *internal* bodily environment is necessary for independent activity in the *external* environment. This idea was later embedded in the concept of **homeostasis** advanced by American physiologist Walter B. Cannon in the 1920s. Homeostasis is the maintenance of a relatively constant internal environment by an array of mechanisms in the body. Clinical and experimental observations starting in the late nineteenth century showed the importance of several glands—including the thyroids, the adrenal cortex, and the pituitary—for maintaining this constant environment inside our bodies.

The term "hormone" was first used in 1905 by the English physiologists William M. Bayliss and Ernest H. Starling, who discovered that the passage of food through the stomach released a substance from the intestines that, in turn, caused the release of pancreatic fluids. This intestinal substance—called secretin—they referred to as a hormone; the term "endocrine" was introduced shortly thereafter.

Earl Sutherland

In the twentieth century new techniques enabled scientists to identify many different hormones. Several Nobel Prizes were given for the determination of the structure of hormones. For example, Vincent du Vigneaud received the 1955 Nobel Prize in Chemistry for synthesizing the hormones oxytocin and vasopressin. Frederick Sanger received the same award in 1958 for establishing the chemical structure of insulin. In 1971, Earl Sutherland received the Nobel Prize in Physiology or Medicine for showing the role of second messengers in the mecha-

Rosalyn Yalow

nisms of hormone action. The discovery of a sensitive technique for measuring small quantities of hormones (called radioimmunoassay) brought Rosalyn Yalow the Nobel Prize in 1978. These techniques, together with earlier ones, give us a powerful set of tools to analyze the reciprocal relations between hormones and behavior.

There Are Several Types of Chemical Communication within and between Organisms

Our knowledge of chemical communication in the body has grown dramatically in the last decade. Many substances are now identified as hormones; even more have hormonelike properties. The following are some categories of chemical signals in the body, classified according to the form of their communication or delivery:

	Group 1	Group 2	Group 3
Appearance of immature roosters			
Manipulation	None	Remove testes	Remove testes and reimplant one in abdomen
Appearance of adult roosters			
Comb and wattles: Mount hens? Aggressive? Crowing?	Normal Yes Yes Normal	Small No No Weak	Normal Yes Yes Normal

7.3　The First Experiment in Behavioral Endocrinology
Berthold's nineteenth-century experiment demonstrated the importance of hormones for behavior. Left undisturbed (Group 1), young roosters grow up to have large red wattles and combs, to mount and mate with hens readily, and to fight one another and crow loudly. Animals whose testes were removed during development (Group 2), displayed neither the appearance nor the behavior of normal roosters as adults. However, if one of the testes was reimplanted into the abdominal cavity immediately after its removal (Group 3), the rooster developed normal wattles and normal behavior. Because the reimplanted testis was in an abnormal body site, disconnected from normal innervation, and yet still affected development, Berthold reasoned that the testes release a humoral, hormonal signal that has widespread effects.

1. Synaptic communication was described in Chapters 5 and 6. In synaptic transmitter function (sometimes called neurocrine function), the released chemical signal diffuses across the synaptic cleft and causes a change in the polarization of the postsynaptic membrane (Figure 7.4a). Typically, synaptic transmitter function is highly localized.

2. **Autocrine** communication involves the release or secretion of a hormone which then acts on the releasing cell itself and thereby affects its own activity (Figure 7.4b). An example of autocrine function is seen in nerve cells which have autoreceptors that are affected by the released synaptic transmitter molecules and thus monitor their own activity. In this case, the signal molecule serves both an autocrine and a synaptic transmitter function.

3. In **paracrine** regulation or communication, the released chemical signal diffuses to nearby target cells through the intermediate extracellular space (Figure 7.4c). The strongest impact is on the nearest cells.

4. In **endocrine** regulation and communication the chemical signal is a hormone released into the bloodstream and taken up selectively by target organs, which may be quite far away (Figure 7.4d). We will see later that some neurons release hormones into the bloodstream in this manner.

5. Hormones can be used to communicate not only within an individual, but also from one individual to another. **Pheromones** (from the Greek *pherein*, "to carry") are hormones produced by one individual and then released outside the body to affect other individuals of the same species (Figure 7.4e).

(a) Synaptic transmission function

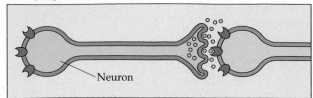

Neuron

(b) Autocrine function

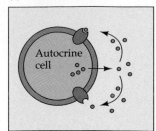

Autocrine cell

(c) Paracrine function

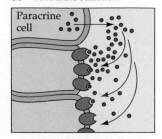

Paracrine cell

(d) Endocrine function

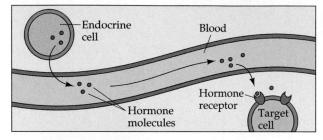

Endocrine cell

Blood

Hormone molecules

Hormone receptor

Target cell

(e) Pheromone function

(f) Allomone function

7.4 Chemical Communication Systems
(a) Synaptic transmitter (neurocrine) mechanisms involve the release of a chemical signal from a neuron's presynaptic terminal and its binding to receptor molecules on a postsynaptic target cell. (b) Autocrine mechanisms refer to the feedback effects of a chemical signal on the very cell from which it was released. Some synaptic transmitters are also autocrine signals in that they affect receptors on the presynaptic terminal (autoreceptors). (c) Paracrine mechanisms involve the diffusion of chemical signals through extracellular space to nearby target cells. The strongest effects are produced in the nearest cells. (d) Endocrine glands produce chemical signals and release them into the bloodstream. Effects are produced in the body wherever receptors for the hormone are found. (e) Pheromones carry a message from one individual of the species to other individuals. The pheromones often indicate whether the individual is ready to mate. (f) Allomones are produced by individuals of one species to communicate with (and affect the behavior of) individuals of other species.

For example, many species of ants produce a wide variety of pheromones that are used to communicate the presence of intruders in the nest, or to mark the trail that leads to a rich food source. Dogs and wolves urinate on various landmarks to designate their "territory"; other dogs smell the pheromones in the urine and either respect or challenge the territory. In Chapter 12 we'll discuss pheromones that hasten or delay sexual maturation and evidence of pheromones that may synchronize menstrual cycles in women.

6. Some chemical signals are released by members of one species and affect the behavior of individuals of another species (Brown, 1968). These hormones are called **allomones** (from the Greek *allo*, "other"). Allomones can carry messages between animal species or from plants to animals (Figure 7.4f). Flowers exude scents to attract insects and birds in order to distribute pollen. Other plant agents inhibit insect growth hormones, thus interfering with potential predators. Skunks may provide the best-known allomone of all.

Hormones Act According to Ten General Principles

Although the many different hormones in the body differ along many dimensions, there are some general principles of hormone action:

1. Hormones frequently act in a gradual fashion, activating behavioral and physiological responses long after the concentrations of hormone in the blood have fallen. This slowness of action complicates our attempts to determine whether a particular change in physiological or behavioral responses has been caused by the hormone per se or by some other factors.

2. When hormones alter behavior they tend to act by changing the intensity or probability of evoked behaviors, rather than acting as a "switch" to turn behaviors on or off regardless of context.

3. Both the quantities and types of hormone released are influenced by environmental as well

as endogenous factors. The relationship between behavior and hormones is clearly reciprocal; that is, hormones change behavior and behavior changes hormone levels or responses. For example, high levels of testosterone are related to aggression, and the "loser" in aggressive encounters shows a reduction in testosterone levels, while the winner in these bouts shows little change in testosterone levels. This is an example of the reciprocal relation between somatic and behavioral events that we discussed in Chapter 1 (see Figure 1.12).

4. Each hormone has multiple effects on different tissues, organs, and behaviors; conversely, a single type of behavior or physiological change can be affected by many different hormones (Figure 7.5).

5. Hormones are produced in small amounts and often are secreted in bursts. This "pulsatile" secretion pattern is sometimes crucial for the small amount of hormone to be effective.

6. The levels of many hormones vary rhythmically throughout the day, and many hormonal systems are controlled by "circadian clocks" in the brain, as we'll see in Chapter 14.

7. Hormones affect metabolic processes in most cells, including the buildup and breakdown of carbohydrates, lipids, and proteins. In this sense, hormones trigger long-term metabolic change.

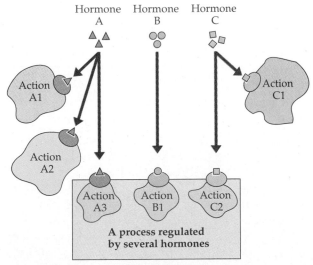

7.5   Multiplicity of Hormone Action
A single hormone often has multiple effects (for example, hormones A and C in this illustration) on several different groups of target cells. Similarly, a single process or bodily organ (box) may be affected by several hormones.

8. Hormones interact; the effect of one hormone can be markedly changed by the actions of another hormone.

9. The chemical structures of hormones in all vertebrates are similar, but the functions served by a particular hormone can vary across species.

10. Hormones can affect only those cells that possess a receptor protein that recognizes the hormone and alters cell function. Among the vertebrates, the same brain regions often possess the same hormone receptors.

Neural and Hormonal Communication Have Similarities and Differences

The nervous system and the hormonal system are the body's major communication mechanisms; these systems interact at many different levels, especially within the brain, where the interactions are referred to as "neuroendocrine."

There Are Four Main Differences between Neural and Hormonal Communication

1. Neural communication works somewhat like a telephone system: messages travel over fixed channels to precise destinations. The anatomical connections between neurons determine the transmission of information from one cell to another. In contrast, hormonal communication works more like a TV broadcasting system: many different endocrine messages spread throughout the body and can then be picked up by scattered cells that have receptors for them. Some hormones broadcast rather locally; for instance, the hypothalamus sends hormones only a few millimeters through the blood vessels to the anterior pituitary gland. Other hormones broadcast throughout the body, but because cells in only a particular organ have the proper receptors, they influence only that organ.

2. Whereas neural messages are rapid and are measured in milliseconds, hormonal messages are slower and are measured in seconds and minutes.

3. Most neural messages are "digitized," all-or-none impulses. Hormonal messages are analog—that is, graded in strength.

4. Neural and hormonal communication also differ in terms of voluntary control. You cannot, at a command, increase or decrease the output of a hormone or a response mediated by the endocrine system, but you can voluntarily lift your arm,

blink your eyelids, or perform many other acts under neuromuscular control. This distinction between neural and hormonal systems, however, is not absolute. Many muscular responses cannot be performed at will, even though they are under neural control. An example is heart rate, which is regulated by the vagus nerve and can meet changing demands during exercise or stress, but which can be altered promptly and directly by very few people. Later in this chapter we will note examples of conditioned responses that involve hormones—the milk letdown response mediated by oxytocin during breast-feeding and the early release of insulin during eating.

There Are Five Main Similarities between Neural and Hormonal Communication

In spite of the differences outlined in the previous section, the neural and hormonal systems show important similarities. The nervous system uses specialized biochemical substances (neurotransmitters) to communicate across synaptic junctions in much the same way that the endocrine system uses hormones (Figure 7.6). Of course, the distance traveled by the chemical messengers differs enormously in the two cases: the synaptic cleft is only about 30 nanometers wide (30×10^{-9} meters) wide, whereas hormones may travel a meter or so from the site of secretion to the target organ. Nevertheless, the analogy between chemical transmission at synapses and hormonal communication holds up in several specific respects:

1. The neuron produces its particular transmitter chemical and stores it for later release, just as an endocrine gland stores its hormone for secretion.

2. Neurons are stimulated, usually by other neurons, to produce an action potential that causes the presynaptic terminal to release transmitter into the synaptic cleft. Similarly, endocrine glands are stimulated to secrete hormones into the bloodstream, some glands responding to neural messages and others to chemical messages.

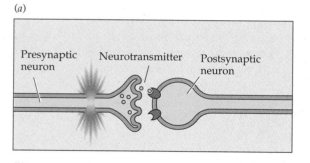

(a)

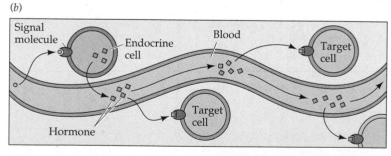

(b)

7.6 Neuroendocrine Cells Blend Neuronal and Endocrine Mechanisms
(*a*) Neurons communicate with other neurons or muscle cells, and signal transmission is determined by the pattern of anatomical connections. (*b*) Hormonal signals are transmitted through the bloodstream and are recognized by appropriate receptors in specific locations in the body. (*c*) Neuroendocrine (or neurosecretory) cells are the interface between neurons and endocrine glands. They receive neural signals from other neurons and secrete a hormone into the bloodstream. Thus, an electrical signal is converted into a hormonal signal.

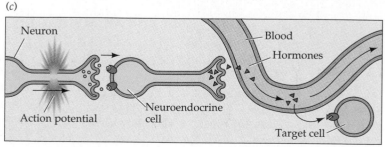

(c)

3. There are many different synaptic transmitter chemicals, and there are many different hormones. In fact, more and more chemicals are being found to serve as both. Examples are norepinephrine and epinephrine, which act as transmitters at many brain synapses but which are also secreted as hormones by the adrenal gland.

4. The synaptic transmitter reacts with specific receptor molecules at the surface of the postsynaptic membrane. Similarly, hormones react with specific receptor molecules, either on the surface or in the interior of their target cells; most organs do not have receptors for a given hormone and therefore do not respond to it.

5. Often when hormones act on receptor molecules on the cell surface, a second messenger is released within the target cells to bring about changes within the cell. This process has been studied extensively in the endocrine system. Some neural effects also involve the release of second messengers in the postsynaptic neuron. Moreover, the same compounds—cyclic AMP and G proteins—act as second messengers in both the nervous and the endocrine systems.

A look at the neurons in the hypothalamus that synthesize hormones and release them into the bloodstream will highlight the similarities between neuronal and hormonal communication. These so-called **neurosecretory** (or neuroendocrine) cells make it hard to draw a firm line between neurons and endocrine cells (see Figure 7.6). In fact, some investigators believe that the endocrine glands may have evolved from neurosecretory cells (Norman and Litwack, 1987).

Findings that certain chemicals—either hormonal peptides or **neuropeptides** (peptides used by neurons)—in vertebrates are also found in single-celled organisms have led to a different hypothesis: that both the nervous system and the endocrine system are derived from chemical communication systems in our remote single-celled ancestors (LeRoith, Shemer, and Roberts, 1992). Much current research is devoted to determining the functions of peptide compounds in the brain (Björklund, Hökfelt, and Kuhar, 1992; Koob, Sandman, and Strand, 1990). Some peptides may be used as neurotransmitters. On the other hand, since peptides typically have a slower onset of effect and a longer duration of action than do other transmitters, it has been suggested that they act as **neuromodulators**, substances that alter the reactivity of cells to the specific transmitters.

Hormones Can Be Classified by Their Chemical Structures

Most hormones fall into one of three categories: protein hormones, amine hormones, and steroid hormones. **Protein hormones**, like all proteins, are composed of strings of amino acids (Figure 7.7*a*). (Recall that a peptide is simply a small protein, i.e., a short string of amino acids. In this chapter we will refer to both protein and peptide hormones as protein hormones). Different protein hormones consist of different combinations of amino acids. **Steroid hormones** are composed not of amino acids, but of four interconnected rings of carbon atoms (Figure 7.7*b*). Different steroid hormones vary in the numbers and kinds of atoms attached to the rings. The distinction between protein and steroid hormones is important because these two classes of hormone interact with different types of receptors and by different mechanisms. **Amine hormones** are compounds composed of a single amino acid (hence their alias, "monoamine" hormones) that has been modified into a related molecule (Figure 7.7*c*). Examples of each class of hormones are given in Table 7.1.

Hormones Act on a Wide Variety of Cellular Mechanisms

Later in the chapter we will be considering the effects of specific hormones on behavior. In preparation for this discussion, let's look briefly at three aspects of hormonal activity: the *effects* of hormones on cells, the *mechanisms* by which hormones exercise these effects, and the *regulation* of hormone secretion.

Hormones Affect Cells by Influencing Their Growth and Activity

Hormones affect many everyday behaviors in people and other animals, and they do so by influencing cells in various tissues and organs. Hormones exert these far-reaching effects by (1) promoting the proliferation, growth, and differentiation of cells, and (2) modulating cell activity. Early developmental processes are promoted by various hormones—for example, the thyroid hormones. Without these hormones, fewer cells are produced in the brain and mental development is stunted. Although proliferation and differentiation occur mainly during early development in the brain, hormones cause cells in some organs to divide and grow at later stages of life, too. For example, male and female hormones cause secondary sex characteristics to appear during

(a) Protein hormone

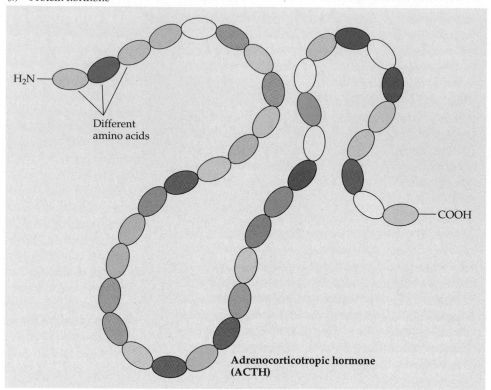

(b) Steroid hormone   *(c)* Amine hormone

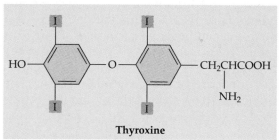

7.7 Chemical Structures of the Three Main Hormone Types
(a) Protein hormones consist of strings of amino acids. If the string of amino acids is short, as is the case of ACTH here, it may be referred to as a peptide hormone. *(b)* Steroid hormones are derived from cholesterol and consist of four interconnected rings of carbon atoms to which are attached different numbers and types of atoms. This structure allows steroids to dissolve readily in lipids, so they can cross cell membranes readily. *(c)* Amine hormones are modified single amino acids. In the case of thyroxine shown here, the shape of the molecule is similar to steroids.

adolescence: breasts and broadening of the hips in women, and facial hair and enlargement of the Adam's apple in men.

In cells that are already differentiated, hormones can modulate the *rate* of function. For example, thyroid hormones and insulin promote the metabolic activity of most of the cells in our body. Other hormones modulate activity in certain types of cells. For example, luteinizing hormone (a hormone from the anterior pituitary gland) promotes the secretion of sex hormones by the testes and by the ovaries.

Hormones Initiate Actions by Binding to Receptor Molecules

The three classes of hormones exert their influences on target organs in two different ways:

Table 7.1

Major Classes of Hormones

CLASS	HORMONE
Amine hormones	Epinephrine (adrenaline)
	Norepinephrine (NE)
	Thyroid hormones
	Melatonin
Protein hormones	Adrenocorticotropic hormone (ACTH)
	Follicle-stimulating hormone (FSH)
	Luteinizing hormone (LH)
	Thyroid-stimulating hormone (TSH)
	Growth hormone (GH)
	Prolactin
	Insulin
	Glucagon
	Oxytocin
	Vasopressin (AVP, ADH)
	Releasing hormones
	Corticotropin-releasing hormone (CRH)
	Gonadotropin-releasing hormone (GnRH)
	Thyrotropin-releasing hormone (TRH)
	Somatocrinin (releases growth hormone)
	Somatostatin (inhibits growth hormone)
Steroid hormones	
Gonadal	Estrogens (e.g., estradiol)
	Progestins (e.g., progesterone)
	Androgens (e.g., testosterone, dihydrotestosterone)
Adrenal	Glucocorticoids (e.g., cortisol)
	Mineralocorticoids (e.g., aldosterone)

1. The protein hormones bind to specific receptors—that is, proteins that recognize only one hormone or class of hormones. Such receptors are usually found *on the surface* of target cell membranes and, when stimulated by the appropriate hormone, cause the release of a second messenger in the cell. (As we saw in Chapter 5, the release of a second messenger can also be caused by some synaptic transmitters.) Protein hormones exert their effects by using this mechanism to alter proteins that already exist within the cell. Most amine hormones also act via surface receptors and second messengers, but as we'll see, the thyroid hormones are an exception.

2. The steroid hormones pass through the membrane and bind to specific receptor proteins *inside* the cell. The steroid–receptor complex then binds to DNA in the cell's nucleus. This binding affects the transcription of specific genes, increasing the production of some proteins and decreasing the production of others. Hence, these hormones act by affecting gene expression and thereby altering the production of proteins (see the Appendix).

Let's look at these two main modes of action in a little more detail and examine the ways in which hormones affect cellular function.

Protein and amine hormones act rapidly. What characteristic of a cell determines whether it responds to a particular protein hormone? Some proteins manufactured by a cell become integrated into the membrane, such as the neurotransmitter receptors discussed in Chapters 5 and 6. Part of the receptor protein faces the outside of the cell to interact with chemical signals, while other parts of the protein re-

7.8   Two Main Mechanisms of Hormone Action

(*a*) Protein hormone receptors are found in the cell membrane. When the hormone binds to the receptor, a second messenger system is activated, which affects different cellular processes. (*b*) Steroid hormones passively diffuse into cells. Inside target cells are large receptor molecules which bind to the steroid hormone. The steroid receptor complex then binds to DNA, causing an increase in the production of some gene products and a decrease in the production of others.

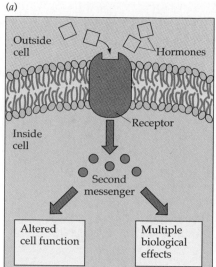

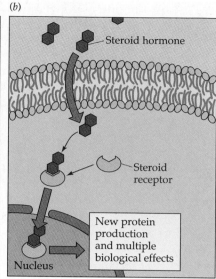

main inside the cell. Some of these proteins serve as receptors for protein hormones rather than for neurotransmitters. Thus, only cells that produce the appropriate receptor proteins and insert them into the membrane will respond to a specific hormone. Hormone receptors can increase or decrease in number, and these changes are sometimes referred to as up-regulation and down-regulation. Sometimes continuous exposure to a specific hormone results in fewer receptors to bind the hormone to a cell; in other cases the reverse condition is noted.

When a hormone binds to the extracellular portion of the receptor, the receptor molecule changes its overall shape. The alteration in the intracellular portion of the receptor then changes the cell's internal chemistry, often by activating a second messenger such as G proteins (Figure 7.8*a*; see Figure 5.11).

One second-messenger compound transmits the messages of many of the peptide and amine hormones: *cyclic* *a*denosine *mono*phosphate, commonly referred to as **cyclic AMP** or **cAMP**. It may seem surprising that the same second messenger can mediate the effects of many different hormones, but recall from Chapter 5 that the same kind of neural impulses can convey all sorts of neural messages. This situation is similar: a change in cAMP can cause very different outcomes depending on which cells are affected, which part of a cell is affected, and on the prior biochemical activity inside the cell.

The specificity of hormonal effects is determined in part by the selectivity of receptors; only a few cells produce the receptor to recognize and react to the hormone, so only those cells respond. For example, adrenocorticotropic hormone (ACTH) interacts with receptors on the membranes of cells in the adrenal cortex, and in these cells an increase in cAMP leads to the synthesis and release of other hormones.

The protein hormones usually act relatively rapidly, within seconds to minutes. (Although rapid for a hormone, this action is, of course, much slower than neural activity.) There can also be prolonged effects. For example, ACTH also promotes the proliferation and growth of adrenal cortical cells, thereby increasing the long-term capacity to sustain production of their hormones.

Steroid hormones act slowly.   Steroid hormones typically act more slowly than the protein hormones, requiring hours to take effect. The specificity of action of steroid hormones is determined by the receptors that reside *inside* target cells. A large "superfamily" of steroid receptor genes has been discovered (Ribeiro et al., 1995). Some of these receptors are "orphans"; that is we don't yet know which steroid hormone binds them. The steroid hormones pass in and out of many cells in which they have no effect. If there are appropriate receptor proteins inside, however, these receptors bind to the hormone, and the receptor–steroid complex then binds to DNA, so that they become concentrated in the nuclei of target cells (Figure 7.8*b*). Thus, one can study where a steroid hormone is active by observing where radioactively tagged molecules of the steroid are concentrated (Box 7.1). For example, when tagged estrogen is administered into the circulatory system, it accumulates not only in the reproductive tract (as you might expect), but also in the nuclei of some neurons throughout the hypothalamus. By altering protein production, steroids have a slow but often long-lasting effect on the development or adult function of cells. We will discuss such effects of steroids further in Chapter 12.

Steroids may be able to affect cells in other ways. For example, there is evidence that estrogen, in addition to its slow, long-lasting action, can also have a rapid, brief effect on some neurons. This rapid effect may involve a separate class of steroid receptors in the membrane of these neurons (Moss and Dudley, 1984). This membrane mechanism may be a way of modulating neural excitability in reproductive behavior. Such multiple mechanisms of hormonal activity are now a subject of intense study.

Feedback Control Mechanisms Regulate the Secretion of Hormones

One of the major features of almost all hormonal systems is that they don't just manufacture a hormone; they also detect and evaluate the effects of the hormone. Thus, secretion is usually monitored and regulated so that the rate is appropriate to ongoing bodily activities and needs. The basic control used is a negative feedback system (see Chapter 5 for an explanation of negative and positive feedback).

The simplest kind of system that regulates hormones is diagrammed in Figure 7.9a. An endocrine cell releases a hormone that acts on target cells to produce a specific set of biological effects. The character of this response—its magnitude or distinctive features—is monitored by some cells in the circuit—either the cells that produced the hormone or the target cells. If the initial effects are too small, additional hormone is released. Thus, for example, the hormone insulin helps control the level of glucose circulating in the blood in the following way: After a meal, glucose from the food enters the bloodstream and extracellular fluid, leading to the release of insulin from the pancreas. The insulin causes extracellular glucose to enter muscle and fat cells and stimulates them to use the glucose. As the level of glucose in the blood falls, the pancreas secretes less insulin, so a balance tends to be maintained. Thus, insulin is normally self-limiting: the more that is secreted, the more glucose is pulled out of circulation and the lower the call for insulin. This negative feedback action of a hormone is like that of a thermostat, and just as the thermostat can be set to different temperatures at different times, the set points of a person's endocrine feedback systems can be changed to meet varying circumstances. We'll encounter negative feedback effects again in Chapter 13.

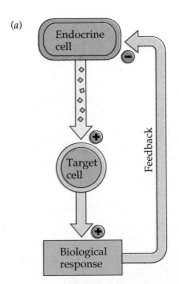 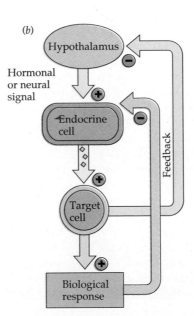 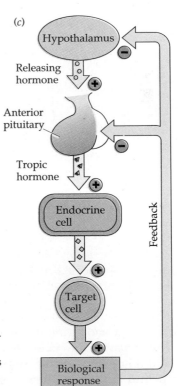

7.9 Endocrine Feedback Loops
(*a*) In the simplest type of negative feedback control, an endocrine gland releases a hormone that acts on target cells to produce a specific set of biological effects. The consequences of these effects are detected by the endocrine gland, which inhibits further hormone release. (*b*) In many feedback systems the brain becomes involved. The hypothalamic region drives the endocrine gland through either neural or hormonal signals. The target organ signals the brain to inhibit this drive. (*c*) Highly complex feedback mechanisms involve the hypothalamus and the anterior pituitary as well as the endocrine gland. Feedback regulation may involve a variety of routes and hormones.

Box 7.1

Techniques of Modern Behavioral Endocrinology

To establish that a particular hormone affects behavior, investigators usually begin with the type of experiment that Berthold performed in the nineteenth century: observing the behavior of the intact animal, then removing the endocrine gland and looking for a change in behavior (see Figure 7.3). Berthold was limited to this type of experiment, but the modern scientist has many additional options available. Let's imagine we are investigating a particular effect of hormones on behavior to see how we might proceed.

First, the investigator must carefully observe the behavior of several individuals, seeking ways to classify and quantify the different types of behavior and place them in the context of the behavior of other individuals. For example, most adult male rats will try to mount and copulate with a female placed in his cage. Sometimes (about every fourth day) the female will respond to the male's advances by lifting her rump and pushing her tail to one side, allowing the male to mate with her. At such times the female is said to be "receptive" to the male. If the testes are removed from the male rat, he will eventually stop copulating with a female, even if she is receptive. We know that one of the hormones produced by the testes is testosterone. Is it the loss of testosterone that causes the loss of male copulatory behavior? To explore this question, we purchase some synthetic testosterone, inject it into castrated males and observe whether the copulatory behavior returns. (It does.)

Next, we might examine individual male rats and ask whether the ones that copulate a lot have more testosterone circulating in their blood than those who copulate only a little. Thus, we measure individual differences in the amount of copulatory behavior, take a sample of blood from each individual and measure levels of testosterone. To take this measure we use radioimmunoassay (RIA), a technique that uses an antibody that binds to a particular hormone. By adding many such antibodies to each blood sample and measuring how many of the antibodies find a hormone molecule to bind, we can estimate the total number of molecules of the hormone per unit volume of blood. (We won't go into detail here about how we determine the number of antibodies that bind to hormone.) It turns out that individual differences in the sexual behavior of normal male rats (and normal human males) do *not* correlate with differences in testosterone levels in the blood. In both rats and humans, a drastic loss of testosterone, as after castration, will result in a gradual decline in sexual behavior. Among normal males, however, everyone appears to make more than enough testosterone to maintain sexual behavior, and something else must modulate this behavior. In other words, the hormone acts in a permissive manner: it permits the display of the behavior, but something else determines how much of the behavior each individual engages in.

What does testosterone do to permit this behavior? One step toward answering this question is to ask another: Which parts of the brain are normally affected by this hormone? We have two methods at our disposal. First, we might inject a castrated animal with testosterone that has been radioactively labeled (one or more of the atoms in the molecule has been replaced with a radioactive atom). After waiting about an hour for the testosterone to accumulate in the brain regions that have receptors for the hormone, we sacrifice the animal, remove the brain, freeze it, and cut thin sections from the brain and place them on photographic film. If the tissue is left in place for a few months, enough radioactive particles from the testosterone will hit the film to expose it. We develop the film to learn which brain regions had accumulated testosterone. This method is known as autoradiography because the tissue "takes its own picture" with radioactivity (see Box 2.1). When the labeled hormone is a steroid like

A more complex endocrine system includes the hypothalamus as part of the circuit controlling an endocrine gland (Figure 7.9b). This control may occur through a neural link, as in control of the adrenal medulla. The secretion of epinephrine by the adrenal medulla affects target cells, and the negative feedback goes directly to the hypothalamus, bypassing the endocrine gland (adrenal medulla) and reducing the demand for further hormone output.

An even greater degree of complexity is encountered when the anterior pituitary becomes involved (Figure 7.9c). As we'll see, there are several anterior

(A) *Androgen autoradiogram*

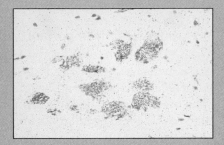

(B) *Oxytocin autoradiogram*

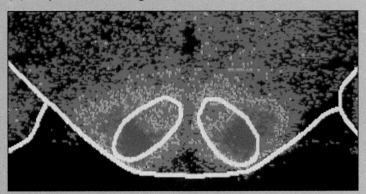

testosterone, the radioactivity accumulates in the nuclei of brain cells, and leaves small black specks on the film, as seen in Figure A. When the radiolabeled hormone is a protein hormone, the radioactivity accumulates in the membranes of cells and appears in particular layers of the brain. Computers can generate color maps that highlight regions with high densities of receptors, as shown in Figure B.

The second method for detecting hormone receptors is immunocytochemistry. In this method we use antibodies that recognize not the hormone but the hormone receptor. This method allows us to map the distribution of the hormone receptors in the brain. We put the antibodies on slices of brain tissue, wait for them to bind to the receptors, wash off the unbound antibodies, and use chemical methods to visualize the antibodies by leaving a tiny dark spot at each antibody. When the antibodies recognize a steroid receptor, chemical reactions cause a brown coloration in the nuclei of target brain cells, as seen in Figure C.

Once we have used either autoradiography or immunocytochemistry (or, better yet, both) to identify brain regions that have receptors for the hormone, those regions become candidates for the places the hormone works to change behavior. Now we can take castrated males and implant tiny pellets of the testosterone into one of those brain regions. We use RIA to insure that the pellets are small enough that they have no effect on hormone levels in the blood. Then we ask whether the small implant in that brain region restores the behavior. If not, then in other animals we can implant pellets in a different region or try placing implants in a combination of brain sites. It turns out that such implants can restore male sexual behavior in rats only if they are placed in the medial preoptic area (mPOA) of the hypothalamus. Thus we have found so far that testosterone does some-

thing to the mPOA to permit individual males to display sexual behavior. Now we can examine the mPOA in detail to learn what changes in the anatomy, physiology, or protein production of this region are caused by testosterone. We have more or less caught up to modern-day scientists who work on this very question. Some of the preliminary answers will be discussed in Chapter 12. (Figure B courtesy of Bruce McEwen.)

(C) *Androgen receptor immunocytochemistry*

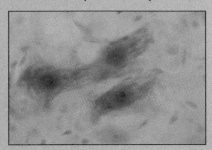

pituitary hormones that affect the secretion of other endocrine glands; all of these pituitary hormones are called **tropic hormones**. ("Tropic," pronounced with a long "o" as in "toe," means "directed toward.") The hypothalamus uses another set of hormones, called **releasing hormones**, to control the pituitary release of tropic hormones. Thus, the brain's releasing hormones affect the pituitary's tropic hormones, which affect the hormone release of another endocrine gland. Feedback in this case goes from the hormone of the endocrine gland to both the hypothalamus and the anterior pituitary (Figure 7.10).

Main Endocrine Glands and Their Hormones

We will restrict our account in this chapter to some of the main endocrine glands, their hormones, and some of their principal effects. Our treatment must be simplified because a thorough treatment would fill an entire book. A more complete listing of hormones and their functions appears in Table 7.2. For

more details see Hadley (1992) and other texts. Keep in mind that most hormones have more functions than are mentioned here and that several hormones may act together in producing effects in the same target cells.

The Pituitary Gland Produces Many Important Hormones

Resting in a depression in the base of the skull is the **pituitary gland**, about 1 cm³ in volume and weighing about 1 gram. The brain region called the hypothalamus sits just above it. The term pituitary comes from the Latin for "mucus," reflecting the outmoded belief that waste products dripped down from the brain into the pituitary, which secreted them out through the nose. (The ancients may have thought you could literally "sneeze your brains out.") A true "mighty mite," the pituitary used to be referred to as the master gland, a reference to its regulatory role in regard to several other endocrine glands. But this master gland is itself enslaved by the hypothalamus above it, as we'll see.

The pituitary gland consists of two main parts: the **anterior pituitary**, or adenohypophysis, and the **posterior pituitary**, or neurohypophysis (Figure 7.11). The term "hypophysis" comes from Greek roots meaning "an outgrowth from the underside of the brain." The adenohypophysis originates from glandular tissue (the root *adeno-* comes from a Greek word meaning "gland"). The neurohypophysis derives from neural tissue. The anterior and posterior pituitary are completely separate in function.

The pituitary is connected to the hypothalamus by a thin piece of tissue called the pituitary stalk (see Figure 7.11a). The stalk contains many axons and is richly supplied with blood vessels. The axons extend only to the posterior pituitary, which we will consider next. The blood vessels, as we will see later, transmit information exclusively to the anterior pituitary.

Hormones of the posterior pituitary. The posterior pituitary gland contains two principal hormones: **oxytocin** and *a*rginine *v*asopressin (**AVP**, sometimes called just vasopressin). Neurons in various hypothalamic nuclei, especially the supraoptic nucleus and the paraventricular nucleus, synthesize these two hormones and transport them along their axons to the axon terminals. Nerve impulses in these hypothalamic neurosecretory cells travel down the axons in the pituitary stalk and reach the axon terminals in the posterior pituitary, causing the release of the hormone from the terminals into the rich vascular bed of the neurohypophysis. The axon terminals abut capil-

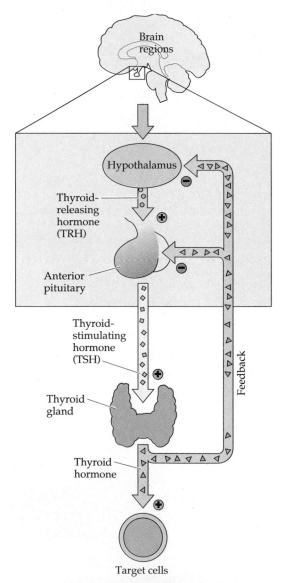

7.10 An Example of Complex Endocrine Regulation The brain funnels information to the hypothalamus which then controls the anterior pituitary which in turn stimulates the thyroid gland. Note that three hormones and at least four cell groups are interacting in this instance.

Table 7.2

Main Endocrine Glands, Their Hormone Products, and Principal Effects of Their Hormones

GLAND	HORMONES	PRINCIPAL EFFECTS
Anterior pituitary	Growth hormone (GH)	Stimulates growth
	Thyroid-stimulating hormone (TSH)	Stimulates the thyroid
	Adrenocorticotropic hormone (ACTH)	Stimulates the adrenal cortex
	Follicle-stimulating hormone (FSH)	Stimulates growth of ovarian follicles and of seminiferous tubules of the testes
	Luteinizing hormone (LH)	Stimulates conversion of follicles into corpora lutea; stimulates secretion of sex hormones by ovaries and testes
	Prolactin	Stimulates milk secretion by mammary glands
	Melanocyte-stimulating hormone	Controls cutaneous pigmentation in lower vertebrates
Posterior pituitary (storage organ for certain hormones produced by hypothalamus)	Oxytocin	Stimulates contraction of uterine muscles; stimulates release of milk by mammary glands
	Vasopressin (antidiuretic hormone; AVP, ADH)	Stimulates increased water reabsorption by kidneys; stimulates constriction of blood vessels (and other smooth muscle)
Hypothalamus	Releasing hormones	Regulate hormone secretion by anterior pituitary
	Oxytocin; vasopressin	*See under* Posterior pituitary
Adrenal cortex	Glucocorticoids (corticosterone, cortisol, hydrocortisone, etc.)	Inhibit incorporation of amino acids into protein in muscle; stimulate formation (largely from noncarbohydrate sources) and storage of glycogen; help maintain normal blood sugar level
	Mineralocorticoids (aldosterone, deoxycorticosterone, etc.)	Regulate sodium and potassium metabolism
	Sex hormones (especially androstenedione)	Regulate facial and bodily hair
Testes	Androgens (testosterone, dihydrotestosterone, etc.)	Stimulate development and maintenance of male primary and secondary sexual characteristics and behavior
Ovaries	Estrogens (estradiol, estrone, etc.)	Stimulate development and maintenance of female secondary sexual characteristics and behavior
	Progestins (especially progesterone)	Stimulate female secondary sexual characteristics and behavior, and maintain pregnancy
Thyroid	Thyroxine, triiodothyronine	Stimulate oxidative metabolism
	Calcitonin	Prevents excessive rise in blood calcium
Pancreas	Insulin	Stimulates glycogen formation and storage; stimulates carbohydrate oxidation; inhibits formation of new glucose
	Glucagon	Stimulates conversion of glycogen into glucose
Mucosa of duodenum	Secretin	Stimulates secretion of pancreatic juice
	Cholecystokinin (CCK)	Stimulates release of bile by gallbladder; may be signal of satiety for food
	Enterogastrone	Inhibits secretion of gastric juice
Pyloric mucosa of stomach	Gastrin	Stimulates secretion of gastric juice

7.11 The Two Major Components of the Pituitary Gland

(*Inset*) The approximate position of the pituitary in relation to the brain. (*a*) Hypothalamic neuroendocrine cells in the supraoptic and paraventricular nuclei synthesize the hormones oxytocin and vasopressin and transmit these hormones along axons to their terminals. From the terminals they are released into the capillaries of the posterior pituitary. (*b*) Other hypothalamic neurosecretory cells produce releasing hormones and inhibiting hormones. When these neurons produce an action potential, these hormones are released into capillaries of the median eminence. The hormones then travel through the portal veins to cells of the anterior pituitary, where they influence the release of anterior pituitary hormones from secretory cells of this gland.

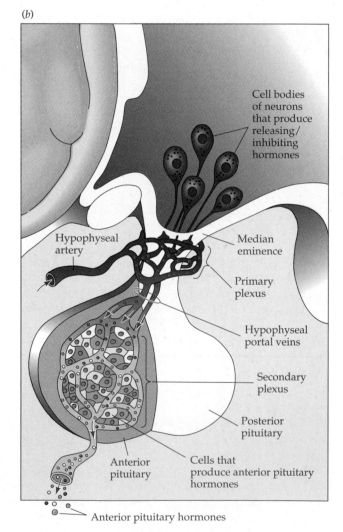

(*a*)

Hypothalamus

Cell bodies of neurons that produce posterior pituitary hormones

Paraventricular nucleus

Optic chiasm

Supraoptic nucleus

Pituitary stalk

Capillaries

Posterior pituitary hormones

Oxytocin
Vasopressin

(*b*)

Cell bodies of neurons that produce releasing/inhibiting hormones

Hypophyseal artery

Median eminence

Primary plexus

Hypophyseal portal veins

Secondary plexus

Posterior pituitary

Anterior pituitary

Cells that produce anterior pituitary hormones

Anterior pituitary hormones

Prolactin
Gonadotropic hormones (FSH and LH)
Thyroid-stimulating hormone
ACTH
Growth hormone

laries (small blood vessels), allowing the hormone to enter circulation immediately (Figure 7.11*a*).

Some of the signals that activate the nerve cells of the supraoptic and paraventricular nuclei are related to thirst and water regulation, which will be discussed in Chapter 13. Secretion of AVP increases blood pressure by causing blood vessels to contract. AVP is also known as *anti*diuretic *h*ormone (ADH) because it inhibits the formation of urine—which is what an "antidiuretic" does. This action of AVP helps conserve water. In fact, the major physiological role of AVP is its potent antidiuretic activity; it exerts this effect with less than one-thousandth of the dose needed to alter blood pressure. Because the name vasopressin was the first one applied to the hormone, however, we will use that name. AVP also acts as a neurotransmitter for some neurons projecting within the brain.

Oxytocin is involved in many aspects of reproductive and parental behavior. One of its functions is to stimulate contractions of the uterine muscles and thus hasten birth (the word "oxytocin" is derived from the Greek *okus*, "rapid," and *tokus*, "birth"). In fact, injections of oxytocin (or the synthetic version, Pitocin) are frequently used to accelerate delivery when prolonged labor threatens the health of the fetus. Oxytocin also triggers **milk letdown**, the contraction of cells in the mammary glands. The mechanism mediating this phenomenon is a good example of the interaction of behavior and hormone release. When an infant or young animal begins to suckle, there is a delay of 30 to 60 seconds before milk is obtained. This delay is caused by the sequence of steps preceding letdown. Stimulation of the nipple activates receptors in the skin, which transmit this information through a chain of neurons and synapses to hypothalamic cells that contain oxytocin. Once these cells have been sufficiently stimulated, the hormone is released from the posterior pituitary and travels via the vascular system to the mammary glands, where it produces a contraction of the cells surrounding the storage sites for milk, thus resulting in the availability of milk at the nipple (Figure 7.12). For human mothers this reflex response to suckling frequently becomes conditioned to baby cries, so milk appears promptly at the start of nursing.

A new perspective on this hormone has emerged, best summarized by a newspaper headline: "A Potent Peptide Prompts an Urge to Cuddle" (Angier, 1992). Oxytocin is active in both sexes and appears to be part of the mechanism mediating both sexual arousal and affectionate responses. Rodents given supplementary doses of oxytocin spend more time in physical contact with each other. Carter (1992) suggests that this hormone is important in the formation of social bonds and social attachment. Because a burst of oxytocin is released during orgasm in both men and women, other researchers have suggested that it is involved in the pleasurable feelings of sexual climax. Oxytocin also serves as a neurotransmitter from hypothalamic cells, projecting widely through the nervous system. Its elaborate role is reflected in the broad distribution of receptors for this hormone in the brain.

Hypothalamic Releasing Hormones Govern the Anterior Pituitary

Different cells of the anterior lobe of the pituitary synthesize and release different tropic hormones (listed in Table 7.3), which we'll discuss in the next section. Synthesis and release of the tropic hormones, however, is under the control of releasing hormones, as we mentioned earlier. The releasing hormones (also listed in Table 7.3) are made by cells of the hypothalamus. We will briefly note some of the properties of these hypothalamic releasing hormones before further consideration of anterior pituitary actions.

Neurons that synthesize different releasing hormones reside in different regions of the hypothalamus; like the neurons that produce oxytocin and AVP, these cells are considered neuroendocrine, or neurosecretory, cells. The axons of the neuroendocrine cells converge on the median eminence just above the pituitary stalk (see Figure 7.11*b*). This region contains an elaborate profusion of capillaries that form the **hypothalamic–pituitary portal system**. Axons in this area contain large granules filled with hormones, which are released not into a synapse, but into the capillaries, where blood carries the releasing hormone a short distance into the anterior pituitary. The blood supply of the anterior pituitary thus contains many different releasing hormones that cause various anterior pituitary cells to change the rate at which they release their tropic hormone. The same kinds of controls apply for all the anterior pituitary hormones: neuroendocrine cells in the hypothalamus make one releasing hormone or another, transport it down their axons to the median eminence, and when an action potential arrives at the terminals, dump the releasing hormone into the hypothalamic–pituitary portal system. When the releasing hormones reach the anterior pituitary, they cause the cells there to release more or less tropic hormone into the bloodstream.

Thus, the hypothalamic releasing hormones are an important control element in the regulation of endocrine secretions. Cutting the pituitary stalk interrupts the blood vessels and the flow of releasing hormones and leads to profound atrophy of the pituitary.

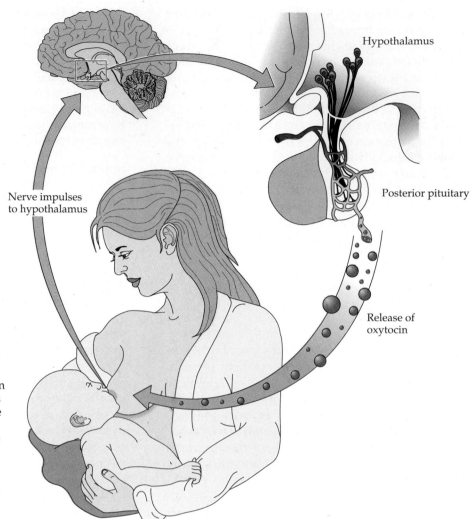

Hypothalamus

Nerve impulses
to hypothalamus

Posterior pituitary

Release of
oxytocin

7.12   The Milk Letdown Reflex
Stimulation of the mother's nipple by the infant's suckling response produces brain activity in the mother that results in inputs to the hypothalamus. Cells there produce and release oxytocin from the posterior pituitary. The oxytocin causes the cells of the mammary glands to contract, thereby releasing milk. The letdown reflex may become conditioned to occur before suckling begins.

The neuroendocrine cells that synthesize the releasing hormones are themselves subject to two kinds of influences:

1. They receive neural impulses from other brain regions via the synaptic contacts of these cells in the hypothalamus. These neural impulses can be either excitatory or inhibitory. In this manner the endocrine system is influenced by a wide range of neural signals originating from both internal and external events. Thus, the outputs of endocrine glands can be regulated in accordance with ongoing events and can be conditioned by learning.

2. They are also directly affected by circulating messages, such as other hormones (especially hormones that have themselves been secreted in response to tropic hormones), and by blood sugar and products of the immune system. In other words, these neuroendocrine cells are not shielded by a blood–brain barrier. (The blood–brain barrier was discussed in Chapter 2).

Tropic hormones of the anterior pituitary.   The anterior pituitary gland secretes six main tropic hormones (Figure 7.13; see also Table 7.2):

1. *Adrenocorticotropic hormone* (**ACTH**) controls the production and release of hormones of the adrenal cortex. The adrenal cortex in turn releases steroid hormones. Measurements of the level of ACTH and adrenal steroids show a marked rhythm in the course of a day (see Chapter 14).

2. *Thyroid-stimulating hormone* (**TSH**) increases the release of thyroid hormones from the thyroid gland and markedly affects thyroid gland size.

Table 7.3

Control and Effects of Anterior Pituitary Hormones

HYPOTHALAMIC RELEASING HORMONE	ANTERIOR PITUITARY HORMONE	MAIN TARGET	HORMONE RESPONSE FROM TARGET
Thyrotropin-releasing hormone (TRH)	Thyroid-stimulating hormone (TSH)	Thyroid	Thyroid hormones (thyroxine and triiodothyronine)
Gonadotropin-releasing hormone (GnRH)	Follicle-stimulating hormone (FSH)	Testes	Testosterone
		Ovaries	Estrogens
	Luteinizing hormone (LH)	Testes	Testosterone
		Ovaries	Progesterone
Corticotropin-releasing hormone (CRH)	Adrenocorticotropic hormone (ACTH)	Adrenal cortex	Glucocorticoids
			Mineralocorticoids
Somatocrinin (stimulates)	Growth hormone (GH)	Throughout body	Somatomedin peptides from liver
Somatostatin (inhibits)			
Prolactin-inhibiting factor (PIF; this may be dopamine)	Prolactin	Mammary glands	None identified

Two tropic hormones of the anterior pituitary influence the gonads. They are:

3. *Luteinizing hormone* (**LH**) stimulates the release of eggs from the ovary in females and prepares the uterine lining for the implantation of a fertilized egg. In males this same hormone stimulates interstitial cells of the testes to produce testosterone (LH used to be called interstitial cell–stimulating hormone when referring to males).

4. *Follicle-stimulating hormone* (**FSH**) stimulates the secretion of estrogen in females and of testosterone in males. It also influences both egg and sperm production.

5. **Prolactin** is named after its role of promoting mammary development for lactation in female mammals. In other vertebrates prolactin plays other roles; for example, in Chapter 12 we'll learn that in ring doves it promotes the secretion of crop milk, which the parents feed to their chicks.

6. *Growth hormone* (**GH**; also known as somatotropin or somatotropic hormone) acts throughout the body to influence the growth of cells and tissues by affecting protein metabolism. The daily production and release of GH is especially prominent during the early stages of sleep. In fact, some sleep stages are required for growth hormone release. Several other factors influence growth hormone release, such as a decrease in blood sugar, starvation, exercise, and stress (see Box 7.2).

Secretion of the tropic hormones is determined largely by releasing hormones that are produced in the hypothalamus and transported to the anterior pituitary by blood vessels of the hypothalamic–pituitary portal system, as discussed earlier. Now let's consider three of the target organs stimulated by anterior pituitary tropic hormones: the adrenal gland, the thyroid gland, and the gonads. Each of these glands secretes hormones of its own in response to the pituitary tropic hormones.

Two Divisions of the Adrenal Gland Produce Hormones

Resting on top of each kidney is an **adrenal gland**, which secretes a large variety of hormones (Figure 7.14). There are two major portions of the adrenal structure in mammals. In many nonmammalian vertebrates, these two portions are separate glands. In mammals, the outer bark of the gland, the **adrenal cortex**, is composed of distinct layers of cells, each producing different steroid hormones. This portion is about 80% of the gland. The core of this gland is the **adrenal medulla**, really a portion of the sympathetic nervous system because it is richly supplied with nerves from the autonomic ganglia.

The adrenal *medulla* releases *amine* hormones—**epinephrine** (adrenaline) and **norepinephrine** (noradrenaline)—in response to nerve impulses of the sympathetic nervous system. In Chapter 6 we saw that epinephrine and norepinephrine are also synaptic transmitters at certain sites in the nervous system.

7.13 Secretions of the Anterior Pituitary

Hormones produced in the anterior pituitary include tropic hormones which control endocrine glands, and hormones that directly affect other bodily organs, such as bones.

Anterior pituitary

Posterior pituitary

ACTH (adrenocorticotropic hormone)

GH (growth hormone)

PRL (prolactin)

LH (luteinizing hormone)

FSH (follicle-stimulating hormone)

TSH (thyroid-stimulating hormone)

Adrenal cortex

Testis

Milk production

Bone growth

Thyroid

Ovaries

Corticosteroids

Thyroxine

Testosterone

Estrogen, progesterone

The adrenal *cortex* produces and secretes a variety of *steroid* hormones, collectively called the **adrenocorticoids** (or adrenal steroids). One subgroup consists of **glucocorticoids**, so named because of their effects on the metabolism of carbohydrates, including glucose. Hormones of this type, such as **cortisol**, increase the level of blood glucose. They also accelerate the breakdown of proteins. In high concentrations

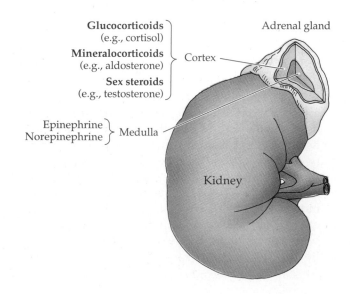

Glucocorticoids (e.g., cortisol)
Mineralocorticoids (e.g., aldosterone)
Sex steroids (e.g., testosterone)
Cortex

Adrenal gland

Epinephrine Norepinephrine } Medulla

Kidney

7.14 The Adrenal Gland

Situated above the kidneys, each adrenal consists of an outer layer (the cortex) and an inner layer (the medulla). The main hormones of the cortical portion are corticosteroids, as well as androgens and estrogens. The cells of the adrenal medulla release epinephrine and norepinephrine as a result of stimulation by the sympathetic nervous system.

Box 7.2

Stress and Growth: Psychosocial Dwarfism

Genie had an extremely deprived childhood. From the age of 20 months until the age of 13 years, she was isolated in a small closed room, and much of the time she was tied to a chair. Her disturbed parents provided food, but nobody held Genie or spoke to her. When released from her confinement and observed by researchers at the age of 13 years 9 months, she looked as if she were only 6 or 7 years old (Curtis, 1977).

Other less horrendous forms of family deprivation have also been shown to result in failure of growth. This syndrome has been referred to as **psychosocial dwarfism** to emphasize that the growth failure arises from psychological and social factors mediated through the CNS and its control over endocrine functions (Green, Campbell, and David, 1984). When such children are removed from stressful circumstances, many begin to grow rapidly. The growth rates of three such "psychosocial dwarfs," before and after periods of emotional deprivation, are shown in the figure (arrows indicate when each child was removed from the abusive situation). These children seem to compensate for much of the growth deficit that occurred during prolonged stress periods.

How do stress and emotional deprivation impair growth?

Growth impairments appear to be mediated by changed outputs of several hormones, including growth hormone (GH), cortisol, and other hormones, called **somatomedins** (which are normally released by the liver in response to GH). GH and the somatomedins normally stimulate cell growth, while high levels of cortisol inhibit growth. Some children with psychosocial dwarfism show virtually no release of GH, which may be caused by an absence of somatocrinin from the hypothalamus (Brasel and Blizzard, 1974). Disturbed sleep has also been suggested as a cause of this failure (Gardner, 1972). GH is typically released during certain stages of sleep, as we will see in Chapter 14, and children under stress show disturbed sleep patterns. Other children with psychosocial dwarfism show normal levels of GH but low levels of somatomedins, and these hormones, along with GH, appear to be necessary for normal growth. Still other psychosocial dwarfs show elevated levels of steroids (probably as a result of stress) which inhibit growth. Some affected children show none of these hormonal disturbances. Thus, there may be other routes through which emotional factors influence growth. Another possi-

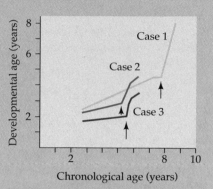

bility is that the hormonal measurements may not have been taken promptly enough. Because growth often resumes rapidly when the child is removed from the stressful environment, delaying even a day or two may cause the investigator to miss the hormonal dysfunction.

Growth is an example of a process that involves a large number of factors—hormonal, metabolic, and dietary—and can therefore malfunction in a variety of ways. Cases of psychosocial dwarfism are more common than once was thought, and investigators who study this syndrome are calling for further awareness of and attention to it (Green, Campbell, and David, 1984). For Genie, relief came in time to restore much of her body growth, but her mental development remained severely limited; she never learned to say more than a few words.

they have a marked anti-inflammatory effect; that is, they inhibit the swelling around injuries or infections. This action normally results in the temporary decrease of bodily responses to tissue injury. However, high levels of corticosteroids can destroy nerve cells, as we'll see shortly and in Chapter 15. Glucocorticoids can also affect appetite and muscular activity.

A second subgroup of adrenal steroids is the **mineralocorticoids**, so named because of their effects on ion concentrations in some body tissues, especially the kidneys. The primary mineralocorticoid hormone is **aldosterone**, which acts on the kidneys to retain sodium and thus reduces the amount of urine produced, conserving water. This action maintains a homeostatic equilibrium of ions in blood and extra-cellular fluids.

The adrenal cortex also produces sex hormones. The molecular structure of these steroids is very similar to that of the adrenal steroids. The chief sex hormone secreted by the human adrenal cortex is **androstenedione**; it contributes to the adult pattern of body hair in men and women. In some females the adrenal cortex produces more than the normal amounts of sex hormones, causing a more masculine appearance (see Chapter 12).

Regulation of the level of circulating adrenal cortical hormones involves several steps (Figure 7.15). The importance of the pituitary hormone ACTH can be demonstrated simply: removal of the pituitary results in shrinkage of the adrenal cortex and drastically reduced hormone secretion from the adrenal gland. ACTH promotes steroid synthesis in the adrenal gland; cortisol is secreted by the adrenal cortex only when ACTH is present. Adrenal steroids in turn exert a negative feedback effect on ACTH release. As the level of adrenal cortical hormones increases, ACTH secretion is suppressed, so the output of hormones from the adrenal cortex diminishes. When the levels of adrenal steroids fall, the pituitary ACTH-secreting cells are released from suppression, and the concentration of ACTH in the blood rises, leading to increased output of adrenal cortical hormones. A prominent influence on ACTH secretion is stress, both physiological and psychological.

Stress is any circumstance that throws us out of homeostatic balance. Such circumstances include unusual physiological states such as exposure to extreme cold or heat and an array of threatening psychological states. A complex array of physiological changes is elicited by stressors; foremost among them is the activation of pathways from the brain to the hypothalamus, the outputs of which lead to activation of the pituitary. As we have noted, hormones released from the pituitary include ACTH, which triggers the release of glucocorticoids from the adrenal cortex. Robert Sapolsky (1992) has found that high levels of glucocorticoids released during stress can actually kill nerve cells in the hippocampus. (Further discussion of stress and ACTH appears in Chapter 15.)

Thyroid Hormones Regulate Growth and Metabolism

Situated just below the vocal apparatus in the throat is the **thyroid gland** (see Figure 7.1). This gland produces and secretes several hormones. Two of these—**thyroxine** and **triiodothyronine**—are usually referred to as "thyroid hormones"; a third—calcitonin—

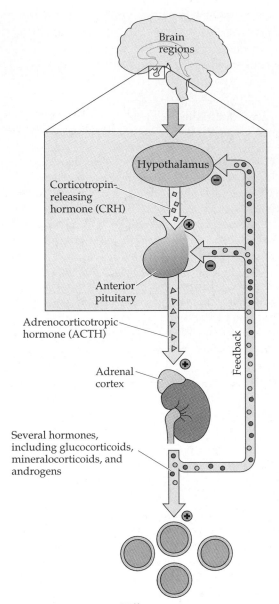

7.15 Adrenocorticoid Hormone Regulation
The level of circulating adrenal cortical hormones is regulated in several steps that involve both corticotropin-releasing hormone from the hypothalamus and adrenocorticotropic hormone secreted by the anterior pituitary.

promotes calcium deposition in bones and will not be discussed further. Certain thyroid cells produce these hormones, and a saclike collection of cells called the thyroid colloid stores them. The thyroid is unique among endocrine glands because it stores large amounts of hormone and releases it slowly; normally the thyroid has at least 100 days' supply of hormones.

Although thyroid hormones are amines—derived from amino acids—they behave like steroids. They bind to specialized receptors (part of the steroid receptor superfamily) found *inside* cells. The thyroid hormone–receptor complex then binds to DNA and regulates gene expression.

The control network for regulating thyroxine levels in blood is shown in Figure 7.10. The major control is exerted by **thyroid-stimulating hormone (TSH)** from the anterior pituitary gland. The secretion of TSH by the pituitary is controlled by two factors. The dominant one is the negative feedback from thyroid hormones circulating in the blood; they directly inhibit the pituitary, reducing TSH release. Second, **thyrotropin-releasing hormone (TRH)** produced by the hypothalamus stimulates TSH release from the pituitary. When the level of circulating thyroid hormone falls, both TRH and TSH are secreted; when TSH reaches the thyroid gland, it stimulates the production and release of thyroid hormones.

Knowledge of the feedback controls of thyroid output is often helpful in diagnosing undersecretion (hypothyroidism) or oversecretion (hyperthyroidism) of the thyroid gland, relatively common disorders. Hypothyroidism is often caused by reduced responsiveness of the thyroid gland to TSH. At first the hypothalamus and pituitary react to this lack of response by producing more and more TSH to bring thyroid hormone levels up to normal. Physicians can sometimes detect the increased TSH levels before levels of thyroid hormones have fallen appreciably.

Thyroid hormones are the only substances produced by the body that contain iodine, and their manufacture is critically dependent on the supply of iodine. In parts of the world where foods contain little iodine, many people suffer from hypothyroidism. In such cases the thyroid gland enlarges, driven by higher and higher TSH levels. In the attempt to produce more thyroid hormones, the gland swells, producing a goiter. The addition of a small amount of iodine to salt—subsequently referred to as "iodized salt"—is now a widespread practice designed to prevent this condition.

The major role of the thyroid is the regulation of metabolic processes, especially carbohydrate use. The thyroid hormones also influence growth; this function is especially evident when thyroid deficiency starts early in life. Besides stunted body growth and characteristic facial malformation, thyroid deficiency produces a marked reduction in brain size and cellular structure (branching of axons and dendrites is reduced). This state is called **cretinism** and is accompanied by mental retardation.

The Gonads Produce Steroid Hormones

Almost all aspects of reproductive behavior, including mating and parental behavior, depend on hormones. Since Chapter 12 is devoted to reproductive behavior and physiology, at this point we will only briefly note relevant hormones and some pertinent aspects of anatomy and physiology. Female and male **gonads** (ovaries and testes, respectively; see figure 7.1) consist of two different subcompartments—one to produce hormones and another to produce gametes (eggs or sperm). Hormone production is critical for triggering both reproductive behavior in the brain and gamete production in the gonads.

The testes.   Within the **testes** are several cell types. Interspersed among the sperm-producing cells (the Sertoli cells) are the Leydig cells, which produce and secrete the hormone **testosterone**. Testosterone and other male hormones are called **androgens** (from the Greek roots *andr-*, "man," and *gen-*, "to produce, create"). Production and release of testosterone is regulated by LH from the anterior pituitary. The pituitary hormone in turn is controlled by a hypothalamic releasing hormone, **gonadotropin-releasing hormone (GnRH)**, also called luteinizing hormone–releasing hormone. Testosterone controls a wide range of bodily changes that become visible at puberty, including changes in voice, hair growth, and genital size. Levels of testosterone vary during the day in adult males, although the connection between these daily rhythms and behavior remains a mystery. In species that breed only in certain seasons of the year, testosterone has especially marked effects on appearance and behavior—for example, the antlers and male–male fighting displayed by many species of deer. The regulation of testosterone secretion is summarized in Figure 7.16*a*.

The ovaries.   The paired female gonads, the ovaries, also produce both the mature gametes (ova [singular: ovum] or eggs) and hormones. However, hormonal secretion by the ovary is more complicated than by the testes. Production of ovarian hormones occurs in cycles, the duration of which varies with the species. In human beings the cycles last about four weeks, whereas in rats they last only four days. The ovary produces two major classes of steroid hormones: the **estrogens** (from the Greek *estrus*, "female sexual receptivity," and *gen-*, "to produce, create") and the **progestins** (from *pro*, meaning "favoring" and *gest* "gestation, pregnancy"). The most important estrogen is **estradiol**; the most influential progestin is **progesterone**. Ovarian production of these hor-

(a)

(b)

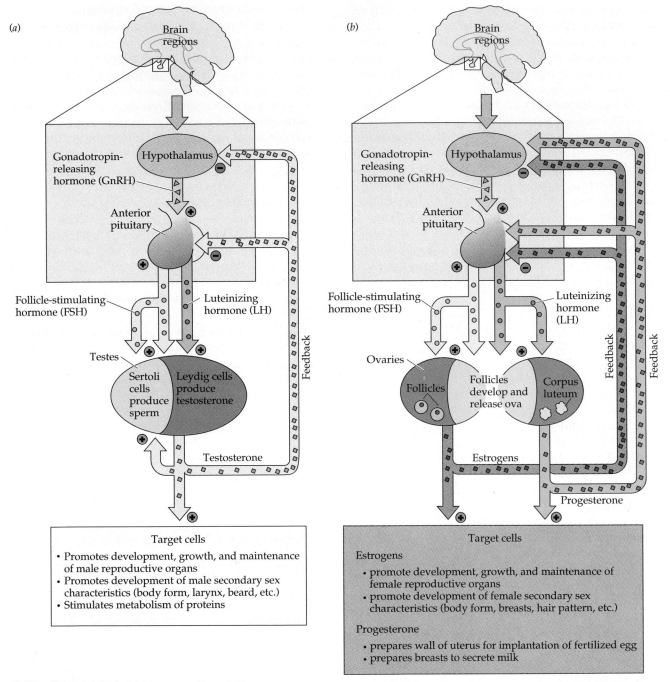

7.16 Gonadal Steroid Hormone Regulation
(a) In males the principal gonadal steroid secreted is testosterone. (b) The female
gonad produces two classes of steroids: estrogens and progestins.

mones is under the control of two tropic hormones of
the anterior pituitary, FSH and LH. The release of
these tropic hormones is controlled by GnRH from
the hypothalamus (Figure 7.16b).

Relations among gonadal hormones. All three classes of sex hormones—androgens, estrogens, and prog-

estins—have closely related chemical structures. They
and the adrenal steroids are all derived from cholesterol, and all have the basic structure of four interconnected carbon rings (see Figure 7.7b). Furthermore, estrogens are synthesized from androgens, and
androgens are synthesized from progestins. Different
organs differ in the relative amounts of these hor-

mones they produce. For example, the testis converts only a relatively small proportion of testosterone into estradiol, whereas the ovary converts most of the testosterone it makes into estradiol. There is no steroid found exclusively in either males or females; rather the two sexes differ in the proportion of these steroids. Some of the testosterone that enters brain cells is converted within those cells to estradiol, as we'll see in Chapter 12.

The Pineal Gland Secretes Melatonin

The **pineal gland** sits atop the brain stem and in mammals is overlaid by the cerebral hemispheres (Figure 7.17a). Whereas other brain structures are paired (left and right), each of us has only one pineal gland. This unique aspect of the pineal may explain why Descartes proposed that it could contain the

soul. Today we know that the pineal is innervated by the sympathetic nervous system, specifically by the superior cervical ganglion (see Figure 7.17a). In response to the activity of cells in this ganglion, the pineal releases an amine hormone called **melatonin.** The melatonin receptor seems to reside in cell membranes and is similar to receptors for peptide hormones. In many vertebrate species, the pineal secretion of melatonin controls whether animals are in breeding condition. Melatonin is released almost exclusively at night (Figure 7.17b). In seasonally breeding mammals such as hamsters, the lengthening nights of autumn affect activity in the superior cervical ganglion, which in turn causes the pineal to prolong its nocturnal release of melatonin. The hypothalamus responds to the prolonged exposure to melatonin by becoming extremely sensitive to the negative feedback effects of gonadal steroids. Consequently, less and less GnRH is released, resulting in less gonadotropin release and atrophy of the gonads. Lesion of the pineal will prevent such regression, whereas prolonged treatment of normal animals with melatonin will induce gonadal regression. In fact, one of the earliest hints of pineal function was the report that a boy with a tumor destroying the pineal underwent puberty early in life.

In birds, light from the environment penetrates the thin skull and reaches the pineal gland directly. Photosensitive cells in the pineal gland monitor daily light durations and direct regression of reproductive function in autumn. In several reptile species the pineal is close to the skull and even has an extension of photoreceptors providing a "third eye" in the back of the head. These photoreceptors do not form images but act as simple photocells, monitoring day length to regulate seasonal functions. In both birds

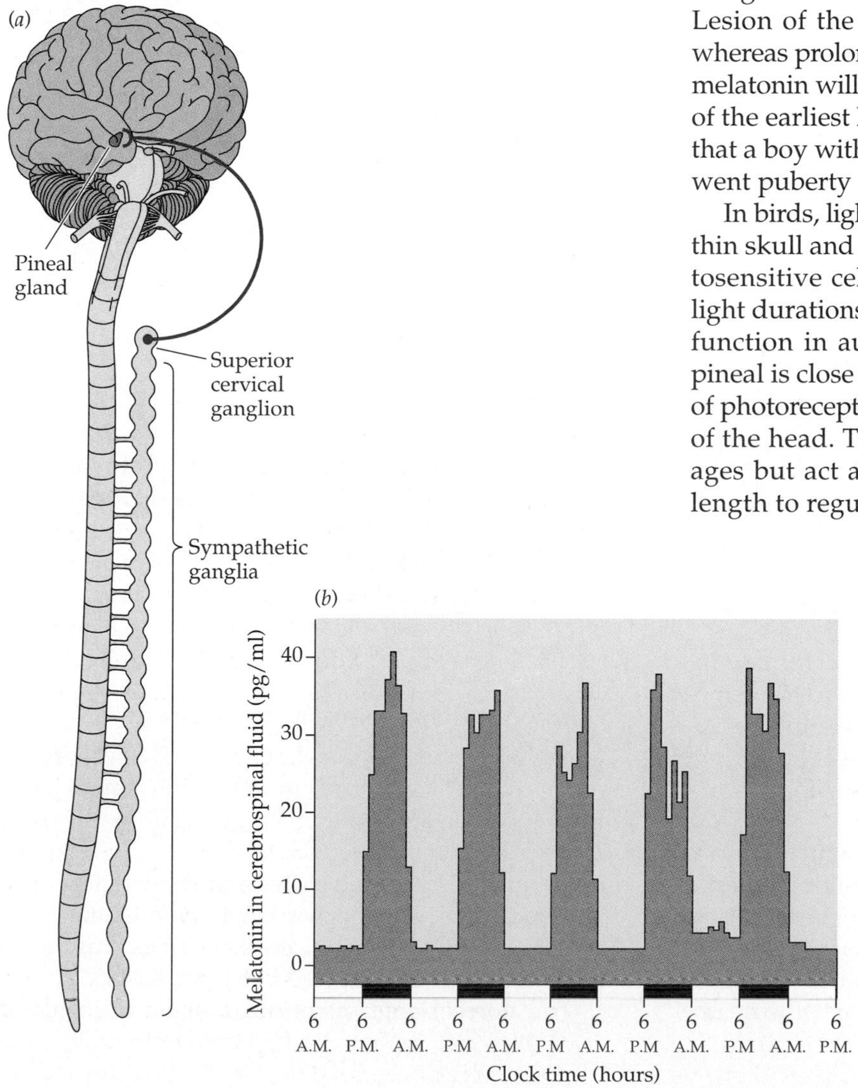

7.17 Regulation of the Pineal Gland
(a) The pea-shaped pineal gland sits close to the floor of the third ventricle, atop the brain stem. Innervated by the sympathetic nervous system, specifically the superior cervical ganglion, the pineal releases melatonin. (b) Melatonin is released almost exclusively during the night in a wide variety of vertebrates, including humans. After Reppert et al., 1979.

and mammals the return of gonadal function is independent of melatonin secretion; after a fixed period of time the hypothalamus becomes less sensitive to the negative feedback effects and the gonads grow and become functional again no matter what the day lengths or amount of melatonin secretion.

Humans are not, strictly speaking, seasonal breeders, but melatonin has been implicated in their daily cycles, such as sleep rhythms. Like other vertebrates, we release melatonin at night, and administering melatonin has been reported to induce sleep sooner at night. In fact, many recent studies indicate a role for melatonin in the timing of sleep. For example, melatonin has been used for treatment of jet lag. Petrie and coworkers (1993) studied the use of melatonin in an international airplane cabin crew. Some of the crew were given melatonin three days prior to international travel and continued to receive it five days after their return home. Other crew members received melatonin for five days after the flight. Both groups were compared to a placebo control. Jet lag, with its associated changes in alertness, was reported diminished for the group receiving melatonin only after the time zone shift. Other studies have shown that melatonin administered to humans shifts circadian rhythms (Lewy et al., 1992). Still other studies have shown that the onset of sleep in humans who work at night is not well synchronized with their melatonin rhythms. This finding might explain the sleep complaints of night workers (Sack, Blood, and Lewy, 1992).

The Pancreas Produces Two Main Hormones

Throughout the **pancreas** (which is located in the back of the abdominal cavity; see Figure 7.1) are clusters of cells called **islets of Langerhans**, which secrete hormones directly into the bloodstream. These endocrine cells are intermingled with other cells that perform an exocrine function, secreting digestive enzymes (such as bile) into ducts leading to the gastrointestinal tract.

Hormones secreted by the islets of Langerhans include **insulin** and **glucagon**, both of which have potent and frequently reciprocal effects on glucose utilization. Insulin is produced in one type of cell within the islets (beta cells), and glucagon is secreted by another type (alpha cells).

Both nonneural and neural factors regulate the release of insulin. The level of glucose in the bloodstream, monitored by cells of the islets of Langerhans, is a critical determinant. As the level of blood sugar rises above a certain concentration, insulin is released. Among the actions of insulin are increased glucose up-take in some tissues, such as muscle, and reduced output of glucose from the liver. These effects produce a lowering of blood glucose. As noted earlier, this reaction is a direct, negative feedback effect that does not involve a tropic hormone from the pituitary.

The effects of insulin directly antagonize those of glucagon, which increases blood glucose levels. The hormonal regulation of insulin and glucagon is summarized in Figure 7.18. In addition, there is paracrine action between adjacent alpha and beta cells of the islets of Langerhans; that is, glucagon and insulin can oppose each other locally within the pancreas as well as by using the endocrine route. The reciprocal action of insulin and glucagon helps keep blood glucose within the range necessary for proper functioning of the brain and other organs.

The release of insulin is also controlled by neural impulses that arrive at the pancreas via the parasympathetic vagus nerve. When a person eats, insulin is released even before glucose reaches the bloodstream. This early release occurs in response to taste stimulation in the mouth. (Other stimuli that are normally associated with eating can also cause the release of insulin.) Cutting the vagus nerve in experimental animals prevents the early release of insulin in response to the taste of food, but it does not interfere with the later response to glucose in the bloodstream, showing that the conditioned response operates via the nervous system.

Hormones Have Many Different Effects on Behavior

As we mentioned earlier, endocrine influences on structural or functional states frequently involve the interaction of several different hormones. In this section we will consider briefly some hormonal effects on homeostasis and on learning and memory; these effects involve several endocrine systems. Hormonal effects on growth are considered in Box 7.2.

Hormones Help Maintain Homeostasis

Many bodily mechanisms have evolved to ensure the relative constancy of the internal environment. Hormones play major roles in regulating many basic homeostatic processes, such as those that govern the distribution of ions and fluids and those that control the concentration of glucose in blood and brain. Consider the regulation of glucose in the blood as an example of the hormonal role in homeostasis.

The normal concentration of glucose in blood

(a) Glucagon regulation

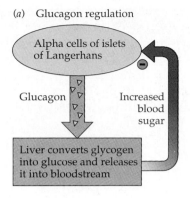

(b) Insulin regulation

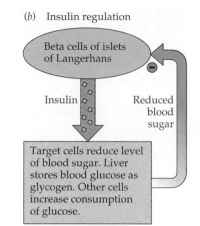

(c) Regulation by both glucagon and insulin

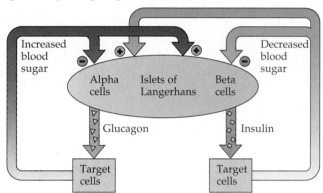

7.18 Regulation of Blood Glucose
Both glucagon and insulin are released by the pancreas, and each affects the availability of glucose in circulation (*a, b*). Normally, both are at work in a reciprocal fashion (*c*).

varies between 80 and 130 milligrams per 100 milliliters. Some hormones—for example, glucagon, growth hormone, and cortisol—lead to an increase in glucose concentration in the blood. Insulin causes a decrease in glucose concentration in blood. The balance among these hormones maintains the glucose concentration of blood within a range that provides for maximal production of energy in a variety of circumstances. The level of blood sugar itself also inhibits the secretion of some hormones.

Failure in these controls has major consequences for bodily organs. In diabetes mellitus, a disorder characterized by insulin deficiency, glucose levels rise. These high blood levels of glucose (hyperglycemia) can produce pathological changes in body tissues leading to symptoms such as diabetic blindness. Such destruction of tissue may arise from the use of metabolic pathways that yield unusual metabolic products.

Homeostatic mechanisms of glucose regulation are particularly prominent during periods of stress or strong exercise. Hormonal changes accompanying

these states enhance the release of glucose from the liver. If insufficient glucose is released, however, the central nervous system is unable to produce its full response. Glucose release is part of the alarm reaction, the prompt "fight or flight" response of the body to any stressor. Prolonged stress leads to long-term reactions that involve several other hormones.

Hormonal mechanisms in homeostatic systems of water balance, energy balance, and body weight will be taken up in Chapter 13.

Hormones Can Affect Learning and Memory

Hormones affect both the early development of capacities to learn and remember, and the efficient use of these capacities after they have been formed. Thyroid hormones, as already indicated, are important in the early development of the nervous system. Insufficient thyroid secretion results in fewer synaptic connections than usual, leading to cretinism. Experimental studies have given us more information about this condition: if a drug that inhibits thyroid function

Table 7.4

Hormonal Disorders and Associated Cognitive, Emotional, and Psychiatric Disorders

HORMONAL DISORDER	IMPAIRED COGNITION[a]	ANXIETY[a]	DEPRESSION[a]	APATHY[b]	DEMENTIA[b]
Hyperthyroidism	+	++	+	++	—
Hypothyroidism	+	+	++	++	+
Hypercortisolism	+	++	++	—	—
Hypocortisolism	—	+	++	+	+
Panhypopituitarism[c]	—	+	++	+	+
Hyperparathyroidism	+	+	++	++	++[d]
Hypoparathyroidism	?	++	+	?	+++
Hyperinsulinism	+	++	—	++	+
Hypoinsulinism	+	—	—	—	—
Excessive vasopressin	+	—	—	+	?
Deficient vasopressin	+	—	—	—	—
Hyperprolactinemia	—	+	++[e]	+[f]	—

[a] + = sometimes; ++ = often.
[b] + = usually mild; ++ = usually moderate; +++ = usually prominent.
[c] Undersecretion of all or nearly all anterior pituitary hormones.
[d] Predominantly in the elderly; may be of short duration.
[e] In females more than in males.
[f] In males.

is administered to infant rats, the results are a decrease in the formation of cortical synapses and significantly impaired learning ability. Giving such "experimental cretin" rats enriched experience as they grow has been reported to diminish their behavioral deficiencies to a large extent (Davenport, 1976). (The effects of enriched experience on the brain will be discussed further in Chapter 17.)

The ability of juvenile or adult animals to learn and remember can be affected by the hypothalamic hormones ACTH, AVP, and oxytocin as well as by particular fractions or analogs of these hormones, and by the catecholaminergic hormones of the adrenal medulla, norepinephrine and epinephrine (Mc-

Gaugh, 1992; Schulteis and Martinez, 1992). Whether these compounds are acting as hormones or neurotransmitters to affect learning is unknown. Some of these studies will be taken up in Chapter 17. One hypothesis being tested in this research is that the emotional aspects of a learning situation affect the release of hormones, and the hormones present during the period following training modulate the formation of memory; that is, the pleasure or pain or stress involved in an episode of learning will, through hormonal aftereffects, help determine how well the situation is remembered. Such hormonal effects may be important in reinforcing learning during crucial situations.

PSYCHOSIS AND DELIRIUM[a]	PSYCHIATRIC DISORDERS WITH SIMILAR SYMPTOMS
+	Anxiety disorder, affective disorder
++	Affective disorder, somatoform disorder, psychotic disorders, dementia
++	Anxiety disorder, affective disorder, somatoform disorder, psychotic disorders
++	Affective disorder, anorexia nervosa, psychotic disorders
++	Anxiety disorder, affective disorder, anorexia nervosa, psychotic disorders
++	Affective disorder, psychotic disorders, dementia
++	Anxiety disorder, somatoform disorder, psychotic disorders, dementia
++	Anxiety disorder, somatoform disorder, psychotic disorders, dementia
+	
+	May exacerbate psychosis
+	Psychogenic polydipsia
—	Affective disorder

Endocrine Pathology Can Produce Extreme Effects on Human Behavior

Both deficient and excessive hormone secretion are associated with a variety of human physiological, anatomical, and behavioral disorders (Erhardt and Goldman, 1992). Some of these disorders have long been known, especially those that include either marked behavioral changes or anatomical abnormalities. Table 7.4 lists an array of hormonal disorders and their associated cognitive, emotional, and psychiatric changes. Many hormonal disorders resemble psychiatric disorders. For example, parathyroid deficiency results in calcium deposition in the basal ganglia and a symptom portrait that resembles a severe psychotic state, schizophrenia. Patients with excessive thyroid release frequently appear intensely anxious; those with decreased thyroid release may show cognitive impairments and depression. Recently, researchers discovered an inherited form of attention deficit disorder in children that involves decreased

sensitivity to thyroid hormone (Hauser et al., 1993). Excessive release of glucocorticoids by the adrenal cortex (Cushing's syndrome) is accompanied by many bodily and psychological changes including fatigue, depression, unusual deposition of hair, and other autonomic changes. Several studies have indicated that affective changes, especially depression, frequently long precede other physiological effects of excessive cortisol secretion. In some people who take excessive amounts of glucocorticoids, such as athletes, psychiatric symptoms can emerge that include periods of intense psychotic behavior.

Endocrine pathology that affects behavior also includes changes in receptor sensitivity to adequate amounts of released hormones. In Chapter 12 we describe dramatic examples of androgen receptor insensitivity in humans.

Hormonal and Neural Systems Interact to Produce Integrated Responses

Although we have focused on the endocrine system in this chapter, the endocrine system participates in interactions with many other organs, including, of course, the brain. Figure 7.19 incorporates the endocrine system into a larger schema of reciprocal relations between body and behavior. Let's examine some of these relations. Incoming sensory stimuli elicit nerve impulses that go to several brain regions, including the cerebral cortex, cerebellum, and hypothalamus. Behavioral responses bring further changes in stimulation. For example, the person may approach or go away from the original source of stimulation, and this action will alter the size of the visual image, the loudness of sound, and so forth. Meanwhile the endocrine system is altering the response characteristics of the person. If evaluation of the stimulus calls for action, energy is mobilized through hormonal routes. The state of some sensory receptor organs may also be altered, thus modifying further processing of stimuli.

Many behaviors require neural and hormonal coordination. For example, when a stressful situation is perceived through neural sensory channels, hormonal secretions prepare the individual to make energetic responses. The muscular movements for the "fight or flight" response are controlled neurally, but the required energy is mobilized through hormonal routes. Another example of neural and hormonal coordination is the milk letdown response (see Figure 7.12).

Four kinds of signals from one cell to another are possible in a system with both nerve cells and endocrine cells: neural-to-neural, neural-to-endocrine, endocrine-to-endocrine, and endocrine-to-neural. All four kinds can be found in the courtship behavior of the ring dove (Friedman, 1977). The visual stimulation and perception of a male dove that sees a female involve (1) neural-to-neural transmission. The particular visual stimulus activates (2) a neural-to-endocrine link, which causes some neurosecretory cells in the male's hypothalamus to secrete LH. (3) Endocrine-to-endocrine signals cause increased production and release of the hormone testosterone. Testosterone, in turn, alters the excitability of some neurons through (4) an endocrine-to-neural link and thus causes the male to display courtship behavior. The female dove

responds to this display, thus providing new visual stimulation to the male and further neural-to-neural signals within his brain. (We will discuss the complex interactions of male and female doves further in Chapter 12, where we will see other examples of the coordination of neural and endocrine activities.)

Our circle schema in Figure 7.19 helps reveal how we discover relations between endocrine activity and behavior. The level of circulating hormones can be altered by chemical intervention, which can affect behavior. For example, since cortisone was introduced as a drug in 1949, occasional cases of Cushing's syndrome have appeared in patients who had been given this glucocorticoid in doses that caused an over-

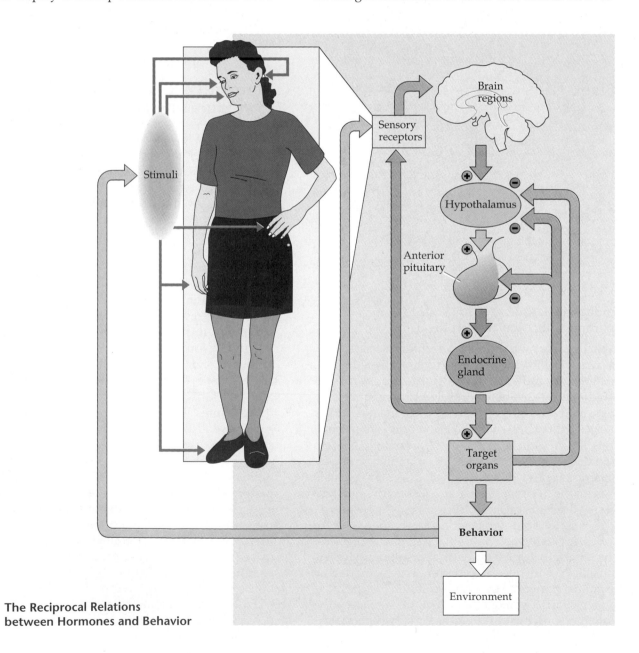

7.19 The Reciprocal Relations between Hormones and Behavior

supply of the hormone. In another example, removal of the adrenals and subsequent deprivation of aldosterone in experimental animals causes excretion of salts, which greatly increases the animals' preference for salty water. In fact, rats lacking adrenal glands show an amazing preference for salt solutions.

Experiential interventions may also cause rapid changes in the output of many endocrine glands. For example, the output of thyroid hormone responds to many environmental influences. Starting to exercise increases the level of thyroxine in the circulation. Putting animals in a cold temperature increases their thyroid activity, and keeping them there increases the size of the thyroid gland. On the other hand, physical stresses, pain, and unpleasant emotional situations decrease thyroid output, probably by modulating the secretion of TRH from the hypothalamus.

Summary

1. Hormones are chemical compounds that act as signals in the body. They are secreted by endocrine glands or specialized cells into the bloodstream and are taken up by receptor molecules in target cells.

2. Neural communication differs from hormonal communication in that neural signals travel rapidly over fixed pathways, whereas hormonal signals spread more slowly and throughout the body.

3. The neural and hormonal communication systems have several characteristics in common: Both utilize chemical messages; the same substance that acts as a hormone in some locations is a synaptic transmitter in others. Both systems manufacture, store, and release chemical messengers. Both use specific receptors and may employ second messengers.

4. Some hormones have receptors in a wide variety of cells and can therefore influence the activity of most cells in the body. Others have receptors in only certain special cells or organs.

5. Hormones act by promoting the proliferation and differentiation of cells and by modulating the activity of cells that have already differentiated.

6. Protein and amine hormones bind to specific receptor molecules at the surface of the target cell membrane and activate second messenger molecules inside the cell. Steroid hormones pass through the membrane and bind to receptor molecules inside the cell.

7. A negative feedback system monitors and controls the rate of secretion of each hormone. In the simplest case, the hormone acts upon target cells, leading them to change the amount of a substance they release; this in turn regulates the output of the endocrine gland.

8. Several hormones are controlled by a more complex feedback system: a releasing hormone from the hypothalamus regulates the release of an anterior pituitary tropic hormone, which in turn controls secretion by an endocrine gland. In this case feedback of the endocrine hormone acts mainly at the hypothalamus and anterior pituitary.

9. Endocrine influences on structures and functions often involve more than one hormone, as in growth, homeostasis, metabolism, and learning and memory.

10. Many behaviors involve the coordination of neural and hormonal components. The transmission of messages in the body may involve neural-to-neural, neural-to-endocrine, endocrine-to-endocrine, or endocrine-to-neural links.

Recommended Reading

Bern, H. 1990. The "new" endocrinology: Its scope and its impact. *American Zoologist* 30:877–885.

Becker, J. B., Breedlove, S. M., and Crews, D. (eds.) 1992. *Behavioral Endocrinology.* MIT Press, Cambridge, MA.

Grossman, A. (ed.) 1992. *Clinical Endocrinology.* Blackwell Scientific Publications, London.

Hadley, M. E. 1996. *Endocrinology.* 4th ed. Prentice Hall, NJ.

Matsumoto, A. and Ishii, S. 1992. *Atlas of Endocrine Organs.* Springer-Verlag, Berlin.

Nelson, R. J. 1995. *An Introduction to Behavioral Endocrinology.* Sinauer Associates, Sunderland, MA.

Wilson, J. D. and Foster, D. W. 1992. *Williams Textbook of Endocrinology.* 8th ed. W. B. Saunders, Philadelphia.

PART 3

Information Processing in Perceptual and Motor Systems

Light from the sun warms our skin and stimulates our eyes. A chorus of sounds, ranging from the songs of insects to the hearty performances of opera singers stimulates our ears. Winds bend the hairs on the skin and carry substances that lead to a sense of pleasant or unpleasant odors. The food we eat affects receptors in the mouth, the stomach, and the brain. All about us there is a wide range of energies and substances that excite our senses and supply our brains with a vast array of information about many external and internal happenings. The success of any animal—including humans—in dealing with the tasks of survival depends on its ability to construct reliable representations of some of the physical characteristics of its environment. In most cases, however, sensory systems are not slavish, passive copiers and reflectors of impinging stimuli—quite the contrary. Evolutionary success calls for far more selective action. For any species, sensory systems construct only partial and selective portraits of the world.

Sensory inputs to the brain do not merely provide "pictures in the head"; they often incite the individual to act. Picture the simple case when a sound occurs suddenly: Our eyes almost automatically turn toward the source of the sound. Some movements are not directly driven or triggered by sensory events but reflect intrinsic programs of action, which may involve sensory inputs only as modulators. How information processing occurs in both perceptual and motor systems is our theme in Part Three.

Lucas Samaras, *Photo-Transformation*, December 17, 1973

Sensory Processing

- *An Overview of the Plan of Sensory Systems*

- *Optimal Sensory Systems Must Meet Five Criteria*

- *Different Species Detect Different Aspects of the World*

- *Change in Electrical Potential in Receptors Is the Initial Stage of Sensory Processing*

- *Principles of Sensory Information Processing*

Touch and Pain

- *Touch Includes a Variety of Sensations*

- *Pain Is an Unpleasant but Adaptive Experience*

- *Pain Can Be Controlled by a Variety of Mechanisms and Pathways*

CHAPTER 8

Principles of Sensory Processing and Experience: Touch and Pain

Orientation

All around us there are many different types of energy that affect us in various ways. Some molecules traveling through the air cause us to note particular odors; we detect waves of compression and expansion of air as sounds. Our abilities to detect, recognize, and appreciate these varied energies depend on the characteristics of sensory systems. These systems include receptors specialized to detect specific energies and the neural pathways of the spinal cord and brain that receive input from these receptors. For each species, however, certain features of surrounding energies have become especially significant for adaptive success. For example, the bat darting through the evening sky is specially equipped to detect ultrasonic cries. Most humans, on the other hand, are hardly able to detect such sounds. Some snakes, such as boa constrictors, have infrared sensing organs that enable them to generate a heat-sensitive image of their surroundings, thus enabling them to locate potential prey. Each species has distinctive windows on the world based on the energy sensitivities of its receptors and on how its nervous system processes information from the receptors. In our discussion of the workings of sensory systems, we will first consider some of the basic principles of sensory processing and then examine how particular sensory systems work.

Sensory Processing

An Overview of the Plan of Sensory Systems

All sensory systems include a basic plan that begins at the sites where energies impinging on the body are converted into a form that activates nerve cells. All animals have specialized body parts that are particularly sensitive to some forms of energy. These body parts—**sensory receptor organs**—act as filters: they detect and respond to some stimuli and exclude others. Furthermore, receptors convert energy into the language of the nervous system—electrical signals. In any animal, the processing of sensory information involves codes. These codes are rules that translate attributes of stimulus energy, such as intensity, into activity of nerve cells.

Knowing these rules, the experimenter should be able to look at a pattern of nerve impulses and distinguish between a beautiful sunset and a tasty bit of food. Of course, we are only slowly gaining understanding of these rules, and up to now our knowledge of coding has been restricted mainly to simple dimensions of stimuli, such as color and spatial location. Sensory systems are complex in part because the processing of sensory neural activity involves many different brain regions, and each may use different transformations of signals. Moreover, the way an event is represented in the nervous system may differ in different brain regions, because each region does not merely passively reflect the barrage of neural inputs, but actively processes these inputs. This processing can be described as filtering, abstracting, and integrating, all of which affect how events are represented in the brain.

All this information processing requires extensive neural circuitry. The evolution of specialized sensory receptors has led to the development of related regions of the brain. In fact, examining the relative sizes of sensory regions of the nervous system in a given species can reveal the degree to which different senses contribute to the adaptation of that species to its environment (see Box 3.1).

Optimal Sensory Systems Must Meet Five Criteria

At the outset of our discussion on the basic principles of sensory mechanisms, it is useful to consider some ideal properties from both biological and engineering perspectives. These perspectives help us understand the characteristics of sensory systems and the evolutionary forces that have generated them. The adaptations of animals to particular environmental niches emphasize the costs and benefits of various sensory mechanisms. Let's consider some of the optimal features and some realistic compromises.

A Sensory System Requires Different Receptors to Discriminate among Forms of Energy

The types of energies and the range of substances in the world are quite broad. Different kinds of energy, such as light and sound, need different receptors to convert them into neural activity, just as you need a camera, not an audiotape recorder, to take a picture. We gain information by distinguishing among types of stimulus energy. We may appreciate the poet who writes, "The dawn came up like thunder," but most of the time we want to know whether a sudden dramatic sensory event was auditory or visual, tactile or olfactory. Furthermore, different senses furnish us with quite different information: we may see a car hurtling toward us, hear the whine of a mosquito circling us, or smell gas escaping, but we might not hear the car until it is too late, and we would not smell the mosquito or see the gas. Thus, our model sensory system should provide us with the means of detecting and distinguishing among different forms of energy.

The pioneer physiologist Johannes Müller explored this requirement of sensory systems early in the nineteenth century. He proposed the doctrine of **specific nerve energies**, which states that the receptors and neural channels for the different senses are independent and operate in their own special ways. For example, no matter how the eye is stimulated—by light or mechanical pressure or by electrical shock—the resulting sensation is always visual. Because Müller formulated his hypothesis before the nature of nervous transmission was known, he could suppose that the different sensory systems of the brain use different kinds of energy to carry their messages. Today, we know that the messages for the different senses—such as seeing, hearing, touch, pain, and sensation of temperature—are kept separate and distinct not by the way systems carry their messages, but by the way they keep their neural tracts separate.

It would be costly, however, for each animal species to be sensitive to all the kinds of energy in its environment. Each species therefore has evolved the sensory detectors it needs to respond to certain forms of stimulation; even the external appearances of receptor organs differ markedly among species (Figure 8.1). However, species are either poorly equipped, or

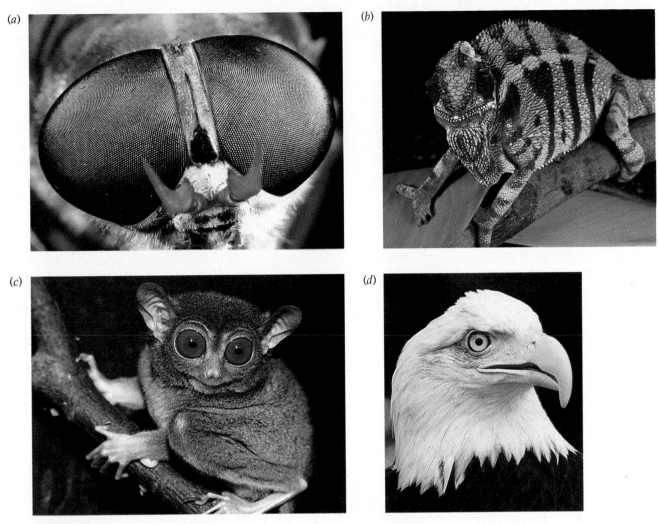

8.1 Variety of Eyes
(*a*) Compound eye of a tabanid fly. (*b*) Panther chameleon, with independent movement of the eyes. (*c*) Philippine tarsier with large eyes specialized for nocturnal foraging. (*d*) American bald eagle with eyes specialized for high acuity.

not equipped at all, for other forms of stimulation. For example, we can hardly detect surrounding electrical fields, but some fish have receptors that are acutely responsive to very small surrounding electrical fields. They rely on detection of electrical fields to guide them in murky water.

A Sensory System Should Discriminate among Different Intensities of Stimulation

Many forms of energy have a broad range of intensities. For example, a sonic boom brings to the ear millions of times more energy than the tick of a watch, and sunlight at noon has 10 million times more energy than the wan light of the first quarter moon. The optimal visual sensory system would be able to rep-

resent stimulus values over these broad ranges so that the viewer could always discriminate accurately, neither groping in the dark nor being blinded by the glare of intense light. However, because sensitivity to very feeble stimuli may require highly specialized, and therefore costly, sensory detectors, we must settle for some realistic lower limit.

If the system is to respond to a wide range of intensities, it should be sensitive to differences in intensity; that is, it should be able to provide large responses for small changes in the strength of a stimulus. The absolute value of a stimulus is seldom of major adaptive significance. In most instances the important signal for adaptive success is sensitivity to *change* in the stimulus. Thus, we respond mainly to changes—whether they are changes in intensity, quality, or location of the stimulus.

A Sensory System Should Respond Reliably

In a reliable sensory system, the relation between any signal in the external or internal environment and the sensory system's response to that signal is consistent. Imagine your confusion if a cold stimulus randomly elicited the responses cold, warm, painful, and slippery. To establish useful representations of the world, our sensory system must work reliably.

A customary way to improve reliability of a system is to increase the number of its components. Using several different circuits to process the same stimulus (parallel processing) is a conventional way to ensure reliability. The backup plans that ensure reliability in engineering designs generally provide such "fail-safe" options. Increasing the number of components in biological systems, however, requires greater metabolic expense and may compromise speed.

A Sensory System Should Respond Rapidly

Optimal adjustment to the world requires that sensory information be processed rapidly. As a driver, you have to perceive the motion of other cars swiftly and correctly to avoid collisions. Similarly, it does not do a predator much good to recognize prey unless it can do so both rapidly and accurately. Thus, we have come up against a conflict between optimal properties: they must be able to respond both reliably and rapidly.

A Sensory System Should Suppress Extraneous Information

Have you ever tried to hold a conversation on a dance floor? Could you hear anything besides the overwhelming input of the music? This example illustrates a paradox. In describing the optimal sensory system, we have emphasized the need for exquisite sensitivity and reliability, but now we are arguing that this extraordinary system should also be able to ignore some of the world! From moment to moment, particular stimuli may be especially important, while other stimuli fade into insignificance. The fragrance of perfume may be quite compelling in an intimate situation but a bit too much when reading a road map. As we will see, different sensory devices suppress stimuli in different ways. These include varying the response thresholds, adaptation, and different forms of direct and indirect controls.

How are the optimal properties we have just discussed realized in the sensory systems of human be-

Table 8.1

Sensory Systems, Their Modalities, and Adequate Stimuli

TYPE OF SENSORY SYSTEM	MODALITY	ADEQUATE STIMULI
Mechanical	Touch	Contact with or deformation of body surface
	Hearing	Sound vibrations in air or water
	Vestibular	Head movement and orientation
	Joint	Position and movement
	Muscle	Tension
Photic	Seeing	Visible radiant energy
Thermal	Cold	Decrement of skin temperature
	Warm	Increment of skin temperature
Electrical	(No common name because humans do not have this sense)	Differences in density of electrical currents
Chemical	Smell	Odorous substances dissolved in air or water in the nasal cavity
	Taste	Taste stimuli; in mammals the categories of taste experience are sweet, sour, salty, bitter
	Common chemical	Changes in CO_2, pH, osmotic pressure

ings and other species? Let's examine some basic principles of all sensory systems.

Different Species Detect Different Aspects of the World

From the physicist's point of view, the stimuli that animals detect are forms of physical energy or chemical substances that can be defined and described by using the scales or measures of physics and chemistry. For example, a sound-level meter can be used to measure the intensity of an acoustic stimulus. But, as we have said, not all the forms of physical energy that the physicist or chemist can describe are necessarily potential stimuli for an animal. Some forms of energy, such as radio waves, cannot be detected by the sensory systems of any existing animal. Table 8.1 classifies sensory systems, giving the kinds of stimuli and receptors related to each system. The term **adequate stimulus** refers to the type of stimulus for which a given sensory organ is particularly adapted. The adequate

stimulus for the eye is photic (light) energy; although mechanical pressure on the eye or an electrical shock can stimulate the retina and produce sensations of light, these are not adequate stimuli for the eye.

Sensory Systems of Particular Animals Have a Restricted Range of Responsiveness

For any single form of physical energy, the sensory systems of a particular animal are quite selective. For example, humans do not hear sounds in the frequency range above 20,000 hertz (Hz), a range we call ultrasonic. To a bat, however, air vibrations of 50,000 Hz would be sound waves, just as would vibrations of 10,000 Hz. Primates in general are deficient in the ability to hear sounds between 20,000 and 80,000 Hz, although many small mammals have good sensory abilities in this range. The range of hearing for larger mammals is even lower than that of humans. Figure 8.2 compares the auditory ranges of a few animals. In the visual realm, too, some animals can detect stimuli that we cannot. For example, bees see in the ultraviolet range of light.

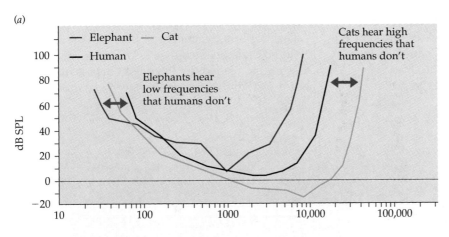

(a)

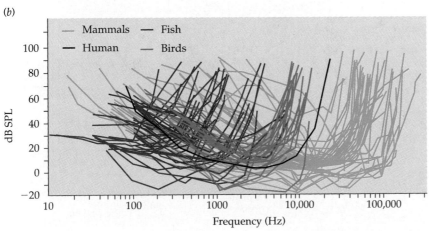

(b)

8.2 Do You Hear What I Hear?
(*a*) Auditory sensitivity ranges of three mammals. (*b*) Auditory sensitivity ranges of many species of fish, birds, and mammals. Note that the species within a class detect a similar range of frequencies.

Receptor Cells Are Responsible for the Initial Stage of Sensory Processing

Detection of energy starts with the properties of **receptor cells**. A given receptor cell is specialized to detect particular energies or chemicals. Upon exposure to a stimulus, a receptor cell converts the energy into a change in the electrical potential across its membrane. Changing the signal in this way is called **sensory transduction** (devices that convert energy from one form to another are known as transducers, and the process is called transduction). Receptors are transducers that are the starting points for the neural activity that leads to sensory perception. Some different receptor cells in skin are shown in Figure 8.3. We will look at these types in more detail later in the chapter.

Most receptors are associated with nerve endings. For example, various kinds of corpuscles are associated with nerve endings in the skin. The eye has specialized receptor cells that convert photic energy into electrical charges that stimulate the fibers of the optic nerve. The inner ear has specialized hair cells that transduce mechanical energy into electrical signals that stimulate the fibers of the auditory nerve.

Across the animal kingdom, receptors offer enormous diversity. A wide array of sizes, shapes, and forms reflects the varying survival needs of different animals. As we have seen already, for some snakes detectors of infrared radiation are essential, and several species of fish depend on receptors of electrical energy. Evolutionary processes have led to the emergence of specialized sensors attuned to the inputs or signals characteristic of particular environmental niches. Thus, we can view receptors as embodying strategies for success in particular worlds. Often receptor characteristics that are optimal from an evolutionary viewpoint closely match the criteria for optimal performance derived from engineering.

Change in Electrical Potential in Receptors Is the Initial Stage of Sensory Processing

The structure of a receptor determines the forms of energy to which it will respond. In all cases the steps between the impact of energy at a receptor and the initiation of nerve impulses in a nerve fiber leading away from the receptor involve local changes of membrane potential; these are referred to as **generator potentials**. (In most instances, the generator potential resembles the excitatory postsynaptic potentials discussed in Chapter 5.) These electrical charges are the necessary and sufficient conditions for generating nerve impulses. They are part of the causal link between stimulus and nerve impulse.

The details of the generator potential process were explored by Loewenstein (1971) in an elegant study on a receptor called the **Pacinian corpuscle**. This receptor is found throughout the body in skin and

8.3 Various Receptors in Skin
The different functions of several of these receptors are compared in Figure 8.14.

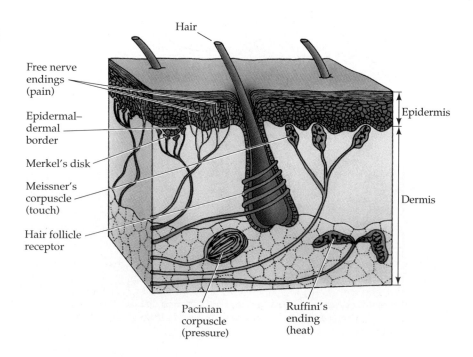

Hair

Free nerve endings (pain)

Epidermal–dermal border

Merkel's disk

Meissner's corpuscle (touch)

Hair follicle receptor

Epidermis

Dermis

Pacinian corpuscle (pressure)

Ruffini's ending (heat)

muscle, but is especially prominent in tissue overlying the abdominal cavity. It is made of a neural fiber that enters a structure resembling a tiny onion consisting of concentric layers of tissue separated by fluid (Figure 8.4*a*).

Mechanical stimuli delivered to the corpuscle produce a graded electrical potential whose amplitude is directly proportional to the strength of the stimulus. When this electrical event reaches sufficient amplitude, the nerve impulse is generated. Careful dissection of the corpuscle, leaving the bared axon terminal intact, shows that this graded potential—the

generator potential—is initiated in the nerve terminal. Pressing the corpuscle bends this terminal, which leads to the generator event. The sequence of excitatory events is as follows:

1. Mechanical stimulation deforms the corpuscle.

2. This deformation leads to mechanical stretch of the tip of the axon.

3. Mechanical effects open pores in the axonal membrane allowing sodium ions to enter (Figure 8.4*b*). When the generator potential reaches threshold amplitude, it can elicit nerve impulses (Figure 8.4*c*).

(*a*)

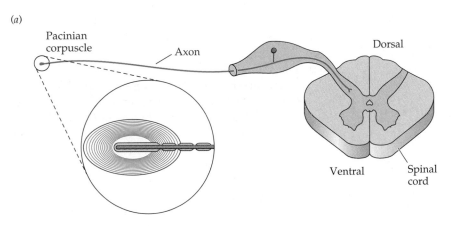

(*b*) Membrane, resting

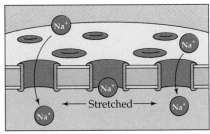

(*c*)

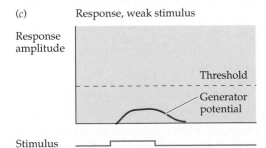
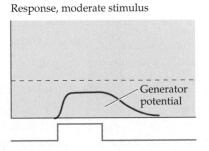
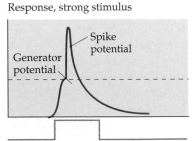

8.4   Structure and Function of the Pacinian Corpuscle
(*a*) Pacinian corpuscle and afferent nerve fiber; nerve ending within the corpuscle. (*b*) Resting membrane of nerve ending. At rest, the ion channels are too narrow to admit sodium (Na⁺) ions. Pressure on the corpuscle stretches part of the neuron membrane, enlarging the ion channels and permitting entry of Na⁺, which initiates an action potential. (*c*) Responses of neuron to stimuli of increasing intensity.

In some receptor systems—for example, hair cells in the inner ear—the generator events are more complicated. Some researchers have suggested the following sequence of events:

1. Mechanical stimulation bends hairs.
2. Membrane deformation creates a receptor potential in the hair cell.
3. A chemical is released at the base of the hair cell.
4. This transmitter flows across the cleft and stimulates the nerve terminal.
5. The generator potential is produced in the nerve cell.

Let's now examine the sensory events that stimuli elicit at sensory receptors.

Principles of Sensory Information Processing

Thinkers in ancient Greece believed that the nerves were tubes through which tiny bits of stimulus objects traveled to the brain, there to be analyzed and recognized. Even after gaining accurate knowledge of neural conduction in the twentieth century, many investigators still thought that the sensory nerves simply transmitted accurate information about stimulation to the brain centers. Now, however, it is clear that the sense organs and peripheral sensory pathways convey only limited—even distorted—information to the centers. The brain is an active processor of information, not a copier. In fact, a good deal of selection and analysis takes place in the peripheral sensory pathways. Here we will examine some basic aspects of the processing of sensory information; coding, sensory adaptation, lateral inhibition, suppression, receptive fields, and attention.

Sensory Events Are Represented by Neural Codes

Information about the world is represented in the circuits of the nervous system by electrical potentials in single nerve cells or groups of cells. We have already considered the first step in this process—the transformation of energy at receptors (that is, transduction). Now we must ask, How are these events represented in the neural pathways? In some manner electrical events in nerve cells "stand for" or represent stimuli impinging on an organism. This process is often referred to as **coding**. (A code is a set of rules for translating information from one form to another. For example, we can code a message in English for telegraphic transmission, by using the set of rules that make up the dot–dash Morse code.) Sensory information can be encoded into all-or-none action potentials according to several criteria: the frequency of the impulses, the rhythm at which clusters of impulses occur, and so forth. We will examine possible neural representations of the intensity, quality, position, and pattern of stimuli.

How Intense Is the Stimulus?

We respond to sensory stimuli over a wide range of intensities. Furthermore, within this range we can detect small differences of intensity. How are different intensities of the same stimulus represented in the nervous system?

Within a single nerve cell the frequency of nerve impulses can represent stimulus intensity (Figure 8.5*a*). However, only a limited range of different sensory intensities can be represented in this manner. As noted in Chapter 5, the maximal rate of firing for a single nerve cell, obtained under highly artificial conditions, is about 1200/impulses per second. Most sensory fibers do not fire more than a few hundred impulses per second. The number of differences in intensity that can be detected in vision and hearing is much greater than this code can offer. Therefore, variations in the firing rate of a single cell simply cannot account for the full range of intensity perception.

Multiple nerve cells acting in a parallel manner provide a broader range for coding the intensity of a stimulus. As the strength of a stimulus increases, new nerve cells are "recruited," and thus intensity can be represented by the number of active cells. A variant of this idea is the principle of intensity coding called **range fractionation** (Figure 8.5*b*). According to this hypothesis, a wide range of intensity values can be accurately noted in the nervous system by cells that are "specialists" in particular segments or fractions of an intensity scale. This mode of stimulus coding requires an array of receptors and nerve cells with a wide distribution of thresholds, some with very high sensitivity (lower thresholds) and others with much less sensitivity (higher thresholds).

What Type of Stimulus Is It?

Within any sensory modality, we can readily discriminate many qualitative differences among stimuli. For example, we can discriminate among wavelengths of light, frequencies of sound, and a variety of skin sensations such as touch, warmth, cold, and pain. What kind of coding underlies these qualitative differences?

An important part of the answer is the concept of **labeled lines**. This view states that particular nerve

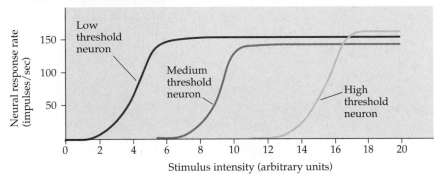

(a) Response rates versus stimulus intensity for three neurons with different thresholds

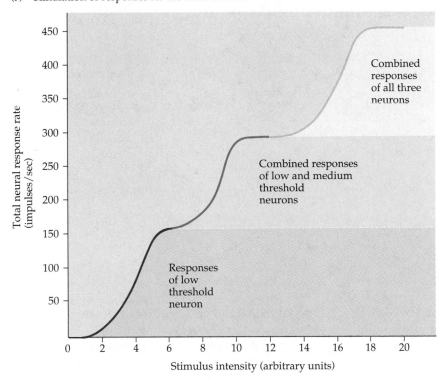

(b) Simulation of responses for the three neurons

8.5   Intensity Coding
(a) Rate of firing in three nerve cells, each with a different threshold: low, medium, or high. Each cell varies its response over a fraction of the total range of stimulus intensities. (b) Although none of these nerve cells can respond faster than 150 times per second, the sum of all three can vary in response rate from 0 to 450 impulses per second, accurately indicating the intensity of the stimulus.

cells are, at the outset, labeled for distinctive sensory experiences (Figure 8.6). Neural activity in this "line" provides the basis for our detection of the experience. Its qualities are predetermined. Clearly major separation of sensory experiences into modalities involves labeled lines; stimulation of the optic nerve, for instance, always yields vision and never gives us sounds or touch sensations. But controversy surrounds the coding for submodalities, as is particularly evident in vision. For example, there does not seem to be a separate labeled line for each discriminable color, although a few main kinds of retinal receptors respond preferentially to some parts of the

visible spectrum. The wealth of different colors appears to result from spatial and temporal activities of only a few different kinds of cells, as we will see in Chapter 10.

Where Is the Stimulus?

The position of an object or event, either outside or inside the body, is an important feature of the information that a person or animal gains by sensory analysis. Some sensory systems reveal this information by the position of excited receptors on the sensory surface. This feature is most evident in the visual and somatosensory ("body sensations") systems.

8.6 Labeled Lines
Each receptor (cold, warmth, touch, pain) has a distinct pathway linking the receptor surface to the brain, so different qualities of skin stimulation can be communicated to distinct places in the brain.

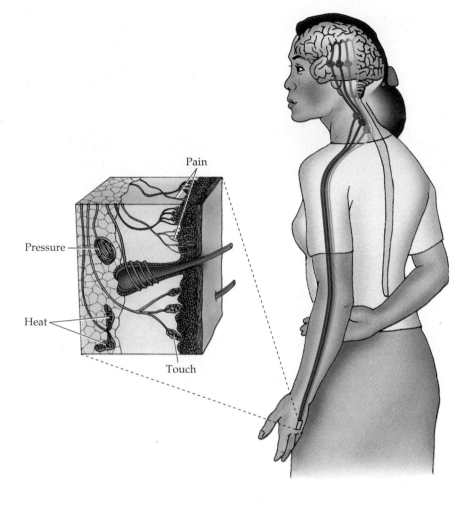

Pain

Pressure

Heat

Touch

Seeing the position of an event or object, and feeling the site of a stimulus on the skin both depend on which receptors are excited. Each receptor in either system activates pathways that convey unique positional information. In these systems the spatial properties of a stimulus are represented by labeled lines that uniquely convey spatial information. In both the visual and the tactile system, cells at all levels of the nervous system—from the surface sheet of receptors to the cerebral cortex—are arranged in an orderly, maplike manner. The map at each level is not exact but reflects both position and receptor density. Thus, more cells are allocated to the spatial representation of sensitive, densely innervated sites like the fovea of the eye, or skin surfaces like the lips, than to sites that are less sensitive, such as the periphery of the eye or the skin of the back.

Information about location is not restricted to sensory systems that are laid out like a map. We all know that we can detect quite accurately the source of a sound or an odor. In neither the hearing nor the olfactory system, however, are the peripheral receptors excited in a manner that corresponds directly to the position or location of the relevant stimulus. Locating a stimulus in these systems can involve unilateral or bilateral receptors—that is, one ear or nostril or both ears or nostrils. The mechanism for detecting position using bilateral receptors differs markedly from that using a unilateral receptor.

Can you tell the direction from which a sound comes if you use only one ear? Research shows that sound position can be determined unilaterally with considerable accuracy if the sound lasts for several seconds, but not if it is sudden and brief. Monaural (one-ear) detection of sound location depends on head movements; it is a sampling, in successive instants, of sound intensity—similar to radar scanning. Some animals with movable external ears (like the cat) can substitute movements of the external ear for head movements. Monaural detection of stimulus location also depends on short-term memory, since successive stimuli are compared for intensity.

With bilateral receptor systems—the two ears or the two nostrils—the relative time of arrival of the stimulus at the two receptors, or the relative intensity, is directly related to the location of the stimulus. For example, the only condition in which both ears are excited identically is when the sound source is equidistant from the ears, in the median plane of the body. As the stimulus moves to the left or right, asymmetrical excitation of receptors of the left and right sides occurs. Our auditory localization circuits allow us to judge accurately whether a sound source is slightly to the right or left of center when the difference in time of arrival at the two ears is only a few millionths of a second. Specialized nerve cells that receive inputs from both left and right ears and measure stimulus disparities between left and right are discussed in Chapter 9.

What Is the Identity of the Stimulus?

Being able to recognize stimuli requires the ability both to perceive patterns of stimulation and to recall patterns that have been learned previously. Usually these abilities go together, but in some cases of brain damage, they can become divorced. In Chapter 19, for example, we will consider some rare cases of people who can see and describe faces but who can no longer recognize familiar faces.

Perceiving patterns requires information about different parts or aspects of the stimulus display; often this information is obtained by movements of the receptor organ. For example, we scan a scene with our eyes. We turn our heads while listening (some other animals turn their ears). To identify an object by touch, we move our fingers to obtain information not only about its shape but also about its firmness, elasticity, and so on. When we taste food, we move it over our tongue, because receptors for different taste qualities are located on different parts of the tongue. Even with smells, we sniff to bring new whiffs of odorous air to the receptors in our nose. Thus we capture different bits of information during our inspection of the stimulus pattern. How these bits are integrated neurally into a unified perception is a question for which we have only partial answers.

Receptor Response Can Decline with Maintained Stimuli

Processing of sensory information also makes use of the adaptation of receptors; **adaptation** is the progressive loss of sensitivity that many receptors show when stimulation is maintained. We can demonstrate adaptation by recording nerve impulses in a fiber leading from a receptor. Observations of the time course of nerve impulses show a progressive decline in the rate of discharges as the stimulus is continued (Figure 8.7).

In terms of adaptation, there are two kinds of receptors:

1. **Tonic receptors** show a slow or nonexistent decline in the frequency of nerve impulses as stimulation is maintained. In other words, these receptors show relatively little adaptation.

2. **Phasic receptors** show a rapid fall in the frequency of nerve impulses.

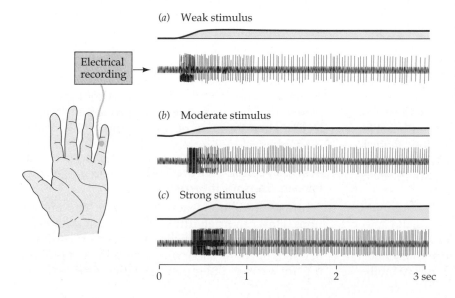

(a) Weak stimulus

Electrical recording

(b) Moderate stimulus

(c) Strong stimulus

0   1   2   3 sec

Figure 8.7 Sensory Adaptation
The rate of firing of this neuron, whose receptive field is located on the fifth finger, is rapid when the stimulus is first applied, but then adapts, slowing to a steady rate. After Knibestol and Valbo, 1970.

Adaptation means that there is a progressive shift in perception and neural activity away from accurate portrayal of maintained physical events. Thus, the nervous system may fail to register neural activity even though the stimulus continues. Such a striking discrepancy does not imply a weakness in the integrity of receptors; rather it emphasizes the significance of changes of state as the effective properties of stimuli. Adaptation is a form of information suppression that prevents the nervous system from becoming overwhelmed by stimuli that offer very little "news" about the world (von Békésy, 1967). For example, the pressing of a hair on the leg by pants may be continuous, but we are saved from a constant neural barrage from this stimulus by several suppression mechanisms, including adaptation.

The bases of adaptation include both neural and nonneural events. For example, in some mechanical receptors, adaptation develops from the elasticity of the receptor cell itself. This situation is especially evident in the Pacinian corpuscle detecting mechanical pressure. Maintained pressure on a corpuscle results in an initial burst of neural activity and a rapid fall to almost nothing. The size of this receptor enables experimenters to remove the corpuscle (the accessory cell) and apply the same constant stimulus to the terminal region of the sensory nerve fiber—that is, to bend the tip of the neuron. In this instance, maintained mechanical stimulation produces a continuing discharge of nerve impulses. This result suggests that for this receptor, adaptation is a mechanical property of the nonneural component, the corpuscle. In some receptors, adaptation reflects a change in the generator potential of the cell. Changes in this electrical property of a receptor may be produced by ionic changes that result in hyperpolarization.

Lateral Inhibition Enhances Contrast Sensitivity

In many cases when a stimulus impinges uniformly on an array of receptors, we perceive the stimulation as being strongest at the edges. For example, Figure 8.8a shows a series of bars. Although each bar is a uniform gray, it appears to be lighter at its left side, where it touches a darker strip. There is contrast with tactile sensation, too. If you press the end of a ruler against the skin of your forearm, you will probably feel the pressure of the corners of the ruler more strongly than the pressure all along the line of contact.

This sharpening of perception is based on a neural process called **lateral inhibition**; that is, the neurons in a region are interconnected, either through their own axons or by means of intermediary neurons (interneurons), and each neuron tends to inhib-

it its neighbors (Figure 8.8b). Many of these lateral inhibitory connections occur at lower levels of sensory systems.

Some Information Must Be Discarded

We have noted that successful adaptation and survival do not depend on exact copying of external and internal stimuli. Rather, our success as a species demands that our sensory systems accentuate, from among the many things happening about us, the important changes of stimuli. Without selectivity we would suffer from an overload of information and would end up with a confusing picture of the world. In addition to minimizing sensory overload, suppression of some sensory inputs may reduce the metabolic expense of nervous system activities.

Information in sensory systems is constrained or suppressed in at least two ways. In many sensory systems, accessory structures can reduce the level of input in the sensory pathway. For example, closure of the eyelid reduces the level of illumination that reaches the retina. In the auditory system, contraction of the middle ear muscles reduces the intensity of sounds that reach the cochlea. In this form of sensory control, the relevant mechanisms change the intensity of the stimulus before it reaches the receptors.

A second form of information control involves neural connections that descend from the brain to lower levels in the sensory pathway, in some cases as far as the receptor surface. For example, higher centers in the pain system (discussed later in this chapter) send axons down the spinal cord, where they can inhibit incoming pain signals. Such central modulation of sensory input is also evident in the auditory system, where a small group of cells in the brain stem sends axons along the auditory nerve to connect with the base of the receptor cells. Stimulation of this pathway can dampen sounds in a more selective manner than the action of middle ear muscles. For years, auditory physiologists have sought a connection between the activities of this efferent pathway and selective attention. Although establishment of this connection has proved elusive, selective attention may be a functional role of these neural fibers.

Successive Levels of the CNS Process Sensory Information

Sensory stimulation leads to responses and perceptions. How? In brief, different levels and regions of the brain process information from receptor surfaces in different ways. These sites of information processing are located along pathways that lead from the

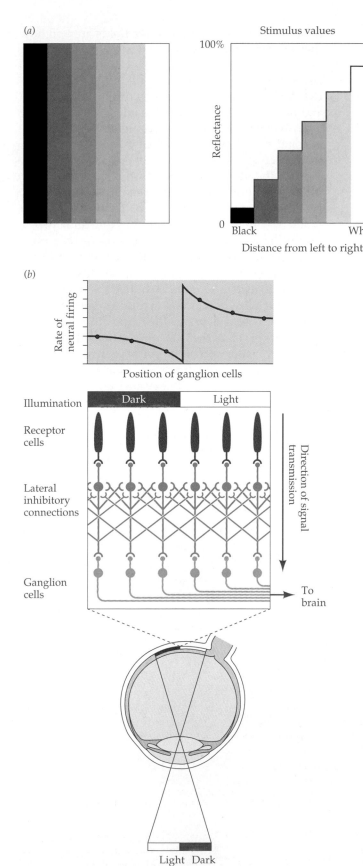

(a)

Stimulus values

Perceived values

Reflectance

100%

0

Black   White

Distance from left to right

Perceived brightness

High

Low

Distance from left to right

(b)

Rate of neural firing

Position of ganglion cells

Illumination   Dark   Light

Receptor cells

Lateral inhibitory connections

Ganglion cells

Direction of signal transmission

To brain

Light   Dark

8.8 Perceptual Consequences of Lateral Inhibition

(a) Each bar in the series at left is actually a uniform color, but appear lighter on the left and darker on the right. The actual values of stimulus intensity are plotted in the center graph. The right-hand graph plots *perceived* intensity; each bar appears brightest at its left edge and darkest at its right.
(b) The circuit of neurons in the eye, which uses lateral inhibition to sharpen contours in this manner.

sensory surface to the highest levels of the brain, and each sensory system has its own distinctive pathways. Specifically, pathways from receptors lead into the spinal cord or brain stem, where they connect to distinct clusters of nerve cells. These cells, in turn, have axons that connect to other nerve cell groups. Eventually the pathway terminates in sets of neurons in regions of the cerebral cortex. Each sensory modality—such as touch, vision, or audition—has a distinct collection of tracts and stations in the brain that are collectively known as the sensory or afferent pathway for that modality.

Each station in any pathway is thought to accomplish a basic aspect of information processing. For example, there is important information processing at the spinal level. Painful stimulation of the finger will lead to reflex withdrawal of the hand, which is mediated by spinal circuits. At the brain stem level, other circuits can turn the head toward the source of stimulation. Presumably the most complex aspects of sensory representations are at the level of the cerebral cortex. A major goal of contemporary studies of sensory processing is to understand the transformations of signals at each level in afferent pathways within the nervous system.

As sensory information enters the nervous system, it travels in divergent pathways, so there is more than one representation of that modality at each level of the nervous system (Figure 8.9). For several senses, information reaches the thalamus before being relayed to the cortex; the somatosensory system is one example. Figure 8.10 shows six different somatosensory regions in the monkey cortex. Each of them is a full, orderly representation of either the body surface or deep body tissues. The neurophysiologist Clinton Woolsey was a pioneer in the mapping of these somatosensory regions. Similar collections of maps are found at different levels of the auditory and visual pathways (Kaas, 1991). One way of studying these brain maps is to record the receptive fields of the cells that constitute

Clinton Woolsey
(1904–1993)

them, so let's see what receptive fields are and how they are measured.

Receptive fields of the sensory neuron. The **receptive field** of a sensory neuron is the stimulus region and the features that cause that cell to alter its firing rate. To determine the receptive field of a neuron, investigators record its electrical responses to a variety of stimuli to learn what makes the activity of the cell change from its resting rate. Figure 8.11 shows an example of such an experiment. Neuron A responds to touch on a region of the forepaw. Neuron B, only a few millimeters away on the somatosensory cortex, responds to stimulation of the tail. In both cases, light touch in the center of the region causes the rate of firing to increase markedly above the resting rate. Light touch in a band that surrounds this central region produces a decrease in firing rate below the resting level. Thus these receptive fields include an excitatory center and an inhibitory surround. Other receptive fields have the reverse organization—inhibitory centers and excitatory surrounds. Receptive

8.9 Levels of Sensory Processing
These levels of processing are involved in all sensory modalities.

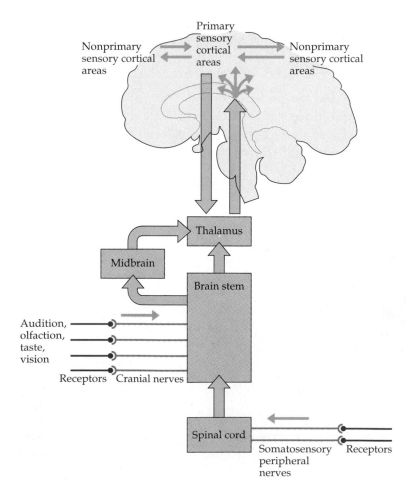

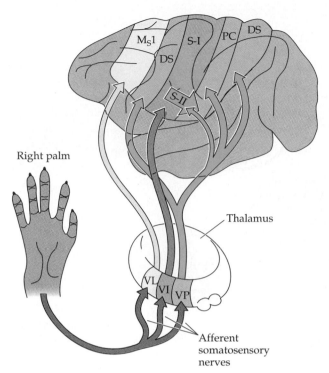

Right palm

Thalamus

Afferent
somatosensory
nerves

8.10 Thalamic Relays
Some of the connections between thalamus and cortex
in the somatosensory system of monkeys. Different divisions of the thalamus—ventrolateral (VL), ventralis
termedius (VI), and ventroposterior (VP)—send axons
to different somatosensory regions of the cerebral cortex. After Merzenich and Kaas, 1980.

Vernon Mountcastle

fields differ also in their sizes and shapes, and in the quality of stimulation that activates them. For example, some cells respond preferen-
tially to light touch, while oth-
er cells respond best to painful
stimuli. Much of the earlier
work on receptor field properties of cerebral cortical somatosensory cells was done
by Vernon Mountcastle. Although we have taken these
examples from neurons in the
cortex, receptive fields have
been studied for cells at all
levels, and we will see examples in other brain regions lat-
er in this chapter and in the next two chapters.

Regions of the cerebral cortex. Several lines of evidence indicate that the different cortical areas that
represent the same receptive surface receive different
inputs, process the information differently, and make

different contributions to perceptual experiences
(Zeki, 1993; Miyashita, 1993). The evidence for different inputs is that these areas receive fibers from
different divisions of the thalamus (see Figure 8.10)
and that the maps, although orderly, differ in internal
arrangement. Some geographic maps exaggerate a
particular aspect; for example, the "New Yorker's
map of the United States" magnifies New York while
shrinking the rest of the country. Similarly, we'll see
that cortical representations of the body surface always enlarge the representation of the hand.

In somatosensory cortical regions, one area (S-I in
Figure 8.10) maps the opposite side of the body. Another area (S-II) maps both sides of the body in registered overlay; that is, the left-arm and right-arm
representations occupy the same part of the map, and
so forth. Neurons within some somatosensory maps
are most sensitive to stimulation of the skin surface,
others to muscles and joints; some neurons are sensitive to stationary stimuli, others to movement
(Mountcastle, 1984).

Probably different cortical regions are simultaneously processing different aspects of perceptual experience, but the details of this processing are not yet
known. In spite of this specialization, it would be incorrect to suppose that a given cortical sensory region
receives a packet of information and processes it
without further communication with other brain regions. For one thing, there are back-and-forth exchanges between cortical and thalamic regions. For
another, the different cortical regions for a given
modality communicate by fibers that make subcortical loops (see Figure 2.23).

Even though each sensory modality is represented by several topographically organized cortical
fields that all have direct thalamic input, there are
reasons for referring to one field as primary for each
sense: the primary area is the main source of input to
the other fields for the same modality, even though
they also have direct thalamic inputs. However, discovering the separate and joint contributions of different sensory regions to perception remains a challenge. Recent findings do not conform to a strict
hierarchical model with its schema of primary, secondary, and association areas.

Variation in cortical maps. Investigators began
mapping cortical sensory and motor representations
in the last quarter of the nineteenth century, using
mainly the techniques of ablation (surgical removal)
and electrical stimulation of the cortex. Other techniques gradually became available: electrical recording, fiber tracing, and noninvasive techniques. By the
1940s, the cortex of several species had been mapped,

8.11 Somatosensory Receptive Fields

Procedures used to record from somatosensory neurons of the cerebral cortex. Changes in the position of the stimulus are related to the rate of response of neural impulses.

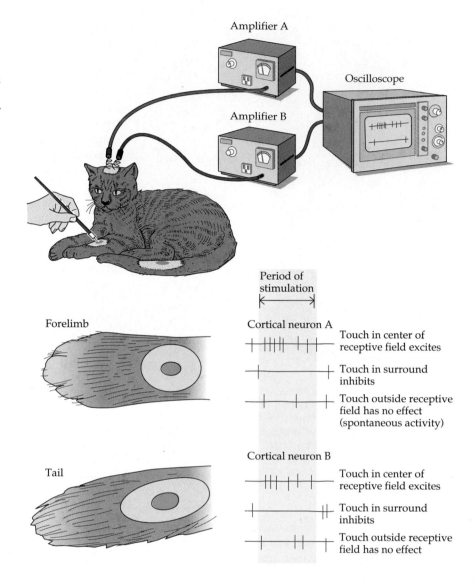

and there was a tendency to regard these maps as being general for a species and being fixed in adults. As early as 1946, however, Lashley and Clark criticized the idea that cortical maps are the same for all members of a species. They showed that the boundaries of the primary visual area differ among monkeys. Because cortical maps differ among humans, neurosurgeons often map the parts of the cortex near the site of an intended operation to ensure that areas responsible for speech are not damaged during surgery.

The idea that cortical maps are fixed in adults took even longer to give way to contrary evidence, although such evidence began to appear in the 1970s (Wall and Egger, 1971; Wall, 1977). Three recent experiments illustrate the plasticity of sensory representation. In the first (Merzenich and Jenkins, 1993), the receptive field of a monkey's hand was mapped

in detail in the somatosensory cortex (Figure 8.12*a* and *b*). Then the nerve to the thumb and index finger was severed. After a few weeks, remapping the same somatosensory cortex revealed that the area representing these fingers had shrunk, while the areas of the neighboring fingers had expanded into their former territory (Figure 8.12*c*). In the second experiment (Merzenich and Jenkins, 1993), the middle finger was surgically removed. This treatment expanded the cortical representation of each adjacent finger (Figure 8.12*d*). In a third experiment, the monkey was trained to maintain contact with a rotating disk with one or two fingers in order to obtain food rewards. After several weeks of training, the hand area was mapped again, and the trained fingers were found to have considerably enlarged representations over their previous areas (Figure 8.12*e*).

(*a*) Location of left hand map on right hemisphere of monkey brain

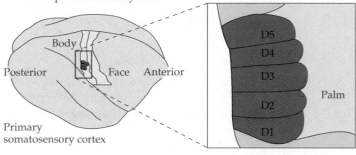

Posterior   Face   Anterior

Body

Primary somatosensory cortex

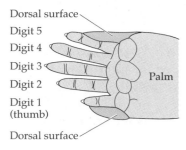

Details of cortical map

(*b*) Normal hand, palmar surface

Dorsal surface
Digit 5
Digit 4
Digit 3
Digit 2
Digit 1 (thumb)
Dorsal surface

Palm

(*c*) Portion deprived by crushing nerve

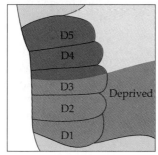

Map immediately after nerve crush

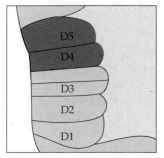

Map of reorganization of cortex, after five months of deprivation caused by nerve crush; dorsal surface now represented in D1–3.

(*d*) Reorganization of cortical map after surgical removal of third finger (D3)

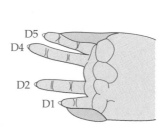

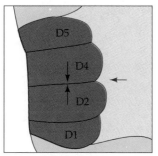

After reorganization of sensory cortex

(*e*) Reorganization of cortical map after discrimination training of two fingertips

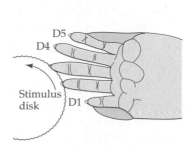

Stimulus disk

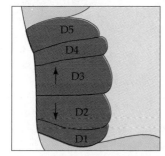

8.12   Plasticity of Somatosensory Representations

In a review of the topic of plasticity of sensory representation, Kaas (1991) reaches the following conclusions:

1. Cortical maps in all sensory systems can change with experience and use.

2. Such plasticity of cortical maps has been found in a wide range of mammalian species, indicating that adult plasticity is a feature of all mammalian brains.

3. Sensory maps at both lower and higher levels in the nervous system show changes with use and disuse, but changes are more dramatic at higher levels, possibly because changes accumulate along the sensory pathways and because the higher levels may have greater potential for plasticity.

4. Some changes in cortical maps occur after weeks or months of use or disuse; they may arise from the production of new synapses (sprouting) or the loss of others. On the other hand, some changes are so rapid, occurring within hours, that they may arise from changes in the strength of existing synapses. Rapid changes in cortical maps may also result from a loss of sustained inhibition of some synapses; these changes could be thought of as the unmasking of synaptic effects that are normally suppressed.

Sensory Systems Influence One Another

Many research observations and individual experiences show that the use of one sensory system influences perception derived from another sensory system (Stein and Meredith, 1993). For example, cats often do not respond to birds unless they can both see and hear them (Figure 8.13); neither sense alone is sufficient to elicit a response (Meredith and Stein, 1983). Such intersensory effects are evident in even the simplest of invertebrates. Many sensory areas in the brain do not exclusively represent a single modality but show a mixture of inputs from different modalities. Individual sensory cells may also respond to stimuli of more than one modality. Some "visual" cells, for instance, also respond to auditory or tactile stimuli. Stimuli converge in such **polymodal cells**, providing a mechanism for intersensory interactions.

Recently investigators have found that many brain cells show very different responses to stimulation of

8.13 Converging Sensory Modalities
A cat often responds to a bird only if it can both see and hear the bird.

two or more modalities than to stimulation of only one modality. This interaction can take any of several forms. For example, some cells respond only weakly or not at all to a sound or a light but respond strongly when both are presented at once. Some cells that respond to lights show a weaker response when a sound is also presented. Although studies of such intersensory effects are much more demanding than are studies of single stimuli, because many different combinations of stimuli must be tested, such investigation is important to our understanding of some perceptual effects.

As with the cat's response to the bird, some perceptions require combinations of different modalities. Flavors, for example, are integrations of both tastes and odors. Much of what we ordinarily think of as "taste" has a large component of odor. If you block your nose, it is hard to discriminate the flavor of a raw potato from that of a raw apple. This explains why food may lose its flavor when you have a bad cold.

When your eyes are open, you normally perceive the position of you body on the basis of both visual and vestibular inputs. If you are looking at a target and your head moves, your eyes move to compensate and keep your gaze on target. In the absence of gravity, as in space flight, the usual correspondence between vision and the pull of gravity on the body is upset, and the lack of this concordance is probably a major factor in the nausea that many astronauts feel during their first days in space.

Sometimes the input from one sensory modality dominates the input from another. For example, in a movie theater you perceive the sound as coming from the person whom you see speaking on the screen, but if you close your eyes you may realize that the sound is actually coming from a speaker located to one side of the screen. With your eyes open in this case, your auditory localization has been overruled by sight. This phenomenon is what allows ventriloquists to work their vocal magic.

Some experiments have shown that visual perception of spatial position, as well as auditory localization, can be strongly influenced by perceived body position (Lackner and Shenker, 1985). In these experiments, subjects sat in the dark and estimated the position of their index finger in space. Each person's arm was restrained in a padded support that fixed the elbow in a bent position with the index finger in the midline of the body, about 50 centimeters in front of the face. The head was also fixed in position, as a result of the subject's clamping his or her jaw on a bite board. Stimulation of the biceps mus-

cle with a mechanical vibrator caused subjects to feel that the arm extended, even though it did not actually move. If a small light was attached to the index finger, in 85% of all trials the subjects reported that the light began to move shortly after they felt that their arm started to extend. The light was seen to move in the same direction as subjects felt their arms moving, although on the average the light was not perceived as moving quite as far. The subjects also reported that their eyes moved to follow the light, even though neither the light nor the eyes actually moved. Similarly, if a small loudspeaker emitting clicks was attached to the finger, subjects reported that the sound began to move shortly after they felt the arm move. And if both a light and a speaker were attached to the finger, both were perceived to move when vibratory stimulation caused the illusion of movement of the arm. The light and sound had some effect on perception of movement of the arm, too; when these stimuli were present, the reported movements of the arm were slightly smaller than when light and sound were absent. Thus, there were reciprocal effects between these senses. Later in this chapter we will see that vibratory tactile stimulation can be used to reduce pain.

Some brain maps appear to have characteristics that favor intersensory integration. In the superior colliculus, usually referred to as the midbrain visual center, many cells in the deeper layers respond to tactile, auditory, or painful stimuli, as well as visual stimuli. The organization of the maps for these different modalities is similar; that is, cells that respond to stimulation at a particular position with regard to the animal are in register—they superimpose exactly— for the visual and somatic representations (Stein and Meredith, 1993). Such a correspondence has been found in reptiles as well as in mammals (Gaither and Stein, 1979). This similarity of organization between reptiles and mammals may represent simply convergent evolution, or it may indicate an ancient plan of brain representation of sensory modalities that was present in their common ancestors more than 180 million years ago. However this correspondence of sensory maps arose, it probably favors intersensory effects and the consistency across the senses of spatial perception.

The maps for the different senses in the colliculus are also in register with a map of motor responses. This arrangement supports quick reflex responses in space, such as quickly swatting a mosquito on the back of your hand whether you see it alight, hear its whine, feel it displace a hair, or feel the prick of its sting.

Attention Is an Enigma That Noninvasive Techniques May Help Us Understand

There are many different aspects of what we call "attention." One view emphasizes the state of alertness or vigilance that enables animals to detect signals. In this view, attention is a generalized activation that attunes us to inputs. According to another view, attention is the process that allows selection of some sensory inputs from among many competing ones. Some investigators view attention in a more introspective manner, arguing that attention is a state of mental concentration or effort that makes it possible to focus on a particular task. As you can see, a notion that may seem self-evident to some has considerable complexity.

Certain regions of the cerebral cortex have been particularly implicated in attention, as evidenced by the impairment of attention in people and animals with localized cortical damage and by recordings of electrical activity of cells in different cortical regions while animals attend to stimuli or await stimuli in order to obtain rewards. One cortical region that appears to play a special role in attention is a part of the posterior parietal lobe. Many cells here are polymodal. Some of them are especially responsive when a trained monkey is expecting the appearance of a stimulus (Mountcastle, Andersen, and Motter, 1981). Lesions of this area in monkeys result in inattention or neglect of stimuli on the opposite side. (In Chapter 19 we will see that this symptom is especially severe in people with lesions of the right parietal lobe.) The frontal eye fields seem to be involved in attentive visual exploration of space. The posterior part of the cingulate cortex (around the posterior part of the corpus callosum) has been implicated in motivational aspects of attention. These three cortical areas have especially prominent anatomical connections with each other, and each receives strong input from sensory fibers (Mesulam, 1989).

Touch and Pain

Touch Includes a Variety of Sensations

Skin envelops our bodies and provides a boundary with our surroundings. This delicate boundary harbors an array of sensors that enable us to detect and discriminate among many types of impinging stimuli. All forms of touch, from the most delicate movement of a single hair to the most forceful pressing of the flesh, are recorded by skin sensors. Among primates an important aspect of skin sensations is the active manipulation of objects by the hands, which enables identification and use of various shapes. The ability to detect differences in temperature adds to the versatility of the skin. More complex aspects of skin sensations are evident in the worlds of pain that we are all too aware of. After examining how skin senses work, we will discuss pain.

Many Different Skin Sensations Arise from All over the Body

Touch is not just "touch." Careful studies of skin sensations using a variety of stimuli reveal that qualitatively different sensory experiences can be provoked by skin excitation. These include pressure, vibration, tickle, "pins and needles," and more complex dimensions, such as smoothness or wetness. Skin sensations vary not only qualitatively but also spatially across the extent of the body surface. For example, studies on the "two-point" threshold reveal spatial discrimination differences on the body surface. This measure is readily obtained by determining how far apart two points, such as the tips of two pencils, must be in order to perceive them as separate points. As the two points of the pencils are brought closer together on the body surface, they are perceived as one point. Some parts of the body, such as the lips and fingers, have very low two-point thresholds (can detect two points even when they are quite close together), whereas other parts, such as the back or leg, have very high two-point thresholds.

Skin Is a Complex Organ That Contains a Variety of Sensory Receptors

The average person has about 10 to 20 square feet of skin. Skin is not a simple structure but is made up of three separate layers (see Figure 8.3); the relative thickness of each layer varies over the body surface. The outermost layer—the **epidermis**—is the thinnest and varies most widely, ranging from a very flexible, relatively thick layer on the surface of the hands and feet to the delicate outer layer of the eyelid. Each day millions of new cells are added to the outermost layer. The middle layer—the **dermis**—contains the rich network of nerve fibers and blood vessels, in addition to the network of connective tissue that is rich in the protein, called collagen, that gives skin its strength. The character of skin is further complicated by other specialized outgrowths, such as hair or feathers, claws, hooves, and horns. The innermost layer—**subcutaneous tissue**—contains fat cells, which act as thermal insulators and cushion internal organs from mechanical shocks.

Within the skin are several receptors with distinctive shapes (Figure 8.14). We have already mentioned the Pacinian corpuscles, which are found deep with-

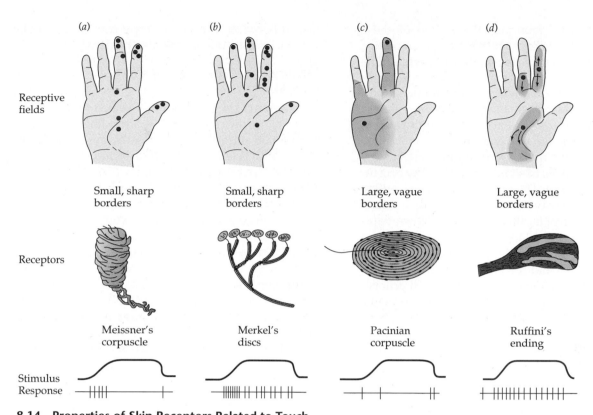

8.14 Properties of Skin Receptors Related to Touch
(*Top row*) Size and type of receptive field; (*middle row*) type of skin receptor; (*bottom row*) electrophysiological response. (*a*) Fast-adapting fibers with small receptive fields. (*b*) Slow-adapting fibers with small receptive fields. (*c*) Fast-adapting fibers with large receptive fields. (*d*) Slow-adapting fibers with large receptive fields. After Valbo and Johansson, 1984.

in the dermis and are the largest receptors in some skin areas, around muscles and joints, and within the gut. These are fast-responding receptors whose excitation is delivered to fast-conducting nerve fibers. The Pacinian corpuscles respond accurately to vibration of the skin over a wide range of stimulus frequencies, but they show little evidence of discrimination of spatial stimuli. Other receptors, called **Meissner's corpuscles**, are especially densely distributed in skin regions where sensitive spatial discriminations are possible, but these receptors respond poorly to vibrating stimuli. The regions where Meissner's corpuscles predominate include the fingertips, tongue, and lips. Also found in these regions are oval-shaped receptors called **Merkel's discs**, which are sometimes found in bundles that are especially sensitive to touch. Detection of heat and cold at the skin has been associated with the activation of two other receptor types: **Ruffini's endings** and **Krause's end bulbs**. Some investigators, however, have cautioned against readily equating sensory categories

and distinct structural classes of receptors. The psychological categories of skin sensations were developed independently of receptor types, and it is not yet clear whether these two can be related to each other in a simple way.

Progress in relating sensations to types of receptors is coming from a new technique for recording from human peripheral nerves—**microneuronography**. Tiny wires are placed in a hypodermic needle and injected into a nerve, then connected to machines to detect nerve impulses. This technique has allowed researchers new insights into mechanisms of touch perception in humans. Now it is possible to relate measures of tactile sensitivity in alert subjects to nerve impulse activity in their peripheral nerves. Within the smooth skin of the hand, it has been estimated that there are 17,000 tactile units of four main types, which are distinguished by the size and shape of their receptive fields and various functional properties, such as the response to maintained stimulation (adaptation) (Valbo and Johansson, 1984). Two of these groups of peripheral nerve fibers have small receptive fields that are especially dense at the fingertips. One of these two groups shows rapid adaptation to maintained skin indentation (Figure 8.14*a*); the other group continues to respond as mechanical stimulation is maintained (Figure 8.14*b*). Each of these groups is believed to involve a different end-organ receptor in the skin. The other two main groups of fibers have very large receptive fields; in some cases they may encompass an entire finger. The fibers with large receptive fields are also subdivided into two groups: a fast-adapting subgroup (Figure 8.14*c*) and a slow-adapting subgroup (Figure 8.14*d*). The slow-adapting nerve fibers with large receptive fields are also especially responsive to stretch and therefore to mechanical stimuli that move across the skin in particular directions.

Microneuronographic studies have revealed some striking insights about tactile sensitivity. Fast-adapting fibers have very low thresholds to mechanical stimuli. In fact, a single nerve impulse in some of these fibers can lead to touch perception. A single brief electrical stimulus can also be detected.

Sensory Information Is Transmitted from Skin to Brain

Inputs from skin surfaces are directed to the spinal cord. Within the cord somatosensory fibers ascend to the brain in at least two major pathways: (1) the dorsal column system and (2) the anterolateral (or spinothalamic) system (Figure 8.15). Inputs to the dorsal column system enter the spinal cord and ascend to the medulla, where they synapse at the gracile and cuneate nuclei. The axons of postsynaptic cells form a fiber bundle that crosses in the brain stem to the opposite side and ascends to a group of nuclei of the thalamus. Outputs of the thalamus are directed to postcentral cortical regions referred to as the somatosensory cortex. The anterolateral, or spinothalamic, system has a different arrangement. Inputs from the skin to this system synapse on cells in the spinal cord, whose axons cross to the opposite

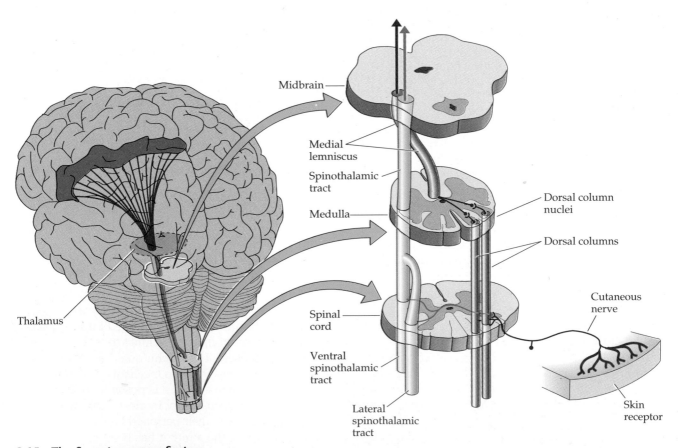

8.15 The Somatosensory System
(*Left*) General view of the system including ascending spinal tracts, thalamic relay, and primary cortical representation. (*Right*) The spinal tracts in greater detail, including crossed and uncrossed spinal pathways. All afferent messages cross before reaching the thalamus.

side and ascend in the anterolateral columns of the spinal cord. At least some of the input to this system mediates pain and temperature sensations.

The skin surface can be divided into bands, or **dermatomes**, according to which spinal nerve carries the most axons from each region (Figure 8.16*a* and *b*). A dermatome (from the Greek *derma*, "skin," and *tomos*, "section") is a strip of skin innervated by a particular spinal root. The pattern of dermatomes is hard to understand in an upright human, but we must remember that an erect posture is a recent evolutionary development in mammals. The mammalian dermatomal pattern evolved among our quadrupedal (four-legged) ancestors. Thus, the dermatomal pattern becomes clear when depicted on a person in a quadrupedal posture (Figure 8.16*b*). There is also a modest amount of overlap between dermatomes (Figure 8.16*c*).

The cells in all brain regions concerned with somatic sensation are arranged according to the plan of the body surface. Thus, each region is a map of the body in which the relative areas devoted to bodily regions reflect the density of body innervations. Since many fibers are involved with the sensory surface of the head, especially the lips, there is a particularly large number of cells concerned with the head; in contrast, far fewer fibers innervate the trunk, so the number of cells that represent the trunk is much lower (Figure 8.17).

Cortical Columns Show Specificity for Modality and Location

We saw in Chapter 2 that the cerebral cortex is organized into vertical columns of neurons; in this section we will examine the functional significance of these cortical columns. It had long been known that the

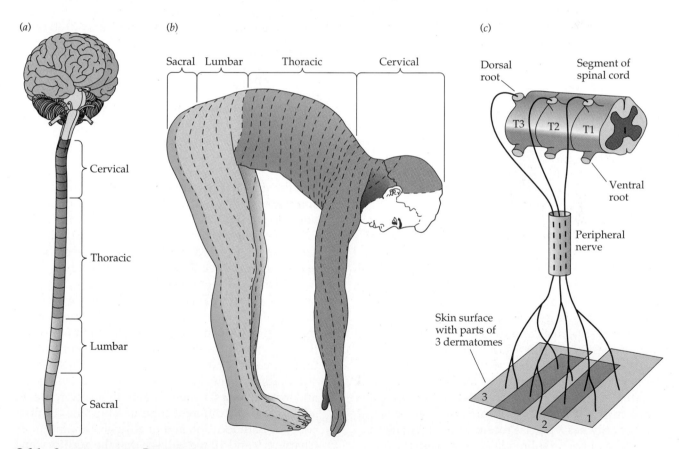

8.16 Somatosensory Dermatomes
(*a*) Bands of skin send their sensory inputs to different dorsal roots of the spinal cord. Each dermatome is the section of the skin that is innervated primarily by a given dorsal root of the spinal cord. (*b*) Side view of the human body in quadrupedal position. Here the pattern of dermatomes is color-coded to correspond to the spinal regions in (*a*), and it appears more straightforward than it would in the erect posture. (*c*) Adjacent dorsal roots of the spinal cord collect sensory fibers from overlapping strips of skin, so the boundaries between the dermatomes overlap.

(a)

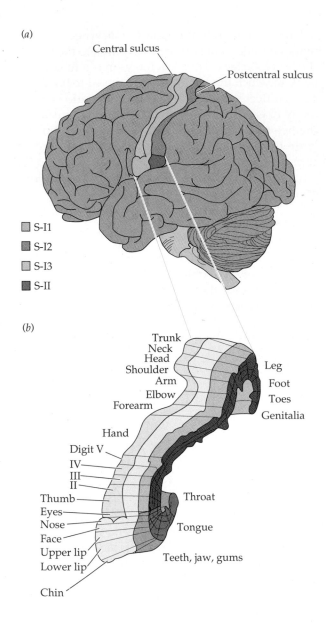

☐ S-I1
☐ S-I2
☐ S-I3
☐ S-II

(b)

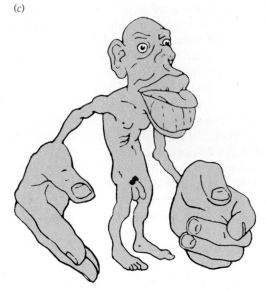

8.17 Representation of the Body Surface in Somatosensory Cortex
(a) Location of primary (S-I) and secondary (S-II) somatosensory cortex on the lateral surface of the human brain. *(b)* The order and size of cortical representations of different regions of skin. *(c)* The homunculus (literally, "little man") depicts the body surface with each area drawn in proportion to the size of its representation in the primary somatosensory cortex.

cortex contains large functional regions, such as the somatosensory areas and the visual areas, and that each of these regions is a sort of map of the sensory world. Then, in pioneering work begun in the 1950s, Mountcastle (1984) mapped the receptive fields of individual neurons in somatosensory cortex using microelectrodes. This work revealed that each cortical cell not only has a precise receptive field, but also responds to only one submodality. For example, a particular cell responds only to a given kind of stimulation, such as light touch, and another cell responds only to deep pressure. Furthermore, Mountcastle found to his surprise that, within a given column of neurons, all the cells respond to the same location and quality of stimulation. All the columns in a band

of adjacent columns respond to the same quality of stimulation, and then another band of columns is devoted to another kind of stimulation (Figure 8.18).

Each column extends from the surface of the cortex (layer I in Figure 8.18) down to the base of the cortex (layer VI). Area 3b of the cortex receives input from both fast-adapting and slow-adapting receptors near the surface of the skin. Each type of receptor feeds information to a different cortical column. Moving the stimulation to a slightly different region on the skin shifts the excitation to a different cortical column. Area 3a of cortex contains cells that respond to stimulation of the stretch receptors in the muscles, and within area 3a each change in location means stimulation of a different column. Thus, the columns code for both location and quality of stimulation. In Chapters 9 and 10 we will see that the auditory and visual areas of the cerebral cortex have the same kind of columnar organization. The discovery of the columnar organization of sensory cortex has been called "perhaps the most important single advance in cortical physiology in the past several decades" (Kandel et al., 1991).

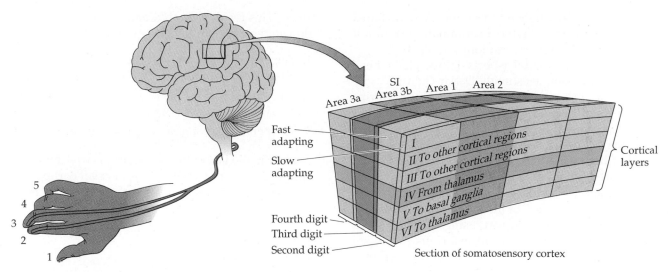

8.18 Columnar Organization of Cortex
This is the region of somatosensory cortex that represents some of the fingers of the left hand. The different regions of somatosensory cortex—Brodmann's areas 3a, 3b, 1, and 2—receive their main inputs from different kinds of receptors. Thus, 3b receives most of its projections from the superficial skin, including both fast-adapting and slow-adapting receptors; these are represented in separate cortical columns or slabs. Area 3a receives input from receptors in the muscle spindles. The cortex is organized vertically in columns and horizontally in layers. In layer IV, input from the thalamus arrives to the cortex. After Kaas et al., 1979.

Neural Maps at Several Levels Represent the Body Surface

The surface of the body is represented at each level of the somatosensory nervous system by an organization of nerve cells that provides a spatial map of the body surface. The first stage of this map of body position is the organization of individual dermatomes (see Figure 8.16) at a spinal level. Although individual dermatomes overlap to some extent, there is an orderly arrangement along the length of the spinal cord. At various levels of the brain, the surface of the body is again represented by an orderly map of nerve cells. Thus, the sensory topography of relevant thalamic cells and cortical areas reflects body topography.

The extreme detail of somatosensory system mapping of certain body surfaces is shown in work on rodents (Harris and Woolsey, 1983). Sections of rat somato-sensory cortex obtained by slicing the cortex in a plane tangential to the surface reveal some unusual groupings of cells in circular patterns. Successive sections of tissue in the same plane resemble the sides of a barrel; thus, these groupings were named **cortical barrels**. The wall of each barrel consists of tightly packed cell bodies surrounding a less dense area.

Electrical recordings of cells in the cortical barrels of a rat revealed the startling fact that each barrel is activated by one whisker on the opposite side of the head. Further, the layout of whiskers on the face of the animal corresponds to the layout of barrels in the cortex. Whiskers are important to a rodent's ability to find its way through narrow passages in the dark. In Chapter 4 we noted the importance of intact facial whiskers for the development or maintenance of cortical barrels. Rats whose whiskers were removed early in life did not form cortical barrels (see Figure 4.21).

Somatosensory Perception of Objects Requires Active Manipulation

The functions of the somatosensory cortex in discriminating forms have been studied in monkeys both by observing effects of lesions in this region and by recording from individual neurons while the monkeys' hands were stimulated. Lesions impaired the ability of the animal to discriminate the form, size, and roughness or smoothness of tactile objects (Norsell, 1980). Each of these impairments could be localized to a subregion of somatosensory cortex: lesions in one area affected mainly the discrimination of texture; lesions in a second area impaired mainly the discrimination of angles; and lesions in a third area affected all forms of tactile discrimination (Randolf and Semmes, Davidson, and Johnson, 1974).

Temporal and spatial aspects of touch have been studied using complex stimuli (Darian-Smith, Davidson, and Johnson, 1980). In this research metal strips of varied widths and spacing were moved at different rates of speed under the fingertips of monkeys while recordings were made from sensory nerves. No single fiber could give an accurate record of each ridge and depression in the stimulus, but the ensemble of fibers provided an accurate representation. Spatial discrimination of more complex stimuli has been studied in a similar way, using stimuli such as Braille dots or other small forms. Cells in the somatosensory cortex were classified in these studies according to the characteristics of their receptive fields (Iwamura and Tanaka, 1978). About one-fourth of the cells responded to simple pressure stimulation of points on the skin. Another fourth responded best to specialized stimulation of the skin (for example, by a moving probe or by a narrow band or rod). Another fourth of the cells could be activated either by stimulation of the skin or by movement of one or more finger joints. About one-eighth of the cells responded specifically to manipulation of joints. The remainder of the cells could not be activated when the experimenter stimulated either skin or joints, but some of these cells responded strongly when the animal grasped an object and manipulated it.

Some of these "active touch" cells had highly specific response characteristics. For example, one unit responded actively when the monkey felt a straight-edged ruler or a small rectangular block, but it did not respond when the monkey grasped a ball or bottle. The presence of two parallel edges appeared to be crucial for effective activation of this cell. In the same electrode penetration, another cell was found that responded best when the monkey grasped a ball, responded well to a bottle, but did not respond at all when the monkey manipulated a rectangular block. Grasping objects causes complex patterns of stimulation of skin receptors and joint receptors. This information about skin and joint stimulation must reach many cortical units. Apparently different cells require particular combinations of input if they are to respond. These units with complex receptive fields in the somatosensory cortex are somewhat like units with complex auditory or visual receptive fields that we will learn about in Chapters 9 and 10.

PET studies have shown that in humans the posterior part of the parietal cortex is activated during exploration of objects by touch (Roland and Larson,

1976). This result was obtained by recording blood flow in the cortex under three conditions:

1. The experimenter moved the passive hand of the observer over the stimulus object.
2. The person moved his or her hand energetically but did not touch an object.
3. The person explored an object by touch.

Only in the last of these conditions was there specific activation of the posterior parietal cortex, suggesting that this region is particularly involved in active touch.

Pain Is an Unpleasant but Adaptive Experience

Because pain is an unpleasant experience that can cause great suffering, it is hard to imagine that it has a "biological role." Clues to the adaptive significance of pain can be gleaned from the study of rare individuals who never experience pain. Such people have a congenital insensitivity or indifference to pain. In some cases they can discriminate between the touch of the point or head of a pin, but a pinprick is painless. Case descriptions note that the bodies of such people show extensive scarring from numerous injuries (Manfredi et al., 1981). Deformation of fingers, hands, and legs from these injuries is common. Most of these people die young, frequently from extreme trauma to the body. These cases suggest that pain guides adaptive behavior by indicating potential harm. Pain is so commonplace for most of us that we easily forget its guiding role: the experience of pain leads to behavior that removes the body from a source of injury.

Advances in human pain research, including the development of effective drug intervention, depend to a great extent on basic research using other animals. In addition, understanding pain in animals offers a distinctive insight into their adaptive behaviors. Comparative observations of pain behavior in humans and other animals led Dennis and Melzack (1983) to some interesting speculations about pain expression. They argue that pain involves two different dimensions—actual tissue trauma and threat. Pain associated with bodily injury or trauma leads to a maintained neural input from the injured region. The role of this signal is to foster behavior that aids the restorative and healing process, which includes a wide array of behavioral changes including sleep, locomotor activity, grooming, feeding, and drinking. Dennis and Melzack suggest that the appropriate behavioral response to trauma may be relative inactivity. In contrast with actual injury or trauma, the pain associated with threat of tissue damage may activate quite a different behavioral system. In the case of threat, pain develops at the initial contact with the noxious stimulus, which if maintained, would damage the tissue. Pain perception in this case can minimize the effect of the offending stimulus by evoking vigorous activity that moves the organism from the stimulus. These two different behavioral dimensions of pain perception may be related to the multiple pain pathways ascending in the spinal cord and brain stem, which we discuss later in this section.

Dennis and Melzack (1983) make another interesting observation: certain aspects of pain expression seem to have value as a social signal to other animals. For example, screeching after a painful stimulus may have significant adaptive value by signaling the potential of harm to genetically related members of the same species or eliciting certain care-giving behavior from others—such as grooming, defending, and feeding—that could mean the survival of the victim.

Human Pain Can Be Measured

In some parts of the world, people endure, with stoic indifference, rituals including body mutilation that would cause most other humans to cry out in pain. Incisions of the face, hands, arms, legs, or chest; walking on hot coals; and other treatments clearly harmful to the body can be part of the ritual. Comparable experiences are common in more ordinary circumstances, such as those occasions when a highly "charged" athlete continues to play a game with a broken arm or leg. War experiences also highlight the complexity of the pain experience. Beecher (1959) reported, for example, that soldiers injured in battle ask for drugs to control pain far less frequently than civilians who have sustained comparable injuries. Beecher's explanation for the difference is that the meaning of the experience is very different to each group. To the soldier a severe injury can signal relief from combat, if only for a while. In contrast, similar injuries to a civilian can signal economic loss and personal inconvenience. Learning, experience, emotion, and culture all seem to affect pain in striking ways.

Detailed psychological studies of the experience of pain further emphasize its complexity. The mere description of pain as mild or intense is inadequate to describe the pain that is distinctive to a particular disease or injury. Furthermore, in order to assess the need for pain-relief intervention, some kind of quantitative measurement is necessary. Several approaches to measuring pain in humans and other animals

appear in contemporary research (Chapman et al., 1985). For example, Melzack (1984) has provided a detailed quantitative rating scale that examines the language of pain. This rating scale—called the McGill Pain Assessment Questionnaire—consists of a list of words arranged into classes that describe three different aspects of the pain experience: (1) the sensory quality, (2) the affective (emotional) quality, and (3) an overall evaluative quality. Patients are asked to select the set of words that best describes their pain, and within the selected sets, to identify the word that is relevant to their condition. Quantitative treatment of this scale includes adding up the number of selected words and the rank value. One of the interesting aspects of the scale is that it can distinguish among pain syndromes, meaning that patients use a distinctive constellation of words to describe a particular pain experience. For example, data obtained from different patient groups show that the pain of toothache is described differently from the pain of arthritis, which in turn is described differently from menstrual pain. The simple query by a physician "Is the pain still there?" may soon be replaced by a more detailed analysis that will provide better clues about the effectiveness of procedures used to control the suffering of pain.

Pain is a complex perception, and our measurement of it needs to recognize this complexity. Laboratory research studies with pain stimulation of normal volunteers has employed methods and measures other than the rating scale developed by Melzack. Early research emphasized the measurement of **pain threshold**, the point on a range of stimuli where pain is first sensed. Other measures in studies where a continuum of pain stimuli is presented include **pain tolerance** level—that is, the most intense stimulus the subject is willing to sustain. Both of these measures are strongly influenced by psychological states such as anxiety, expectancy, and the subtle aspects of instructions from experimenters. In addition, some researchers believe that these laboratory measures are not very sensitive to pain-relief interventions that are very effective in clinical situations. Recently, laboratory research methods have relied more on the type of assessments and measures that are found in clinical research. A simple scenario in this type of research includes asking the subject to rate a pain stimulus on a scale of pain intensity. In some situations the subject indicates the extent of pain by moving a lever over a range from "no pain" to "severe pain." The subject moves the lever whenever he or she feels a change, and this adjustment provides an assessment of the temporal course of pain and the changes produced by pain-relief efforts. More elaborate psychophysical techniques have also been employed in laboratory studies of pain, including signal detection methods.

Pain Information Is Transmitted through Special Neural Systems

Contemporary studies of pain mechanisms have described the characteristics of receptors in the skin that transmit pain information and the relevant pathways of the central nervous system. There remain many unknowns in our understanding of pain pathways, and research continues to elaborate on the complexity of the distribution of neural activity initiated by pain stimuli. In this section we will discuss some features of peripheral and central nervous system pathways that mediate pain.

The periphery. Pain information originates in the periphery. In most cases the initial stimulus for pain is the partial destruction of or injury to tissue adjacent to certain nerve fibers. This tissue change results in the release of a chemical substance or substances that most likely activate pain fibers in the skin. Various substances have been suggested as the chemical mediators of pain. They include neuropeptides, serotonin, histamine, various proteolytic (protein-metabolizing) enzymes, and prostaglandins—a group of unusual hormones (Figure 8.19). Some researchers have isolated other substances that are associated with the inflammation that accompanies pain (Granstrom, 1983). This area of research is very important because it may lead to the development of new pain-relief drugs that act at the periphery.

Are there peripheral receptors and nerve fibers that are specialized for the signaling of noxious stim-

ulation? Over the years this issue has generated considerable controversy. Some researchers have argued that there are no specialized receptors or fibers that respond to noxious stimulation but rather that pain is initiated by some pattern of stimulation of a broad class of peripheral afferent fibers. Other researchers have argued that pain involves a specialized class of afferent fibers that conduct more slowly. Perl (1980) has clarified this issue by showing that several populations of peripheral afferent fibers respond to noxious stimulation. One class includes myelinated, high-threshold mechanoreceptors. The most common pain receptors of the skin, however, are the terminals of a group of thin, unmyelinated fibers (called C fibers). These fibers respond to strong mechanical stimulation and other noxious stimuli, such as heat. Repetitive activation of these fibers by noxious stimulation can lower thresholds considerably, a kind of sensitization to noxious stimuli. Thus, contemporary research has clearly established that there are specific groups of **nociceptors**—receptors that respond selectively to noxious stimulation. Information about pain is then transmitted in specialized pain fibers.

CNS pathways. In the central nervous system (CNS), special pathways mediate pain. Afferent fibers from the periphery that carry nociceptive information terminate on neurons in the superficial layers of the dorsal horn of the spinal cord. Several distinct tracts in the spinal cord ascend to the brain carrying pain information (Figure 8.20). Especially prominent among these is the spinothalamic tract. Pain fibers entering the spinal cord synapse on dorsal horn neurons whose axons cross the midline and ascend the

8.19   Peripheral Mediation of Pain

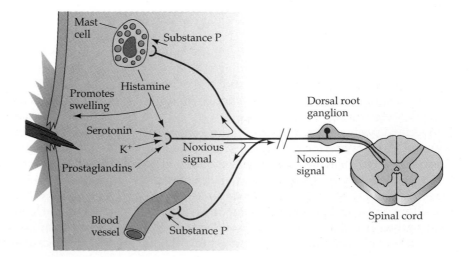

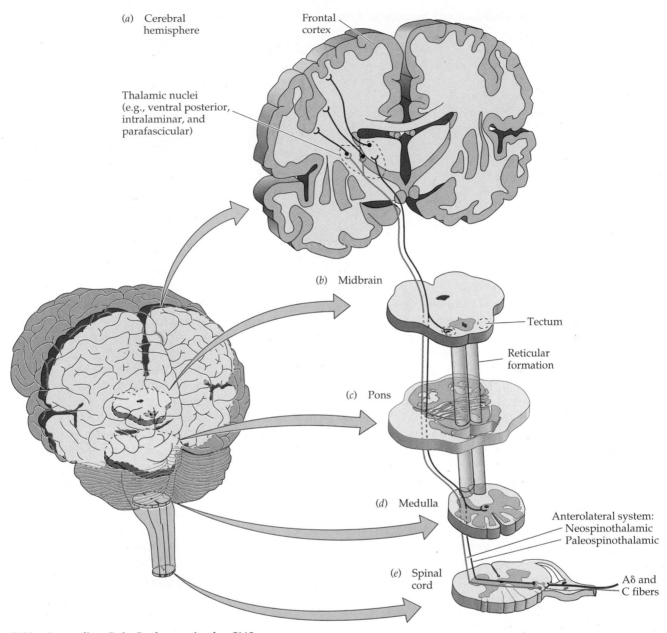

(*a*) Cerebral hemisphere

Frontal cortex

Thalamic nuclei (e.g., ventral posterior, intralaminar, and parafascicular)

(*b*) Midbrain

Tectum

Reticular formation

(*c*) Pons

(*d*) Medulla

Anterolateral system:
Neospinothalamic
Paleospinothalamic

(*e*) Spinal cord

Aδ and C fibers

8.20   Ascending Pain Pathways in the CNS

spinal cord to terminate in several nuclei of the thalamus. Several other pain pathways have been identified within the spinal cord. The pain-response properties of various parts of these pathways have been clearly established; as with peripheral labeled lines (see Figure 8.6), cells at different levels of the central nervous system respond preferentially to intense mechanical stimuli and other noxious stimuli. One interesting and persistently puzzling aspect of pain pathways is that their interruption reduces pain perception only temporarily. After a pathway in the

spinal cord is cut, pain is diminished, but returns after an interval of weeks or months. The usual way of interpreting these data is that nociceptive input from the remaining intact pathways becomes abnormally effective. However, there is more to the story of pain pathways, as we will see.

Additional complexity of the central nervous system pain pathways is related to the complexity of the pain experience itself. Some researchers have suggested that pain experience is multifaceted (Figure 8.21). One aspect is the "sensory–discriminative" fea-

8.21   The Multifaceted Character of Pain

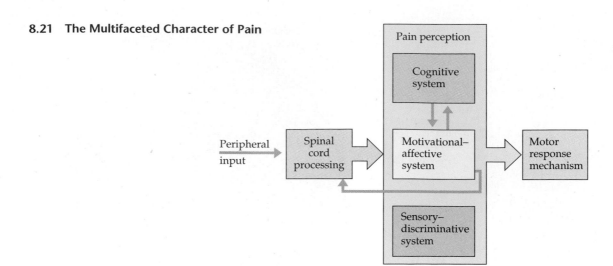

ture—the perception that a painful event has occurred, the detection of the place(s) where it was initiated, and the character of the event that produced the noxious experience. Another aspect of the perception of noxious events has been referred to as the "motivational–affective" component of pain—the emotional feature that leads to species-typical defense and escape behaviors (Casey, 1980). A third aspect of the pain experience is the cognitive evaluation of pain stimuli. The combined techniques of brain stimulation and nerve cell recording have shown that the brain pathways mediating these different aspects of pain are separated, at least to some degree. Some researchers have shown that there are sites within the brain stem where electrical stimulation elicits escape behavior much like that provoked by pain stimuli. Furthermore, nerve cells in this region are preferentially sensitive to noxious stimulation. Finally, the depiction of brain pathways for pain is also complicated by an array of brain sites that modulate pain in a profound manner. The description of endogenous pain-control systems has led to new hope that we may eventually be able to control pain. The remainder of this chapter is devoted to this theme.

Pain Can Be Controlled by a Variety of Mechanisms and Pathways

Relief from the suffering of pain has long been a dominant concern of humans. Throughout history different remedies have been offered. Pain relief received renewed attention after the publication of an insightful paper by Melzack and Wall (1965). They suggested that pain is subject to many modulating influences, including some that can close spinal "gates" controlling the flow of pain information from the spinal cord to the brain (Figure 8.22).

Additional control is exerted by higher centers in the pain system, which send axons down the spinal cord, where they terminate on the first synapses of the pain system in the superficial layers of the dorsal horn. The modulatory signals above the spinal cord can inhibit the transmission of incoming pain impulses. Figure 8.23 shows both the ascending pain system and the descending pain-control system. The discov-

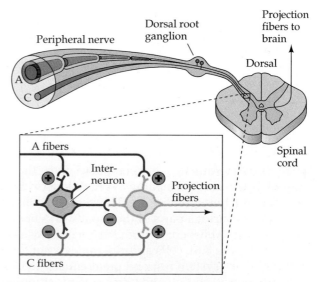

8.22   The Gate Control Theory of Pain Perception This circuitry could explain why cutaneous stimulation of A fibers could reduce the transmission of pain signals originating in C fibers.

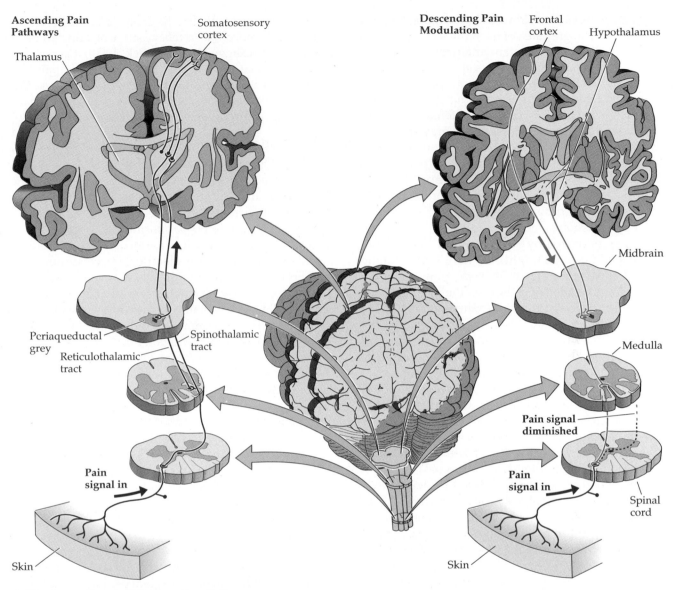

Ascending Pain Pathways

Somatosensory cortex

Thalamus

Periaqueductal grey

Reticulothalamic tract

Spinothalamic tract

Pain signal in

Skin

Descending Pain Modulation

Frontal cortex

Hypothalamus

Midbrain

Medulla

Pain signal diminished

Pain signal in

Skin

Spinal cord

8.23 Ascending and Descending Pathways
Pain sensation is projected up to the brain (*left*) but the brain can inhibit those signals to control pain (*right*). After Basbaum and Fields, 1984.

ery of the brain's power to control the flow of pain signals has inspired many new approaches for the alleviation of pain. In the sections that follow, we will discuss some of these strategies, which are examples of the interaction between basic research and application.

Opiate Drugs Activate a Pain-Relief System in the Body

Over the centuries opium has been admired for its pain-relieving effects. For years researchers attempted to determine how opiate drugs such as morphine control pain; finally they successfully showed that the brain contains natural opiatelike substances. This finding suggested that the brain has built-in mechanisms to control the transmission of pain information. In effect, the brain might modulate pain in a manner akin to that produced by exogenous opiates such as morphine. Several classes of endogenous opioids have now been discovered (see Chapter 6), and various ideas about how these substances fit into the circuitry of pain information have been presented (Basbaum and Fields, 1984).

Early observations showed that stimulation of the periaqueductal gray area of the brain stem in rats (see Figure 8.23) produced potent **analgesia** (loss of pain sensation; from the Greek roots *an-*, "not," and *algesis*, "feeling of pain"). Injection of opiates into this area also relieved pain, suggesting that the region contains synaptic receptors for opiatelike substances. Neural inputs to the periaqueductal gray area are diverse, including axons that arise from some cerebral cortical sites, the amygdala, and the hypothalamus. Most important, there is a strong input from the spinal cord, which presumably delivers nociceptive information. According to the model of the control of pain transmission in the spinal cord by the brain stem that was proposed by Basbaum and Fields (1978, 1984; see Figure 8.23 right), excitation of periaqueductal gray neurons leads via endorphin-containing axons to stimulation of neurons in the medulla. These medullary neurons have serotonin-containing axons that innervate the spinal cord and *inhibit* neurons that transmit information from the periphery. In this way, pain information is blocked by a direct gating action in the spinal cord. Electrical stimulation of the descending tract elicits inhibition of the response of spinal cord sensory relay cells to noxious stimulation of the skin. Considerable evidence supports this model, including the anatomical and physiological demonstration of pathways that descend from the brain stem to various levels of the spinal cord.

In addition to their beneficial pain-relieving effects, opiates and other analgesics often produce side effects such as confusion, drowsiness, vomiting, constipation, and depression of the respiratory system. Now that we know the circuitry of the pain-relief system, why give large doses of the drug systemically—that is, throughout the body? Instead, physicians can now administer very small doses of opiates directly to the spinal cord to relieve pain, thus avoiding many of the side effects. The drugs can be administered epidurally (just outside the spinal cord's dura mater) or intrathecally (between the dura mater and the spinal cord). Both routes are somewhat invasive and therefore are restricted to surgical anesthesia, childbirth, or the management of severe chronic pain (Landau and Levy, 1993).

In the clinical context there have been long-standing concerns about the use of morphine and other opiates for the relief of pain because of their addictive potential. Low doses and infrequent use have been the common standard. However, a recent report of the Agency for Health Care Policy and Research urges swift and aggressive use of painkillers after surgery to relieve pain and speed recovery. Several recent studies show that the danger of addiction from the use of morphine to relieve surgical pain had been vastly overexaggerated (Melzack, 1990); it is now estimated to be 0.04%. Moreover, once chronic pain develops, it is extremely difficult to overcome, so the best approach is to prevent the onset of chronic pain by early, aggressive treatment.

Stimulation of the Skin Can Relieve Pain

Human history is filled with examples of the use of strange techniques to achieve relief from pain. One of the more unusual procedures is the administration of electrical currents to the body. Centuries ago this technique included the application of electric fish or eels to sites of pain. More recently, a new procedure called **transcutaneous electrical nerve stimulation (TENS)** has gained prominence as a way to suppress certain types of pain that have proven difficult to control. TENS involves the delivery of electrical pulses through electrodes attached to the skin, which excite nerves that supply the region that hurts. The stimulation itself produces a sense of tingling rather than pain. In some cases dramatic relief of pain can outlast the duration of stimulation by a factor of hours. The best pain relief is produced when the electrical stimulation is delivered close to the source of pain. TENS has been especially successful in the treatment of patients whose pain is derived from peripheral nerve injuries. The analgesic action of this technique is at least partially mediated by endogenous opioids, since administration of naloxone, an opioid antagonist, partially blocks the analgesic action of TENS.

Painful accidental injuries to the body are a common feature of our existence. Recall, for example, the last time you stubbed your toe on a piece of furniture. In addition to a string of expletives, a frequent result of such incidents is the self-administration of skin stimulation; that is, you react by vigorously rubbing the injured area. Of course, there are many physiological aspects to such "first aid," but is it possible that skin stimulation following an injury has an analgesic response? A special type of tactile stimulus—vibratory stimulation—can alleviate some types of clinical and experimental pain in humans. A large-scale study by Lundeberg (1983) using patients with either chronic or acute pain systematically explored pain alleviation by vibratory stimulation applied to the skin. In this study, acute-pain patients were defined as those suffering from pain for less than 14 days, while chronic-pain patients were those who had been experiencing pain for 6 months to 22 years. Pain was assessed in several ways. Patients filled out the McGill Pain Assessment Questionnaire and rated their pain on a simple seven-point scale (0 = no pain, 6 = excruciating pain). Pain was also measured subjectively by a rating system that consisted of a simple lever that patients could move from a neutral position to one side when pain was reduced or to the other side when pain was increased. The treatment in these studies consisted of the application of an electromechanical vibrator to different body sites depending on the apparent origin of the pain. The study included a wide array of disorders. The pain relief achievedby this method was compared with the effectiveness of three other treatments: administration of aspirin, electrical stimulation of the skin (TENS), and use of an apparent vibrator that produced the sounds of vibration but not actual vibration. Vibratory stimulation was applied for prolonged periods, usually 45 minutes. In a large percentage of both chronic- and acute-pain patients, pain was reduced; the duration of pain relief ranged from 3 to 12 hours. The best results were obtained with 100- to 200-Hz stimuli applied with moderate pressure to the skin surface. This method of pain relief was as effective as the TENS procedure, which is commonly used in pain-treatment programs throughout the United States (Landau and Levy, 1993).

A detailed psychophysical study of the effects of vibration on pain, conducted by Bini and colleagues (1984), used normal subjects. Pain was induced in volunteer subjects by electrical stimulation through an electrode placed directly into the median nerve at the wrist. The subjects usually perceived pain induced by this method as coming from one finger. Vibratory stimuli were applied to the region of the finger where pain was perceived. Subjects reported their estimates of the magnitude of the pain by moving a lever along a scale from 0 to 5. Nerves were stimulated at an intensity that the subject indicated was the highest "bearable." The skin was then stimulated by vibration, and subjects indicated any change in pain by movements of their rating lever. Striking analgesia was evident when vibratory stimuli were applied in the region of the skin where pain was felt. Analgesic effects were not evident when the skin stimulated was outside the area of perceived pain. Other skin treatments, such as brushing, pressure, or cooling, had much less of an analgesic effect, leading to the conclusion that vibratory stimulation is extremely effective in alleviating pain.

Placebos Work through Both Opioid and Nonopioid Mechanisms

The search for relief from pain has led people to consume many unusual substances; even chemically in-ert pills have been reported to alleviate pain in many patients. The term **placebo** (from the Latin for "I shall please") has been applied to such inert substances or other treatments that have no obvious direct physiological effect. Whenever a placebo appears to alleviate pain, investigators try to determine the indirect effects of the placebo treatment or of the circumstances in which it is administered.

Recent research has yielded striking observations providing clues about why placebos relieve pain in some patients. In one study, Levine, Gordon, and Fields (1978) used volunteer subjects who had just had their wisdom teeth extracted—an especially painful procedure that one could expect to produce some miserable people. These patients were told that they were being given an analgesic but were not told what kind. Some of these patients received morphine-based drugs, and some were given saline solutions—the placebo. One out of three patients given the placebo experienced pain relief. (Of course, morphine produced relief in most of the patients who received it.) To explore the mechanisms of the placebo effect, these researchers gave naloxone to other patients who were also administered the placebo. Recall that naloxone blocks the effects of both exogenous opiates and endogenous opioids or opiate-like substances. Patients given the placebo and naloxone did not experience pain relief; this result implies that placebo relief of pain is mediated by an endogenous opioid system.

A critical analysis of studies of the mechanisms of placebo effects by Grevert and Goldstein (1985) has pointed to a number of deficiencies in these studies. Factors such as suitable control groups and the dose level of naloxone have proved critical in placebo research. Furthermore, we now know that there are several types of opioid receptors in the brain, and the affinity of naloxone for these various receptors is quite different. Thus, a negative effect of naloxone administration is not definitive in excluding the possible mediation of endogenous opioids. Moreover, in a study designed to deal with criticisms of previous placebo research, Grevert, Albert, and Goldstein (1983) showed that naloxone did not completely prevent placebo-induced analgesia but rather reduced the effectiveness of a placebo. This relationship was established in experiments involving normal subjects in whom pain was induced by the inflation of a pressure cuff on their arm. The results suggest that both opioid and nonopioid mechanisms contribute to placebo analgesia; the same conclusion comes from studies of stress-induced analgesia that we will discuss shortly. Future studies dealing with this phenomenon will increase our understanding of the multifaceted character of pain relief.

Acupuncture May Control Pain by Causing the Release of Opioids

Visitors to China during recent decades have described in glowing terms the relief from pain produced by **acupuncture**, a practice based on insertion of needles at designated points on the skin, but others have greeted these procedures with skepticism. The earliest description of acupuncture is at least 3000 years old. In some acupuncture procedures, the needles are manipulated once in position, and in other instances electrical or heat stimulation is delivered through the inserted needles. The points at which needles are inserted are related to the locus of pain and some of the characteristics of the pain condition.

Acupuncture has gained popularity but detailed clinical assessments have tended to be more reserved and emphasize that only a small number of people achieve continued relief from chronic pain. At least part of the pain-blocking character of acupuncture appears to be mediated by the release of endorphins (Pert et al., 1981). Administering opioid antagonists prior to acupuncture blocks or reduces its pain-control effects. More research is needed in clinical settings to identify the limits of this type of pain control. Animal models of the procedures used with human patients are also promoting an understanding of this ancient but enduring remedy.

Stress Can Induce Analgesia

Inhibition of pain has been shown in many laboratory situations that involve unusual treatments, such as brain electrical stimulation. Such studies demonstrate the existence of pain-control circuitry, but they do not provide information about the customary ways in which inhibitory systems are activated. What are the conditions that activate endorphin-mediated pain control? To answer this question, researchers have examined pain inhibition that might arise in stressful circumstances. Some researchers have suggested that stress-provoked activation of the brain systems that produce analgesia might come about when pain threatens to overwhelm effective coping strategies. Studies concerned with how pain might control pain itself have revealed some new perspectives on mechanisms mediating these effects.

Several years ago researchers showed that exposure of rats to mild foot shock produced analgesia. Some other forms of stress, such as swimming in cold water, also produced inhibition of pain responses. Other observations suggested that such stress-in-

duced analgesia was mediated by brain endogenous opioids. In fact, the analgesia produced by stress was similar in several respects to that produced by opiates (Bodnar et al., 1980). Like opiates, repeated exposure to stress resulted in declining analgesic effectiveness. In addition, cross-tolerance is observed between opiates and stressors; that is, diminished analgesia to repeated stress also results in reduced pain inhibition by opiate drugs. However, antagonists to opiates, such as naloxone, have had variable effects on stress-induced analgesia, suggesting that some part of stress-produced analgesia is not mediated by endogenous opioids. More recent research has explored this theme more completely.

John Liebeskind—a leading researcher in the area of pain—and his colleagues have studied rats in stress situations that consisted of inescapable foot shock (Terman et al., 1984). Different groups of rats were exposed to different regimens of foot shock, and changes in pain threshold were assessed using a technique called the tail-flick test. This assessment is a measure of the level of radiant heat that produces a quick flick of the tail of the rat. In these studies the role of endorphins was assessed by the administration of an opiate antagonist—naltrexone. In this experimental situation, the stress of inescapable shock produces an increase in tail-flick latency, which shows that the shock stress produces an analgesic effect. However, administration of naltrexone produces a curious complication. When analgesia is produced by short periods of foot shock, naltrexone reverses the analgesic response, a result that demonstrates that the source of analgesia is an opioid system in the brain. However, antagonists to opiates have little effect on stress-produced analgesia if it is produced by prolonged periods of foot shock. This finding demonstrates that stress activates both an opioid-sensitive analgesic system and a pain-control system that does not involve opioids. Relatively precise parameters of the stress-inducing stimuli seem to determine which system is activated. Similar elements are probably involved in both pain-control circuits, since spinal lesions disrupt both forms of stress-induced analgesia. But the pathways must be separated to some extent, for some brain stem lesions can affect the opiate-mediated analgesia without affecting the nonopiate-mediated analgesia (Terman et al., 1984). These findings are very important in suggesting clinical strategies for pain-relief intervention in humans. Further research should clarify whether there are additional forms of pain relief controlled by other circuits.

Figure 8.24 summarizes the many types of pain-relief strategies and interventions, including surgical and pharmacological strategies, psychological brain and spinal cord stimulation, and sensory stimulation. The elusive nature of pain is evident in this range of potential interventions, some of which reflect desperation in the face of great anguish.

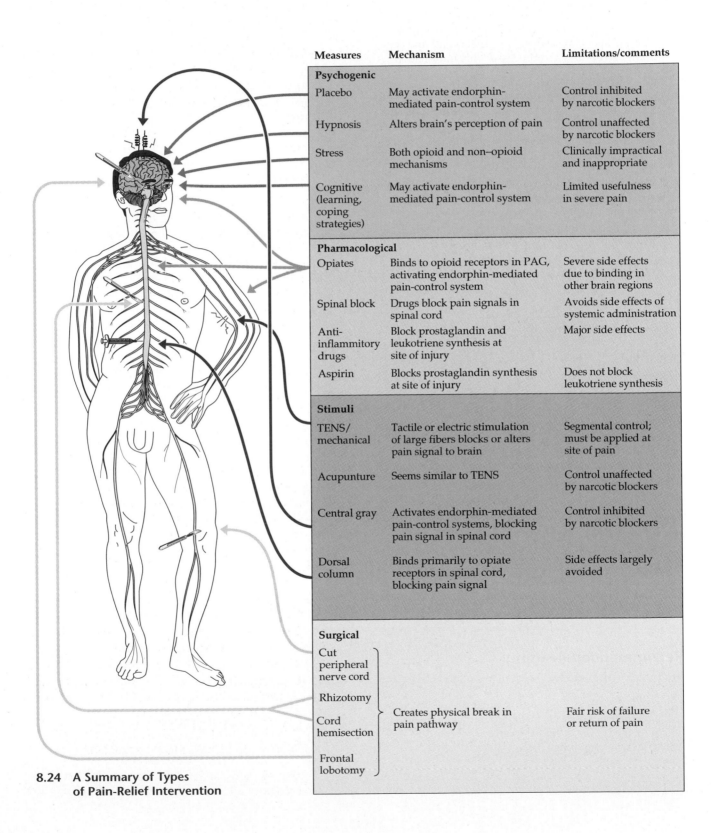

Measures	Mechanism	Limitations/comments
Psychogenic		
Placebo	May activate endorphin-mediated pain-control system	Control inhibited by narcotic blockers
Hypnosis	Alters brain's perception of pain	Control unaffected by narcotic blockers
Stress	Both opioid and non–opioid mechanisms	Clinically impractical and inappropriate
Cognitive (learning, coping strategies)	May activate endorphin-mediated pain-control system	Limited usefulness in severe pain
Pharmacological		
Opiates	Binds to opioid receptors in PAG, activating endorphin-mediated pain-control system	Severe side effects due to binding in other brain regions
Spinal block	Drugs block pain signals in spinal cord	Avoids side effects of systemic administration
Anti-inflammitory drugs	Block prostaglandin and leukotriene synthesis at site of injury	Major side effects
Aspirin	Blocks prostaglandin synthesis at site of injury	Does not block leukotriene synthesis
Stimuli		
TENS/mechanical	Tactile or electric stimulation of large fibers blocks or alters pain signal to brain	Segmental control; must be applied at site of pain
Acupuncture	Seems similar to TENS	Control unaffected by narcotic blockers
Central gray	Activates endorphin-mediated pain-control systems, blocking pain signal in spinal cord	Control inhibited by narcotic blockers
Dorsal column	Binds primarily to opiate receptors in spinal cord, blocking pain signal	Side effects largely avoided
Surgical		
Cut peripheral nerve cord		
Rhizotomy	Creates physical break in pain pathway	Fair risk of failure or return of pain
Cord hemisection		
Frontal lobotomy		

8.24   A Summary of Types of Pain-Relief Intervention

Summary

Sensory Processing

1. A sensory system furnishes selected information to the brain about internal and external events and conditions. It captures and processes only information that is significant for the particular organism.

2. Ideal sensory systems discriminate among some of the available forms of energy, respond over a wide range of intensities, are highly sensitive to a change of stimuli, respond reliably and rapidly, and suppress unwanted information.

3. Stimuli that some species detect readily have no effect on other species that lack the necessary receptors.

4. Some receptors are simple free nerve endings, but most include cells that are specialized to transduce particular kinds of energy.

5. Transduction of energy at sensory receptors involves the production of a generator potential that stimulates the sensory neurons.

6. Coding is the translation of receptor information into patterns of neural activity.

7. Adaptation refers to the progressive decrease in the rate of impulses as the same stimulation is maintained. This decline is slow in the case of tonic receptors but rapid for phasic receptors. Adaptation protects the nervous system from redundant stimulation.

8. Mechanisms of information suppression include accessory structures, descending pathways from neural centers to the receptor, and central circuits.

9. The receptive field of a cell is the stimulus region that changes the response of the cell.

10. The succession of levels in a sensory pathway is thought to allow for different and perhaps successively more elaborate kinds of processing.

11. Attention refers to the temporary enhancement of certain sensory messages during particular states of the individual. Attention is thought to involve the reticular activating system in the reticular formation of the brain stem.

Touch and Pain

1. The skin contains several distinct types of receptors that have specific sensitivities. Inputs from the skin course through distinct spinal pathways, including the dorsal column system and the anterolateral (spinothalamic) system.

2. The surface of the body is represented at each level of the somatosensory system, and at the level of the cerebral cortex there are multiple maps of the body surface.

3. Pain guides adaptive behavior by providing indications of harmful stimuli. Pain is a complex state that is strongly influenced by cultural factors and many aspects of individual experience.

4. Pain sensation is subject to many controlling or modulating conditions. These include circuitry within the brain and spinal cord that employs opioid synapses. One component in the modulation of pain is descending pathways arising in the brain stem that inhibit incoming neural activity at synapses within the spinal cord.

5. Pain control has been achieved using drugs (including placebos), electrical and mechanical stimulation of the skin, acupuncture, and surgery, among other methods.

Recommended Reading

Fields, H. L. 1988. *Pain*. McGraw-Hill, New York.

Johnson, K. O., Hsiao, S. S., and Twombly, I. A. 1995. Neural mechanisms of tactile form recognition. In M. S. Gazzaniga (ed.), *The Cognitive Neurosciences*. pp. 253–269. MIT Press, Cambridge, MA.

Stein, B. and Meredith, M. A. 1993. *The Merging of the Senses*. MIT Press, Cambridge, MA.

Valbo, A. B. 1995. Single-afferent neurons and somatic sensation in humans. In M. S. Gazzaniga (ed.), *The Cognitive Neurosciences*. pp. 237–253. MIT Press, Cambridge, MA.

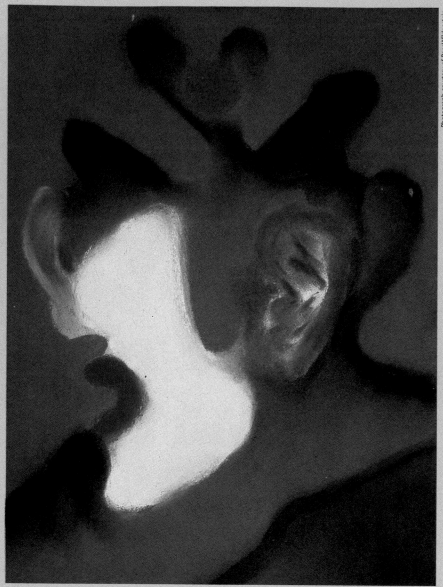

Lucas Samaras, *Untitled*, February 16, 1961

Hearing

Vestibular Perception

The Chemical Senses: Taste and Smell

CHAPTER 9

Hearing, Vestibular Perception, Taste, and Smell

Orientation

You exist only because your ancestors had keen senses that allowed them to find food and to avoid predators and other dangers. In this chapter we continue our consideration of sensory worlds by discussing the perception of distant signals, including hearing (audition) and smell (olfaction). We will also explore two related sensory systems: (1) the vestibular system, which detects orientation and movement of the body, and which is related to the auditory system, and (2) the sense of taste, which, like smell, is a chemical sense. Recent discoveries have greatly expanded our understanding of both receptor mechanisms and central processing, especially in audition and olfaction. Both of these senses are extremely acute, and we will explore some of the special mechanisms that make them so sensitive. We begin with hearing, because audition evolved from special mechanical receptors akin to the somatosensory elements we discussed in Chapter 8.

Hearing

Hearing is an important part of the adaptive behavior of many animals. For humans, the sounds of speech form the basic elements of the thousands of our languages and therefore of our social relations. Helen Keller, who was both blind and deaf, said, "Blindness deprives you of contact with things; deafness deprives you of contact with people."

The sounds of any one language are only a small subset of the enormous possibilities for sounds that can be produced by human vocal cavities. The sounds produced by animals—from insects to whales—also have a wide range of complexity. The adaptive successes of many animals are linked to their ability to make and perceive these sounds, with which they probe the environment. For example, the melodic songs of some male birds and the chirps of male crickets attract females of their species. The grunts, screeches, and burbly sounds of primates signal danger or the need for comfort or satisfaction. Owls and bats exploit the directional property of sound to locate prey and avoid obstacles in the dark. Whales communicate with each other using sounds that can travel hundreds of miles in the ocean. Unlike sights, sounds can turn corners and go around obstacles, and they work as well in the dark as in the light.

The use of sounds by all these different animals depends on distinct features of auditory information processing that discriminate aspects of acoustic signals with great accuracy. Your auditory system can detect rapid changes of sound intensity (measured in decibels) and frequency (measured in hertz). In fact, the speed of auditory information processing is so good that the analysis of frequency by the human ear rivals that of modern electronic gadgets. Your ear is also as sensitive as possible to weak (low-decibel) sounds at frequencies in the range from 1000 to 2000 hertz (1 to 2 kilohertz). If it were any more sensitive, you would be bothered by the random movement of air molecules bouncing against each other in your external ear canal.

The Impact of Sounds Is Shaped by the External and Middle Ears

How do the small vibrations of air particles become the speech, music, and other sounds we hear? By shaping the mechanical forces that act on auditory end organs, the peripheral components of the auditory system determine the beginnings of auditory perception. In this section we will discuss these initial stages of auditory excitation. Box 9.1 reviews the basic characteristics of the auditory stimulus, sound.

The External Ear Captures, Focuses, and Filters Sound

Sound waves are collected by the **external ear**, which consists of the part we readily see, called the **pinna**, and a canal that leads to the eardrum (Figure 9.1*a*). The external ear is a distinctly mammalian characteristic, and mammals show a wide array of ear shapes and sizes. The acoustic properties of the external ear are important because its shape physically transforms sound energies. The "hills and valleys" of the pinna modify the character of sound that reaches the middle and inner ear. Some frequencies of sound are enhanced; others are dimmed. For example, the shape of the human ear especially increases the efficiency of sounds in the frequency range of 2 to 5 kilohertz (kHz), a range that is important for speech perception. The shape of the external ear is also important in sound localization—that is, identifying the direction and distance of the source of a sound (which we discuss later in the chapter).

Very few humans can move their ears, but many other mammals have an elaborate set of muscles associated with the external ear, enabling them to change the shape of the pinna and to point it to the source of sound. Animals with acute auditory localization abilities, such as bats, have especially mobile ears. Of course, animals with mobile ears have to take into account the position of the pinna when interpreting sounds around them. Information about the position of the external ear in such animals is conveyed to the auditory pathways in several forms, including feedback information from receptors in the muscles around the pinna.

In addition to their auditory function, the size and shape of the external ear reflect evolutionary adaptations to environmental factors related to heat dissipation. Consider, for example, the small ears of an arctic fox compared with the large ears of a fox living in a warm climate (see Figure 13.6). Elephants dissipate heat by waving their huge external ears.

The Middle Ear Concentrates Sound Energies

Between the external ear and the receptor cells of the inner ear is a group of structures, including bones and muscles, that constitute the **middle ear** (Figure 9.1*c*). A chain of three tiny bones, or **ossicles**, connects the eardrum (**tympanic membrane**) at the end of the ear canal to an opening of the inner ear called the

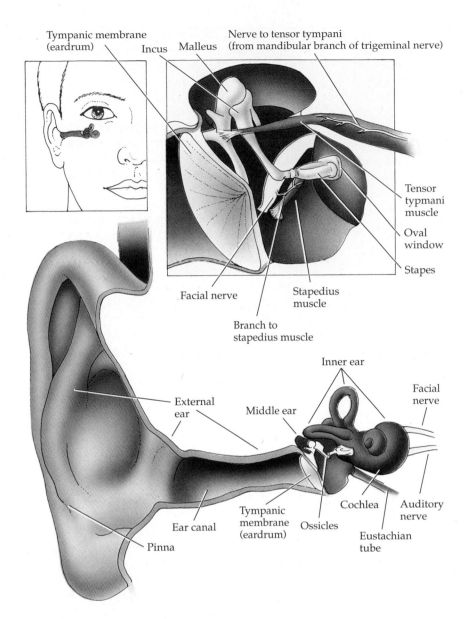

Tympanic membrane (eardrum)

Incus

Malleus

Nerve to tensor tympani (from mandibular branch of trigeminal nerve)

Tensor typmani muscle

Oval window

Stapes

Facial nerve

Stapedius muscle

Branch to stapedius muscle

Inner ear

Facial nerve

External ear

Middle ear

Auditory nerve

Cochlea

Pinna

Ear canal

Tympanic membrane (eardrum)

Ossicles

Eustachian tube

9.1   The Human Ear
(*Top left*) Orientation figure of the ear canal and middle and inner ears within the head. (*Bottom*) An enlargement of these auditory structures. (*Top right*) The middle ear.

oval window. These ossicles are the smallest bones in the body; they are called the **malleus** (hammer), **incus** (anvil), and **stapes** (stirrup). Small displacements of the tympanic membrane move the ossicular chain. These bones help the minute mechanical forces of air particles perform the extremely difficult task of compressing the fluid in the inner ear by focusing the pressures at the relatively *large* tympanic membrane onto the *small* oval window. This arrangement vastly amplifies the sound pressure so that it is capable of stimulating the fluid-filled inner ear.

The mechanical linkage of the ossicles is not fixed and invariable; it is modulated by two muscles in ways that improve auditory perception and protect

the delicate receptor cells of the inner ear from loud, potentially damaging sounds. One of these muscles, the **tensor tympani** (see Figure 9.1*c*), is attached to the malleus, which is connected to the tympanic membrane. The other muscle of the middle ear is attached to the stapes and thus is called the **stapedius**. When activated, these muscles make it harder to move the middle ear bones, thus limiting the effectiveness of sounds.

The muscles of the middle ear are activated by sounds that are 80 to 90 decibels above a person's hearing threshold (see Box 9.1)—about as loud as a noisy street. A simple circuit in the brain stem evokes the muscle contraction (Borg and Counter, 1988). Fig-

Box 9.1
The Basics of Sound

Sound is a repetitive change in the pressure of some medium, commonly air or water. In air the change arises because air particles are moved by a vibrating mechanical system, such as the glottis of the larynx in speech, the cone of loudspeaker, or a tuning fork. In the latter case, as the tuning fork moves away from a resting position, it compresses air particles, causing the air pressure to rise above atmospheric pressure. As the tuning fork swings to the other side of its resting position, air particle density is briefly reduced with respect to atmospheric pressure. A single alternation of compression and expansion of air is called one **cycle**. Figure A illustrates the changes in the spacing of air particles produced by a vibrating tuning fork. Because the sound produced by a tuning fork has only one frequency of vibration, it is called a **pure tone** and can be represented by a sine wave. A pure tone is described physically in terms of two measures:

1. **Frequency**, or the number of cycles per second, measured in hertz (Hz). For example, middle A on a piano has a frequency of 440 Hz.

2. **Amplitude**, or **intensity**—the distance of particle movement in

a defined period of time, usually measured as pressure, or force per unit area, in dynes per square centimeter (dyn/cm^2).

Most sounds are more complicated than a pure tone. For example, a sound made by a musical instrument contains a "fundamental"

frequency and "harmonics." The fundamental is the basic frequency, and the harmonics are multiples of the fundamental. Thus, if the fundamental is 440 Hz, the harmonics are 880, 1320, 1760, and so on. When different instruments play the same note, they differ in the relative intensities of the various harmonics; this difference is what gives each instrument its characteristic sound quality, or timbre. Any complex pattern can

(A)

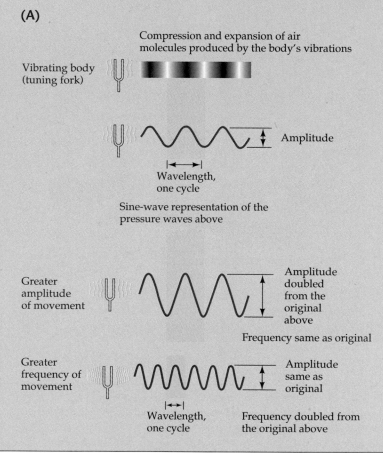

loud, self-produced vocalizations (Avan et al., 1992). For example, some birds and some bats (and some babies) produce vocalizations at intense levels of sound pressure; activation of the stapedius muscle dramatically reduces the effect of the vocalization on the animal's own auditory receptors. In the case of sounds produced by one's own body, the stapedius muscle contracts automatically just *before* the sound-produc-

ure 9.2*a* shows the electrical response of the stapedius muscle beginning about 200 milliseconds *after* the onset of a loud external sound. The muscles of the middle ear also become active during body movement, swallowing, and vocalization; they are the reason we hear few of the sounds produced by the workings of our own bodies. In some animals, activation of these muscles prevents damage to receptors from very

be analyzed into a sum of sine waves, a process called **Fourier analysis** after the French mathematician who discovered it. (We will see in Chapter 10 that Fourier analysis can also be applied to visual patterns.) Figure B shows how a complex wave form can be analyzed into component sine waves of different frequencies.

Most animals produce sound. Hearing enables us to detect energies that we and other animals produce, either for communication or incidentally to other activities.

Since the ear is sensitive to a huge range of sound pressures, sound intensity (a measure of the difference between two pressures) is usually expressed in decibels (dB), a logarithmic scale. The definition of a decibel is as follows:

$$N(dB) = 20 \log P_1/P_2$$

where N is the number of decibels and P_1 and P_2 are the two pressures to be compared. The common reference level, or threshold, in hearing studies (P_2 in the notation above) is 0.0002 dyn/cm^2; this is the least amount of pressure necessary for an average human observer to hear a 1000-Hz tone. In this scale a whisper is about 10 times as intense as 0.0002 dyn/cm^2, and a jet airliner 500 feet overhead about a million times as intense. In decibel notation the whisper is about 20 dB above threshold, and the jetliner is about 120 dB above threshold. Normal conversation is about 60 dB above the reference level.

(B)

(a) Part of a black and white grid

(b) Stimulus intensity across the grid, a square wave

(c) First harmonic

(d) Third harmonic, 1/3 amplitude

(e) Fifth harmonic, 1/5 amplitude

(f) Sum of (c) + (d) + (e)

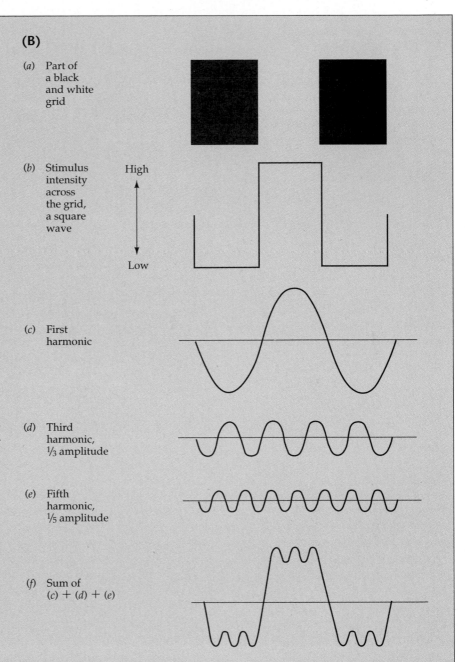

ing movement, as Figure 9.2*b* shows. People whose middle-ear muscles have been damaged by disease complain about the annoying loudness of sounds they formerly ignored. The middle-ear muscles have a greater effect on sounds of low frequency than on sounds of high frequency. Since the most important speech sounds are relatively high in frequency (1 to 2 kHz) and many noises are predominantly low in fre-

quency, the reflex contraction of the muscles to noise often helps us hear speech above noise.

The Inner Ear Transduces Mechanical Energy into Neural Activity

The complex structures of the **inner ear** (see Figure 9.3) convert the mechanical character of sound into neural activity. To understand how the inner ear ac-

9.2 The Stapedius Muscle Modifies Loudness

(*a*) About 200 milliseconds after the onset of a loud external sound, the stapedius muscle starts to contract, thus decreasing the intensity of the stimulus to the inner ear. (*b*) Shortly *before* a person starts to speak, the stapedius contracts, so the voice doesn't overwhelm the auditory system.

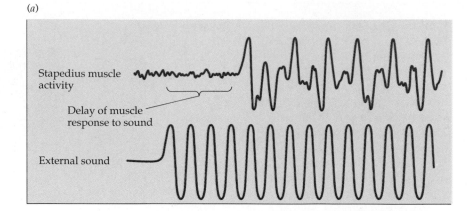

(*a*)

Stapedius muscle activity

Delay of muscle response to sound

External sound

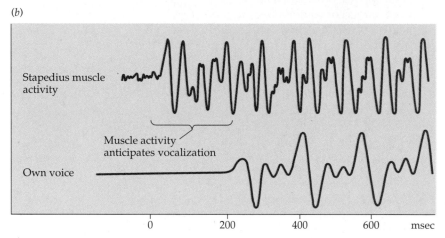

(*b*)

Stapedius muscle activity

Muscle activity anticipates vocalization

Own voice

complishes this transduction, let's look at the details of the inner ear. In mammals the auditory portion of the inner ear is a coiled structure called the **cochlea** (from the Greek *kochlos*, "snail"; Figure 9.3*a*). The human cochlea (Figure 9.3*b*) is embedded in the temporal bone of the skull, and is a marvel of miniaturization. In an adult, the cochlea measures only about 4 mm in diameter—about the size of a pea. Unrolled, the cochlea would measure about 35 to 40 mm in length. The region nearest the oval window membrane is the base of the spiral; the other end, or top, is referred to as the apex. Along the length of the cochlea are three parallel canals: (1) the **tympanic canal**, (2) the **vestibular canal**, and (3) the **cochlear duct** (Figure 9.3*c*). Because the entire structure is filled with noncompressible fluid, movement within the cochlea in response to a push on the oval window requires the presence of a movable outlet membrane. This membrane is the **round window**, which separates the cochlear duct from the middle ear.

The principal elements for converting sounds into neural activity are found on the **basilar membrane**, a flexible structure that separates the tympanic canal

from the cochlear duct (see Figure 9.3*c*). This membrane vibrates in response to sound. It is about five times wider at the apex of the cochlea than at the base, even though the cochlea itself narrows toward its apex. Within the cochlear duct and atop the basilar membrane is the **organ of Corti**—the collective term for all the elements involved in the transduction of sounds. The organ of Corti includes three main structures: (1) the sensory cells (**hair cells**), (2) an elaborate framework of supporting cells, and (3) the terminations of the auditory nerve fibers (Figure 9.3*d*).

Each ear contains two sets of sensory cells, a single row of about 3500 **inner hair cells** (**IHCs**; called inner because they are closer to the central axis of the cochlea) and about 12,000 **outer hair cells** (**OHCs**) in three rows (see Figure 9.3*d*). The IHCs are flask-

9.3 Structures of the Inner Ear

Illustrations at successively higher magnifications of (*a*) the location of middle-ear structures in relation to the external ear; cut-away views of the cochlea (*b, c*); the organ of Corti (*d*); and a single inner hair cell (*e*).

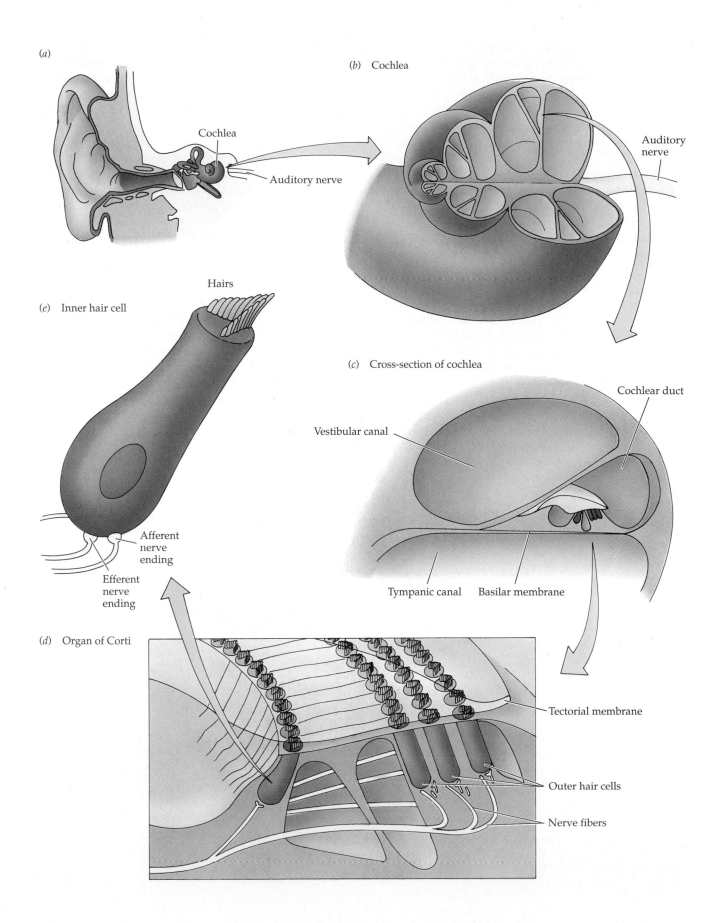

(a)

Cochlea

Auditory nerve

(b) Cochlea

Auditory nerve

(e) Inner hair cell

Hairs

Afferent nerve ending

Efferent nerve ending

(c) Cross-section of cochlea

Cochlear duct

Vestibular canal

Tympanic canal   Basilar membrane

(d) Organ of Corti

Tectorial membrane

Outer hair cells

Nerve fibers

shaped and the OHCs are cylindrical, with a diameter of approximately 5 micrometers (μm) and a length of 20 to 70 μm. From the upper end of each hair cell protrude tiny hairs whose length ranges from about 2 to 6 μm (Figure 9.3*e*). Each hair cell has 50 to 200 of these relatively stiff hairs, which are called **stereocilia** (from the Greek *stereos*, "solid," and the Latin *cilium*, "eyelash"). The heights of the stereocilia increase progressively across the hair cell, so that the tops approximate an inclined plane. Atop the organ of Corti is the **tectorial membrane** (see Figure 9.3*d*). The stereocilia of the OHCs extend into indentations in the bottom of the tectorial membrane. (IHCs do not seem to make direct contact with the tectorial membrane.)

Auditory nerve fibers contact the base of the hair cells (Figure 9.4). Each IHC is associated with about 20 auditory nerve fibers; relatively few nerve fibers contact the many OHCs. In fact the nerve fibers running from the IHCs account for 90 to 95% of the afferent auditory fibers, suggesting that the IHCs convey most of the information about sounds to the brain. The OHCs have a different function: *modulating* acoustic stimulation. They send messages out the auditory nerve to the CNS, but they are also contacted by efferent nerve fibers from the CNS—centrifugal fibers. When these efferent nerve fibers are excit-

ed, the OHCs change their length, thereby influencing the mechanics of the cochlea. Changes in length of the OHCs during the basic responses to sound sharpen the tuning to different frequencies, as we will see later in this chapter (Ashmore, 1994). The IHCs also receive efferent messages, perhaps to inhibit some of the input from loud sounds. Further evidence of the different roles of the inner and outer hair cells comes from studies of a mutant strain of mice that lack IHCs but have normal OHCs; these mice appear to be deaf (Deol and Glueksohn-Waelsch, 1979).

Synapses in the Organ of Corti Convey Messages to and from the Brain

The organ of Corti has four kinds of synapses and nerve fibers. Two of these (1 and 3 in Figure 9.4*a*) convey messages from the hair cells to the brain; the other two (2 and 4 in Figure 9.4*a*) convey messages from the brain to the hair cells. Different synaptic transmitters are active at each type of synapse, as histological, pharmacological, and electrophysiological studies have gradually made clear (Eybalin, 1993). The four types and the synaptic transmitters associated with them are as follows (numbers correspond to those in Figure 9.4*a*):

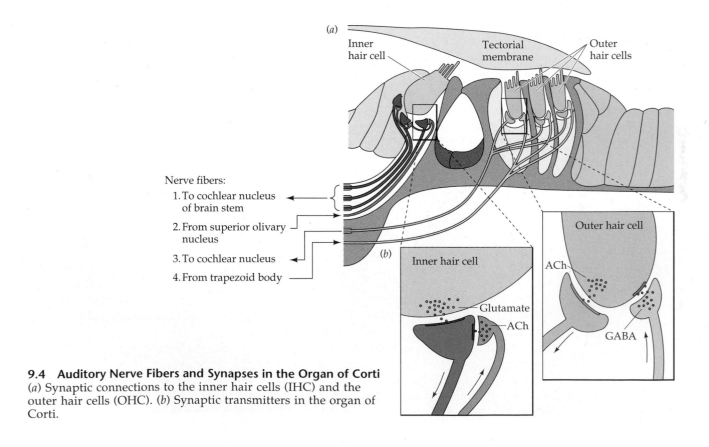

9.4   Auditory Nerve Fibers and Synapses in the Organ of Corti
(*a*) Synaptic connections to the inner hair cells (IHC) and the outer hair cells (OHC). (*b*) Synaptic transmitters in the organ of Corti.

1. *IHC/afferent fiber.* These afferent fibers, which synapse at the IHCs, are the relatively large-diameter fibers that carry to the brain the auditory messages that result in hearing. These are the main fibers in the auditory nerve. The associated transmitter appears to be the excitatory amino acid glutamate, as shown by several kinds of complementary evidence: the presence of glutamate in the IHCs; synthesis of glutamate in the IHCs; release of glutamate upon stimulation of the IHCs; glutamate receptors (both AMPA and NMDA) at these synapses; local neurophysiological effects of release of glutamate; and inactivation of glutamate by glial uptake. As well as glutamate, another excitatory amino acid, aspartate, may also serve as a synaptic transmitter at these junctions.

2. *IHC/efferent fiber.* Efferent fibers, carrying information from the brain, have presynaptic inhibitory endings on the main afferent fiber terminals at the IHCs. Acetylcholine (ACh) is the transmitter released by these efferent fibers.

3. *OHC/afferent fiber.* Using ACh as the transmitter, the OHCs stimulate small-diameter fibers carrying information to the brain.

4. *OHC/efferent fiber.* Efferent fibers that end on the OHCs use gamma-aminobutyric acid (GABA) as their transmitter.

Sounds Produce Waves of Fluid in the Cochlea

When the stapes moves in and out as a result of acoustic vibrations, it exerts varying pressure on the fluid of the vestibular canal, which in turn causes oscillating movements of the cochlear duct and the basilar membrane. late in the nineteenth century, it was suggested that the cochlea might be "tuned"—that is, that different parts of the basilar membrane might be affected by different frequencies of auditory stimulation. In the 1930s and 1940s the Hungarian scientist Georg von Békésy tested this hypothesis, using ingenious physical techniques to make direct observations on cochleas that had been surgically removed from cadavers or dead animals. Von Békésy found that sounds initiate traveling waves that sweep along the basilar membrane, and the site of the largest amplitude of dis-

Georg von Békésy
(1899–1972)

placement of the basilar membrane depends on the frequency of the stimulus (Figure 9.5). For high frequencies the displacement of the basilar membrane peaks in the region where the basilar membrane is narrow—the base of the cochlea. For low-frequency stimuli the amplitudes of membrane displacement peak at the widest portion of the basilar membrane—the apex. Modern research techniques have enabled a closer look at the mechanical changes produced in the cochlea by sound (Ashmore, 1994), and these findings have implications for pitch perception, which we discuss later in this chapter.

The Hair Cells Transduce Auditory Vibrations into Electrical Signals

The processes that link the elaborate mechanical events within the cochlea to auditory nerve fiber excitation remain something of a puzzle even after years of intense investigation. The inner ear is particularly difficult to study because it is relatively inaccessible, buried within the temporal bone, and because the receptor cells are very small. In addition, the cochlea is quite vulnerable, so even delicate experimental manipulations can affect the way it functions.

Recent techniques have overcome these difficulties and revealed intimate details of the principal elements of transduction—the hair cells (Hudspeth, 1989, 1990). The movements of fluid in the cochlea, excited by sounds, produce vibrations of the basilar membrane. These vibrations bend the hair cell cilia that are inserted into the tectorial membrane (see Figure 9.3e). Recordings by Hudspeth (1990) from isolated individual hair cells showed that very small displacements of hair bundles cause rapid changes in ionic channels of the stereocilia. These changes initiate the excitation of the hair cells and then of the afferent neurons.

The ion channels in the stereocilia are the subject of much recent work. They are believed to be gated by mechanical energy, as are those in touch receptors (see Chapter 8), but the gates in the channels for hearing are also specialized for rapid response: they can open and close as often as 1000 times per second. This rapidity rules out the use of second messengers, which are found in receptors for smell, taste, and sight (as we'll see later in this chapter and in Chapter 10).

The characteristics and mechanisms of hair cell action are inferred from various experiments rather than observed directly, because the ion channels are relatively sparse and, unlike some other receptor channels, they have not yet been isolated. The num-

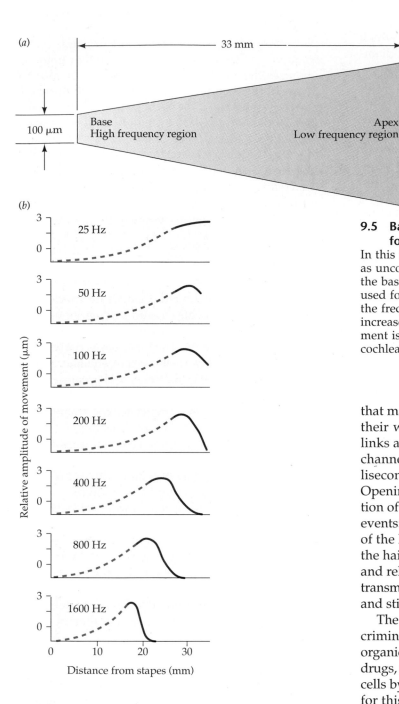

(a)

33 mm

100 μm

Base
High frequency region

Apex
Low frequency region

500 μm

(b)

25 Hz

50 Hz

100 Hz

200 Hz

400 Hz

800 Hz

1600 Hz

Relative amplitude of movement (μm)

Distance from stapes (mm)

9.5 Basilar Membrane Movement for Sounds of Different Frequencies

In this illustration the basilar membrane is represented as uncoiled. (*a*) The diagram shows the dimensions of the basilar membrane; note that different scales are used for length and width. (*b*) The graphs show that as the frequency (Hz = cycles per second) of stimulation increases, the position of the peak of membrane movement is displaced progressively toward the base of the cochlea.

that makes the hair cells sway only a few percent of their width increases the tension on the elastic tip links and pulls open a "trapdoor," opening the ion channel, which closes again in a fraction of a millisecond as the hair cell sways back (Figure 9.6*b*). Opening of the channels causes a rapid depolarization of the entire hair cell, leading to a succession of events: rapid influx of calcium ions (Ca^{2+}) *at the base* of the hair cell, synaptic vesicles within the base of the hair cell fusing with the presynaptic membrane and releasing their chemical contents—the synaptic transmitter glutamate—from the base of the hair cell, and stimulation of the afferent nerve fiber.

The ion pores in the cilia are large and do not discriminate among kinds of ions. They let even small organic molecules pass through, which is why some drugs, such as aspirin and antibiotics, can impair hair cells by attacking their mitochondria. Susceptibility for this kind of damage to the receptor is inherited maternally, as are the mitochondria.

Active Electromechanical Processes in the Cochlea Enhance Frequency Discrimination

As von Békésy realized, the broad peaks of tuning for different frequencies he observed along the basilar membrane (see Figure 9.5) are not sharp enough to account for our ability to discriminate frequencies only 2 Hz apart. Von Békésy and others suggested that the broad patterns of excitation along the basilar membrane were "sharpened" by higher neural cen-

ber of channels has been estimated by measuring the ability of response in relation to the size of response. These measures suggest that there are about 100 ion channels per hair cell, or about one or two per stereocilium. Directing an extremely fine jet of inhibitory chemical at different parts of the bundle of stereocilia indicates that the ion channels are near the top of the cilia, because that is where the inhibitor is effective. Fine, threadlike fibers called **tip links** run along the tips of the stereocilia (Figure 9.6*a*). According to one current model (Hudspeth et al., 1989), a sound

(a)

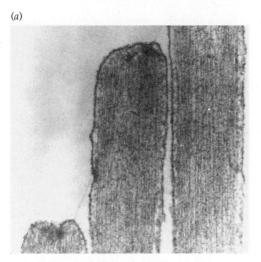

(b)

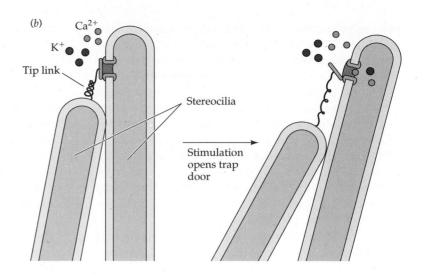

9.6 How Auditory Stimulation Affects the Stereocilia on Cochlear Hair Cells

(*a*) Micrograph of stereocilia showing tip links as threadlike structures. (*b*) The model of hair cell stimulation proposed by Hudspeth (1989). *a* courtesy of A. J. Hudspeth.

ters. That is, they hypothesized that the neural response to a particular sound frequency (at some level of the auditory nervous system) could be largely confined to a small, specific region; this small neural region would represent the exact place along the basilar membrane where the amplitude of the traveling wave is greatest.

Even in the 1940s, recordings from auditory nerve fibers showed much more precise tuning than von Békésy had found in his measurements of the basilar membrane. The **tuning curves** (or receptive fields) of single auditory nerve fibers were studied by recording their responses to sounds that varied in frequency and intensity (Figure 9.7). Each neuron responds to a very precise frequency at its threshold, but as more intense stimuli are used, the neuron responds to a broader range of frequencies. For example, the fiber shown in red in Figure 9.7 has its "best frequency" at 1200 Hz—that is, it responds to a very weak tone at 1200 Hz. When sounds are 20 decibels stronger however, the fiber responds to any frequency from 500 to 1800 Hz. Thus, an auditory nerve fiber is not a labeled line of the sort we discussed in Chapter 8; that is, it does not respond to just one frequency of stimulation. If the brain received a signal from only one such fiber, it would not be able to tell whether the stimulus was a weak tone of 1200 Hz or a stronger tone of 500 or 1800 Hz or any frequency in between. Rather, the auditory system appears to code pattern *across fibers:* It needs signals from many au-

ditory neurons to determine the frequency of the stimulus.

The fact that auditory nerve fibers are tuned much more precisely than is the basilar membrane suggests that the cochlea itself must have a way of enhancing the tuning. In the 1980s technical advances made it possible to record the movements of the *live* basilar membrane, rather than using cochleas removed from cadavers, as von Békésy had to do. In addition, it became possible to record from individual hair cells.

We mentioned earlier that OHCs show the sur-

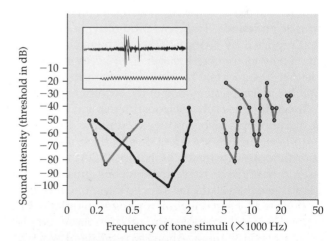

9.7 Examples of Tuning Curves of Auditory Nerve Cells

The curves are obtained by measuring neural responses (inset) to sounds of different intensities and frequencies. These curves are threshold measurements. The graph illustrates responses of six neural units recorded from the auditory nerve of the cat. After Kiang, 1965.

prising property of changing length when they are stimulated electrically—an electromechanical response (Brownell et al., 1985). Hyperpolarization causes the OHCs to increase in length, while depolarization causes them to shorten. These changes, which amount to as much as 4% of the length of the cell, occur almost instantaneously. Investigators hypothesize that these mechanical responses of the OHCs amplify the movements of the basilar membrane and thereby sharpen its tuning (Ashmore, 1994; Hubbard, 1993). Other evidence of the active nature of the cochlea is that the ear can *emit* sounds, as discussed in the next section.

The ability to discriminate frequencies is probably even sharper at higher stations of the auditory nervous system, as von Békésy hypothesized. At the medial geniculate nucleus and the auditory cortex, neurons are excited by certain frequencies and inhibited by neighboring frequencies. This interplay of excitation and inhibition sharpens the frequency responses.

The Ears Emit Sounds

The cochlea is not only the first stage in the analysis of sounds; in most people it also *produces* sounds. If you make a brief sound—a click or a short burst of tone—in the external ear canal, a few milliseconds later a similar sound comes back from the inner ear. This is not just an echo from the eardrum or middle ear, although such echoes exist. The cochlea produces this sound (although not if impaired by drugs or exposure to loud noise). The sounds the cochlea produces in response to acoustic stimulation are called **evoked otacoustic emissions**. These ear-produced sounds were first reported by Kemp (1978) and have since been studied by many investigators. They occur in all people that have normal hearing and are thought to reflect the active participation of the cochlea in hearing.

In addition to *evoked* otacoustic emissions, the ears of many people also produce continuous low-level sounds at one or more frequencies; these are called **spontaneous otacoustic emissions (SOAEs)** (Kemp, 1979; Zurek, 1981). These spontaneous emissions are usually less than 20 decibels above threshold; they can be detected by sensitive microphones in quiet environments, but the people who produce these sounds do not perceive them. About two-thirds of women and half of men under 60 have SOAEs, and SOAEs occur more often in the right ear than in the left (McFadden, 1993a). Since they are observed in infants as well as in adults, they don't seem to require prior auditory experience. Usually people who have SOAEs have more sensitive hearing than persons without them, and the right ear (which is more likely to produce SOAEs) has a slightly lower threshold for sound than the left in most people (McFadden, 1993b).

McFadden (1993b) has reported a startling finding in twins where one twin is female and one is male: females with a male twin show significantly fewer SOAEs than singleton females or females with a female twin. McFadden suggests that the reason for the lower incidence of SOAEs in females with male twins is that in the womb, the female is exposed to androgens secreted by the male—a prenatal masculinizing effect. (We will see some other prenatal masculinizing effects in Chapter 12.)

Since their discovery, otacoustic emissions have inspired hundreds of studies (reviewed by Probst, Lonsbury-Martin, and Martin, 1991). Because they are naturally occurring responses that can be recorded from outside the head, they offer many advantages for research and application, including these: (1) They provide a technique to study the mechanisms of the cochlea without interfering with the delicate relationships of its tiny components. (2) They offer a way to study the effects of noise exposure and the influences of drugs on hearing. (3) They provide a means of testing hearing in infants and other hard-to-test subjects. In fact, a few states require testing all infants for evoked otoacoustic emissions in the first three months of life, in the hope that early detection of deafness will avert problems of learning and development.

The Auditory Nervous System Uses Multiple Pathways from Brain Stem to Cortex

On each side of the human head, about 30,000 to 50,000 auditory fibers from the cochlea make up the auditory part of the eighth cranial nerve. Recall that most of these are afferent fibers carrying messages from the IHCs, each of which stimulates several nerve fibers. Input from the auditory nerve is distributed in a complex manner to both sides of the brain (Figure 9.8). Each auditory nerve fiber divides into two main branches as it enters the brain stem. Each branch goes to separate segments of cells in the dorsal and ventral cochlear nuclei (see Figure 9.8). The output of the cochlear nuclei also involves multiple paths. One set of paths goes to the **superior olivary complex**, which receives inputs from both right and left cochlear nuclei. The bilateral input to this set of cells is the first level for binaural interaction (using two ears) in the auditory system and is therefore of primary importance for mechanisms of auditory lo-

9.8 Auditory Pathways of the Human Brain

View from the front of the head showing the first interaural interactions in the brain stem and increasing interaural interaction at the higher levels of the auditory system.

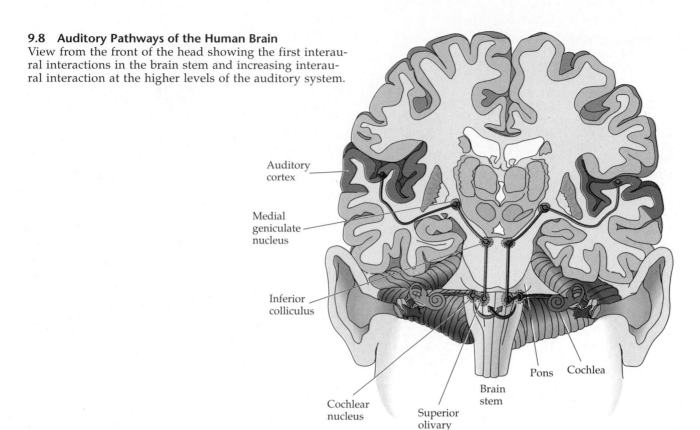

Auditory cortex

Medial geniculate nucleus

Inferior colliculus

Cochlear nucleus

Superior olivary nucleus

Brain stem

Pons   Cochlea

calization, which we'll discuss shortly. Several other parallel paths converge on the **inferior colliculus**, which is the auditory center of the midbrain. Outputs of the inferior colliculus go to the **medial geniculate nucleus** of the thalamus. At least two different pathways from the medial geniculate extend to several auditory cortical areas.

At each level of the auditory system, from cochlea to auditory cortex, a major feature is that the neurons are arranged in an orderly map that reflects the frequencies of stimuli; cells responsive to high frequencies are located at a distance from those responsive to low frequencies. This mapping of neural regions of the auditory system according to stimulus frequency is called **tonotopic organization**. To find the representation of a frequency in the inferior colliculus of the cat, an animal was injected with 2-deoxyglucose (2-DG) and was then exposed to a tone of a particular frequency. 2-DG is taken up by cells as though it were glucose, but 2-DG is not metabolized, so it remains in the cells. The neurons that were most active at the time 2-DG was injected take up more 2-DG than other cells, so post-mortem staining for 2-DG reveals the regions of greatest activity (Figure 9.9).

The auditory cortex of many animals has been

studied in order to determine its principles of organization and its functional features. These studies have mapped the extent and the character of responses to auditory stimulation. Most animals seem to have several auditory cortical fields. Merzenich and Schreiner (1993) suggest that input to each region of auditory cortex includes both a tonotopically arranged system and a second, nontonotopic system projected from other subcortical areas. That is, different fields of the auditory cortex may be specialized for location of sounds in space, movement of sound sources, species-specific sounds, and so on (Figure 9.10). In the next chapter we will see that different visual cortical areas specialize in representation of color, movement, and object recognition.

The human auditory cortex has been studied with noninvasive imaging techniques, including positron emission tomography (PET) and functional magnetic resonance imaging (fMRI; see Chapter 2 for a review of these techniques). Stimulation with pure tones or noise activates chiefly the primary auditory cortex on the superior temporal lobe, Figure 9.11*a*. Speech activates this and other auditory areas (Figure 9.11*b–d*). As in other mammals, the primary auditory area shows tonotopic organization in people.

9.9 Mapping Auditory Frequencies in the Cat Inferior Colliculus

(*a*) Lateral view of cat brain, showing plane of section through inferior colliculi. (*b*) Transverse section through inferior colliculus. (*c*) Location of the 2-DG labeled cells with 2000-Hz stimulation, and (*d*) 20,000-Hz stimulation. (*e*) Complete tonotopic mapping. After Serviere, Webster, and Calford, 1984.

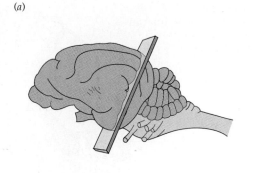

(*a*)

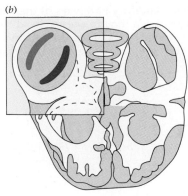

(*b*)

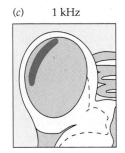

(*c*)   1 kHz

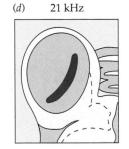

(*d*)   21 kHz

(*e*)

1 kHz
6.5
13.5
15.0
21.0

There Are Two Main Theories about How We Discriminate Pitch

Most of us can discriminate very small differences in frequency of sound over the entire audible range—from 20 Hz to the range from 15,000 to 20,000 Hz. The ability to detect a change in frequency is usually measured as the **minimal discriminable frequency difference** between two tones. The detectable difference is about 2 Hz for sounds up to 2000 Hz, at which point it grows larger. Note that pitch and frequency are not synonymous terms. **Pitch** relates solely to sensory *experience*—that is, the responses of subjects to sounds; **frequency** describes a physical property of sounds (see Box 9.1). The reasons for emphasizing this distinction are many, including the fact that frequency is not the sole determinant of pitch experience (at some frequencies, sounds seem to increase in pitch as they become more intense), and changes in pitch do not precisely parallel changes in frequency.

How do we account for the ability to discriminate pitches? Two main theories have been offered. One, described as **place theory**, argues that our perception of pitch depends on where the sound causes maximal displacement of the basilar membrane. "Place," ac-

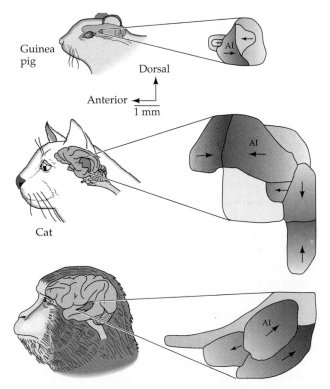

Guinea pig

Dorsal

Anterior

1 mm

AI

Cat

AI

AI

9.10 Tonotopic Organization of Auditory Cortical Regions in Three Species of Mammals

After Merzenich and Schreiner, 1993.

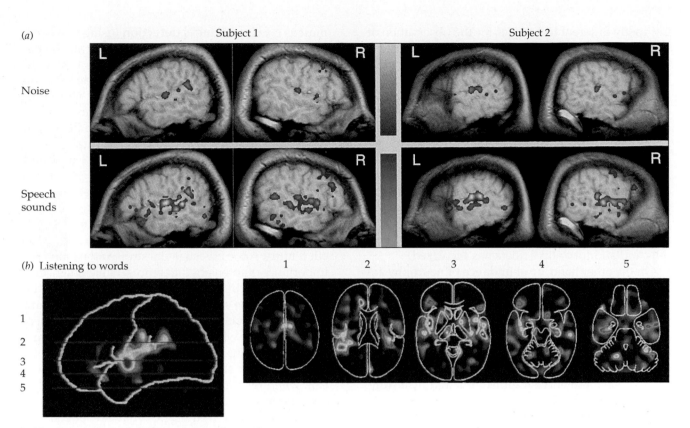

9.11 Responses of the Human Auditory Cortex
(*a*) MRI scans of the cerebral hemispheres show that pure tones or noise (*top*) activate chiefly the primary auditory area on the superior aspect of the temporal lobe, while listening to speech sounds (*bottom*) activates other auditory cortical regions as well as the primary auditory area. (*b*) Lateral (*left*) and horizontal (*right*) PET scans show that listening to words activates not only several regions of the cerebral cortex but also regions of the thalamus and cerebellum. The numbered horizontal lines in the left panel correspond to the levels of the horizontal sections in the right panel. *a* from Binder et al., 1994; *b* from Posner and Raichle, 1994. Courtesy of Jeffrey Binder, Marcus Raichle.

cording to this view, also includes which neurons are stimulated in the central auditory pathways; that is, particular nerve cells receive excitation from a particular part of the basilar membrane and therefore respond to particular stimulus frequencies. The alternative theory, commonly known as **volley theory**, emphasizes the relations between the frequency of auditory stimuli and the pattern or timing of neural discharges. According to this perspective, the firing pattern of a single nerve cell reveals the frequency of the stimulus, because each time the stimulis changes frequency, the pattern of neuronal discharge is altered. The crudest representation of this idea suggests a one-to-one relationship; that is, a 500-Hz tone is represented by 500 nerve impulses per second, and a 1000-Hz tone stimulating this same neuron is represented by a frequency of 1000 nerve impulses per second. In both

cases the firing of the nerve impulse is "phase-locked" to the stimulus; that is, it occurs at a particular portion of the cycle. Such a phase-locked representation can be accomplished more accurately by several fibers than by a single fiber—hence the term "volley," as in a volley of nerve impulses. Are these views—place and volley theories—necessarily antagonistic? No. In fact, the best contemporary view of pitch perception incorporates both perspectives. This combined view is referred to as **duplex theory**. Let's examine some experimental results that support each theory.

As already noted, the region of maximal vibration along the basilar membrane varies with the frequency of the stimulus, a change of frequency is accompanied by a change in the region of maximal disturbance (see Figure 9.6). Von Békésy reported clear tuning for frequencies. More recent studies employing vastly different techniques for the observation of basilar membrane movement show that the relations between the location of maximal displacement on the basilar membrane and frequency of the stimulus are considerably sharper than von Békésy had observed, especially for sounds above 1000 Hz (Rhode, 1984). For complex sounds with several frequency components, the cochlea accomplishes a sort of Fourier analysis (see Box 9.1), with the different frequencies represented by peaks of vibration at different places along the basilar membrane. The accuracy of such place representation of auditory frequency has improved over the course of evolution as the basilar membrane has lengthened and the number of hair cells and auditory nerve fibers has increased.

On the other hand, an abundance of neurophysiological data suggests that pitch sensation also involves the temporal *patterns* of nerve discharge, as volley theory predicted. Thus, single neurons may be able to convey frequency information over a broad range. In these experiments the measurement of temporal pattern is usually the distribution of the intervals between the nerve impulses elicited by a stimulus. A neuron can be said to code the frequency of the sound if this distribution is either the same as the interval between successive cycles of the sound or some integral multiple of it. This kind of coding is quite prominent at frequencies below about 1500 Hz, although it has also been noted for sounds with frequencies up to 4000 Hz.

It would seem, then, that the frequency properties of a sound can be coded in the auditory pathway in terms of both (1) the distribution of excitation among cells—that is, place coding or tonotopic representation—and (2) the temporal pattern (volley) of discharge in cells extending from the auditory nerve to the auditory cortex. With complex sounds, such as speech, that contain mixtures of frequencies, the auditory system makes a useful, although incomplete, Fourier analysis, so we respond to the presence of different frequencies in a complex sound. For example, we discriminate vowel sounds because each vowel sound has its own characteristic frequency bands, and we identify musical instruments by the relative intensities of different harmonic frequencies (see Box 9.1).

One Ear Can Localize Sounds, but Two Ears Are Better

Under special circumstances—when sounds are of long duration and the head is free to move—**monaural detection** (using one ear) of acoustic sources is al-

most as good as **binaural detection** (using two ears). Normally, however, we use two ears to locate the position of a sound source, with great accuracy (within about one degree). This ability usually depends on the interaction between the two ears, or more precisely, on the interaction of neural messages from the two ears. What features of the stimulus are important for binaural localization? Two main binaural cues for auditory localization are (1) the difference in sound *intensity* at the two ears and (2) the difference in the *time of arrival* of sound at the two ears.  (More complex binaural differences also play a part, such as the frequency spectrum and phase differences.) Early in the twentieth century, some investigators stressed the importance of intensity differences, while others emphasized time differences. Research showed that the properties of the sound (especially its frequency) and the acoustic environment (for example, sound reflection) determine which of these interaural cues is most important in binaural sound localization.

Some sounds show intensity differences at the two ears when they are not in the median plane of the body, because the head casts a sound shadow (Figure 9.12). The sound frequencies that are effectively blocked depend on the size of the head, since long waves of low-frequency sounds go around the head. At low frequencies, no matter where sounds are presented in the horizontal plane, there are virtually no intensity differences between the ears. For these frequencies, differences in times of arrival are the principal cues for sound position. At higher frequencies, the sound shadow cast by the head produces significant binaural intensity differences. We cannot tell by monitoring our own performance that we are using one cue to localize high-frequency sounds and another cue to localize low-frequency sounds. In general we are aware of the *results* of neural processing but not of the processing itself.

How are the binaural features of an acoustic environment analyzed by the nervous system? There are many opportunities for binaural interaction at various levels of the brain stem—regions where single nerve cells receive inputs derived from both ears. The lowest level of the auditory system at which there are binaural effects is the superior olivary complex. Cells within the superior olivary region are particularly sensitive to binaural differences of time or intensity. The inferior colliculus receives inputs from several brain stem nuclei with binaural inputs.

Are there neurons at the inferior colliculus that respond to some sound positions but not others? The answer differs depending on the species. In mam-

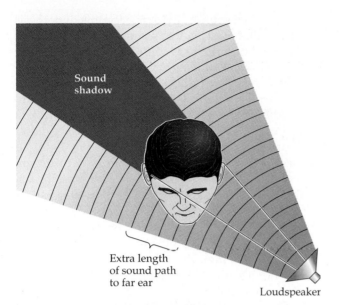

9.12 Cues for Binaural Hearing

The two ears receive somewhat different information from sound sources located to one side or the other of the observer's midline. The head blocks frequencies greater than 1000 Hz, producing binaural differences in sound intensity. Sounds also take longer to reach the more distant ear, resulting in binaural differences in time of arrival.

mals, little evidence supports this idea (Masterton and Imig, 1984). One might conclude either that the detection of acoustic position is the product of the summation of many cells active in particular spatial and temporal patterns, or that sounds are localized at a higher level.

Middlebrooks and Pettigrew (1981) tested for spatial selectivity in cortical neurons of the cat, using a setup like that shown in Figure 9.13*a*. About half the neurons showed some spatial selectivity (Figure 9.13*b*). Some of these neurons responded to a sound that originated anywhere in the opposite hemifield. Other location-sensitive neurons had relatively small receptive fields that responded only to sounds at a particular location on the side of the opposite ear. There was no indication of a systematic map of sound space in cats, but such mapping does occur in the brain of the owl.

In the owl—whose livelihood (hunting at night) depends on accurate auditory localization—detailed and elaborate neural representations of auditory space are found. In the avian equivalent to the inferior colliculus some cells are arranged in a roughly spherical representation of space; that is, each space-specific cell has a receptive field that includes sounds coming from a small cone of space centering on the

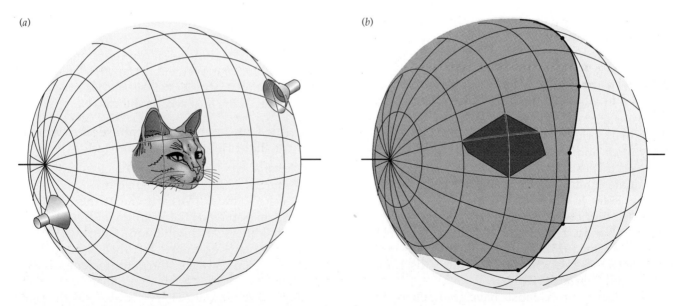

9.13 Spatial Sensitivity of the Auditory Neurons in Cat Cortex

(*a*) A loudspeaker emitting sound was moved along the surface of an imaginary sphere with a radius of 1 meter, while the responses of individual neurons were recorded. (*b*) About half the neurons showed some spatial sensitivity. One-fourth responded to sounds that originated anywhere in the opposite hemifield (tan). The other fourth showed relatively small receptive fields, responding only to sounds at a particular location on the side of the opposite ear (brown). After Middlebrooks and Pettigrew, 1981.

owl's head. Successive cells in the nucleus represent neighboring regions of auditory space (Knudsen, 1984b; Knudsen and Konishi, 1979).

In the tectum (dorsal part of the midbrain) of the owl, auditory *and* visual space are represented, and the maps for the two senses correspond closely (Knudsen, 1981). Most cells in this region respond to both auditory and visual stimuli, and all of the auditory cells respond specifically to spatial direction. In most cases the visual receptive field of a cell is enclosed within the auditory receptive field of the same cell. Perhaps this close alignment of auditory and visual maps of space provides signals for motor responses with regard to the position of the stimulus. A little later in this chapter we will see how early experience in owls affects auditory mechanisms of the tectum.

What Are the Functions of the Auditory Cortex?

Most investigators of hearing, from the late nineteenth century until recently, believed that auditory sensation and discrimination depend on the auditory cortex. The noncortical auditory nuclei were considered to be mere relay stations or stepping stones in a pathway to the cortex (Masterton, 1993). Clinical and experimental neurology seemed to support this idea. Patients with injury to the auditory cortex and animals with extensive lesions of the auditory cortex often appeared to ignore sounds, but little attempt was made to find what such patients or animals *could* hear or discriminate. Even after such attempts were made with experimental animals, beginning in the 1940s, the unexpected results were long resisted. Careful experiments combining ablation (surgical removal) of auditory cortex and behavioral testing showed that cats do *not* need auditory cortex to discriminate intensity (Raab and Ades, 1946; Rosenzweig, 1946), frequency (Butler, Diamond, and Neff, 1957), or duration of tones (for a review of all three kinds of sound discrimination, see Neff, Diamond, and Casseday, 1975). If the auditory cortex is not involved in these basic kinds of auditory discrimination, what then *does* it do?

Auditory neuroscientists have gradually become more interested in how the nervous system discriminates among natural sounds and sound sources than among physically simple but unnatural pure tones (Masterton, 1993). Most of the sounds in nature are brief and change rapidly—such as vocalizations of animals, footsteps, snaps, crackles, and pops—and it is likely that the auditory nervous system evolved to

deal with such sounds. Evidence for this hypothesis is the fact that most central auditory neurons habituate rapidly to continuous sound, ceasing to respond after only a few milliseconds, but brief sounds or abrupt onsets of sound usually evoke responses from a wide array of neurons from the cochlear nuclei to the auditory cortex. Ablation of auditory cortex in cats does impair discrimination of temporal *patterns* of sound (Neff, Diamond, and Casseday, 1975). In monkeys, bilateral ablation of the auditory cortex impairs the ability to discriminate species-specific vocalizations (Heffner and Heffner, 1989). As investigators follow up on these observations, they may find that different auditory cortical areas are specialized for particular kinds of information—for example, movement and identity—that animals need to gain about sound sources. But that remains a challenge for further research.

If the different regions of auditory cortex are not required for discriminating *frequency*, why are that many of them tonotopic in their layout? Quite possibly, since the cochlea responds to different frequencies in a regular manner along its length, it is orderly and economical for the afferent projections from the 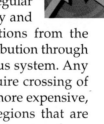 cochlea to maintain a tonotopic distribution through the successive stations of the nervous system. Any other kind of projection would require crossing of fibers and more complex, and thus more expensive, organization. But auditory brain regions that are tonotopic in one dimension can represent such aspects as space or movement in the other dimension, or even complex aspects such as species-specific vocalizations, as the next section indicates.

Does the Left Cerebral Hemisphere Hear Words and the Right Hemisphere Hear Music?

The left and right auditory cortical areas appear to play somewhat different roles in human perception of speech and music. An early clue to this difference came from a study of the anatomy of the temporal lobes in adults (Geschwind and Levitsky, 1968); in 65% of the brains examined, the upper surface of the lobe—a region known as the **planum temporale**—was larger in the left hemisphere than in the right (Figure 9.14b). In only 11% of adults was the right side larger. The region examined includes part of the area known as Wernicke's area; damage to this area impairs the perception of speech (see Chapter 19). Presumably the difference in size of this region between the two hemispheres reflects the specialization (dominance) of one hemisphere for speech; in most people the left hemisphere is specialized for speech.

The difference in size of the planum temporale is even more evident in newborns than in adults; it appeared in 86% of the infant brains examined. The difference in size develops in about the 30th week of gestation (Witelson and Pallie, 1973). This evidence suggests an innate basis for cerebral specialization for language and speech perception, since the asymmetry occurs before any experience with speech.

In the case of music, studies indicate a major role for the auditory areas of the *right* hemisphere. These studies show that musical perception is impaired particularly by damage to the right hemisphere (Samson and Zatorre, 1994) and that music activates the right hemisphere more than the left (Zatorre, Evans, and Meyer, 1994). But a recent study indicates that perfect pitch (the ability to identify any musical note without comparing it to a reference note) involves the *left* rather than the right hemisphere. Schlaug and colleagues (1995) made MRI measurements of the planum temporale in three kinds of subjects, all right-handed (because the larger size of the left planum temporale is seen especially in right-handed individuals): (1) musicians with perfect pitch, (2) musicians without perfect pitch, and (3) nonmusicians. The size of the left planum temporale was twice as large in musicians with perfect pitch than in nonmusicians (Figure 9.14*b*). The size of the left planum temporale in musicians without perfect pitch was intermediate, but closer to that of nonmusicians. Since perfect pitch requires both verbal ability (to name the pitch) and musical ability, perhaps it is not surprising to find that, like language, it is associated with the left hemisphere.

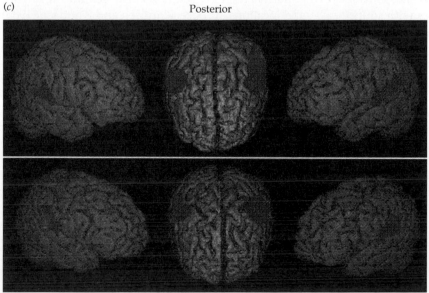

9.14 Structural Asymmetry of the Human Planum Temporale
(*a*) Orientation diagram for brain section in (*b*). (*b*) The planum temporale shown in green and blue on the upper surface of the human temporal lobe. (*c*) MRI images from the brain of a musician with perfect pitch (*top*) and of a nonmusician (*bottom*). Note the larger size of the left planum temporale in the musician. After Schlaug et al., 1995. *c* courtesy of Gottfried Schlaug.

(*a*)

(*b*)

Posterior

Right hemisphere auditory cortex

Left hemisphere auditory cortex

Secondary

Secondary

Primary

Primary

Anterior   Temporal pole

(*c*)

Posterior

Right hemisphere   Anterior   Left hemisphere

Despite these data, we cannot assign the perception of speech and pitch entirely to the left hemisphere and the perception of music entirely to the right hemisphere. We will see in Chapter 19 that the right hemisphere can play a role in speech perception even in people in whom the left hemisphere is speech-dominant. Furthermore, although damage to the right hemisphere can impair perception of music, it does not abolish it, but damage to *both* sides of the brain can completely wipe out musical perception (Samson and Zatorre, 1991). Thus, even though each hemisphere plays a greater role than the other in different kinds of auditory perception, the two hemispheres appear to collaborate in these as well as in many other functions.

Experience Affects Auditory Perception and the Auditory Pathways

People and other animals acquire information from and about auditory stimuli throughout life. At the same time, aspects of auditory discrimination and the neural circuits involved in hearing change. In this section we will see examples of such changes during early development and in adults.

At birth the human infant has diverse hearing abilities. In fact, good evidence suggests that the fetus responds to sounds. Postnatal developments involve elaborate structural changes throughout the auditory pathways. Accompanying these changes are progressive improvements in the perception of complex sounds, such as speech. Since the world after birth is filled with a complex array of sounds, it is reasonable to ask whether the infant's experiences with sound have any impact on the progressive structural and physiological development of the auditory system. Does experience in some way shape or modulate the formation of connections in the auditory system? One aspect of auditory experience that is especially interesting in this regard is auditory localization. At birth, many animals show a coarse ability to localize sounds. Human infants often move their eyes toward the side where a sound stimulus occurs. Changes in the size of the ears and head, however, change the character of information used for auditory localization, and various studies have shown that animals improve their localization abilities as they mature.

The role of auditory experience in the development of sound localization is implied by observations in bilaterally deaf children who were fitted with different types of hearing aids (Beggs and Foreman,

1980). The children in one group were given a hearing aid that delivered the same sounds to both ears. In a second group the children were fitted with a separate hearing aid for each ear so that they experienced different cues at the two ears (dichotic stimuli). Of course, both groups experienced impoverished auditory environments. When examined years later, the children who had been fitted with dichotic hearing aids were able to localize sounds with significantly greater accuracy than the children who experienced comparable overall levels of sounds but were deprived of dichotic stimuli.

Knudsen and Esterly (1984) performed some of the most elegant studies in this area, using an especially acute binaural perceiver—the owl. To assess the impact of early deprivation of binaural inputs, the investigators placed a plug in one ear of the owl, which reduced sound intensity in that ear by 20 to 40 decibels. This treatment was applied to owls of various ages. When the plug was first placed in the ear, the animal made large localization errors to the side of the open ear. For example, if a sound was made directly in front of the owl, the owl responded as if the sound came from the side of the open ear—presumably because it was more intense in that ear, which would normally mean that it came from that side. Owls that were younger than eight weeks at the time of plugging slowly began to compensate for the binaural disparity produced by the blockage of one ear. Then, when the ear plugs were removed, these animals made large localization errors to the opposite side. Older animals are less likely to show adjustment during this postplug period in which the animal is experiencing new relations between auditory cues and locations in space. Knudsen and Knudsen (1985) showed the critical role of vision in this process of adjustment of auditory localization. Barn owls with one ear plugged did not correct their auditory localization errors if deprived of vision. Furthermore, if these animals were fitted with prisms that deviate vision by 10 degrees, the adjustment of auditory localization was matched to this visual error.

Neurophysiological studies of these owls reveal some features of the underlying mechanisms (Knudsen, 1985). As we mentioned earlier, within the optic tectum of barn owls, there are nerve cells that are bimodal; that is, they respond to both visual and auditory stimuli. These neurons are selective for sound source locations and visual spatial information. The auditory and visual spatial sensitivities are similarly aligned; that is, they correspond to approximately the same positions in space. When the correspondence between auditory localization cues and visual position is changed by the use of an ear plug, an interesting finding is noted. Despite the fact that correspondence was altered by the ear plug, when tested months later, the auditory receptive fields align well with the visual receptive fields. But removal of the ear plug causes the cells' most sensitive auditory receptive areas to shift away from the alignment with the visual fields of a nerve cell. These changes in auditory spatial tuning did not occur in an adult animal that had been similarly treated, which suggests that this experience-dependent process involves a critical period during early development. Thus, these neurophysiological data correspond with the data obtained in the behavioral studies of sound localization already noted. These changes might arise from either structural modifications of growing neural circuits or from modulations of synaptic effectiveness.

Even in adult mammals, experience can change auditory mechanisms. Adult sensory cortex shows plastic changes both in the receptive fields of cells and in maps of the sensory fields. Weinberger (1995) states the following law: "Behaving (i.e., waking) animals can continually acquire and retain information about (a) individual sensory stimuli, (b) relationships between various sensory stimuli and (c) relationships between their own behavior and its sensory consequences." Similarly, neuroscientists can find changes in cortical representations of stimuli as a consequence of (1) presenting individual sensory stimuli, (2) presenting pairs or groups of sensory stimuli, or (3) inducing behavior that has its own sensory consequences. Let's look at a few examples.

Repeated presentation of a behaviorally uninteresting tone (one with no consequences for the animal) causes habituation, with decreased response of cortical cells to that tone compared with other tones that have not been repeated frequently. This plasticity of the receptive field is the result of learned inattention rather than of sensory adaptation or fatigue, because it develops even when the rate of presentation of the stimulus is too slow to cause adaptation or fatigue (Condon and Weinberger, 1991). On the other hand, if presentations of a particular tone are followed regularly by mild electrical shock or food reward, the response to a tone of that frequency is enhanced, while responses to other tones either show little change or decrease. Pairing the tone with a shock yields such cortical effects very quickly, after only five to ten pairings (Lennartz and Weinberger, 1992).

Maps of the auditory areas also show plasticity. For example, monkeys were trained by means of a food reward to perform a difficult auditory frequency discrimination task. After several months of training, during which the performance of the monkeys improved, the cortical surface area representing the frequency band in which they had learned to discriminate had increased. Other subjects that heard the same tones but were *not* required to engage in the discrimination task, did not develop an enlarged representation for these frequencies (Recanzone, Schreiner, and Merzenich, 1993). Although this experiment demonstrates plasticity of the auditory cortex, it certainly does not prove that the cortex is necessary for frequency discrimination. The changes observed at the cortex may only reflect changes in subcortical regions that are necessary for frequency discrimination.

Deafness Is a Major Disorder of the Nervous System

Health surveys indicate that there are about 18 million cases of deafness or hearing impairment in the United States (Travis, 1992). These disabilities range in severity from occasional difficulties in speech perception (a drop in sensitivity of 41 to 55 decibels between 500 and 2000 Hz) to the inability to hear anything (a 90-decibel drop between 500 and 2000 Hz). Many severe hearing impairments arise early in life and impair the acquisition of language. Most of these impairments involve changes in the end organ—the hair cells. In many cases, direct stimulation of the auditory nerve by electrical signals controlled by auditory stimuli can provide useful partial substitutes for natural sounds.

There Are Three Main Types of Hearing Disorder

Hearing disorders are usually classified on the basis of the site of pathological changes. The principal classes are these:

1. **Conductive deafness**, hearing impairments associated with pathology of the external or middle ear cavities, usually involving the ossicles of the middle ear.

2. **Sensorineural deafness**, hearing impairments originating from lesions of the cochlea or auditory nerve. Usually these disorders involve the loss of hair cells.

3. **Central deafness**, hearing impairments related to lesions in auditory pathways or centers, including sites in the brain stem, thalamus, or cortex.

Conductive deafness. Conductive deafness is hearing loss that results from a failure of mechanical stimulation to reach the cochlea. The cause may be as simple as an earwax obstruction, or it may be a more complex condition that affects movement of the middle ear bones. Infections of the middle ear can also affect the transmission of mechanical energies. Since the middle ear is connected (through the Eustachian tube; see Figure 9.1*a*) to the upper respiratory tract, throat infections can, under some conditions, gain access to the middle ear. This phenomenon is especially a problem with young children because the length of the tube connecting the middle ear with the pharynx is short early in life. The loss of sensitivity that is characteristic of conductive deafness extends across all frequencies, although there is a tendency for a greater loss at higher frequencies.

Sensorineural deafness. Sensorineural deafness, which results from the destruction of cochlear mechanisms (especially the integrity of hair cells), accounts for the largest class of deaf individuals—more than 14 million in the United States. The conditions that cause cochlear impairment are quite varied and include hundreds of hereditary disorders, metabolic dysfunctions, exposure to toxic substances, trauma, and loud sounds. The end result is the same: auditory nerve fibers are unable to become excited in a normal manner.

Drug-induced deafness results particularly from the toxic properties of a group of antibiotics that includes streptomycin and gentamicin. The ototoxic (ear-damaging) properties of these substances were first discovered in the treatment of tuberculosis with streptomycin. Although this antibiotic was remarkably effective in the treatment of the disease, it became evident soon after its introduction that there was a tremendous price to pay for the cure: many patients showed severe cochlear and/or vestibular damage. In some patients streptomycin produced total, irreversible loss of hearing caused by the virtually complete destruction of hair cells in the cochlea. Generally the highest frequencies are the first to be affected. This result conforms to the histological observations of the progression of destruction; that is, the first signs of change appear in the basal region of the cochlea. Because the endings of the auditory nerve near the hair cells remain viable, however, some new types of electronic prostheses (see below) can be of some use in treating cochlear damage.

Noise-induced hearing impairments also involve primarily inner-ear mechanisms. Noise pollution and the advent of intense recreational sounds—such as those derived from music, motorcycles and other loud engines, and especially the firing of guns—have made this a prominent problem and have given audiologists (hearing therapists) and otologists (ear doctors) a lot of business (Clark, 1991). The cochlea can be damaged by exposure to intense sudden sounds or to chronic sounds of high intensity. The initial histological changes in the inner ear involve primarily hair cells; the outer hair cells are more susceptible to sound trauma than are the inner cells. The progression of changes with continued sound exposure leads in some individuals to destruction of the organ of Corti and the nerve fibers that innervate it. Figure 9.15 shows such destruction in a region of the cochlea surrounded by intact tissue. In time, damage to the cochlea spreads out from the initial site, even without additional acoustic trauma.

Recent research suggests that loud sounds coupled with the use of some over-the-counter drugs can have profound effects on hearing. For example, it is common clinical knowledge that aspirin can impair hearing (McFadden and Champlin, 1990). The hearing loss caused by chronic use of aspirin can be impressive—a reduction of up to 40 decibels for high tones, coupled with the development of **tinnitus**, a sensation of noises or ringing in the ears (Brien, 1993).

Can the hair cells damaged in sensorineural deafness be regrown in mammals? Although fish and amphibians produce hair cells throughout life and are thus able to replace damaged hair cells, mammals were generally thought to be incapable of regenerating hair cells. But recent findings are beginning to call this traditional idea into question. First, researchers discovered that birds can regenerate hair cells damaged by acoustic overstimulation or by ototoxic chemicals (Cotanche, 1987). Later, chemical stimulation was found to induce the regenerations of hair cells in cultures of the organ of Corti that had been surgically removed from young rats (Lefebvre et al., 1993). Such research may lead to way of restoring hair cells in humans with sensorineural deafness, but clinical treatment of this sort is at least a decade away.

Central deafness. Hearing loss that is caused by brain lesions or impairments is seldom a simple loss of sensitivity (Bauer and Rubens, 1985). An example of the complexity of changes in auditory perception following cerebral cortical damage is **word deafness**, a disorder in which people show normal speech and hearing for simple sounds but cannot recognize spoken words. Some researchers have suggested that the basis of word deafness is an abnormally slow analysis of auditory inputs. Another example of central deafness is **cortical deafness**, in which patients have

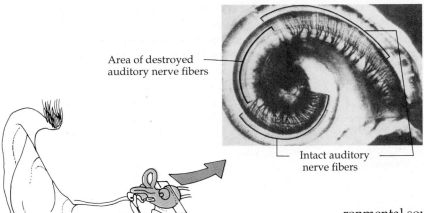

9.15 Noise Can Destroy the Auditory Receptor Cells
Right cochlea of a person who died at age 71 after long-term exposure to intense noise. The cochlea shows marked degeneration of auditory nerve fibers. This view was obtained after the removal of overlying temporal bone. From Bredberg, 1968.

Area of destroyed auditory nerve fibers

Intact auditory nerve fibers

difficulty recognizing both verbal and nonverbal auditory stimuli. Cortical deafness is a rare syndrome that arises from a bilateral destruction of inputs to the auditory cortex. Persistent cortical deafness has been noted when strokes involve white matter in addition to temporal parietal cortex. Case reports by Tanaka and colleagues (1991) show persistent deafness when strokes appear to interrupt *all* of the projection fibers (white matter) from the medial geniculate nucleus to the various auditory cortical regions. Figure 9.16 shows the brain regions that are destroyed. These patients still show various acoustic reflexes mediated by the brain stem—such as bodily responses to environmental sounds—although they deny hearing the sounds they react to. In contrast, patients with bilateral destruction of the primary auditory cortex often have less severe hearing loss; presumably, other auditory cortical regions maintain hearing.

Electrical Stimulation of the Auditory Nerve Can Alleviate Deafness

In recent years researchers have tried to restore hearing in profoundly deaf individuals by directly stimulating the auditory nerve with electrical currents (Loeb, 1990; Miller and Spelman, 1989). Progress in this endeavor has been rapid, resulting in the development of an electronic device that has been approved by the U.S. Food and Drug Administration for widespread clinical use (Figure 9.17). About 5,000 people in the United States are equipped with this kind of prosthetic device. A newer type of stimulator delivers electromagnetic stimulation from outside the skull and brain (Conner, 1993).

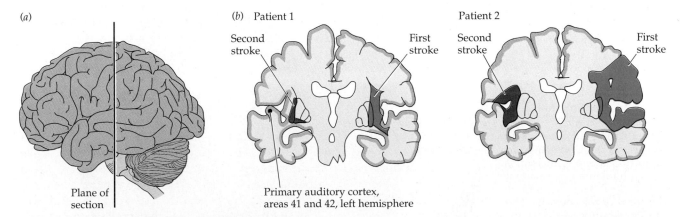

(*a*)

Plane of section

(*b*) Patient 1

Second stroke

First stroke

Primary auditory cortex, areas 41 and 42, left hemisphere

Patient 2

Second stroke

First stroke

9.16 Brain Lesions that Caused Deafness
(*a*) Lateral view of the brain, showing position of the coronal sections in part *b*. (*b*) Diagrams made from coronal MRI sections of two patients, showing damage in the right (blue) and left (red) hemispheres caused by stroke. These lesions resulted in cortical deafness. After Tanaka et al., 1991.

Who will gain by the use of such devices? In several types of sensorineural hearing loss, including those caused by ototoxic drugs and childhood meningitis, the damage that produces deafness involves the hair cells. Often, however, although the hair cells may be completely destroyed, the electrical excitability of the auditory nerve remains unchanged. Some of the most enthusiastic recipients of this clinical aid are patients who became deaf prior to the acquisition of language (Loeb, 1990). However, some deaf people and advocates of deaf people oppose the use of such prostheses. They believe that deaf people should accept their disability and use sign language to communicate, rather than become imperfect hearers.

What kinds of sensory responses does electrical stimulation of the auditory nerve provoke? The usu-

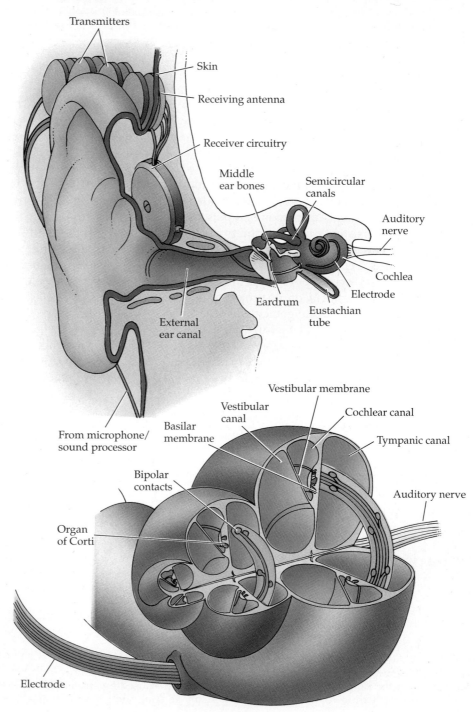

9.17 An Experimental Hearing Aid
(*Top*) Hearing aid developed by workers at the University of California at San Francisco, is shown implanted in a patient's ear. (*Bottom*) An enlarged interior view of the cochlea. (The rows of sensory hair cells, included in this view, would be absent in a typical patient with sensorineural deafness.) After Loeb, 1985.

al technique employed in these studies is the insertion of a small group of wires through the cochlea to the endings of the auditory nerve. In these patients electrical stimulation produces pitch sensations that are partially related to the tonotopic organization of the cochlea. Unfortunately, the effective number of channels is limited by technical factors, so the range of frequencies that can be excited is also limited. With successive technical advances, the number has increased from 6 different frequencies to 20, but this range is still very limited compared with the range of frequencies we appreciate in normal hearing. Dynamic range is also limited because intensities of electrical stimulation barely above the thresholds for sound produce discomfort. Nevertheless, when stimulation is controlled by the sounds picked up by a microphone, the resulting pattern of electrical stimulation of the auditory nerve greatly facilitates some acoustically mediated behaviors and aids speech perception. For example, this treatment makes it possible to distinguish voiced and unvoiced speech sounds (for instance, "f" and "v") which cannot be distinguished in lip reading. This partial replacement for mechanical-to-neural transduction also enables deaf people to detect some important environmental sources of sounds, such as an automobile or the approach of another individual.

Auditory excitation produced by cochlear electrical stimulation in deaf individuals markedly increases the metabolic rate of the auditory cortex of these patients, as revealed by PET studies (Ito et al., 1993). This finding indicates that such electrical stimulation may activate the speech comprehension systems of the auditory cortex.

Deafness Leads to Brain Reorganization

In Chapter 8 we noted that a major reorganization of somatosensory cortex in primates follows loss of sensory input from digits, as neurons accept new inputs to make up for missing inputs from lost digits. This form of sensory cortex reorganization, which reveals remarkable neural plasticity, also occurs in auditory cortex. Making a localized lesion in the cochlea of an adult guinea pig increases the thresholds of neurons in certain cortical regions—these were the regions that represented the sound frequencies corresponding to the damaged part of the cochlea (Robertson and Irvine, 1989). A month after the lesions are made, however, the neurons in the affected regions of the cortex respond with normal sensitivity to sound frequencies *adjacent* to those transduced by the damaged part of the cortex. Thus, the auditory cortical map remains plastic even in adult mammals.

Vestibular Perception

The **vestibular system** provides information about the force of gravity on our body and the acceleration of our head. When you go up in an elevator, you feel the acceleration clearly. When you turn your head or when you ride in a car going around a tight curve, you feel the change of direction. If you are not used to these kinds of stimulation, sensitivity to motion can make you "seasick." The receptors of the vestibular system inform the brain about mechanical forces, such as gravity and acceleration, that act on the body.

The Receptor Mechanisms for the Vestibular System Are in the Inner Ear

The receptors of the vestibular system lie within the inner ear next to the cochlea. (The term "vestibular" comes from the Latin *vestibulum*, "entrance hall" and reflects the fact that the system lies in hollow spaces in the temporal bone.) In mammals one portion of the vestibular system consists of three **semicircular canals**, fluid-filled tubes, each oriented in a different plane (Figure 9.18*a* and *b*). The three canals are connected at their ends to a saclike structure called the **utricle** (literally, "little uterus"). Lying below this is another small fluid-filled sac, the **saccule** ("a little sac").

Receptors in these structures, like those of the auditory system, are groups of hair cells whose bending leads to the excitation of nerve fibers. In each semicircular canal, the hair cells are in an enlarged region, the **ampulla**, that lies at the junction between canal and utricle (Figure 9.18*c* and *d*). Here the cilia of the hair cells are embedded in a gelatinous mass (Figure 9.18*e*). The orientation of the hairs is quite precise and determines the kind of mechanical force to which they are especially sensitive. The three semicircular canals are at right angles to each other; thus, one or another detects angular *acceleration* in any direction. The receptors in the saccule and utricle respond to *static positions* of the head. Small bony crystals on the gelatinous membrane, called **otoliths** (from the Latin roots for "ear" and "stone"), increase the sensitivity of these receptors to movement (Figure 9.18*e* and *f*). At the base of the hair cells in these receptors are nerve fibers whose connections to the hair cells are much like the connections in the auditory portions of the inner ear.

Evolution Has Shaped the Auditory and Vestibular End Organs

The long evolutionary history of the auditory-vestibular system is better known than that of other sensory systems because the receptors are encased in bone, which can fossilize. Combined studies of fos-

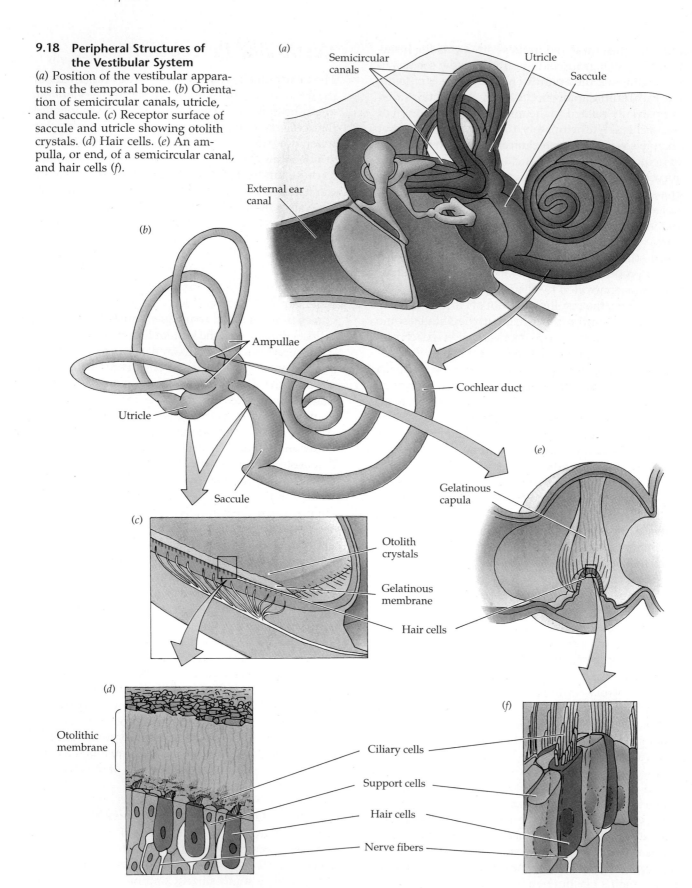

9.18 Peripheral Structures of the Vestibular System

(a) Position of the vestibular apparatus in the temporal bone. (b) Orientation of semicircular canals, utricle, and saccule. (c) Receptor surface of saccule and utricle showing otolith crystals. (d) Hair cells. (e) An ampulla, or end, of a semicircular canal, and hair cells (f).

(a)

Semicircular canals

Utricle

Saccule

External ear canal

(b)

Ampullae

Cochlear duct

Utricle

Saccule

(c)

Otolith crystals

Gelatinous membrane

Hair cells

(e)

Gelatinous capula

(d)

Otolithic membrane

Ciliary cells

Support cells

Hair cells

Nerve fibers

(f)

sils and of many living animals have yielded a detailed story of the origins of hearing and vestibular sensation (van Bergeijk, 1967; Wever, 1974).

It is generally accepted that the auditory end organ evolved from the vestibular system. In turn, the vestibular system evolved from the **lateral-line system**, a sensory system found in many kinds of fish and some amphibians. The lateral-line system is an array of receptors along the side of the body; tiny hairs emerge from sensory cells in the skin. These hairs are embedded in small gelatinous columns called **cupulae**. In aquatic animals with lateral-line systems, movements of water in relation to the body surface stimulate these receptors so that the animal can detect currents of water and movements of other animals, prey, or predators. Information from the lateral line helps schools of fish stay in formation; each fish feels the currents made by the others. A specialized form of lateral-line organ is the lateral-line canal, a groove that partially encloses the cupulae. It is speculated that the first semicircular canals developed from a stretch of lateral-line canal that migrated into the body. This gave the animal a sensor for turns to the right or left, and this receptor, being away from the surface of the body, was free of effects of stimulation of the skin. Sensitivity to *change* of direction was optimized when the canal developed into a roughly circular form.

The inner ear developed in fish through the evolution of an organ, the **swim bladder**, that served an entirely different function, aiding balance. Many species of fish have this gas-filled cavity in the abdomen. Vibrations in water cause the air bladder to contract and expand, which increases sensitivity to such vibrations. In some families of fish the sac extended and made contact with the vestibular labyrinth; in others a series of bones connected the swim bladder with the labyrinth. In both cases the animals acquired increased sensitivity to vibrations in the environment, and a new part of the labyrinth evolved in conjunction with this vibratory sense. This flask-shaped duct, the **lagena** (Latin for "flask"), is found in bony fishes, amphibians, reptiles, and birds. It corresponds to the cochlea found in mammals.

Thus, the auditory system evolved out of the vestibular system, which in turn arose from the lateral-line system (Figure 9.19). Animals with more advanced characteristics show longer auditory ducts with greater numbers of hair cells and auditory nerve fibers. Presumably this larger system is the basis for the excellent ability of animals with these advanced characteristics to discriminate frequencies and auditory patterns.

Nerve Fibers from the Vestibular Portion of the Eighth Nerve Synapse in the Brain Stem

The structural arrangements of brain pathways dealing with vestibular excitation reflect its close connection to muscle adjustments in the body. Nerve fibers from the vestibular receptors of the inner ear enter lower levels of the brain stem and synapse in a group of nuclei, called the **vestibular nuclei**. Some of the fibers bypass this structure and go directly to the cerebellum, a center for motor control. The outputs of the vestibular nuclei are complex, as is appropriate to their influences on the motor system. These outputs go to the motor nuclei of the eye muscles, the thalamus, and the cerebral cortex, among others.

Some Forms of Vestibular Excitation Produce Motion Sickness

There is one aspect of vestibular activation that many of us would prefer did not exist. Certain types of body acceleration—such as those we experience as a passenger in an oceangoing boat, an airplane, a car, or an amusement park ride—can produce distress known as **motion sickness**. Caloric stimulation—the pouring of warm water into one ear canal—produces the same effect by initiating movements of inner ear fluids that simulate mechanical stimulation. Motion sickness is caused especially by low-frequency movements that an individual cannot control. For example, passengers in a car suffer from motion sickness, but the driver does not.

One major theory of motion sickness—**sensory conflict theory**—says that the malady arises from contradictory sensory messages, especially a discrepancy between vestibular and visual information. To illustrate, as an airplane suddenly moves up, the vestibular system is excited but the eyes see the constancy of the plane's interior; the resulting disorientation is distressing. Some investigators have pointed out that there can also be conflicts of information within the vestibular system. For example, going quickly around a sharp curve can produce conflicts between information about acceleration and forces related to gravity (Benson, 1982).

Why do we experience motion sickness at all? The experimental psychologist Michel Treisman (1977) hypothesized that the sensory conflict of some conditions of motion sets off responses that evolved to rid the body of swallowed poison. According to this hypothesis, sensory inputs from the eyes, nose, and taste receptors signal danger and cause dizziness and vomiting to eliminate potential toxin. Such a response has obvious significance for preservation of life, although it is not helpful as a response to movements

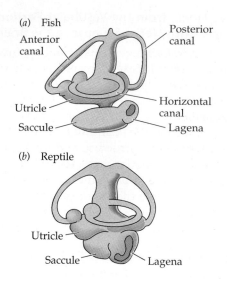

(a) Fish

Anterior canal

Posterior canal

Horizontal canal

Utricle

Saccule

Lagena

(b) Reptile

Utricle

Saccule

Lagena

(c) Bird

Utricle

Saccule

Lagena

(d) Mammal

Utricle

Saccule

Cochlea

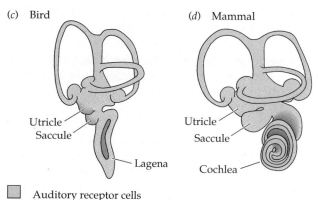

■ Auditory receptor cells

9.19 Evolution of the Vestibular and Auditory End Organs

of vehicles. A person whose vestibular system has been destroyed by toxic drugs or by side effects of antibiotics does not experience motion sickness.

The Chemical Senses: Taste and Smell

Sensitivity to chemical stimuli in the environment is vital for the survival of organisms throughout the animal kingdom. The sense of taste provides "quality control" of foods (Lindemann, 1995): sweet indicates high-calorie foods; salty and sour relate to important aspects of homeostasis; and bitter warns of toxic constituents. Many animals also use chemical sensitivity to detect the odor trails of other animals, thus informing themselves about prey and predators and guiding themselves to mates. This section will show examples of the many roles of the chemical

senses—taste and smell—in guiding behavior. Although the chemical senses are acute, some toxic substances do not have taste or smell and others have tastes or smells that do not warn us of their dangers. Manufacturers of some such toxic substances add an unpleasant taste or smell to alert us to their presence.

We will start our review of the chemical senses with taste, which is somewhat simpler and in some ways has been more thoroughly investigated than smell. Smell is a more complicated and puzzling chemical sense, although recent discoveries are greatly increasing our understanding of it, as we will see.

Taste

Humans Detect Only Four Basic Tastes

Because we recognize many substances by their distinct flavor, we tend to think that we can discriminate many tastes. But humans detect only four basic tastes: salty, sour, sweet, and bitter. (We can qualify that limitation a bit, because, as we will see, there is probably more than one sweet taste, and there are probably several bitter tastes.) The sensations aroused by foods such as an apple, a steak, or an olive are *flavors* rather than simple tastes; they involve smell as well as taste. Block your nose, and a potato tastes the same as an apple. Our ability to respond to many odors—it is estimated that humans can detect more than 10,000 different odors and can discriminate as many as 5000 (Ressler, Sullivan, and Buck, 1994)—is what produces the complex array of flavors that we normally think of as tastes. Most mammals share the four basic tastes that we discriminate, but members of the cat family have only three: cats are not sensitive to sweet. Other animals may have more tastes than we do.

The ability to taste many substances is already well developed at birth. Even premature infants show characteristic responses to different tastes, sucking in response to a sweet substance, but trying to spit out a bitter substance. Newborns seem to be relatively insensitive to salty tastes, but a preference for mildly salty substances develops in the first few months. This preference does not seem to be related to experience with salty tastes but probably indicates maturation of the mechanisms of salt perception (Beauchamp et al., 1991).

Taste Involves Specialized Receptor Cells on the Tongue

In mammals, most taste receptor cells are located on small projections from the surface of the tongue;

these little bumps are called **papillae** (Latin for "nipples"). Each papilla holds one or more clusters of 50 to 150 cells, which are the **taste buds** (Figure 9.20*a*). At the surface end of the taste bud is an opening, the taste pore. The taste cells extend fine cilia into the taste pore, and they come into contact with **tastants**—substances that can be tasted. Not all the sensory cells in taste buds signal taste sensations; some are pain receptors, responding to stimuli such as "hot" red pepper, and others are touch receptors. With a lifespan of only 10 to 14 days, taste cells are constantly being replaced. A single taste bud has receptor cells that are at many different stages of development (see Figure 9.20*a*).

There are three kinds of taste papillae; Figure 9.20*b* shows their distribution on the tongue. The most numerous are **fungiform papillae** which resemble button mushrooms in shape (*fungus* is Latin for "mushroom"). There are hundreds of fungiform papillae on the tongue, but the numbers vary greatly among individuals. A fungiform papilla usually contains only a single taste bud. Each of the few **circumvallate papillae** and **foliate papillae** contains several taste buds. Many books show a map of the tongue indicating that each taste is perceived mainly in one region (sweet at the tip of the tongue, bitter at the back, and so on), but Linda Bartoshuk, a specialist in taste psychophysics, states that this map is erroneous and explains, "The [usual] tongue map has become an enduring scientific myth" (1993:253). Work of Collings (1974) and Yanagisawa and colleagues (1992) shows that all four basic tastes can be perceived anywhere on the tongue where there are taste receptors. The areas do not differ greatly in the strength of taste sensations they mediate (see Figure 9.20*b*).

Other animals have taste receptors in quite different parts of the body. For example, flies have taste receptors on their feet so that they can tell whether material they land on may be good to eat.

Different Cellular Processes Transduce the Four Basic Tastes

The tastes of salty and sour are evoked when taste cells are stimulated by simple ions acting on ion channels in the membranes of the taste cells. Sweet and bitter tastes involve specialized receptor molecules and second messengers. We will examine the mechanisms of each taste, proceeding from simple to complex.

Salty. Sodium ions (Na^+) are transported across the membranes of taste cells by sodium-ion channels. Blocking these channels by the use of a drug prevents the salty taste of sodium chloride in both humans and rats; facilitating the passage of Na^+ across the membrane with another drug intensifies salty tastes (Schiffman, Lockhead, and Maes, 1983; Schiffman et al., 1986). The entry of sodium ions partially depolarizes the taste cells and causes them to release neurotransmitters that stimulate the afferent neurons that relay the information to the brain.

Sour. An acid tastes sour, whether it is a simple inorganic compound, such as hydrogen chloride, or a more complex organic compound, such as lactic acid. The property that all acids share is that each releases a hydrogen ion (H^+). The hydrogen ions block potassium channels in cell membranes, preventing the release of potassium ions (K^+) from taste cells. The buildup of K^+ in the cell leads to depolarization and to neurotransmitter release. The afferent fibers stimulated by these taste cells report the acidic stimulation to the brain.

Sweet. The molecular mechanisms in the transduction of sweet and bitter tastes are more complex than those responsible for salty and sour tastes. There are good reasons to believe that sweet and bitter tastants stimulate specialized receptor molecules on membranes of the taste cells, causing a cascade of internal cellular events involving G proteins and second messengers (see Chapter 5 for a review of G proteins). These receptors are probably like the slow, metabotropic synaptic receptors we considered in Chapter 5. Some known G proteins are synthesized in great numbers in taste cells. Also, a novel G-protein alpha subunit has recently been isolated in taste cells (McLaughlin and Margolskee, 1994). Investigators have not yet identified the receptor molecules for sweet or bitter tastes, but some receptor molecules for *odors* have recently been isolated, as we will discuss a little later. A variety of molecules taste sweet, and psychophysiological experiments show that there is probably more than one kind of sweet taste.

Bitter. Bitter sensations are evoked by even more different tastants than are sweet sensations. The bitter taste of many toxic substances—such as nicotine, caffeine, strychnine, and morphine—provided strong evolutionary pressure to develop a high sensitivity to bitterness. Findings that different bitter substances can be discriminated from each other—in psychophysical work with human tasters (McBurney, Smith, and Shick, 1972) and with animal subjects (Lush, 1991)—are evidence of more than one receptor for bitterness.

Further evidence that there is more than one re-

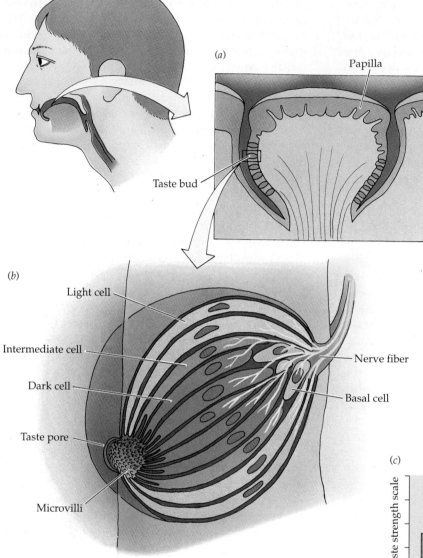

(a)

Papilla

Taste bud

(b)

Light cell

Intermediate cell

Dark cell

Taste pore

Microvilli

Nerve fiber

Basal cell

9.20 A Taste Bud and Taste Receptor Cells

(*a*) A single papilla from the surface of the tongue. (*b*) Diagram of a taste bud; cells at several different stages of development are present. (*c*) Map of locations of papillae and sensitivity to different tastes on the tongue. *a* after McLaughlin and Margolskee, 1994; *c* after Bartoshuk, 1993.

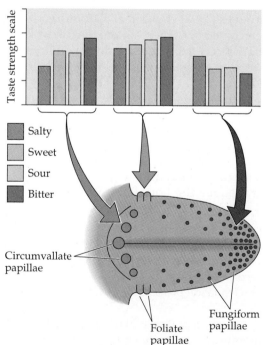

(c)

Taste strength scale

Salty
Sweet
Sour
Bitter

Circumvallate papillae

Foliate papillae

Fungiform papillae

ceptor for bitterness is the specific inability of some individuals to taste certain bitter substances. For example, about 25% of people in the United States cannot taste the chemical phenylthiocarbamide (PTC) and the related compound 6-*n*-propylthiouracil (PROP), even though they can taste other bitter substances. Family genetic studies have suggested that the ability to taste PTC and PROP requires a gene that can take two forms (alleles), *T* and *t*. Individuals with the *T* allele can taste these substances. Individuals with two *tt* alleles are nontasters. Those with one gene, *Tt*, are tasters, which is why the *T* gene is called dominant. Recent psychophysical evidence indicates that the tasters can be divided into two groups— medium tasters and supertasters, the latter representing about 25% of the total population (Bartoshuk et al., 1992). This breakdown suggests the possibility that medium tasters have one dominant allele, *Tt*, and supertasters have two dominant alleles, *TT*. Supertasters perceive stronger taste intensities not only from some bitter compounds but also from some sweet compounds (Bartoshuk et al., 1992). Counts of the number of taste buds in people with varying sensitivity to PROP show that nontasters have the fewest taste buds (averaging 96 per cm^2) on the tongue tip, medium tasters an intermediate number (averaging 184), and supertasters the most (averaging 425) (Reedy et al., 1993). These differences are striking, but numbers of taste buds alone cannot explain the observation that supertasters experience only certain substances more intensely than do medium tasters (Bartoshuk and Beauchamp, 1994).

Neural Coding for Tastes Is Complex

Since different taste cells appear to be responsible for each of the four main tastes, it might seem obvious that each afferent axon from the taste buds carries information about only one taste. This idea is known as the labeled-line, or **specific pathway hypothesis**. (Recall our discussions of labeled lines for the skin senses in Chapter 8 and for auditory frequencies earlier in this chapter.) According to another hypothesis, **pattern coding**, each axon responds to some extent to more than one taste, and taste discrimination requires central processing based on relative activity coming from different afferent axons.

Recording from individual taste axons shows that each responds to a low concentration of one taste stimulus but also responds to higher concentrations of other tastes (Pfaffmann, Frank, and Norgren, 1979). For example, one axon responds most readily to sweet stimuli but also responds to a concentrated salt or bitter solution. Thus, the fact that this cell is active does not tell whether it is responding to a dilute sugar solution or a strong salt solution. Only central analysis of the pattern of responses across several neurons reveals the identity of the stimulus. This situation is similar to what we saw in audition, where the response of a single axon could be evoked by a weak stimulus at its best frequency or by stronger stimuli anywhere in a surrounding frequency in a range of more than 1000 Hz.

Taste Information Is Transmitted to Several Parts of the Brain

The gustatory system (from the Latin *gustare*, "to taste") extends from the taste receptor cells through brain stem nuclei and the thalamus to the cerebral cortex (Figure 9.21). Each taste cell transmits information to several afferent fibers, and each afferent fiber receives information from several taste cells. The afferent fibers run along three different cranial nerves—the facial (VII), glossopharyngeal (IX), and vagal (X) nerves (see Figure 2.11). The gustatory fibers in each of these nerves run to the medulla. Here they synapse with second-order gustatory fibers that run to the ventral posterior medial nucleus of the thalamus. After another synapse, third-order gustatory fibers run to the cortical taste areas in the somatosensory cortex.

Smell

Chemicals in the Air Elicit Odor Sensations

We have already noted that many aspects of an animal's world are determined by chemicals carried in the air. Information about human abilities to detect and identify odors comes from a survey sponsored by the *National Geographic* magazine that elicited responses from more than 1.5 million individuals (Gilbert and Wyslocki, 1987). Scents were affixed to pages of the magazine and were released when the paper surface was scratched. Readers were asked to detect the odors, to identify them, and to mail in response sheets. Six odors were presented to sample some aspects of the wide variety of odors that humans can detect. Figure 9.22 presents some results from a large sample of the responses. Half the respondents were able to detect all six odors, and only about 1% were unable to smell three or more samples. But there was widespread partial **anosmia** (odor blindness): 35% of the respondents could not detect androsterone, and 29% could not detect galaxolide; most individuals who could not detect one of these odors could not detect the other either. For each odor, the questionnaire gave 12 possible identifying words; the most common choice for each odor was the correct one, but many people made wrong choices. Thus, although 99% detected isoamyl acetate, only half identified it as banana. Women were slightly better than men in both detecting and identifying odors. The ability to detect odors declined somewhat with age. This age-related drop was greatest in the number of elderly people who rated mercaptans—the foul smell added to natural gas—as extremely unpleasant; this trend indicates a possible danger for elderly people. Smokers showed a dulled sense of smell; they found pleasant odors to be less pleasant and unpleasant odors less unpleasant than nonsmokers did.

9.21 Anatomy and Main Pathways of the Human Taste System

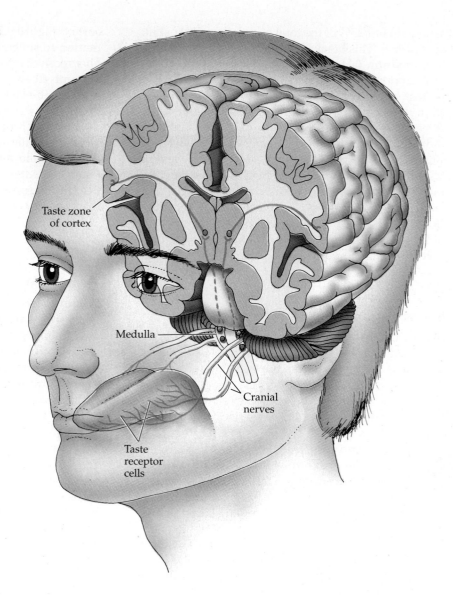

Taste zone of cortex

Medulla

Cranial nerves

Taste receptor cells

The Sense of Smell Starts with Receptor Neurons in the Nose

In humans, a sheet of cells called the **olfactory epithelium** lines the dorsal portion of the nasal cavities and adjacent regions, including the septum that separates the left and right nasal cavities (Figure 9.23). Other regions of the nasal cavity are lined with respiratory epithelium. Within the olfactory epithelium of the nasal cavity are three types of cells: (1) receptor neurons, (2) supporting cells, and (3) basal cells. At least 6 million olfactory receptor neurons are found in the 2-cm^2 area of human olfactory epithelium; in many other mammals this number is an order of magnitude greater, for example, rabbits have about 40 million receptor neurons in the olfactory epithelium. Each receptor cell has a long slender apical dendrite that extends to the outermost

layer of the epithelium, the mucosal surface. There numerous cilia emerge from the dendritic knob and extend along the mucosal surface. At the opposite end of each bipolar olfactory receptor cell, a fine unmyelinated axon, which is among the smallest-diameter axons in the nervous system, runs to the olfactory bulb. The olfactory neurons are the only sensory neurons in vertebrates in which the cell bodies are located so close to the surface of the body. This and other features, including the lack of a myelin sheath, suggest that the mammalian olfactory system retains some of the characteristics of ancestral animals.

In contrast to many other receptor neurons in the body, olfactory receptor neurons are constantly degenerating and being replaced by new receptor cells,

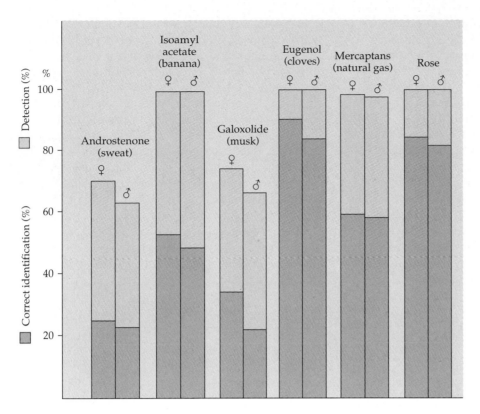

9.22 **Results of a** *National Geographic* **Smell Survey** After Gilbert and Wyslocki, 1987.

even in adults (Costanza, 1991). It is easy to understand why they degenerate; these neurons are in direct contact with the external environment and are therefore exposed to a wide array of irritants, such as chemicals and viruses. But we do not yet understand exactly how they are replaced. After an olfactory receptor cell degenerates, an adjacent basal cell differentiates into a neuron and extends dendrites to the mucosal surface and an axon into the brain. Thus, the olfactory system is constantly being rewired; the functional capability of these new connections has been clearly demonstrated in both behavioral and electrophysiological studies of animals with completely regenerated olfactory epithelium. Investigators are trying to determine how these neurons can regenerate whereas those in most other parts of the nervous system cannot. A related unresolved question is how the new neurons are able to establish the correct connections in the olfactory bulb.

Chemicals Excite Specialized Receptor Molecules on Olfactory Receptor Cells

Odorants enter the nasal cavity during inhalation and especially during periods of sniffing; they also rise to the nasal cavity from the mouth when we chew food. The direction of airflow in the nose is determined by complex curved surfaces called **turbinates** that form the nasal cavity (the turbinates in the rat's nasal cavity are designated by Roman numerals in Figure 9.26). Airborne molecules initially encounter the fluids of the mucosal layer, which con-

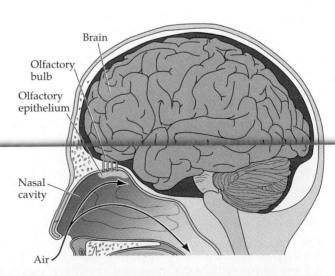

9.23 **Location of the Human Olfactory Epithelium**

tain binding proteins that transport odorants to receptor surfaces (Farbman, 1992). These stimulus-binding proteins have been found in a wide array of animals, including insects and mammals. The viscosity (stickiness) of the mucous layer determines how rapidly odorants reach the cilia of olfactory receptor cells (Kinnamon and Getchell, 1991).

The odorant stimulus then interacts with receptor sites located in the cilia and dendritic knob of the receptor cells. These receptors are members of a superfamily of G-protein–linked receptors. Interactions with the receptor trigger the synthesis of second messengers, including cyclic AMP (cAMP)and inositol trisphosphate (IP_3). Cyclic AMP opens a cation channel to elicit the generator current that depolarizes the olfactory receptor cell, and the depolarization, in turn, leads to action potentials. Inositol trisphosphate opens calcium channels, and calcium entering these channels modulates the generation of cAMP, thus af-

fecting the sensitivity of receptors (Anholt, 1993). This sensory transduction process, portrayed in Figure 9.24, is similar to the activation of other sensory systems, such as those for sweet and bitter tastes, and those in the eye (see Chapter 10).

The number and variety of these specific receptor protein molecules is debated. Some investigators have suggested that our sense of smell depends on a small number of different receptor molecules somewhat analogous to the three-color vision receptor processes that furnish all the hues we can see, as we will discuss in Chapter 10. An alternative hypothesis suggests that there are a large number of different receptor molecules, each detecting a different odor. Discoveries in the 1990s have strongly supported the hypothesis of many specific olfactory receptor molecules (Buck and Axel, 1991; Buck, 1993). This research has revealed a large, novel family of genes for G-protein receptors ex-

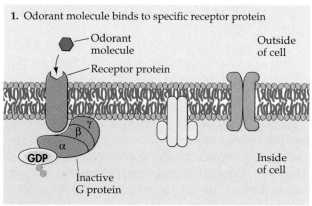

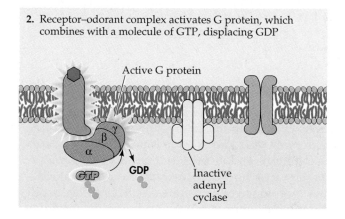

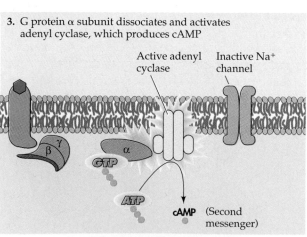

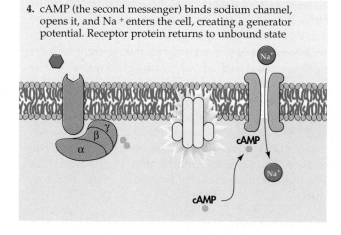

9.24 Steps in Olfactory Sensory Transduction
The diagram shows the main steps from the binding of an odorant molecule to a specific receptor protein to the creation of a generator potential. Note in steps 2 and 3 the role of a G protein as a second messenger.

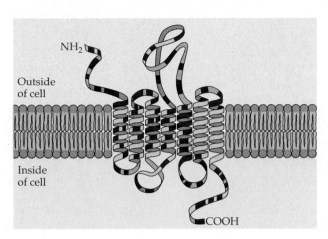

9.25 Structure of an Olfactory Receptor Molecule
The molecule has seven transmembrane regions. The amino acids that are the same in most olfactory receptor molecules examined to date are shown in orange; more variable positions are shown in black. After Buck and Axel, 1991.

pressed in the olfactory epithelium; these receptors all have seven regions that are believed to span the cell membrane (Figure 9.25). These apparent receptor molecules are synthesized only in the olfactory receptor cells and not in the neighboring supporting cells or basal cells. The members of this family of receptors are diverse, although they have certain regions in common. There are subfamilies whose members are very similar, and they may recognize subtle differences between structurally related odorants.

It is now estimated that there are about 500 to 1000 different odorant receptor genes in the human genome (Ressler, Sullivan, and Buck, 1994). Comparisons with the estimated 5000 odors that humans can discriminate suggests that each odorant receptor probably interacts with a small number of different odorants. Although some odorants may be "recognized" by a single kind of receptor molecule, most probably are recognized by a combination of a few different kinds of receptor molecules.

Neurons that express the same receptor gene are not closely clustered in the olfactory epithelium, but they are limited to distinct regions of the epithelium (Figure 9.26). Each subfamily of receptors is synthesized in several different bands of the epithelium (Vassar, Ngai, and Axel, 1993).

Olfactory Axons Connect with the Olfactory Bulb, Whose Output Projects to Several Brain Regions

The numerous axons of the olfactory nerve terminate in a complex structure at the anterior end of the brain called the **olfactory bulb**. The projection from the epithelium to the bulb maintains the zonal distribution evident in the epithelium (see Figure 9.26). The olfactory bulb has several distinct layers and an elaborate circuit. The activities of these cells are modulated by other types of neurons in the olfactory bulb; the intrinsic circuitry of the olfactory bulb contributes to an elaborate feedback control and modulation of olfactory bulb activity. The size of the olfactory bulb, in relation to the rest of the brain, is much smaller in humans than in animals such as rats and dogs that depend extensively on olfaction.

Outputs from the olfactory bulb extend to prepyriform cortex, the amygdala, and the hypothalamus, among other brain regions. The human olfactory system is diagrammed in Figure 9.27. Note that the olfactory system is the only sensory system in vertebrates that does not synapse in the thalamus on its way to the cortex.

Many Vertebrates Possess a Second Olfactory System: the Vomeronasal System

Many vertebrates have a second olfactory system that appears to specialize in detecting pheromones, the odor signals or trails that many animals secrete (see Chapter 7). This **vomeronasal system** (Box 9.2), as it is called, is present in most terrestrial mammals, amphibians, and reptiles but is usually said to be absent or vestigial in fishes, birds, and higher primates, including humans. However, recent research shows evidence–both anatomical (Moran, Jafek, and Rowley, 1991) and electrophysiological (Monti-Bloch et al., 1994)–of a vomeronasal system in adult humans. In reptiles, the vomeronasal receptor (vomernasal organ) is located above the roof of the mouth; in other animals, it is in the nasal cavity.

Sex pheromones enable males of many species to discriminate ovulating from nonovulating females, and mothers and their offspring recognize each other through odors. Many of the odors of importance in these adaptive acts are emitted in urine and distinctive body glands. Although odor-related species-typical acts are common in many other animals, the role of olfaction in human social behavior is less obvious. Humans have distinctive odors, as shown by the ability of police dogs to readily distinguish one person from another, but do *people* respond to human odors? It is known that human infants recognize their mothers by odors of the breast, and human mothers can distinguish the odors of their babies from others. In contrast with other animals, humans show no clear role for pheromones in their copulatory behavior, but the allure of perfumes and

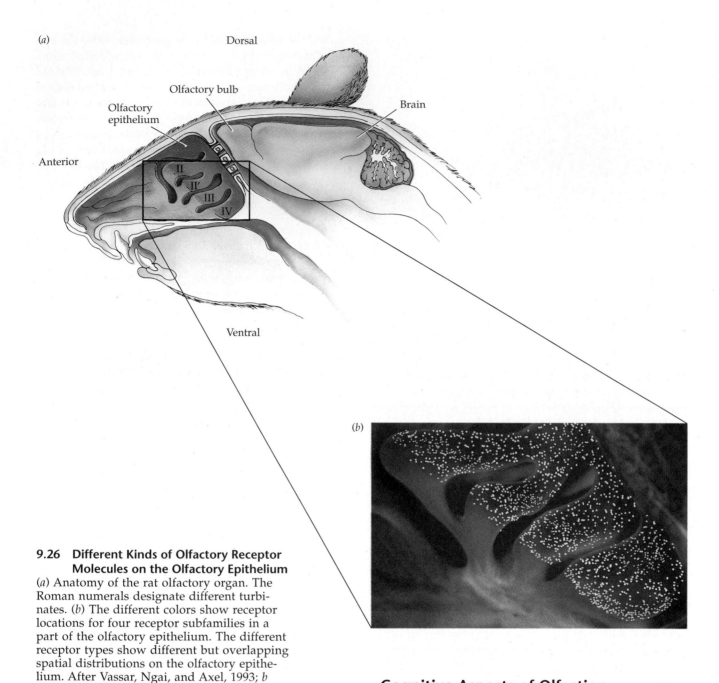

9.26 Different Kinds of Olfactory Receptor Molecules on the Olfactory Epithelium
(*a*) Anatomy of the rat olfactory organ. The Roman numerals designate different turbinates. (*b*) The different colors show receptor locations for four receptor subfamilies in a part of the olfactory epithelium. The different receptor types show different but overlapping spatial distributions on the olfactory epithelium. After Vassar, Ngai, and Axel, 1993; *b* courtesy of Robert Vassar.

colognes provides a clue that humans might not be all that different from other animals (Takagi, 1988). (In fact, "Pheromone" is used as the name of a perfume!) The role of odors in mediating the emotional tone of humans is well documented. Some odors provoke a sense of comfort and others can be distressing, especially the odors of substances that could produce food poisoning.

Cognitive Aspects of Olfaction

Some animals have species-specific responses to certain odors, such as pheromones, but human responses to odor are learned. From a whiff, we can often identify and name an odorant, an ability that depends on learning. Adult rats readily learn in a laboratory apparatus to choose the correct side based on odor cues (Staubli, Le, and Lynch, 1995). Rat pups develop an attraction to artificial odors that are paired with reinforcing stimuli like those they receive from maternal care; such reinforcing

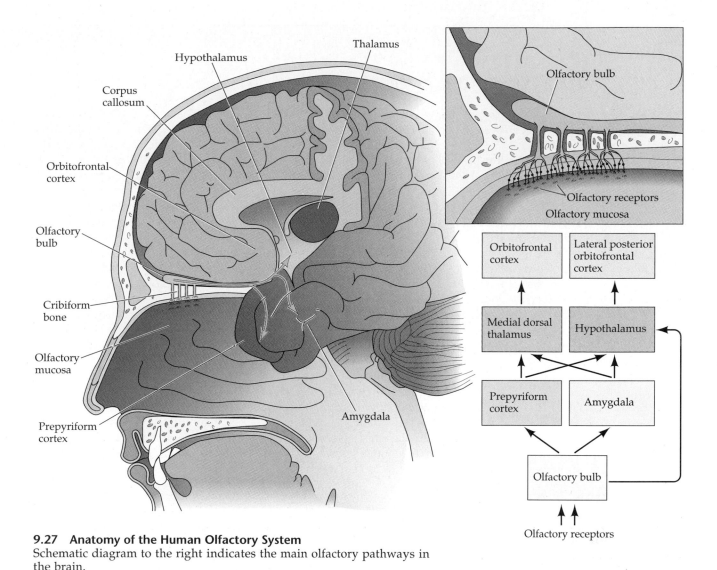

9.27 Anatomy of the Human Olfactory System
Schematic diagram to the right indicates the main olfactory pathways in
the brain.

stimuli include grooming and infusions of milk or
sucrose solution into the mouth (Leon et al., 1977;
Caza and Spear, 1984). The pairing of a reinforcing
tactile stimulus and an unfamiliar odor, peppermint,
resulted in enhanced uptake of 2-deoxyglucose in
certain dendritic lattices (glomeruli) in the olfactory
bulb of rat pups (Sullivan and Leon, 1986). The enhanced uptake was associated with a 21% enlargement of the individual glomeruli affected (Woo and
Leon, 1987). None of these changes occurred in the
bulbs of animals exposed to the peppermint odor
alone or to the tactile stimulation alone. Thus training results in measurable, localized changes in the
olfactory bulb.

It is commonly believed that emotional memories
can be evoked by exposure to distinct odors. Evidence for this idea was obtained in the *National Geographic* odor survey (Gilbert and Wyslocki, 1987).
Half the respondents aged 40 or less reported such
occurrences, but the frequency declined with age,
reaching about 30% for those 80 or more. This decline
may be related to the clear loss of olfactory responsiveness seen with aging and with neurological disorders that affect memory, such as Alzheimer's
disease (Solomon, 1994). Women report more odor-
induced memories than men do, more intense odors
are more likely than weaker ones to evoke memories,
and both pleasant and unpleasant odors kindle more
memories than do odors that the respondents consider neutral.

Box 9.2

Why Do Snakes Have Forked Tongues?

The forked tongue of snakes has intrigued people for millennia, inspiring many hypotheses (Schwenk, 1994). In many cultures and religions the forked tongue symbolizes malevolence and deceit. The first person known to inquire about the functional significance of the forked tongue was Aristotle; he suggested that it would double the pleasure of gustatory sensations. By the beginning of the twentieth century, the consensus was that the snake's tongue is a tactile organ; that is, the snake uses it to tap the ground much as a blind person uses a cane.

In 1920, Browman suggested what seemed to be a winning hypothesis: When the snake retracts its tongue, the tips (or tines) of the forked tongue are inserted into openings on both sides of the roof of the mouth; through these openings chemical stimuli reach special olfactory organs—the vomeronasal organs (VNO). These organs are highly developed in snakes, lizards, and many mammals. They are a second olfactory system that appears to have evolved specifically to detect pheromones, the chemical signals that animals secrete as messages to other animals of their species. (We will refer to the VNO again in Chapter 12, on sex.) Browman suggested that the forked tongue flicks out, picking up chemical signals, and then delivers these to the VNO. This hypothesis was widely accepted into the 1980s. Then X-ray movie studies of tongue flicks in snakes and lizards with forked tongues disproved the hypothesis; they showed that when the tongue is withdrawn into the mouth, it enters a sheath and the tips do not go into the openings to the VNO (Gillingham and Clark, 1981). Instead, the chemical molecules are deposited on pads at the bottom of the mouth, and closing the mouth presses the pads and molecules against the VNO openings.

If the tongue is not forked to fit into the VNO, then what function could the forked shape serve? Schwenk (1994) proposes a solution that encompasses observations from several fields—animal behavior, ecology, sensory physiology, and neuroanatomy. He hypothesizes that the forked tongue allows the snake to sense chemical stimuli at two points simultaneously, thereby giving it the ability to detect gradients in an odor trail. Obtaining two simultaneous readings enhances the ability of the snake to follow pheromone trails accurately, as depicted in the fig-

---

Summary

Hearing

1. The external ear captures, focuses, and filters sound. The sound arriving at the tympanic membrane (eardrum) is focused by the ossicles of the middle ear onto the oval window to stimulate the fluid-filled inner ear (cochlea).

2. Sound arriving at the oval window causes traveling waves to sweep along the basilar membrane of the inner ear. For high-frequency sounds, the largest displacement of the basilar membrane is at the base of the cochlea, near the oval window; for low-frequency sounds, the largest amplitude is near the apex of the cochlea.

3. The organ of Corti has both inner hair cells (about 3500 in humans) and outer hair cells (about 12,000 in humans). The inner hair cells convey most of the in

formation about sounds; each is associated with about 20 nerve fibers. The outer hair cells amplify the movements of the basilar membrane in response to sound, thus sharpening the frequency tuning of the cochlea.

4. Vibration of the hair cells causes the opening and closing of ion channels, thereby transducing mechanical movement into changes in electrical potential. These changes in potential stimulate the nerve cell endings that contact the hair cells.

5. Discrimination of auditory frequency involves two kinds of neural coding. For low frequencies, each cycle of the sound can be represented by nerve impulses (the volley principle); higher frequencies are represented mainly by the site of maximal stimulation along the basilar membrane (the place principle). The duplex theory relies on both of these types of coding.

ure. This ability is important in seeking both prey and mates.

This accurate spatial chemical perception is like other systems for spatial perception that are based on simultaneous stimulation of two separated sense organs—for example, auditory localization, which depends on differential stimulation at the two ears, as we discussed earlier in this chapter. Similarly, the use of the two eyes permits stereovision (see Chapter 10).

Several kinds of evidence support the hypothesis that forked tongues evolved as chemosensory edge detectors to enhance the ability to follow odor trails: (1) Snakes and lizards spread the tines of their tongue apart when they retrieve odor molecules, then draw the tines together when retracting the tongue. The greater the distance between sampling points, the better the animals sample a chemical gradient. (2) Lizards that forage widely have forked tongues, whereas lizard species

without forked tongues tend not to forage widely. (3) Forked tongues have evolved independently at least twice in different families of reptiles (Schwenk, 1994), indicating their value as an adaptation. (4) In the snake nervous system, each tine of the tongue projects to a nucleus in the other side of the brain, and the two nuclei are linked across the two hemispheres. This arrangement is similar to the anatomy of auditory centers in mammals and birds that permits the computation of binau-

ral differences and mediates auditory localization.

Species in other orders have also evolved paired chemical receptors to guide individuals to mates or prey. For example, male gypsy moths have large, elaborate, odor-detecting antennae with which they track potential mates over large distances. And the ant nest beetle has spoon-shaped antennae extending from each side of the head with which it detects and follows the pheromones of the ants that are its food.

6. Beginning with the cochlea and continuing into the neural centers for audition, sound frequencies are mapped in an orderly succession; this is called tonotopic mapping.

7. Auditory localization depends on differences in the sounds arriving at the two ears. For low-frequency sounds, differences in *time of arrival* at the two ears is especially important. For high-frequency sounds, differences in *intensity* are especially important.

8. Sound experiences early in life can influence later auditory localization and the responses of neurons in auditory pathways. Experiences later in life can also lead to changes in responses of auditory neurons.

9. Deafness can be caused by pathological changes at any level of the auditory system. Conductive deafness consists of impairments in the transmission of sound to the cochlea that are produced by changes in the external or middle ears. Sensorineural deafness is hearing loss that arises in the cochlea or auditory nerve. Central deafness arises in the brain.

10. Some forms of deafness can now be alleviated by direct electrical stimulation of the auditory nerve through an implanted prosthesis. This electrical stimulation is controlled by devices (cochlear implants) that record and transform acoustic stimuli.

Vestibular Perception

1. The receptors of the vestibular system lie within the inner ear next to the cochlea. In mammals the vestibular system consists of three semicircular canals, the utricle, and the saccule.

2. Within each of these structures, the receptors, like those of the auditory system, are groups of hair cells whose bending leads to excitation of nerve fibers.

3. The vestibular system appears to have evolved from the lateral-line system, found in many kinds of fish and some amphibians. It is generally accepted that the auditory end organ evolved from the vestibular system.

Taste

1. Humans detect only four main tastes: salty, sour, sweet, and bitter.

2. In mammals, most taste receptor cells are located in clusters of cells called taste buds. The taste cells extend fine cilia into the taste pore of the bud, where tastants come into contact with them. The taste buds are on small projections from the surface of the tongue called papillae.

3. The tastes of salty and sour are evoked by simple ions acting on ion channels in the membrane of taste cells. Sensing sweet and bitter tastes involves specialized receptor molecules and second messengers.

4. Each taste axon responds most strongly to one taste but also to other tastes. Taste discrimination requires central processing based on relative activity coming from different afferent axons.

5. Each taste cell transmits information to several afferent fibers, and each afferent fiber receives information from several taste cells. The afferent fibers run along three different cranial nerves to brain stem nuclei. The gustatory system extends from the taste receptor cells through brain stem nuclei to the thalamus and then to the cerebral cortex.

Smell

1. We can detect thousands of different odors, in contrast to only four tastes. Many species depend more on smell than humans do; such species have larger numbers of olfactory receptor cells, larger olfactory bulbs, and lower thresholds for odorants.

2. Each olfactory receptor cell is a small bipolar cell whose dendrites extend to the olfactory epithelium in the nose. The fine, unmyelinated axon runs to the olfactory bulb. An olfactory receptor cell dies after about two weeks and is replaced by an adjacent basal cell.

3. There appears to be a large family of odor-receptor molecules. These molecules all have seven transmembrane regions, and they utilize G proteins and second messengers.

4. Neurons that express the same receptor gene are not closely clustered in the olfactory epithelium, but they are limited to distinct regions of the epithelium. Each subfamily of receptors is synthesized in several different bands of the epithelium.

5. The axons of the olfactory nerve terminate in the olfactory bulb. The projection from the epithelium to the bulb maintains a zonal distribution for different kinds of receptor molecules.

6. The olfactory bulb has several distinct layers and an elaborate circuit.

7. Outputs from the olfactory bulb extend to prepyriform cortex, the amygdala, and the hypothalamus, among other brain regions.

8. Many responses to odors are learned, even by young animals. Training results in measurable, localized anatomical and physiological changes in the olfactory bulb.

Recommended Reading

Altschuler, R. A., Bobbin, R. P., Clopton, B. M., and Hoffman, D. W. (eds.) 1991. *Neurobiology of Hearing: The Central Auditory System.* Raven, New York.

Bartoshuk, L. M. and Beauchamp, G. K. 1994. Chemical senses. *Annual Review of Psychology* 45:419–449.

Ciba Foundation. 1993. *The Molecular Basis of Taste and Smell. Ciba Foundation Symposium* 179. Wiley, New York.

Farbman, A. I. 1992. *Cell Biology of Olfaction.* Cambridge University Press, Cambridge.

Masterton, R. B. 1993. Central auditory system. *Journal of Otorhinolaryngology.* 55:159–163.

Popper, A. N. and Fay, R. R. (eds.) 1992. *The Mammalian Auditory Pathway: Neurophysiology.* Springer-Verlag, New York.

Weinberger, N. M. 1995. Dynamic regulation of receptive fields and maps in the adult sensory cortex. *Annual Review of Neuroscience* 18:129–158.

Yost, W. A. 1994. *Fundamentals of Hearing.* 3rd ed. Plenum, New York.

Mary Joan Waid, *Dream Series V*, 1983.

- *Vision Provides Information about the Form, Color, Location, and Movement of Objects*

- *The Eye Is Both an Optical Device and a Neural Organ*

- *Eyes with Lenses Have Evolved in Several Phyla*

- *Neural Signals Travel from the Retina to Several Brain Regions*

- *Neurons at Different Levels of the Visual System Have Very Different Receptive Fields*

- *Why Acuity Is Best In Foveal Vision*

- *Area V1 Is Organized in Columns*

- *Color Vision Depends on Special Channels from the Retinal Cones through Cortical Area V4*

- *Perception of Visual Motion Is Analyzed by a Special System That Includes Cortical Area V5*

- *The Magnocellular and Parvocellular Pathways Are Not Completely Separate*

- *Visual Neuroscience Can Be Applied to Improve Some Visual Deficiencies*

CHAPTER 10

Vision: From Retinal Processes to Perception

Orientation

Vision plays a key role in the lives of many animals. Even animals that inhabit relatively dark ecological niches—such as owls, bats, and deep-sea fish—need information from light receptors. Some nocturnal animals have huge eyeballs in comparison to their body size; presumably the large pupils help them capture the small amounts of light available at night. Some invertebrates are so greedy for light that they have multiple light receptors scattered about the body, and some amphibians have photoreceptors directly in their brains.

The visual *perceptions* of each species depend on how their brains process the information they receive from the eyes about the spatial distribution of various wavelengths of light. Different kinds of processing of the stimulus input allow us to see the form, color, position, and distance of objects in the visual field. Research on visual information processing is one of the most active fields of biological psychology and neuroscience, as it should be, since about one-third of the human brain is devoted to visual analysis and perception. Our aim is to convey some of the major challenges, accomplishments, and excitement of this field; in the space available we can only sample from the full range of this intriguing subject.

After introducing some of the main phenomena of visual perception, we will examine the bases of vision—structures and functions of the visual system, from the eye to the nervous system to the regions of the cerebral cortex specialized for vision. The visual system has several main processing stations and pathways, and the neurons in each have different properties and functions. On the basis of evidence connecting specific impairments of vision with brain lesions, we will see that different parts of the brain process different aspects of visual perception.

Vision Provides Information about the Form, Color, Location, and Movement of Objects

Although we're familiar with vision because we use it every day, we should note some features of visual perception that are not immediately apparent. Some of these features are surprising, but a good grasp of the visual system (which we will discuss shortly) helps us understand many of these phenomena.

Perception of Form and Identification of Objects Are Complex Accomplishments

The whole area that you can see without moving your head or eyes is called your **visual field**. In a single glance, you can perceive the details of objects accurately only in the center of your visual field. We are usually not aware of this phenomenon because we move the direction of our gaze rapidly as we scan a scene or read a line of print. Thus we build up a sort of collage of detailed views. But try keeping your eyes fixed on a letter in the center of a line and then attempt to read a word in the opposite column. You'll find it difficult because **visual acuity** (the sharpness of vision) falls off rapidly from the center of the visual field toward the periphery. This difference in acuity across the visual field is the reason your gaze

10.1   Recognition at a Distance
This coarsely reproduced portrait loses its graininess if viewed using only peripheral vision or from a distance of a few meters.

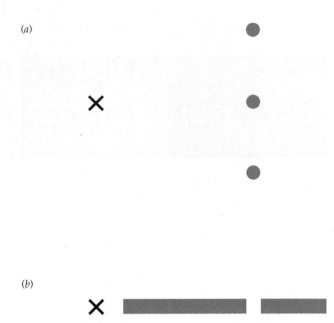

(a)

(b)

10.2   The Blind Spot
To locate your blind spot, hold the page about 10–12 cm away (you may need to adjust the page closer or further), close your left eye, and focus your right eye on the X's. In (a), the middle dot on the right should disappear. In (b), when the gap in the line is placed at your blind spot, you should see the line as solid rather than broken.

has to jump from place to place in a line as you read. Figure 10.1 illustrates another example of this phenomenon. If you fixate on a point 10 cm to the left or right of this portrait, you no longer detect the coarse graininess; the image is indistinct but seems regular. From several feet away you cannot distinguish this portrait from a detailed photograph.

If a stimulus suddenly appears away from the center of the visual field, we shift our direction of view, placing the new stimulus in the center of the visual field, where we can see it clearly. When we examine the circuitry of the retina and of higher stations of the visual system a little later, we will learn why vision is so much more acute in the center of the visual field. Most of us don't have to worry about having acute vision only in the center of our visual field, but many older people have a condition (called macular degeneration) in which the receptor cells at the center of the retina degenerate; they are left at best with only the fuzzy, indistinct vision of the peripheral visual field.

If we examine the visual field of each eye separately, we find a **blind spot** about 16° to the temporal (lateral) side of the fixation point, where a stimulus cannot be seen. This blind spot is relatively large, about 5° in diameter. Use Figure 10.2a to find the blind spot in the visual field of your right eye. The reason for the blind spot is that the fibers of the optic nerve exit the eye in a region called the **optic disc** about 16° to the *nasal* (medial) side of the retinal center. Because there are no receptors in this region, nothing can be seen in the corresponding *temporal* part of the visual field. The reason that the optic disc on the nasal side of the retina causes the blind spot in the temporal side of the visual field is that the pupil and lens reverse the retinal image, left to right, as Figure 10.3 shows; the retinal image is also inverted top to bottom.

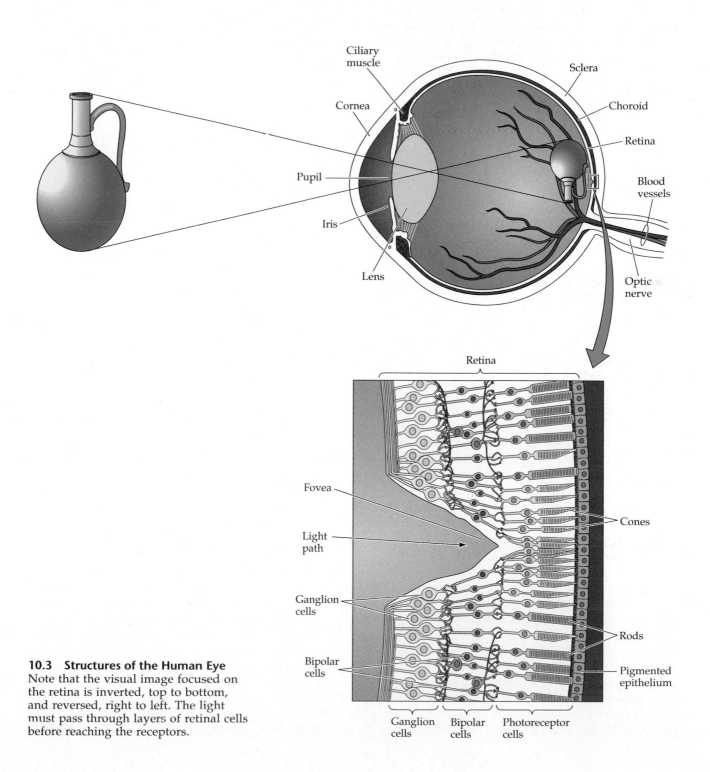

10.3 Structures of the Human Eye
Note that the visual image focused on the retina is inverted, top to bottom, and reversed, right to left. The light must pass through layers of retinal cells before reaching the receptors.

The blind spot does not appear as a dark spot; it is simply a region from which we cannot get any visual information. Find your blind spot again using Figure 10.2a and place a pencil so that its center runs vertically through the blind spot. Is there a gap in the pencil where it intersects the blind spot? No. You receive no information from the blind spot, yet you perceive a complete pencil because your perceptual system fills in from the surrounding area. If you place the broken line in Figure 10.2b in your blind spot, you will see the line as complete because the gap is invisible. Similarly, if you keep your left eye closed and look at a uniform area or most patterns with your right eye, you will not be aware of any discontinuity in the region of the blind spot. An isolated stimulus, however, may disappear in the blind spot. King Charles I of England is said to have amused himself by "beheading" some courtiers in this way.

We perceive a simple form like a triangle or recognize the face of a friend so rapidly and easily that we do not appreciate that these are exceedingly complex events that require processing in several parts of the brain. Most of the forms we see are embedded in complicated fields of objects; separating out a particular form for attention and identification requires practice and skill. It has been very difficult to achieve even primitive object recognition with artificial systems such as computers. Furthermore, recognition requires more than the accurate perception of objects. For example, as we will see later in this chapter, some people with brain damage lose their ability to recognize familiar faces even though they can still describe them accurately.

Consider the complexity of visual perception at the level of the nervous system: Each photoreceptor at each instant is in a particular state of membrane polarization, which is signaled to the neural units by a certain rate of transmitter release. In effect, each receptor is signaling a quantitative index of excitation that can be represented by a number. The nervous system takes in, about three times per second, a number from each of the approximately 100 million photoreceptors, and it faces the stupendous task of trying to figure out what in the outside world could have produced that particular array of values. Figure 10.4 illustrates a much simpler example of such a task. The numbers in this array represent shades of gray from lightest (2) to darkest (9). As you inspect this grid, you may notice that the darker shades appear mainly in the upper half of the array, but you don't perceive a form. Now look again at Figure 10.1, which shows the shades of gray that correspond to

```
99888888888888888888888888888776
99889898888888657795788888887777
99899999999974333344468888887777
99889999998533443334436888888777
99988888874338996433333488777777
99988888843369999864333488877777
99999888864349999999843446777777
99888888533699999999964555777777
99888888423889999999986646777777
99888888223679999999889864467777
99888884323467854578888634667777
99888883354268644348634344766777
99888874664377564468533357777776
99988777478388876588854477666666
98877774677357877777865566666666
98777776476435677677766465666666
98777777553434466653434455555565
98777776652446556774232555555555
98777666764446665655324555555555
97777666665336656434224555555555
97777766665424435565323555555555
97777766664622223322245555555454
97776766652752222222224555555444
97777767632476222222245555555454
97777764222277653224545555554454
97776222222246436666624555544454
97632222233222322222322555544454
84222222333333333222222244544554
82222222233322243342222222345554
82222222233322235432222222223455
62222222222222237665553222222223
62222222222222222466666622222222
```

10.4 Can You Identify the Subject?
This array of numbers represents the point-to-point illumination of a picture, from lightest (2) to darkest (9).

the numbers in the array in Figure 10.4—the form leaps out! Your nervous system processes those data to achieve the perception in an instant. How the nervous system processes so much data so quickly is the staggering problem that confronts anyone who tries to understand vision. We will consider current research and theories that attempt to resolve this absorbing question.

Color Is Created by the Visual System

For most of us, the visible world has several distinguishable hues: blue, green, yellow, red, and their intermediates. For about 8% of human males and about 0.5% of females, some of these color distinctions are either absent or at least less striking. Although the term "color blindness" is commonly used to describe impairments in color perception, most people with impaired color vision distinguish *some* hues. Complete color blindness in humans is extremely rare, although it can be caused by brain lesions. Animals exhibit different degrees of color vision. Many species of birds, fish, and insects have excellent color vision. Humans and Old World monkeys also have an excellent ability to discriminate wavelengths, but many other mammals (for example, cats) cannot discriminate wavelengths very well. We'll see more about the distribution of color vision among mammals later in this chapter.

A patch of light has other aspects besides hue. The color solid shown in Figure 10.5 illustrates the basic dimensions of our perception of light when the visual system is adapted to daylight illumination; the figure is deliberately asymmetrical, for reasons we will mention. The three dimensions of color are:

1. **Brightness**, which varies from dark to light; it is the vertical dimension in figure 10.5. The middle plane of the figure is tipped up for yellow and down for blue because yellow in the spectrum is perceived as brighter and blue as darker than the other hues.

2. **Hue**, which varies continuously around the color circle through blue, green, yellow, orange, and red. (This is what most people mean when they say "color.")

3. **Saturation**, which varies from rich full colors at the periphery of the color solid to gray at the center. For example, starting with red at the periphery, the colors become paler toward the center, going through pink to gray. Yellow is shown closer to the central axis than the other saturated hues because yellow is perceived as less saturated than the other spectral hues.

It is important not to equate a particular hue with a particular wavelength of light because, depending on the intensity of illumination and on the surrounding field, a patch illuminated by a particular wavelength is seen as various different hues. As illumination fades, the blues in a painting or a rug appear more prominent and the reds appear duller, even though the wavelength distribution in the light has not changed. Also, the hue perceived at a particular point is strongly affected by the pattern of wavelengths and intensities in other parts of the visual field. Another important distinction is that between the stimulus (light rays) and the response (color perception).

Brightness Is Created by the Visual System

The brightness dimension of visual perception is also created by the visual system rather than being determined entirely by the amount of illumination reflected. The arrows in Figure 10.6a point to two patches that clearly differ in brightness, but *they reflect the same amount of light.* If you use your hands to cover the surrounding pattern to the left and right of the two patches, then they appear the same. Figure 8.9 illustrated a similar phenomenon. How are such puzzling effects produced? The contrast effect we saw in Figure 8.9 is determined, at least in part, by interactions among adjacent retinal cells, but areas a_1 and a_2 in Figure 10.6a are not adjacent, so the effect must be produced higher in the visual system.

The visual system operates over a very wide range of intensities of light, Figure 10.6b illustrates. At any given time, however, you can discriminate over a range of light intensity that is only about one-fifth the size of the total range. We will discuss the mechanisms by which the eye adapts to the prevailing level of illumination later in this chapter.

Motion Can Enhance the Perception of Objects

The visibility of moving objects, which are especially important to many animals, is enhanced by their movement. Predators and prey both must be sensitive to moving objects in order to survive. In the periphery of our visual field, we may not be able to see stationary objects. But visibility is aided by motion only within a range of angular displacement that is

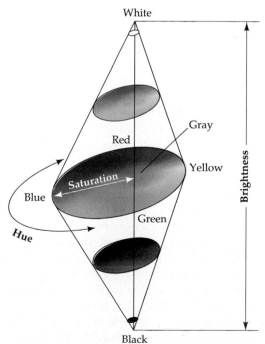

10.5 The Color Solid
This diagram illustrates the three basic dimensions of the perception of light: brightness, hue, and saturation.

(a)

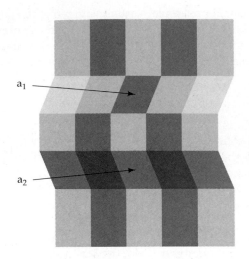

a_1

a_2

(b)

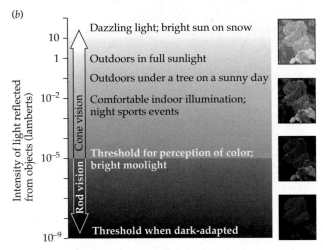

Intensity of light reflected from objects (lamberts)

10

1

10^{-2}

10^{-5}

10^{-9}

Cone vision

Rod vision

Dazzling light; bright sun on snow

Outdoors in full sunlight

Outdoors under a tree on a sunny day

Comfortable indoor illumination; night sports events

Threshold for perception of color; bright moolight

Threshold when dark-adapted

10.6 Perceiving Brightness
(a) Shading around a patch of light affects the perception of brightness. For example, patch a_1 appears darker than a_2, even though they are the same shade of gray. If you don't believe this, view them through two holes two centimeters apart. (b) The remarkably wide range of the human eye's sensitivity to light intensity.

appropriate to locomotion of animals. Anything that moves faster is a blur or may be invisible, as is a bullet speeding by. Anything that moves too slowly—such as the hands of a clock—is not seen as moving, although we can note from time to time that it has changed position. A succession of still pictures, presented at the proper rate, can cause apparent motion, as in motion pictures. The investigation of apparent visual motion by psychologist Max Wertheimer (1925) led to the Gestalt movement in psychology. Perception of motion is analyzed by special areas of the brain, as we will see later in this chapter.

The Eye Is Both an Optical Device and a Neural Organ

The eye is an elaborate structure with optical functions (capturing light and forming detailed spatial images) and neural functions (transducing light into neural signals and beginning the processing that enables us to perceive objects and scenes). The optical functions of the eye require both internal and external muscles under delicate neural control. The eye transduces light into neural activity through a series of steps in receptor cells of the retina, starting with photochemical transformations. Our examination of the eye will lead us to a discussion about how this elaborate organ evolved.

The Vertebrate Eye Acts in Some Ways Like a Camera

Our ability to discriminate visual objects and scenes depends on a number of structures and processes. First among these are the structures and processes that enable the eye to form relatively accurate optical images on the light-sensitive cells of the retina. (Box 10.1 describes some of the features of the optical stimulus.) Accurate optical images are necessary for us to be able to see the shapes of objects; that is, light from a point on a target object must end up as a point—rather than a blur—in the retinal image. Without optical images, light-sensitive cells could detect only the presence or absence of light and could not see forms, just as exposing photographic film to light outside a camera will not produce an image of the surroundings.

To produce optical images the eye has many of the features of a camera, starting with a lens to focus light (see Figure 10.3). Light travels in a straight line until it encounters a change in the density of the medium, which causes light rays to bend. This bending of light rays, called **refraction**, is the basis of such instruments as eyeglasses, telescopes, and microscopes. The **cornea** of the eye, whose curvature is fixed, bends light rays, and is primarily responsible for forming the image on the retina. The **lens**, whose shape is controlled by the **ciliary muscles** inside the eye, makes further adjustments. As the degree of contraction of the ciliary muscles varies, the lens focuses images of nearer or farther objects so that they form sharp images on the retina; this process of focusing is called **accommodation**. In many people the shape of the eyeball is such that the lens cannot bring images into sharp focus on the retina. Eyeglasses or contact lenses can correct such conditions. As mammals get older, their lenses become less elastic and therefore less

Box 10.1

The Basics of Light

The physical energy to which our visual system responds is a band of electromagnetic radiation. This radiation comes in very small packets of energy called **quanta** (singular: quantum). Each quantum can be described by a single number, its **wavelength** (the distance between two adjacent crests of vibratory activity). The human visual system responds only to quanta whose wavelengths lie within a very narrow section of the total electromagnetic range, from about 400 to 700 nanometers (nm; as shown in the figure). Such quanta of light energy are called **photons** (from the Greek *phos*, "light"). The band of radiant energy visible to animals may be narrow, but it must provide for accurate reflection from the surface of objects in the size range that matters for survival. Radio waves are good for imaging objects of astronomical size; X rays penetrate below the surfaces of objects.

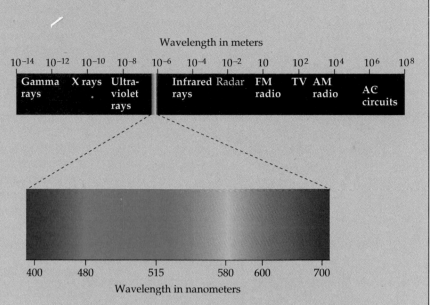

Each photon is a very small amount of energy; the exact amount depends on its wavelength. A single photon of wavelength 560 nm contains only a tiny amount of energy. A 100-watt (W) light bulb gives off only about 3 W of visible light; the rest is heat. But even the 3 W of light amounts to 8 quintillion (8×10^{18}) photons per second! When quanta within the visible spectrum enter the eye, they can evoke visual sensations. The exact nature of such sensations depends both on the wavelengths of the quanta and on the number of quanta per second.

---

able to change their curvature to bring near objects into focus. Humans correct this problem by wearing bifocal or trifocal eyeglasses, in which segments of the lens refract differently, permitting accurate viewing at various distances.

The amount of light that enters the eye is controlled by the size of the **pupil**, just as the aperture controls the light that enters a camera. The pupil is an opening in the structure called the **iris**. In Chapter 2 we mentioned that dilation of the pupils is controlled by the sympathetic division of the autonomic system, and constriction by the parasympathetic division. Since both divisions usually are active, pupil size reflects a balance of influences. During an eye examination, the doctor may use a drug to block acetylcholine transmission in the parasympathetic synapses of your iris; this drug relaxes the sphincter muscle fibers and permits the pupil to open widely. One drug that has this effect, belladonna (which is Italian for "beautiful lady"), got its name because it was thought to make a woman more beautiful by giving her the wide open pupils of an attentive person. Some drugs, such as morphine, stimulate the sympathetic division; intensely constricted pupils are a sign of overdose of such drugs.

The movement of the eyes is controlled by the **extraocular muscles**, three pairs of muscles that extend from the outside of the eyeball to the bony socket of the eye (Figure 10.7); fixating (focusing on) still or moving targets requires delicate control of these muscles. When we view distant objects, the muscles move the two eyes in parallel, but when we view a nearby object, the muscles make the directions of gaze of the two eyes converge precisely on the target.

Thus, delicate and elaborate control of both ciliary (intraocular) and extraocular muscles is important in finding, focusing, and following visual stimuli. Some of these processes—such as control of pupil size by

(a) Left eye and its muscles

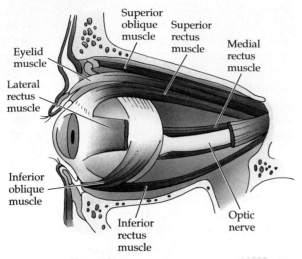

Superior oblique muscle

Superior rectus muscle

Medial rectus muscle

Eyelid muscle

Lateral rectus muscle

Inferior oblique muscle

Inferior rectus muscle

Optic nerve

(b) Up/down movement

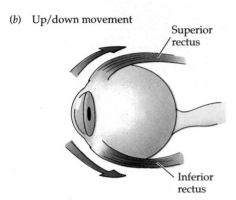

Superior rectus

Inferior rectus

(c) Rotation

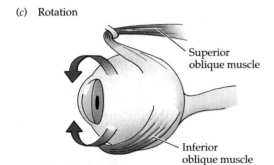

Superior oblique muscle

Inferior oblique muscle

(d) Right/left movement

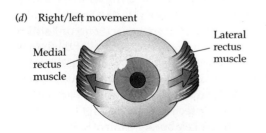

Lateral rectus muscle

Medial rectus muscle

10.7 The Three Pairs of Extraocular Muscles
(*a*) These muscles, shown here in their relative positions, are responsible for movements of the eye. (*b*) The superior and inferior rectus muscles control vertical movement. (*c*) The superior and inferior obliques control rotation. (*d*) The medial and lateral recti control horizontal movement.

the level of ambient illumination—are controlled largely through brain stem reflexes. Others depend on feedback involving the perceptions that result from processing visual information. For example, the contractions of the ciliary muscles adjust the shape of the lens until a target object is in sharp focus, and continual interaction between muscular activity and perception keeps the object in focus. All the visual processes depend on stimulation of the light-sensitive cells of the retina.

There Are Three Classes of Eye Movements

The eyes perform different kinds of movements as you examine stationary or moving targets. Special techniques devised to record and study eye movements reveal many of the mechanisms of visual perception.

As we mentioned earlier, when you read a line of type, you make quick eye movements to transfer your gaze from one fixation point to another. These quick, accurate movements are called **saccades**, or **saccadic movements** (from the French *saccade,* "twitch, jerk"). As children start to read, their saccades have short spans because they must examine each word. As children improve their skill and learn to read several words at once, without shifting gaze, the saccades increase in extent. You also make use of saccades when you direct your attention to a stimulus that appears suddenly in the periphery of your visual field.

Because the direction of gaze is controlled by active contraction of the extraocular muscles, even when you try to keep your eyes still they always show fine, involuntary, to-and-fro movements. In cases of dizziness or some diseases, the eye may show large oscillatory movements, a condition is called **nystagmus**. The fine normal oscillatory movements are called **physiological nystagmus**, with "physiological" meaning "normal." Physiological nystagmus has an important function: If an image is held *absolutely stationary* on the retina by artificial means (such as a special small projector mounted on a contact lens), the image fades out in a minute or less because the visual system adapts rapidly to constant stimulation. Physiological nystagmus moves the eye enough to prevent such adaptation, so we are not bothered by images fading from view (like a Cheshire cat) as we try to gaze steadily at them.

When your gaze smoothly and continuously follows a moving object, you are making use of **pursuit movement**. Some people are unable to perform smooth, accurate pursuit movements; their gaze lags behind the target or it undershoots, then overshoots, the moving position of the target. Some investigators report that deficiency in pursuit movements appears to be a genetic trait linked to schizophrenia (Levy et al., 1993), as we will discuss in Chapter 16.

Visual Processing Begins in the Retina

The first stages of the processing of visual information occur in the **retina**, the receptive surface inside the back of the eye (Figure 10.8*a*). The retina is only 200 to 300 μm thick—not much thicker than the edge of a razor blade—but it contains several types of cells in distinct layers (Figure 10.8*b*). The receptive cells are modified neurons; some are called **rods** because of their relatively long, narrow form, and the others are called **cones** (Figures 10.8*c* and *d*). The rods and cones release neurotransmitter molecules that modulate the activity of the **bipolar cells** that synapse with them (10.8*e*). The bipolar cells in turn connect with **ganglion cells**. The axons of the ganglion cells form the **optic nerve**, which carries information to the brain. **Horizontal cells** and **amacrine cells** (Figure 10.8*f*) are especially significant nerve cells in interactions within the retina. The horizontal cells contact both the receptor cells and the bipolar cells; the amacrine cells contact both the bipolar and the ganglion cells.

The rods, cones, bipolar cells, and horizontal cells generate only graded local potentials; they do not generate or conduct action potentials. In this respect they are like other small cells that we mentioned in Chapter 5. These cells affect each other through the *graded* release of neurotransmitters in response to *graded* changes in electrical potentials. The amacrine cells and the ganglion cells, on the other hand, do conduct action potentials. Because the ganglion cells have action potentials and are relatively large in size, they were the first retinal cells to have their activity recorded electrically. From the receptive cells to the ganglion cells there is overall an enormous convergence and compression of data; the human eye contains about 100 million rods and 4 million cones but there are only 1 million ganglion cells to transmit that information to the brain. The multitude of retinal cells and the connections among them permit a great deal of information processing at the first level of the visual system.

Studies of human sensitivity to light reveal the existence of two different functional systems corresponding to the two different populations of receptors and associated neural elements in the retina. One system works in dim light and involves the rods and highly convergent neural processing; this system is called the **scotopic system** (from the Greek *skotos*, "darkness"). The scotopic system does not see colors, which is the basis for the saying "At night, all cats are gray." The other system requires more light and involves much more detailed neural processing; in some species, it shows differential sensitivity to wavelengths, enabling color vision. This system involves the cones and is called the **photopic system** (from the Greek *phos*,"light"). At moderate levels of illumination, both rods and cones function, and some ganglion cells receive input from both rods and cones. Having these two systems enables us to see over a wide range of light intensities. Table 10.1 summarizes the characteristics of the photopic and scotopic systems.

The extraordinary sensitivity of rods and cones is the result of their unusual structure and biochemistry. A portion of their structure, when magnified, looks like a large stack of pancakes or discs (see Figure 10.8*e*). The stacking of discs increases the probability of capturing quanta of light, an especially important function, since light is reflected in many directions by the surface of the eyeball, the lens, and the fluid media inside the eye. The reflection of light from all these surfaces means that only a fraction of the light that strikes the cornea actually reaches the retina.

The quanta of light that strike the discs are captured by special photopigment receptor molecules. In the rods this photopigment is **rhodopsin** (from the Greek *rhodos*, "rose" or "red," and *opsis*, "vision"). Cones use a few main photopigments, as we will see later. All the photopigments in the eye consist of two parts: **retinal** (an abbreviated form of *retinaldehyde*, which is vitamin A aldehyde) and **opsin**. (We will print the noun "retinal" in small capital letters—RETINAL—to distinguish it from the adjective "retinal.") The pioneering studies of George Wald (1964) established the chemical structure of rhodopsin and the related visual pigments of the cone receptors. Wald received the 1967 Nobel Prize in Physiology or Medicine for this research. The visual receptor molecules have structures that are similar to those of G protein–coupled receptor molecules for synaptic transmitters that we discussed in Chapter 6. Figure 10.9 shows the hypothesized structure of the rhodopsin molecule spanning the membrane of a disc.

When light activates a rhodopsin molecule, the RETINAL dissociates rapidly from the opsin, revealing

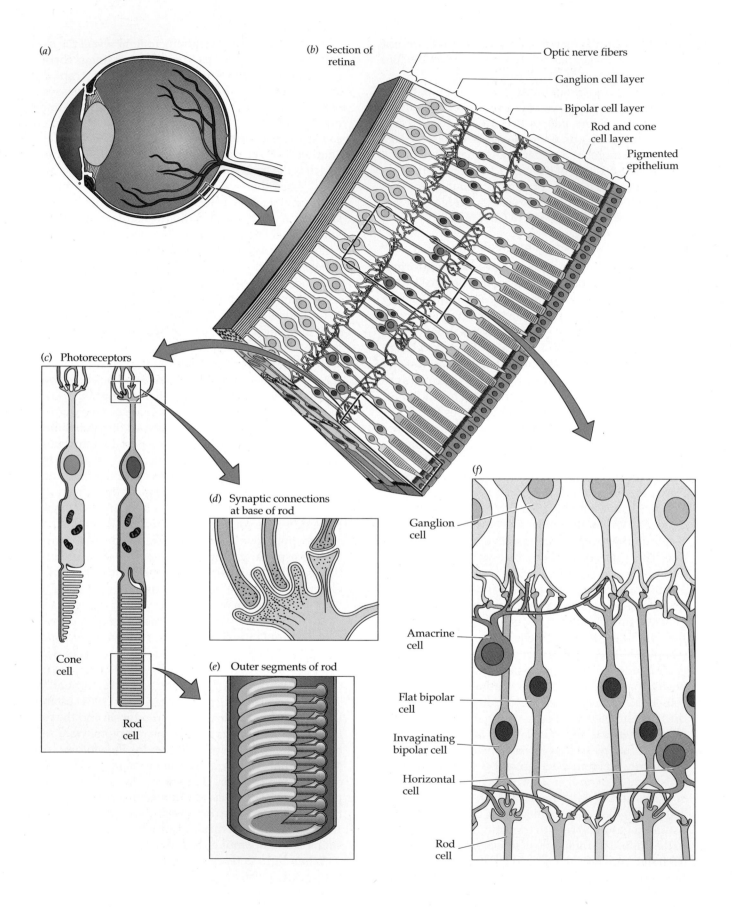

(a)

(b) Section of retina

Optic nerve fibers

Ganglion cell layer

Bipolar cell layer

Rod and cone cell layer

Pigmented epithelium

(c) Photoreceptors

Cone cell

Rod cell

(d) Synaptic connections at base of rod

(e) Outer segments of rod

(f)

Ganglion cell

Amacrine cell

Flat bipolar cell

Invaginating bipolar cell

Horizontal cell

Rod cell

◀ 10.8 Anatomy of the Eye and Retina

(*a*) The eye in cross section. (*b*) Cross section of the retina, showing its layered structure. (*c*) Structure of a single rod and single cone. (*d*) Synaptic connections at the base of a rod. (*e*) Outer segments of a rod. (*f*) Synaptic connections of rods to other retinal cells. Note the two classes of bipolar cells, those that make invaginating connections to photoreceptors and those that make flat connections.

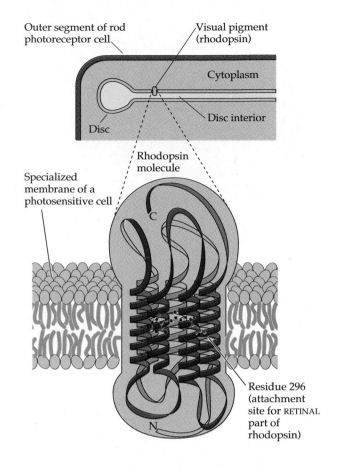

an enzymatic site on the opsin molecule. The activated opsin combines rapidly with many molecules of the G protein called transducin (Fibure 10.10*b*). Transducin in turn acts through an enzyme, phosphodiesterase (PDE), to transform cyclic GMP (guanosine monophosphate) to 5'-GMP. In the dark, cyclic GMP holds channels for sodium ions (Na$^+$) open; light stimulation initiates a cascade of events that closes Na$^+$ channels. Capture of a single quantum of light, under dim light conditions, can lead to the closing of hundreds of sodium channels in the photoreceptor

10.9 The Structure of Rhodopsin

The rhodopsin molecule includes seven segments that transverse the disc membrane. Note the location of one molecule of rhodopsin in the disc membrane (*top*).

Table 10.1

Properties of the Human Photopic and Scotopic Visual systems

PROPERTY	PHOTOPIC SYSTEM	SCOTOPIC SYSTEM
Receptors[a]	Cones	Rods
Approximate number of receptors per eye	4 million	100 million
Photopigments[b]	Three classes of cone opsins; the basis of color vision	Rhodopsin
Sensitivity	Low; needs relatively strong stimulation; used for day vision	High; can be stimulated by weak light intensity; used for night vision
Location in retina[c]	Concentrated in and near fovea; present less densely throughout retina	Outside fovea
Receptive field size and visual acuity	Small in fovea, so acuity is high; larger outside fovea	Larger, so acuity is lower

[a]Cones and rods are illustrated in Figure 10.8.
[b]Figure 10.25 shows the spectral sensitivities of the photopigments.
[c]See Figure 10.21.

(a)

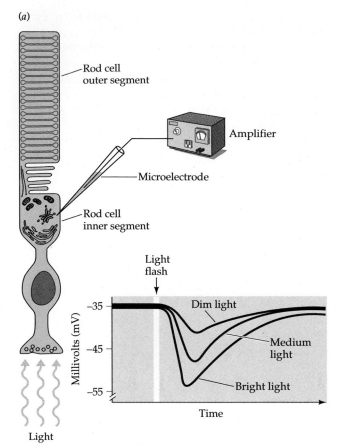

10.10 Light Causes Photoreceptors to Hyperpolarize
(a) Light stimulation causes hyperpolarization of the visual receptor cells, as shown here for a rod receptor. (b) The hyperpolarization is caused by a cascade of neurochemical events that enormously multiply the effect of each photon of light captured by a receptor cell.

membrane and block the entry of a million Na⁺ ions (Schnapf and Baylor, 1987). Closing the Na⁺ channels creates a hyperpolarizing generator potential (Figure 10.10a). This change of potential represents the initial electrical signal of activation of the visual pathway. The size of the photoreceptor potential regulates the release of synaptic transmitter.

It may seem puzzling at first that light stimulation hyperpolarizes vertebrate retinal photoreceptors, since sensory stimulation depolarizes most other receptor cells. But remember that the visual system responds to *changes* in light. Either an increase or a decrease in light intensity can stimulate the visual system, and hyperpolarization is just as much a neural signal as is depolarization. Stimulation of the cone pigments hyperpolarizes the cones, just as stimulation of rhodopsin hyperpolarizes the rods.

(b)

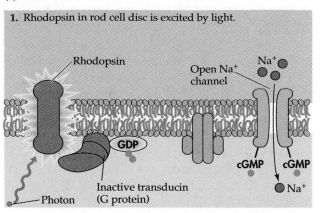

1. Rhodopsin in rod cell disc is excited by light.

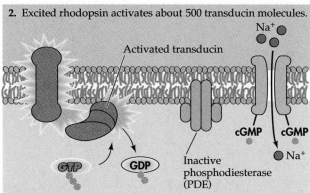

2. Excited rhodopsin activates about 500 transducin molecules.

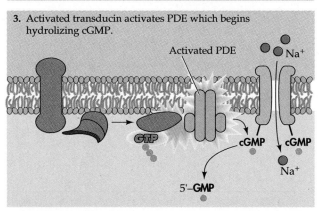

3. Activated transducin activates PDE which begins hydrolizing cGMP.

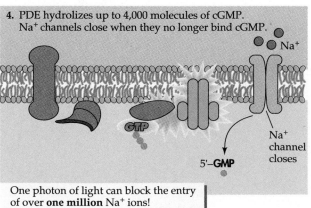

4. PDE hydrolizes up to 4,000 molecules of cGMP. Na⁺ channels close when they no longer bind cGMP.

One photon of light can block the entry of over **one million** Na⁺ ions!

Photoreceptors Excite Some Retinal Cells and Inhibit Others

Each cone in the central retina connects to four bipolar cells (Figure 10.11). Two are **midget bipolars**, which connect to just this one cone; the other two are **diffuse bipolars**, which connect to several neighboring cones as well. In the dark, the photoreceptor is depolarized and steadily releases its synaptic transmitter, probably glutamate. This transmitter depolarizes (excites) one midget and one diffuse bipolar cell but hyperpolarizes (inhibits) the other midget and diffuse bipolar cells (Daw, Brunken, and Parkinson, 1989). We saw in Chapter 5 that the same neu-rotransmitter can have opposite effects when it acts at different chemical receptor molecules in the neuronal membrane; the retinal bipolar cells are an example. Some agonists of glutamate stimulate one class of bipolar cells—the **on-center bipolars**, which respond with depolarization to light in the center of their receptive fields—without affecting the **off-center bipolars**, those that respond to light offset from the center of their receptive fields. Other agonists of glutamate, acting at different membrane receptor molecules, have the reverse action: they depolarize off-center bipolars and hyperpolarize on-center bipolar cells.

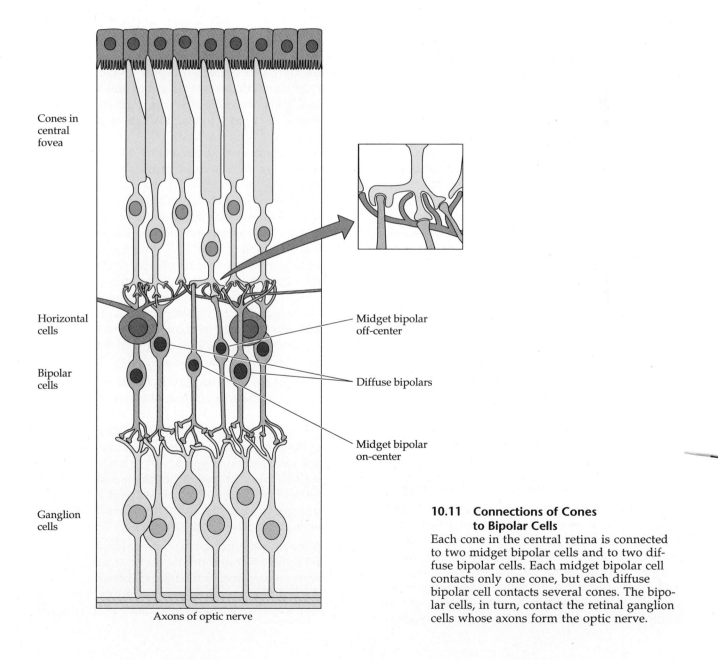

Cones in central fovea

Horizontal cells

Bipolar cells

Ganglion cells

Axons of optic nerve

Midget bipolar off-center

Diffuse bipolars

Midget bipolar on-center

10.11 Connections of Cones to Bipolar Cells

Each cone in the central retina is connected to two midget bipolar cells and to two diffuse bipolar cells. Each midget bipolar cell contacts only one cone, but each diffuse bipolar cell contacts several cones. The bipolar cells, in turn, contact the retinal ganglion cells whose axons form the optic nerve.

Normally in the dark the photoreceptor transmitter depolarizes the bipolar cells that report "light off," or "dark," to ganglion cells, which relay the message to higher visual centers. At the same time, the same photoreceptor transmitter hyperpolarizes the other bipolar cells and prevents them from reporting "light on." When a particular region of the retina is illuminated, some bipolar cells that were being hyperpolarized by the photoreceptor transmitter agent are now released from hyperpolarization, so they depolarize and report "light" to the ganglion cells. The stimulated ganglion cells then fire nerve impulses and report "light" to higher visual centers.

The story is more complicated, however, because each bipolar cell has a concentric receptive field with a roughly circular center and a doughnut-shaped ring surrounding it (Figure 10.12). The center and the surround are antagonistic; that is, if one part is stimulated by an increase of light, the other is inhibited. Thus, an on-center cell is also an off-surround cell (see Figure 10.12). Input to the center of a bipolar cell's receptive field comes from the photoreceptor; input to the surround comes from the horizontal cells. Each bipolar cell responds to the transmitter from the horizontal cell in the opposite way that it responds to the transmitter from the cone. The center of a bipolar cell's receptive field has somewhat more influence than the surround, so if light increases in both the center and the surround of an on-center/off-surround bipolar, the bipolar cell signals an increase of light. At higher stations of the visual system, the surround portion of receptive fields gains increasing importance.

Retinal ganglion cells normally fire at a low rate in the absence of stimulation. If you are in a place with no light, you don't see "black." You see a sort of dim flickering, which is caused by the spontaneous activity of the retinal ganglion cells. As we will see in more detail later, some ganglion cells fire more impulses when illumination increases, some fire at a higher rate when illumination decreases, and some fire in response to both increases and decreases.

Different Mechanisms Enable the Eyes to Work over a Wide Range of Light Intensities

Many sensory systems have to work over wide ranges of stimulus intensity, as we learned in Chapter 8. This is certainly true of the visual system, where a very bright light is about 10 billion times as intense as the weakest lights we can see (see Figure 10.6b).

One way the eye deals with a large range of intensities is by adjusting the size of the pupil. In bright light the pupil contracts to admit only about one-tenth as much light as when illumination is dim. Another mechanism for handling different light intensities is range fractionation; that is, different receptors—some with low thresholds, and others with high thresholds—handle different intensities. Figure 8.6 illustrated this mechanism for the somesthetic system. The visual system uses this mechanism by dividing the receptors into two systems: the scotopic (rod) and photopic (cone) systems. But additional range fractionation would carry an unacceptable cost: If, at a particular light level, several sets of receptors were not responding, acuity would be impaired. If only a fraction of the receptors responded to the small changes of light intensity around a given level, the active receptors would be spaced apart from each other in the retina, and the "grain" of the retina would be coarse. The eye solves this problem by having receptors *adapt* to the prevailing level of illumination; that is, each receptor adjusts its sensitivity to match the average level of ambient illumination. Thus the visual system is concerned with *differences*, or *changes*, in brightness, not with the absolute level of illumination.

As we mentioned earlier, at any given time a photoreceptor operates over a range of intensities of about two log units (1 to 100); that is, it is completely depolarized by a stimulus about one-tenth (one log unit below) the ambient level of illumination, and a light ten times more intense than (one log unit above) the ambient level will completely hyperpolarize it. The fact that the sensitivity of the visual receptors adapts to the level of illumination means that the receptors can shift their whole range of response to work around the prevailing level of illumination. Three main factors help account for this adaptation of sensitivity; the second and third of these mechanisms are specific to the visual system.

1. Probably the most important factor is one shared by other sensory modalities—the role(s) of calcium (Ca^{2+}) ions (Pugh and Lamb, 1990). When intracellular Ca^{2+} ions are bound experimentally and thus made unavailable for reactions, the visual system can no longer adapt to higher levels of illumination. Several processes seem to be involved here, and the precise ways in which Ca^{2+} ions participate in adaptation are still being worked out (Pugh and Lamb, 1990).

2. When the photoreceptor pigment is split apart by light, its two components—RETINAL and opsin—slowly recombine, so the balance between the rate of breakdown of the pigment and its rate of recombination determines how much photopigment

(*a*) An on-center/off-surround cell

(*b*) An off-center/on-surround cell

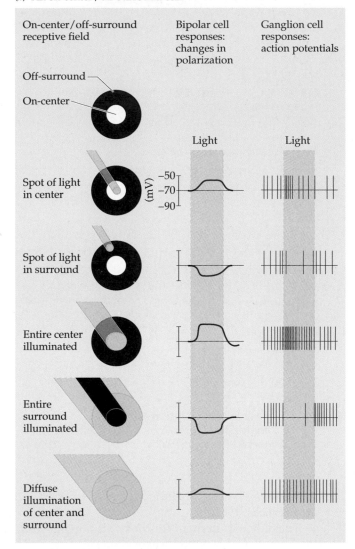

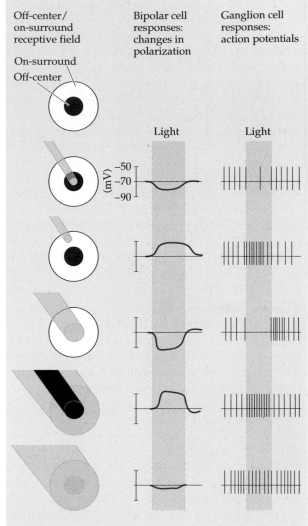

10.12 Retinal Cell Receptor Fields

Each primate retinal bipolar cell and each retinal ganglion cell has a concentric receptive field, with antagonistic center and surround. Bipolar cells respond by changes in local membrane potentials whereas ganglion cells respond with action potentials. (*a*) An on-center/off-surround cell is excited by an increase of illumination in the center of its receptive field and inhibited by an increase of illumination in the surround. (*b*) Changes in illumination have the opposite effects on an off-center/on-surround cell.

is available at any given time to respond to stimulation by light. If you go from bright daylight into a dark theater, it takes several minutes until enough rhodopsin becomes available to restore your dark vision.

3. The photoreceptors have limited numbers of molecules of the enzyme phosphodiesterase (PDE) and Na⁺ channels, both of which are needed for the response to light, as we have described. PDE

molecules and Na⁺ channels tend to be available at low levels of illumination, so stimulation by only a few photons can activate a molecule of PDE and lead to the closing of Na⁺ channels and hyperpolarization of the receptor. But available PDE molecules and Na⁺ channels tend to be increasingly rare at higher levels of illumination, so increasing numbers of photons are required to activate them and hyperpolarize the receptors.

Eyes with Lenses Have Evolved in Several Phyla

When we look at a complex organ like the eye of a mammal, an octopus, or a fly, it is hard to imagine how it could have evolved. But inspection of different living species reveals a gradation from very simple light-sensitive cells to increasingly complex organs with focusing devices. Some of the steps in the evolution of eyes like those of a mammal or an octopus were the following (Land and Fernald, 1992):

1. Concentrating light-sensitive cells into *localized groups* that serve as photoreceptor organs (Figure 10.13a). Animals with such photoreceptor organs have better chances to survive and reproduce than do similar animals with scattered receptor cells, because photoreceptor organs facilitate responding differently to stimuli that strike different parts of the body surface.

2. Clustering light receptors at the bottom of *pitlike or cuplike depressions* in the skin (Figure 10.13b). Animals with this adaptation can discriminate better among stimuli that come from different directions. They also perceive increased contrast of stimuli against a background of ambient light.

3. Narrowing the top of the cup into a *small aperture*, so that, like a pinhole camera, the eye can focus well (Figure 10.13c).

4. Closing over the opening with *transparent skin* or filling the cup with a *transparent substance* (Figure 10.13d). This covering protects the eye against the entry of foreign substances that might injure the receptor cells or block vision.

5. Forming *a lens* either by thickening the transparent skin or by modifying other tissue in the eye (Figure 10.13e). This adaptation improves the focusing of the eye while allowing the aperture to be relatively large to let in more light; thus, vision can be acute even when light is not intense.

Phylogenetic studies of the structure and development of eyes led investigators to conclude that eyes evolved independently in many different phyla. The evolution of an organ of vision thus is not unusual in the history of animal forms (Salvini-Plawen and Mayr, 1970). A competent optical system with a lens, however, has evolved in only 6 of the 33 phyla of multicellular animals. These few phyla have been very successful; they account for about 96% of known species of multicellular animals. An effective optical

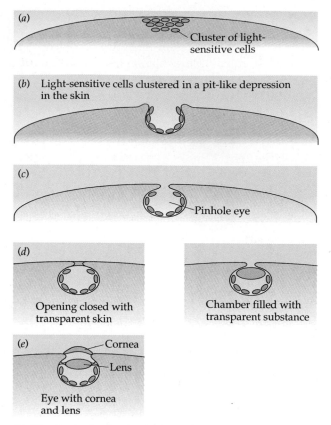

10.13   Steps in the Evolution of Single-Chambered Eyes with a Lens
After Land and Fernald, 1992.

system may have contributed to this success (Land and Fernald, 1992:7).

The only requirement for the evolution of eyes to begin appears to be the existence of light-sensitive cells. Natural selection then favors the development of auxiliary mechanisms needed to improve vision. Many kinds of cells show some light sensitivity, and different phyla have modified different types of cells for specialized photoreceptors. The most common starting point has been cells of epidermal (skin) origin, but several lines (including our chordate-vertebrate ancestors) derived their visual receptors from cells of neural origin. All known visual systems use a light-receptor molecule similar to rhodopsin, indicating a basic similarity among them.

Three basic structures for forming a visual image are a lens (a camera eye), a pinhole aperture, or a compound eye formed of narrow tube receptors (called ommatidia) that fan out to point in different directions. Animals that use lenses include not only vertebrates and some cephalopods (like the octopus) but also some insects and some bivalve molluscs. These three main structures for forming visual images do not exhaust the mechanisms that have evolved: some animals (for example, scallops) use mirrors to form images, and in one microscopic marine animal (*Copilia*), its few light receptors sweep back and forth and scan the image formed by the lens (Land, 1984).

The fact that the cephalopods (such as squid and octopus) evolved a visual system that in many ways resembles that of vertebrates (from fish to humans) suggests that there are major constraints on the development of a visual system for a large, rapidly moving animal. Let's look at some of the major similarities and differences between the eyes of cephalopods and those of vertebrates. In both, the eyes are relatively large, allowing for many receptors and the ability to gather large amounts of light. The incoming light is regulated by a pupil and focused by a lens. In both cephalopods and vertebrates, three sets of extraocular muscles move the eyeballs (see Figure 10.7). An important difference in eye structure is the organization of the retina. In the vertebrate eye, light must travel through neurons and blood vessels to reach the receptors, and the area where the neural axons and blood vessels enter and leave the retina forms the blind spot. In cephalopods the organization is more efficient in some respects: light reaches the receptors directly, and the neurons and blood vessels lie *behind* the receptors; thus there is no blind spot. The detailed structure of the receptor cells is quite different in cephalopods and vertebrates. In addition, the visual stimulus causes depolarization of cephalopod (and most invertebrate) retinal receptor cells, but it causes hyperpolarization of fish and mammalian retinal receptors.

The major similarities between cephalopod and vertebrate eyes have often been cited as examples of convergent evolution, showing ways in which similar functions can be achieved with different structures and processes, starting from different origins. Recent research suggests, however, that the eyes of all seeing animals share at least one important genetic feature: the compound eye of the fruit fly *Drosophila*, the vertebrate eye, and the cephalopod eye all develop using genes of the *Pax* family. The finding that highly homologous molecules are key regulators of eye development in different phyla argues that eyes in all phyla share a common origin (Zuker, 1994).

The opsins—photopigment molecules—go back in evolutionary history even beyond the earliest structures that we would recognize as an eye (Land and

Fernald, 1992). Opsin molecules resemble each other in all multicellular animals—animals as diverse as vertebrates, insects, and molluscs, whose ancestors diverged from each other about half a billion years ago in the Cambrian era (Goldsmith, 1990). This molecule has been conserved for hundreds of millions of years probably because of two remarkable properties: (1) Absorption of a single photon can significantly change the structure of the RETINAL so it can detect incredibly small amounts of energy. (2) When light causes RETINAL to dissociate from opsin, opsin turns into an enzyme that sets off a chemical cascade large enough to initiate neural activity.

Neural Signals Travel from the Retina to Several Brain Regions

The results of visual processing in the retina *converge* on the ganglion cells, from which they then *diverge* to several brain structures (see Figure 5.15). The optic nerves, which are made up of the axons of the ganglion cells in each eye, convey visual information to the brain (Figure 10.14a). In all vertebrate animals, some or all of the axons of each optic nerve cross to the opposite cerebral hemisphere. The optic nerves cross at the **optic chiasm** (named from the Greek letter χ [chi] because of its crossover shape), which is located just anterior to the stalk of the pituitary gland. In humans, axons from the half of the retina toward the nose (the nasal retina) cross over to the opposite side of the brain. The half of the retina toward the side of the head (the temporal retina) projects its axons to its own side of the head. Proportionally more axons cross over in animals, such as rodents, that have laterally placed eyes with little binocular overlap in their fields of vision. After they pass the optic chiasm, the axons of the retinal ganglion cells are known collectively as the **optic tract**.

Most optic tract axons terminate in the **lateral geniculate nucleus (LGN)**, which is the visual part of the thalamus. Most of the axons of postsynaptic cells in the lateral geniculate form the **optic radiations**, which terminate in the visual areas in the **occipital cortex** at the back of the brain. In addition to the **primary visual cortex** shown in Figure 10.14, numerous surrounding regions of the cortex are also largely visual in function. The primary visual cortex is often called the **striate cortex** because a broad stripe or striation is visible in anatomical sections through this region; the stripe represents the layer of the cortex where the optic radiation fibers arrive. In-

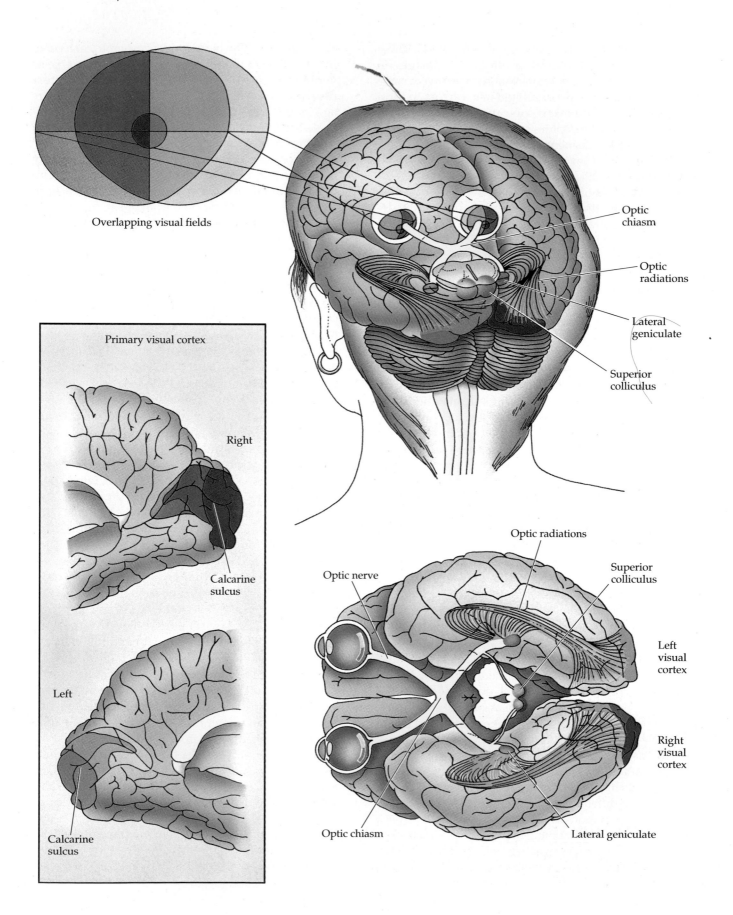

Overlapping visual fields

Optic chiasm

Optic radiations

Lateral geniculate

Superior colliculus

Primary visual cortex

Right

Calcarine sulcus

Left

Calcarine sulcus

Optic radiations

Superior colliculus

Optic nerve

Left visual cortex

Right visual cortex

Optic chiasm

Lateral geniculate

puts from the two eyes converge at the cortical level, making binocular effects possible. Visual cortical areas outside the striate cortex are sometimes called extrastriate cortex. As Figure 10.14*b* shows, the visual cortex in the right cerebral hemisphere receives its input from the left half of the visual field, and the visual cortex in the left hemisphere receives its input from the right half of the visual field. Because of the orderly mapping of the visual field (known as retinotopic mapping) at the various levels of the visual system, damage to parts of the visual system can be diagnosed from defects in perception of the visual field.

Figure 10.14*a* shows that some axons leave the optic tract to reach sites other than the LGN. Some retinal ganglion cells send their optic tract axons to the superior colliculus in the midbrain. In Chapter 8 we saw that cells in the deeper layers of the superior colliculus form maps of visual, somatosensory, and auditory space, as well as of the motor system—and that all these maps are aligned with each other. The superior colliculus helps coordinate rapid movements of the eyes toward a target. Other ganglion cells send relatively small bundles of optic tract axons to nuclei in the diencephalon that are involved in the control of daily cycles of behavior (circadian rhythms), which we will discuss in Chapter 14. Optic tract axons from still other ganglion cells go to the midbrain nuclei that regulate the size of the pupil and help coordinate the movements of the eyes. Some of the midbrain visual nuclei also project axons to the cerebellum where the activity maps visual space.

Investigators have found several cortical areas for each sensory modality, and most of these areas are laid out in an orderly topographic map of the receptor surface (Woolsey, 1981a, b, c). Examination of the cortex of the macaque (an Old World monkey) reveals more than 30 visual areas, each of which is a topographic representation of the retina. Evidence is accumulating that different cortical regions work in parallel to process different aspects of visual perception, such as form, color, location, and movement, as we will take up later in this chapter.

Investigators have used a variety of techniques to map the visual system: anatomical tracing of fibers, electrophysiological recording of activity evoked by specific kinds of visual stimulation, PET and other noninvasive measures of regional activity in the brain, and experimental and clinical lesions of the visual system. Integrating the findings of these techniques provides us with our current understanding of the structure and functions of the visual system.

Neurons at Different Levels of the Visual System Have Very Different Receptive Fields

Spots of light that are lighter or darker than surrounding areas are sufficient to activate cells in the retina or LGN, but many cells in the visual cortex are more demanding and respond only to more complicated stimuli. The nature of a cell's receptive field gives us good clues about its function(s) in achieving various aspects of perception. In this research, investigators ask to what extent we can understand certain phenomena of visual perception on the basis of properties of neurons at a given level in the nervous system. Moreover, we want to know to what extent other phenomena require combinations or circuits of cells instead. In the next sections we will see cases in which neurons at a given level in the visual system seem to account for particular perceptual phenomena and other cases in which solutions need to be sought at higher levels in the visual system.

Neurons in the Retina and LGN Have Concentric Receptive Fields

Two scientists discovered the main features of the receptive fields of vertebrate retinal ganglion cells independently within a few months of each other: Stephen Kuffler (1953), using the cat, and Horace Barlow (1953), using the frog. They recorded from single ganglion cells while they moved a small spot of light across the receptive field, keeping the animal's eye still. Results showed that the receptive fields of retinal ganglion cells are concentric, consisting of a roughly circular central area and a ring around it. Similar results were later obtained for retinal bipolar cells (see Figure 10.12), but whereas the responses of the bipolar cells are changes in polarization (depolarization or hyperpolarization), the responses of the ganglion cells are nerve impulses. Ganglion cells were studied before bipolar cells because they are larger and easier to record from. Like bipolar cells, ganglion cells have two basic types of retinal receptive fields: on-center/off-surround and off-center/on-

◀ **10.14 Visual Pathways in the Human Brain** The visual fields are represented on the retinas and project to the cerebral hemispheres. The right visual field projects to the left cerebral hemisphere, and the left visual field projects to the right cerebral hemisphere.

surround. The center and its surround are always antagonistic and tend to cancel each other's activity.

Stephen Kuffler
(1913–1980)

Horace Barlow

These effects explain why uniform illumination of the visual field is less effective in activating a ganglion cell than is a well-placed small spot or a line or edge passing through the center of the cell's receptive field.

Later work found that the receptive fields of ganglion cells in the cat are actually elongated (Hammond, 1974) and that different cells respond selectively to different orientations of stimulation (Thibos and Levick, 1985). In primates, however, the ganglion cells do not appear to show orientation specificity.

Although the visual mechanisms of cats have been studied extensively, cats have little or no color vision, so we will focus on research with primates, which possess good color vision as well as good form vision. Investigators who study primate visual systems take the organization of the LGN as their key. The anatomy of the primate LGN is different from that of the cat. Whereas the LGN of the cat has only four layers, the primate LGN has six layers, as shown in Figure 10.15. This figure also shows why the structure is called geniculate—the layers are bent like a knee ("geniculate" is derived from the Latin *genu*, "knee"). The four dorsal, or outer, layers of the primate LGN are called **parvocellular** (from the Latin *parvus*, "small") because their cells are relatively small. The two ventral, or inner, layers are called **magnocellular** because their cells are large. Most of the neurons in the magnocellular layers have relatively large receptive fields whose input can be traced back to the diffuse retinal bipolar cells that contact several neighboring photoreceptor cells. Many cells of the magnocellular layers do not show differential wavelength responses; that is, they are not involved in color discrimination. The neurons of the parvocellular layers have relatively small receptive fields whose input is derived from the midget bipolar cells; these neurons

discriminate wavelengths. The LGN cells of all six layers have concentric receptive fields. At the LGN, the importance of stimulation of the surround becomes relatively more important than at the retina, so it is harder to stimulate an LGN cell with uniform illumination of the visual field. At the cerebral cortex it is even more difficult to arouse a response by altering the overall illumination.

Discovery of the difference between the parvocellular and magnocellular neurons of the primate LGN led investigators to take a fresh look at primate ganglion cells; they found two main types (Leventhal,

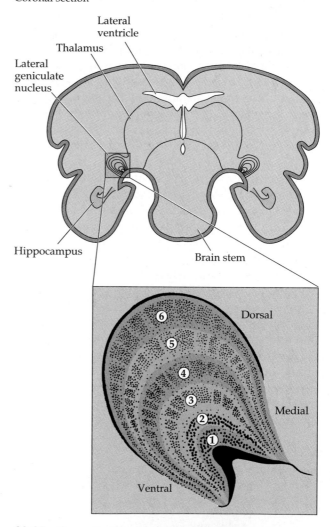

10.15   Cross Section of the Monkey LGN
In the four dorsal (parvocellular) layers, the cells are relatively small; in the two ventral (magnocellular) layers, the cells are relatively large. Cells with input from the opposite eye are in layers 1, 4, and 6 (pink); cells with input from the eye on the same side are in layers 2, 3, and 5 (blue).

1979; Perry, Oehler, and Cowey, 1984). The two types are sometimes called M and P ganglion cells because they project their axons, respectively, to the *Magno*cellular or *Parvo*cellular layers of the LGN. The M ganglion cells are relatively large cells with large dendritic fields that contact many bipolar cells; consequently they have large receptive fields. The M ganglion cells can detect stimuli with low contrast and are sensitive to motion; they respond transiently, and have large-diameter axons that conduct very rapidly. They make up about 10% of the primate retinal ganglion cells. About 80% of the primate retinal ganglion cells send their axons to the P layers of the LGN. These P ganglion cells are relatively small and have small dendritic and receptive fields. Several properties of the P ganglion cells distinguish them from the M ganglion cells: (1) The P cells require high contrast to be stimulated, and they are relatively insensitive to motion. (2) Most of them show differential responses to different wavelengths, so they provide a basis for color vision. (3) They have sustained or tonic responses. The remaining 10% of the primate ganglion cells that are neither M nor P consist of various types that will not concern us here.

Neurons in the Visual Cortex Have Varied and Complicated Receptive Fields

The next station, the primary visual cortex, provided a puzzle. Neurons from the LGN send their axons to cells in the primary visual cortex (called visual area 1, or **area V1**), but the spots of light that are effective stimuli for LGN cells are not very effective at the cortical level. After much unfruitful work, success in stimulating cortical visual cells was finally announced in 1959: David Hubel and Torsten Wiesel reported that visual cortical cells require more specific, elongated stimuli than those that activate LGN cells. Most cells in area V1 (see Figure 10.20) respond best to lines or bars in a particular position and at a particular orientation in the visual field (Figure 10.16*b*). Some cortical cells also require movement of the stimulus to make them respond actively. For some of those cells, any movement in

David Hubel

their field is sufficient, while others are even more demanding, requiring motion in a specific direction (Figure 10.16*c*). For this and re-

lated research, Hubel and Wiesel were awarded the Nobel Prize in Physiology or Medicine in 1981.

The ability of special stimuli to evoke vigorous responses in visual cortical cells was soon verified by other investigators, and it led to a great amount of productive research. Although the success of this research also led many to accept the theoretical model proposed by Hubel and Wiesel, challenges to this model have emerged. Let's examine a few more of Hubel and Wiesel's findings and look at their theoretical model.

Torsten Wiesel

Hubel and Wiesel categorized cortical cells into four classes according to the types of stimuli required to produce maximum responses. So-called **simple cortical cells** responded best to an edge or a bar of a particular width and with a particular orientation and location in the visual field. These cells were therefore sometimes called bar detectors or edge detectors. Like the simple cells, **complex cortical cells** had elongated receptive fields, but they also showed some latitude for location; that is, they would respond to a bar of a particular size and orientation anywhere within a particular area of the visual field. Cells called **hypercomplex 1** had inhibitory areas at the two ends; that is, the best response occurred if the bar was of limited length, and extending the length beyond this limit reduced the response. (Later work showed that even simple and complex cortical cells possess this property, at least to some extent.) Finally, **hypercomplex 2** cells responded best to two line segments meeting at a particular angle. Hubel and Wiesel mentioned this type only briefly, but it gave rise to a great amount of theorizing.

Hubel and Wiesel's theoretical model can be described as hierarchical; that is, more complex events are built up from inputs of simpler ones. For example, a simple cortical cell can be thought of as receiving input from a row of LGN cells. A complex cortical cell can be thought of as receiving its input from a row of simple cortical cells. Other theorists extrapolated from this model of Hubel and Wiesel, suggesting higher-order circuits of cells to detect any possible form. Thus it was suggested that by integrating enough successive levels of analysis, a unit could be constructed that would enable a person to recognize his or her grandmother, and there was frequent mention in the literature of such hypothetical

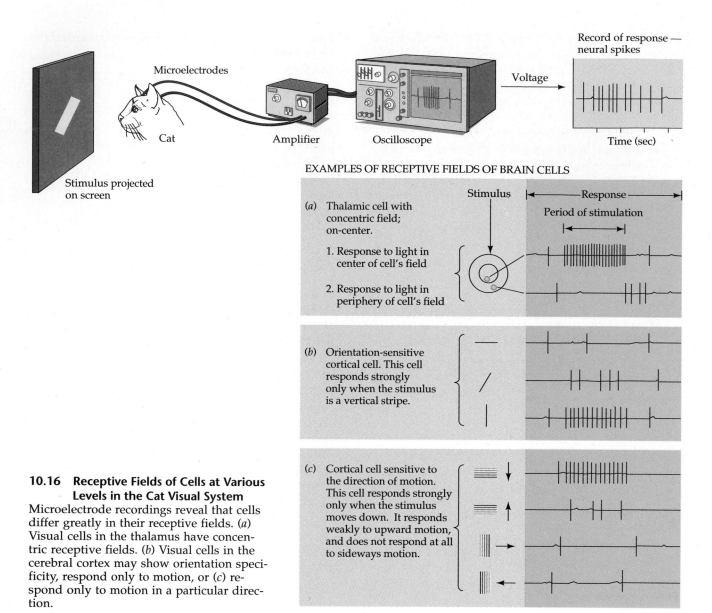

10.16   Receptive Fields of Cells at Various Levels in the Cat Visual System
Microelectrode recordings reveal that cells differ greatly in their receptive fields. (*a*) Visual cells in the thalamus have concentric receptive fields. (*b*) Visual cells in the cerebral cortex may show orientation specificity, respond only to motion, or (*c*) respond only to motion in a particular direction.

"grandmother cells." According to this view, any time such a cell was excited, up would pop a picture of one's grandmother. This hypothesis was given as a possible explanation for facial recognition.

Critics soon pointed out problems with the hierarchical model, some of a theoretical nature and others arising from empirical observations. For one thing, a "grandmother-recognizing" circuit would require vast numbers of cells, perhaps even more than the number available in the cerebral cortex. Each successive stage in the hierarchy is obviously built on the preceding one, but Hoffman and Stone (1971) found that the complex cells had slightly *faster* responses, al-

though the hierarchical theory requires the simple cells to respond earlier. Furthermore, complex cells were found to receive direct input from LGN cells, whereas the hierarchical theory would have them obtain input from simple cortical cells. At the same time that difficulties with this model were being shown (for example, by Stone, Dreher, and Leventhal, 1979), an alternative model was emerging.

Most Cells in the Primary Visual Cortex Are Tuned to Particular Spatial Frequencies

Concepts of pattern analysis in terms of lines and edges at various orientations have largely given way to what is known as the **spatial frequency filter model**. To discuss this model, we must become familiar with a way of regarding spatial vision that is quite different from our intuitive thinking (Westheimer, 1984; De Valois and De Valois, 1988). By the spatial frequency of a visual stimulus, we mean the number of light/dark (or color) cycles it shows per degree of visual space. For example, Figure 10.17*a* and *b* differ in the spacing of the bars; Figure 10.17*a* has twice as many bars in the same horizontal space and is therefore said to have double the spatial frequency of Figure 10.17*b*. The spatial frequency technique applies Fourier analysis (see Box 9.1) or linear

systems theory rather than analyzing visual patterns into bars and angles.

When we discussed the auditory stimulus in Box 9.1, we saw that any complex, repeating auditory stimulus can be produced by adding together simple sine waves. Conversely, using Fourier analysis, we can determine which sine waves would be needed to make any particular complex wave form. The same principle of Fourier analysis can be applied to visual patterns. If the dimension from dark to light is made to vary according to a sine wave function, we get visual patterns like the ones in Figure 10.17*c* and *d*. A series of dark and light stripes, like those in Figure

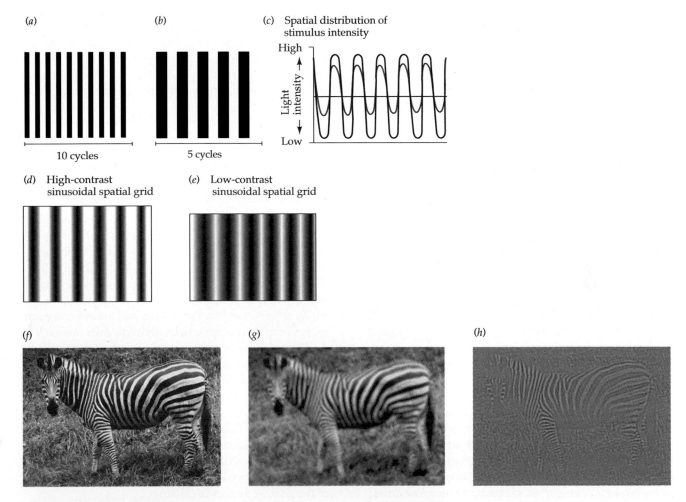

10.17 Spatial frequencies
(*a, b*) The spacing between dark and light stripes shows that part *a* has double the spatial frequency of part *b*. (*c*) Visual grids with sinusoidal modulation of intensity. (*d*) high-contrast sinusoidal spatial grid. (*e*) low-contrast sinusoidal spatial grid. (*f–h*) Zebras subjected to spatial filtering: (*f*) normal photograph; (*g*) high spatial frequencies filtered out; (*h*) low spatial frequencies filtered out.

10.17*a* and *b*, can be analyzed into the sum of a visual sine wave and its odd harmonics, that is, multiples of the basic frequency. A complex visual pattern or scene can also be analyzed by the Fourier technique; in this case frequency components at different angles of orientation are also used. A given spatial frequency can exist at any level of contrast; Figures 10.17*d* and *e* show examples of high and low contrast, respectively. To reproduce or perceive the complex pattern or scene accurately, the system has to handle all the spatial frequencies that are present in it. If the high frequencies are filtered out, the small details and sharp contrasts are lost; if the low frequencies are filtered out, the large uniform areas and gradual transitions are lost. Figure 10.17*f–h* show how filtering spatial frequencies affects a photograph. The photograph is still recognizable after the high visual frequencies are filtered out (Figure 10.17*g*) or when the low frequencies are filtered out (Figure 10.17*h*). (Similarly, speech is still recognizable, although it sounds distorted, after either the high audio frequencies or the low frequencies are filtered out.)

Campbell and Robson (1968) suggested that the visual system includes many channels that are tuned to different spatial frequencies, just as the auditory system has channels for different acoustic frequencies. The term "channel" is used here to mean a mechanism that accepts or deals with only a particular band or class of information. A particular radio or television station transmits its information through an assigned channel or band of wavelengths; to receive this information, you must tune your receiving device to the particular channel. The suggestion that the nervous system has different spatial frequency channels was soon supported by results of experiments on selective adaptation to visual frequency (Pantle and Sekuler, 1968; Blakemore and Campbell, 1969). In these experiments a person spent a minute or more inspecting a visual grating with a given spacing (or spatial frequency), such as those in Figure 10.17*a* and *b*. Looking at the grating made the cells that are tuned to that frequency adapt (become less sensitive). Then the person's sensitivity to gratings of different spacings was determined. The results showed that sensitivity to the subsequent gratings was depressed briefly at whatever frequency the person had adapted to. According to Russell De Valois and Karen De Valois (1980:320), the suggestion of multiple spatial frequency channels

had revolutionary impact because it led to entirely different conceptions of the way in which the visual system might function in dealing with spatial stimuli. It suggests that rather than specifically detecting

such seminaturalistic features as bars and edges, the system is breaking down complex stimuli into their individual spatial frequency components in a kind of crude Fourier analysis. . . . Irrespective of the eventual judgment of the correctness of this particular model, Campbell and Robson's conjecture will remain pivotal in having opened the eyes of vision researchers to the many ways in which the visual system could analyze the world using elements not akin to our verbal descriptions of scenes.

The responses of cortical cells to spatial frequency stimuli were found to be tuned more accurately to the dimensions of spatial frequency grids than to the widths of bars (De Valois, Albrecht, and Thorell, 1977; Hochstein and Shapley, 1976; Maffei and Fiorentini, 1973). The concept of multiple spatial frequency channels does not require a thorough Fourier analysis of the optical image (Westheimer, 1984). In fact, the receptive field of a cortical cell typically shows only an excitatory axis and one clear band of inhibition by the surround on each side, but the spacing of these components shows the frequency tuning. The spatial frequency approach has proved useful in analyzing many aspects of human pattern vision (De Valois, De Valois, and Yund, 1979).

Neurons in Visual Cortex beyond Area V1 Have Complex Receptive Fields and Contribute to Identification of Forms

Area V1 is only a small part of the cortex devoted to vision. Area V1 sends axons to other visual cortical areas, including areas that appear to be involved in the perception of form: area V2, area V4, and the inferior temporal area (Figure 10.18). Some of these extrastriate areas also receive direct input from the LGN. Many cells of these extrastriate visual areas have even more complex receptive fields than do cells in area V1. As Figure 10.18*a–c* reflect, on the basis of anatomical, physiological, and behavioral investigations with macaque monkeys, we know that more than 30 distinct cortical areas are directly involved in visual function (Van Essen, Anderson, and Felleman, 1992). The visual areas of the human brain (Figure 10.18*d* and *e*) have been less thoroughly mapped than those in the monkey brain, but the general layout appears to be similar in the two species. We will discuss only a few of the main visual cortical areas.

Area V2 is adjacent to V1, and many of its cells show properties similar to those in V1. Many V2 cells can respond to illusory contours, which may help explain how we perceive contours such as the boundaries of the upright triangle in Figure 10.19 (Peterhans and von der Heydt, 1989). Clearly such cells respond

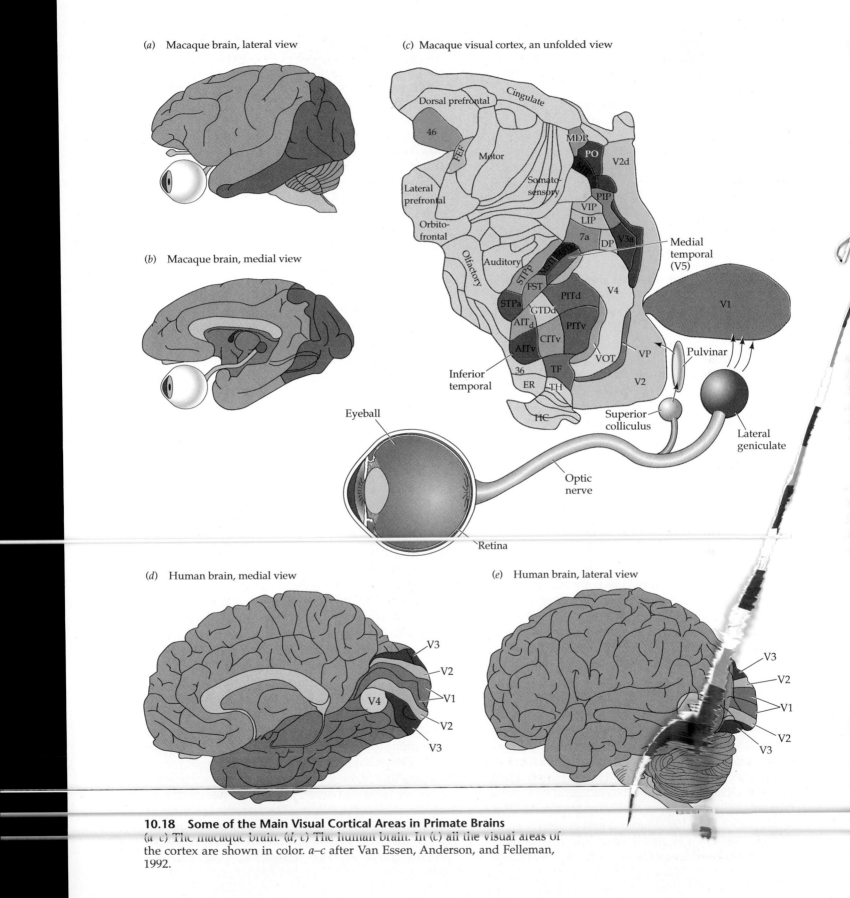

(a) Macaque brain, lateral view

(b) Macaque brain, medial view

(c) Macaque visual cortex, an unfolded view

Dorsal prefrontal
Cingulate
46
MDP
FEF
Motor
PO
V2d
Lateral prefrontal
Somato-sensory
PIP
VIP
Orbito-frontal
LIP
7a
DP
V3a
Medial temporal (V5)
Olfactory
Auditory
STPp
V4
V1
FST
PITd
STPa
GTDd
AIT d
PITv
AITv
CITv
VOT
VP
Pulvinar
36
TF
ER
TH
V2
Superior colliculus
Lateral geniculate
Inferior temporal
HC
Eyeball
Optic nerve
Retina

(d) Human brain, medial view

V3
V2
V4
V1
V2
V3

(e) Human brain, lateral view

V3
V2
V1
V2
V3

10.18 Some of the Main Visual Cortical Areas in Primate Brains
(a–c) The macaque brain. (d, e) The human brain. In (c) all the visual areas of
the cortex are shown in color. *a–c* after Van Essen, Anderson, and Felleman,
1992.

**10.19   A Geometric Figure with "Illusory"
or "Subjective" Contours**
Cells have been found in visual cortical areas that respond to illusory contours such as those forming the white upright triangle in this figure. The perception of such contours thus has a neurophysiological basis.

to complex relations among the parts of its receptive field. Recent work has shown that some V1 cells can also respond to illusory contours (Grosof, Shapley, and Hawken, 1993), but this feature is more common in area V2. The presence of such cells in V1 shows that the perception of illusory contours begins at a lower level in the visual system than investigators expected.

Area V4 receives axons from V2 and has cells that give their strongest responses to the sinusoidal frequency gratings that we discussed in the previous section. Many V4 cells respond even better, however, to concentric and radial stimuli, such as those in Figure 10.20*a* (Gallant, Braun, and Van Essen, 1993). Investigators suggest that these V4 cells show an intermediate stage between the spatial frequency processing in V1 and V2 cells and the recognition of pattern and form in cells of the inferior temporal area. Area V4 also has many cells that respond preferentially (most strongly) to wavelength differences, as we will see later in this chapter when we discuss color vision. Area V5 appears to be specialized for the perception of motion, as we will also discuss later in this chapter.

Finally, the inferior temporal (IT) visual cortex has many cells that respond best to particular complex forms, including forms the subject has learned to recognize. We saw one example in Figure 1.3: a cell that responded best to a monkey face in lateral view. Area IT is subdivided into areas that some anatomists (Von Bonin and Bailey, 1947) have called posterior IT, or TEO, and anterior IT, or TE. Area V4 projects many fibers to TEO and fewer fibers to TE. TE sends its ax-

ons to structures outside the visual areas and appears to be involved in visual contributions to emotion and control of action.

Because many cells in IT have highly specific receptive fields, it is hard to find the exact stimuli that can activate a particular cell. Experimenters start by presenting many three-dimensional animal and plant objects (Desimone et al., 1984; Tanaka, 1993). When a stimulus elicits a strong response, the experimenters then simplify the image by sequentially removing parts of the features to determine the necessary and sufficient features for maximal activation of the cell. Most cells in TE do not require a natural object such as a face to activate them; instead they require moderately complex shapes, sometimes combined with color or texture, such as those in Figure 10.20*b*. Tanaka (1993) reports that TE has a columnar organization like that of V1 (as we will see shortly) , with adjacent cells often having similar receptive fields. He proposes that simultaneous activation of tens of such cells may be sufficient to specify a natural object. The complex receptive fields in TE probably develop through experience and learning. When a monkey was trained for a year to discriminate a set of 28 moderately complex shapes, 39% of the cells in TE gave a large response to some of these shapes, whereas in control monkeys only 9% of the cells in TE gave strong responses to these forms (Kobatake and Tanaka, 1994).

Recognition of Familiar Objects Requires More Than Accurate Perception of Forms

A common result of stroke is the inability to identify familiar objects. This condition is called **visual agnosia** (from the Greek roots *a-*, "without," and *gnosis*, "knowledge"). In some cases the disability is restricted to the recognition of faces. One extraordinary account describes the precise onset of this disability in a French radio announcer (Lhermitte et al., 1972). He had a stroke in the left hemisphere that affected his speech, and he was undertaking speech therapy. One day during a session, he felt uncomfortable and closed his eyes for a few minutes. Upon opening his eyes and looking across the table at the therapist, he exclaimed, "But mademoiselle, I no longer recognize you!" From that time on, he could no longer recognize any face, even those of his family members. He could see faces and describe them accurately, but he could not recognize them. The specific inability to recognize familiar faces is called **prosopagnosia** (from the Greek *prosop*, "face"). Most cases of prosopagnosia involve damage to both cerebral

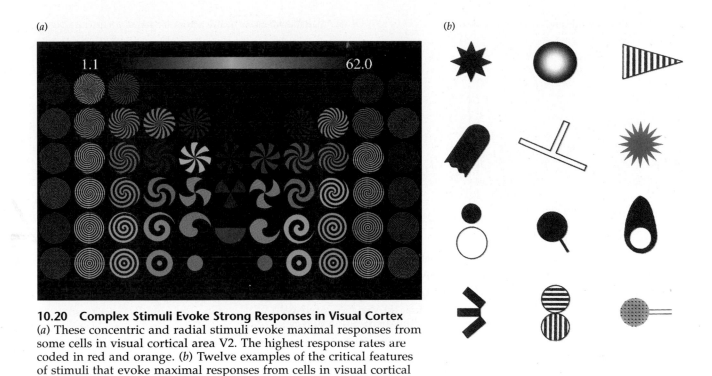

10.20 Complex Stimuli Evoke Strong Responses in Visual Cortex
(*a*) These concentric and radial stimuli evoke maximal responses from some cells in visual cortical area V2. The highest response rates are coded in red and orange. (*b*) Twelve examples of the critical features of stimuli that evoke maximal responses from cells in visual cortical area TE (the anterior inferior temporal area). *a* from Gallant, Braun, and Van Essen, 1993; *b* from Tanaka, 1993.

hemispheres (Damasio et al., 1990). The radio announcer probably had a second small stroke while his eyes were closed, this time in his right hemisphere, causing him to lose his ability to identify faces. The term prosopagnosia is often used more generally to refer to difficulty in recognizing some specific category of forms other than faces. We will consider prosopagnosia further in Chapter 19.

The existence of specific deficits after brain damage suggests that particular abilities or skills depend on particular regions of the brain that are not required for other kinds of ability or performance. In subsequent chapters we will consider other dissociations between abilities that depend on different brain regions.

Why Acuity Is Best in Foveal Vision

We noted early in this chapter that acuity is especially fine in the center of the visual field and falls off rapidly toward the periphery. Reasons for this difference have been found in the retina and in the successive levels of the visual system, each of which is a detailed map of the visible world. Although the neural maps preserve the *order* of the visual field, each emphasizes some regions at the expense of others;

that is, each map is topographic. One reason that the maps are topographic is that the center of the retinal surface has a denser concentration of receptors than does the periphery. The central region, called the **fovea** (which in Latin means "small depression" or "pit"), has a dense concentration of cones and provides for maximal acuity (Figure 10.21). The data on cone concentration in Figure 10.1 come from a classic study by Østerberg (1935), but they are based on only one retina. More recently Curcio and coworkers (1987) measured four other retinas. Østerberg's data fall in the same range, but the four retinas differed by as much as three to one in the number of cones per square millimeter in the fovea. Very likely this variation is related to individual differences in visual acuity. Species differences in visual acuity are also related to the density of cones in the fovea. For example, hawks, whose acuity is much greater than ours, have much narrower and more densely packed cones in the fovea than we do.

The rods show a different distribution; they are absent in the fovea but are more numerous than cones in the periphery of the retina. They are the most concentrated in a ring about 20° away from the center of the retina. That is why, if you want to see a dim star, you do best to search for it about 20° away from your

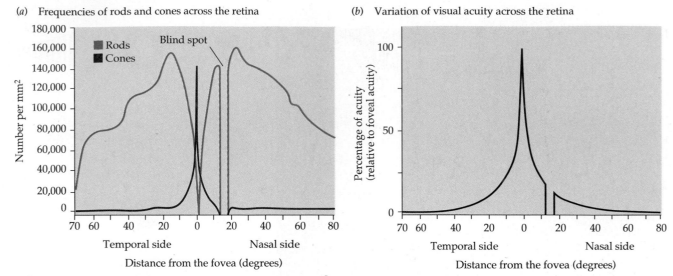

(a) Frequencies of rods and cones across the retina

(b) Variation of visual acuity across the retina

10.21 Frequencies of Retinal Receptors and Visual Acuity
(a) Distribution of rods and cones across the retina. (b) Variation of visual acuity across the retina, which closely resembles the distribution of cones.

central gaze. As mentioned earlier, there are no rods or cones in the optic disc where the axons of the ganglion cells leave the retina and where blood vessels enter the retina. In the brain, a major part of the projection of visual space onto the topographic brain maps is devoted to the foveal region, as Figure 10.22*a* and *b* (Tootell et al., 1982). Although area V1 of the macaque is located on the lateral surface of the occipital area, the human primary visual cortex is located mainly on the medial surface of the cortex. A map of the visual field onto the human visual cortex is shown in Figure 10.22*d* and *e*. The fact that, as in the monkey, about half of the human primary visual area is devoted to the fovea and the retinal region just around the fovea does not mean that our spatial perception is distorted. Rather this representation makes possible the great acuity of spatial discrimination in the central part of the visual field. Although our acuity falls off about as rapidly in the horizontal as in the vertical direction, species that live in open, flat environments (such as the cheetah and the rabbit) have fields of acute vision that extend much farther horizontally than vertically.

Studying the regions of blindness caused by brain injuries reveals the extreme orderliness of the mapping of the visual field. If we know the site of injury in the visual pathway we can predict the location of such a perceptual gap, or **scotoma**, in the visual field. Although the word "scotoma" comes from the Latin word for "darkness," a scotoma is not perceived as a dark patch in the visual field; rather it is a spot where

nothing can be perceived, and usually rigorous testing is required to demonstrate the existence of a scotoma. Although a person cannot perceive, in the usual sense, within a scotoma, in some cases some visual discrimination in this region is still possible.

Area V1 Is Organized in Columns

Area V1 is organized into columns with a richness undreamed of only a few years ago. More complicated than the organization of the somatosensory cortex (see Chapter 8), the primary visual cortex has separate representations for at least four dimensions of the visual stimulus: (1) location in the visual field, with larger, finer mapping of the central region of the visual field than of the periphery; (2) orientation; (3) color; and (4) ocular dominance (**ocular dominance columns** [ODCs] are alternating bands or stripes of cells that represent each of the two eyes separately).

ODCs were first discovered by electrophysiological recording of the receptive fields of individual neurons when one eye or the other was stimulated by visual targets. This recording revealed the existence of elongated bands of cells that responded preferentially (that is, most strongly) to stimulation of one eye. Each band was 350 to 500 μm (10^{-9} m) wide. A given point in the visual field elicited responses in adjacent ODCs. The ocular dominance is especially clear in the broad layer 4 of area V1 where each cell responds to only one eye; above and below layer 4, most cells re-

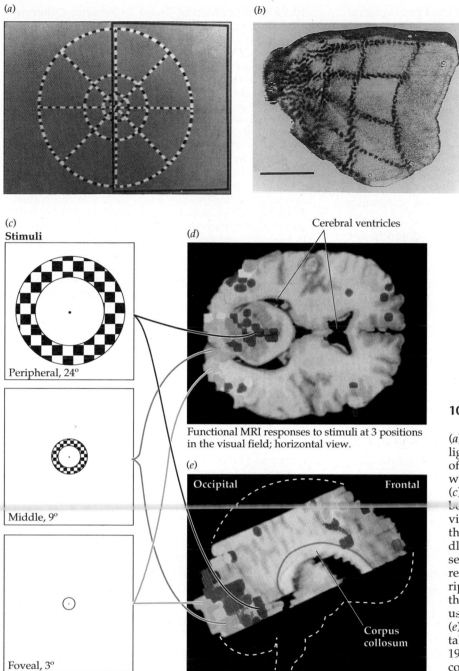

(a)

(b)

(c)
Stimuli

Peripheral, 24°

Middle, 9°

Foveal, 3°

(d)

Cerebral ventricles

Functional MRI responses to stimuli at 3 positions in the visual field; horizontal view.

(e)

Occipital   Frontal

Corpus collosum

Functional MRI responses; mid–sagittal view.

10.22 Maps of the Visual Field onto Area V1
(*a*) When a pattern of flickering lights was shown in the visual field of a macaque, a map of striate cortex was revealed by 2-DG uptake (*b*). (*c*) Patterns of flickering checkerboard rings presented to human viewers at various distances around the fixation point (peripheral, middle, and foveal). (*d*) Horizontal fMRI section of the human brain, showing regions activated by stimuli in peripheral, middle, or foveal parts of the visual field, with false colors used to separate the responses. (*e*) Similar mapping on a mid-sagittal section. *a, b* from Tootell et al., 1988; *c–e* from E. DeYoe, personal communication.

spond to stimulation of both eyes; so ocular dominance is less strongly expressed than in layer 4.

Anatomical tracing techniques that proliferated beginning in the 1970s furnished additional information about ODCs. For example, when a small dose of radioactive amino acid is injected into one eye, some of it is transported along neurons, crossing synapses and reaching the visual cortex. Autoradiographic examination of the cortex then reveals parallel bands of radioactivity in layer 4 that correspond to the ODCs of the injected eye. Activation of neurons *outside* layer 4 was demonstrated by use of the 2-deoxyglucose autoradiographic technique that we described in Box 2.1. In these experiments, a monkey had one eye covered and the other eye open while radioactive 2-deoxyglucose was administered. Subsequent autoradiography of the cortical tissue showed not only bands about 350 μm wide in layer 4 but also dots of radioactivity about 150 μm wide in the other layers, showing responses to stimulation of the one eye. These dots ran along the centers of the ocular dominance columns. The presence of these dots shows that some of the neurons in other layers of the columns are also mainly monocular.

Recently developed techniques of optical imaging of cortical activity (Bonhoeffer and Grinvald, 1991; Ts'o et al., 1990) allow us to see the ocular dominance columns in the primary visual cortex of an awake monkey when visual patterns are presented to one eye (Figure 10.23). The imaging is based on small changes in the light reflected from the cortex during activity (Figure 10.23*a*). These changes are of two types: (1) changes in blood volume, probably in the capillaries of the activated area; and (2) changes in cortical tissue, such as movements of ions and water or the expansion and contraction of extracellular spaces. Experimenters can combine optical imaging with electrophysiological recording to obtain visual guidance for placing microelectrodes in particular parts of ODCs. Figure 10.23*b* shows the ODCs activated when one eye was stimulated. The investigators suggest that this recording technique may prove useful as a mapping tool in human neurosurgery.

Within the ocular dominance columns are narrower **orientation columns** 30 to 100 μm in diameter. Microelectrode recording has shown that all the cells within each orientation column share the same preference for stimuli at a given orientation within the visual field. As the recording electrode is moved from one column to the next, the preferred axis of orientation shifts by about 10°. That is, in one column all the cells are "tuned" to upright stimuli (at an orientation of 0°); in an adjacent column, all cells respond best to stimuli at 10° from the vertical; in the next column, at 20°; and so forth. In Figure 10.23*d* and *e* we see the indications of activity at the surface of the cortex produced by presenting stimuli of four different orientations (see Figure 10.23*c*). Inspection reveals regularly spaced "pinwheels" in which responses to the different stimulus orientations pivot around a center.

Also within the ocular dominance columns of primate visual areas are vertical "blobs" or "pegs." Early experiments suggested that the blobs were related to color vision (Hendrickson, 1985; Livingstone and

10.23   Visualization of Ocular Dominance Columns and Orientation Columns by Optical Imaging ▶
(*a*) In a method for visualization of ocular dominance columns (ODCs), bands of neurons that represent the left or right eye in area V1, a camera records light reflected from the cortex when the monkey views a twinkling checkerboard pattern with one eye. Small differences in the reflected light are amplified and intensity is coded with color (red for strong intensity, green for weak intensity). (*b*) After the recording is processed, ODCs for the active eye are seen as green stripes. (*c*) In a method for visualization of orientation columns, stimuli at different orientations (vertical, horizontal, diagonal) are presented to find cortical areas that respond most strongly to a particular orientation. These stimuli are usually black or white, but are color coded here to correspond to (*d*), color-coded responses to four different orientations combined into a single pattern. Although the pattern initially appears disorderly, closer inspection reveals several regions where all four orientations converge in a "pinwheel" pattern; a typical pinwheel is shown in the enlarged view of one section of the pattern. Note that foci of pinwheels occur at regular intervals, that each orientation is represented only once within each pinwheel, and that the sequence of orientations is consistent across pinwheels. After Ts'o et al., 1990; Bonhoeffer and Grinvald, 1991.

Hubel, 1984), but later work has cast doubt on this hypothesis, as we will see shortly. These pegs extend above and below layer 4 but are not seen in layer 4 itself. Figure 10.24 is a diagrammatic representation of the organization of the primate visual cortex, including the large ocular dominance columns, the orientation columns, and the pegs. (Compare with Figure 8.18, which shows the similar columnar organization of the somatosensory cortex.) The orientation columns in this diagram are arranged radially, like the "pinwheels" in Figure 10.23. Some investigators suggest that the orientation columns are laid out in a rectangular arrangement, like city blocks; this question is not yet settled.

Color Vision Depends on Special Channels from the Retinal Cones through Cortical Area V4

For most of us, different hues are a striking aspect of vision. The color solid in Figure 10.5 shows relations of hue to brightness and saturation. The system for color perception appears to have at least three stages (De Valois and De Valois, 1993). The first stage involves the cones, the retinal receptor cells that are

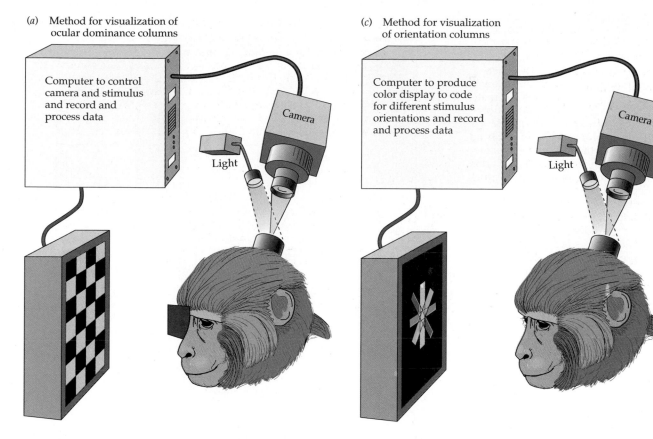

(*a*) Method for visualization of ocular dominance columns

Computer to control camera and stimulus and record and process data

Camera

Light

(*c*) Method for visualization of orientation columns

Computer to produce color display to code for different stimulus orientations and record and process data

Camera

Light

(*b*) Cortical regions driven by left eye reflect light differently, here coded in red

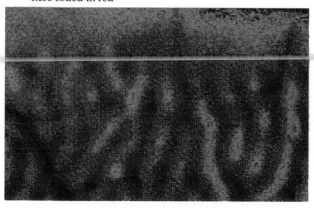

(*d*) Cortical regions driven by stimuli in four different orientations are each coded in a different color

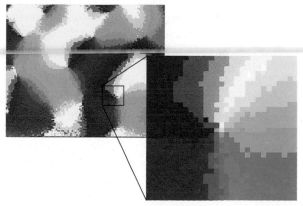

specialized to respond to certain wavelengths of light. The second stage is the processing of this information by neurons in the local circuits of the retina, leading to retinal ganglion cells that are excited by light of some wavelengths and inhibited by light of other wavelengths. The ganglion cells send the wavelength information via their axons to both the magnocellular and parvocellular layers of the LGN; from there it goes to area V1, from which it is relayed

to other visual cortical areas. The third stage of color perception takes place in the cortex.

Color Perception Requires Receptor Cells That Differ in Their Sensitivities for Different Wavelengths

At the start of the nineteenth century, the English scientist Thomas Young hypothesized that three separate kinds of receptors in the retina provide the basis

10.24 Organization of Primate Striate Cortex

Ocular dominance columns (ODCs) represent the left and right eyes; parts of two ODCs are shown here. Pegs extend vertically through layers 1 to 3 and 5 to 6 of the ODCs. Small columns represent the preferred orientations of groups of cells; these orientation columns radiate out from the centers of the pegs. The orientation is color coded here, as in Figure 10.23. In order to avoid complicating the figure further, this diagram does not represent spatial frequency (higher spatial frequencies are represented at the edges of the blocks and lower frequencies in the centers) nor does it represent the spectrally opponent cells which occur irregularly in the columns.

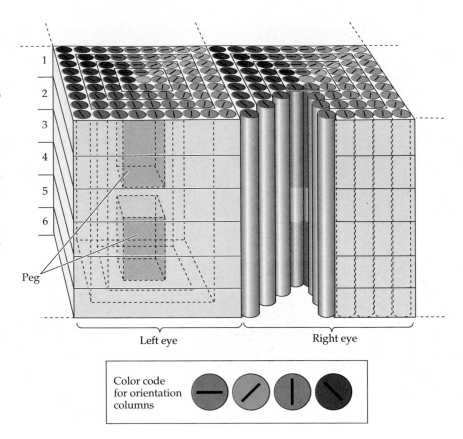

Left eye   Right eye

Color code for orientation columns

for color vision. This **trichromatic hypothesis** (from the Greek *tri-*, "three," and *chroma*, "color") was endorsed in 1852 by the great physiologist-physicist Hermann von Helmholtz and became the dominant position. Helmholtz predicted that blue-sensitive, green-sensitive, and red-sensitive cones would be found, that each would be sharply tuned to its part of the spectrum, and that each type would have a separate path to the brain. The color of an object would be recognized, then, on the basis of which color receptor was activated. This system would be like the mechanisms for discriminating touch, cold, and warmth, on the basis of which skin receptors and labeled neural lines are activated (see Chapter 8).

The physiologist Ewald Hering proposed a different explanation. He argued on the basis of visual experience that there are three opposed pairs of colors—blue and yellow, green and red, and black and white—and that three physiological processes with opposed positive and negative values must therefore be the basis of color vision. As we will see, both this **opponent-process hypothesis** and the trichromatic hypothesis are encompassed in current color-vision theory, but neither of the old hypotheses is sufficient by itself.

Are there three classes of cones with different color properties? Recent measurements of photopigments in cones have borne out the trichromatic hypothesis in part. Each cone of the human retina has one of three classes of pigments. These pigments do not, however, have the narrow spectral distributions that Helmholtz predicted. The color system that Helmholtz postulated would have given rather poor color vision and poor visual acuity. Color vision would be poor because only a few different hues could be discriminated; within the long-wavelength region of the spectrum there would be only red, and not all the range of hues that we see. Acuity would be poor because the grain of the retinal mosaic would be coarse; a red stimulus could affect only one-third of the receptors. (Actually, acuity is as good in red light as in white light.)

The human visual system does not have receptors that are sensitive to only a narrow part of the visible spectrum. Two of the three retinal cone pigments give some response to light of almost any wavelength. The pigments have different *peaks* of sensitivity, but the peaks are not as far apart as Helmholtz predicted. As Figure 10.25 shows, the peaks occur at about 420 nanometers (in the part of the spectrum where we usually see blue under photopic conditions), at about 530 nm (where most of us see green), and at about 560 nm (where most of us see yellow-green). Note that, despite Helmholtz's prediction, none of the curves peaks in the long-wavelength part of the spectrum where most of us see red (around 700 nm). Under ordinary conditions almost any visual object stimulates at least two kinds of cones, thus ensuring high visual acuity and good perception of form. The spectral sensitivities of the three cone types differ from each other, and the nervous system detects and processes these differences to extract the color information. Thus, certain ganglion cells and certain cells at higher stations in the visual system are color-specific, even though the receptor cells are not. Similarly, visual receptors are not form-specific, but form is detected later in the visual centers by comparing the outputs of different receptors. Since the cones are not color detectors, the most appropriate brief names for them can be taken from their peak areas of wavelength sensitivity: short (S) for the receptor with peak sensitivity at about 420 nm, middle (M) at 530 nm, and long (L) at 560 nm. There are roughly equal numbers of M and L receptors, but far fewer S receptors; this difference explains why acuity is much lower with short-wavelength illumination than in the other parts of the visible spectrum.

The genes for wavelength-sensitive pigments in the retina have been located on human chromo-somes, and the amino acid sequences for the cone pigments have been determined (Nathans, 1987). The similarities in structure of the three genes suggests that they are all derived from a common ancestral gene. In particular, the genes for the middle and long wavelength pigments occupy adjacent positions on the X chromosome and are much more similar to each other than either is to the gene for the short wavelength pigment on chromosome 6. The fact that humans and Old World monkeys have both M and L pigments whereas most New World monkeys have only a single longer wave pigment suggests that differentiation of the M and L pigments was rather recent, in evolutionary terms. Furthermore, the genes for the M and L pigments are variable among individuals, and particular variants in these pigment genes correspond to variants in color vision, so-called colorblindness. Thus, detailed examination of a person's photopigment genes can now show whether the person has normal color vision or has one of the recognized deficiencies of color discrimination. In animal experiments, antisera that have been developed for the S, M, and L cones can be dyed distinctively, and this makes it relatively easy to locate the different kinds of cones and to study their distribution over the retina (Wikler and Rakic, 1990).

The fact that the genes for the M and L pigments are on the X chromosome explains why defects of color vision are much more frequent in human males than in human females. Because males have only one X chromosome, a mutation in the genes for the M or L pigments can impair color vision. But if a female has a defective photopigment gene in one of her two X chromosomes, a normal copy of the gene on the other X chromosome can compensate. Only very rarely do both of a female's X chromosomes have defective genes for color receptors.

Some Retinal Ganglion Cells and Parvocellular LGN Cells Show Spectral Opponency

Recordings made from retinal ganglion cells in Old World monkeys, which can discriminate colors as humans with normal color vision do, reveal the second stage of processing. Most ganglion cells and cells in the parvocellular layers of the LGN fire in response to some wavelengths and are inhibited by other wavelengths. LGN cells show the same response characteristics that retinal ganglion cells show. Leading this research are Russell and Karen De Valois, whose results provide much of the information in this discussion.

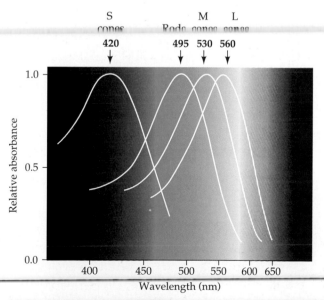

10.25 Spectral Sensitivities of Human Photopigments
Note that each pigment responds to a wide range of wavelengths.

Figure 10.26*a* shows the response of a parvocellular LGN cell as a spot of light centered on the cell's receptive field is changed from one wavelength to another. Firing is inhibited by wavelengths from about 420 to 600 nm, then stimulated from about 600 nm on. A cell exhibiting this response pattern is called a plus L/minus M cell (+L/−M). Since two regions of the spectrum have opposite effects on the cell's rate of firing, this is an example of what is called a **spectrally opponent cell**. Figure 10.26 shows examples of responses of the four main kinds of spectrally opponent cells.

Karen De Valois

Russell De Valois

Each spectrally opponent ganglion cell presumably receives input from two different kinds of cones through bipolar cells. The connections from one type of cone are excitatory, and those from the other type are inhibitory (Figure 10.27). The spectrally opponent ganglion cells thus record the difference in stimulation of different populations of cones. For example, a +M/−L cell responds to the difference in excitation of M minus L cones. (Recall from Chapter 6 that a neuron can process information by subtracting one input from another; spectral opponency is an example of such information processing.) Although the peaks of the sensitivity curves of the M and L cones are not very different, the M-minus-L *difference* curve shows a clear peak around 500 nm (in the green or blue-green part of the spectrum). The L minus M difference function shows a peak around 650 nm (in the reddish-orange part of the spectrum; see Figure 10.25). Thus, +M/−L and +L/−M cells yield distinctly different neural response curves. The spectrally opponent neurons are the second stage in the system for color perception, but they still cannot be called color cells for the fol-

10.26 The Four Main Types of Spectrally Opponent Cells in the Monkey LGN
Each type is excited by one band of wavelengths and inhibited by another.

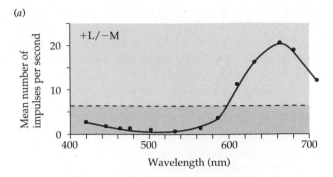

(a)

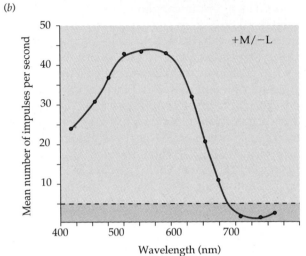

(b)

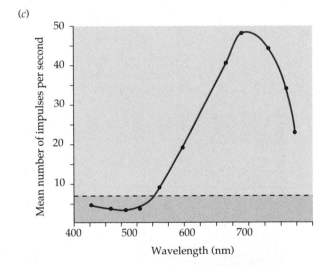

(c)

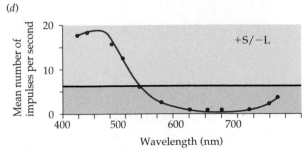

(d)

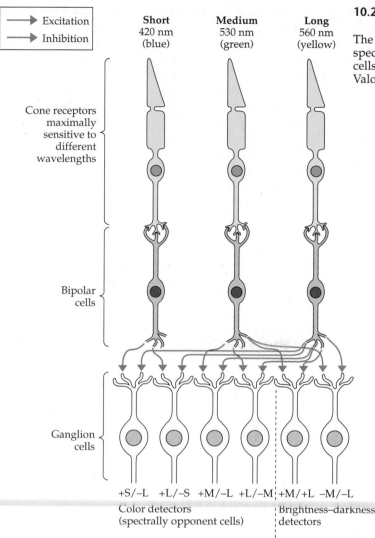

Excitation
Inhibition

Short
420 nm
(blue)

Medium
530 nm
(green)

Long
560 nm
(yellow)

Cone receptors
maximally
sensitive to
different
wavelengths

Bipolar
cells

Ganglion
cells

+S/–L +L/–S +M/–L +L/–M +M/+L –M/–L

Color detectors
(spectrally opponent cells)

Brightness–darkness
detectors

10.27 A Model of the Wavelength Discrimination Systems in the Primate Retina
The connections from the cones yield four kinds of spectrally opponent ganglion cells and also ganglion cells that detect brightness or darkness. After De Valois and De Valois, 1975.

lowing reasons: (1) they send their outputs into many higher circuits—for detection of form, depth, and movement as well as hue; and (2) their peak wavelength sensitivities do not correspond precisely to the wavelengths that observers choose as representing the principal hues.

In addition to the four kinds of spectrally opponent ganglion cells, Figure 10.27 also diagrams the presumed inputs of ganglion cells that detect brightness and darkness. The brightness detectors receive stimulation from both M and L cones (+M/+L), whereas the darkness detectors are inhibited by both the M and L cones (–M/–L). The S cones contribute little to perception of brightness or darkness.

In the monkey LGN, 70 to 80% of the cells are spectrally opponent, whereas in the cat very few spectrally opponent cells are found—only about 1%.

This difference explains the ease with which monkeys discriminate wavelengths and the difficulty of training cats to discriminate even large differences in wavelength.

Some Visual Cortical Cells and Regions Appear to be Specialized for Color Perception

In the cortex, spectral information appears to be used for various kinds of information processing. Forms are segregated from their backgrounds by differences in color or intensity (or both). The most important role that color plays in our perception is in denoting which parts of a complex image belong to one object and which belong to another. Some animals use displays of brightly colored body parts to call attention to themselves, but color can also be used as camouflage. Some spectrally opponent cortical cells contribute to perception of color, providing the third stage of the color vision system. De Valois and De Valois (1993) have suggested how adding and subtracting the outputs of spectrally opponent ganglion cells could yield cortical cells that are perceptually opponent: red versus green and blue versus yellow. The spectral responses of these cells correspond to the wavelengths of the principal hues specified by human observers, and their characteristics also help to explain other color phenomena.

Many of the cells in the peg-shaped regions of area V1 are double-opponent cells; that is, both the center and the surround show spectral opponency. For example, the center of the receptive field may respond with excitation to long wavelengths and with inhibition to middle wavelengths, while the surround responds with excitation to middle wavelengths and with inhibition to long wavelengths. The receptive fields of some of the peg cells are round, with no axis of orientation, but others are elongated and show orientation preference. The cortical pegs are situated along the centers of ocular dominance columns (see Figure 10.24), and they are more plentiful and larger in regions of cortex that map the center of the visual field. Chemical techniques suggest that neurons in the pegs are prepared for higher rates of activity than are the cells outside the pegs (interpeg cells). For example, the pegs can be revealed anatomically by using a stain for an enzyme (cytochrome oxidase) that is characteristic of mitochondria and whose activity varies with the level of the cellular activity of neurons. The fact that the pegs stain more darkly for this mitochondria-related enzyme than does surrounding tissue indicates that the pegs are rich in energy-supplying mitochondria. Enzymes of both the ACh and GABA transmitter systems also are found preferentially in the pegs.

Although recordings in macaque monkeys indicate that many neurons in the pegs are associated with color perception, this is not a strict association. In fact, recent quantitative studies show that neurons in the pegs cannot be readily distinguished from neurons outside the pegs on the basis of either chromatic tuning (Lennie, Krauskopf, and Sclar, 1990) or orientation tuning (Leventhal et al., 1995). Other evidence also challenges the attempt to associate cortical pegs with color vision: (1) even nocturnal primates, whose retinas are poor in cones, and cats, which have little or no color vision have pegs; and (2) cone-rich rodents, such as ground squirrels, do *not* have pegs.

Visual cortical region V4 is particularly rich in color-sensitive cells. Evidence that this area is normal-

ly involved in the perception of color in humans comes from studies using positron-emission tomography (PET). Thus, area V4 is activated when subjects view colored stimuli but not when they view black and white stimuli (Zeki et al., 1991).

Some human patients have lost color vision completely after sustaining brain lesions that included area V4 (Damasio et al., 1980; Zeki, 1993). One poignant case is an artist who could no longer see the hues in the impressionist paintings he had once admired (Sacks and Wasserman, 1987); he could still make black-and-white sketches but could no longer paint in color. Such lack of color vision is called **achromatopsia** (from the Greek *a-*, "not," or "without"; *chroma*, "color"; and *opsis*, "vision"). Since each half of the visual field is seen by the opposite side of the brain, unilateral damage to area V4 can cause loss of color vision in half of the visual field (a condition called hemiachromatopsia) (Kölmel, 1988).

Most Mammalian Species Probably Have Some Degree of Color Vision

In 1942 Gordon Walls concluded from his survey that "within the mammals, color vision is by no means widespread," and this conclusion has been repeated in many books and articles. A much more extensive recent survey by Gerald Jacobs (1993), however, indicates that almost all mammals probably have at least *some* color vision, which he defines as the ability to discriminate between stimuli that differ in wavelength distributions of spectral energy (Table 10.2). Among mammals, only the primates have good trichromatic color vision (based on three classes of cone photopigments), but many species have dichromatic color vision (based on two classes of cone pigments). Most so-called colorblind humans have dichromatic vision and can distinguish short-wavelength stimuli from long-wavelength stimuli.

How does one measure the ability of animals to discriminate on the basis of wavelength? The only direct method is a behavioral test of ability to discriminate among stimuli that differ in wavelength but not in brightness (Neitz, Geist, and Jacobs, 1989). An indirect approach is to determine whether the necessary cone types are present by measuring the electrical responses of the eye to flashes of different stimuli, a method called **electroretinography**; (Goldsmith, 1986; Neitz and Jacobs, 1984). The presence of multiple cone pigments can also be determined by measuring the pigment in individual photoreceptors, using a technique called **microspectrophotometry** (Bowmaker, 1984; Levine and MacNichol, 1985). No

Table 10.2

Categories of Color Vision in Some Mammalian Species

Temporal niche	Order family common name *species*	Excellent trichromatic	Robust dichromatic	Weak dichromatic	Minimal color vision (rod/cone wavelength discrimination)
Diurnal	**Primates** Hominidae Human *Homo sapiens*	✓			
Diurnal	**Primates** Cercopithecidae Rhesus monkey *Macaca mulatta*	✓			
Diurnal	**Primates** Cebidae Squirrel monkey *Saimiri sciurensis*	4/5 of females ✓	All males ✓		
Nocturnal	**Primates** Cebidae Owl monkey *Aotus trivirgatus*				✓
Nocturnal	**Primates** Galagidae Bush baby species *Galago* sp.				✓
Diurnal	**Primates** Tupaidae Tree shrew *Tupaia belangeri*		✓		
Diurnal/ Nocturnal	**Carnivora** Canidae Domestic dog *Canis familiaris*		✓		
Diurnal/ Nocturnal	**Carnivora** Felidae Domestic cat *Felis cattus*			✓	
Diurnal	**Carnivora** Procyonidae Coati *Nasua*			✓	
Nocturnal	**Carnivora** Procyonidae Raccoon *Procyon lotor*				✓
Diurnal/ Nocturnal	**Artiodactyla** Suidae Domestic pig *Sus domestica*		✓		

species that possesses multiple cone pigments has been found to lack the central neural mechanisms for using them in color vision. In a few species, all three of the methods mentioned here—behavioral testing, electroretinography, and microspectrophotometry—have been used to study color vision, and because in these test cases the results of the three methods agreed, clear evidence from any one of these methods is accepted as proof of color vision.

On the basis of his survey, Jacobs (1993) suggests that it may be better to think of a continuum of color capabilities rather than use an all-or-none criterion, and proposes that four categories probably cover all mammalian species: (1) the excellent trichromatic color vision of primates, (2) the robust dichromatic vision of species that have two kinds of cone photopigments and a reasonably large population of cones, (3) the feeble dichromatic vision of species that have two kinds of cone pigments but only a small population of cones, and (4) the minimal color vision of species that have only a single kind of cone pigment and that must rely on interactions between rods and cones to discriminate wavelength. Table 10.2 gives examples of these four categories. Note that when both diurnal and nocturnal species of a given taxonomic family are shown in the table (for example, the coati and the raccoon), the diurnal species usually has the better color vision.

Investigators uncovered a perplexing problem in attempts to characterize the color vision of squirrel monkeys (*Saimiri sciureus*). Monkeys of this species showed a great deal of variability among individuals when they took behavioral tests of color vision: about half were dichromats (among this group there were six different kinds of red–green vision), but the other half were trichromats. After puzzling over the data, the investigators found an unexpected pattern: all the male squirrel monkeys were dichromats, whereas about four-fifths of the females were trichromats (Jacobs, 1984; Jacobs, Neitz, and Neitz, 1993). A study of variation in cone pigments in a sample of 78 squirrel monkeys supported the conclusion from the behavioral tests (Jacobs and Neitz, 1987). Imagine the arguments about choices of clothing and interior decoration if all men were dichromats and most women were trichromats!

Perception of Visual Motion Is Analyzed by a Special System That Includes Cortical Area V5

Some retinal ganglion cells respond preferentially to a certain *direction* of motion of objects; for example,

certain ganglion cells respond to stimuli that move to the left but not to stimuli that move to the right (Barlow and Levick, 1965). Investigators have hypothesized that the direction-selective responses require retinal circuits involving both excitation and inhibition: movement in the preferred direction stimulates excitatory units before inhibitory units, whereas movement in the nonpreferred direction reaches inhibitory units first. More recently, the synaptic transmitter GABA has been found to be involved in inhibition in the retina, and the transmitter ACh is involved in excitation in the retina. Treating the retina with drugs that block either GABA or ACh impairs the activity of the directional circuits (Poggio and Koch, 1987).

Movement of an image across the retina is not necessarily interpreted as movement of an object. Because we continually move our eyes in pursuit or saccadic movements, the movement of the eyes must be taken into account in interpreting movement of an image across the retina. The analysis of motion is accomplished by the cortex, partly in regions close to those that control eye movements. All the neurons in area V5 (also called the medial temporal [MT] area in the monkey; see Figure 10.18) respond to moving visual stimuli, but they do not respond differentially to the wavelength of stimulation. A variety of studies provide converging evidence that area V5 is specialized for perception of motion and of direction of motion. PET scan studies with human subjects show that moving stimuli, rather than colored stimuli, evoke responses in area V5. A stationary pattern that nevertheless causes perceptions of motion in human observers also evokes responses in an area that overlaps area V5 (Zeki, 1993:280). When monkeys are trained to report the direction of perceived motion, experimental lesions of area V5 impair their performance, at least temporarily (Newsome et al., 1985). Electrical stimulation of clusters of V5 neurons with similar preferred directions of motion can affect the monkeys' judgments of direction of motion: weak stimulation biases the judgments toward the neurons' preferred direction (Salzman et al., 1992); stronger stimulation impairs performance, presumably because its effects spread to neurons representing all directions of motion (Murasugi, Salzman, and Newsome, 1993).

A single but quite convincing report describes a woman who lost the ability to perceive motion after a stroke that had damaged the medial temporal region, area V5, of her brain (Zihl, von Cramon, and Mai, 1983). The woman was unable to perceive continuous motion, and saw only separate, successive positions. This impairment led to many problems in her daily life. She had difficulty crossing streets because she could not follow the positions of automobiles in motion: "When I'm looking at the car first, it seems far away. But then, when I want to cross the road, suddenly the car is very near." She complained of difficulties in following conversations because she could not see the movements of speakers' lips. And she had trouble pouring tea into a cup because the fluid appeared to be frozen; she could not stop pouring at the right time because she was unable to see the movement in the cup as the fluid rose. Except for her inability to perceive motion, this person's visual perception appeared to be normal in all other respects.

The Magnocellular and Parvocellular Pathways Are Not Completely Separate

Investigators in the latter 1980s suggested that the parvocellular (P) system is mainly responsible for analysis of color and form and for recognition of objects, whereas the magnocellular (M) system is mainly responsible for perception of depth and movement (Livingstone and Hubel, 1988). From the LGN, the different divisions were thought to project to different layers and areas of the cerebral cortex. In area V1, the P and M projections are segregated but intertwined with each pathway leading to a different region of layer 4 in area V1. In area V2 as well, the M and P systems occupy separate but intermixed small regions. Beyond area V2, the two systems were thought to segregate completely—the P pathway going to inferiortemporal regions of the cortex, the M pathway to parietal regions (Figure 10.28*a*).

 A recent review of this topic states, "The notion of parallel visual subsystems has been broadly disseminated and popularized . . . and has quickly become widely accepted, owing in part to its great explanatory power and its appealing simplicity" (Merigan and Maunsell, 1993:370). But there is now increasing evidence—anatomical, neurophysiological, and behavioral—that the two systems overlap and intermingle considerably, so "it is increasingly difficult to know whether it is appropriate to consider the visual system as made up of subsystems" (Merigan and Maunsell, 1993:370). Interconnections between the two pathways begin in layer 4B of area V1 (Figure 10.28*b*). Further interconnections between the M and P pathways occur in other visual cortical regions, so the systems become increasingly merged. Since Figure 10.28 shows only a small part of the visual cortical regions and their interconnections, the idea of *completely* separate M and P pathways has to be abandoned.

The main pathways of the visual system appear to be determined genetically. For example, some features of cellular anatomy and neurochemistry of the monkey visual cortex develop even without input from the photoreceptors (Kuljis and Rakic, 1990). However, many aspects of the visual system develop in interaction with the environment and visual experience. We discussed this topic in Chapter 4, where we considered the effects of depriving one or both eyes of light during the first months after birth (see Figure 4.20). In Chapter 4 we also considered the misalignment of the two eyes, which can lead to the condition called amblyopia or "lazy eye," in which acuity is poor in one eye. We'll learn more about amblyopia in the next and final section of this chapter.

Visual Neuroscience Can Be Applied to Improve Some Visual Deficiencies

Vision is so important that many investigators have sought ways of restoring sight to the blind and of improving inadequate vision. In the United States half a million people are blind. Recent medical advances have reduced some causes of blindness but have increased blindness from other causes. For example, improved treatment resulting in the increased survival of diabetics does not overcome all effects of this disease, one of which in many cases is blindness. Three main approaches to overcoming some of the problems of blindness or weak vision are: (1) bypassing nonfunctioning eyes by stimulating the visual cortex directly; (2) substituting another sense for vision; and (3) exercising and training a weak eye.

Direct Stimulation of the Visual Cortex Can Evoke Visual Sensations

Mapping of the human brain in studies of epilepsy has shown that mild electrical stimulation of the visual cortex can cause the patient to see localized flashes of light. Changing the site of stimulation within the visual cortex causes the perceived light to move its position in a way that is predictable from mapping of the brain (see Figure 10.22). Visual sensations caused by stimuli other than light are called **phosphenes** (from the Greek, *phos*, "light," and *phainein*, "to cause to appear"). The first kinds of phosphenes to be studied were caused by mechanical or electrical stimulation of the eyes. For example, if you close your eyes, turn them to the left, and press the side of your right eye, you will probably perceive an arc of light. If you move the pressure up on the side of your eye, the arc goes down. Thus you bypass the cornea and lens and stimulate the retina directly. By placing electrodes on the cortex, investigators can bypass all the lower stations of the visual system.

10.28 Parallel Pathways in the Visual System
(a) Broad locations of the temporal ("what") and parietal ("where") pathways. (b) The magnocellular and parvocellular pathways, from the retina to the higher levels of the visual cortex. These pathways are separate at the lower levels of the visual system but show increasingly greater overlap at the higher levels.

(a) Broad locations of the temporal and parietal pathways in monkey brain

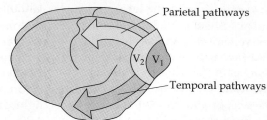

(b) The magnocellular and parvocellular pathways, from the retina to the higher levels of the visual cerebral cortex.

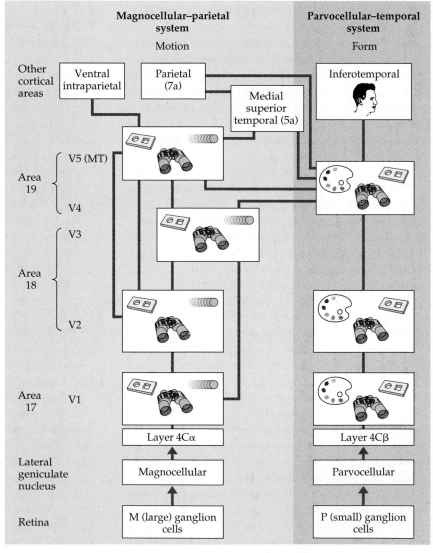

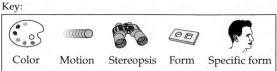

Investigators are attempting to find whether some useful vision can be obtained by placing an array of electrodes on the cortex and producing patterned stimulation controlled by computer programs (Bak et al., 1990). Only crude images can be expected from this method, since each electrode stimulates millions of cortical neurons at once; such nonspecific stimulation can hardly replace the detailed processing of refined cortical circuits. Nevertheless, this technique may permit some blind people to read and to gain useful cues for locomotion. Such systems have been simulated by restricting the vision of normal observers to punctated spots of light from a visual simulator (Cha, Horch, and Normann, 1992). When an array of about 1000 points of lights is delivered, observers are able to avoid obstacles and to read. The investigators propose that implanting "625 electrodes . . . in a 1 cm by 1 cm area near the foveal representation of the visual cortex should produce a phosphene image with visual acuity of approximately 20/30" (Cha, Horch, and Normann, 1992:439). Trials of such systems with patients date back to the 1970s, but many problems remain to be solved if such prostheses are to become useful.

Other Senses Can Substitute for Vision

Some investigators are exploring to what extent touch or hearing can substitute for vision. For example, an optical scanning device and related equipment can turn a spatial array of light signals into an array of electrical or vibratory signals that stimulate a patch of skin (Kaczmarek et al., 1991). With practice, subjects can use such equipment to scan the environment and detect obstacles or read words. Since the nineteenth century blind people have been using their fingertips to "read" Braille books; optical scanners with tactile outputs may make it possible for the blind to read ordinary books or get information from computer screens. Researchers continue to try to make such devices practical (Kaczmarek et al., 1991).

Auditory devices can also substitute for some aspects of vision. You have probably seen blind people tap the tips of their canes to produce sounds whose echoes can reveal the presence of obstacles. Computer-controlled optical reading systems now convert written text to speech in understandable fashion, and improvements are constantly being made.

All three modalities—touch, hearing, and vision—provide for perception of space and spatial relations, and to some extent, space can be translated from one sense into another, but there are limitations. Sonar systems, for example, do not have high acuity in detecting patterns and shapes, because the wavelengths of sound are so much longer than those of light, and although tactile perception of the vibrations from optical scanning can detect simple forms, it cannot resolve even moderately cluttered or complicated stimuli (Easton, 1992). The improvements in vision that *are* possible with sensory substitution indicate the value in pursuing related research, but this technique of improving vision has a long way to go.

Increased Exercise Can Restore Function to a Previously Deprived or Neglected Eye

Attempts to alleviate amblyopia ("lazy eye") by training have produced mixed results and a great deal of controversy. The treatment recommended most often is, beginning at as early an age as possible, give the "weak" eye extensive training and experience while obstructing the good eye (American Academy of Ophthalmology, 1994). (Although we follow the usual practice in referring to the "good" eye and the "weak" eye, the difference is generally believed to lie not in the eyes but in the higher visual centers to which they send their neural messages. Even in an eye deprived of experience of visual patterns, the retinal cells often have normal receptive fields.) Children with amblyopia often wear a patch or opaque contact lens over their good eye to force use of the weak eye. Some investigators conclude that only treatment during the first few years of life can be effective (Epelbaum et al., 1993). Others report considerable improvement, even with adults, if they exercise the weak eye sufficiently and if the amblyopia is not too severe. One study reported considerable recovery from long-standing amblyopia when the good eye was lost or severely damaged (Romero-Apis et al., 1982). In all eight patients in this study, aged 16 to 69 at the time they lost their good eye, the vision in the amblyopic eye improved markedly, thus revealing plasticity of the adult brain.

A remarkable study by Chow and Stewart (1972) encouraged much subsequent work on rehabilitation even in adult animals and people. Chow and Stewart studied kittens, depriving one or both eyes of pattern vision for about the first 20 months after birth, longer than the critical period for development of visual function (from about 3 to 12 weeks of age). When a unilaterally deprived kitten was then tested for pattern perception with the previously deprived eye, it showed almost no discrimination on formal tests and it was not able to guide its locomotion visually, although it performed well using its other eye. The investigators then undertook an intensive program of rehabilitation with some of the kittens. They "gentled" and petted these animals frequently to keep them working on the demanding program. Over time the kittens developed some pattern discrimination with the previously deprived eye, and they could use it to guide their locomotion. Furthermore recovery of vision was accompanied by morphological changes in the LGN. After monocular deprivation the LGN cells that received input from the deprived eye were about one-third smaller than those that had been stimulated by pattern vision. When the previously deprived eye was retrained, the difference in size of LGN cells disappeared. Electrical recording showed that retraining also increased the numbers of binocu-

lar cells in the visual cortex (those that respond to stimulation of either eye), in comparison with kittens that were not retrained. Such animal research, and research with human patients, provide encouraging examples for programs of rehabilitation (Bach-y-Rita, 1992).

The evidence for continuing plasticity in the visual system is consistent with similar evidence from the somesthetic system presented in Chapter 8 and the auditory system presented in Chapter 9. Evidence of plasticity in other parts of the adult nervous system will be presented in Chapter 18.

Summary

1. Perception of forms and recognition of objects are complex accomplishments that require processing in many parts of the visual system.

2. The vertebrate eye is an elaborate structure that forms detailed and accurate optical images on the receptive cells of the retina.

3. Many different phyla have independently evolved photoreceptor organs; several have evolved eyes with lenses to focus light.

4. Visual information processing begins in the retina, where cells that contain photopigments capture light and initiate neural activity. Two kinds of retinal receptor cells, rods and cones, are the initial stages of two systems—the scotopic (dim light) and photopic (bright light) systems, respectively.

5. Each receptor reports only how strongly it has been excited, so at any given instant the visual nervous system receives an enormous array of quantitative information and has to determine what patterns in the outside world could have produced a particular set of "numbers." About one-third of the brain is devoted to this computation.

6. Brain pathways of the visual system include the lateral geniculate nucleus in the thalamus, the primary visual cortex (striate cortex), and other cortical regions. Some axons of retinal ganglion cells extend to the superior colliculus in the midbrain.

7. As one records from cells at successively higher levels in the visual system, the receptive fields change in two main ways: (a) they become larger (occupy larger parts of the visual field), and (b) they require increasingly specific stimuli to evoke responses.

8. The cortex contains several visual areas, each presenting a topographic map of the visual field, but each processing one or more different aspect of visual information, such as form, color, or movement.

9. Like the somatosensory and auditory cortices, the primary visual cortex is organized in columns perpendicular to the surface. Columns and groups of columns provide separate representations of the two eyes, angular orientation of stimuli, position in the visual field, and color.

10. For perception of visual patterns and forms, the stimulus pattern is analyzed at the primary visual cortex according to the orientation and spatial frequency of stimuli.

11. Discrimination of hue in Old World primates and in humans depends on the existence of three different cone photopigments and on the fact that retinal connections yield four different kinds of spectrally opponent retinal ganglion cells.

12. Location of visual stimuli in space is aided by detailed spatial maps at every level of the visual system.

13. In both cats and primates, parallel magnocellular and parvocellular projective systems from the retina to the brain mediate different aspects of visual projection, but these systems show increasing overlap in the cortical visual areas.

14. Clinical evidence supports the concept of parallel processing, because genetic anomalies or injury to the brain may impair some aspects of visual perception while leaving others intact. Examples include prosopagnosia (the inability to recognize formerly familiar faces even though the faces are seen clearly) and achromatopsia (the inability to see hues).

15. The main pathways of the visual system appear to be determined genetically, but many aspects of the visual system develop in interaction with the environment and visual experience.

16. Research to aid the blind includes bypassing non-functioning eyes by stimulating the visual cortex directly and substituting another sense (touch or audition) for vision.

17. Attempts to treat amblyopia work best when retraining starts early in life, but success with some older patients demonstrates that the visual nervous system remains plastic even in adults.

Recommended Reading

De Valois, R. L. and De Valois, K. K. 1988. *Spatial vision*. Oxford University Press, New York.

Land, M. F. and Fernald, R. D. 1992. The evolution of eyes. *Annual Review of Neuroscience*, 15:1–29.

Merigan, W. H. and Maunsell, J. H. R. 1993. How parallel are the primate visual pathways? *Annual Review of Neuroscience*, 16:369–402.

Wandell, B. A. 1995. *Foundations of Vision*. Sinauer Associates, Sunderland, MA.

Zeki, S. 1993. *A Vision of the Brain*. Blackwell, London.

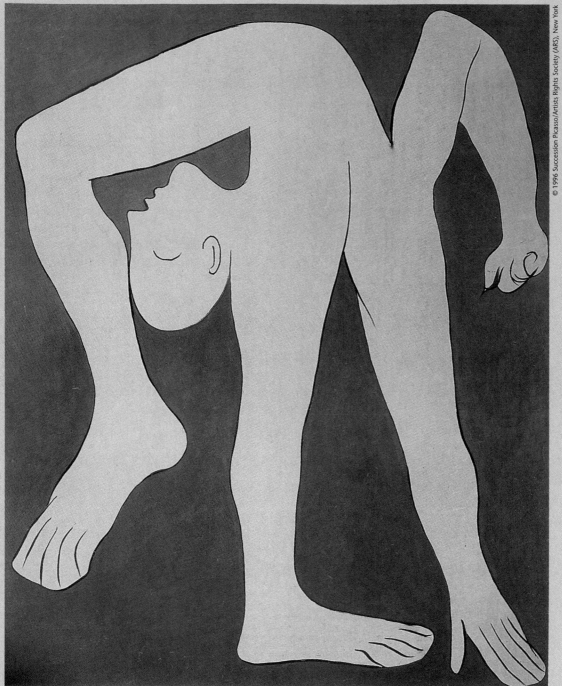

Pablo Picasso, *Acrobat*, 1930

- *The Behavioral View*

- *The Control Systems View*

- *The Neurobiological View*

- *Human Movement Disorders*

- *Changes over the Lifetime*

CHAPTER 11 Movements and Actions

Orientation

Our movements and acts seem effortless; we hardly think about what it takes for us to reach out and pick up an object, walk across a room, or even to talk. It just happens! Some of our movements and acts show the effects of careful honing of a skill, such as the finger movements of the concert pianist or the coordination of highly skilled athletes. But even everyday movements require an intricate sequence of muscle activity. Think, for example, of all the muscles involved when you say a single word. The tongue, larynx, throat, lips, chest, and diaphragm must work in a highly coordinated manner to produce even the simplest speech sound. And there is little room for error if you are to be understood. The difference between saying "time" and "dime," for example, depends mainly on whether your vocal cords are relaxed or tensed during the start of the word.

What enables us to perform the movements and acts that make up our behavior? Any coordinated movement implies that there are underlying neural mechanisms for choosing the appropriate muscles and how they should act. These mechanisms require that motoneurons are activated in the proper order. Voluntary behavior adds another level of complexity: how the initial *idea* for a movement or act is translated into the selection of muscles. This process must involve at some places in the nervous system a plan for action—a motor plan.

We begin our discussion by looking at movements and their coordination from different points of view—the behavioral view, the control systems view, and especially the neurobiological view.

The Behavioral View

Crawling, walking, flying, and swimming are some of the many ways to move from one place to another. Close analysis of different animals offers some notions about the underlying mechanisms of these behaviors. For example, the vigorous, regular beating of insect or bird wings suggests that the nervous system contains a rhythm generator, an oscillator. The varied gaits of four-legged animals suggest that different oscillators are coupled in precise but flexible ways to produce coordinated movement. The great versatility of learned movements in humans shows the range of complex adjustments possible in the motor system (Figure 11.1).

Movements and Actions Can Be Classified into Categories

Efforts to classify movements began with the distinction between the "machinelike" actions of nonhuman animals and the "voluntary" behavior of humans. In the seventeenth century the philosopher René Descartes particularly emphasized this distinction, and in the eighteenth and nineteenth centuries

it was advanced by discoveries of the basic properties of the spinal cord. During this time scientists noted that the dorsal roots of the spinal cord serve sensory functions and the ventral roots contain motor fibers; sensorimotor connections seemed to provide the basis for simple movements.

Sir Charles Sherrington
(1857–1957)

In the late nineteenth and early twentieth centuries the British physiologist Charles Sherrington conducted extensive studies of spinal animals (animals whose spinal cord has been disconnected from the brain). He showed that skin stimulation, such as pinching, provoked simple acts such as limb withdrawal. Many such observations led him to argue that the basic units of movement are **reflexes**, which he defined as simple, highly stereotyped, and unlearned responses to external stimuli. He showed that the magnitude of a reflex is directly related to the intensi-

11.1 Running Is a Complex Act

ty of the stimulus. Sherrington's work ushered in an era of intensive attempts to identify the different reflexes and to chart their pathways in the nervous system, particularly in the spinal cord. Some reflexes involve only pathways in the spinal cord linking dorsal and ventral roots; others involve longer loops connecting spinal cord segments or even brain regions.

Are reflexes the basic units of more complex movements and acts? Can every act be broken down into reflexes? The reflex perspective appropriately invited criticism when it tried in a rather simple fashion to explain complex behaviors. For instance, Sherrington thought that complex acts were simply combinations of simpler reflexes strung out in some temporal order. The limitations of this perspective are apparent in attempts to analyze complex sequences of behavior, such as speech, in reflex terms. For example, explanations of speech in terms of reflexes are based on the claim that the movements and sounds associated with each element of speech provide the stimuli that instigate the next element. If this were true, speech would be a series of stimulus–response units chained together, each response triggering off the next unit. But, on the contrary, it appears that the speaker has a *plan* in which several units (speech sounds) are placed in a larger pattern. Sometimes the units get misplaced, although the pattern is pre-

served: "Our queer old dean," said English clergyman William Spooner, when he meant, "Our dear old queen." Or "You hissed all my mystery lectures." (Spooner was so prone to mix up the order of sounds in his sentences that this type of error is called a spoonerism.) Such mistakes reveal a plan: The speaker is anticipating a later sound and executing it too soon. A chain of reflexes would not be subject to such an error.

Notions of a **motor plan** or motor program have been strongly advanced by researchers in this field, although not without criticism (Rosenbaum, 1991). These terms are loose metaphors that convey the view that complex movements and acts are controlled and produced by a set of commands to muscles that is established *before* an act occurs. Pearson (1993) suggests that the role of feedback from movements is to inform the motor program about how the execution is unfolding. Examples of this kind of internal plan for action range from skilled movements, such as piano playing, to a wide repertoire of simple escape behaviors of animals such as crayfish.

Table 11.1 gives a scheme for classifying movements and acts that focuses on their functional properties rather than on their exact muscle relations. We can use this table to distinguish between movements and acts. Simple reflexes include brief, unitary activi-

Table 11.1

A Classification of Movements and Examples of Each

I. **Simple Reflex**
Stretch, knee jerk, sneezing, startle, eye blink, pupillary contraction

II. **Posture and Postural Changes**
Standing, rearing, lying, balancing, sitting, urination posture

III. **Locomotion**
Walking, creeping, running, crawling, swimming, stalking, flying, hopping

IV. **Sensory Orientation**
Head turning, touching, eye fixation, sniffing, ear movement, tasting

V. **Species-Typical Action Patterns**
Ingestion: tasting, chewing, biting, sipping, drinking
Courtship display: sniffing, chasing, retreating
Escape and defense: hissing, spitting, submission posture, cowering
Grooming: washing, preening, licking
Gestures: grimacing, tail erection, squinting, tooth baring, smiling

VI. **Acquired Skills**
Speech, tool use, dressing, painting, sculpting, driving a car, sports, dancing

ties of muscle that we commonly call **movements**. These events are discrete, in many cases limited to a single part of the body, such as a limb. The lower parts of the table list complex, sequential behaviors, frequently oriented toward a goal. Different movements of several bodily parts might be included in such behavior. These more complex events we distinguish as **acts**, or action patterns.

Movements and Acts Can Be Analyzed and Measured in a Variety of Precise Ways

Movements and acts are readily visible in motion pictures, and high-speed photography provides an intimate portrait of even the most rapid events. To deal with the excessive data furnished by high-speed photography, methods of simplification or numerical analysis have been devised. Photographic techniques such as multiple exposures offer simple portraits of human movement. Continuing developments in computer graphic simulation techniques also provide striking examples of the representation of movements. For example, the world of sports uses detailed analyses of athletic acts (Figure 11.2). The data that generate these portraits are either time-lapse photographs or information derived from sensors attached at joints. Computer programs process digitized photos to help quantify movements and acts, thereby enabling detailed measurement of the position of different body parts in successive instants and an array of quantitative data about rates of changes of different components of acts.

Another approach to the fine-grain analysis of movements is to record the electrical activity of muscles, a procedure referred to as **electromyography**. Since the contraction of muscles involves electrical potentials generated by the muscle fibers, fine needle electrodes placed in a muscle or electrodes placed on the skin over a muscle can provide electrical indications of muscle activity (Figure 11.3). If we put electrodes in many different muscles, we get an electrical portrait of the contraction of the different muscles involved in a distinct act, including the progressive buildup and decay of activity in the different muscles. This technique is useful in diagnosing neuromuscular disorders.

The Control Systems View

Engineering descriptions of the regulation and control of machines provide a useful way of looking at the mechanisms that regulate and control our movements. In designing machines, engineers commonly encounter two problems: (1) accuracy—how to prevent or minimize error—and (2) speed—how to accomplish a task quickly and efficiently. Two forms of control mechanisms—closed-loop and open-loop—are commonly employed to optimize performance according to these criteria. In **closed-loop control mechanisms**, information flows from whatever is being controlled back to the device that controls it. The control of en-

11.2 Digitized movement
A computerized representation of a runner's movements.

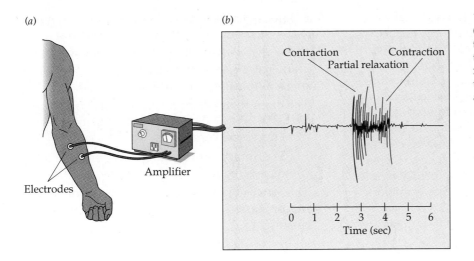

11.3   Electromyography
(*a*)Electrodes on the arm detect action potentials that trigger contraction in underlying muscles. (*b*) The resulting electromyogram shows activity with contraction and relaxation.

docrine secretion, which we discussed in Chapter 7, is a closed-loop mechanism (see Figure 7.9 and 7.10). We can consider a more complex example of a closed-loop system: someone driving a car. In this case the variable being controlled is the position of an automobile on the road (Figure 11.4). Continuous information is provided by the driver's visual system, which guides correcting movement.

The only way the car could stay on the road without feedback control (as, for example, driving with your eyes closed) would be with the aid of accurate memory of all the turns and bends in the road. But the car would not be able to deal with anything new, such as other moving cars. Such a memory system could be considered a form of open-loop control. **Open-loop control mechanisms** do not involve external forms of

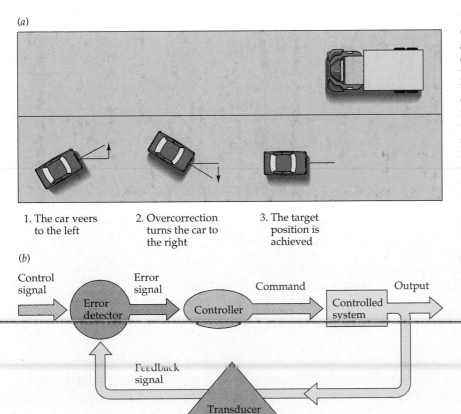

11.4   A Closed Loop System
(*a*) Example of feedback control in auto driving. (*b*) Formal description of closed-loop systems. In our example, the controlled system is the automobile. The input is the position of the steering wheel, and the output is the position on the road. The transducer is an element that measures output, and the error detector measures differences between actual output and desired output (control signal). In this example the transducer (visual system), error detector (perceptual system), and controller (muscles) all refer to properties of the person driving the car. The actual position of the car is compared with its desired position on the road, and the driver makes corrections to minimize the discrepancy. Closed-loop systems emphasize accuracy and flexibility at the expense of speed.

feedback; output is measured by a sensor but the activity is preprogrammed. Open-loop controls are needed in systems that must respond so rapidly that no time is available for the delay of a feedback pathway. Elevators are a familiar example of the open-loop control system: their rates of acceleration and deceleration are preset. Pressing the button for a given floor sets off the whole predetermined program. Because there is no feedback, open-loop systems need other ways to reduce error and variability. They employ devices that supply a control signal that *anticipates* potential error. In living systems accurate anticipation may arise from prior learning (Box 11.1).

The Neurobiological View

Adaptive acts are produced by instructions generated by neural processing in the brain and spinal cord; these in turn lead to neural activity in motoneurons connected to muscles. Neuroscientists have distinguished four different levels of hierarchically organized motor control systems in the central nervous system:

1. The spinal cord deals with reflex responses. Processing at this level is relatively rigid and involves many automatic mechanisms.

2. The brain stem integrates motor commands from higher levels of the brain and transmits inputs from the spinal cord.

3. In the **primary motor cortex** some of the main commands for action are initiated.

4. The areas adjacent to motor cortex, **nonprimary motor cortex**, initiate another level of cortical processing.

We will examine each level of neural control after we have considered some of the characteristics of muscles and bones that determine the properties of movements. Other brain regions—the cerebellum and basal ganglia—modulate the activities of these hierarchically organized control systems. The orga-

---

Box 11.1
Movements and Acts Are Shaped and Modified by Learning

We don't have to learn how to withdraw a hand from a hot stove, or how to breathe, or how to swallow. These and many other acts are highly stereotyped, "involuntary" reflexes; no aspect of a person's attention changes their essential character. In contrast, we need explicit training to play tennis, use a keyboard, and perform many other trivial to extraordinary acts. The characteristics of these acts are highly variable, frequently idiosyncratic, and show considerable variability among individuals. These acts are commonly referred to as "voluntary" motor skills. How are such skills acquired? A comprehensive review of motor learning has been provided by Ivry (1993), who notes that the number of variables that affect skill acquisition or mo-

tor learning are many. This variability may account for why there are so many theoretical views in this field.

A simple example using a single subject in a task that involved using a joystick to move a cursor on a screen to follow a moving spot of light helps focus issues in motor learning. Large errors are evident in the initial presentation; the subject is slow to change course and overshoots the path of the spot. On successive presentations of this simple stimulus, the subject tracks the spot faster and with very little errors. What has happened during the acquisition of this motor skill? According to Paul Fitts (Fitts and Posner, 1967), a pioneer in the modern study of motor learning, there are three stages in skill acquisition:

1. The cognitive stage, in which the subject develops thoughts about different features of the task and the effects of actions.

2. The associative stage, during which trial-and-error solutions are attempted and successful strategies are defined.

3. The automatic stage, during which acts are performed with little conscious recognition and variability in performance is reduced. In this stage behavior relies less on continuous feedback, and it has become more "open-loop" in character.

Another view about skill acquisition is that it involves the development of a **schema** for action—the formation of some kind of higher-level program. The performance of any skilled movement shows that

11.5 Hierarchy of Movement Control

Primary motor cortex receives information from other cortical areas and sends commands to the brainstem, which passes commands to the spinal cord. Both the cerebellum and the basal ganglia provide adjustments to these commands.

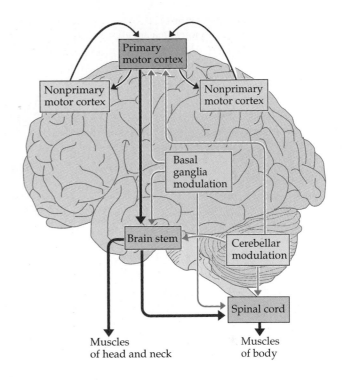

nizational scheme outlined in Figure 11.5 will form the basis of our discussion.

The Skeletal System Enables Particular Movements and Precludes Others

Some properties of acts arise from characteristics of the skeleton and muscles themselves. For example, the length, form, and weight of the limbs shape an animal's stride. The skeletal system of any vertebrate consists of many separate bones of different shape, weight, and length. Through painful experience we know that bones themselves do not bend, although their shape may change as the result of sustaining un-

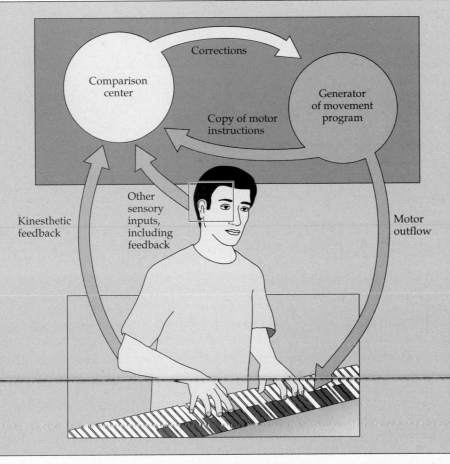

several types of information are essential to acquiring a motor skill. One model of skill learning (Keele and Summers, 1976) posits that input to muscles is provided by a hypothetical movement program in the brain that directs the timing and force of neural outputs to muscles (the motor outflow). Feedback from receptors in joints and other modes of information about movements—visual or auditory—are matched to a model of skilled performance, as shown in the figure. Feedback information thus provides input about errors, which are gradually reduced; in some cases the need for monitoring the movement is eliminated—that is, Fitts' third stage is reached. At this stage of learning a skilled movement, the subject becomes unaware of the act; execution is automatic. Faster performance becomes possible because feedback control loops exert less impact.

11.6 Joints and Movements

Next to each enlarged joint is a mechanical model that shows the kinds of movements the joint can perform. (*a*) The wrist joint moves in two principal planes: lateral and vertical. (*b*) The hip joint is a "universal" joint, moving in all three planes. (*c*) The knee joint has a single plane of motion.

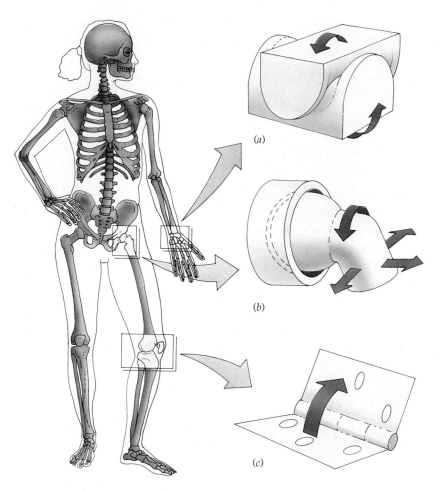

(*a*)

(*b*)

(*c*)

usual use or weight. The primary sites for bending are at the joints, where bones meet. Figure 11.6 illustrates the human skeleton and shows examples of some joints and their possible movements. Some joints, such as the hip, are almost "universal" joints, permitting movement in many planes. Others, like the elbow or knee, are more limited and tolerate little deviation from the principal axis of rotation.

Muscles Control the Actions of the Skeletal System

Our bare skeleton must now be clothed with muscles. The distribution of muscles in the body—their size and how they attach to bones—is a direct indication of the forms of movement that they mediate. By contracting (under instructions from motoneurons), some muscles produce forces that sustain body weight, and others produce actual movement around a joint. In contrast, other muscles do not act on the skeleton at all—for example, the muscles that move the eyes, lips, and tongue and those that contract the abdomen. Muscles have some springlike properties that influ-

ence the timing of behavior, and the rate and force of muscular contractions limit some responses.

A muscle is composed of thousands of individual muscle fibers. The contraction of muscle fibers leads to movements or to the maintenance of posture according to the ways in which the muscle is mechanically attached to a bone or bones. The arrangement around a typical joint is illustrated in Figure 11.7. Muscles are connected to bone by **tendons**. Around a joint, different muscles are arranged in a reciprocal fashion: when one muscle group contracts (shortens), the other is extended; that is, the muscles are **antagonists**. (Muscles that act together are said to be **synergists**.) Coordinated action around a joint may require that one set of motoneurons be excited while the antagonistic set is inhibited. The limb can be locked in position by graded contraction of the opposed muscles.

The molecular machinery of muscles. Each muscle fiber is made up of many filaments of two kinds arranged in a very regular manner (Figure 11.8*a*). Bands of relatively thick filaments alternate with

(a)   (b)

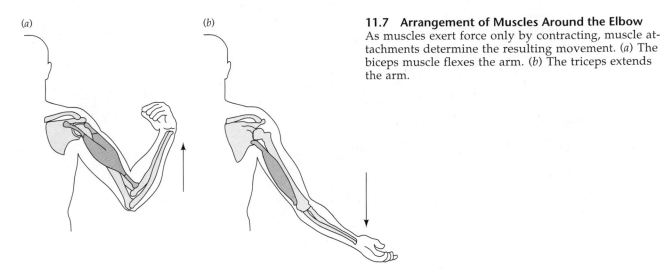

11.7   Arrangement of Muscles Around the Elbow
As muscles exert force only by contracting, muscle attachments determine the resulting movement. (*a*) The biceps muscle flexes the arm. (*b*) The triceps extends the arm.

bands of thinner filaments, giving the fibers a striped appearance. The thick and thin filaments (made up of the complex proteins myosin and actin, respectively) always overlap. Contraction of the muscle increases the overlap: the filaments slide past each other, shortening the overall length of the muscle fiber.

What causes the fibers to move past each other? Magnification shows that the thick filaments have paddle-shaped extensions of cross bridges that make contact with the thin filaments (Figure 11.8*b*). During contraction these cross-bridges rotate, pushing the thin filaments (Taylor, 1993). Actually a cross-bridge moves through a certain distance and then breaks contact; it moves back, makes a new contact, and pushes again. Rotation of the myosin head causes the filaments to slide over one another. A single muscular contraction involves several cycles of such paddling actions. In summary, what generates force in this molecular mechanism is changes in the cross-bridges between actin and myosin filaments. The movement of the cross-bridges is initiated when calcium ions contact the muscle filament proteins. We'll discuss shortly how nerves arrange for calcium ions to reach the muscle filament proteins.

Muscle types.   Speed, precision, strength, and endurance are all desirable qualities in movements, but the requirements for these qualities differ depending on the behavioral act. Matched to these requirements are at least two main types of muscle fibers, "fast" and "slow." Eye movements, for example, must be quick and accurate so that we can follow moving objects and shift our gaze from one target to another. But fibers in the extraocular muscles do not have to maintain tension for long periods of time because the neur-

al program uses them in rotation; that is, it allows some fibers to relax while others contract. The extraocular muscles are therefore made up of **fast muscle fibers**. In leg muscles fast fibers react promptly and strongly but fatigue rapidly; they are used mainly for activities in which muscle tension changes frequently, as in walking or running. Mixed in with them are **slow muscle fibers**, which are not as strong but have greater resistance to fatigue; they are used chiefly to maintain posture.

Neural Messages Reach Muscle Fibers at the Neuromuscular Junction

Once a motoneuron has integrated all the information bombarding it through hundreds or thousands of synapses (Figure 11.9*a*), it may produce an action potential. As the axon splits into many branches near the target muscle (Figure 11.9*b*), each branch carries an action potential to its terminal, which then (in vertebrates) releases acetylcholine (ACh). Then all the muscle fibers innervated by that motoneuron respond to the ACh by producing action potentials of their own. The action potentials travel along each muscle fiber, permitting sodium (Na^+) and calcium (Ca^{2+}) ions to enter and then trigger the molecular changes that produce contraction. The region where the motoneuron terminal and the adjoining muscle fiber meet—and produce distinctive structures for communication—is called the **neuromuscular junction** (Figure 11.9*c*). The neuromuscular junction is large and very effective: every action potential that reaches the axon terminal releases enough ACh to cause a large enough depolarization (called an **end-plate potential**) in the muscle fiber to produce an action potential. Thus, normally every action potential

(a)

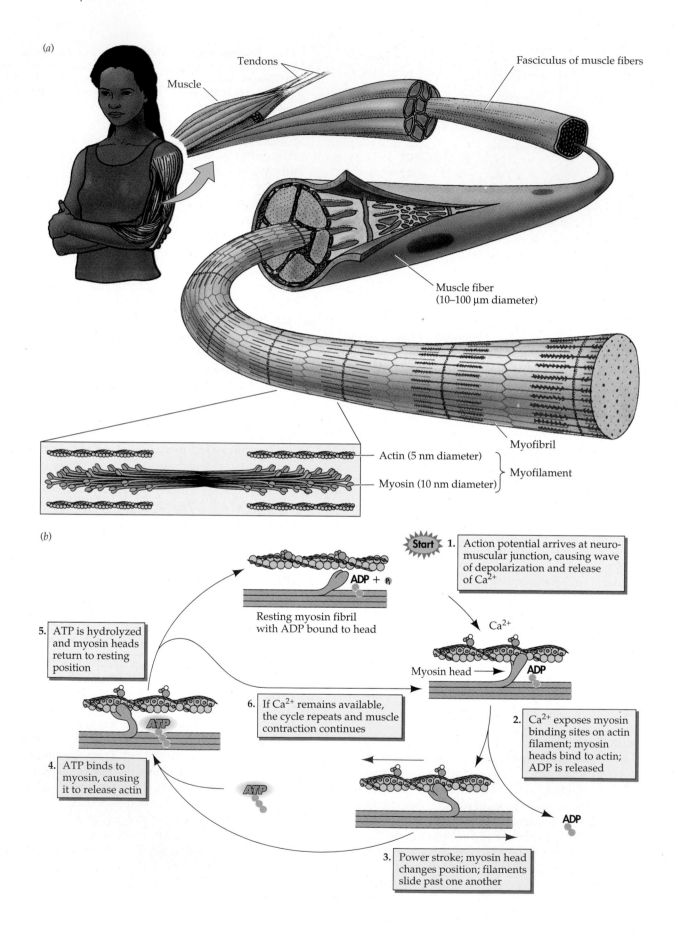

Muscle

Tendons

Fasciculus of muscle fibers

Muscle fiber
(10–100 μm diameter)

Myofibril

Actin (5 nm diameter)

Myosin (10 nm diameter)

Myofilament

(b)

Start **1.** Action potential arrives at neuro-muscular junction, causing wave of depolarization and release of Ca^{2+}

5. ATP is hydrolyzed and myosin heads return to resting position

ADP + P_i

Resting myosin fibril with ADP bound to head

Ca^{2+}

Myosin head → ADP

6. If Ca^{2+} remains available, the cycle repeats and muscle contraction continues

2. Ca^{2+} exposes myosin binding sites on actin filament; myosin heads bind to actin; ADP is released

4. ATP binds to myosin, causing it to release actin

ATP

ATP

ADP

3. Power stroke; myosin head changes position; filaments slide past one another

11.8 The Composition of Muscles

(a) Views of muscle fibers at progressively greater magnifications, from life-size to 2 million times. (b) How actions of myosin and actin cause muscle contraction.

in the motoneuron elicits a contraction in the postsynaptic fiber. Because it is large and accessible, the neuromuscular junction is a very well studied synapse, and much of what we know about synapses and synaptic plasticity was first established at the neuromuscular junction.

Even though the neuromuscular junction is a large

and reliable synapse, its properties can change with use. All of us are familiar with muscle fatigue from extended use; some of the reduced responsiveness of the fatigued muscle is due to diminished effectiveness of neuromuscular junctions. Another well-known example of neural plasticity is **posttetanic potentiation**. When a rapid series of action potentials (a tetanus) is induced in a motor nerve, the neuromuscular junctions are altered for a period so that subsequent single action potentials cause a stronger end-plate potential in the muscle. This potentiation is caused by a build up of Ca^{2+} ions in the presynaptic terminal and therefore the release of more ACh. The study of several types of neuromuscular junction

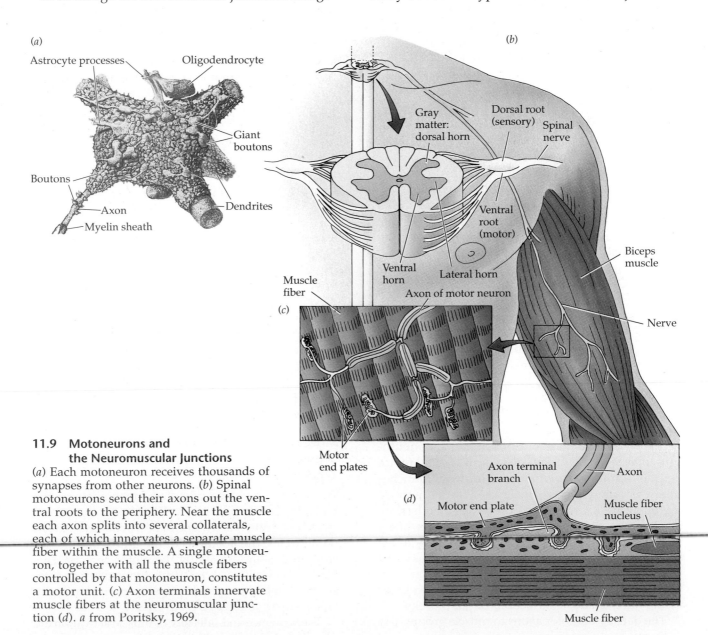

11.9 Motoneurons and the Neuromuscular Junctions

(a) Each motoneuron receives thousands of synapses from other neurons. (b) Spinal motoneurons send their axons out the ventral roots to the periphery. Near the muscle each axon splits into several collaterals, each of which innervates a separate muscle fiber within the muscle. A single motoneuron, together with all the muscle fibers controlled by that motoneuron, constitutes a motor unit. (c) Axon terminals innervate muscle fibers at the neuromuscular junction (d). a from Poritsky, 1969.

plasticity led to other studies of synaptic plasticity that may underlie learning, as will be discussed in Chapter 18. In vertebrates, all neuromuscular junctions are excitatory because they all release ACh and all muscle fibers are excited by ACh. Among invertebrates, some muscles are innervated by two neurons, one of which uses an inhibitory neurotransmitter to prevent muscle contraction.

Early in embryogenesis, young muscle fibers have ACh receptors along their entire length, so application of ACh anywhere along the fiber causes a response. But as the growing axon tip (the growth cone; see Figure 4.11) from a motoneuron contacts the fiber, ACh receptors migrate from other parts of the muscle fiber to cluster opposite the axon tip. (Remember that receptors and ion channels "float" in the fatty membrane of cells.) From this point on, the muscle fiber preferentially inserts additional ACh receptors beneath the motoneuron terminal at the newly formed neuromuscular junction. Vertebrate motoneurons sometimes also release other chemicals, including peptides such as calcitonin gene-related peptide. One hypothesis is that these peptides tell the muscle fiber where to insert ACh receptors (Laufer and Changeux, 1989). In adulthood, if muscle fibers are denervated (that is, deprived of a nerve supply, as when the motor nerve to the muscle is cut), the muscle fibers again produce ACh receptors along their entire length. Thereafter the fibers are said to show **denervation supersensitivity** because contractions can be produced by applying ACh anywhere along the fiber, as in the embryo. Once the regenerating motoneuron axons reach the muscle fiber, the fiber again provides ACh receptors only at the point of contact. Although a different motoneuron may come to innervate a given fiber, regenerating motoneurons prefer to return to the site of the original neuromuscular junction (Sanes, Marshall, and McMahan, 1978).

Another interesting aspect of the development of the neuromuscular junction is that, early in life, every muscle fiber is contacted by several motoneurons (Redfern, 1970). During a postnatal period of **neuromuscular synapse elimination**, however, all motoneurons withdraw some of their terminal branches until every muscle fiber is innervated by only a single motoneuron (see Figure 4.3*f*). Many scientists are studying how the motoneurons and muscle fibers eliminate just the right number of synapses to accomplish this task (Purves, 1988; Jordan, Letinsky, and Arnold, 1988). The net result is that each motoneuron has exclusive control of a pool of muscle fibers, enabling finely graded contractions of our muscles.

The density of motor axons to muscle groups also affects the precision of control of movements. Fine neural control results when each axon connects to only a few muscle fibers. To understand this concept better, let's look at the motor unit. The **motor unit** is a single motor axon and all the muscle fibers that it innervates (see Figure 11.9*b*). The term **innervation ratio** refers to the ratio of motor axons to fibers. Low innervation ratios characterize muscles involved in fine movements, like those of the eye (1:3 ratio). Muscles that act on large body masses such as those of the leg have innervation ratios of one neuron to several hundred muscle fibers; thus, the same call for contraction goes to hundreds of leg muscle fibers at the same time.

The Motoneuron Integrates Information from the Brain and Spinal Cord

Muscles contract because motoneurons of the spinal cord and cranial nerve nuclei initiate neural activity that travels along motor axons to muscles. These motoneurons are the **final common pathway** that links the activity of the rest of the spinal cord and brain to our many muscles. Because they respond to inputs from so many sources, motoneurons often have very widespread dendritic fields, and are the largest cells in the spinal cord. Furthermore, motoneurons must respond to a tremendous variety of synaptic transmitters, both excitatory and inhibitory.

Motor cells of the spinal cord are not uniform in size or electrophysiological properties. Large motoneurons have axons of wide diameter and therefore conduct impulses faster. In general, small motoneurons innervate slow muscles and are more easily excited by synaptic currents; therefore they are activated before large motoneurons (Jones et al., 1994). Large motoneurons innervate fast muscles and tend to respond after small cells because, being large, they are less readily excited by synaptic currents. Their discharge characteristics are more phasic or abrupt. All spinal levels contain both large and small motoneurons.

Movements Are Monitored by Sensory Feedback from Muscles, Tendons, and Joints

To produce rapid coordinated movements of the body, the integrative mechanisms of the brain and spinal cord must have information about the state of the muscles, the positions of the limbs, and the instructions being issued by the motor centers. This kind of information about bodily movements and positions is called **proprioceptive** (from the Latin *proprius*, "own," and *recipere*, "to receive").

The sequence and intensity of muscle activation are

monitored by sensory receptors, which report the state of muscles and joints, and this information is used by the circuits that initiate and guide movements. Several kinds of sensory receptors can provide information about the state of muscle length or contraction. Two major kinds of receptors are **muscle spindles**, which lie in parallel with the muscle fibers (Figure 11.10*a* and *c*), and **Golgi tendon organs**, which lie in series with muscles, one end attached to tendon, the other to muscle (Figure 11.10*b*). The mechanical sensitivities of the spindles and tendon organs differ. The stretching of a muscle, which occurs in most movements, activates especially the spindles and transiently the tendon organs. The shortening of a muscle during contraction activates the tendon organs because they lie in series with the muscle. Together these two kinds of receptors transmit to the central nervous system a range of information about muscle activities.

Classical studies in physiology, especially those of Sherrington, emphasized the importance of these receptors for movement. Mott (1895) and Sherrington (1898) showed that after they cut the afferent fibers from muscles, monkeys failed to use the deafferented limb, even if the efferent connections from motoneurons to muscles were preserved. The deafferented limb is not paralyzed, since it can be activated, but lack of information from the muscle leads to relative disuse. This picture has been qualified: monkeys can flex a deafferented limb in response to a visual signal to avoid shock, even though during free behavior the arm looks paralyzed.

Although deafferenting one forearm leads to *apparent* paralysis of that limb, the result is quite different if both forearms are deafferented. In that case the monkey recovers coordinated use of its forearms over a few months (Taub, 1976); when one limb is deafferented, the monkey makes do with the other, but when both are deafferented, the monkey has to learn to use them and is able to do so. Even if only one arm is deafferented, forced use of it can lead to the return of coordinated use of the two arms. This result was shown in experiments in which the hand of the *intact* limb was placed inside a ball, which prevented the monkey from grasping objects with it but allowed finger movements and thus prevented atrophy. Slowly the deafferented limb gained dexterity, and over the course of several weeks fine movements like those needed for feeding were achieved. After several months the ball on the intact hand was removed, and the monkey made coordinated movements of both limbs. However, if the forced usage lasted less than four months, movements of the deafferented limb regressed rapidly.

The portrait of deafferentation in humans provides some striking insight into the significance of sensory feedback. One patient suffered loss of sensory input from muscles, joints, and skin, but his motor functions were spared (Marsden, Rothwell, and Day, 1984). He engaged in a wide range of manual activities, including repetitive alternating hand movements and some grasping movements. A striking example of preserved motor skills was his ability to drive his manual shift car. On the other hand, the disabilities of this patient were not insignificant. Fine movements of the fingers, such as writing or fastening buttons, were drastically impaired. In addition, it was quite difficult to acquire *new* movements of the hand. For example, after buying a new car, the patient found that he was unable to acquire the arm movements necessary to drive it and had to revert to his old car. Thus, sensory feedback is an important ingredient in skilled performance and in motor learning.

The muscle spindle. The muscle spindle of vertebrates is a complicated structure consisting of both afferent and efferent elements (see Figure 11.10*c*). The spindle gets its name from its shape—a sort of cylinder that is thicker in the middle and tapers at its two ends. The Latin for "spindle," *fusus,* is used to form adjectives referring to the muscle spindle; thus the small muscle fibers *within* each spindle are called **intrafusal fibers**, and the ordinary muscle fibers that lie *outside* the spindles are referred to as **extrafusal fibers**.

There are two kinds of receptors in the muscle spindle: (1) primary or central sensory endings (also called annulospiral endings) and (2) secondary or distal sensory endings (also called flower spray endings). These endings are related to different parts of the spindle (see Figure 11.10*c*). The primary ending wraps in a spiral fashion around a region called the nuclear bag (the central region of the intrafusal fiber). The secondary fibers terminate toward the thin ends of the spindle.

How do these elements become excited? Suppose a muscle is stretched, as when a load is placed on it. For example, if you were trying to hold your arm straight out in front of you, palm up, and someone put a book in your hand, that would put an additional load on your biceps. Your arm would move down transiently, stretching the biceps muscle. The muscle spindle would also stretch, and the resulting deformation of the endings on the spindle would set up nerve impulses in the afferent fibers. These afferents inform the spinal cord, and the spinal cord then informs the brain about the muscle stretch and therefore about the load imposed (Figure 11.10*d*).

Two important factors affect the stretch of the mus-

(a)

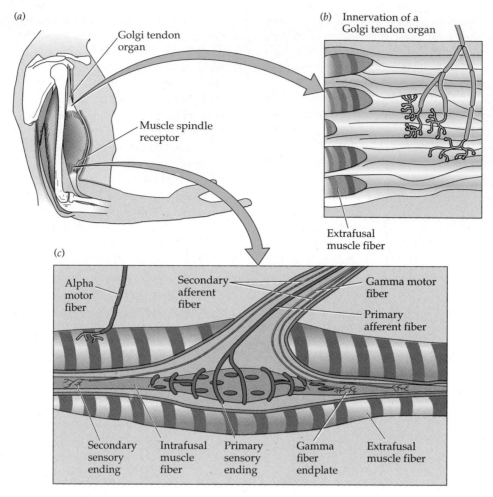

Golgi tendon organ

Muscle spindle receptor

(b) Innervation of a Golgi tendon organ

Extrafusal muscle fiber

(c)

Alpha motor fiber

Secondary afferent fiber

Gamma motor fiber

Primary afferent fiber

Secondary sensory ending

Intrafusal muscle fiber

Primary sensory ending

Gamma fiber endplate

Extrafusal muscle fiber

(d)

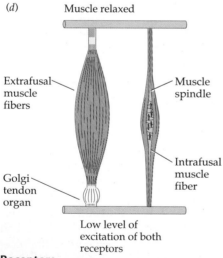
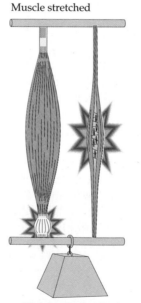

Muscle relaxed

Extrafusal muscle fibers

Muscle spindle

Golgi tendon organ

Intrafusal muscle fiber

Low level of excitation of both receptors

Muscle stretched

High level of excitation of both receptors

Muscle contracted

Tendon organ excited; spindle not excited

11.10 Muscle Receptors

(a) Location of muscle spindles in the body of the muscle and of Golgi organs in the tendons. (b) Typical sensory ending of Golgi tendon organ. (c) Typical structure of a muscle spindle. Two types of receptor endings are shown: primary and secondary. Gamma motor fibers control a contractile portion of the spindle. (d) The excitation of muscle receptors when a load is imposed.

cle. One is the *rate of change* of muscle length. In our example the rate of change is jointly a function of the weight of the load and the rate at which it is applied. The second factor is the *force* you must continually exert with the muscle to prevent dropping the load. In our example this force is a function only of the weight of the book. The different receptor elements of the muscle spindle are differentially sensitive to these two features of muscle length changes. The primary (central) endings show a maximum discharge early in stretch and then adapt to a lower discharge rate. In contrast, the secondary (distal) endings are maximally sensitive to maintained length and are slow to change their rate during the early phase of stretch. Because of this differential sensitivity, the primary endings are called *dynamic* and the secondary endings are called *static* indicators of muscle length. This distinction probably arises from the difference in how these receptors are embedded in the spindle rather than from a difference in the nerve fibers themselves.

Regulation of muscle spindle sensitivity.　Muscle spindles not only help to maintain posture but also coordinate movement. Spindles are informed of planned and ongoing actions through innervation by special motoneurons that alter the tension within the spindle and thus control the sensitivity of its receptors. These motoneurons are called **gamma efferents**, or gamma motoneurons, to distinguish them from the faster-conducting **alpha motoneurons**, which go to extrafusal muscle fibers (see Figure 11.10c). The cell bodies of gamma efferents are found in the ventral horns of the spinal cord. The gamma efferent axon fibers connect to a contractile region of the spindle (called the myotube region). The activity in the gamma fibers causes a change in the length and tension of the spindle, which modifies its sensitivity to changes in the length of adjacent extrafusal muscle fibers. Hence the number of impulses elicited in the spindle afferents is a function of two factors: (1) muscle stretch, and (2) the resting tension in the muscle spindle.

How do the gamma efferents help coordinate movements? Suppose that instead of continuing to hold your arm out straight ahead, you move your forearm up and down. If the muscle spindle had only one fixed degree of internal tension, it could not help monitor and coordinate this movement. As the forearm moves up, the extrafusal and intrafusal fibers both shorten. Shortening the spindle, as we have noted, removes the tension, so the sensory endings should no longer respond. But the real situation is more complicated and more effective. As the muscle shortens, the gamma efferents must correspondingly increase the tension on the intrafusal fibers, if they are to maintain their sensitivity. One reflection of the importance of the gamma efferent system is the fact that about 30% of all efferent fibers are gamma efferents (the rest being alpha motoneurons).

The muscle spindles are responsive primarily to *stretch;* the other receptors that respond to muscle tension—Golgi tendon organs—are especially sensitive to muscle *contraction* or shortening. Golgi tendon organs are rather insensitive to passive muscle stretch because they are connected in series with an elastic component. They detect overloads that threaten to tear muscles and tendons. Stimulation of these receptors inhibits the muscles that pull on the tendon and thus, by relaxing the tension, prevents mechanical damage.

Movements Are Controlled at Several Nervous System Levels

The nerve cells directly responsible for excitation of muscle are the motoneurons in the ventral region of the spinal cord and in the brain stem nuclei of several cranial nerves. (See Figures 2.11 and 2.12 for the anatomy of the spinal cord and cranial nerves.) This is the simplest level in the neural control of motoneurons. Firing patterns of these cells determine the onset, coordination, and termination of muscle activity. To understand the physiology of movement, we need to know the source of the inputs to motoneurons. A variety of influences converge on the motoneurons. Some arise solely at a spinal level from muscle afferents and the intrinsic circuitry of the spinal cord. Other influences are directed to motor cells from several brain pathways. This is another reason that spinal and cranial motoneurons are called the final common pathway.

Spinal reflexes.　One way to study spinal mechanisms is to sever the connections between the brain and spinal cord (producing a spinal animal) and then observe the forms of behavior that can be elicited below the level of the cut. (All voluntary movements that depend on brain mechanisms are lost, of course, as is sensation from the regions below the cut.) Immediately after the cord is severed, there is an interval of decreased synaptic excitability in spinal cord neurons because they are isolated from brain communication. This condition is known as **spinal shock**. The period may last for months in humans, although for cats and dogs, it may last only a few hours. During this period no reflexes mediated by the spinal cord can be elicited by either skin stimulation or excitation of muscle afferents.

As spinal shock fades, various kinds of reflexes can be elicited; their properties help us understand the basic functional organization of the spinal cord. The spinal animal can show various stretch reflexes that may function well enough to support the weight of a standing animal for brief periods. Stimulation of the skin of a spinal animal can also elicit reflex effects, which can be readily demonstrated in a spinal cat or dog with intense stimulation of the toe pad. This stimulation results in abrupt withdrawal of the stimulated limb, a response called the **flexion reflex**. Unlike the stretch reflex, which involves a monosynaptic pathway, as we'll see in the next section, the flexion reflex involves a multisynaptic pathway within the

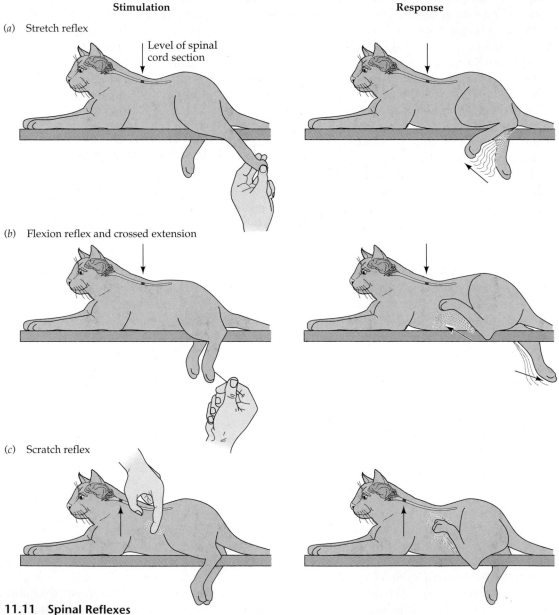

Stimulation   Response

(a) Stretch reflex

Level of spinal cord section

(b) Flexion reflex and crossed extension

(c) Scratch reflex

11.11 Spinal Reflexes
The site where the spinal cord was cut is shown in red. (*a*) Stretching the hind limb evokes muscle contraction to oppose the stretch. (*b*) Noxious stimulation of the pad elicits hind limb flexion on the same side of the stimulation and extension of the opposite hind limb. (The animal feels no pain because the brain never receives a pain signal from the foot). (*c*) Scratching the flank below the level of section elicits accurate, rhythmic scratching movements.

spinal cord. Other reflexive behaviors evident in the spinal animal include bladder emptying and penile erection. Thus, some very basic properties of movement are "wired in" to the organization of the spinal cord itself and do not require the brain (Figure 11.11).

The behavior of the spinal animal also reveals the presence of pattern generator circuits in the spinal cord, which we'll describe at the end of this chapter. For example, mechanical stimulation of the feet or electrical stimulation of the spinal cord can elicit rhythmic movements of the legs. If the cut is high on the spinal cord, the alternating movements of the limbs are coordinated as in walking; this coordination indicates that the pattern generators for the different limbs are linked within the spinal cord (Grillner, Hill, and Grillner, 1991).

Spinal reflexes do not usually function in isolation. They are integrated and modulated by the activity of brain circuits. Control of movements involves **selective potentiation** of spinal neural circuits; that is, activity of certain spinal circuits is enhanced by the brain, while the activity of other spinal circuits is inhibited.

The stretch reflex. A good example of automatic control at the spinal level is the **stretch reflex**—the contraction that results when a muscle stretches. The physiological condition for muscle stretch can be readily understood under conditions of an imposed weight or load. For example, in Figure 11.12 a weight (disturbance) added to the hand imposes sudden stretch on muscle 1 (M1). Such a disturbance can be imposed on many joints simply by the weight of the body. The circuit that keeps us from dropping the load or simply falling from the weight of our body is one that links muscle spindles and the relevant muscles. The simplest depiction of the events portrayed in Figure 11.12 is the following (parts 1 to 3 we already saw when we described the activity of the muscle spindle):

1. A disturbance is imposed.

2. The muscle is stretched.

3. Muscle spindle afferent elements are excited.

4. Excitatory synaptic potentials in motoneurons are produced by muscle spindle afferents. (These afferents connect directly—that is, monosynaptically—to the motoneurons that control the stretched muscle.)

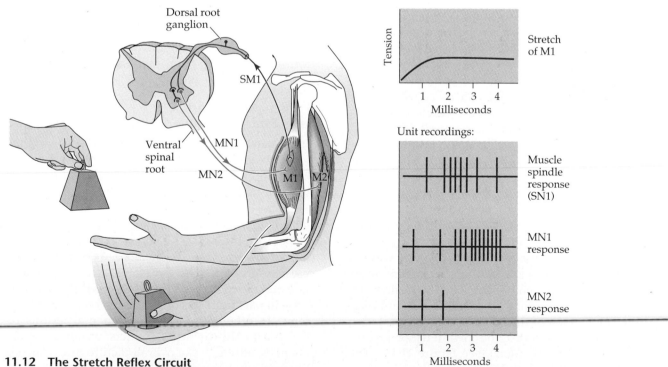

11.12   The Stretch Reflex Circuit
MN1 is the motor nerve to muscle 1 (M1) and MN2 is the motor nerve to muscle 2 (M2), an antagonist to muscle 1. SN1 is the sensory nerve from the muscle spindle of M1. Characteristic responses at different stages in the circuit are shown at right.

5. The muscle is stimulated by motoneuron output, contracting to oppose muscle stretch.

This sequence describes a simple negative feedback system that tends to restore the limb to its "desired" position. Additional influences exerted by the activation of the muscle spindle system include the inhibition of the motoneurons supplying the antagonistic muscle (M2). Two synapses are involved. Thus, in the situation illustrated in Figure 11.12, spindle information terminates on the interneuron whose output goes to the motoneuron supplying M2, at which junction inhibitory postsynaptic activity is produced. During this action, then, the spindle excites the stretched muscle (and its synergists) and inhibits the antagonistic muscles. The relaxation of antagonistic muscles ensures that they are not injured by the sudden movement. A familiar example of the stretch reflex is the knee jerk used in medical examinations to test the integrity of a neural circuit (see Figure 5.14).

Pathways from the Brain Control Different Aspects of Movements

Pathways from the brain to cranial and spinal motoneurons are many and complex (Figure 11.13). Complex movements clearly involve programs of the brain, which are a major focus of research. (Refer to Figure 11.5 to review the relations of major brain regions associated with the control of movement.) Some pathways deliver discrete information; for example, the vestibulospinal tract provides important information about head position, and this information influences postural muscles to effect body adjustments.

Ideas about the different roles of each pathway in integrating and controlling movement have relied heavily on observations of changes in posture and locomotion produced by natural or experimental interferences in these regions. Clinical data from people with brain damage have generated useful anatomical and functional distinctions between two major divisions of the motor system: the pyramidal and extrapyramidal motor systems.

The **pyramidal system** (or corticospinal system) refers to neuron cell bodies within the cerebral cortex and their axons, which pass through the brain stem, forming the pyramidal tract to the spinal cord (Figure 11.13a). Many of these cell bodies are located in the primary motor cortex, the cortical region just anterior to the central sulcus (see Figure 11.14). The pyramidal tract is most clearly seen where it passes through the anterior aspect of the medulla. In a cross section of the medulla, the tract is a wedge-shaped anterior protuberance (pyramid) on each side of the midline. The pyramidal tract consists of large-diameter (and therefore fast-conducting) axons and is a relatively recent development in evolution. It has been likened to a superhighway pushed through after the network of local routes had been established.

In addition to the corticospinal outflow through the pyramidal tract, many other motor tracts run from the brain to the brain stem and spinal cord. Since these tracts are outside of the pyramids of the medulla, they and their connections are called the **extrapyramidal system**.

Brain Stem Nuclei and Tracts Control Movements

Several brain stem components are critical for the control of movements. First, scattered throughout this region are cranial motor nuclei whose axons innervate muscles of the head and neck (Figure 11.13b). Second, pathways originating at higher levels course through the brain stem and, in some cases, connect to regions in the brain stem. Finally, within the brain stem the extensive pool of interconnected neurons called the reticular formation modulates various aspects of movements. Some zones of the reticular formation facilitate movements; other zones are inhibitory. These effects are transmitted in descending tracts known as **reticulospinal tracts** that arise from the reticular formation and connect to spinal interneurons, where they influence the excitability of spinal motor circuitry. Some neurons of the reticular formation also help regulate the activation of muscles responsible for breathing.

Primary Motor Cortex Is an Executive Motor Control Mechanism

In humans, brain injuries involving the primary motor cortex produce partial paralysis on the side of the body opposite the brain lesion. This disturbance is greatest in distal muscles, such as those of the hand. Humans with these lesions are generally "disinclined" to use the affected limb.

Because human lesions arise from accidental injury or disease, they are usually not limited to a single neural system. The symptoms of corticospinal injury and the complexity of the observed changes may arise in part from loss of adjacent motor control systems. In other primates, experimental lesions restricted to the pyramidal tracts produce similar changes, although the overall picture is less severe. Six weeks following the bilateral interruption of the pyramidal tracts, monkeys can run, climb, and reach accurately for food. The persistent deficits they display are a limited ability in individual finger move-

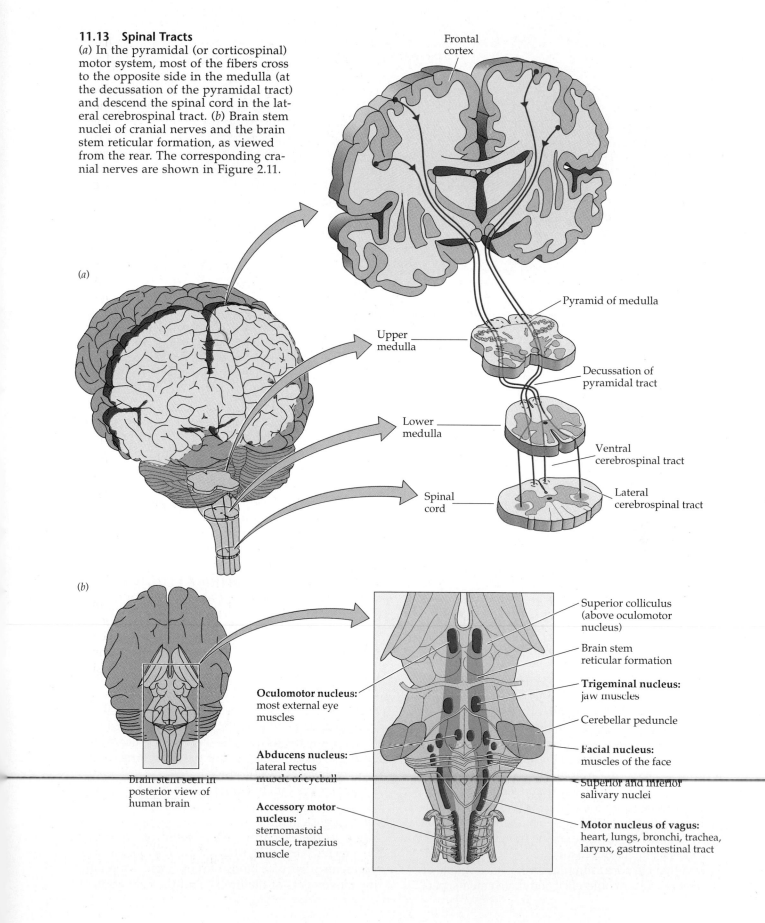

11.13 Spinal Tracts

(*a*) In the pyramidal (or corticospinal) motor system, most of the fibers cross to the opposite side in the medulla (at the decussation of the pyramidal tract) and descend the spinal cord in the lateral cerebrospinal tract. (*b*) Brain stem nuclei of cranial nerves and the brain stem reticular formation, as viewed from the rear. The corresponding cranial nerves are shown in Figure 2.11.

Frontal cortex

Pyramid of medulla

Upper medulla

Decussation of pyramidal tract

Lower medulla

Ventral cerebrospinal tract

Spinal cord

Lateral cerebrospinal tract

Brain stem seen in posterior view of human brain

Superior colliculus (above oculomotor nucleus)

Brain stem reticular formation

Oculomotor nucleus: most external eye muscles

Trigeminal nucleus: jaw muscles

Cerebellar peduncle

Abducens nucleus: lateral rectus muscle of eyeball

Facial nucleus: muscles of the face

Superior and inferior salivary nuclei

Accessory motor nucleus: sternomastoid muscle, trapezius muscle

Motor nucleus of vagus: heart, lungs, bronchi, trachea, larynx, gastrointestinal tract

(a)

Central sulcus

Primary motor cortex

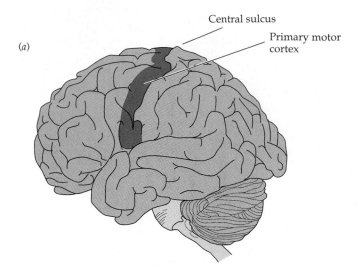

(c)

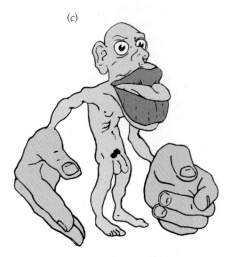

(b)

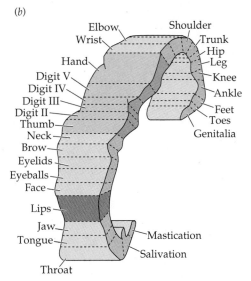

Elbow
Wrist
Hand
Digit V
Digit IV
Digit III
Digit II
Thumb
Neck
Brow
Eyelids
Eyeballs
Face
Lips
Jaw
Tongue
Throat

Shoulder
Trunk
Hip
Leg
Knee
Ankle
Feet
Toes
Genitalia

Mastication
Salivation

11.14 Human Primary Motor Cortex
(a) Lateral view of the human brain, showing the location of primary motor cortex. (b) The sequence and sizes of regions controlling motor responses of different parts of the body. (c) The proportions of this homunculus show the relative sizes of motor representations of parts of the body.

ments and an overall tendency for slower-than-normal movements, which rapidly "fatigue." Although they have difficulty releasing food from the hand, they can readily release their grip while climbing. In mammals other than primates, the impairments following pyramidal lesions are even less severe.

What do the differences in these deficits mean in terms of the overall role of the corticospinal system? This problem has plagued many investigators, and definitive answers have not yet been found. In attempts to provide answers, investigators have made recordings from pyramidal cells during various movements and have closely examined the anatomical relations between the motor cortex and other levels of movement control systems. We will consider briefly some of the ideas emerging from these studies.

In the late nineteenth century, several experimenters showed that electrical stimulation of some regions of the cerebral cortex could elicit body movements, par-

ticularly flexion of the limbs. These early findings—and other converging experiments—have helped scientists to develop maps of movements elicited by cortical stimulation. A map of the human motor cortex is shown in Figure 11.14. The largest motor regions in these maps are devoted to the most elaborate and complex movements in any species. For example, humans and other primates have extremely large cortical fields concerned with hand movements. More recent studies have shown that "colonies" of cells are related to particular muscle groups, and they seem to form vertical columns in the cortex (Ghez, Hening, and Gordon, 1991), an organizational principle similar to that of cortical sensory systems (see Chapter 10). About one-third of the human pyramidal tract fibers originate in the so-called motor area of the cortex. Another one-fifth come from the postcentral gyrus (somatosensory cortex). The remaining pyramidal fibers arise from many other cortical regions. Thus control of motor function is dispersed among cortical areas, leading to controversies about the boundaries of the primary motor cortex (Rothwell, 1994).

Converging data from clinical observations, studies involving motor cortex stimulation, and PET scans suggest that the motor cortex–pyramidal tract system is the executive mechanism for voluntary movements. According to this view, the motor cortex represents particular kinds of movement, especially fine movements of the limbs, and the activation of

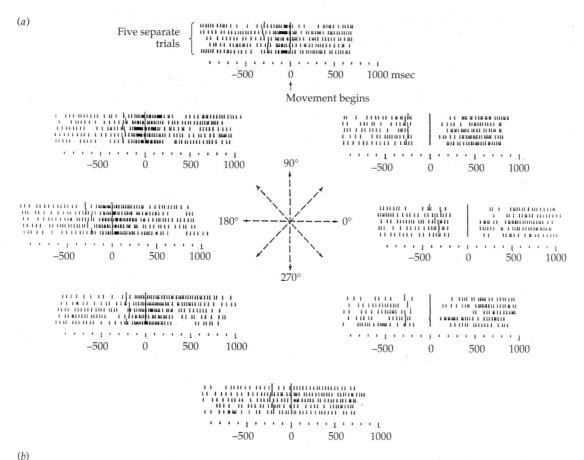

(a)

Five separate trials

−500   0   500   1000 msec

Movement begins

−500   0   500   1000

−500   0   500   1000

90°

180°   0°

270°

−500   0   500   1000

−500   0   500   1000

−500   0   500   1000

−500   0   500   1000

−500   0   500   1000

(b)

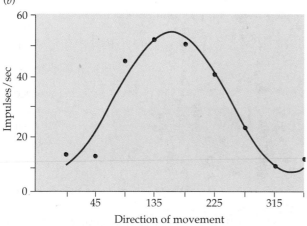

11.15 Directional Tuning of Motor Cortex Cells

(*a*) Neural activity of a neuron during arm movement in one of eight directions on five separate trials. Note that this cell consistently fires before the arm moves in the direction between 90° to 180° to 270°, and is silent before movements in the other directions. (*b*) The average frequency of discharge during the interval before movement in the various directions. From Georgopoulos et al., 1982.

these cells commands the excitation of rele- vant spinal and cranial motoneurons. In primates the pyramidal tract does have some monosynaptic con- nections with spinal motoneurons, particularly those relevant to the control of distal segments of the upper limbs (the hands, wrist, and fingers). However, most pyramidal tract neurons influence spinal motoneur- ons through polysynaptic routes and share control of these motor cells with other descending influences.

The functional properties of motor cortex neurons have been studied by recording from these cells dur- ing movements. In some experiments monkeys are trained to make particular movements such as reach- ing or pressing levers, while activity from single mo- tor cortex cells is monitored (Evarts, Shinoda, and Wise, 1984). For some types of movement—especial- ly those involving gross movements of a limb, in con- trast to the fine movements of a hand—it is very dif- ficult to see a relationship between the firing pattern of a single cell and measures of movement. Geor- gopoulos has focused on the properties of *populations* of motor cortex neurons (see Georgopoulos, Taira, and Lukashin, 1993). He recorded from the motor cortex neurons of monkeys that were trained to make free arm movements in eight possible target direc- tions (Figure 11.15*a*). Many cells changed their firing rates according to the direction of the movement, and for any one cell, discharge rates were highest in a particular direction (Figure 11.15*b*). Although different cells prefer different directions, each cell carries only partial information about the direction of reaching. When the activity of several hundred neurons is combined, their overall vector shows a good relation to the actual direction of the reaching arm. Given the millions of neurons in this region, a larger sampling would presumably provide an even more accurate prediction (Georgopoulos et al., 1993).

Nonprimary Motor Cortex Aids Learned Responses

Recordings of single nonprimary motor cortex neurons in awake monkeys have shown that many nerve cells in nonprimary motor cortex change their discharge rate just before the onset of conditioned movements, such as pressing a key in response to a sensory stimulus. Some nerve cells in these regions also respond to a sensory stimulus without evidence of elicited movement (Wise and Strick, 1984). Such data suggest that these regions are involved in the sensory guidance of movements. Records from single neurons also reveal that the nonprimary motor cortical areas are especially active during the preparation of skilled movements.

Nonprimary motor cortex consists of two main regions: the **supplementary motor cortex**, which lies mainly on the medial aspect of the hemisphere, and the **premotor cortex**, which is anterior to the primary motor cortex (Figure 11.16). The supplementary motor cortex receives input from the basal ganglia, and the premotor cortex receives input from the cerebellum. In the sections that follow we will discuss the roles of the basal ganglia and the cerebellum in modulating movements.

Patients with unilateral lesions of premotor cortex retain fine motor control of the fingers but are impaired in the stability of stance and gait and in the coordination of the two hands. Patients with bilateral damage to the supplementary motor cortex are unable to move or speak voluntarily, although some automatic and reflex movements remain. These long-lasting effects suggest that this region is involved in the conception and initiation of movement (Freund, 1984).

Studies of localized cerebral blood flow and metabolism reveal important aspects of cortical motor control (Roland, 1980, 1984). In simple tasks, such as keeping a spring compressed between two fingers of one hand, blood flow increases markedly in the hand area of the opposite primary motor cortex and in the adjacent somatosensory area. Increasing the complexity of motor tasks extends the area of blood flow increase to the supplementary motor cortex. Finally, when the subjects mentally *rehearse* the complex movement sequence, the enhanced blood flow is restricted to the supplementary motor cortex.

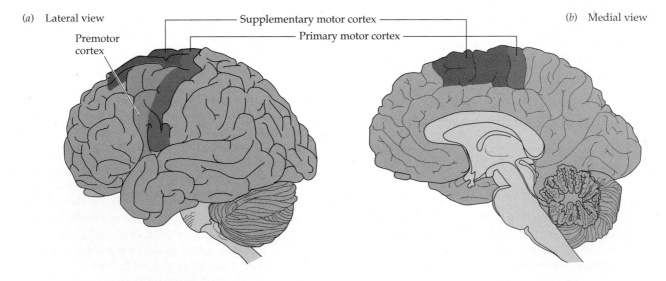

(a) Lateral view   Supplementary motor cortex   *(b)* Medial view
Premotor cortex   Primary motor cortex

11.16   Human Motor Cortical Areas
The primary motor cortex (pink) lies just anterior to the central sulcus. Anterior to the primary motor cortex are the premotor cortex (green) and the supplementary motor cortex (purple), which together make up the nonprimary motor cortex.

These data illustrate the significance of nonprimary motor cortex in governing complex motor activities. Presumably the activities of these areas are integrated with those of the primary motor cortex to produce coordinated behavior.

The Basal Ganglia Modulate Movements

The **basal ganglia** include a group of forebrain nuclei—the caudate, putamen, and globus pallidus. Closely associated with these structures are some nuclei in the midbrain—the substantia nigra and subthalamic nucleus. The locations and major connections of these structures are shown in Figure 11.17. The term **striatum** refers to the caudate nucleus and putamen together. Each of these structures has subcomponents whose characteristics and connections have been described in detail (Graybiel, 1995). These structures receive input from wide areas of the cerebral cortex and send much of their output right back to the cerebral cortex in what can be described as a

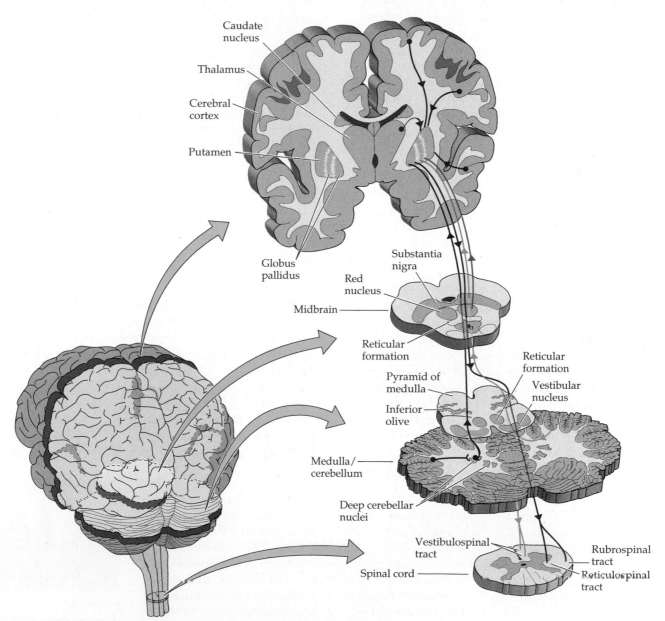

11.17　The Basal Ganglia, Cerebellum, and Their Connections
Final commands are delivered to the spinal cord via several tracts, including the rubrospinal, reticulospinal, and vestibulospinal tracts indicated here.

cortex–basal ganglia–cortex loop. Lesions of these regions in humans produce movement impairments that seem quite different from those following interruption of the pyramidal system. We will discuss these impairments later in the chapter.

Inputs to the basal ganglia come from an extensive region of the cerebral cortex, as well as from thalamic nuclei and the substantia nigra. The sources of inputs suggest a subdivision of the basal ganglia into two major systems. One includes the caudate nucleus, whose inputs are especially derived from frontal association cortex. The other system includes the putamen; inputs to this system are from sensorimotor cortical zones. Lesions within these subdivisions have different effects (DeLong et al., 1984). Lesions of the caudate impair relatively complex behavior, as, for example, in dealing with spatial aspects of behavior—*where* to respond. In contrast, the effects of lesions in the putamen are more exclusively motor, affecting the strength and rate of response, rather than the direction of response.

Animal studies of the basal ganglia use both lesions and recordings of single neurons during motor responses (DeLong et al., 1984). Each structure of the basal ganglia contains a topographic representation of body musculature. Studies suggest that the basal ganglia may play a role in determining the amplitude and direction of movement rather than affecting the initiation of actions. The basal ganglia networks thus seem to modulate the patterns of activity initiated in other brain circuits that control movements, such as motor and premotor cortical systems (see Figure 11.5). Experiments also indicate that basal ganglia are especially important in the generation of movements influenced by memories, in contrast to those guided by sensory control (Evarts, Shinoda, and Wise, 1984). This point is also emphasized by Graybiel and colleagues (1994), who indicate that the multiple loops that connect the basal ganglia and neocortex are important in sensorimotor learning.

The Cerebellum Affects Programs, Timing, and Coordination of Acts

The cerebellum in higher vertebrates is a sheet with many folds (see Figure 2.24). This brain structure is found in almost all vertebrates. In some vertebrate groups its size varies according to the range and complexity of movements. For example, the cerebellum is much larger in fish with extensive locomotor behavior than it is in less active fish; it is also large in flying birds, as compared with bird species that do not fly.

The cell types and basic circuitry of the cerebellum are shown in Figure 11.18a and b. Recall that the out-

11.18   Cerebellar Circuitry   ▶
(*a*) A folium of the cerebellum. (*b*) The basic neural circuits of the cerebellum. All Purkinje cells project to the deep cerebellar nuclei, which project to the rest of the brain. (*c*) A model for the modification of Purkinje cell activity. Simultaneous activation of the parallel fibers and the climbing fibers results in a reduced Purkinje response to parallel fibers up to 30 minutes later. *c* after Ito, 1987.

er layers of the cerebellum are called the cerebellar cortex and are dominated by a sheet of large multipolar cells called Purkinje cells. All output of the cerebellar cortex travels via the axons of Purkinje cells, all of which synapse with the deep cerebellar nuclei. At this synapse they produce only postsynaptic inhibitory potentials. Hence, all the circuitry of the extensive cortical portion of the cerebellum, which also includes 10 to 20 billion granule cells in humans, acts to inhibit motor cells.

Inputs to the cerebellar cortex are derived from both sensory sources and other brain motor systems. Sensory inputs include the muscle and joint receptors, and the vestibular, somatosensory, visual, and auditory systems. Both pyramidal and nonpyramidal pathways contribute inputs to the cerebellum and in turn receive outputs from the deep nuclei of the cerebellum. Thus, the cerebellum receives elaborate information both from systems that monitor movements and from systems that execute movements. For this reason the cerebellum has long been believed to play a role in the feedback control of movements. It has also been suggested that the cerebellum elaborates neural "programs" for the control of skilled movements, particularly rapid, repeated movements that become automatic. This role of the cerebellum in the acquisition and retention of learned motor responses will be discussed in Chapter 18.

Various theories and experiments have suggested that cerebellar circuitry includes memorylike devices that might be important for motor learning. Ito (1987) has described a long-term depression of Purkinje cell activity that occurs when both the climbing fiber and parallel fiber inputs to these cells are stimulated to-

Masao Ito

gether (Figure 11.18c). The depression of firing can last as long as one hour. This kind of memory change in

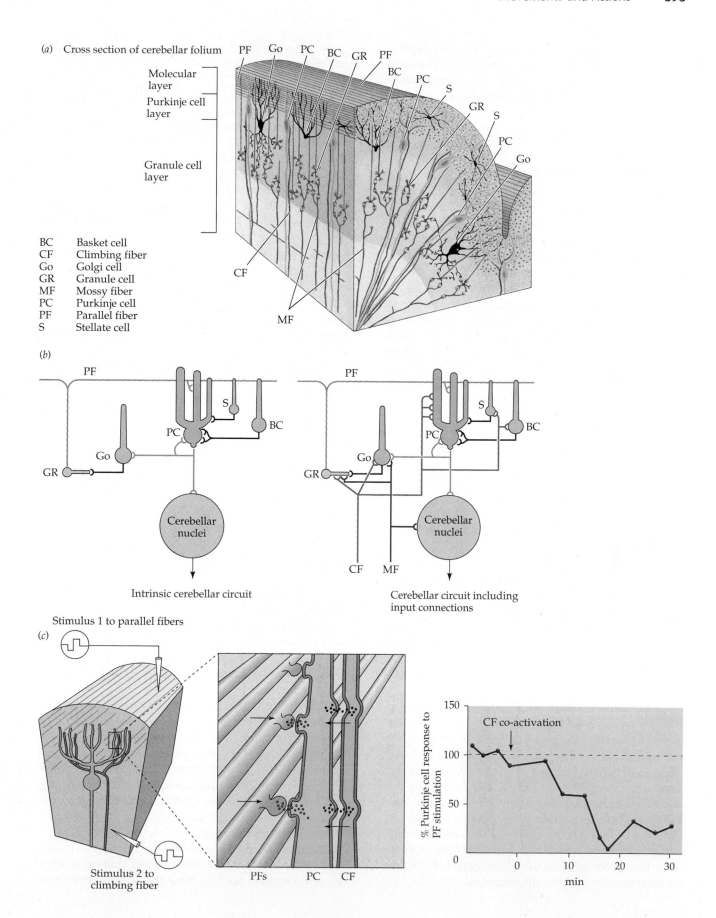

(a) Cross section of cerebellar folium

Molecular layer
Purkinje cell layer
Granule cell layer

BC   Basket cell
CF   Climbing fiber
Go   Golgi cell
GR   Granule cell
MF   Mossy fiber
PC   Purkinje cell
PF   Parallel fiber
S   Stellate cell

(b)

Intrinsic cerebellar circuit

Cerebellar circuit including input connections

(c)

Stimulus 1 to parallel fibers

Stimulus 2 to climbing fiber

PFs   PC   CF

CF co-activation

% Purkinje cell response to PF stimulation

the cerebellar cortex might be important for adaptive changes that involve interactions between the vestibular and visual systems, such as those that accompany the changing orientation of the head.

Human Movement Disorders

Some Muscle Disorders Are Inherited

Many metabolic conditions can affect the chemistry and structure of muscle. In Chapter 7 we noted that several hormones—especially thyroid hormones—affect muscle chemistry and function. Chronically low levels of thyroid hormone produce muscle weakness and slowness of muscle contraction. Several muscle diseases are particularly mysterious, seemingly involving biochemical abnormalities that lead to structural changes in muscle; these disorders are referred to as **muscular dystrophy**. As the name implies, a symptom that the various muscular dystrophies share is the wasting away of muscles. Many muscular dystrophies are hereditary; because of recent advancements, Duchenne's muscular dystrophy is the best understood.

Duchenne's muscular dystrophy strikes almost exclusively boys, beginning at the age of about four to six years and leading to death within a decade. Pedigrees suggested that the disorder is a simple Mendelian trait—caused by a single gene, in this case carried on the X chromosome. When researchers began examining the X chromosomes in members of families afflicted with the disorder, they found that a single gene was indeed abnormal in all the boys carrying the disorder, and on one of the two X chromosomes carried by their mother, but was normal in the fathers and in all unafflicted brothers. The gene and its normal protein product were named **dystrophin**. In some ways the name is unfortunate, because this is the protein that, when

normal, does *not* lead to dystrophy. Dystrophin is normally produced in muscle cells and may play a role in regulating internal calcium (Ca^{2+}) stores. Because females have two X chromosomes, even if one carries the defective copy of the dystrophin gene, the other X chromosome can still produce normal dystrophin. But about half the sons of such females will receive the defective gene and be afflicted with the disease. No one knows why the defective dystrophin protein shows no effects during the first few years of life. Mice with a mutation in this gene also show normal muscle function early in life and dystrophy in adulthood, but unlike humans with Duchenne's dystrophy, the mice recover without intervention.

Results from studies of the gene that produces dystrophin suggest a very promising therapy for Duchenne's muscular dystrophy. Since females who carry the defective gene on only one of their X chromo- somes are unafflicted by the disease, administering dystrophin protein to afflicted boys may enable their muscles to function properly. The fact that muscles are particularly willing to accept new genes facilitates such treatment; sometimes the mere injection of messenger RNA causes muscle cells to translate the RNA and produce the protein for a while (Barr et al., 1991). Other gene therapies may lead to the permanent establishment of a functional dystrophin gene in the muscles of Duchenne's patients.

The Immune System May Attack Neuromuscular Junctions

Movement disorders involving the neuromuscular junction include a variety of reversible poison states. For example, snake bites can cause neuromuscular blocks because the venom of some highly poisonous snakes contains substances (such as bungarotoxin, which we discussed in Chapter 6) that block postsynaptic receptor sites for acetylcholine. Studies on the mechanisms of action of this venom have led directly to an understanding of one of the more debilitating neuromuscular disorders, **myasthenia gravis** (from the Greek *mys*, "muscle," and *asthenes*, "weak"; and the Latin *gravis*, "grave" or "serious"). This is a disorder characterized by a profound weakness of skeletal muscles. The disease often first affects the muscles of the head, producing symptoms such as drooping of the eyelids, double vision, and slowing of speech. In later stages paralysis of the muscles involved in swallowing and respiration can become life-threatening.

Physiological studies of myasthenia gravis have shown abnormalities in synaptic transmission (Rowland, 1987). The main defect observed in these studies is a reduction in end-plate potentials recorded at the neuromuscular junction. Studies by Drachman (1983) showed that the neuromuscular junctions of myasthenic patients had a markedly reduced number of acetylcholine receptor sites. In addition, these junctions in patients are flattened and simplified in comparison to normal synaptic junctions. These changes at the neuromuscular synapse result in much less effective transmission, and presynaptic action potentials are frequently unable to trigger postsynaptic muscle action potentials.

Basic research in animals and continuing studies in human patients have established that antibodies directed against acetylcholine receptors cause these changes. Apparently myasthenic patients spontaneously develop these antibodies, which attack their own postsynaptic membranes. Serum taken from patients and injected into animals can produce the same effect. Cells in the thymus may generate the anti-acetylcholine receptor antibody (Engel, 1984), and there is clinical evidence that removal of the thymus helps patients. Temporary depletion of antibodies by filtering the plasma from blood of patients—a procedure called plasmapheresis—is another successful clinical intervention.

Some Motor Impairments Reflect Pathology of the Spinal Cord

Pathological changes in motoneurons also produce movement paralysis or weakness. Virus-induced destruction of motoneurons—for example, by the disease polio—was once a frightening prospect, especially in the United States and western Europe. Polio viruses destroy motoneurons of the spinal cord and, in more severe types, cranial motoneurons of the brain stem. Since the muscles can no longer be called upon to contract, they atrophy.

War, sports, and accidents cause many forms of human spinal injuries that result in motor impairment. Injuries to the human spinal cord commonly develop from forces to the neck or back that break bone and compress the spinal cord. Sudden acceleration of the head with respect to the back, such as occurs in car accidents, can also injure the spinal cord.

If the spinal cord is severed completely, immediate paralysis results, and reflexes below the level of injury are lost—a condition known as **flaccid paralysis.** Flaccid paralysis generally occurs only when a considerable stretch of the spinal cord has been destroyed. When the injury severs the spinal cord without causing widespread destruction of tissue, reflexes below the level of injury frequently become excessive because the intact tissue lacks the dampening influence of brain inhibitory pathways.

In many spinal injuries, the spinal cord is not severed but is bruised or compressed. Physiological changes in the spinal cord after injury, such as the buildup of calcium or excitotoxic transmitters, vastly amplify the direct effects of an accident. Inflammatory states such as swelling, hemorrhaging, and a sharp drop in blood flow accentuate the injury. Drugs are used to limit the spreading effects of injury. For example, the fact that endorphins released at the time of injury seem to contribute to the intensity of acute trauma led investigators to try administering endorphin blockers to experimental animals at the time of injury; they found that this treatment limits the long-term effects of spinal trauma. Other drugs, given shortly after a spinal injury, limit the secondary consequences of spinal cord injury, helping restore movement more quickly.

The hope of reconnecting the injured spinal cord no longer seems as far-fetched as it did a few years ago. Investigators working on the spinal cord of lampreys have shown that months after the spinal cord is severed, these animals can swim again (Cohen et al., 1989). Anatomical studies on lampreys using marker dyes have demonstrated that axons grow across the surgical gap in the spinal cord. In rats and cats, axon sprouting is seen at the site of spinal trauma and may mediate some aspects of spinal reflex recovery (Goldberger and Murray, 1985). In rats, implants of peripheral nerve or fetal nervous tissue into the gap produced by injury to the spinal cord promote anatomical indications of reconnection of the cord (Bernstein-Goral and Bregman, 1993). These observations buoy the hope that regeneration is possible in the injured human spinal cord. Perhaps the accuracy of the regenerative process in humans with spinal injury can be controlled by using grafts of nerve tissue as "guide wires." The use of enzymes to prevent scar formation might also remove an obstacle to adaptive forms of reconnection in the injured human spinal cord. Putting the spinal cord back together after injury would render obsolete the wheelchairs that today signal a tragic limitation in rehabilitation.

Some Motor Impairments Reflect Pathology of the Brain Stem

In the late 1930s the sad end of the brilliant baseball career of New York Yankees star Lou Gehrig brought public awareness to an unusual degenerative disorder in which the motoneurons of the brain stem and spinal cord are destroyed and their target muscles waste away. This syndrome is formally known as **amyotrophic lateral sclerosis** (**ALS**), although journalists more commonly refer to it as Lou Gehrig's disease. The plight of the late Senator Jacob Javits (1904–1986) drew attention to the personal struggles that accompany this disease, which progressively paralyzes a person while leaving their intellectual abilities intact. Characteristic symptoms at the start of the disorder depend on the level of the nervous system at which motoneuron destruction begins (Tandan and Bradley, 1985). The origins of the disease remain a mystery, but a wide range of causal factors are under investigation, including premature aging, toxic minerals, viruses, immune responses, and endocrine dysfunction.

About 10% of ALS cases are hereditary; that is, there is a clear family history of the disease which indicates that gene defects are involved. The pedigrees of several afflicted families indicate a single gene disorder. The particular gene has been isolated (Andersen et al., 1995) and found to encode an enzyme—copper/zinc superoxide dismutase—that can convert highly reactive compounds (carrying what chemists call a free radical) into more ordinary compounds that can react in only a few ways. Some investigators speculate that this enzyme protects the muscles and/or motoneurons from the cellular damage that free radicals might cause. Thus, the nonhereditary cases of ALS might stem from the buildup of similar damage from other sources, and this damage may accumulate despite the efforts of such enzymes. But this plausible hypothesis appears to have been disproved by an experimental test. When scientists produced transgenic mice that, in addition to their own normal copies of the enzyme, carry a copy of the defective 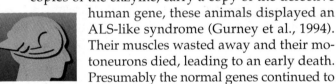 human gene, these animals displayed an ALS-like syndrome (Gurney et al., 1994). Their muscles wasted away and their motoneurons died, leading to an early death. Presumably the normal genes continued to protect these animals from free radical damage, yet they succumbed to the disease. Thus the abnormal gene may actively damage part of the neuromuscular system. These molecular genetic changes may also lead to high levels of the transmitter glutamate (Dean, 1994). In high concentrations this excitatory amino acid can cause neurons to die.

Some Motor Impairments Reflect Pathology of the Cerebral Cortex

Motor impairments that follow strokes or injury to the human cerebral cortex are familiar to clinical investigators. The most common change is a paralysis or partial paralysis (paresis) of voluntary movements on one side of the body, usually the result of injury to the cerebral cortex of the hemisphere opposite to the side of the body displaying symptoms. In addition, there is some spasticity, especially increased rigidity in response to forced movement of the limbs. The spasticity reflects the exaggeration of stretch reflexes. Abnormal reflexes occur, such as the flaring and extension of the toes elicited by stroking the sole of the foot (the Babinski reflex). In the months following cerebral cortical injury, the clinical picture changes. The initial paralysis slowly diminishes, with some return of voluntary movements of the proximal portion of limbs, although fine motor control of fingers is seldom regained. As we noted previously, in humans the symptoms are more severe than in many other mammals.

Damage to nonmotor zones of the cerebral cortex, such as some regions of parietal or frontal association cortex, produces more complicated changes in motor control. Box 11.2 describes one such condition—**apraxia**.

Parkinson's Disease Reflects Impoverished Movement Resulting from Lack of Stimulation of the Basal Ganglia

Diseases of the basal ganglia can produce a variety of effects, some almost opposite to others. Some disorders reflect release from the constraints that the basal ganglia usually impose on motor control. In the absence of these constraints, the activity initiated by other brain regions appears unchecked and yields dramatic, persistent excesses of movement. Other basal ganglia disorders produce slowness of movement and marked changes in muscle tone.

Almost 200 years ago, physician James Parkinson noted a small group of patients on the streets of London who moved quite slowly, showed regular tremors of the hands and face while at rest, and walked with a rigid bearing. Another feature of what is now known as **Parkinson's disease** is a loss of facial muscle tone, which gives the face a masklike appearance. Parkinson's patients also show few spontaneous actions and have great difficulty in all motor efforts, no matter how routine. These changes are progressive and may take years to reach a maximally disabled state.

Parkinson's patients show progressive degeneration of dopamine-containing cells in the substantia nigra of the brain. The loss of cells in this area is continuous; symptoms appear only after a major loss (Figure 11.19). The causes of this disorder remain a mystery, although the discovery of a form of the disorder induced by illicit drugs (described in Box 11.3) has suggested to some researchers that subtle exposures to toxins over a prolonged period may underlie the development of the disorder (Tetrud et al., 1994).

For years, there was no treatment for Parkinson's disease. A pharmacological therapy emerged from the discovery in the late 1960s that these patients show a loss of dopamine levels in the substantia nigra, which projects to the corpus striatum. This treatment was the administration of a precursor to dopamine to enhance the dopamine levels of surviving cells. This substance, called L-dopa, markedly reduces symptoms in Parkinson's patients, including a decrease in tremor and an increase in the speed of movements.

Box 11.2
Sometimes I Can Move, Sometimes I Can't

A patient is seated in front of an examiner who is assessing the impact of a recent stroke. Simple inquiries reveal a startling deficit. When asked to smile our patient is unable, although he certainly attempts to. If asked to use a comb placed in front of him, he seems unable to figure out what to do. But things aren't as simple as they might appear. At one point in the discussion our patient spontaneously smiles, and at another point he retrieves a comb from his pocket and combs his hair with ease and accuracy. Our

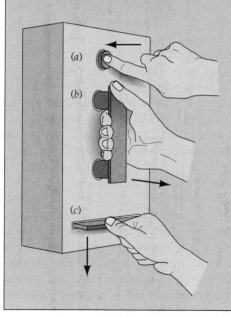

patient is displaying a syndrome called apraxia (from the *a*, "not," and *praxis*, "action"). Apraxia is the inability to carry out certain acts even though paralysis or weakness is not evident and comprehension and motivation are intact. Apraxia was first described by the nineteenth-century neurologist Hughlings Jackson, who noted that some patients could not protrude their tongue on command even though they could use it in a variety of spontaneous acts such as speech, licking their lips, and eating. Apraxia is a symptom of a variety of disorders, including stroke, Alzheimer's disease (Benke, 1993), and developmental disorders of children (Dewey, 1993).

Neurologists studying stroke patients have discovered several different types of apraxia. **Ideomotor apraxia** is characterized by the inability to carry out a simple motor activity in response to a verbal command (for example, "smile," or "use this comb"), even though this same activity is readily performed spontaneously. Some researchers emphasize that this type of apraxia is characterized by the inability to select responses, arrange them in an appropriate order, and orient them

properly; these processes are crucial in gestures. Other researchers emphasize the connection between this disorder and aphasia (disturbances of language that follow injury or diseases of the cerebral hemispheres). An example of a task that assesses this form of apraxia is shown in the figure.

Ideational apraxia is an impairment in the carrying out of a *sequence* of actions that are components of a behavioral script, although each element or step can be done correctly. A patient was asked to go through the sequence of acts in order to light a candle with a match. The patient was unable to comply, but when the lights went out during a storm, she found a candle and lit it (Kosslyn et al., 1992). Such patients have difficulty pushing a button, then pulling a handle, then depressing a switch in sequence (see figure), but can do each of these tasks in isolation.

One anatomical explanation of apraxia focuses on the disconnection of primary motor areas from nonprimary motor areas. Other anatomical interpretations emphasize the importance of injury to parietal areas, which include representations of various sensory features of actions.

Although L-dopa can reverse some symptoms of Parkinson's disease, nerve cell degeneration in the substantia nigra is relentless. Since the cell bodies in the brain stem degenerate, dopamine-containing terminals in the caudate nucleus and putamen also disappear. Eventually, there are not enough dopamine-containing neurons in the substantia nigra to be influenced by the intake of L-dopa. Until recently, there were no treatments to address this terminal

condition. By the 1980s, however, researchers had begun to use transplants of dopamine-containing cells as a form of treatment in humans. Initially they transplanted dopamine cells of the adrenal gland into the cerebral ventricles of patients. It was believed that these cells would act as a "chemical factory" and release dopamine into the surrounding area, which includes the caudate nucleus. But clinical benefits with this intervention were minimal.

11.19 The Relations between Parkinsonism and Dopamine

Initially, the loss of dopamine cells is compensated for by increased production of dopamine receptors. But continued loss of cells eventually leads to declines in striatal dopamine levels and a worsening of parkinsonian symptoms. Dotted lines represent estimates based on values obtained in nonparkinsonian patients. After Jankovic and Calne, 1989.

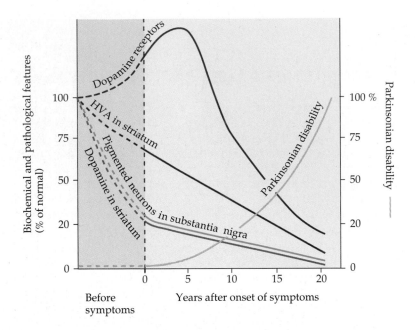

The refinement of techniques led to the transplantation of human fetal cells derived from the brain stem (see Figure 1.3). Direct injection of these cells into the corpus striatum produces remarkable relief of some parkinsonian symptoms (Figure 11.20; Peschanski et al., 1994). In addition to the improved quality of movements, this graft increases the efficacy of L-dopa treatment. Animal research with such grafts indicates that these fetal brain stem cells become integrated into the circuitry of the corpus striatum; thus, transplants result in a rewiring of the damaged brains in addition to whatever effects they produce by the release of synaptic transmitter. Such transplants appear to have helped patients who suffer from drug-induced Parkinson's disease (see Box 11.3). Because there are ethical problems with the use of fetal cells, some researchers hope to produce cells that are genetically engineered to make dopamine; these cells may substitute for fetal cells as effective donor grafts.

An aspect of Parkinson's disease that might be independent of the degree of motor impairment is the appearance of cognitive and emotional changes. An unusual number of Parkinson's patients show marked cognitive decline during the course of their illness (Cummings, 1995). Depression in Parkinson's patients is also common; some researchers have attributed it to the consequences of diminished movement capabilities and the general stress of such incapacity. Other researchers have attributed this depression to a diminished responsiveness of the serotonergic system (Sano et al., 1991). Depressed Parkinson's patients show lower levels of the metabolites of serotonin than do nondepressed Parkinson's patients. Reduced activity in prefrontal cortex in these patients also suggests that their altered mood is associated with frontal lobe impairments. Studies of mood and emotions in Parkinson's patients has laid the groundwork for research on the role of basal ganglia in emotional regulation in psychiatric disorders, which we will consider in Chapter 16.

Huntington's Disease Involves Excessive Movement Caused by Deterioration of the Basal Ganglia

George Huntington was a young physician whose only publication (1872) was a description of a strange motor affliction of a nearby family. He correctly noticed that this disorder was inherited, passed from generation to generation. We now know that **Huntington's disease** is transmitted by a single dominant gene, so each child of a victim has a 50% chance of developing the disease. The first symptoms of this disease are subtle behavioral changes: clumsiness, twitches in fingers and the face. Subtlety is rapidly lost as the illness progresses; a continuing stream of involuntary jerks engulf the entire body. Aimless movements of the eyes, jerky leg movements, and writhing of the body turn the routine challenges of the day into insurmountable obstacles. Worse yet, as the disease progresses, marked behavioral changes include intellectual deterioration,

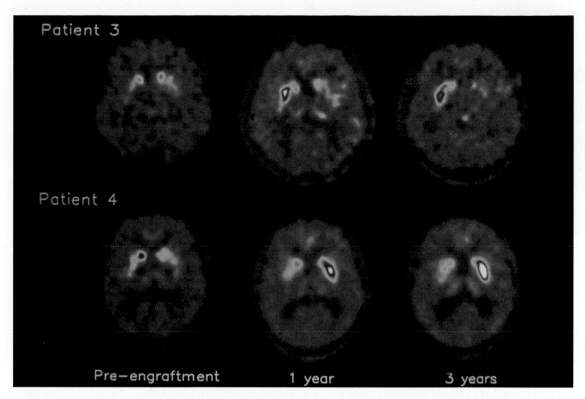

Patient 3

Patient 4

Pre—engraftment   1 year   3 years

11.20   Brain Implants for Parkinson's Disease
The injection of cells into a patient with Parkinson's disease leads to increased dopamine receptors in the striatum one and three years later, as these PET scans reveal. From Lindvall et al., 1994.

depression, and in a minority of patients, a psychotic state that resembles schizophrenia. Both memory disruption and changes in visuospatial organization are common in this disorder (Shoulson, 1992). In some patients, cognitive and emotional changes may appear many years before obvious motor impairments (Wexler, Rose, and Housman, 1991). Huntington's disease usually develops over a period of 15 to 20 years.

The neuroanatomical basis of this disorder is the profound, progressive destruction of the basal ganglia, especially the caudate nucleus and putamen (Figure 11.21). Several types of cells are particularly vulnerable; this includes neurons that contain the transmitter GABA. Perhaps death of these cells results from a transmitter or transmitterlike substance in the brains of patients. One model for the progression of motor symptoms emphasizes the destruction of inhibitory circuitry as the essential characteristic of the disorder (Wexler, Rose, and Housman, 1991). Acetylcholine-containing neurons are relatively spared.

Because the symptoms of Huntington's disease usually first appear between the ages of 30 and 45 years, many victims have children before knowing whether they will ultimately come down with the disease. Until quite recently this meant that there would be continuing generations of ravaged individuals. In a massive effort to help avert this tragic cycle, psychologist Nancy Wexler pieced together a pedigree map of more than 10,000 individuals, including more than 300 Huntington's patients, from a community in Venezuela. After years of work, she and her collaborators (including David Housman, James Gusella, and Venezuelan physician Ernesto Bonilla) were able to pinpoint the gene, on chromosome 4,

Nancy Wexler

Box 11.3
The Frozen Addicts

Parkinson's disease has been very difficult to study because until recently it was not possible to find or produce a similar disorder in laboratory animals. Mistakes in the synthesis of drugs for illegal sale have led to the first valuable model of Parkinson's disease. This saga began when several drug addicts were admitted to a hospital in California with an unusual array of symptoms. Especially puzzling was the fact that they were in their twenties yet presented an unmistakable portrait of Parkinson's disease, which is usually restricted to people 50 or older. The movements of these young patients were slow, they had tremors of the hands, and their faces were frozen without expression. In addition, the diagnosis of Parkinson's disease in these cases was confirmed by the therapeutic response to the drug L-dopa. All of these drug addicts had recently used a "home-brewed" synthetic form of heroin. That fact, coupled with the recollection of a report of an unusual disorder that had arisen from a laboratory accident several years earlier, led to the conclusion that the synthetic heroin contained a neurotoxin that produced brain damage typical of Parkinson's disease (Kopin and

Markey, 1988; Langston, 1985).

Moving step by step in a trail that resembles a detective story, researchers pieced together what had happened. Chemical studies led to the identification of a contaminant in the synthetic heroin, now known as MPTP (an abbreviation of the much longer chemical name). Many addicts have been exposed to this substance, but relatively few come down with this parkinsonian disorder. Patients with symptoms show a decline in dopamine concentrations in the brain, as revealed by PET scans (top panels of figure; Martin and Hayden, 1987).

The injection of MPTP into various research animals yielded a startling result: although rats and rabbits showed only minimal and transient motor impairments, monkeys were as sensitive to the toxin as are humans and developed a permanent set of motor changes identical to those of humans with Parkinson's disease. Furthermore, the sites of damage in the brain were identical to those in the frozen addicts and in Parkinson's patients. MPTP accumulates in the substantia nigra and caudate nucleus because it binds selectively to a form of the enzyme monoamine

oxidase (MAO), which is plentiful in these regions. MPTP interacts with this enzyme to form a highly toxic metabolite: MPP$^+$. Researchers have suggested that the natural pigment neuromelanin, found in the substantia nigra, accounts for the selectivity of damage produced by MPTP (Snyder and D'Amato, 1985). They have shown that MPP$^+$ binds with a special affinity to this pigment. Thus, cells with neuromelanin accumulate MPP$^+$ to toxic levels, and since cells of the substantia nigra contain large amounts of the pigment, they are particularly vulnerable to the destructive impact of MPP$^+$. In other parts of the brain, MPP$^+$ levels decline following exposure; in contrast, MPP$^+$ levels in substantia nigra cells may continue to increase for some time following exposure. In view of this binding mechanism, differences among species become more comprehensible. Nigral cells of monkeys and humans have pigment, while those of rodents are unpigmented.

Monkeys can be protected against the toxic effects by oxidase inhibitors and certain other drugs (D'Amato et al., 1987). This drug model has already resulted in new drug treatments that hold consider-

that is responsible for the disorder (Gusella and MacDonald, 1993). The gene had not been cloned before and the function of the protein is still unknown, but the nature of the mutation in this gene (called *HD* for Huntington's disease) provides unexpected insight into the inheritance of Huntington's disease. In afflicted individuals the *HD* gene is interrupted by a series of three nucleotides—CAG—repeated over and over (see the Appendix). This **trinucleotide repeat** can vary in length; if there are fewer than 30 repeats, no symptoms appear, but if there are 38 or

more trinucleotide repeats in the *HD* gene, the person will develop Huntington's disease (Young, 1993). The longer the string of trinucleotide repeats, the earlier in life Huntington's disease symptoms commence. When the repeats are carried by the mother, the gene with its repeats is copied faithfully in eggs and transmitted to the offspring, but in the production of sperm, a father may transmit more or fewer repeats than he himself carries. Unfortunately, it is more common for the father to transmit more repeats than fewer repeats. Thus, in some cases an

Preoperative PET scans of two patients suffering from MPTP-induced parkinsonism

PRE-OPERATIVE   PRE-OPERATIVE

Scans of the same two patients after transplant procedure

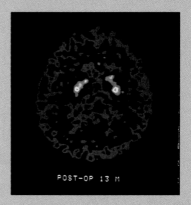

POST-OP 13 M   POST-OP 12 M

able promise for human sufferers. For example, the MAO inhibitor deprenyl slows the progression of Parkinson's disease.

Discovering a primate model of this disease opened an exciting set of research opportunities that is removing the shroud of mystery that has enveloped Parkinson's disease. Primate experiments have also provided an opportunity to test other therapies, such as neural transplants. This research has led to apparently successful transplants in human patients (bottom panels of figure), including some of the original frozen addicts. Some research-ers have speculated that Parkinson's disease in humans may arise from exposure to an unknown toxin. In two cases involving laboratory workers, MPTP-induced disease has arisen from either inhalation or skin contact with MPTP, suggesting that a brief and almost trivial contact with MPTP may be sufficient to begin the disease. Some environmental toxins, such as certain herbicides, may provide exposure to MPP^+ (Snyder and D'Amato, 1986). (Figures courtesy of J. William Langston.)

asymptomatic father may transmit Huntington's disease to his offspring.

How does carrying a copy of *HD* with extended repeats cause degeneration of the striatum and the symptoms of Huntington's disease? One hypothesis was that only striatal cells normally make the HD protein, so only they die when it is defective. But the *HD* gene, whether normal or defective, is expressed not just in the striatum, but throughout the brain, by both neurons and glia. The *HD* gene is also expressed in muscle, liver, pancreas, and testes (Young, 1993). Thus, why the defective *HD* gene appears to affect only striatal cells remains a mystery. Study of the function of normal and defective *HD* genes in laboratory animals may suggest why striatal cells succumb in Huntington's disease and what therapies might preserve them.

The example of Huntington's disease, with its increased movements, demonstrates the major role that inhibition plays in normal motor control. Without adequate inhibition a person is compelled to perform a variety of unwanted movements.

(a)

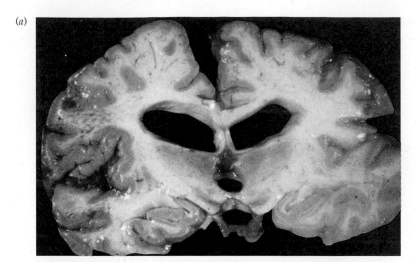

(b)

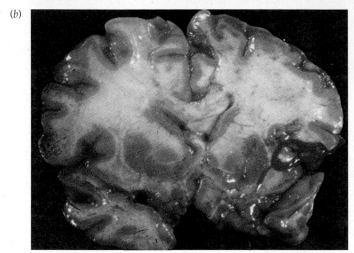

11.21 Brain Regions Affected by Huntington's Chorea

A coronal section through the brain of a Huntington's patient (*top*) shows marked atrophy of the caudate and putamen compared to a normal brain (*bottom*). Courtesy of W. W. Tourtellotte.

Cerebellar Damage Leads to Many Motor Impairments

Since the cerebellum modulates many aspects of motor performance, it is not surprising that its impairment leads to many abnormalities of behavior. These symptoms permit an examiner to tell with considerable accuracy what part of the cerebellum is involved (Dichgans, 1984).

A relatively common lesion of the cerebellum results from a tumor that usually occurs in childhood. The tumor damages a part of the cerebellum—the vermis—with close connections to the vestibular system and therefore causes disturbances of balance. The patient walks as if drunk and has difficulty even standing erect. Often the feet are placed widely apart in an attempt to maintain balance. The abnormalities usually involve the legs and trunk but not the arms. Normally the world seems to hold still as we walk because movements of our eyes compensate for movements of the head. Some patients with lesions

of the cerebellum, however, see the world around them move whenever they move their heads. If normal subjects wear prismatic lenses, they learn to compensate for the new relationship between movement of the eyes and perceived change of direction. Patients with lesions of the vestibular part of the cerebellum cannot make this adjustment, suggesting that this part of the cerebellum is important for such learning.

Some alcoholic patients show degeneration of the cortex of the anterior lobe of the cerebellum. When this region is damaged, abnormalities of gait and posture are common. The legs show **ataxia** (loss of coordination), but the arms do not. Loss of coordination and swaying indicate that the patient is not compensating normally for the usual deviations of position and posture. Several investigators have proposed that the cerebellum works like a comparator in a negative feedback circuit, comparing ongoing movements with target levels and sending corrective instructions to overcome any departures from planned values. (Such a feedback system is diagrammed in Figure 11.4.) The cerebellar cortex has motor and sensory maps of the body that are in register (that is, that are perfectly superimposed), which may allow the comparison of ongoing acts with planned positions and motions of body parts.

Some diseases of the cerebellum may cause difficulties in speaking; this is mainly a motor rather than a cognitive problem. A posterior region just to the left of the midline is most often involved in cerebellar speech disorders (Gilman, Bloedel, and Lechtenberg, 1981). Difficulties of motor coordination are common after damage to the lateral aspects of the cerebellum. One such problem is called *decomposition of movement*, because gestures are broken up into individual segments instead of being executed smoothly. A patient who had this problem after damage to his right cerebellar hemisphere described his condition in this way: "The movements of my left hand are done subconsciously, but I have to think out each movement of my right arm. I come to a dead stop in turning and have to think it out before I start again." Thus the cerebellum is not needed to initiate acts or to plan the sequence of movements but to facilitate activation and to "package" movements economically (Brooks, 1984).

Changes over the Lifetime

Fetal Activity May Influence Development

Developmental views of movements must start with the womb, since the life of the fetus is not passive and quiet. Indeed, some pregnant mothers have been almost thrown out of bed by a surprising and vigorous kick of a fetal child. We study human fetal movements using ultrasonic echograms (Birnholtz, 1981; Birnholtz and Farrell, 1984). This technique permits even small movements, such as isolated eye movements, to be seen in early fetal life. Localized reflexes begin to develop about 11 to 12 weeks after conception. These reflexes are selective motor changes that do not involve the entire body. Mouth opening and swallowing are evident at this stage. Tongue movements appear at 14 weeks.

The functional role of the vast range of fetal reflexes has been debated for many years. A thoughtful discussion by Hall and Oppenheim (1987) distinguishes among three different potential roles of fetal movements:

1. These movements may simply reflect the fact that a neural circuit is being formed that will be functionally significant later.

2. These movements may be a necessary ingredient in the shaping of subsequent, more elaborate responses. For example, the "spontaneous" movements of a fetal human may be necessary for the subsequent orderly development of walking.

3. These movements may serve an immediate adaptive function.

Decisive evidence is lacking for the second hypothesis that fetal rehearsal influences later motor control. Hall and Oppenheim (1987) cite several studies that show that giving amphibian embryos drugs that block neural activity does not measurably affect the later emerging swimming ability of a tadpole. However, they note that fetal behavioral responses are important to fetal development itself (hypothesis 3), especially musculoskeletal development: skeletal muscles do not develop normally when fetal movements are impaired.

Human Infants Acquire Motor Skills through the Interaction of Neural Maturation, Physical Changes, and Experience

Motor abilities of human infants have been the focus of many studies in child psychology. A common way of describing the development of motor skills is to specify the ages at which infants and children reach typical motor accomplishments, such as standing, running, and handling objects. The lengthening of bones and the acquisition of muscle mass, along with other biomechanical changes, account for the progression of many early skills (Freedland and Bertenthal, 1993). For example, the neural program for walking is available at birth, as you can see by holding a newborn infant erect (supporting its weight) and bringing its feet in contact with a solid surface. Under this condition the infant will make stepping movements of the feet. However, independent walking does not appear until 12 to 18 months, because neither the skeletal system nor muscle organization are sufficiently developed until this time.

Motor Skills Change with Aging

As we get older, we grow weaker and slower. This common observation may dismay us, but it is amply supported by experimental observations. The only debate concerns the magnitude of these changes. Strength in humans reaches its peak in the age range 20 to 29 years and shows accelerating decline in each subsequent decade. Almost all motor outputs change in strength, and this decline seems to arise from changes in the properties of muscles and joints. Human performance studies in work settings indicate that this decline is less evident in people who engage in strenuous work.

Speed is also affected by age. Both simple and complex motor tasks take longer after the peak period of 20 to 29 years. Over the life span and across many tasks this decline is from 20 to 40%. Changes in the muscle system and in information-processing networks that command movements are the cause. Some relatively simple tasks, such as writing, show major changes. The slowing of writing and many similar tasks that involve small muscle movements arises not from muscular limitations but from changes in central processing that guide movements. This is demonstrated in studies showing that the effects of aging are reduced when special warning signals prepare the subject for the intended movement. One benefit of slowing is increased *accuracy* of movement, provided the tasks do not involve complex perceptual information.

The physiological bases of motor decline are evident at many levels of the neuromotor system. In the brain both neurochemical and neuroanatomical changes have been shown. For example, in normal adults the levels of enzymes that synthesize dopamine decline with age, and the amount of dopamine in the basal ganglia decreases by about 13% per decade of life (Figure 11.22).

Locomotion Is Controlled by Oscillatory Circuits

Comparisons of particular acts by various animals can provide a useful perspective for understanding the anatomy and physiology of movement. Some differences depend on anatomical specializations in bones; for example, long hind limb bones aid in jumping. Other differences emphasize neural specializations such as the fineness of forelimb innervation, which allows primates the dexterous use of their forelimbs.

Animals move from one place to another in a variety of ways. Some animals move by changing body shape. Picture the sweeping curves of a snake's body moving through the grass or the oscillations of the tail of a fish in water. More dramatic examples of changes in body shape as the basis for locomotion are the jet propulsion of squid and the backward, darting escape movements of crayfish produced by rapid tail flexions. Many other animals, such as humans, move by using specialized limb structures that provide the force required.

However it is accomplished, most locomotion is rhythmic. For all animals, moving about consists of repetitive cycles of the same act, be it the beating of

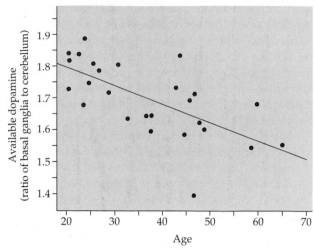

11.22   The Normal Loss of Dopamine
The normal decline in striatal dopamine availability with aging indicates that everyone who lives long enough will manifest some Parkinsonian symptoms.

wings or the repetitive swinging of legs. Contemporary neuroscience has devoted considerable attention to the possible neural basis of the repetitive cycles of locomotion. Do these repetitive cycles develop from the sensory impact of movement itself, or do they reflect endogenous oscillators that provide the basic locomotor programs that motoneurons obligingly obey? Earlier we presented an example of a basic neural circuit that could act as an **endogenous oscillator** (Figure 5.17). This circuit could generate regularly repeating sequences of behavior.

Early theories of locomotion suggested a reflex chain. According to this view, each act provides the sensory feedback from muscles that is the stimulus to the next component. As with Sherrington's attempt to reduce complex behavior to a series of reflexes (which we discussed earlier in this chapter), this explanation is inadequate. Early experiments showed that eliminating the sensory feedback in locomotor acts such as walking or flying did *not* affect the basic rhythmic aspect of the act. Rhythmic movements are generated by mechanisms within the spinal cord. These endogenous rhythms are independent of brain influences and afferent inflow. The term **central pattern generators** has been used to refer to the neural circuitry responsible for generating rhythmic patterns of behavior as seen in walking.

Examples of neural circuitry for locomotion are shown in Figure 11.23. A key feature of all these networks is the potent role of inhibitory connections. Pattern-generating networks probably can be reorga-

(a)

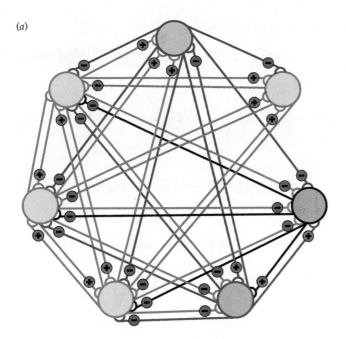

11.23 Pattern-Generating Networks
Both of these networks mediate rhythmic swimming in (a) an invertebrate, the mollusc Tritonia, and (b) a vertebrate, the lamprey. Note the symmetrical patterns of innervation and extensive use of inhibitory synapses in each case.

(b)

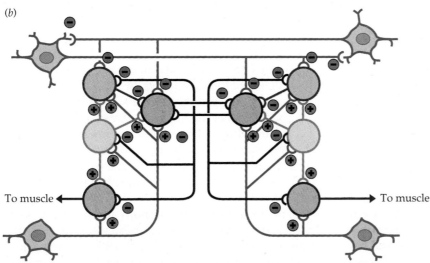

To muscle ←   → To muscle

nized to function in more than one task; that is, they are flexible (Pearson, 1993). Some of this flexibility emerges because of the role of higher levels of nervous system control. The term **command neuron** has been used to refer to higher-level nerve cells that can selectively activate specific behaviors such as walking. These cells, when activated, initiate acts but do not participate in the production of the movements. They act as triggers that command the neurons that are needed in the execution of the actual movements.

Central pattern generation in locomotor rhythms has been studied by Grillner and colleagues (Grillner, 1985; Grillner, Hill, and Grillner, 1991). Their electromyographic records of hind limb muscles of cats with

spinal cord section and dorsal root cuts reveal a "walking" pattern that lasts for seconds when a single dorsal root is briefly stimulated electrically (Figure 11.24). This response has been referred to as **fictive locomotion**. Outputs from spinal motoneurons also show different types of coordination that are variants of typical locomotor patterns, like galloping. The activity of the relevant muscles shows phase relations similar to characteristic muscle time differences observed in the movements of intact animals. Three intact adjacent spinal segments provide the minimal amount of spinal processing necessary for generation of part of the locomotor rhythm. Thus, the brain does not generate the essential rhythm in the

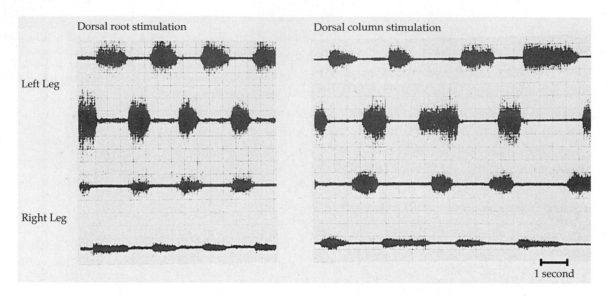

Dorsal root stimulation   Dorsal column stimulation

Left Leg

Right Leg

1 second

11.24   Spinal Generation of Patterns for Walking
The pattern of walking shown in electromyograms of hind limb muscles in
an acute spinal and deafferented cat demonstrate a spinal pattern-generator.
From Grillner and Zangger, 1979; courtesy of Sten Grillner.

spinal cord, but may control onset and provide corrections arising from other influences registered by
the brain. The generation of locomotor rhythms has
been demonstrated especially clearly in invertebrate
preparations (Selverston and Moulins, 1985).

Speech and Vocalization Require Delicate Motor Control

In many animals, including humans, structures used
for breathing also produce species-typical sounds. In
most cases these sounds are produced by forcing air
across a structure that can vibrate when stretched in
particular ways. Coordination of muscle activity is essential at several steps. In mammals, these steps include control of expiration from the lung, which determines airflow across the vocal folds (or cords),
pressure on the vocal folds, and changes in the shape
of the vocal cavities, such as the throat and mouth.
Human speech, like many other animal vocalizations,
is complicated and demands extremely delicate coordination of many muscles to keep it from sounding
like gibberish.

Muscles that control the vocal folds and the shape
of the vocal cavities in the mouth and throat help
shape sounds. Many of the relevant muscles, such as
those of the lips, have a low innervation ratio of muscle fibers to motoneurons, since delicate control is required for sounds to become intelligible signals. Note

the very small differences in tongue position in the
production of the consonants "d" and "t" or effects of
timing of voice and lip positions in the production of
"b" and "p." Feedback control in speech is particularly interesting because it is multimodal; it involves
muscle receptors, tactile receptors, and sounds. The
neural organization of speech—the representation in
the brain of programs of movements—is presented in
Chapter 19.

The vocal repertoire of many young animals includes the sounds of crying. As a motor activity, crying is a complex sequence of acts that are relatively
stereotyped. In human infants each "unit" of crying
ranges from one-half to one second repeated 50 to 70
times per minute. This basic oscillatory pattern is evident at birth and remains the same until later infancy, when there is greater variability among individuals. The sound pattern of human crying at birth
provides an indication of the developmental integrity of the central nervous system (Lester et al., 1985).
For example, infants who have experienced birth
trauma have cries that include an increase in the basic sound frequency and variability in this fundamental frequency. Pitch that varies widely may signal that brain activity is disordered, perhaps lacking
fine inhibitory controls. Sound spectrographic analysis of infant cries is opening the door to a new approach to diagnostic assessment of human infants.

Summary

1. All behavior consists of either the secretion of glands or muscle contractions. Muscle contractions are regulated by neural impulses that arrive at the muscles over motor nerve fibers, which are axons from motoneurons.

2. Reflexes are patterns of relatively simple and stereotyped movements that are elicited by stimulation of sensory receptors; their amplitude is proportional to the intensity of the stimulation.

3. Many reflexes are controlled by closed-loop, negative feedback circuits. Some behaviors are so rapid, however, that they are controlled by open-loop systems; that is, the pattern is preset and does not respond to feedback.

4. Many learned, skilled acts such as typing or playing a musical instrument also have open-loop control and are not influenced by stimulus intensity, so long as the intensity exceeds the threshold.

5. When a muscle is stretched, a reflex circuit often causes contraction, which works to restore the muscle to its original length; this response is called the stretch reflex. The stretch of the muscle is detected by special receptors, called muscle spindles, that are located among the muscle fibers.

6. The sensitivity of the muscle spindle can be adjusted by efferent impulses that control the length of the muscle spindle. This adjustment allows flexible control of posture and movement.

7. The final common pathway for impulses to skeletal muscles consists of motoneurons, whose cell bodies in vertebrates are located in the ventral horn of the spinal cord and within the brain stem. The motoneurons receive impulses from a variety of sources, including sensory input from the dorsal spinal roots, other spinal cord neurons, and descending fibers from the brain.

8. Circuits within the spinal cord underlie the spinal reflexes, which can occur even when the cord is cut and connections to the brain are severed.

9. The corticospinal tract is especially well developed in primates and is mainly involved in controlling fine movements of the extremities. Its fibers originate mainly in the primary motor cortex and adjacent regions, and they run directly to spinal motoneurons or to interneurons in the spinal cord.

10. Brain regions that modulate movement include the basal ganglia (caudate, putamen, and globus pallidus), some major brain stem nuclei (substantia nigra, thalamic nuclei, and red nucleus), and the cerebellum.

11. Movement disorders can result from impairment at any of several levels of the motor system: muscles, neuromuscular junctions, motoneurons, the spinal cord, brain stem, cerebral cortex, basal ganglia, or cerebellum. The characteristics of the movement disorders depend on and permit diagnosis of the locus of the impairment.

12. Many locomotor acts depend on oscillatory pattern generators in the nervous system. Some acts, such as speech, require very delicate coordination of many muscles.

Recommended Reading

Brooks, V. B. 1986. *The Neural Basis of Motor Control.* Oxford University Press, New York.

Requin, J. and Stelmach, G. E. (eds.) 1991. *Tutorials in Motor Neuroscience.* Kluever, Dordrecht, Netherlands.

Rosenbaum, D. A. 1991. *Human Motor Control.* Academic Press, San Diego.

Rothwell, J. 1994. *Control of Human Voluntary Movement.* (2nd ed.) Chapman and Hall, London.

PART 4

Control of Behavioral States: Motivation

We have now reviewed the basic structure and function of the nervous system, the specialized organs that gather information about the environment and the specialized motor systems that allow us to respond to that information. Now we come to a problem—given the information we have, which response should we make? The number of possible responses is, for all practical purposes, infinite. But natural selection favors some responses in one situation, other responses in others. From the point of view of natural selection, a food deprived animal should eat, an animal that's lost water should drink, an animal that is not adapted to function in darkness should sleep at night, and so on. When an animal consistently displays the same response, even in slightly inappropriate circumstances, we can infer that the animal is motivated to make that response. Of course the brain is pivotal in making the decision about which response to make. To some extent, we can find the different brain regions that are involved in deciding whether to reproduce (Chapter 12), eat, drink, seek shelter (Chapter 13), sleep (Chapter 14), be afraid, panic, or fight (Chapter 15). In each of these cases, we can catalog the situations that usually elicit a particular response from members of a particular species, and can ask which brain regions are required for the response to be elicited, which brain regions are activated by the situation, and how various responses are integrated. As we'll see, many brain regions are involved in each of these responses, which is a recurring theme in this book.

George Tooker, *Lovers II*, 1960

Sexual Behaviors

- *There Are Four Stages of Reproductive Behavior*
- *Copulation Brings Gametes Together for Reproduction*
- *Human Reproduction*
- *Pheromones Both Prime and Activate Reproductive Behaviors*

The Evolution of Sexual Reproduction

- *Sexual Reproduction Helps Combine Beneficial Mutations*
- *Males and Females Often Adopt Different Reproductive Strategies*
- *There Are Four Basic Types of Mating Systems*
- *Sexual Selection Accentuates Differences between the Sexes*
- *Many Vertebrates Depend on Their Parents for Survival*

Sexual Differentiation

- *The Sex of an Individual Is Determined Early in Life*
- *Sex Chromosomes Direct Sexual Differentiation of the Gonads*
- *Gonadal Hormones Direct Sexual Differentiation of the Rest of the Body*
- *Departures from the Orderly Sequence of Sexual Differentiation Result in Predictable Changes in Development*
- *How Shall We Define Gender—by Genes, Gonads, Genitals, or the Brain?*
- *Gonadal Hormones Direct Sexual Differentiation of the Brain and Behavior*
- *Social Influences Affect Sexual Differentiation of the Nervous System*
- *Do Early Gonadal Hormones Masculinize Human Behaviors in Adulthood?*

CHAPTER Sex

12

Orientation

Sexuality is such an important part of our lives that we take for granted some of its most basic properties—for example, that two and only two sexes are required for reproduction, that males tend to be somewhat larger and more aggressive than females, and that an adult human is, in some core sense, either a man or a woman. In this chapter we will learn that there are exceptions to each of these rules. We divide the chapter into three main sections: (1) First, we'll review sexual behaviors, which includes the sex act itself, copulation. (2) The bewildering variety of sexual behaviors across species (and within our own species) will lead us to consider next why such a messy and confusing process as sexual reproduction evolved. We'll find that sexual reproduction eventually gave rise to two sexes, which can sometimes be remarkably divergent in structure and behavior. (3) The evolution of two different sexes will lead us to the final topic, sexual differentiation—the process by which an individual's body and brain develop in a male or female fashion.

Sexual Behaviors

We wish we could explain exactly why and how humans and other animals engage in the "three Cs"—courting, copulating, and cohabitating—but very little practical knowledge of such matters exists, as James Thurber and E. B. White lamented in 1929 (Figure 12.1). You may feel that there has been little improvement in the years since. Two main barriers have blocked our understanding of sexual behavior: (1) a deep-seated reluctance within our culture to disseminate knowledge about sexual behavior and (2) the remarkable variety of sexual behaviors in existence. We are therefore forced to discuss the aspects of sexual reproduction that are common across vertebrate species with only a little attention to the aspects that are particular to a species.

There Are Four Stages of Reproductive Behavior

Sexual attraction is the first step in bringing the male and female together. In many species an individual is attractive to others, and is itself attracted *to* others, only when its body is ready to reproduce. We can gauge how attractive a female is by observing how males respond to her—how rapidly they approach, how hard they work to gain access to her, and so on. These same measures show how attractive

a male is to females. By manipulating the appearance of females, we can deduce which features males find attractive. Such methods have demonstrated that in many species of apes and monkeys the male is attracted by the sight of the female's "sex skin," which swells under the influence of the steroid hormone estrogen. You have probably seen such swellings on the rumps of female baboons at the zoo. Most male mammals are also attracted by particular odors emitted by females of their species; in many cases such odors are also the result of estrogen's action. Thus estrogen simultaneously instigates the release of eggs (ovulation) and attracts males to fertilize them. In many species, estrogen also stimulates the production of vaginal lubricants to facilitate copulation. Of course, the female may find some of the males that approach her unattractive and refuse to mate with them. Despite a few descriptions of what may or may not be rape in nonhuman animals, for most species, copulation is not possible without the female's active cooperation.

If the animals are mutually attracted, they may progress to the second stage of reproductive behavior: **appetitive behaviors** (Figure 12.2). Appetitive behaviors establish, maintain, or promote sexual interaction. A female mammal that engages in such behaviors is said to be **proceptive**. She may approach males, remain close to them, or show alternating approach and retreat behavior. In rats, the female may slap the male's face with her forepaws then run away

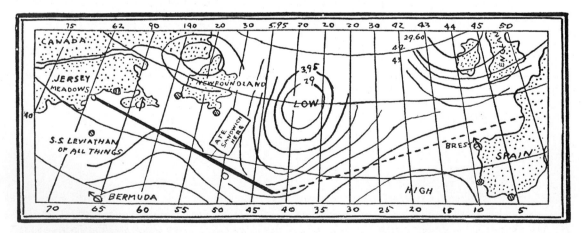

12.1 Sex According to Thurber and White
In *Is Sex Necessary?*, written in 1929, James Thurber and E. B. White explain, "It is customary to illustrate sexology chapters with a cross section of the human body. The authors have chosen to substitute in its place a chart of the North Atlantic, showing airplane routes. The authors realize that this will be of no help to the sex novice, but neither is a cross section of the human body."

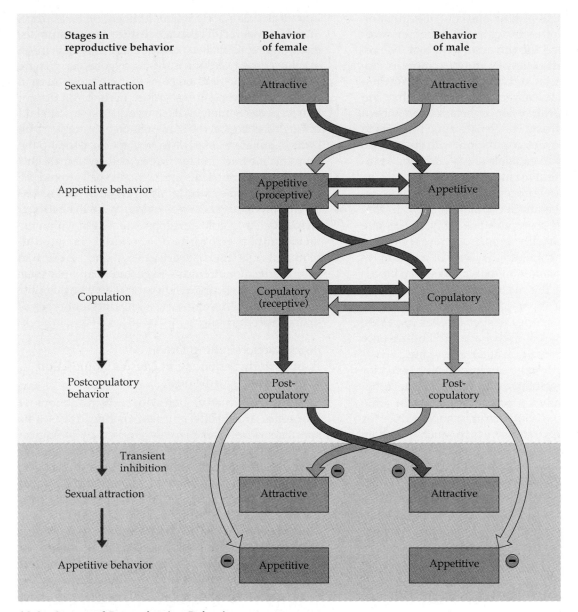

12.2   Stages of Reproductive Behavior
Interaction between male and female partners is extensive. The postcopulatory phase includes a temporary decrease in the sexual attractiveness of the partner and inhibition of appetitive behavior. After Beach, 1977.

from the male with a distinctive hopping and darting gait, to which the male often responds by mounting the female. Male appetitive behaviors usually consist of staying near the female. In many mammals the male may sniff around the female's face and vagina. Male birds may engage in elaborate songs or nest-building behaviors.

If both animals display appetitive behaviors, they may progress to **copulation**, also known as **coitus**. In

many vertebrates, including all mammals, copulation begins when the male puts his **penis** inside the female's **vagina**—a behavior referred to as **intromission**. Then the male **ejaculates**, rhythmically squirting a fluid mixture called **semen** inside the female. Not all species engage in intromission; however, the term "copulation" refers to the acts that sexual species engage in to provide the male's semen to the female. The semen contains reproductive cells called sperm (see below) for reproduction. After one bout of copulation the animals will not mate again for some period of time, which is called the **refractory period**. The refractory period varies from minutes to months, depending on the species and circumstances. Many animals show a shorter refractory period if they are provided with a new partner, a phenomenon known as the **Coolidge effect**. The female often appears to choose whether or not copulation will take place; when she is willing to copulate she is said to be **sexually receptive**, **in heat**, or **in estrus**. In some species, the female may show proceptive behaviors days before she will participate in copulation itself. In that case she is said to be proceptive but not (yet) receptive (see Figure 12.2). Usually females are receptive only during periods when mating is likely to result in reproduction. Because most animals are seasonal breeders (see Chapter 14), this means females are usually receptive only during the breeding season, which varies considerably from species to species. Many species, such as salmon, octopus, and cicadas, reproduce only once, during a single season at the end of life.

Finally, the fourth stage of reproductive behavior consists of **post-copulatory behaviors**. These behaviors are especially varied across species. In some mammals—dogs and southern grasshopper mice for example—the male's penis swells so much after ejaculation that he can't remove it from the female for a while (10 to 15 minutes in dogs), and the animals are said to be in a **copulatory lock** (Dewsbury, 1972). (Despite wild stories you may have heard or read, humans do *not* experience copulatory lock.) Post-copulatory behaviors also include parental behaviors which we'll discuss later in this chapter.

Copulation Brings Gametes Together for Reproduction

Sexually mature females are animals that can produce **gametes** called eggs, or **ova** (singular: ovum); sexually mature males produce gametes called **sperm**. Successful reproduction requires a sperm cell to contact and fuse with an egg cell, a process known as **fertilization**. The resulting single cell is called a fertilized egg, or **zygote**, and will eventually divide and grow to make a new individual. For many vertebrates, fertilization takes place outside the female's body, a process known as **external fertilization**. In most fishes and frogs, for example, males and females release their gametes in water, where fertilization takes place. In some fishes, such as guppies and swordtails, the male uses a modified fin to direct his sperm to swim

into the female's body where fertilization takes place. Such **internal fertilization**, a feature of all mammals, birds, and reptiles, allows the gametes to remain moist even in a desert, and the resulting zygotes can gain resources from the mother. Note that birds use internal fertilization even though most male birds do not have a penis. Semen is discharged and eggs are laid through the **cloaca**, the same passage through which birds eliminate wastes. After the sperm swim up the reproductive tract and fertilize an egg, the female bird assembles rich nutrients and a tough shell around the zygote, which she extrudes as an egg that hatches later. This process is known as **oviparity**. In live birth, or **viviparity**, the zygote develops extensively within the female until a well-formed individual emerges. All mammals use internal fertilization and all but two species (the monotremes—the echidna and platypus of Australia—which are oviparous) give birth to live young. Table 12.1 summarizes the different types of sexual reproduction.

Reproduction in Ring Doves Is an Orderly Sequence of Mutual Stimulation Regulated by Hormones

Because reproductive behavior and the actions of hormones are tightly coupled in ring doves, this species has been extensively studied by biological psychologists. Ring doves look like slender pigeons with a black semicircle around the back of the neck. Although males and females look very similar, when a pair with breeding experience are placed in a cage together, they show different behaviors (Figure 12.3). The male appears to be attracted first, as he almost immediately begins courtship. He struts around the female, bowing, cooing and chasing her. After a few days the female must find the male attractive, because she starts showing proceptive behaviors—flipping her wings in a special way and approaching the male. The sight of the male's courtship behavior and the sound of his cooing can bring about this change in the female even through a glass partition. Soon the animals show new proceptive behaviors—they crouch on a nest site (a glass bowl in the laboratory) and utter distinctive "nest coo" sounds. Once the female begins nest cooing in earnest, the male starts gathering nesting materials, which the female accepts and uses to build the nest. After a week or so, when the nest is nearly complete, the birds copulate. The female squats low; the male mounts her back, flapping his wings to keep his balance, pushes his cloaca

12.3   Reproductive Behavior in the Ring Dove ▶

1. A male and female are placed together in a cage.

2. Courtship activity begins shortly thereafter with "bowing coos" from the male.

3. The male and the female utter distinctive "nest coos" at their selected nest site (here, the glass bowl).

4. The pair spends a week building a nest.

5. When the nest is ready, the male and the female copulate.

6. The female lays the fertilized eggs.

7. The adults take turns incubating the eggs.

8. The eggs hatch after about 14 days.

9. The adults feed the hatchings (squabs) crop milk.

10. As the young birds learn to peck grain for food, the parents become increasingly reluctant to feed them.

11. When the young are 2 to 3 weeks old, the adults ignore them and may start a new cycle of breeding.

Table 12.1

Types of Sexual Reproduction in Animals

TYPE	ANIMALS THAT FOLLOW THIS PATTERN
External fertilization (requires aquatic environment)	Many invertebrates, many fishes, amphibians
Internal fertilization Oviparity (laying of fertilized eggs)	Insects, birds, many reptiles, monotremes
Viviparity (live birth)	Some fishes, some reptiles, all mammals except monotremes

against hers, and squirts in the semen. A few days later the female lays the first of two eggs and the birds take turns sitting on them.

The eggs hatch after a few weeks and the parents feed the young crop milk, a thick liquid secreted from their crop (a pouch in their throat). The young doves (squabs) leave the nest when they are about 10 to 12 days old, continuing to beg for food. Over the next few days the parents feed them less and less while the squabs learn to eat more and more grain on their own. When the young are 15 to 25 days old the parents may start the cycle over again (Cheng, 1977).

Each phase of the reproductive cycle is influenced by a particular hormone. The level of the hormone affects the behavior and the behavior in turn stimulates hormone release (Figure 12.4). In Chapter 7 we mentioned that such bidirectionality—behaviors altering hormone secretion and hormone secretion altering behaviors—is common. In the ring dove we can see how such bidirectionality results in a coordinated, orderly sequence of reproductive behaviors. The male displays his courtship behaviors only if he has some circulating testosterone, the steroid hormone from the testes. The courtship behavior and the presence of the female, however, cause the testes to release more testosterone. This additional testosterone will facilitate later male proceptive and copulatory behaviors. In the meantime the sights and sounds of the male's courtship behaviors have been detected by the female's brain, which directs her ovaries to produce estrogen (see Chapter 7 if you need a reminder about how the brain controls estrogen production). The estrogen acts on the brain to facilitate proceptive behaviors such as wing flipping and the receptive behaviors of copulation. Within a few days the ovaries also produce progesterone, which facilitates nest building and egg laying. Thus, the behaviors of each

animal stimulate hormone secretion in its partner, paving the way for later behaviors in the sequence. Incubating the eggs causes each parent to produce prolactin, which stimulates the crop to produce crop milk for the squabs. For a limited time, the begging behavior of the squabs helps maintain prolactin secretion, but eventually the parents' brains stop prolactin release so that the cycle may begin again.

Copulation in Rats Is a Brief Interlude

Rats, like most other rodents, do not engage in lengthy courtship, nor do the partners tend to remain together after copulation. Rats are attracted to each other largely through odors. Females are spontaneous ovulators; that is, even when left alone they ovulate every four to five days. For a few hours during each cycle, the female seeks out a male and displays proceptive behaviors—hopping and darting, which we mentioned earlier, and ear-wiggling. Both animals produce vocalizations at frequencies too high for us to detect but audible to each other. These behaviors prompt the male to mount the female from the rear, grasp her hind flanks with his forelegs, and rhythmically thrust his hips. If the female is receptive, she stands still and assumes a posture that allows intromission: she lifts her head and rump and moves her tail to one side. This posture is called **lordosis** (Figure 12.5). Once intromission is achieved, the male rat makes a single thrust lasting half a second or so and then springs back off the female. During the next six to seven minutes the male and female will orchestrate seven to nine such intromissions; then, instead of a springing dismount, the male will vocalize a squeak (audible to humans) and raise the front half of his body up for a second or two while he ejaculates. Then he falls backward off the female. The male almost immediately begins grooming his penis with his tongue

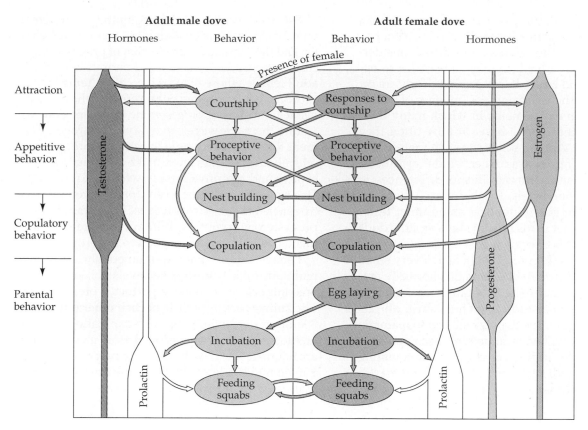

12.4 Hormonal Control of Reproduction in Ring Doves
Summary of behavioral and hormonal changes during the reproductive cycle of ring doves. Note the reciprocal relationship between the male and female and between behavioral and hormonal variables. After Lehrman, 1964.

12.5 Copulation in Rats
The raised rump of the female and her deflected tail (the lordosis posture) make intromission possible. After Barnett, 1975.

and forepaws, while the female typically remains still for a few minutes before grooming her vagina. The male pays little attention to the female for the next five minutes or so until, often in response to the female's proceptive behaviors, he will mount for another round of multiple intromissions and another ejaculation. In other rodent species, intromission may be accompanied by more prolonged thrusting, or the penis may swell to form a copulatory lock. The northern pygmy mouse has only a single ejaculation during a mating session. In some rodent species a male and a female live together before and long after copulation; such animals are said to form **pair bonds**.

As with ring doves, hormones play an important role in rat mating behaviors. Testosterone increases the male's interest in females, causes him to mount them more rapidly and more often, and allows him to achieve ejaculation. If castrated (if its testes are removed), an adult male rat will stop ejaculating within a few weeks and will eventually stop mounting receptive females. Although testosterone disappears from the bloodstream within a few hours after castration, whatever effects the hormone had upon the nervous system take several days to dissipate. Treating a castrated male with testosterone eventually restores mating behavior; thus testosterone is an example of a steroid that has an **activational effect** on behavior.

Interestingly, although male rats differ considerably in the vigor with which they mate with a receptive female, blood levels of testosterone clearly are *not* responsible for these differences. Evidence of this effect comes from experiments in which many male rats are classified on the basis of how often they mount females. Among scientists such males (rats, we mean) are referred to as either "studs" or "duds." These groups show no significant differences in blood testosterone levels. Furthermore, when castrated males are given identical amounts of testosterone, the former studs remain studs and the duds are still duds. This effect was first demonstrated for male guinea pigs (Figure 12.6). In fact, a very small amount of testosterone—one-tenth that normally produced by the animals—is enough to maintain the mating behavior of stud rats. Thus, since all rats make more testosterone than is required to maintain their copulatory behavior, something else appears to be responsible for individual differences in mating activity. As we will see shortly, testosterone plays a similar role in human mating behavior.

Estrogen secreted at the beginning of the female rat's ovulatory cycle facilitates her proceptive behavior, and the subsequent production of progesterone increases proceptive behavior and permits lordosis. An adult female whose ovaries have been removed will show neither proceptive nor receptive behaviors, and neither estrogen nor progesterone treatment alone will restore them. However, two days of estrogen treatment followed by a single injection of progesterone will, about six hours later, make the female rat proceptive and receptive for a few hours (Figure 12.7). One reason the rat must receive progesterone after estrogen is that the estrogen causes the brain to make progesterone receptors. Without estrogen pretreatment, the brain cannot respond to the progesterone.

Female rats ovulate spontaneously and males maintain high testosterone levels throughout the breeding season, whether a partner is present or not. The animals see very little of each other outside the 30 minutes or so taken up with copulation. However, the multiple intromissions before an ejaculation are not mere idle dawdling on the part of the male. If a male rat ejaculates the first time he enters the female (say, because a researcher arranged for him to

12.6 Androgen Permits Male Copulatory Behavior
But hormone level does not completely determine the amount of sex behavior, even in rodents. After castration caused the sex activity of male guinea pigs to decrease, the same amount of testosterone was given to each animal, beginning at week 26. Each group returned to the level of sex activity it had exhibited before castration. Doubling the amount of hormone at week 36 did not increase the mating activity of any group. After Grunt and Young, 1953.

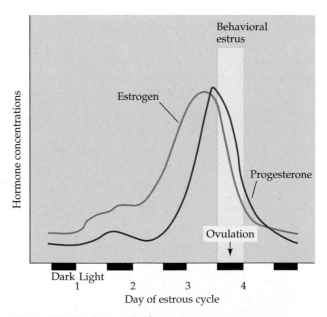

12.7 Rat Ovulatory Cycle
Changes in hormonal levels indicate when the female rat will display lordosis responsiveness. This behavioral receptivity, or estrus, occurs after the animal has been exposed first to estrogen then to progesterone. In spontaneous ovulators such as rats, the cycle of hormone secretion will repeat unless eggs are fertilized. In that case, the embryos secrete hormones to interrupt the cycle and maintain pregnancy.

enter another female several times first), the female will not become pregnant. Only if the female receives enough vaginal stimulation from multiple intromissions will her brain later cause the release of prolactin at a crucial stage for maintaining pregnancy. In this instance, then, the behavior of one rat (the male) affects the hormonal secretions of its mate.

Human Reproduction

In women, ovaries produce eggs and, every 28 days or so, release one of them, a process known as **ovulation**. The released egg falls into the adjacent **fallopian tube**, the walls of which have specialized hairs, or cilia, that wave back and forth, moving the egg into the **uterus** (Figure 12.8*a*). The walls of the uterus are specialized to allow implantation of a developing embryo and support the **placenta**, which will nourish the embryo and fetus. If the egg is to result in a baby, it must be fertilized in the fallopian tube; thus, copulation must take place during a particular phase of the cycle or the fertilized egg (zygote) will not have enough time to divide to form an embryo sufficiently developed to implant into the walls of the uterus. If not implanted, the embryo will drift into the connecting vagina and outside the body. Surrounding the opening of the human vagina are folds of skin known as **labia**, and rostral to the vaginal opening is a mound of tissue called the **clitoris**. This region surrounding the vaginal opening is sometimes called the **vulva**. In all mammals the walls of the uterus thicken before ovulation to allow implantation of a newly formed embryo. In some mammals, including humans and dogs, so many cells lining the walls of the uterus are shed between ovulations that a visible flow of cells and blood exits through the vagina, a process known as **menstruation**. In most mammals, however, many fewer cells are shed and there is no visible flow. Thus, although all vertebrate species have ovulatory cycles (that is, the periodic release of eggs), only a few mammalian species display menstrual cycles.

In males, the sperm are produced in the testis and mature in the adjacent, crescent-shaped **epididymis**

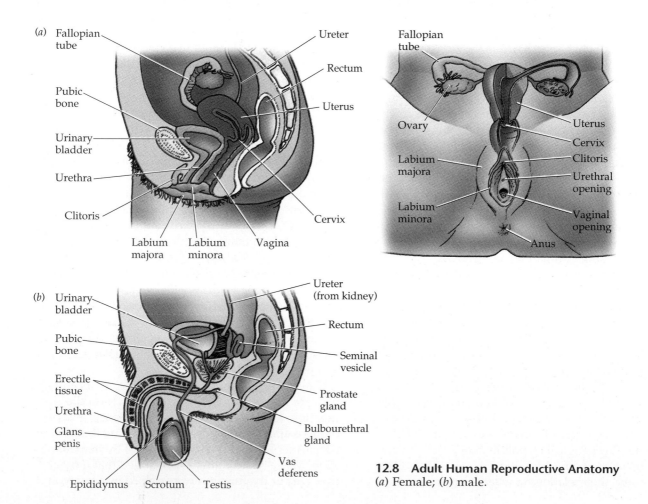

12.8 Adult Human Reproductive Anatomy (*a*) Female; (*b*) male.

(Figure 12.8b). Attached to the epididymis is a small tube called the **vas deferens**. Muscles lining the vas deferens contract to propel sperm to the **urethra**, a tube that travels through the penis to reach the outside. (The urethra also connects to the bladder and conducts urine outside the body.) At the point at which the vas deferens from the left and right testes join with the urethra, several glands are attached: the **seminal vesicles** produce and store a cloudy, viscous fluid; the **prostate**, which encircles the urethra at this point, produces a clear, astringent fluid; and other glands contribute other fluids. During copulation sperm are expelled from the epididymis via the vas deferens and mixed with these various fluids in the urethra; the mixture (semen) is expelled from the penis during ejaculation.

The Hallmark of Human Sexual Behavior Is Diversity

There was little objective information about human sexual behavior until the 1940s, when biology professor Alfred Kinsey began to ask friends and colleagues about their sexual histories. Kinsey constructed a standardized set of questions and procedures to obtain information for representative samples of the U.S. population categorized by sex, age, religion, and education. Eventually he and his collaborators were able to publish extensive surveys (based on tens of thousands of respondents) of the sexual behavior of American males (Kinsey, Pomeroy, and Martin, 1948) and females (Kinsey et al., 1953). Controversial in their time, these surveys indicated that nearly all men masturbated, that college-educated people were more likely to engage in oral sex than were noncollege-educated people, that many people had at one time or other engaged in homosexual behaviors, and that as much as 10% of the population preferred homosexual sex. Although recently it has been suggested that the last figure is an overestimate, these surveys revealed much about human sexual behavior.

A further step is to make behavioral and physiological observations of people engaged in sexual intercourse or masturbation, but such studies are perilous for a scientist: John B. Watson, the founder of behaviorism, attempted such studies in the early 1920s, and the ensuing scandal cost him his professorship. After Kinsey's surveys were published, however, physician William Masters and psychologist Virginia Johnson began a large, well-known project of this kind (1965, 1966, 1970; Masters, Johnson, and Kolodny, 1994) which greatly increased our knowledge about the physiological responses that occur in various parts of the body during intercourse, their time courses, and their relations to what is experienced.

Among most mammalian species, including nonhuman primates, the male mounts the female from the rear, but among humans, face-to-face postures are most common. A great variety of coital postures have been described, and many couples vary their postures from session to session or even within a session. This variety of reproductive behaviors, both within and between individuals, is a characteristic that differentiates humans from all other species.

Masters and Johnson (1965) summarized the typical response patterns of men and women as consisting of four phases: increasing excitement, plateau, **orgasm** (the extremely pleasurable sensations experienced by most men during ejaculation and by most women during copulation), and resolution (Figure 12.9). In spite of the basic similarity, there are some typical differences between male and female responses. One important difference is the greater variety of commonly observed sequences in women. Whereas men have only one basic pattern, women have three typical patterns (see Figure 12.9b). The second main difference between the sexes is that most men, but not women, have an absolute refractory period following orgasm. That is, most men cannot achieve full erection and another orgasm until some time has elapsed, the length of time varying from minutes to hours, depending on individual differences and other factors. Many women, on the other hand, can have multiple orgasms in rapid succession.

Male sexual response pattern. In males, sexual excitement mounts in response to stimulation, which may be mental or physical or both, and is accompanied by blood engorging the penis, making it erect. The rate of rise of excitement varies with many factors, and what may enhance excitement in some men may reduce excitement in others. If stimulation continues, the level of excitement reaches a high plateau, which many people seek to extend as long as possible. Eventually a reflexive orgasmic response is triggered and accompanied by ejaculation. Then excitement gradually dissipates and the penis loses its erection during the resolution phase. Usually the excitement phase and resolution phase are the longest parts of the cycle. Typically the plateau phase lasts only a few minutes, the orgasm less than a minute.

The two most common sexual complaints among men are failure to achieve an erection (**erectile dysfunction**, formerly referred to as impotence) and **premature ejaculation**—ejaculating before the man or his partner have achieved the level of excitement desired. Masters and Johnson concluded that most cases of erectile dysfunction were caused by anxiety, and

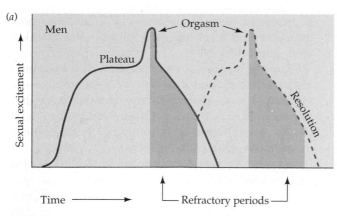

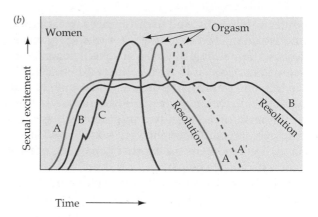

12.9   Human Sexual Response Cycles
These are schematic diagrams and do not represent a particular physiological measure, although heart rate varies in roughly this manner. The patterns vary considerably from one individual to another. (*a*) The typical male pattern, with an absolute refractory period after orgasm. (*b*) Three patterns often observed in women. After Masters and Johnson, 1965.

they recommended several techniques to help men reduce their fears and relax to enable full erection. Because some medical conditions also can interfere with erection, however, any men experiencing repeated difficulty maintaining an erection during sex or masturbation should consult a physician. Premature ejaculation is also usually a result of anxiety; Masters and Johnson developed several techniques to help couples focus on the pleasures of foreplay and to help men learn to recognize the sensations preceding orgasm so that they can adjust their behavior or their partner's behavior to forestall ejaculation.

Female sexual response patterns.   The most common pattern in women (pattern A in Figure 12.9*b*) is similar to the male pattern. During the excitement phase the clitoris, like the penis, swells by congestion of blood vessels. Furthermore, vaginal secretion of lubricating fluids is increased, and the muscles surrounding the vagina relax. As in males, orgasm is marked by rhythmic muscular contractions—in women, of the muscles surrounding the vagina. Stimulation of the clitoris facilitates orgasm in most women. Women and men differ in their temporal patterns of response. Women are usually somewhat slower than men to reach orgasm during intercourse and have no absolute refractory period. Two other patterns are common in women. In pattern B, the high level of excitement of the plateau phase does not quite trigger an orgasmic release; after a prolonged plateau period, sexual excitement gradually dissipates. In pattern C, the woman experiences a rapid and explosive arrival at orgasm, with only a brief plateau or resolution phase. Orgasm in this pattern tends to be both longer and more intense than in pattern A or pattern B.

The two most common sexual complaints among women are discomfort during intromission (**dyspareunia**, from the Greek *dys*, "bad," and *pareunos*, "bedfellow"!) and difficulty achieving orgasm. Dyspareunia is commonly the result of failing to relax sufficiently or to engage in the excitement phase long enough to allow adequate lubrication of the vagina and loosening of the muscles around the vagina. The muscles around the opening of the vagina may spasm painfully, a condition known as **vaginismus**. Water-based lubricants can be purchased to augment natural lubrication. For women who reach the age at which they stop menstruating (menopause), restoring estrogen levels can improve lubrication during coitus. Not all women feel the need to achieve orgasm to be satisfied with intercourse, but for those seeking more frequent orgasm, treatment often consists of relaxation techniques and using masturbation to identify the sensations of orgasm and the techniques that facilitate orgasm for the particular individual.

The similarities and differences in sexual responses exemplify the generalization of Chapter 1 that in some ways each person is like all other people, in some ways like some other people, and in some ways like no other person. The existence of differences among groups and individuals does not contradict or lessen the value of research into biological determinants of such behavior. Some behavioral differences are related to differences in genetic makeup; some may be related to differences in hormone levels. But some are certainly due to differences in experience and learning; sexual therapy, for example, usually consists of helping the person relax, recognize the sensations associated with coitus, and learn the behaviors that produce the desired effects in both partners. Masturbation during adolescence, rather than being harmful as suggested in previous times, may help avoid in adulthood the very sexual problems we have discussed here. As in other behaviors, practice, practice, practice helps.

Finally, we feel compelled to include in any discussion of human sexuality a reminder that many serious diseases, including syphilis and gonorrhea, can be communicated through sexual intercourse. The **human immunodeficiency virus**, or **HIV**, can be passed through genital, anal, or oral sex and causes **acquired immune deficiency syndrome** (**AIDS**), an insidious, fatal disease without cure. Proper use of **condoms** (rubber sheaths fitted over the penis to trap semen) during sexual intercourse can prevent the transmission of HIV. Condoms can also be effective birth control devices, preventing unwanted pregnancies that lead to serious social and moral problems.

Hormones Play Only a Permissive Role in Human Sexual Behavior

Recall that in male rodents a little bit of testosterone must be in circulation for the male to initiate mating, but additional testosterone has no effect on the vigor of mating. Consequently, there is no correlation between the amount of androgen produced by an individual and his tendency to copulate. The same relations seem to hold for men. Some boys fail to undergo puberty because an inability to release gonadotropins prevents the testes from being stimulated to make testosterone. To develop normally, these males must be treated with androgen. These and other men who have lost their testes as the result of cancer or accidents have made possible double-blind tests (where neither subjects nor investigator know which subjects are receiving the drug and which are receiving a placebo) of whether androgens affect human copulatory behavior. These studies indicate that androgen indeed stimulates sexual activity in men (Davidson, Carmago, and Smith, 1979). As with testosterone in rats, blood levels below normal were sufficient for this effect, and no one has ever found a correlation between systemic androgen levels and sexual activity among men who have some androgen. Low androgen levels sometimes cause infertility in men and may be due to reduced release of gonadotropin-releasing hormone or of gonadotropins, or reduced sensitivity of the testes to gonadotropins. In men over

60 years old, testosterone levels gradually decline as gonadotropin levels rise, indicating that the decline is in gonadal function.

You might be surprised to learn that androgen may also activate sexual interest in women. Some women report reduced interest in sex after menopause. There are many possible reasons for such a change, including several hormonal changes. As we mentioned earlier, estrogen increases a woman's ability to produce lubricants, and indeed estrogen treatment of menopausal women aids lubrication, but it does not change their interest in sex. On the other hand, a very low regimen of androgen is sometimes reported to revive menopausal women's interest in sexual relations. There have been several attempts to determine whether women's interest in or participation in sexual behavior varies with the menstrual cycle. Some researchers have found a slight increase in sexual behavior around the time of ovulation, but the effect is small, and several studies have failed to see any significant change in interest in sex across the menstrual cycle.

Pheromones Both Prime and Activate Reproductive Behaviors

When steroid hormones from the gonads affect the brain to activate mating behavior, the activation is not absolute; individuals are simply more likely to engage in mating behaviors when gonadal steroid levels are adequate. This activation can be thought of as communication between the gonad and the brain: by producing steroids to make gametes, the gonads also inform the brain that the body is ready to mate. This signaling takes place inside the individual, but hormones can also provide information *between* animals. For example, during ovulation, female goldfish produce a hormone called F prostaglandin. Some F prostaglandin escapes the female's body and passes through the water to a male. The F prostaglandin is detected by the male and stimulates his mating behavior (Sorensen and Goetz, 1993). The most likely scenario for the evolution of this relationship is that long ago females released F prostaglandin only as a by-product of ovulation, but because the presence of the hormone conveyed important information about the female's condition, natural selection favored males who detected the hormone and began courting in response to the signal. As we learned in Chapter 7, a chemical that is released from one individual and affects another individual is called a **pheromone.** In the case of the goldfish, a single chemical acts both as a hormone (in the female) and as a pheromone. This pheromone quickly activates another individual's behavior, but other pheromones act more gradually to affect the other individual. In the latter case the pheromone is said to act as a "primer"—priming the potential mate for copulation. Even very simple unicellular organisms, such as yeasts, prepare each other for mating by releasing and detecting pheromones (Fields, 1990).

Because most mammals do not live in an aquatic environment, pheromones must either pass through the air (so-called volatile chemicals) or must be passed by contact between individuals. The olfactory system may detect some such signals, but an accessory sensory system has developed specifically to detect pheromones: the vomeronasal system (see Chapter 9). The **vomeronasal organ** consists of specialized receptor cells near but separate from the olfactory epithelium. These sensory cells detect pheromones and send electrical signals to the accessory olfactory bulb in the brain. Two well-characterized pheromonal systems in mammals are the activation of aggression in mice and blocking of pregnancy in several rodent species. Male mice placed in a cage together will often fight; pheromones in the urine of one mouse determine whether the other mouse will attack. If one of the mice is a female or a male that has been castrated, the normal male mouse will not attack. If the castrated male is smeared with urine from an intact male (or from a female who has been injected with androgen), however, other males will attack him. Thus, circulating androgens appear to cause chemical(s) to be released in the urine (Novikov, 1993), and other male mice can detect this signal. Male mice attack only mice who produce these pheromones, because only they are rivals for mating with females.

Pheromones in the urine of male mice can accelerate puberty in young females (Price and Vandenbergh, 1992; Drickamer, 1992) and can halt pregnancy in mature females (Brennan, Kaba, and Keverne, 1990). Female mice can even identify an individual male by the particular mix of pheromones in his urine. When prairie voles mate, the female is exposed to pheromones from her mate's mouth and urine. If she is then isolated and exposed to urine from that male or any other male, pregnancy will be blocked; the fetuses are resorbed by the female and she is soon ready to mate again. Yet, if left with the original male, pregnancy continues, apparently because the female is careful not to apply her mate's urine to her vomeronasal organ (Smale et al., 1990). The female not only distinguishes males by their pheromones, but remembers which male mated with her and avoids using his urine to interrupt pregnancy. Resorption of the young in the presence of a new male may be an attempt to make the best of a bad situation: if her original mate is gone, she may be better off beginning a new litter with a new male.

Do Pheromones Synchronize Menstrual Cycles in Women?

Martha McClintock (1971) reported that women residing together in a college dormitory were more likely to have their menstrual cycles in synchrony than would be expected by chance. Women who spend more time with each other are more likely to menstruate at the same time; McClintock hypothesized that pheromones passing between the women might serve as a signal of the ovulatory cycle, enabling synchronization. It has been difficult even to prove that women show menstrual synchrony, but most studies confirm this idea (Weller and Weller, 1993). Whether the synchronization relies on social signals or pheromonal signals between the women has been even more difficult to determine. Perhaps the most compelling evidence that pheromones may play some such role is the acceleration or delay of menstrual cycles in women who have extracts of sweat from other women applied to their upper lip (Presti et al., 1986), but both the effects and the sample sizes in these studies are small.

The Evolution of Sexual Reproduction

Now that we've talked about sex and some of its many complications, we may wonder how such an outlandish system ever got started. In fact, many animals come in two sexes. Author William Tenn (1968) imagines an exotic animal species that has *seven* different sexes. The sexes have wildly divergent bodies and behavior, allowing each to occupy a particular ecological niche. One problem with such an arrangement is reproduction: how do you get a member of each of the seven sexes together for mating when some are predators, some prey? Well, one of the seven sexes is highly adapted for the tricky diplomacy of arranging suitable orgies. In real life, no creatures have more than two sexes, so perhaps even natural selection cannot solve diplomatic problems involving more than two parties. As we'll see next, however, species with only one sex reproduce perfectly well. Why should any species bother with two?

Sexual Reproduction Helps Combine Beneficial Mutations

If in a given population of animals one individual has a very rare, *beneficial* mutation, the mutation can be spread to other individuals in only two ways. One way is for that individual to make clones of itself, to give birth to individuals that have only its genes, including the mutated one. In unicellular organisms this process is known as **fission**, the simple splitting of one individual cell into two. In multicellular animals this process is known as **parthenogenesis** (meaning "virgin birth"; the Parthenon was a temple to the virgin goddess Athena). If the mutation is especially useful, future generations will consist mostly of this individual's progeny. Eventually other beneficial mutations may arise. Thus it is possible for a species to evolve without sexual reproduction. But consider the other method of spreading the new gene—sexual reproduction. In this process the original holder of a helpful new gene produces offspring that have both the new gene and genes from other individuals. Some of those other genes may also be beneficial. By reproducing sexually, many beneficial genes, each arising from different individuals, can come *together* in later individuals. Although this mixing of beneficial genes is undoubtedly accomplished by sexual reproduction, evolutionary theorists still debate about why any particular individual, if capable of either parthenogenesis or sexual reproduction, would benefit by producing offspring that carry only half of its genes.

Some animals can reproduce by either method. Aphids, the small green insects that probably infest your garden every year, reproduce by parthenogenesis when there is ample food and favorable conditions for growth and unchecked reproduction. When conditions worsen, though, the aphids begin sexually reproducing, effectively swapping genes to produce offspring that begin migrating away, looking for a more hospitable environment. Perhaps the advantage of reproducing sexually is that you halve your gene contribution to the next generation, thus enhancing the chance of at least some offspring surviving by producing new combinations of genes that might better survive the new conditions. Nevertheless, parthenogenesis has been documented to occur on rare occasions in some vertebrate species, such as chickens and turkeys, and there are several species of whiptail lizards in the southwestern United States in which all individuals are females that reproduce exclusively via parthenogenesis (Crews, 1994; Figure 12.10). Aquarium fanciers know a species of tropical fish, the Amazon molly, that consists solely of females reproducing by parthenogenesis. Apparently, then, nothing inherent in the vertebrate body *requires* sexual reproduction, but this method of reproduction among vertebrates is so pervasive that it must convey some advantage.

But even sexual reproduction does not require that animals come in two different sexes. In many sexually reproducing species, each individual produces both sperm and eggs, and sex consists of donating sperm to a partner while accepting sperm in return.

12.10 Are Males Necessary?
Whiptail lizards (*left*) and Amazon mollies (*right*) are two of the rare vertebrate species that reproduce by parthenogenesis. All individuals are females who produce daughters with only the mother's genes. Nevertheless, these animals exhibit mock mating behaviors (such as those displayed by the lizards abovethat greatly resemble the mating behaviors of related species that reproduce sexually. Courtesy of David Crews, Michael Ryan.

In these species, every individual is the same sex. Individuals that can reproduce as either males or females are called **hermaphrodites** (from the Greek gods Hermes and Aphrodite, the exemplars of masculinity and femininity). Although hermaphrodites, such as the sea slug *Aplysia*, are common among the invertebrates, very few vertebrates (all of them are fishes) are true hermaphrodites. Early in the evolution of our prevertebrate ancestors, the roles of males and females became so divergent that the sexes eventually split, with some individuals reproducing exclusively via sperm while others produced only eggs. This inference about evolution is reminiscent of the ancient Greek notion that humans were once hermaphrodites whom the gods tore into separate males and females. This legend was purported to explain why we are each looking for our other half to make us whole again.

In many species of fish, individuals may spend some parts of their life behaving and reproducing as females and other parts of their life reproducing in a male fashion. Although these individuals never produce both sperm and eggs *at the same time,* they may be regarded as "serial" hermaphrodites. In some cases the switch in sex has obvious reproductive advantages: most such fish reproduce as females when young and switch to the more aggressive, territorial behavior needed to reproduce as males only after they grow large enough to compete with others (Francis, 1992). In other fishes, social stimuli may drive the sexual switch. In black mollies, for example, a male may

defend a feeding territory from other males and share its resources with many female mates. If the male is removed and no other male appears, one of the females will undergo the transformation into a male and replace him. The female that undergoes this change is usually the largest and most aggressive member of the harem. Since any female is capable of this change (as can be shown when one removes all larger females), but only one at a time completes the transformation, the social interactions between the females must accelerate the change in one and inhibit the change in the others. Table 12.2 reviews the various reproductive strategies.

Males and Females Often Adopt Different Reproductive Strategies

When our ancestors began reproducing through separate male and female individuals, it became possible for the two sexes to diverge in form and behavior (Figure 12.11). Today many species are **sexually dimorphic**, the term Darwin used to describe species in which males and females have very different bodies. Species in which the sexes look very similar are referred to as sexually monomorphic, despite the fact that they are different internally, for example, in the production of eggs or sperm. The most obvious sexual dimorphism is the larger body size of males in many vertebrate species (see Figure 12.11). Later in

---

Table 12.2

Reproductive Strategies of Animals

TYPE OF REPRODUCTION	STRATEGY	EXAMPLES OF ANIMALS THAT USE THE STRATEGY
Asexual	Fission	Unicellular animals
	Parthenogenesis (virgin birth)	
	Obligatory	Amazon mollies, some whiptail lizards
	Occasional	Aphids
Sexual	Hermaphroditism (each individual produces sperm and eggs)	
	Simultaneous	Many invertebrates (e.g., *Aplysia*)
	Serial	Many fishes
	Gonochorism (separate sexes; each individual produces either sperm or eggs)	
	Sexually monomorphic	Many birds (e.g., seagulls, ring doves
	Sexually dimorphic	Most mammals

(a) Mandrill baboons

(b) Peafowl

(d) Praying mantises

(c) Ring doves

(e) Jacanas

12.11 Which Is the Female in Each Pair?
In mandrill baboons (*a*) and peafowl (*b*), the male is larger and more
brightly colored than the female. In ring doves (*c*), males and females have
identical appearances, but behave differently. Among praying mantises (*d*)
and jacanas (*e*), the female is larger than the male.

this chapter we will learn that the nervous systems of
rats, humans, and other vertebrates also display sexual dimorphism. One example of sexual dimorphism
that appears to have had profound effects on vertebrate evolution is the difference in the size of male gametes (sperm) and female gametes (ova).

Male gametes are small and cheap; female gametes
are large and expensive. Figure 12.12 demonstrates
the difference in size between male and female gametes, but perhaps you had not realized the difference
in cost. Every animal must gain scarce resources to

live, including nutrients to support growth. Unless individuals budget their use of nutrients and energy
wisely, they cannot succeed at reproduction. An individual specialized for producing sperm can produce
many millions of gametes for the same cost, in terms
of nutrients and energy, as a single egg.

Many Males Are Promiscuous, Many Females Are Choosy

Because of the low cost of producing sperm, a single
male individual can gather enough energy and nu-

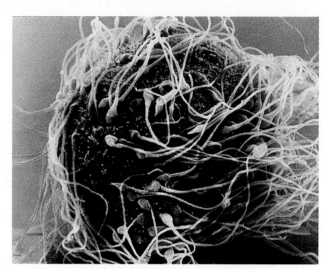

12.12 Male Gametes are Small and Cheap
Sperm and an ovum are magnified about 450 times. Note that sperm are much smaller than ova, and are therefore easier to produce.

trients to produce sufficient sperm to inseminate millions of females, potentially providing the entire next generation. Females, on the other hand, must be more selective in order to reproduce successfully. Females that carefully nurture their costly eggs (in whatever manner is appropriate for that species) reproduce more often than less cautious females and come to predominate in future generations. One of the most important ways that females of any species can nurture their egg investments is to *choose a mate carefully*. Males that carry many beneficial genes are more likely to provide the female's offspring with favorable genes. Therefore, females that discover and mate with such males should come to predominate in future generations, while females that mate indiscriminately will have fewer descendants.

The difficulty for a female, of course, is how to determine whether a potential mate has beneficial genes. Until recently, she could not count on training in molecular biology. Instead, the female must observe the appearance and behavior of the male carefully. A vigorous, healthy male must be doing something right, and in general, an unhealthy looking male is more likely (although by no means certain) to carry harmful genes. On the other hand, inseminating a female is rarely dangerous to a male (except for species such as black widows and preying mantises in which the female kills the male after mating, and with respect to sexually transmitted diseases). Even if the offspring do not survive, ample sperm will be left for the next female.

From this perspective, **courtship** is a period during which the female indirectly assesses the genetic makeup of a male to judge his suitability as a mate. The female need not be aware of this process, but females who choose genetically able males will predominate in future generations. For mammalian females, which carry their young *in utero* for a prolonged period and then provide milk for an additional time, the investment in each fertilized egg is tremendous, and therefore the pressure to select a good mate is intense. In most vertebrates, nearly all the females who reach reproductive age manage to mate, but only a minority of the males who reach reproductive age succeed in mating. Some interesting exceptions are described in the next section.

There Are Four Basic Types of Mating Systems

The different mating strategies of males and females across species can be classified into four different mating systems: promiscuity, polygyny, polyandry, and monogamy. These different systems seem to be related to species differences in the investment of males and females in their offspring.

1. Recall that among mammals, most females are very selective in mating and most males never mate. That means a few males are doing most of the mating, and since the number of males and females is roughly equal, these males must be mating with more than one female. But most female mammals also mate with more than one male. Such a mating system, in which animals mate with several partners and do not establish long-lasting associations, is said to reflect **promiscuity**.

2. With some animals, such as elephant seals and gorillas, a long-lasting association between mates develops, with one male mating with a group of females (a harem). Each female mates with only one male, but that male mates with several females. This system is called **polygyny** (from the Greek *polys*, "many," and *gyne*, "woman").

3. Much more rare than polygyny are cases of **polyandry** ("many husbands"), where each female of the species mates with several males, but each male mates with only one female. The jacana (see Figure 12.11) is an example; in this species it is the females who compete for mates. The females are larger and more colorful than males and they defend the nest site from other females. Once the female jacana lays the eggs, she departs, leaving the

male to incubate the eggs and raise the young. The term **polygamy** ("many spouses") is sometimes used to refer to polygyny and polyandry collectively. (*Bigamy* means "having *two* spouses.")

4. **Monogamy** ("one spouse"), is the mating system characterized by one male and one female forming a breeding pair and mating exclusively (or almost exclusively) with one another. Monogamy is far more common among birds than among mammals (Figure 12.13). It has been suggested that because birds have a high metabolic rate and their young tend to be very immature at hatching, a single parent could not provide enough food for the chicks to survive (Figure 12.14). In that case, males that did not care for eggs and chicks would make little or no contribution to the next generation; thus, you would expect monogamy to become common. Different human cultures have adopted each of these four mating systems (Box 12.1).

Sexual Selection Accentuates Differences between the Sexes

As we learned in Chapter 3, Charles Darwin was the first to recognize that competition between males and the tendency of females to be very selective in mating would affect the course of natural selection. He coined the term **sexual selection** to refer to the selective pressures that each sex exerts on the other.

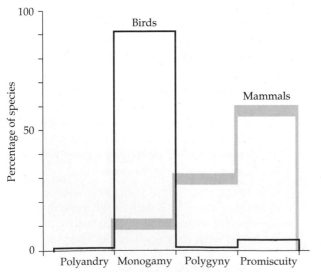

12.13   Mating Systems in Mammals and Birds
Estimates for birds are based on data from Lack, 1968; estimates for mammals from Daly and Wilson, 1978. Both should be regarded as only rough estimates.

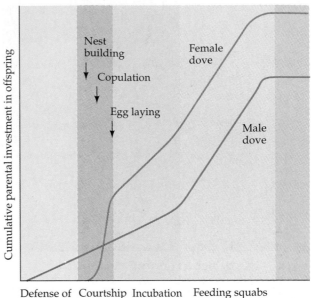

12.14   Parental Investment in Offspring
Hypothetical curves of the cumulative investment of a female and a male ring dove in their offspring throughout the reproductive cycle. (Adapted from Erickson, 1978, and Trivers, 1972.)

Darwin regarded sexual selection as a special type of natural selection and used the concept to explain certain features that were not easy to explain on the basis of natural selection alone. For example, why do male lions have manes, male birds of paradise display elaborate tail feathers, and male moose sport enormous antlers? These features do not seem to help the animal gather food, elude predators, or find shelter. Indeed, in many cases they seem to hinder those functions.

The only advantage Darwin could imagine these features might confer on animals was in procuring mates. Why? Because members of the other sex display a preference for mates with those features. Darwin also realized that sexual selection, by exerting *different* selective pressures on males and females, would impel the two sexes to diverge more and more in their appearance. Thus, sexual reproduction provides the pressure to select mates with advantageous genes. In some insect species the sexes are so dimorphic that zoologists originally classified them as different species. Of course, there is a limit to the influence of sexual selection, because other selective pressures also apply. A male who is overly ornamented, for example, may be unable to find food or

Box 12.1

Can Sociobiology Explain Human Reproductive Behavior?

Humans share the major adaptations of all mammals for reproductive behavior: sperm are cheap, mothers must invest much more heavily than fathers to produce a newborn, and men tend to be larger than women. But humans have also been molded by their culture. Almost all humans depend on social relations to survive. Dependence on specialized personnel to provide us with food, clothing, and shelter is especially obvious in our society. Even in less technologically advanced societies, however, the division of labor is almost always crucial for survival. Thus for humans the basic facts of mammalian reproductive biology have long been tempered by the basic facts of cultural survival. Anthropologists have studied marriage practices in hundreds of human societies (Bourguignon and Greenbaum, 1973) and have found much variety. When the findings are grouped into large categories (see figure), the mammalian tendency to polygyny is apparent. Polyandry is exceedingly rare. Monogamy is the only accepted form in many societies, but it is actually far more prevalent than this statement suggests: even in societies that accept polygamy, most marriages are monogamous.

Evolution has given us large brains that are specialized for communication and learning. This heritage is undoubtedly responsible for the wide range of behaviors that human societies permit and the wide range of behaviors people display within a given society. Our tendency to communicate and learn, within the context of complex social networks, is also related to the wide variety of sexual behaviors among individuals and displayed by a given individual at different times.

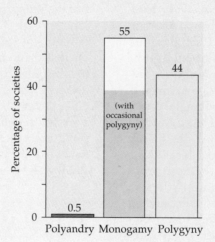

evade predators (Figure 12.15), activities that are crucial for survival.

In sexual selection, individuals who demand that potential partners display certain characteristics or perform certain behaviors before mating benefit by passing genes that favor such behaviors on to their offspring. Once a particular species begins showing such partiality—for manes on male lions, elaborate tails on birds, balding in men, and so on—the prejudice tends to be self-perpetuating. For example, once a population of females comes to favor mating with maned lions, a female who mates with a male without a mane leaves her offspring (especially her sons) at a distinct disadvantage. Natural selection thus favors the maintenance of such mating preferences.

One interesting way in which females of several species enforce these demands is in the control of ovulation (the physical release of an egg from the ovary so that it can be fertilized). In frogs, for example, exposure to courting males facilitates ovulation in the female; the more such behavior the males display, the more eggs are released and made available

12.15 Results of Sexual Selection
A tail display by a male raggiana bird of paradise. Although such a tail may interfere with the bird's ability to avoid predators, it definitely attracts female birds of paradise. Courtesy of Bruce Beehler.

for fertilization. Rats provide another example, as we saw earlier. In other species, courtship and/or copulation is *required* for ovulation. In lions, only very vigorous copulation over several days will induce the female to ovulate. The lionesses' reproductive physiology enforces strict evolutionary pressure on male behavior.

Remember the parthenogenetic whiptail lizards and Amazon mollies we discussed earlier? In both cases, closely related species reproduce sexually, and in these sexual species courtship and mating behaviors facilitate ovulation. Some remnant of this courtship-facilitated ovulation must remain in the parthenogenetic females because they too will release more eggs if they are courted and go through mating behavior. But who do you mate with when there are only females of your species? With whiptail lizards, females take turns mating with one another. A given female may play the role of a male one moment—wrapping her body around the other female, pressing their cloacae together, biting her neck, and so on—and play the role of a female later (see Figure 12.10). Two females in a cage alone will literally take turns. Such mock mating increases the number of eggs released and laid. Mollies are among the fish species in which the eggs are fertilized and hatched inside the mother. The Amazon mollies "mate" not with one another, but with males of the closely related sailfin molly species. These males court Amazons, insert their modified fin into the female, and deposit sperm. The sperm do not fertilize the eggs, but the Amazon will release more eggs and later give birth to more daughters for having gone through the mock mating. Why should the male sailfins bother? Perhaps the cost to the male is very low, and perhaps the rehearsal will improve later mating with a sailfin female. But another reason that has been suggested is that sailfin females, seeing the male mate with another female (of either species), may regard him as more attractive and be more likely to mate with him (Schlupp, Marler, and Ryan, 1994).

Many Vertebrates Depend on Their Parents for Survival

Many young vertebrates, and all newborn mammals, require parental attention to survive. Animals that are born or hatched with well-developed sensory and motor systems (for example, chickens, guinea pigs, horses) are said to be **precocial**; species in which the young begin life with poorly developed motor or sensory systems (for example, songbirds, cats, humans)

are said to be **altricial**. Among birds it is common for both the female and male to feed and care for the eggs and young. Among mammals, in which offspring must receive milk by nursing after birth, it is often the female alone who raises the offspring. The factors that facilitate such maternal behavior have been studied extensively in rats. Rat mothers (called dams) show four easily measured maternal behaviors: nest building, crouching over pups, retrieving pups, and nursing. A virgin female or a male will not normally display these behaviors toward rat pups. Almost any rat, however, whether virgin female, experienced dam, or even a male, will show the first three behaviors (all but the nursing) if they are exposed to a nest of pups long enough—a few hours a day for a few days. Apparently the sights and sounds of newborn pups help elicit such attentions from adults. A rat dam that has just delivered a litter of pups shows these behaviors almost instantly. The complicated changes in the levels of several hormones at the end of pregnancy prepare the female to show these maternal behaviors (and to produce milk) right away, but the sight and sounds of the pups are needed to maintain the dam's willingness to show these behaviors.

Sexual Differentiation

For species such as our own, in which the only kind of reproduction is sexual reproduction, and in which sexual selection has generated sexual dimorphism, each individual must become either a male or a female to reproduce. **Sexual differentiation** is the process by which individuals develop either male or female bodies and behavior. In mammals this process begins before birth and continues until the individual becomes capable of reproducing.

The Sex of an Individual Is Determined Early in Life

For mammals sex is determined at the time of conception, when a sperm penetrates the egg and contributes either a Y chromosome or an X chromosome. From that point on, the path of sexual differentiation is set. We will describe that path and its occasional exceptions shortly. In mammals the individuals that receive an X chromosome from their father will become females; those who receive a Y will become males. (The mother always contributes an X chromosome.) Males are said to be the **heterogametic** sex because they have two different **sex chromosomes** (XY), while females are homogametic (XX). In birds it is the females who are heterogametic. The sex of some reptiles is determined by sex chromosomes; in other reptile species the factor determining whether an individual will develop as a male or female is the temperature at which the egg is incubated. No matter what the mechanisms, the developmentally early event that normally decides whether the individual will become a male or female is known as **sexual determination**. In vertebrates the first visible consequence of sexual determination is in the **gonads**. Very early in development each individual has a pair of indifferent gonads, glands that vaguely resemble both testes and ovaries. During the first month of gestation in humans, the indifferent gonads begin changing into either ovaries or testes.

Sex Chromosomes Direct Sexual Differentiation of the Gonads

In mammals the Y chromosome contains a gene called the **sex-determining region on the Y gene (*Sry*)** that is responsible for the development of testes. If an individual has a Y chromosome, the cells of the indifferent gonad begin making the Sry protein. The Sry protein causes the cells in the core of the indifferent gonad (the medulla) to proliferate at the expense of the outer layers (the cortex), and the indifferent gonad develops into a testis. If the individual has no Y chromosome (or if it has a Y chromosome but the *Sry* gene is defective), no Sry protein is produced, and the indifferent gonad takes a different course: cells of the cortical layers proliferate more than those of the medullary layers, and an ovary forms. (In reptiles that lack sex chromosomes, the temperature at which the egg is incubated appears to determine whether or not an *Sry*like gene product is made.) For all vertebrates, this early decision of whether to form testes or ovaries has a "domino effect," setting off a chain of events that result in either a male or a female.

Gonadal Hormones Direct Sexual Differentiation of the Rest of the Body

The most important way the gonads influence sexual differentiation is through their hormonal output. Developing testes produce several hormones, while early ovaries produce very little hormone. If other cells of the embryo receive the testicular hormones, they begin developing masculine characters; if the cells are not exposed to testicular hormones, they develop feminine characters.

We can chart masculine or feminine development by examining the structures connecting the gonads to the outside of the body. The conduits that allow gametes to exit the body are quite different in males and females (see Figure 12.8), so the proper development of these structures is crucial for sexual reproduction. At the embryonic stage, all individuals have the precursor tissues that could form either the female or male apparatus. For example, the early fetus has a genital tubercle that can form either a clitoris or a penis, as well as two sets of ducts that connect the indifferent gonads to the outer body wall: the **Wolffian ducts** and the **Müllerian ducts** (Figure 12.16*a*). The early fetus has both sets of ducts, but in females the Müllerian ducts develop into the fallopian tubes, uterus, and inner vagina (Figure 12.16*c* and *e*), and only a remnant of the Wolffian ducts remains. In males, hormones secreted by the testes orchestrate the converse outcome: the Wolffian ducts develop into epididymis, vas deferens, and seminal vesicles (Figure 12.16*b* and *d*), while the Müllerian ducts shrink to mere remnants.

The development of the Wolffian ducts is promoted by the steroidal androgen **testosterone**; the shrinkage of the Müllerian ducts is caused by the protein hormone **Müllerian regression hormone (MRH)**. If there is no testis to produce testosterone and MRH, the Wolffian ducts fail to develop and the Müllerian ducts develop unimpeded. Testosterone also masculinizes other, non-Wolffian-derived structures. Testosterone causes tissues around the urethra to form the prostate gland. Furthermore, testosterone acts on the epithelial tissues around the urethra to form a scrotum and penis. These effects are aided by the local conversion of testosterone into another steroidal androgen, dihydrotestosterone (DHT). The epithelial cells have the enzyme 5-α-reductase to convert testosterone to DHT, and the DHT binds the androgen receptors even more readily than testosterone, resulting in greater gene activation and further masculine development. Without steroidal androgens, the prostate fails to form and the external skin grows into the female labia and clitoris (Figure 12.17).

Departures from the Orderly Sequence of Sexual Differentiation Result in Predictable Changes in Development

There is a condition called **sex-reverse (*Sxr*)** in mice that is caused by a bit of the Y chromosome, including the *Sry* gene, attaching itself to an X chromosome. When an egg, with its single X chromosome from the

12.16 Sexual Differentiation in Humans
(*a*) Undifferentiated fetus. (*b, d*) Male fetus.
(*c, e*) Female fetus.

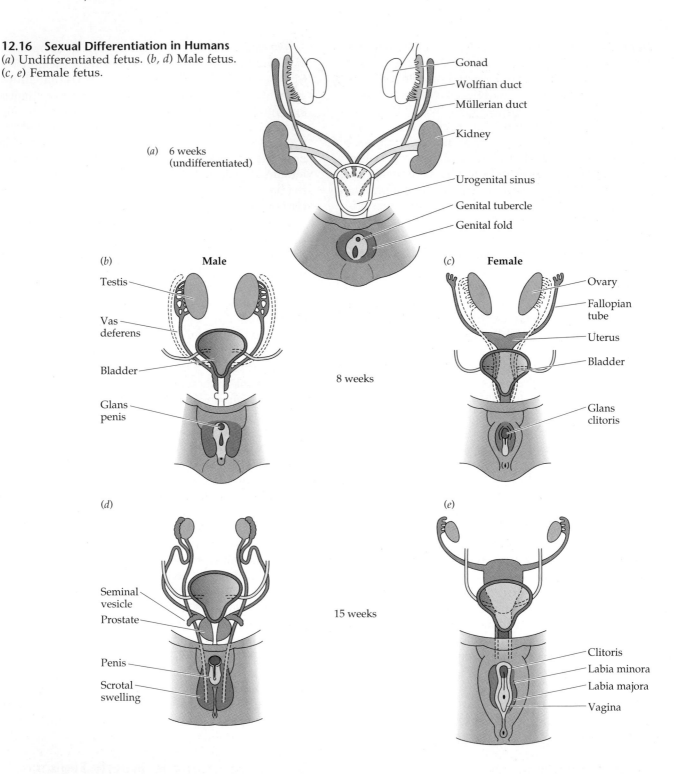

(*a*) 6 weeks
(undifferentiated)

Gonad
Wolffian duct
Müllerian duct
Kidney
Urogenital sinus
Genital tubercle
Genital fold

(*b*) **Male**

Testis
Vas deferens
Bladder
Glans penis

8 weeks

(*c*) **Female**

Ovary
Fallopian tube
Uterus
Bladder
Glans clitoris

(*d*)

Seminal vesicle
Prostate
Penis
Scrotal swelling

15 weeks

(*e*)

Clitoris
Labia minora
Labia majora
Vagina

mother, is fertilized by a sperm carrying this X-plus-*Sry*-gene chromosome, the developing mouse forms testes. The testes then release hormones to masculinize the rest of body development. Such mice look like normal males, but they have two X chromosomes (one of which is a little longer than normal because it's carrying the bit of Y chromosome material). There

have been several examples of humans who look very much like males but turn out to have two X chromosomes and no (apparent) Y chromosome. These human cases appear to mirror the *Sxr* mice.

A more common chromosomal abnormality is the possession of no Y chromosome and only

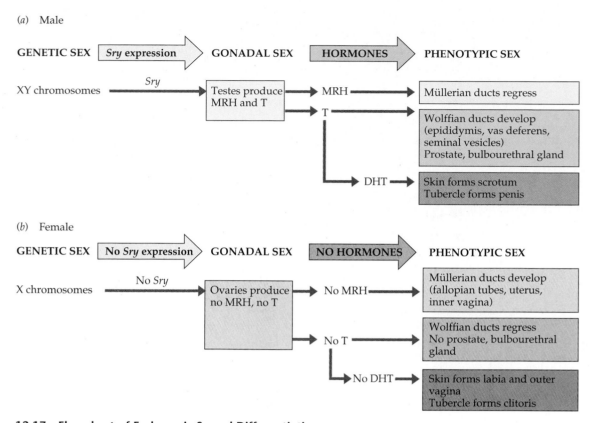

(*a*) Male

GENETIC SEX → *Sry* expression → **GONADAL SEX** → HORMONES → **PHENOTYPIC SEX**

XY chromosomes —*Sry*→ Testes produce MRH and T → MRH → Müllerian ducts regress

→ T → Wolffian ducts develop (epididymis, vas deferens, seminal vesicles) Prostate, bulbourethral gland

→ DHT → Skin forms scrotum Tubercle forms penis

(*b*) Female

GENETIC SEX → No *Sry* expression → **GONADAL SEX** → NO HORMONES → **PHENOTYPIC SEX**

X chromosomes —No *Sry*→ Ovaries produce no MRH, no T → No MRH → Müllerian ducts develop (fallopian tubes, uterus, inner vagina)

→ No T → Wolffian ducts regress No prostate, bulbourethral gland

→ No DHT → Skin forms labia and outer vagina Tubercle forms clitoris

12.17 Flowchart of Embryonic Sexual Differentiation
(*a*) Male. (*b*) Female. DHT = dihydrotestosterone; MRH = Müllerian regression hormone; T = testosterone.

one X chromosome. Such genetic makeup (referred to as XO) results in **Turner's syndrome**—an apparent female with poorly developed but recognizable ovaries, as you would expect since no *Sry* gene is available.

Other sex chromosomal anomalies have predictable results: if one or more Y chromosomes is present, Sry will be available, testes will form, and testicular secretions will masculinize the rest of the body. If no Y chromosome is present, the gonads will develop as ovaries and the rest of the body, in the absence of testicular secretions, will follow suit. So the role of the sex chromosomes is to determine the sex of the gonad; gonadal hormones then drive sexual differentiation of the rest of the body. Figure 12.18 charts the series of events in mammalian sexual differentiation.

Androgen Sometimes Reaches Developing Females

XX individuals with well-formed ovaries are sometimes exposed to androgen in utero, and depending on the degree of exposure, they may be masculinized. For example, most fetal rats develop in the uterus sandwiched between two siblings. If a female is surrounded by brothers, some of the androgen from the siblings must reach the female because, although her gross appearance will be feminine at birth, her anogenital distance (the distance from the tip of the phallus to the anus) will be slightly greater (that is, more malelike) than that of a female developing between two sisters (Clemens, Gladue, and Coniglio, 1978). In Chapter 9 we saw an example of a similar phenomenon in humans: women who have a male twin produce otoacoustic emissions that are slightly more typical of males than of females.

In humans there are several genetic mutations that can result in a female being exposed to androgen *in utero*. What these various conditions, known as **congenital adrenal hyperplasia** (**CAH**), have in common is that the adrenal glands, which normally produce small amounts of androgenic steroids, produce a considerable amount of androgen. (The condition is called adrenal hyperplasia because at birth the adrenal glands are swollen from excessive cell division. The word "congenital" means "present at birth.") In

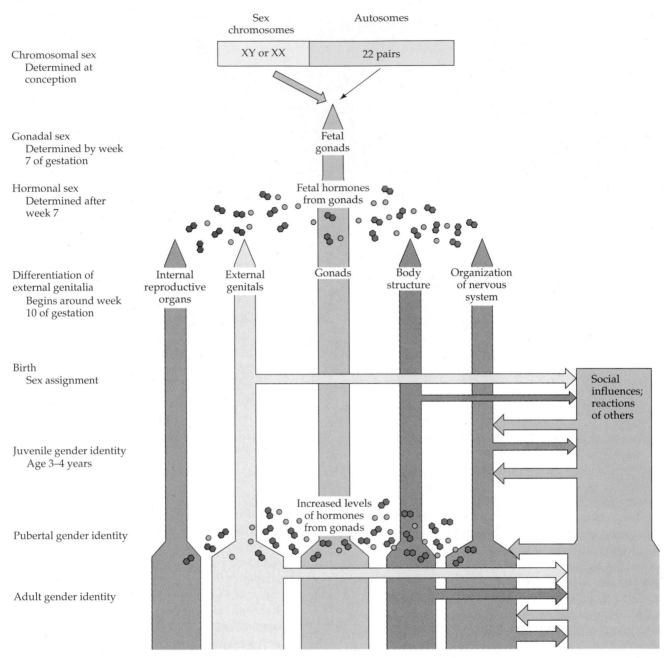

12.18 Steps Toward Adult Gender Identity

XX individuals with this condition, the androgen levels produced are usually intermediate between those of normal females and males, and the newborn has an "intersex" appearance—a phallus that is intermediate in size between a normal clitoris and a normal penis, and skin folds that resemble both labia and scrotum (Figure 12.19). Sometimes the opening of the vagina fails to form (although the internal portion of the vagina is present), and sometimes the opening of the urethra is somewhere along the base or length of the phallus (rather than below the clitoris as in normal females). Such individuals are readily recognizable at birth because, even in severe cases in which penis and scrotum are fully formed, no testes are present in the "scrotum." The ovaries of such individuals, as you would expect, are normal and remain in the abdomen. The Müllerian duct structures are fully developed. The treatment for such individuals is

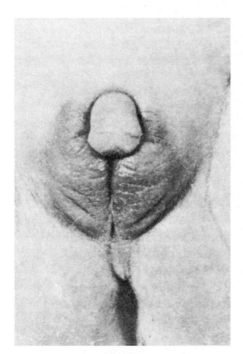 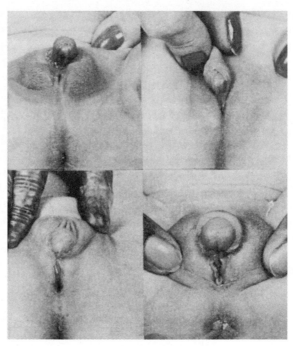

12.19   An Intersex Phenotype
Genitalia of newborn girls with congenital adrenal hyperplasia (CAH).
Courtesy of John Money.

surgical correction of the external appearance and medication to inhibit androgen production by the adrenals. CAH females are much more likely to be described by their parents (and themselves) as "tomboys" than are other girls. In adulthood, most CAH females describe themselves as heterosexual, but they are somewhat more likely to report a homosexual orientation than are other women.

In rats and other mammals, experimenters have deliberately exposed developing females to androgenic steroids, and the results are quite uniform: given sufficient testosterone during development, XX individuals will form Wolffian duct structures—prostate, scrotum, and penis. Because the testosterone has no effect on Müllerian ducts, these structures—fallopian tubes, uterus and (internal) vagina—also develop. The gonads develop as ovaries, apparently ignoring the androgens. As we will see later in the chapter, the adult behavior of such androgenized females provided the first clues that early androgens could masculinize the brain as well as the body.

A Defective Androgen Receptor Can Block the Masculinization of Males

An interesting demonstration of androgen's influence on sexual differentiation is provided by the condition known as **androgen insensitivity**. The gene for the androgen receptor is found on the X chromosome. If this gene is defective on one of the X chromosomes of a female, she can still produce functional androgen receptors from the gene on the other X chromosome. But when the X chromosome of an XY individual has a defective androgen receptor gene, that person is incapable of producing the androgen receptor and is therefore unable to respond to androgenic hormones. The gonads of such people develop as normal testes, and the testes produce MRH, which inhibits Müllerian duct structures, and plenty of testosterone. However, in the absence of working androgen receptors, the Wolffian ducts fail to develop and the external epithelia form labia and a clitoris. Such individuals look like normal females at birth and at puberty develop breasts. (Breast development in humans appears to depend on the ratio of estrogenic to androgenic stimulation at puberty, and since androgen-insensitive individuals receive little androgenic *stimulation*, despite ample androgenic hormones, the functional estrogen-to-androgen ratio is high.) Androgen-insensitive individuals may be recognized when their menstrual cycles fail to commence, because neither ovaries nor uterus are present to produce menstruation. Such women are infertile and, lacking a Müllerian contribution, may have a slightly shallow vagina, but otherwise they look like other women (Figure 12.20) and, as we'll see next, behave like women. Later in this chapter we will describe another mutation that causes some people to appear to change their sex (without surgery) at adolescence.

How Shall We Define Gender—by Genes, Gonads, Genitals, or the Brain?

Most humans are either male or female, and whether we examine their chromosomes, gonads, external genitalia, or internal structures, we will see a consistent pattern: each will be either feminine or masculine in character. Behavior is much more difficult to define as feminine or masculine. The only behavior displayed *exclusively* by one sex is childbirth. Even behaviors that are very rarely displayed by members of a sex (for example, sexual assault by women or breast feeding by men) occur sometimes. As for behaviors that can be measured and made amenable to

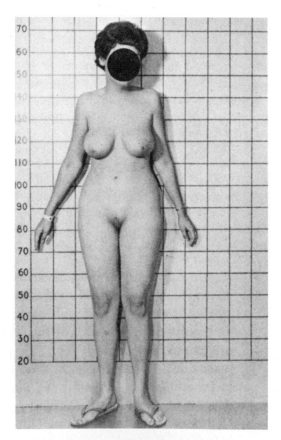

12.20 A Woman with Testes
Although this person has the male XY chromosome pattern and therefore testes (undescended), she also has complete androgen insensitivity. Therefore her body has developed in a feminine fashion. Courtesy of John Money.

experimental study in humans or other animals, we have to resort to group means and statistical tests to see the differences. A given individual will almost always display *some* behaviors that are more common in the opposite sex.

Androgen-insensitive individuals show us that even morphological features can be confusing criteria by which to judge sex. Androgen-insensitive humans have a male chromosome and testes. Like most males, they do not have fallopian tubes or a uterus, but they do have a vagina and breasts and in many respects behave like females. They dress like females, are attracted to and marry males, and perhaps most important, even after they learn the details of their condition, they call themselves women (Money and Ehrhardt, 1972).

As we will see next, parts of the brain are also typically different between the sexes in humans and other animals. In androgen-insensitive rats, some brain regions are masculine and others are feminine. Thus, from a scientific standpoint we cannot regard an animal, especially a human, as simply masculine or feminine. Rather, we must specify which structure or behavior we are talking about when we say it is typical of females or of males.

Gonadal Hormones Direct Sexual Differentiation of the Brain and Behavior

As scientists began discovering that testicular hormones direct masculine development of the body, behavioral researchers found evidence for a similar influence on the brain. In 1959, Phoenix, Goy, Gerall, and Young described the effect of fetal hormones on the sexual behavior of guinea pigs. Recall that a female guinea pig, like most rodents, normally displays the lordosis posture in response to male mounting for only a short period around the time of ovulation, when her fertility is highest. If a male mounts her at other times, she does not show lordosis. An experimenter can induce the female to display lordosis by removing her ovaries and injecting ovarian steroids in the sequence they normally follow during ovulation—giving her estrogen for a few days and then progesterone. A few hours after the progesterone injection, the female will display lordosis in response to male mounting.

Phoenix and collaborators knew that when this same regimen of steroids was given to an adult male guinea pig, whether or not he was allowed to keep his testes, he almost never showed lordosis in response to mounting males. In the 1959 study, the experimenters exposed female guinea pigs to testosterone *in utero*. As adults these females did *not* show lordosis. Even if their ovaries were removed and they were given the steroidal regimen that reliably activated lordosis in normal females, these fetally androgenized females did not show lordosis. In response to these data, Young and his young colleagues proposed the **organizational hypothesis**: The same testicular steroids that masculinize the genitalia also masculinize the developing brain and thereby permanently alter behavior. This **organizational effect** of steroid hormones stood in contrast with the **activational effect** we mentioned earlier (such as when adult females are given estrogen and progesterone to activate lordosis). Whereas steroids have an organizational influence only during early development and the effect is permanent, in adulthood they exert an activational effect, temporarily influencing behavior. Steroids have an organizational effect only when present during a **sensitive period** in development—the exact age depending on which behavior and which species. For rats, which are altricial, androgen given just after birth (during the neonatal period) can affect later behavior; guinea pigs, which are precocial, must be exposed to androgens prenatally (before birth) for adult behavior to be affected. Often, as in the demonstration by Phoenix, one must provide an activational dose of steroid in order to detect the organizational effect.

Early Testicular Secretions Result in Masculine Behavior in Adulthood

The organizational hypothesis provides a unitary explanation for sexual differentiation: the same steroidal signal that masculinizes the body (androgen) also masculinizes parts of the brain, ensuring that an individual's behavior usually is appropriate for its sex. From this point of view the nervous system is just another type of tissue listening for the androgenic signal that will instruct it to organize itself in a masculine fashion. If the nervous system does not detect androgen, it will organize itself in a feminine fashion. In fact, outside of the gonads and Müllerian ducts, all tissues that develop differently in males and females have been shown to do so under the influence of androgenic steroids. This is one of the functions that steroid hormones, with their capacity to infiltrate the entire body, can fulfill: sending a single message to disparate parts of the body to coordinate an integrated response.

What was demonstrated originally for the lordosis behavior of guinea pigs has been observed in a variety of vertebrate species and a variety of behaviors. Female rats must also display lordosis for mating to

take place; experiments have shown that exposing female pups to testosterone either just before birth or during the first ten days after birth greatly reduces their lordosis responsiveness as adults. Such results explain the previous findings that adult male rats show very little lordosis even when given estrogen and progesterone. Male rats that are castrated during the first week of life, however, display very good lordosis responses after a treatment of estrogen plus progesterone in adulthood. In rats, many behaviors were shown to be consistent with the organizational hypothesis. Animals exposed to either endogenous or exogenous androgens early in life behaved like males, while animals not exposed to androgens early in life behaved like females.

Some sex differences in behavior seem indifferent to early exposure to androgens. For example, male rhesus monkeys yawn more often than do females, but this behavior seems to be the result of *adult* exposure to androgens. If rhesus males are castrated in adulthood, they yawn about as often as normal females, and treating adult females with androgens activates yawning. Androgen exposure during development has no effect on later yawning behavior, so this sex difference in behavior seems to respond solely to activational rather than to organizational effects of androgens.

In other cases androgen seems to be needed both in development (to organize the nervous system to enable the later behavior) and in adulthood (to activate that behavior). For example, as we learned earlier, the copulatory behavior of male rats can be quantified in terms of how often they mount a receptive female and how often such mounting results in intromission. Androgen must be present in adulthood to activate this behavior: adult males that have been castrated stop mounting in a few weeks; injecting them with testosterone eventually restores masculine copulatory behavior. Such androgen treatment has *some* effect on adult female rats as well, causing them to mount other females more often, but they rarely manage intromission of their phallus (the clitoris) into the stimulus female's vagina. To see the full range of masculine copulatory behavior in a female rat, you must treat her with androgens just before birth, just after birth, *and* in adulthood. Such females not only mount receptive females, but they achieve intromissions regularly and ejaculate a spermless fluid (Ward, 1969)! Conversely, castrating a male rat at birth will result in very few intromissions later, no matter how much androgen you give in adulthood.

Thus, masculine copulatory behavior in rats and

several other rodent species seems to depend on both organizational and activational influences of androgen. An early criticism of this conclusion was offered by Frank Beach, who pointed out that the failure of fe-

Frank Beach (1911–1988)

males and neonatally castrated male rats to achieve intromission could well be due to the small size of the phallus rather than any differences in the nervous system (Beach, 1971). Indeed, there is remarkable correlation between the size of the penis and intromission success in male rats castrated at various ages (Beach and Holz, 1946). Thus, although there is excellent evidence that steroids present at birth masculinize the body, Beach found no proof that they masculinize the brain.

However, an unexpected development soon made it clear that steroids do indeed organize the developing nervous system of rodents to display male copulatory behavior, as we will see next.

The Estrogenic Metabolites of Testosterone Masculinize the Nervous System and Behavior of Rodents

Soon after the organizational hypothesis was published, some researchers reported a paradoxical finding. When newborn female rats were treated with small doses of estrogen, they failed to show lordosis behavior in adulthood (Feder and Whalen, 1965). In fact, a very small dose of estrogen, as little as 10 micrograms (10 µg), could permanently masculinize these behaviors, while a higher dose of testosterone (100 to 1,000 µg) was required for the same effect. The fact that a steroid such as estrogen, regarded as a "female hormone," could have such a profoundly masculinizing influence on later behavior was very puzzling. The results were especially strange because during development *all* rat fetuses are exposed to high levels of estrogen that originate in the mother and cross the placenta. If estrogens masculinize the developing brain, why aren't all females masculinized by maternal estrogens?

A closer look at the synthesis of steroid hormones reveals the explanation. The major androgen (testosterone) and the major estrogen (estradiol) differ by only one molecule. In fact, testosterone is often used as a precursor for the manufacture of estradiol in the ovary (see Figure 7.8). In a single chemical reaction, called **aromatization**, the enzyme **aromatase** converts testosterone to estradiol and other androgens to other estrogens. The ovaries normally contain a great deal of aromatase, and the brain was found to have high levels of aromatase as well. From this evidence arose the **aromatization hypothesis**, which suggested that testicular androgens enter the brain and are converted there into estrogens, and that these estrogens are what masculinize the developing nervous system. Why, then, aren't the brains of females masculinized by maternal estrogens? A protein found in the plasma of rat fetuses, called **alphafetoprotein**, binds estrogens and prevents them from entering the brain. Although both male and female fetuses produce alphafetoprotein, it does not bind androgens. The male rat is masculinized when his testes produce testosterone, which traverses the bloodstream (unimpeded by alphafetoprotein), and enters the brain, where aromatase converts the testosterone to estrogen, the estrogen binds to estrogen receptors, and the steroid–receptor complex regulates gene expression to cause the brain to develop in a masculine fashion. If no androgens are present, no estrogens reach the brain, and the fetus develops in a feminine fashion. The lack of aromatase also seems to play a role in the unusual sexual differentiation of the spotted hyena (Box 12.2).

The aromatization hypothesis was soon shown to apply even to masculine copulatory behavior in rats. If male rats were castrated at birth, they would grow up to have a small penis and to show few intromissions even when given testosterone in adulthood. If the males were castrated at birth and given the androgen dihydrotestosterone (DHT), which cannot be converted into estrogen, as adults they would have a penis of normal size, but would still show few or no intromission behaviors when given androgen. On the other hand, males castrated as newborns and treated with estrogen achieve intromission regularly when treated with androgen as adults, despite having a very small penis (no larger than in untreated castrated males). Thus Frank Beach's playful explanation of why female rats achieve few intromissions—"you can't  be a carpenter if you don't have a hammer"—was disproved. Rather, early testicular secretions seemed to organize the developing nervous system to masculinize later behavior. This idea was amply confirmed later, when sex differences in the structure of the nervous system were found.

Several Regions of the Nervous System Display Prominent Sexual Dimorphism

Because male and female rats behave differently, researchers assumed that their brains were different, and

Box 12.2

The Paradoxical Sexual Differentiation of the Spotted Hyena

Scientists of antiquity believed that spotted hyenas were hermaphrodites. The mistake is understandable because the female hyena has a clitoris that is as large as the penis of males (as shown in the figure), and like males, she urinates through her phallus. What's more, she appears to have no vagina, because during mating the male puts his penis inside the tip of her clitoris and later the pups come into the world through the clitoris. A group of scientists in Berkeley, California, has begun to understand how this remarkable situation could come about. Since hyenas are born with this sexually monomorphic exterior (although females tend to have larger bodies than do males), either both sexes are exposed to prenatal androgens, or their epithelial tissues develop in the masculine fashion whether androgens are present or not. Studies of steroid metabolism in the hyena placenta suggest the former. In other mammals the placenta rapidly aromatizes androgens into estrogens; this conversion may be a way to protect mother and female fetuses from androgens produced by fetal males. (Remember that in rodents a plasma protein prevents circulating estrogens from masculinizing the brain). But the hyena placenta is remarkably deficient in the aromatase enzyme (Licht et al., 1992). Because the hyena mother produces large amounts of the androgen androstenedione (Glickman et al., 1987), and the placenta fails to convert the androstenedione to estrogens, all the fetuses receive considerable androgen, and this may be the cause of their masculine appear-ance. One test of this hypothesis would be to see whether the placenta of the striped hyena (in which females do *not* have a masculine appearance) has enzymatic activities more like other mammals than like the spotted hyena.

Is the spotted hyena *brain* affected by these early androgens? Possibly, because females grow faster than males and are more aggressive than males. The social lives of hyenas center around the adult females. All adult females are dominant over all males, which means that females always get to eat first and, except during the breeding season, do not tolerate males getting close. There is also a dominance hierarchy among the females, and the daughters of high-ranking females tend to get first access to food and other resources. Thus there is considerable selective pressure for females to be aggressive, especially with other females. One of the remarkable findings from the captive-bred hyenas at Berkeley is that female pups begin fighting immediately after birth. They are born with teeth and use them to attack their siblings. Female pups are especially aggressive, and especially so toward a sister. At Berkeley, investigators intervene to prevent serious injury, but field studies indicate that in the wild it is very common for one pup to kill its sibling (Frank, Glickman, and Licht, 1991). It remains to be seen whether this extreme aggression is due to prenatal androgen stimulation of the brain. Even if the extreme aggressiveness of the female hyena is due to fetal androgen, females do mate with males, so their brains have not been made permanently unreceptive (as would happen in prenatally androgenized rats). Just the same, mating in the spotted hyena seems a tense affair, as the female seems to just barely tolerate the male's proximity, and the male alternates between approaching and retreating from his more powerful mate. (Photograph courtesy of Stephen Glickman.)

the organizational hypothesis asserted that early androgens masculinize the developing brain. But these neural differences can be very subtle; the same basic circuit of neurons connected together will produce very different behavior if the strength of the myriad synapses varies. However, sex differences in the *number* of synapses were identified in the preoptic area (POA) of the hypothalamus as early as 1971 (Raisman and Field, 1971). As we will see, later demonstrations of sexual dimorphism in the nervous system would include differences in the number, size, and shape of neurons, as well as the number of synapses.

Brain regions that control song in male songbirds.

Fernando Nottebohm and Arthur Arnold were studying the brain regions that control singing in canaries and zebra finches when they noticed something unexpected. Brain sections from males and females showed that the nuclei that control song are much larger in males than in females (Nottebohm and Arnold, 1976; Figure 12.21). Measuring the sections revealed that the nuclei are 5 to 6 times larger in volume in males (which produce elaborate songs) than in females (which produce only simple calls). Let's briefly discuss these brain nuclei and their sexual dimorphism.

Birds produce song through a specialized muscular organ called the **syrinx**, which is wrapped around the air passage. The muscles of the syrinx control the frequency of sounds produced by changing the tension of membranes around the air passage. These muscles are controlled by motoneurons of the twelfth cranial nerve (the cranial nerve that controls the tongue in mammals). The corresponding nucleus receives most of its innervation from a brain nucleus called the robustus archistriatum (RA). The RA receives most of its innervation from a nucleus that is both literally and organizationally higher, the higher vocal center (HVC). Lesions of the HVC abolish complex song in canaries and zebra finches, and electrical stimulation of the nucleus elicits song snippets. Lesions of the RA also severely disrupt song, as you would expect from the circuitry we've described. Collectively the various brain regions supporting song are sometimes referred to as vocal control regions or VCRs, presumably because of their resemblance to complicated machines.

As the organizational hypothesis would suggest, the early action of steroid hormone masculinizes the brains of zebra finches; exposing a hatchling female to either testosterone or estradiol will cause the HVC and the RA to be larger in adulthood. If such a female is also given testosterone as an adult, the VCR will become larger still, and she will sing much like a

male zebra finch (Gurney and Konishi, 1981). Female zebra finches treated with androgen only in adulthood do not sing. Thus, in zebra finches early hormone *organizes* a masculine song system and adult hormone *activates* the system to produce song.

The song of canaries is also affected by androgens, but in this species early steroids seem unimportant. A female canary will begin singing after a few weeks of androgen treatment in adulthood. Androgen also causes the HVC and the RA to become larger in volume and the dendrites of neurons in those regions to grow, making new synaptic connections. This difference in hormonal control of song in zebra finches and canaries may relate to the ecological niche occupied by each. Zebra finches, originally from the Australian

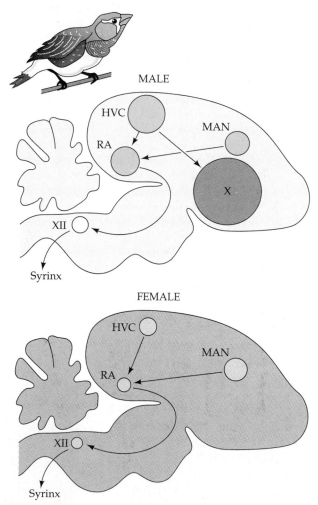

12.21 Neural Regions Involved in Bird Song
In this schematic, the area of each circle is proportional to the volume of the brain region. These regions have been magnified so that their relative sizes can be seen more clearly. After Arnold, 1980.

desert, are opportunistic breeders; they are ready to breed at any time of the year, awaiting rainfall that will provide additional food. Canaries are seasonal breeders; their reproductive apparatus (including the testes) shuts down in the fall. Therefore, male canaries have high androgen levels in spring and summer and low androgen levels in fall and winter. With this ebb and flow of androgen, singing and the volume of the HVC and the RA also vary: the nuclei grow in the spring as the animal resumes courtship singing and shrink in the fall as singing declines. Unlike zebra finches, which have only a single, relatively simple song, male canaries produce many, highly elaborate songs, learning additional songs each spring. Thus we can think of male canaries as having brains that remain sensitive to the organizational influences of androgen even in adulthood, and this continual reorganization may help them produce large repertoires to gain a mate.

The preoptic area of rats. The discovery that the brains of songbirds display such obvious sexual dimorphism inspired researchers to look for other neural sex differences. The laboratory of Roger Gorski examined the preoptic area (POA) of the hypothalamus in rats because of an earlier report that the number of synapses in this region was different in males and females and because lesions of the POA disrupt ovulatory cycles in female rats and reduce copulatory behavior in males. Sure enough, there was an easily identifiable nucleus within the POA, and this nucleus was three to five times larger in volume in males than in females (Gorski et al., 1978). This nucleus, dubbed the sexually dimorphic nucleus of the POA (SDN-POA), was so much more prominent in male rats that Gorski and colleagues could tell male from female brain sections just by glancing at the slides without a microscope (Figure 12.22). Yet, despite intense anatomical study of this brain region for almost a century, no one had noticed the SDN-POA until the birdsong work inspired a search.

Like the song control nuclei in zebra finches, the SDN-POA conformed beautifully to the organizational hypothesis: Males castrated at birth had much smaller SDN-POAs in adulthood, while females androgenized at birth had large, malelike SDN-POAs as adults. Castrating male rats in *adulthood*, however, did not alter the size of the SDN-POA, and neither did androgen treatment of adult females. Thus, testicular androgens somehow alter the development of the SDN-POA, resulting in a permanently larger nucleus in males than in females. Later experiments demonstrated that testosterone convert-

ed to estrogens in the brain masculinize the SDN-POA, so this nucleus conforms to the aromatization hypothesis as well. For example, androgen-insensitive rats have a masculine SDN-POA, despite their feminine exterior, because their *estrogen* receptors are normal.

The function of the SDN-POA is still not completely understood. Lesions of the SDN portion of the POA in rats cause only a slight, temporary decline in male copulatory behavior. A similarly obvious sexually dimorphic nucleus has been described and studied in gerbils (Yahr and Gregory, 1993), and lesions of this SDN-POA significantly reduce the typical scent marking behavior of male gerbils.

The spinal cord in mammals. The birdsong work inspired a search for sexual dimorphism in the spinal cord, where neural elements controlling sexual re-

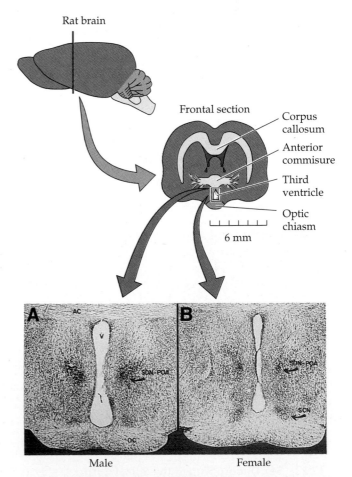

12.22 Hypothalamic Sex Difference
The sexually dimorphic nucleus of the preoptic area (SDN-POA) is much larger in male rats than in females.

sponse should be different for males and females. In rats, for example, the striated bulbocavernosus (BC) muscles (absent in females) that surround the base of the penis are innervated by motoneurons in the spinal nucleus of the bulbocavernosus (SNB; Figure 12.23). Male rats have about 200 SNB cells, but females have far fewer motoneurons in this region of the spinal cord. There has been considerable progress in understanding how the sexual dimorphism in the SNB system develops. On the day before birth, female rats have BC muscles attached to the base of the clitoris that are nearly as large as those of males and that are innervated by motoneurons in the SNB region (Rand and Breedlove, 1987). In fact, a few days before birth, females have as many SNB cells as males do (Nordeen et al., 1985). In the days just before and after birth, however, many SNB cells die, especially in females, and the BC muscles of females die. A single injection of androgen, either testosterone or dihydrotestosterone, delivered to a newborn female rat will permanently spare some SNB motoneurons and their muscles. Castration of newborn males, accompanied by prenatal blockade of androgen receptors, causes the BC muscles and SNB motoneurons to die as in females. Similarly, androgen-insensitive rats have very few SNB cells and no BC muscle, so aromatization seems to be unimportant for masculine development of this system.

Several lines of evidence indicate that androgen acts on the BC muscles to prevent their demise and that the SNB motoneurons do not themselves respond to the androgen, but are spared as a consequence of their target's survival. For example, although the BC muscles possess androgen receptors by the day of birth (Fishman, et al., 1990), SNB motoneurons do not acquire androgen receptors until the second week of life (Jordan, Breedlove, and Arnold, 1991), well after the fate of the motoneurons is determined. Thus, the muscles are competent to respond to androgen during the sensitive period, but the motoneurons are not. It is hypothesized that androgen spares the muscles and that the muscles then provide the motoneurons with a neurotrophic substance (a chemical that "feeds" neurons to keep them healthy and alive). Recall from Chapter 4 that about half of all the spinal motoneurons produced early in development normally die, that the death of the motoneurons can be prevented if they are provided with enough muscle target, and that the muscles are thought to provide a neurotrophic factor to keep the appropriate number of motoneurons alive into adulthood. No one knows yet what neurotrophic substance muscles provide to motoneurons to keep them alive. Theoretically, that substance or one like it may be regulated by androgen in the BC muscles and thereby control SNB fate (Forger et al., 1993).

All male mammals have BC muscles, but in nonrodents their motoneurons are found in a slightly different spinal location and are known as Onuf's nucleus. The rat studies suggest that Onuf's nucleus should be sexually dimorphic—that males should have more Onuf's motoneurons than do females.

(a)

(b)

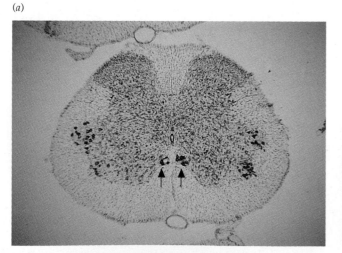
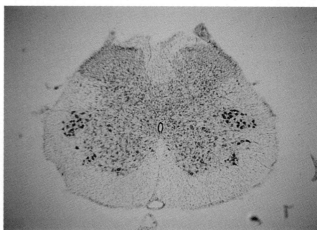

12.23 Sex Dimorphism in the Spinal Cord
The spinal nucleus of the bulbocavernosus (SNB) consists of large, multipolar motoneurons. Male rats (*a*) have more SNB cells (arrows) than do females (*b*).

Surprisingly, most female mammals retain a BC muscle into adulthood. For example, in women the BC surrounds the opening of the vagina, and contractions of the BC slightly constrict the opening (hence the muscle is sometimes referred to as the constrictor vestibule in women). Nevertheless, the BC is larger in men than in women, and men have more Onuf's motoneurons than do women (Forger and Breedlove, 1986; Figure 12.23). Dogs also display sexual dimorphism in Onuf's nucleus, and early androgenization of females leaves them with a very malelike BC and a male number of Onuf's motoneurons. The rat studies suggest that the sexual dimorphism in Onuf's nucleus is the result of androgenic action on the muscles that rescues motoneurons from death. Motoneuron counts in the human spinal cord indicate that we all normally lose some of these motoneurons before the 26th week of gestation (Forger and Breedlove, 1987; see Figure 4.14*c*), a time during which male fetuses produce androgen. Females lose more Onuf's motoneurons during that period, apparently because they have lower androgen levels.

Social Influences Affect Sexual Differentiation of the Nervous System

The SNB system offers an illuminating example of how social factors can mediate the masculinization produced by steroids. Newborn rat pups can neither urinate nor defecate on their own; the mother (dam) must lick the anogenital region of each pup to elicit a spinal reflex to empty the bladder and colon. (Incidentally, the dam ingests at least some of the wastes and thereby receives pheromones from the pups that affect the composition of her milk as the pups mature. Another reason not to be a rat!) Celia Moore and colleagues noticed that dams spend more time licking the anogenital region of male pups than of females. If the dam is made temporarily anosmic (unable to smell) by chemical treatment of the olfactory epithelium (see Chapter 9), she licks all the pups less and does not distinguish between males and females. Males raised by anosmic mothers thus receive less anogenital licking and, remarkably, fewer of their SNB cells survive the period around birth (Moore, Dou, and Juraska, 1992). The dam's stimulation of a male's anogenital region helps to masculinize his spinal cord.

On the one hand, this masculinization is still an effect of androgen because the dam detects male pups by smelling androgen metabolites in their urine. On the other hand, this effect is clearly the result of a so-

cial influence: the dam treats a pup differently because he's a male and thereby masculinizes his developing nervous system. Perhaps this example illustrates the futility of trying to distinguish "biological" and "social" influences.

What about humans? Humans are at least as sensitive to social influences as are rats. In every culture most people treat boys and girls differently, even when they are infants. Such differential treatment undoubtedly has some effect on the developing human brain and contributes to later sex differences in behavior. Of course this is a social influence, but testosterone instigated the influence when it induced formation of a penis in some fetuses. If prenatal androgen has even a very subtle effect on the fetal brain, then older humans interacting with the baby might detect such differences and treat the baby differently. Thus, originally subtle differences might be magnified by early social experience. Such interactions of steroidal and social influences are probably the norm in the sexual differentiation of human behavior.

Do Early Gonadal Hormones Masculinize Human Behaviors in Adulthood?

Since men and women do behave differently, something about them, probably something about their brains, *must* be different. The only remaining question is whether men and women behave differently because they are raised in a culture that treats them differentially or because they develop with different biological processes, which might be immune to cultural influences. Of course these are not mutually exclusive hypotheses. In fact, because sex roles vary in different societies (and have changed dramatically in our own society in the past few decades), there seems little doubt that society affects sexual differentiation of the brain and behavior. But do prenatal steroids alter the adult behavior of humans?

Answering this question is difficult. Prenatal androgens may or may not act on the brain, but they certainly act on the periphery. If we expose a female fetus to enough androgen, she will look entirely male on the outside at birth and will be treated by family and society as a male. If she (?) behaves as a male in adulthood, we won't know whether that's because of what androgen did to the outside or to the brain. We saw earlier that CAH females, exposed prenatally to an-

Box 12.3

What Determines a Person's Sexual Orientation?

Some people develop romantic attachments to and yearn to have sex with a person of the same sex. Researchers have offered two explanations for this sexual orientation. Some suggest that infants observe the adults around them and use them as role models for their later sexual orientation as homosexual or heterosexual; sometimes, by accident or circumstance, they choose to model the opposite sex. Others believe that something happens before birth to determine later orientation ("some people are born gay"). For the latter camp, it is tempting to explain homosexual behavior as an example of the organizational action of early steroids that has been demonstrated in animals. After all, the more androgens the young male rat receives neonatally, the more male copulatory behaviors he'll display as an adult. Furthermore, by depriving a male rat of androgen at birth, we can be sure that (with adult steroid treatment) he will display lordosis (a female behavior) in response to another male in

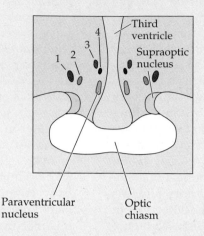

adulthood. Superficially, the behavior of the male rat deprived of androgen at birth resembles homosexual behavior, but all we have measured is which sexual motor pattern the animal will display. A neonatally androgenized animal will mount any rat—male or female. A female rat given estrogen and progesterone will display the lordosis posture in response to mounting by any rat—or in response to the investigator's hand! In other words, the animals show

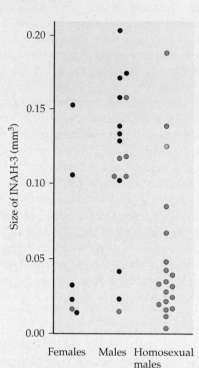

these behaviors regardless of who or what their partner is. In contrast, we humans are much more concerned about what sort of partner we have than what particular

---

drogen, play more like boys than do normal females. Is that because androgen directly masculinized their brains or because, with their ambiguous genitalia, they

or their parents have some doubts about their "real" gender? Much controversy surrounds the debate over whether hormones or social influences determine sexual orientation (Box 12.3). We will close this chapter with a discussion of a fascinating phenomenon that demonstrates again the difficulty of distinguishing prenatal from social influences.

Some People Seem to Change Sex at Puberty

A rare genetic mutation affects the enzyme (5-α-reductase) that converts testosterone to dihydrotestosterone (DHT). If an XY individual cannot produce this enzyme, the internal structures still develop in a masculine fashion. Testes develop, Müllerian ducts regress, and Wolffian duct structures, under the influence of testosterone, are masculinized. However, the genital epithelium, which normally possesses 5-α-reductase, is unable to amplify the androgenic signal by converting the testosterone to the more active DHT. Consequently, the phallus is only slightly masculinized and resembles a large clitoris, and the genital folds resemble labia, although they contain the testes. There usually is no vaginal opening. Babies in a particular village in the Dominican Republic occasionally are born with this type of appearance (Figure 12.24). These children seem to be regarded as girls in the way they are dressed and raised (Imperato-McGinley et al., 1974). At puberty, however, the testes increase androgen production and the external genitalia become more fully masculinized. The phallus

sexual behavior we perform. It is possible to measure what sort of rat companion a given rat would like to have available, but such studies paint a more complicated picture. There is more variability in steroid effects on a rat's partner preference than on lordosis or mounting behaviors.

Simon LeVay reported (1991) that the POA (preoptic area) of humans contains a nucleus (the third interstitial nucleus of the anterior hypothalamus, or INAH-3) labeled "3" in the figure's left panel) that is larger in men than in women and larger in heterosexual men than in homosexual men (right panel of figure). For the public, this sounds like strong evidence that sexual orientation is "built in." Those of us studying biological psychology, however, know that early experience can alter the structure of the brain to have an influence on later behavior. It's possible, then, that early social experience affects the development of INAH-3 to determine later sexual orientation. Furthermore, sexual experiences as an adult could affect INAH-3 structure, so the smaller nucleus in some homosexual men may be the result of their homosexuality,

rather than vice versa. LeVay himself was careful to point out these alternatives, but most journalists know so little about the brain that they have never quite caught on. Michael Gorman (1994) suggested that the popular media also focused on LeVay's findings because they could be interpreted as conforming to a popular but very much oversimplified view of gay men—that they are like women.

The reports that sexual orientation is heritable (Bailey and Bell, 1993) also do little to resolve the controversy. Estimates are that about half the variability in sexual orientation is due to differences in the genome, which leaves ample room for early social influences. Indeed, this evidence indicates quite strongly that both genetic and environmental influences affect sexual orientation in humans. Members of a very select subpopulation of homosexual men—pairs of homosexual brothers—are likely to have each inherited the same region of their X chromosome from their mother (Hamer et al., 1993). But even in this subpopulation there are exceptions; that is, some of the homosexual brothers received from their mother different genes from

that region of the X, so co-inheritance of those genes could not account for their being alike. Finally, monozygotic twins, who have exactly the same genes, do not always have the same sexual orientation (Buhrich, Bailey, and Martin, 1991).

From a political viewpoint, the controversy—whether sexual orientation is determined before birth or determined by early social influences—is irrelevant. Many religions practiced in Western culture regard homosexuality as a sin that some people choose to commit, and this view forms the prime basis for laws and prejudices against homosexuality. But scientists representing each viewpoint agree that sexual orientation, especially in males, is set very early in life—by age four or so. Almost all homosexual and heterosexual men report that from the beginning their interest and romantic attachments matched their adult orientation. Furthermore, despite sometimes heroic efforts, no one has come up with a way to change a person's sexual orientation (LeVay, 1993). Thus, all research indicates that sexual orientation is not a matter of choice, thus challenging the validity of discrimination against homosexuals.

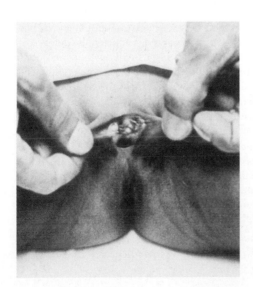
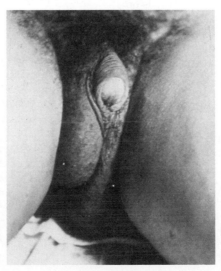

12.24   *Guevedoces*
In the Dominican Republic some individuals, called *guevedoces*, are born with ambiguous genitalia (*left*) and are raised as girls. At puberty, however, the phallus grows into a recognizable penis (*right*) and the individuals begin acting like young men. Courtesy of Julianne Imperato-McGinley.

grows into a recognizable penis, the body develops narrow hips and a muscular build, without breasts, and the individuals begin acting like young men. The villagers have nicknamed such individuals *guevedoces,* meaning "eggs (testes) at twelve (years)." These men never develop facial beards, but they usually have girlfriends, indicating that they are sexually interested in women. Examinations have confirmed that the men are deficient in 5-α-reductase.

There are two possible explanations for why these people raised as girls would later behave as men. First, prenatal testosterone may have masculinized their brains; thus, despite being raised as girls, when they reach puberty, their brains lead them to seek out girls for mates. This explanation suggests that the social influences of growing up—assigning oneself to a gender and mimicking role models of that gender, gender-specific playing, dressing—are unimportant

for later behavior and sexual orientation. An alternative explanation is that early hormones have no effect—that this culture simply recognizes and teaches children that some people can start out as girls and change to boys later. If so, then the social influences on gender role development might be completely different in this society from those in ours, and it is not possible to state with certainty whether prenatal hormonal influences or early social influences are more important for sexual differentiation of human behavior. The reports of sexual dimorphism in the adult human brain, often touted as proof of the predominance of "biological" influences, do not really address the issue. Despite the absence of any airtight demonstrations that prenatal hormones directly affect human brain and behavior, it seems likely that hormones have at least some effect on the developing brain and that society reinforces and accentuates sex differences.

Summary

Sexual Behavior

1. Reproductive behaviors are divided into four stages: attraction, appetitive behaviors, copulation, and postcopulatory behaviors, including parental behaviors in some species.

2. The brain decides when the organism should reproduce and uses protein hormones to induce the gonads to produce gametes. The gonads in turn produce steroid hormones that activate the brain to increase the probability of reproductive behaviors.

3. In humans very low levels of testosterone are required for either men or women to display a full interest in mating, but additional testosterone has no additional effect. Therefore there is no correlation between circulating androgen levels and reproductive behaviors in men. Nor is there any strong correlation between copulatory behavior and stage of the menstrual cycle in women.

4. Human copulatory behavior is remarkably varied. Attempts at classification of the stages of copulation in humans suggest that most men show a single pattern while most women display one of three basic patterns of sexual response.

The Evolution of Sexual Reproduction

5. Sexual reproduction brings together in a single individual the beneficial mutations that arose in separate individuals.

6. In some species, sexual reproduction has led to the evolution of individuals specialized to reproduce as either a male or a female. Sexual differentiation during development then allows males and females to develop different bodies and brains.

7. Male and female vertebrates make different investments in their offspring; consequently, most males of most species are promiscuous and most females of most species are very discriminating in choosing mates. This situation leads to sexual selection pressures that can over time exaggerate sexual dimorphism.

Sexual Differentiation

8. In vertebrates, genetic sex (determined by the presence or absence of a Y chromosome in mammals) determines whether testes or ovaries will develop, and hormonal secretions from the gonads determine whether the rest of the body, including the brain, will develop in a feminine or masculine fashion. In the presence of testicular secretions a male will develop; in the absence of testicular secretions a female will develop.

9. The brains of vertebrates are masculinized by the presence of testicular steroids during early development. Such organizational effects of steroids permanently alter the structure and function of the brain and therefore permanently alter the behavior of the individual.

10. Among the prominent sexual dimorphisms in the nervous system (including the song system of birds, the sexually dimorphic nucleus of the preoptic area in rats, and the spinal nucleus of the bulbocavernosus in mammals), gonadal steroids have been shown to alter cellular processes such as neuronal size, neuronal survival, dendritic growth, and synapse elimination to engender sex differences in neural structure and in behavior.

11. Several regions of the human brain are sexually dimorphic. However, we do not know whether these dimorphisms are generated by fetal steroid levels or by sex differences in the early social environment. Neither do we know whether any of the identified sex differences in neural structure are responsible for any sex differences in human behavior.

12. There seems to be no reliable animal model of sexual orientation, which is such a salient aspect of human experience. However, all research indicates that sexual orientation is determined early in life and, especially in men, is not a matter of individual choice.

Recommended Reading

Becker, J. B., Breedlove, S. M. and Crews, D. 1992. *Behavioral Endocrinology*. MIT Press, Cambridge.

Fausto-Sterling, A. 1985. *Myths of Gender*. Basic Books, New York.

Gerall, A. A., Moltz, H. and Ward, I. L. 1992. *Handbook of Behavioral Neurobiology*. Vol. 11: *Sexual Differentiation*. Plenum Press, New York.

LeVay, S. 1993. *The Sexual Brain*. MIT Press, Cambridge.

Nelson, R. J. 1995. *An Introduction to Behavioral Endocrinology*. Sinauer Associates, Sunderland, MA.

Barbara Friedman, *Hidden Head*, 1986

- *Homeostasis Maintains Internal States within a Critical Range*

Temperature Regulation

- *Body Temperature Is a Critical Condition for All Biological Processes*

- *Some Animals Generate Heat, Others Must Obtain Heat from the Environment*

- *The Brain Monitors and Regulates Body Temperature*

- *Many Behaviors Can Adjust Body Temperature*

- *Some Endotherms Have a Wide Range of Body Temperatures*

Fluid Regulation

- *Our Cells Evolved to Function in Seawater*

- *Two Internal Cues Trigger Thirst*

- *We Don't Stop Drinking Just Because Our Throat and Mouth Are Wet*

- *Homeostatic Regulation of Salt Is Required for Effective Regulation of Water*

Food and Energy Regulation

- *Nutrient Regulation Requires the Anticipation of Future Needs*

- *Insulin Is Crucial for the Regulation of Body Metabolism*

- *Experience Normally Guides Us to a Healthful Diet*

- *There Is Apparently No Single Satiety Center or Single Hunger Center in the Brain*

- *Brain Peptides May Mediate Some of the Signals for Hunger*

- *Anorexia Nervosa and Bulimia Are Compulsive, Life-Threatening Eating Disorders*

CHAPTER 13

Regulation of Internal States

Orientation

If we asked you what you need to survive, you would probably quickly mention shelter, water, and food. If you had only these three things, plus air to breathe, you might not be happy, but you would survive. Your brain stem and autonomic nervous system take care of your breathing, but the other three necessities—warmth, water, and food—all require active, goal-directed behaviors. Too much of something can be nearly as harmful as too little. Our bodies must keep temperature, water supplies, and nutrient supplies somewhere between a high level that would make us unhealthy and a low level that would prove fatal. In other words, there is a critical range for each of these parameters, and many of the basic principles of regulation that we discuss in this chapter apply to all three regulatory systems. After a brief discussion of the general regulatory properties shared by these three systems, we will describe each one in more detail.

Homeostasis Maintains Internal States within a Critical Range

Because warmth, water, and food are both vital and scarce, elaborate physiological systems have evolved to monitor and maintain them. One hallmark of all three systems is redundancy: there are several different means of monitoring our stores, of conserving remaining supplies, and of shedding excesses. Therefore the loss of function of one part of the system can be compensated for by the remaining portions. This redundancy helps keep us alive, but it also makes it difficult for us to figure out how the body regulates temperature, water, and food. Another hallmark of these three regulatory systems is that each exploits the organism's behavior to regulate and to acquire more heat, water, or food.

The nervous system coordinates these regulatory systems. The brain closely monitors temperature, water supply, and nutrient supply, and uses a variety of neural and hormonal mechanisms to keep them within the critical range. If we have a surplus of any of the three, our bodies have ways to shed the excess, usually without our being aware of it. But when supplies are running out, we must display active behaviors to gain more; the nervous system initiates these behaviors. If we are losing body heat, our nervous system directs us to seek warmth. When our internal water supplies are low we seek water, and when our internal nutrient supplies are low we seek food. Our conscious experience is that we feel cold, thirsty, or hungry. Other animals are unable to use words to tell us how they feel, so for the rest of this chapter we will assume that an animal that seeks water is thirsty, and that an animal seeking food is hungry. Probably such animals feel much the same way we do when we say we are thirsty or hungry, but we will not be addressing that issue. Without making any assumptions about the animal's experience, we will say that an animal seeking shelter has an internal drive to conserve heat; an animal seeking water has an internal drive (thirst) for water; and an animal seeking food has an internal drive (hunger) for food. In each case the animal is showing **motivated behavior**. The particular behaviors they display may vary depending on the circumstances but nevertheless serve the goal of gaining warmth, water, or food.

The homeostatic mechanisms that regulate temperature, body fluids, and metabolism are all **negative feedback** systems. That is, in each case a desired value or zone is established; this desired value is called the set point, by analogy with the setting of a thermostat (Figure 13.1*a*). (We have already dis-

cussed negative feedback systems in connection with neural circuits in Chapter 5 and regulation of hormone secretion in Chapter 7.) A drop in temperature below the set point activates the thermostat, which turns on the heating system. When the thermostat registers a sufficient rise in temperature, it turns off the heating system. (Note that there is a small range of temperature between the "turn on" and "turn off" signals, otherwise the heating system would be going on and off very frequently. Thus there is really a **set zone** rather than a set point.) The setting of the thermostat can be changed; for example, it can be turned down at night to save energy. The building may also have a cooling system that is thermostatically controlled with set temperatures that cause it to go on when temperatures are too high. Thus two active, negative feedback systems prevent the internal temperature from going too high or too low.

All such negative feedback systems must possess three characteristics:

1. a means of accurately monitoring the relevant state or variable (temperature, fluid levels, or nutrient levels)

2. a means of adjusting the variable (gaining heat, water, or food), pushing it back to the set range

3. the ability of the monitor to trigger incremental increases when the variable falls too low and inhibit further gains when the variable has returned to the proper range; this inhibition is what constitutes negative feedback (Figure 13.1*b*).

The nervous system is intimately involved in all three components. First, the brain itself monitors these variables to some degree, and it integrates information from other parts of the body about temperature, water, and nutrients. Second, the nervous system organizes the behaviors that ultimately return the body to homeostasis—heat generation, drinking, and eating. Finally, the brain decides when we've had enough.

The body temperature for most mammals and birds is usually held within a narrow range—about 36 to 38°C (97 to 100°F)—though the set zone can be altered depending on overall conditions and current goals of the organism. The total amount of water in our bodies varies more widely because, as we'll see later, water can move between different compartments inside us. This shifting between compartments complicates the regulation of water, but there is still a narrow set range in the amount of water that cells can contain and still function properly. Food intake is even more complicated, partly because the delay between when we eat and when our bodies can finally make use of the food forces us to ingest nutrients in

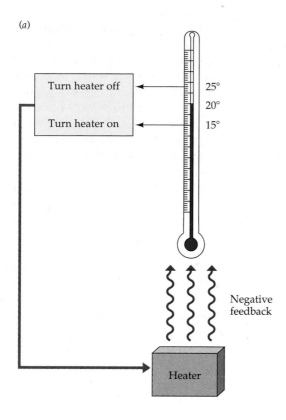

(a)

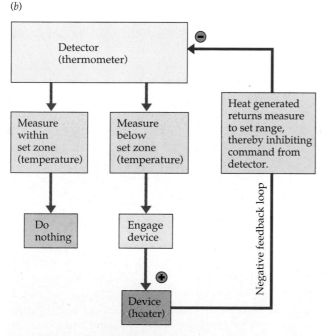

(b)

13.1 Negative Feedback

(a) The thermostatically controlled heating system found in homes is an example of a negative feedback system. (b) All such systems have a detector to monitor the variable and a device to change the variable. By changing the variable (for example by heating the room) the device sends a negative feedback signal to the detector, turning it off.

anticipation of future needs. Also there are different classes of nutrients, each of which must be provided if we're to remain healthy. Yet our bodies integrate all these demands for nutrients and water to result in a set range of body weight that is often remarkably narrow. We will see examples of animals vigorously defending their body weight—maintaining a particular weight in the face of physiological challenges. Thus, this chapter will show that all three regulatory systems—for body temperature, water balance, and body weight—are **homeostatic**, which means they maintain relatively constant values.

Unavoidable Losses Require Us to Gain Heat, Water, and Food

The regulation of internal resources is complicated by the fact that staying alive requires us to give some of them up. Because external temperatures rarely hover at 37°C (98.6°F) for long, we must actively heat or cool our bodies. We lose water vapor with each breath, and through sweating, and because various biochemical processes produce waste chemicals that can be disposed of only with a little water, through urination. Food provides us with energy and nutrients (chemicals needed for growth, maintenance, and repair of the body), but our behavior uses up energy and incurs wear and tear on our bodies, so more energy and nutrients are continuously needed. Our homeostatic mechanisms are constantly challenged by these **unavoidable losses** (sometimes called obligatory losses), which require us to gain and conserve heat, water, and food constantly.

Important Body Variables Are Maintained through Redundant Homeostatic Systems

For guaranteed performance of vital mechanical and electrical functions, NASA designed space capsules with multiple monitoring units and with parallel systems or backup devices. Thus the failure of one unit or system is not lethal, since other systems can guarantee the same objective. Evolution has similarly endowed our bodies with multiple systems. This endowment has complicated researchers' efforts, because interfering with one or another mechanism often produces little or no effect, since parallel or alternative mechanisms assume the burden. For example, unlike most homes, the body has at least three different thermostats; when one is not working, the others continue to regulate temperature. For water regulation there are two different, fairly independent cues that warn the brain when we need to drink. As for eating, no single brain center controls either hunger or its opposite—satiety.

Temperature Regulation

Body Temperature Is a Critical Condition for All Biological Processes

Adult humans cannot survive if the temperature of their bodies falls outside a fairly narrow range around 37°C. As we will see, some animals can survive much greater changes in body temperature, but even these species have a critical range of body temperature.

What we intuitively describe as "temperature" is a reflection of the motion of molecules making up an object. Chemical reactions rely on the constant motion of molecules to bring atoms together (or push them apart). When cells are warm, almost all chemical reactions proceed faster. As the interior of a cell becomes cooler, chemical reactions slow down. The enzyme systems of mammals and birds are most efficient within a narrow range around 37°C. At lower temperatures, reactions slow down and some stop altogether. At higher temperatures, protein molecules fold together improperly, and thus do not function as they should. At very high temperatures, the amino acids that form proteins begin to break apart and fuse together more or less at random, and we say the tissue is "fixed" (or, if it is edible tissue, we say it is "cooked"). Brain cells are especially sensitive to high temperatures. A very prolonged, high fever can cause brain centers that regulate heart rate and breathing to die, thus killing the patient.

At very low temperatures, the bilipid layers that make up cellular membranes become so disrupted by the formation of ice molecules that they cannot reform even when thawed. Some animals that cannot avoid subfreezing temperatures—shrimp-like krill (Figure 13.2*a*) in the Arctic Ocean, for example—produce "antifreeze" consisting of special molecules that disrupt the formation of ice crystals and prevent damage to membranes (Ahlgren et al., 1988). Arctic ground squirrels, however, achieve body temperatures below 0°C during hibernation and apparently do not have antifreeze molecules in their plasma (Barnes, 1989). How they avoid the formation of ice crystals is not yet understood (Figure 13.2*b*). For most animals, even moderately cool body temperatures—which, like prolonged high temperatures, adversely affect the brain—can be fatal.

Some Animals Generate Heat, Others Must Obtain Heat from the Environment

For centuries it has been recognized that mammals and birds differ from other animals in the way they

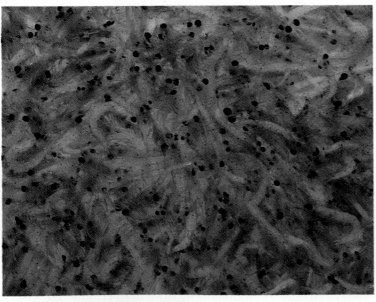

13.2 Braving the Cold
Arctic krill (*left*) and golden-mantled ground squirrels (*right*) are two species that sometimes have body temperatures below 0°C. The krill produce an "anti-freeze" in body fluids to prevent ice crystals from forming in cell membranes. The ground squirrels do not have such anti-freeze, so how they avoid damaging ice crystal formation is unknown.

regulate body temperature. Our ways of characterizing the difference have become more accurate and meaningful over time, but popular terminology still reflects the old division: mammals and birds are called warm-blooded; all other creatures are called cold-blooded. But this classification is misleading. A fence lizard or a desert iguana—both "cold-blooded"—usually has a body temperature only a degree or two below ours, so it is not really "cold." The next set of terminology distinguished animals that maintain a constant body temperature, called homeotherms (from the Greek *homos*, "same," and *therme*, "heat"), from those whose body temperature varies with their environment, called poikilotherms (from the Greek *poikilos*, "varied"). This classification also proved inadequate, because some mammals (homeotherms) vary their body temperatures during hibernation. Furthermore, many invertebrates in the depths of the ocean (poikilotherms) never experience a change in the chill of the deep waters, so their body temperatures remain quite constant.

The modern distinction is between endotherms and ectotherms. **Endotherms** (from the Greek *endon*, "within") regulate their body temperature chiefly by internal metabolic processes. **Ectotherms** (from the Greek *ectos*, "outside") get most of their heat from the environment. Most ectotherms do regulate their body temperature, but through behavioral means, such as moving to favorable sites or changing their exposure to external sources of heat. Endotherms (mainly mammals and birds) also choose favorable environments, but primarily they regulate body temperature by making internal adjustments. Whether an animal is an ectotherm or an endotherm, if it is placed in a laboratory situation where there is a gradient of temperature from warm to cold, it will spend most of its time at its preferred environmental temperature. The **preferred temperature** differs from species to species.

The Advantages of Endothermy Come at a Cost

No one knows whether endothermy arose in a common ancestor of the birds and mammals or arose separately in these two lines. What we do know is that endotherms pay substantial costs for maintaining a high body temperature and keeping it within narrow limits. Much food must be obtained and metabolized, elaborate regulatory systems are required, and departures of body temperature of a few degrees in either direction impair functioning. What benefits led to the evolution of such a complicated and costly system in comparison with that of the ectotherms, who get along with somewhat lower mean body temper-

atures and have more tolerance for changes in environmental temperature?

An increased capacity to sustain a high level of muscular activity over prolonged periods may have been the principal gain in the evolution of endothermy (Bennett and Ruben, 1979). A person's metabolic rate (or heat production) can rise almost tenfold between resting and very strenuous exercise (see Table 13.1). Apparently a tenfold increase above the resting level is about the greatest that vertebrates can achieve, whether ectotherms or endotherms. Ectotherms are capable of such bursts of high activity for only a few minutes; in this case anaerobic metabolism—chemical reactions that do not require oxygen—contributes most of the energy. A high level of anaerobic metabolism can be maintained for only a few minutes; then the animal must rest and repay the oxygen debt. Ectotherms can escape from and sometimes even pursue endotherms over short distances, but in a long-distance race the endotherm will win. Probably the capacity for internal thermoregulation evolved along with increasing capacity to sustain a high level of muscular activity through aerobic metabolism. On the other hand, ectotherms such as fishes and reptiles require much less food than endotherms do.

Human evolution shows particular adaptations for thermoregulation. There has been much speculation on why human beings have hair on only part of the body surface, whereas other primates have full coats of hair. Perhaps humans evolved into "naked apes" to facilitate the rapid dissipation of heat during prolonged pursuit of prey in their original tropical homelands. We may never be sure of the answer, but some present-day differences among human groups may be related to thermoregulation. For example, the nostrils of people living in Arctic regions tend to be narrower, which aids conservation of heat (Roberts, 1973). The eyelid shape of some Asian peoples is believed to have evolved in the north to protect against loss of heat by evaporation from the eyes. Eskimo have fewer sweat glands on their limbs and trunk than do Europeans, but they have more sweat glands on the face. This distribution may prevent sweat from the limbs or trunk from defeating the insulation of heavy clothing. When Eskimo are active, the face is the only uncovered surface that can dissipate heat, so the face has to be richly supplied with sweat glands.

Endotherms Generate Heat through Metabolism

Metabolism is the utilization of stored food in the body. Because the breaking of chemical bonds in metabolic processes releases energy as heat, all living (and thus metabolizing) tissues produce heat. Table 13.1 shows the amount of heat produced per hour by an adult person engaging in different activities, from sleep to strenuous exercise. (The unit of heat is a kilocalorie [kcal]; 1 kcal is enough heat to raise the temperature of 1000 cubic centimeters of water 1°C.) When the body is at rest, about a third of the heat is produced by the brain. As bodily activity increases, the heat production of the brain does not rise much, but that of the muscles can increase nearly tenfold, so when we are active our bodies produce a much high-

er percentage of the heat we generate. Like mechanical devices, muscles produce a good deal of heat while they are accomplishing work. Muscles and gasoline engines have about the same efficiency; each produces about four or five times as much heat as mechanical work. Some of the main ways the human body gains, conserves, and dissipates heat are shown in Figure 13.3.

The rate of heat production can be adjusted to suit conditions, particularly in certain organs. Deposits of brown adipose tissue (also called **brown fat**) are found especially around vital organs in the

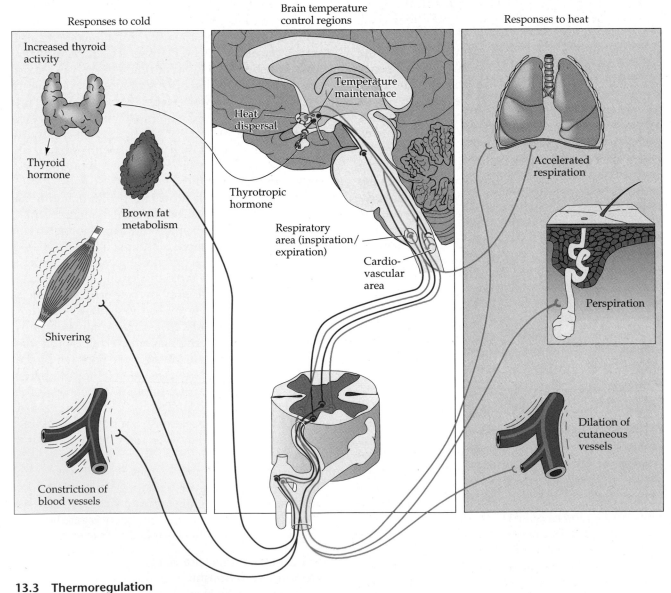

13.3 Thermoregulation
Some of the primary ways our body gains, conserves, and loses heat and their neural controls.

Table 13.1

Influence of Activity on Heat Production of an Adult Person

ACTIVITY	HEAT (kcal/hr)
Resting or sleeping	65
Awake, sitting quietly	100
Light exercise	170
Moderate exercise	290
Strenuous exercise	450
Very strenuous exercise	600

trunk and around the cervical and thoracic levels of the spinal cord. These fat cells look brown because they are full of mitochondria that break down molecules and produce heat. Under cold conditions the sympathetic nervous system stimulates metabolism within the brown fat cells, producing heat. A more conspicuous means by which heat is generated is muscular activity. At low temperatures nerve impulses cause muscle cells to contract out of synchrony, producing shivering rather than coordinated movements. Humans start to shiver when their body temperature approaches 36.5°C. This response spreads from facial muscles to the arms and legs. The fivefold increase in oxygen uptake that accompanies extreme shivering shows how metabolically intense this response is.

Body Size and Shape Affect Heat Production and Heat Loss

Heat production is closely related to the surface area of the body, because heat is exchanged with the environment primarily at the surface of the body. A big animal like an elephant has relatively little skin surface compared with the volume of its body; a small animal like a canary has a large surface-to-volume ratio. As volume increases, the ratio of surface to volume decreases (Figure 13.4a). A high surface-to-volume ratio means a greater capacity to dissipate heat. You may have noticed that small food items such as peas cool off faster than large objects such as baked potatoes. That's because the surface-to-volume ratio of the potato is much less than that of the pea.

Table 13.2 shows the body sizes of several species

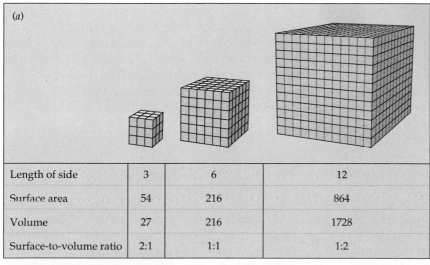

Length of side	3	6	12
Surface area	54	216	864
Volume	27	216	1728
Surface-to-volume ratio	2:1	1:1	1:2

3.8:1	2.0:1

13.4　Surface-to-Volume Ratios
(*a*) For a given shape, the ratio of surface to volume of a solid decreases as the volume increases. (*b*) However, forms with different shapes can have very different surface areas, even if the volume is the same.

Table 13.2
Body Size and Heat Production of Some Birds and Mammals

SPECIES	BODY WEIGHT (kg)	BODY SURFACE (m²)	SURFACE-TO-WEIGHT RATIO (m²/kg)	ENERGY OUTPUT PER DAY TOTAL (kcal)	PER UNIT OF BODY WEIGHT (kcal/kg)	PER UNIT OF BODY SURFACE (kcal/m²)
Canary	0.016	0.006	0.375	5	310	760
Rat	0.2	0.03	0.15	25	130	830
Pigeon	0.3	0.04	0.13	30	100	670
Cat	3.0	0.2	0.07	150	50	750
Human	60	1.7	0.03	1,500	25	850
Elephant	3,600	24	0.007	47,000	13	2,000

in terms of weight, surface area, and heat production. Smaller animals, because of their larger surface-to-volume ratio, lose heat more rapidly to the environment, so they must produce more heat in relation to body size than do larger animals. For example, from the data of Table 13.2, we see that it takes 20 cats to equal the weight of a human, but the 20 cats produce twice the heat of that person. (That's why we have to buy so much cat food!) Small mammals also tend to maintain slightly higher body temperatures than do large mammals. Small mammals lose heat more easily than larger mammals do. Large animals, on the other hand, lose heat more slowly and thus have lower metabolic rates.

The effect of surface-to-volume ratio on heat conservation is evident in the distribution of species across environments. Within a group of closely related mammals or birds, for example, those living in cold climates are larger than those in warm environments. Even in a temperate zone, though, a very small mammal like the shrew has to eat almost incessantly to meet its metabolic needs.

Shape also affects the conservation of heat and therefore energy. The humanoid form in Figure 13.4*b* has exactly the same volume as the squat figure beside it, but the more slender form has almost twice as much surface area as the compact form. Because of its lower surface-to-volume ratio, the more compact body conserves heat better and therefore is better able to protect its internal temperature in a cold climate. Among human groups, taller, more slender body forms have evolved in the tropics and shorter, stockier physiques are more typical of the colder regions (Figure 13.5). Migrations and the intermingling of human groups blur this tendency, and of course other

factors also influence stature, as the pygmies of tropical Africa illustrate. Among many animal groups, body appendages are smaller in Arctic species than in related tropical species (Figure 13.6). Smaller appendages mean a lower surface-to-volume ratio and thus less heat loss.

Fur of mammals and feathers of birds are special adaptations of the skin that insulate the body from the environment. In cold environments large mammals usually have a thick coat of fur, but thick fur on small animals would interfere with their locomotion. To insulate properly, fur or feathers must be kept in good condition—one reason why many mammals and birds spend a great deal of time grooming and preening. For an animal like the sea otter, which spends its life in cold water, insulation is vital; even a small area of matted fur allowing heat loss could be fatal. Most species of birds have a preen gland or oil gland near the base of the tail; the bird uses its beak to distribute oil from the gland to dress the feathers and waterproof them. Of course, sometimes an animal needs to lose heat, and different species have different adaptations for doing so (Figure 13.7).

The Brain Monitors and Regulates Body Temperature

The nervous system controls and regulates all the processes of heat production and heat loss, with assistance in some cases from the endocrine system. What parts of the nervous system are active in these processes?

In the 1880s physiologists found that small lesions in the hypothalamus of dogs elevated body temper-

(a)

(b)

13.5 Adaptations to Extreme Climates
Such adaptation include changes in behavior, physiology, and anatomy. Examples are seen in comparing (*a*) an Eskimo from arctic Alaska with (*b*) a Nilotic inhabitant of tropical Africa.

ature. Barbour (1912) manipulated the temperature of the hypothalamus in dogs by implanting silver wires. When the wires were heated, body temperature fell; when the wires were cooled, body temperature rose. These results suggested that body temperature is monitored in the hypothalamus and that

(a)

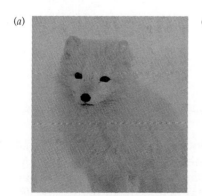

(b)

(c)

13.6 Ear Adaptations to Climate
Variation in the size of the external ear in foxes from (*a*) arctic, (*b*) temperate, and (*c*) tropical climates.

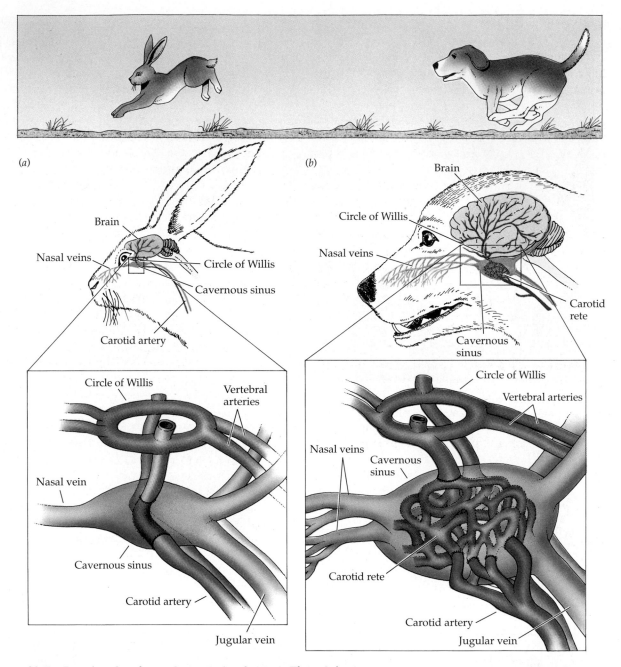

13.7 Exertion Overheats Some Animals More Than Others
Exercise produces heat, but some species, such as the dog, have a special heat exchange cooling system (*bottom*). Other species, such as the rabbit, do not possess this special cooling system.

when temperature there departs in either direction from the desired level, compensatory actions are triggered. In the 1950s, electrical recording from single cells revealed that some changed their discharge rate in response to small increases or decreases of brain temperature; these cells are scattered throughout the preoptic area (POA) and the anterior hypothalamus.

Lesion experiments in mammals indicate that there are different sites for two kinds of regulation: (1) regulation by locomotor and other behaviors common to both endotherms and ectotherms and (2) physiological regulation characteristic of endotherms. Lesions in the lateral hypothalamus of rats abolished behavioral regulation of temperature but did not affect the autonomic thermoregulatory responses such as shivering and vasoconstriction (Satinoff and Shan, 1971; van Zoeren and Stricker, 1977). On the other hand, lesions in the POA of rats impaired the autonomic responses but did not interfere with such behaviors as pressing levers to turn heating lamps or cooling fans on or off (Satinoff and Rutstein, 1970; van Zoeren and Stricker, 1977). Here is a clear example of parallel circuits for two different ways of regulating the same variable.

Receptors at the surface of the body also monitor temperature. If you enter a cold room, you soon begin to shiver—long before your core temperature falls. If you enter a hot greenhouse or a sauna, you begin to sweat before your hypothalamic temperature rises. The skin provides information to central circuits, which promptly initiate corrective action in anticipation of a change in core temperature.

Does a Single, Master Thermostat Monitor and Regulate Body Temperature?

It would be simple to think that a single, integrating center accounts for thermoregulation. However, evidence has accumulated to suggest that a single "thermostat" is inadequate to account for all the facets of thermoregulation. For one thing, as we saw in the previous section, there appear to be different brain sites for behavioral and autonomic regulation of temperature. Even two thermoregulatory circuits may not be sufficient. For example, Roberts and Mooney (1974) warmed small sites in the diencephalon and mesencephalon of rats. Normally a rat exposed to increasing heat shows successive potentiation of three different responses: first it grooms, then it moves about

actively, and finally it lies quietly in a sprawled-out position. Grooming allows the rat to lose heat by evaporation of saliva from the skin, activity normally helps the rat locate a cooler spot, and sprawling out helps the rat dissipate heat without generating more through activity. Local heating of the brain does not produce this sequence; instead, each of these behaviors tends to be elicited by the heating of a different brain region. These observations are not consistent with the hypothesis of a single thermostat.

In addition, there seems to be a hierarchy of thermoregulatory circuits, some located at the spinal level, some centered in the midbrain, and others in the hypothalamus. For example, spinal animals (with the brain disconnected from the spinal cord) can regulate body temperature somewhat, indicating that some temperature monitor is available to the spinal cord and/or body. Such animals die in cold or heat, however, because they do not respond until body temperature deviates 2 to 3°C from normal values. Satinoff (1978) suggests that the thermal set ranges are broader in "lower" regions of the nervous system (Figure 13.8). The thermoregulatory systems at the hypothalamic level have the narrowest neutral zones, and they normally coordinate and adjust the activity of the other systems. This arrangement can give the impression of a single system, although in reality there are multiple interlinked systems. Figure 13.9 summarizes the basic thermoregulatory system—receptors in the skin, body core, and hypothalamus detect temperature and transmit that information to three neural regions (spinal cord, brain stem, and hypothalamus). If body temperature moves outside the set range, each of these neural regions can initiate autonomic and behavioral responses to return body temperature to the set range.

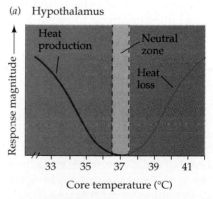

(a) Hypothalamus

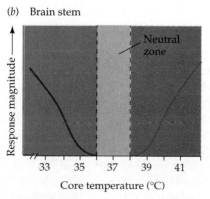

(b) Brain stem

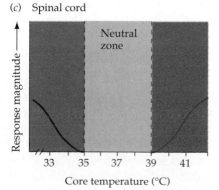

(c) Spinal cord

13.8 Multiple Thermostats in the Nervous System
Thermal neutral zones of thermoregulatory systems are narrower at the higher levels of the nervous system than at the lower levels. After Satinoff, 1978.

**13.9   The Basic Elements of the
Thermoregulatory System**

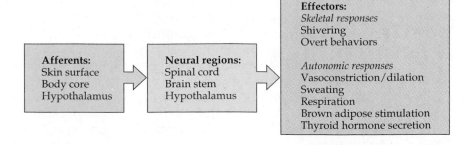

Many Behaviors Can Adjust Body Temperature

Ectotherms generate little heat through metabolism and therefore must rely heavily on behavioral methods to regulate body temperature. The marine iguana of the Galápagos Islands eats seaweed under water for an hour or more (occasionally coming up for air) in water that is 10 to 15°C cooler than its preferred body temperature. After feeding, the iguana emerges and lies on a warm rock to restore its temperature. While warming up, it lies broadside to the sun to absorb as much heat as possible (Figure 13.10*a*). When its temperature has reached 37°C, the iguana turns to face the sun and thus absorb less heat, and it may extend its legs to keep its body away from warm surfaces (Figure 13. 10*b*). Many other ectotherms regulate their temperature in similar ways. Some snakes, for example, adjust their coils to expose more or less surface to the sun and thus keep their internal temperature relatively constant during the day. Bees regulate the temperature inside the hive by their behavior, keeping the temperature in the brood area at 35 to 36°C. When the air temperature is low, the bees crowd into the brood area and shiver, thus generating heat. When the air temperature is high, the bees reduce the temperature in the brood area by fanning with their wings and by evaporative cooling (Heinrich, 1981).

Even endotherms such as mammals and birds control their exposure to the sun and to hot or cold surfaces to avoid making excessive demands on their internal regulatory mechanisms. In hot desert regions many small mammals, such as the kangaroo rat, remain in underground burrows during the day and appear above ground only at night, when the environment is relatively cool. Humans have devised many cultural practices to adapt to conditions of cold or heat. For example, Eskimo learned to design clothing that insulates well but permits the dissipation of heat through vents. Other Eskimo cultural adaptations include the design of efficient shelters, sharing

of body heat, choice of diet, and use of seal oil lamps (Moran, 1981).

Behavioral thermoregulatory responses of ectotherms and endotherms can be divided into three categories:

1. Changing exposure of the body surface, for example, huddling or extending limbs

2. Changing external insulation, for example, by using clothing or nests

3. Selecting a surround that is less thermally stressful, for example, by moving to the shade or into a burrow

Humans seldom wait for the body to get cold before putting on a coat. We anticipate homeostatic signals based on experience. As any parent will tell you, shivering reflects a lapse of intelligent behavior.

Even Birds and Mammals Begin Life as Ectotherms

Fetuses maintained in the mother's body and fertilized eggs must rely on their parents to provide warmth and regulate temperature. Most birds keep their eggs warm by using a specially vascularized area of skin (the brood patch), which transfers heat efficiently to the eggs. Even after hatching or birth, the young of many species cannot regulate their temperatures well and must continue to be protected by their parents. Rat pups are born without hair and cannot maintain body temperature when exposed to cold. The rat mother keeps her pups protected in a warm nest, and this response of the mother is related to her own thermoregulation. By the time their eyes open and they begin to stray from the nest at about 13 days of age, rat pups have developed physiological thermoregulatory reflexes and have grown a coat of fur. Other rodents, such as guinea pigs, are born in a more mature state. They show endothermic regulation from birth and do not need maternal protection.

Although newborn rats are not capable of endothermic regulation, they do show ectothermic reg-

(a)

(b)

13.10 Behavioral Control of Body Temperature

(*a*) A Galápagos marine iguana, upon emerging from the cold sea, raises its body temperature by hugging a warm rock and lying broadside to the sun. (*b*) Once its temperature is sufficiently high, the iguana reduces its surface contact with the rock and faces the sun to minimize its exposure. These behaviors afford considerable control over body temperature.

ulation. They huddle together and vary their positions in the huddle in accordance with changes in temperature (Figure 13.11). Rectal temperatures and oxygen consumption were measured in pups of different ages placed in a cool chamber (23 to 24°C), either singly or in a group of four. In five-day-old rats, the temperature of the isolated pups fell below 30°C in less than an hour, whereas those in the group maintained their temperatures above 30°C for four hours (Alberts, 1978). Huddling also significantly reduced oxygen consumption. The form of the huddle changes according to ambient temperatures; it is

loose in warm temperatures but tightly cohesive in the cold. Each pup frequently changes positions in the clump, sometimes being inside and at other times at the periphery, effectively regulating its temperature. In effect, pups share the costs and benefits of this group activity. Thus, early in the rat's development its thermoregulation depends on social interaction; later the rat becomes capable of individual endothermic regulation. The early period of ectothermy may be related to the ability of young rats and humans (unlike older rats and humans) to survive having their body core reach much lower than normal

High temperature

Low temperature

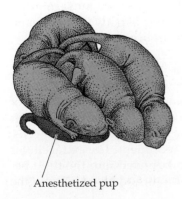

Anesthetized pup

Anesthetized pup

13.11 Social Thermoregulation

A litter of rat pups manages some degree of thermoregulation by huddling together to conserve heat. Animals push to the center to gain heat and move to the periphery to cool off. Thus an anesthetized pup will be left in the center during high temperatures and pushed to the periphery when temperatures are low. After Alberts and Brunjes, 1978.

temperatures. In fact, lowering body temperature has been used as a method of surgical anesthesia for young of both species.

Some Endotherms Have a Wide Range of Body Temperatures

All endotherms show some variation in body temperature. There's usually a daily fluctuation in body temperature that constitutes a circadian rhythm, which we'll discuss in Chapter 14. When we are ill we may have a fever. This fever is brought on by the body to help fight off infection (Box 13.1). But some endotherms that occupy habitats with extreme seasonal variations in temperature succumb periodically to the cold. For example, golden-mantled ground squirrels in the far north survive long, cold winters by staying in their burrow, curling up in a tight ball, and allowing their body temperature to plummet! An animal in this state, called **torpor**, is cold to the touch and appears not to breathe, but it does take a breath every few moments or so. Its heart still beats, but only very slowly. No one knows how these animals evolved the ability to survive this drop in body temperature, which would certainly kill a human, but it seems clear that they save a great deal of energy while in torpor. The state does not last the entire winter; once a week or so the animals arouse from torpor by raising their body temperature, move about the burrow, check on the outside conditions, and if things look grim, reenter torpor. The arousal episode requires energy but lasts less than an hour, so the animals save a good deal of energy over the winter (Heldmaier and Ruf, 1992). Reduced glucose availability, which indicates a shortage of available energy, can trigger an episode of torpor (Dark, Miller, and Zucker, 1994).

Fluid Regulation

Our Cells Evolved to Function in Seawater

The first living creatures on Earth were single-celled organisms that arose in the sea. In this setting—a large body of water with fairly uniform concentrations of salts and minerals—most basic cellular reactions evolved, including DNA production and replication, the manufacture of proteins from amino acids, and the storing and harnessing of chemical energy from ATP.

These various reactions evolved by natural selection to proceed efficiently only in a particular concentration of salt water. For these creatures, maintaining the proper concentration of salts in the water was effortless—simply let seawater inside the cell membrane and let it out again. But when multicellular animals began coming out of the water, they either had to evolve all new cellular processes to work without water or they had to bring the water with them. Only the latter solution (no pun intended) was feasible.

Land animals had to prevent dehydration (excessive loss of water) so that their cells would work properly. Thus, they needed a more or less watertight outer layer of cells, and they had to maintain the proper concentration of salts and other molecules in the water. The composition of the fluid inside your body, once proteins and the like have been removed, is similar to that of seawater. During evolution, diversity has arisen across species in the concentration of salt in plasma. For example, in closely related fish species, those that inhabit fresh water have lower salt concentration in the plasma than those that inhabit seawater. For a given species, if the concentration of molecules is altered even a small amount, the most basic cellular functions cease working properly and the animal dies. A very few species, such as salmon, have adaptations that allow them to live in fresh water at hatching, to grow up in saltwater, and to return again to fresh water to breed.

We cannot seal ourselves from the outside world, hoarding our "precious bodily fluids" without alteration. For one thing, completely watertight outer layers are difficult to make and cumbersome. More important, many body functions require that we use up some water (and some salt molecules), as, for example, when we produce urine to rid ourselves of waste molecules. Furthermore, giving up some water molecules can be a very good way to shed excess body heat, as we saw earlier. We are obliged to lose some water molecules, and therefore we are obliged to get some more (Table 13.3). Once we begin relinquishing and replacing our body's water, we must monitor and regulate the composition of body fluid to maintain basic cellular processes in order to live.

The Water in Our Body Moves Back and Forth between Two Major Compartments

Most of our water is contained within the billions of cells that make up our body—this is the intracellular compartment. But some fluid is outside of our cells, in the extracellular compartment. The extracellular compartment can be subdivided into the fluid between cells (interstitial fluid), and blood plasma (the

Box 13.1

Fever Is an Important Ally to Combat Infection

During a typical day, our body temperature varies less than one degree. This variation is quite regular, with the low points reached during early morning and the high points reached in late afternoon or early evening. Striking disturbances in the regularity of temperature control become evident during some illnesses and exposure to some environments. Fever is a familiar accompaniment of disease caused by bacteria or viruses. What causes fever? Fever begins with the invasion of the body by microbes and the mobilization of body defense mechanisms. Cells of the immune system, such as white cells in the blood, release endogenous **pyrogens**—substances that elevate body temperature. These substances are the same ones that mediate inflammatory and immunological responses. They are carried to the brain, where they act directly on nerve cells of the preoptic area and anterior hypothalamus. However, fever can be evoked even after lesion of these cells. In fact, injection of endogenous pyrogens into several other brain regions can produce fever (Blatteis et al., 1984). The impact of pyrogens is not to obliterate temperature control. Rather, many studies suggest that with fever, temperature becomes regulated at a higher level, just as though the setting of the "thermostat" was suddenly

raised. Observations of diseased persons suggest that there is an upper limit to fever of approximately 41°C. This upper level ensures that the body is not exposed to high temperatures that might cause widespread cellular damage. In rare instances prolonged fever breaks away from this limit, or is maintained too long, damaging neural centers and leading to death.

Is normal fever biologically advantageous, or is it simply the "sting" of aggressive microbes?

The adaptive value of body temperatures above normal has been shown in experiments on ectotherms such as reptiles. For example, Kluger (1979) described experiments in which desert iguanas were injected with bacterial pyrogens. These animals showed different survival rates depending on the temperature to which they were exposed. Animals with higher body temperatures (as a consequence of exposure to heat) showed higher survival rates following microbe exposure than did those with lower body temperatures. These results hold true over a range of 34 to 42°C, the usual body temperatures of endotherms. Survival at higher body temperatures is enhanced because elevated temperatures are harmful to the survival of microbes in the body. Thus, fever promotes recovery from illness

following exposure to infectious agents by producing an environment that is lethal to viruses and bacteria.

Injection of pyrogens also leads animals to seek out a warmer environment. Ectotherms such as reptiles are valuable for this type of research because the rise in body temperature that follows pyrogen injection can be prevented simply by keeping the animal in a cool environment. (However, not all reptiles show responses to bacterial pyrogens [Kluger, 1986].) Research with animals that do respond clearly illustrates the adaptive value of fever. For example, rabbits injected with a pathogen that produces fever showed better survival rates if the magnitude of the increase in fever was about 2.25°C. Above or below that amount, there was increased mortality. The mechanism mediating this effect of fever may involve several of the body's defense mechanisms, including the production of the proteins known as interferons.

This work has clear implications for therapeutic procedures used with humans, especially the use of drugs to combat fever. Antipyretic drugs, such as aspirin, may actually prolong illness by reducing fever! Moderate fever is, in view of this research, beneficial and is an "inexpensive," natural way of combating disease.

protein-rich fluid carrying red and white blood cells). By convention, water in the stomach or elsewhere in the gastrointestinal tract is considered to be outside the body—in neither of these compartments. Water must leave the gastrointestinal tract and enter the

body before we can make use of it. Similarly, water that has reached the bladder cannot be returned to the body and so is effectively outside the body as well. A simplified version of the basic systems regulating fluid intake is presented in Figure 13.12. Water

Table 13.3

Average Daily Water Balance of an Adult Person

APPROXIMATE WATER INTAKE (ml)		APPROXIMATE WATER OUTPUT (ml)	
Fluid water, including beverages	1200	Urine	1400
Water content of food	1000	Evaporative water loss	900
Water from oxidation of food	300	Feces	200
Total	2500	Total	2500

continually migrates between the intracellular and extracellular compartments. To understand the forces driving this migration, we must understand osmosis.

Osmosis is the passive movement of molecules from one place to another. The motive force behind osmosis is the constant vibration and movement of molecules. If we put a drop of food coloring in a beaker of water, the molecules of dye meander about because of this jiggling until they are more or less uniformly distributed throughout the beaker. If the water is hot, the dye molecules spread out more quickly. If we divide the beaker of water in half with a solid barrier that is impermeable to water and dye, and put the dye in the water on one side, the molecules distribute themselves only within that half. If we divide the beaker with a barrier that impedes dye molecules only a little, then the dye first distributes itself within the initial half and then slowly invades and distributes itself across both halves. In this case we say the barrier is permeable to the dye. A barrier such as a cell membrane that is permeable to *some* molecules but not others is referred to as **semipermeable**.

Before we look at what happens with semipermeable membranes, let's review a few terms. The liquid in our discussion of membranes is referred to as a **solvent**; the solid (for example, salt) dissolved in the solvent is called a **solute**. A semipermeable membrane that allows water to pass through it but prevents the passage of salt (NaCl) molecules demonstrates the principles of osmosis (Figure 13.13). If salty water is on one side of the semipermeable membrane and pure water on the other, the motion of the salt molecules pulls in water from the other compartment. The tendency to equalize salt concentrations across the membrane causes some of the water molecules to overcome gravity, raising the level of the liquid on the salt side (see Figure 13.13*c*).

Put another way, molecules have a tendency to spread out—to move *down* concentration gradients (from an area of greater concentration to an area of lower concentration). In the case we have outlined here, the water molecules are moving into the compartment where they are less concentrated (because the salt molecules are there). The force that pushes or pulls water across the membrane (that is, the force that the solutes exert on the membrane that is impermeable to them) is called **osmotic pressure**.

Cell membranes are not as passive as you might think; they strongly resist the passage of some molecules and allow other molecules to pass freely. Recall from Chapter 5, for example, that neurons normally allow very few sodium (Na^+) ions to pass through their membrane unless the voltage-sensitive Na^+ channels are opened, beginning the action potential. We refer to the concentration of solute in a solution as **osmolality**. Normally the concentration of

13.12   The Basics of Fluid Regulation

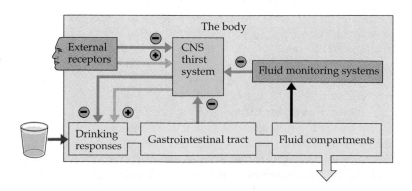

13.13 Osmosis
The same movement of water between compartments goes on inside us.

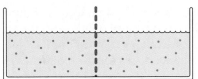

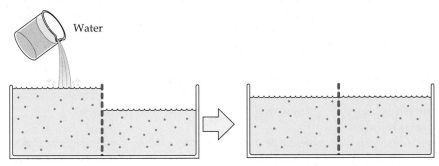

(a) Equal concentration of solute on both sides, so no net change.

Water

(b) Add water to one side.

Water molecules pass through semipermeable membrane leading to equal concentration of solute on both sides. Concentration of solute is lower (on both sides) than it was before.

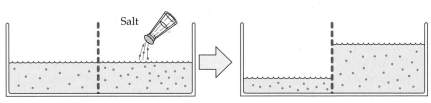

Salt

(c) Add salt (NaCl) to one side.

Water molecules on left cross membrane to reach equal solute concentration on both sides.

NaCl in the extracellular fluid of mammals is about 0.9% (weight to volume, which means there's about 0.9 grams of NaCl for every 100 milliliters of water). A solution with this concentration of salt is called physiological saline and is described as **isotonic**, having the same concentration of salt as mammalian fluids. A solution with more salt is **hypertonic**; a solution lower in salt is **hypotonic**. These solutions differ in osmolality. Before being administered, injected drugs are usually mixed in isotonic solution rather than in pure water because if pure water were injected into a muscle, the water would be pulled inside cells (which are filled with ions) by osmotic pressure and rupture the cells. At the other extreme, if hypertonic saline were injected, water would be pulled out of the cells, and that too could prove lethal for the cells. These fates could befall any cells exposed to wa-

ter of the wrong tonicity, so it is crucial that we prevent the fluid surrounding our cells from becoming either too concentrated or too dilute.

The Extracellular Fluid Compartment Serves as a Buffer

The volume of a cell probably can change slightly as proteins are made or degraded, or as new membrane is added. At any one time, however, each cell has a particular volume and is filled with enzymes and other proteins carrying out the biochemical business of living cells. Because these proteins cannot pass through the cell's external membrane, the cell needs to take in enough water molecules to keep the internal concentrations of salts and proteins within the range at which biochemical reactions run smoothly. Normally water molecules can pass out of the cell freely, but if a process such as osmotic pressure forces water *into* the cell too quickly it will rupture and die. From this viewpoint, the extracellular fluid is a "buffer"—a reservoir that provides and accepts water molecules so that cells can maintain proper internal conditions. The nervous system is responsible for ensuring that the extracellular compartment has about the right amount of water and solute to allow cells to absorb or shed water molecules readily, as conditions dictate.

Two Internal Cues Trigger Thirst

In addition to acting as a buffer, the extracellular fluid is an indicator of conditions in the intracellular compartment. In fact, the nervous system carefully monitors the extracellular compartment to determine whether we should seek water. There are two cues that more water may be needed: low extracellular volume (hypovolemic thirst), and high extracellular solute concentration (osmotic thirst). We'll consider each in turn.

Hypovolemic Thirst Is Triggered by a Loss of Water Volume

The example of hypovolemic thirst that is most easily understood is one we hope you never experience—blood loss (hemorrhage). Any animal that loses a significant amount of blood has a lowered total blood volume. Thus, blood vessels that would nor-

mally be full and slightly stretched no longer contain their full capacity. Blood pressure drops, and the individual (unless unconscious) becomes thirsty. Note that losing water from blood loss (or from diarrhea or vomiting) does not change the concentration of the extracellular fluid, because salts and other ions are lost with the fluid. Rather, only the volume of the extracellular fluid is affected in these instances (Figure 13.14a). However, continued loss in the extracellular compartment leads to fluid passing out of the intracellular compartment. So when the brain is informed of the initial drop in extracellular volume (by pressure receptors in major blood vessels and the heart known as **baroreceptors**) it initiates thirst to replace the water and salt hunger to replace salts.

The role of vasopressin.   When baroreceptors detect a drop in blood pressure (probably by detecting change in the tension in artery walls) they communicate that information through the autonomic nervous system. Selective potentiation of certain responses counteracts that drop in pressure. The sympathetic portion of the autonomic nervous system stimulates muscles in the artery walls to constrict, which reduces the size of the vessels, compensating for the reduced volume. The brain also receives information from the autonomic nervous system and in response releases the peptide hormone vasopressin from the posterior pituitary gland. The vasopressin further constricts blood vessel walls and instructs the kidneys to reduce the flow of water to the bladder. The

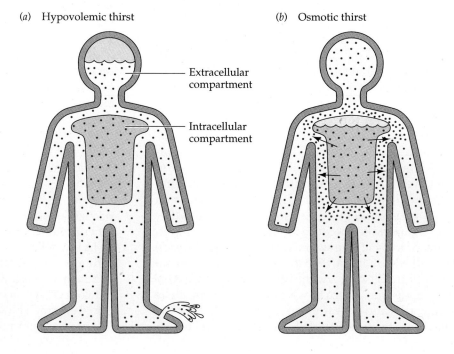

(a) Hypovolemic thirst   (b) Osmotic thirst

Extracellular compartment

Intracellular compartment

13.14 Two Kinds of Thirst
(*a*) Hypovolemic thirst is triggered by the loss of blood, which includes both solutes and water. In this case, extracellular fluid is depleted without changing the solute concentration in either the intracellular or extracellular compartments, so there is no osmotic pressure to push water from one compartment to the other. (*b*) Osmotic thirst is triggered when the total volume of water is constant, but a sudden increase in the amount of solute in the extracellular compartment (as after a very salty meal) exerts osmotic pressure that pulls water out of the intracellular compartment.

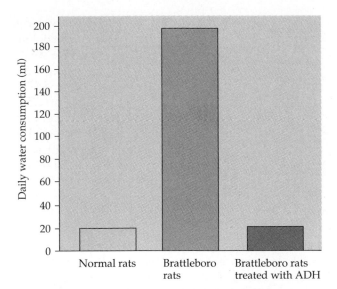

13.15 Inherited Diabetes Insipidus in Rats
The amount of water consumed daily by normal rats, and in Brattleboro rats before and after treatment with exogenous vasopressin (ADH).

latter function explains why this hormone is sometimes called anti-diuretic hormone, as we saw in Chapter 7. (A diuretic is something that causes excessive urination.)

In the disease **diabetes insipidus**, the production of vasopressin ceases, and the kidneys retain less water; they send more urine to the bladder and that urine is very pale and dilute. A consequence of all that urination is that the person is chronically thirsty and must drink a lot of water. Treatment with vasopressin relieves the symptoms. Some rats have a mutation that keeps them from producing functional vasopressin. These Brattleboro rats (so called because they were first isolated in Brattleboro, Vermont) show the symptoms of diabetes insipidus (Figure 13.15).

(Note that when people talk about diabetes, they usually do not mean diabetes insipidus, but are referring to another type of diabetes, which we'll discuss later in this chapter).

The renin–angiotensin system. The kidneys also detect the reduced blood flow accompanying hypovolemia and release a hormone called renin into circulation, triggering a cascade of hormones (Figure 13.16). The renin reacts with a protein called angiotensinogen to form the protein angiotensin I. The angiotensin I is converted to angiotensin II, which seems to be the active product. (The first demonstrated effect of this protein was to increase blood pressure, which is how it got its name: the Greek *angeion*, "blood vessel," and the Latin *tensio*, "tension or pressure.") Angiotensin II has several water-conserving actions. In addition to constricting blood vessels, angiotensin II triggers the release of vasopressin. In addition, very low doses of angiotensin II injected into the preoptic area are extremely effective in eliciting drinking, even in animals that are not deprived of water (Epstein, Fitzsimons, and Rolls, 1970). When administered to rats that had been deprived of food but not water, angiotensin II caused them to stop eating and start drinking; thus, its effect is highly specific. It appears, then, that angiotensin II can also act on the brain to trigger the sensation of thirst, prompting the animal to drink.

Where in the brain does angiotensin II act? Although the original work found the preoptic area to be the most sensitive site, it was difficult to see how angiotensin II could reach receptors in this region, since the protein does not penetrate the blood–brain barrier. Attention then focused on the **circumventricular organs**. As their name suggests, these organs lie in the walls of the cerebral ventricles (Figure 13.17). The blood–brain barrier is somewhat "leaky"

13.16 The Angiotensin Cascade
A drop in blood volume is detected by the kidneys. The kidneys then release renin, which catalyzes the conversion of angiotensinogen (already present in blood) into angiotensin I. Angiotensin I is converted into angiotensin II, the most biologically active of the angiotensions, and angiotensin III.

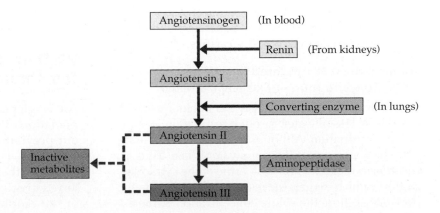

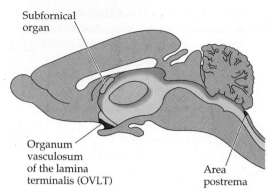

13.17 Circumventricular Organs
The circumventricular organs, here seen in a mid-sagittal view of the rat brain, mediate between the brain and the cerebrospinal fluid. The blood–brain barrier is weak in these regions and neurons within the subfornical organ and OVLT seem to monitor the osmolality of blood.

in these regions, so the neurons there have access to blood proteins that other brain regions never see. The circumventricular organs also contain receptor sites that can be affected by substances in the cerebrospinal fluid, and information about stimulation of these sites is carried by axons of the circumventricular cells into other parts of the nervous system. The neurons in one of these regions, the subfornical organ, rapidly respond to intravenous injections of angiotensin II by showing increased metabolic activity (Kadekaro et al., 1989) and expressing immediate early gene products (Lebrun et al., 1995). Thus, the subfornical organ may be one of the brain sites responding to angiotensin II by triggering thirst. There is some doubt about whether angiotensin II regulates thirst in normal situations, because blood volume reductions that induce thirst do not always produce a measurable change in blood concentration of angiotensin II (Abraham et al., 1975; Stricker, 1977). Of course, there may be more subtle changes in the concentration or distribution of angiotensin II that are not detected by present blood measures.

Osmotic Thirst Is Triggered by a Change in the Concentration of Extracellular Fluid

A more common way to trigger thirst than by loss of blood is by loss of water, through respiration, perspiration, or urination. Although some salt is lost along with the water, generally more water is lost. Thus, in addition to the reduction in volume of the extracellular fluid, which triggers the responses described in the previous section, the solute concentration of the ex-

tracellular fluid increases. The result is that water is pulled out of cells as the body tries to balance the intracellular and extracellular concentrations. The solute concentration can be increased without an accompanying increase in volume—for example, by eating salty food. Such an increase in solute concentration triggers a thirst that is independent of extracellular volume: **osmotic thirst** (see Figure 13.14*b*). Osmotic thirst causes us to seek water to protect the intracellular compartment from becoming so depleted of water that its cells are damaged.

In the 1950s it was shown that injecting a small amount of hypertonic (salty) solution into regions of the hypothalamus caused animals to start drinking. This observation suggested that some cells there might be **osmoreceptors**—that is, cells that respond to changes in osmotic pressure. Electrical recordings from single nerve cells have revealed osmotically responsive neurons spread widely throughout the preoptic area, the anterior hypothalamus, the supraoptic nucleus, and the organum vasculosum of the lamina terminalis (OVLT), a circumventricular organ (see Figure 13.17). Perhaps these cells themselves detect the change in osmolality and are themselves osmoreceptors, or perhaps they are informed by other, true osmoreceptors. If there are neuronal osmoreceptors, they may be more "elastic" than other cells and change their rate of firing based on whether they are full (when the extracellular fluid concentration is normal) or "deflated" (when more concentrated extracellular fluid draws water out of the cell). Any osmoreceptor cells may also reside among the circumventricular organs, including the OVLT and the subfornical organ, where the blood–brain barrier is weak. In any case, the neural circuits through which osmoreceptors trigger drinking have yet to be fully defined. The two types of thirst (hypovolemic and osmotic), the two fluid compartments, and the multiple methods to conserve water make for a fairly complicated system for the regulation of water (Figure 13.18).

We Don't Stop Drinking Just Because Our Throat and Mouth Are Wet

Although plausible, the most obvious explanation of why we stop drinking—that our previously dry throat and mouth are now wet—is quite wrong. In one test of this hypothesis, thirsty animals were allowed to drink water, but had the water diverted out of the esophagus through a small tube. They re-

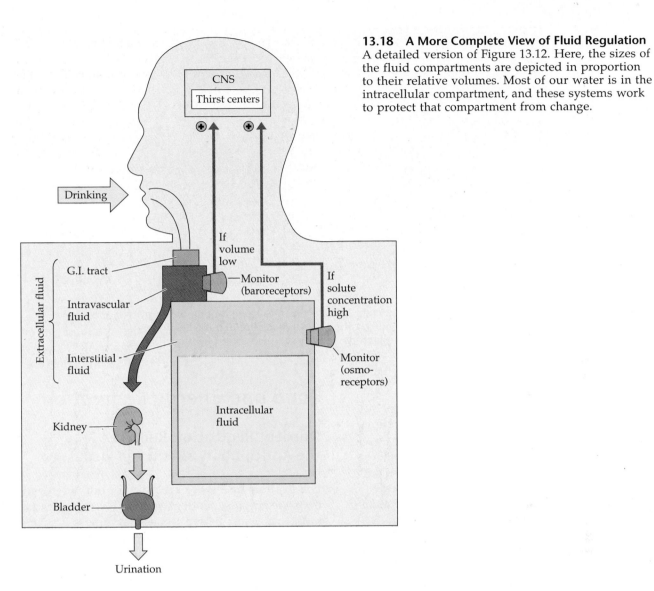

13.18   A More Complete View of Fluid Regulation
A detailed version of Figure 13.12. Here, the sizes of the fluid compartments are depicted in proportion to their relative volumes. Most of our water is in the intracellular compartment, and these systems work to protect that compartment from change.

mained thirsty and continued drinking. Thus, we conclude that moistening the mouth is not sufficient to stop the behavior of drinking or the sensation of thirst. Furthermore, we stop drinking before water has left the gastrointestinal tract and entered the extracellular compartment. Somehow we monitor how much water we have ingested and stop in *anticipation* of correcting the extracellular volume and/or osmolality. Experience may teach us and other animals how to gauge accurately whether we've ingested enough to counteract our thirst (hypovolemic or osmotic). Normally all the signals—blood volume, osmolality, moisture in the mouth, estimates of the amount of water we've ingested that's "on the way"—register agreement, but the cessation of one signal alone will not stop thirst; in this way animals insure against dehydration.

Homeostatic Regulation of Salt Is Required for Effective Regulation of Water

Animals may travel great distances to eat salt (Figure 13.19) and the sodium (Na^+) is particularly important to fluid balance. Why? Because we cannot maintain water in the extracellular compartment without solutes; if the extracellular compartment contained pure water, osmotic pressure would drive it into the cells, killing them. The number of Na^+ ions we possess primarily determines how much water we can retain. Thus, thirsty animals may prefer slightly salty water (as long as it's hypotonic) over pure water, and this preference may be adaptive for conserving water. Some Na^+ loss is inevitable, as during urination. But when water is at a premium, when an animal is

13.19 Hungry for Salt
Rabbits inhabiting sodium-deficient habitats, such as these rabbits living in
alpine regions of Australia, will devour wooden pegs impregnated with sodium. Rabbits in sodium-rich habitats ignore such pegs. From Denton, 1982.

thirsty, the body tries to conserve Na⁺ in order to retain water. The mineralocorticoid, steroid hormone
aldosterone is crucial to Na⁺ conservation. Like vasopressin, aldosterone acts directly upon the kidneys,
but aldosterone induces the kidneys to conserve Na⁺
(while vasopressin acts to conserve water). Aldosterone conserves some sodium to aid water retention,
but animals must find salt in their diets to survive.

You might think that, since some Na⁺ aids water
retention, seawater should quench thirst—but it
doesn't. Seawater is hypertonic—it has too much
Na⁺. We lose some water each day without Na⁺
(through our skin, with our breathing) and that sodi-
um-free water must be replaced. Adding isotonic water will not help restore the water-to-sodium ratio. If
we could excrete lots of sodium ions in our urine, we
could drink seawater, use some of the water molecules to replace the day's loss, and excrete the excess
salt. But our kidneys cannot excrete enough additional Na⁺ in the urine to allow this. Obviously, marine mammals have found a means of excreting excess
salt, via kidneys that can produce very concentrated
urine. Many species of desert rodents can produce
highly concentrated urine to help conserve water.
Some seabirds, including gulls and petrels, have specialized salt glands near the nostrils that can excrete
highly concentrated salt solutions (Schmidt-Nielsen,
1960); thus, they can drink seawater. Perhaps most
impressive are the fishes that can adapt to either a
saltwater or freshwater environment.

Food and Energy Regulation

Nutrient Regulation Requires the Anticipation of Future Needs

Feast or famine—these are poles of human experience. We are so dependent on food for energy and to
build and maintain our bodies that hunger is a compelling motive and flavors are powerful reinforcements. The need to eat shapes our daily schedules and
molds our activities. Our newspapers are full of food-
related information—news of successes or failures of
food crops; famines and droughts; laws and treaties
governing import and export of foods; hunger strikes;
recipes and articles about food; advertisements for
restaurants and kitchen appliances; effects of diet and
obesity on health; clinics to treat weight problems. A
major part of any economy is devoted to the raising,
processing and preparing, packaging, transporting,
and distributing of food. Although much of our involvement with food has purely human cultural aspects, our basic reliance on food for energy and nutrition is shared with all other animals. In the
remainder of this chapter we will look at the general
needs and physiological regulation of feeding and energy expenditure, as well as some species-specific aspects of food-related behavior and regulation.

The regulation of eating and of body energy is intimately related to the regulation of body temperature and water, which we have already considered,

but is more complicated. One reason for the greater complexity is that food is needed not only to supply energy but also to supply nutrients. **Nutrients**, in the technical meaning of the term, are chemicals that are not used as sources of energy but that are required for the effective functioning of the body; for example, they are needed for the growth, maintenance, and repair of bodily structures. We do not know all the nutritional requirements of the body—even for humans. Of the 20 amino acids found in our bodies, 9 are difficult or impossible for us to manufacture, so we must find them in our diet. These 9 are thus called essential amino acids. Similarly, we must obtain a few fatty acids from food. Other nutritional requirements include about 15 vitamins and several minerals.

One reason that eating and nutrient regulation are complicated is that no animal can afford to run out of energy or nutrients; there must be a reserve on hand at all times (Figure 13.20). If the reserves are too large, though, mobility (for avoiding predators or securing prey) will be compromised. Thus, the neurobiology of feeding requires us to understand how the organism anticipates the need for energy and nutrients, as well as how these resources are moved in and out of various body reservoirs.

The Digestive System Breaks Down Food in Four Stages

For the cells of the body to receive and use vital nutrients, ingested food must be converted into simpler chemicals. These simpler substances are the products of **digestion**, a series of mechanical and chemical processes that take place in the digestive tract. A brief review of the four main processes of digestion will set the stage for our consideration of the control of feeding behavior.

1. The digestive tract begins at the mouth, where food is broken down mechanically in preparation for the chemical processes of digestion. Saliva dissolves food and contains an enzyme that initiates the chemical breakdown of carbohydrates. Tasting and chewing produce signals that start the secretion of digestive enzymes in the stomach.

2. Food passes to the stomach with the act of swallowing, a complex reflex involving an elaborate set of muscles of the mouth and throat. The esophagus is a tube that connects the mouth and stomach. Within the esophagus, waves of movements (peristalsis) propel food toward the stomach. The most intense digestion occurs in the stomach. Structural characteristics of the stomach vary among animals; especially elaborate morphology

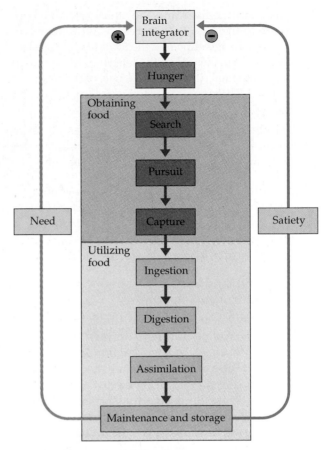

13.20 The Stages of Feeding
While the goal of feeding is to gather energy and nutrients, all of these events themselves require the expenditure of energy, so an animal that does not retain sufficient energy reserves to initiate the sequence is doomed. During development, animals are given a "head-start" by their parents who provide the initial energy needed to gather our first meal.

is found in grazing animals (herbivores) because of their diet of tough grasses. Within the stomach, waves of movements keep food mixed while enzymes break down the substances. One enzyme breaks down protein into its constituents, amino acids; another changes the proteins characteristically found in milk; a third aids in the digestion of fats. Since the stomach also acts as a reservoir for food being digested, the presence and amount of food in the stomach could be expected to influence the timing of eating.

3. The contents of the stomach are directed in spurts, through a muscular valve, the pyloric sphincter, into the small intestine. Within the small intestine, enzymatic action continues. Enzymes from the pancreas act on proteins, carbohydrates, and fat. Secre-

tions from the liver and the small intestine contribute to the digestive process. Rhythmic movements of the intestine mix the food to aid digestive processes. Further along the length of the small intestine, the final simplified products of digestion are absorbed. These substances pass into capillaries and enter the bloodstream leading to the liver.

4 A sludge with the remaining, undigestible substances collects in the large intestine, which reabsorbs much of the water, leaving feces.

In addition to enzymes, hormones secreted by cells of the stomach regulate certain aspects of the digestive process. Some gut hormones regulate enzyme production; others may also act on brain cells to influence feeding behavior, as we will see later.

Most of Our Food Is Used to Provide Us with Energy

All the energy we need to move, think, breathe, and maintain body temperature is derived in the same way: it is released as the chemical bonds of complex molecules are broken to form smaller, simpler compounds. In a sense we "burn" food just as a car burns gasoline for energy. To raise body temperature we release the bond energy as heat. For other bodily processes, such as those in the brain, the energy is utilized by more sophisticated biochemical processes. In either case we assess the amount of energy used in terms of calories. (Recall that, in physics, a calorie is the amount of energy it takes to raise the temperature of 1 milliliter of water by 1°C.) When nutritionists talk about calories in food, they are describing the potential energy available. Unfortunately, what a nutritionist calls a calorie is actually 1000 calories (a kilocalorie) as defined by physicists. By convention, nutritionists simply leave off the "kilo-" prefix. To avoid confusion, we will use kilocalories (kcal) as defined in physics. We can gauge metabolic rate, the amount of energy we use during a given period, in terms of kcal/day.

Some of the energy in food cannot be converted to metabolizable form and is excreted. In a study of metabolism in the laboratory rat, about 75% of the ingested energy became available for use in bodily functions (Corbett and Keesey, 1982). The available energy is used in one of three ways:

1. Some energy is used simply to process newly ingested food. Typically both metabolic rate and heat production rise just after a meal, and this rise has been interpreted as reflecting energy used to process food. The energy utilization for processing food amounts to about 8%.

2. The greatest part of the energy—about 55%—is used for basal metabolism—that is, for maintaining bodily heat and other resting functions, such as neural potentials.

3. Only about 12 to 13% of the energy is spent on active behavioral processes. In an environment more conducive to activity than the small metabolic chamber used to take these measurements in the laboratory, the percentage of energy spent on active behavioral processes would probably be larger.

It used to be thought that only the expenditure of energy for active behavioral processes showed much elasticity and that basal metabolism and heat production caused by feeding were fixed. In fact, basal metabolism is known to follow a rule that relates energy expenditure to body weight (Kleiber, 1947):

$$\text{kcal/day} = 70 \times \text{weight}^{0.75}$$

where weight is expressed in kilograms. This rule has been shown to apply from the largest mammals to mice—a range in size greater than 3000 to 1 (Figure 13.21).

Although this relation holds for baseline conditions, if an animal or person is not at its optimum body weight, basal metabolism departs from the value predicted by the Kleiber equation. For example, food-deprived people have lower basal metabolism as well as a lower weight (Keys et al., 1950). In fact, severe restriction of caloric intake affects metabolic rate much more than it affects body weight (Figure 13.22). Animal studies show similar disproportions (Keesey and Corbett, 1984). Thus the resting rate of energy expenditure is really "basal" only for animals and people who are in energy balance. The expenditure of energy at rest drops substantially below "normal" (that is, the level predicted by the Kleiber formula) when body weight is reduced from the normally maintained level. Such adjustments in the rate of energy expenditure play a significant role in maintaining energy balance and in keeping an individual's body weight relatively constant (Keesey and Powley, 1986).

Since people and animals adjust their energy expenditures in response to under- or overnutrition, they tend to resist either losing or gaining weight. This tendency helps explain why it is so difficult for some people to lose weight and for others to gain. The relation between metabolic rate and body weight may also indicate when an individual is at his or her physiologically normal target weight (Keesey and Corbett, 1984). Only at this weight will the person's resting metabolism be at the level predicted by the

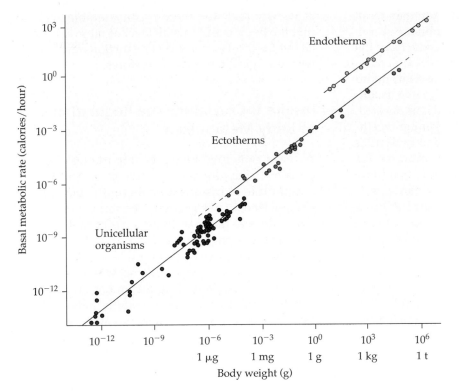

13.21　Relation Between Body Size and Metabolism
Note that over a wide range of body weights, basal metabolic rate increases in a very regular, predictable fashion. However, endotherms have a higher metabolic rate than ectotherms of a similar body weight. After Hemmingsen, 1960.

Kleiber equation. A lower metabolic rate than predicted by the equation indicates that the person is below his or her physiologically normal weight. People who hold their weight down by dieting may remain hypometabolic as long as their weight stays below the level that they used to maintain (Leibel and

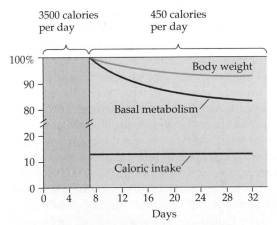

13.22　Why Losing Weight Is So Difficult
After seven days on a diet of 3500 kcal per day, the intake of six obese subjects was restricted to 450 kcal per day, a drop of 87%. However, basal metabolism also declined, by 15%, so that after 3 weeks body weight had declined by only 6%. After Bray, 1969.

Hirsch, 1984), and thus they must continue dieting to remain at a body weight that would be normal for someone else.

Carbohydrates Provide Energy for Body and Brain

What molecules provide energy to the body, and how does the body regulate that energy? Large carbohydrate molecules can be broken down into simple carbohydrates, including sugars. The most important sugar used by our body is **glucose**. In fact, the brain is quite dependent on glucose for energy, while the rest of the body can use both glucose and more complicated molecules, such as fatty acids, for energy. Because a readily available supply of glucose is crucial for brain function and for survival, the liver stores glucose by combining excess glucose molecules to form a more complex carbohydrate called glycogen. When the concentration of glucose molecules in circulation falls, the liver can convert the glycogen back into glucose molecules and release them into circulation as needed. This shuttling of energy supplies back and forth is controlled by two protein hormones from the pancreas: Glucagon promotes the breakdown of glycogen to glucose; insulin promotes the conversion of glucose into glycogen. Thus the pancreas determines the balance of ready energy (glucose) from a short-term energy source (glycogen). (You may recall from Chapter 7 that glucagon and insulin are secreted from the alpha and beta cells, respectively, of the islets of Langerhans within the pancreas.)

For long-term energy storage, we use fat, maintained in fat cells, which form what is known as **adipose** tissue. Fat molecules are large and complicated. You may think of them as the result of joining together many different sugars and other small molecules into a large molecule that is not soluble in water. Fat either comes directly from our food or is manufactured in the body from glucose and other nutrients. If the glycogen store becomes depleted, our body can convert fat into fatty acids to supply energy to the body and into glucose to provide energy to the brain (Figure 13.23). When an animal or person is deprived of food, little or no energy gets stored in fat deposits. When an animal eats liberally, some of the energy is laid down in fat supplies so that it will be available in the future. The factors that regulate how much energy is stored in fat are not well understood. However,

as we will see later, there is considerable evidence that the body maintains its level of fat in the face of all but the most extreme diet restrictions and even after the surgical removal of fat stores.

Insulin Is Crucial for the Regulation of Body Metabolism

We've already mentioned the importance of insulin for converting glucose into glycogen. Another important role of insulin is enabling the body to use glucose. Most cells regulate the import of glucose molecules via **glucose transporters** that span the cell's external membrane and bring glucose molecules from outside the cell into the cell for use. The glucose transporters must interact with insulin in order to function. (Brain cells are an important exception; they can use glucose without the aid of insulin.) Each time you eat a meal, the foods are broken down and glucose is released into the bloodstream. Most of your body requires insulin to make use of that glucose, so three different, sequential mechanisms stimulate insulin release. First, the stimuli from food (sight, smell, and taste) evoke a conditioned release of insulin in anticipation of glucose arrival in the blood. This release, because it is mediated by the brain, is called the cephalic phase of insulin release. Next, during the digestive phase, food entering the stomach and intestines causes them to release gut hormones, some of which stimulate the pancreas to release insulin. Finally, during the absorptive phase, glucose enters the bloodstream, and special cells in the liver, called **glucodetectors** (or glucostats), detect this circulating glucose and signal the pancreas to release insulin. The newly released insulin allows the body to make use of some of the glucose immediately, and other glucose is converted into glycogen. The liver and the pancreas communicate via the nervous system. Autonomic afferents from the liver deliver nerve impulses up the vagus nerve to the brain stem. Efferent fibers carry signals from the brain stem out a different vagus nerve route to the pancreas. These efferent fibers modulate hormonal secretions from the pancreas.

Lack of insulin causes the disease **diabetes mellitus**. The simplest and deadliest form of diabetes mellitus is Type I, also called juvenile-onset diabetes. In this disease, the pancreas stops producing insulin. While the brain can still make use of glucose from the diet, the rest of the body cannot and is forced to use energy from fatty acids. The result is that lots of glucose is left in the bloodstream because the brain

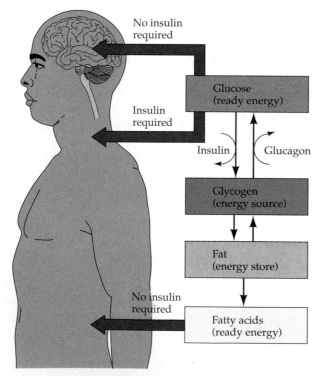

13.23 The Role of Insulin in Energy Utilization
The body can make use of either fatty acids or glucose for energy, while the brain can make ready use only of glucose. So the brain requires a constant supply of glucose, which it can use without the need of insulin. On the other hand, the body can make use of glucose only with the aid of insulin, so in the absence of insulin our bodies must use fatty acids for energy.

cannot use it all and the lack of insulin means there is no way to put it into glycogen storage. Some of the glucose is secreted into the urine, making the urine sweet, hence the name diabetes mellitus ("passing honey").

Untreated Diabetics Eat Ravenously yet Lose Weight

The body did not evolve to gather all its energy efficiently from fatty acids, so an untreated (Type I) diabetic is chronically undernourished. Although untreated diabetics eat a great deal, because their bodies cannot make much use of the food, they lose weight anyway. Tissues begin showing signs of degradation as a result of relying so heavily on the less efficient fatty acids for energy. The urine, in addition to being sweet, is also copious as the kidneys try to dump the excess glucose; consequently untreated diabetics are also chronically thirsty. Finally, the excess glucose in circulation may itself damage some tissues. The treatment is obvious: provide exogenous insulin. Unfortunately, insulin normally is not secreted just once during the day; the pattern of secretion across the day is complex and varies depending on what is eaten, when it is eaten, and what other behaviors are displayed. Thus, exogenously providing the proper amount of insulin at the proper time is tricky.

There has long been evidence that Type I diabetes has a genetic component, and recent research indicates that there are many different genes that can affect the probability of developing diabetes. One hypothesis suggests that diabetes is an autoimmune disorder—that diabetics produce antibodies that attack their own pancreatic cells, stopping the insulin supply. Why would this happen? After all, the immune system is supposed to help us. Scientists have found that some viruses that cause upper respiratory infections have a protein that resembles glutamic acid decarboxylase (GAD). When this viral protein is injected into mice, some of the mice produce antibodies that recognize both the viral protein and their own GAD. Because GAD is found on the surface of the pancreatic cells, the antibodies attack and destroy the cells, which leads to a loss of insulin and the development of diabetes. Some strains of mice are much more likely to suffer these effects of viral exposure than others (Atkinson et al., 1994). Some people exposed to this virus may produce antibodies to defeat the virus that also destroy their own insulin source. In support of this theory, some people in the early stages of diabetes have been found to have circulating antibodies that recognize GAD (Atkinson and

Maclaren, 1994). Many different genes could influence whether a person makes these particular antibodies. If this hypothesis proves correct, it may be possible to inoculate children (with *other* proteins from these viruses) so that, when they are exposed to the virus, they already have antibodies to defeat the infection without making the harmful antibodies.

There is another, more common type of diabetes mellitus, called Type II, or adult-onset diabetes. This milder version can be caused either by a gradually decreasing sensitivity to insulin or by gradually decreasing production of the hormone. This condition is far more common in obese people, and, because the individuals still produce some insulin, can usually be treated by reducing the amount of glucose in the diet and by giving a drug that stimulates the pancreas to produce more insulin, without resorting to insulin injections.

Despite Its Importance, Insulin Provides neither the Hunger nor the Satiety Signal

Given the crucial role of insulin in mobilizing and distributing food energy, you might think that the brain monitors circulating insulin levels to decide when it is time to eat and when it is time to stop eating. For example, if the insulin level is high, there must be food in the pipeline and the fat stores will be increased, so the brain might produce the sensation of satiety so that we stop eating. If insulin levels are low, the brain might signal hunger to impel us to find food and eat. Experiments have shown that forc- 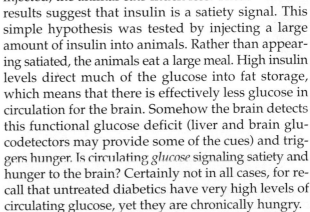 ing an animal's blood insulin levels to be low causes it to become hungry and eat a large meal. If moderate levels of insulin are injected, the animal eats much less. These results suggest that insulin is a satiety signal. This simple hypothesis was tested by injecting a large amount of insulin into animals. Rather than appearing satiated, the animals eat a large meal. High insulin levels direct much of the glucose into fat storage, which means that there is effectively less glucose in circulation for the brain. Somehow the brain detects this functional glucose deficit (liver and brain glucodetectors may provide some of the cues) and triggers hunger. Is circulating *glucose* signaling satiety and hunger to the brain? Certainly not in all cases, for recall that untreated diabetics have very high levels of circulating glucose, yet they are chronically hungry.

Studies of diabetic rats provide more evidence that insulin is not the only satiety signal. Like untreated human diabetics, these rats eat a great deal. But if the rats are fed a high-fat diet, they eat normal amounts (Friedman, 1978), probably because their body can make immediate use of the fatty acids without insulin. Thus, the circulating levels of neither insulin nor glucose are sufficient to explain all the cases when an animal is hungry or satiated. Somehow the brain makes use of both insulin and glucose levels and other sources of information, then integrates this information to decide whether to initiate eating. This seems to be the theme of hunger research—that the brain integrates many different signals rather than relying exclusively on any one signal to trigger hunger. Another of the possible cues the brain may use to signal satiety is discussed next.

Do Gut Peptide Hormones Signal Satiety?

We mentioned earlier that when food arrives in the stomach and intestines, they release several peptide hormones. Among them is cholecystokinin (CCK). The release of CCK is especially pronounced if the food has a high content of fat and/or proteins. CCK seems to have widespread effects, including stimulating the pancreas to release insulin, a function we alluded to before. Thus, CCK meets the first criterion for a circulating satiety signal: levels are high when food is already in the intestines and low when the intestines are empty (Gibbs and Smith, 1986). CCK also acts as a neurotransmitter in the brain, so we know that some neurons respond to CCK and that circulating CCK could communicate satiety to the brain. When CCK is administered to humans, however, they report experiencing nausea and even vomiting (Miaskiewicz, Stricker, and Verbalis, 1989). Apparently exogenous CCK acts on the intestines themselves, increasing the muscular contractions, producing cramping and nausea. Does CCK make rats

nauseated? It's difficult to know because, for one thing, rats cannot vomit, even when they are very sick. But one indication that exogenous CCK may make rats nauseated is that pairing a new food with CCK treatment causes rats to avoid the food in the future (Chen et al., 1993). This phenomenon, called **taste aversion** (which is described in the next section), indicates that the CCK made the rats uncomfortable and that they avoided the food thereafter under the (mistaken) assumption that the food was responsible for the unpleasant feelings. We must interpret the effects of exogenous CCK on food intake with some suspicion: it may make rats feel nauseated rather than satiated, but of course the normally secreted CCK triggered by a meal does not cause us to feel nauseated. Therefore either the amount of CCK and/or the corelease of presently unidentified compounds must prevent the production of nausea. Whether the endogenously released CCK, alone or in conjunction with other intestinal hormones, contributes to the sensation of satiety remains to be seen.

Experience Normally Guides Us to a Healthful Diet

Learning has a profound effect on the feeding behavior of animals. We've already mentioned the cephalic phase of feeding, during which the stimuli of food evoke a conditioned release of insulin so that we will make quick use of the food. Another example of conditioning is the preference that many species show for foods to which they were exposed during development. Normally such a preference would be adaptive. Some moths prefer to lay their eggs on the leaves of whichever plant that moth ate as a caterpillar. This seems sensible: if it was good enough for me to survive to adulthood on, it should do for my offspring. One can influence the food preferences of adult rats by exposing them to the food as nursing pups. Rats normally prefer plain water over garlic-flavored water, but if a rat mother has only garlic-flavored water to drink, she will drink it. Her offspring, nursing for the first 21 days of their life, will prefer garlic water over plain. This preference is strengthened if they are exposed to such water just after weaning (Capretta, Petersik, and Stewart, 1975). Many adult humans prefer the cuisine provided them by their parents while growing up.

Another important means by which experience shapes feeding is conditioned taste aversion, which we mentioned in our discussion of CCK. A young, inexperienced blue jay will readily snap up and eat a monarch butterfly. Score one for the blue jay. A few minutes later, however, the bird will vomit up the butterfly and wipe its bill repeatedly as if to remove any traces (Figure 13.24). That bird will eat other butterflies, but will not eat another monarch (Wiklund and Sillén-Tullberg, 1985), even when hundreds are available. Score several hundred for the monarchs. Why does the blue jay vomit up the monarch? Because the monarch, as a caterpillar, fed on milkweed and gathered from that plant toxins that offend other caterpillars, but which monarch caterpillars tolerate. The toxins remain in the adult's body and also offend birds, making them nauseated. The bird learns to associate the monarch with illness and, to avoid becoming ill again, avoids that food.

Discovered by John Garcia, conditioned taste aversion is sometimes referred to as the Garcia effect.

(a)

(b)

13.24   Taste Aversion
(a) A blue jay immediately before and (b) a few minutes after eating a monarch butterfly and becoming sick from the toxins such butterflies contain. The animal regurgitates the butterfly, wipes its beak repeatedly and will in the future avoid eating other monarchs. Courtesy of Lincoln Bower.

Garcia's original work, which involved making rats sick using X rays, was only very slowly accepted by

John Garcia

scientists because the learning psychologists of the day believed that any stimulus could be paired with any other stimulus equally well, and that repeated trials would be necessary for the animal to associate one stimulus with the other. The assertion that animals could learn, with a single trial, to avoid food associated with illness, but would require many trials to avoid food associated with foot shock, was a heresy. Another reason for the hesitation was the common belief that the interval between presentation of the stimuli could not exceed seconds if the association was to be made (see Chapter 17), but the illness effects occur moments to hours after ingestion. We now know that animals from snails to humans readily associate food with illness that occurs even hours later and use this learning ability to avoid poisons. The selective advantage of this propensity seems obvious.

A related phenomenon is **neophobia**, the avoidance of new things—in this case new foods. Rats are quite reluctant to eat any new food, and when they do eat the food, they tend to eat a small amount and

wait a period before eating more. If they become ill after the first sample, conditioned taste aversion prevents them from taking more.

In some instances individuals choose to eat exactly those foods that are needed, and it is not clear that experience teaches these preferences. In the 1920s and 1930s, so-called cafeteria experiments found that children who were offered a variety of nutritious foods encompassing all known dietary requirements would efficiently balance their own diets. These studies persuaded generations of physicians to reassure parents that finicky eaters would be fine. However, the experiments did not offer the children high-sugar foods 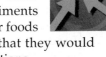 as an alternative, so it is not clear that they would gain a proper diet under such conditions.

A wide variety of species, including humans, can show very specific changes in preferences when they are suffering from a deficiency of a particular nutrient. We mentioned salt hunger earlier; people who are experiencing a deficiency in salt prefer their food more heavily salted than other people. The person may not be aware of the deficiency; salt simply tastes better. An even more compelling example is cod liver oil. Most children hate the taste of cod liver oil, but children suffering from rickets, a disease caused by insufficient vitamin D and improper metabolism of calcium and phosphorus, actually like it, but only until the rickets is dispelled! Animals have demonstrated a remarkable ability to select the diet that most effectively corrects specific dietary deficiencies.

There Is Apparently No Single Satiety Center or Single Hunger Center in the Brain

Just as no single molecule in the bloodstream always triggers hunger or satiety, it appears that no single brain region has exclusive control of these sensations. Discoveries of the early 1950s gave support for a time to a "dual-center theory" of the control of eating. According to this theory, the hypothalamus contained the primary control centers for hunger and satiety: A hunger center in the lateral hypothalamus (LH) facilitated eating, and a satiety center in the ventromedial hypothalamus (VMH) inhibited eating. Information from all the other brain regions, and from other factors (such as circulating hormones) that influence eating, were presumed to funnel into and to act through these hypothalamic control centers. Further research aimed at filling in the details of this picture soon dethroned the hypothalamic regions from their exclusive status, and even the concept of a center or centers was challenged, as we will see.

The Ventromedial Hypothalamus Appeared for a Time to Be the Satiety Center

Occasionally a person develops a pathologically voracious appetite and soon becomes obese. In the nineteenth century, physicians found that some of these patients had tumors at the base of the brain. In 1940, Hetherington and Ranson reported that bilateral lesions of the ventromedial hypothalamus (Figure 13.25) cause rats to become obese. VMH lesions produced obesity in all the species that were tested— monkeys, dogs and cats, several species of rodents, and some species of birds.

The VMH was promptly called a satiety center because destroying it seemed to prevent animals from ever being satiated with food, but this characterization was soon seen to be inadequate. Destruction of the VMH does not simply cause the rats to become feeding machines. Rather, the eating habits of VMH-lesioned rats are still controlled by both the palatability of food and body weight, but these controls are no longer exerted in normal ways. If palatable food of high caloric content is available, VMH-lesioned rats typically show two phases of weight gain. At first they show an amazing increase in consumption, eating two or three times as much as normal; this condition is called **hyperphagia** (from the Greek, *hy-*

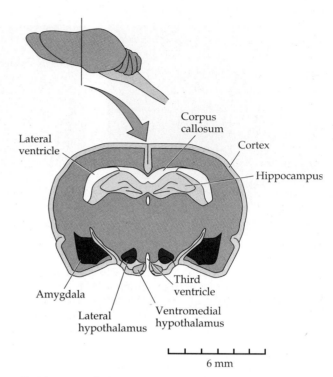

13.25 Hypothalamic Regions Implicated in Eating

per, "over," and *phagein*, "to eat"). Body weight shoots up, a stage called the dynamic phase of weight gain (Figure 13.26). But after a few weeks, weight stabilizes at an obese level, and food intake is not much above normal; this stage is called the static phase of obesity. Once animals have reached this new weight, they seem to display normal satiety in response to their food. Since the VMH is gone from these animals, it cannot be responsible for their satiety; therefore it seems likely that some other brain regions normally contribute to satiety.

Some observations indicate that the obese VMH-lesioned rat regulates its weight at a new target value. If an obese rat in the static phase is force-fed, its weight will rise above the plateau level (see Figure 13.26); but when it is again allowed to eat on its own, body weight actually falls back to the plateau level. Similarly, after an obese rat has been deprived of food and has lost weight, when given free access to food, it will regain its plateau level. Furthermore, the plateau body weight also depends on the palatability if the diet. If VMH-lesioned rats are kept on a diet of laboratory chow pellets (rather than a high-fat diet), their weight does not rise much above that of control animals. If the food is adulterated with qui-

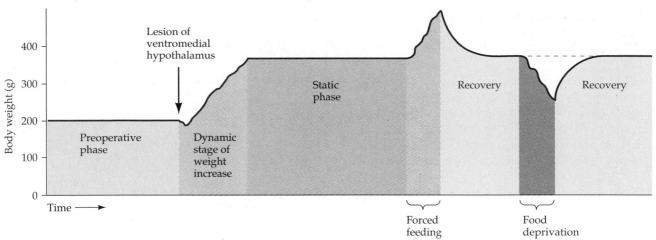

13.26 Lesion-Induced Obesity
After receiving a lesion of the ventromedial hypothalamus (VMH), rats overeat and gain weight until they reach a new, higher body weight, which they defend in the face of either forced feeding or food deprivation. Thus they continue to regulate body weight, but at a higher set point. After Sclafani, Springer, and Kluge, 1976.

nine to make it bitter, then the body weight of the VMH-lesioned rats may fall *below* that of controls (Sclafani, Springer, and Kluge, 1976). These results suggest that VMH-lesioned rats are finicky and therefore show exaggerated reactions to palatability.

The Lateral Hypothalamus Appeared for a Time to Be the Hunger Center

In 1951 Anand and Brobeck announced that bilateral destruction of the lateral hypothalamus (LH) caused rats or cats to stop eating. This refusal to eat, known as aphagia, was so severe in some cases that animals died of starvation even when their usual food was present. The investigators proposed that the LH contains a "feeding center" and that the VMH normally acts as a brake on feeding by inhibiting the LH. Two important features of the effects of LH damage soon emerged (Teitelbaum and Stellar, 1954). First, the rats refused not only to eat but also to drink (they showed adipsia as well as aphagia). If the experimenters placed a bit of food or a drop of water on the lips or in the mouth of the rat, it spat out the food or water as if it were distasteful. Second, the aphagia and adipsia were not necessarily permanent. A few rats began to eat and drink spontaneously after about a week. Most rats would eventually eat spontaneously if they were kept alive meanwhile by having food and water pumped through a tube directly into the stomach. Thus, just as VMH destruction does not abolish all inhibition of eating, LH destruction does not perma-

nently prevent eating and drinking. Therefore, some other brain region must be able to monitor feeding and signal satiety in LH-lesioned rats. Presumably this other region contributes to satiety in normal animals.

Recovered LH-lesioned rats regulate their new body weight with precision. The larger the size of the LH lesion, the lower the target level of body weight. If food is restricted, the weights of LH-lesioned and control rats fall in parallel, and the pre-deprivation level is regained when free access to food is restored (Figure 13.27). Similarly, if the only food available is eggnog (year-round!), both lesioned and control rats gain weight in parallel; and when the usual diet is restored, both groups fall to their previous level. When food is adulterated with quinine, the LH-lesioned rats again show changes strictly in parallel with normal controls (Keesey and Boyle, 1973). (Recall that VMH-lesioned rats displayed an exaggerated reaction to quinine.) Thus the LH-lesioned rats are said to defend a lowered weight target or set point (Keesey, 1980). Human beings may become emaciated if they suffer from lesions or tumors of the lateral hypothalamus. Bilateral damage to the LH through accident or disease is rare, but even unilateral damage to the LH sometimes produces aphagia and adipsia in animals. Cases of anorexia (absence of appetite) induced by LH lesions in humans are about a quarter as frequent as cases of hypothalamic obesity (White and Hain, 1959).

13.27 Lesion-Induced Weight Loss
Both normal rats and rats that have recovered from lesions of the lateral hypothalamus (LH) regulate body weight quite well. The LH-lesioned rats regulate around a lowered target weight, but in parallel with normal rats. After Keesey and Boyle, 1973.

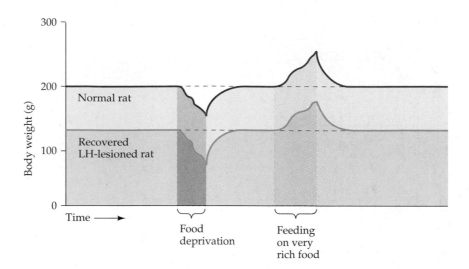

Satiety and Hunger Functions Are Spread throughout the Brain

The dual-center hypothesis was challenged by many observations. As we saw, animals exhibited some capacity for hunger and satiety despite losing the LH or VMH, respectively. Controversies arose about whether the lesions were effective because they destroyed integrative centers, as originally believed, or because they interrupted fiber tracts that passed through these regions (Marshall, Richardson, and Teitelbaum, 1974). In addition, many brain regions outside the hypothalamus were found to be involved in the regulation of feeding behavior, and they do not contribute solely by their connections to the hypothalamus. Among the regions whose destruction impairs the regulation of feeding are the amygdaloid nuclei, the frontal cortex, and the substantia nigra. Taken together, these data suggest that hunger and satiety are not centered in any single brain region, but that a network of cells distributed across the brain is responsible for these functions.

Scientists have become increasingly aware that peripheral structures, notably the liver, also play a crucial role in monitoring energy and nutrient balance and signaling the brain to activate or inhibit eating. In the extreme, it could be the peripheral structures that weigh the variables and send commands to the brain, while the brain has little latitude in whether or not to initiate food seeking and eating. This view may be discomfiting to neuroscientists because it deemphasizes the role of the brain in deciding whether to eat, but in any case the brain organizes the behavior.

Genes Can Affect Target Weight

Genes can result in a high target weight, as, for example, in rats of the Zucker strain (Zucker and Zuck-er, 1961). Similarly, mice that receive two copies of the gene called obese (abbreviated *ob*) regulate their body weight at a high level, as you might have guessed from the gene's name (Figure 13.28). These mice have larger and more numerous fat cells than their heterozygous littermates (*ob/+*). Like Zucker rats, the fat mice (*ob/ob*), maintain their obesity even on diets strongly adulterated with quinine or when they are required to work hard to obtain food (Cruce et al., 1974). When the mouse *ob* gene was cloned recently, it was found that normally only fat cells produce the protein, and the sequence of that protein suggests that it may be secreted (Zhang et al., 1994). If so, then fat cells may release this protein to signal the brain and the rest of the body about the level of body fat. This mechanism may be how the body regulates total body fat (Box 13.2). If so, the defect in the ob protein may "underreport" body fat, leading the animal to overeat, especially high-fat or sugary foods.

Injecting the obese mice with the normal ob protein causes them to lose weight dramatically (Halaas et al., 1995). Since the protein is much more effective when provided to the hypothalamus (Campfield et al., 1995), it appears that a hormonal signal is what tells the brain when there is enough body fat. Behavior genetic analyses indicate a strong genetic contribution to obesity in humans (representing the effect of many genes, not just one; Price and Gottesman, 1991), but whether variation in the human homolog of the obese gene has a major effect has not yet been determined. Nevertheless, injecting ob protein also caused normal mice to lose weight, so such treatment may alleviate human obesity no matter what the cause. Certainly none of the present dietary, surgical, or

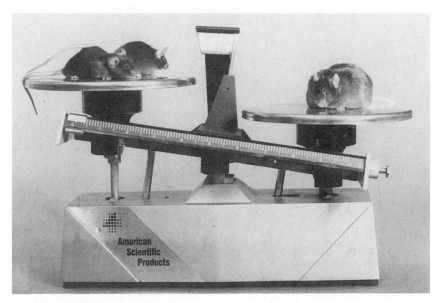

13.28 Inherited Obesity
As you can see, a single obese (*ob/ob*) mouse weighs more than two of his normal (heterozygote) siblings. Courtesy of Jeffrey Friedman.

pharmacological interventions reliably reverse obesity for long periods of time. A few individuals improve; many others do not.

Brain Peptides May Mediate Some of the Signals for Hunger

Recent studies have suggested that the peptide neurotransmitter neuropeptide Y (NPY) carries some of the signals for feeding (Morley, 1987). Most hypothalamic NPY is made by neurons of the arcuate nucleus, which send their axons to other hypothalamic sites, including the paraventricular nucleus. When NPY is infused into the hypothalamus, rats that seemed satiated begin eating again (Stanley et al., 1987). In contradiction of the idea that the lateral hypothalamus is a hunger center, NPY infusions are most effective in other nearby hypothalamic sites, such as the paraventricular nucleus (Leibowitz, 1991). When animals are deprived of food and lose weight, NPY levels increase in the paraventricular nucleus (Sahu, Kalra, and Kalra, 1988). Such animals are certainly hungry, and the increased hypothalamic NPY may be responsible for that sensation. The fact that obese Zucker rats have more hypothalamic NPY than do normal rats (Sanacora et al., 1990) might explain their exaggerated appetite.

Perhaps the most striking correlation between hypothalamic NPY and eating is seen in golden-mantled ground squirrels, which even in the laboratory show a seasonal cycle of weight gain and loss (Zucker, 1988; see Box 13.2). When in situ hybridization (see Appendix) is used to detect the mRNA for NPY, neurons of the arcuate are heavily labeled. Ground squirrels that are in the hyperphagic overeating phase produce more arcuate NPY than do animals in the hypophagic phase (Boswell et al., 1993). There is even a significant positive correlation across individual squirrels: those that eat more food have higher arcuate levels of NPY mRNA.

Now you might think that the paraventricular nucleus is the hunger center and NPY is the neurotransmitter that stimulates this nucleus and therefore hunger. But lesions of the paraventricular nucleus have little effect on body weight. Thus, although this nucleus may contribute to the activation of hunger, in its absence other neural centers can and will regulate eating. We warned you about the redundancy of vital systems near the chapter's beginning. Apparently natural selection has favored distributing the regulation of eating across several brain regions. Furthermore, these regions have more than one job. For example, remember that the paraventricular nucleus also contains the neurons that release vasopressin from the posterior pituitary to regulate water. Another reflection of the redundancy in feeding systems is that in both rats and ground squirrels, another peptide, galanin, appears to act much like NPY in promoting

Box 13.2

Body Fat Stores Are Tightly Regulated, Even After Surgical Removal of Fat

We've already seen that animals maintain a fairly constant body weight, even when given more food than they can eat, and that various lesions may change the body weight the animal defends but do not abolish weight regulation completely. Certainly most of us who have tried dieting can attest that our body seems to know how much it wants to weigh, despite our efforts. There is ample evidence that body fat is carefully regulated. Perhaps the most striking demonstration is in golden-mantled ground squirrels. In the wild, these animals show a seasonal variation in body weight. Every spring, as the food supply increases, the animals fatten up considerably. You might think that this extreme seasonal variation in body weight is simply the result of having food available at some times but not others. However, when these squirrels are brought into the laboratory, they continue to show an annual rhythm in body weight, even when food is always available (Zucker, 1988; Figure A). (We'll discuss annual cycles further in Chapter 14.) Experimenters can increase or decrease the squirrels' body weight either by force-feeding the animals or by restricting their food. When food is abundant, the squirrels eat just enough to achieve not the body weight they had before the manipulation, but the body weight that is appropriate for the present point in their circannual cycle. The return to their normal body composition is not simply a matter of altering diet. The way the squirrels partition what they eat—how much goes into fat, how much goes into glycogen, how much is defecated—also changes back to normal.

For example, they lower their metabolic rate during the fattening phase so that more food can be shuttled into fat (Dark, 1984).

Golden-mantled ground squirrels also show a seasonal cycle in body fat. Although some of the fat can be surgically removed, after the surgery, just as with body weight, the animals eat until they regain, with remarkable precision, the amount of fat they would have had without surgery (Dark, Forger, and Zucker, 1984; Figure B). Interestingly, some of the body fat depots from which fat was removed cannot regenerate new fat cells, but when such a non-regenerating depot is removed, other fat depots increase production in compensation, restoring the animal's total body fat. Needless to say, these results are not encouraging to humans considering liposuction. Usually the fat simply returns after the procedure, which is not without risks. It appears that the brain of humans, and certainly that of ground squirrels, can somehow measure body fat and that appetite is altered in order to maintain a particular amount of fat.

---

eating. A human engineer building an organism might choose to make a single center for integrating all hunger signals, another for collecting satiety cues, and a third for promoting water conservation. To the regret of most scientists (and students), evolution did not follow this strategy.

Anorexia Nervosa and Bulimia Are Compulsive, Life-Threatening Eating Disorders

Some young people become obsessed with their body weight and become extremely thin. They usually accomplish this by eating very little and may in addition regurgitate food, take laxatives, or drink large amounts of water to suppress appetite. This condition, which is more common in adolescent girls and women than in males, is called **anorexia nervosa**. Usually the menstrual cycle of female anorexics is disrupted or stops altogether. The name indicates (1) that the patients have no appetite (*anorexia*) and (2) that the origin of the disorder is in the nervous system (*nervosa*). But the disorder is so poorly understood that both of these assumptions could be mistaken. For example, anorexics sometimes think about food a good deal, and physiological evidence suggests that they respond even more than normal subjects to the presentation of food (Broberg and

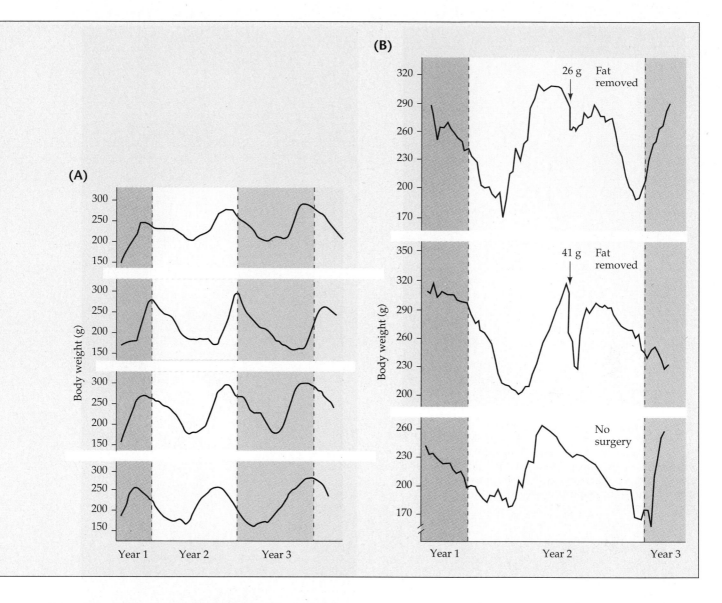

Bernstein, 1989), so their appetite may be normal or even exaggerated. Yet they deny themselves food. The idea that anorexia is primarily a nervous disorder stems from the distorted body image of the patients (they may consider themselves fat when others see them as emaciated) and from the fact that their diet is self-imposed. **Bulimia** (or bulimia nervosa) is a related disorder. Bulimics may also believe themselves fatter than they are, but they periodically gorge themselves, usually with "junk food," and then either vomit the food or take laxatives to avoid weight gain. Like anorexics, bulimics may be obsessed with food and body weight, but not all bulimics become emaciated. Either disorder can be fatal, because the patients' lack of nutrient reserves damages various organ systems and/or leaves them unable to battle otherwise mild disease.

Our present culture emphasizes that women, especially young women, must be thin to be attractive. It has been suggested that anorexics and bulimics are the victims of a mismatch between what their biological makeup wants them to weigh and what society expects them to weigh (Figure 13.29). In earlier times, however, when plump women were considered the most beautiful (witness Renaissance paintings), some women still fasted severely and may have been anorexics. The origins of these disorders are still elusive, and to date the available therapies cure only a minority of patients.

(a)

(b)

13.29 Two Ideals of Female Beauty
Supermodel Kate Moss (*a*) and *Helena Fourment as Aphrodite* (ca. 1630) by Rubens (*b*) exemplify ideal feminine forms of their respective eras. It has been suggested by some that our weight-conscious notions of female beauty are responsible for some cases of anorexia nervosa.

Summary

1. The nervous system plays a crucial role in maintaining the homeostasis that the body requires for proper functioning. Temperature, fluid concentration, chemical energy, and nutrients must all be maintained within a critical range.

2. Several mechanisms that normally act in synchrony can be dissociated experimentally, revealing a redundancy of physiological methods of ensuring homeostasis.

Temperature Regulation

1. Endotherms generate most of their body heat through metabolizing food; ectotherms obtain most of their body heat from the environment. Both endotherms and ectotherms regulate body temperature, but ectotherms are more dependent on behaviors to capture heat.

2. Endotherms can remain active longer than ectotherms can, but endotherms are also obliged to gather more food than ectotherms to generate their body warmth.

3. Body size and shape drastically affect the rate of heat loss; thus, small endotherms use more energy (relative to body size) than do large endotherms.

4. Several regions of the nervous system monitor and help regulate body temperature, including the preoptic area of the hypothalamus and the spinal cord.

Fluid Regulation

1. Our cells function properly only when the concentration of salts and other ions (the osmolality) of the intracellular compartment is within a critical range. The extracellular compartment is a source of replacement water and a buffer between the intracellular compartment and the outside world.

2. Thirst can be triggered either by a drop in the volume of the extracellular compartment (hypovolemic thirst) or by an increase in the osmolality of the extracellular compartment (osmotic thirst). Either signal indicates that the volume or osmolality of the intracellular compartment may fall outside the critical range. Because of the importance of osmolality, we must regulate salt intake in order to regulate water balance effectively.

3. A drop in blood volume triggers at least three responses. (1) Baroreceptors in the major blood vessels detect any volume drop and signal the brain via the autonomic nervous system. (2) The brain in turn releases vasopressin from the posterior pituitary. Vasopressin reduces blood vessel volume and reduces the amount of water lost through urination. (3) The kidneys release renin, providing circulating angiotensin II. Angiotensin II reduces blood vessel volume to maintain blood pressure and may also signal the brain that the blood volume has dropped.

Food and Energy Regulation

1. Our digestive system breaks down food and uses most of the food for energy, especially because we are endotherms. The brain must have glucose for energy; the body can use either glucose or fatty acids as fuel.

2. Although brain cells can use glucose directly, body cells can import glucose only with the assistance of insulin secreted by the pancreas. Insulin also promotes the storage of glucose in fat. Another pancreatic hormone, glucagon, mobilizes fats to release glucose.

3. Manipulations of either glucose or insulin can affect whether an animal experiences hunger, but experimental studies have indicated that neither glucose nor insulin alone can be the single indicator of hunger or satiety. The nervous system integrates information about these compounds and others to determine whether an animal should eat.

4. Within the nervous system are several regions that seem to contribute to the sensations of hunger or satiety, but animals can regulate body weight reasonably well even without any one of these regions. Thus there does not seem to be a single brain center for either satiety or hunger.

5. There are powerful genetic and seasonal influences on body weight, and body weight is very tightly regulated around a set range, despite extensive dietary, behavioral, or surgical interventions

Recommended Reading

Le Magnen, P. 1991. *Neurobiology of Feeding*. Academic Press, New York.

Stricker, E. M. (ed.) 1990. *Handbook of Behavioral Neurobiology*, Vol. 10. Plenum Press, New York.

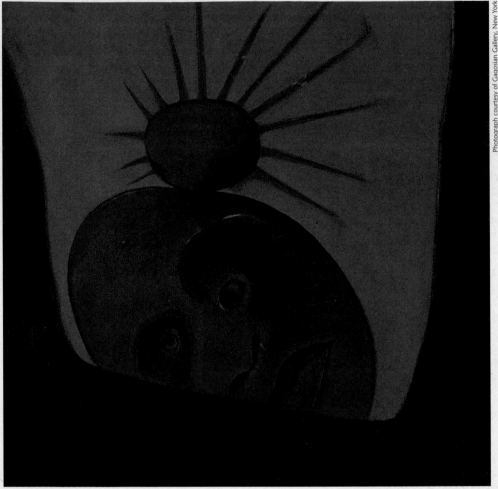

Francesco Clemente, *Head*, 1990/1991

Biological Rhythms

- *Many Animals Show Daily Rhythms in Activity and Physiological Measures*

- *The Endogenous Circadian Clock Seems to Be in the Hypothalamus*

- *The Circadian Clock of the Fruit Fly Can Be Dissected Genetically*

- *Many Biological Events Display Rhythms Shorter Than a Day*

- *Animals Use Circannual Rhythms to Anticipate Seasonal Changes*

- *Human Sleep Displays Circadian Rhythmicity*

Sleeping and Waking

- *There Are Five Stages of Human Sleep*

- *Sleep Stages Appear in a Pattern during the Night's Sleep*

- *Some Humans Sleep Remarkably Little, yet Function Normally*

- *The Sleep of Different Species Provides Clues about the Evolution of Sleep*

- *Our Sleep Patterns Change across the Life Span*

- *Manipulating Sleep Reveals an Underlying Structure*

- *We Do Our Most Vivid Dreaming during REM Sleep*

- *There Seems to Be a Relationship between Learning and Sleep*

- *Several Neurobiological Systems Are Activated during Sleep*

- *What Are the Neural Mechanisms of Sleep?*

- *The Search for Sleep-Promoting Substances*

- *What Are the Biological Functions of Sleep?*

- *Sleep Disorders*

CHAPTER

Biological Rhythms and Sleep

14

He made the moon for the seasons;
The sun knows the place of its setting.
Thou dost appoint darkness and it becomes night
In which all the beasts of the forest crawl about.
The young lions roar after their prey
And seek their food from God.
When the sun rises they withdraw
And lie down in their dens.
Man goes forth to his work
And to his labor until evening.
                    Psalm 104:19–23

Orientation

All living systems show repeating, predictable changes over time. The frequency of these oscillations varies from rapid, such as brain potentials, to slow, such as annual changes like hibernation. Daily rhythms have an intriguing "clocklike" regularity, which is the first topic of this chapter. Other rhythms range from minutes to seconds, and some extend from a month to years. One familiar and important daily rhythm is the sleep–waking cycle: by age 60, most of us have spent 20 years asleep! (Some, alas, on either side of the classroom podium.) Since sleep accounts for so large a slice of our lives, it is surprising that the behavioral and biological features of sleep remained unstudied for so long. Since the early 1960s, however, sleep has been a major focus of investigation in biological psychology. Sleep is not just nonwaking, but rather the interlocking of elaborate cyclical processes, an alternation of several different states. The behavioral correlates of these different sleep states range from tiny finger twitches to a galaxy of images and dreams. In this chapter we'll discuss biological rhythms and patterns of sleep in human beings and other animals, the factors that influence sleep patterns, and the physiological events of sleep.

Biological Rhythms

Many Animals Show Daily Rhythms in Activity and Physiological Measures

Most functions of any living system display an approximately 24-hour rhythm. Since these rhythms last about a day, they are called **circadian rhythms** (from the Latin *circa*, "about," and *dies*, "day"). By now circadian rhythms have been studied in a host of creatures at behavioral, physiological, and biochemical levels. One favorite way to study circadian rhythms in the laboratory takes advantage of the penchant of rodents to run in activity wheels (Figure 14.1*a*). A switch attached to the wheel connects to a computer that registers each complete revolution. This revolution can be displayed on a recorder as a brief flick of a pen. The activity rhythm of a hamster in a running wheel is displayed in Figure 14.1*b*. Like most other rodents, hamsters are **nocturnal**—active during the dark periods. Humans and most other primates are **diurnal**—active during the day. Almost all other physiological measures—hormonal levels, body temperature, drug sensitivity—change across the course of the day. These circadian activities show extraordinary precision: the beginning of activity may vary only a few minutes from one day to another. For humans who attend to watches and clocks, this regularity may seem uninteresting, but other animals also display remarkable regularity. It turns out that they are attending to a "biological clock."

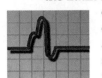

Circadian Rhythms Are Generated by an Endogenous Clock

If a hamster is blinded or placed in a constantly darkened environment, it continues to show a daily rhythm in wheel running and other measures, despite the absence of a light–dark cycle. This suggests that the animal must have an internal clock to regulate these activities. On the other hand, even though the low level of light is constant, the animal may detect other external cues (outside noises, temperature, gravitational changes) about the time of day. Arguing for the internal clock, however, is the fact that the hamster shows a bit of imprecision in its cycle: activity starts a few minutes later each day, so eventually the hamster is active while it is daytime outside (see the bottom of Figure 14.1*b*). The animal is said to be **free-running**, continuing a cycle that is not exactly 24 hours long in the absence of external light cues. The free-running period is the animal's natural

rhythm. (A **period** is the time between two similar points of successive cycles, such as sunset to sunset.) Since this free-running period does not quite match the period of the earth's rotation, it cannot simply be reflecting some external cue but must be generated inside the animal. So the animal has some sort of endogenous oscillator, which we can call a "clock," and in the hamster this clock runs a bit slow.

Normally the internal clock is set by light. If we expose a free-running nocturnal animal to periodic light and dark, the onset of activity soon becomes synchronized to the beginning of the dark period. The shift of activity produced by a synchronizing stimulus is referred to as a **phase shift**, and the process of shifting the rhythm is called **entrainment**. Not all environmental stimuli have the ability to entrain circadian rhythms. Light is by far the most powerful entrainment cue, so it is sometimes called the **zeitgeber** (German for "timegiver"). The fact that light stimuli can entrain circadian rhythms implies that the endogenous oscillatory circuit has inputs from the visual system, as we'll discuss shortly. In humans, circadian rhythms probably are also entrained by social stimuli.

Circadian Rhythms Allow Animals to Anticipate Changes in the Environment

Why are circadian rhythms valuable to an organism? The major significance of circadian rhythms is that they synchronize behavior and bodily states to changes in the environment. The cycle of light and dark during the day has great significance for survival. For example, picture the small nocturnal rodent who can avoid many predators during the day by remaining hidden, and who moves about hurriedly in the dark. An endogenous clock allows animals to *anticipate* periodic events, such as the appearance of darkness (note the onset of activity slightly *before* the dark period in Figure 14.1*b*), and to engage in appropriate behavior before conditions change. In other words, circadian rhythms provide the temporal organization of an animal's behavior. Biological clocks allow for resource partitioning; diurnal animals are adapted for obtaining food during the daytime, and thus do not compete with nocturnal animals, whose adaptations favor an active life during dark periods.

The Endogenous Circadian Clock Seems to Be in the Hypothalamus

Where in the body is the clock (or clocks) that drives circadian rhythms, and how does it work? One way

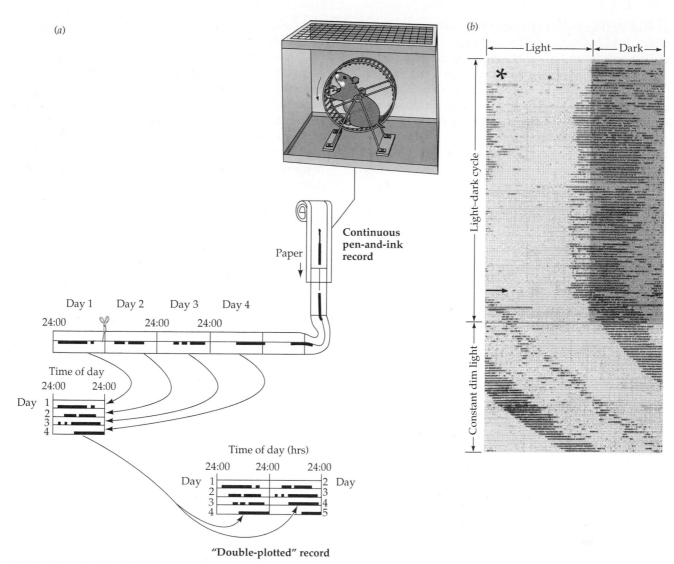

14.1 How Activity Rhythms Are Measured
(*a*) Typical setup for a single hamster, with a running wheel monitored by an event recorder. Each revolution of the wheel produces a brief pen deflection, which forms a dark vertical mark on the slowly moving paper. The paper strips are cut up and duplicated so that each resulting line shows 48 hrs of activity in a so-called "double-plot." (*b*) Normally, a hamster becomes active shortly before the start of the dark phase of the daily cycle and remains active during the dark period. After several weeks, the optic tract in this hamster was severed (arrow); the hamster then ignored light cues and became active a few minutes later each day. This "free-running" activity rhythm indicates that the hamster has an endogenous clock that has a period slightly greater than 24 hours. After Zucker, 1976; based on Rusak, 1975.

to establish the locus of circadian oscillators is to remove different organs and examine behavioral or physiological systems for any changes in circadian organization. A pioneer in the field, Curt Richter, established that the brain must be the site of the relevant oscillators. Richter removed various endocrine glands

and showed that these surgeries had no effect on the free-running rhythm of blinded rats (Richter, 1967). Although Richter did show that gross hypothalamic lesions appeared to interfere with circadian rhythms, he did not pursue this work anatomically. In 1972, two groups of researchers clearly showed that a small region of the hypothalamus—the **suprachiasmatic nucleus**, or **SCN** (Figure 14.2)—is the location of the circadian oscillator. The SCN gets its name from its location above the optic chiasm. Stephan and Zucker (1972) showed that lesions of the SCN interfere with circadian rhythms of drinking and locomotor behavior, and Moore and Eichler (1972) showed that such

lesions interfere with daily rhythms of adrenal corticosteroid secretion.

The clocklike activity of the SCN is also revealed in metabolic studies using autoradiographic techniques (see Box 2.1). Figure 14.3 shows the circadian variation in the metabolic activity of the SCN. This metabolic tracing technique has also revealed some properties of fetal circadian clocks. In both rats and monkeys, the fetal SCN shows a regular circadian rhythm of metabolic activity as revealed by the 2-deoxyglucose technique. In these studies pregnant animals were injected with 2-deoxyglucose, and the metabolic activity of the SCN of both the parent and the fetal animals was measured. In rat fetuses a circadian rhythm is evident in the SCN shortly after it forms, well before birth. Unidentified signals from the mother appear to synchronize fetal SCN activity (Reppert, 1985). Maternal control continues for a short time following birth. Although researchers do not yet know the source of the maternal entrainment signal, they have eliminated some candidates. The fetal rhythm survives removal of the mother's pineal, adrenal, pituitary, thyroid, and ovaries. If the maternal SCN is lesioned early in gestation, however, the SCN metabolic activity of the fetuses is temporally scattered; a circadian rhythm remains, but the fetuses are no longer in synchrony with each other. This evidence reinforces the view that the fetal clock is entrained by the mother.

Studies of **brain explants**—small pieces of brain tissue isolated from the body—reveal some fascinating properties of the SCN. Brain slices containing the

14.2   The Effect of Lesions in the SCN
Circadian rhythms were normal and synchronized to the light–dark period before an SCN lesion was made (asterisk). After the lesion the animal showed some daily rhythms in activity in synchrony with the light–dark cycle, but when placed in continuous (dim) light, its activity became completely random, indicating that the lesion had eliminated the endogenous rhythm. Note that the lesioned animal does not show a free-running rhythm of activity, but is arrhythmic, running at very different times each day. From Zucker, 1976; based on Rusak, 1975.

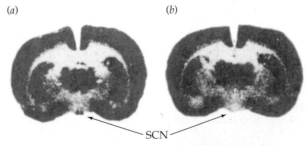

14.3   A Circadian Rhythm in the Metabolic Activity of the SCN
Autoradiograms of coronal sections of rat brains (see Box 2.1). In a section taken from an animal during a light phase, greater metabolic activity in the SCN is represented by the darkly stained regions; at the base of the brain (*a*); this dark staining is not evident in a section taken from an animal during a dark phase (*b*). From Schwartz, Smith, and Davidsen, 1979.

SCN are placed in a dish with fluids resembling the brain extracellular environment and provided with a mixture of oxygen and carbon dioxide gases to permit approximately normal metabolic activities. Electrical recordings from these slices indicate that single cells of the SCN show discharge rates that are synchronized to the light–dark cycle the animal had previously experienced. This is striking evidence for the endogenous character of the circadian oscillators in the SCN. Circadian oscillations are also evident in the neural activity of the isolated SCN—an SCN still inside an animal, but which is isolated from other brain areas by knife cuts (a hypothalamic "island"; Inouye, cited in Turek, 1985). As we'll see shortly, transplants of SCN from one animal to another have proved that the SCN generates a circadian rhythm.

In Mammals, Light Information from the Eyes Reaches the SCN Directly

What pathways entrain circadian rhythms to light–dark cycles? The pathway varies depending on the species (Rusak and Zucker, 1979). Some vertebrates have photoreceptors outside the eye that are part of the mechanism of light entrainment. For example, the pineal gland of some amphibians is itself sensitive to light and helps entrain circadian rhythms to light. Be-

cause the skull over the pineal is especially thin in some of these species, we can think of them as having a primitive "third eye" in the back of their head. In some birds, circadian rhythms can be entrained by light even if the eyes are removed, so other photosensitive receptors must be involved in entrainment. Again, it is the pineal that possesses these receptors, which detect daylight through the skull! In mammals, however, *retinal* pathways clearly mediate photoentrainment, because severing the optic nerves ends the role of light in circadian rhythms of all varieties.

Extensive research on the projections of the optic nerve to various brain regions laid the groundwork for systematic research that identified the entrainment pathway. Piece by piece the puzzle was assembled. In experiments with rodents, lesions of the primary visual cortex and accessory pathways did not alter entrainment to a light–dark cycle although these animals appeared "blind" and showed no indication of visually guided orientation or discrimination behavior. Robert Moore (1983) established the existence of a direct retinohypothalamic pathway—retinal ganglion cells that project out of the optic chiasm to synapse within the SCN (Figure 14.4). Lesions of this tiny pathway interfere with photic (light-induced) entrainment. A pathway from the lateral geniculate nu-

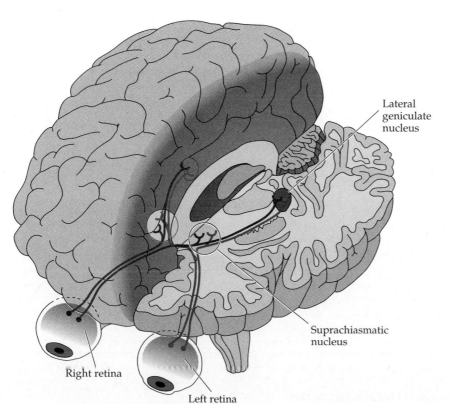

14.4 The Retinohypothalamic Pathway
This pathway carries information about the light–dark cycle in the environment to the SCN. This information synchronizes, or entrains, the endogenous daily rhythm to external conditions. For clarity of synaptic connections, the SCN is shown proportionately larger than other features.

Lateral geniculate nucleus

Suprachiasmatic nucleus

Right retina

Left retina

cleus to the SCN may also facilitate photic entrainment (Rusak et al., 1981). Figure 14.5 provides a schematic outline of the circadian system, including entrainment components.

Transplants Prove That the SCN Produces a Circadian Rhythm

Ralph and Menaker (1988) found a male hamster that exhibited an unusually short free-running activity rhythm in constant conditions. Normally hamsters free-run at a period slightly longer than 24 hours, but this male showed a period of 22 hours that was stable for three weeks. They bred this male and by studying his offspring concluded that he possessed a mutation that affected the endogenous circadian rhythm. Animals with two copies of the mutation had an even shorter period—20 hours. The mutation was named *tau,* after the Greek symbol used by scientists to represent the period of a rhythm. All these animals could be entrained to a normal 24-hour light–dark period; only in constant conditions was their endogenous circadian periodicity revealed.

Dramatic evidence that this endogenous period is contained within the SCN was provided by transplant experiments. Hamsters with a lesioned SCN were placed in constant conditions; as expected, they showed arrhythmicity in activity (Figure 14.6, middle; Ralph et al., 1990). Then the investigators transplanted into the hamsters an SCN taken from a fetal hamster with two copies of the mutant *tau* gene.

About a week later the hamsters that had received the transplants began showing a free-running activity rhythm again, but the new rhythm matched that of the donor SCN—it was 19.5 hours rather than the original 24.05. Reciprocal transplantations gave comparable results: the endogenous rhythm always matched the genotype of the *donor* SCN, further demonstrating that the circuitry that produces this circadian rhythmicity is within the SCN.

The SCN Is Not the Only Endogenous Oscillator

The work we have mentioned to this point shows that there is at least one major circadian oscillator in the brain that governs a number of circadian systems, especially motor activity. Is this the *only* master oscillator? No. If you look at measures other than wheel running, you observe some free-running and entrained rhythms even after suprachiasmatic lesions. Moore-Ede (1982) suggests that the circadian timing system of mammals consists of *two* master pacemakers that drive many other secondary, passive oscillators. He hypothesizes that there are two categories of circadian rhythms, each driven by a different master oscillator, one of which is found in the SCN. This suggestion is based on the desynchronization of various circadian rhythms that occurs in humans when they live (temporarily) in isolation without time cues such as daily light–dark cycles (Figure 14.7). Researchers interpreted such desynchronization as the spontaneous uncoupling of two internal clocks. Moore-Ede's conception of the underlying mechanisms is presented in Figure 14.8. The issue of oscillators and what function each controls continues to be a major focus of current research on circadian rhythms.

The Circadian Clock of the Fruit Fly Can Be Dissected Genetically

As we have mentioned in previous chapters, the fruit fly *Drosophila melanogaster* has been studied extensively by geneticists. Fruit flies display circadian rhythms in activity (they are diurnal) and in the time at which they emerge from their pupal skins as adults (in the morning). Screening of mutant flies revealed animals that, when transferred to constant dim light, failed to "free-run" in either locomotor activity or emergence as adults. These flies were found to have a mutation that disabled a gene on the X chromosome. Subtle mutations of this same gene could, de-

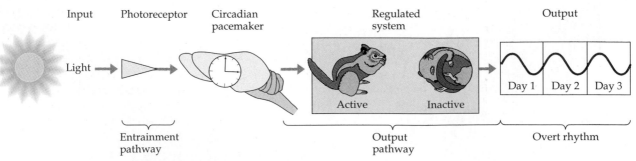

14.5   Schematic Model of the Components of a Circadian System

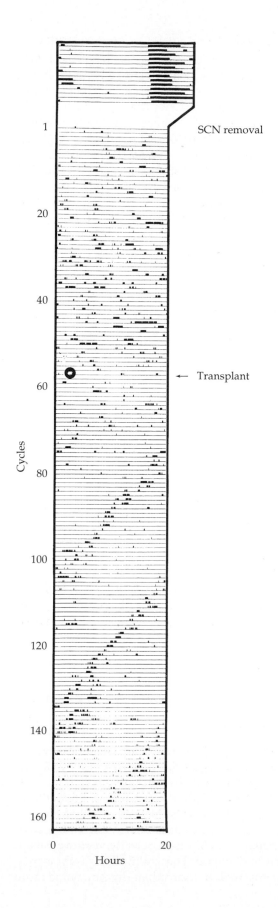

SCN removal

← Transplant

Cycles

Hours

14.6 Brain Transplants Prove That the SCN Contains a Clock

A wild-type hamster, when kept in constant dim light, displays an endogenous circadian rhythm, 24.05 hours in duration (*top*). After the SCN was lesioned, the animal became arrhythmic. Later, a SCN from a fetal hamster with two copies of the *tau* mutation was transplanted into the adult hamster (*circle*). Soon thereafter the adult hamster began showing a free-running activity rhythm of 19.5 hours, matching the SCN of the donor animal, showing that the period of the clock is determined within the SCN. From Ralph, 1990.

pending on the exact change in the gene, cause the animals to have a longer or shorter than normal free-run period; thus the gene was dubbed *per*, for "period" (Konopka and Benzer, 1971).

The protein normally produced by the *per* gene is found in the nuclei of cells in the flies' eyes and brain. This nuclear localization suggests that the per protein is itself regulating the transcription of other genes, and several studies have confirmed this idea. In fact, one of the genes regulated by the per protein is the *per* gene itself! Even more interesting is the fact that there is a circadian rhythm in the appearance of per protein in the brain and eyes: more of the protein is present at night than in the daytime. Of course, when the *per* gene is deleted from an animal, there is no per protein and the flies are arrhythmic, as we mentioned before. But when the gene is *slightly* altered to produce animals with either shorter or longer circadian periods, the circadian rhythm in per protein production is also correspondingly shorter or longer. This correlation between the periods of per protein production and several behaviors suggests that the circadian rhythmicity in *per* gene expression is in fact *responsible* for the circadian rhythm in behavior.

Studies of another fly mutant support this idea. Animals with a disruption of the *tim* ("timeless") gene also fail to show an endogenous circadian rhythm when transferred into constant dim light (Sehgal et al., 1994). Examination of such mutants revealed no circadian rhythm in the appearance of the per protein. Thus the product of the *tim* gene seems to be necessary for the *per* gene to be expressed rhythmically, and when per protein is not rhythmically produced, the circadian rhythms in behavior are blocked. How does the tim protein block the circadian rhythm in per protein production? In the absence of the tim protein, the per protein apparently fails to bind to DNA (Vosshall et al., 1994). This result also suggests that the rhythm in per production is a result of feedback of the per protein on the expression of its own gene, which re-

Time of day (hours)

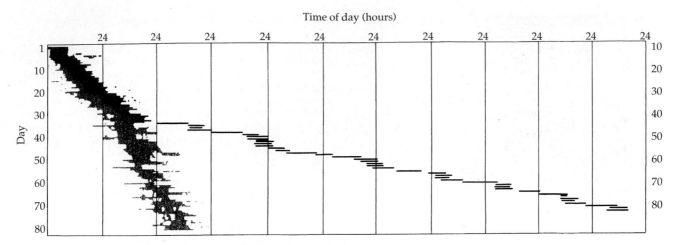

14.7 Controversial Evidence that Humans Have Two Clocks

In this human subject, bed rest episodes and body temperature were entrained to a 24-hour day-night cycle on days 1 to 5. When the person was placed in temporal isolation, both rhythms free-ran but maintained synchrony until day 35, then spontaneously desynchronized. After day 35 the period of the body temperature rhythm shortened, and that of the rest-activity cycle lengthened, indicating that these two rhythms rely on different clocks. From Czeisler et al., 1980.

sults in an oscillation of per production, which somehow drives behavior in a rhythmic fashion.

Recently scientists have discovered a mouse mutant that, while able to entrain to a light–dark rhythm,

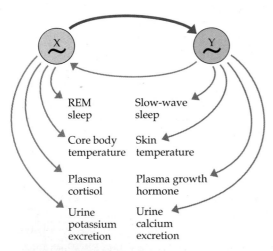

14.8 How Two Endogenous Clocks Might Interact

Pacemaker X drives the rhythms of REM sleep, core body temperature, plasma cortisol concentration, and urinary potassium excretion. Pacemaker Y drives the rest-activity cycle and the rhythms of slow-wave sleep, skin temperature, plasma growth hormone concentration, and urinary calcium excretion. The coupling force exerted by X on Y is approximately four times greater than that of Y on X. (REM sleep and slow-wave sleep are discussed later in this chapter.) After Moore-Ede, 1982.

fails to display an endogenous circadian rhythm—that is, to free-run—in constant dim light (Vitaterna et al., 1994). These mice have a mutation in a gene that was named *Clock* (*C*ircadian *L*ocomotor *O*utput *C*ycles *K*aput). The *Clock* gene is found on the fifth chromosome, and only animals that have both copies of their *Clock* gene disrupted show severe arrhythmicity in constant conditions. If only one copy of the gene is disrupted, the animals free-run for a few days but then suddenly stop showing any circadian rhythmicity (Figure 14.9). The nucleotide sequence of the *Clock* gene has not yet been determined, so it is not known whether *Clock* resembles the *per* or *tim* genes in *Drosophila*, or the *tau* gene in hamsters, or whether the *Clock* protein is normally expressed in a circadian rhythm (Takahashi, 1995).

Many Biological Events Display Rhythms Shorter Than a Day

Among the many diverse rhythmic biological events, a large group have periods that are *shorter* than circadian rhythms. Such rhythms are referred to as **ultradian** ("ultra" designates a frequency greater than once per day), and their periods are usually from several minutes to hours. Ultradian rhythms are seen in such behaviors as bouts of activity, feeding, sleep, and hormone release. These ultradian rhythms may be superimposed on a circadian rhythm. Some more

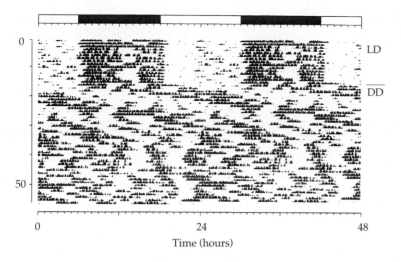

14.9 When the Endogenous Clock Goes Kaput
This homozygous *Clock/Clock* mouse showed a normal circadian rhythm when given normal light cues (LD). When put in constant dim light conditions (DD), it maintained an activity period of 27.1 hours for the first ten days but then lost circadian rhythmicity. Note, however, than an ultradian rhythm with a period of just over 5 hours remains. From Takahashi, 1994.

complex human behaviors also display ultradian rhythms. Human subjects either isolated from cues about time of day or in their normal environment show a 90-minute cycle of daydreaming characterized by vivid sensory imagery (Lavie and Kripke, 1981). Ultradian rhythms in the performance of various tasks may reflect fluctuations in alertness, which may account for the ultradian rhythm in the performance of poorly motivated subjects (Broughton, 1985). One indication of an ultradian rhythm in alertness is that EEG indices of alertness (as defined later in this chapter) also vary in an ultradian rhythm.

The periods of ultradian rhythms seem to be correlated with measures such as brain and body size: more rapid cycles are typical of smaller animals (Gerkema and Daan, 1985). Several manipulations can make ultradian rhythms more apparent (and perhaps more regular), including examining the subject early in development, exposing the subject to constant illumination (which dampens the circadian rhythm), and destroying the subject's SCN. The functional advantage of nonrandom timing of such events within a single day is obvious in some cases. For example, animals that flock together are better served by synchronizing their foraging behavior so that individuals are not isolated and subject to predation; synchrony of grazing and rumination in herbivores is evident on any ranch. In many other instances the ultradian rhythmicity and synchrony of social behavior among animals have advantages for survival.

Hormone levels often display ultradian rhythms. For example, luteinizing hormone seems to be released every 60 minutes (Knobil and Hotchkiss, 1985). Electrical activity in the hypothalamus (medial basal region) of monkeys shows rhythmic bursts every hour (Wilson et al., 1984).

Two broad classes of generators for ultradian rhythms have been suggested by Gerkema and Daan (1985). One type involves a renewal or homeostatic process, which means that the *behavior is part of the mechanism controlling the timing* of that behavior. For example, rhythms in foraging and feeding behavior may emerge from the alternation of hunger and satiety in species that eat frequently during the day. A second type of generator of ultradian rhythms is an *endogenous* oscillator that drives regular physiological and behavioral events. Destruction of the SCN, which destroys circadian timing of activity in voles, does *not* affect their ultradian feeding rhythms. However, lesions to other hypothalamic areas break up ultradian rhythmicity. These areas include parts of the rostral and basal hypothalamus. Interestingly, the mutations in flies and mice discussed earlier, which can abolish circadian rhythms, do *not* abolish ultradian rhythms. Also, there remains an ultradian periodicity after the loss of the circadian rhythm in a *Clock/Clock* mouse (see Figure 14.9). These findings indicate that separate clocks control circadian and ultradian rhythms. We still do not know whether all ultradian rhythms reflect the operation of a single clock, or many different oscillators separately control a variety of ultradian events. Sleep cycles show an ultradian character, as we'll see later in the chapter.

Animals Use Circannual Rhythms to Anticipate Seasonal Changes

Recall that many animals display a seasonal cycle in body weight (see Box 13.2). Many other behaviors of animals are also characterized by annual rhythms.

Some of these rhythms are driven by exogenous factors, such as food availability and temperature. In the laboratory, however, many annual rhythms, including body weight, persist under constant conditions. Like circadian rhythms in constant light, animals in isolation show free-running annual rhythms of a period not quite equal to 365 days. Thus there also seems to be an endogenous **circannual** oscillator. Obviously this is a realm of research that requires considerable patience. Such rhythms are sometimes called **infradian** because their frequency is less than once per day. (A familiar infradian rhythm is the 28-day human menstrual cycle.) The relevance of annual rhythms to human behavior is becoming evident in striking seasonal disorders of behavior (see Chapter 15).

The possibility that the SCN might control circannual rhythms of ground squirrels maintained in constant conditions of photoperiod and temperature was assessed by Zucker, Boshes, and Dark, (1983). These researchers measured activity rhythms, reproductive cycles, and body weight cycles of animals that were free-running in both their circadian and annual rhythms. SCN lesions clearly disrupted *circadian* activity cycles, but there were at least some animals in which these lesions did not affect *circannual* changes in body weight and reproductive status. Circannual cycles, then, do not arise from a transformation of circadian rhythms (for example, simply counting 365 circadian cycles) and seem to involve an oscillatory mechanism separate from the SCN.

Although seasonal rhythms do not arise from a transformation of the circadian oscillator, it is important to note that circannual changes in circadian rhythms can be demonstrated. Lee, Carmichael, and Zucker (1986) found annual changes in the daily pattern of wheel-running behavior of golden-mantled ground squirrels. These squirrels ordinarily hibernate with a six-month period of relative inactivity. Animals kept in constant temperature conditions and a light–dark cycle of 14 hours light and 10 hours dark did not hibernate, but they did maintain activity cycles for several years. Every spring, however, the onset of activity started earlier in the 24-hour period than during the fall.

Pronounced seasonal rhythms in gonadal hormone concentrations are evident in many animals. Could

changes in these hormones, such as testosterone, account for annual cycles? Zucker and Dark (1986) report that annual cycles of body weight are not affected by gonadectomy in male ground squirrels. Annual cycles

of hibernation and gonadal function in these animals also survive early removal of the pineal gland. Thus neither the testes nor the pineal are required for the endogenous circannual rhythms to persist.

Human Sleep Displays Circadian Rhythmicity

Most of us enjoy a single period of sleep starting late in the evening and lasting until morning. The onset and termination of sleep seem synchronized to many external events, including light and dark periods. What happens to sleep when all the customary synchronizing or entraining stimuli are removed? One way to get away from such stimuli is to find deep caves and to spend weeks there with all cues to external time removed. Under such conditions a circadian rhythm of the sleep–waking cycle remains evident, although the biological clock slowly shifts from 24 to 25 hours. In other words, people have free-running periods just as a hamster does in constant dim light (Figure 14.10). Some people adopt much longer days, lasting up to 35 hours. Only one subject out of 147 displayed a period shorter than 24 hours in isolation (Wever, 1979). The free-running periods of a little more than 24 hours indicate that we have an endogenous circadian clock shaped by evolutionary forces that is very similar to our customary 24-hour rhythm. External cues then entrain this endogenous rhythm to 24 hours. The animal research already cited suggests that the relevant timer is the SCN.

You may think of sleep as a simple event in your life, but for biological psychologists sleep has turned out to be a remarkably complex, multifaceted set of behaviors. We devote the remainder of the chapter to this fascinating phenomenon.

Sleeping and Waking

There Are Five Stages of Human Sleep

Sleep seems to be characterized by the *absence* of behavior—a period of inactivity with raised thresholds to arousal by external stimuli. Sleep research gained momentum in the early 1960s when experimenters found that brain potentials recorded from electrodes on the human scalp (electroencephalography, or EEG; see Box 5.1) provided a way to define, de-

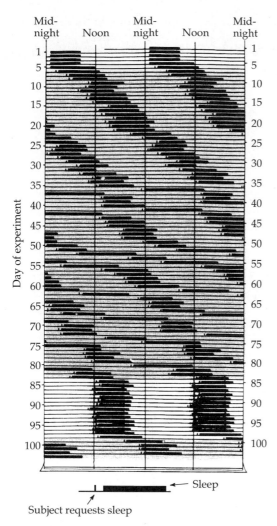

14.10 Humans Free-Run, Too
These are the sleep–waking patterns of a subject who, after 5 days, was isolated from cues about the time of day for the next 77 days. During this period the subject drifts away from a 24-hour daily cycle, getting the equivalent of 74 "nights" of sleep. From Weitzman et al., 1981.

scribe, and classify levels of arousal and states of sleep. This measure of brain activity is usually supplemented with recordings of eye movements and muscle tension. These methods reveal two main classes of sleep: **slow-wave sleep** (**SWS**) and **rapid-eye-movement sleep**, or **REM sleep**. In humans, slow-wave sleep can be divided further into four distinct stages.

What are the electrophysiological distinctions that define different sleep states? To begin, the pattern of electrical activity in the fully awake, vigilant person is a desynchronized mixture of many frequencies dominated by waves of relatively fast fre-

quencies (greater than 15 to 20 cycles per second, or hertz [Hz]) and low amplitude. When you relax and close your eyes, a distinctive rhythm appears, consisting of a regular oscillation at a frequency of 9 to 12 Hz, known as the **alpha rhythm**. As drowsiness sets in, the amplitude of the alpha rhythm decreases, and the EEG shows events of much smaller amplitude and irregular frequency (Figure 14.11*b*). This stage 1 SWS is accompanied by a slowing of heart rate and a reduction of muscle tension. Many subjects awakened during this stage do not acknowledge that they have been asleep, even though they failed to respond to instructions or signals. This period usually lasts for several minutes and gives way to stage 2 sleep, which is defined by 14 to 18-Hz waves called **sleep spindles** that occur in periodic bursts (Figure 14.11*c*). Someone in stage 2 sleep is quite unresponsive to the external environment, and under the closed eyelids the eyes begin to roll about in a slow, uncoordinated manner. In the early part of a night of sleep, this stage leads to stage 3 sleep, which is defined by the appearance of spindles mixed with large-amplitude, very slow waves (so-called delta waves, about one per second; Figure 14.11*d*). Stage 4 sleep, which follows, is defined by a continuous train of these high-amplitude slow waves (Figure 14.11*e*). Stages 1 through 4 are all classified as SWS.

After about an hour, the time usually required for progression through these stages, with a brief return to stage 2, something totally different occurs. Quite abruptly, scalp recordings display a pattern of small-amplitude, high-frequency activity similar in many ways to the pattern of an awake individual, but tension in the postural neck muscles has disappeared (Figure 14.11*f*). (Because of this seeming contradiction—the brain waves look awake, but the musculature is deeply relaxed and unresponsive—one name for this state is paradoxical sleep.) Breathing and pulse rates become fast and irregular. The eyes now show rapid movements under the closed lids, so this stage is usually referred to as REM, or rapid-eye-movement, sleep. These movements are much like the rapid movements characteristic of waking behavior. Once you've entered REM sleep, many distinctive physiological changes occur while you remain recumbent and, in terms of common behavioral descriptions, decidedly asleep. It is during REM sleep that we experience vivid dreams. Thus, the EEG portrait shows that sleep consists of a sequence of states instead of just an "inactive" period. Table 14.1 compares the properties of slow-wave sleep and REM sleep.

14.11 Physiological Correlates of Consciousness

These are the characteristic EEG patterns seen during different stages of sleep in humans. The arrow in (*b*) points to a sharp wave called a vertex spike that appears during stage 1 sleep. The arrow in (*c*) points to a brief period of sleep spindles characteristic of stage 2 sleep. Note the similarity of activity during waking and REM sleep. After Rechtschaffen and Kales, 1968.

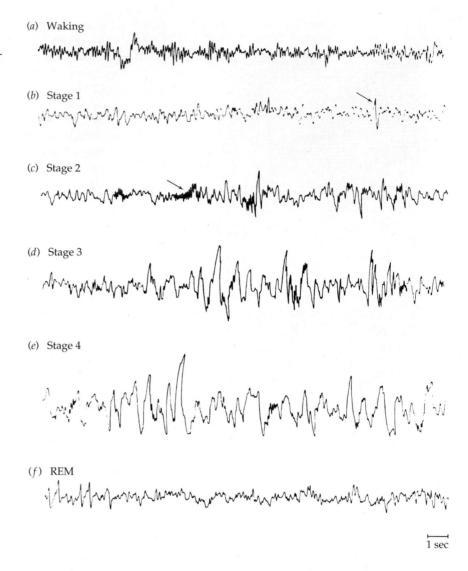

(*a*) Waking

(*b*) Stage 1

(*c*) Stage 2

(*d*) Stage 3

(*e*) Stage 4

(*f*) REM

1 sec

Sleep Stages Appear in a Pattern during the Night's Sleep

Many people have exposed their sleep life to researchers in sleep laboratories. The bedroom you walk into in the experimental setup differs little from the usual sleep environment except for the presence of many wires. These lead to an adjacent room where machines record brain waves and experimenters observe. You go to sleep in a usual way except that electrodes are pasted in position on your scalp. In addition, electrodes near the eye record eye movements, and the tension of muscles is noted by electrical recordings from the skin surface above muscles. Although the onset, pattern, duration, and termination of sleep are affected by many variables, there is a regularity that allows a portrait to be drawn of the typical sleep pattern of adults.

The total sleep time of young adults usually ranges from seven to eight hours, and 45 to 50% of sleep is stage 2 sleep. REM sleep accounts for 25% of total sleep. A typical night of adult human sleep shows repeating cycles about 90 to 110 minutes long, recurring four or five times in a night (Figure 14.12). These cycles change in a subtle but regular manner through the night. Cycles early in the night are shorter and are characterized by greater amounts of stages 3 and 4 SWS. The latter half of a typical night's sleep is virtually bereft of stages 3 and 4. In contrast, REM sleep is typically more prominent in the later cycles of sleep. The first REM period is the shortest, sometimes lasting only 5 to 10 minutes, while the last REM period just before awaking may last 40 minutes.

REM sleep is normally preceded by stage 2 SWS

Table 14.1

Properties of Slow-Wave and REM Sleep

	SLOW-WAVE	REM
Autonomic activities		
Heart rate	Slow decline	Variable with high bursts
Respiration	Slow decline	Variable with high bursts
Thermoregulation	Maintained	Impaired
Brain temperature	Decreased	Increased
Cerebral blood flow	Reduced	High
Skeletal muscular system		
Postural tension	Progressively reduced	Eliminated
Knee-jerk reflex	Normal	Suppressed
Phasic twitches	Reduced	Increased
Eye movements	Infrequent, slow, uncoordinated	Rapid, coordinated
Cognitive state	Vague thoughts	Vivid dreams, well organized
Hormone secretion		
Growth hormone secretion	High	Low
Neural firing rates		
Cerebral cortex	Many cells reduced and more phasic	Increased firing rates; tonic (sustained) activity
Event-related potentials		
Sensory-evoked	Large	Reduced
Drug effects		
Effects of antidepressants	Increased	Decreased

(except in infants and in a disorder called narcolepsy, which we describe at the end of the chapter). Brief arousals occasionally occur immediately after an REM period, and you may shift your posture at this transition (Aaronson et al., 1982). The sleep cycle of 90 to 110 minutes has been viewed by some researchers as the manifestation of a basic ultradian rest–activity cycle (Kleitman, 1969); cycles of similar duration occur

during waking periods. Recall that cycles of day-dreaming during waking have an interval of approximately 90 minutes (Lavie and Kripke, 1981). Many other psychological and physiological properties show a 90- to 110-minute cycle, including eating and drinking, play behavior of children, changes in heart rate, and the relative dominance of one cerebral hemisphere over the other (Cohen, 1979).

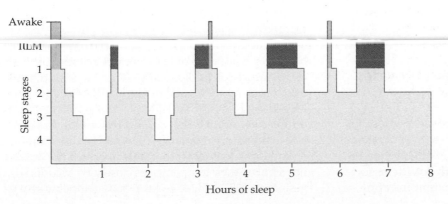

14.12   A Typical Night's Sleep in a Young Adult. Note the progressive lengthening of REM episodes (blue) and the loss of stage 3 and 4 sleep as the night goes on. After Kales and Kales, 1970.

Some Humans Sleep Remarkably Little, yet Function Normally

The portrait of human sleep shows many variations. Some differences can be clearly related to maturational status, functional states like stress, the effects of drugs, and many other external and internal states. Some departures from the "normal" state of human sleep can be quite marked, including unusual people who hardly sleep at all. These cases are more than just folk tales. Dement (1974) described a Stanford University professor who slept only three to four hours a night for over 50 years and died at age 80. Reports of nonsleeping humans verified by scientific observations are quite rare. After searching for that exotic type of person and about to give up the quest, sleep researcher Ray Meddis (1977) found a cheerful 70-year-old retired nurse who said she had slept little since childhood. She was a busy person who easily filled up her 23 hours of daily wakefulness. During the night she sat on her bed reading or writing, and at about 2:00 A.M. she fell asleep for an hour or so, after which she readily awakened. For her first two days in Meddis's laboratory she did not sleep at all because it was all so interesting to her! On the third night she slept a total of 99 minutes, and her sleep contained both SWS and REM sleep periods. Later her sleep was recorded for five days. On the first night she did not sleep at all, but on subsequent nights she slept an average of 67 minutes. She never offered complaints about not sleeping more and did not feel drowsy during either the day or the night. Meddis described several other people who sleep either not at all or for about one hour per night. Some of these people report having parents who slept little.

Other people sleep longer than the normal seven to eight hours per night. Such "long sleepers" have more REM and stage 2 sleep, resulting from extra sleep cycles. In some human cultures a nap in the late afternoon is common—the siesta. Modern industrial societies may inhibit a natural tendency (shared with many other primates) to nap during the day.

The Sleep of Different Species Provides Clues about the Evolution of Sleep

Behavioral and EEG descriptions of sleep states let us make precise comparisons of different sleep stages in a variety of animals. This ability has resulted in the description of sleep in a wide assortment of mammals and to a lesser extent in reptiles, birds, and amphibians (Campbell and Tobler, 1984). Species differ widely in various measures of sleep. What factors control the timing and periodic properties of sleep?

Not All Mammals Display REM Sleep

The amount of daily life occupied by sleep and the percentage of sleep devoted to REM sleep for a variety of animals are shown in Figure 14.13. We can make several generalizations. Among mammals, all that have been investigated thus far, with the exception of the echidna (spiny anteater) and dolphin, display both REM and SWS. The spiny anteater is an egg-laying mammal, a **monotreme** (the only other surviving monotreme is the platypus), that shows prolonged SWS but no REM sleep. Its near rival for antiquity among existing mammals is the opossum—a **marsupial** (that is, an animal that is born at a very early developmental stage and spends a period of its development in a pouch). The other mammals, including humans, are so-called **placental mammals**. Marsupials such as the opossum display both SWS and REM sleep with EEG characteristics that are not distinguishable from those of placental mammals. Recall that in Chapter 3 we discussed the correlations between brain size and sleep in placental mammals. Among the other vertebrates, only birds display both SWS and REM sleep. These comparisons suggest that SWS developed more than 150 million years ago in an ancestor common to birds and mammals. For REM sleep there are two possibilities. Either REM sleep arose later independently in birds and mammals (and after the divergence of monotremes from other mammals), or REM sleep was also present in the ancestor common to birds and all mammals. In that case, monotremes for some reason lost REM sleep after their divergence from the rest of the mammalian line. Reports that reptiles may display an REM-like sleep support this second possibility.

Meddis (1979) offers another interesting argument that REM is at least as ancient as SWS. He notes that cycles of the two main stages of sleep (REM and SWS) have been confirmed only in animals that regulate their temperature physiologically—that is, endotherms. Since temperature regulation during REM sleep is poor, Meddis suggested that REM sleep was derived from ectotherms, animals that could survive with less accurate temperature regulation. It would be disastrous for endotherms to remain in a state in which they could not regulate their temperatures closely. So Meddis suggests that SWS evolved to keep body temperature reg-

14.13 Comparisons of Sleep States in Various Mammals

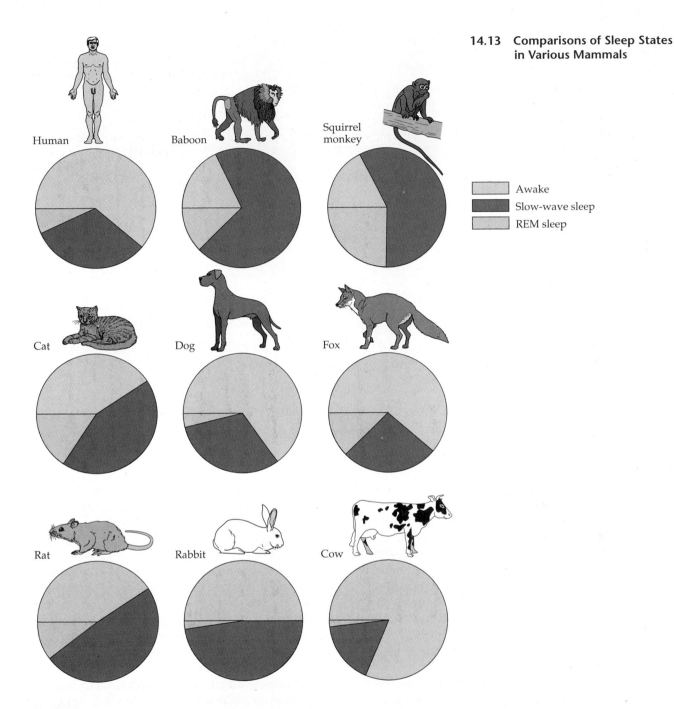

ulated during sleep, and that REM sleep was the only type of sleep prior to the development of endothermy. This hypothesis predicts that vertebrate ectotherms would display REM sleep, but there are conflicting opinions about whether they do.

Sleep in marine mammals (dolphins, whales, and seals) is especially intriguing because they must continually emerge at the surface of the water to breathe. Sleep in the dolphin is characterized by the complete absence of REM sleep periods, and SWS

on only one side of the brain (Mukhametov, 1984). It's as if one whole hemisphere is asleep while the other is awake! EEG data that illustrate this unusual phenomenon are presented in Figure 14.14. During these periods of "unilateral sleep," the animals continue to come up to the surface to breathe; hence their sleep is not characterized by relative motor immobilization. Some seals show REM sleep and normal (bilateral) SWS, usually when they are out of the water.

14.14   Sleep in the Porpoise
(*a*) EEG patterns in right (R) and left (L) brain hemispheres in a porpoise from recording of roughly symmetrical areas of the parietal cortex. (*b*) Diagrams of EEG stages in right (R) and left (L) brain hemispheres of a bottlenose dolphin during a 24-hour session. The two cerebral hemispheres seem to "take turns" sleeping. From Mukhametov, 1984.

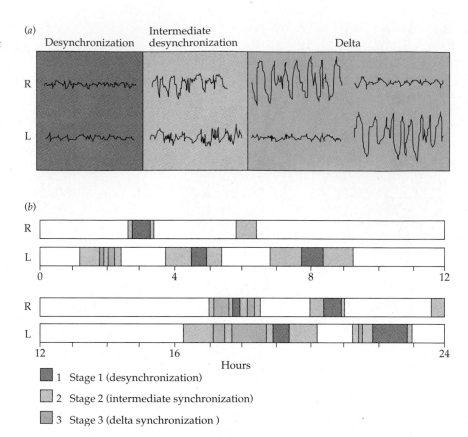

(*a*)

| Desynchronization | Intermediate desynchronization | Delta |

(*b*)

3 Stage 3 (delta synchronization)

Hours

1 Stage 1 (desynchronization)

2 Stage 2 (intermediate synchronization)

The EEG waves look very similar across the primates and can be classified into the same stages of SWS and REM sleep. Stages 1 and 2 of SWS predominate in the sleep of a baboon species that sleeps way out on the ends of smaller limbs of trees. Bert (1971) suggests that this location, which protects the baboon from predators, makes the total muscular relaxation of REM sleep more dangerous—the animal could fall out of the tree. Higher amounts of REM sleep are shown by the chimpanzee, which builds temporary nests on large branches. Studying animal sleep in the laboratory might tend to minimize the distinctive features of sleep for particular species. However, comparison of sleep patterns of primates in the laboratory and in the field has failed to show significant differences.

Vertebrate Species Differ in Their Patterns and Types of Sleep

A **sleep epoch** is a period of one episode of SWS followed by an episode of REM sleep. For the laboratory rat, one sleep epoch lasts an average of 10 to 11 minutes, while for humans it lasts 90 to 110 minutes. In fact, across species epoch duration is inversely related to metabolic rate; that is, small animals, which tend to have high metabolic rates (see Chapter 13), have short sleep epochs. Large species have long sleep epochs. Demands other than high metabolic rate can also cause short epochs. Some birds, such as the swift and the sooty tern, sleep briefly while gliding. The swift spends almost all its time in the air, except during the nesting season, and the sooty tern spends months flying or gliding above water, never alighting, catching fish at the surface. Sleep epochs must of necessity be short in such birds, if they sleep at all.

Except for some such sea birds, *all* vertebrates appear to show (1) a circadian distribution of activity, (2) a prolonged phase of inactivity with (3) raised thresholds to external stimuli, and (4) a characteristic posture during inactivity. REM sleep is found in mammals (except monotremes), birds, and (perhaps) reptiles, but not in amphibians or fishes. Slow waves associated with sleep are evident only in mammals and birds. Many insects have clear periods of behavioral quiescence that include heightened arousal thresholds and distinctive postures (Hartse, 1989), but invertebrate nervous systems do not allow EEG measures.

Our Sleep Patterns Change across the Life Span

In any mammal the characteristics of sleep–waking cycles change during the course of life. These changes are most evident during early development. In fact, the characteristic EEG picture of different stages of SWS is not evident until five or six years of age in humans. After this age EEG data can be classified into stages just as adult EEG data are. Even infant sleep, however, can be generally classified into SWS and REM sleep. SWS of infants is characterized by slower EEG patterns, strong sucking, and irregular respiration. REM sleep is defined by phasic increases in respiration accompanying bursts of eye movements, EEG patterns of very low amplitude, facial grimacing, and occasional smiles. Let's look at the changing sleep patterns over the life span.

Mammals Sleep More during Infancy Than in Adulthood

A clear cycle of sleeping and waking takes several weeks to become established in human infants (Figure 14.15). A 24-hour rhythm is generally evident by 16 weeks of age. Infant sleep is characterized by shorter sleep epochs than those of adulthood. These features of the sleep of infants seem to be due to the relative immaturity of the brain. For example, premature infants have even shorter epochs than do full-term children. Some animals born in an advanced state of development (precocial animals), such as the guinea pig, show a more mature sleep pattern at birth. The sleep patterns of mentally retarded children are different from those of normal children, with fewer eye movements during sleep and reduced amounts of REM sleep (Petre-Quadens, 1972).

Infant mammals show large percentages of REM sleep. For example, Figure 14.16 shows that in humans within the first two weeks of life, 50% of sleep is REM sleep. The percentage of REM sleep is even greater in premature infants: about 80% of the sleep of infants born after only 30 weeks gestation is REM sleep. Unlike normal adults, human infants can move directly from an awake state to REM sleep. By four months of age, REM sleep is entered through a period of SWS. REM sleep of infants is quite active, with muscle twitching, smiles, grimaces, and vocalizations. These behaviors during REM are not related to any aspect of waking behavior; rather they seem to be endogenously generated (Challamel, Lahlou, and Jouvet, 1985).

The preponderance of REM sleep early in life led some investigators to suggest that this state provides stimulation that is essential to the maturation of the

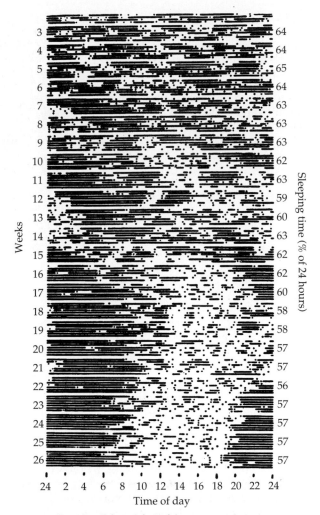

14.15 The Trouble with Babies
Note that a stable pattern of sleep consolidated at night does not appear until about 16 weeks of age. The dark portions indicate time asleep, the blank portions time awake. From Kleitman and Engelmann, 1953.

nervous system. This hypothesis has not been developed in any detail. Some support for this idea comes from observations of the effects of REM deprivation in rats starting 11 to 12 days after birth. Elimination of this stage of sleep in rats is associated with reduced cerebral cortex size akin to that sustained by sensory-deprived animals (Mirmiran, 1986). Mirmiran also asserts that REM sleep deprivation in infancy interferes with the beneficial consequences of environmental enrichment for brain structures in rats. Another hypothesis we'll consider shortly is that REM sleep is important for the consolidation of long-term memories. Since infancy is a time of much learning, this hypothesis may provide an account for the large amount of REM sleep early in life.

14.16 Human Sleep Patterns Change with Age

Early in life we sleep a great deal and about half of sleep time is spent in REM sleep. By adulthood, we average about 8 hours sleep a night, 20% of which is in REM. After Roffwarg, Muzio, and Dement, 1966.

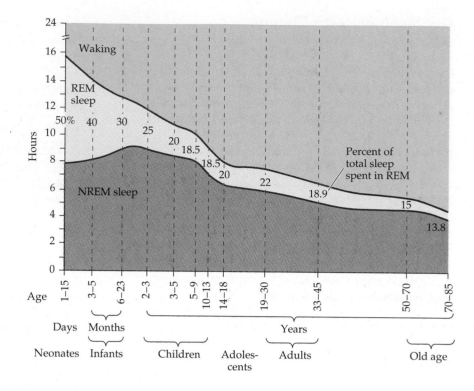

Most People Sleep Appreciably Less When They Reach Old Age

The parameters of sleep change more slowly in old age than in early development. Figure 14.17 shows the pattern of a typical night's sleep in an elderly person. A decline in the total amount of sleep is evident, as is an increase in the number of arousals during a night (compare with Figure 14.12). Lack of sleep, or insomnia (which we discuss at the end of this chapter), is a common complaint of the very elderly (Miles and Dement, 1980), although daytime naps may contribute to nighttime sleep difficulties. The most dramatic progressive decline is in stages 3 and 4 sleep; their amounts at age 60 are only 55% of what they are at age 20. The decline of stages 3 and 4 SWS starts

quite early in life, perhaps as early as the third decade (Bliwise, 1989). By age 90 virtually all stages 3 and 4 sleep has disappeared. This decline in stages 3 and 4 sleep in the aged may be related to diminished cognitive capabilities. There is an especially marked reduction of stages 3 and 4 sleep in aged humans who show senile dementia. An age-associated decrease in stages 3 and 4 SWS is also seen in other mammals.

Are the changes in the sleep patterns of the elderly directly related to the aging process? A study by Reynolds and colleagues (1985) examining healthy seniors shows REM features comparable to those of young adults. Webb (1992) has emphasized the wide range of variability in the sleep of aged individuals, although a central difference between the young and

14.17 The Pattern of Sleep in the Elderly

Records such as this are characterized by frequent awakenings, absence of stage 4 sleep, and a reduction of stage 3 sleep. Compare this with the young adult pattern shown in Figure 14.12. After Kales and Kales, 1974.

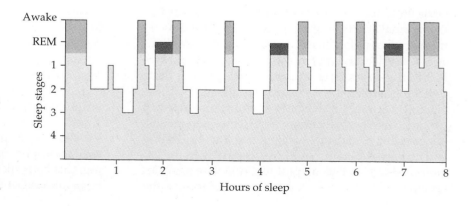

the old is the older person's inability to *maintain* sleep, which causes their sleep "dissatisfaction." In Chapter 18 we'll see that there are also individual differences among rats and humans in the shrinkage of brain structures with aging and that some of these differences are correlated with declines in learning ability.

Manipulating Sleep Reveals an Underlying Structure

Sleep is affected by many environmental, social, and biological influences. From one viewpoint, though, sleep is an amazingly stable state: major changes in our waking behavior have only a minor impact on subsequent sleep. For example, exercise before sleep seems to help us fall asleep more quickly (Horne, 1981), but except in highly trained athletes (Shapiro et al., 1981), it has no impact on any other sleep parameter. But some conditions do produce major shifts in sleep measures. The effects of sleep deprivation and various drugs on sleep are especially interesting because they give insight into its underlying mechanisms.

Sleep Deprivation Drastically Alters Sleep Patterns

All of us at one time or another have been willing or not-so-willing participants in informal **sleep deprivation** experiments. Thus, we are all aware of the effect of partial or total sleep deprivation: it makes us sleepy! But the study of sleep deprivation is also a way to explore the potential regulatory mechanisms of sleeping and waking. Most of the studies concern **sleep recovery**, asking questions such as, Does a sleep-deprived organism somehow "keep track" of the amounts and types of lost sleep? When the organism is given the opportunity to compensate, is recovery partial or complete? Can you pay off sleep debts? How many days of recovery sleep are necessary for compensation?

The effects of sleep deprivation. Early reports from sleep deprivation studies emphasized a similarity between instances of "bizarre" behavior provoked by sleep deprivation and features of psychosis, particularly schizophrenia. Partial or total sleep deprivation has been examined in the hope that it might illuminate some aspects of the genesis of psychotic behavior. A frequent theme in this work has been the functional role of dreams as a "guardian of sanity." But examination of schizophrenic patients does not seem to confirm this view. For example, these patients can

show sleep–waking cycles similar to those of normal adults, and sleep deprivation does not exacerbate their symptoms.

The behavioral effects of prolonged, total sleep deprivation vary appreciably and may depend on some general personality factors and age. In several studies employing prolonged total deprivation—205 hours (8.5 days)—*some* subjects showed *occasional* episodes of hallucinations. But the most common behavior changes noted in these experiments are increases in irritability, difficulty in concentrating, and episodes of disorientation. During each deprivation day, the effects are more prominent in the morning; by late afternoon and early evening, the subjects seem much less affected by the accumulating sleep loss. The subject's ability to perform tasks is best described by L. C. Johnson (1969:216): "His performance is like a motor that after much use misfires, runs normally for a while, then falters again." Tasks that elicit strong motivation and are brief in duration may show almost no impairment, even with prolonged sleep deprivation. Sleep deprivation is accompanied by a progressive decline in the prominence of the alpha rhythm. The EEG of these subjects takes on an appearance resembling stage 1 sleep, although the subjects move about. Prolonged sleep deprivation can provoke EEG signs similar to those of people with seizure disorders.

Sleep recovery. Figure 14.18 provides data on sleep recovery in a young man following 11 days of sleep deprivation. No evidence of a psychotic state was noted, and the incentive for this unusually long act was simply the young man's curiosity. Researchers got into the act only *after* the subject started his deprivation schedule, which is the reason for the absence of predeprivation sleep data.

In the first sleep recovery night, stage 4 sleep shows the greatest relative difference from normal. This increase in stage 4 sleep is usually at the expense of stage 2 sleep. However, the rise in stage 4 sleep during recovery never completely makes up for the deficit accumulated over the deprivation period. In fact, it is no more than for deprivation periods half as long. REM sleep after prolonged sleep deprivation shows its greatest recovery during the second postdeprivation night. Eventually, the REM debt comes closer to being paid off, but it requires more recovery nights.

Experiments of the early 1970s dealing with the "repayment of sleep debts" involved short-term deprivation effects—either total sleep deprivation or, more usually, REM deprivation. The latter condition

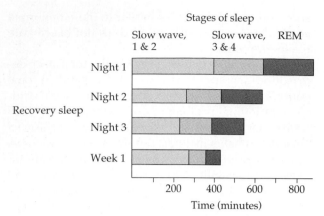

14.18 Sleep Recovery After 11 Days Awake
After Gulevich, Dement, and Johnson, 1966.

was achieved by forcefully awakening a subject whenever EEG signs of REM sleep appeared. These short-term, early REM deprivation studies generally showed that in postdeprivation recovery sessions subjects made up for the loss of REM sleep in the form of REM episodes of longer-than-normal duration. With more prolonged REM deprivation, the debt is paid off somewhat differently. Recovery of the number of hours of REM sleep is not complete, but other forms of REM recovery are evident. For example, the loss of tension of postural muscles, which is part of the signature of REM sleep, may appear in SWS following prolonged deprivation. Thus the usual properties of REM sleep seem to be reallocated to other stages of sleep, as observed in both humans and cats. REM recovery may also involve another form of compensation—greater intensity; recovery night REM sleep is more "intense" than normal, with more rapid eye movements per period of time.

Although Many Drugs Affect Sleep, There Is No Perfect Sleeping Pill

Throughout recorded history humans have reached for substances to enhance the prospects of sleep. Early civilizations discovered substances in the plant world that induced sleep (Hartmann, 1978). Ancient Greeks used the juice of the poppy to obtain opium and used products of the mandrake plant that we recognize today as scopolamine and atropine. Modern sleep pharmacology started with the synthesis of morphine from opium at the beginning of the nineteenth century. The preparation of barbituric acid in the mid-nineteenth century by the discoverer of aspirin, Adolph von Bayer, began the development of an enormous number of substances—barbiturates—that continue to be used for sleep dysfunctions. Un-

fortunately, none of these substances can provide a completely normal night's sleep in terms of time spent in various sleep states such as REM sleep, and none of them remains effective when used repeatedly. For example, one of mankind's oldest and simplest drugs is alcohol. Its effects on sleep seem to be typical of a larger class of depressants: a relatively moderate dosage (comparable to two shots of whiskey within an hour) may help initiate sleep, but it also depresses REM sleep time.

The effects of certain substances generally regarded as sleep inducers depend on dosage and on whether the assessment of effect is made during a single night or over an extended period of time. As our knowledge of some of the underlying neurochemical events increases, some of the variability of results may become more understandable. Beware of assessments of the effects of drugs on sleep that use normal young subjects without sleep complaints. The use of such subjects may limit the validity of the results. To provide an analogy: If you were interested in the antitubercular properties of a drug, would you assess this substance using subjects *without* tuberculosis?

Antidepressant drugs (or "pep pills") markedly suppress REM sleep. Amphetamine addicts may show a virtual absence of REM sleep during the period of drug use. Following cessation of drug use, rebound REM sleep in some cases may amount to 75% of the night's sleep and may occur very quickly after the onset of sleep, without the normal latency of 40 to 90 minutes. The preponderance of REM sleep in the withdrawal sleep of amphetamine addicts may be related to the terrifying dreams they have during withdrawal. Some other antidepressants inhibit REM sleep without a subsequent rebound.

Reliance on sleeping pills, including the currently popular benzodiazepine, triazolam (Halcion), poses many problems (Rothschild, 1992). Viewed solely as a way to deal with sleep problems, current drugs fall far short of being a suitable remedy for several reasons. First, continual use of sleep medication results in a loss of the sleep-inducing property of these substances. Declining ability to induce sleep frequently leads to increased dosages that are self-prescribed and pose a health hazard. A second major drawback in the use of sleeping pills is that they produce marked changes in the pattern of sleep, both during the period of drug use and for a period following drug use that may last for days. Most commonly during the initial phase of drug use a reduction of REM sleep occurs, especially during the first half of a night's sleep. A gradual adaptation to drug use is evident in the return of REM sleep with continued use of sleeping pills. Sudden withdrawal of sleeping pills results in a period of REM rebound with an intensity that many people experience as unpleasant and that may lead to a return to reliance on sleeping pills. A final major problem in the frequent use of sleeping pills is their impact on waking behavior. A persistent "sleep drunkenness" coupled with drowsiness, despite intense efforts at maintaining vigilance, may impair productive activity during waking hours.

These problems have led to other biochemical approaches to sleep disorders. Because melatonin is normally released from the pineal at night (see Figure 7.17*b*), it has been suggested that taking exogenous melatonin could aid the onset of sleep. In fact, melatonin does have a weak hypnotic effect, perhaps because it causes a lowering of body temperature, reducing arousal and causing drowsiness (Dawson and Encel, 1993). Another approach is to promote increases in the concentration and release of neurotransmitters that may be involved in sleep induction. Hartmann (1978) has emphasized serotonin as an important transmitter in this process. Serotonin levels in the brain can be strongly influenced by the administration of tryptophan, which is a precursor in the synthesis of serotonin. Low doses of the precursor under double-blind conditions (neither experimenters nor subjects know which subjects receive the drug and which take the control until after the study is over) reduced sleep latency without changing the basic pattern of sleep in humans (Hartmann, 1978). This observation in normal subjects has been confirmed in a population with mild insomnia. Further promise for tryptophan is shown by the absence of long-term tolerance effects and the absence of daytime effects on vigilance. Larger doses, however, can lead to other health problems. Meanwhile, Grandmother's suggestion to drink a glass of warm milk before sleep may be sound, since milk is a good source of tryptophan.

We Do Our Most Vivid Dreaming During REM Sleep

One exciting aspect of the psychobiology of sleep is the thinking and imagery that accompany sleep. We can record the EEG of subjects, awaken them at a particular stage—1, 2, 3, 4, or REM—and question them about thoughts or perceptions immediately prior to awakening. Early data strongly indicated that dreams were largely restricted to REM sleep. Subjects reported dreams 70 to 90% of the time when they were awakened in this stage—in contrast to an incidence of 10 to 15% for non-REM sleep periods. At first it was even thought that the rapid eye movements characteristic of this period were related to "viewing" dream scenes. In other words, if you were dreaming of watching a ping-pong match, your eyes would reveal the rapid to-and-fro movement of real-life observations of such a match. This scanning theory of eye movements during REM dreams now seems unlikely, because there are many differences between the characteristics of eye movements during actual viewing of scenes and those of REM sleep.

Although all studies report a large percentage of dream reports upon awakening from REM sleep, some investigators have increasingly questioned whether REM is the sole sleep state associated with dreams. With careful, more persistent questioning, subjects can report dreams upon awakening from SWS. Dream reports of REM sleep are characterized by visual imagery, whereas the dream reports of SWS are of a more "thinking" type. REM dreams are apt to include a story that involves odd perceptions and the sense that "you are there" experiencing sights, sounds, smells, and acts. SWS dreams, on the other hand, are characterized more as thoughts than sights. Subjects awakened from this state report thinking about problems rather than seeing themselves in a stage presentation. Cartwright (1979) has shown that the dreams of these two states are so different that judges reading a dream description can indicate the sleep state from which it arose with 90% accuracy. REM sleep dreams during the first half of the night are oriented toward reality. The dreams incorporate the day's experience, and the sequence of events is ordinary. Dreams during the second half of sleep are more unusual and less readily connected with the day's events, becoming more emotionally intense and bizarre. Dreams of depressed patients are emotionally bland, with very reduced activity and mood. Terrifying dreams have become the subject of close scrutiny (Hartmann, 1984). **Nightmares** are defined as long, frightening dreams that awaken the sleeper from REM sleep. They are occasionally confused with **night terror**, which is a sudden arousal from stage 3 or 4 SWS marked by intense fear and autonomic activation. In night terror the sleepers do not recall a vivid *dream* but rather remember a sense of a crushing feeling on their chest as though being suffocated. Night terrors are common in children during the early part of an evening's sleep.

Nightmares are quite prevalent, and some people are especially plagued by them (Figure 14.19). At least 25% of college students report having at least one nightmare per month. (A common one, shared

Photograph © 1995 by the Detroit Institute of Arts. Gift of Mr. and Mrs. Bert L. Smokler and Mr. and Mrs. Lawrence A. Fleischman.

14.19 Henry Fuseli, *The Nightmare*, ca. 1791

with Freud, is suddenly remembering a final exam in progress.) During some illnesses people are more likely to experience nightmares. Medications that enhance the activity of dopamine systems, such as L-dopa, also make nightmares more frequent. Individuals with frequent nightmares may be a more creative group, with "loose" personal boundaries (Hartmann, 1984). Perhaps these people are prone to either a greater or more rapid activation of dopamine systems.

Dreams Have Intrigued Humans for Centuries

The functional role of dreams is a very ancient and persistent riddle that is not likely to be answered by currently available experimental approaches. In the history of humans, dreams have been viewed in many different lights. Van de Castle (1994) provides some interesting illustrations from societies around the world. For example, Cuna Indians off the coast of Panama viewed dreams as predictors of imminent disaster, and their dream "analysts" had a variety of objects to ward off both dreams and their presumed

consequences. For instance, a tomahawk-like object was used to treat dreams of thunder and lightning. In early Western societies, the origin of dreams was attributed to external stimulation or states of the body, especially the stomach. By the nineteenth century, dreams had come to be attributed to endogenous events in the *brain* that the dreamer cannot control. Sigmund Freud (1900) regarded dreams as an opportunity for our mind to fulfill our inner wishes, but the events are distorted by other parts of our mind to avoid conflict and guilt. Thus, Freud and other psychoanalysts, such as C. G. Jung, regarded these nightly adventures as clues to our deepest conflicts.

For psychiatrists Alan Hobson and Robert McCarley (1977), dreams are considered an innocent by-product of basic bodily restorative processes and have no significance by themselves. From the perspective of their "activation-synthesis" hypothesis, there is no way to accomplish the biological role of sleep without the "accidental" provocation of dreams. Certain brain stem regions produce phasic activation that affects the visual cortex. This activation excites visual cortical neurons to produce the perceptual elements of a dream. These random bursts are synthesized by the cognitive activity of the dreamer, so that upon awakening she remembers a narrativelike weaving together of the disparate elements.

Perhaps "we dream in order to forget," speculate Crick and Mitchison (1983), who bring to the study of REM sleep some concepts of information theory and computer sciences. The essence of their argument is that REM sleep is a period of reverse learning, in which false or irrelevant memories that are routinely accumulated during the day are erased—a kind of mental housecleaning. According to this theory, the cerebral cortex is a rich matrix of interconnected cells that might become overloaded with bizarre or unusual associations. REM sleep weakens the irrelevant synapses by "zapping" them! Let's consider the relationship between sleep and learning in more detail.

There Seems to Be a Relationship between Learning and Sleep

Every now and then we are confronted with newspaper reports and advertisements that herald a new technique or gadget that will enable us to learn during sleep. The appeal of such possibilities is overwhelming to some, including those who begrudgingly accept sleep as a necessary interference with the pursuit of knowledge and those who sport the fantasy that information can be transmitted by the deep embrace of a book. More seriously, sleep is a state in which many neurons are active. Can we learn during this state? Even if we can't learn *during* sleep, can sleep help us consolidate what we learned today? If so, then sleep deprivation may interfere with learning. Students participating in the ritual of overnight cramming for exams would want to know. Conversely, do the learning experiences of a day influence the pattern of a night's sleep?

Only the Simplest Types of Learning Can Occur during Sleep

The idea that we can learn while sleeping is a controversial area beset with many conflicting claims (Aarons, 1976). The only overall conclusion one can confidently draw from a large range of studies is that if you are relying on acquiring and retaining complex information during sleep, you had best find a backup system (Druckman and Bjork, 1994). Although several nonhuman experiments indicate that simple

conditioned responses can be acquired during various sleep stages, evidence of people learning verbal materials while asleep is quite modest.

Studies that ensured that subjects were asleep during presentation of verbal material—by recording EEG patterns, muscular potentials (electromyogram, EMG), and eye movements—provided no convincing evidence that people could recall the material later when awake. Until recently all such experiments used *explicit* recall or recognition; that is, the subjects were asked to recall or recognize the material. Investigators of learning now differentiate this from *implicit* memory—that is, where subjects reveal memory through their performance. (We will take up this distinction further in Chapter 17.) A type of implicit memory is seen in **priming**, where recent use of a word makes it more likely that the subject will offer that word in a response. For example, subjects listen to a list of paired words, where the first word is a homophone (for example, hair, hare) and the other word provides context for one of the spellings (for example, tortoise). In the recall test ten minutes after the presentation, the subjects are asked to spell words from a list that includes the homophones presented earlier. Subjects who heard the word pairs in the waking state showed clear priming effects: they were significantly more likely to spell the homophones in accordance with the context word (in our example, "hare"), but subjects who heard the words either in REM or stage 2 SWS showed no evidence of priming (Wood et al., 1992). Thus it appears that neither explicit nor implicit memories for verbal material are formed during sleep.

Some less complicated forms of learning are possible in both humans and other animals, as shown by habituation experiments in which a stimulus is repeated without consequence over some period of time. For example, if a sudden loud sound is presented during SWS, the subject—human or cat—will show EEG signs of arousal. Repetition of the stimulus makes the arousal result less likely. In some sense this response is not sleep learning, since arousal is produced. However, this phenomenon indicates that the novelty of a stimulus can be detected in the sleeping state.

A peculiar property of dreams is that, unless we tell them to someone or write them down soon after waking, we tend to forget them (Dement, 1974). It is probably beneficial that most dreams are never stored in long-term memory, since it would pose difficulties to store permanent traces of events that may not be accurate descriptions of the world. Perhaps one of the roles of the SWS that follows REM episodes is to provide the neural condition that precludes lasting storage of the events of REM periods. Or perhaps the random, incoherent chain of events in most dreams makes them difficult to consolidate or retrieve.

Sleep May Help Consolidate What We Learn While Awake

In 1924, Jenkins and Dallenbach reported an experiment that continues to provoke research. They trained subjects in a verbal learning task at bedtime and tested them eight hours later on arising; they trained other subjects early in the day and tested them eight hours later as well. The results showed better retention when a period of sleep occurred *between* a learning period and tests of recall. What accounts for such an effect? Several differing psychological explanations have been offered. One suggests  that during the waking period between learning and recall, diverse experiences interfere with accurate recall. Sleep during this interval appreciably reduces interfering stimulation. A second explanation notes that memory tends to decay and that this relentless process simply occurs more slowly during sleep. These two explanations posit sleep as a passive process in consolidating memory. A third explanation emphasizes an active, functional contribution of sleep to learning. This view says that sleep includes processes that consolidate the learning of waking periods. Sleep is then seen as providing the conditions to allow a firm "printing" of enduring memory traces. A possible neurophysiological correlate of such consolidation has been described in the rat hippocampus (Wilson and McNaughton, 1994).

Ekstrand and collaborators (1977) compared the magnitude of memory loss in three groups, all of whom learned lists of paired associates. Group 1 learned a list in the evening and was tested for retention after an interval of eight hours of no sleep; group 2 slept for half the night, was then awakened, learned the list, and had four hours of sleep before retention testing; group 3 learned the list, slept four hours, and was awakened and tested for retention. Group 2 showed the best recall. The experimenters' interpretation is that SWS favors retention, but other interpretations are possible. Idzikowski (1984) showed that eight hours sleep (16 hours after learning) leads to better verbal retention than no sleep. A control experiment showed that this effect was not due to the stress of sleep deprivation (Horne, 1985).

Many animal studies have explored the notion that sleep—especially REM sleep—is important for learning and retention (Smith, 1985). One approach has been to examine the qualitative and quantitative character of sleep following training experiences. The most consistent finding in this type of study is that the amount of REM sleep increases considerably after learning. In several studies the increased REM sleep occurred immediately at the onset of sleep following training. Increases in the amount of REM sleep result either from longer REM episodes or from more frequent REM episodes. In a few enriched environment exposure experiments, not only REM but also SWS is enhanced. If learning extends over several days, the increase in REM sleep is largest during the steepest part of the learning curve (Bloch, 1976).

The functional significance of increases in REM sleep following learning has been explored by using REM sleep deprivation. In these studies the subjects are deprived of REM sleep during the period in which REM increments are normally seen after learning. As little as three hours of such deprivation retards the rate of learning in some cases (Smith, 1985). REM sleep deprivation following learning has also produced results open to more than one interpretation. No doubt, this kind of study is difficult to perform because REM sleep deprivation entails many physiological changes that might overwhelm more subtle effects that are pertinent to learning and associated phenomena. Some of the tasks employed may be too simple to require the REM mechanism. Or perhaps only certain types of learning processes are sensitive to REM deprivation. For example, in humans certain "perceptual learning" tasks, such as learning to discriminate different textures visually, show little improvement in a single training session but show considerable improvement eight to ten hours after the session. Karni and colleagues (1994) found that if people were deprived of REM sleep after a session, they failed to show improvement the next day. In contrast, depriving them only of SWS had no effect. So perhaps REM sleep is important only for very particular types of tasks.

Several Neurobiological Systems Are Activated during Sleep

During sleep, many nervous and hormonal functions are dramatically modified. Some of these changes have strong implications for hypotheses about the presumed restorative role of sleep. In this section we will discuss some of the major physiological modifications that occur during sleep.

The Brain Inhibits Spinal Motoneurons, Immobilizing Us during Sleep

For many animals, sleep means the absence of activity of the skeletal musculature. How does the motor system become quiescent? This feature is especially puzzling since at the same time much of the brain is quite active. This contrast implies that motor pathways become reversibly uncoupled from the rest of the brain. Another motor system puzzle is the unusual episodic activity in nonpostural muscles during REM sleep—the rapid eye movements and sudden twitches of fingers, hands, and other muscle groups.

During SWS monosynaptic and polysynaptic spinal reflexes decrease. In REM sleep these reflexes are almost nonexistent, resulting in profound loss of muscle tone. Some of this motor decrement must depend on influences descending from the brain to the spinal cord, because reflexes during sleep are not depressed if the spinal cord has been disconnected from the brain. Recordings from spinal motoneurons during sleep reveal inhibitory postsynaptic potentials that prevent the cells from reaching threshold and producing an action potential. The usual loss of muscle tone during sleep can be abolished by lesions near a part of the pons called the locus coeruleus (see Figure 14.24), suggesting that this region plays a role in uncoupling the motor system during sleep (Morrison, 1983). Cats with such lesions seem to act out their dreams. After a bout of SWS, the EEG from the cats becomes desynchronized as it does during waking and REM sleep, and the animals stagger to their feet. Are they awake or in REM sleep? They move their heads as though visually tracking moving objects (that aren't there), bat with their forepaws at nothing, and ignore objects that are present. This behavior is accompanied by an EEG phenomenon (called PGO waves, for *p*ons, *g*eniculate, and *o*ccipital; Figure 14.20) that is normally seen only in REM sleep. In addition, the cats' "inner eyelid," the translucent nictitating membrane, partially covers the eyes. Thus, although the cats appear to be in REM sleep, motor activity is not inhibited by the brain. Many cells in this region use norepinephrine as a neurotransmitter, whose possible role in sleep we discuss later in this chapter.

Some view sleep as a period of restoration following the demands of a prolonged waking period. From this viewpoint we would expect nerve cells of sensory and motor regions to show reduced firing rates during sleep, but studies of single nerve cells in the cerebral cortex reveal that nerve cells actually *increase* their firing rates during sleep. In the autonomic nervous system, functions such as heart rate,

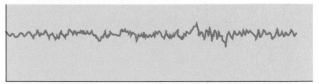

(*a*) Slow-wave sleep

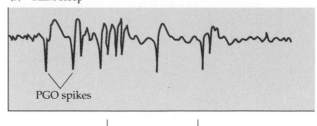

(*b*) REM sleep

PGO spikes

| 2 seconds |

14.20 PGO Waves Associated with REM Sleep in Cats
Such PGO waves are especially prominent in lateral geniculate recordings such as these, but only during REM sleep.

blood pressure, and respiration show progressive declines during SWS but marked *increases* during REM sleep (see Table 14.1). During REM sleep cerebral blood flow increases in some areas—another example of the increased metabolic demands of REM sleep. These data emphasize that the brain does not stop working during sleep.

Some Hormones Are Normally Secreted during Sleep

Daily rhythms are apparent in the secretion of many hormones, including various pituitary hormones. A specific link to sleep processes has been established for growth hormone, which, in addition to being involved in growth processes, participates in governing the metabolism of proteins and carbohydrates. The highest concentrations of growth hormone in blood are evident during sleep (Figure 14.21). Release normally occurs only during SWS, particularly stages 3 and 4. The exact nature of the control or regulation of hormone release by sleep remains to be explored. For instance, is SWS the exclusive causal condition for growth hormone release? And how are these events synchronized? Recent studies suggest that growth hormone may have direct effects on the brain and thus influence sleep (Martin, Wyatt, and Mendelsohn, 1985). We mentioned earlier that the hormone melatonin is secreted by the

14.21 Growth Hormone Is Secreted While We Sleep

Note the correlation between slow-wave sleep and growth hormone release. After Takahashi, 1979.

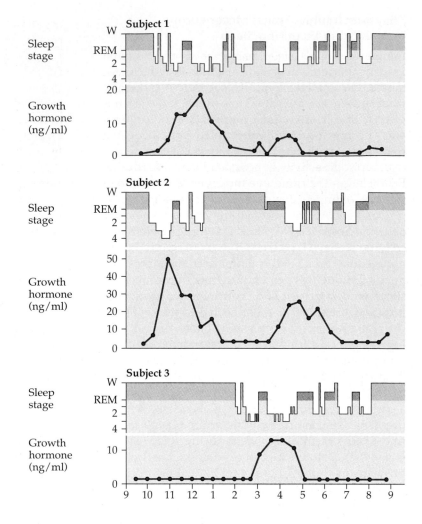

pineal during the dark period in vertebrates, both in nocturnal and diurnal species; there is some evidence that melatonin can aid the induction of sleep in humans.

What Are the Neural Mechanisms of Sleep?

Any complete theory of nervous system mechanisms that control sleep must explain the following basic questions:

1. Why and how does sleep start?
2. What accounts for the periodic properties of sleep, including the daily sleep–waking cycle and the timing of successive episodes of SWS and REM?
3. What stops a prolonged period of sleep?

Various hypotheses, guesses, and conjectures have been offered, but there is still no comprehensive the-

ory that successfully deals with these major questions. We will explore a variety of hypotheses. Some of them appear increasingly plausible; others, however tantalizing, still yearn for confirmation. Some hypotheses are exclusively anatomical, dealing with neural circuits of sleep; others are neurochemical.

We can roughly classify sleep theories into two broad categories:

1. Sleep as a passive process. From this perspective, sleep starts because the mechanisms promoting waking simply run down from a period of use.
2. Sleep as an active process. From this perspective, sleep starts because the mechanisms promoting waking are actively inhibited.

Although the passive view dominated among ancient philosophers and early scientists, current research views sleep as an active process. To understand why, let's briefly review the progression of research and theories since the 1930s.

Early Research Suggested That Sleep Is a Passive Phenomenon

In the late 1930s the Belgian neurophysiologist Frédéric Brémer performed experiments that became the foundation of the view that sleep onset and maintenance are passive. In one group of cats, Brémer examined cortical electrical activity after the brain stem was isolated from the spinal cord by a cut below the medulla. He called this physiological preparation an **encéphale isolé** ("isolated brain"; Figure 14.22*a*). The EEGs of these animals showed signs of waking and sleeping. During EEG-defined wakeful periods, the pupils were dilated and the eyes followed moving objects. During EEG-defined sleep, the pupils were small, as is characteristic of normal sleep. (Brémer did not distinguish between SWS and REM sleep; this distinction was not discovered until the 1950s. By sleep Brémer meant SWS.) In another group of animals, Brémer examined cortical electrical activity following a cut at the upper level of the midbrain (between the inferior and superior colliculi). This preparation was called the **cerveau isolé** ("isolated forebrain"; Figure 14.22*b*). These animals displayed persistent EEG sleep patterns with no instance of wakefulness in terms of either the EEG or pupil size and eye movements. At the time, these data were interpreted to mean that sleep starts and is maintained by the loss of sensory input, a state of deafferentation. The cerveau isolé animals showed no signs of wakefulness, according to this interpretation, because cutting across the upper brain stem reduced the normal flow of sensory input, which, according to this view, is a prerequisite for the waking condition.

In the late 1940s, Brémer's experiments were reinterpreted on the basis of experiments involving electrical stimulation of the extensive region of the brain stem known as the **reticular formation** (Figure 14.23). The reticular formation consists of a diffuse group of cells whose axons and dendrites course in many directions, extending from the medulla through the thalamus. Moruzzi and Magoun, two scientists prominent in the study of the reticular formation, found that they could awaken sleeping animals by electrical stimulation of the reticular formation; the animals showed rapid arousal. Lesions of these regions produced persistent sleep in the animals, although this phenomenon was not observed if the lesions interrupted only the sensory pathways in the brain stem. This latter observation led to new views about the phenomena displayed in Brémer's experiments. The effects noted by Brémer were now interpreted as arising not from loss of sensory input alone, but from the interruption of an activating system within the brain stem. This mechanism remained intact in the encéphale isolé animal, but its output was precluded from reaching the cortex in the cerveau isolé animal. The "reticular formation" school argued that waking results from activity of brain stem reticular formation systems and that sleep is the passive result of a decline in reticular formation activity.

Some Brain Regions Seem to Inhibit Arousal Centers

Many influences were found to dampen the brain stem mechanisms of arousal. These include blood pressure, receptor afferent inputs, deactivation influences from the cerebral cortex, and influences from caudal regions of the brain stem. The existence of a caudal brain stem mechanism that can inhibit rostral activating mechanisms was shown in experiments in which sections were made between these two systems. Animals subjected to this treatment display

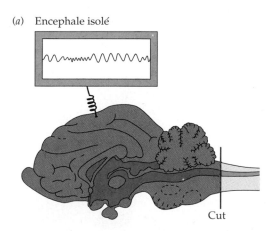

(a) Encephale isolé

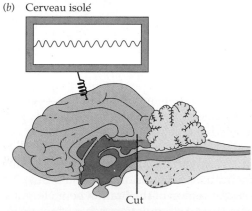

(b) Cerveau isolé

14.22 Brain Transections Reveal Sleep Mechanisms
The levels of brain section in encéphale isolé *(a)* and cerveau isolé *(b)* preparations and the patterns of sleep seen in the front of the brain.

14.23   The Brain Stem Reticular Formation
This system is thought to activate the rest of the brain.

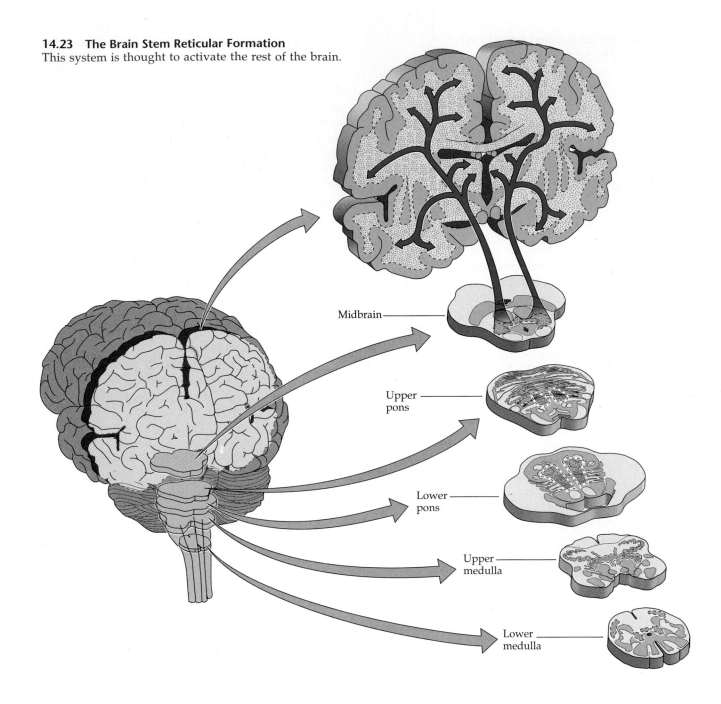

Midbrain

Upper pons

Lower pons

Upper medulla

Lower medulla

persistent signs of wakefulness, suggesting that caudal regions have a dampening effect on the upper levels of the reticular formation. Stimulation of this caudal brain stem region also inhibits motor systems. Such observations suggest that sleep actively takes over the waking brain.

Michel Jouvet (1967), a major sleep researcher, particularly emphasized a system of neurons coursing in the midline of the brain stem, called the **raphe nucleus** (Figure 14.24). These neurons use the neurotransmitter serotonin, as we will discuss shortly. Oth-

er regions that have been implicated in the onset and maintenance of sleep, particularly SWS, include portions of the medial thalamus, whose stimulation can produce sleep behavior in cats. Similar results have been produced by excitation of a group of forebrain regions, including the anterior hypothalamus. No one has found a region of the brain where electrical or pharmacological stimulation can induce REM sleep. However, cuts through the brain stem that are intermediate to the cerveau isolé and encéphale isolé make it clear that the pons is crucial for this state. If a cut is made below the pons, the rostral brain (still

14.24 The Raphe Nucleus, Locus Coeruleus and Their Projections

Raphe neurons use serotonin as a transmitter; locus coeruleus cells use norepinephrine.

● Raphe

● Locus coeruleus

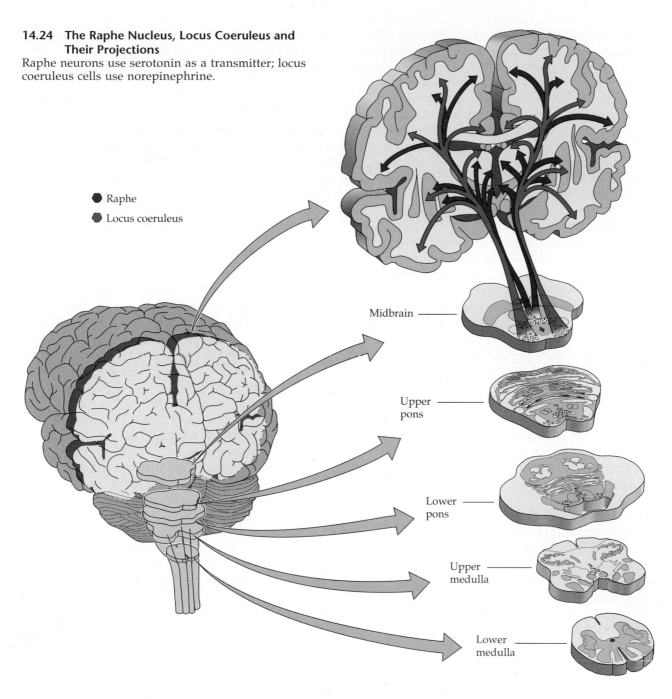

Midbrain

Upper pons

Lower pons

Upper medulla

Lower medulla

connected to the pons) displays REM sleep. Conversely, if the cut is made rostral to the pons, leaving the pons attached to the caudal nervous system (medulla and spinal cord), then the caudal half of the animal shows REM sleep (J. Siegel, 1989). Furthermore, lesions of a small region of the pontine reticular formation appear to abolish REM sleep (Friedman and Jones, 1984). The integration of these various regions, in terms of a more defined circuit that encompasses the forms of interaction in these diverse systems, has yet to be accomplished. For the moment many regions of the brain appear to be capable of actively controlling or modulating the induction of various sleep states.

The Search for Sleep-Promoting Substances

The complexity of the circuitry relevant to control of the sleep–waking cycle led to a neurochemical perspective. Many years ago it was thought that sleep might result from the accumulation in the brain and body of a sleep-producing substance, a so-called

hypnogen. The existence of such a substance was suggested by the experiments of Henri Piéron (1913), who showed that the injection of cerebrospinal fluid from fatigued dogs into rested animals resulted in sleep in the rested animals. This basic kind of experiment has been done in many ways since that time, and some recent observations have renewed an interest in endogenous sleep factors, substances produced by the organism that induce or promote sleep. These substances are sought in blood, urine, cerebrospinal fluid, or extracts of the brain. Because the concentration of hypnogen is presumed to increase in response to lack of sleep and to build up progressively during the awake period, some of the proposed sleep factors are obtained following sleep deprivation. After their collection, these substances are injected into other test animals to determine whether they change the base level of sleeping behavior.

Factor S is the name given to a sleep-inducing substance that Pappenheimer and collaborators (1975) extracted from the cerebrospinal fluid of sleep-deprived goats. Injections of Factor S into the cerebral ventricles or basal forebrain of cats or rats increased SWS (Garcia-Arraras and Pappenheimer, 1983). A factor collected from human urine closely resembles Factor S (Krueger et al., 1984). This human-derived factor, which was isolated and found to consist of muramyl peptides, also increases SWS when injected into rats. The surprise is that although muramyl peptides are *found* circulating in virtually all mammals, they are not *made* by the mammals themselves (Johannsen et al., 1991). Rather, these peptides are released from the degraded cell walls of bacteria destroyed by the immune system. Perhaps Factor S does not normally control sleep onset. The brain may somehow detect these indicators of infection and promote sleep to help combat the infection. On the other hand, several factors released by the immune system induce the proliferation of immune cells. These factors, which include the interleukins and interferons, are known as **cytokines**, and they, too, have a somnogenic effect (Kimura et al., 1994), which probably helps the fight against infections (Krueger and Majde, 1995). Thus, the muramyl peptides may promote sleep indirectly by inducing cytokine release.

Sleep-promoting substances have also been sought from sleeping animals; some investigators use a filtrate of blood obtained from animals in whom sleep has been induced by electrical stimulation of the thalamus. In rabbits, low-frequency electrical stimulation of a thalamic region called the in-tralaminar nuclei induces SWS. The sleep-inducing substance produced is a chain of nine amino acids and has been named **delta-sleep-inducing peptide** (**DSIP**). Studies have shown that DSIP can increase sleep in humans suffering from chronic insomnia (Schneider-Helmert, 1985). Circulating levels of DSIP vary in a circadian fashion in humans and closely follow the rhythm in body temperature (Friedman et al., 1994). The peptide appears to be present in presynaptic terminals of hypothalamic regions near the pituitary stalk, but the cells that produce DSIP have not yet been identified (Skagerberg et al., 1991). This work supports the idea that onset of sleep is controlled by the accumulation of a "sleep factor" that may act as a neuromodulator.

Although the data we have just discussed seem promising in terms of the possibility of endogenous sleep-promoting substances, some observations with human conjoined twins do not seem to support this view. Most so-called Siamese twins do not share vascular systems to any great extent, so there are few opportunities for the exchange of fluids. In an interesting but seldom cited paper, however, Webb (1978) described a set of twins joined along the chest and abdomen who shared a single heart. Two weeks after birth, the behavior of these children was observed to assess the timing of sleep and waking. The following categories were scored minute by minute: quiet sleep, active sleep, crying, quiet awake, and active awake. The data revealed a relative independence of these states in the twins. Some of the time one twin was asleep while the other was awake. Even when both were asleep, there were considerable periods in which one twin was in a state of quiet (slow-wave) sleep while the other was in a state of active (REM) sleep. These data, reinforced by later observations in another set of conjoined twins (Sackett and Korner, 1993), seem to oppose the theory that sleep onset or maintenance is controlled by an endogenous substance. Perhaps, however, the very young age at which these ob- servations were made minimized the opportunity for adequate assessment of possible sleep factors. Or perhaps such factors only alter the probability of sleep rather than force the onset of sleep.

Synaptic Transmitters May Control Sleep and Waking

The levels of several synaptic transmitters vary in a circadian manner, suggesting that sleep onset and maintenance are controlled by changes in the relative activity of different transmitter systems. Newer techniques have enabled a large-scale effort to map the changes in transmitters that might be related to sleep processes. Manipulations of several neurotransmitters can influence sleep states, and general relationships exist between the activity of certain neurotransmitters and particular sleep states. Here, we'll discuss the possible roles of serotonin and norepinephrine in sleep.

Serotonin. Research accomplishments since the mid-1960s show that many dimensions of sleep are affected by serotonergic activity (Koella, 1985). Converging evidence supports this view, including the effects on sleep of lesions of serotonin-containing neurons, behavioral effects of chemical enhancement or inhibition of these neurons, and electrical recordings relating sleep behavior to neural activity of brain stem serotonergic nerve cells. To give you the flavor of these manipulations, which have also been applied to other neurotransmitter systems, let's briefly consider examples of each of these types of evidence.

Much of the serotonin innervation of the brain arises from the raphe nuclei (see Figure 14.24). Lesions of these cell bodies lead to a profound drop in concentrations of serotonin in the forebrain. In experimental animals such lesions also produce an immediate, profound drop in the amounts of SWS and REM sleep. Similarly, a neurotoxin, 5,6-dihydroxy-tryptamine, injected into the cerebral ventricles produces a selective impairment of serotonin-containing neurons and a marked drop in the level of SWS and REM sleep. These effects on sleep continue for as long as ten days after a single treatment. The drug parachlorophenylalanine, abbreviated PCPA, blocks the synthesis of serotonin, producing a decrease in transmitter levels and a reduction in sleep, although repeated administration of PCPA becomes progressively less effective in reducing sleep levels. Pharmacological *enhancement* of serotonin activity frequently leads to prolongation of sleep. Serotonin activity can be enhanced by direct injection of the transmitter into the cerebral ventricles or by the use of drugs that enhance serotonin concentrations—for example, by the administration of the precursor tryptophan, as we mentioned earlier in this chapter.

Measurement of brain serotonin levels in awake animals is now possible using a technique called differential pulse **voltametry**—an electrical method of determining biochemical levels. Data obtained with this technique add complexity to the story. Measuring at various brain sites that receive serotonergic nerve endings, investigators showed that levels of serotonin are high in the waking state and become

lower during SWS and REM sleep (Cespuglio et al., 1984). This finding is consistent with neurophysiological observations of raphe nucleus cells, which halt neuronal discharge when SWS begins. How can these data be reconciled with observations such as the effects of PCPA, which blocks synthesis of serotonin and causes insomnia? Jouvet and his collaborators suggest that serotonin plays a role in the synthesis of a sleep-inducing factor that is the direct agent responsible for sleep. Depletion of serotonin precludes the development of this factor. Supporting evidence for this view is that the reversal of PCPA-induced insomnia takes about an hour—the time apparently necessary for the synthesis of the sleep-inducing factor. Serotonin clearly plays a role in *some* aspect of sleep regulation. However, the broad controlling role once attributed to serotonin in neurochemical models of sleep must now be tempered by the recognition that other transmitters also seem to be part of the sleep story (Table 14.2).

Norepinephrine. Given the complexity of the organization of brain stem norepinephrine cell groups and pathways (see Chapter 6), it is not surprising that noradrenergic roles in sleep are also quite complex. One general theme in recent research is that norepinephrine is involved in the control of both waking and REM sleep. An increase in this transmitter accompanies or causes waking behavior. REM sleep appears only when norepinephrine activity decreases, suggesting that norepinephrine normally inhibits REM sleep (Gaillard, 1985).

A particular focus of sleep researchers is the noradrenergic cells in the locus coeruleus (see Figure 14.24). As we saw earlier, selective lesions near this area in cats cause them to retain muscle control even during REM sleep. Such findings are interpreted to mean that noradrenergic neurons of the locus coeruleus are not needed for the initiation or maintenance of REM sleep, but rather control some of the phasic and tonic *accompaniments* of this state. Drug inhibition of norepinephrine synthesis in the brain decreases waking EEG activity in animals, while drugs that enhance noradrenergic activity increase EEG signs of waking activity. Neurotoxins, such as 6-hydroxydopamine, that damage norepinephrine terminals, produce some reduction of waking and REM sleep, although the effect is temporary. The complexity of effects observed with treatments of noradrenergic systems has led to the view that this transmitter system is not part of the executive system controlling sleep, but exerts an important neuromodulatory influence (Monti, 1987).

Table 14.2

Neurotransmitters That Affect Sleep

NEUROTRANSMITTER	CELL BODIES OF ORIGIN	MANIPULATION	EFFECTS ON SLEEP
Serotonin	Raphe nuclei	Increase	Promotes sleep
		Decrease	Reduces sleep
Norepinephrine	Locus coeruleus	Increase	Promotes waking, inhibits REM sleep
		Lesions	Abolish loss of muscle tone in REM sleep
Dopamine	Basal ganglia	Increase	Arousal
		Decrease	Biphasic effects on sleep
Acetylcholine	Basal forebrain	Increase	Induces REM
		Decrease	Suppresses REM

Neurotransmitters and Sleep: An Integration

As the list of transmitters in the brain gets longer (see Table 14.2), so does the bibliography of papers dealing with transmitters and sleep (Gillin et al., 1985; Wauquier, 1985). Earlier efforts to provide a comprehensive neurochemical model of sleep (for example, Jouvet, 1972), although elegant in their simplicity, now fly in the face of a brain that seems much more complicated than was envisaged not long ago. Is there a way to begin to put together the many facts so that they tell a story? Koella (1985) bravely sought to outline a systematic model of the neurochemical character of sleep. He suggested that several transmitters act as vigilance-enhancing agents in different compartments. Such a role especially characterizes the actions of adrenergic, cholinergic, and dopaminergic systems. According to this broad model, vigilance-suppression mechanisms involve serotonin along with several other neurotransmitters, which we did not include in this discussion. Sleep factors are viewed as feedback elements carrying information about the current state of both the body and the brain and affecting the central coordination of the vigilance control system. This model is still portrayed in only general terms; perhaps further refinements will provide a more detailed integration of neurochemical and other psychobiological data.

What Are the Biological Functions of Sleep?

Why do most of us spend one-third of our lifetime asleep? Furthermore, why is sleep divided into two dissimilar states with distinct physiological attributes? The functions of sleep are a subject of great debate; our discussion here emphasizes only the major ideas. Keep in mind that the proposed functions or biological roles of sleep are not mutually exclusive; sleep may play many roles. As with other processes, sleep may have acquired more than one function during evolution. The four functions most often ascribed to sleep are:

1. Sleep conserves energy
2. Sleep helps animals avoid predators
3. Sleep restores our bodies
4. Sleep aids learning

Having already discussed the connections between sleep and learning, we now turn our attention to the other three hypotheses. None of these four proposed functions has yet been proved, and no theory has been proposed to explain why some people who sleep very little show apparently normal intellect and personality.

Energy conservation. We consume less energy when we sleep. For example, SWS is marked by reduced muscular tension, lowered heart rate, reduced blood pressure, and slower respiration. Reduced metabolic processes are also related to the characteristic lowered body temperature of sleep. This diminished metabolic activity during sleep suggests that one role of sleep is to conserve energy. From this perspective sleep enforces the cessation of ongoing activities and thus ensures rest.

The importance of this function can be seen by

looking at the world from the perspective of small animals. Small animals have very high metabolic rates, so activity for them is metabolically expensive. Demand can easily outstrip supply. Periods of reduced activity can be especially valuable if they occur when food is scarce. Some support for the view that sleep conserves energy can be seen in comparative sleep data, which reveal a high correlation between total amount of sleep per day and waking metabolic rate: small animals sleep more than large species (see Chapter 3). The energy savings may not be as great as you think, however, since at least part of sleep is characterized by intense metabolic expenditure, such as the phasic events of REM sleep.

Predator avoidance. Intense evolutionary pressures have generated a variety of tactics for avoiding predators. Diurnal animals are well adapted to survive in the daytime; nocturnal animals are adapted for surviving the night. Meddis (1975) suggests that sleep helps animals stay out of harm's way during the part of the day when each is most vulnerable to predation. In this manner, sleep can enable effective sharing of an ecological niche—survival without becoming a meal. From a similar perspective, Snyder (1969) suggested that REM sleep is a periodic quasi-arousal to make sure the sleep site is still safe.

Body restoration. If someone asked you why you sleep, chances are you would answer that you sleep because you're tired. Indeed, one of the proposed functions of sleep is simply the rebuilding or restoration of materials used during waking, such as proteins (Moruzzi, 1972). Growth hormone release during SWS, which we mentioned earlier, supports a restorative hypothesis. Hartmann (1973) suggests that there are two types of restorative needs that sleep deals with differently—physical tiredness and the tiredness associated with emotional activation.

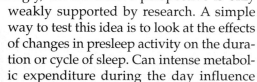 Surprisingly, the restorative perspective is only weakly supported by research. A simple way to test this idea is to look at the effects of changes in presleep activity on the duration or cycle of sleep. Can intense metabolic expenditure during the day influence sleep duration? As we mentioned earlier, for most people exercise may cause them to fall asleep more quickly, but not to sleep longer. On the other hand, prolonged and *total* sleep deprivation, either forced on rats or as a result of inherited pathology in humans, interferes with the immune system and leads to death (Box 14.1). Recall, too, that immune system cytokines promote sleep. The widespread belief that sleep helps us recover from illness (which cannot ethically be tested in humans) is well supported by animal research.

Sleep Disorders

The peace and comfort of regular, uninterrupted sleep each day may occasionally be disturbed by such occurrences as an inability to fall asleep, prolonged sleep, or unusual awakenings. The assessment of sleep is a major focus of sleep disorder clinics, which have become common in major medical centers. The Association for Sleep Disorder Clinics provides a forum for analysis of research needs and accomplishments. Table 14.3 lists the main diagnostic classes of sleep disorders with examples of each (Weitzman, 1981; American Academy of Neurology, 1992).

Among the dysfunctions associated with sleep are the nightmares we mentioned earlier and other events that are more common in children than in adults. **Somnambulism** (sleepwalking) can consist of getting out of bed, walking around the room, and appearing awake. In most children these episodes last from a few seconds to minutes, and the child usually does not remember the experience. Because such episodes occur during stages 3 and 4 SWS, they are more common in the first half of the night (when those stages predominate). The belief that sleepwalkers are acting out a dream is not supported by data (Parkes, 1985). The main problem is the inability of sleepwalkers to awaken into full contact with their surroundings. SWS is also related to two other common sleep disorders in children—night terrors (mentioned earlier) and **sleep enuresis** (bed-wetting). Most people grow out of somnambulism, night terrors, or enuresis without intervention, but pharmacological approaches can be used to reduce the amount of stages 3 and 4 sleep (as well as REM time) while increasing stage 2 sleep. For enuresis some doctors prescribe a nasal spray of the hormone vasopressin before bedtime, which decreases the amount of urine collecting in the bladder.

REM sleep can actually aggravate some health problems. Intense activation of autonomically innervated visceral organs during REM sleep can increase the severity of impairments. Gastric ulcer patients secrete 3 to 20 times more acid during REM episodes than do normal subjects, and many ulcer patients report intense pain that awakens them from sleep. Cardiovascular patients experience similar attacks of illness. Hospital reports show that cardiac patients are most likely to die between the hours of 4:00 and 6:00 A.M., the period of most intense and prolonged REM

Box 14.1
Sleep Deprivation Can Be Fatal

"Sleep that knits up the ravell'd sleave of care"

William Shakespeare, *Macbeth*, Act II, Scene 2.

Although some people seem to need very little sleep, for those of us who need the normal seven to eight hours a night, sleep is crucial. In fact, sustained sleep deprivation in rats causes them to increase their metabolic rate, lose weight, and, within an average of 19 days, die (Everson, Bergmann, and Rechtschaffen, 1989). Allowing them to sleep prevents their death. After the fatal effect of sleep deprivation had been shown, researchers undertook studies in which they terminated the sleep deprivation before the fatal end point and looked for pathological changes in different organ systems. No single organ system seems affected in chronically sleep-deprived animals, but early in the deprivation they develop sores on their bodies. These sores seem to be the beginning of the end; shortly thereafter the rats' plasma reveals infections from a host of bacteria, which probably enter through the sores (Everson, 1993). These bacteria are not normally fatal for rats because their immune system and body defenses keep them in check, but severely sleep-deprived rats fail to develop a fever in response to these infections. In

fact, the animals show a *drop* in body temperature, which probably speeds bacterial infections, which in turn leads to diffuse organ damage. (Recall from Chapter 13 that fever is generated by our bodies to help repel infections.) The decline of these severely sleep-deprived rats is complicated, but if the sequence of events we have described is responsible for their death, then we should ask why the skin develops the sores that permit bacteria to enter. One observation is that the skin of these rats fails to show an inflammatory response to the infections. Inflammation is the local dilation of blood vessels, which enables greater blood flow and thus allows more immune cells to reach and attack an infection. Signs of inflammation include a reddening of the skin, a rise in local temperature, and swelling. We have no idea how sleep deprivation impairs inflammatory response, but such response is crucial for maintaining the integrity of our skin. So perhaps Shakespeare's folk-theory of the function of sleep, quoted above, isn't so far from the truth. This connection between sleep deprivation and lack of an inflammatory response to infection confirms the close relationship between sleep and the immune system that was implied by the somnogenic effect of cytokines described earlier.

But what about those rare humans who sleep only an hour or two a night? Why aren't their immune systems and inflammatory responses compromised? Of course we don't know, but since what distinguishes these people is that they don't *need* much sleep, perhaps their immune and inflammatory systems don't need much sleep either. Or perhaps the small amount of sleep they have almost every night is more efficient at doing whatever sleep does.

Some unfortunate humans inherit a defect in the gene for the prion protein, and although they sleep normally at the beginning of their life, in midlife they simply stop sleeping—with fatal effect. People with this disease, called **fatal familial insomnia**, die 7 to 24 months after the insomnia begins (Medori et al., 1992). Autopsy reveals degeneration of the thalamus; this lesion may be responsible for the insomnia (Manetto et al., 1992). (Recall that electrical stimulation of the thalamus can induce sleep in animals.) As in sleep-deprived rats, the humans seem to die not from the loss of any single organ system, but from diffuse organ damage. While no one is certain, these patients may die *because* they are chronically sleep-deprived. Research with rats certainly supports the idea that prolonged insomnia is fatal.

---

episodes. Kales (1973) found that 32 out of 39 episodes of angina (chest pain caused by artery disease) occurred during REM episodes. Appropriate medical care for some patients might include reducing REM sleep.

Insomniacs Have Trouble Falling Asleep or Staying Asleep

All of us experience an occasional inability to fall asleep, and a very few individuals die apparently because they stop sleeping altogether (see Box 14.1). But

Table 14.3

A Classification of Sleep Disorders

1. **Disorders of initiating and maintaining sleep (insomnia)**

   Ordinary, uncomplicated insomnia
   > Transient
   > Persistent

   Drug-related
   > Use of stimulants
   > Withdrawal of depressants
   > Chronic alcoholism

   Associated with psychiatric disorders

   Associated with sleep-induced respiratory impairment
   > Sleep apnea

2. **Disorders of excessive drowsiness**

   Narcolepsy

   Associated with psychiatric problems

   Associated with psychiatric disorders

   Drug-related

   Associated with sleep-induced respiratory impairment

3. **Disorders of sleep–waking schedule**

   Transient
   > Time zone change by airplane flight (jet lag)
   > Work shift, especially night work

   Persistent
   > Irregular rhythm

4. **Dysfunctions associated with sleep, sleep stages, or partial arousals**

   Sleepwalking (somnambulism)

   Sleep enuresis (bed-wetting)

   Night terror

   Nightmares

   Sleep-related seizures

   Teeth grinding

   Sleep-related activation of cardiac and gastrointestinal symptoms

After Weitzman (1981).

many people persistently find it difficult to fall asleep and/or stay asleep as long as they would like. Estimates of the prevalence of **insomnia** from surveys range from 15% of the adult population of Scotland to one-third of the people in Los Angeles (Parkes, 1985). Insomnia is commonly reported by people who are older, female, or users of drugs like tobacco, coffee, and alcohol. Insomnia seems to be the final common outcome for a number of situational, neurological, psychiatric, and medical conditions. It is not a trivial disorder; adults who regularly sleep for short periods show a higher mortality rate than those who regularly sleep seven to eight hours each night (Wingard and Berkman, 1983).

Sometimes there is a discrepancy between a person's *reported* failure to sleep and EEG indicators of sleep. This discrepancy has been labeled "sleep state misperception" (McCall and Edinger,1992). Such insomniacs report that they did not sleep when actually they showed EEG signs of sleep and failed to respond to stimuli during the EEG-defined sleep state. Other insomniacs show less REM sleep and more stage 2 sleep than normal sleepers. No differences are evident in the amounts of stages 3 and 4 sleep.

Situational factors that contribute to insomnia include shift work, time zone changes, and environmental conditions such as "novelty" (that hard motel bed). Usually these conditions produce transient **sleep-onset insomnia**—a difficulty in falling asleep. Drugs and neurological and psychiatric factors seem especially relevant to **sleep-maintenance insomnia**, which is a difficulty in remaining asleep. This type of sleep is punctuated by frequent nighttime arousals. This form of insomnia is especially evident in disorders of the respiratory system.

During sleep, respiration becomes unreliable in some people. In these cases respiration can cease or slow to dangerous levels; blood levels of oxygen show a marked drop. This syndrome, called **sleep apnea**, arises from either the progressive relaxation of muscles of the chest, diaphragm, and throat cavity or changes in the pacemaker respiratory neurons of the brain stem. In the former instance, relaxation of the throat obstructs the airway—a kind of self-choking. This mode of sleep apnea is common in very obese people who sleep lying on their back. Each episode of apnea arouses the person enough to restore breathing, but the frequent nighttime arousals mean they are sleepy in the daytime. Insertion of a removable tube in the throat can restore a normal sleep pattern and eliminate excess daytime sleepiness. For others, breathing through a special machine maintains air pressure in their airways and prevents the collapse. Investigators have speculated that **sudden infant death syndrome** (crib death) arises from sleep apnea as a result of a reduction in the brain stem neural activity that normally paces respiration. Continuous monitoring of the sleep of infants at risk for crib death can save the lives of some children.

Narcoleptics Are Always Sleepy

Although some of us might find it difficult to consider excessive sleeping an affliction, many people are either drowsy all the time or suffer sudden attacks of sleep. In these cases sleep is not viewed as welcome rest but rather as an encumbrance that endangers and compromises the quality of life.

One of the largest groups of patients found at sleep disorder clinics consists of people who suffer from narcolepsy. **Narcolepsy** is an unusual disorder that involves frequent, intense attacks of sleep, which last from 5 to 30 minutes and can occur at any time during the usual waking hours. Uncontrollable attacks of sleep occur several times a day—usually about every 90 minutes (Dantz, Edgar, and Dement, 1994). Narcoleptics feel drowsy all the time. Individuals with this sleep disorder are distinguished from others by the appearance of REM sleep at the onset of sleep. In fact, the duration of a narcoleptic attack is similar to the usual period of an REM sleep episode. At night, however, narcoleptics exhibit a relatively normal sleep pattern. Some investigators consider this disorder to be the result of a brain stem dysfunction that involves the failure of a waking mechanism to suppress the brain stem centers controlling REM sleep.

Many narcoleptics also show **cataplexy**, a sudden loss of muscle tone, leading to collapse of the body without loss of consciousness. These episodes, like narcoleptic attacks, are triggered by sudden, intense emotional stimuli, including both laughter and anger. At sleep onset, some narcoleptics report **sleep paralysis**, which includes the (temporary) inability to move or talk; in this state they may experience sudden sensory hallucinations. This disorder usually manifests itself between 15 and 25 years of age and continues throughout life. No structural changes in the brain have been connected to narcolepsy. Several studies have shown a familial factor; one human narcolepsy-susceptibility gene has been identified and is an immune-related gene (Mignot et al., 1993). An inherited form of narcolepsy has also been found in dogs.

Several strains of dogs have been shown to exhibit the properties of narcolepsy (Aldrich, 1993). These animals show sudden motor inhibition (cataplexy) and very short latencies to sleep onset (Figure 14.25). Many instances of sleep-onset REM episodes are evident, just as in human narcoleptics. Cataplexy in these animals is suppressed by the same drugs that are used to treat human cataplexy. These narcoleptic dogs have abnormally high acetylcholine receptor levels in the pons (Aldrich et al., 1993). More-

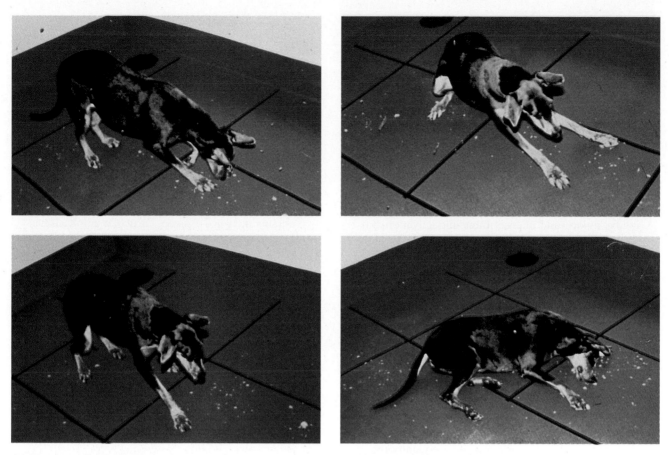

14.25 Narcolepsy in Dogs
A narcoleptic dog that suffers cataplexy when excited is offered a food treat
(*top left*), becomes drowsy (*bottom left*), lies down (*top right*), and finally falls
asleep (*bottom right*). Courtesy of Seiji Nishino.

over, inducing cataplexy in these animals (by offering very desirable food) causes an increase in the release of acetylcholine in the pontine reticular formation (Reid et al., 1994). The mutant gene at work in
one of these strains has been named *canarc,* and as
with the human gene for narcolepsy, the *canarc* gene

seems to be a part of the immune system
(Mignot et al., 1991). How an alteration of
the immune system could lead to narcolepsy remains a mystery, but a relationship between the immune system and
sleep is not a new concept.

Summary

Biological Rhythms

1. Many living systems show circadian rhythms that can
   be entrained by environmental stimuli, especially
   light. These rhythms synchronize behavior and bodily states to changes in the environment.

2. Neural pacemakers in the suprachiasmatic nucleus
   (SCN) of the hypothalamus are the basis of many (but

not all) circadian rhythms. The basis of light entrainment in many cases is a pathway from the retina to
the SCN.

3. Rhythms shorter than 24 hours—ultradian rhythms—
   are evident in both behavior and biological processes.
   The underlying mechanism does not involve clocks in
   the SCN.

Sleep and Waking

1. During sleep almost all mammals alternate between two main states, slow-wave sleep (SWS) and rapid-eye-movement (REM) sleep.

2. Human SWS shows several stages defined by EEG criteria that include bursts of spindles and persistent trains of large, slow waves. During SWS, there is a progressive decline in muscle tension, heart rate, respiratory rate, and temperature.

3. REM sleep is characterized by a rapid EEG of low amplitude—almost like the EEG during active waking behavior—and intense autonomic activation, but the postural muscles are profoundly relaxed.

4. In adult humans SWS and REM sleep alternate every 90 to 110 minutes. Smaller animals have shorter sleep cycles and spend more time asleep.

5. The characteristics of sleep–waking cycles change during the course of life. Mature animals sleep less than the young, and REM sleep accounts for a smaller fraction of their sleep.

6. The prominence of REM sleep in infants suggests that REM sleep contributes to development of the brain and to learning.

7. Mental activity does not cease during sleep. Vivid perceptual experiences (dreams) are frequently reported by subjects awakened from REM sleep; reports of ideas or thinking are often given by subjects awakened from SWS.

8. Formation of memory is impaired when sleep deprivation—particularly REM sleep deprivation—follows learning sessions, so sleep may aid consolidation of memory. Little or no learning, however, can take place during sleep.

9. Deprivation of sleep for a few nights in a row leads to impairment in tasks that require sustained vigilance. During recovery nights following deprivation, the lost SWS and REM sleep are partially restored over several nights.

10. Many drugs used to induce sleep inhibit REM sleep during the first few nights. When the drug is withdrawn, there is a rebound increase of REM sleep on the following nights. No pill repeatedly provides a normal night's sleep.

11. Many brain structures are involved in the initiation and maintenance of sleep. Particular emphasis has been placed on brain stem structures, including the reticular formation, the raphe nucleus, and the locus coeruleus. The synaptic transmitters serotonin, acetylcholine, and norepinephrine are prominent in these structures and are involved in the control of sleep. In addition, other transmitters play a modulating role.

12. Researchers have suggested several biological roles for sleep, including conservation of energy, avoidance of predators, restoration of depleted resources, and consolidation of memory.

13. The immune system interacts with sleep in several ways. Cytokines released from the immune system (to marshal immune cell attacks on bacteria and viruses) also promote sleep. This sleep probably helps combat infections, since prolonged insomnia fatally compromises the ability to combat infection.

14. Sleep disorders fall into three major categories: (1) disorders of initiation and maintenance of sleep (for example, insomnia); (2) disorders of excessive drowsiness (for example, narcolepsy); and (3) disorders of the sleep–waking schedule.

Recommended Reading

Carskadon, M. A. (ed.) 1993. *Encyclopedia of Sleep and Dreaming*. Macmillan, New York.

Cooper, R. (ed.) 1994. *Sleep*. Chapman & Hall Medical, New York.

Kryger, M. H., Roth, T. and Dement, W. C. (eds.) 1989. *Principles and Practice of Sleep Medicine*. W. B. Saunders, New York.

Takahashi, J. S. 1995. Molecular neurobiology and genetics of circadian rhythms in mammals. *Annual Review of Neuroscience*, 18:531–554.

Thorpy, M. J. and Yager, J. (eds.) 1991. *The Encyclopedia of Sleep and Sleep Disorders*. Facts on File, New York.

PART 5

Emotions and Mental Disorders

So far in this text we have discussed a wide variety of behaviors which individuals display under particular circumstances, and in each case the behaviors seem adaptive to those circumstances. We detect stimuli that surround us, drink when body fluids are low, eat when energy supplies are depleted, sleep at night when moving about may be dangerous. It is a little more difficult to understand why we are sometimes angry, terrified, or joyful, but these emotions are clearly an important part of our lives. Chapter 15 takes up research that attempts to explain how emotions are generated and why they are indeed adaptive, even if we sometimes resent experiencing them. Other behaviors are clearly not adaptive, and in these cases we refer to them as disorders. It will not help us to survive or reproduce if we hear voices that are not present, are driven to suicide by depression, or persistently relive dreadful memories. Chapter 16 deals with the origin of these and other disorders and the modest means so far available to combat them.

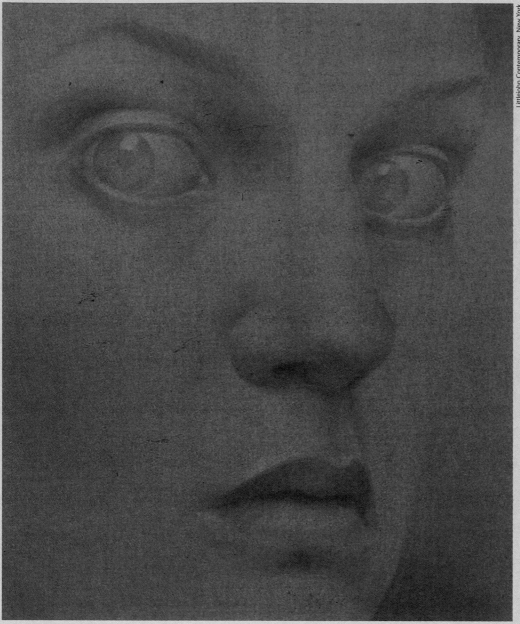

Diane Kepford, *Self Portrait #2*, 1987

CHAPTER Psychobiology of Emotions

15

Orientation

The sound of unexpected footsteps in the eerie quiet of the night brings fear for many of us. But the sound of music we enjoy and the voice of someone we love summons feelings of warmth. For some of us, feelings and emotions can become vastly exaggerated; fears can become paralyzing attacks of anxiety and panic. No story about our behavior is complete without consideration of the many events in a single day that involve feelings.

The psychobiological study of emotions has progressed in several directions. One traditional area focuses on bodily responses during emotional states, especially changes in facial expression, and visceral responses such as changes in heart rate. Another focus of research on emotion is maladaptive activation related to stress, such as that which accompanies some health impairments. The study of brain mechanisms related to emotional states has especially emphasized aggression, both because it is important for human existence and because its lack of subtlety makes it relatively easy to examine experimentally in nonhumans. Emotions are closely identified with many aspects of mental disorders, since marked emotional changes are among the more striking characteristics of many of these conditions. We explore the connections between emotions and mental disorders in Chapter 16.

What Are Emotions?

The complicated world of emotions includes a wide range of observable behaviors, expressed feelings, and changes in body state. This diversity—that is, the many meanings of the word "emotion"—has made the subject hard to study. For many of us emotions are very personal states, difficult to define or identify except in the most obvious instances. Moreover, many aspects of emotion seem unconscious to us. Even simple emotional states seem much more complicated than states such as hunger and thirst. Even more puzzling are emotions in nonhuman animals. Is the hissing cat frightened, angry, or perhaps enjoying the experience of tormenting another cat or its solicitous but apprehensive owner?

There Are Three Different Aspects of Emotions

At least three aspects of emotion are evident in the psychobiological research literature:

1. Emotion is a *feeling* that is private and subjective. Humans can report an extraordinary range of states, which they say they "feel" or experience. Some such reports are accompanied by obvious signs of enjoyment or distress, but frequently these reports of subjective experience have no overt indicators. In many cases, the emotions we note in ourselves seem to be blends of different states.

2. Emotion is a state of *physiological arousal*—an expression or display of distinctive somatic and autonomic responses. This emphasis suggests that emotional states can be defined by particular constellations of bodily responses. Specifically, these responses involve autonomically innervated visceral organs, such as the heart, stomach, and intestines. Presumably these responses are provoked by distinctive emotional stimuli. This second aspect of emotion allows us to examine emotion in nonhuman animals as well as in human beings.

3. Emotions are *actions* commonly deemed "emotional," such as defending or attacking in response to a threat. This aspect of emotion is especially relevant to Darwin's view of the functional roles of emotion. He suggested that emotions had an important survival role because they aided in generating appropriate reactions to "emergency" events in the environment, such as the sudden appearance of a predator. The "psychoevolutionary theory of emotions," advanced by Plutchik (1994), argues that emotions increase individual survival by eliciting reactions to emergency events in the environment (such as flight produced by fear) or by signaling the intention of future actions (as evident in facial displays and body gestures). According to Plutchik, emotions have a genetic basis and can be thought of as a chain of events that move an individual to a state of behavioral homeostasis. The chain of events that defines fear (Figure 15.1) illustrates this aspect of emotion.

To these three aspects of emotion—subjective feeling, physiological arousal, and behavioral expression—some researchers add two others: motivational state and mode of cognitive processing (Scherer, 1993).

Psychologists Have Defined Different Categories of Emotion

An ongoing discussion about the study of human emotions focuses on whether a basic core set of emotions underlies the more varied and delicate nuances of our world of feelings. From a biological perspective, one reason for interest in this question is the possibility that distinctly separate brain systems are related to parts of this core set. The question has not suffered from a lack of debate. Wilhelm Wundt, the great nineteenth-century psychologist, offered the view that emotion consists of three basic dimensions, each one a pair of opposing states: pleasantness/unpleasantness, tension/release, and excitement/relaxation. This listing has become more complex over time. Plutchik suggests that there are eight basic emotions grouped in four pairs of opposites: (1) joy/sadness, (2) acceptance/disgust, (3) anger/fear, and (4) surprise/anticipation. In Plutchik's view all other emotions are derived from combinations of this basic array, which he believes is quite similar across all human societies. According to this view, the different intensities of core emotions and their combinations contribute to emotional diversity. This hypothesis can be represented by a three-dimensional cone with the vertical dimension reflecting emotional intensity (Figure 15.2). The number of emotions and how discrete they are remain active topics of psychological theorizing.

Classical Theories of Emotion Emphasize Bodily Responses

In many emotional states, we can sense our heart beating fast, our hands and face feeling warm, our palms sweating, and a queasy feeling in our stomach. Several theories have tried to explain the especially close tie between the subjective psychological phe-

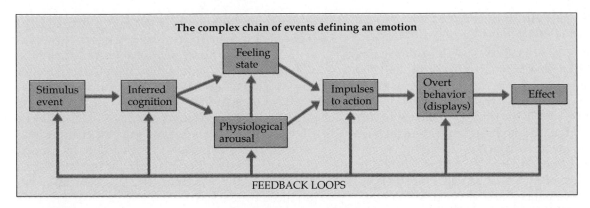

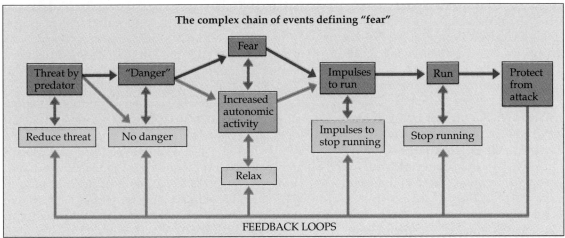

15.1 The Chain of Events That Defines an Emotion
The top panel illustrates the chain of events for emotions in general; the bottom panel specifies these events in terms of a particular emotion: fear. After Plutchik, 1994.

nomena we know as emotions and the activity of visceral organs controlled by the autonomic nervous system. These theories ask whether we can experience emotions *without* the activity of visceral organs.

Among the many theories of emotion, some focus on peripheral bodily events, some focus on central brain processes, and some seek to integrate both kinds of events. In this section we will discuss prominent examples of these respective theories—the James–Lange theory, the Cannon–Bard theory, and Schachter's cognitive theory. Later in this chapter we will focus on brain theories of emotion.

15.2 The Dimensions of Emotion
This representation of emotion in a three-dimensional model suggests there are eight primary emotions with at least three discernible levels of intensity.

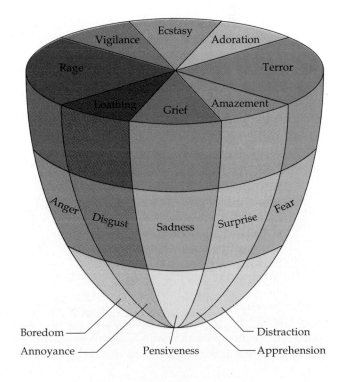

William James and Carl Lange Regarded Emotions as the Perception of Bodily Changes

Strong emotions are virtually inseparable from activation of the skeletal muscle and/or autonomic nervous systems. Common expressions capture this association: "trembling with rage," "with all my heart," "hair standing on end," "a sinking feeling in the stomach." William James, the leading figure in American psychology around the turn of the twentieth century, suggested that emotions are the perceptions of bodily changes provoked by particular stimuli. From this perspective fear is evident because particular stimuli produce changes in bodily activity, and these changes constitute an emotion. About the same time that James was developing his theories of emotion, a Danish physician, Carl Lange, proposed a similar view, which he boldly stated as follows: "We owe all the emotional side of our mental life, our joys and sorrows, our happy and unhappy hours, to our vasomotor system. If the impressions which fall upon our senses did not possess the power of stimulating it, we would wander through life, unsympathetic and passionless, all impressions of the outer world would only enrich our experience, increase our knowledge, but would give us neither care nor fear" (Lange, 1887).

The James–Lange theory thus emphasizes peripheral physiological events in emotion. The theory initiated many studies that attempted to link emotions to bodily responses, a focus of lasting interest in the field. Questions such as "What are the responses of the heart in love, anger, fear?" continue to form a prominent part of the biological study of emotions. Although the James–Lange theory initiated this research, however, it has not survived critical assessment.

The Cannon–Bard Theory Emphasizes Central Processes

If body states are emotions, then provoking changes in the body by experimental treatments such as surgical procedures or drugs should change emotional responses. In addition, different emotions should be characterized by different bodily responses. The simplicity of the James–Lange theory presented ready opportunity for experimental assessment. Physiologists Walter Cannon and Philip Bard studied relations between the autonomic nervous system and emotion and offered strong criticism of the James–Lange theory.

Humans with a spinal injury that prevents sensation from most of the body are ideal subjects on whom to study the role of visceral changes in emotion. Unfortunately, the few studies that have been reported have inconsistent results. One investigator reported that paraplegics do not have a reduced level of emotions following spinal injury (McKilligott, 1959, cited in Van Toller, 1979). Another researcher studying the same patients, however, concluded that although patients with high spinal injuries have not lost emotions, they do report a reduction in the intensity of their feelings (Hohman, 1966). Cannon argued that visceral changes may be similar in different emotions and that some visceral changes may have very different emotional consequences, depending on the context. For example, the tearfulness produced by sadness is markedly different from that produced by tear gas.

Cannon's theory stressed the cerebral integration of emotional experience and emotional response. Noting that emotional states involve a considerable expenditure of energy, Cannon (1929) emphasized that some emotions are an emergency response of an organism to a sudden threatening condition. According to Cannon, the response produces maximal activation of the sympathetic component of the autonomic nervous system. Thus, emotions produce bodily changes, such as increased heart rate, glucose mobilization, and other effects mediated by the sympathetic division of the autonomic nervous system. The viscera are activated by the sympathetic system, according to this theory, because emotional stimuli excite the cerebral cortex, which in turn releases thalamic control mechanisms from inhibition. Activation of the thalamus produces further cortical excitation, resulting in emotional experiences and autonomic nervous system activity. Cannon's theory provoked many studies of the effects of brain lesions and electrical stimulation on emotion.

Stanley Schachter Proposed That Cognitive States Are Important in Interpreting Stimuli and Visceral States

We have noted in our criticism of the James–Lange theory that activation of a physiological system by itself is not sufficient to provoke an emotion. For example, tears produced by a noxious gas do not ordinarily provoke sadness. Schacter (1975) suggests that individuals interpret visceral activation in terms of the eliciting stimuli, the surrounding situations, and their cognitive states. An emotion is thus not relentlessly driven by physiological activation—especially that controlled by the sympathetic nervous system. Rather, bodily states are *interpreted* in the context of cognitions and are molded by experience. According to Schachter, emotional labels—anger, fear, joy—depend on the interpretations of a situation, interpretations that are controlled by internal cognitive systems. Thus, an emotional state is the result of an interaction between physiological activation and cognitive interpretation of physiological arousal. According to this view, emotion depends not only on the interaction of arousal and cognitive appraisal but also on the perception that a causal connection exists between physiological arousal and emotional cognition (Reisenzein, 1983).

Schachter's theory has not been without its critics (Reisenzein, 1983; Leventhal and Tomarken, 1986). For example, the theory asserts that physiological arousal is "nonspecific," affecting only the intensity of a perceived emotion but not its quality, yet recent data suggest that each different emotion exhibits a specific pattern of autonomic arousal (Cacioppo et al., 1993). When subjects were asked to pose facial expressions distinctive for particular emotions, autonomic patterns of the subjects were different for several emotions, such as fear and sadness (Levenson, Ekman, and Friesen, 1993). Another criticism is that reducing or blocking the physiological arousal may not affect emotion. Studies that support this idea use agents that block adrenergic beta receptors and thus reduce physiological arousal, such as the level of blood pressure or heart rate. These agents do *not* appear to reduce emotion in healthy individuals (Reisenzein, 1983). Many other predictions from Schachter's theory have failed to be substantiated (Leventhal and Tomarken, 1986). The few positive data, such as those cited at the beginning of this section, may be limited to novel contexts that elicit low to moderate autonomic arousal. Overall, peripheral feedback seems to have little impact on emotion.

The theories we have just discussed focus on relations between bodily events and emotion in healthy people. Other types of theoretical views originate from observations of changes in emotional expression and responsiveness that result from brain injury or disease.

Facial Expressions Reveal Emotional States

Our bodies reveal emotions in many ways. Overt expressions of emotion are evident in posture, gesture, and facial expression; all these dimensions are well cultivated by actors and actresses. The human face, which is hard to hide from view, is a ready source of information. Its elaborate and finely controlled musculature provides for an enormous range of expressions, thus enhancing the prospect for communication. In this section we discuss the variety of facial expressions and their neural control.

Facial Expressions Have Complex Functions in Communication

In his book *The Expression of the Emotions in Man and Animals* (1872), Charles Darwin catalogued the facial expressions of humans and other animals and emphasized the universal nature of these expressions. He noted especially that facial expressions are connected to distinctive emotional states both in humans and in nonhuman primates. In part he viewed facial expressions as information communicated to other animals.

Paul Ekman has provided rich insight into the properties of facial expressions. He and his collaborators have developed an array of analytic tools that enable objective description and measurement of facial expressions among humans of different cultures (Ekman, 1981, 1983). Analyses of facial expressions reveal that both static features of the face, such as the structure of facial bones, and rapidly changing features of the face produced by facial muscles provide information.

How many different emotions can be detected in facial expressions? According to Ekman (1973), there are distinctive expressions for anger, happiness, sadness, disgust, fear, contempt, and surprise (Figure 15.3). Facial expressions of these seven emotions are interpreted similarly across many cultures. No explicit training is needed to interpret the expressions in any of these cultures. Cross-cultural similarity is also noted in the *production* of expressions specific to particular emotions. For example, people in a preliterate New Guinea society, when posing particular emotions, show facial expressions like those of advanced societies. This "universality" hypothesis of facial expression has come under strong criticism. Fridlund (1994) suggests that universal expressions do not account for the full complement of human facial expressions. Cultural differences may emerge in culture-specific display rules, which stipulate social contexts for facial expression. Some anthropologists have suggested that cultures that prescribe rules for facial expression and control and enforce those rules by cultural conditioning might mask the universal property of facial expressions. A model of this process is presented in Figure 15.4; the stimuli for expression may differ among cultures.

Early on, infants show facial expressions that resemble particular adult expressions. For example, newborn humans show smiles during periods of REM sleep. By three to four months of age, infants show differential responses to various facial expressions of adults (Figure 15.5). Much research indicates that by the ages of four to five years, children have acquired full knowledge of the appearance and meaning of many common facial expressions.

Anger Sadness Happiness Fear

Disgust Surprise Contempt

15.3 Universal Facial Expressions of Emotion.
According to Paul Ekman and colleagues, the seven basic emotional facial
expressions shown here are displayed in all cultures. Courtesy of David
Matsumoto.

Facial expression in nonhuman primates permits
the study of cross-species emotional displays. Redican
(1982) described distinctive primate expressions labeled as (1) grimace, perhaps analogous to human expressions of fear or surprise; (2) tense mouth, akin to
human expressions of anger; and (3) play face, similar

in form to the human smile. In nonprimates the range
of facial expressions is more limited since the muscles
of the face resemble a continuous sheet of poorly differentiated muscles.

Facial displays are usually regarded as expressions or indicators of emotion; each primary emotion

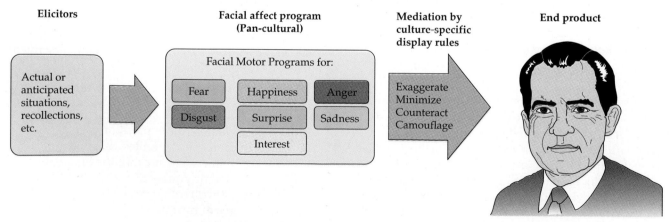

Elicitors

Actual or
anticipated
situations,
recollections,
etc.

Facial affect program
(Pan-cultural)

Facial Motor Programs for:

Fear Happiness Anger

Disgust Surprise Sadness

Interest

Mediation by
culture-specific
display rules

Exaggerate
Minimize
Counteract
Camouflage

End product

15.4 Model for Emotional Facial Expressions across Cultures

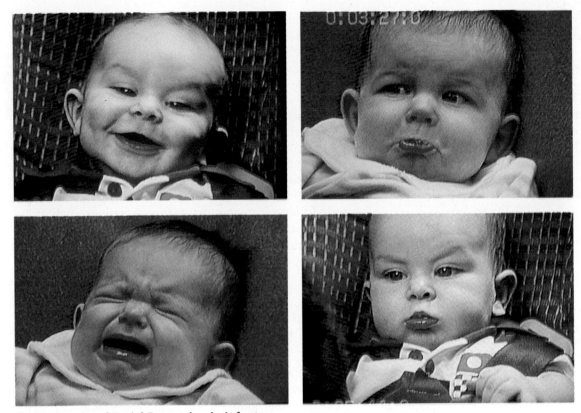

15.5 Emotional Facial Expression in Infants
The early appearance of facial expressions such as smiling, pouting, interest, and crying (*clockwise from top left*) suggests that they are not learned from parents or others. From Oster and Rosenstein, *Baby FACS Coding Manual*.

is said to be connected to a pattern of facial muscle activation. However, Fridlund (1994) notes several studies that suggest that faces do not portray emotions per se; rather, they occur in a social context with distinct social motives. According to Fridlund, a major role of facial expression is "paralinguistic"; that is, the face is accessory to verbal communication, perhaps providing emphasis and direction in conversation. Fridlund also notes the display func-tion of facial expressions. For example, Gilbert et al. (1986) showed that subjects display few facial responses to odor when smelling alone but significantly more in a social setting. In support of the social-display role of facial expression, Kraut and Johnston (1979) noted that bowlers seldom smile when making a strike but smile frequently when they turn around to meet the faces of others watching them. Clearly the face is a final common pathway for many different functions.

Facial Expressions Are Mediated by a Set of Muscles, Two Cranial Nerves, and Varied CNS Pathways

How are facial expressions produced? Within the face is an elaborate network of finely innervated muscles whose functional roles in addition to facial expression include production of speech, eating, and respiration, among others. Facial muscles can be divided into two categories: (1) Superficial muscles attach to facial skin (Figure 15.6). They act as sphincters, changing the shape of the mouth, eyes, or nose, for example, or they pull on their attachment to the skin. One superficial facial muscle, the frontalis muscle, wrinkles the forehead and raises the eyebrow. (2) Deep facial muscles attach to skeletal structures of the head. These muscles enable movements such as chewing. An example of a deep muscle is the masseter, a powerful jaw muscle.

Human facial muscles are innervated by two cranial nerves: (1) the facial nerve, which innervates the superficial muscles of facial expression; and (2) the trigeminal nerve, which innervates muscles that move the jaw. Studies of the facial nerve reveal that the right and left sides are completely independent. As Figure 15.6 shows, the main trunk of the facial nerve divides into an upper and lower division shortly after entering the face. These nerve fibers originate in the brain stem in a region called the nucleus of the facial nerve. Distinct subgroups of neurons within this nucleus form specific branches of the facial nerve, which in turn connect to distinct segments of the face. Within the facial nerve nucleus, cells that control the muscles of the lower face are clearly separated from those that control the muscles of the upper face.

Brain pathways that control facial expression are complex. Both direct and indirect inputs from the cerebral cortex activate the cells of the facial nucleus. The face is represented extensively in the human motor cortex (see Figure 11.14). The cerebral cortex innervates the facial nucleus both bilaterally and unilaterally: the lower half of the face receives input from the opposite side of the cortex; the upper half receives input from both sides. This pattern of innervation is evident in our ability to produce one-sided movements of the lips (the unilateral movement of an eyebrow is a more exotic talent shared by few).

Some investigators suggest that the brain control of voluntary facial movements is very different from

that of facial movements induced by emotion (Rinn, 1984). Whereas voluntary activation of the facial nerve nucleus is achieved through the corticospinal system, emotional activation of the face is presumed to involve subcortical systems. Support for this view comes from studies of patients who have sustained unilateral damage to the motor cortex. Such patients are unable to retract the corner of the mouth opposite to the damaged hemisphere when asked to do so, but both corners retract during a period of spontaneous, happy laughter or amusement. The reverse syndrome follows damage to subcortical regions such as the basal ganglia, as in Parkinson's disease. Such patients are able to move the facial muscles voluntarily but lose spontaneous emotional expression of the face.

Autonomic Responses Are Elicited by Emotion-Provoking Stimuli

Although the changing expressions of the face are easy to see, the detection of visceral changes requires electronic gadgets. A subject who is connected to devices that measure heart rate, blood pressure, stomach contractions, dilation or constriction of blood ves-

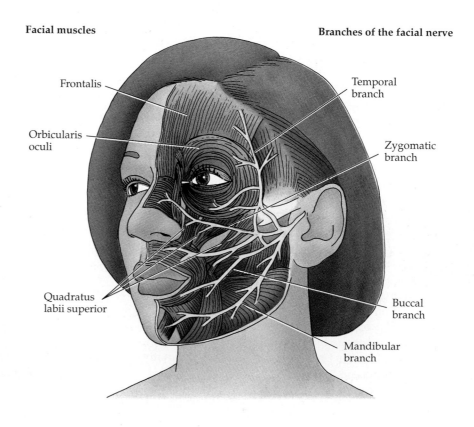

Facial muscles

Frontalis

Orbicularis oculi

Quadratus labii superior

Branches of the facial nerve

Temporal branch

Zygomatic branch

Buccal branch

Mandibular branch

15.6 Facial Muscles and Their Neural Control

sels, skin resistance, or sweating of the palms or soles exhibits many changes in response to emotional states. Devices that measure several of these bodily responses are called **polygraphs**, popularly known as "lie detectors." The use of polygraphs to detect lying in individuals accused of crimes is controversial, with most psychophysiologists arguing against such use (Cacioppo et al., 1993).

Does the pattern of bodily response indicate the kind of emotion being experienced? This question, arising from the James–Lange theory, continues to intrigue investigators. Experimental studies explore whether people show patterns of reactions that are specific to particular events or stimuli. For example, if we recorded heart activity, stomach contractions, skin temperature, respiration, and blood pressure during states of anger and fear, we would expect to see profiles distinctive for each state. Ax (1953) reported an oft-quoted experiment that shows such specificity in response to anger- and fear-provoking stimuli. In this study, wires connected to the subjects recorded several physiological measures. A collaborator in the experiment provoked anger by insulting the subjects and fear by acting worrisome and incompetent in the presence of sparks deliberately contrived to elicit fear of electrocution. However hesitant one might now be about this kind of subject manipulation, it produced potent emotional states. Several differences in physiological patterns were observed, including greater increases in pulse rate and blood pressure in fear than in anger. After reviewing a large array of data from studies of the last 30 years, Cacioppo and colleagues (1993) concluded that the evidence on autonomic differentiation of emotions remains inconclusive. Distinct emotional stimuli do not invariably elicit a distinct pattern of autonomic responses. Some autonomic responses, such as changes in heart rate, provide better autonomic differentiation of emotions than others.

Individuals Show Their Own Patterns of Autonomic Responses

Responses of various bodily systems reveal distinct patterns that are characteristic of the individual. Lacey and Lacey (1970) refer to this characteristic as **individual response stereotypy**. Their work involved longitudinal (extending over many years) studies of people, from early childhood to adulthood. The stimuli they used to provoke autonomic responses included stress conditions such as immersion of the hand in ice-cold water, performance of rapidly paced arithmetic calculations, and exposure to intense stimuli on the skin. Across these conditions the investigators observed an individual profile of response that is

evident even in newborns. For example, some newborns respond vigorously with heart-rate changes, others with gastric contractions, still others with blood pressure responses. Response patterns are remarkably consistent throughout life. This observation may provide the basis for understanding why the same intense stress might cause pathology of different organs in different individuals. Constitutional factors appear to lead some of us to develop ulcers and others to develop high blood pressure in similar emotion-provoking situations. The concept of individual response stereotypy is therefore of considerable significance in the field of psychosomatic medicine, which we will explore later in this chapter.

Endocrine Changes Accompany Emotions

Humoral theories of emotion—those related to internal bodily secretions—have a long history and have involved many body organs, including liver, spleen, and endocrine glands. This relationship is reflected in words used to express emotion, such as "bilious" (derived from "bile"), meaning irritable, cranky, or unpleasant, and "phlegmatic" (from "phlegm"), meaning apathetic or sluggish (see Figure 7.2). Current research explores the relations between hormones and emotions using the following techniques:

1. Observing changes of hormone levels in the blood during experimentally or naturally produced emotional states. The technology of biochemical measurement of hormones has become quite precise and can detect minute changes.

2. Observing changes in emotional states after administering hormones or after a period of hormone deficiencies produced by endocrine disease. In the former case, a frequent area of study has been mood changes produced by hormone treatments (generally from birth control pills) in women.

Endocrine changes accompanying emotional experiences have generally been measured in terms of the levels of (1) epinephrine, released by the adrenal *medulla* and reflecting sympathetic activation of this gland; and (2) 17-hydroxycorticosteroids in blood or urine, which reflect the activities of the pituitary–adrenal *cortical* systems. Clearly, emotional stimuli or situations are accompanied by hormone secretions. Urinary and blood levels of epinephrine or norepinephrine are elevated both prior to and during stressful and energetic activities such as professional sports encounters, military maneuvers, and many other anxiety-provoking situations. Studies by Elmadjian and collaborators (Elmadjian, Hope, and Lamson, 1957) show that norepinephrine levels might be related to the *intensity* of the emotional encounter. Data from these experiments reveal elevated norepinephrine levels for individuals who react to an interview situation with intense emotional responses, including aggression, in contrast with those who respond more passively. However, norepinephrine levels may not distinguish the *type* of emotional display, since Levi (1965) has found similar norepinephrine increases in women presented with film material that elicits pleasant or unpleasant responses. Adrenocortical responses also do not seem to differentiate the type of emotion. Films that were either erotic or suspenseful both produced elevated cortisol levels in blood (Brown and Heninger, 1975).

Various measures of fear and avoidance behavior of nonhuman primates and other animals have been investigated. Figure 15.7 shows a series of measures obtained in monkeys (Mason, 1972). These animals engaged in an extended period of avoidance behavior in which they pressed a lever to avoid shock. The only cue controlling this behavior was time; responses had to be presented at a particular rate (for example, once per minute) to avoid shock. Hormones that showed an increase during these avoidance periods include epinephrine, 17-hydroxycorticosteroids, thyroid secretions, and growth hormone; insulin and testosterone levels decreased.

Diminished hormone output produced by disease also influences emotional responses. Decreased thyroid output is frequently associated with depression. Depression is also associated with Addison's disease, an adrenal gland disorder that is accompanied by decreased glucocorticoid secretions. Hormonal relationships to affective disorders are discussed in Chapter 16.

Distinct Brain Circuits Mediate or Control Emotions

Are particular neural circuits for emotions localized in particular regions of the brain? This question has been explored in studies involving either localized brain lesions or electrical stimulation. Neuropharmacological studies have tried to determine the role of specific transmitters in particular emotions. Brain lesion studies, involving clinical observations in humans or experimentally produced lesions in nonhu-

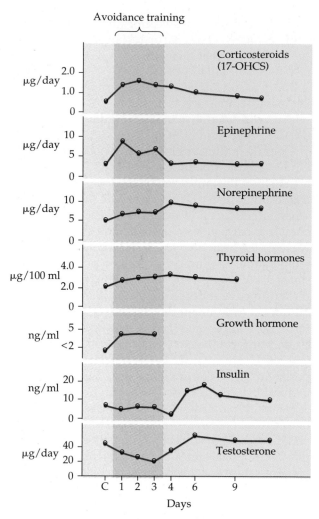

15.7   Hormonal Responses to Stress in a Monkey
These graphs show hormone levels before, during, and after a three-day period of avoidance training. Note that after the stressful task is over, some stress-induced hormone effects, such as increased norepinephrine and insulin levels, persist. After Mason, 1972.

man animals, have focused on some dramatic syndromes of emotional change, such as the taming of monkeys following lesions of the temporal lobe. Brain stimulation studies have generated brain maps for various emotional responses, especially those involving aggression. In this section we will look at both types of studies and their results.

Brain Lesions Affect Emotions

Many studies have explored the brain mechanisms of emotion by investigating how the destruction of brain regions affects behavior. These studies include both clinical investigations of injured humans and surgical experiments with animal subjects.

Decorticate rage. Surgical removal of the neocortex provided the oldest experimental demonstration of brain mechanisms and emotion. Early in the twentieth century, decorticate dogs were shown to respond to routine handling with sudden intense rage—sometimes referred to as "sham rage" because it lacked well-directed attack. Snarling, barking, and growling were provoked by ordinary handling, and this behavior included strong visceral responses. Clearly, emotional behaviors of this type are organized at a subcortical level. These observations suggested that the cerebral cortex helps inhibit emotional responsiveness.

The Klüver–Bucy syndrome. Studies of brain mechanisms and emotion were advanced by the work of Klüver and Bucy (1938), who described a most unusual syndrome in primates following temporal lobe surgery. During studies on the cortical mechanisms of perception, these investigators removed large portions of the temporal lobe of monkeys. The behavior of these animals changed dramatically after surgery; the highlight was an extraordinary taming effect. Animals that had been wild and fearful of humans prior to surgery became tame and showed neither fear nor aggression. In addition, they showed strong oral tendencies, ingesting a variety of objects, including some that were inedible. Frequent mounting behavior was observed and was described as hypersexuality. Because lesions restricted to the cerebral neocortex did not produce these results, deeper regions of the temporal lobe, including sites within the limbic system, were implicated. This syndrome has also been observed in humans

following a variety of disorders that damage the temporal lobes, including degenerative hereditary disorders (Lanska and Lanska, 1994), Alzheimer's disease (Forstl et al., 1993), and brain inflammation. Initial observations on the Klüver–Bucy syndrome formed a cornerstone for subsequent attempts to understand the role of subcortical structures in emotion.

Several Models Explain the Role of the Brain in Emotion

Studies of brain lesions and emotion have led to several anatomical models of brain circuits that mediate emotional behaviors. In this section, we will present two examples of models that seek to synthesize many empirical findings.

Papez's neural circuit. Knowledge about brain anatomy and emotion has been derived from both experimental and clinical sources. In 1937, James W. Papez, a neuropathologist, proposed a neural circuit of emotion. Papez (rhymes with "capes") reached his conclusions from brain autopsies of humans with emotional disorders, including psychiatric patients. He also studied the brains of animal subjects, such as rabid dogs. He noted the sites of brain destruction in these cases and concluded that the destruction necessary for impairment of emotional feelings involved a set of interconnected pathways in the limbic system. According to Papez's circuit model, emotional expressions involve hypothalamic control of visceral organs, and feeling arises from connections to a circuit that includes the hypothalamus, the mammillary bodies, the anterior thalamus, and the cingulate cortex. The progression of activity in this circuit, as hypothesized by Papez, is shown in Figure 15.8.

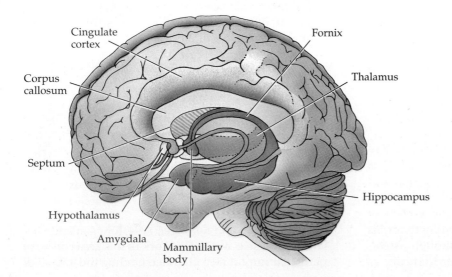

Cingulate cortex

Fornix

Corpus callosum

Thalamus

Septum

Hypothalamus

Amygdala

Mammillary body

Hippocampus

15.8 Papez's Circuit of Emotion These various components of the limbic system make extensive connections with one another and have been implicated in emotional responses.

Papez's proposed circuit has been the source of much experimental work. Each region in the circuit has been lesioned or electrically stimulated to determine its relation to emotional processing. Aggression in particular has been a focus of many studies of the Papez circuit, because of its importance in human affairs and the ease with which it can be observed in nonhumans. These studies have expanded the complexity of the circuitry, especially by adding roles for other limbic structures, including the amygdala and the septal area.

The triune brain. A broad, speculative neural model of emotion has been presented by Paul MacLean (1970). His model arises from a diverse array of observations, including the study of limbic-system seizures in humans, the mapping of behavior elicited by brain stimulation in monkeys, and an interpretation of the research literature on the evolution of the vertebrate brain.

According to MacLean, the human brain can be viewed as a three-layered (or triune) system, with each layer marking a significant evolutionary development. The oldest and deepest layer, in the brain stem, represents our reptilian brain heritage. It mediates highly stereotyped acts that are part of a limited repertoire, including acts that creatures have to perform to survive, such as breathing and eating. Routine maintenance is one way of describing these functions. In time, another layer wrapped around the reptilian core; this two-layered system is seen in some "lower" mammals. This additional layer, MacLean argues, deals with the preservation of the species and the individual and includes the neural apparatus that mediates emotions, feeding, pain escape and avoidance, fighting, and pleasure seeking. The set of relevant structures in this layer is the limbic system. Further evolution brought a final, third layer, consisting of the dramatic elaboration of the cerebral cortex and providing the substrate for rational thought, according to this speculative model.

MacLean views his model as providing an understanding of the common features of emotional responses among many animals and an understanding of changes evident with progressively "higher" animals. From the standpoint of understanding the advantage of the development of the limbic system, he sees the elaboration of these structures as offering the reptilian brain freedom from stereotyped behavior and a flexibility that is driven by emotions. Many aspects of MacLean's speculation suggest interesting thoughts about neural aspects of emotions, although assessments of the broad scope of his model are difficult.

Electrical Stimulation of the Brain Can Produce Emotional Effects

Another productive approach to understanding the neuroanatomy of emotion is electrical stimulation of sites in the brains of awake, freely moving animals and observation of the effects on behavior. Such stimulation may produce either rewarding or aversive effects or may elicit sequences of emotional behavior.

Positive reinforcement. In 1954, psychologists James Olds and Peter Milner reported a remarkable experimental finding: rats could learn to press a lever when the reward or reinforcement was a brief burst of electrical stimulation of the septal area within the limbic system. Another way to describe this phenomenon is brain "self-stimulation." Heath (1972) reported that patients receiving electrical stimulation in this region feel a sense of pleasure or warmth, and in some instances stimulation in this region provokes sexual excitation.

Peter Milner

The report of Olds and Milner (1954) is one of those rare scientific discoveries that starts a new field; many investigators have since employed techniques of brain self-stimulation. Some research has focused on mapping the distribution of brain sites that yield self-stimulation responses (Figure 15.9). Other studies have analyzed the similarities and differences between positive responses elicited by brain stimulation and those elicited by other rewarding situations, such as the presentation of food to a hungry animal or water to a thirsty animal (reviewed by White and Milner, 1992). Perhaps electrical stimulation taps in on the circuits mediating these more customary rewards. Research in this area has also moved in a neurochemical direction, with many efforts made to identify the relevant transmitters in brain pathways that mediate self-stimulation behavior (Ranaldi and Beninger, 1994; Johnson and Stellar, 1994; Wise et al., 1992). Work in this area can be of particular importance in understanding the impact of

James Olds

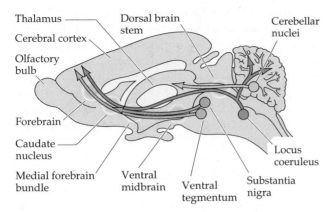

Thalamus
Cerebral cortex
Olfactory bulb
Dorsal brain stem
Cerebellar nuclei
Forebrain
Caudate nucleus
Medial forebrain bundle
Ventral midbrain
Ventral tegmentum
Substantia nigra
Locus coeruleus

15.9 Self-Stimulation Sites in the Rodent Brain
Animals will work very hard pressing a bar in return for a mild electrical stimulation at any of these sites, which seem to represent four neural tracts.

many drugs on the emotional responses of humans.

Self-stimulation is not a peculiar property of rat brains. It can be shown in diverse mammals, including cats, dogs, monkeys, and humans. Nevertheless, it has been studied the most extensively in rats. In these animals self-stimulation by lever pressing can go on for hours; response rates vary with the amount of electrical current and the brain site being stimulated. Early studies comparing self-stimulation with natural rewards—such as food and water—seemed to reveal significant differences in reinforcement properties. For example, sudden extinction was observed with behavior reinforced by direct brain stimulation: as soon as the electrical stimulation was interrupted, lever pressing ceased. However, studies directly comparing responses for food, water, and electrical stimulation of the brain show similar features, no matter which reinforcing condition is employed (White and Milner, 1992).

Self-stimulation is observed with electrical stimulation of many different subcortical sites and a few frontal cortical regions. Cerebral cortical stimulation in most regions, however, does not have positive reinforcement properties. Positive brain sites are concentrated in the hypothalamus, although these sites also extend into the brain stem. A large tract that ascends from the midbrain to the hypothalamus—the **medial forebrain bundle**—contains many sites that yield strong self-stimulation behavior. This bundle of axons is characterized by widespread origins and an extensive set of brain regions where terminals of these axons can be found. The anatomical arrangements of self-stimulation sites seem similar in different species, although positive sites are spread more

extensively in the rat brain than in the cat brain.

Comparing maps of self-stimulation sites to those of neurotransmitters gave rise to the hypothesis that dopamine is the transmitter for reward circuits (Wise, 1984). On the other hand, Gallistel and colleagues (1985) failed to corroborate this conclusion using a metabolic mapping technique with 2-deoxyglucose. They reported that a map of the circuitry aroused by self-stimulation of the medial forebrain bundle did not coincide with a more extensive map of the dopaminergic systems activated by stimulation of the substantia nigra. But this result may mean only that some dopaminergic fibers and sites are engaged in functions other than reward. The role of dopamine is emphasized in several drug studies. Dopamine agonists reduce the threshold for brain stimulation reinforcement, and changes in extracellular dopamine levels in rats are directly related to the strength of the reward (Fiorino et al., 1993). This relationship was noted in the nucleus accumbens, which is part of the mesolimbic dopamine system. Neurons in this area are activated during self-stimulation of the ventral tegmental area (Wolske et al., 1993). Dopamine pathways certainly are significant in the mediation of reward although they may not be the only relevant synaptic transmitter.

Emotional effects. Electrical stimulation of the brains of alert cats and monkeys implanted with electrodes has provided maps of the distribution of emotional responses. This work has especially emphasized limbic-system sites and has focused particularly on aggression (which we discuss a little later in the chapter). An example of the integration of behavioral and autonomic responses provoked by stimulation of the hypothalamus is shown in Figure 15.10, (Kaada, 1967). These maps show that very discrete components of both autonomic and behavioral responses are represented at selected sites in the limbic system and the hypothalamic regions. The types of responses produced by direct electrical stimulation of limbic-system sites are described by Panksepp (1982) as "expectancy," "anger," "fear," and "panic." Observations of the varied behaviors elicited by brain stimulation suggest that the limbic system has three main levels: (1) various zones of the hypothalamus, including critical connecting pathways such as the medial forebrain bundle, which connects to mesencephalic limbic structures; (2) a second level consisting of olfactory zones, septal area, amygdaloid complex, and the hippocampal formation; and (3) the limbic lobe, which consists of the cingulate gyrus and

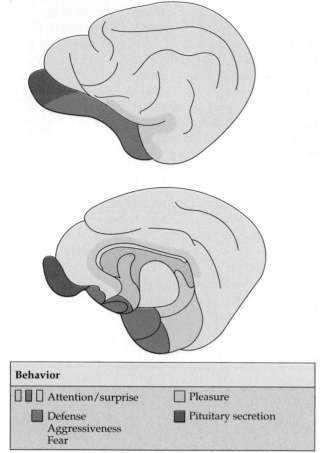

Behavior

▯▮▯ Attention/surprise   ▯ Pleasure

▮ Defense   ▮ Pituitary secretion
   Aggressiveness
   Fear

15.10 Brain Sites That Can Produce Emotional Responses

Mild electrical stimulation of these various components of the limbic system can elicit specific emotional responses in both cats (shown here) and monkeys.

the parahippocampal gyrus. Figure 15.10 shows the effects of stimulation of these three tiers of the limbic system. No emotional response was elicited by stimulation of the cerebral cortex.

The Cerebral Hemispheres Process Emotion Differently

The fact that the two cerebral hemispheres play different roles in cognitive processes in humans is well established by many experimental and clinical observations (see Chapter 19). Recently researchers have investigated the possibility that there are hemispheric differences in emotion processing. Differences between the cerebral hemispheres have been explored from several perspectives. One focuses on the special role of the right hemisphere in the perception of emotional states. Another aspect concerns the lat-

eralization of emotional expression, especially in displays of facial expression (Fridlund, 1988). Finally, a clinical contribution concerns affective disorders associated with unilateral brain diseases, such as stroke, and departures from the usual portrait in hemispheric specializations seen in psychiatric populations. Contributions from each of these perspectives lead to the tentative assertion that emotions involve the hemispheres to different extents.

Emotional syndromes. A major theme to emerge from studies with patients who have sustained injury or disease confined to one hemisphere is that the hemispheres differ in emotional tone. A program of observations in stroke patients summarized by Starkstein and Robinson (1992) reveals that patients with strokes involving the left anterior cerebral hemisphere have the highest frequency of depressive symptoms; the closer the lesion is to the frontal pole, the more intense is the depressive portrait. In these patients, injury-produced language deficits are not correlated with severity of depression. In contrast, patients with right-hemisphere lesions are described as unduly cheerful and apathetic. Similar observations are seen in left-handed individuals, suggesting that poststroke mood disorders are independent of cerebral lateralization for handedness and language. Table 15.1 summarizes the clinical syndromes involving emotional changes following cerebrovascular disorders. Bear (1983) has suggested that patients with right-hemisphere injuries show a deficit in emotional surveillance (the detection of events that ordinarily elicit emotional responses, such as threat). Hemispheric differences in the site of the initiation of epileptic discharges also seem related to differences in emotional dimensions. In some cases right temporoparietal injury that includes seizures can lead to psychosis. This result has been observed in several patients, all of whom showed no psychiatric disorders prior to brain injury. Intense delusional and hallucinatory symptoms characterize this disorder. Many other clinical observations related to hemispheric differences have been summarized by Heilman and Watson (1983).

Results of unilateral injections of sodium amytal into a single carotid artery offer additional data about hemispheric differences in emotion. This procedure, described in Box 19.1, is used to determine the hemisphere that is dominant for language. Generally, injection of sodium amytal into the "dominant" hemisphere (for most people, the left hemisphere) produces a depressive aftereffect, while an identical injection into the carotid artery on the

Table 15.1

Clinical Syndromes Associated with Cerebrovascular Disease

SYNDROME	CLINICAL SYMPTOMS	ASSOCIATED LESION LOCATION
Catastrophic reaction	Anxiety, tears, aggressive behavior, swearing, displacement, refusal, renouncement, and compensatory boasting	Left hemisphere
Indifference reaction	Undue cheerfulness or joking, anosognosia, minimization, loss of interest, and apathy	Right hemisphere
Major depression	Depressed mood, daily mood variation, loss of energy, anxiety, restlessness, worry, weight loss, decreased appetite, early morning awakening, delayed sleep onset, social withdrawal, and irritability	Left frontal lobe; left basal ganglia
Minor depression	Depressed mood, anxiety, restlessness, worry, daily mood variation, hopelessness, loss of energy, delayed sleep onset, early morning awakening, social withdrawal, weight loss, and decreased appetite	Right or left posterior patietal and occipital regions
Aprosody		
Motor	Poor expression of emotional prosody and gesturing, good prosodic comprehension and gesturing, and denial of feelings of depression	Right posterior inferior frontal lobe
Sensory	Good expression of emotional prosody and gesturing, poor prosodic comprehension and gesturing, and difficulty empathizing with others	Right posterior inferior parietal lobe and posterior superior temporal lobe
Pathological laughing and crying	Frequent, usually brief laughing and/or crying; crying not caused by sadness, or out of proportion to it; social withdrawal secondary to emotional outbursts	Frequently bilateral hemispheric lesions; can occur with almost any lesion location
Anxiety disorder	Symptoms of major depression, intense worry and anxious foreboding in addition to depression, associated light-headedness or palpitations and muscle tension or restlessness, and difficulty concentrating or falling asleep	Left cortex, usually dorsal lateral frontal lobe
Mania	Elevated mood, increased energy, increased appetite, decreased sleep, feeling of well-being, pressured speech, flight of ideas, grandiose thoughts	Right basotemporal or right orbitofrontal region
Bipolar mood disorder	Symptoms of major depression alternating with mania	Right basal ganglia or right thalamus

nondominant side elicits a feeling of euphoria and smiling.

Davidson (1994) has presented a different view of the role of the cerebral hemispheres in emotion processing. According to this view, anterior regions of the right and left hemispheres are specialized for approach and withdrawal processes, respectively. Thus, damage to the left frontal region results in a deficit in approach, as evident in the loss of interest and pleasure in other people and the difficulty in initiating behavior. The diminished activation of this area is associated with sadness and depression. In contrast, activation of the right anterior region is associated with withdrawal-related emotions, such as fear and disgust. Deficits in right anterior activation produced by lesions or injury will reduce withdrawal behavior and related negative emotions. Relevant evidence includes the results from an array of electrophysiological experiments with humans. For example, in one study (Davidson et al., 1990), subjects were presented with film clips while their facial expressions and brain electrical activity were recorded. The film excerpts were intended to produce either happiness or disgust. Disgust was associated with greater electrophysiological activation on the right side; the reverse was noted for happiness. Davidson (1994) further suggests that individual differences in the degree of hemispheric asymmetry are related to characteristic affective style.

Processing of emotional stimuli.

Dichotic listening techniques (see Chapter 19) have shown that the cerebral hemispheres might function differently in how they recognize emotional stimuli. An example of the use of this technique is the work of Ley and Bryden (1982), who presented normal subjects with brief sentences spoken in happy, sad, angry, and neutral voices. The sentences were presented through headsets—a different sentence in each ear. Subjects were instructed to attend to one ear and report both the content of the message and its emotional tone. Subjects showed a distinct left-ear advantage for identifying the emotional tone of the voice and a right-ear advantage for understanding the meaning of the brief message. Since each ear projects more strongly to the opposite hemisphere, these results indicate that the right hemisphere is better than the left in interpreting emotional aspects of vocal messages. Some critics suggest that both hemispheres process emotional stimuli but that stimuli directed to the right hemisphere are more likely to produce emotional reactions (Silberman and Weingartner, 1986).

The presentation of different visual stimuli to each

eye has also revealed hemispheric differences in the perception of emotional states or stimuli. The stimuli in these studies usually consist of faces displaying different emotional expressions. In a variety of tasks that emphasize either reaction time or identification, the common finding is that emotional stimuli presented to the left visual field (projecting to the right hemisphere) result in faster reaction times and more accurate identification of emotional states (Bryden, 1982). These effects can be modified by instructions to subjects. For example, hemispheric differences can be enhanced by instructions that emphasize an empathic response, such as "Try to feel like the face depicted."

Asymmetry of facial expressions.

By cutting a photograph of the face of a person displaying an emotion down the exact middle of the face, we can create two new composite photos, one made by combining two left sides (one of which is printed in mirror image) and the other made by combining two right sides of the face (Figure 15.11). The results reveal that facial expressions are not symmetrical. Furthermore, the two photos produced from the same original photo elicit different responses from people looking at them. In several studies subjects judged the left-sides photo as more emotional than the right-sides photo (Sackheim, Gur, and Saucy, 1978). Campbell (1982) showed that composite photos constructed of the left side of the face are judged as happier, and composites of the right side of the face are judged as sadder.

Critics of this type of experiment have noted that such studies fail to distinguish between photographs of posed emotions and those of genuinely emotional expressions (Hager, 1982). The asymmetry of facial expression becomes much less evident when photos of spontaneous, genuine emotions are used as stimuli, although when subjects are asked to relate an emotional experience from their lives, they  show more expressive movements on the left side of their face than on the right side (Moscovitch and Olds, 1982). Ekman and colleagues (1983) emphasize that judgments of facial expression include complex assessments that involve both static features of the face, such as bony landmarks, and dynamic features, such as those produced by facial musculature.

In some studies subjects have been instructed to produce facial asymmetries by moving parts of one side of their face. Schiff and Lamon (1989) asked subjects to lift one corner of their mouth and describe their emotion when those facial muscles were al-

(a) 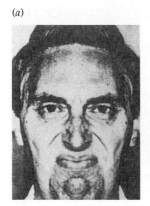   *(b)*    *(c)*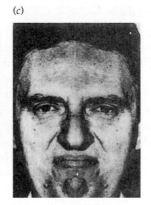

15.11 Emotions and Facial Asymmetry Comparison of the intensity of emotional expression in composite faces. Photographs constructed by using only the left side of the face (*a*); these are judged to be more emotional than either the original face (*b*), or a composite of the right side of the face (*c*). Courtesy of Ruben C. Gur.

lowed to relax. Feelings of sadness were associated with left-side facial muscle contraction, and positive feelings were associated with deliberately induced right-side facial muscle contraction.

Asymmetry in psychiatric patients. Patients with psychiatric disorders have been tested in various cognitive and perceptual tasks to determine whether their cerebral lateralization differs from that of normal subjects. Studies involving schizophrenic patients, which have yielded many debatable findings, suggest an association between schizophrenia and impaired cerebral laterality (Marin and Tucker, 1981). Although no single finding seems pivotal, inferences formed from many observations buoy this view. For example, Wexler and Heninger (1979) assessed the performance of psychotic patients on dichotic listening tests and found that laterality scores increased as the psychiatric condition of the subject improved.

This story has many variables, and it is sometimes difficult to disentangle unpredictable patient behavior from hemispheric effects. Data from PET scans, however, support the idea that cerebral laterality is related to emotion. Depressed patients, for example, show increases in cerebral blood flow in the left prefrontal cortex (Drevets et al., 1992).

Neural Circuitry, Hormones, and Synaptic Transmitters Mediate Violence and Aggression

Violence, assaults, and homicide exact a high toll in many human societies; for example, homicide is the most prominent cause of death in young adults in the United States. Many different approaches have investigated the psychological, anthropological, and bi-

ological dimensions of aggression. These concerted efforts have clarified many aspects of aggression, including its biological bases in hormonal and neurophysiological mechanisms. In this section we examine the results of these studies.

What Is Aggression?

Surely we all know aggression! Alas, a more sustained consideration suggests that this all-too-familiar term has many different meanings. In common usage, "aggression" refers to an emotional state that many humans describe as consisting of feelings of hate and a desire to inflict harm. This perspective emphasizes aggression as a powerful inner feeling. However, when we view aggression as an overt response—overt behavior that involves actual or intended destruction of another organism—we see several different forms. Some view the attack behavior of an animal directed at natural prey as predatory aggression. Glickman (1977), however, has argued that this behavior is more appropriately designated as feeding behavior.

Aggression between males of the same species is observed in virtually all vertebrates. The relevance to humans may be the fact that the ratio of males to females arrested on charges of murder in the United States is 5:1. Further, aggressive behavior between boys, in contrast to that between girls, is evident early in the form of vigorous and destructive play behavior. Some animals display maternal aggression; an extreme form of this behavior is the cannibalism of young by rodent mothers. Animals that are cornered and unable to escape display fear-induced aggression. Some forms of aggression are considered a component of sexual behavior. Finally, one form of aggression is referred to as irritable aggression; it can emerge from frustration or pain and frequently has the quality described as uncontrollable rage.

Androgens Seem to Increase Aggression

Male sex hormones play a major role in some forms of aggressive behavior, especially in social encounters between males (Nelson, 1995). One set of data relates levels of circulating androgens to different measures of aggressive behavior. With the advent of sexual maturity, intermale aggression markedly increases in many species. McKinney and Desjardins (1973) have shown changes in aggressiveness in mice that start at puberty. Immature mice treated with androgen display increased aggression. Levels of testosterone change seasonally in many species, and increases in testicular size seem related to increased aggression in animals as diverse as birds and primates. Androgen levels are also influenced by the history of success or failure in aggressive encounters. In mice and monkeys the loser in aggressive encounters shows reduced androgen levels (Lloyd, 1971; Bernstein and Gordon, 1974). In birds, androgen levels are elevated when intermale competition is high (Wingfield et al., 1987).

Observations of the behavioral effects of castration give additional evidence for the relation between hormones and aggression. Reductions in the level of circulating androgen produced in this manner are commonly associated with a profound reduction in intermale aggressive behavior. Restoring testosterone by injection in castrated animals increases fighting behavior in mice in a dose-related manner (Figure 15.12).

The aggressive behavior of female mammals can also depend on reproductive hormones. Although the prevailing view among researchers is that males of most mammalian species are typically the more aggressive sex, there are examples of species where such dimorphism is not evident. For example, among spotted hyenas females are typically larger than males and rule a clan that can consist of up to 80 hyenas (Kruuk, 1975). Further, observations of aggression in encounters between the sexes suggest that females might specialize in types of aggression that are dissimilar from the aggression displayed by males. For example, female aggressive behavior is particularly evident in ter-

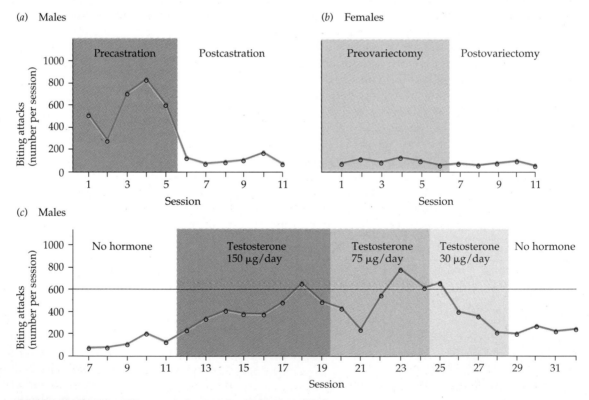

15.12 Androgen Effects on Aggressive Behavior of Mice.
The number of biting attacks on an inanimate object is counted. (*a*) Male behavior before and after castration. (*b*) Female behavior before and after the removal of the ovaries. (*c*) The effects of hormone replacement on the attack behavior of castrated males; testosterone reinstates aggressive behavior in the castrated males. From Wagner, Beuving, and Hutchinson, 1980.

ritorial defense and mate selection, whereas male aggression is more likely to be seen in situations where males are pitted against each other to determine dominance. Female aggressive behavior shows changes in the course of the estrous cycle in some rodent species. For example, estrous hamsters are less aggressive than nonestrous females in response to members of the same species of either sex. Studies of changes in aggression during the menstrual cycle in primates are steeped in controversy (Brain, 1994). At present there is no clear evidence linking hostility changes in women, including the syndrome of premenstrual tension, to the menstrual cycle.

The idea of a relationship between hormones—especially androgens—and human aggression is also very controversial. Arguments summoned in legal briefs frequently cite the literature on nonhuman animals. Some human studies have shown a positive correlation between testosterone levels and the magnitude of hostility, as measured by behavior rating scales. One study of prisoners (Kreuz and Rose, 1972), however, shows no relation between testosterone levels and several measures of aggressiveness; another study (Ehrenkranz, Bliss, and Sheard, 1974) shows positive relations. Comprehensive studies of military veterans suggest that testosterone is related to antisocial behavior (Dabbs and Morris, 1990). Nonaggressive tendencies in males are associated with satisfaction in family functioning and with low levels of serum testosterone (Julian and McKenry, 1989). Among females, testosterone concentrations are highest in women prisoners convicted of unprovoked violence and lowest among women convicted of defensive violent crimes (Dabbs et al., 1988).

Nevertheless, several attempts to modify the aggressive behavior of male criminals have involved the manipulation of sex hormones. Castration studies generally show that violence in sex offenders is reduced by this surgical procedure, especially where "excessive libido" is considered the instigator of sexual assaults (Brain, 1994). The administration of antiandrogen drugs, such as cyproterone acetate, which exerts its impact by competing with testosterone for receptor sites, acts as reversible castration. Several studies on criminals convicted of sexual assault show that administration of these substances reduces sexual drive and interest (Brain, 1994). However, some researchers have suggested that the effects of antiandrogens on aggressive behavior are less predictable than their effects on sexual behavior. Many ethical issues are involved in this approach to the rehabilitation of sex offenders, and the intricacies of such intervention have yet to be worked out.

Distinct Neural Circuits Mediate Aggression

For many years researchers seeking to map aggressive behavior have electrically stimulated various brain regions in awake, behaving animals. This work started with the pioneering experiments of Walter Hess in the 1920s. The dramatic character of feline aggressive behavior made cats a favorite experimental animal. Most of the sites that elicit aggressive behavior in cats are in the limbic system and connected brain stem regions. Regions differ in the patterns of elicited behavior and the emphasis on particular components. Brain stem stimulation in the central gray area produces piloerection (hair standing up), hissing, claw retraction, and especially prominent, loud, characteristic vocalizations.

The Synaptic Transmitter Serotonin is Associated with Aggression

Aggressive behavior in various animals, including humans, seems especially connected to serotonin mechanisms. Studies show a negative correlation between brain serotonin activity and aggression. For example, Higley and collaborators (1992) studied 28 monkeys chosen from more than 4500 monkeys maintained on an island off the coast of South Carolina. These animals roamed freely, and researchers collected observations of aggressive behavior and noted body wounds from fights; animals were ranked from least to most aggressive by researchers who knew nothing of the animals' neurochemical activity. Data from this study show a significant negative correlation between magnitude of aggression and serotonin activity measured in cerebrospinal fluid.

Many other observations support the view that diminished cerebrospinal concentrations of serotonin metabolites such as 5-HIAA are correlated with human aggression and violence. Diminished serotonin activity (as measured by 5-HIAA concentration in cerebrospinal fluid) is seen in humans who become violent with alcohol use (Virkkunen and Linnoila, 1993), in U.S. Marines expelled for excessive violence (Brown et al., 1979), in children who torture animals (Kruesi, 1989), and in children whose poor impulse control produces disruptive behavior. Certain types of suicide are also correlated with diminished serotonin activity. Diminished cerebrospinal serotonin metabolite levels are seen in suicides that are violent in character; these same individuals also show diminished functional serotoninergic terminals in the frontal cortex, as revealed by studies of binding by the drug imipramine. Serotonergic activity also predicted eventual suicide in a group of persons whose initial suicide attempt was unsuccessful.

We must caution that serotonin levels are not inflexible quantities that are indifferent to social stimuli and contexts. Quite the contrary! Examining primate groups, Raleigh and colleagues (1992) have shown that low-ranking male primates have low levels of serotonin but that serotonin levels increase with social ascent. When the dominant male loses his high status, his serotonin levels decline. Further, serotonin is not the "aggression" transmitter. Other substances have been implicated in various forms of aggression in both humans and other animals. The list includes noradrenergic and GABA systems, as well as neuropeptides that might act as modulators of aggression. In addition, a group of knockout mice, in which a gene needed for the production of the neurotransmitter nitric oxide was disabled, are extremely aggressive (Nelson et al., 1995), so this neurotransmitter may normally serve to inhibit or limit aggressive behavior.

The Neurology of Human Violence Is a Topic of Controversy

Some forms of human violence are characterized by sudden intense physical assaults. In a very controversial book, *Violence and the Brain,* Mark and Ervin (1970) suggested that some forms of intense human violence are derived from temporal lobe seizure disorders. They offered horrifying examples from newspaper accounts as preliminary evidence. For example, in 1966 Charles Whitman climbed a tower at the University of Texas and murdered by random shooting a number of passing individuals. Earlier he had killed family members, and letters he left behind revealed a portrait of a bewildered young man possessed by an intense need to commit violence. Postmortem analysis of his brain suggested the presence of a tumor deep in the temporal lobe. Other, more formal data cited by Mark and Ervin include the common occurrence of aggression in temporal lobe seizure patients and the long-controversial claim that a large percentage of habitually aggressive criminals display abnormal EEGs that indicate likely temporal lobe disease. Mark and Ervin argued that temporal lobe disorders may underlie many forms of human violence and produce a disorder they labeled **dyscontrol syndrome**. They presented several detailed clinical reports of humans with possible temporal lobe seizure disorders. These patients had depth electrodes implanted within the temporal lobe. Electrical stimulation of various sites along the electrode tracts resulted in seizures typical of the patient. Intense assaultive behavior was directly relat-

ed to elicitation of temporal lobe seizure. In some patients, neurosurgical intervention—the removal of some temporal lobe regions, especially the region of the amygdala—profoundly reduced both seizure activity and reports of assaultive behavior.

Much of the controversy surrounding Mark and Ervin's book has to do with the claim that a large proportion of human violence has this neuropathological origin (Valenstein, 1973). Vigorous controversy is also promoted by the implicit argument that neurosurgery can alleviate forms of violent behavior that many feel are more readily understood as products of social distress and developmental impairment.

Many other studies have linked violence in humans with some forms of seizure disorders or other clinical neurological pathology (Lewis, 1990). A high percentage of both juveniles and adults arrested for violent crimes have abnormal EEGs (Lewis, Shankok, and Pincus, 1979; Williams, 1969). Devinsky and Bear (1984) examined a group of patients with seizures involving emotion-controlling structures of the limbic system. These patients showed aggressive behavior that occurred after the development of an epileptic focus localized within this system. None of these patients had a history that included traditional sociological factors linked to aggression, such as parental abuse, poverty, or use of drugs. In these patients aggression is an event between seizures; directed aggression is seldom seen during an actual seizure involving the limbic system (Delgado-Escueta et al., 1981). Although the relation of violence and aggression to epilepsy remains controversial, a growing set of clinical observations supports this association in some individuals. Some of these observations are case histories that show an unequivocal link between a seizure and a violent act. For example, a babysitter killed the child in her charge in a most violent manner. Studies done after she was arrested showed that her violent response to the child was elicited during a temporal lobe seizure provoked by the child's laughter—a specific seizure-eliciting stimulus for this person. Many other observations point to complex forms of aggression that might arise as a function of a history of temporal lobe seizures (Engel, 1992).

Discussions about the biology of human violence have also focused on certain abnormalities of human sex chromosomes. This interest was partially fostered by the observation that a murderer who had killed a group of nurses in their home had the rare XYY chromosome pattern. Some investigators, noting the link to male hormones established in studies of hormones and aggression, suggested a connection between an extra Y chromosome and violence. Because this chromosome disorder is very rare, testing of this relation has proved difficult. A group of investigators using the very thorough birth and life history data in Denmark pursued a thorough analysis of the relation between human aggression and the XYY chromosome type (Mednick and Christiansen, 1977). To the surprise of some, they found that although XYY chromosome males were more likely to be in jail than were normal males, the crime that resulted in imprisonment was less likely to have been violent in nature. In fact, the cause for jailing was usually petty theft or a similar offense; diminished social intelligence of many of these men seemed to preclude the ability to hide their crimes. Meyer-Bahlburg and Ehrhardt (1982) express the view that there is no good evidence that XYY males have any gross abnormalities of androgen or gonadotropin production, although there is some evidence that prior to puberty they are more aggressive than normal males.

Undoubtedly human violence and aggression stem from many sources. In recent years biological studies of aggression have led to vigorous criticism from both politicians and social scientists. Both have argued that emphasizing biological factors such as genetics or brain mechanisms could lead to a failure to focus on the most evident origins of human violence and aggression, and to odious forms of biological controls of social dysfunction. However, violence envelops the behavior of only a few individuals. Furthermore, it is important to understand the possible roles of biological factors, especially since the quality of life of some violent persons might be significantly improved by addressing biological problems such as diminished serotonin activity. Treatments that enhance brain serotonin activity may be an important addition to a social–environmental or psychotherapeutic intervention (Coccaro and Siever, 1995).

Fear Is Mediated by Circuitry That Involves the Amygdala

There is nothing very subtle about fear. The awareness of danger may impel the prospect of defense or flight and escape, or it may provoke the opposite response—freezing in one's tracks. Many animals share similar appearances under conditions that provoke fear, such as danger to one's life posed by either an animal predator or the modern predator that confronts us in the city streets. The neuroscience of fear has been explored using tools whose simplicity

makes them appealing (LeDoux, 1995). Notable is classical fear conditioning in which the subject or animal is presented with a stimulus such as light or sound that is paired with a brief aversive stimulus such as mild electric shock. After several such pairings, the response to the sound or light is the typical fear portrait; in rats, this portrait includes freezing and autonomic signs such as cardiac and respiratory changes.

Studies of such fear conditioning using an auditory stimulus, and the techniques of experimental brain lesions have provided a portrait of the mediating circuitry (Figure 15.13*a*). This type of study shows that a key structure in the mediation of conditioned fear is the amygdala. The amygdala is located at the anterior medial portion of each temporal lobe and is composed of about a dozen distinct nuclei, each with a distinctive set of connections. Some of the connections with the rest of the brain include direct projections from sensory cortex. Lesions of the central nucleus of this structure prevent blood pressure increases and constrain freezing behavior in response to the conditioned fear stimulus. Interconnections within the amygdala form an important part of the story. Information about the conditioned stimulus—the sound—reaches the lateral portion of the amygdala first and is then transmitted to two other small subregions of the amygdala—the basolateral and basomedial portions—and then goes to the central nucleus (Figure 15.13*b*). Glutamate is a probable transmitter in this pathway.

The data from this type of experiment fit well with observations that humans with temporal lobe seizures that include the amygdala commonly report intense fear as a prelude or warning about the immediate prospect of a seizure (Engel, 1992). In addition, stimulation of various sites within the temporal lobe of humans—a procedure performed to identify seizure-provoking sites—elicits fear in some patients (Bancaud et al., 1994). In Chapter 16 we consider another aspect of fear: clinical states of anxiety.

The role of the amygdala in emotions is more elaborate than mere involvement with fear. Earlier we discussed the Klüver–Bucy syndrome, which is characterized by marked changes in emotional responses. Contemporary studies with monkeys show a role for the amygdala in learning the emotional significance of external events, especially social actions (Aggleton, 1993). A case description of a patient without an amygdala illustrates the role of this structure in mediating recognition of emotion in human facial expressions (Adolphs et al., 1994). This patient suffers

(a)

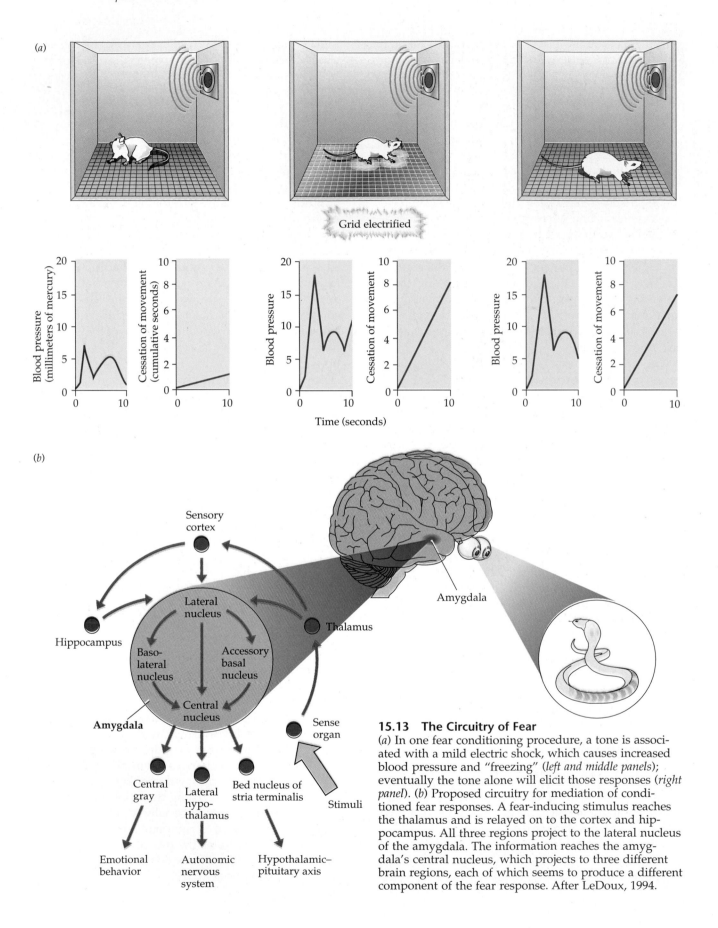

15.13 The Circuitry of Fear

(a) In one fear conditioning procedure, a tone is associated with a mild electric shock, which causes increased blood pressure and "freezing" (*left and middle panels*); eventually the tone alone will elicit those responses (*right panel*). (b) Proposed circuitry for mediation of conditioned fear responses. A fear-inducing stimulus reaches the thalamus and is relayed on to the cortex and hippocampus. All three regions project to the lateral nucleus of the amygdala. The information reaches the amygdala's central nucleus, which projects to three different brain regions, each of which seems to produce a different component of the fear response. After LeDoux, 1994.

from a rare medical condition that results in the bilateral loss of the amygdala without damage to the surrounding hippocampus or overlying neocortex. She was shown photos of facial expressions that represented six basic emotions: happiness, surprise, fear, disgust, sadness, and anger. She showed a marked impairment of the recognition of fear, although she could select faces of people she knew and learn the identity of new faces. In addition, this patient could not appreciate similarities between emotional expressions; for example, she did not evaluate faces showing surprise and happiness as more alike than faces displaying sadness and happiness. The amygdala thus appears important in mediating features of social cognition in which subtle emotional discriminations are significant.

Stress Activates Many Bodily Responses

We all experience stress, but what is it? Attempts to

Hans Selye

define **stress** have always danced around a certain vagueness implicit in this term. Some researchers emphasize that stress is a multidimensional concept that includes the stress stimuli, the processing system including the cognitive assessment of the stimuli, and the stress responses. The early use of the concept "stress" is closely identified with the work of Hans Selye, who popularized the term and defined it in a broad way as "the rate of all the wear and tear caused by life" (Selye, 1956). In

many studies over the course of almost 40 years, Selye described the impact of "stressors" on the responses of different organ systems of the body. He emphasized the connection between stress and disease in his "general adaptation syndrome." According to this scheme, the initial response to stress—called the alarm reaction—is followed by a second stage—the adaptation or resistance stage—which includes the successful activation of the appropriate response systems and the reestablishment of homeostatic balance. If stress is prolonged or frequently repeated, the exhaustion phase sets in, and it is characterized by increased susceptibility to disease.

In contemporary studies, this concept of stress and disease has been modified; some investigators note that the common ingredient to stressful stimuli is uncertainty or unpredictability about how to gain positive outcomes in response to these stimuli (Levine and Ursin, 1980). This perspective focuses on the evaluation of a stress stimulus as a key feature of the stress response (Figure 15.14). This model, which considers a broad array of factors relevant to stress and disease, including the roles of coping strategies and learning, emphasizes that stress per se does not inevitably lead to dysfunction or illness, and helps account for the variability in health histories of humans exposed to similar stressful life experiences.

Laboratory studies of human stress have used painful stimuli such as exposure to electric shock or immersion of the hand in ice-cold water. Researchers of stress have frequently criticized the artificiality of such laboratory studies. Placing a hand in a bucket of ice cubes certainly pales in comparison to dangerous situations that threaten life or produce psychological trauma. Some researchers have sought to use real-life situations to explore the biology of stress. Since most human stress situations are not predictable, however, baseline prestress assessments are not available. A

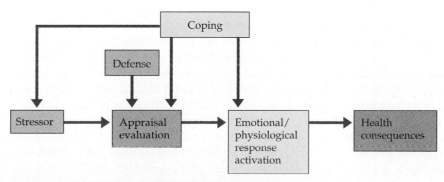

15.14   How Stress May Affect Health

few studies avoid this difficulty and offer controlled observations of baseline conditions and prolonged observations during a continuing potentially harmful situation. The most commonly studied real-life stress situation is military training, especially aviator training and parachute training, where stress involves fear of bodily harm and fear of failure.

The classical work by Grinker and colleagues (1963) provided a comprehensive study of stress in parachute training, involving both tower training and airplane jumps. However, this pioneering study took place long before the development of modern chemical assessments of substances circulating in the body, such as hormones. Ursin, Baade, and Levine (1978) took advantage of contemporary analytic tools that allow the study of minute changes of hormone levels in blood. A group of young recruits in the Norwegian military were studied by a variety of psychological and physiological measures before and during the early phase of parachute training. This training period involved a sliding ride along a long sloping wire suspended from a tower 12 meters high. Recruits were dressed in a suit equipped with a hook to the guide wire, and they slid along its course. This parachute training evokes an experience somewhat like that of free fall. Initial apprehension is high, and at first the sense of danger is acute, although recruits know that they are not likely to lose their lives in this part of the training.

Physiological measures were obtained during a basal period prior to training and with successive jumps. On jump day 2, samples of blood were drawn to chart the time course of neuroendocrine events. Autonomic activation in this situation (Figure 15.15) resembles the pituitary activation of the adrenal cortex during stress that is observed in many animal experiments, as noted earlier. Initially, cortisol levels were elevated in the blood, but successful jumps during training quickly led to a decrease in the pituitary–adrenal response. On the first jump, testosterone levels in the plasma fell below those of controls, but they also returned to normal with subsequent jumps. Other substances that showed marked increases in concentration at the initial jump included urinary epinephrine and growth hormone.

Less dramatic real-life situations also evoke clear endocrine responses, as shown by the research of Frankenhaeuser and associates (1978). For example, riding in a commuter train was found to provoke the release of epinephrine; the longer the ride and the more crowded the train, the greater is the hormonal response (Figure 15.16a). Factory work also leads to the release of epinephrine; the shorter the work cycle—that is, the more frequently the person has to repeat the same operations—the higher are the levels of epinephrine. The stress of a Ph.D. oral exam leads to a dramatic increase in both epinephrine and norepinephrine (Figure 15.16b, c).

Stress experienced by animals in the wild has become an interesting area of study for investigators who are trying to understand the stress response of humans. Robert Sapolsky (1992) studies baboons living freely in a natural reserve in Kenya. At first appearance, these animals seem to have a good life; food is abundant, predators are rare. The stresses they experience are the impacts they exert on each other. For males, this stress is the vigorous competition that surrounds courtship and the establishment of dominance hierarchies. 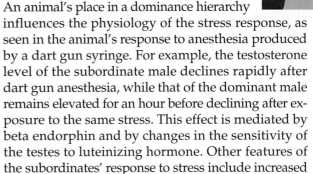 An animal's place in a dominance hierarchy influences the physiology of the stress response, as seen in the animal's response to anesthesia produced by a dart gun syringe. For example, the testosterone level of the subordinate male declines rapidly after dart gun anesthesia, while that of the dominant male remains elevated for an hour before declining after exposure to the same stress. This effect is mediated by beta endorphin and by changes in the sensitivity of the testes to luteinizing hormone. Other features of the subordinates' response to stress include increased levels of circulating cortisol, which results in a change in the profile of the immune response of the subordinate baboon.

Stress and Emotions Are Related to Some Human Diseases

During the past 50 years many psychiatrists and psychologists have strongly emphasized the role of psychological factors in disease. This field came to be known as **psychosomatic medicine** after an eminent psychoanalyst, Thomas French, suggested that particular diseases arise from distinctive sets of psychological characteristics or personality conflicts. From this perspective ulcers are related to frustration of "oral" needs and the development of "oral dependency," hypertension is seen as arising from hostile competitive activities, and migraine headaches represent repressed hostile needs or impulses. Each disease state or illness is thought to be associated with a specific set of psychological characteristics—those that generate some form of unresolved conflict. Although these ideas were prominent in the early de-

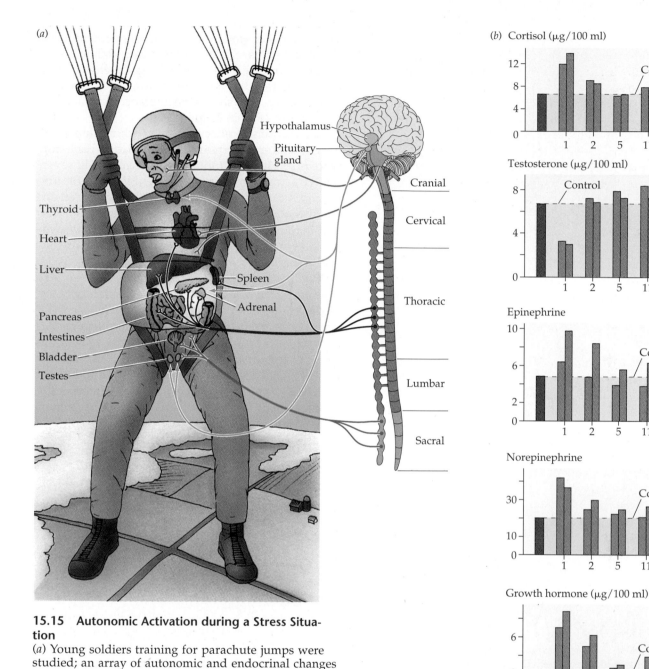

15.15   Autonomic Activation during a Stress Situation

(*a*) Young soldiers training for parachute jumps were studied; an array of autonomic and endocrinal changes accompanies such stressful experiences. (*b*) Note the hormone changes during parachute training, especially during the first jumps. After Ursin, Baade, and Levine, 1978.

velopment of psychosomatic medicine, current views make fewer claims for highly particular associations. Instead they emphasize that emotional responsiveness is only one factor among many that determine the onset, maintenance, and treatment of bodily disorders.

Emotional stimuli activate a diversity of neural and hormonal changes that influence pathological processes of bodily organs. Studies in psychosomatic medicine have broadened in scope and now range from evaluating emotions, stress, and sickness on a global scale to unraveling particular relations be-

(a)

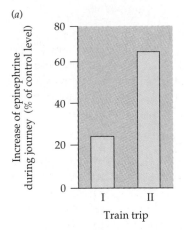

(b)

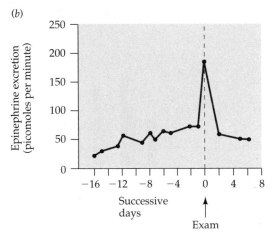

(c)

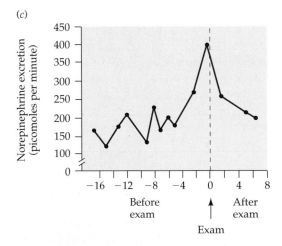

**15.16   Hormone Changes in Humans
from Social Stresses**
(a) Effects of small changes in crowding on a morning
commuter train ride. A 10% increase in the number of
passengers during a period of gasoline rationing (trip
II) resulted in a much higher increase in epinephrine
secretion. Levels of epinephrine (b) and norepinephrine (c) in a graduate student during a two-week period before, during, and after a thesis exam. After
Frankenhaeuser, 1978.

tween emotions and bodily responses or conditions.
A field called psychological medicine (or behavioral
medicine or health psychology) has developed from
this interest (Adler and Matthews, 1994; Sapolsky,
1994). Figure 15.17 shows the interaction of the many
factors that result in human disease.

Connections between stress and human disease
have been drawn in many different ways. Each new
piece of evidence is tantalizing but generally several steps away from being conclusive. Perhaps the ambiguity is caused by the vast range of individual differences among people with regard to susceptibility
to different diseases. Some of us are more constitu-
tionally prone than others to failure in certain organs.
Further, research on stress and human disease is be-
deviled by the fact that stress is only a contributory
condition to most disease states. Health habits, including nutritional variables, and patterns of coping
with stress are probably of equal significance. Although this area is difficult to study, it is of major importance to human life (Rodin and Salovey, 1989).

One global approach to linking stress and human
disease is to study the covariation between precisely
defined stressful life events and the incidence of particular diseases over a long period of time. Cancer and

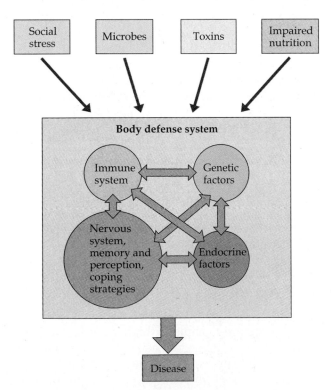

**15.17   Factors That Interact during the
Development and Progression of Disease**

heart disease are leading causes of death and misery in human beings. The toll of these diseases in many countries has generated large-scale studies of the health habits, quality of life, and personal adjustment of large samples of people, including whole communities. Most of these studies have been retrospective; that is, participants have been asked to report and rate experiences and emotional responses prior to the interview. In some instances relatives of deceased subjects provide this information. Behavior scales allow a quantitative assessment of the frequency and number of stressful events that precede an illness.

Although many methodological problems are evident in this approach, some consistent relations between stressful events and illness have been found (Adler and Matthews, 1994). For example, men who report frequent and severe stress in a period of one to five years prior to interviews are more likely to experience heart disease over a 12-year period following the interview than those who report little stress (Rosengren et al., 1991). A study of naval shipboard personnel by Rahe and collaborators (1972) provides another example. Navy personnel were asked to report major life events associated with stress (such as death of family members or divorce) and a history of illness for a ten-year period. Results showed that subjects who reported few stressful events for a particular period had few episodes of illness in the following years. In contrast, subjects who experienced many stressful events reported a much higher level of illness for the following year. However, some other studies fail to find this association between stressful life events and subsequent disease (Hollis et al., 1990). The social network within which stress occurs may be a more important determinant of disease outcome than stress itself. Evidence related to this hypothesis has been presented in many different research contexts (Adler and Matthews, 1994).

Mere frequency of stressful life events may be less related to serious illness than earlier studies emphasized. In a study of stressful events and heart attack, Byrne and White (1980) compared a group of coronary patients with a "control" group of people who were admitted to emergency rooms with suspected heart difficulties but who were rapidly diagnosed as not being heart attack cases. Questionnaires completed by the patients gave researchers an estimate of the frequency and intensity of stressful life events for the year prior to hospitalization. Analysis of these data show that heart attack patients did not have a higher frequency of stressful events during the year prior to ill-

ness than did the controls. Nor was the intensity of stress events a factor that distinguished these groups. However, heart attack patients were significantly more distressed by stressful life events and tended to be more anxious. The emotional impact of stress appears to have greater significance for future serious illness than does the mere occurrence of stressful events.

Stress Affects the Stomach

Many of us have felt stomach upset during moments of stress and emotion. Stress is accompanied by many changes in the gastrointestinal system. Secretion of digestive enzymes stops, motility of the gastrointestinal tract is slowed, and blood flow to the stomach is reduced so that more is available for skeletal muscular activity. There are many different disorders of the human gastrointestinal system that physicians have long believed to be exacerbated by stress. During the 1930s psychosomatic medicine focused on a key set of gastrointestinal disorders, especially stomach ulcers, that were believed to be intimately connected to psychological stress. A connection between stress and ulcers was also suggested by observations of a patient known as Tom, by the neurologist Harold Wolff in the 1940s. Tom had swallowed a caustic solution that had seared his esophagus, so he could not eat normally. To enable Tom to take in food, surgeons made a hole through the body wall into his stomach; a tube through this hole provided a route for nutrient fluids. The tube also let Wolff and collaborators directly observe the surface lining of the stomach during the course of interviews that provoked emotional responses. During intensely emotional phases of these interviews, Tom showed marked changes in the gastric mucosa, along with a dramatic buildup of stomach acid. Subsequent studies of humans with ulcers have shown a marked elevation of hydrochloric acid in the stomach.

An ulcer is an erosion in the wall of the stomach itself (gastric ulcer) or in adjacent intestinal areas (peptic ulcer) (Figure 15.18). Ulcers may form because of excessive secretion of unneutralized acid, which might result from a failure in mechanisms that ordinarily govern the levels of hydrochloric acid secretion in the stomach. Other factors implicated include the dramatic drop in stomach blood flow that accompanies stress which might result in changes in stomach cells. Recently evidence has accumulated that an unusual type of bacterium (called *Helicobacter pylori*) is found in the stomachs of people with ulcers; administering antibiotics to such patients helps heal ulcers. Stress might change the immune properties of the stomach and allow this bacterium to proliferate. Stress

15.18 A Pit in the Stomach
Cross-section of a gastric ulcer showing the erosion of the outer layer of cells.

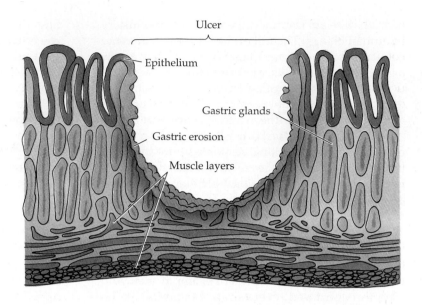

also interferes with the synthesis of prostaglandins, a type of hormone that influences stomach blood flow and gastric acid secretion (Kauffman et al., 1990).

The role of stress in ulcer formation can be studied in laboratory animals, especially rats. Various experimental conditions generate ulcers in these animals. Preventing rats from moving by using a body restraint is one of the oldest methods. The effect is especially evident in younger animals, particularly those separated early from their mother (Weiner, 1992). This effect might be due to a failure of thermoregulation in young, restrained rats, since cooling normal rats increases acid secretion in the stomach. Cutting the vagus nerve leading to the stomach (which lowers stomach acid secretion) reduces the number of gastric lesions. Another determinant of ulcer formation in this experimental context is the level of the digestive substance pepsinogen that is secreted into the stomach. High levels in the stomach increase the probability of stomach lesions in rats.

A classic experiment in this field that is more directly related to ulcer formation came to be known as the "executive monkey" experiment (Brady et al., 1958). Pairs of monkeys in primate restraint chairs were placed next to each other. One animal, the "executive" monkey, had to press a lever every 20 seconds to avoid shock. Whenever this monkey failed to press the lever within this interval, it received a shock. The second monkey received shocks at the same time, but it could not perform any response that prevented shocks. Executive monkeys in this experiment developed ulcers, whereas their adjacent partners failed to show gastric lesions. This experiment, in the years af-

ter its initial presentation, stimulated many research efforts, most of which have failed to confirm Brady's finding. Indeed, in some rat experiments, the responding animal is *less* likely to get ulcers, especially if shock is preceded by a warning signal. Weiss (1977) has claimed that unpredictable electric shocks are more likely to contribute to gastric ulcer formation than are predictable shocks. Gastrointestinal pathology in rats may be related to high levels of motor activity seen in response to stressful stimuli. High activity either causes ulcers or is related to a mechanism common to disease susceptibility.

Ulcer formation can also be understood as a "brain-driven" event—that is, the end product of information processing related to emotions and stress. The role of the brain in ulcer formation has been established in drug, lesion, and recording studies (Glavin, 1991). For example, lesions of the medial portions of the amygdala exacerbate stress-induced gastric lesions in rats, whereas lesions of the centromedial amygdala attenuate stress effects on ulceration. High doses of dopamine agonists attenuate stress-produced gastric lesions (Puri et al., 1994).

Emotions and Stress Influence the Immune System

For a long while, researchers viewed the immune system as an automatic mechanism: a pathogen, such as a virus, arrived on the scene, and soon the defense mechanisms of the immune system went to work, usually prevailing with their armory of antibodies and other immunological devices. Few thought of the nervous system as having an important role in this process, although the notion that the mind can influence well-being has been a persistent theme in human history. In the 1980s a new field, **psychoneuroimmunology** appeared; its existence signals a new awareness that the immune system, with its collection of cells that recognize intruders, interacts with other organs, especially hormonal systems and the nervous system. Studies with both human and non-human subjects now clearly show psychological and neurological influences on the immune system. These interactions go in both directions: the brain influences responses of the immune system, and immune cells and their products affect brain activities.

The immune system.   To understand this intriguing story we need to note some of the main features of the immune system. There are two basic types of immunological responses mediated by two different classes of cells called **lymphocytes**. One type, called **B lymphocytes**, mediates **humoral immunity**, which occurs when these cells produce proteins called **antibodies**, or immunoglobulins, that either directly destroy antigens (foreign molecules) such as viruses or bacteria or enhance their destruction by other cells. A second type of immunological response is called **cell-mediated immunity** and involves another class of cells, known as **T lymphocytes.** These cells directly attack various antigens. They act as "killer cells," forming a strong part of the body's attack against substances that can cause tumors. T cells are also involved in the rejection of organ transplants. In addition, T cells interact with humoral reactions mediated by B cells. Some of these interactions involve enhancement of antibody reactions, and this response requires special T lymphocytes called helper T cells. Other T lymphocytes suppress humoral reactions and are referred to as suppressor T cells.

These basic components of the immune system also interact with other bodily substances and cells in defending the body against disease and harmful substances. The organs of the body where these immune system cells are formed include the thymus, bone marrow, spleen, and lymph nodes. Figure 15.19 illustrates the main components of the immune system and their interactions. More details about this complex process can be found in a special issue of *Scientific American* entitled "Life, Death and the Immune Systems" (September 1993).

Bidirectional communication.   The potential for interactions between the brain and immune system is revealed in many anatomical and physiological studies (Felten et al., 1993; Ader et al., 1990; Ader and Cohen, 1993). The nervous system influences the immune system either through the autonomic nervous system or through the hypothalamic–pituitary–neuroendocrine system. Anatomical studies have noted the presence of nerve fibers from the autonomic nervous system in immune organs such as the spleen and thymus gland. Within these organs nerve endings are found among groups of lymphocytes, but the potential impact of their activity is still mysterious. These fibers are usually noradrenergic, sympathetic postganglionic axons. Other transmitters are also found in immune-system tissues, including various neuropeptides. Receptors for neurotransmitters have been found on immune cells such as lymphocytes; these substances probably exert their effects via a second-messenger system. Noradrenergic innervation is claimed to affect antibody production and immune cell proliferation, among other immune-system effects (Bellinger et al., 1992). These same cells are also affected by the hormones released through the hypothalamic–pituitary–neuroendocrine system. Neural activity in these organs might directly affect the responsiveness of immune-system cells by either enhancing or depressing various immune cell functions.

The bidirectional character of relations between the immune system and the brain is also seen in other studies that show the effects of antibodies on the firing rates of brain neurons, especially in regions within the hypothalamus (Besedovsky et al., 1985; Besedovsky and del Rey, 1992). Other immune-system products, such as the hormones interferon and interleukins, also affect brain activity. Thus the brain seems to be directly informed about the actions of the immune system. In fact, it has been suggested that "the immune system serves as a sensory organ for stimuli not recognized by the classical sensory system" (Blalock, 1984), or as a kind of receptor sensorial system (Besedovsky and del Rey, 1992).

Another way to show the brain's role in immune-system responsiveness is to examine the effects of brain lesions on immune responses. Lesions of the hypothalamus in experimental animals can influence immune processes, such as antibody production (Stein, Keller, and Scheifer, 1981). Some of these effects are quite specialized, involving responses to some antigens but not others. Furthermore, the specific hypothalamic site of the lesion also determines the character of immune effects. Some ways in which the hypothalamus influences immune-system processes involve neuroendocrine mechanisms mediated through the pituitary gland. Under stressful conditions the hypothalamus produces corticotropin-releasing factor, which causes the release of adrenocorticotropic hormone (ACTH) from the pituitary. ACTH causes the release of corticosteroid hormones from the adrenal cortex, and one of the effects of

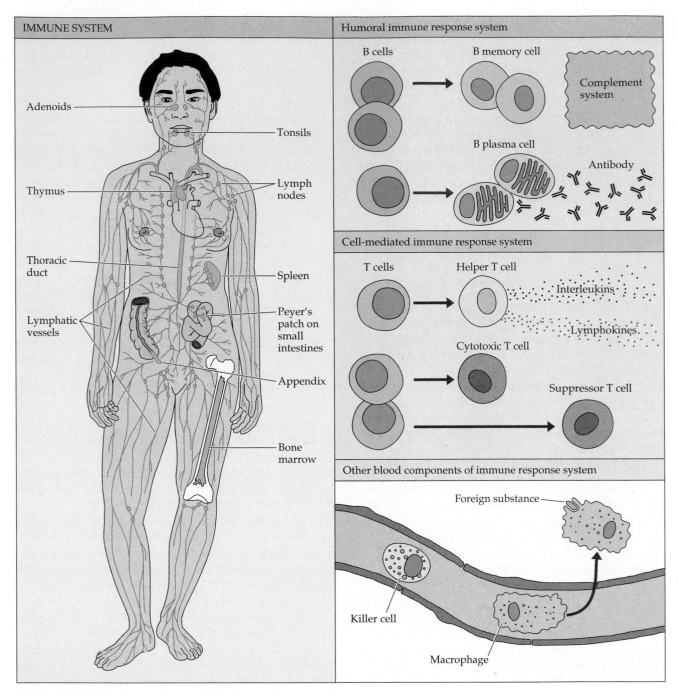

IMMUNE SYSTEM

Adenoids

Tonsils

Thymus

Lymph nodes

Thoracic duct

Spleen

Lymphatic vessels

Peyer's patch on small intestines

Appendix

Bone marrow

Humoral immune response system

B cells

B memory cell

Complement system

B plasma cell

Antibody

Cell-mediated immune response system

T cells

Helper T cell

Interleukins

Lymphokines

Cytotoxic T cell

Suppressor T cell

Other blood components of immune response system

Foreign substance

Killer cell

Macrophage

15.19   The Main Components of the Human Immune System.
The various components of the immune system (*left*) protect us through
three classes of cells: B lymphocytes (*top right*) produce antibodies to attack
invading microbes. T lymphocytes (*middle right*) release hormones to stimulate B cells to divide. T cells also form killer cells which, together with
macrophages (*bottom right*) directly attack foreign tissues or microbes.

these hormones is to suppress immunological responses by inhibiting the proliferation of some lymphocytes
and triggering the death of others.

Psychological stress and immunity.   The anatomical
and physiological data described in the previous section suggest some bases for the role of psychological

factors in immune-system responses. How can we determine whether psychological factors such as emotions and stress affect either susceptibility or responses to infectious diseases? One approach is to examine unusual immunological responses or disease history in emotionally disturbed populations. For example, several lines of evidence suggest that the competence of the immune system is decreased during depression (Stein, Miller, and Trestman, 1991). Such a compromise of the immune system would increase susceptibility to infectious diseases, cancer, and autoimmune disorders. Altered immune function is also observed in people who are grieving the death of a relative, especially a spouse (Stein and Miller, 1993).

Another way to assess the impact of stress on the immune system is to search for emotional factors in diseases that involve a failure or change in the immune system, especially autoimmune disorders such as arthritis, some types of thyroid disorder, inflammatory bowel disease, and multiple sclerosis, among others. This approach focuses on searching for social and psychological factors that influence the emergence and outcomes of these disorders. For example, psychological factors have been associated with the onset and course of arthritis, which involves a failure of the immune system.

The most common current approach is to study the effects of stress on the immune system of humans and nonhuman populations. These various strategies are revealing the importance of emotions and stress in the susceptibility to and outcome of disorders of the immune system. Here are some examples.

Psychological factors have been related to the susceptibility to and progression of many infectious diseases (Kiecolt-Glaser and Glaser, 1995). For example, the relation between academic stress and immunological functioning has been examined in several studies of medical or dental students during exam periods (which presumably involve high levels of stress) and in subsequent periods of no exams or low levels of stress. Stressful exam periods usually produce a decline in natural killer cell activity (Glaser et al., 1986) and gamma interferon, a glycoprotein that helps regulate the immune system. Most important, some studies have noted that the student's *perception* of the stress of the academic program was a predictor of the level of circulating antibody; those who perceived the program as stressful showed the lowest levels. Observations of immune function during marital disruption, such as separation and divorce, show decreases in immune function, as well as increased mortality rates (Kiecolt-Glaser and Glaser, 1995). Indeed, all forms of impaired personal relationships seem associated with immunological changes. However, healthy subjects show considerable variability and much overlap with stressed subjects in measures of immunological competence.

Studies using nonhumans allow more precise intervention and yield intriguing data. For example, Ader (1987) was able to condition immunosuppression in rats. This result was demonstrated in studies that involved the pairing of saccharin solution with the administration of a chemical immunosuppressive drug. Continued pairings of this type led to the ability of saccharin alone to reduce the response to pathogens.

In similar experiments, Spector and colleagues (1987) have shown that it is possible to use classical conditioning techniques to *enhance* the activity of natural killer cells. In their research they exposed mice to the odor of camphor for several hours. This treatment by itself had no impact on the immune system. Some mice were then injected with a chemical that increased the activity of natural killer cells. After the tenth session of pairings of odor and chemical, mice presented with the odor of camphor alone showed a large increase in natural killer cell activity. This kind of Pavlovian conditioning of immune-system responsiveness might be important as a treatment in some human disorders. It might substitute for injection of drugs that are used to enhance immune-system responses and thus enable reduced exposure to toxic treatments.

Another connection between the nervous and immune systems was described in Chapter 14, where we learned that sleep deprivation impairs the responsiveness of the immune system. Ader and Cohen (1993) comment that the mediators of changes in the immune system are multiple mechanisms that involve the bidirectional character of interactions between the nervous system and the immune system. Clearly a new era of observations of neural modulation and control of immune-system responses has begun.

Immunosuppression as a defense mechanism.   In a delightful book entitled *Why Zebras Don't Get Ulcers*, Robert Sapolsky (1994) considers a variety of evolutionary hypotheses about why immunity is suppressed during stress. To the extent that stress might be a sudden emergency, the temporary suppression of immune responses makes some sense, because the stress response demands a rapid mobilization of energy; immune responses extend longer than the immediacy of a demanding situation would require. However, Sapolsky points out that stress actively modifies the properties of the immune system, rather

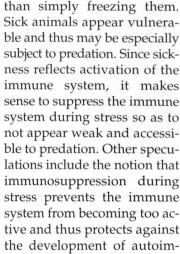

Robert Sapolsky

than simply freezing them. Sick animals appear vulnerable and thus may be especially subject to predation. Since sickness reflects activation of the immune system, it makes sense to suppress the immune system during stress so as to not appear weak and accessible to predation. Other speculations include the notion that immunosuppression during stress prevents the immune system from becoming too active and thus protects against the development of autoimmune disorders. It remains a mystery why some species have evolved suppression of immunity during stress, while others have not.

Handedness and immune disorders.   An unusual association of handedness with immune-system defects in humans was noted by researchers interested in cerebral hemisphere specialization of function. Geschwind and Galaburda (1985) proposed that left-handed people are more likely than right-handed people to suffer from immune-system defects. A high degree of association between left-handedness and asthma, hay fever, and eczema—all dysfunctions of the immune system—was reported by these researchers. Left-handers were more than ten times more likely to report these disorders at some point in their life. The presumed vulnerability of left-handers has also been claimed by Coren (1992), who argues that left-handers die earlier than right–handers. This finding was derived initially from studying the mortality figures of baseball players; subsequent studies relied on vital statistics from California and Canada. However, some researchers have failed to confirm both immune relations to handedness and the differential effects of handedness on mortality. For example, Bishop (1986) found that the distribution of frequencies of immune disorders of 10,000 children in Great Britain is unrelated to handedness. Multiple sclerosis is believed to be an autoimmune disorder, yet the incidence of left-handedness among MS patients is similar to that of age- and sex-matched controls (Hering et al., 1994). This area of study remains steeped in controversy.

Animal models have added more data to the puzzle of laterality and immune-system functioning. The two sides of the mouse brain exert different effects on the immune system. Lesions of right or left neocortex produce opposite effects on such immune measures as interleukin production, natural killer cell activity, and macrophage activation (Neveu, 1993). A connection to immune-system functioning and paw preference in these animals can also be demonstrated. Mice can be classified as "right-pawed" or "left-pawed" based on observations of reaching for food pellets through a narrow opening. This attribute is consistent, and mice are evenly divided according to paw preference. Left-pawed male mice show lower natural killer cell activity compared with right-pawed or ambidextrous male mice (Betancur et al., 1991). These data emphasize that laterality preferences are yet another way to show the interaction between the brain and the immune system.

Stress and Emotions Might Influence Cancer

Every now and then a newspaper or magazine article blares out a warning to readers about links between emotions and cancer. Mystery envelops many aspects of cancer, and its victims often feel "chosen" by evil forces, so it is not surprising that subtle factors, such as emotions, have come under scrutiny in the attempt to discover the cause of cancer. This realm of research is fraught with many contradictory claims. One focus of work concerns the potential role of psychological factors as *causes* of cancer. A second direction of research has explored the impact of psychological influences on the *course and outcome* of cancer (Greer, 1983).

Do emotional states promote the *onset* of cancer? Most studies fail to reveal any direct relation between stressful experiences and the onset of cancer. Some personality studies, however, reveal relations between particular personality attributes and the likelihood of coming down with cancer. One study involved a large collection of students who entered Johns Hopkins School of Medicine between 1948 and 1964 (Thomas, Duszynski, and Shaffer, 1979). Psychological tests and yearly questionnaires about health status were given to this population, and the data were related to disorders that appeared many years later. The group of 48 students who ultimately developed cancer were strikingly similar in personality attributes to those who committed suicide. They were described as "low-gear" people with little display of emotion and whose relation to their parents was characterized as cold and remote. In other studies, prior depression and feelings of hopelessness have been associated with cancers even after statistical adjustments for smoking habits. Some researchers have related breast cancer to a lifelong suppression of anger (Greer, 1983).

The influence of psychological factors on the *course* of cancer has been explored in studies of the reactivation of cancer after a long period of dormancy. Some researchers believe that reactivation in these instances can follow a period of severe emotional stress. Debate also surrounds another psychological aspect of outcome that has emerged from studies of survival time following the diagnosis of cancer. Several investigations have shown that long-term survivors had close personal relationships and coped better with illness-related problems; short-term survivors were characterized as responding with passivity, stoic acceptance, and attempts to forget (Weisman and Worden, 1977). The patient's response three months after mastectomy for breast cancer is also related to the outcome five years after surgery, according to Greer, Morris, and Pettingale (1979). These investigators believe that survival without recurrence is associated with "fighting spirit or denial." Causal connections are difficult to draw in these efforts to relate psychological factors to the many aspects of cancer. Although methodological problems remain to be dealt with, current data clearly point to potentially important psychobiological interactions.

Clues to mechanisms that might account for the links between psychological factors and cancer are found in animal research on stress and the immune system. Research using nonhumans shows that various types of stress produce increased amounts of circulating adrenal cortical hormones, especially corticosterone. Researchers have shown that corticosterone has potent effects on the immune system, including decreased circulating lymphocytes, shrinkage of the thymus gland, and some loss of tissue mass of lymph nodes. Thus, the effectiveness of the immune system is reduced in stress states, and Riley (1981) has suggested that stress enhances vulnerability to cancer-causing agents such as viruses. In one study, this researcher stressed mice into which tumors had been implanted by giving them a brief period of forced body rotation. Following this treatment the tumors grew to four times the size of those in control animals. A similar effect is produced by the direct administration of corticosterone without a stress experience, a finding that lends support to the view that stress-activated release of adrenal cortical hormones can increase susceptibility to cancer or speed its progression.

Emotions and Stress Influence Cardiac Disease

Each day several thousand Americans suffer heart attacks, and many more suffer from other vascular disorders. About one-half of all cardiac-related deaths occur within a few minutes of the onset of symptoms. For many of these individuals, death appears to be caused by the influence of the nervous system on mechanisms that control rhythms of the heart. One part of the story of the origin and progression of heart disease has focused on emotions and psychological stress. Common views of causes of heart attacks emphasize the role of emotions. Many an excited person has heard the admonition, "Calm down before you blow a fuse!" In this section we consider psychological and physiological data that examine the connections among emotions, stress, and heart disease. Many psychological and sociological variables have been examined in studies of behavior patterns related to heart disease.

A major theme instigated by the initial studies of Friedman and Rosenman (1974) has focused on differences between two behavior patterns—Type A and Type B—in the development and maintenance of heart disease. Type A behavior is characterized by excessive competitive drive, impatience, hostility, and accelerated speech and movements; in short, life is frantic, hectic, and demanding for such individuals. In contrast, Type B behavior patterns are more relaxed, with little evidence of aggressive drive or an emphasis on getting things done fast. Of course, this is a crude dichotomy; many individuals have some of each pattern in their characteristic style. For many years research seemed to indicate that Type A individuals show a substantially higher incidence and prevalence of coronary heart disease than do Type B individuals. In the Western Collaborative Group study, following subjects for eight and a half years revealed that those who showed Type A behavior at the beginning of the study were twice as likely as Type B subjects to develop heart disease (Rosenman et al., 1975). This difference was evident even after controlling for cigarette smoking, alcohol use, and nutritional differences. However, studies since 1985 have cast doubt on this association, and some researchers have suggested that the Type A concept is too broad (Steptoe, 1993).

A strong association between *hostility* and heart disease has been noted in these recent studies (Almada et al., 1991). Excessive expression of hostility may also be related to social isolation, which has been implicated as a risk factor for heart disease in several studies. For example, men who are socially isolated and have experienced significant recent life stress, such as family separation, have a much higher mortality rate than do socially integrated controls (Ruberman et al., 1984). In normal young subjects, the presence of a friend during a demanding task lessens the magnitude of cardiovascular responses to this type of stress.

Sudden cardiac death, especially in younger people, highlights another aspect of the link between emotions and heart disease. For example, cardiac disease is common with various brain disorders, especially those that involve destruction in the hypothalamus. Studies of people who have experienced life-threatening arrhythmias also reveal that a period of acute emotional distress preceded the attack in two-thirds of the patients. In addition, psychological stress produces unusual heartbeats in this population. An increased rate of sudden cardiac deaths is also seen following large-scale environmental disasters such as earthquakes. Experimental studies of patients after heart attacks have revealed a group of these patients who respond to mental arithmetic and reaction time tasks with pronounced restriction of blood flow in heart vessels. This effect is regarded as rare in normal individuals. Clearly, sudden cardiac death might arise from brain activities initiated by stress.

Laboratory studies in guinea pigs show that stress can markedly reduce the threshold for heart arrhythmias that are elicited by the drug digitalis (Natelson, 1985). (This drug is often used to regulate heart rate, but at toxic levels it can prove fatal.) Abnormal heart rhythms are evident in rats exposed to conflict stress and inescapable shock. Comparing two different primate species, Hennessy and colleagues (1995) has shown a possible relation between species-characteristic response patterns and disease. They note that squirrel monkeys are excitable, restless, and frequently on the move. In contrast, titi monkeys are more low-key. At rest the squirrel monkey shows a much higher heart rate and higher levels of the hormone cortisol in blood than does the titi monkey. Long-term studies of these animals reveal that squirrel monkeys are susceptible to heart disease, while titi monkeys, in contrast, are more prone to disorders of the immune system. These and other studies show the role of central nervous system influences on cardiac arrhythmias. Various hormones and transmitters also influence cardiac rhythms in ways that suggest their role in the emergence of heart disease (Bohus and Koolhaas, 1993).

Biofeedback Can Control Autonomic Responses

Heart rate, blood pressure, and respiration, among other autonomic responses, are influenced by many internal and external conditions. Yogis (people who practice yoga) and others have dramatically demonstrated ways to control some internal conditions. Stories of their success in reducing heart rate and respiration to death-defying levels are part of the folklore surrounding these mystics. Laboratory observations have documented unusual autonomic control in some of these individuals. Efforts of this sort powerfully demonstrate learned modulations of physiological systems that were at one time thought to be controlled by automatic mechanisms that could not be affected by experience.

Miller (1979) has described biofeedback procedures that result in sustained elevation of blood pressure in patients when they are moved to an upright position. Subjects are instructed to try to increase their blood pressure. Although they can make only tiny changes at the start, training that involves direct knowledge of results has been successful in many cases. Blood pressure information is continuously provided to the patient, and increases of systolic pressure cause a tone to sound. The patient is told to try to make the sound come on as frequently as possible. With success at one blood pressure level, the criterion is changed so that the sound comes on only with yet higher blood pressure responses. Following such a regimen, spinal humans (people whose spinal cord has been severed) can learn to increase their blood pressure when moved to an upright posture, enabling some to be fitted with braces and crutches and thus to become mobile. This learned increase in blood pressure becomes highly specific; that is, eventually it is not accompanied by changes in heart rate.

Summary

1. The term "emotion" includes private subjective feelings, as well as expressions or displays of particular somatic and autonomic responses.

2. Psychologists have generated different category systems to account for the varieties of emotions.

3. The James–Lange theory considered emotions to be the perceptions of stimulus-induced bodily changes, whereas the Cannon–Bard theory emphasized the integration of emotional experiences and responses in the brain. A cognitive theory of emotions argues that activity in a physiological system is not enough to provoke an emotion; rather, the key feature in emotion is the interpretation of visceral activities.

4. Distinct facial expressions represent anger, happiness, sadness, disgust, fear, and surprise, and these expressions are interpreted similarly across many cultures. Facial expressions are controlled by distinct sets of facial muscles controlled by the facial nerve and trigeminal nerve.

5. Particular brain circuits and interconnected regions mediate and control emotions. Relevant regions include limbic-system sites described in the Papez circuit and other related regions, including the amygdala.

6. Electrical stimulation of some brain regions is rewarding. Dopamine is an important transmitter at brain sites involved in reward.

7. The left and right cerebral hemispheres process emotions differently. In normal people, the right hemisphere is better at interpreting emotional states or stimuli.

8. Aggressive behavior is increased by androgens. Brain regions of the limbic system and related sites differ in their relationship to aggressive behavior; stimulation of some regions readily elicits a full, species-typical pattern of aggression.

9. Fear is mediated by circuitry that involves the amygdala, which is directly connected to cortical sensory regions.

10. Assessment of stress in real-life situations shows that stress produces elevations in several hormones, such as cortisol, growth hormone, and epinephrine.

11. Stress affects human health and influences the outcome of disease. Reports of illness tend to be higher in people who sustain prolonged stress, although constitutional factors, as well as strategies for coping with stress, are also important.

12. Ulcer formation, some aspects of cardiac disease, and cancer are affected by stress.

Recommended Reading

Lewis, M. and Haviland, J. M. (eds.) 1993. *Handbook of Emotions*. Guilford Press, New York.

Sapolsky, R. 1994. *Why Zebras Don't Get Ulcers*. W. H. Freeman, New York.

Stanford, S. C. and Gray, J. A. (eds.) 1993. *Stress—From Synapse to Syndrome*. Academic Press, San Diego.

Weiner, H. 1992. *Perturbing the Organism: The Biology of Stressful Experience*. University of Chicago Press, Chicago.

Max Coyer, *Self Portrait #4*, 1985

- *The Toll of Psychiatric Disorders Is Huge*

- *Schizophrenia Is the Major Neurobiological Challenge in Psychiatry*

- *Depression Is a Major Psychiatric Disorder*

- *There Are Several Types of Anxiety Disorders*

- *Neurosurgery Has Been Used to Treat Psychiatric Disorders*

- *There Are Many Different Biological Models of Mental Disorders*

CHAPTER 16

Psychobiology of Mental Disorders

Orientation

Brain researchers have achieved a detailed understanding of the basic workings of nerve cells—especially of molecular events. The rapid accumulation of knowledge in basic neuroscience underlies efforts to understand disordered behaviors. There is a particular urgency to find out more about these afflictions because neurological and psychiatric disorders produce some of the more poignant aspects of human debility. They frequently envelop all aspects of an individual's existence and, in some instances, rob people of the precious sense of personal identity. Most important, those afflicted with these disorders are not an exotic few. Recent surveys show that at least 50 to 75 million persons in the United States suffer from neurological and psychiatric diseases. On the optimistic side, in a relatively short time major developments have offered new insights into disorders such as schizophrenia, anxiety, epilepsy, and other afflictions that have traveled along with human history.

Within the past decade the biological sciences have advanced our understanding of many human afflictions. An explosion of information about the "broken brain" (Andreasen, 1984) gives us the sense that some long-standing mysteries, such as the nature of schizophrenia, are going to be solved and that effective treatments will be based on genuine psychobiological understanding of causes, processes, and mechanisms. Our aim in this chapter is to weave a story; we will restrict our focus to those disorders for which biological research seems to be providing a more complete understanding—to those disorders for which the tale seems to have a beginning, a middle, and the prospect of an end.

The Toll of Psychiatric Disorders Is Huge

Since the beginning of the twentieth century, the mental health movement in the United States has supported large-scale studies that try to determine the number and distribution of psychiatric cases. How many and who among us are or have been psychiatrically ill? All epidemiological studies depend on the clarity of a diagnosis. In psychiatric epidemiology these problems become particularly pressing because there has been much argument about the definition of different psychiatric disorders. During the 1970s, work by psychiatrists to achieve greater agreement about diagnostic judgments led to a major psychiatric epidemiology study; sponsored by the National Institute of Mental Health, it was titled the "Epidemiologic Catchment Area Study" (Robins and Regier, 1991). The most comprehensive look at the psychiatric health of the United States that has ever been accomplished, this study employed thousands of interviewers, researchers, and respondents. Armed with a carefully developed questionnaire and clearly defined diagnostic categories, interviewers went to five different communities across the country. These communities were selected on the basis of several considerations, including the proximity of a major psychiatric research unit, environmental distinctions including the rural/urban difference, and ethnographic features that enabled attention to minority mental health issues.

This large-scale survey provides a definitive portrait of the extent of psychiatric problems in the United States. Risk factors such as social class, level of education, race, and sex are exhaustively reported. Prevalence is described for different time periods, including one month, six months, and lifetime (Table 16.1). The lifetime rates for psychiatric disorder in this study range from 28 to 38%; that is, about one-third of the U. S. population at some point during a typical lifetime reports symptoms that fulfill the defining features of a major psychiatric disorder. Within a six-month period almost 20% of adult Americans suffer from at least one type of disorder classified as psychiatric, at least 8% of us suffer from anxiety disorders, and another 6 to 7% are involved in drug dependency or abuse, especially involving alcohol consumption. In the same time period, depression and related disorders affect 6% of the adult population, and at least 1 in 100 is schizophrenic. Rates for total mental disorders in men and women are comparable, although the proportions of disorders are slightly different for the two sexes. Depression is far more prevalent among females, and drug dependency and alcoholism are more frequent in males. Certain psychiatric disorders—for example, drug abuse and schizophrenia—tend to appear relatively early in life. The age range 25 to 44 shows peaks for depression and antisocial personality, whereas cognitive impairment occurs especially in people older than 65.

Another national study of lifetime and 12-month prevalence of psychiatric disorders offers an even graver portrait of the mental health of the U. S. population (Kessler et al., 1994). About 8100 nonhospitalized persons participated in this survey. They were given a detailed, standardized psychiatric interview that contained more sensitive probes of psychological state than the "Epidemiologic Catchment Area Study" had. According to this new study, almost half the population reported at least one lifetime psychiatric disorder; 30% reported at least one disorder in a twelve-month period (Table 16.2). Although almost half of this sample has a lifetime history of at least one disorder, this population also includes many people who have multiple psychiatric disorders over a lifetime. In fact, almost 15% of this sample has a lifetime history of three or more psychiatric disorders. Furthermore, a majority of severe disorders afflict people with a history of three or more disorders. The most common disorders were major depression and alcohol dependence, with 17% of the sample indicating a history of depression. At least one in four had a lifetime history of anxiety. As in other studies, men were much more likely to have substance use disorders and women were more likely to have affective disorders and anxiety. Psychiatric disorders are most prevalent in the group aged 25 to 34; this declines monotonically with age. Rates of almost all disorders decline with education and income.

Clearly, mental disorders exact an enormous toll on our lives. Efforts to understand these disorders depend on research in diverse areas ranging from cell biology to sociology. Although in the past many psychiatric dysfunctions have been approached from an exclusively psychological framework, current efforts have become more distinctly biological. This orientation aids not only understanding but also therapeutic intervention. Some seeds for a biological perspective in psychiatry were sown around the beginning of the twentieth century. At that time, one widely prevalent psychosis accounted for 20 to 25% of the patient population in mental hospitals. Descriptions of these patients emphasized: profound delusions, grandiosity and euphoria, poor judgment,

Table 16.1

Standardized One-Month, Six-Month, and Lifetime Prevalence of DIS/DSM-III Disorders in Persons 18 Years and Older[a]

DISORDERS	RATE (%)		
	1 MONTH	6 MONTHS	LIFETIME
Any DIS disorder covered	15.4	19.1	32.2
Any DIS disorder except cognitive impairment, substance use disorder, and antisocial personality	11.2	13.1	19.6
Any DIS disorder except phobia	11.2	14.0	25.2
Any DIS disorder except substance use disorders	12.6	14.8	22.1
Any DIS disorder except substance use or phobia	8.3	9.4	13.8
Substance use disorders	3.8	6.0	16.4
Alcohol abuse/dependence	2.8	4.7	13.3
Drug abuse/dependence	1.3	2.0	5.9
Schizophrenic/schizophreniform disorders	0.7	0.9	1.5
Schizophrenia	0.6	0.8	1.3
Schizophreniform disorder	0.1	0.1	0.1
Affective disorders	5.1	5.8	8.3
Manic episode	0.4	0.5	0.8
Major depressive episode	2.2	3.0	5.8
Dysthymia[b]	3.3	3.3	3.3
Anxiety disorders	7.3	8.9	14.6
Phobia	6.2	7.7	12.5
Panic	0.5	0.8	1.6
Obsessive–compulsive	1.3	1.5	2.5
Somatization disorder	0.1	0.1	0.1
Personality disorder, antisocial personality	0.5	0.8	2.5
Cognitive impairment (severe)[b]	1.3	1.3	1.3

[a]The rates are standardized to the age, sex, and race distribution of the 1980 noninstitutionalized population of the United States aged 18 years and older. DIS indicates Diagnostic Interview Schedule.

[b]Dysthymia and cognitive impairment have no recency information; thus, the rates are the same for all three time periods.

impulsive and capricious behavior, and profound changes in thought structure. This disorder was known in virtually all societies of the world and had been noted for centuries. Many people regarded it as a psychosis derived from the stresses and strains of personal and social interactions. Then, in 1911, the microbiologist Hideyo Noguchi discovered the cause of this profound psychosis. Examining the brains of patients during autopsy, he established that extensive brain changes were wrought by *Treponema pallidum*, a bacterium of the class Spirochaeta. This psychosis was produced by syphilis, a venereal infection that has journeyed through history with humans and has appeared in almost all cultures. Noguchi's discovery ushered in an era of biological psychiatry that many believe is now reaching its golden age.

Table 16.2

Lifetime and 12-Month Prevalence of UM-CIDI/DSM-III-R Disorders[a]

DISORDERS	MALE (%)		FEMALE (%)		TOTAL (%)	
	LIFETIME	12 MONTHS	LIFETIME	12 MONTHS	LIFETIME	12 MONTHS
Affective disorders						
Major depressive episode	12.7	7.7	21.3	12.9	17.1	10.3
Manic episode	1.6	1.4	1.7	1.3	1.6	1.3
Dysthymia	4.8	2.1	8.0	3.0	6.4	2.5
Any affective disorder	14.7	8.5	23.9	14.1	19.3	11.3
Anxiety disorders						
Panic disorder	2.0	1.3	5.0	3.2	3.5	2.3
Agoraphobia without panic disorder	3.5	1.7	7.0	3.8	5.3	2.8
Social phobia	11.1	6.6	15.5	9.1	13.3	7.9
Simple phobia	6.7	4.4	15.7	13.2	11.3	8.8
Generalized anxiety disorder	3.6	2.0	6.6	4.3	5.1	3.1
Any anxiety disorder	19.2	11.8	30.5	22.6	24.9	17.2
Substance use disorders						
Alcohol abuse without dependence	12.5	3.4	6.4	1.6	9.4	2.5
Alcohol dependence	20.1	10.7	8.2	3.7	14.1	7.2
Drug abuse without dependence	5.4	1.3	3.5	0.3	4.4	0.8
Drug dependence	9.2	3.8	5.9	1.9	7.5	2.8
Any substance abuse/ dependence	35.4	16.1	17.9	6.6	26.6	11.3
Other disorders						
Antisocial personality	5.8	—	1.2	—	3.5	—
Nonaffective psychosis[b]	0.6	0.5	0.8	0.6	0.7	0.5
Any NCS disorder[a]	48.7	27.7	47.3	31.2	48.0	29.5

[a]UM-CIDI indicates University of Michigan Composite International Diagnostic Interview; NCS, National Comorbidity Survey.

[b]Nonaffective psychosis includes schizophrenia, schizophreniform disorder, schizoaffective disorder, delusional disorder, and atypical psychosis.

Schizophrenia Is the Major Neurobiological Challenge in Psychiatry

Throughout the world, some persons are recognized as unusual because they hear voices, feel intensely frightened, sense persecution from unseen enemies, and act strangely. People with schizophrenia seem to have been a part of all the cultures of the world since the dawn of civilization, although the antiquity of this condition is debated (Bark, 1988; Hare, 1988). For many, this state lasts a lifetime; for others, it appears and disappears unpredictably. Of all the psychiatric disorders, schizophrenia has summoned the most intense public interest and research efforts because it seems such a cruel exaggeration of the human condition. Although most epidemiological surveys of schizophrenia reveal an incidence of less than 1% of the population, this disorder has long commanded a huge portion of community health resources because of its chronic and overwhelming character. Its similarity to some disorders that arise from acknowledged brain disease has long contributed to the view that neurobiological research will provide a thorough understanding of schizophrenia.

Schizophrenia Is Characterized by an Unusual Array of Symptoms

The modern story of schizophrenia starts with Emil Kraepelin (1856–1926), a distinguished German psychiatrist whose book *Dementia Praecox and Paraphrenia* (1919) became the cornerstone of this field. Kraepelin searched for coherent patterns in the many symptoms of psychiatric disorders. His work reflected the zeal in medicine for categorization of disease states. The acuity of his observational skills is evident in his description of the many features of schizophrenia, which reads like notes from the "psychic underworld." Kraepelin's description was rich with details, and he argued that the elements of schizophrenia fit into 11 distinct clinical forms. Features common to the varied forms of **schizophrenia** included bizarre disturbances in thought, paranoid and grandiose delusions, auditory hallucinations, and an odd array of emotional changes. His use of the term "dementia praecox" embodies his view that this disorder begins during adolescence ("praecox" is from the Latin for "early") and moves relentlessly to a chronic state of cognitive impairment ("dementia" is from the Latin *mens*, "mind," and *de*, "without"). According to Kraepelin, the cause must be partly genetic, although the relationship to inheritance is not simple.

In the early twentieth century another major work introduced the term "schizophrenia" (from the Greek, *schizein*, "to part" or "split," and *phren*, "mind"). In 1911, Eugen Bleuler's monograph *Dementia Praecox, or the Group of Schizophrenias* examined more closely the underlying psychological processes of schizophrenia. Although he agreed with Kraepelin that this disorder was a chronic and persistent condition, he did not consider it a "dementia" and he argued that it did not necessarily arise early in life. While agreeing with Kraepelin's description of the disease, he identified the key symptom as **dissociative thinking**. Bleuler also distinguished between primary (fundamental) and secondary (accessory) symptoms. Fundamental symptoms, according to Bleuler, included the four A's: loosening of associations, autism (unmindfulness of reality), affective disturbance, and ambivalence. Accessory symptoms included delusions and hallucinations.

The qualitative character of the descriptions offered by Kraepelin and Bleuler left much room for controversy. During the 1980s and 1990s researchers have continued to refine diagnostic and descriptive categories so that both convey a common understanding of the basic features and withstand the rigors of reliability assessments. The need for clearly defined categories was especially keenly felt among researchers such as Irving Gottesman who believe that some of the inconsistency in data is a consequence of diagnostic categories that have ill-defined boundaries (Gottesman, 1991). Some of the modern reexamination of diagnostic categories is derived from a major shift in diagnostic focus that started with the work of the German psychiatrist Kurt Schneider (1959), whose pragmatic orientation gave primacy to a few major symptoms referred to as "first-rank" symptoms of schizophrenia. These included several forms of auditory hallucinations, delusional interpretations that are highly personalized, and changes in affect. This symptom-oriented approach led to efforts to delineate the highly discriminating signs with clear criteria for diagnosis. The *Diagnostic and Statistical Manual IV* (1993) of the American Psychiatric Association incorporates this view.

Irving Gottesman

Some investigators have proposed a major division of schizophrenic symptoms into two separate groups: positive and negative (Andreasen, 1991). **Positive symptoms** refer to abnormal states such as hallucinations, delusions, and excited motor behavior. **Negative symptoms** reflect insufficient functioning; some examples are emotional and social withdrawal, blunted affect, slowness, and impoverishment of thought and speech. Although researchers continue to question whether schizophrenia is a single entity or a family of related disorders, biological research is helping to clarify the issue.

Defined according to modern criteria, schizophrenia is not distinctive to any particular society; it is a universal disorder found throughout the world. Long-term epidemiological studies of the World Health Organization present some relevant findings (Sartorius et al., 1986; Jablensky et al., 1992). Recently the WHO compared the incidence of schizophrenia in specific cities in ten different countries. These locations included advanced, industrialized communities (Rochester, New York; Moscow, Russia; Aarhus, Denmark) and impoverished cities in developing nations (Agra, India; Cali, Colombia; Ibadan, Nigeria). Data from the report show that the incidence of schizophrenia in all these cities was similar. Symptom pictures in all the varied cultures were also similar, although the prominence of some symptoms appears to show the effects of culture. There were major differences in the mode of onset of the disorder. In developing nations, onset is acute for about 50% of patients, whereas acute onset characterizes only 26% of the patients in developed nations. Follow-up studies conducted over a two-year period revealed that the outcome of schizophrenia is better in less industrialized countries, an intriguing finding that may relate to some of the social support networks available in developing nations or the complex cognitive demands of industrialized societies.

There Is a Genetic Contribution to the Development of Schizophrenia

For many years genetic studies of schizophrenia were controversial, although the notion of inheritance of mental illness is quite old. Data and speculations in this research area sparked vigorous interchanges for several reasons. For one, early researchers in psychiatric genetics seemed to couple presentation of data with advocacy for eugenics measures that were repugnant to many. These included forced sterilization, planned marriages, and the use of positive and negative incentives for having children. Early researchers also failed to appreciate that environments are major modifiers of gene actions. For any genotype there is often a large range of alternative outcomes that are determined by both developmental and environmental factors.

The basic aim of studies in this area is to understand the role of genetic factors in causing and maintaining schizophrenic states. If population studies establish that inheritance plays a significant role, then it becomes important to search for the mechanisms of such effects, including the neurochemical, neurophysiological, and neuroanatomical processes that have gone awry. This type of study includes modern techniques for identification of relevant chromosomes and genes. Genetic studies are also important in the development of preventive programs. For example, if a genetic contribution is established as a significant ingredient in the genesis of schizophrenia, then it would be important to generate programs to aid the at-risk population.

The world population of schizophrenics is estimated at about 10 million. Because of the large number of patients, scientists have been able to conduct a variety of genetic studies (Gottesman, 1991; Kendler et al., 1991a, b), including family or pedigree studies, twin studies, and adoption studies. Let's look at each in turn.

Family studies.   If schizophrenia is inherited, then relatives of schizophrenic patients should show a higher incidence of schizophrenia than is found in the general population. In addition, the risk of schizophrenia among relatives should increase the closer the relationship, since close relatives share a greater number of genes. In general, parents and siblings of patients have a higher risk of being or becoming schizophrenic than do individuals in the general population (Figure 16.1). The risk is greater the closer the biological relatedness. The conclusion of many family studies is that the mode of inheritance of schizophrenia is not simple; that is, it does not involve a single recessive or dominant gene (Tamminga and Schulz, 1991). Most likely, multiple genes play a role in the emergence of schizophrenia.

It is easy to find fault with family studies. First, they confuse hereditary and experiential factors, since members of a family share both. Second, the data usually depend on the recollections of relatives whose memories are likely to be clouded by zealous efforts to attribute "blame" for the disorder. "Funny," departed aunts and uncles are easily designated as the agents responsible for the mental disorder. More reliable family studies restrict data to professionally diagnosed cases.

Although genetic linkage studies in large families have been successful in identifying the specific cause of some disorders (for example, Huntington's disease, as described in Chapter 11), they have been disappointing in the study of schizophrenia, especially since there is little likelihood that a single genetic locus underlies this disorder. Other techniques used in studies of genetic mechanisms of schizophrenia have yielded data that either fail to reveal genetic sites or fail to be confirmed in other studies. Current studies—including those that deal with genes for various transmitter receptors, such as dopamine receptors—should clarify the genetic mechanisms.

Twin studies.   In twins, nature provides researchers with what would seem to be the perfect conditions for a genetic experiment. Human twins can arise either from the same egg (**monozygotic**, or identical, twins) or from two different eggs (**dizygotic**, or fraternal, twins). In addition, many twins have other siblings. Studies of schizophrenia in twins are especially concerned with determining the difference in the rate of occurrence between identical and fraternal twins. When both individuals of a twin pair are schizophrenic, they are described as being **concordant** for this trait. If only one member of the pair is schizophrenic, the pair is described as **discordant**. Table 16.3 compares concordance rates in identical and fraternal twins, as reported in several early studies. It is clear that the concordance rates are much higher in identical (monozygotic) twins.

Contemporary studies of twins continue to confirm

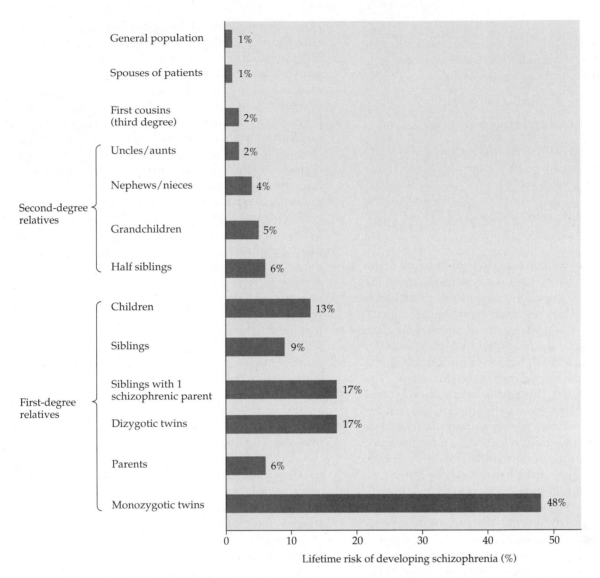

16.1   Schizophrenia Is Heritable
The more closely related a person is to a schizophrenic patient, the greater his or her chances of also developing schizophrenia.

these findings. One recent study (Kendler and Robinette, 1983) used an unusual twin registry established many years ago. This extensive registry was developed from a search of birth certificates in 39 states for twins born during the years 1917 to 1927. The resultant list of 54,000 multiple births was then matched against an index of names maintained by the Veteran's Administration of people who had served in the armed forces. This process identified the twins who were soldiers around the time of World War II; an examination of their medical records revealed 590 individual twins who had a recorded diagnosis of schizophrenia. An analysis of this population revealed that concordance for schizophrenia was greater in monozygotic (30.9%) than in dizygotic (6.5%) twins.

Can we accept such data as reflecting the heritability of schizophrenia? Studies of schizophrenia in twins have been criticized on several grounds. For example, some data indicate that twins are unusual from a developmental perspective in that they usually show lower birth weights and different developmental progress than nontwins. In addition, parental treatment of identical twins differs considerably from their interaction with fraternal twins, thus generating a confounding environmental variable.

Table 16.3

Concordance Rates of Schizophrenia for Monozygotic and Dizygotic Twins

	CONCORDANCE RATE (%)	
STUDY	MONOZYGOTIC	DIZYGOTIC
A	61	10
B	82	15
C	75	14
D	42	9
E	38	10

Despite these weaknesses, studies of twins do indicate the importance of genetic mechanisms in the development of psychotic disorders, particularly schizophrenia. They regularly show higher concordance rates for schizophrenia in identical twins than in fraternal twins or in nontwin siblings. Kendler (1983) notes that the behavior of identical twins is more similar than that of fraternal twins, even when they are mistakenly thought to be fraternal by parents and themselves. Even with identical twins, however, the concordance for schizophrenia is far less than 100%. Although identical twins have the same genetic constitution, one member of the identical twin pair may be schizophrenic and the other normal. The most striking case of schizophrenia in multiple births is presented in Box 16.1.

Studies of identical twins discordant for schizophrenia can provide useful information about the possible factors that lead to schizophrenia and those that protect against its emergence. Many studies emphasize that the twin that developed schizophrenia tended to be the one who was more abnormal throughout life. The symptomatic twin frequently weighed less at birth and had an early developmental history that included more instances of physiological distress (Wahl, 1976). This developmental history is connected with the parents' view of the symptomatic twin as more vulnerable. During development this twin was more submissive, tearful, and sensitive than the identical sibling. Still in its infancy, this type of study may yet suggest how to prevent schizophrenia. We mention this aspect of genetic studies to show that a genetic tendency does not mean that schizophrenia is inevitable; rather such studies may provide ways of preventing onset of the disorder.

Identical twins discordant for schizophrenia have been exhaustively studied in a recent major research report by E. Fuller Torrey and associates (Torrey et al., 1994). Extensive psychological, neuroanatomical,

neurochemical, and developmental data were obtained from both the well and sick twins. This study included 66 pairs of identical twins, of which 27 pairs were discordant for schizophrenia, 13 pairs were concordant, 8 pairs were normal controls, and the rest included either affective disorders or other diagnoses. Family history for schizophrenia did not distinguish monozygotic from dizygotic twins nor either group from normal controls. Early developmental factors, including some related to birth and pregnancy, were evident in the histories of 30% of the twins with schizophrenia. These factors included obstetrical complications such as bleeding during pregnancy, prolonged labor, forceps delivery, prematurity, and initial difficulties in breathing. During childhood, the developmental difficulties of twins who would later become schizophrenic continued in behavioral, cognitive, and other neurological signs such as motor coordination. Other studies have confirmed such childhood developmental dif-

E. Fuller Torrey

Elaine Walker

ferences in future schizophrenics. For example, Elaine Walker showed that, by watching home films of children, observers can pick out the child who became schizophrenic in adulthood with uncanny accuracy (Walker, 1991).

The distinctions between schizophrenics and nonschizophrenics in this study included several neuropsychological characteristics, such as eye tracking. Eye-tracking measurements record eye movements as they follow a moving target on a screen. Many studies show abnormal eye tracking in schizophrenic patients (Levy et al., 1993). In smooth pursuit movements, such as those we perform as we follow the slow to-and-fro movements of the pendulum of an old clock, schizophrenic patients are unable to keep up with the moving object and show the intrusion of the rapid eye movements called saccades (see Chapter 10). Figure 16.2 compares normal and schizophrenic eye tracking. In some studies, eye-tracking dysfunction has also been observed in the relatives of schizophrenic patients, suggesting that this measurement might be a

Box 16.1

Four Copies of Schizophrenia: The Genain Quads

The ultimate"twin" study examined an unusual multiple birth that was first described in the book *The Genain Quadruplets* (Rosenthal, 1963). These identical quadruplets all became schizophrenic by their early twenties. Based on current epidemiological data, this event is extraordinarily rare; only once in one and a half billion births is one likely to find a set of monozygotic quadruplets, all of whom are schizophrenic. It is no surprise, then, that these quads were studied intensively, and that 25 years after their initial evaluation at the National Institute of Mental Health, they were reexamined. Several reports provide a longitudinal perspective on schizophrenia in what can be described as four copies of the same genes (Buchsbaum et al., 1984; DeLisi et al., 1984; Mirsky et al., 1984).

Although identical genetically, from the earliest age the quads showed behavioral differences. The quad that seemed to lag in behavioral development and educational accomplishments would ultimately become the most severely ill of the group. As children they were described as sweet and well mannered, although their teachers noted that they did not display the investigative curiosity typical of young children. They seldom separated and seemed to lack distinctive individual personalities. An ab-

sence of fun and humor was noted in the home environment. Each quad became ill in her early twenties; the clinical description revealed withdrawal, hallucinatory experiences, delusional features, and other elements that were idiosyncratic to each quad. Thus, although the quads are concordant for the diagnosis of schizophrenia, they are not identical in the clinical manifestations of the disorder. The clinical picture since the initial diagnosis has changed very little. All four had psychotic periods during the 25 years between research evaluations, although the severity of recurrent episodes varies. One quad remained for ten years in a mental hospital. The quads vary in their response to antipsychotic medication: when drugs are removed, two of the quads show obvious exacerbation of symptoms while one of them shows little change.

Technical advances allowed more specialized neurological assessments at the second evaluation than were possible 25 years earlier. For example, PET scan studies revealed relatively low glucose utilization in frontal cortical areas in comparison to normal people. In contrast, the quads had higher *posterior* cerebral glucose use than did normal controls. EEG data revealed reduced alpha rhythm amplitude, a finding similar to that observed with other schizophrenic patients. However,

CT scan studies, which show ventricular enlargement in many other schizophrenic patients, did not reveal such abnormalities in the quads. Sluggish response of the autonomic nervous system to arousing stimuli was also noted. Biochemical studies revealed some unusual features. The concentration of dopamine beta hydroxylase, the enzyme that converts dopamine to norepinephrine, was lower in all the quads than in controls. This finding has been seen in at least one other study of chronic schizophrenics. An elevated concentration of phenylethylamine (PEA) was found in the urine of all four. PEA has been thought to be a potential endogenous hallucinogen. Several other biochemical measures that assess aspects of dopamine and norepinephrine metabolism did not differ from controls. The long years of intensive scrutiny of this unique group did not reveal a particular biological fault with any striking or vivid clarity.

The differences among the quads underscore the fact that genes are not the sole basis of schizophrenia. Rather, many environmental variables probably also play a part. The gains won in the quest for a biological understanding of schizophrenia come slowly. Perhaps tomorrow's new findings will offer a perspective on the Genain quads that is missing in today's efforts.

genetic marker for schizophrenia. In the twin study by Torrey and colleagues, however, unaffected identical twins showed no eye-tracking dysfunction, which casts doubt on this measure as a genetic marker. In a following section we will describe neuroanatomical differences in discordant identical twins.

Adoption studies.   Criticisms of twin studies led to adoption studies, which have produced substantial support for the significance of genetic factors in many psychiatric disorders. Most of the relevant data have come from Denmark, where follow-up studies of adoptees are quite complete. Studies by

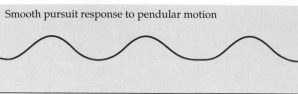

Smooth pursuit response to pendular motion

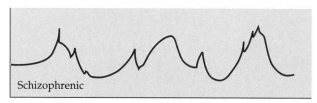

Schizophrenic

16.2 Eye-Tracking in Schizophrenics and Normals
Schizophrenic patients have greater difficulty making
smooth eye pursuits.

Kety and his collaborators (1975) identified the biological and adopting parents of all children in
Copenhagen, Denmark, given up for
adoption early in life during a particular
time period, and identified those who had
been hospitalized for psychiatric difficulties. Psychiatric disorder was found to a
higher degree among the offspring of schizophrenic
parents than in a control group of children of non-
schizophrenic parents. Further, if we change the
point of reference and look at comparisons of the biological and foster parents of schizophrenic
adoptees, striking evidence is displayed. The biological parents of schizophrenic adoptees are far
more likely to have been schizophrenic than are the
adopting parents. It should be emphasized that the
rearing of these patients was almost entirely by
adopting parents, and therefore social influences
from a schizophrenic parent were virtually nil. Although the group of parents giving children up for
adoption early in life is more likely to have psychiatric problems than the general population, the differences between control and patient groups remain
striking. The findings provide conclusive evidence
for genetic factors that predispose to schizophrenia.
A reexamination of these data using current diagnostic criteria continues to show a concentration of
schizophrenia and related disorders among biological relatives of adoptees who developed schizophrenia (Kety, 1983).

These pioneering adoption studies of schizophrenia have now been extended to include the entire country of Denmark (Kety et al., 1994). Figure
16.3 shows pedigrees of adoptees with chronic
schizophrenia and the pedigrees of control subjects.
Once again, the key finding is the significant concentration of cases of schizophrenia in the biological relatives of adoptees with schizophrenia—5.6 %
of relatives versus 0.9 % for adoptees free of schizophrenia. This disorder was more common in first
degree relatives (12 %) than second degree relatives
(2.2%). The frequency of schizophrenia in relatives
of schizophrenic adoptees is similar to that in relatives of nonadoptee schizophrenic patients, suggesting that there is nothing unique about the
adoptee population and strengthening the assertion
that genetics plays a significant part in the emergence of schizophrenia. In addition, these latest
studies show that the increased risk for psychiatric
illness in the biological relatives of schizophrenic
adoptees is limited largely to schizophrenia and a
closely associated diagnosis of latent schizophrenia;
biological relatives do not show an increased likelihood for psychopathology in general. Although
low socioeconomic status (SES) has been associated
with heightened risk of schizophrenia, this study
showed that adoptees from biological parents of low
SES or placed in families of low SES were no more
likely to develop schizophrenia than were adoptees
placed in families of higher SES or from biological
parents of higher SES.

Family, twin, and adoption studies provide consistent evidence that genetics contributes to the incidence of schizophrenia. But many questions remain unanswered: (1) How is the
disorder transmitted? (2) What is being
inherited? (3) What genes are related to
this disorder and what processes do they

control? Although the evidence for genetic transmission of a predisposition to schizophrenia is
clear, there is controversy about alternative genetic
models. Neither single gene models nor multifac-
torial models fit all the data (Faraone and Tsuang,
1985), making genetic counseling difficult. A better
understanding of the environmental and biological
factors that enhance the risk of schizophrenia will
aid the genetic counseling of individuals who are at
risk because of their close relationship to a schizophrenic patient.

(a) (b)

16.3 Schizophrenic Adoptees

The biological relatives of people who were adopted as children and developed schizophrenia in adulthood, are much more likely to develop schizophrenia than are the biological relatives of non-schizophrenic adoptees.

Structural Changes Occur in the Brains of Some Schizophrenics

Since in many patients the symptoms of schizophrenia are so marked and persistent, investigators have wondered whether schizophrenics' brains show a measurable structural change—that is, whether schizophrenia can be localized in the brain (Trimble, 1991). Postmortem investigations of the brains of schizophrenics during the past 100 years occasionally have yielded exciting findings that have been rapidly challenged by better controlled studies. Studies in this field usually have involved aged patients or those who have been hospitalized for long periods. The advent of CT and MRI scans has enabled the study of brain anatomy in living patients at all stages of their illness. Within the last ten years an enormous amount of data from patients at all stages of this disorder have shown that schizophrenic patients do have

structural abnormalities of the brain (Hyde and Weinberger, 1990). Furthermore, there is a growing belief that these brain changes are primary to the disease. The schizophrenic brain is indeed broken!

Ventricular abnormalties. Studies of schizophrenic patients have consistently revealed an enlargement of cerebral ventricles, especially the lateral ventricles (Figure 16.4; Hyde and Weinberger, 1990). Ventricular enlargement is not related to length of illness or to duration of hospitalization. Weinberger and colleagues (1980) indicate that the degree of ventricular enlargement predicts the patient's response to antipsychotic drugs. Patients with more enlarged ventricles show poorer response to these drugs. Although many studies have confirmed that schizophrenic patients have enlarged lateral ventricles, the findings must be qualified: patients with this anatomical characteristic form a distinct subgroup of schizophrenics. Attempts to characterize the patients with enlarged ventricles have revealed other general features, some of them controversial. Some researchers have shown that this group is characterized by a high degree of cognitive impairment and social maladjustment (Kemali et al., 1985). Some researchers have also suggested that patients with enlarged ventricles have more first-degree relatives with schizophrenia than do patients with normal ventricular size.

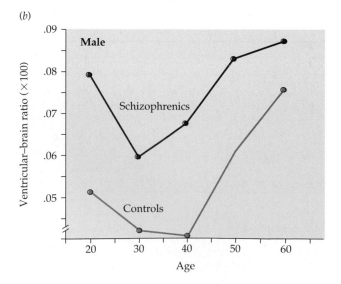

(a)

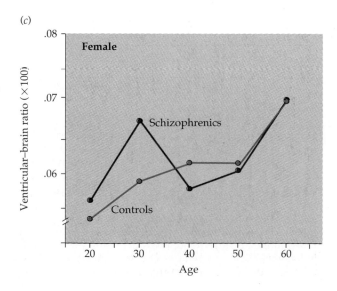

(c)

16.4 Ventricular Enlargement in Schizophrenia
The volume of the cerebral ventricles, relative to overall brain volume, is greater in schizophrenics than in control subjects. Interestingly, this difference is seen almost exclusively in males.

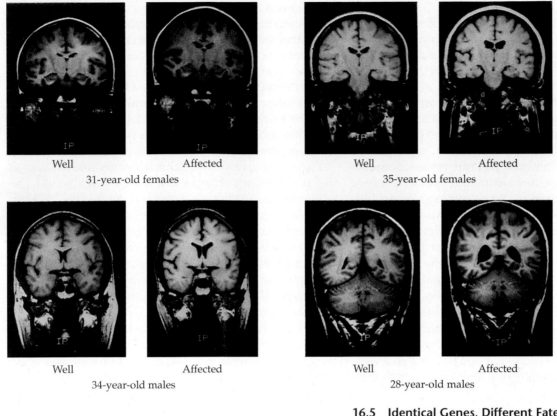

Well · Affected
31-year-old females

Well · Affected
35-year-old females

Well · Affected
34-year-old males

Well · Affected
28-year-old males

16.5 Identical Genes, Different Fates

(*Top*) Although each member of these pairs of monozygotic twins has the exact same genes, only one of each of the twins developed schizophrenia (the twin with larger ventricles). (*Bottom*) Measurements of these subjects' ventricles. After Torrey et al., 1994. MRIs courtesy of E. Fuller Torrey.

breakdown. A study of identical twins discordant for schizophrenia yielded startlingly clear results: the schizophrenic twin had decidedly enlarged lateral ventricles, but the ventricles of the well twin were of normal size (Figure 16.5; Torrey et al., 1994). This twin study also revealed that more than 75% of discordant pairs show a marked difference in the size of the hippocampus and amygdala, with these structures *smaller* in the schizophrenic twin. This observation suggests that the ventricular enlargement in schizophrenics arises from atrophy or destruction of adjacent neural tissue. When brain cells in the regions adjacent to the cerebral ventricles shrink or die, the

Nancy Andreasen

Neuropsychiatrist Nancy Andreasen has used MRI to greatly expand the data in this area and confirm earlier observations that were made using other techniques (Andreasen, 1994). This technique shows that enlargement of the ventricles is a static trait in patients, remaining for many years after the initial

ventricles expand to fill those regions. Some of these changes might arise early in development, even in the prenatal period. This suggestion is supported by the developmental data that we noted earlier, such as the tendency for lower birth weight in the twin who becomes schizophrenic.

Another direction of research that considers a developmental origin for these changes in the schizophrenic brain focuses on viral exposures during pregnancy (Mednick, Huttunen, and Machon, 1994). This area is controversial. Some researchers have shown the possible role of viral exposures by examining relationships between the incidence of schizophrenia and unusual flu epidemics that occurred during the period of the second trimester of the brain development of patients. Other data are based on the distribution of birth dates of schizophrenic patients; there is a slight correlation between the incidence of schizophrenia and a birthdate that falls in the winter or spring months rather than during summer or fall. Some researchers believe that this finding is evidence of a possible enhanced likelihood that patients were exposed in the womb to viral agents that could affect brain development.

Limbic system abnormalties. Neuropathological studies of the limbic system of schizophrenic patients have revealed differences between patients and controls in several areas, including the hippocampus, amygdala, and parahippocampal regions. Kovelman and Scheibel (1984) noted changes in the hippocampus of chronic schizophrenics. These investigators compared the brains of chronic schizophrenics with those of medical patients of the same age that did not exhibit brain pathology. A sample of the typical cellular differences is shown in Figure 16.6. The pyramidal cells of chronic schizophrenics were disoriented, a type of cellular disarray. Presumably the lack of normal cellular polarity is related to abnormal synaptic linkages, including both inputs and outputs of these cells. The degree of disorientation was positively related to the severity of the disorder. A more recent study by this group (Conrad et al., 1991) extends and corroborates the earlier work and establishes that disorientation of hippocampal pyramidal cells is evident in both the right and left hippocampus. According to these authors, this cellular derangement probably arises during early cell development and might reflect maternal exposure to an influenza infection during the second trimester of pregnancy. These abnormalities of cellular arrangement in the hippocampus are said to resemble

those of mutant mice that show disordered neurogenesis in the hippocampus (Scheibel and Conrad, 1993). Other studies have noted differences between patients and controls in the entorhinal cortex, parahippocampal cortex, and cingulate cortex (Shapiro, 1993).

Some cellular observations have focused on the basal ganglia because schizophrenic patients often show unusual body postures and mannerisms in addition to other abnormal movements. In addition, some metabolic disorders that destroy basal ganglia sites as the result of calcium deposits result in psychiatric changes that resemble schizophrenia. Although structural studies reveal inconsistent differences between patients and controls, neurochemical studies of these structures show an increase in dopamine D_2 receptors in the caudate and putamen of some schizophrenic patients. Unfortunately, antipsychotic drugs drastically modify D_2 receptors; most patients who are not taking antipsychotic drugs do not have elevated levels of D_2 receptors (Hietala et al., 1994). A dramatic sixfold increase in dopamine D_4 receptors in schizophrenic patients has drawn renewed attention to basal ganglia structures, which contain extensive dopaminergic connections (Seeman, Guan, and Van Tol, 1993). A little later in this chapter we will discuss the hypothesis that abnormal levels of dopamine underlie schizophrenia.

Regional and cellular abnormalities. Once there were very few reliable findings of brain structural pathology in schizophrenia. Now an overabundance of positive findings overwhelms the effort toward an integrative portrait of the regional and cellular pathology of schizophrenia.

Deficits shown by schizophrenic patients in tests that are sensitive to frontal cortical lesions have drawn attention to possible frontal cortical abnormalities. Although some studies show reduced frontal cortical volume in patients, others have failed to show major abnormalities of the frontal cortex (Wible et al., 1995). However, altered gene expression relevant to inhibitory neurons of the frontal cortex has been shown in the prefrontal cortex of schizophrenics without the loss of neurons. These cells show reduced activity for an enzyme involved in GABA synthesis (Akbarian et al., 1995). Several studies have noted marked shrinkage of the vermian region of the cerebellum in chronic patients, and have shown that this abnormality is not related to prolonged antipsychotic drug use (Heath et al., 1979; Snider, 1982). Chronic schizophrenics whose disorder started early in life have thicker regions in the corpus callosum, both in

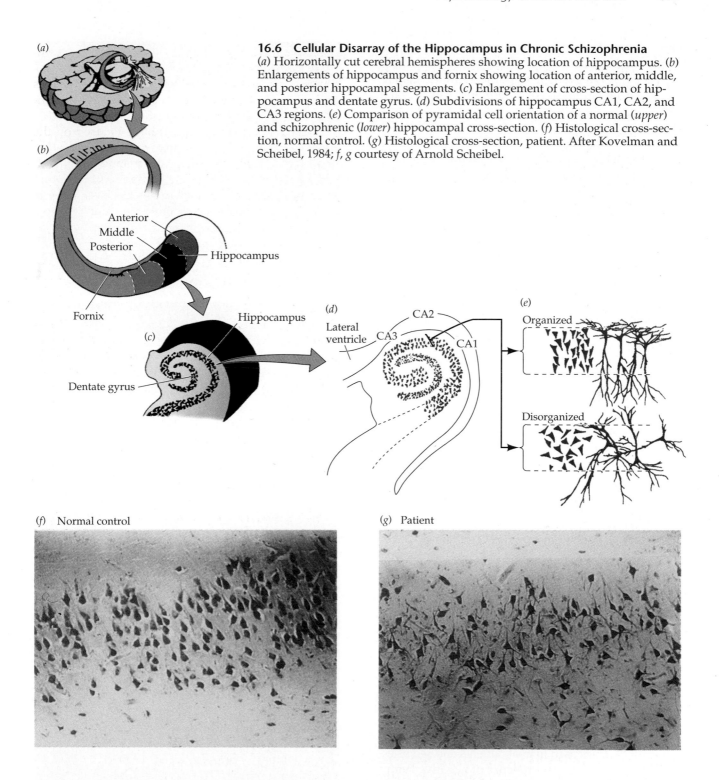

16.6   Cellular Disarray of the Hippocampus in Chronic Schizophrenia
(*a*) Horizontally cut cerebral hemispheres showing location of hippocampus. (*b*) Enlargements of hippocampus and fornix showing location of anterior, middle, and posterior hippocampal segments. (*c*) Enlargement of cross-section of hippocampus and dentate gyrus. (*d*) Subdivisions of hippocampus CA1, CA2, and CA3 regions. (*e*) Comparison of pyramidal cell orientation of a normal (*upper*) and schizophrenic (*lower*) hippocampal cross-section. (*f*) Histological cross-section, normal control. (*g*) Histological cross-section, patient. After Kovelman and Scheibel, 1984; *f*, *g* courtesy of Arnold Scheibel.

anatomical preparations and in some CT scans (Bigelow, Nasrallah, and Rauscher, 1983).

Several hypotheses that link anatomical plasticity of the brain to schizophrenia have a developmental focus. One researcher has proposed that a fault in the normal course of synapse elimination (see Chapter 4) during adolescence gives rise to a major rearrangement of brain structures that results in schizophrenia (Feinberg, 1982). Another researcher has suggested that genetic factors predispose schizophrenic brains to show unusual plastic changes in response to the routine stresses of life (Haracz, 1984).

This suggestion is derived from observations that brain structures can be modified by experience (see Chapter 18). Whereas the hypotheses that we mentioned earlier emphasized abnormalities in prenatal development, these hypotheses refer to development in adolescence or later. Effects at one period in development do not necessarily preclude effects at another, and schizophrenia may be a blanket term for a collection of disorders, as we'll see.

Functional Maps Reveal Differences in Schizophrenic Brains

The advent of positron emission tomography (PET), functional magnetic resonance imaging (fMRI), and single photon emission computerized tomography (SPECT) has provided an abundance of new windows to view the schizophrenic brain. (These methods were introduced in Chapter 2.) The most common measures in these studies have been regional blood flow and cerebral rate of glucose metabolism.

Schizophrenia may involve an alteration in the functional lateralization of the cerebral hemispheres, according to some blood flow imaging studies. Left hemisphere overactivation during resting states has been suggested (Gur et al., 1987), but other data suggest that this effect may be restricted to overactivation of left frontal lobe (Berman and Weinberger, 1990).

Early observations using PET scan techniques revealed an unusual metabolic feature of schizophrenic brains: patients show relatively less metabolic activity in frontal lobes as compared with their posterior lobes than do normal subjects (Buchsbaum et al., 1984). This observation, sometimes referred to as the **hypofrontality hypothesis,** has generated controversy and has fueled interest in the role of the frontal lobes in schizophrenia (Weinberger et al., 1994). Some experiments related to this hypothesis show this effect only during difficult cognitive tasks that particularly activate the frontal area (Figure 16.7) and at which frontally damaged patients often fail. Unlike control subjects, schizophrenic patients fail to increase their prefrontal activation above basal levels (Weinberger et al., 1994). This deficit is behavior-specific; other tasks do not elicit this phenomenon. This effect does not appear to be the result of drugs used to treat patients and seems especially related to the prominence of negative symptoms (Andreasen et al., 1992). Studies of discordant identical twins show that the hypofrontal blood flow levels are low only in the schizophrenic twin. Changes in frontal lobe structure and function are also found in EEG studies and MRI observations of schizophrenic patients (Andreasen et al., 1986; Morihisa and McAnulty, 1985).

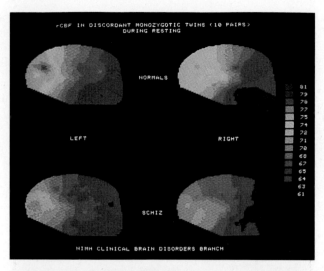

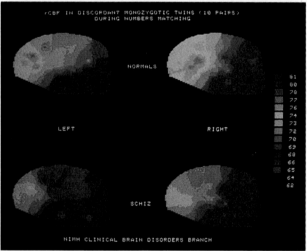

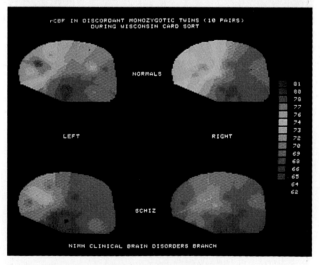

16.7 Hypofrontality in Schizophrenia
Regions of increased cerebral blood flow during a number-matching task (*middle*) and the Wisconsin Card Sort (*bottom*) is more restricted in schizophrenics. Courtesy of Karen Berman.

Many of the pathological changes in the brains of schizophrenic patients are found in regions of the limbic system that are involved in neural mechanisms of emotion. Some of these anatomical observations are generating a more useful classification system for schizophrenia, because they reveal that frank structural pathology is not a characteristic of all schizophrenic patients. Some researchers (for example, Crow, 1990) have suggested that there are two types of schizophrenia. One type is characterized by the prominence of widespread anatomical changes, negative symptoms, and nonresponsiveness to drug treatments. A second type is characterized by the absence of anatomical changes in the brain, greater prominence of positive symptoms, and successful intervention with antipsychotic drugs. Some facts fit this model and some do not. There are methodological problems in this work and the reliability of some observations may prove weak, but these studies are opening a productive era of research. There is light at the end of this tunnel!

The Brains of Schizophrenics Change Neurochemically

Throughout history explanations of mental disorder have emphasized biological origins. Bodily factors assumed to be related to schizophrenia have included injury, infection, diet, and brain disease. As knowledge about the neurochemistry of the brain has grown, hypotheses about the bases of schizophrenia have become more precise. Several major views of the biological origins of schizophrenia are backed by large amounts of experimental data and clinical observation. One view holds that schizophrenia arises from faulty metabolic processes in the brain that lead to excesses or insufficiencies of neurochemicals that are normally found in the brain. In most cases these substances are neurotransmitters or neuromodulators; the most prominent example in current research is dopamine. The functional effect of this type of change would be under- or overactivity of some brain circuits. A second general perspective proposes that schizophrenia develops from faulty metabolic processes in the brain that produce abnormal substances that generate psychotic behavior. Such hypothetical substances, called **psychotogens** or **schizotoxins**, might be similar in some ways to hallucinogenic agents. We will examine each of these two main hypotheses in the sections that follow.

Although exciting ideas and data are apparent in the research, several problems continue to frustrate major progress. First, it is very hard to separate neurochemical events that are primary causes of psychiatric disorder from those that are secondary effects. Secondary effects arise from the profound impairments of social behavior and may range from dietary limitations to prolonged stress. Treatment variables, especially the long-term use of antipsychotic substances, can mask or distort primary causes, because they frequently produce marked changes in brain and body physiology and biochemistry. A second major problem in neurochemical research of schizophrenia is the definition of schizophrenia itself. Is it a single disorder, or many disorders with different origins and outcomes? Although evident in other areas of schizophrenia research, this problem is especially acute for neurochemical research because of the variability of the neurochemical findings.

The dopamine hypothesis. Many clinical and basic experimental findings have suggested that abnormal levels of dopamine form the basis of schizophrenia. In Chapter 6 we learned that dopamine is a synaptic transmitter in the brain; in Chapter 15 we discussed its role in brain reward circuits. The first clues suggesting that dopamine plays a role in schizophrenia came from observations of amphetamine psychosis, the effects of antipsychotic drugs, and Parkinson's disease.

Part of the dopamine story starts with the search for experimental models of schizophrenia. Basic scientific advances in the understanding of human disease frequently depend on the development of a controllable model of the disorder, usually an animal replica that can be turned on and off by experimenters. Some scientists involved in psychiatric research have suggested the effects of certain hallucinogenic agents as models of the symptoms of schizophrenia. Although many drugs, such as LSD and mescaline, produce profound perceptual, cognitive, and emotional changes, some of which resemble aspects of psychoses, several features of the behavioral effects of these drugs are quite dissimilar from symptoms of schizophrenia. Most drug-induced psychoses are characterized by confusion, disorientation, and frank delirium; these are not typical symptoms of schizophrenia. Hallucinations produced by these drugs are usually visual, in contrast to the predominantly auditory hallucinations of schizophrenia. Schizophrenic patients given LSD report that the experience produced by the drug is very different from the experiences of their disorder, and psychiatrists can readily distinguish taped conversations of schizophrenics from those of subjects given hallucinogenic agents. One drug state, however, comes close to replicating the schizophrenic state—amphetamine psychosis.

Some individuals use amphetamine on an every-day basis as a stimulant. To maintain the same level of euphoria, however, the self-administered dose must be progressively increased and may reach as much as 3000 milligrams (mg) per day. Contrast this level with the usual 5 mg taken to control appetite or prolong wakefulness. Many of these individuals develop paranoid symptoms, often involving delusions of persecution with auditory hallucinations, and exhibit suspiciousness and bizarre postures. The similarity of amphetamine psychosis to schizophrenia is also supported by the finding that amphetamine exacerbates symptoms of schizophrenia. Neurochemically, amphetamine promotes the release of catecholamines, particularly dopamine, and prolongs the action of the released transmitter by blocking reuptake. Rapid relief from amphetamine psychosis is provided by injection of **chlorpromazine**—a substance that brings us to the second part of the story of the dopamine hypothesis.

Chlorpromazine has been used much more widely than as an antidote to amphetamine psychoses. In the early 1950s, there were about half a million psychiatric hospitals in the United States. This number has decreased dramatically since then. Several factors contributed to this reduction, the most significant being the introduction of chlorpromazine in the treatment of schizophrenia. In the search for a substance to produce muscle relaxation for surgery, French surgeon Henri Laborit in the 1940s discovered that chlorpromazine not only achieved these effects but also reduced worry and preoperative tension. An insightful investigator, Laborit collaborated with psychiatrists in trying this substance on psychiatric patients; they found remarkable antipsychotic effects. Chlorpromazine was then introduced on a large scale in psychiatric hospitals around the world, with a profound impact. By now a massive number of well-controlled studies point to the fact that chlorpromazine and many other substances related to it (called **phenothiazines**) have a specific antipsychotic effect. Neurochemical studies show that this substance acts in the brain by blocking postsynaptic receptor sites for dopamine (Figure 16.8), specifically, the D_2 type. As we noted in Chapter 6, there are several major dopamine-containing pathways. Investigators believe that a major site of action of antipsychotic drugs (also called neuroleptics or tranquilizers) is dopamine terminals in the limbic system. These cells originate in the brain stem, near the substantia nigra. The clinical effectiveness of antipsychotic agents is directly related to the magnitude of postsynaptic receptor blockage of dopamine sites, as we saw in Table 6.4. This result suggests that schizophre-

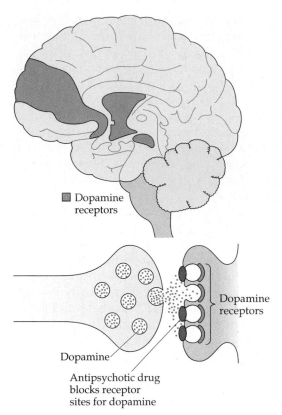

■ Dopamine receptors

Dopamine receptors

Dopamine

Antipsychotic drug blocks receptor sites for dopamine

16.8   Mechanisms of Drug Action at a Dopamine Synapse
Overactivation of dopamine receptors may cause symptoms of schizophrenia.

nia may be produced either by abnormal levels of available and released dopamine or by excessive postsynaptic sensitivity to released dopamine, which might involve an excessively large population of postsynaptic dopamine receptor sites.

Another trail leading to the dopamine hypothesis of schizophrenia involves Parkinson's disease (see Chapter 11). Parkinson's disease is caused by the degeneration of nerve cells located in the brain stem (in a region called the substantia nigra). These cells contain dopamine, and administering the substance L-dopa, a precursor for the synthesis of dopamine, increases the amount of released dopamine, which thus provides some relief of parkinsonian symptoms. Two observations of Parkinson's patients connect this disease with schizophrenia and the dopamine hypothesis. First, some patients given L-dopa to relieve parkinsonian symptoms become psychotic. Second, some schizophrenic patients receiving chlorpromazine develop parkinsonian symptoms. In fact, treatment with antipsychotic drugs can result in permanent movement disorders (see Box 16.2). Some studies show a

Box 16.2

Long-Term Effects of Antipsychotic Drugs

Few people would deny that drugs like chlorpromazine have had a revolutionary impact on the treatment of schizophrenia. With such treatment, many people who might otherwise have been in mental hospitals their whole lives can take care of themselves in nonhospital settings. Drugs of this class can justly be regarded as antipsychotic.

Antipsychotic drugs often have other effects that bring their use into question. Soon after beginning to take these drugs, some users develop maladaptive motor symptoms (dyskinesia). Although many of these symptoms are transient and disappear when the dosage of drug is reduced, some drug-induced motor changes emerge only after prolonged drug treatment—after months, sometimes years. This condition is called **tardive dyskinesia** (from the Latin *tardus*, "late"). The motor effects of tardive dyskinesia include many involuntary movements, especially involving the face, mouth, lips, and tongue. Elaborate uncontrollable movements of the tongue are particularly prominent, including incessant rolling movements and sucking or smacking of the lips. Some patients show twisting and sudden jerking movements of the arms or legs (Casey, 1989). Antipsychotic substances affect a

large percentage of patients—as much as one-third—in this way. The drugs usually affect females more severely than they do males (Smith et al., 1979). The relationship between drug parameters and the likelihood of such side effects is complex. In some patients, these effects become apparent only after prolonged use of the drug; in others, relatively brief use of the drug causes these motor changes (Toenniessen, Casey, and McFarland, 1985). What is alarming is that this motor impairment frequently becomes permanent, even if drug treatment is halted.

The underlying mechanism for tardive dyskinesia continues to be a puzzle. Some researchers claim that it arises from chronic blockade of dopamine receptors, which results in receptor site supersensitivity. Critics of this view point out that tardive dyskinesia frequently takes a long time to develop and may be irreversible, a time course that is different from dopamine receptor supersensitivity. In addition, there is no difference in D_1 or D_2 receptor binding between patients with tardive dyskinesia and those without these symptoms. A GABA deficiency hypothesis of tardive dyskinesia has been offered by Fibiger and Lloyd (1984). They believe that tardive dyskinesia is

the result of drug-induced destruction of GABA neurons in the corpus striatum. Neuroleptic-induced changes in enzymes related to GABA have been observed in experimental animals. A noradrenergic hypothesis of this disorder has also been presented, based on evidence that the cerebrospinal fluid concentration of norepinephrine is correlated with tardive dyskinesia (Kaufmann et al., 1986).

Long-term treatment with antipsychotic drugs has another unusual effect: prolonged blockage of dopamine receptors seems to increase the number of dopamine receptors and lead to receptor supersensitivity. In some patients discontinuation of the drugs or a lowering of dosage results in a sudden, marked increase in positive symptoms of schizophrenia, such as delusions or hallucinations. The effect is often reversible by increasing the dosage of dopamine-receptor blocking agents. Some data suggest, however, that this "supersensitivity psychosis" might be enduring. Both tardive dyskinesia and supersensitivity psychosis are pressing problems for research, since they may limit the effectiveness of phenothiazines and related substances in the treatment of schizophrenia.

link between schizophrenic brain atrophy and disturbed dopamine metabolism: schizophrenic patients with enlarged ventricles show a marked reduction in spinal fluid levels of dopamine beta hydroxylase, an enzyme involved in the conversion of dopamine into norepinephrine (Sternberg et al., 1982).

The earliest, simplest dopamine model of schizophrenia argued that this disorder arises from the hy-

perfunctioning of dopamine circuits. This hyperfunctioning could develop from excessive release of dopamine—a presynaptic effect—or an excess of dopamine receptors—a postsynaptic effect. For years, the strongest evidence for this simple hypothesis was the remarkable clinical success of dopamine blockers in treating schizophrenia. Indeed, the clinical effectiveness of the many neuroleptic drugs introduced

16.9 Anti-Psychotic Drugs That Affect Dopamine Receptors

Drugs vary widely in the affinity with which they bind to various neurotransmitter receptors. Those drugs that block dopamine receptors, specifically the D_2 variety, are more effective at combating symptoms of schizophrenia.

Receptor affinity key

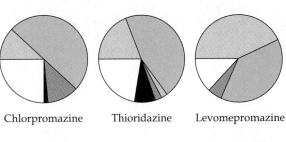

Sulpiride Pimozide Haloperidol

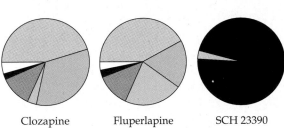

Flupentixol Clopenthixol Perphenazine

Chlorpromazine Thioridazine Levomepromazine

Clozapine Fluperlapine SCH 23390

over the past 40 years has been directly related to their effectiveness in blocking or antagonizing dopamine (Figure 16.9; see also Table 6.4). Drugs that have the opposite effect—*increasing* dopamine activity—worsen schizophrenic symptoms.

Criticisms of a dopamine model of schizophrenia began to emerge in the 1980s (Alpert and Friedhoff, 1980). Clinical observations revealed that some schizophrenic patients show no changes with drugs that affect dopamine; more recently, some of these patients have been shown to derive benefit from drugs such as clozapine that affect serotonin levels. Other clinical observations indicate that dopamine antagonists do little to alleviate the negative symptoms of schizophrenia. More directly related to an assessment of the simple dopamine hypothesis is the fact that studies of dopamine metabolites in blood, cerebrospinal fluid, or urine have provided inconsistent evidence regarding the possible hyperfunctioning of dopamine terminals. For example, many schizophrenic patients have normal levels of metabolites of dopamine in their cerebrospinal fluid.

Some postmortem and PET studies of schizophrenic brains reveal an increase in dopamine receptors, especially the D_2 type (Figure 16.10; Davis et al., 1991). This elevated level of dopamine receptors is evident even in patients who have been off neuroleptic drugs for some time. PET studies of D_2 receptor density in schizophrenics are inconsistent, as are efforts to relate a D_2 receptor gene to schizophrenia. Another problem with the dopamine hypothesis is the lack of correspondence between the time at which drugs block dopamine (quite rapidly) and the behavior changes that signal the clinical effectiveness of the drug (usually on the order of weeks). Thus, the relation of dopamine to schizophrenia may be more complex than that envisioned in the simple model of hyperactive dopamine synapses. Perhaps dopamine impairment accounts for only some aspects of the schizophrenic syndrome (Carlton and Manowitz, 1984).

A reformulation of the simple dopamine hypothesis adds another dimension to the story. Davis and colleagues (1991) speculate that schizophrenia might be related to both hypo- and hyperfunctioning of dopamine. They suggest that activity is diminished in the dopamine synapses of the prefrontal cortex, but excessive in mesolimbic dopamine pathways. In fact, low prefrontal dopamine activity leads to abnormal excessive subcortical dopamine activity and D_2 receptors. Negative symptoms, they suggest, arise from low prefrontal dopamine activity. Complicating the dopamine story further is the recent discovery of the marked increase in D_4 receptors in schizophrenic brains.

The schizotoxin hypothesis. The chemical structure of some manufactured hallucinogens resembles that of some endogenous substances of the brain. This finding suggested that the brain might accidentally produce a psychotogen—a chemical substance that causes psychotic behavior. Metabolic faults in particular pathways

Control   Blocked

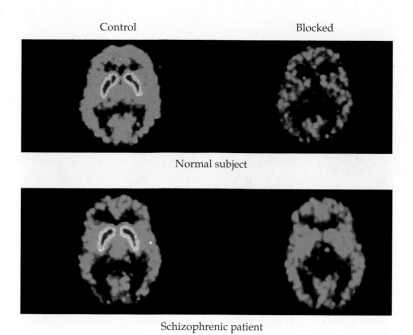

Normal subject

Schizophrenic patient

16.10   Distribution of Dopamine Receptors in Schizophrenia
These PET scans indicate distribution of dopamine binding in the brain of a normal (*top*) and schizophrenic subject (*bottom*). In the control condition (*left*), the normal subject shows greater and more widely distributed receptors than the schizophrenic subject. Injecting the D2 dopamine blocker haloperidol (*right*) abolishes nearly all binding in the normal subject but not in the schizophrenic. Courtesy of Dean F. Wong.

might cause the brain to convert an innocuous molecule into a behaviorally maladaptive substance capable of producing schizophrenic symptoms. The **transmethylation hypothesis** suggests that the addition of a methyl group (CH_3) to some naturally occurring brain compounds can convert the substances into known hallucinogenic agents. This hypothesis was initiated in the 1950s by Osmond and Smythies, who showed hallucinogenic properties for a substance called adrenochrome. This substance was viewed as a possible metabolic product of norepinephrine—now known to be a neurotransmitter in the brain as well as in the peripheral autonomic nervous system.

More recent experiments have tested the idea that transmethylation could produce a compound that might act as a substance that produces schizophrenia—a schizotoxin. One way to test this idea is to administer substances (methyl donors) that provide a good supply of methyl groups. When administered to schizophrenic patients, some of these substances exacerbate the symptoms, although the effect is not general to all such substances. This inconsistency, coupled with problems in understanding how the mechanism could account for the effects of antipsychotic drugs, limits the current credibility of the proposal A modification of the transmethylation hypothesis (Smythies, 1984) suggests that the fault in schizophrenia is an impairment in the transmethylation mechanism itself, rather than the generation of an unusual schizophrenia-producing substance. To

support this idea, Smythies presents evidence that the rate of transmethylation in some patients is slower than in normal subjects.

Can the body produce amphetamine-like substances by metabolizing norepinephrine? The amphetamine molecule resembles the molecules of catecholamine transmitters. Since amphetamine psychosis resembles paranoid schizophrenia, an endogenous amphetamine-like substance would be a very interesting finding. Recently several investigators have argued that phenylethylamine (PEA)—a substance with amphetamine-like properties—is produced in small quantities by the metabolism of norepinephrine. Current work seeks to assess levels of this metabolite in the bodies of schizophrenics. (Recall that PEA was elevated in the Genain quads; see Box 16.1.)

As we learned in our discussion of the dopamine hypothesis, drug-induced psychoses do not make good models of schizophrenia because the psychological and behavioral changes that they produce do not mimic schizophrenia with great fidelity. One powerful psychotogen, however, comes close to producing a schizophrenia-like state. Initially developed to produce a "dissociative" anesthetic state (one in which an animal was insensitive to pain but showed some types of arousal or responsiveness), this substance, called phencyclidine (PCP), produces auditory hallucinations, strange depersonalization, disorientation, and intense assaultive behavior. In some cases, prolonged psychotic states can develop from

(a)

(b)

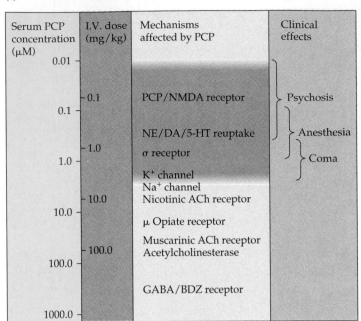

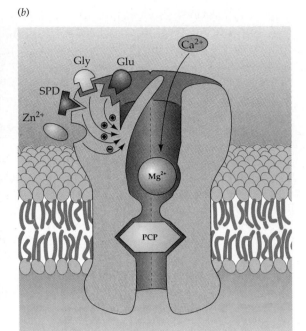

Serum PCP concentration (μM)	I.V. dose (mg/kg)	Mechanisms affected by PCP	Clinical effects
0.01 —			
	0.1	PCP/NMDA receptor	Psychosis
0.1 —			
	1.0	NE/DA/5-HT reuptake	Anesthesia
		σ receptor	
1.0 —			Coma
		K⁺ channel	
	10.0	Na⁺ channel	
		Nicotinic ACh receptor	
10.0 —			
		μ Opiate receptor	
	100.0	Muscarinic ACh receptor	
		Acetylcholinesterase	
100.0 —			
		GABA/BDZ receptor	
1000.0 —			

16.11   PCP Affects the NMDA Receptor
Because the serum concentrations of PCP which elicit clinical effects are the same concentrations that result in PCP binding of the NMDA receptor, the clinical effects may be caused by NMDA receptor binding.

the use of this substance. The mechanism of action of PCP involves the NMDA receptor complex (see Box 5.3), as illustrated in Figure 16.11. Thus PCP can disturb glutamate neurotransmission; a glutamate hypothesis of schizophrenia has been advanced by some researchers, although research findings about this transmitter in the brains of schizophrenics have been inconsistent.

Neurochemicals and Schizophrenia: A Commentary

The development of neurochemical tools since the mid-1970s has provided many opportunities to describe the metabolic activities of the brain. Some of this work is limited by the fact that clues to brain events are derived primarily from analysis of metabolic products found in blood, urine, or cerebrospinal fluid. These fluids are remote from the sites at which significant changes may occur. Recent developments in PET scans using radiolabeled drugs may provide a more direct view of the neurochemical events in the schizophrenic brain. Another issue in examining the neurochemistry of schizophrenia is that our conceptions of the chemical machinery of the brain are rapidly changing, so a simplistic single-transmitter

view, such as the dopamine hypothesis, is difficult to reconcile with the elaborate picture of interactive influences that modern research depicts.

An Integrative Psychobiological Model of Schizophrenia

At times it seems as though research on schizophrenia has given us many pieces of a large puzzle whose overall appearance is still unknown. Some recent efforts at integrating the many psychological and biological findings in the field have resulted in important new views about the origins of schizophrenia. One such model, presented by Mirsky and Duncan (1986), views schizophrenia as an outcome of the interaction of genetic, developmental, and stress factors. According to this model, at each life stage specific features contribute to an enhanced vulnerability to schizophrenia. Genetic influences can be expressed as "brain abnormalities" that provide the basic neurological substrate for schizophrenia. Intrauterine and birth complications—often evident in schizophrenic patients—may also contribute to schizophrenia-generating brain abnormalities. Mirsky and Duncan suggest that through childhood and adolescence, neurological deficits are manifested by behaviors such as impaired cognitive skills, attention deficits, irritability, and delayed gross motor development. Similar neurological deficits are evident in the non-schizophrenic relatives of schizophrenic patients, which lends further support to the idea that a genetic factor contributes to schizophrenia (Kinney, Woods, and Yurgelum-Todd, 1986).

According to the model of Mirsky and Duncan, the emergence of schizophrenia and related disorders depends on the *interaction* of a compromised biological substrate with environmental stressors (Figure 16.12). The magnitude of brain abnormalities in vulnerable individuals determines how much stress is needed to produce a schizophrenic disorder. Schizophrenia emerges, according to this model, when the combination of stress and brain abnormalities exceeds a threshold value. People with many schizophrenic brain abnormalities may become symptomatic with relatively minor environmental stresses. Sources of stress may include some types of family interactions, the consequences of impaired attentional or cognitive skills, and the stress of "being different" during development, especially during adolescence. Models like this offer the opportunity to appreciate differences among patients. They also sug-

gest the possibility of strategies for decreasing the likelihood of schizophrenia for the at-risk child. New biological aids, such as PET scans and genetic tools, might help us identify and understand the at-risk child at a stage early in life, when biological and environmental interventions might reduce the prospects of schizophrenia later in life.

Depression Is a Major Psychiatric Disorder

It would seem as though no person now alive nor any of our forebears has been a stranger to depression. In the engraving shown in Figure 16.13, medieval artist Albrecht Dürer gives us a powerful portrait of the posture and sense of emptiness of this condition. Many of us go through periods of unhappiness that we commonly describe as depression. In some people, however, a depressive state is more than a passing malaise and occurs over and over with cyclical regularity. Such people are usually over 40 years old, and women are two to three times as likely to suffer from depression as men. The depression is characterized by an unhappy mood; loss of interests, energy, and appetite; difficulty in concentration; and restless agitation. Pessimism seems to seep into every act. Periods of such **unipolar depression** (that is, depression that alternates with normal emotional states) can occur with no readily apparent stress. Without treatment, the depression lasts for several months. Depressive illnesses of this sort afflict 13 to 20% of the population at any one time (Cassens, Wolfe, and Zola, 1990).

Some individuals have depressed periods that alternate with periods of excessively expansive moods that include sustained overactivity, talkativeness, increased energy, and strange grandiosity. This condition is called **bipolar illness** (also known as **manic-depressive psychosis**). Men and women are equally affected, and the age of onset is usually much younger than that of unipolar depression.

Inheritance Is an Important Determinant of Depression

Genetic studies of unipolar and bipolar disorders reveal strong hereditary contributions (Moldin et al., 1991). Concordance is much higher for monozygotic (identical) than for dizygotic (fraternal) twins. The concordance rates for monozygotic twins are similar whether the twins are reared apart or together. Adoption studies show high rates of affective illness in the biological parents in comparison to foster parents. Al-

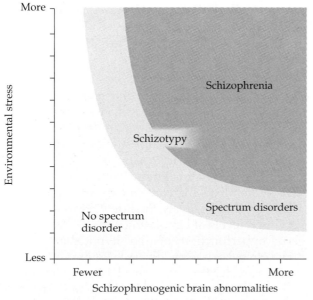

16.12 Model of Interaction of Stress and Brain Abnormalities in Schizophrenia
Environmental stress and certain brain abnormalities may both contribute to producing a schizophrenic disorder. Disorders ranging from more mild to more severe are called, respectively, spectrum disorders, schizotypy, and schizophrenia. Adapted from Mirsky and Duncan, 1986.

16.13 *Melancholia*
This engraving by Albrecht Dürer (1471–1528) vividly depicts the symptons of depression.

though several early studies implicated specific chromosomes, subsequent linkage studies have failed to identify the locus of any relevant gene.

Depression Can Be Lethal

Depression often leads to suicide. Most estimates indicate that about 80% of all suicide victims are profoundly depressed. Unlike the incidence of schizophrenia, suicide rates show great variability across time, age, and places in the world. Although the trend during the twentieth century in the United States and western Europe shows an overall progressive decline in the incidence of suicide, there is a disturbing trend toward an increase in suicide in younger populations (Figure 16.14). Several studies have associated the younger age of suicide victims with the frequent use of drugs in this age group (Rich, Young, and Fowler, 1986; Sigurdson et al., 1994).

Studies of suicide victims consistently show low-er concentrations of serotonin or its metabolites in the brain (Asberg et al., 1986). Low levels of the metabolites of serotonin are also found in the cerebrospinal fluid of people who attempt suicide. Furthermore, suicide attempters with lower levels of serotonin metabolites are ten times more likely to die of suicide later in their lives than are suicide attempters with higher metabolite levels. Suicide victims also show very high levels of circulating cortisol, which suggests hyperfunction of the hypothalamic–pituitary–adrenal axis (Roy, 1992; see Figure 16.16). (Later in the chapter we will look at the hypothalamic–pituitary–adrenal system in more detail.)

Some Affective Disorders Are Associated with Medical Conditions

In some individuals, depression develops secondarily to other bodily disorders, especially endocrine and brain disorders. For example, **Cushing's syndrome** is characterized by high levels of serum cortisol,

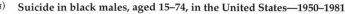

(*a*)   **Suicide in black males, aged 15–74, in the United States—1950–1981**

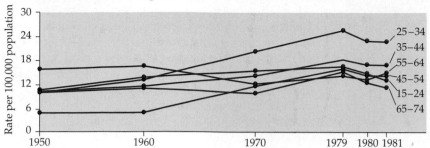

16.14   Recent Trends in Suicide in the United States
Note the alarming increase in suicide rates for young men, black or white.

(*b*)   **Suicide in white males, aged 15 and older, in the United States—1950–1981**

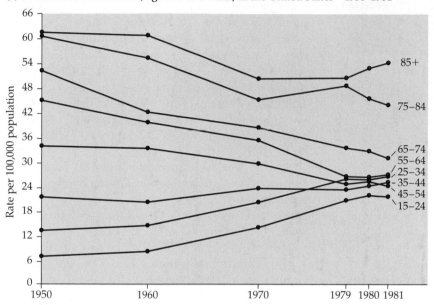

which arise from pituitary tumors that produce excessive amounts of ACTH (adrenocorticotropic hormone), adrenal tumors, or deliberate therapy involving corticosteroids. In more than 85% of patients with Cushing's syndrome, depression appears quite early in the disorder, even before other signs such as obesity or unusual growth and distribution of bodily hair (Haskett, 1985; Krystal et al., 1990). Depression also accompanies brain disorders such as Parkinson's disease (see Chapter 11). Earlier in the chapter we noted that most researchers attribute Parkinson's disease to insufficient production of dopamine. But some argue that Parkinson's patients develop depression in reaction to the motor disabilities of the disorder; others assert that depression accompanies this disorder because this disease state affects emotional circuitry and associated transmitters (Sano et al., 1990).

About 50% of Parkinson's patients are in a state of depression that is unrelated to either the duration or the severity of the motor disability. Research suggests that serotonin plays a strong role in the depression of Parkinson's patients. Cerebrospinal fluid levels of metabolites of serotonin are lower in Parkinson's patients than in controls of the same age (Sano et al., 1990). Administering the precursor for serotonin synthesis alleviates depression in Parkinson's patients. Some of the effects of serotonin in this disorder might arise from a common anatomical lesion in such patients—the loss of large neurons in the dorsal raphe nucleus, which contain large amounts of serotonin.

Functional Maps of the Brain Show Changes with Depression

PET scans of depressed patients show increases in blood flow in the frontal cortex compared with controls (Figure 16.15; Posner and Raichle, 1994). (To make these illustrations, scans of control subjects were subtracted from scans of depressed patients). In

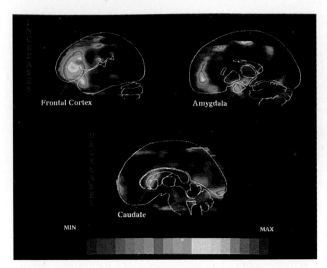

16.15   Brain Activity Patterns in Depression
These PET scans reveal increased activity in the frontal cortex and amygdala (*top*) of depressed patients. These images were made by subtracting brain scans from control subjects from those of depressed subjects. The caudate was significantly less active (*bottom*) in the depressed subjects. Courtesy of Marcus Raichle.

addition to increasing in the frontal cortex, blood flow decreases in the parietal and posterior temporal cortex—systems that have been implicated in attentional networks and language. Blood flow also increases in the amygdala—a structure involved in mediating fear (see Chapter 15). Changes in this structure remain even after the alleviation of depression over time. Patients treated with antidepressants, however, show normal blood flow in the amygdala.

There Are Several Neurochemical Theories of Depression

Work on the psychobiology of affective illness has been greatly influenced since the 1960s by a theory offered by Joseph Schildkraut and Seymour Kety (1967)—the **monoamine hypothesis of depression**. According to this view, depressive illness is associated with a decrease in synaptic activity of connections that employ the transmitters norepinephrine and serotonin. This decrease is especially characteristic of hypothalamic and associated limbic system circuitry. Support for this hypothesis comes from the clinical effectiveness of two forms of treatment: antidepressant drugs and electroconvulsive therapy. Some antidepressant drugs inhibit monoamine oxidase—the enzyme that inactivates norepinephrine, dopamine, and serotonin—thus raising the level of available monoamines. In contrast, the drug reserpine, which depletes the norepinephrine and serotonin of the

brain (by releasing intraneuronal monoamine oxidase, thereby breaking down these transmitters), results in profound depression. Electroconvulsive treatment is especially valuable in many depressed patients, and these seizures have a strong impact on biogenic amines. This hypothesis continues to be offered as a biological explanation of affective illness, although the clinical effectiveness of many other drugs is not easily related to the monoamine system. An alternative hypothesis is that antidepressant drugs work by blocking neural receptors for histamine (Kanof and Greengard, 1978). Table 16.4 lists drugs commonly used to treat depression.

Simple increases or decreases in transmitter release may not account for the breadth of changes that constitute depression. Mood, sleep, eating, and activity are but part of the changes. A simple monoamine hypothesis no longer seems reasonable; in fact, some researchers have even argued the reverse state—increased catecholaminergic activity—as a factor in depression.

A very interesting broader view of changes in transmitters like norepinephrine—the **dysregulation hypothesis of depression**—has been presented by Siever and Davis (1985). They hold that depression is not simply related to depletion of a transmitter but reflects failure in a regulatory mechanism that governs transmitter operations. This dysregulation results in erratic transmitter activities; they are no longer governed reliably by external stimuli, time of day, or their own actions. Such governance could fail at several different levels in the pathway of noradrenergic system activity. For example, there is evidence that noradrenergic activity is governed by inhibitory feedback that stabilizes noradrenergic neurons. Long-term stabilization of adrenergic synapses also accompanies maintained stress, which can enhance the basal activity of noradrenergic synapses. Dysregulation can emerge from these steps or others. In any case, the consequence of impairment of the regulatory devices, according to Siever and Davis, is a transmitter system that is inappropriately responsive to external or internal needs; that is, it becomes maladapted to environmental needs. The dysregulation hypothesis can lead investigators to search for changes that are quite different from those customarily sought in chemical assessments of patients. The clinical effects of some newer antidepressants seem to fit this formulation because their mechanism of action appears more elaborate than simply modifying a single parameter of transmitter function or a single transmitter (Tyrer and Marsden, 1985).

Table 16.4

Drugs Used to Treat Depression

DRUG CLASS	MECHANISM OF ACTION	EXAMPLES[a]
Monoamine oxidase inhibitors	Inhibit the enzyme monoamine oxidase, which breaks down serotonin, norepinephrine, and dopamine	Marplan, Nardil, Parnate
Tricyclics and heterocyclics	Inhibit the reuptake of norepinephrine, serotonin, or dopamine	Elavil, Wellbutrin, Aventyl, Ludiomil, Norpramin
Selective serotonin reuptake inhibitors	Block reuptake of serotonin. Serotonin is normally removed from the synapse either by degradation by monoamine oxidase or by transportation back into presynaptic terminals	Prozac, Paxil, Zoloft

[a]We give here the more commonly used trade names rather than chemical names.

Why Do More Females Than Males Suffer from Depression?

Studies all over the world show that more women than men suffer from major depression. The National Institutes of Health (NIH) epidemiological survey mentioned at the start of this chapter documents this sex difference for five areas in the United States—New Haven, Baltimore, St. Louis, Los Angeles, and Piedmont, North Carolina (Robins et al., 1991). All sites revealed a twofold difference for major depression. For example, New Haven had a rate of 2.2% for males and 4.8% for females. Similar recent findings have been noted in Sweden. What accounts for these sex differences? The answer to this question is especially important for achieving an understanding of the causes of depression.

Several hypotheses have been advanced. Some researchers argue that the sex differential arises from differences in how males and females seek help, notably, that women use health facilities more than men do. But even though the NIH survey was a door-to-door survey, not an assessment of appearance at health centers, significant sex differences were apparent. This fact appears to rule out the hypothesis that the sex difference in the incidence of depression is caused by sex differences in help-seeking patterns.

Several psychosocial explanations have been advanced. One view emphasizes that depression in women arises from the social discrimination that prevents them from achieving mastery by self-assertion. According to this view, inequities lead to dependency, low self-esteem, and depression. Another psychosocial focus leans on the learned helplessness model. According to this view, stereotypical images of men and women produce in women a cognitive set of classic feminine values, reinforced by societal expectations, of which helplessness is one dimension.

A genetic interpretation of the gender difference in depression is that depression is an inherited disorder linked to the X chromosome. But relatives of male and female depressives show no differences in depression rates (which would be expected with X-linking). Thus, although there is a strong genetic determinant for depression in general, there does not seem to be a genetic basis for sex differences in depression.

Some researchers have emphasized gender differences in endocrine physiology. The occurrence of clinical depression often is related to events in the female reproductive cycle—for example, before menstruation, while using contraceptive pills, following childbirth, and during menopause. Although several hormones have been linked to depression, there is little relation between circulating levels of hormones related to female reproductive physiology and measures of depression.

Epidemiological studies of Amish communities (Egeland and Hostetter, 1983) provide a different slant on the mystery of gender differences in depression. An exhaustive survey of this religious community, which prohibits the use of alcohol and shuns modernity, reveals *no* sex difference in major depression. This finding suggests that in the general population heavy use of alcohol masks depression in many males, making it appear as if fewer males than females suffer from depression. Epidemiological data on alcoholism shows another major gender difference, only this time males are more affected.

The Hypothalamic–Pituitary–Adrenal Axis Is Involved in Depression

For many years researchers have sought easily measurable biochemical, physiological, or anatomical indicators of various mental disorders. These indicators, called biological markers, may reflect factors relevant to the causes of a disorder or its current state. The development of such laboratory tests is important especially because some behavioral assessments may not provide clues to genetic mechanisms or differential responses to drugs. Thus, two patients might present a similar portrait of depression but respond differently to antidepressant drugs. An appropriate biological marker could suggest what drug to use for a particular patient. Depression research has been especially productive in generating potential biological markers, in particular several that are linked to hormonal responses to stress that involve the hypothalamic–pituitary–adrenal system (Figure 16.16a). Another reason that investigators studying depression are interested in the hypothalamic–pituitary–adrenal system is that it is activated by stress, which is also believed to activate depression in susceptible individuals.

Early work in this area focused on the hypothalamic–pituitary–adrenal system because observations showed elevated cortisol levels in hospitalized depressed patients. This finding suggested that ACTH (adrenocorticotropic hormone) was released in excessive amounts by the anterior pituitary. One method for analyzing the pituitary–adrenal function in Cushing's syndrome (an endocrine abnormality characterized by high levels of circulating corticosteroids) is the **dexamethasone suppression test**. Dexamethasone is a potent synthetic corticoid that ordinarily suppresses the typical early morning rise in ACTH. Generally given late at night, dexamethasone seems to "fool" the hypothalamus into believing that there is a high level of circulating cortisol (Figure 16.16b). In normal individuals, dexamethasone clearly suppresses cortisol levels, but in many depressed individuals it fails to suppress circulating levels of cortisol. As depression is relieved, dexamethasone again suppresses cortisol normally. The normalization is claimed to occur no matter what the cause of relief—lapse of time, psychotherapy, pharmacotherapy, or electroconvulsive shock therapy. One possible

mediating mechanism is that in depressed people the cells of the hypothalamus are subject to abnormal excitatory drive from limbic system regions, resulting in sustained release of ACTH. Some evidence suggests that depression causes a reduction of cellular corticosteroid receptors, resulting in defective feedback control of this system (Barden, Reul, and Holsboer, 1995). Genes controlling the production of these receptors are stimulated by antidepressants. Many questions have been raised about the generality of this test of depression, its specificity, and its sensitivity to clinical strategies that affect depression. It may be especially valuable in some types of depression but not others (Schatzberg et al., 1983).

Other hormonal systems explored in depression marker research include growth hormone and thyroid hormones. Depressed patients secrete twice as much growth hormone as controls do over a 24-hour period (Kalin et al., 1987). Both hypo- and hyperthyroid conditions have been associated with affective changes. Thyroid hormone supplementation can enhance the responsiveness of patients to antidepressant drugs. However, additional studies are needed to determine whether any components of the hypothalamic–pituitary–thyroid axis are sensitive and reliable markers of depression.

Sleep Characteristics Change in Affective Disorders

The fact that sleep is disturbed in depression is not news, but the character of the change and the fact that induced changes in sleep might influence depression are new pieces in the puzzle. Difficulty in falling asleep and inability to maintain sleep are common in major depression. EEG sleep studies of depressed patients show certain abnormalities that go beyond difficulty in falling asleep. The sleep of patients with major depressive disorders is marked by a striking reduction in stages 3 and 4 of slow-wave sleep (SWS) and a corresponding increase in stages 1 and 2 of SWS (Figure 16.17a); compare to Figure 14.12. REM sleep changes include a shortened time from sleep onset to the first REM episode (Figure 16.17b). Furthermore, the temporal distribution of REM sleep is altered, with an increased amount of REM during the first half of sleep, as though REM had been displaced toward an earlier period in the night (Wehr et al., 1985). REM sleep in depressives is also more vigorous, as shown by very frequent rapid eye movements.

Are these sleep abnormalities specific to depression? This question remains steeped in controversy. Some of the abnormalities are seen in other psychiatric states, and most likely some are nonspecific. However, alterations of REM seem to have a special

(a)

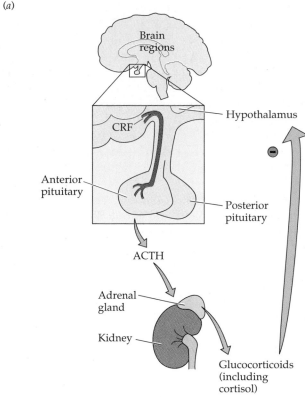

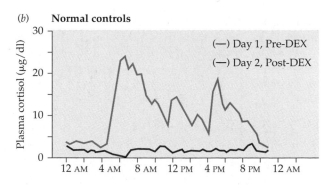

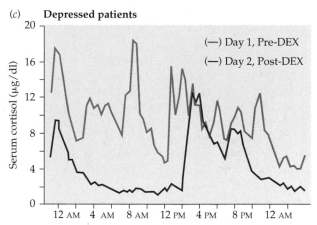

16.16 Hypothalamic–Pituitary–Adrenal Axis in Depression

(*a*) The hypothalamic–pituitary–adrenal system. (*b*) The normal circadian rhythm in the secretion of cortisol (Day 1) is abolished by treatment with the synthetic glucocorticoid, dexamethasone (Day 2). (*c*) The same dose of dexamethasone is far less effective in depressed patients. (*d*) Circulating cortisol levels are usually higher in depressed subjects versus psychiatric and normal controls.

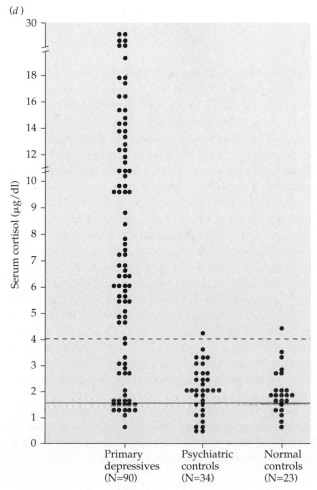

connection to depression; shortened REM latency correlates significantly with the severity of depression. The role of REM in depression is also supported by the clinical effectiveness of various types of sleep therapy. Vogel and colleagues (1980) focused on the fact that REM seems misplaced and extended in the sleep of depressives; depressives almost seem to start sleep where normals leave off. This analysis generated studies on the effect of selective REM deprivation on the symptoms of depression. A marked antidepressant effect of REM deprivation has been noted in several studies with patients suffering from major affective disorders. Patients were awakened as they entered REM sleep, which reduced the overall amounts of REM sleep; the procedure was continued for two to three weeks. A control group of depressed patients was awakened from non-REM sleep. Depression was evaluated using a clinical rating scale. At the end of three weeks, the REM-deprived group showed a sig

(a)

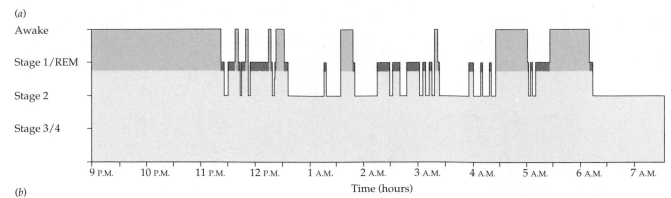

Time (hours)

(b)

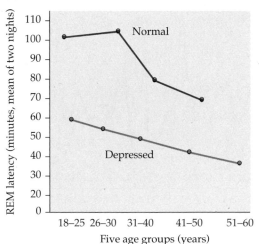

16.17 Sleep and Depression

Depressed subjects spend less time in REM sleep over the course of the night than do normal subjects (*a*). Yet depressed people enter their first REM period earlier in the night (*b*). Thus REM sleep seems distributed differently in depressed people.

1. The cholinergic–aminergic hypothesis suggests that a change in the balance of cholinergic and aminergic synaptic transmission may account for both depression and the accompanying changes in REM sleep. Basic to this hypothesized state is an increased sensitivity of cholinergic receptors. A pharmacological test that measures how long it takes a cholinergic agonist to induce REM sleep shows that depressed individuals respond to the drug much faster than do normal people. The fact that this rapid response is evident in depressed patients even after the remission of depressive symptoms suggests that cholinergic sensitivity is a trait marker for depressed patients.

2. The phase advance hypothesis proposes that depression is related to an impairment in the mutual interaction of oscillators that control REM sleep, temperature, and other physiological rhythms. Consequences seem to be both the phase advance of REM sleep and the flattened circadian rhythms of depressives.

3. The S-deficiency hypothesis suggests that the propensity for sleep is governed by the buildup during wakefulness of a sleep factor (process S). The sleep process is thought to be deficient in depressives, resulting in changes in REM sleep. Disturbances in sleep that are characteristic of major affective disorders may provide a way of examining some of the biological bases of depression. It remains unclear whether these deficits cause or are caused by depression. Intensive current research is seeking to clarify the connections and to use measures of sleep as a prognostic tool in depression treatments.

nificantly lower depression score than the non-REM-deprived group. Three weeks later, the treatments were reversed, and by the end of another three weeks, the effect had also switched. Several antidepressant drugs, like monoamine oxidase inhibitors, suppress REM sleep for extended periods. Vogel asserts that REM deprivation improves severe depression to the extent that it modifies REM sleep abnormalities.

Another sleep therapy approach has emerged from the analysis of circadian rhythms of sleep in depressed patients. Wehr and colleagues (1983) found that depressed patients show abnormal phase relationships in some body rhythms, in addition to alterations in REM cycles. As Figure 16.18 shows, a shift in phase relations between body temperature and sleep was found in depressed patients. This analysis generated a type of circadian treatment for depression. Wehr and colleagues (1982) had patients go to bed six hours before their usual time and reported that several patients showed a rapid improvement in their depression

Sleep studies of depression have generated several intriguing speculations about the relation between sleep and depression. Three major hypotheses have been assessed by Wehr and colleagues (1985):

(*a*) **Depressed**

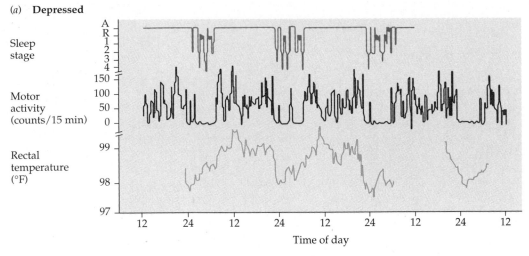

Sleep
stage

Motor
activity
(counts/15 min)

Rectal
temperature
(°F)

Time of day

(*b*) **Recovered**

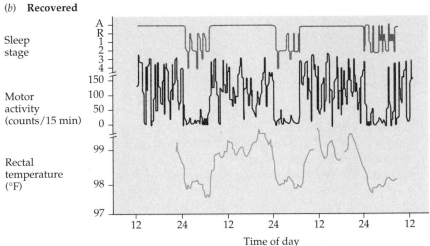

Sleep
stage

Motor
activity
(counts/15 min)

Rectal
temperature
(°F)

Time of day

16.18 Sleep and Body Temperature during Depression
The low in body temperature occurs at the beginning of sleep during depression (*a*) and the end of the sleep period after recovery from depression (*b*). After Wehr et al., 1983.

In addition to these links between daily rhythms and depression, seasonal rhythms have also been implicated in a particular depressive condition known as seasonal affective disorder, or SAD (Box 16.3).

Seizures Can Relieve Depression in Some Patients

About 50 years ago treatments in psychiatry were few, yet the needs were enormous. The title of a book by Elliot Valenstein (1986)—*Great and Desperate Cures*—captures the general thinking: try anything in the face of an overwhelming absence of knowledge about the brain. During this period several desperate cures were introduced with little rationale. One of them was the induction of seizures to treat schizophrenia. Initially, convulsions were produced chemically, using the convulsant drug Metrazol. Beginning in the late 1930s convulsions were produced by electricity delivered through two large electrodes placed on the skin above the skull.

Although this treatment had no clinical impact on schizophrenia, frequent use of this technique showed that such induced seizures could rapidly reverse severe depression. The advent of antidepressant drugs led to the temporary retirement of this clinical tool. However, there proved to be a class of patients for whom antidepressant drugs were relatively ineffective. Furthermore, patients in imminent danger of committing suicide need a treatment that works faster to relieve depression than do most antidepressant drugs (although new types are constantly being developed and made available for clinical trials). Starting in the 1980s, electroconvulsive shock treatment was resumed to treat suicidal patients who failed to respond to antidepressant drugs. Although somewhat different from its original form, this treatment still elicits a large-scale seizure (Weiner, 1994). The mechanisms that make electroconvulsive shock therapy an effective treatment of depres-

Box 16.3
The Season to Be Depressed

Seasonal rhythms characterize the behavior and physiology of many animals, including humans. For some unfortunate people winter inevitably brings a low period, which may become a profound depression. For many of these people, the winter depression alternates with summer mania (Blehar and Rosenthal, 1989). In wintertime affected people feel depressed, slow down, generally sleep a lot, and overeat. Come summer they are elated, energetic, active, and become thinner. This syndrome—**seasonal affective disorder** (**SAD**)—appears predominantly in women and generally starts in early adulthood. Some studies have reported a positive correlation between latitude and the frequency of SAD, but a recent study in a country at a far northern latitude—Iceland—failed to confirm this relationship (Magnusson and Stefansson, 1993). On the contrary, this study revealed a much lower rate for SAD in Iceland. Perhaps population selection over centuries has tended to diminish the reproductive prominence of individuals susceptible to SAD in Iceland and has led to greater tolerance of prolonged periods of winter darkness. Some support for this idea comes from studies of SAD in descendants of Icelandic emigrants in Canada. In this population, SAD is lower than in other populations along the eastern coast of the United States (Magnusson and Axelsson, 1993).

In nonhuman animals, many seasonal rhythms are controlled by the length of the day. For example, migration or hibernation may be triggered by changes in the duration of daylight. Some researchers have suggested that SAD in humans may show a similar dependence. To examine that prospect, researchers have explored whether exposure to light that simulates sunlight can act as an antidepressant. In one investigation (Rosenthal et al., 1985), a group of patients was secured by a newspaper ad that described the typical features of seasonal affective disorder. The patients selected for the study had at least two winter episodes of depression. The level of depression was evaluated quantitatively using the Hamilton Rating Scale, a self-administered scale consisting of a number of items describing different features of depression. Experimental treatment consisted of two one-week exposures to additional light separated by one week of no additional light. During the treatment periods, patients were exposed to bright light twice during the day: from 5:00 A.M. to 8:00 A.M., and from 5:30 P.M. to 8:30 P.M. This distribution extended normal daylight and thus tended to simulate the long daylight period characteristic of summer. The results of such light exposure, as measured by the Hamilton Rating Scale, showed that bright lights have a significant antidepressant effect that is reversed upon withdrawal of the lights. No significant effects were noted following exposure to dim lights. The improvement in mood appears after a few days and generally persists through the week of treatment. Removal of light quickly produces relapse. Is the timing of the light exposure during a typical day an important factor? Studies by Wehr and colleagues (1986) compared the differences in two light exposure regimens in persons with seasonal affective disorder: a light distribution that simulated long summer days, or the same amount of light concentrated over a few hours as in short winter days. Both light regimens were equally effective as antidepressants.

One important biological effect of light is that it suppresses melatonin, a hormone found in the pineal gland that affects gonadotropins and may be of importance in controlling sleep. Exposure to darkness stimulates melatonin synthesis, whereas light suppresses it. People with SAD have been shown to have a high threshold for melatonin suppression. However, as we just saw, experiments by Wehr and collaborators (1986) in which patients with SAD were exposed to different light schedules failed to demonstrate that phototherapy acts by suppressing melatonin secretion. (Oral administration of melatonin did not influence this treatment.) Other neurochemical mediators may be involved with this antidepressant effect of light. Serotonin may be relevant since it has a marked seasonal rhythm in humans, with lower values in winter and spring than in summer or fall (Ergrise et al., 1986). Attention to the SAD syndrome arose primarily because of animal research dealing with photoperiodic behavior and circadian control systems—another example of the significance of such basic research in alleviating the distresses and diseases of humans.

sion remain elusive, although recently developed imaging techniques are being used to gain insight into possible mediating changes in brain function (Nobler et al., 1994).

There Are Various Animal Models for Depression

Because it is difficult to ask a monkey or a cat or a rat if they have delusions of persecution or if they hear voices accusing them of awful crimes, animal models of schizophrenia are limited. But many of the signs of depression are behaviorally overt—such as decreased social contact, problems with eating, and changes in activity. An animal model for the study of depression can provide the ability to evaluate the proposed neurobiological mechanisms, a convenient way to screen potential treatments, and the ability to explore possible causes experimentally (Lachman et al., 1993). Table 16.5 lists the characteristics of animal models used in studies of depression.

In one type of stress model—"**learned helplessness**"—an animal is exposed to a repetitive stressful stimulus, such as an electric shock that it cannot escape. Like depression, learned helplessness has been linked to a defect in serotonin function (Petty et al., 1994). Removing the olfactory bulb from rodents creates an anatomical model of depression: the animals display irritability, hyperactivity, preferences for alcohol, elevated levels of corticosteroids, and deficiency in passive avoidance conditioning—all of

which are reversed by many antidepressants. A genetically developed line of rats—the Flinders-sensitive line—has been proposed as a model of depression because these animals show reduced locomotor activity, reduced body weight, increased REM sleep, learning difficulties, and exaggerated immobility in response to chronic stress (Overstreet, 1993). These varied animal models may be useful in finding the essential paths that cause and maintain depression (Lachman et al., 1993).

There Are Several Types of Anxiety Disorders

All of us have at times felt apprehensive and fearful. Some experience this state with an intensity that is overwhelming and includes irrational fears; a sense of terror; unusual bodily sensations, such as dizziness; difficulty in breathing; trembling; shaking; and a feeling of loss of control. For some, anxiety comes in sudden attacks of panic that are unpredictable and last for minutes or hours. And anxiety can be lethal: a follow-up of patients with panic disorder reveals an increased mortality in men with this disorder resulting from cardiovascular disease and suicide (Coryell, Noyes, and House, 1986) The American Psychiatric Association distinguishes two major groupings of

Table 16.5

Characteristics of Animal Models of Depression

	ACTIVITY CHANGE	ANHEDONIA[a]	SENSITIVITY TO ANTIDEPRESSANTS	DECREASED SOCIAL CONTACT
Stress models				
Learned helplessness	+	+	+	—
Chronic mild stress	—	+	+	—
Behavorial despair separation models (e.g., primate separations)	+	—	+	+
Pharmacological models (e.g., reserpine reversal)	+	—	+	—
Anatomical models (e.g., olfactory bulbectomy)	+	—	+	—
Genetic models (e.g., Flinders-sensitive line)	+	—	+	—

[a]A reduction in the ability to experience pleasure.

anxiety disorders: phobic disorders and anxiety states. **Phobic disorders** are intense, irrational fears that become centered on a specific object, activity, or situation that the person feels he or she must avoid. **Anxiety states** include recurrent panic states, generalized, persistent anxiety disorders, and posttraumatic stress disorders.

Panic Can Be Provoked Chemically

Several decades ago psychiatrists observed that some patients experience intense anxiety attacks during or after vigorous physical exercise. This effect was thought to be caused by a buildup of blood lactate. This observation stimulated Pitts and McClure (1967) to administer sodium lactate to anxiety patients. The infusions produced immediate panic attacks in some patients which resembled the naturally occurring episodes; this chemical treatment did not produce panic attacks in normal people. Margraf and Roth (1986) contested the study on the grounds that it fails to exclude confounding psychological factors: patients show a certain level of panic even when infused with placebo. PET scans (which we will discuss in the next section), however, do support the lactate-induction effect.

In an attempt to account for chemically induced panic, Liebowitz and collaborators (1986) have considered mechanisms that include adrenergic systems. They note that the effect is not produced by calcium levels, changes in blood pH, or increases in plasma levels of epinephrine. The notion that lactate-induced panic is produced by an action on beta-adrenergic synapses is not supported by their observation that blocking these synapses did not prevent lactate-induced panic. These researchers believe that the lactate-induced panic may involve central noradrenergic mechanisms of the locus coeruleus and its outputs. This suggestion is partially supported by the observation that another locus coeruleus stimulant—inhalation of 5% carbon dioxide—produces panic in clinically vulnerable individuals.

Anxiety and Panic Disorders Involve Structural and Functional Changes in the Temporal Lobes

Because many of the features of panic attacks resemble seizure disorders that involve the temporal lobes, MRI studies of panic have focused on temporal lobe structures. Many patients who suffer from recurrent panic attacks have temporal lobe abnormalities according to MRI studies. Ontiveros and colleagues (1989) found temporal lobe abnormalities—including small lesions in white matter and dilation of the lat-

eral ventricles—in 40% of patients with panic disorder. The magnitude of neuroanatomical anomalies correlated significantly with the total number of spontaneous attacks and the age of onset of panic (patients whose episodes of panic began at an earlier age have more anomalies).

Intriguing PET scan observations have provided a portrait of the anatomy of anxiety. These studies by Reiman and collaborators (1986) revealed abnormalities in the resting, nonpanic state. They compared patients whose panic disorder could be induced by injection of sodium lactate, patients who were not vulnerable to lactate-induced panic, and normal controls. Those who were vulnerable to lactate-induced panic showed a markedly abnormal increase in blood flow in the right parahippocampus. This region contains the major input and output pathways of the hippocampus. In addition to this regional effect, lactate-vulnerable panic patients also had abnormally high oxygen metabolism in the brain. Reiman and collaborators relate these findings to a theory of Gray (1982) that emphasizes septohippocampal connections in the neurobiology of anxiety. They also cite observations by Gloor and colleagues (1982) that electrical stimulation of this region in awake patients commonly elicits sensations of strong fear and apprehension. The work of Reiman and collaborators raises the possibility that a biological indicant—PET scan data—can distinguish two major anxiety groups: those vulnerable to lactate-induced panic and those not vulnerable to this form of induced attack. This distinction might reflect a fundamental difference in underlying biological mechanisms. Although these PET observations were criticized because of the possible confound of temporal muscle activity (Posner and Raichle, 1994), more recent metabolic studies also point to the role of temporal lobe structures in the elicitation and maintenance of anxiety states (Rauch et al., 1995).

Drug Treatment of Anxiety Provides Clues to Its Mechanisms

Throughout history people have imbibed all sorts of substances in the hopes of controlling anxiety. The list includes alcohol, bromides, scopolamine, opiates, and barbiturates. But not until 1960 was a drug introduced that would forever change the treatment of anxiety. Molecular changes in an antibacterial substance produced the drug meprobamate, which, under the trade name Miltown, became famous as a tranquilizing agent. Competition among drug companies led to the development of a class of substances called **benzodiazepines**, which have become the most common drugs used in the treatment of anxiety. One type of benzodiazepine—diazepam (trade name Valium)—is one of the most prescribed drugs in history. These drugs are commonly described as anxiolytic, although at higher doses they also have anticonvulsant and sleep-inducing properties.

Early behavioral and electrophysiological data established that the benzodiazepines are associated in some way with the action of GABA synapses (see Chapter 6; recall from Chapter 5 that GABA is the most common inhibitory transmitter in the brain.) In the late 1970s many investigators showed that benzodiazepines exert their therapeutic effects by interacting with special receptors in the brain. It was rapidly established that the benzodiazepine receptor interacts with receptors for GABA, an interaction that results in enhancement of the action at inhibitory synapses in the brain that use GABA. Thus GABA-mediated postsynaptic inhibition is facilitated by benzodiazepines. Benzodiazepine receptors are widely distributed throughout the brain and are especially concentrated in the cerebral cortex and some subcortical areas, such as the hippocampus and amygdala (Figure 16.19). The ultimate function of the benzodiazepine/GABA receptor complex is to regulate the permeability of neural membranes to chloride ions. When GABA, upon release from a presynaptic terminal, activates its receptor, chloride ions are allowed to move from the outside to the inside of the nerve

cell, hyperpolarizing and therefore inhibiting the neuron from firing. Benzodiazepines alone do little to chloride conductance, but in the presence of GABA, they markedly enhance GABA-provoked increases in chloride permeability. Research also suggests that specific anxiety peptides occur naturally in the brain and act in association with the benzodiazepine receptor (Marx, 1985). Early work indicated that a brain extract could decrease the binding of diazepam to its receptor, implying that the brain extract works this way because it contains a material that also binds to this receptor. A compound derived from some of this work—beta-carboline—behaves like the natural anxiety-producing compound and can induce anxiety in experimental animals. When administered to human volunteers, a carboline compound produced motor tension, autonomic hyperactivity, and bodily effects that were described as severe anxiety (Dorow et al., 1983). By now a vast array of information implicates the GABA/benzodiazepine receptor complex as a key ingredient in the mechanism of anxiety.

In Posttraumatic Stress Disorder Horrible Memories Won't Go Away

For some people, life has some especially awful moments that seem indelible, resulting in vivid impressions that accompany them through the rest of their lives. Persons exposed to sustained periods of unrelieved horrors, such as the "killing fields" of war, may find it intensely difficult to shut out these events even long after they have passed. The kind of event that seems particularly likely to produce subsequent stress disorders is one that is intense and usually associated with witnessing abusive violence and death. Other such events may be the sudden loss of a close friend, torture, kidnapping, and profound social dislocation, such as in forced migration. Memories of horrible events intrude into consciousness and produce the same intense visceral arousal—the fear and trembling—that the original event caused. These traumatic memories are easily reawakened by stressful circumstances and even by innocuous stimuli. An ever watchful and fearful stance becomes the portrait of individuals afflicted with what is called **posttraumatic stress disorder** (once called combat fatigue, war neurosis, or shell shock).

Recent studies on risk factors associated with posttraumatic stress disorder in Vietnam war veterans have clarified the interaction of genetic and environmental factors in this disorder. The disorder is particularly prevalent among those who served in the most intense combat areas (True et al., 1993). Familial factors also affect vulnerability, as shown in twin

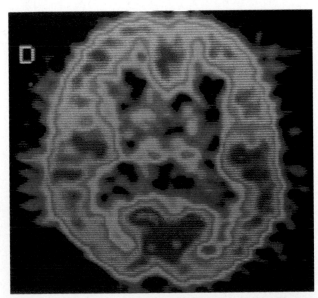

16.19   Distribution of Benzodiazepine Recepters
PET scan of benzodiazepine receptors showing their wide distribution in the brain. Highest concentrations are coded as orange and red. Courtesy of Goran Sedvall.

studies of Vietnam era veterans. Researchers compared twins—both monozygotic and dizygotic—who served in combat zones with other veterans who did not serve in Southeast Asia. The twin pairs were compared according to distinct posttraumatic stress symptoms such as persistent reexperiencing of the painful experience, nightmares, avoidance of stimuli associated with the trauma, and signs of overall increased arousal, such as persistent insomnia. On all of these dimensions, monozygotic twins were more similar than dizygotic twins, and the specific contribution of inheritance to this disorder is claimed to account for one-third of the variance.

A comprehensive psychobiological model of the development of posttraumatic stress disorder draws connections between the symptoms and the neural mechanisms of fear conditioning, extinction, and behavioral sensitization (Table 16.6; Charney et al., 1993). The investigators argue that patients learn to avoid a large range of stimuli associated with the original trauma. A kind of emotional numbing is the conse-

quence of this avoidance, which can also be seen as a type of conditioned emotional response. Work in animals has revealed that this type of memory—fear conditioning—is very persistent and involves the amygdala and some brain stem pathways that are part of a circuit of startle response behavior. NMDA receptor- mediated mechanisms in the amygdala are important for the development of fear conditioning. The persistence of memory and fear in posttraumatic stress disorder may also depend on the failure or fragility of extinction mechanisms. In experimental animals, NMDA antagonists delivered to the amygdala prevent the extinction of fear-mediated startle. Sites projecting to the amygdala, such as the hippocampus and prefrontal cortex, may also lose their effectiveness in suppressing learned fear responses. The third element of this model—behavioral sensitization mechanisms—enhances response magnitude after exposure to a stimulus. The neural mechanisms probably involve dopamine, since repeated stressors increase

---

Table 16.6

Neural Mechanisms Related to Primary Symptoms of Posttraumatic Stress Disorder (PTSD)

MECHANISM	DESCRIPTION	NEUROCHEMICAL SYSTEMS	BRAIN REGIONS
Fear conditioning	Animals exposed to emotionally neutral stimulus (conditioned stimulus [CS]) in conjunction with an aversive stimulus (unconditioned stimulus [UCS]) will subsequently exhibit a conditioned fear response (CR) to the CS in the absence of the UCS	NMDA, noradrenergic, opiate receptors	Amygdala, locus coeruleus, thalamus, hippocampus
Extinction	There is a reduction in the CR when the CS is presented repeatedly in the absence of the UCS; this may result from learning a new inhibitory memory that opposes the original memory	NMDA receptors	Sensory cortex, amygdala
Sensitization	Increase in response magnitude following repeated administration of a stimulus or presentation of a different strong stimulus	Dopaminergic, noradrenergic, NMDA receptors	Nucleus accumbens, striatum, hypothalamus, amygdala

dopamine function in the forebrain. A large-scale portrait of this intriguing neural model is presented in Figure 16.20. One important implication of this model is that it might direct clinical intervention. For example, it suggests a potentially important use for drugs that block conditioned responses.

Exposure to stress leads to high levels of circulating glucocorticoids, which some researchers have suggested might lead to cell loss in the hippocampus (Sapolsky et al., 1990). Patients with combat-related posttraumatic stress disorder show memory changes such as amnesia for some war experiences, flashbacks, and deficits in short-term memory (Bremner et al., 1993). Reports of such psychological changes have led to MRI studies of the brains of combat veterans with posttraumatic stress disorder. Measurements of the right hippocampus reveal an 8% reduction in the volume of this structure without any changes in other brain regions. Patients with the smallest right hippocampus show the worst performance in verbal memory tasks (Bremner et al., 1995).

CLINICAL RELEVANCE

Fear conditioning may account for the common clinical observation in patients with PTSD that sensory and cognitive stimuli associated with or resembling the original trauma elicit symptoms, including anxiety, flashbacks, and hyperarousal; this results in the frequent reexperiencing of the traumatic event, a persistent avoidance of such stimuli, and a compensatory numbing of general responsiveness

A failure in extinction in PTSD may relate to the persistence in recalling traumatic memories

Sensitization may explain the increased responsiveness of patients with PTSD to stress both related and unrelated to the original trauma; dopaminergic and noradrenergic dysfunction may account for persistent symptoms of increased arousal and the potentiated responses to cocaine; alcohol, opiates, and benzodiazepines may be used to reduce symptoms associated with fear conditioning and socialization

In Obsessive–Compulsive Disorders Thoughts and Acts Keep Repeating

Neatness, orderliness, and similar traits are attributes we tend to admire, especially during those chaotic moments when we realize we have created another tottering pile of papers, bills, or whatever. What, then, constitutes what we call **obsessive–compulsive disorders (OCD)**? In her book *The Boy Who Couldn't Stop Washing* (1989), Judith Rapoport, a psychiatrist at the National Institutes of Health with extensive experience in researching and treating people afflicted with this disorder, describes a remarkable group of people whose lives have become riddled with repetitive acts that are carried out without rhyme, reason, or the ability to stop. Routine acts that we all engage in, such as checking whether the door is locked when we leave our home, are repeated over and over. Recurrent thoughts, such as fears of germs or other potential harms in the world invade consciousness. Table 16.7 summarizes the symptoms of OCD. These symptoms progressively isolate a person from ordinary social engagement with the world. For many patients, hours of each day are consumed by compulsive acts such as repetitive hand washing.

Determining the number of persons afflicted with OCD is difficult, especially since many persons with this disorder tend to hide their symptoms. It is estimated that there are more than 4 million affected persons in the United States (Rapoport, 1989). In many cases, the initial symptoms of this disorder appear in childhood; the peak age group is 25 to 44 years. For a long time, this disorder was thought of as a psychiatric dysfunction associated with psychological conflict. More recently, evidence has accumulated that this disorder is rooted in the neurobiology of the brain. Rapoport (1989) suggests that the features of this disorder reflect "subroutines" associated with grooming and territoriality that have evolved gradually. Symptoms arise when brain malfunction causes these programs to be executed without the usual provoking stimuli, such as the loss of cleanliness. The first step in examining this hypothesis is to establish that brain circuits malfunction in these patients, as PET studies are doing.

The basal ganglia, frontal cortex, and OCD. PET scan studies of OCD patients show significantly higher metabolic rates in the left orbital gyrus and bilaterally in the caudate nucleus. The basal ganglia have also been implicated in other disorders related to OCD, such as Tourette's Syndrome (Box 16.4). Regional cerebral blood flow studies of patients in

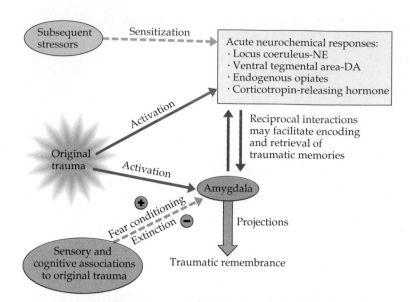

16.20 Neural Model of Posttraumatic Stress Disorder

The original trauma activates two systems—one in the brain stem, which sensitizes the subject to related stimuli in the future, and another in the amygdala which conditions a long-lasting fearful reaction.

Symptom	Brain region
Flashbacks, intrusive memories	Cortex, hippocampus
Anxiety, fear, hypervigilance	Locus coeruleus, ventral tegmental area
Facial expression of fear	Trigeminal, facial motor nuclei
Anhedonia, depression	Nucleus accumbens
Startle	Reticular formation
Hyperventilation	Medullary respiratory center
Sympathetic activation: tachycardia, increased blood pressure	Lateral hypothalamus
Parasympathetic activation: diarrhea, increased urination	Vagal nerve nucleus

whom OCD symptoms have been provoked support this finding. In a recent study investigators provoked a symptomatic state by using stimuli that patients reported provoked OCD symptoms (Rauch et al., 1994). Brain images obtained in response to an innocuous stimulus were subtracted from those obtained when symptoms were provoked. Statistically significant increases in regional blood flow were seen in the right caudate nucleus, left anterior cingulate cortex, and bilateral orbitofrontal cortex. This pattern of enhanced blood flow supports an anatomical model of obsessive–compulsive disorders proposed by Insel (1992) that emphasizes a circuit involving a loop among frontal, striatal, and thalamic structures.

The role of serotonin in OCD. The basic observation behind the serotonin hypothesis of obsessive–compulsive disorders is that clomipramine, a tricyclic antidepressant (see Table 16.4), markedly reduces the symptoms of this disorder. Although OCD is classi-

fied as an anxiety disorder, some clinicians have long believed that this disorder is related to depression. For example, studies of the incidence of OCD and depression show some overlap between the two. Furthermore, as in depressed patients, dexamethasone fails to suppress circulating levels of cortisol in OCD patients (recall our discussion of the dexamethasone suppression test earlier in this chapter). OCD patients, whether depressed or nondepressed, also exhibit decreased REM latency. Neither the DST nor the REM sleep data, however, predict the response of OCD patients to antidepressants.

Comparisons of antidepressants used to treat OCD generally show that clomipramine has greater anti-obsessional effects than most other antidepressants. What sets clomipramine apart? One significant difference between clomipramine and other antidepressants is the potency of its ability to block serotonin uptake. Blocking the reuptake of serotonin has significant anti-obsessional effects.

Table 16.7

Symptoms of Obsessive–Compulsive Disorders

	PERCENT
Obsessions	
Dirt, germs or environmental toxins	40
Something terrible happening (fire, death or illness of self or loved one)	24
Symmetry, order, or exactness	17
Scrupulosity (religious obsessions)	13
Bodily wastes or secretions (urine, stool, saliva)	8
Lucky or unlucky numbers	8
Forbidden, aggressive, or perverse sexual thoughts, images, or impulses	4
Fear might harm others or oneself	4
Household items	3
Intrusive nonsense sounds, words, or music	1
Compulsions	
Excessive or ritualized handwashing, showering, bathing, toothbrushing, or grooming	85
Repeating rituals (going in or out of a door, up or down from a chair)	51
Checking (doors, locks, stove, appliances, emergency brake on car, paper route, homework)	46
Removing contaminants from contacts	23
Touching	20
Preventing harm to self or others	16
Ordering or arranging	17
Counting	18
Hoarding or collecting	11
Cleaning household or inanimate objects	6
Miscellaneous rituals (such as writing, moving, speaking)	26

Zohar and colleagues (1988) report that MCPP, a selective serotonin agonist, when given to patients who have had clomipramine treatment for four months, does not affect obsessional symptoms. They suggest that clomipramine treatment produces adaptive subsensitivity to serotonin agonists —that is, that treatment produces down regulation of the serotonin responsiveness.

Neurosurgery Has Been Used to Treat Psychiatric Disorders

Through the ages, the mentally disabled have been treated by methods limited only by the human imag-ination. Some methods have been gruesome, inspired by views that people with mental disorders are con-trolled by demonic forces. Although twentieth-cen-tury psychiatry has been purged of such moralistic views, until recently treatment was a trial-and-error affair, and inspiration for new efforts came from di-verse sources. In the 1930s experiments on frontal lobe lesions in chimpanzees inspired psychiatrist Egas Moniz to attempt similar operations in patients. He was intrigued by the report of a calming influence in nonhuman primates, and at the time he tried frontal surgery little else was available. His observa-tions led to the beginning of **psychosurgery**, defined as the use of surgically produced brain lesions to modify severe psychiatric disorders. Its use has provoked vigorous debate, which continues to the present (Valenstein, 1980, 1986).

During the 1940s frontal lobe surgery (lobotomy) was forcefully advocated by several neurosurgeons and psychiatrists. A presidential commission on psychosurgery estimated that during this period 10,000 to 50,000 patients underwent this surgery (National Commission for the Protection of Human Subjects in Biomedical and Behavioral Research, 1978). During the most intense period of enthusiasm, patients of all diagnostic types were operated on, and different varieties of surgery were employed. Interest in psychosurgery arose from the saddening sight of many people in mental hospitals living empty, disturbed lives without hope of change. No drug to that point had aided chronic schizophrenics, and the population of the permanently hospitalized continued to grow. Today frontal surgery is limited to controlling emotional arousal accompanying intense pain. Its use in psychiatry has practically ended, although the commission on psychosurgery urged further consideration of the role of surgery in psychiatry. (Recall from Chapter 15 that temporal lobe surgery has also been used to treat violent behavior attributed to seizures.)

Assessments of the value of frontal lobe surgery in psychiatric treatment are steeped in controversy. William Sweet (1973) argued that more localized brain lesions might significantly relieve particular psychiatric disorders. Strong support for this view was offered by Ballantine and colleagues (1987), who recently reported on the treatment of depression and anxiety disorders by stereotaxic cingulotomy (lesions that interrupt pathways in the cingulate cortex). This operation is based on observations of overactivation of the cingulate cortex (as noted earlier). Clinical evaluations reported positive outcomes of this procedure in many chronically depressed patients who were not aided by other treatments. For example, a follow-up study on a group of severely disabled OCD patients (Jenike et al., 1991) indicated that one-third of patients who underwent cingulotomy benefitted substantially from this intervention. However, the use of drugs has overshadowed psychosurgery, especially since surgical results are generally not reversible.

The development of techniques for accurate placement of depth electrodes in humans has encouraged some surgeons to use subcortical lesions to treat psychiatric disorders. Neurosurgical intervention continues to be used in some patients who do not respond to any other treatment. Figure 16.21 shows the placement of lesions to treat OCD (Martuza et al., 1990).

There Are Many Different Biological Models of Mental Disorders

In this chapter we have described several examples of human mental illnesses and some of the biological information that relates to the origins and character-

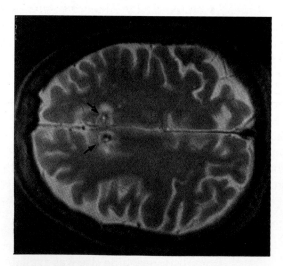
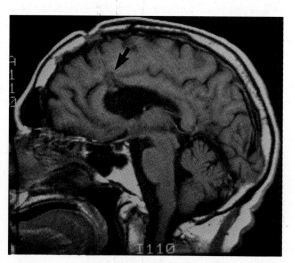

16.21 Neurosurgery for Obsessive Compulsive Disorder
Horizontal (*left*) and sagittal (*right*) MRIs of a patient who received a cingulotomy, disconnecting cingulate cortex connections (arrows), in an attempt to treat OCD. Courtesy of Robert L. Martuza.

Table 16.8

Some Biological Models of Mental Disorders

MODEL	CAUSE(S)
Anatomical models	
Destructive/deficiency/loss of neural components	Fault in development produced by genetic mechanisms or exposure to toxins or microbes such as viruses or bacteria
	Brain injury
	Vascular interference, such as stroke
	Excessive excitation of nerve cells (excitotoxic effects)
	Deficiency of growth regulators/maintainers
Hyperconnection	Developmental failure or synaptic pruning at any stage
	Cell death in early embryonic development
	Perturbed or faulty regenerative events
Cellular disorganization	Developmental errors during early prenatal development
Synaptic communication models	
Interference at the level of the presynaptic compartment	Failure to produce or release transmitter
	Excessive release of transmitter
	Failure in feedback regulation
Interference at the level of the postsynaptic compartment	Failure to terminate action of transmitter
	Reduced or excessive receptors
	Excessive excitation produced by inhibitory failure
	Failure in transmitter balance

istics of these disorders. Many different forms of biological data have been presented by researchers in these fields. In one sense, each research perspective is a model of the disorder. In most cases, comprehensive integration of different research approaches is yet to be achieved. Given the vast range of data, it is useful to summarize the different models, as we do in Table 16.8.

The two major categories are anatomical models and synaptic communication models. Anatomical models suggest that mental disorders arise from miswiring of the brain, generally a loss of some component. In many cases, such as schizophrenia, the deficiency is suspected to have arisen during early development. Synaptic communication models suggest that changes in synaptic communication are the basis of mental disorders. These changes include decreased or increased synaptic activity that could arise from the failure of one or more transmitter systems. These biological models of mental disorder are based on a vast array of psychopharmacological data, which show how various substances change the course of the disorders. Of course the two are not mutually exclusive and undoubtedly a full understanding of any mental disorder will reveal both anatomical and neurochemical changes. We can hope that such knowledge will provide a means of relieving or preventing these cruel states.

Box 16.4

Tics, Twitches, and Snorts: The Unusual Character of Tourette's Syndrome

Their faces twitch in an insistent way, and every now and then out of nowhere, they blurt out an odd sound or, quite suddenly, an obscene word. At times they fling their arms, kick their legs, or make violent shoulder movements. Also a part of **Tourette's syndrome** is heightened sensitivity to tactile, auditory, and visual stimuli (Cohen and Leckman, 1992). Many patients also sense the buildup of an urge to emit verbal or phonic tics; they report that these acts relieve this powerfully felt need. Professionals have long argued about whether this collection of symptoms forms a psychiatric disturbance derived from the stresses of life or emerges from a disturbance in brain structures and/or function.

Tourette's syndrome begins early in life; the mean age of diagnosis is 6 to 7 years (de Groot, Janus, and Bornstein, 1995). A portrait of the chronology of symptoms is shown in the figure. Associated behavioral disturbances include attention deficit hyperactivity disorder, problems in school, and obsessive–compulsive disorder (Park et al., 1993).

Genetics appears to play a potent role in this disorder. The most common contemporary view is that Tourette's syndrome is mediated by a single gene inherited in a dominant manner (Eapen, Pauls, and Robertson, 1993). Twin studies of the disorder reveal an identical twin concordance rate of 53 to 77%, contrasted with a dizygotic twin concordance rate of 8 to 23 % (Price et al., 1985; Hyde et al., 1992). (The variation depends on the narrowness of the diagnostic

definitions.) An unusual view of genetic factors in Tourette's is provided by a study of a set of triplets who were reared apart after the age of two months (Segal et al., 1990). The triplets consisted of a pair of identical female twins and a dizygotic male who were reunited when they were 47 years old. The male had a history of eye blinking, facial tics, and repetitive arm and finger movements that began at age 4. Eye blinking persisted into adulthood. The female twins showed a more severe set of symptoms: frequent motor and phonic tics, head jerks, shoulder jerks, and kicking leg movements.

The symptoms of Tourette's patients resemble some of those seen in patients with basal ganglia disease. MRI studies show subtle changes in some basal ganglia structures in Tourette's patients.

Summary

1. Biological approaches have enabled better distinctions within large classes of mental disorders such as schizophrenia and anxiety.

2. There is strong evidence for a genetic factor in the origin of schizophrenia. Consistent evidence comes from the study of the incidence of schizophrenia in families, twins, and adoptees.

3. There are structural changes in the brains of schizophrenics that may arise from early developmental problems.

4. Biological theories of schizophrenia include two general classes of ideas: (1) the view that schizophrenia comes about because of a failure at some level in the operation of neurotransmitters at synapses, and (2) the view that schizophrenia develops from a metabolic fault that results in the production of a toxic substance, a psychotogen with properties similar to known hallucinogenic agents.

5. The dopamine hypothesis attributes schizophrenia to excess release of or sensitivity to dopamine. Supporting evidence comes from studies on the effects of antipsychotic drugs, amphetamine psychosis, and Parkinson's disease.

6. According to an integrative psychobiological model, the emergence of schizophrenia depends on the interaction of a vulnerable biological substrate and environmental stressors. The greater the biological vulnerability of an individual, the less stress is needed to precipitate a schizophrenic disorder.

7. Biological studies of affective disorders reveal a strong genetic factor and the importance of levels of various neurotransmitters.

8. The hypothalamic–pituitary–adrenal axis is involved in depression. REM sleep changes in depression include shortened onset to REM and larger percentages of REM in overall amounts of sleep. Some sleep treatments appear to act as antidepressants.

For example, normal subjects usually show asymmetry in the volumes of left and right basal ganglia structures, but Tourette's patients fail to show this asymmetry and show lower overall volumes of basal ganglia such as the caudate nucleus and globus pallidus (Peterson et al., 1993).

Advances in the pharmacological treatment of Tourette's syndrome have laid the foundations for a neurochemical understanding of the disease. Several drugs that affect dopamine functioning have proved quite successful in reducing the frequency of some of the motor features (Peterson and Azrin, 1992). Halperidol, a dopamine antagonist, significantly reduces tic frequency and is the primary treatment of this disorder. Unfortunately, side effects limit the duration of this treatment. Behavior modification techniques that aim at reducing the frequency of some symptoms, especially tics, are claimed to have promising potential (Peterson and Azrin, 1992).

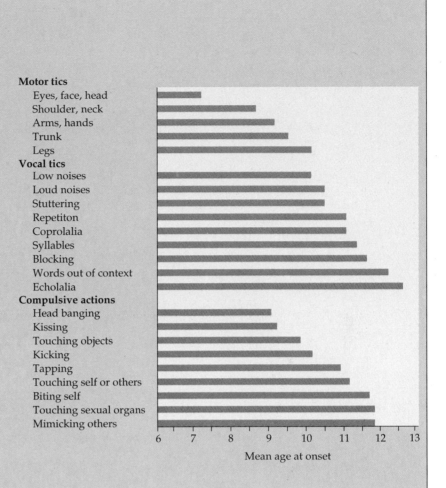

9. Anxiety states involve functional changes in the temporal lobes that can be revealed by PET scans.

10. Anti-anxiety drugs affect receptors for the transmitter GABA. These drugs enhance the inhibitory influence of this neurotransmitter.

11. Obsessive–compulsive disorder is characterized by changes in basal ganglia and frontal structures and has a strong link to serotonin activities.

12. Neurosurgery continues to be used as a form of psychiatric treatment in a limited number of instances.

Recommended Reading

Bloom, F. E. and Kupfer, D. J. (eds.) 1995. *Psychopharmacology: The Fourth Generation of Progress.* Raven Press, New York.

Gottesman, I. I. 1991. *Schizophrenia Genesis.* W. H. Freeman, New York.

Torrey, E. F., Bowler, A. E., Taylor, E.H. and Gottesman, I. I. 1994. *Schizophrenia and Manic Depressive Disorder.* Basic Books, New York.

Yudofsky, S. C. and Hales, R. E. (eds.) 1992. *Textbook of Neuropsychiatry.* American Psychiatric Press, Washington, D.C.

PART 6

Learning, Memory, and Cognition

Learning and memory, language, and cognition are the fascinating focal points of much current research. In this part of the book, we start with a top-down approach, beginning in Chapter 17 by describing learning and memory in whole organisms and identifying the neural regions and systems that are involved. In Chapter 18 we investigate the neuronal and synaptic mechanisms and the neural networks that may underlie learning and memory. In Chapter 19 we will discuss the most elaborate products of brain function—the biology of language and cognitive states that are so distinctively human.

Striking cases of impaired memory start off our discussion. We can discover a great deal about learning and memory by examining how they fail. Clinical cases show that memory can fail in quite different ways, and these observations support the conclusion that there are different kinds of learning and memory in normal subjects. The clinical cases also provide clues about the brain regions that are especially involved in processing memory. Carefully designed animal research has delved deeper into this question. After examining several cases of impaired learning and memory, we propose ten challenges that any successful theory about the biology of memory must meet At the end of Chapter 18 we evaluate how well these challenges are being met and what problems remain.

Joe Baker, *Office Stress*, 1992

- *Many Kinds of Brain Damage Can Impair Memory*

- *Ten Challenges for a Neuroscience of Learning and Memory*

- *Even "Simple" Learning Can Be Complex*

- *Memory Has Temporal Stages: Short, Intermediate, and Long*

- *Different Regions of the Brain Process Different Aspects of Memory*

- *Memory Processes Extend from Acquisition to Retrieval*

- *Emotion Can Modulate Memory Formation*

- *Comparative Approaches Yield Insights about the Evolution of Learning and Memory*

- *Learning and Memory Change throughout Life*

CHAPTER 17

Learning and Memory: Biological Perspectives

Orientation

Investigating learning and memory and their biological mechanisms is one of the most active and exciting areas of biological psychology. All the distinctively human aspects of our behavior are learned: the languages we speak, how we dress, the foods we eat, and how we eat them. Much of our own individuality depends on learning and memory. Research on learning and memory gives us a better understanding of almost all the topics we have taken up so far, because almost every aspect of behavior and cognition requires learning: how we perceive, the skilled acts we perform, our motivations, and the ways we achieve our goals. Conditions that impair memory are particularly frightening; they make it impossible to take part in normal social life and can rob us of our identity.

Nonhuman animals also depend upon learning, as we have seen in previous chapters. They learn how to obtain food (in some cases remembering where to retrieve food they have hidden weeks or months earlier) and how to get back to dens or nests. Many animals learn how to mate and how to parent effectively. Investigators are becoming steadily more impressed by the amount and complexity of learning that even relatively simple animals can and must accomplish.

Valuable research on learning and memory is being done at all the levels of organization of the nervous system, from the intact organism to subcellular mechanisms. To find the neural regions involved in learning and memory, investigators use a variety of techniques, including studying people with impaired memory, examining the effects of precise, experimental brain lesions in animals on learning and memory, and noninvasive brain scans of people with normal abilities.

Many Kinds of Brain Damage Can Impair Memory

Many kinds of brain damage, caused by disease or accident, impair learning and memory. Newer brain imaging techniques are providing much new information about the involvement of brain regions in learning and memory (Figure 17.1), but longer-established methods provide powerful lessons, and we start with them. The different types of impairment have been scrutinized to find clues to the mechanisms of memory. Study of such cases has revealed the existence of different classes of learning and

memory, which we will discuss later in the chapter. First, let's look at a few cases of memory impairment that have posed puzzles for investigators. Some cases—certainly the first one we will consider—have stimulated a great deal of controversy.

Patient H.M.:
The Present Vanishes into Oblivion

H.M. had suffered from epileptic seizures since the age of 16. His condition became steadily worse and could not be controlled by medication; he had to stop work at the age of 27. His symptoms indicated that the seizures began in the medial basal regions of both

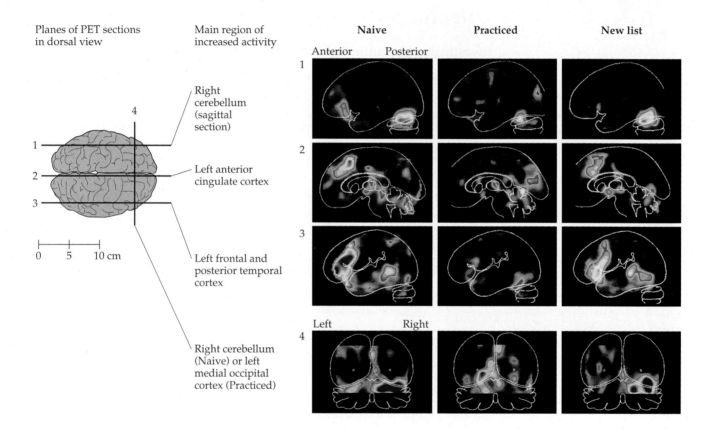

17.1   Training Can Lead to Rapid Changes in Brain Activity

Adults saw a list of 40 nouns, one presented every 1.5 seconds, and were told to speak an appropriate verb as rapidly as possible for each noun (for example, knife/cut, horse/gallop). The control task was speaking each word after it was presented on screen. The "Naive" column shows sites of increased brain activity during generation of verbs, found by subtracting PET scans made during the control task from scans made during the experimental task (see Box 2.3). After the task was repeated a few times, the sites of brain activity changed, as seen in the "Practiced" column. Then, when a new list of stimulus nouns was presented, generating appropriate responses caused specific brain activity in the same regions as seen in the Naive condition. Areas of highest activation are coded as orange and red. After Raichle et al., 1994; PET scans courtesy of Marcus Raichle.

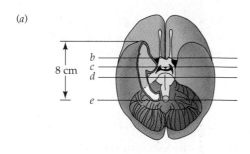

(a)

8 cm

b
c
d

e

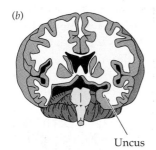

(b)

Uncus

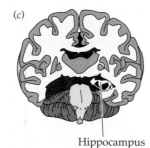

(c)

Hippocampus

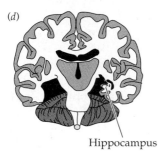

(d)

Hippocampus

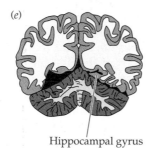

(e)

Hippocampal gyrus
(posterior part)

**17.2 Brain Tissue Removed in the Operation
on Patient H.M.**

After the operation, H.M. was no longer able to form
some kinds of long-term memory. (*a*) Basal view of the
brain showing the extent of the operation and the levels
of the transverse sections, *b–e*. The operation was performed bilaterally, but the diagrams show only unilateral removal on the left side so the forms of the structures
can be seen on the right. After Scoville and Milner, 1957.

temporal lobes, so in 1953 a neurologist removed this
tissue, including much of the amygdala and hippocampus, on both sides (Figure 17.2; Scoville and
Milner, 1957; Hilts, 1995). Similar operations had been
performed before without harmful effects, although
in those cases less tissue had been removed. Upon recovery from the operation, H.M.'s seizures were
milder, and they could be controlled by medication.
But this relief came at a terrible, unforeseen price:
H.M. was found to suffer from a peculiar kind of amnesia. (**Amnesia**—from the Greek *amnesia*, "forgetful-

ness"—is a severe impairment of memory; however,
most patients with amnesia retain some memories.)

Most of H.M.'s old memories remained intact, but
H.M. had difficulty retrieving memories that had
formed during the ten years before the operation.
Such memory loss is called **retrograde amnesia**
(from the Latin roots meaning "to go backward").
Retrograde amnesia is not rare. What was striking
about H.M. was his apparent inability to retain *new*
material for more than a brief period. When he met
someone new, almost as soon as that person left the
room, H.M. was unable to recall the person's name or
even that he had met someone. The inability to form
new memories after the onset of an illness is called
anterograde amnesia (from the Latin roots meaning
"to go forward").

Even now, years after the operation, H.M. retains
a new fact only briefly; as soon as he is distracted, the
newly acquired information vanishes. H.M. doesn't
know his age or the current date, and doesn't know
that his parents (with whom he lived) died several
years ago. But H.M. does converse easily, and his IQ
remains a little above average (Corkin, 1984).

There are a few indications that H.M. has formed
some bits of long-term memory in the years since his
operation. For example, when asked where he is, he
sometimes guesses M.I.T., the place where he has
been interviewed and tested many times in the last
40 years. And when H.M. has been awakened at
night in the laboratory and asked what he was just
dreaming, perhaps it is a distorted memory that occasionally leads him to say, "I was just dreaming I
was a brain surgeon" (Hilts, 1995).

H.M. recognizes that something is wrong with
him because he has no memories of the past several
years or even of what he did earlier in the same day.
His description of this isolation from his own past is
poignant (Milner, 1970:37):

> Every day is alone in itself, whatever enjoyment I've
> had, and whatever sorrow I've had. . . . Right now,
> I'm wondering, have I done or said anything amiss?
> You see, at this moment everything looks clear to me,
> but what happened just before? That's what worries
> me. It's like waking from a dream. I just don't re-
> member.

Testing shows that H.M.'s short-term memory is
normal. For example, if he is given a series
of digits and is asked to repeat the list immediately, he, like most of us, can usually
repeat a list of seven digits without error.
But if he is given a list of words to study
and is tested on them after other tasks have inter-

vened, he cannot repeat the list; in fact, he does not even remember having studied the list! Thus, H.M.'s case gives clear evidence that short-term memory (STM) differs from long-term memory (LTM). Psychologists have recognized the distinction between STM and LTM on behavioral/cognitive grounds ever since the time of William James (1890). Short-term memory is usually considered to last only for about 30 seconds, or as long as a person rehearses the material; it holds only a limited number of items (Brown, 1958; Peterson and Peterson, 1959). Long-term memory is an enduring form that lasts for hours, days, weeks, or more; it has very large capacity. We will discuss long- and short-term memory in more depth later in this chapter.

After publication of H.M.'s case, similar cases were reported that resulted not from brain surgery but from disease. On rare occasions, herpes simplex virus destroys tissue in the medial temporal lobe. This destruction can produce a severe failure to form new long-term memories, although acquisition of short-term memories is normal (Damasio et al., 1985a). Rupture of the anterior cerebral arteries that damages basal forebrain regions, including the hippocampus, can cause amnesia (Damasio et al., 1985b). An episode of reduced blood supply to the brain (ischemia), such as can be produced by a heart attack, can also damage the medial temporal lobe and memory formation. Within this general region of the brain, can we pinpoint a specific site as the cause of the memory problems of H.M. and similar patients?

At first, H.M.'s memory deficit was ascribed to bilateral destruction of much of the hippocampus, because other surgery patients who had received the same type of damage to more anterior structures, including the amygdala, but less damage to the hippocampus, did not exhibit memory impairment. To test this hypothesis, investigators began to remove the hippocampus from experimental animals to reproduce H.M.'s deficit. But after a decade of research, brain scientists had to confess failure: neither in rats nor in monkeys did widespread failure of memory consolidation follow bilateral destruction of the hippocampus; the effects that were observed could not be distinguished from possible effects of motivational or perceptual factors (Isaacson, 1972).

Different investigators attempted to account for this puzzling discrepancy between human and animal results in different ways. Some investigated the roles of various structures in the medial temporal lobe and the diencephalon; others looked more carefully into the behavioral tests used to measure memory. This broadened research produced major gains

in knowledge—about amnesia in people and ways to test memory, about functions of the hippocampus and neighboring structures, and about brain mechanisms of memory.

Later in this chapter we will review research with both human and animal subjects that reveals more precisely the structures in the medial temporal lobe where damage causes symptoms like those of H.M. Before such research could yield useful results, however, it was necessary to define more exactly what was impaired and what was spared in H.M.'s memory.

An early hypothesis to explain why human results differed from those in other animals was that the impairment caused by damage to the medial temporal lobe in humans involves chiefly *verbal* material and that animals, of course, could not be tested for such deficits. An interesting finding suggested that H.M.'s memory deficit is restricted mainly to verbal material and may not hold for motor learning. Milner (1965) presented a mirror-tracing test to H.M. (Figure 17.3a), and H.M. showed considerable improvement over several trials. The next day the test was presented again. When asked if he remembered it, H.M. said no, but his performance was better than at the start of the first day (Figure 17.3b). Over three successive days, H.M. never recognized the problem, but his tracings showed memory. If an animal subject with the same type of brain damage showed similar proof of memory, we would have no doubt that the animal had normal memory, because we do not ask our animal subjects whether they *recognize* the test.

Two other types of findings, however, indicate that the memory problems of H.M. and other similar patients cannot be attributed solely to difficulties with verbal material. First, such patients also have difficulty in reproducing or recognizing pictures and spatial designs that are not recalled in verbal terms. Second, although the patients have difficulty with the specific content of verbal material, they can learn some kinds of information *about* verbal material (Cohen and Squire, 1980). For example, they can learn to read words printed mirror-reversed. No motor skill is involved, but rather the ability to deal with abstract rules or procedures. If some words are used repeatedly, normal subjects come to recognize them and to read them easily. Patients of several kinds—those with temporal-lobe amnesia, those who suffer from Korsakoff's syndrome (described in the next section), and those who have recently received electroconvulsive shock therapy—learn the *skill* of mirror reading well but show impaired learning of the specific words and do not recognize the task on successive occasions.

(a) The mirror-tracing task

17.3 H.M.'s Performance on a Mirror Tracing Task

(a) The mirror tracing task. (b) Performance of H.M. on 3 successive days shows progressive improvement and thus, long-term memory. After Milner, 1965.

(b) Performance of H.M. on mirror-tracing task

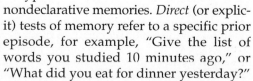

Thus, the important distinction is probably not between motor and verbal performances but between two kinds of memory: (1) **Declarative memory** is directly accessible to conscious recollection. It is what we usually think of as memory: facts and information acquired through learning. (2) **Nondeclarative memory** is shown by performance rather than by conscious recollection. It is sometimes called procedural memory. The two kinds of memory can be distinguished as follows: declarative memory deals with *what;* nondeclarative memory deals with *how.* Thus, an animal's inability to speak is probably not what accounts for its apparent immunity to the effects of medial temporal lesions on memory storage. Rather, the culprit is the difficulty in measuring declarative memory in animals.

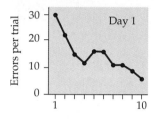 Different types of tests measure declarative and nondeclarative memories. *Direct* (or explicit) tests of memory refer to a specific prior episode, for example, "Give the list of words you studied 10 minutes ago," or "What did you eat for dinner yesterday?" They also have been defined as requiring conscious recognition of the material. *Indirect* (or implicit) tests of memory do not refer to a specific prior episode and do not require conscious recognition; the memory is inferred from performance. For example, memory for the recent presentation of certain words may be inferred from ease of recognizing them, versus control words, in blurred or very rapid presentation or from the probability of using them in a word-completion test.

Patient N.A.: Damage to the Medial Diencephalon Can Prevent Formation of New Memories

The medial temporal lobe is not the only brain region involved in the formation of declarative memories. Damage to the midline diencephalic region was first linked to amnesia in humans a century ago, and evidence of the involvement of this brain region has continued to accumulate. For example, the case of patient N.A. indicates that damage to the dorsomedial thalamus can impair memory formation (Squire and Moore, 1979; Teuber, Milner, and Vaughan, 1968). N.A. became amnesic as a result of a bizarre accident in which a miniature fencing foil entered his brain through the nostril. N.A. is markedly amnesic, primarily for verbal material, and he can give little information about events since his accident in 1960, but he shows almost normal recall for events of the 1940s and 1950s. An MRI study of N.A. (Figure 17.4) shows damage to the left dorsal thalamus, bilateral damage to the mammillary nuclei, and probable damage to the mammillothalamic tract (Squire et al., 1989). The devastating effects of this deficit on N.A.'s daily life are described in Box 17.1. Like H.M., N.A. shows normal short-term memory but impaired long-term memory, and the difficulty in long-term memory is in forming declarative, but not nondeclarative, memories. The similarity in symptoms raises the question of whether the medial temporal region and the midline diencephalic region are parts of a larger system. We will return to this question in Chapter 18.

Patients with Korsakoff's Syndrome Show Damage to Midline Diencephalic Structures and to Frontal Cortex

In the 1880s a Russian neurologist published a paper about a syndrome in which impaired memory was a major feature. This paper became a classic, and the condition was subsequently named after him: **Korsakoff's syndrome**. Sufferers of Korsakoff's syndrome fail to recall many items or events of the past; if such an item is presented again or if it happens to be recalled, the patient does not feel familiar with it. Korsakoff's patients frequently deny that anything is wrong with them. They often show disorientation for time and place, and they may confabulate, that is, fill a gap in memory with a falsification that they seem to accept as true.

The main cause of Korsakoff's syndrome is lack of the vitamin thiamine. Alcoholics who obtain most of their calories from alcohol and neglect their diet often exhibit this deficiency. Treating such a person with thiamine can prevent further deterioration of memory functions; if the treatment is started before the person has become a full-blown Korsakoff's case, the condition can be remedied. Animal models of Korsakoff's syndrome involve either drug-induced thiamine deficiency (Langlais, Mandel, and Nair, 1992) or surgical lesions.

Mair, Warrington, and Wieskrantz (1979) examined two Korsakoff's patients for several years, using a battery of behavioral tests; later they examined the brains of these patients in detail. Both brains showed shrunken, diseased mammillary bodies, as well as some damage in the dorsomedial thalamus. Temporal lobe structures, including the hippocampus and the temporal stem, were normal. Thus these cases confirm the less precise, earlier studies. Mair

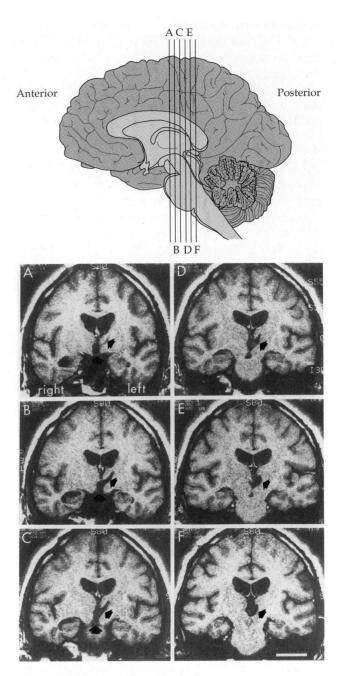

17.4 MRI Images Show Brain Damage in Amnesia Patient N.A.

Successive scans were made through the diencephalic region (*top*); note that right and left are reversed in these scans, as if you were face-to-face with the patient. A prominent lesion on the left side of the brain is indicated by the blue arrows. The floor of the third ventricle also appears to be missing throughout much of the caudal two-thirds of the hypothalamus, as indicated by the red arrows in A–C. Where the mammillary nuclei should be present in B and C, there is no indication of intact tissue. From Squire, et al., 1989; MRI scans courtesy of Larry Squire.

and coworkers characterize the mammillary bodies as "a narrow funnel through which connections from the midbrain as well as the temporal lobe neocortex and limbic system gain access to the frontal lobes" (1979:778). Damage to the basal frontal lobes, also found in Korsakoff's patients, is probably what differentiates them from other amnesia patients.

Patient K.C.: Damage to the Cerebral Cortex Can Impair Retention or Retrieval of Memories

Damage to the cerebral cortex impairs memory in many cases, perhaps by destroying some memory stores or by preventing access to memories. Sensory maps in the cortex change with experience (see Chapter 8), and some investigators believe that these changes reflect cortical storage of memories. Cortical damage may destroy the ability to recognize certain kinds of stimuli. One example is the loss of ability to recognize faces (prosopagnosia) after damage to the inferotemporal cortex (see Chapter 10); another is the specific inability to understand words after damage to cortical language areas, which we will take up in Chapter 19. Each region of the cerebral cortex may store the kinds of information it processes.

A striking case involving cortical damage shows profound effects on memory. It also supports an important distinction betweeen two kinds of memory that cognitive psychologist Endel Tulving (1972) had defined: semantic memory and episodic memory. **Semantic memory** is generalized memory, such as knowing the meaning of a word without knowing where or when you learned that word. **Episodic memory** is autobiographical memory that pertains to a person's own history; you show episodic memory when you recall a particular episode or relate an event to a particular time and place (such as remembering where and when you last saw a particular friend).

Biological evidence for the distinction between semantic and episodic memory appeared in studies of a man known as K.C., who suffered extensive damage to the anterior cerebral cortex in a traffic accident and can no longer retrieve any personal memory of his past, although his general knowledge remains good (Tulving, 1989). He converses easily and plays a good game of chess, but he cannot remember where he learned to play chess or from whom. K.C. has difficulty acquiring new semantic knowledge, but he can acquire some, *if* care is taken to space out the trials to prevent interference among items (Tulving, Hayman, and Macdonald, 1991). Even with this method he cannot acquire new episodic knowledge. Studies of normal human subjects indicate increased blood flow in the anterior regions of the cortex during recall of episodic memories, and increases in posterior regions during recall of semantic materials (Tulving, 1989).

Ten Challenges for a Neuroscience of Learning and Memory

Surveying some of the main aspects of learning and memory poses major challenges for any theory that attempts to explain learning and memory in biological terms. Ten of these challenges are stated in this section. In the rest of this chapter and in Chapter 18 we will see how well these challenges are being met.

1. Memory storage is huge. The memory of human beings, and of many other animals, has enormous capacity, even though most of what an individual experiences never enters long-term memory. How can such a large amount of information be stored in the nervous system?

2. Long-term memories can be formed for some brief experiences. By what means can a brief experience be stored in the nervous system and remembered for a lifetime?

3. There appear to be several different kinds of learning and memory. Some investigators and theorists in the field of learning and memory like to lump together as many phenomena as they can, while others like to make fine distinctions. Both "lumpers" and "splitters" agree on at least some different kinds of learning and memory. Which proposed distinctions among kinds of learning and memory are confirmed by biological research, and which are not? (Some differences among kinds of learning and memory are confirmed by the clinical cases we have reviewed.)

4. Relatively simple learning includes both nonassociative forms—habituation, dishabituation, and sensitization—and associative forms, such as classical (Pavlovian) conditioning and instrumental learning (Box 17.2 reviews the basic terminology and concepts that relate to learning and memory). But even these relatively simple kinds are more complex than originally supposed. Conditioning involves learning relations and predictability among events. Close temporal pairing of stimuli is neither necessary nor sufficient for conditioning to occur. Can neuroscience research provide adequate models for these kinds of learning?

Box 17.1

How Do You Live When You Can't Form New Memories?

What is life like for a person who becomes severely impaired in the ability to form memories? Some people suffer such a fate as a consequence of disease, brain operations, or injury to the brain. The description of daily life for one of these people is illuminating (Kaushall, Zetin, and Squire, 1981).

N.A. did well in school both scholastically and athletically; he graduated from high school in 1958. After a year of junior college, he joined the Air Force. One day in 1960 while N.A. was assembling a model airplane, a roommate took a miniature fencing foil from the wall, tapped N.A. from behind, and thrust forward as N.A. turned around. The blade entered his right nostril and penetrated the left hemisphere of N.A.'s brain. N.A. reports memories of the acci-

dent and of the minute or two afterward until he lost consciousness. During hospitalization several not uncommon neurological symptoms were noted, and they cleared up. But there was one unusual symptom that persisted: N.A. was practically unable to form new long-term memories, especially for verbal material.

After several months N.A. was returned to the care of his parents. During the several years after the accident, psychologist H. L. Teuber and colleagues followed his case (Teuber, Milner, and Vaughan, 1968). Since 1975 a psychological-medical team has tested N.A. frequently and has visited his home often (Kaushall, Zetin, and Squire, 1981).

Upon first meeting N.A., visitors are impressed with his nor-

mality. He is relaxed and amiable, and is polite and hospitable. He invites you to inspect his collection of guns and model airplanes and hundreds of souvenirs that he has acquired on trips with his parents. He describes the objects lucidly and intelligently, although he is sometimes unsure where he obtained a particular object. He does not exhibit confusion, and during a visit he does not show the same object twice.

But when you return for repeated visits, N.A. apologizes each time for not remembering your name and asks each time whether he has shown you his collections. By the third or fourth visit, these repetitions and other aspects of N.A.'s behavior "come to reveal a devastated life and an isolated mental world" (Kaushall, Zetin, and Squire, 1981:384).

Although N.A. has an IQ of 124, he can neither hold a job nor form close personal relationships. N.A. has attended an outpatient treatment center for many years and is

---

5. Experience and memory have several main dimensions (or attributes), which include *space, time, sensory perception, response,* and *affect* (that is, emotional tone or content). Are the different attributes of memory processed in separate brain regions? If so, how are the different attributes of memory assembled in the retrieval of memory?

6. Information processing often becomes easier and more automatic with practice, as in the experiment shown in Figure 17.1. Do neural circuits and brain regions thus change as actions and processing become practiced?

7. Species differ in their needs to learn and remember depending on their ecological niches and lifestyles. How do species differ in their neural mechanisms of learning and memory, and how did these differences evolve?

8. Conditions that follow an event, such as emotional reactions, can alter the strength of the memory for that event. By what mechanisms can post-

training conditions modulate the strength of memory?

9. In animals with large and varied stores of memories, how can memories be retrieved accurately and rapidly enough to serve ongoing behavior? Furthermore, how can retrieval be effective not only in the original situations in which the memories were acquired but also in novel contexts? In many cases memories are not just recall or reenactments of past experiences and actions; often they are new combinations—*re*-collections, *re*-membering of information.

10. Because every animal species appears capable of some learning and memory, learning, which permits prompt adaptation to the environment, must be required for survival. Are the mechanisms of learning and memory basically the same in all animals, or do they represent convergent evolution in response to similar environmental pressures?

popular among staff and patients, but he cannot remember their names or their histories. He is alert and enjoys humor, but his socializing is limited by his inability to keep a topic of conversation in mind, especially if there are interruptions. His failure to acquire knowledge about current events or people prevents him from contributing much to conversations. Although N.A. was sexually active before his accident, he has had virtually no sexual contact since. He once made a date with a young woman he met at a picnic, but he failed to remember the appointment until two weeks afterward, and did not pursue the acquaintanceship further. His relationship with his mother is the dominant feature of his emotional life. He has said that he would have had a wife and family if he had not been injured but now believes that he will not be able to do so.

The only routines that N.A. can perform reliably are ones that he has learned through years of prac-

tice. Cooking or other activities that require correct sequencing of steps are very difficult for him. Even watching television is a problem because a commercial interruption may cause him to forget the subject. N.A. spends much of his time tidying around the house, doing small woodworking projects, and assembling models. He constantly arranges objects and shows obsessive concern that everything be in its right place. He is irritated if he finds that anything has been moved. N.A.'s mother says that his obsessiveness and irritability developed since the accident. Probably he strives for a rigorously stable environment to compensate for his deficient memory.

Despite his handicap, N.A. maintains a generally optimistic view of his life. In part this attitude may reflect the fact that he remembers mainly experiences prior to 1960, when he was successful socially, athletically, and scholastically. Although he has had many

frustrating experiences since his accident, these are not remembered in detail, and apparently they do not lead to depression. N.A.'s inability to form memories is as severe as that of patients with Korsakoff's syndrome, but he does not show the apathy, blandness, and loss of initiative that characterize them.

N.A. has formed some verbal memories after the accident, but they are spotty. He knows that "Watergate" signifies some political scandal that took place in "Washington or Florida" but he cannot give any details or tell who was involved. Only occasionally does he write notes or instructions to himself as memory aids, and he tends to lose track of such notes. At one session when N.A.'s memory was being tested, he repeatedly tried to recall a question that he wanted to ask the investigator. Finally he searched his pockets and found a poignant note that he had written to himself: "Ask Dr. Squire if my memory is getting better."

Even "Simple" Learning Can Be Complex

Experimenters often try to keep learning situations as simple as possible in order to control all aspects and interpret the results clearly. But even relatively simple learning situations may be rather complex. A few examples will illustrate. (Review Box 17.2 for some basic definitions of types of learning.)

Conditional Learning Depends on Context

The fact that typical learning involves a number of dimensions is revealed by conditional learning. In **conditional learning**, you learn that a particular response to a particular stimulus is appropriate in one setting but not in another. More formally, the conditioned stimulus (CS) or unconditioned stimulus (US) becomes associated with the conditions or context in which it occurs. A CS evokes a US in one context but does not (or not as strongly) in another. Conditional learning does not require a big brain, or any brain at

all; the relatively simple mollusc *Aplysia* can do it, as the following experiment shows (Colwill, Absher, and Roberts, 1988).

Each of several *Aplysia* was trained in both of two enclosures: a shiny, smooth white bowl filled with lemon-flavored seawater (Figure 17.5*a*), and a dark gray, rectangular enclosure with a ribbed surface, filled with unflavored seawater (Figure 17.5*b*). Each *Aplysia* spent 20 minutes a day in each of these enclosures, during which it received one CS and one US, with at least 5 hours between the sessions in the two enclosures. The CS was a light touch to the siphon of the mollusc; the US was an electric shock to its mantle shelf that caused the siphon and mantle shelf to withdraw. For each *Aplysia*, the CS and US were paired in one enclosure (CS preceding US by 0.5 seconds), but unpaired in the other, occurring at least 5 minutes apart. Half the *Aplysia* received the paired training in enclosure *a* and the unpaired training in enclosure *b*, while the other half received the un-

Box 17.2

Learning and Memory: Some Basic Concepts and Definitions

Since you probably have studied learning and memory in one or more psychology courses, here we only briefly review some of the basic concepts and definitions. Basic experiments on learning and memory, as described for neuroscientists by Rescorla (1988), involve the organism's experience and behavior at two separate times. At the first time (t_1), the organism is exposed to a particular experience—a sensory stimulus or some other opportunity to learn. At a later time (t_2), the investigator assesses the organism to determine whether the t_1 experience has modified its behavior. The aim is to determine whether a particular t_1 experience produces an outcome at t_2 that would be absent without the t_1 experience. Therefore, studies of learning usually compare *two* organisms (or two groups of organisms) at t_2: those that were exposed to the t_1 experience and those that did not have that experience but instead had a "control" experience at t_1. The basic learning paradigms can be organized in terms of the different types of experience they provide at t_1 and the different techniques of assessment they use at t_2.

There are three main experimental paradigms:

1. A single stimulus (S1), without any other event or constraint, is presented to the organism. The result may be habituation, dishabituation, or sensitization (defined below).

2. One stimulus (S1) is presented in relation with another stimulus (S2). This paradigm (called Pavlovian, or classical, conditioning) allows us to study how the organism learns about the structure of its environment and the relations among stimuli in its world.

3. The stimulus (S1) is delivered in such a way as to reinforce a certain behavior. Called instrumental, or operant, conditioning, this paradigm allows us to study how an organism learns about the impact of its *own* actions on the world.

Nonassociative learning involves only a single stimulus at t_1. Three kinds of nonassociative learning are: habituation, dishabituation, and sensitization. **Habituation** refers to a decrease in response to a stimulus as the stimulus is repeated (when the decrement cannot be attributed to sensory adaptation or motor fatigue). When the response to a stimulus has become habituated, a strong stimulus (of the same sort or even in another sensory modality) will often cause the response to the habituated stimulus to increase sharply in amplitude; it may become even larger than the original response. The increase in response amplitude over the baseline level is called **dishabituation** (the habituation has been removed). Even a response that has not been habituated may increase in amplitude after a strong stimulus. This effect is known as **sensitization**: the response is greater than its baseline level because of prior stimulation.

Learning that involves *relations* between events—for example, between two or more stimuli, between a stimulus and a response, or between a response and its consequence—is called **associative learning**. In one form, **classical conditioning** (also called **Pavlovian conditioning**), an initially neutral stimulus comes to predict an event. At the end of the nineteenth century, Ivan Pavlov (Figure A) found that a dog would salivate when presented with an auditory or visual stimulus *if* the stimulus came to predict an event that normally caused salivation. Thus, if the experimenter rang a bell just before putting meat powder in the dog's mouth, repeating this sequence a few times would cause the dog to respond to the bell itself by salivating. In this case the sound is called the **conditioned stimulus** (**CS**) and the meat powder in the mouth is the **unconditioned stimulus** (**US**); the meat powder already evokes an **unconditioned response** (**UR**), and the acquired response to the CS is called the **conditioned response** (**CR**).

In **instrumental conditioning** (also called **operant conditioning**) an association is formed between the animal's behavior and its consequence(s). The first inves-

paired stimuli in *a* and the paired in *b*. Thus, in one setting the light touch foretold that a shock was coming, but in the other setting the touch and shock were uncorrelated. After eight days of training—eight trials in each enclosure—each animal received the CS alone in each enclosure. As Figure 17.5*c* shows, the withdrawal response lasted significantly longer ($p <$ .05) in the context where the CS had been paired with

(A) *Pavlov and spectators in his laboratory*

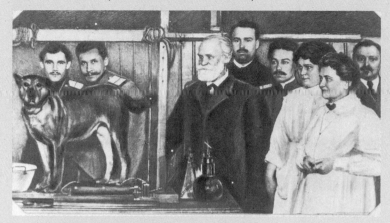

(B) *Thorndike's puzzle box*

tween the conditioned auditory stimulus (the bell) and the meat powder, but they also learned many other aspects of the situation. They learned the location of the test apparatus and the rewarding features of the test situation, so when the dogs came into the test room, they would eagerly leap onto the test stand. They also learned when in the day to expect to be tested. Thorndike's cats learned sensory aspects of the test situation as well as the correct motor responses. Different brain regions may process different dimensions or attributes of a learning/memory situation: space, time, sensory dimensions, response, and emotional aspects (Kesner, DiMattia, and Crutcher, 1987; Kesner, Bolland, and Dakis, 1993). Later in the chapter we will consider some experiments performed to test this so-called **attribute model** of memory.

(C) *A "Skinner box"*

tigation of instrumental learning was Thorndike's report (1898) of cats learning to escape from a puzzle box (Figure B). When placed in a small box with a latch inside, a cat would initially engage in a variety of behaviors and take quite a bit of time to free itself. But after several trial-and-error sequences, the cat learned to perform skillfully and economically the specific response (the conditioned instrumental response) that permitted escape (the reward). A modern example of an apparatus designed to study instrumental learning is an operant conditioning apparatus, often called a Skinner box (Figure C). Here the conditioned instrumental response is pressing a bar to gain the reward of a food pellet.

Some investigators emphasize that typical learning events have a number of dimensions or attributes. For example, Pavlov's dogs learned not only the relation be-

shock US than in the context where the CS and US had been unpaired.

The investigators point out, "Such findings highlight the potential complexity of Pavlovian conditioning processes. Moreover, they demonstrate the inadequacy of accounts of associative learning that appeal exclusively to close temporal proximity of the CS and the US for learning to occur" (Colwill, Absh-

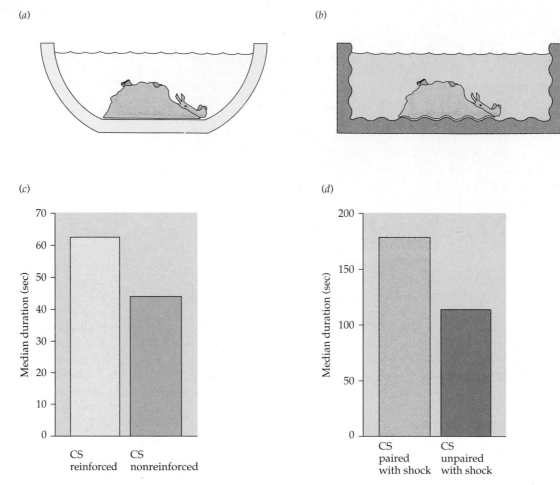

17.5 Conditional Learning in *Aplysia*
(*a*) Behavioral condition: shiny, smooth, white bowl filled with lemon-flavored seawater. (*b*) Contrasting behavioral condition: dark gray rectangular enclosure with ribbed surface, filled with unflavored seawater. (*c*) Median duration of *Aplysia* siphon withdrawal was significantly longer in response to the tactile CS when tested in the context where the CS was paired with shock US than in the context where the CS was presented without any US. (*d*) Median duration of siphon withdrawal was also longer when a CS had been paired with shock than to the same stimulus that had not been paired with shock. After Colwill, Absher, and Roberts, 1988.

er, and Roberts, 1988:4443). In the next section we will see further evidence that temporal proximity of CS and US is not necessary for conditioning.

Close Temporal Pairing of Stimuli Is Not Necessary for Conditioning

Neuroscientists have often assumed that close temporal proximity of CS and US is required for conditioning, but several experiments during the 1960s demonstrated that such pairing is neither necessary nor sufficient. Although proximity is important in some experiments, such as the eye-blink conditioning of

mammals that we describe shortly, it would be wrong to overgeneralize from these examples. As we will see, proximity does not guarantee conditioning, and conditioning does not necessarily require proximity.

Pavlov (1927) described a phenomenon referred to as "overshadowing," in which pairing does not guarantee conditioning. In these experiments he presented both a light and a tone shortly before the US during training, then tested responses to the light or tone separately. Most animals gave the CR to either the light or the tone but not to both, even though both stimuli were strong enough that either would have become conditioned if it had been presented alone during training. If CS1 is clearly stronger than CS2, then CS2 does not become associated with the US. The presence of CS1 prevents CS2 from becoming conditioned even though CS2 is paired regularly with the US. The overshadowing effect described by Pavlov went largely unnoticed until Kamin (1969) published similar experiments.

An already established CS1 can block conditioning of another stimulus, CS2, that is presented along with it (Kamin, 1968). Even though each presentation of CS2 is paired with the US, just as CS1 is, CS2 does not supply new information and it never becomes conditioned. The animal's nervous system seems to ignore the redundant information in CS2.

In another paradigm, pairing a CS with a US does not produce conditioning *if* the US occurs with equal frequency when the CS is absent; this situation is referred to as the effect of background conditioning (Rescorla, 1988). Thus, proximity does not guarantee conditioning; in order for conditioning to occur, the CS must be a reliable *predictor* of the US—in fact, the most reliable predictor available.

The best-known results that raise doubts about the necessity for temporal pairing of CS and US are from experiments on the ability of animals to learn to avoid poisons; these experiments were conducted by psychologist John Garcia and his collaborators (Garcia and Levine, 1974; Revusky and Garcia, 1970; see Chapter 13). They showed that if a rat tasted a novel food and then several hours later was given X-irradiation or an injection that caused a nauseous illness, the rat would refuse to sample that food again. Garcia initially had a hard time getting these results published; they were greeted with incredulity because they departed sharply from the widely held belief that close temporal contiguity was necessary for conditioning. In fact, these experiments on "bait-shyness" or taste aversion conform to the well-known ability of rats to avoid being poisoned by sampling any novel food cautiously and in small amounts, then waiting before returning to it. Many people have also reported the experience of becoming ill hours after tasting a novel food and then being unwilling to try it again, even if it was very unlikely that the food had caused the illness. This effect could be induced when the treatment that caused illness followed tasting the food by as much as 12 hours, thus raising the question of what is meant by the requirement of contiguity.

Several kinds of conditioning have an optimal CS–US interval, but the optimum varies considerably depending on the task. For conditioning the eye-blink reflex in mammals, the interval is about 200 millisec-

onds; for the siphon- or gill-withdrawal reflex in *Aplysia,* about 0.5 seconds; for operant-conditioned bar pressing in rats, about 2 seconds; and for taste aversion in rats, an hour or more. This wide variation in optimum CS–US interval raises the question of whether it is meaningful to insist on the temporal pairing of stimuli as a requirement for conditioning.

There Are Many Response Aspects of Conditioning

In conditioning, both the response and the stimulus tend to have multiple dimensions. Consider the example of eye-blink conditioning, which is studied in both human and animal subjects. In these experiments a tone or buzzer (the conditioned stimulus) precedes a puff of air to the eye (the unconditioned stimulus) that causes the subject to blink. After a few trials, the subject begins to blink to the CS, *before* the puff of air is delivered. Blinking early protects the eye from the mildly unpleasant air puff. But even before subjects develop the specific conditioned response (CR) of blinking to the CS, they show a number of unspecific CRs that may include increases in heart rate and blood pressure, changes in respiration, and changes in electrical resistance of the skin. These nonspecific autonomic responses develop earlier than the appearance of the specific CR in many situations, especially if the US is aversive; perhaps they help prepare the subject to respond to a novel or threatening situation.

Because the nonspecific CRs appear earlier in the conditioning process than the specific CR, some investigators suggested that conditioning involves two processes, and that the specific CR (eye-blink) develops from the nonspecific CRs. Others held that the two kinds of conditioning are independent of each other. Recent research demonstrates a double dissociation between the brain regions required for the conditioned eye-blink and conditioned heart rate responses in animal subjects (Supple et al., 1989; Supple and Leaton, 1990). That is, brain lesions that prevent eye-blink conditioning do not prevent heart rate conditioning, and lesions that prevent heart rate conditioning do not prevent eye-blink conditioning. This research thus disproves (at least for eye-blink conditioning) the two-process theory that nonspecific conditioning is a necessary prerequisite for specific conditioning. We will take up the particular brain regions involved when we discuss brain localization of conditioning.

Animals Form Cognitive Maps

A pioneer in the study of representational memory in humans and other animals was the American psychologist Edward C. Tolman. Tolman and his students showed that when rats explore a maze, they are not learning a series of turns, but instead they form a cognitive map. For example, after rats had run a maze several times, the experimenters removed a section of wall, thus opening up a shortcut to the goal area. Most rats took the shortcut as soon as it became available, thus showing their knowledge of the overall layout of the maze.

Edward C. Tolman
(1886–1959)

Tolman and his students also demonstrated that rats' performance may not reveal all they know unless the test situation is appropriate to reveal the knowledge. One kind of evidence for this is the phenomenon called "latent learning" (Tolman and Honzik, 1930). Rats were divided into two groups and were allowed to gain experience in a maze. One group received food when they reached the goal area of the maze; they ran to that area more and more quickly in successive daily trials. Animals of the other group were allowed to explore the maze for a few daily sessions without receiving any reward and without any region being marked as a special area. Then, in one session, they found food in the goal area. The next time they were placed in the maze, they raced to the goal, reaching it just as rapidly as the rats that had been rewarded on each trial. If the experimenter hadn't offered the reward, he would not have realized that the previously unrewarded group had learned the maze as well as the uniformly rewarded rats.

At a time when most American psychologists were studying only instrumental learning or conditioning, and were trying to find THE laws of learning, Tolman (1949) wrote an article entitled "There Is More than One Kind of Learning." He suggested that investigators should be looking for the different laws that govern different kinds of learning. A quarter century passed before many workers began to follow this suggestion.

Memory Has Temporal Stages: Short, Intermediate, and Long

The terms "learning" and "memory" are so often paired that it sometimes seems as if one necessarily implies the other. We cannot be sure that learning has

occurred unless a memory can be elicited later. (Here we are using "memory" in the common meaning of anything that shows that learning has occurred.) Even demonstrating that something has been learned, however, does not guarantee that the memory for the learned material will be retrievable again in the future. A long-lasting memory may later be absent for a variety of reasons: it may never have formed, it may have decayed with time, it may have been impaired by injury to the brain, or it may be temporarily unretrievable because of the particular state of the subject. Some kinds of memory, classified by duration, are shown in Figure 17.6.

Investigators often contrast short-term and long-term memories, but like many twofold distinctions, this differentiation is probably too simple. The briefest memories are called **iconic** (from the Greek *eikon*, "image"). An example would be your impressions of a scene that is illuminated for only a moment. You may be able to grasp one part of the display, but the rest vanishes in seconds. (A very brief auditory memory is called echoic, as if you could still hear it ringing in your ears.) These brief memories are thought to reflect the continuation of sensory neural activity, the so-called "sensory buffers" (Figure 17.6).

Somewhat longer than iconic memories are **short-term memories (STM)**. For example, suppose you want to call a person on the telephone using a number that you have never used before. You look up the number, and if nothing distracts or interrupts you, you call the number successfully, displaying an STM of the telephone number. If the line is busy, however, and you want to call back a minute later, you may have to look the number up again unless you have

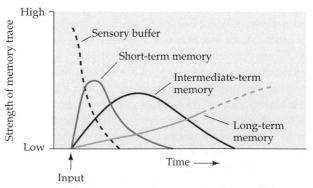

17.6　A Multiple-Trace Hypothesis of Memory
According to this hypothesis, there is first a brief sensory buffer, then a short-term memory trace, which may be followed by an intermediate-term memory trace. If the learning is sufficiently strong, a long-term memory trace may also result. After McGaugh, 1968.

been repeating it to yourself in the meantime. If you rehearse or use the number, then it can remain in STM until you turn to some other activity. Unfortunately, the label "STM" is not used consistently among investigators from different fields. Cognitive psychologists, who first used the term STM, have found that if subjects are not allowed to rehearse, STM lasts only about 30 seconds (Brown, 1958; Peterson and Peterson, 1959).

As an example of memory that lasts somewhat beyond STM as defined by psychologists, suppose that you drive to school or work and park your car in a different place each day. If things go well, you remember each afternoon where you parked your car that morning, but you may not recall where you parked your car yesterday or a week ago. You are also likely to recall today's weather forecast, but not that of a few days ago. These are examples of what is sometimes called **intermediate-term memory (ITM)**, that is, a memory that outlasts STM but that is far from being permanent (Rosenzweig et al., 1993).

Beyond ITM are memories that last for weeks, months, and years; these are called **long-term memories (LTM)**. Because many memories that last for days or weeks do, however, become weaker and may even fade out completely with time, some investigators use the term **permanent memory** to designate memories that appear to continue without decline for the rest of the life of an organism, or at least as long as the organism remains in good health.

The fact that some memories last only for seconds and others for months is not proof that short-term memories are based on cognitive processes or biological mechanisms that differ from those of long-term memories. The scientist's task is to find out whether these memories are based on the same or different processes and mechanisms. As we will see, there are good reasons—both clinical and experimental—to conclude that the cognitive processes and biological mechanisms that underlie STM storage are different from those that underlie LTM storage.

Early behavioral evidence for differences between short-term and long-term memory stores came from the performance of subjects who learned lists of words or numbers. If you see or hear a list of ten words presented one at a time, and then 30 seconds later you try to repeat the list, you will probably remember best the first and the last items of the list. Figure 17.7 shows typical results from such an experiment—a U-shaped serial position curve. The superior performance at the start of the list is called the **primacy effect**. The superior performance at the end of the list, which is attributed to STM, is called the **re-**

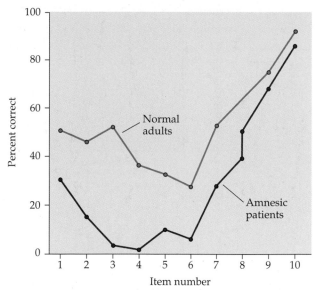

17.7 Serial Position Curves of Human Subjects
The curves show percent correct for immediate recall of a list of 10 words. The amnesic patients perform as well on the most recent items (8 through 10) as do the normal adults, but they are significantly worse on earlier items. After Baddeley and Warrington, 1970.

cency effect. If subjects try to recall the list a few *minutes* after having seen or heard the items, there is no recency effect; it is short-lived and reflects STM. The primacy effect, however, lasts longer and is usually attributed to LTM.

Experimental animals also show U-shaped serial position functions. These results provide one type of behavioral evidence to separate STM from a longer-lasting memory store (or stores) in animal subjects, and they offer the possibility of relating behavioral and biological mechanisms of memory stages in the same subjects. Wright and coworkers (1985) gave similar recognition memory tests to pigeons, monkeys, and humans. For each test, the material consisted of four sequentially presented color slides. Each slide was presented for 1 second for monkeys and humans and 2 seconds for pigeons, with a 1-second interval between items. After a delay interval that varied from trial to trial, a probe item was presented; on half the trials the probe item matched one of the four test patterns. Subjects demonstrated their memory by making one response if the probe matched a test item and another response if it was new. All three species showed primacy and recency effects in their serial position curves (Figure 17.8). The human subjects showed both primacy and recency effects when the delay between presentation of the

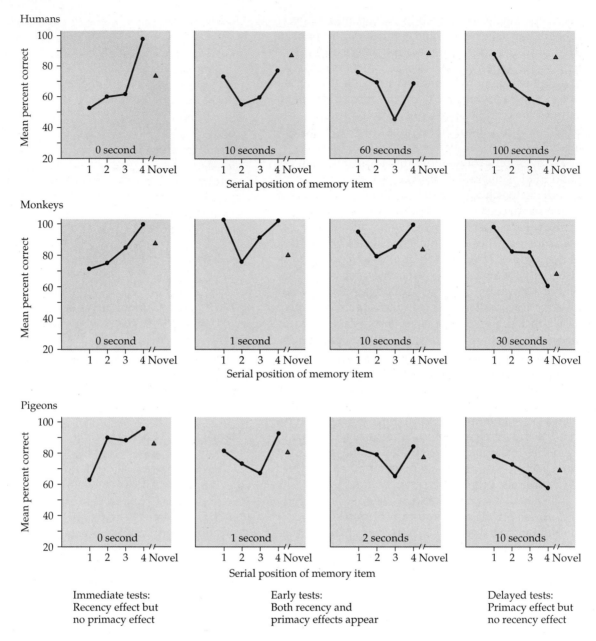

17.8 Recognition Memory Test Results for Humans, Monkeys, and Pigeons
The curves show percent correct responses to a probe item for four positions in the stimulus series, for humans (*a*), monkeys (*b*), and pigeons (*c*). "Novel" indicates an item that matched none of the four list items. After Wright et al., 1985.

items and the test varied from 10 to 60 seconds. If the test occurred earlier than 10 seconds after the items were seen, no primacy effect was seen; this result was attributed to retroactive interference from the test items. If the test occurred later than 60 seconds after

the items were seen, then no recency effect was present, but the primacy effect still occurred. Monkeys showed both primacy and recency effects for delays from 1 to 10 seconds, and pigeons showed both effects at delays of 1 and 2 seconds, but not at shorter or longer delays. Thus, results for all three species provide evidence for two distinct memory processes: a transient STM that accounts for the short-lived recency effect and a longer-lasting memory store that accounts for the primacy effect.

Brain lesion studies corroborate the parallel between humans and experimental animals: rats with hippocampal lesions exhibit the recency but not the primacy effect (Figure 17.9; Kesner and Novak, 1982). Similarly, amnesia patients, particularly those whose amnesia is caused by impairment of the hippocampus, show a reduced primacy effect but retain the recency effect (see Figure 17.7).

Unfortunately, there are no standard definitions of STM and LTM. Many biological psychologists and other biologists define STM as memory that is not permanent but that lasts for minutes or hours, or even up to a day. Thus, Kandel et al. (1987) wrote that in the sea slug *Aplysia*, "A single training trial produces short-term sensitization that lasts from minutes to hours" (p. 17), and that long-term memory is "memory that lasts more than one day" (p. 35). The lack of agreement on the duration of STM and LTM weakens attempts to find biological mechanisms of the temporal stages of memory.

The Capacity of Long-Term Memory Is Enormous

A fascinating case study of a man who remembered almost everything he had experienced from child-

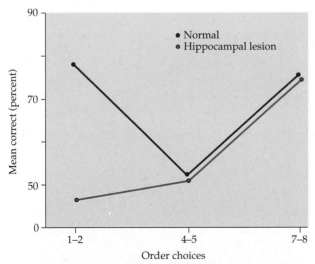

17.9 Hippocampal Lesions in Rats Eliminate the Primacy Effect in the Serial Position Curve
Normal rats and those with hippocampal lesions were tested for memory of early, middle, and late choices in an 8-arm radial maze. After Kesner and Novak, 1982.

hood on and was burdened by his total recall is presented by Russian psychologist Alexander Luria in his book *The Mind of a Mnemonist* (1987). Even the fallible memory stores of most of us hold huge numbers of memories and can acquire enormous amounts more. For example, American college students can recognize, on the average, about 50,000 different words. Many people who master several languages readily acquire even vaster vocabularies. Beyond the words, a person who speaks a language knows its grammar and grammatical forms, its idioms, and its familiar phrases; it is estimated that learning a language means acquiring on the order of 100,000 items of knowledge. Most of us recognize hundreds or thousands of faces and countless visual scenes and objects, hundreds of voices and many other familiar sounds, and hundreds of different odors. Depending on our interests, we may be able to recognize and sing or play many tunes and identify and supply information about a great many athletes, actors, or historical characters.

Such memories can be acquired rapidly and retained well. For example, Canadian psychologist Lionel Standing (1973) presented subjects with color slides for 5 seconds each in blocks of 20 to 1000 or more slides. Recognition memory was tested a few days later by presenting pairs of slides, one previously seen and one new, and requiring subjects to indicate which of the pair they had seen before. After an early study showed 90% recognition for 2560 items, Standing increased the number of items to 10,000 and found little decrease in scores. He concluded that, for all practical purposes, "there is no upper bound to memory capacity" (1973).

Of course, these results do not mean that the subjects learned all the details of the pictures; the two-alternative, forced-choice procedure only guarantees that *something* about the picture makes it more familiar than the paired item. Nevertheless, the amount of information acquired and the rapidity of acquisition are impressive. And it doesn't require a human brain to accomplish such a task; pigeons readily learned 320 slides in a picture-recognition test with no indication that this amount approached their capacity, and they retained many of the discriminations over a two-year period (Vaughan and Greene, 1984). An example of such memory retention in nature is the Clark nutcracker, a bird that can go back to locate several thousand cache sites months after hiding food in them (Vander Wall, 1982). What kind of memory mechanisms provide for the extensive storage exhibited by the enormous capacity of long-term memory?

Different Regions of the Brain Process Different Aspects of Memory

Any particular memory is composed of features or aspects that are specific and unique to that learning experience. As we mentioned earlier, some of the main features (or attributes) of memories are *space, time, sensory perception, response,* and *affect* (that is, emotional tone or content). For example, as you look at this book, you are aware of spatial aspects of your experience—where the book is in relation to you and where you are; you know the approximate or even the exact time; you are experiencing a particular affect or emotional state—feeling content, eager, happy, or sad; you perceive the color, shape, and other aspects of the book; and you are aware of making certain responses, such as holding the book, turning the page, and writing notes. The multiple aspects of experience and of memory are a focus of the work of biological psychologist Raymond Kesner (1980, 1992), which is based on earlier suggestions by Underwood (1969) and Spear (1976). Kesner is attempting to test the hypothesis that the different attributes of memory are processed by different regions of the brain. Drawing on the reports of many other investigators, he has designed a program of experiments with rats, as well as experimental and observational studies of people with various kinds of brain damage. Figure 17.10 shows the basic attributes of memory and the brain regions that are believed to process them.

17.11 Experiments to Test Specific Attributes of Animals' Memory ▶

a, c, and *e* show the experimental setups, and *b, d,* and *f* show effects of different brain lesions on the test results. (*a, b*) Spatial recognition. (*c, d*) Response recognition. (*e, f*) Object recognition. After Kesner, Bolland, and Dakis, 1993.

In the animal research, Kesner tried to design a series of tasks, each of which would make the animals focus especially on a particular attribute of experience. Only working, short-term memory was tested. Thus, for a *spatial recognition task,* Kesner, Bolland, and Dakis, (1993) used the well-known eight-arm radial maze (Figure 17.11*a*). Appropriate pretraining taught the rat to expect to find a bit of food at the end of each arm of the maze. For the spatial recognition task, each trial consisted of a study phase and a test phase. In the study phase, the rat was allowed to run down any arm. When it returned to the central platform, all doors to the arms were closed, confining the rat for a period of 1 to 30 seconds. Next, two doors were opened, allowing the rat a choice between the arm it had recently entered and another arm; the rat found food only if it chose the arm it had entered on the study phase of the trial. In each of the four daily trials, different arms were used. Different groups of animals were tested after having received a sham lesion or a lesion in the hippocampus, the caudate nu-

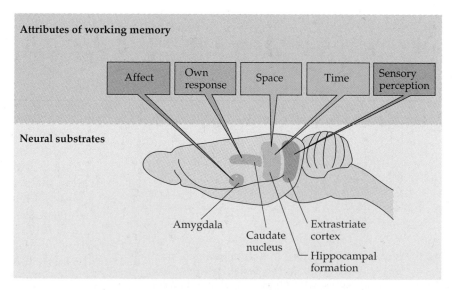

17.10 Basic Attributes of Memory and the Specific Brain Regions That Are Thought to Process Them
After Kesner, 1980, 1991.

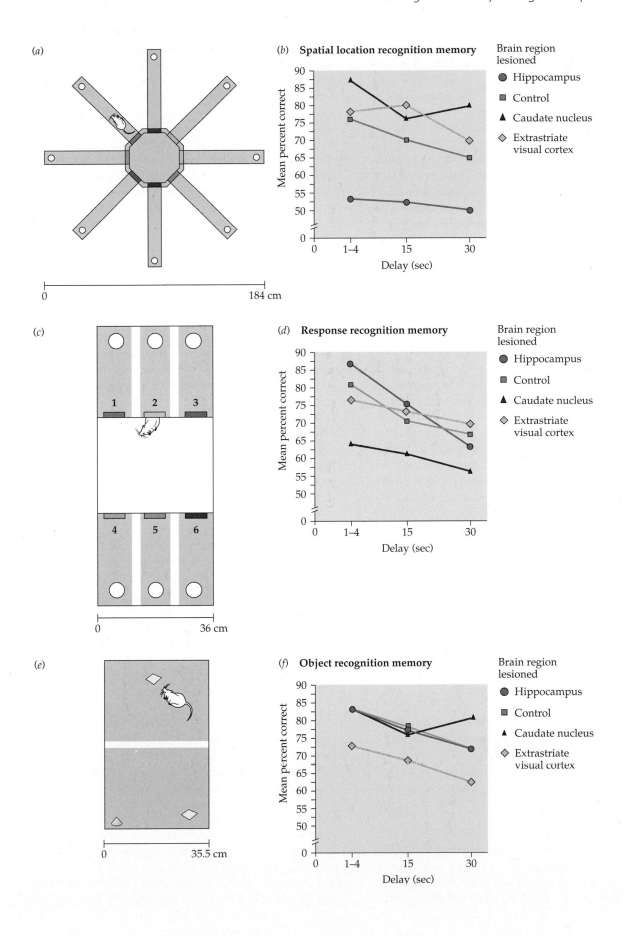

cleus, or the extrastriate (visual) cortex. The results of this experiment (Figure 17.11*b*) showed that only the animals with hippocampal lesions made fewer correct responses than the controls (the animals with sham lesions) on this predominantly spatial task.

To emphasize memory for the animal's own *response,* the investigators ran trials in a different apparatus (Figure 17.11*c*). On the study phase of a trial, the rat was placed in the middle arm on one side (for example, 2), where it could make an initial turn to its left (3) or right (1). Then it was placed in a different starting location (5), and was rewarded only if it made a turn to the same side of its body as before, not to the same direction in space. Performance on this task, which depends on memory of the previous response, was impaired by lesions of the caudate nucleus, but not by lesions of the hippocampus or extrastriate visual cortex (Figure 17.11*d*).

A task that emphasizes *sensory perception* is the object recognition (or non-matching-to-sample) test. Using the experimental setup shown in Figure 17.11*e*, the rat was first rewarded each time it pushed aside the sample object over the center depression (top). In the test phase of the experiment (Figure 17.11*e*, bottom), the rat was presented with two objects, one like the sample object that had been presented during the study phase and one novel object; the rat was rewarded only if it chose the object that did *not* match the sample. Only lesions of the extrastriate visual cortex, and not those of the hippocampus or caudate, significantly impaired performance on this visual memory task (Figure 17.11*f*).

Thus, Kesner, Bolland, and Dakis (1993) found a triple dissociation among brain regions and the tests. That is, lesions of each of three brain regions affected memory performance on only one of the three tests, and performance on each test was affected by lesions in only one of the three brain regions. This dissociation is good evidence that these different aspects of working memory are processed separately and, in part at least, by the brain regions indicated. Of course, an even more complete set of brain regions remains to be tested, if only to try to exclude them as important in processing these aspects of memory. Further work by Kesner and Williams (personal communication) on memory involving *affect* indicates that this attribute of memory is impaired by lesions of the amygdala, but not by lesions in the hippocampal formation or in the cerebral cortex dorsal to the hippocampus.

A similar research project in another laboratory found similar results (McDonald and White, 1993). This study used three different problems, all run in the radial maze, and found a triple dissociation of memory systems that require, respectively, the hip-

pocampus, the dorsal striatum (mainly the caudate nucleus), and the amygdala. The authors conclude that the mammalian brain is capable of acquiring different kinds of information with more-or-less independent neural systems: (1) a neural system that includes the hippocampus, which acquires information about relationships among stimuli and events (declarative memories); (2) a different neural system that includes the dorsal striatum, which mediates the formation of reinforced stimulus–response associations (habits, or non-declarative memories); and (3) another system that includes the amygdala, which mediates rapid acquisition of behaviors based on biologically significant events with affective properties.

Since different attributes appear to be processed in different regions of the brain, how are the attributes brought together during retrieval? Because the neural representations of the different attributes of an experience are activated at the same time, they tend to form links to each other, as we will see in Chapter 18, and the linkages help bind them together.

Memory Processes Extend from Acquisition to Retrieval

Psychologists who study learning and memory suggest that several successive processes are necessary to guarantee recall of a past event: **encoding, consolidation,** and **retrieval** (Figure 17.12). The original information must enter sensory channels and then be encoded rapidly into a form that passes into short-term memory. Some of this information may then be consolidated in long-term storage.

Some cognitive psychologists hold that there is no essential difference between short-term and long-term storage; they claim that more deeply processed information is stored longer. Others claim that the neural processes for short-term and long-term memory storage differ; we will see both neurological and neurochemical evidence for this hypothesis. For example, some patients with brain damage retain new items in short-term storage but show no long-term memory for them. The final stage of processing is retrieval, that is, the use of information that was stored earlier.

With these stages in mind, investigators have tried to find out whether particular examples of failure of recall in normal subjects involve failure of encoding, of consolidation, or of retrieval, and whether pathological impairments of memory selectively involve one or another of these main processes. Experimental studies show that performance on a memory test can be either enhanced or impaired by varying the

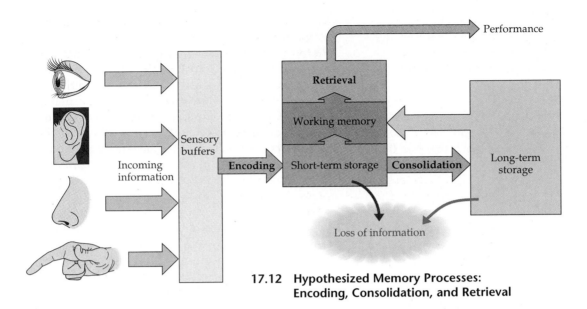

17.12 **Hypothesized Memory Processes: Encoding, Consolidation, and Retrieval**

conditions of acquisition, of consolidation, or of retrieval. In Chapter 18 we will see that some conditions or treatments impair encoding, some impair consolidation, and some impair retrieval.

Normally recent memories are stronger than older ones, but French psychologist Théodule-Armand Ribot (1881) concluded on the basis of published cases of amnesia that impairment of memory caused by disease or injury to the brain harms recent memories more severely. As more observations accumulated, this conclusion became known as Ribot's law, but not all investigators were convinced it was correct (Rozin, 1976b). In the 1970s work on the problem was revived; questionnaires were used to measure recall or recognition of events or faces from different decades of the past (Warrington and Silberstein, 1970; Squire and Slater, 1975). A problem with this research is the uncertainty that materials learned at different times in the past were equivalent in difficulty or that the learning was equally strong. To avoid this problem, four groups of investigators recently and independently designed experiments in which animals learned equivalent material at various times before they sustained lesions of the hippocampal formation. These studies were done with rats (Winocur, 1990; Kim and Fanselow, 1992), mice (Cho et al., 1991), and monkeys (Zola-Morgan and Squire,

Larry Squire

1990). Psychologist-neuroscientist Larry Squire has studied this problem and many other aspects of memory with both human and nonhuman subjects.

In the monkey experiment, the animals learned to discriminate between two objects in 20 different pairs at each of five periods (16, 12, 8, 4, and 2 weeks before surgery)—a total of 100 pairs. Eleven of the monkeys were then given bilateral lesions of the hippocampal formation, including the subicular complex and the entorhinal cortex; seven monkeys formed the control group, receiving no lesions.

Two weeks after surgery, the investigators showed the animals each of the 100 previously presented pairs in a mixed order. The control monkeys remembered more of what they had learned most recently (Figure 17.13). The lesioned monkeys, however, performed significantly worse than the controls on the object pairs they had learned 2 and 4 weeks before surgery; they did not differ from the controls for pairs learned earlier. Note also that the lesioned monkeys performed worse on items learned 2 and 4 weeks before surgery than on the items learned earlier. Experiments with rodents have yielded similar results, except that the temporal gradient is measured in days rather than in weeks.

These results show that the medial temporal system is not a repository of long-term memory. In each of the animal experiments, it was possible to identify a time after learning when damage to this system had no effect on memory for the learning. Thus, the information that initially depends on the medial temporal system for processing does not depend on it for long-term (or permanent) storage. Permanent storage is thought to occur in regions of the neocortex where

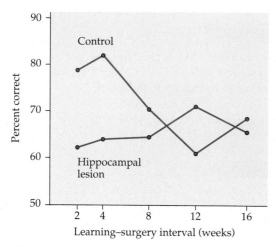

17.13 Retention by Monkeys of Object-Discrimination Problems
Equal numbers of items were learned 2, 4, 8, 12, and 16 weeks before the experimental animals had hippocampal surgery. Note that for the control animals memory is best for the most recently learned items, whereas for the lesioned animals memory is significantly worse for the items learned 2 and 4 weeks prior to surgery. After Zola-Morgan and Squire, 1990.

the information is first processed and held in short-term memory; after further processing that involves the medial temporal region (and probably the midline diencephalic region as well), the permanent storage serves memory independently of the medial temporal–diencephalic region.

The fact that memories require consolidation for long-term storage may help explain the retrograde amnesia that is common with injury to the brain. Memories that have not yet been completely consolidated in the cortex may be seriously impaired by interruption of processing. Conditions that follow learning can also modulate the strength of memory, as we will see in the next section.

Emotion Can Modulate Memory Formation

Most of us would agree that emotionally exciting experiences tend to be well remembered. Over a century ago William James (1890:670) wrote, "An experience may be so exciting emotionally as almost to leave a scar on the cerebral tissues." Recently investigators have found much evidence that emotions can modulate memory formation in several ways. For example, they often enhance memory for aspects of an event or story that are closely tied to the emotional

aspects, but they can also weaken memories that are not central to the emotional theme (Reisberg and Heuer, 1995). Several investigators are attempting to find the neural mechanisms that may be involved in emotional modulation of memory (for example, Mc-Gaugh, 1994; Pitman and Orr, 1995).

A recent report demonstrated that an emotionally arousing story was remembered significantly better than a closely matched but more emotionally neutral story; it also showed that the emotional enhancement of memory was caused by activation of α-adrenergic stress hormones (Cahill et al., 1994). In this experiment some subjects were given the emotional version of a story, and some were given the neutral version; both versions were accompanied by the same 12 slides. The first four items of both stories were identical, with four slides showing a mother and son going to visit the father's workplace in a hospital. In the second phase the two narratives differed, but the same five slides were shown: in the neutral version, the boy saw wrecked cars in a junkyard and then witnessed a disaster drill at the hospital; in the emotional version, the boy was badly injured in a traffic accident and was treated in the emergency room and in the surgery. In the third phase (three slides), the mother went to pick up her other child at preschool. The subjects heard the narratives and saw the slides while connected to heart rate and blood pressure monitors and were told that the study concerned physiological responses to different types of stimuli. One hour before the story presentation, all subjects received injections; some received a control injection of physiological saline solution, while the others received propranolol, a α-adrenergic receptor antagonist. (Propranolol and other "α-blockers" are used to combat high blood pressure.) A week later, without expecting any further contact with the stories, the subjects were asked to recall as many of the slides as possible and then took an 80-item multiple choice recognition memory test that assessed memory for both visual and narrative story elements.

Subjects who had received the control injection remembered the second, emotionally arousing phase of the story significantly better than the first or third phases. Subjects who had received the propranolol injection scored about the same as those with the control injection on the first and third phases of the story but did not show better memory for the second phase than for the first and third phases. Thus, the drug did not affect memory in general but blocked only the enhancement related to emotional arousal.

Did the propranolol affect memory strength by preventing the subjects from having an emotional reaction to the stories? To test this question, the investigators had each subject rate his/her degree of emotion in response to the story just after it was presented. The "emotional" version was rated significantly more arousing than the neutral version by subjects given the α-blocker as well as by subjects given the control injection, so it was not the failure of emotional experience that prevented enhancement of memory. Another hypothesis was that propranolol acted after training to block enhancement of the processes of memory formation. This hypothesis is supported by animal research that we will review in Chapter 18. In fact, the human experiment just described was based on earlier animal research.

Comparative Approaches Yield Insights about the Evolution of Learning and Memory

Learning and memory exist throughout the animal kingdom—from short-term learning in single-celled animals through all the variety of learning we have noted in multicellular animals. Although there has been a good deal of speculation about the early evolution of abilities to learn and remember, we cannot research this subject directly, since we cannot measure the behavior of extinct animals. The fact that learning is so widespread throughout the animal kingdom suggests that it was an early evolutionary development, with changes occurring as animals evolved to occupy new niches and meet new challenges. A fruitful approach is to compare the learning and memory of related species in which differences in ecological niche and lifestyle have caused different selection pressures for specific kinds of learning and therefore changes in brain structure.

As we consider attempts at comparing learning ability among existing species, we will see that it is not a simple matter. Just as it is difficult and perhaps impossible to devise a "culture-free" intelligence test for human beings, so it has been difficult to devise tests for animals that do not favor the sensory and/or motor capacities of some species and work against others. The problem has become even more complicated now that recent research has shown that relatively simple animals are capable of a greater variety of learning than was suspected only a few years ago (Carew and Sahley, 1986; Krasne and Glanzman, 1995). In part, these findings have come from attempts to use "simple systems" to investigate the basic neural processes involved in learning and memory formation. Thus, associative learning and conditional learning have been

found in the mollusc *Aplysia,* as we noted earlier in this chapter, and complex conditioning has been found in the garden slug. On the other hand, many kinds of animals show specialized kinds of learning that seem to be restricted to particular combinations of events and are not able to encompass other relations. The wide distribution of learning throughout the animal kingdom, as well as restrictions in these abilities, has suggested implications for the evolution of abilities to learn and remember.

Learning Abilities Are Widely Distributed throughout the Animal Kingdom

Nonassociative learning appears to be very widespread in the animal kingdom. Rather simple animals with small nervous systems readily habituate to repeated mild stimuli and become sensitized to strong stimuli. Furthermore, the time courses and other features of habituation and sensitization are similar, whether studied in an earthworm, a mollusc, or a mammal. Some investigators have reported nonassociative learning even in paramecia and bacteria, single-celled animals that, of course, do not have a nervous system. Apparently all animals show some kinds of learning and memory.

The fact that learning and memory are so widespread among animal species has led to attempts to study basic mechanisms of learning and memory in animals without nervous systems or with relatively simple nervous systems. It is tempting to suppose that all animals share some basic processes of learning and memory storage, so that relatively simple animals can be taken as model systems to study processes that all animals use. Perhaps, however, learning arose separately in some of these diverse animal forms; similar learning behaviors may represent convergent evolution in the face of common demands of the environment, but all animals may not use the same mechanisms to accomplish learning and memory storage. We will have to examine critically claims that findings with relatively simple animals can be extrapolated directly to other forms. Neuroscientist Seymour Kety (1976:321) urged the search for varieties of mechanisms in learning and memory:

> So profound and powerful an adaptation as learning and memory is not apt to rest upon a single modality. Rather, I suspect that advantage is taken of every opportunity provided by evolution. There were forms of memory before organisms developed nervous systems, and after that remarkable leap forward it is likely that every new pathway and neural complexity, every new neurotransmitter, hormone, or

metabolic process that played upon the nervous system and subserved a learning process was preserved and incorporated.

Until recently associative learning was believed to have a more restricted distribution than nonassociative learning in the animal kingdom. For example, *Aplysia* had been used for many years to investigate the neural mechanisms of habituation, and investigators had sought in vain for evidence of associative learning until it was discovered in 1980. Evidence for learning in the fruit fly, *Drosophila*, was long sought in order to try to relate learning to genetic factors, which are very well known in *Drosophila*, but only in 1974 did investigators first announce successful training in these animals.

Part of the difficulty in assessing the capacity of a species to learn and remember is that these capacities may be highly specific. Certain species can learn particular associations well even though they are very poor at other tasks that do not seem more difficult to us. Evidence for specificity has accumulated since the 1960s and has led to two successive and quite different concepts.

First came the concept of **genetic constraints on learning**, which was prominent from the 1960s into the early 1980s. This formulation held that species-typical genetic factors restrict the kinds of learning that a species can accomplish, or at least accomplish readily. For example, bees readily learn to come to a particular station to feed on a 24-hour schedule, which of course occurs in nature, but they cannot learn to come on an 8- or 12-hour schedule. Birds of some species do not learn the pattern of markings or even the color of their eggs even though they turn the eggs over frequently, yet they learn to recognize their young individually within three days after they hatch, just the time at which the chicks begin to wander about.

The interpretation of such observations changed in the 1980s. Rather than supposing that the genes of certain species constrain their general ability to learn and thus make them selectively stupid, investigators now believe that the evolution of **specific abilities to learn and remember** in response to selective pressures in particular ecological niches is more likely (Gould, 1986; Sherry and Schacter, 1987). Let's consider an example of a specific learning ability.

Selection for Spatial Memory Is Associated with Increased Hippocampal Size in Mammals and Birds

Selection of animals for a particular ability can improve that ability markedly in successive generations.

A current research program involves both naturalistic observations and experimental studies with birds and rodents to find out what effects natural or artificial selection for spatial ability may have on brain measures. Sherry, Jacobs, and Gaulin (1992:298) state the basic concept of this program as follows: "If a particular neuroanatomical feature occurs in different species exposed to the same selective pressure, and is better accounted for by this selective pressure than by the phylogenetic relations among the species, then it is reasonable to conclude that the feature is indeed an adaptation—the result of convergent evolution in response to natural selection."

We saw one example of this research in Chapter 3: species of birds that store or cache food for retrieval days or weeks later have hippocampal regions larger than those of related species that do not cache food (see Figure 3.4). The differences in size of hippocampus among these species could not be accounted for by other factors that were tested, including migratory behavior, social organization, diet, mode of development, nest dispersion, or habitat (Sherry et al., 1989; Krebs et al., 1989). Furthermore, ablation of the hippocampus in a food-storing species disrupts the birds' ability to retrieve cached food and to solve other spatial problems, without obvious effects on storing food, feeding, or other behaviors (Sherry and Vaccarino, 1989). Thus, the larger hippocampus in food-storing species of birds seems to be an adaptive modification that makes it possible for them to retrieve cached food.

Comparison of two related species of kangaroo rats provided an independent test of this hypothesis. Both species are small, nocturnal, seed-eating, desert rodents from the same genus. One species, Merriam's kangaroo rat (*Dipodomys merriami*) hoards food in scattered locations and requires spatial memory to relocate its caches. In contrast, the bannertail kangaroo rat (*Dipodomys spectabilis*) hoards seeds in its burrow and thus needs no specialized spatial memory to retrieve them. *D. merriami* has a significantly larger hippocampus than does *D. spectabilis* (Jacobs and Spencer, 1994).

People have long bred animals selectively to enhance certain traits; such artificial selection can produce results similar to those of natural selection, and more rapidly. For example, pigeons have been bred for their ability to fly rapidly and accurately to their home lofts. Pigeons of these strains have larger hippocampi than breeds of pigeons not selected for homing ability (Rehkamper, Haase, and Frahm, 1988).

In interweaving information about the hippocampus of birds and mammals, we have to recognize that the hippocampus differs in its location and connections in these two classes of animals. Nevertheless, comparative neuroanatomists consider the hippocampus to be homologous in these two classes of animals, and the results of recent behavioral-anatomical research appear to bear this assumption out (Bingman, 1993).

Investigators who test the spatial learning and memory of laboratory rats and mice have often observed that males perform better than females, and human males perform better on many spatial tasks than do human females (Halpern, 1986). Some have suggested that males in general are superior in spatial learning and memory, but others have hypothesized that the behavioral roles of the two sexes determine whether a sex difference in spatial memory exists in a given species, and if it does, which sex is superior in this behavior. An instructive comparison has been made between two species of North American voles (Figure 17.14).

Pine voles (*Microtus pinetorum*) are monogaous, and field observations show that the males and females travel over ranges that are equal in size. In contrast, meadow voles (*Microtus pennsylvanicus*) are highly polygynous (that is, a male mates with several females), and the males have ranges that are several times larger than the females' ranges. In this polygynous mating system, males compete in order to include within their home range as many female ranges as possible. The polygynous male meadow voles, in comparison with females of the same species, have significantly better scores on laboratory tests of spatial learning and memory. The monogamous pine voles show no sex differences on these tests. Furthermore, the polygynous male meadow voles have a significantly larger hippocampus than do the females, whereas among the monogamous pine voles, there is no significant difference in hippocampal size between the sexes (Jacobs et al., 1990).

When the size of the hippocampus differs between the sexes, it is not invariably the male who shows the larger size. For example, as investigators predicted, the hippocampus of the female brown-headed cowbird (*Molothrus ater*) is significantly larger than that of the male (Sherry, Jacobs, and Gaulin, 1993). The prediction was based on sex differences in spatial ability related to the breeding behavior of this species. The female cowbird is parasitic; that is, she lays her eggs in the nests of other species, who then do the work of hatching and feeding the cowbird chick. In order to do this, the female cowbird has to find and keep track of nests so that she can slip in and lay an egg when the other birds are away. The male cowbird does not participate in this spatial sleuthing and gets

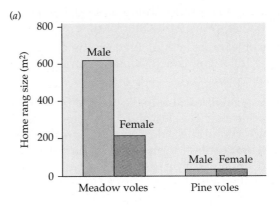

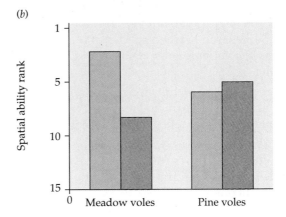

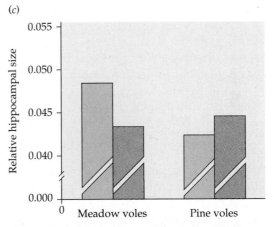

17.14   Sex, Memory, and Hippocampal Size
Comparison of males and females of two species of voles on three variables: (*a*) size of home range; (*b*) score on spatial learning task; (*c*) size of hippocampus. After Jacobs et al., 1990.

along with a smaller hippocampus. No sex difference in hippocampal size was found in two closely related species that are not parasitic. This example is one of the few indications that spatial ability can influence the size of the hippocampus when other factors—such as sex, breeding system, or foraging behavior—have been ruled out.

Differences in Learning Ability among Species Are Both Qualitative and Quantitative

A review of learning and intelligence among species led to the following conclusions (Rosenzweig and Glickman, 1985):

1. Nonassociative learning and certain kinds of associative learning (classical and instrumental conditioning) occur throughout the vertebrates; among invertebrates these forms of learning are widespread among arthropods and molluscs and perhaps in other phyla.

2. Cognitive learning (formation of "memories," in William James's sense of the word) occurs in primates and some other, but perhaps not all, mammals. Some large-brained species of other phyla, such as the cephalopods, also exhibit cognitive learning.

3. Not only qualitative, but also quantitative differences in abilities to learn and remember can be important for individual behavior and therefore also for evolution.

4. The hypothesis that particular complex cognitive abilities are found only within a few selected species warrants further investigation.

These conclusions are based on the work of many psychologists and other neuroscientists who have attempted, since the beginning of this century, to compare the learning abilities of different species. If valid comparisons of learning ability could be found, they would contribute to our understanding of the evolution of these abilities and to relating intelligence to brain measures such as brain weight.

How Learning and Intelligence May Have Evolved

From our survey of comparative aspects of learning and intelligence, we can draw some tentative conclusions about how these capacities may have evolved. We saw in earlier chapters that simpler animals with more primitive characteristics have specific sensory and motor abilities that are adapted to their particular environmental niches. Sometimes these abilities are keen and precise, such as the ability of bees to distinguish patterns of blossoms (although their ability to distinguish form is not as acute as ours) and wavelengths (including some in the ultraviolet part of the spectrum that we cannot see). The learning abilities of such animals may also be good in some ways but restricted in others, compared with the more general learning abilities of more complex animals. An example of such specificity has already

been mentioned: the ability of bees to learn to come to a particular location for food on a 24-hour schedule, but not on an 8- or 12-hour schedule. These shorter schedules do not occur in a bee's world.

It has been argued that learning and intelligence evolved because of the survival value in being able to predict events in the environment. An animal that can predict where it is likely to find food will have an advantage over one that wanders randomly in search of food; an animal that can predict that a particular response to a particular stimulus will be followed by pain is less likely to damage itself. A male pine vole that learns the locations of several females and keeps track of their reproductive status will probably have more offspring than another male with poorer learning and memory; this has probably led to progressive improvements in abilities to learn and remember. Because learning and memory confer obvious advantages for survival and reproduction, one theorist hypothesizes that the ability to form associations "evolved very early and proved so powerful as a predictive mechanism that subsequent improvements in problem solving have arisen largely from the undoubted improvements in the quality of sensory processing and in the variability and skill of motor responses available" (Macphail, 1985:285). This hypothesis assumes that the neural circuits that underlie learning and memory storage are the same for all animals with nervous systems, and for all kinds of learning, which is far from the case, as we will discuss here and in Chapter 18.

In order for an associative link to be formed, information of the different kinds to be associated must be available in the same neurons, or at least in closely neighboring neurons, and that is not usually the case. Rather, simpler animals seem to have evolved specific circuits in which particular kinds of associations can be formed, and during the course of further evolution these specific circuits have come to be used in more general and plastic ways in higher animals (Rozin, 1976a). This view of events is consistent with the hypothesis already mentioned from comparative studies of animal behavior that specific abilities to learn and remember evolved where they had survival value. In other words, particular circuitry that evolved to handle particular problems (such as memory for food location) was initially accessible only to those input and output systems that it was designed to serve. With evolution, some of these systems became connected to other systems; thus they became components in a hierarchy and could be used more widely. Also, circuits that were successful in a particular context probably served as models for circuits in related systems. An example that supports this idea is the modular structure of the cerebral cortex, where similar basic circuits are replicated many times to fit into different networks, some to serve vision, some to mediate language, and so forth. This replication of basic units in complex brains is one of the causes of the increase in brain size with evolution, as we considered in Chapter 3.

Learning and Memory Change Throughout Life

It is easier for us to form some kinds of new memories when we are in the middle of our lives, as young or mature adults, than when we are infants or elderly. Can these changes in ability over the life span be explained in neural terms? Do they provide clues about the neural mechanisms of learning and memory? To answer these and other questions, investigators conduct developmental studies of learning and memory with a variety of species, ranging from humans to molluscs.

Many kinds of animals must be ready to learn as soon as they are born or hatch. For example, newly hatched chicks eagerly sample objects in their environment to find what is edible. Their yolk sacs provide nourishment, so they can sample small bits without having to ingest much. By the time the yolk sac is used up three to four days after hatching, the chicks must have learned what is safe and good to eat. Thus, chicks are good subjects for some kinds of learning experiments, as we will see in Chapter 18. Chicks are precocial—able to locomote and care for themselves from the time they emerge—but even altricial animals (those that are helpless at birth) must learn to adapt to their environments. For example, rat pups' eyes and ears are closed for about the first two weeks after birth, but each pup in a litter learns which of the mother's nipples is "its own." In laboratory experiments, young rat pups learn rapidly which of two artificial nipples provides milk; they can use cues of texture or odor to learn this distinction (Woo and Leon, 1987). Human infants learn quickly to distinguish the faces of their main caregivers from those of others. And human infants can be conditioned to turn their heads to one side or the other at the sound of a tone in order to find the nipple of a nursing bottle (Papousek, 1992). Learning can thus be studied in newly born or newly hatched animals without the complicating effects of prior learning. Careful recent testing shows that young nervous systems can accomplish some kinds of

learning that we used to think only older animals could.

Some kinds of learning are not required until an animal passes the stage of infancy. We mentioned that food-storing species of birds have a larger hippocampus than do related species that do not store food. A recent study measured hippocampal size in nestlings (5 to 25 days after hatching) and adult birds of two species in the crow family (Healy and Krebs, 1993): the food-storing magpie (*Pica pica*) and the non-food-storing jackdaw (*Corvus monedula*). In the nestlings, the relative volume of the hippocampus did not differ between the two species, but in the adults, the food-storing magpies had significantly greater hippocampal volume and cell number than the non-food-storing jackdaws had. Healy and Krebs (1993) suggested that the differences between adults of the two species are related to the *use* of spatial memory in retrieving stored food. This hypothesis was tested by Clayton and Krebs (1994), who raised crows in the laboratory, giving some birds the opportunity to store and retrieve food whereas other birds ate from feeders and had no opportunity to store food. The birds who stored and retrieved food developed hippocampal formations that were larger than those of the birds who did not store and retrieve food.

Habituation, Dishabituation, and Sensitization Appear Successively during Development in *Aplysia*

Since the 1960s the mollusc *Aplysia* has become a popular subject of studies on the neural mechanisms of habituation and sensitization. Psychologist Thomas Carew (1989) has shown that *Aplysia* is also well suited to investigations of the emergence during development of different forms of learning and their neural mechanisms.

The youngest *Aplysia* that experimenters have been able to use for behavioral studies are about 45 days old (stage 9 of their development) but only about 1 millimeter long. At this stage *Aplysia* already show habituation, but only if the stimuli are repeated at short intervals, 1 second or less. As *Aplysia* mature, the stimuli can be spaced increasingly farther apart and still cause habituation (Figure 17.15*a*). But at stage 9, neither dishabituation nor sensitization can be evoked. A few days later, at developmental stage 10, *Aplysia* can be habituated to stimuli delivered at an interval of 5 seconds, and for the first time, a strong stimulus leads to dishabituation, but sensitization still does not occur. That is, a strong stimulus does not increase the size of subsequent responses

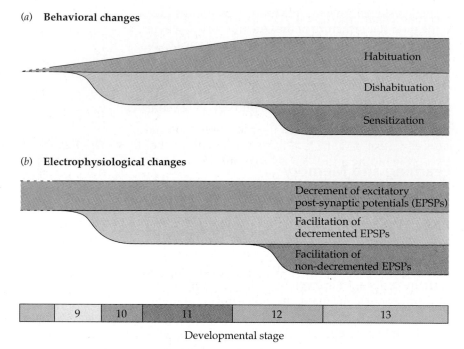

(a) **Behavioral changes**

Habituation

Dishabituation

Sensitization

(b) **Electrophysiological changes**

Decrement of excitatory
post-synaptic potentials (EPSPs)

Facilitation of
decremented EPSPs

Facilitation of
non-decremented EPSPs

| 9 | 10 | 11 | 12 | 13 |

Developmental stage

**17.15 Development of Learning
and Its Electrophysiological Correlates in *Aplysia***
(*a*) Habituation appears at an early age, but can be elicited at longer intertrial
intervals with increasing age. Dishabituation first appears at stage 10 and sensitization at stage 12. (*b*) Development of electrophysiological correlates of learning in *Aplysia* shows parallels with behavioral developments. After Carew,
1989.

unless the animal has first been habituated. Only in
stage 12, about 100 days after *Aplysia* has hatched,
does sensitization first appear. At this age, stimuli
presented as far apart as 30 seconds can cause habituation. It has not yet been reported whether associative learning also appears at stage 12 or whether it
requires additional maturity. Pinpointing when different kinds of learning emerge is an important technique because it allows investigators to differentiate
among the kinds of learning and to search for
changes in the nervous system that occur at each of
those times.

Electrophysiological correlates of different aspects
of learning appear in parallel with the stages of learning in *Aplysia* (Figure 17.15*b*). Repeated weak stimulation causes the excitatory postsynaptic potentials
(EPSPs) to decrease in size (decrement) even in very
young *Aplysia*. A strong stimulus can enhance or facilitate decremented EPSPs starting at stage 10, just
when behavioral dishabituation emerges. Non-
decremented EPSPs can be facilitated at stage 12,
when sensitization first occurs.

At the same time that sensitization appears, strik-

ing neuroanatomical changes take place: the number
of neurons multiplies several times, and there is a
150-fold increase in the volume of neural connections,
significantly increasing the opportunity for synaptic
interactions (Cash and Carew, 1989). It is not yet
known what roles the increases in neurons and in synaptic connections may play in capacities for learning.

Does Immaturity of Certain Brain Regions Prevent Some Kinds of Learning?

Young animals have difficulty learning certain kinds
of problems. Investigators have tried to determine
whether these difficulties are related to the immaturity of the specific brain regions required to process
these kinds of learning. In some cases hypotheses
have been verified, but experiments have forced the
abandonment of other hypotheses, as the following
examples show.

Spanning a temporal separation. A classic test of
cognitive development devised by Swiss psychologist Jean Piaget now appears to require development
of the dorsolateral prefrontal cortex. This "A not B"

test requires an infant to uncover a toy that she sees hidden in one of two possible locations (A or B); both locations are used in a series of trials. After the toy is hidden, the infant's visual fixation is broken so that she does not look at the location during the delay. Human infants will not reliably reach for a hidden object until they are 7 to 8 months old. At this age, an infant will reach correctly to either location *if* there is no delay (except for breaking visual fixation) between the hiding and the reaching. But with a delay of only 1 to 5 seconds during which the infant is prevented from reaching, she tends to reach for the object in the last location where she reached successfully, even if that is not the location where she just saw the object hidden.

Given these observations one might conclude that with a short delay, the *habit* of successful reaching is stronger than the *representational memory* of the hidden object. No long-term memory is required in either case; only short-term working memories are involved. Testing of infants every two weeks shows a steady rise in their ability to perform successfully at longer delays. This improvement is due to maturation, not experience, because infants of a given age test equally well whether or not they were given prior tests. By age 12 months, most infants perform successfully with a delay of 10 seconds between seeing the object hidden and reaching for it. Later in this chapter, we'll see that some adult amnesia patients also fail the "A not B" test.

Investigators who confirmed these observations with human infants (Diamond and Goldman-Rakic, 1989) also studied monkeys, using a similar test. They used both intact monkeys and monkeys with lesions of either dorsolateral prefrontal cortex or parietal cortex (Figure 17.16). The dorsolateral prefrontal cortex was chosen because other research had shown impairment in performance after a delay with lesions in this area. The parietal cortex was chosen because it has been implicated in spatial processing and because it is large enough that lesions of comparable size could be made in the two regions. Normal monkeys performed well on the test at delays of 10 seconds and more, as did monkeys with lesions of parietal cortex, but monkeys with lesions of dorsolateral cortex made errors similar to those of 7- to 8-month-old

Patricia Goldman-Rakic

human infants (Figure 17.17). Thus, it appears that a normal, relatively mature dorsolateral prefrontal cortex is required for representational memory of the hidden object to be retained as long as 10 seconds. Further research by Patricia Goldman-Rakic on the roles of prefrontal cortex in memory will be discussed in Chapter 18.

Hippocampal immaturity.   In the 1980s several investigators proposed that young primates do not have access to declarative memories because the hippocampus is not yet sufficiently mature (Nadel and Zola-Morgan, 1984; Schacter and Moskovitch, 1984; Bachevalier and Mishkin, 1984). Recall that several lines of research have shown that the hippocampus is required to process new declarative memories. The delayed non-matching-to-sample task can be used to test the ability of animals to form and use declarative memories. In this test, as we described earlier, an animal sees a sample object and then, a few seconds later, is offered a choice of that object and another; if it moves the object that does *not* match the sample, it finds a reward underneath. If the delay between the sample and the test is 10 seconds or more, human and monkey infants perform poorly on the task, as do amnesic humans and adult monkeys with lesions of the hippocampus. This is a test of declarative memory because, to recognize the sample successfully, the subject has to form and employ a representation of it. To investigate the hypothesis that immaturity of the hippocampus prevents young primates from employing such memory, investigators have used a different test of representational memory, and they have studied development of the primate hippocampus.

A simple test of representational declarative memory is to observe whether the subject prefers to look at the sample object or at a novel object (the visual paired-comparison test). The experimenter presents a sample object, then, after a short delay, presents the sample object and a novel object and records whether the subject spends more time looking at the sample object or the other object. In this visual paired-comparison test, human infants reliably *look at* the novel stimulus by the age of 4 months after delays of 10 seconds or more, but in the delayed non-matching-to- sample test, they do not reliably *reach for* the novel object until 21 months of age, and then only after a delay of 5 seconds or less. Similarly, infant monkeys look at the novel stimulus by 2 weeks of age after delays of at least 10 seconds, but they do not reliably reach for the novel stimulus after delays of 10

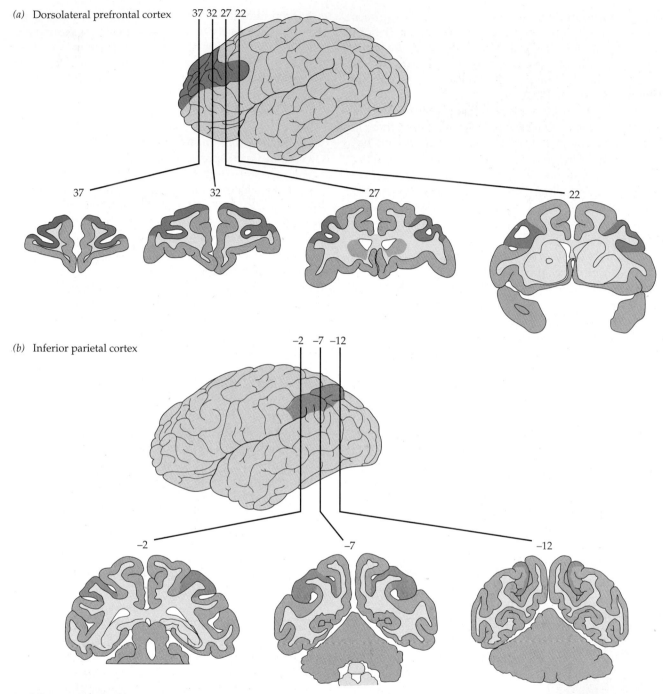

17.16 Cortical Regions Tested for Roles in Representational Memory
Sites of brain lesions in monkeys, in experiments on cortical regions involved in
representational memory. (*a*) Dorsolateral prefrontal cortex. (*b*) Parietal cortex.
After Diamond and Goldman-Rakic, 1989.

seconds until 4 months of age (Diamond, 1990b).
Thus, young primates show recognition memory by
looking, even at ages when they cannot readily combine the two operations of looking and reaching. We
can conclude that success on the delayed visual

paired-comparison test depends on the hippocampus, because hippocampal lesions seriously impair
performance on this test.

The investigators who thought that young primates could not use declarative memories also be-

Trial at well "A"

Human infant

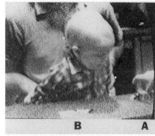 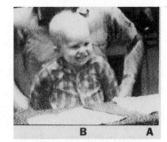 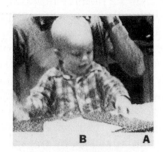

Prefrontal monkey

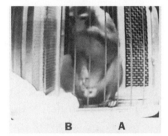 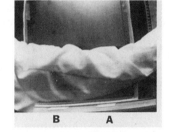 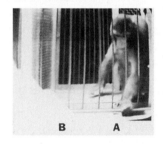

Cueing	**Delay**	**Response**
Subject watches as experimenter hides bait in well "A."	Wells are covered, then subject's visual fixation on the correct well is broken.	Subject reaches correctly to well "A."

Trial at Well "B"

Human infant

Prefrontal monkey

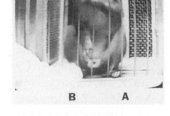 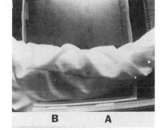 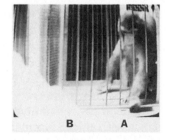

Cueing	**Delay**	**Response**
Subject watches as experimenter hides bait in well "B."	Wells are covered, then subject's visual fixation on the correct well is broken.	Subject reaches incorrectly to well "A," which is now empty.

17.17 Memory for Location of a Hidden Object
A typical human infant's memory for the location of a hidden object resembles that of an adult monkey with lesions of dorsolateral prefrontal cortex. After Diamond and Goldman-Rakic, 1989.

lieved that the primate hippocampus is slow to mature, basing this assumption on development of the hippocampus in the rat. However, Adele Diamond (1990c:400–401) cites a variety of evidence to show that the hippocampus in humans and monkeys is relatively well developed at birth, and much further developed than that of the rat. The precocious development of the hippocampus in primates may be responsible for their early ability to form declarative memories, as shown by the visual recognition test. Thus the hypothesis relating inability to use declarative memory and immaturity of the hippocampus was wrong on both counts: infants can form and use declarative memories, as shown by other tests, and the primate hippocampus matures relatively early!

Aging Impairs Some Aspects of Learning and Memory

The capacity of older people to learn and remember has become a topic of heightened interest in recent years. This awareness stems in part from the growing proportion of elderly people in the population of developed countries and the recognition that some reductions in capacity accompany normal aging. It also reflects attention to pathological forms of cognitive impairment that are more likely to affect older people, such as Alzheimer's disease (see Chapter 19). Most investigators agree that older people in normal health show some decrements in abilities to learn and to remember (Craik, 1986), and reviews of both human and animal studies show declines with age in both abilities (Kubanis and Zornetzer, 1981; Gallagher, Nagahara, and Burwell, 1995). Accurate comparisons of learning and memory in people of different ages are difficult because of confounding factors. For example, differences in learning ability may be caused not by age, or not by age alone, but by other factors, such as educational level, how recently the subjects have experienced formal learning, or motivation. After correcting for such factors, differences related to age usually accompany only some tasks, not all.

What kinds of tasks usually show decrements in performance with aging? Normal elderly people tend to show some memory impairment in tasks of con-

scious recollection that require effort (Hasher and Zacks, 1979) and that rely primarily on internal generation of the memory rather than on external cues (Craik, 1985). In such cases giving the elderly subjects easily organized task structures, or cues, or both can often raise their performance to the level of the young. Thus the type of task helps determine whether impairment is observed. Recent neuroimaging studies show impairment in both the encoding and the retrieval of information in old subjects compared with young, as we will see in Chapter 18. There is greater variability among old subjects than among young, and for many tasks some elderly subjects perform as well or almost as well as the young.

With pathological forms of aging, such as Alzheimer's disease, some memory systems deteriorate, and it has been suggested that what remains are memory processes similar to those of infants (Moscovitch, 1985). In fact, testing the implications of this idea led Morris Moscovitch to discover a cognitive disability in amnesia patients similar to the failure on the "A not B" test that Piaget described for 8-month-old infants. Most amnesia patients, presented with a familiar object in a new location, B, continue to search for it at A, even passing by the object in plain sight in order to search for it at A. They appear to remember the search procedure and not the object being sought.

Studies of the effects of aging on memory are difficult with human subjects, partly because of the variability among people resulting from genetic and environmental factors. Therefore, some investigators use animal subjects to obtain an intimate and detailed understanding of how aging affects memory. Here again experiments must be designed in such a way as to overcome the effects of potentially confounding variables, such as differences in strength of motivation with age or differences in sensory acuity (Ingram, 1985). Evidence of slower learning with advanced age has been reported by some of these investigators (for example, Gallagher, Nagahara, and Burwell, 1995). We will see in Chapter 18 that certain neurochemical and neuroanatomical changes correlate closely with the impairments in behavior. Further research may suggest effective therapeutic measures.

Summary

1. The abilities to learn and remember affect all behaviors that are characteristically human. Since every animal species appears capable of some learning and memory, the ability to learn must be *required* for survival. Whereas evolution by natural selection brings about adaptation over successive generations, learning permits prompt adaptation within the lifetime of the individual.

2. Learning includes both nonassociative forms, such as habituation, dishabituation, and sensitization, and associative forms, such as classical (Pavlovian) conditioning and instrumental learning.

3. Conditioning involves learning relations and predictability among events. Close temporal pairing of stimuli is neither necessary nor sufficient for successful conditioning.

4. Some learning results in the formation of habits (gaining nondeclarative knowledge, or "learning how"), whereas other learning results in the formation of representational memories (gaining declarative knowledge, or "learning what"). Abilities to form habits and memories appear to depend on different brain circuits.

5. Declarative memory tends to be flexible—accessible to many response systems. Nondeclarative memory tends to be inflexible—the information is not readily expressed by response systems that were not involved in the original learning.

6. Memories are often classified by how long they last. Frequently used classifications include iconic, short-term, intermediate-term, and long-term. Some disorders prevent the formation of long-term declarative memory while not impairing short-term memory.

7. Although capacity of long-term memory is huge, most of what we experience is not remembered. Attention, reinforcement, and emotional responses help determine what is held in memory beyond the short term.

8. The capacity for associative learning is very widespread among animal species. The evolution of powerful and flexible brain mechanisms of learning and memory may have resulted from the earlier development of precise and elaborate systems to handle specific sensorimotor adjustments and then from the extension of these systems for more general use.

9. Patients with Korsakoff's disease show gaps in memory, which they may attempt to fill by confabulation; this syndrome involves severe retrograde as well as anterograde amnesia and impairment in encoding new information. Patients show damage to the mammillary nuclei, midline thalamus, and frontal cortex.

10. Some patients with damage to the medial temporal lobe or medial diencephalon show particular impairment in consolidation of long-term representational memories. Recent research has focused both on the type of memory test and on the sites of brain damage. Hippocampal lesions in people and animals impair the formation of representational long-term memories but spare the formation of habits (nondeclarative or procedural memories).

11. The hippocampal region is required for processing but not for storage of long-term declarative memory. Long-term (or permanent) memory is stored in the neocortex.

12. Abilities to learn and remember change throughout life. For some aspects of these changes, biological correlates have been found, but other aspects continue to pose questions.

Recommended Reading

Baddeley, A. 1990. *Human Memory: Theory and Practice.* Allyn and Bacon, Needham Heights, MA.

Cohen, N. J. and Eichenbaum, H. 1993. *Memory, Amnesia, and the Hippocampal System.* MIT Press, Cambridge, MA.

Luria, A. R. 1987. *The Mind of a Mnemonist.* Harvard University Press, Cambridge, MA.

Squire, L. R., Knowlton, B. and Musen, G. 1993. The structure and organization of memory. *Annual Review of Psychology,* 44:453–495.

Zola-Morgan, S. and Squire, L. R. 1993. Neuroanatomy of memory. *Annual Review of Neuroscience,* 16:547–563.

Ellen Carey, *Untitled*, 1987

- *Progress in Memory Research*

- *Changes in Synapses May Be Mechanisms of Memory Storage*

- *The Nervous System Could Form and Store Memories in Various Ways*

- *Cerebral Changes Result from Training*

- *Training Produces Electrophysiological Changes in Cerebral and Neural Activity*

- *Sites of Plasticity Can Be Located in an Invertebrate Nervous System*

- *Mechanisms of Associative Learning Have Been Found in Invertebrate Central Nervous Systems*

- *Long-Term Potentiation: A Model System to Study Mechanisms of Learning and Memory?*

- *The Mammalian Cerebellum Houses the Brain Circuit for a Simple Conditioned Reflex*

- *The Cerebral Sites of Encoding and Retrieval Can Be Localized*

- *Memories of Different Durations Form by Different Neural Mechanisms*

- *Several Model Systems for the Study of Learning and Memory Show Similar Cascades of Neurochemical and Anatomical Processes*

- *Memory Formation Can Be Modulated by Several Processes*

- *Some Brain Measures Correlate with Age-Related Impairments of Memory*

- *To What Extent Have the Ten Challenges Been Met?*

CHAPTER 18

Neural Mechanisms of Learning and Memory

Orientation

This chapter presents some of the main advances that have led to the current optimism of many investigators. Whereas Chapter 17 stressed behavioral aspects of learning and memory and the general regions of the nervous system where plastic changes that underlie learning and memory occur, this chapter deals mainly with detailed sites and neural mechanisms. We will focus on three main topics:

1. What are the basic biological mechanisms for long-term storage of memories in the nervous system? To what extent are the same mechanisms used in different species, and in different sites in the nervous system of the same species?

2. What are the storage mechanisms for memories of different durations (short-term and intermediate-term, in contrast to long-term memory)? What are the stages in the formation of long-term memory?

3. What mechanisms modulate (facilitate or inhibit) learning and memory formation? (Some neural, hormonal, and transmitter systems that do not play a *direct* role in learning and memory storage have been implicated in *modulating* these processes.)

In reviewing this field, we must be careful not to overgeneralize. Some investigators have been so happy to find a specific site or precise mechanism of change for one kind of memory that they have proposed that their finding accounts for many or all kinds. Other investigators recognize that learning and memory and their biological substrates take many forms. Careful work is needed to find what mechanisms may be common among different forms of learning and what mechanisms are specific to particular forms of learning.

Progress in Memory Research

I sometimes feel, in reviewing the evidence on the localization of the memory trace, that the necessary conclusion is that learning just is not possible. It is difficult to conceive of a mechanism which can satisfy the conditions set for it. Nevertheless, in spite of such evidence against it, learning does sometimes occur.

Karl S. Lashley (1950:477)

In the past generation, understanding of the biological basis of learning and memory has undergone a revolution. It now seems possible to identify the circuits and networks that participate in learning and memory, localize the sites of memory storage, and analyze the cellular and molecular mechanisms of memory. The roots of this new understanding lie in advances made by several different disciplines: psychology, behavioral neuroscience, network analysis and cognitive science, and neurobiology.

Richard F. Thompson (1986:941)

There is a dramatic contrast between the statements above, made a generation apart by two prominent investigators.

For a long time the only method available to investigators was somatic intervention; that is, they could study how damage to the nervous system or interference with neural activity affected learning and memory. Much of the material in Chapter 17 came from the study of effects of localized damage to the nervous system, and some of those observations go back to the nineteenth century.

Only in the twentieth century, and especially in the last few decades, have investigators discovered how to use behavioral intervention, coupled with biological measures, to study the mechanisms of learning and memory—that is, to study changes in the nervous system as a result of training (see Figure 1.12 for definitions of somatic and behaviorial intervention). A variety of techniques, with a steady increase in their spatial and temporal resolution, have become available. Now the combined use of somatic and behavioral interventions is yielding rapid progress in understanding the neural mechanisms of learning and memory. This approach is revealing how a brief experience can lead to a cascade of neurochemical events that may, in some cases, include protein synthesis and structural changes at synapses.

Changes in Synapses May Be Mechanisms of Memory Storage

Soon after experiments on memory began in the 1880s, and as information accumulated on the phys-
iology and anatomy of the nervous system, investigators speculated that changes in neuronal junctions could be a mechanism to store memories. Italian neurophysiologist Eugenio Tanzi suggested in 1893, even before the synapse had been named, that both development and learning depend on changes in neuronal junctions. In the same publication in which British neurophysiologist Charles S. Sherrington proposed the name "synapse," he stated that such changes were likely to be important for learning (1897:1117):

> Shut off from all opportunity of reproducing itself and adding to its number by mitosis or otherwise, the nerve cell directs its pent-up energy towards amplifying its connections with its fellows, in response to the events which stir it up. Hence, it is capable of an education unknown to other tissues.

The great Spanish neuroanatomist Santiago Ramón y Cajal (1894) also suggested that neurons extend their axons and dendrites to make new connections with other neurons in both development and learning.

Early in the twentieth century, when Ivan Pavlov sought to explain conditioning in neural terms, it was natural to think that neurons in the sensory cortex, representing the conditioned stimulus (CS), developed or strengthened their connections to neurons in the motor cortex, where the unconditioned response (UR) is represented; thus CS–UR linkages would develop. These linkages would form or strengthen neural chains, such as we saw in Figure 5.15. Later, however, it was discovered that cortical lesions that should have interrupted such cross-cortical connections did not abolish conditioned responses or memories for other kinds of learning. This finding appeared to invalidate the hypothesis that memories depend on direct neural chains, or at least cross-cortical chains. Investigators then began to consider other kinds of neural circuits and even to speculate about other mechanisms, such as the interaction of electrical fields in the brain.

Different Kinds of Neural Circuits May Underlie Memories

It will be helpful for us to organize much of the varied and active research on neural mechanisms of learning and memory according to the kinds of neural circuits investigators consider, which range from simple neural chains to parallel distributed circuits (Figure 18.1). We will define each kind of circuit briefly here; these definitions will become more meaningful as we discuss research related to them. Most theorizing about circuits locates the site(s) of memory storage in one or more plastic synapses shown in Figure 18.1 in orange).

The neural chain (Figure 18.1a), at its simplest, can be a monosynaptic reflex arc, as in the knee-jerk reflex (see Figure 5.14). Some studies indicate that even the simplest variety—a monosynaptic neural circuit—can show some learning (habituation), as we will see a little later.

Many simple neural circuits also receive input from **superordinate circuits** (Figure 18.1b), as we saw in the case of the motor system, where the activity of spinal reflex circuits is modulated by higher-order circuits at the level of the brain stem, basal ganglia, and motor cortex. We will see an example (eye-blink conditioning) of plasticity in a higher-order circuit, while the basic reflex circuit shows no change during training.

Many kinds of learning may require the establishment of relatively complex networks of neurons—"cell assemblies," as psychologist Donald O. Hebb called them in his influential book *The Organization of Behavior* (1949). In Figure 18.1c several plastic synapses are involved in the formation of a neural network.

Many current hypotheses suggest that the same group or ensemble of neurons can encode many different memories (Figure 18.1d), each neuron participating to a greater or lesser extent in a particular memory (McNaughton and Morris, 1987). Encoding memories in an ensemble of neurons also depends on plasticity of the synapses involved.

Before we look at the research on different kinds of neural circuits, we will consider two topics that provide important background: (1) In the next section we will examine the ways in which synapses can change and thereby store information. (2) In the following section we will discuss technological developments of the 1940s to 1960s that encouraged research on the neural mechanisms of memory: the ability to measure changes in electrical activity, neurochemistry, and neuroanatomy in response to training. Finding such changes encouraged research on neural mechanisms of memory.

The Nervous System Could Form and Store Memories in Various Ways

As knowledge of synaptic anatomy and chemistry increased, hypotheses about plastic synaptic changes became more numerous and precise. Changes in existing synapses and changes in numbers of synapses have been proposed as mechanisms of information storage (Figure 18.2).

(a)   Plasticity in a neural chain

(b)   Plasticity in a superordinate circuit

(c)   Plasticity in a cell assembly

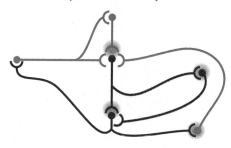

(d)   Plastic sites in an ensemble of neurons

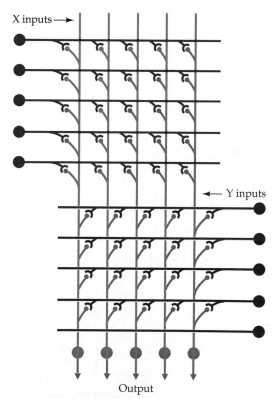

18.1   Sites of Synaptic Plasticity in Neural Networks
(a) A neural chain with a plastic synapse. (b) Plasticity in a higher-order segment of a circuit. (c) A cell assembly with many plastic sites. (d) All the synapses may be plastic in a parallel distributed circuit of neurons. Changes at such sites could underlie memory storage.

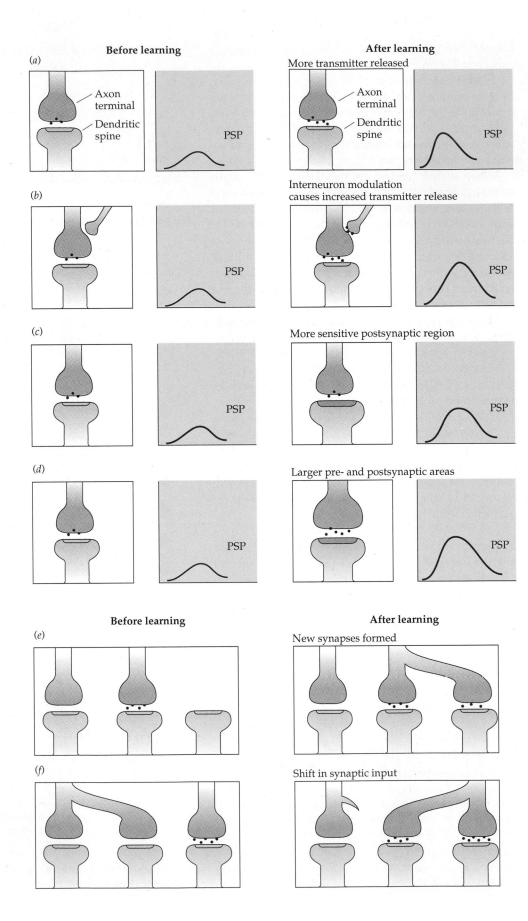

Physiological Changes at Synapses Could Store Information

Some of the changes that could store information can be measured physiologically. The changes could be presynaptic, postsynaptic, or both. One possibility is that the number of transmitter molecules released per nerve impulse could increase, thus altering the response of the postsynaptic cell (Figure 18.2*a*). A change in release of transmitter could be caused by chemical changes within the end bouton.

The amount of neurotransmitter released could also be affected by the influence of terminals from other neurons on the end boutons, as shown in Figure 18.2*b*. That is, impulses from other neurons could alter the polarization of the boutons and thus affect the amount of neurotransmitter released.

The responsiveness or sensitivity of the postsynaptic endings could also change, for example, by an increase in the number of receptor molecules, so that the same amount of transmitter release would initiate a larger effect (Figure 18.2*c*). Changes in the rate of inactivation of the transmitter could produce a similar effect.

Because synapses in the central nervous system are not as reliable as neuromuscular junctions, changes such as those described here could have important influences on the activity of the nervous system.

Structural Changes at Synapses Could Provide Long-Term Storage

Many investigators believe that long-term memories require changes in the nervous system so dramatic that they can be seen by microscopic techniques. Structural changes resulting from use are apparent in other parts of the body. For example, exercise changes the mass and/or shape of muscles and

bone. In a similar way, the synaptic contact area could increase or decrease as a function of training (Figure 18.2*d*).

We do not have to limit ourselves to existing synapses. Training could lead to an increase in the number of terminals for the pathway being used (Figure 18.2*e*), or it could cause a more used pathway to take over endings formerly occupied by a less active competitor (Figure 18.2*f*).

What Conditions Are Required to Induce Memory-Related Changes at Synapses?

Psychologist Donald O. Hebb suggested conditions that might be required to produce changes at synapses that could account for the development of the nervous system and for learning. Hebb (1949:62) proposed that the functional relationship between a presynaptic neuron (A) and a postsynaptic neuron (B) could change if A frequently took part in exciting B:

> When an axon of cell A is near enough to excite a cell B and repeatedly or persistently takes part in firing it, some growth process or metabolic change takes place in one or both cells such that A's efficacy, as one of the cells firing B, is increased.

Many investigators have sought to determine whether Hebb's hypothesis is correct, and synapses that appear to obey this rule are called **Hebbian synapses**. Hebb later expressed some amusement that his formulation attracted so much attention, because he thought it was only a formal expression of ideas that many theorists had held for many years and that other aspects of his theory were more original (Milner, 1993:127).

Hebb also restated what he called the old idea "that any two cells or systems of cells that are repeatedly active at the same time will tend to become 'associated,' so that activity in one facilitates activity in the other" (1949:70). Thus two cells, C and D, that both send impulses to the same region will tend to make connections to intermediate cells and then no longer act independently of each other. This is an extension of the preceding hypothesis, and it can be used to explain phenomena such as sensori-sensory conditioning and conditional learning (see Chapter 17). Both of these mechanisms

Donald O. Hebb
(1904–1985)

◀ **18.2   Synaptic Changes That Could Store Memories** (*a*) After training, each nerve impulse in the relevant neural circuit causes increased release of transmitter molecules (red dots). The postsynaptic potential (PSP) therefore increases in size (as indicated in the graph). (*b*) An interneuron modulates the polarization of the axon terminal and causes the release of more transmitter molecules per nerve impulse. (*c*) Increase in size of the postsynaptic receptor membrane causes a larger response to the same amount of transmitter release. (*d*) The size of the synaptic contact area increases with training. (*e*) A neural circuit that is used more often increases the number of synaptic contacts. (*f*) A more frequently used neural pathway takes over synaptic sites formerly occupied by a less active competitor.

can be summed up by the following expression: Neurons that fire together wire together (Löwel and Singer, 1992:211).

To explain how neural activity could lead to the formation of new synaptic connections as a result of experience, Hebb proposed the **dual trace hypothesis**. According to this hypothesis, formation of a memory involves first a relatively brief transient process: learning experience sets up activity that tends to reverberate through the activated neural circuits. This activity holds the memory for a short period. If sufficient, the activity helps build up a stable change in the nervous system, which is a long-lasting memory trace.

Negative Changes Could Also Store Information in the Nervous System

We have mentioned only *increases* in synaptic effects with training, and Hebb wrote only about "strengthening" synaptic connections, never about weakening them. Changes in the opposite direction, however, could just as well mediate learning and memory, since both making and breaking contacts alter circuits. Later theorists added "weakening connections" to Hebb's formulations, thus greatly increasing their power to account for features of learning and memory. Thus, our list of the ways of increasing synaptic activity or numbers (see Figure 18.2) should be considered shorthand notation for "increasing or decreasing."

Computing What to Remember Requires Circuits of Neurons

For many aspects of learning and memory it may not be possible to find correlates in the responses of individual neurons or synapses; it may be necessary to study the activities of sets or ensembles of neurons. Consider, for example, the cards that a cheering section at a football game holds up: looking at one or a few cards cannot reveal the pattern made by all the cards. Hebb therefore proposed the concept of **cell assemblies**—that is, large groups of cells that tend to be active at the same time because they have been activated simultaneously or in close succession in the past. Such groups would include cells that are widely dispersed in the brain and that do not necessarily show any orderly spatial arrangement. Excitation of cells in one part of the assembly would tend to activate other cells in the assembly and so to excite the whole assembly. Such cell assemblies could represent "perceptual elements" that could be grouped into more complex ensembles to give rise to perceptions. Certainly the behavior of neural ensembles depends on unit activity, but it may not be entirely reducible to the activity of units.

In Chapter 17 we found that various kinds of learning require specialized circuits to compute particular features of what is to be remembered. For example, some experiments have demonstrated that different regions of the brain are necessary to process and store different attributes of memory. Each of these brain regions possesses its own particular anatomy of circuits, which differs from that of the other regions, and each processes an aspect of information that the other regions do not. Several experiments revealed that the temporal pairing of stimuli is neither necessary nor sufficient for conditioning to occur; here, too, complex networks are necessary to process the information, and monosynaptic circuits do not suffice. The distinction between *computation* by neural networks and *storage* of information is stressed by Gallistel (1990), who notes that neuroscientists have been much more concerned with storage than with neural computation.

Cerebral Changes Result from Training

Training Produces Electrophysiological Changes in Cerebral and Neural Activity

The first electrophysiological observations of training were made by accident on a human subject. The French neurophysiologists Gustave Durup and Alfred Fessard (1943) were studying how the alpha rhythm of the electroencephalogram (EEG; see Box 5.1) is blocked when the subject's field of vision is illuminated. After switching on the light several times one day and seeing the subject's alpha rhythm disappear from the record each time, the experimenters again threw the light switch, but the bulb failed and the room remained dark; nevertheless the alpha rhythm again disappeared! Ordinarily it wouldn't take a neuroscientist much time to screw in a new lightbulb and get on with the experiment, but this team took time to ponder the puzzling occurrence. They hypothesized that the sound of the switch had become a conditioned stimulus predicting the appearance of light and thus had caused the EEG to respond as if light were present. Tests with other subjects soon demonstrated that the sound of the switch did not block the alpha rhythm in naive subjects but came to do so after pairings of sound and light.

After this work became known, many investigators undertook studies of EEG correlates of various kinds of conditioning in the late 1940s and 1950s. Because of the overlying skull and tissue, however, precise localization of EEG activity in the human cortex is difficult. In addition, the critical events might be occurring not in the cortex, but in deeper brain structures. Thus, the focus of research shifted to recording from the brains of alert, behaving animal subjects, often with implanted electrodes. Later in this chapter we will review a program of research to find the sites of plastic neural changes that accompany eye-blink conditioning. The invention of microelectrodes around 1950 made it possible to record the activity of single neurons during training. We will see this technique applied to investigating cellular activity during conditioning of a variety of animals, including relatively simple molluscs. Let's begin, however, with some other relatively early findings of ways in which the nervous system changes as a consequence of training.

Training and Experience May Cause the Brain to Change Chemically and Anatomically

In the early 1960s two experimental programs announced that they could show that the brain can be altered by training or differential experience. First was the demonstration by an interdisciplinary team (Figure 18.3) that either formal training or informal experience in varied environments led to measurable changes in the neurochemistry and neuroanatomy of the rodent brain (Rosenzweig, Krech, and Bennett, 1961; Bennett et al., 1964; Renner and Rosenzweig, 1987; Rosenzweig, 1984). Soon thereafter came the announcement by Hubel and Wiesel that depriving one eye of light in a young kitten, starting at the age at which the eyes open, reduced the number of cortical cells responding to that eye (see Chapter 4; Hubel and Wiesel, 1963, 1965; Wiesel and Hubel, 1965). Although depriving an eye of light is a severe condition whereas giving animals different degrees of experience without depriving them of any sensory modal-

ity is a mild and natural treatment, both approaches lead to measurable changes in the nervous system.

In some experiments, animals have differential opportunities for informal learning (Figure 18.4). Littermates of the same sex were assigned by a random procedure to various laboratory environments. The three most common environments were:

1. The **standard colony** (SC). Three animals were kept in a standard laboratory cage and provided with food and water (Figure 18.4a). This is the typical environment for laboratory animals.

2. The **enriched condition** (EC). A group of 10 to 12 animals was kept in a large cage containing a variety of stimulus objects, which were changed daily (Figure 18.4c). This environment is considered enriched because it provides greater opportunities for informal learning that does the SC.

3. The **impoverished**, or isolated **condition** (IC). A single animal was housed in an SC-sized cage (Figure 18.4b).

In the initial experiments of this series, rats were assigned to the different conditions at weaning (about 25 days after birth), and they were kept in the conditions for 80 days. In later experiments both the age at assignment and the duration of the period of differential experience were varied.

At the end of the period of differential experience, each brain was dissected into standard samples for chemical analysis. In the initial experiments, animals in the enriched condition (EC) were found to develop greater activity of the enzyme acetylcholinesterase (AChE) in the cerebral cortex than their littermates in IC. (Recall that AChE breaks down the synaptic transmitter ACh and clears the

18.3 Pioneer Investigators of Effects of Training and Differential Experience on Brain Chemistry and Brain Anatomy
From left to right: Edward L. Bennett, neurochemist; Marian C. Diamond, neuroanatomist; David Krech, biological psychologist; Mark R. Rosenzweig, biological psychologist. Photograph taken around 1965.

(a)

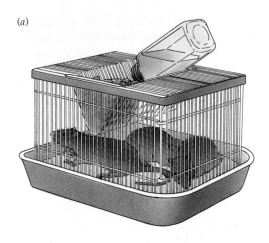

(b)

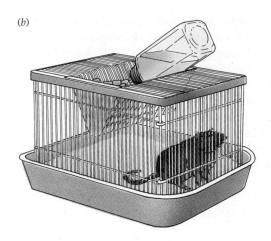

(c)

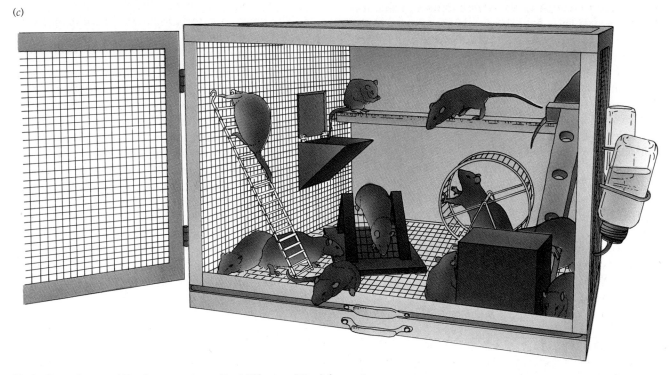

18.4 Experimental Environments to Test Effects of Enrichment on Learning and Brain Measures

(*a*) Standard colony; (*b*) impoverished condition; (*c*) enriched condition. Interaction with an enriched environment has measurable effects on brain measures, on stress reactions, and on learning.

synapse for renewed stimulation.) Control experiments showed that this effect could not be attributed to either greater handling of the EC animals or greater locomotor activity in the EC situation (Rosenzweig, Krech, and Bennett, 1961). Scrutiny of the data then revealed that the experimental groups dif-

fered not only in total enzymatic activity but also in weight of the cortical samples: the EC animals developed a heavier cerebral cortex than did their littermates in IC (Rosenzweig et al., 1962). This result was a real surprise, because since the beginning of the twentieth century brain weight had been considered a very stable characteristic and not subject to environmental influences.

Further experiments showed that the differences in brain weight were extremely reliable, although small. Moreover, these differences were not distributed uniformly throughout the cerebral cortex. They were largest in the occipital cortex and smallest in the adjacent somesthetic cortex. The rest of the brain outside the cerebral cortex tended to show very little effect.

The differences in cortical weights among groups were caused by differences in cortical thickness: animals exposed to the EC environment developed slightly but significantly thicker cerebral cortices than their littermates in the other conditions (Diamond, 1967; Diamond, Krech, and Rosenzweig, 1964). More refined neuroanatomical measurements were then undertaken on pyramidal cells in the occipital cortex; these included counts of dendritic spines, measurements of dendritic branching, and measurements of the size of synaptic contacts. Each of these measurements showed significant effects of differential experience, as we will see shortly.

Experience in the EC environment promotes better learning and problem solving in a variety of tests. It also aids recovery from or compensation for brain damage (Will et al., 1977). As we will see later in this chapter, enriched experience appears to protect against age-related declines in memory, both in laboratory animals and in humans.

Learning Can Produce New Synaptic Connections

The idea that learning and memory can be mediated by the formation of new synaptic contacts has had its ups and downs over the last century. Proposed in the 1890s, this idea was supported by such eminent investigators as Ramón y Cajal (1894) and Sherrington (1897). Because no concrete evidence was produced to back it up, however, support for the hypothesis waned. Hebb (1949) helped to revive the synaptic hypothesis of learning, but in 1965 John C. Eccles (the neurophysiologist who shared the Nobel Prize in 1963) remained firm in his belief that learning and memory storage involve "growth just of bigger and better synapses that are already there, not growth of new connections." Not until the 1970s did experiments with laboratory rats assigned to enriched or impoverished environments provide evidence that learning can produce new synaptic connections.

We saw in Chapters 2 and 3 that growth of dendritic spines is a late aspect of the development of neurons and is affected by experience. When dendritic spines were counted in EC–IC experiments, the numbers of spines per unit of length of dendrite were found to be significantly greater in EC than in IC animals (Globus et al., 1973). This effect was not uniform over the dendritic tree; it was most pronounced for basal dendrites. Different aspects of the dendritic tree receive inputs from different sources, and the basal dendrites of pyramidal cells receive input especially from adjacent neurons in the same region. Thus it appears that enriched experience leads to the development of increased numbers of synaptic contacts and richer, more complex intracortical networks.

Psychologist William Greenough also placed laboratory rats in SC, EC, and IC environments and quantified **dendritic branching** by the methods shown in Figure 18.5. EC animals developed dendritic branching significantly greater than that of IC animals (Greenough and Volkmar, 1973; Volkmar and Greenough, 1972). The SC values fell between the IC and EC values and tended to be closer to the IC values. With enriched experience, each cell did not send its dendrites out farther, but instead tended to fill its allotted volume more densely with branches. These results, together with the dendritic spine counts, indicate that the EC animals develop more elaborate information processing circuits. More direct measures of numbers of synapses and neurons were then made by more refined techniques (Turner and Greenough, 1985). In layers I to IV of the occipital cortex, the EC rats had about 9400 synapses per neuron versus about 7600 for the IC rats—a difference of more than 20%. The value for SC rats was intermediate, but closer to the IC level. A study on the effects of formal training used split-brain rats and gave training to only one eye so that it reached a single cerebral hemisphere (Chang and Greenough, 1982); effects of training on dendritic branching appeared mainly in the trained hemisphere. These results provide strong support for the view that learning and long-term memory involve the formation of new synaptic contacts.

The *size* of synaptic contacts also changes as a result of differential experience. The mean length of the postsynaptic thickening in synapses of the occipital cortex is significantly greater in EC rats than in their IC littermates (Diamond et al., 1975; Greenough and West, 1972). Such increased size and number of synaptic contacts may increase the certainty of synaptic transmission in the circuits where changes occur.

Experiments with several strains of rats showed similar effects of EC and IC environments on both brain values and problem-solving behavior. Similar effects on brain measurements have been found in

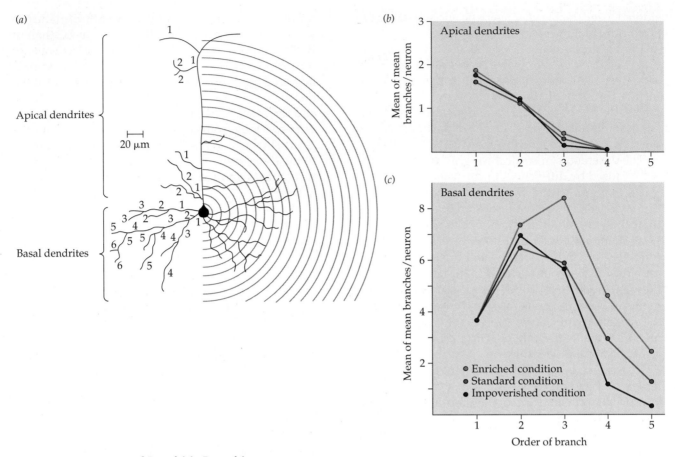

18.5 Measurement of Dendritic Branching

An enlarged photograph of a neuron is used to quantify branching either by counting the number of branches of different orders (*a, left*), or by counting the number of intersections with concentric rings (*a, right*). (*b, c*) Results obtained by counting the number of branches. There are significant differences in branching among rats kept for 30 days in enriched, standard colony, or impoverished environments. From Greenough, 1976.

several species of mammals: mice, gerbils, ground squirrels, cats, and monkeys (Renner and Rosenzweig, 1987:54–59); effects of training on brain measurements have also been found in birds. Thus, the cerebral effects of experience that were surprising when first found in rats have been generalized to several mammalian and avian species. The fruit fly *Drosophila* also shows greater branching of neuronal processes when placed in an enriched environment with leafy branches and other *Drosophila*, in comparison with *Drosophila* kept in isolation in small food vials (Technau, 1984). Further work has confirmed the effects of enrichment versus deprivation in the *Drosophila* brain, although the precise roles of different environmental factors have not yet been determined (Heisenberg, Heusipp, and Wanke, 1995). The latter investigators conclude that most regions of the

Drosophila brain that show extensive neuronal branching "are continuously reorganized throughout life in response to specific living conditions."

The finding that measurable changes could be induced in the brain by experience, even in adult animals, was one of several factors that led increasing numbers of investigators to ask in more detail how the nervous system reacts to training and how new information can be stored by the nervous system. Another factor was the growing knowledge of development of the nervous system on a cellular level, and the long-held surmise that changes accompanying learning might be similar to those that occur in development. Increasing technical capacities to examine nerve cells—electrophysiologically, neuroanatomically, and neurochemically—also favored this trend.

Sites of Plasticity Can Be Located in an Invertebrate Nervous System

The relative simplicity of the central nervous systems of some invertebrates led several investigators to try to find in them the neural circuits necessary and sufficient for learning, with the goal of studying plastic synaptic changes in these circuits. Invertebrate preparations, such as the large sea slug *Aplysia* (Figure 18.6), appeared to offer several advantages for this research, although we will see later that some of these were overestimated:

1. The number of nerve cells in an *Aplysia* ganglion is relatively small compared with that in a mammalian brain or even brain region, although the number in the invertebrate ganglion is still on the order of 1000.

2. In the invertebrate ganglion, the cell bodies form the outside and the dendritic processes are on the inside. This arrangement, the opposite of that in mammals, makes it easy to identify and record from cells of invertebrates.

3. Many individual cells in invertebrate ganglia can be recognized, both because of their shapes and sizes and because the cellular structure of the ganglion is uniform from individual to individual (see Figure 18.6). Thus it is possible to identify certain cells and to trace their sensory and motor connections. Merely isolating a ganglion in a particular *Aplysia* tells you the basic connections of many of the larger cell bodies. The neurotransmitters in some large, identifiable cells are also known.

A well-known example of studies on neural plasticity in invertebrates is the program of research initiated by Eric R. Kandel that investigated sites and mechanisms of plasticity for both nonassociative and associative learning in *Aplysia* (Kandel et al., 1987). Much of Kandel's research indicated that learning takes place within a straight sensorimotor chain that controls the behavior being studied (see Figure 18.1*a*). Many interesting results have been reported from this program, but since the mid-1980s some investigators have voiced reservations about the methods and findings of this research. We will review the work of the Kandel group and recent criticisms of this research.

The Nervous System of *Aplysia* Shows Habituation and Sensitization

Kandel and his colleagues first investigated nonassociative forms of learning—habituation and sensitization—because for many years they were unable to

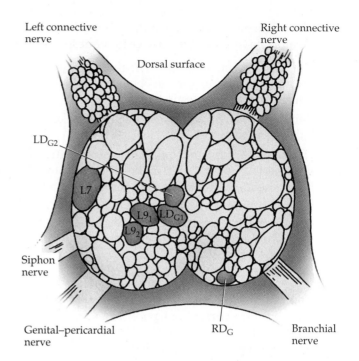

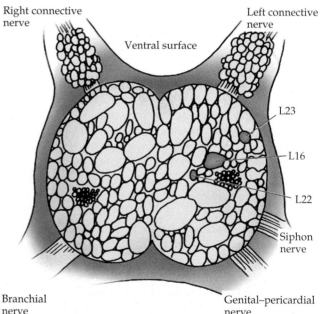

18.6 Identified Cells in the Abdominal Ganglion of *Aplysia*
Some of the neurons involved in gill-withdrawal conditioning, as indicated by electrophysiological recording, are shown in pink (*top*) and blue (*bottom*).

demonstrate associative learning in *Aplysia*. Habituation and sensitization are probably the simplest and most ubiquitous forms of learning, and they are important in everyday life. In attempting to analyze these two forms of learning at the cellular level, investigators have sought to answer four questions:

1. Are the crucial changes distributed diffusely through the circuit for the behavior, or are they limited to specific sites in the circuit?

2. Can the mechanisms be specified in molecular and anatomical terms?

3. How do the sites and mechanisms of relatively short-term habituation (lasting from minutes to hours) relate to those of long-term habituation (lasting from days to weeks)?

4. Can the mechanisms of associative learning be derived from the mechanisms of nonassociative learning?

Habituation, you will recall, means becoming insensitive to stimuli that have no special significance or consequence for current behavior. The mechanisms of habituation have been studied in intact mammals, in spinal preparations of mammals, and in relatively simple invertebrate systems.

How *Aplysia* Shows Habituation

As *Aplysia* moves across the bottom of a shallow body of seawater, its gill (respiratory organ) is usually spread out on its back, protected only by a light mantle shelf; the siphon is extended in order to draw in water and circulate it over the gill (Figure 18.7*b*). If anything touches the mantle shelf or the siphon, the animal retracts them and its delicate gill to protect them (Figure 18.7*c*). The gill-withdrawal response habituates readily upon repeated stimulation, following rules similar to those of habituation in human beings and other animals.

Aplysia also shows sensitization; when the animal is given a strong stimulus to the head, the gill-withdrawal response to a touch of the mantle shelf or siphon is greatly enhanced. The close correspondence between the characteristics of habituation and sensitization in *Aplysia* and these behaviors in mammals justifies our looking further into the neural mechanisms of these behaviors in *Aplysia*, even if we are not particularly interested in this sea slug in itself. We saw in Chapter 17 that habituation appears earlier in the development of *Aplysia* than does sensitization, an indication that their mechanisms differ, at least in part.

To study habituation, investigators usually measure the amplitude of the gill-withdrawal response in an *Aplysia* fixed in position so that it cannot locomote. Unfortunately, the usual methods ignore the complexity of gill movements. Gill withdrawal in *Aplysia* "varies in form and amplitude within as well as be-

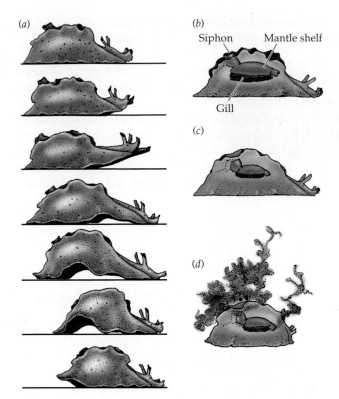

18.7   Characteristic Behaviors of *Aplysia*
(*a*) Locomotion. (*b*) Usual posture. The siphon is extended and the gill is spread out on the back. Ordinarily only the tip of the siphon would be visible in a lateral view; here the rest of the siphon and the gill are shown as if the animal were transparent. (*c*) The siphon and the gill retract in response to light touch. (*d*) The head retracts and the animal releases ink in response to a strong stimulus. After Kandel, 1976.

tween preparations and is therefore a heterogeneous collection of action patterns, not a reflex" (Leonard, Edstrom, and Lukowiak, 1989:585). The gill of *Aplysia* consists of about 16 fanlike structures (pinnules) and two veins; each of these parts can move independently of the others (Figure 18.8). There are at least four main action patterns, which are combinations of ten different actions. Because all of these actions are under separate neural control, we must reevaluate studies that are based on the assumption that the gill-withdrawal response involves a single type of movement under the same neural control.

Kandel and colleagues used diagrams like Figure 18.9 to describe the basic neural circuits controlling the gill-withdrawal response (Kupfermann, Carew, and Kandel, 1974). All the neurons in this diagram are within the abdominal ganglion, but the diagram does not begin to reflect the number of cells involved or the much greater number of their interconnections. More recent research has also shown that neurons outside  the ganglion should not be ignored, because the gill-withdrawal response persists after surgical removal of the abdominal ganglion (Mpitsos and Lukowiak, 1985). In addition, the central nervous system of *Aplysia* enters a suppressed state after the animal has eaten or engaged in sexual activity, but even when the CNS is inactivated, the animal shows the gill-withdrawal response, mediated by the peripheral nervous system. Thus, the neural circuitry of the gill-withdrawal response includes small, diffuse cells of the peripheral nervous system that are inaccessible to the neurophysiologist.

Eric R. Kandel

Convinced that they had located the circuit responsible for the gill-withdrawal response in the central nervous system of *Aplysia,* Kandel and his colleagues then made "reduced preparations" consisting of the siphon, mantle shelf, gill, and the sensory and motor nerves connecting these structures to the abdominal ganglion. With these structures fixed in position, the experimenters stimulated the siphon or mantle with calibrated jets of water at precisely de-termined times, and they recorded the size of the gill-withdrawal response. To test for possible sites of plasticity in the CNS circuit they had described, they explored several possible loci of altered activity during habituation.

Sites of Short-Term Habituation

Habituation in the *Aplysia* preparation was not caused by receptor adaptation, or fatigue of the muscles, or depression of the neuromuscular junctions. In the ganglion, intracellular recordings from the motor neurons showed decreased firing rates during habituation. Tests indicated that decreased synaptic input to the motor neuron was responsible for habituation: The excitatory postsynaptic potentials (EPSPs) to synaptic input decreased progressively during repeated sensory stimulation, and this decrease could account for the decreased firing rate of the motor neuron. With a period of rest and no stimulation, the amplitude of the EPSPs recovers. Since depression of the EPSPs caused by repeated stimulation of one part of the receptive field (such as the siphon) did not cause a decrease of the EPSPs caused by stimulation of another part of the sensory field (for instance, the mantle), the depression is strictly localized. The contribution of the interneurons to the EPSPs of the motor cells was small relative to that of the monosynaptic sensorimotor pathway, so the investigators concluded that the effect must be localized chiefly at the monosynaptic sensorimotor junctions.

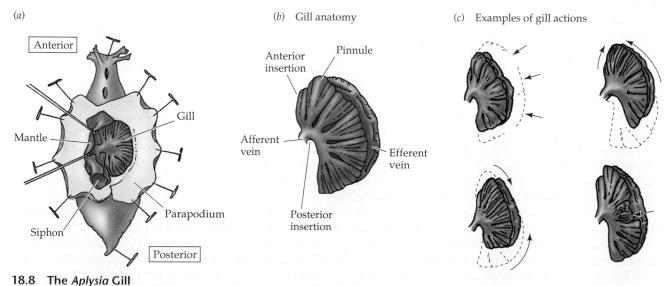

18.8 The *Aplysia* Gill
(*a*) There are 16 pinnules and two veins in the *Aplysia* gill. (*b*) Each pinnule can move independently; some possible gill motions are shown. After Leonard, Edstrom, and Lukowiak, 1979.

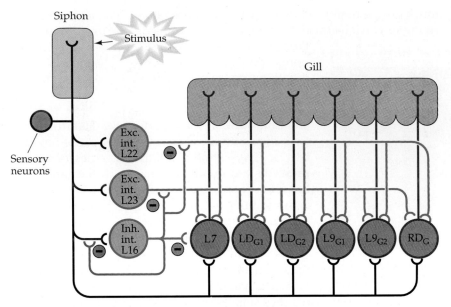

18.9 *Aplysia* Abdominal Ganglion Neurons That May Control the Gill-Withdrawal Reflex
Some investigators propose that a monosynaptic reflex arc consisting of sensory neurons and large identifiable motor neurons control the gill-withdrawal reflex. After Kupfermann, Carew, and Kandel, 1974.

The depression of the EPSPs was found to be caused by a decrease in the *number* of quanta (packets) of synaptic transmitter released by each sensory impulse; the *size* of the individual quanta remained constant. Recall that a change in the amount of transmitter released upon arrival of a nerve impulse is one of the hypothesized mechanisms of memory (see Figure 18.2*a*). Thus, the investigators claimed to have localized precisely the site of the alteration that had resulted from habituation; habituation appeared to occur mainly at one site: the presynaptic terminals on the motor nerve. Therefore, although the *anatomy* of the circuit is fixed, it appears that the *effectiveness* of the sensorimotor synapses can be modified.

The depression in transmitter release at the synapses involves, at least in part, a decrease in the number of calcium ions (Ca^{2+}) that flow into the terminals of the sensory neurons with each action potential. Repeated stimulation of the sensory neuron produces moderately long inactivation of the channels by which Ca^{2+} enters the neuron. Since Ca^{2+} influx helps determine how many vesicles bind to release sites and therefore how many quanta of transmitter are released by each action potential, a decrease in Ca^{2+} influx results in diminished transmitter release and therefore in decreased excitatory postsynaptic potentials (Klein, Shapiro, and Kandel, 1980).

Mechanisms of Long-Term Habituation

Long-term habituation in the central nervous system of *Aplysia* involves a change in the anatomy as well as in the neurochemistry of the sensory neuron synapses. These presynaptic terminals have active zones—that is, regions of the membrane from which the synaptic transmitter is released. These active zones can be quantified in three ways: (1) number (in nonhabituated *Aplysia*, only about half the terminals in this part of the abdominal ganglion have active zones) (2) area, and (3) the number of synaptic vesicles clustered within them. The higher the score on each of these measures, the greater the capacity of the animal to transmit neural signals in this path.

Bailey and Chen (1983) examined the terminals of sensory neurons in long-term habituated *Aplysia* and in control *Aplysia*; all three measures in the habituated animals were found to be significantly lower than in the controls (Figure 18.10). Some *Aplysia* in this study were also stimulated to induce long-term sensitization; the active zones of the synapses in the sensitized animals were significantly greater than those of the controls on all three measures. In another study, Bailey and Chen (1984) found that long-term habituated animals have fewer presynaptic sensory terminals in the ganglion than do controls. The fact that both numbers and sizes of synaptic junctions vary

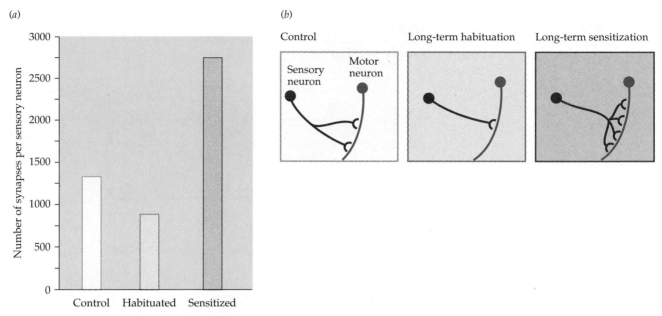

18.10 Structural Synaptic Changes in *Aplysia* Induced by Long-Term Habituation and Sensitization
(*a*) Long-term habituation leads to decreases in number and size of synaptic connnections, whereas long-term sensitization leads to increases. (*b*) A schematic rendering of these changes. After Bailey and Chen, 1983.

with training in *Aplysia* is similar to previous findings with mammals (Diamond et al., 1975; West and Greenough, 1972). Moreover, the work with *Aplysia* shows that at least some of the anatomical changes in learning occur specifically in neurons that are part of a circuit involved in the reflex, which the mammalian research had not been able to do. The finding that in *Aplysia,* as in mammals, long-term memory involves changes in numbers of synaptic contacts refutes the earlier claim of some investigators that neurochemical events at existing synapses are sufficient to account for learning and long-term memory.

The similarity in results obtained with *Aplysia* and with rats indicates that over a wide range of species, information can be stored in the nervous system by changes in both size and number of synaptic contacts. These findings confirm the hypotheses diagrammed in Figure 18.2*d* and *f.* Thus, even in a relatively simple animal like *Aplysia,* the structural remodeling of the nervous system that we considered early in development (see Chapter 4) probably continues to some extent throughout life and can be driven by experience.

Sites and Mechanisms of Sensitization

A diagram of the circuit proposed by Kandel and associates for the sensitization of the gill-withdrawal re-

sponse of *Aplysia* is shown Figure 18.11. Strong (presumably painful) stimulation of the head activates sensory neurons that, among other connections, excite facilitating interneurons. These interneurons end on the synaptic terminals of the sensory neurons from the siphon or the mantle. Thus, sensitization is a somewhat more complex form of nonassociative learning than habituation, because it involves two kinds of stimuli: the effect of the sensitizing stimulus alters the response to the touch stimulus.

The cellular neurochemical mechanism of sensitization in the abdominal ganglion is also somewhat more complex than is that of habituation. It involves, at least in part, the same locus as habituation—the synapses that sensory neurons make on the motor neurons—as well as an alteration in transmitter release by the sensory neurons. Furthermore, the neural circuit suggested for sensitization in *Aplysia* includes elements in addition to those in the circuit that has been proposed to underlie habituation. In particular, as Figure 18.11 shows, information about strong stimulation of the head or tail is mediated by **facilitator interneurons** that form presynaptic endings on the terminals of the sensory neurons from the mantle shelf or siphon; that is, the facilitating interneurons can modulate the activity of the sensory neurons that synapse on the motor neurons controlling the gill.

18.11 A Proposed Neural Circuit for Short-Term Sensitization in *Aplysia*

This circuit is similar to that for habituation (Figure 18.9) but adds facilitator interneurons that can modulate the activity of the motor neurons. After Hawkins and Kandel, 1983.

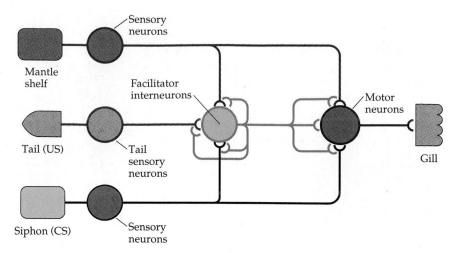

Kandel and colleagues have suggested a neurochemical model for the processes that underlie so-called short-term sensitization in the *Aplysia* preparation. Later we will see a related account for the processes that underlie associative learning. The model for short-term sensitization in the abdominal ganglion includes at least seven steps, each of which is consistent with experimental tests (Figure 18.12). In brief, (1) strong stimulation of the head or tail of *Aplysia* activates facilitator interneurons whose presynaptic contacts on the sensory terminals are thought to use serotonin as their transmitter. (2) Activation of the serotonin receptors in the sensory neurons leads to synthesis of cyclic AMP (cAMP) within these neurons.

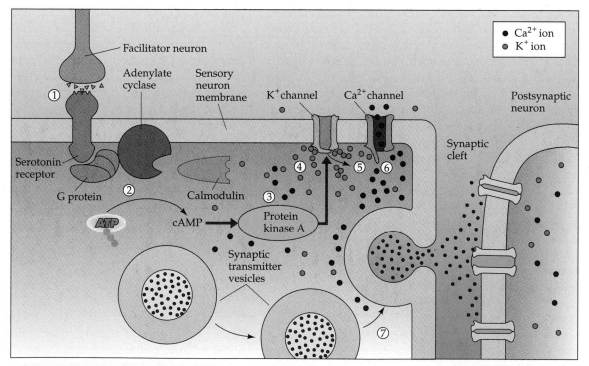

18.12 A Neurochemical Model Proposed for Short-Term Sensitization in *Aplysia*

The model proposed for short-term sensitization includes at least seven neurochemical steps (detailed in the text) leading to increased release of neurotransmitter by the sensory neuron. After Kandel et al., 1986.

(3) Increased levels of cAMP lead to the activation of an enzyme, protein kinase A, which (4) catalyzes a reaction that closes potassium (K^+) channels in the membrane. (5) Delaying the outflow of K^+ ions during action potentials prolongs the potentials, which (6) opens more calcium channels. (7) The greater influx of Ca^{2+} increases transmitter release by the sensory neurons.

Mechanisms of Long-Term Sensitization in *Aplysia*

Long-term sensitization in the abdominal ganglion of *Aplysia*, as mentioned earlier, causes increases in the number and size of active zones of the sensory terminals (see Figure 18.10). Whereas so-called short-term sensitization can be accomplished by purely neurochemical processes, long-term retention involves structural changes in the synapses. Later we will consider how neural activity can lead to structural changes.

Mechanisms of Associative Learning Have Been Found in Invertebrate Central Nervous Systems

Years of attempts to condition the gill-withdrawal response of *Aplysia* were unsuccessful until Carew, Walters, and Kandel (1981*a*, *b*) discovered the following method: if a light touch to the mantle is promptly followed by a strong shock to the tail, after a few trials the touch alone elicits a strong withdrawal response. The touch (CS) and shock (US) must be paired and the interval between them kept brief for this kind of conditioning to occur; tests demonstrate that this response is conditioning and not sensitization. Now it is possible to compare the mechanisms of conditioning and of nonassociative learning in the same relatively simple preparation. Other invertebrate preparations are also being used in the study of mechanisms of learning and memory. These include the nudibranch mollusc *Hermissenda* (Alkon, 1985, 1988) and the marine gastropod mollusc *Pleurobranchaea* (Mpitsos et al., 1980). In the sections that follow we will consider research on conditioning in some invertebrate preparations.

Aplysia Form Conditioned Responses Readily

The ability of *Aplysia* to display conditional learning was described in Chapter 17 (see Figure 17.5). Some related but earlier research on conditioning utilized **differential classical conditioning** of the siphon-withdrawal response (Carew et al., 1983). Here two conditioned stimuli (CS) are used in the same animal: one (CS+) is *paired* with the US; the other (CS)

is *unpaired* and has no consequence for the animal. With such training each animal can serve as its own control in comparing responses to CS+ and to CS–. In the study by Carew, Hawkins, and Kandel (1983), weak tactile stimuli to two parts of the body were the discriminative stimuli (CS+ to the siphon and CS– to the mantle, or the reverse), and tail shock was the US. Differential conditioning is rapid in *Aplysia* and increases in strength with increased numbers of trials.

Investigation of the neurochemical mechanisms of classical conditioning in *Aplysia* suggested to Kandel and his associates that they are similar to those involved in sensitization. Differential conditioning produced a significantly greater enhancement of the duration of action potentials with paired (CS+) than with unpaired (CS–) stimulation. Furthermore, the activity-dependent facilitation in conditioning involves modulation of the same type of ion channel as in sensitization (Hawkins and Abrams, 1984). Figure 18.13 presents hypothesized events in the sensory terminal under CS– and CS+ conditions. Compare this diagram with Figure 18.12 (the hypothesized mechanisms of sensitization).

Challenges to Research on Learning in *Aplysia*

As we have noted, some investigators have shown that the gill-withdrawal response is not a simple unitary reflex and is not controlled only by cells in the abdominal ganglion; in fact, the gill-withdrawal response occurs even when the central nervous system of *Aplysia* has been inactivated or removed. Colebrook and Lukowiak (1988) further pointed out that in experiments on conditioning in *Aplysia*, no one had recorded the electrical activity of both the motor neurons and the gill responses in the same animals. When they carried out such an experiment, they found that while both the neural responses and the gill-withdrawal amplitudes to the CS showed mean increases as a result of conditioning, more than one-third of the animals showed an increase in one but not in the other measure. That is, the behavioral response and its supposed neural cause did not necessarily act in the same way. Colebrook and Lukowiak (1988) concluded that many loci and neural mechanisms are likely to be involved in conditioning of the gill-withdrawal response, with both the ganglia and peripheral sites combining their effects.

Recently Kandel and associates have moved in this direction: they have used a reduced preparation for simultaneous behavioral and cellular studies of plasticity of the gill-withdrawal response, and they

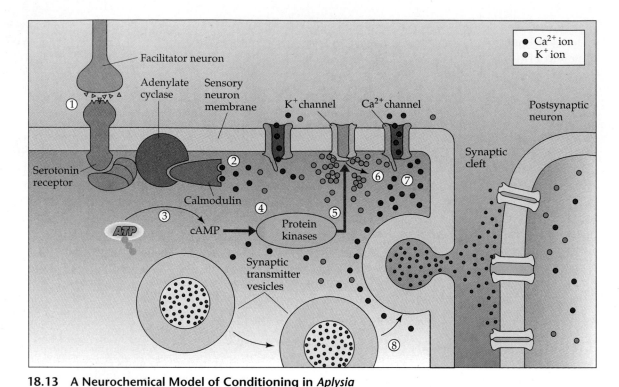

18.13   A Neurochemical Model of Conditioning in *Aplysia*
(1) The CS activates facilitator neurons. If this occurs shortly prior to US activation (not shown) of the sensory neuron, then (2) the increased Ca^{2+} influx activates calmodulin (CaM), which was not involved in sensitization. (3) CaM causes increased cAMP. (4) cAMP activates protein kinases which (5) phosphorylate K^+ channels, closing them. (6) This causes a build-up of intracellular K^+. (7) The increased concentration of K^+ causes prolonged opening of Ca^{2+} channels. (8) Greater influx of Ca^{2+} increases transmitter release by the sensory neuron. Because calmodulin remains active until specifically deactivated, the neurons remain in the altered (conditioned) state. After Kandel et al., 1986.

have published preliminary reports on nonassociative learning with this preparation (Cohen et al., 1991; Hawkins, Cohen, and Kendel, 1992). To investigate the role of different motor neurons in the ganglion, they inactivated one or another neuron by hyperpolarization; they report that one motor neuron, LD_{G1}, is responsible for about 70% of the gill-withdrawal response. They then recorded responses of LD_{G1} during habituation, dishabituation, and sensitization. The "results suggest that habituation in this preparation is largely due to depression at central synapses, whereas dishabituation and sensitization are due to central and peripheral facilitation with different time courses" for the central and peripheral components (Hawkins, Cohen, and Kendel, 1992). Further work on the sites involved in conditioning has not yet appeared, but probably both conditioning and sensitization involve the peripheral as well as the central nervous system of *Aplysia*.

These results force us to reject the earlier reports that plasticity is located exclusively in the ganglia of *Aplysia*. However, there seems to be no reason to question that the proposed synaptic mechanisms of plasticity occur at least in a few large neurons in the abdominal ganglion. In Box 18.1 we consider research with *Drosophila* mutants that are impaired in learning and memory. These mutants have deficiencies in some of the same neurochemical steps (outlined in Figure 18.13) identified by Kandel and his associates, providing independent support for the generality of their hypotheses.

Even in the ganglion the story is far from complete, because a single touch to the siphon can activate electrical responses in about 150 different neurons (Zecevic et al., 1989), and many of these probably play roles in the complex gill movements. Since different neurons in the ganglion employ different synaptic transmitters, at least part of the neurochemical cascade involved in plasticity probably differs among central neurons. Other investigators have recently reported that approximately 200 abdominal ganglion neurons are involved in the gill-withdrawal response, and most of them are also involved in respiratory movements (Wu, Cohen, and Falk, 1994). Study of the different kinds of responses mediated by these neurons suggests that the different behaviors are generated by altered activities of a single, large distributed network rather than by separate small networks, each dedicated to a particular response (Figure 18.14).

18.14 One Large Ensemble of Neurons Mediates The Gill-Withdrawal Response and Other *Aplysia* Behaviors
Each line represents one neuron in the abdominal ganglion; each vertical tick on the line indicates the timing of an action potential in the neuron. (*a, f* = gill-withdrawal responses; *b, d* = gill contractions; *c, e* = respiratory pumping episodes. After Wu, Cohen, and Falk, 1994.

Countering the claim that a few identified sensory neurons account for 58% of the input to the gill motor neurons (Byrne, Castellucci, and Kandel, 1978), which would indicate a major simple component of the gill-withdrawal circuit, Wu, Cohen and Falk (1994) report that the contribution of these neurons is much smaller, probably less than 10%. Beyond these problems at the *central* sites, the mechanisms of plasticity at *peripheral* neural sites in *Aplysia* have not yet been studied, so there is still much to find out about the mechanisms of learning, even in what some investigators hoped would be a "simple" kind of learning in a "simple" organism.

Hermissenda Displays a Different Mechanism of Conditioning

Visitors to tide pools sometimes see slim, attractively colored molluscs several centimeters long, without shells and with gills rising from their backs. One such mollusc, *Hermissenda*, is the subject of extensive research on mechanisms of conditioning by neuroscientist Daniel Alkon and his colleagues (Alkon, 1985, 1988; Farley and Alkon, 1985; Alkon, 1992). In the laboratory, pairing light with rotation on a turntable causes conditioned suppression of the tendency to approach the light. In fact, the plasticity in this system is in the eyes of *Hermissenda*, which contain only five photoreceptor cells.

The work with *Hermissenda*, which has revealed important changes with training in the neuronal membrane, affords quite a different picture of basic mechanisms of conditioning from that furnished by the research with *Aplysia*, which focuses on changes that occur at the presynaptic side of the synaptic junction. Clark and Schuman (1992) compare the neurochemical mechanisms of learning in *Aplysia* and *Hermissenda*. In addition to noting important similarities, they point out some distinctions: "Compared with plasticity in *Aplysia* siphon sensory cells, plasticity in *Hermissenda* Type B photoreceptors involves a different sensory modality (light rather than touch), different types of potassium conductances (I_A and I_{K-Ca}, rather than I_S), primarily a different second-messenger system (protein kinase C, rather than cAMP-dependent kinase), and an inhibitory rather than an excitatory synaptic potential, among other differences. These are meaningful distinctions, and their existence suggests that each preparation will provide unique insights into cellular mechanisms of learning" (Clark and Schuman, 1992:598). The next few years should demonstrate how well either or both of these pictures will be validated by further investigation in the two species. These may be only

Box 18.1

Studies with Drosophila: *A Genetic Approach to Mechanisms of Learning and Memory*

Because much is known about its genetics, the fruit fly *Drosophila* brings distinct advantages to the study of mechanisms of learning and memory, even though its central nervous system (with about 100,000 very small neurons) is more complex than that of *Aplysia* or *Hermissenda*. Geneticists William Quinn, W. A. Harris, and Seymour Benzer (1974) developed a method to condition groups of *Drosophila*. They put about 40 flies in a glass tube and let them move upward toward one of two odors that normally are equally attractive. Reaching the upper part of one tube brought an electrical shock, whereas the other odor was not associated with shock. The group could then be tested after various time intervals for approach to each of the odors. As the procedure was refined, about 90% avoided the odor associated with shock (Jellies, 1981). The geneticists then tested mutant strains of *Drosophila*. In 1976 they an-

nounced the isolation of the first mutant that failed to learn to discriminate the odors, and they named it *dunce* (Dudai et al., 1976).

Tests showed that *dunce* had a real problem with learning; its deficiency was not in olfaction, locomotion, or general activity. Three more learning mutants were isolated and named *cabbage, turnip,* and *rutabaga*; another mutant, *amnesiac,* learned normally but forgot more rapidly than normal flies (Quinn, 1979). Mutants found in other laboratories were also deficient in learning. One had been named for the enzyme in which it is deficient, dopa decarboxylase (*DDC*). Tests with other procedures showed that the failures of these mutants were not restricted to odor–shock training but occurred as well in other tests of associative learning, although the mutants appeared normal in nonlearning behaviors.

Another kind of training—for sucrose reward—was remem-

bered for days rather than hours by normal flies (Tempel et al., 1983). The sucrose test showed that *dunce* and *rutabaga* could learn but forgot within an hour. The mutants with poor learning or memory were also examined with regard to nonassociative learning: habituation and sensitization (Duerr and Quinn, 1982). *Dunce* and *turnip* showed low habituation; *dunce, rutabaga,* and *amnesiac* showed unusually brief sensitization. These observations supported the idea that nonassociative and associative learning share some of the same mechanisms, since mutations of single genes affected both.

The investigators determined which genes were disrupted in each of these mutants (Tully, 1987; Dudai, 1988). In each case the deficiency can be related to the schema of Kandel that we saw in Figure 18.13 and that is reproduced here with information about *Drosophila* mutants (shown in the figure). The enzyme dopa

---

two of a wide variety of possible mechanisms of learning, or either one or both may prove to be typical of a number of species (see Box 18.1 on learning and memory in *Drosophila*).

Long-Term Potentiation: A Model System to Study Mechanisms of Learning and Memory?

Investigators have long sought a way of isolating a vertebrate brain circuit in which learning occurs so that they could study the mechanisms in detail, much as invertebrate "reduced preparations" are being studied. Some researchers claim that **long-term po-**

tentiation (LTP) in the mammalian brain has the advantages necessary for studying mechanisms of synaptic plasticity that may also be important for memory. Long-term potentiation is a stable and enduring increase in the magnitude of the response of neurons after afferent cells to the region have been stimulated with bursts of electrical stimuli of moderately high frequency. LTP was first discovered in 1973 in the hippocampus of

Timothy Bliss

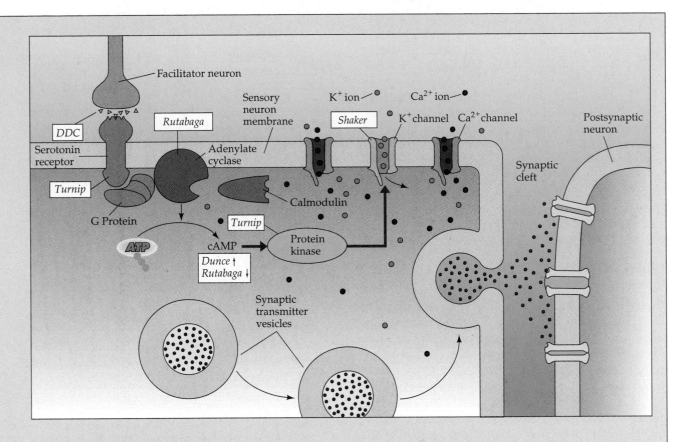

decarboxylase is necessary for the synthesis of the transmitters dopamine and serotonin, so its deficiency impairs stimulation by serotonergic fibers (*DDC*). The deficiency of *turnip* impairs both the serotonin receptor and protein kinase. The *rutabaga* mutation decreases cAMP levels and adenylate cyclase levels. The deficiency of *dunce* is in the enzyme that splits cAMP.

The finding that these genetic defects all fit into the schema of Kandel and associates provides independent support for their hypotheses about mechanisms of plasticity. In evaluating this striking convergence of findings, remember that the mutants had been isolated *behaviorally* without knowledge of their genetic deficiencies and independently of Kandel's hypotheses.

Terje Lømo

the intact rabbit by British neurophysiologist Timothy Bliss and Norwegian Terje Lømo, then a psychology student. The surprising aspect of their finding was the long-lasting nature of the increase in response magnitude. A shorter-term effect of this sort had long been known under the name of posttetanic potentiation (PTP); PTP occurs at neuromuscular junctions (see Chapter 11) and in the nervous system.

The 1973 report of Bliss and Lømo has become one of the most frequently cited papers on brain mechanisms of memory. Soon after this report, other investigators demonstrated that LTP could also be studied in slices of rat hippocampus maintained in a tissue chamber (Schwartzkroin and Wester, 1975). LTP can be observed in awake and freely moving animals, in anesthetized animals, or in tissue slices, on which most of the research is now being done. Although most of the work on LTP has been done in the hippocampus of the rat, it has been observed in many other brain areas in several species of mammals, and even in fishes. A recent paper reports LTP in sensorimotor synapses of *Aplysia* in a cell culture (Lin and Glanzman, 1994).

Bliss and Lømo (1973) were cautious as to whether LTP bears any relation to normal behavior. But LTP does resemble memory in several ways: LTP can be induced within seconds, it may last for days or weeks (Bliss and Gardner-Medwin, 1973), and it shows a labile "consolidation" period that lasts for several minutes after induction (Barrionueveo, Schottler, and Lynch, 1980). Such properties attracted many investigators to the study of LTP. After reviewing some other findings about LTP, we will consider more critically how well LTP may serve as a mechanism of memory. We'll follow our discussion of LTP by looking at an opposite phenomenon: long-term depression (LTD). LTD has recently attracted attention and may also be important as a mechanism of learning.

Different Kinds of LTP Occur at Different Sites in the Hippocampal Formation

Even within the hippocampal formation, there is more than one kind of LTP, although for some time LTP was assumed to be a unitary phenomenon. The different forms of LTP occur in different sites in the hippocampal formation (Figure 18.15). The hippocampal formation consists of two interlocking C-shaped regions, the hippocampus and the **dentate gyrus**, and includes the adjacent **subiculum** (also called the subicular complex or hippocampal gyrus). The strange shapes of the structures in the hippocampal formation earned them picturesque names: "hippocampus" is Latin for "seahorse," as we noted in Chapter 2. But other neuroanatomists called it by the Latin name of cornu ammonis ("Ammon's horn"), from the horn of the ram that represented the Egyptian deity Ammon. One region where LTP is investigated is known as CA1 (cornu ammonis 1), another as CA3. The dentate gyrus got its name from its toothlike projections. The term *subiculum* (Latin) means "underlayer" or "support"; the subiculum can be seen as a support for the rest of the hippocampal formation.

Main inputs to the hippocampal formation come from the nearby entorhinal cortex via the axons of the **perforant pathway** that push through ("perforate") the subiculum (see Figure 18.15). The site at which LTP was originally demonstrated consists of synapses from the perforant path to the dentate gyrus. From the dentate gyrus, so-called **mossy fibers** run to the hippocampus, where they synapse in area CA3. Until recently, LTP was not much studied at these synapses, possibly because this projection has relatively few synapses, and induction of LTP there requires special conditions, as we will see later. Neurons in CA3 send their axons, called **Shaffer collaterals**, to area CA1; LTP has been studied intensively at these synapses. The CA1 and CA3 regions also receive inputs from the corre-

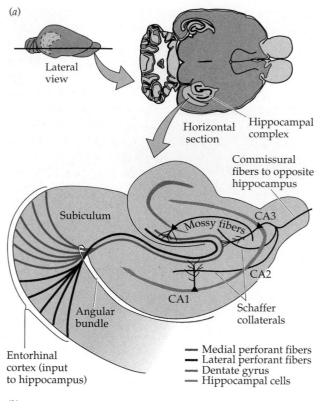

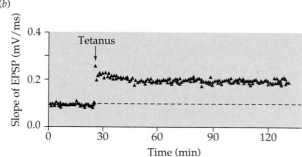

18.15 Hippocampal Regions Where LTP Has Been Studied
(*a, top*) Location of the hippocampal formation in whole rat brain and a horizontal section. (*a, bottom*) Diagram of the right hippocampal formation showing input fibers from the entorhinal cortex via the perforant pathway. (*b*) An example of LTP: after brief tetanic stimulation, the slope of EPSP responses increases markedly and remains high throughout the recording period.

sponding regions of the hippocampus in the other hemisphere of the brain via **commissural fibers**, that is, fibers that cross over through the corpus callosum.

The discovery of selective agonists for different kinds of glutamate receptors in the 1980s allowed investigators to characterize the pharmacology of synaptic transmission in the hippocampus and to study the neurochemistry of hippocampal LTP. LTP in area CA1 was found to require the kind of glutamate receptors that respond to the glutamate agonist N-methyl-D-aspartate (the NMDA receptors that we introduced in Box 5.3). Blocking of these receptors by antagonists of NMDA made it impossible to induce LTP in CA1, even though the NMDA antagonists did not affect other glutamate receptors, the AMPA receptors (also introduced in Box 5.3). Although NMDA antagonists prevent induction of LTP, they do not affect LTP that has already been established. For a time it appeared that induction of all hippocampal LTP and many kinds of learning might depend on NMDA receptors, but then it was found that NMDA antagonists did not prevent induction of LTP in some afferents of the dentate gyrus or CA3. Both of these regions obtain their inputs from the lateral perforant path, whereas the NMDA receptor–dependent form of LTP receives its input via the medial perforant path.

NMDA Receptors and AMPA Receptors Play Separate Roles in Induction of LTP in the CA1 Region

When the neurotransmitter glutamate is released at a synapse that has both AMPA and NMDA receptors, a moderate level of stimulation activates only the AMPA receptors, which handle most of the normal traffic of messages at these synapses. The NMDA receptors do not respond because magnesium ions (Mg^{2+}) block the NMDA receptor channel (Figure 18.16) so that few Ca^{2+} ions can enter the neuron. Sufficient activation of AMPA receptors or other excitatory receptors in the same neuron can partially depolarize the membrane to less than –35 millivolts. This partial depolarization removes the Mg^{2+} block (see Figure 18.16*b*); the NMDA receptors now respond actively to glutamate and admit large amounts of Ca^{2+} through their channels. Thus, the NMDA receptors are fully active only when they are gated by a combination of voltage and the ligand. The large influx of Ca^{2+} can lead to the next steps in induction of LTP, as we will see shortly.

Opioid Peptides Modulate Induction of LTP in the CA3 Region

At the synapses between mossy fibers and CA3 neurons (see Figure 18.15), LTP can be induced even in the presence of an NMDA antagonist, so the NMDA receptors are not needed here (Harris and Cotman, 1986). On the other hand, induction of LTP in region CA3 can be blocked by the presence of the opioid antagonist naloxone (Derrick and Martinez, 1994). The amount of inhibition depends on the dose: the greater the dose of the opioid receptor antagonist, the greater the blockage of LTP. In other regions of the hippocampus, opioid receptor–dependent LTP occurs in perforant pathway fibers arising from the lateral en-

torhinal cortex and projecting to several regions (see Figure 18.15)—the dentate gyrus, area CA3, and possibly area CA1—via the lateral temperoammonic tract, as well as in the mossy fiber projection from the dentate region to area CA3. Thus the opioid-dependent form of LTP may be the predominant form of LTP in fibers that convey information from cortex to hippocampus (Derrick, 1993).

LTP in the CA3 region differs markedly from LTP in CA1, both in the rate of induction—that is, the time over which the responses rise in amplitude—and in the duration of the enhancement. LTP rises more slowly but lasts longer in the CA3 region than in CA1. Thus these two forms of LTP differ in their temporal characteristics as well as in their neurochemical mechanisms.

In other parts of the brain, too, LTP can be induced without activating NMDA receptors. For example, in the visual cortex of adult rats, LTP can be induced in the presence of a strong antagonist of NMDA (Aroniadou, Maillis, and Stefanis, 1993). But administering blockers of other Ca^{2+} channels prevents induction of LTP. NMDA activity is known to diminish in the mature neocortex. Aroniadou, Maillis, and Stefanis (1993) conclude that with maturity, the role of the NMDA receptors becomes less important, whereas voltage-gated Ca^{2+} channels assume increasing importance in maintaining synaptic plasticity.

Induction of LTP Involves a Cascade of Neurochemical Steps

Several neurochemical steps have been identified in the induction of LTP, and we will see that some of these steps have also been implicated in other kinds of memory formation. In fact, many of these steps are seen whenever a signal leads cells to change the kind of compounds they synthesize or the rate of synthesis.

As Figure 18.17 shows, the entry of Ca^{2+} ions into neurons activates some **protein kinases**, enzymes that catalyze **phosphorylation**, the addition of phosphate groups (PO_4) to protein molecules. Phosphorylation changes the properties of many protein molecules. Several protein kinases are present in relatively large amounts in neurons, including protein kinase A (PKA), protein kinase C (PKC), calcium–calmodulin kinase (CaM kinase), and tyrosine kinase. Blockage of any of these kinases can prevent the induction of LTP. CaM kinase has the interesting property of remaining activated once it is put into that state by Ca^{2+}, even if the level of Ca^{2+} subsequently falls; only a specific enzyme can cause CaM kinase to revert to its inactive state. Thus CaM kinase could play a role in maintaining LTP. Research on learning in vertebrates shows that inhibitors of CaM kinase inhibit the formation of intermediate-term memory (ITM), whereas inhibitors

(a) Normal synaptic transmission

(b) Induction of LTP

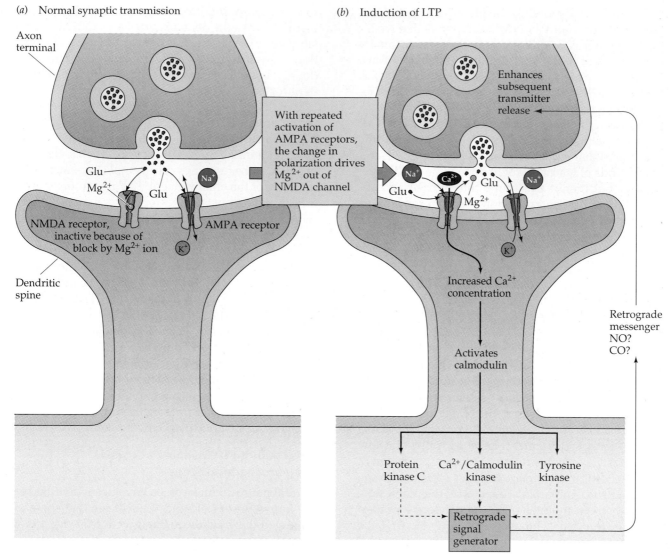

18.16 The Roles of the AMPA and NMDA Receptors in the Induction of LTP in the CA1 Region
(a) Normally the NMDA channel is blocked by a Mg^{2+} molecule and only the AMPA channel functions in excitation of the neuron. (b) With repeated activation of AMPA receptors, the depolarization of the neuron drives Mg^{2+} out of the NMDA channel and CA^{2+} ions enter. The rapid increase of CA^{2+} ions triggers processes that lead to LTP.

of PKC prevent the formation of long-term memory (LTM) (Rosenzweig et al., 1992, 1993; Serrano et al., 1994). Recently Huang and Kandel (1994) reported a similar finding concerning LTP in the CA1 region of the hippocampus: one train of 100-hertz stimuli induces a form of LTP that lasts 1 to 3 hours and is blocked by an inhibitor of CaM kinase, but not by an inhibitor of PKA or of protein synthesis; three trains of 100-hertz stimuli induce LTP that lasts 6 to 10 hours and is blocked by inhibitors of PKA or of protein synthesis. Thus, what Huang and Kandel (1995) call two

kinds of LTP resemble, respectively, ITM and LTM.

The activated protein kinases, in turn, not only catalyze the phosphorylation of proteins but also trigger the synthesis of proteins. First they lead to increases in **immediate early genes (IEGs)**, a class of genes that show rapid but transient increases in response to extracellular signals such as neurotransmitters and growth factors. Many IEGs code for transcription factors that govern the growth and differentiation of cell types by regulating the expression of other genes. Only a few studies to date have sought to relate IEGs

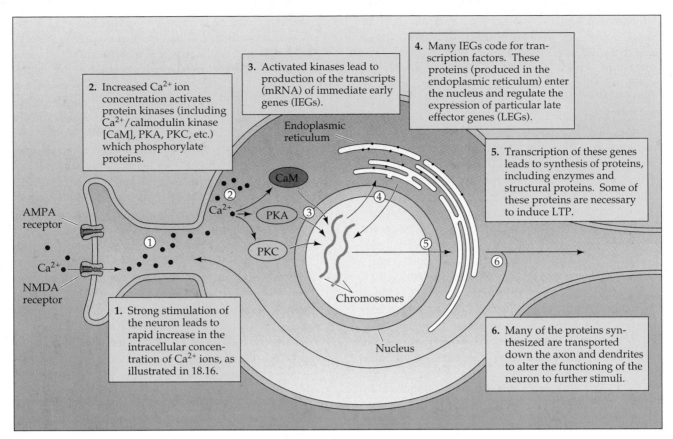

2. Increased Ca^{2+} ion concentration activates protein kinases (including Ca^{2+}/calmodulin kinase [CaM], PKA, PKC, etc.) which phosphorylate proteins.

3. Activated kinases lead to production of the transcripts (mRNA) of immediate early genes (IEGs).

4. Many IEGs code for transcription factors. These proteins (produced in the endoplasmic reticulum) enter the nucleus and regulate the expression of particular late effector genes (LEGs).

5. Transcription of these genes leads to synthesis of proteins, including enzymes and structural proteins. Some of these proteins are necessary to induce LTP.

1. Strong stimulation of the neuron leads to rapid increase in the intracellular concentration of Ca^{2+} ions, as illustrated in 18.16.

6. Many of the proteins synthesized are transported down the axon and dendrites to alter the functioning of the neuron to further stimuli.

Endoplasmic reticulum

CaM

PKA

PKC

AMPA receptor

Ca^{2+}

NMDA receptor

Chromosomes

Nucleus

18.17   Steps in the Neurochemical Cascade during Induction of LTP
This is based on LTP induction in the CA1 region of the hippocampus.

to induction of LTP. Some investigators have reported that induction of LTP is accompanied by increases in IEGs (Abraham, Dragunow, and Tate, 1991; Demmer et al., 1993), but others have concluded that activation of IEGs is neither necessary nor sufficient for the induction of LTP (Schreiber et al., 1991). This point remains to be settled.

It is clear that induction of LTP involves protein synthesis. The earlier stage(s) of LTP, lasting an hour or so, appears not to require protein synthesis, but thereafter inhibition of protein synthesis prevents longer-lasting LTP (Krug, Lössner, and Ott, 1984; Frey, Huang, and Kandel, 1993). Three hours after induction of LTP, certain proteins increase while others decrease, indicating a complex pattern of changes in proteins (Fazeli et al., 1993). Some of these changes may be involved in structural changes in synapses.

In spite of the considerable amount of research devoted to this preparation, there are still many disagreements about the processes involved in LTP. Some investigators suggest that the main changes occur in the

presynaptic terminals that show increased release of the transmitter glutamate after LTP (Dolphin, Errington, and Bliss, 1982; Skrede and Malthe-Sorenssen, 1981). Others hold that the main events are *postsynaptic*, involving increased intracellular levels of Ca^{2+} (Bekkers and Stevens, 1990; Malinow and Tsien, 1990) and exposure of greater numbers of glutamate receptors (Lynch and Baudry, 1984). Both presynaptic and postsynaptic processes may participate in LTP, and at present there seems to be no compelling evidence for the exclusive location of changes at either site. Recently evidence has accumulated that induction of LTP requires a **retrograde signal**, from the postsynaptic neuron to the presynaptic neuron. The postsynaptic site is thought to release the signal when conditions of LTP are met, and the presynaptic neuron responds to the signal by increasing transmitter release. Thus, Colley and Routtenberg (1993) speak of the pre- and postsynaptic neurons as being engaged in a "synaptic dialog" in forming LTP. Both nitric oxide (Schuman and Madison, 1991) and arachidonic acid (Lynch, Errington, and Bliss, 1989) are possible retrograde messengers.

Changes in synapse morphology have also been reported when LTP is induced both in intact animals (Lee et al., 1980) and in slice preparations (Chang and Greenough, 1984; Fifkova et al., 1982). An inhibitor of protein synthesis, anisomycin, was reported not to affect the initiation of LTP in freely moving rats but to prevent LTP from continuing more than a few hours (Krug, Lössner, and Ott, 1984). This result is consistent with studies suggesting that long-term memory, but not short-term memory, depends the synthesis of proteins in the brain, a topic we consider later in this chapter.

Some of the complexity and discrepancy in the results of experiments on long-term potentiation may come from the fact that several different phenomena seem to be involved. Reviews of the evidence suggest the existence of four or five overlapping but separable effects of prior stimulation on the amplitude of responses of hippocampal cells (Abraham and Goddard, 1985; Bliss and Collingridge, 1993). Depending how and when the experimenter measures the responses and the treatments that are used to affect them, one or another phenomenon may predominate in the results. We have also seen significant differences between LTP induced in region CA1 and LTP in CA3. Further work is needed to sort out these complex phenomena and to decide the extent to which any of them can help us understand the mechanisms of various kinds of learning.

Is LTP a Mechanism of Memory Formation?

Several reviewers support the claim that LTP is a mechanism of memory formation because of similarities between LTP and examples of learning and memory (Lynch et al., 1991; Staubli, 1995; Teyler and Discenna, 1986). As we have noted, LTP can be induced within seconds, it may last for days or weeks, and it shows a labile "consolidation" period that lasts for several minutes after induction. These properties of LTP have suggested to some investigators that LTP is a kind of synaptic plasticity that underlies certain forms of learning and memory. They have therefore sought to test this hypothesis by examining (1) whether other properties of LTP are reflected in properties of learning and memory, and vice versa, and (2) whether various treatments (for example, drugs) have similar effects on LTP and on learning and memory.

Many additional similarities between LTP and learning have emerged from this research, as the following examples show: LTP can be induced by stimulation at rates that are normal in the nervous system. There is a positive correlation between the speed with which individual rats, young or old, learn a maze and the degree to which LTP can be induced in them (Barnes, 1979). Also, allowing rats to explore a complex

environment, which improves spatial learning, is reported to produce LTP in the hippocampus (Sharp, McNaughton, and Barnes, 1983). Application of high-frequency stimulation to a hippocampal input, which produces LTP, facilitates the acquisition of eye-blink conditioning in the rabbit (Berger, 1984). Conditioning the hippocampus facilitates induction of LTP 48 hours later, and posttraining stimulation of the reticular formation enhances both conditioning and LTP and makes them last longer (Bloch and Laroche, 1984).

Apparently contradicting the last two points are reports that induction of LTP in the hippocampus of rats "saturates" the hippocampus and thus impairs the ability to acquire spatial information, although it does not disrupt the use of previously learned spatial information (McNaughton et al., 1986; Castro et al., 1989). The difference between the two sets of results may not be a contradiction, because the learning in the latter experiments is spatial, which is not the case in the studies of Berger (1984) and Bloch and Laroche (1984).

Some investigators have reported an inability to reproduce the saturation effect; recent evidence suggests that these efforts may have failed because the stimulation of the hippocampus was not sufficiently strong to involve most of the cells (Korol et al., 1993). Even a small proportion of hippocampal cells may be sufficient to process some kinds of spatial learning. Thus, while there is some evidence that LTP and spatial learning utilize the same hippocampal neurons, the issue is still not settled.

Other evidence for a similarity between LTP and learning comes from experiments in which a particular gene is disrupted to produce so-called "knockout" mice—mice in which one gene has been made nonfunctional. Two laboratories have produced knockout mice lacking one of the enzymes crucial to the LTP cascade, then studied the animals to assess their ability to learn a maze. Kandel's group (Grant et al., 1992) disrupted four different kinases in four different groups of mice. They found that hippocampal LTP was reduced only in the mice missing the kinase gene *fyn*, and that these were the only mice that showed a deficit in maze learning. This result strongly suggests that the fyn protein is important in both LTP and maze learning, and that the electrophysiological phenomenon of LTP is related to learning. The other group of investigators (Silva et al., 1992) produced knockout mice lacking the CaM kinase II gene; these mice were also slower at learning spatial relations. Interestingly, all of the knockout mice were able to learn the task eventually, indicating that none of these genes is absolutely necessary for learning.

Several drugs have been used to test for the similarity of effects on LTP and on learning. A recent review (Staubli, 1995) focuses on the effects of antagonists of the NMDA receptor on both LTP and learning. Administration of an agent that blocks the NMDA receptor prevents induction of LTP in some experiments (Huber, Mauk, and Kelly, 1995) and prevents at least some forms of spatial learning (Morris et al., 1986; Robinson et al., 1989). Inhibitors of protein synthesis have long been known to block the formation of long-term memory (Flood et al., 1975), and they have been shown to block the formation of LTP that lasts more than a few hours (Krug, Lössner, and Ott, 1984).

Such findings support the idea that LTP is a kind of synaptic plasticity that underlies or is similar to certain forms of learning and memory and that it can therefore be used to investigate the mechanisms of those forms of learning and memory. The variety of forms of LTP, however, shows that it cannot serve as a general model for learning and memory; rather, certain kinds of LTP may be responsible for certain kinds of learning and memory, but this has yet to be proved. Thus some investigators maintain the prudent doubt expressed by Bliss and Lømo in their initial paper that LTP has anything to do with normal behavior. Martinez and Derrick (1996) conclude a recent review about whether LTP is a memory mechanism by conceding that convincing proof that LTP is involved in memory does not exist; nevertheless, they believe that after 20 years of research, "LTP remains the best single candidate for the primary cellular process of synaptic change that underlies learning and memory in the vertebrate brain" (Martinez and Derrick, 1996:198).

Long-Term Depression May Be a Reversal of LTP

We noted early in this chapter that negative as well as positive changes can store information in the nervous system. Recently several investigators have shown that **long-term depression** (**LTD**) may play a role in memory (Bear and Malenka, 1994; Linden, 1994). LTD is the converse of LTP: it is a lasting *decrease* in the magnitude of responses of neurons after afferent cells have been stimulated with electrical stimuli of relatively *low* frequency. In the CA1 region of the hippocampus, induction of LTD appears to require the entry of Ca^{2+} through NMDA receptors, just as induction of LTP does. How can the entry of Ca^{2+} call for induction of both LTP and LTD? The *amount* of change of Ca^{2+} is critical. A large surge of Ca^{2+} in the postsynaptic neuron appears to trigger the induction of LTP by activating Ca^{2+}-dependent protein kinases. In contrast, small increases of postsynaptic Ca^{2+} cause induction of LTD by selectively activating the opposite kind of enzyme—protein phosphatases that catalyze the removal of phosphate groups (Lisman, 1989; Mulkey, Herron, and Malenka, 1993). Figure 18.18 diagrams the symmetrical nature of this model, in which high-frequency stimulation causes phosphorylation of a synaptic protein and low-frequency stimulation causes dephosphorylation of the same synaptic protein; the state of phosphorylation of this protein helps to control synaptic strength.

The Mammalian Cerebellum Houses the Brain Circuit for a Simple Conditioned Reflex

While many investigators studied learning in the apparently simpler nervous systems of invertebrates and others probed the phenomenon of LTP, some tried to

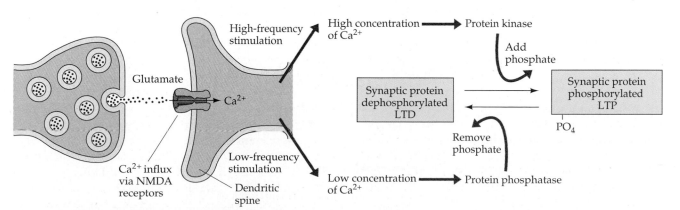

18.18 A Model of the Induction of LTP and LTD
High-frequency stimulation causes phosphorylation of a synaptic protein, and low-frequency stimulation causes dephosphorylation of the same synaptic protein; the state of phosphorylation of this protein helps to control synaptic strength. After Bear and Malenka, 1994.

define a circuit for learning in intact mammals. Psychologist Richard F. Thompson and his colleagues have been studying the neural circuitry of eye-blink conditioning since the 1970s (Thompson, 1990; Lavond, Kim, and Thompson, 1993). Much behavioral research has produced a great deal of knowledge about how the eye-blink reflex of the rabbit becomes conditioned when a puff of air to the cornea (US) follows an acoustic tone (CS). A stable conditioned response (CR) develops rapidly: the rabbit comes to blink when the tone is sounded. This response is similar to eye-blink conditioning in humans.

The basic circuit of the eye-blink reflex is simple, involving two cranial nerves and some interneurons that connect their nuclei (see Figure 18.20, where these are shown in black). Sensory fibers from the cornea run along cranial nerve V (the trigeminal nerve) to its nucleus in the brain stem. From there some interneurons go to the nucleus of cranial nerve VII (the facial nerve), which is also in the brain stem. Motor fibers in nerves VI and VII activate the muscle fibers that cause the eyelids to close.

Early in their work, Thompson and colleagues found that during conditioning, the hippocampus develops neural responses whose temporal patterns resemble closely those of the eye-blink responses (Figure 18.19). Although the hippocampal activity closely

Richard F. Thompson

(a) Single-trial analysis of the first block of conditioning trials

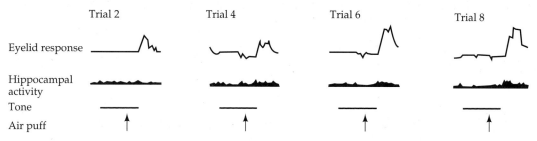

(b) Development of hippocampal response during training

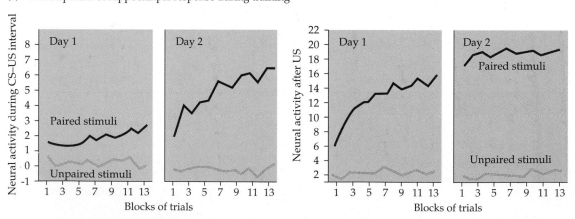

18.19 Appearance and Growth of the Hippocampal Response during Eye-Blink Conditioning

(a) Analysis of single trials during the first block of eight paired presentations of CS and US. Although the puff of air elicits a blink of the eyelid from the first trials, the hippocampus shows no response until trial 8. (b) Further growth of the hippocampal response during two days of training. The amplitude of the response grows steadily, but more slowly in the interval between CS and US (left) than after the US (right). Note the difference in scale on the y-axes of the two graphs. Animals receiving an unpaired presentation of the tone and puff of air show no response in the hippocampus. Adapted from Berger and Thompson, 1978.

parallels the course of conditioning, this result does not prove that the hippocampus is required for conditioning. In fact, destruction of the hippocampus has little effect on the acquisition or retention of the conditioned eye-blink response in rabbits (Lockhart and Moore, 1975). Therefore the hippocampus is not *required* for this conditioning. It may, however, participate in the conditioning, as indicated by the finding that abnormal hippocampal activity can disrupt the acquisition of conditioning.

Thompson and his coworkers then searched further, mapping in detail the brain structures where neurons are electrically active during conditioning. They found that learning-related increases in the activity of individual neurons are prominent in the cerebellum, in both its cortex and deep nuclei, and in certain nuclei in the pons (Figure 18.20).

Deep Cerebellar Nuclei Are Necessary for Eye-Blink Conditioning

In the cerebellum there are only negligible responses to the CS and the US before the stimuli are paired, but a neuronal replica of the learned behavioral response emerges during conditioning. These responses, which precede the behavioral eye-blink responses by 50 milliseconds or more, are found in the deep cerebellar nuclei on the same side as the eye that is trained. The interpositus nucleus appears to be particularly involved. Figure 18.21 shows how the cerebellar response predicts and corresponds with the form of the CR (McCormick and Thompson, 1984).

Lesion experiments were undertaken to determine whether the cerebellar responses are required for conditioning or whether, like the hippocampal responses, they only correlate with the CR. In an animal that had already been conditioned, destruction of the interpositus nucleus on the side that had been trained abolished the CR. (Whereas the cerebral cortex and basal ganglia govern activity on the *opposite* side, each hemisphere of the cerebellum governs motor activity on the *same* side of the body.) The CR could not be relearned on the same side, but the opposite eye could be conditioned normally. In a naive animal, prior destruction of the interpositus nucleus on one side prevented conditioning on that side. The effect of the cerebellar lesions could not be attributed to interfer-

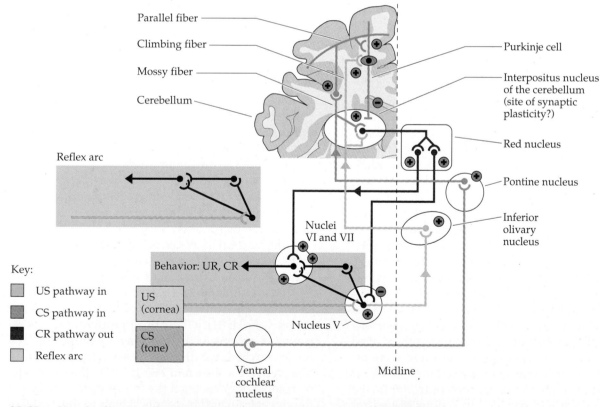

18.20   Sites in the Neural Circuit for Conditioning of the Eye-Blink Reflex
The pathway of the CS (tone) input to the cerebellum is shown in orange; the pathway of the US (corneal air puff) input is shown in yellow. The two inputs converge at both the Purkinje cells and the interpositus nucleus of the cerebellum. After Thompson, 1986.

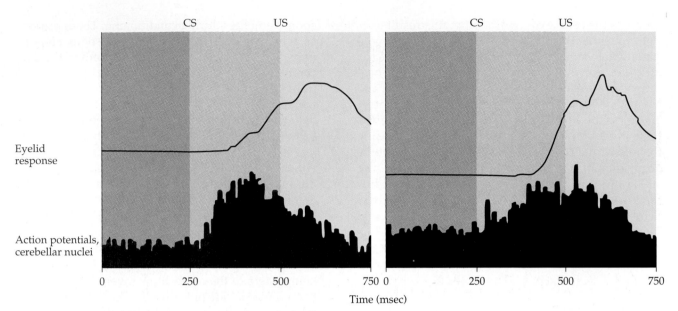

18.21 The Cerebellar Response and the Form of the Eye-Blink Reflex
Action potentials were recorded at two sites in the dentate and interpositus nuclei of the cerebellum. The cerebellar response shows the activity of several neurons summated over the trials of a training session. Note that the cerebellar activity precedes the eyelid response by about 100 msec and resembles it in form. After McCormick and Thompson, 1984.

ence with sensory or motor tracts, because the animal still showed a normal unconditioned blink when a puff of air was delivered to its eye.

The circuit of the conditioned reflex was mapped in further detail using a combination of methods: electrophysiological recording, localized lesions, localized stimulation of neurons, localized infusion of small amounts of drugs, and tracing of fiber pathways. For example, prior work showed that the inhibitory synaptic transmitter GABA is the main transmitter in the deep cerebellar nuclei. Using well-conditioned rabbits, the investigators injected a small amount of a blocking agent for GABA into the deep cerebellar nuclei on the side of the conditioned response. The injection resulted in the disappearance of the behavioral CR and of its electrophysiological neuronal replica. This effect was reversible: as the blocking agent wore off, the CR returned.

What would happen if the experimenters tried to condition naive animals while the blocking agent was present in the cerebellum and then tested them after it had worn off? In this experiment there were no signs of conditioning in six daily sessions in which the blocking agent was used; the control animals, however, which had received injections of neutral saline solution, acquired the CR by the third daily session (Krupa, Thompson, and Thompson, 1993).

Figure 18.22 compares the performances of the two groups. After training, the rabbits were given three days of rest without any injection to make sure that the effects of the drug had completely worn off. No injections were given on experimental days 7 through 10, and on these days the animals that had previously received the drug learned just as rapidly as the saline group had learned on days 1 to 3. This result showed that the series of drug administrations had not harmed the cerebellum, and that once it was free to function, the animal could acquire the eye-blink CR. On day 11 of the experiment, both groups of rabbits were given the blocking agent in the cerebellum; this treatment abolished the CR in both groups.

A third group that was included in the experiment helps us see the difference between a brain region that is required as the locus of plasticity in conditioning and one that is in the circuit of the memory trace and is required for the CR to occur, but is not the site of plasticity. This third group of rabbits received injections of the blocking agent into the red nucleus, which we discussed as a motor nucleus in Chapter 11. As shown in Figure 18.20, the red nucleus receives signals from the interpositus nucleus of the cerebellum and transmits signals to the nuclei of cranial nerves VI and VII, which control the eye-blink muscles. When the animals in this group received the

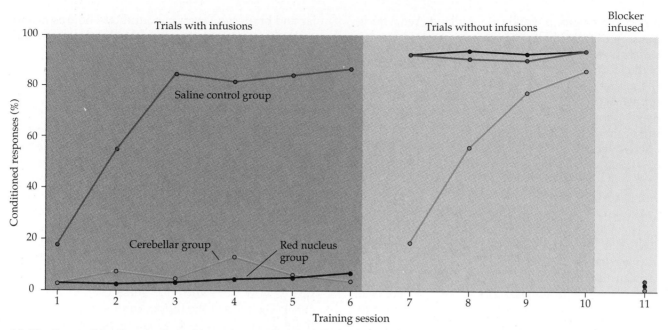

18.22 Reversible Chemical Blocking of Eye-Blink Conditioning
All animals received localized infusions before training sessions 1 to 6. The saline control group received localized infusions of neutral saline solution into the lateral cerebellum on the side of the trained eye. The cerebellar group received infusions of a GABA blocker into this site. The red nucleus group received localized infusions of the blocker into the red nucleus on the opposite side from the trained eye. No infusions were administered on days 7 to 10, and the text interprets the differential effects observed then. All animals received infusions of the GABA blocker on day 11, eliminating conditioned responses. After Krupa, Thompson, and Thompson, 1993.

blocking agent on days 1 to 6, they gave no CRs, thus showing the same behavior as the group that had received the agent in the interpositus nucleus. But on day 7, when no injection was given, the third group immediately gave CRs as soon as the CS sounded. Thus these animals had learned on days 1 to 6, but the drug had prevented them from showing the CR. In contrast, inhibition of the interpositus nucleus prevented learning, rather than just the performance of the CR. We should also mention that on days 1 to 6, all animals were given air puffs to the eye from time to time without the preceding tone; the amplitudes of the reflex blinks were the same in all groups, demonstrating that the drug did not affect the US or CR, even though the CR circuit was interrupted at either the interpositus or the red nucleus.

Based on these experiments, Thompson proposed a simplified schematic circuit for the conditioned eye-blink response (see Figure 18.20). This circuit includes the input and output parts of the eye-blink reflex circuit, shown in black at the lower left of the figure. This pathway ensures the eye-blink reflex, but additional

pathways are required to bring together information about the US and the CS. The pathway that carries information about the corneal stimulation (US), shown in yellow, goes to the inferior olivary nucleus of the brain stem, from where it is carried into the cerebellum by way of axons called climbing fibers, which go to the deep cerebellar nuclei and to cells of the cerebellar cortex, including granule cells and Purkinje cells. The same cerebellar cells also receive information about the auditory CS by a pathway (orange in Figure 18.20) through the cochlear nucleus in the brain stem and the pontine nuclei; the latter send axons called mossy fibers into the cerebellum. Efferent information controlling the CR travels along another pathway (purple), which runs from the interpositus nucleus of the cerebellum to the red nucleus. From there it goes to the cranial motor nucleus of nerves VI and VII, which control the eye-blink response.

Since the main input to the deep cerebellar nuclei comes from the cerebellar cortex, lesions of the cortex would be expected to abolish the eye-blink CR just as lesions of the deep nuclei do. Such a finding has been reported by a group working in England (Yeo, Hardiman, and Glickstein, 1985). Thompson and his associates, however, have not found lesions of the cerebellar cortex to interfere with the CR unless the lesions are very large. Perrott, Ruiz, and Mauk (1993) report that lesions of the anterior cerebellar cortex make it impossible for rabbits to acquire accurate timing of the CR. They propose that motor learning involves two sites of plasticity in the cerebellum: the CS–US association occurs at the synapses between mossy fibers and cerebellar nuclei, whereas the cerebellar cortex (synapses between granule cells and Purkinje cells) mediates temporal discrimination.

The role of the cerebellum in conditioning is not restricted to eye-blink conditioning. The cerebellum is also needed for the conditioning of leg flexion; in this task, an animal learns to withdraw its leg when a tone sounds in order to avoid a shock to the paw (Donegan et al., 1983; Voneida, 1990). On the other hand, the cerebellum is not required for all forms of conditioning of skeletal muscular responses: Thompson and colleagues have found that cerebellar lesions do not prevent operant conditioning of a treadle press response in the rabbit (Holt, Mauk, and Thompson, unpublished, cited in Lavond, Kim, and Thompson, 1993:328).

Studies with human subjects are consistent with the animal research and add further information. Patients with unilateral cerebellar lesions show normal eye-blink reflexes with both eyes, but they can acquire a conditioned eye-blink response only on the side where the cerebellum is intact (Lye et al., 1998; Papka, Ivry, and Woodruff-Pak, 1994). A recent PET study with humans who had been conditioned using the paired tone and puff of air used both behavioral intervention and the correlational approach (Logan and Grafton, 1995). During the first, control session of the experiment, PET scans were taken while subjects received an unpaired tone and puff of air to the right eye. In the second session, 1 to 6 days later, the stimuli were paired. In the third session, 2 to 7 days after the first, PET scans were made while the subjects received paired stimuli. Comparison of the scans from this third session with the first showed increased activity in several regions of the brain (Figure 18.23*a*): the right and left inferior cerebellum, anterior cerebellar vermis, left cerebellar cortex, and left cerebellar deep nuclei or pontine tegmentum; right inferior thalamus/red nucleus, right hippocampal formation, right and left ventral striatum, right cortical middle temporal gyrus, left cortex occipitotemporal fissure. Activity in some of these regions correlated significantly with conditioning behavior (Figure 18.23*b*). Thus the neural network involved in human eye-blink conditioning includes not only the cerebellar and brain stem regions found by Thompson and colleagues, but also the hippocampus, the ventral striatum, and regions of the cerebral cortex.

The Hippocampus Is Required for Some Kinds of Eye-Blink Conditioning

The hippocampus is not required for animals to acquire a simple form of eye-blink conditioning, specifically, when little or no time passes between the end of the CS and the US. But when the time intervals are longer (in what is called trace conditioning), animals from which the hippocampus has been removed are not able to form conditioned eye-blink responses (Moyer, Deyo, and Disterhoft, 1990). Removal of the hippocampus also prevents the formation of discrimination reversal conditioning, that is, conditioning in which the stimulus that previously served as CS+ is now CS–, and vice versa (Berger and Orr, 1983). The roles of the hippocampus and cerebellum in this conditioning could be interpreted as follows: the cerebellum represents the direct or obligatory circuitry required for conditioning, and the hippocampus is a modulatory circuit that can facilitate the conditioning. (Later in this chapter we will discuss how learning and memory formation are modulated.)

Points to Note about the Investigation of Brain Substrates of Aversive Classical Conditioning

Thompson and colleagues stress three points about their program of investigation of the mammalian brain substrates of classical conditioning (Lavond, Kim, and Thompson, 1993); here we add two others:

1. The investigation was deliberately restricted to a relatively simple form of conditioning, in the hope that a good understanding of simple conditioning would aid in the study of more complex forms of learning.

2. Learning involves regions of the brain other than just the cerebellum. At the very least, the hippocampus and cerebral cortex are important in more complex learning, and the amygdala appears to be involved in the learning of fear; all three regions probably are involved in aversive classical conditioning.

3. The evidence for localization of plasticity in aversive classical conditioning relies not on a single technique, but on converging results from various techniques.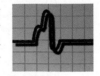

4. Research using electrophysiological recording demonstrates that brain circuits involved in learning can be located even in the complex mammalian brain.

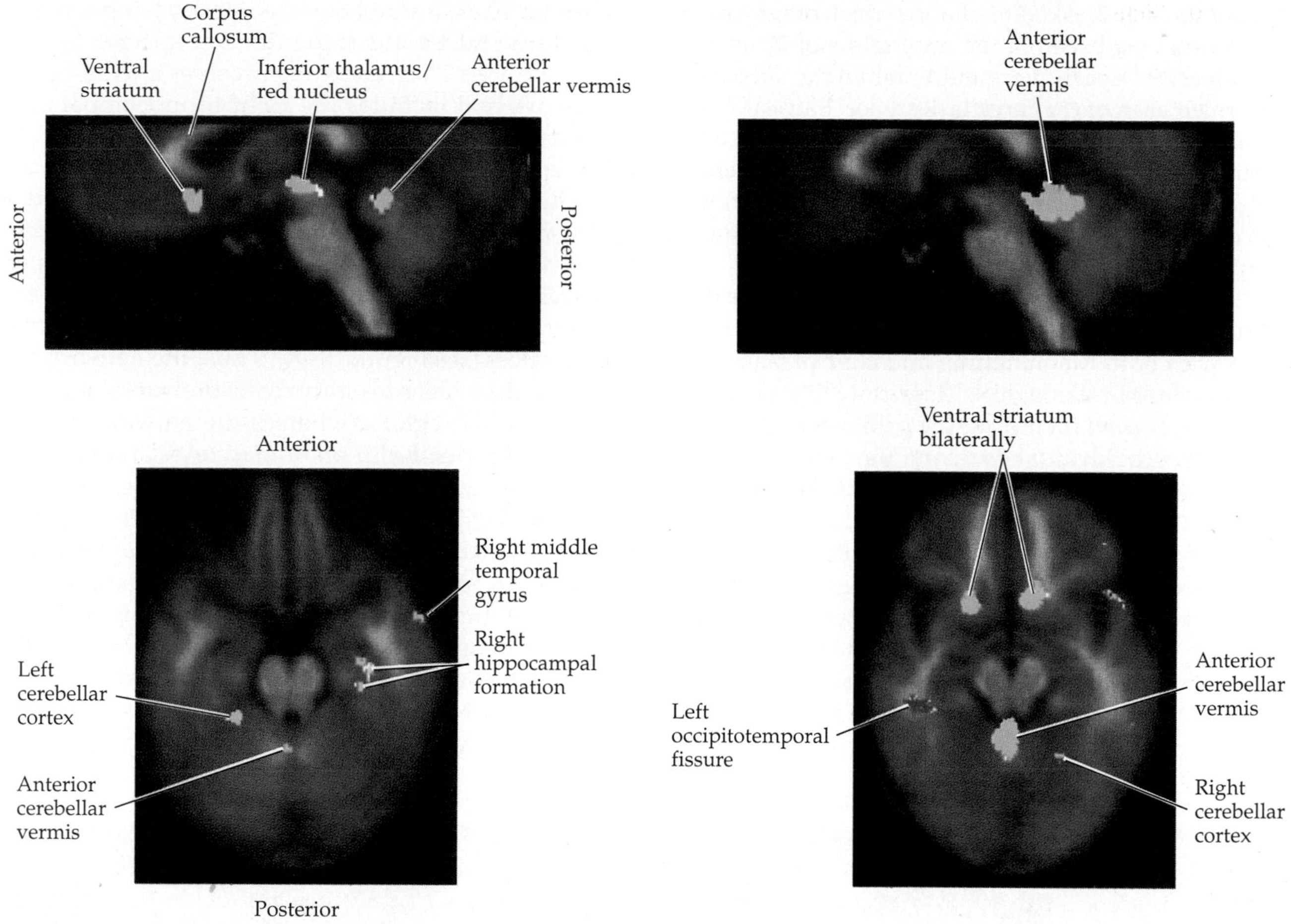

(a)   Areas showing increased activity with conditioning

Corpus
callosum

Ventral
striatum

Inferior thalamus/
red nucleus

Anterior
cerebellar vermis

Anterior

Posterior

(b)   Areas showing correlations with learning performance

Anterior
cerebellar
vermis

Anterior

Right middle
temporal
gyrus

Right
hippocampal
formation

Left
cerebellar
cortex

Anterior
cerebellar
vermis

Posterior

Ventral striatum
bilaterally

Left
occipitotemporal
fissure

Anterior
cerebellar
vermis

Right
cerebellar
cortex

**18.23   Changes in Human Brain Activity with Conditioned Eye-Blink
Responses**

(*a*) Areas showing metabolic changes versus the control condition; areas of
increased activity relative to the unpaired stimulus condition are shown in
yellow. (*Top*) Midsagittal view; (*bottom*) horizontal view. (*b*) Areas whose relative metabolic change is significantly correlated with learning performance;
positive correlations are shown in yellow. (*Top*) Midsagittal view; (*bottom*)
horizontal view. Note the negative correlation (blue) in the left occipitotemporal fissure. From Logan and Grafton, 1995.

5. In this case at least, plasticity does not occur in the
circuit of the unconditioned reflex; the reflex circuit remains unaffected, but the response can be
conditioned through a somewhat complex circuit
that is, in a sense, superimposed on the circuit of
the unconditioned reflex (see Figure 18.20).

The Cerebral Sites of Encoding
and Retrieval Can Be Localized

Noninvasive scans of brain activity can be used to reveal brain regions of extensive neural networks in-

volved in learning and memory, as we saw in the
case of eye-blink conditioning. Similarly, positron
emission tomography (PET) has been used to study
the cerebral localization of processes involved in encoding and in retrieval, as shown in a recent study
of face recognition (Grady et al., 1995).
During the encoding (acquisition) task, the
subjects were shown photographs of 32
unfamiliar faces and asked to memorize
them. Then they performed a face matching (perception) test: they were shown faces not in
the memorization set, and for each face they had to
choose the same face from another pair of faces. For

the recognition (retrieval) task, they were shown pairs of faces and asked to choose which member of the pair they had seen in the original set of 32 faces. Repeated PET scans were made while the subjects performed each of the three tasks twice. Each subject also performed a sensorimotor control task at the beginning and end of each scanning session. The cerebral blood flow during encoding and recognition was compared with that during the matching and control tasks.

During encoding, young subjects (mean age 25 years) showed increased cerebral blood flow, compared with both the matching and control tasks, in the following brain regions (Figure 18.24): the left prefrontal cortex, including the orbitofrontal, inferior, and medial frontal gyri; and the temporal cortex, extending over the middle and inferior temporal gyri. In addition, but not shown in the figure, they had increased activation in the anterior cingulate cortex. In the right hemisphere, significant activation during encoding, compared with both the matching and control tasks, was limited to the medial temporal region, including the hippocampal region and the parahippocampal gyrus (see Figure 18.24). Earlier in this chapter we saw that the pre-

frontal cortex is involved in working memory, and in Chapter 10 we learned that the inferior temporal cortex is involved in the recognition of specific forms, such as faces. Thus, encoding involves a widespread network that includes the right hippocampal and medial temporal regions and the left prefrontal cortex, among other regions.

During recognition, the young subjects showed a different pattern of enhanced activity from that displayed during encoding. The areas activated during recognition included the *right* prefrontal cortex, the right parietal cortex, and the bilateral ventral occipital cortices (see Figure 18.24). Thus, the network for recognition includes the *right* prefrontal cortex, among other regions; whereas the network for encoding includes the *left* prefrontal cortex and the right hippocampal region, among other regions.

Older subjects (mean age 69 years) were given the same series of tasks. During encoding, no brain region showed activation that exceeded that of both the matching and control tasks (see Figure 18.24). During recognition, the old people showed a significant increase in cerebral blood flow in the right prefrontal cortex, although over a less extensive region than in the young people. The old people did not

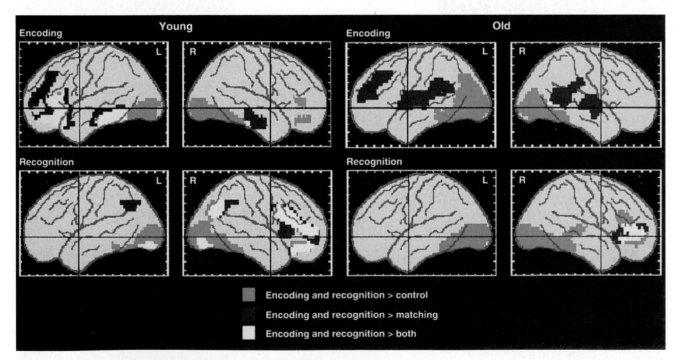

18.24   Active Brain Regions during Encoding and Recognition Tasks in Young and Old People
Lateral views of the cerebral hemispheres show regions of enhanced cerebral blood flow caused by encoding and retrieving information. From Grady et al., 1995. Courtesy of Cheryl Grady.

show the significant increases in the right parietal cortex or the bilateral inferior occipital regions that characterized the young people. Behavioral scores showed the older subjects to be significantly poorer in face recognition than the young subjects (66% versus 80% correct, respectively), but only slightly poorer in face matching.

The results of this study agree with previous observations that old people are less likely than young to use effective strategies for encoding. They also indicate that the old subjects failed to engage the appropriate neural network for encoding, which in young people includes the hippocampal formation and the anterior cingulate cortex. Furthermore, the old people failed to employ as extensive a network for recall as the young people. These conclusions hold for the average old and young subjects; as is often the case, the old subjects showed a wider spread of behavioral and blood flow values than the young subjects, and the values for some old subjects overlapped those for young subjects.

Memories of Different Durations Form by Different Neural Mechanisms

Memories differ markedly in how long they last, from iconic and short-term memories to long-term and permanent memories, as we saw in Chapter 17. Behavioral evidence suggests that memories of different lengths reflect the operation of different neural processes. For example, individuals who have no trouble forming short-term memories may have an impaired ability to form long-term memories. In the cases of habituation and sensitization, we saw earlier that the formation of relatively short-term memories in *Aplysia* involves merely neurochemical changes at existing synapses, whereas the formation of long-term memories also involves structural changes in existing synapses and changes in the number of synapses.

Since the 1950s pharmacological agents have been used extensively to study memory formation; this approach has led to many interesting discoveries and to new concepts. Unlike brain lesions or other permanent interventions, many chemical treatments are advantageous for this research because they are reversible. Chemical treatments can produce relatively brief, accurately timed effects, and subjects can be tested in their normal state both before and after treatment. Chemical agents can be given systemically or locally. Systemic administration permits the study of a whole system of widely separated neurons, such as neurons that employ a particular synaptic transmitter. Local injection into a specific brain site can be used to investigate localized processes.

Various agents appear to affect different stages of memory formation: short-term, intermediate-term, and long-term. This result has given rise to the concept of sequential neurochemical processes in memory formation. In addition, the same chemical or pharmacological agent may aid memory formation under certain conditions but impair it under other conditions, suggesting that memory formation can be modulated. We will discuss the modulation of memory formation later in this chapter.

Recall that Hebb proposed the dual trace hypothesis, according to which a learning experience sets up activity that tends to reverberate through the activated neural circuits and that holds the memory for a short period. The activity constitutes the first memory trace; if sufficient, it helps build up a stable change in the nervous system, which is a long-lasting memory trace. Electrophysiological recording from cells in the lateral frontal cortex may have found an early, active memory trace. This work indicates that maintained neural firing may hold memories for periods lasting from seconds up to a minute—from the time an animal receives a signal to be ready to give a certain response to the time the response is called for (Goldman-Rakic, 1995a; Funahashi, Chafee, and Goldman-Rakic, 1993).

Since about 1960, much research on the formation of long-term memory has centered on the hypothesis that long-term memory cannot form without increased protein synthesis during the minutes (perhaps hours) that follow training (for example, Flood et al., 1977; Davis and Squire, 1984; Rosenzweig, 1984). More recently investigators have studied the neurochemical processes involved in earlier stages of memory formation—short-term and intermediate-term memories (Gibbs and Ng, 1977; Mizumori, Rosenzweig, and Bennett, 1985; Rosenzweig et al., 1992). In the sections that follow we examine some of this research.

The Formation of Long-Term Memory Requires Protein Synthesis

Experiments to test the hypothesis that the formation of long-term memory (LTM) requires protein synthesis have employed both behavioral intervention (in the form of training) and somatic intervention (in the form of agents that inhibit protein synthesis). Training produces increased branching of dendrites and increased numbers of synaptic contacts (Black and Greenough, 1991). The enlarged outgrowths of the neurons are made, in part, of proteins. Furthermore, direct measures of protein in the cerebral cortex of rats showed a significant increase with enriched experience (Bennett, Rosenzweig, and Diamond, 1969). Experiments in the laboratory of neurochemist Steven Rose (Schleibs et al., 1983) have shown that after a chick is trained briefly, parts of its brain can be removed and the training-induced increase in protein synthesis can be followed within a tissue chamber; brain samples from control (untrained) chicks show a significantly lower rate of protein synthesis.

The other side of the story is that inhibiting the synthesis of proteins in the brain at the time of training can prevent the formation of LTM even though it does not interfere with acquisition or with retrieval during tests of short-term or intermediate-term memory. This field of investigation is a good example of the rigorous testing and elimination of alternatives that characterize an advancing area of research.

Effects of antibiotics. Many new antibiotic drugs are created each year. Some have been found to inhibit the formation of memory, but many have been abandoned for memory research because of toxic side effects. Furthermore, even strong inhibition of protein synthesis seemed to prevent memory only for rather weak training, so investigators wondered whether there was a real effect of inhibition on memory formation. Use of the protein synthesis inhibitor anisomycin helped overcome previous problems.

Anisomycin was first used in memory experiments when Schwartz, Castelluci, and Kandel (1971), studying *Aplysia*, showed that inhibiting more than 95% of protein synthesis did not affect neuronal functioning and did not affect *short-term* neural correlates of habituation or sensitization. Then anisomycin was found to prevent LTM storage in mice, although it did not affect short-term memory (Bennett, Orme, and Hebert, 1972; Flood et al., 1973). This inhibitor is an effective **amnestic** (amnesia-causing) agent at low doses; 25 times the effective amnestic dose is nonlethal. Because anisomycin is safe, it can be given in repeated doses; administering it every 2 hours keeps cerebral protein synthesis at about 10% of normal. It may seem strange that the brain can get along with protein synthesis almost completely blocked for hours, but cells contain large supplies of proteins; existing enzymes, for example, can continue directing the cell's metabolism. With repeated administration of anisomycin, Flood and coworkers (1975, 1977) demonstrated that even relatively strong training could be overcome by inhibition of protein synthesis; the stronger the training, the longer the inhibition had to be maintained to cause amnesia.

Inhibition of protein synthesis prevents formation of LTM for positive as well as negative reinforcements. When rats ran a radial maze for food rewards, pretrial administration of anisomycin did not prevent the acquisition of short-term memory, but it did prevent the formation of long-term memory (Mizumori, Rosenzweig, and Bennett, 1985). Similarly, when mice ran a Y maze for water rewards, inhibition of protein synthesis prevented LTM (Patterson, Rosenzweig, and Bennett, 1987). Thus, inhibition of protein synthesis during the period following learning prevents the formation of LTM for a wide variety of training situations, including learning for both positive and negative reinforcements and situations that involve active and passive avoidance.

Short-Term and Intermediate-Term Memories Appear to Form by Different Neurochemical Mechanisms

Even when an experience does not result in LTM, a person or animal may be able to respond correctly during a period of minutes before memory vanishes. Such short-term (STM) and intermediate-term (ITM) memories are useful in dealing with the flow of events. Since protein synthesis is not required for these brief memories, as we have just seen, what neural processes maintain them?

A hypothesis that has inspired quite a bit of research holds that memory formation consists of three sequentially linked biochemical stages. Australian psychologists Marie Gibbs and Kim Ng (1977) found evidence that memory in chicks includes at least three temporal components, which they labeled short-term, intermediate-term, and long-term. Their experiments employed a single-trial peck avoidance test: chicks pecked at a small, shiny bead coated with an aversant liquid; after a single peck they usually avoided a similar bead whether it was presented minutes, hours, or days later. (Some investigators refer to the aversant bead as "bitter," but bitter taste alone is not enough to cause chicks to form a strong LTM [Paul J. Colombo, personal communication].) Formation of memory for the unpleasant experience could be impaired if an amnestic agent was administered close to the time of training. Gibbs and Ng reported that different families of amnestic agents caused memory to fail at different times after training (Figure 18.25). The agents that caused memory failure by about 5 minutes after training were considered to prevent the formation of STM, those that caused failure about 15 minutes after training were thought to prevent the formation of ITM, and those that caused memory to fail by about 60 minutes after training were thought to be affecting LTM.

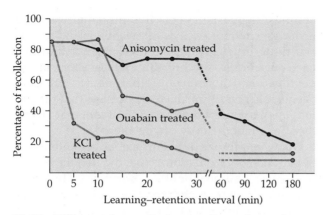

18.25 Different Amnestic Agents Cause Amnesia at Different Times After Training
Different amnestic agents are thought to impair different stages of memory. They therefore provide a means of observing the duration of the preceding stages. After Gibbs and Ng, 1977.

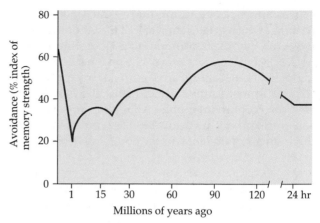

18.26 Four Components of Retention Strength After Weak Training
The components of this smoothed curve may reflect, successively, the sensory buffer, STM, ITM, and LTM. After Rosenzweig et al., 1993.

Memory Appears to Form in Stages

Gibbs and Ng (1979) also reported dips in the strength of memory of untreated chicks at about 15 minutes and 55 minutes after training. They suggested that the dips marked the times of transition between STM and ITM, and between ITM and LTM, respectively. They also found that preventing the formation of one stage of memory inhibited the formation of the following stage(s). These results support the concepts that memory forms in stages and that each stage of memory depends on the preceding one(s).

Further evidence for successive stages of memory formation comes from experiments with relatively weak training. After weak training, achieved by using a weak solution of the aversant substance, the retention function for control chicks (with no drug treatment) shows four components (Figure 18.26); these may reflect, successively, the sensory buffer (the immediate continuation of sensory input [see Figure 17.6]), STM, ITM, and LTM (Rosenzweig et al., 1993). If these do represent successive stages, then it should be possible to inhibit each of them with specific agents. The final rise in memory strength, beginning about 60 minutes after training and hypothesized to reflect LTM, was abolished by inhibitors of protein synthesis, in conformity with the hypothesis. Inhibitors of STM abolished all stages after the initial descending limb of the function (the presumptive sensory buffer), thus supporting the hypothesis that the stages are sequentially dependent. So far it has not been possible with an amnestic agent to inhibit the formation of the presumptive ITM stage after weak training.

Some Steps in the Neurochemical Cascade Underlying Memory Formation Are Reflected in the Stages of Memory Formation

Some agents that inhibit neurochemical processes also impair the formation of different stages of memory; thus, they can be used to relate the neurochemical processes to the stages of memory. Both the NMDA receptor antagonist AP5 and lanthanum chloride, which inhibits the influx of Ca^{2+} ions, prevent the formation of STM (and therefore of the succeeding ITM and LTM stages). Ouabain, which inhibits Na^+–K^+ ATPase, prevents the formation of ITM (and therefore also of LTM). Protein synthesis inhibitors, such as anisomycin, prevent the formation only of LTM. Some **calcium-dependent enzymes** that have been investigated in regard to memory are protein kinases.

Protein kinase inhibitors (PKIs) were known to be amnestic, but until recently it was not known which stage(s) of memory formation they affected. Serrano found that two classes of PKIs affect two different stages of memory formation (Rosenzweig et al., 1993; Serrano et al., 1994): PKIs that act on calcium/ calmodulin kinase (CaM kinase) but not on protein kinase C (PKC) impair the formation of ITM; those that act on PKC but not on CaM kinase impair the formation of LTM. (As noted earlier, these two kinds of PKIs have a similar differential effect on long-term potentiation in the hippocampus [Huang and Kandel, 1994].)

Not all effects of amnestic agents conform to the three predicted times of the onset of amnesia or to the stage they would be expected to affect (Rosenzweig et al., 1993). For example, the opioid leu-enkephalin causes amnesia beginning more than 4 hours after training, which is later than the LTM stage as defined by other findings. MK801, an inhibitor of NMDA receptors, causes amnesia 3 to 4 hours after training, in contrast to the almost immediate effect of the NMDA receptor antagonist AP5. Thus, unsettled issues remain, but most of the data confirm at least three stages of memory formation.

Several Model Systems for the Study of Learning and Memory Show Similar Cascades of Neurochemical and Anatomical Processes

Several other model systems have been proposed for studying the mechanisms of neural plasticity, including (1) changed responsiveness to drugs, including both tolerance and sensitization (Nestler and Duman, 1995); (2) increased susceptibility to epileptic seizures (kindling) (Post and Weiss, 1995); and (3) change in the timing of circadian rhythms by exposure to a brief light (Taylor, 1990). Without going into detail about research on these models, we should note here that the resulting findings about cellular mechanisms of plasticity show some of the same neurochemical processes as those obtained from research on conditioning in invertebrate systems, the formation of memory in vertebrates, and long-term potentiation (see Figure 18.17).

Memory Formation Can Be Modulated by Several Processes

Many agents and conditions other than those we have already discussed also affect the formation of memory. For example, the general state of arousal of an organism affects its ability to form memories; a moderate state of arousal is optimal (Bloch, 1976). Rapid-eye-movement (REM) sleep in the hours following learning has long been known to improve the formation of LTM in animals (Bloch, 1976), and investigators have recently demonstrated a similar effect in human perceptual learning (Karni et al., 1994). The emotional state immediately following the learning experience also affects the formation of memory for that experience. Specific agents that affect memory formation include stimulants (such as amphetamine and caffeine), depressants (such as phenobarbital and chloral hydrate), neuropeptides, so-called neuromodulators that affect the activity or "gain" of

neurons (including agents that elsewhere serve as neurotransmitters, such as acetylcholine and norepinephrine), drugs that affect the cholinergic transmitter system or the catecholamine transmitters, opioid peptides, and hormones. Experiments with such agents and conditions have suggested that the formation of memory can be modulated—that is, that the strength of memory can be altered.

Many conditions or agents can either enhance or impair memory formation, depending on the time or strength of treatment or other conditions. This variation implies that some biological processes are essential in the formation of memories and that others are modulatory, superimposed on the basic processes. The fact that many treatments that follow training affect memory formation supports other evidence that the cascade of events underlying memory formation takes considerable time.

Emotions Can Affect Memory Storage

Emotion appears to enhance the formation of memory, as we saw in Chapter 17. In research with humans, however, it is difficult to separate effects on memory formation from effects on attention at the time of learning or on rehearsal after the learning session. Research with animal subjects has clarified these effects and has investigated the neurochemical systems and the brain regions involved in emotional enhancement of memory formation (see reviews by McGaugh et al., 1993, 1995).

Considerable experimental research dating back to the 1960s and 1970s shows that postlearning treatments affect memory storage in rodents. For example, posttraining electrical stimulation of the brain (McGaugh, 1960) and some drugs (McGaugh and Herz, 1972) cause retrograde amnesia. Retention can be enhanced by posttraining electrical stimulation of some brain regions (Bloch, 1970), as well as by some drugs that affect neuromodulatory systems that can be activated by training experiences (Denti et al., 1970). Usually such treatments are effective if administered within minutes after training, but not if given an hour or longer after training. Effects on memory do not require that the treatments act as rewards or punishments. Substances effective in modulating memory storage include neurotransmitters and hormones such as acetylcholine, epinephrine, norepinephrine, vasopressin, the opioids, and GABA, as well as agonists and antagonists of these agents.

Several lines of evidence suggest that epinephrine affects memory formation by influencing the amygdala. Posttraining electrical stimulation of the amygdala can enhance or impair memory formation, depending on the experimental conditions. Lesions of the amygdala induced by the excitotoxin NMDA block the memory-enhancing effects of systemic injections of epinephrine (Cahill and McGaugh, 1991). Injection of epinephrine into the amygdala enhances memory formation at doses too small to be effective elsewhere in the brain. This treatment appears to cause the release of norepinephrine within the amygdala, as do emotional experiences. Injections of propranolol, a blocker of beta-adrenergic receptors, into the amygdala block the memory-enhancing effects. Opioid peptides also block the release of norepinephrine, in the amygdala and elsewhere in the brain.

From a variety of experimental findings on the effects and interactions of several families of agents—adrenergic, opioid, GABA-ergic, and cholinergic—on memory storage, McGaugh and coworkers (1993) propose the following model (Figure 18.27): The amygdala influences memory formation in certain brain regions to which it sends axons, including the hippocampus and the caudate nucleus. The amygdala integrates the influences of several neuromodulatory systems that act on it, including adrenergic, opioid, GABA-ergic, and cholinergic. Because several different neurotransmitter systems are involved in this model, a number of agents can affect the influences of emotion on memory formation; some of these agents and their synaptic sites of activity are shown in Figure 18.27. An intact amygdala is not required for either the acquisition or the long-term storage of memory, although it may be a temporary locus of memory storage for a few days after training. The long-term storage of memory may occur in brain regions influenced by amygdala activity.

The amygdala appears to play more than one role in memory formation. We saw in Chapter 15 evidence that the amygdala may be required for fear conditioning. In Chapter 17 we saw that the amygdala appears to play a special role in learning about rewards and punishments. In addition to these *direct* roles in some kinds of learning, the amygdala can *modulate* learning in which other brain regions play more direct roles. Thus, it can enhance declarative learning mediated by the hippocampus, and it can enhance nondeclarative learning mediated by the

James L. McGaugh

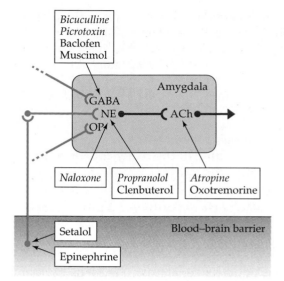

18.27   A Model of Neuromodulatory Interactions in the Regulation of Memory Storage
The diagram shows sites of activity of drugs that affect different neuromodulatory and neurotransmitter systems in the amygdala. ACh = acetylcholine; GABA = gamma aminobutyric acid; NE = norepinephrine; OP = opioids. Antagonists of the transmitters are shown in italics; agonists are not italicized. Adapted from McGaugh, 1993.

caudate nucleus.

Whether the amygdala can, reciprocally, be modulated in its memory-forming activity by regions such as the hippocampus and the caudate nucleus does not yet appear to have been explored. Earlier, however, we saw indications that the hippocampus, as well as playing a direct role in formation of declarative memories, can modulate the activity of the cerebellum in eye-blink conditioning.

Some Brain Measures Correlate with Age-Related Impairments of Memory

In Chapter 17 we saw that some measures of learning and memory decline with aging, even when there is no obvious impairment of the nervous system. Investigators are trying to find changes in the nervous system that may explain such age-related declines in learning and memory. Some of this work is being done with laboratory animals, in which both behavioral measures and brain measures can be obtained from the same individuals. This method is much more powerful than obtaining behavioral and brain measures in separate groups and trying to draw inferences from group means, as earlier studies had done. Also beginning to appear are studies that correlate changes in the anatomy of the human brain with age-related impairment in memory. We will review one such study with laboratory rats and one with human subjects. Recall also the PET study mentioned earlier on encoding and retrieval of memory for faces in young and old subjects (see Figure 18.24).

Learning-Impaired Aged Rats Show a Localized Decline in the Acetylcholine System

Some studies of age-related changes focus on brain regions that provide inputs to the hippocampal formation. One such region is the **septal complex**, which provides input from subcortical structures to the hippocampus. The neurons of the septal complex are located in the medial septal nucleus and the vertical limb of the diagonal band (Figure 18.28). Many of these neurons use acetylcholine as their transmitter. These regions of the septohippocampal pathway, along with neurons of the nucleus basalis, appear to be involved in the neuropathology of Alzheimer's disease (McGeer et al., 1984; Rossor et al., 1982), and

they have also been implicated in declines of memory associated with normal aging (Drachman and Leavitt, 1974).

Recent experiments by Gallagher, Naaghara, and Burwell (1995) compare brain measures in two groups of aged rats: (1) those that perform about as well as young rats on tests of learning and memory, and (2) those that show impairment on these tests. Rats of three age groups—young (4 to 7 months), middle-aged (16 to 18 months) and aged (25 to 29 months)—were trained on a water maze. Special measures of performance taken on every fifth trial showed the number of animals that had reached a designated level of performance (the criterion) by that trial (Figure 18.29). Most young rats reached criterion by the second trial, most middle-aged rats by the third trial, and most aged rats by the fourth trial. No young rat required more than four trials, but some aged rats did not reach criterion by the sixth trial. However, more than one-fourth of the aged rats reached criterion by the second trial and thus performed as well as the young rats. The aged rats showed much greater variability in their scores than did the young rats, as has been found in many other studies.

The investigators then measured the activity of the enzyme choline acetyltransferase (ChAT) in the septal region; this enzyme catalyzes the synthesis of acetylcholine. Any rats that showed pathology in the gross anatomy of the nervous system were eliminat-

Frontal section through
the septal complex

Corpus
callosum

Cerebral
cortex

Caudate
Putamen

Septal
complex

Diagonal   Optic
band   nerve

18.28.   The Septal Region in the Rat
This is a site of studies of changes related to defects in memory that occur with aging.

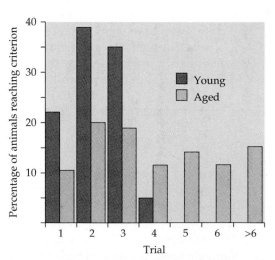

18.29   Performance of Young and Aged Rats in the Water Maze
All young rats reached criterion by the fourth test trial; many aged rats required more trials to reach criterion, but some were as quick to learn as the young rats. After Gallagher, et al., 1995.

ed from the study. ChAT activity in the septal region was as high in aged rats that performed well as it was in young rats, but the aged rats that performed poorly showed significantly lower ChAT activity than the unimpaired aged rats or the young rats. ChAT activity decreased not intrinsically with age, but only when aging was associated with impaired performance. This study thus suggests (but does not prove) that the decrease of ChAT *causes* impaired performance with age. Further research may reveal more conclusively the factors that lead to impairment and may suggest interventions that can preserve cognitive functions during aging.

In Humans, Age-Related Decline in Memory Correlates with Shrinkage of the Hippocampal Formation

A recent study of medically healthy and cognitively normal people, aged 55 to 87, sought to determine whether mild impairment in memory is specifically related to reduction in size of the hippocampal formation (HF) or is better explained by generalized shrinkage of brain tissue (Golomb et al., 1994). The loss of HF tissue has been reported in mild cases of Alzheimer's disease and in elderly individuals with cognitive impairment (Convit et al., 1993; de Leon et al., 1993; Killiany et al., 1993), but it was unclear to what extent atrophy of the HF could account for the milder decline in memory that many neurologically healthy older people experience. In this study, volunteers took a series of memory tests and were scored for both immediate recall and delayed recall; the delays between learning and recall ranged from 5 to 30 minutes. Ten coronal magnetic resonance images (MRI) for each subject were measured for three variables (see Figure 4.22):

1. Volume of the HF.

2. Volume of the supratemporal gyrus. This region was chosen because it is close to the HF and is known to shrink with age but has not been implicated in memory.

3. Volume of the subarachnoid cerebrospinal fluid— that is, the fluid-filled space between the meninges that line the interior of the skull and the surface of the brain. This volume yields a measure of overall shrinkage of the brain.

Immediate memory showed very little decline with age, but delayed memory did decline. When effects of sex, age, intelligence, and overall brain atrophy were eliminated statistically, HF volume was the only brain measure in this study that correlated significantly with the delayed memory score. Of course,

brain regions not included in this study may also correlate with memory, so other areas of the brain should be included in future experiments. Furthermore, the techniques used in this experiment were unable to measure small regions, such as the entorhinal cortex, that animal experiments show to be important for memory; the roles of such regions in aging should also be investigated as more refined anatomical techniques become available.

Can Effects of Aging on Memory Be Prevented or Alleviated?

The hippocampus is more susceptible than most brain regions to some kinds of pathology. It can be attacked by certain kinds of encephalitis, and it is easily injured by hypoxia (lack of oxygen), which may occur during major surgery. In Chapter 15 we saw that glucocorticoids—adrenal hormones secreted during stress—can damage the hippocampus, which is particularly rich in glucocorticoid receptors. Experiments with rats show that early handling, as opposed to isolation, lowers the concentration of glucocorticoids in adults and retards signs of aging of the hippocampus (Sapolsky, 1993). Rats raised in an enriched condition (EC), as opposed to those in an isolated condition (IC), have lower basal levels of corticosterone and, when challenged by a stressful situation, show a more rapid return of glucocorticoids to low basal levels (Black et al., 1989; Mohammed et al., 1993). Thus, adequate early experience may help protect the hippocampus.

Some research focuses on whether decreased production of nerve growth factor (NGF) causes decline of the hippocampus (Hefti and Mash, 1989). Rats with EC experience show a greater expression of NGF in the hippocampus than do IC rats (Mohammed et al., 1993; Ottoson et al., 1994). On the basis of these results, investigators in some clinical studies are infusing NGF into the brains of Alzheimer's patients (Nordberg, 1993; Seiger et al., 1993) in an attempt to prevent or alleviate impairment to the hippocampus and thus preserve memory.

Although it does not pinpoint the hippocampus, longitudinal research with people indicates that enriched experience throughout life can help reduce the risk of cognitive decline in old age. Schaie (1994), summarizing a 35-year-long study of more than 5000 individuals, lists the following among seven factors that reduce the risk of "normal" cognitive decline:

1. Living in favorable environmental circumstances (for example, above-average education, occupational pursuits that involve high complexity and

low routine, above-average income, and the maintenance of intact families).

2. Involvement in activities typical of complex and intellectually stimulating environments (for example, extensive reading, travel, attendance at cultural events, continuing education activities, and participation in clubs and professional associations).

3. "Being married to a spouse with high cognitive status" (Schaie, 1994:310).

Enriched experience may also cushion the brain and intellectual function against decline in old age. Masliah and colleagues (1991) report that loss of synapses correlates strongly with the severity of symptoms in Alzheimer's disease. Enriched experience produces richer neural networks in the brains of all species that have been studied in this regard, as we noted earlier in this chapter. If similar effects occur in humans, as seems likely, then this may set up reserves of connections that protect intellectual function from Alzheimer's disease.

To What Extent Have the Ten Challenges Been Met?

In Chapter 17 we stated ten major challenges for attempts to explain learning and memory in biological terms. Let's review how well investigators have been able to respond to these challenges.

1. *How can very large amounts of information be stored in the nervous system?*

Information is stored in the nervous system in terms of changes at synapses. Because the nervous system contains enormous numbers of synapses, even in relatively simple animals, it can store large amounts of information. Furthermore, there are several different ways to encode the strength of synaptic connections. Thus, the capacity for memory storage is enormous.

2. *How can at least some memories be stored rapidly in the nervous system yet last a lifetime?*

Memory formation starts very rapidly and easily, at least in some cases, because a brief

experience can initiate a cascade of neuro-chemical events that leads to long-term, self-perpetuating changes in neurons. Nevertheless, full consolidation of long-term memories takes considerable time, and the strength of memory can be modulated by events during the consolidation period.

3. *Which proposed distinctions among kinds of learning and memory have been confirmed by biological research?*

Some distinctions among kinds of learning and memory are confirmed both by clinical cases and by animal experiments in which one kind of learning or memory is impaired while another kind is spared. Confirmed distinctions include short-term versus long-term memories, declarative versus nondeclarative memories, and episodic versus semantic memories.

4. *Can neuroscience research provide adequate models for even relatively simple kinds of learning, such as conditioning, which involves learning relations and predictability among events and which does not require close temporal pairing of stimuli?*

It does not seem possible to account fully for the phenomena of conditioning with a model that depends solely on synaptic processes, but models based on neural circuitry may be able to do so.

5. *Are the different dimensions (or attributes) of memory (for example, space, time, sensory perception, response, and affect) processed in separate brain regions? If so, how are the different attributes of memory assembled into a unified experience during retrieval?*

The different dimensions (or attributes) of memory appear to be processed in separate brain regions, because lesions of different regions impair memories for which specific dimensions are salient. During retrieval, the assembly of different attributes of a memory into a unified experience may involve neural linkages (cell assemblies) formed because the responses to different attributes were activated simultaneously.

6. *With practice, information processing often becomes easier and more automatic. Do the neural circuits and brain regions involved thus change?*

Noninvasive monitoring of activity in the human brain during repeated or novel performances indicates that the practicing of information processing changes the underlying neural circuits and brain regions (see Figure 17.1).

7. *Do species that differ in their needs to learn and remember according to their ecological niches have different neural mechanisms of learning and memory?*

Some species that differ in their needs to learn and remember have been found to differ in neural mechanisms of learning and memory. For example, birds that cache food have a larger hippocampus than related species that do not cache food.

8. *By what mechanisms can posttraining conditions modulate the strength of memory?*

Posttraining stimulation can activate brain regions, such as the amygdala, that enhance the activity of other regions, such as the hippocampus and the caudate nucleus, which mediate the formation of declarative and nondeclarative

memories, respectively. Thus, the neural activity that leads to memory formation can be more intense and/or last longer.

9. *How can memories be retrieved accurately and rapidly enough to serve ongoing behavior? How can retrieval be effective not only in the original situations in which memories were acquired but also in novel contexts?*

Even in animals with large and varied stores of memory, memories are retrieved accurately and rapidly because activation of part of a memory circuit can lead to activation of the whole circuit. Since only part of the original pattern of stimulation is required for effective retrieval, memories can be used not only in the original situations in which they were acquired but also in contexts that are somewhat different. This flexibility can yield not just recall or reenactment of past experiences and actions, but also new combinations—*re*-collections—of information.

10. *Are the mechanisms of learning and memory basically the same in all animals, or are they different, suggesting that the behavioral similarities represent convergent evolution in response to similar environmental pressures?*

Neural mechanisms of learning and memory have not yet been studied in enough species and families of animals to provide a clear answer to this question, but among those that have been investigated, the mechanisms of synaptic storage of information are rather similar. This similarity suggests that in most species, memory storage uses parts of the same cascade of neurochemical events that extend from initial stimulation to protein synthesis.

Summary

1. Memory storage has long been hypothesized to involve changes in neural circuits. Research since the 1960s has demonstrated both functional and structural synaptic changes related to learning.

2. Much current research on neural changes related to learning and memory is based on two hypotheses stated by D. O. Hebb in 1949: (1) The functional relationship between neuron A and neuron B changes when A frequently takes part in exciting B. (2) Any two cells or systems of cells that are repeatedly active at the same time tend to become "associated"; that is, activity in one facilitates activity in the other.

3. An early indication that training affects brain measures was the finding that formal training or enriched experience in rats leads to structural changes, including alterations in the number and size of synaptic contacts and in the branching of dendrites.

4. Mechanisms of two kinds of nonassociative learning, habituation and sensitization, have been studied in the relatively simple nervous system of the mollusc *Aplysia*, especially at identified neurons of the abdominal ganglion. Habituation of the gill-withdrawal response reduces the influx of Ca^{2+} ions and transmitter release at presynaptic endings and thereby decreases excitatory postsynaptic potentials. Long-term habituation causes a decrease in the number and size of synaptic contacts.

5. Sensitization of the gill-withdrawal response leads to changes in presynaptic K^+ and Ca^{2+} channels that cause increased release of transmitter and increased EPSPs. Long-term sensitization causes an increase in the number and size of synaptic contacts.

6. Conditioning in *Aplysia* leads to changes in the same kinds of ion channels as in sensitization. Conditioning to a light stimulus in another mollusc, *Hermissenda*, causes changes in different kinds of ion channels and in membrane potentials. Mechanisms of conditioning in the fruit fly *Drosophila* have been studied by genetic techniques. Mutants that learn or remember poorly have biochemical deficits that are related to steps that appear to function in the *Aplysia* system.

7. The apparent advantages of *Aplysia* for research on mechanisms of learning and memory formation have recently been challenged on several counts: (1) The gill-withdrawal response is a heterogeneous collection of action patterns, each of which is under somewhat different neural control. (2) When the CNS is inactivated, the gill-withdrawal response still occurs, mediated by small, peripheral neurons that are poorly suited for neurophysiological research. (3) Even in the abdominal ganglion, about 200 neurons participate in the gill-withdrawal response, rather than just

a few, and these neurons also participate in controlling other behaviors, probably in a large, distributed network.

8. Long-term potentiation (LTP) of neural responses is a lasting increase in amplitude of the response of neurons caused by brief high-frequency stimulation of their afferents. It can be studied in intact animals or in isolated slices of brain tissue; the tissue slice preparation favors electrophysiological and neurochemical investigations. Some of the many different forms of LTP may be components of or models for various kinds of learning. Long-term depression (LTD) may be a reversal of LTP.

9. Conditioning of the eye-blink response in the rabbit is crucially dependent on the cerebellum on the same side of the head; the hippocampus may facilitate acquisition of this response. The cerebellar cells show little initial response to the US or the CS, but during conditioning a neuronal replica of the learned behavioral response emerges along with the CR. Inactivation of the cerebellum on the same side of the head as the stimulus during training prevents conditioning. Eye-blink conditioning in humans involves not only cerebellar and brain stem regions, but also the hippocampus and regions of the cerebral cortex, as revealed by noninvasive recordings.

10. Locations of cerebral activation during encoding and retrieval of information are being studied by noninvasive recordings. Encoding involves the left prefrontal cortex, among other regions; recognition involves the right prefrontal cortex, among other regions. Old subjects have less efficient encoding and use a less extensive neural network than do young subjects.

11. Neurochemical mechanisms are being investigated for successive stages of memory formation: short-term memory (STM), intermediate-term memory (ITM), and long-term memory (LTM). Each stage appears to be linked to a different part of the cascade of neurochemical events that underlie memory formation. LTM appears to require protein synthesis in the posttraining period: training induces increased synthesis of protein in certain brain regions, and blocking protein synthesis prevents the formation of LTM, although it does not prevent learning, or the formation of STM or ITM.

12. STM and ITM formation may depend on two different mechanisms of polarization of neurons. Different drugs that affect these mechanisms can cause specific failure at one or the other time period. The stages of memory formation appear to be sequentially linked, because failure of one stage causes failure of the succeeding stage.

13. Memory formation can be modulated (facilitated or impaired) by neural states and by a variety of agents, including stimulants, depressants, certain neurotransmitters, opioid peptides, hormones, and sensory stimulation.

14. A variety of findings suggest that a number of neural structures and mechanisms are involved in learning and memory. Different brain circuits and different neurochemical mechanisms may be found for such different aspects as habits versus memories, associative versus nonassociative learning, different attributes of memory, and different stages of memory formation.

15. Among the species in which neural mechanisms of memory storage have been studied, the mechanisms

have been found to be similar, though not identical. This similarity suggests that learning and memory formation use parts of the basic cascade of neurochemical events that extends from initial stimulation of neurons to protein synthesis.

16. Some neurochemical and neuroanatomical measures correlate with declines in learning and memory that occur in some, but not all, elderly subjects. The biological changes occur only in those subjects who show behavioral decline.

17. The incidence of memory impairments in old age can be reduced by adequate early environment and continuing enriched experience.

Recommended Reading

Lavond, D. G., Kim, J. J. and Thompson, R. F. 1993. Mammalian brain substrates of aversive classical conditioning. *Annual Review of Psychology*, 44: 317–342.

Martinez, J. L. and Derrick, B. E. 1996. Long-term potentiation and learning. *Annual Review of Psychology* 47: 173–203.

Martinez, J. L. and Kesner, R. P. (eds.) 1991. *Learning and Memory: A Biological View.* 2nd ed. Academic Press, New York.

McGaugh, J. L., Weinberger, N. M. and Lynch, G. (eds.) 1995. *Brain and Memory: Modulation and Mediation of Neuroplasticity.* Oxford University Press, New York.

Rose, S. P. 1992. *The Making of Memory: From Molecules to Mind.* Anchor Books-Doubleday, New York.

Squire, L. R. and Butters, N. (eds.) 1992. *Neuropsychology of Memory.* 2nd ed. Guilford Press, New York.

David Hockney, *Steve Cohen, Ian, Gary, Lindsay, Doug, Anthony, + Ken, Los Angeles, March 8, 1982*

- *There Are Many Ideas about the Evolution of Speech and Language*

- *Language Disorders Result from Region-Specific Brain Injuries*

- *Electrical Stimulation of the Brain Provides Information about Brain Organization of Language*

- *Functional Neuroimaging Portrays Brain Organization for Speech and Language*

- *The Left Brain Is Different from the Right Brain*

- *The Frontal Lobes of Humans Are Related to Higher-Order Aspects of Cognitive and Emotional Functions*

- *The Anatomy of the Frontal Lobe Forms a Basis for Understanding Its Complex Roles*

- *Spatial Perception Deficits Follow Some Types of Parietal Lobe Injury*

- *Some Functions Show Recovery Following Brain Injury*

CHAPTER 19 Language and Cognition

Orientation

Inspection of the week's best-seller list confirms the impression that only humans write books, though chimps may dabble in paint, and rats may occasionally eat books. By this and many other measures, human mental life is distinctive in the animal world, and the biological foundations of these abilities, especially language, are beginning to be known. Clues to the workings of the brain related to human cognition come from individuals with brain disorders, and from hemispheric differences in the brain functions of normal individuals. Specific brain regions are related to particular classes of cognitive disorders, especially of language. Imaging techniques such as PET provide interesting views of the brain during cognitive states.

In the late nineteenth century, the neurologist Paul Broca discovered that lesions in the left hemisphere impair speech and language. More than a hundred years later, studies of normal humans at all ages still provide us with interesting ideas about brain organization and cognition. Starting with simple observations of handedness, we readily note an asymmetry of brain mechanisms. Only 5 to 10% of humans are left-handed. Do these individuals differ from right-handed people in functional organization of the cerebral hemispheres? Many investigators point to a large range of hemispheric differences in complex cognitive functions. Extreme arguments suggest that within a single brain there are two forms of consciousness that may vie with each other for expression. In this chapter we seek clues about brain processes and structures involved in human mental life.

There Are Many Ideas about the Evolution of Speech and Language

There are 5,000 to 10,000 languages in the world and countless local dialects. All these languages have similar basic elements, and each is composed of a set of sounds and symbols that have distinct meanings. These elements are arranged in distinct orders according to rules characteristic of that language. Thus, anyone who knows the sounds (**phonemes**), symbols, and rules (**grammar**) of a particular language can generate sentences that convey information to others with similar knowledge. The acquisition of language in children is remarkably consistent across all human languages. The ability to produce language seems to be inherent in the biological structure of human brains.

Over the centuries, scholars have speculated about the origins of language, but data are scarce. The oldest written records available are clay tablets only about 6000 years old. The absence of older records has promoted a sense of mystery and elaborate tales about the beginnings of language. At one point more than a hundred years ago, the French Academy of Sciences banned speculation about the origin of languages, claiming that such speculation was fruitless and incapable of being verified. Nevertheless, a recently revived notion is that speech and language originally developed from gestures, especially those involving facial movements. Even today, hand movements often accompany speech. Anthropologist Gordon Hewes (1973) suggested that gestures came under voluntary control early in human history and became an easy mode of communication before the emergence of speech. Perhaps tongue and mouth movements slowly came to replace grosser body movements. In time, sounds connected to these tongue and mouth movements may have provided the substrate of speech. Other speculations note that primitive humans were surrounded by sounds. Sounds caused by the wind, such as the rustling of leaves, or vocalizations by other animals are always part of our surroundings. Human imitations of these sounds might have formed the beginning of vocal communication, which, in time, came to be speech.

Some Nonhumans Engage in Elaborate Vocal Behavior

Chirps, barks, meows, songs, and other sounds are among the many produced by nonhuman animals.

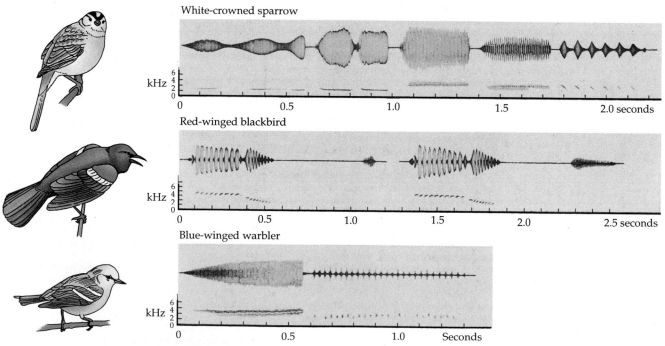

19.1 Songs of Three Bird Species
For each species, the top trace shows the exact sound pattern detected by a sensitive microphone. The bottom trace shows this same pattern analyzed by a sound spectrograph which reveals the amount of energy in different sound frequencies at each moment. After Greenewalt, 1968.

Many mammals, especially primates, have a large repertoire of species-typical vocalizations that seem to be related to distinct situations significant for adaptive behavior. Many of these sounds, especially calls that separate species or signal readiness to mate, accompany reproductive behavior. Other vocalizations alert the group to danger. Could the vocal behavior of nonhuman animals be related to the biological history of human speech and language? Are some attributes of nonhuman vocal behavior akin to human speech? We will explore these questions by focusing on the songs of birds and the sounds of nonhuman primates.

Bird song.   Many birds sing pleasant tunes, and these songs offer some intriguing analogies to human speech. Bird songs vary in complexity; some repeat a simple basic unit, while others are more elaborate (Figure 19.1). The intricate patterning of some songs suggests a connection to human speech. Parallels between human speech and bird song include the importance of early experience and the similarities of neural mechanisms controlling sound production. No investigator believes that bird song is an evolutionary *precursor* to human speech. Rather, the hope is that bird song can provide an interesting analogy that could be useful as an experimental tool. Peter Marler of the University of California at Davis has been an influential proponent of this viewpoint (Marler, 1970.)

Some birds have simple vocal behavior that is not affected by early deafening or by rearing in isolation; ring doves are an example (Nottebohm, 1987). In contrast, song development in canaries, zebra finches, and white-crowned sparrows, and many other species depends on exposure to sounds at particular developmental stages—much as human speech does (De-Voogd, 1994). Only males of such species sing, and the acquisition of song involves several distinct stages: (1) an initial exposure to the song of a tutor, (2) a period of successive approximation of the produced song to the stored model, and (3) the fixing or crystallization of the song in a permanent form. Song learning is complete by sexual maturity (90 days). These birds show quite abnormal song if they are deafened during the second stage before they have learned how to produce the final song. Male songbirds raised in acoustic isolation also fail to develop a normal song (Figure 19.2). However, if such isolated birds are exposed to tape recordings of species-typical vocalizations during an early "critical" period, they acquire normal song; if the birds are exposed to taped songs only later in life, the song acquired is abnormal. When a bird is exposed to synthetic songs, that are composed

Peter Marler

of notes both of the same species and of another, it copies only the song of its own species (Marler, 1991; Marler and Peters, 1982). There is an innate preference for the species' own song.

SWAMP SPARROW   SONG SPARROW

Normal song

Isolate song: hearing intact

Isolate song: deafened before singing

19.2   Effects of Isolation on Bird Song
(*Top*) Sonograms of the typical adult song patterns of two sparrow species. (*Middle*) Songs produced by males reared in isolation. (*Bottom*) Songs produced by males deafened in infancy. Either form of early auditory isolation results in abnormal song, but note that the two species still produce different patterns. Deafening has a more profound effect because the animal is prevented from hearing its own song production as well as that of other males. After Marler and Sherman, 1983, 1985.

The zebra finch song system in the brain and periphery has been well described as a series of brain nuclei and their connections (DeVoogd, 1994; Arnold and Schlinger, 1993; Figure 19.3). Lesions of some components of this circuit during *development* result in severe song deficits; similar lesions during *adulthood* may not affect song production. In Chapter 12 we discussed the role of hormones in the neural development of birdsong circuitry. Song development is paralleled by changes in the sizes and organization of these nuclei. Regions of the brain that control song are larger in individual birds that have more elaborate songs. Furthermore, comparisons of different species of songbirds reveal that larger song repertoires are related to larger control regions in the brain (Brenowitz and Arnold, 1986). Brain studies of bird song now include molecular genetics. Researchers identified a gene (named *ZENK*) that is expressed in some nerve cells when a male canary or zebra finch is exposed to the songs of other males of its species (Mello, Vicario, and Clayton, 1992). Gene expression is noted in a region of the bird's brain that had not been thought to be important for song processing or production. This finding will help researchers chart the sequence of steps in the brain as a bird learns the songs of its species.

Some birds show a striking similarity to humans in the neurology of vocal control. The sound-production machinery of birds consists of a voice organ, the **syrinx**, from which sound originates. Changes in membranes of this organ are produced by adjacent muscles innervated by the right and left hypoglossal nerves—cranial nerves that control the musculature of the neck. When these nerves are cut, the effects on song differ markedly depending on whether the right or the left nerve is cut. Cutting the right hypoglossal nerve produces almost no change in song. Cutting the left hypoglossal nerve produces a virtually silent bird; such birds "look like actors in silent cinema

film" (Nottebohm, 1987). All the correct body movements are made, but no sound comes out. This observation indicates left dominance of vocal-control mechanisms in these birds.

Peripheral dominance is matched by differences in brain hemispheres. Fernando Nottebohm (1980) has mapped the vocal-control centers of the canary brain (Figure 19.3), showing that lesions of the vocal-control regions in the left hemisphere markedly impair production of song; singing becomes unstable and monotonous. But minimal changes are seen following lesions in right-hemisphere structures. There is an interesting parallel to recovery from human language impairment following brain injury: In birds with damage to the left hemisphere, some song elements are recovered months after lesions as the right hemi-

Fernando Nottebohm

sphere takes over vocal control. As we'll discuss later in this chapter, cortical lesions are also more likely to disrupt human speech if they occur in the left hemisphere (Table 19.1).

Some investigators have expressed reservations about viewing the localization of bird song to one hemisphere as analogous to human speech lateralization (Konishi, 1985). One suggestion is that lateralization in songbirds includes peripheral factors. Examination of the syrinx reveals that the left side is larger than the right. Further, studies of hemispheric asymmetry in the sizes of vocal-control nuclei in the brain show only a small difference for the nucleus of the hypoglossal nerve, but no difference for any oth-

19.3   Vocal Control Centers of the Songbird Brain
HVC, higher vocal center; LMAN, lateral magnocellular nucleus of anterior neostriatum; RA, nucleus robustus of the archistriatum; X, area X of the locus parolfactorium; n XII ts, nucleus of the XIIth cranial nerve. From Arnold, 1980

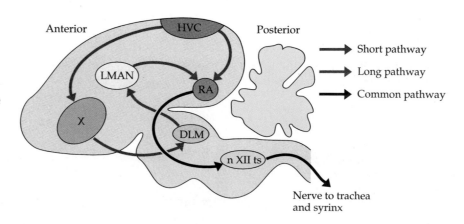

Table 19.1
Proposed Cognitive Modes of the Two Cerebral Hemispheres in Humans

LEFT HEMISPHERE	RIGHT HEMISPHERE
Phonetic	Nonlinguistic
Sequential	Holistic
Analytic	Synthetic
Propositional	Gestalt
Discrete temporal analysis	Form perception
Language	Spatial

er vocal-control area. The absence of right/left differences in electrical recordings of activity of the hemispheres during song production also suggests that lateralization of function is not complete.

Vocalization in nonhuman primates. The calls of nonhuman primates have been examined intensively in both field and laboratory studies (Jurgens, 1990). Many nonhuman primate vocalizations seem preprogrammed, including infant crying and the emotional vocalizations of adults, such as shrieking in pain and moaning. Understanding the context of primate vocalizations depends on learning the meaning of the vocal outputs. Ploog and his collaborators in Munich (Ploog, 1992) studied the vocal behavior of squirrel monkeys, cataloging the calls they produce and the communication properties of those sounds in a social context. The monkeys' calls include shrieking, quacking, chirping, growling, and yapping sounds. Many of these calls can penetrate a forest for some distance, communicating alarm, territoriality, and other emotional statements. Direct electrical stimulation of subcortical regions can elicit some calls, but stimulation of the cerebral cortex generally fails to elicit vocal behavior (Figure 19.4). Brain regions that elicit vocalizations also seem to be involved in defense, attack, feeding, and sex behaviors. These regions include sites in the limbic lobe and related structures. Some investigators have shown that removing parts of the cerebral cortex of nonhuman primates has little effect on vocalization, whereas in humans it can dramatically affect language. Thus we conclude that human speech requires the cortex, whereas animal cries do not.

Nonhuman primate vocalizations differ from human speech in several other ways. In most cases these vocalizations seem elicited by emotional stimuli and are bound to particular situations. Further, even in the most talkative nonhuman primate, the number of distinct sounds is small.

A further look at nonhuman primate vocal behavior has pointed to versatility that was overlooked in earlier studies that had emphasized the dissimilarity between human and nonhuman primate vocal behavior. Struhsaker (1967) noticed that the alarm calls of vervet monkeys differ depending on the source of danger (leopard, eagle, snake) and elicit different adaptive responses from other vervet monkeys. For example, the call warning of leopards leads other monkeys to run into trees, while the alarm call warning of eagles leads other monkeys to look up at the sky. Using tape recordings of these alarm calls, Seyfarth and Cheney (1984) confirmed that different alarm calls elicit different behavioral responses, suggesting parallels to human words. Seyfarth and Cheney also reported on the calls monkeys use in more relaxed social situations. Humans listening to these calls may not detect small differences that are differentially appreciated by the monkeys. Discrimination experiments showed that some species seem predisposed to divide a continuum of sounds into special categories that are species-typical. Further, each species showed cerebral lateralization for processing their own species-typical vocal behavior but not for analyzing the sounds of other species.

Some Aspects of Speech Mechanisms Might Form Fossils

The use of sound for communication often has advantages over the use of other sensory channels. For example, sound enables animals to communicate at night or in other situations in which they cannot see each other. The development of oral communication clearly has survival value. Of course, sounds do not fossilize. However, parts of the skull concerned with speech sounds do form fossils and provide clues about the origins of language.

On the basis of the probable shape and length of the vocal tract of various ancient human specimens, Lieberman (1994) suggested that the capability of *Homo sapiens* to produce speech may be only 50,000 years old. About 50,000 years ago, the human vocal tract developed a size and shape that could generate signals adequate for complex communication. This development may have enabled a switch from a language dominated by gesture to one dominated by sound production. The increase in the size and shape of the vocal tract, according to Lieberman, enabled the production of certain key vowel sounds, like "i" and "u." The ability to produce these sounds probably evolved along with the development of percep-

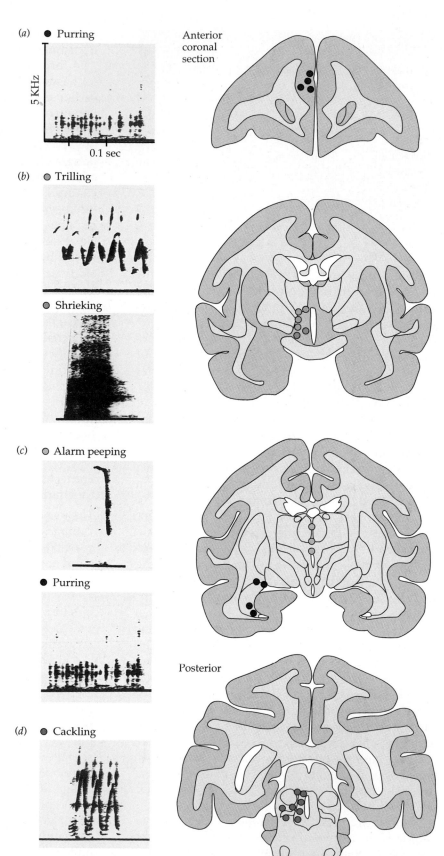

19.4 Electrical Stimulation of Monkey Brain Elicits Vocalizations
Stimulation at different sites in the monkey brain results in different, species-typical vocalizations. The left column shows spectrograms of different vocalizations, and the coronal sections in the right column show brain sites at which the different vocalizations are elicited. After Ploog, 1992; spectrograms courtesy of Uwe Jürgens.

tual detectors that were especially sensitive to them. Lieberman further argues that the vocal tracts in human infants and in nonhuman primates are shaped in such a way that they cannot produce all the sounds that speech requires. A computer reconstruction of the Neanderthal vocal tract suggests that they

too were incapable of producing vowel sounds similar to those of modern humans. These interesting speculations have been criticized. There is a great deal of uncertainty in reconstructing the position of the larynx based on so few bones. Further, although such an adaptation allows for a richer potential sound repertoire, Wang (1991) has pointed out that the languages of the world vary widely in the number and complexity of sounds. He notes that no human language exploits all the sound-production resources available from the vocal tract. Larynx descent during language evolution may have had some advantages, but this adaptation may not have been necessary for language emergence.

Whether Nonhuman Primates Can Acquire Language Is a Controversial Issue

Throughout history people have tried to teach animals to talk. In most cases, however, any communication between animal and human resulted because the person learned to meow, grunt, or bark rather than because the animal learned to produce human speech. Many such efforts have led to the conclusion that in order to speak like a human, an animal must have a vocal apparatus like that of a human.

Since both the vocal tracts and the vocal repertoires of nonhuman primates are different from those of humans, scientists have given up attempting to train animals to produce human speech. Can nonhuman primates be taught other forms of communication that have features similar to human language, including the ability to represent objects with symbols and to manipulate these symbols according to rules of order? Can animals other than humans generate a novel string of symbols, such as a new sentence?

Allen and Beatrice Gardner (1969, 1984) successfully trained chimpanzees to acquire a gestural language called American Sign Language (ASL)—the sign language used by the deaf in the United States. The chimps learned many signs and appear to be able to use them spontaneously and to generate new sequences of signs. Patterson (1978) claims to have taught a gorilla a vocabulary of several hundred ASL words.

David Premack (1971) used another approach. He taught chimpanzees a system based on an assortment of colored chips (symbols) that could adhere to a magnetic board. After extensive training, the chimpanzees could manipulate the chips in ways that may reflect an acquired ability to form short sentences and to note various logical classifications.

At the Yerkes Primate Center, Project Lana has involved teaching "Yerkish" to chimpanzees (Rumbaugh, 1977). Yerkish is a computer-based language in which different keys on a console represent words. Apes are quite good at acquiring many words in this language and appear to string together novel, meaningful chains. Savage-Rumbaugh (1990) claims that pygmy chimpanzees do much better than other chimps in learning the meaning of symbols and in using them to communicate (Figure 19.5). On the basis of studies such as these, Savage-Rumbaugh and collaborators (1993) claim that language comprehension preceded the appearance of speech by several million years. Thus, although nonhuman primates (at least those as intelligent as the chimpanzee) do not have a vocal system that permits speech, they appear to have a capacity for learning at least some components of language.

Debate about the extent to which chimpanzees learn language has been vigorous, including both methodological and theoretical issues. One of the main critics of the conclusion that chimps can acquire language is Herbert Terrace (1979), who raised a young chimp and taught it many signs. Terrace tested

carefully to see whether his chimp or others really could construct sentences. According to linguists, grammar is the essence of language, so investigators

19.5 Chimp Using Symbols
While there is no doubt that chimpanzees can learn to use signs and/or symbols to communicate, some researchers still question whether this usage is equivalent to human language. Courtesy of Sue Savage-Rumbaugh.

look for the ability of sign-using chimps to generate meaningful and novel sequences of signs. As we noted, the studies by Gardner and Gardner suggested that sign-using chimps make distinctive series of signs, just as though they were using words in a sentence. Terrace, however, argues that strings of signs have been explicitly presented to the chimps and that the animals merely imitate rather than generate new combinations. He suggests that the imitation is quite subtle and may involve cuing practices of which the experimenter is unaware.

Savage-Rumbaugh, Rumbaugh, and Boysen (1980) have opened a broader debate emphasizing the nature of language. True symbolization, they argue, involves something more than the representation of objects or action. True symbolization involves an intention to communicate an internal representational process akin to thought. This process may not be a component of language learning in chimpanzees, although, of course, questioning the animals about this feature of language use is difficult. More recently, Savage-Rumbaugh (1993) has argued that apes can comprehend spoken words, produce novel combinations of words, and respond appropriately to sentences arranged according to a syntactic rule. She now believes that the ape's linguistic capacity has been underestimated. This debate is far from settled, but the accomplishments of the trained chimpanzees have at least forced investigators to sharpen their criteria of what constitutes language. Whether nonhuman primates are really capable of language is not yet clear. Pinker (1994) asserts, "Even putting aside vocabulary, phonology, morphology, and syntax, what impresses one the most about chimpanzee signing is that fundamentally, deep down, chimps just don't 'get it.'"

Language Disorders Result from Region-Specific Brain Injuries

Much of our early understanding of the relationship between brain mechanisms and language was derived from observation of language impairments following brain injury resulting from accidents, diseases, or strokes. The history of this topic extends almost to the earliest written records. Early Egyptian medical records known as the *Edwin Smith Surgical Papyrus*, written at least 3,000 years ago, describe people who became speechless after blows to temporal bone (Finger, 1994). The modern era of the study of language impairments following brain injury started in the nineteenth century. Particularly important was the observation by Paul Broca of a man who had lost the ability to speak. Postmortem study of this patient revealed damage to the left inferior frontal region—a region now known as **Broca's area** (Figure 19.6). Studies of many patients in the following years found that some common syndromes of language impairment appear to be related to distinct brain regions. Specifically, in approximately 90 to 95% of the cases of language impairment due to brain injury—called **aphasia**—the damage is to the *left* cerebral hemisphere. Damage to the right hemisphere is responsible for the remaining 5 to 10% of the cases of aphasia. Studies using the so-called Wada test (Box 19.1) on humans who have not suffered a stroke confirm that most of us use our left cerebral hemisphere to control language. In this section we'll examine the signs and types of aphasia.

Aphasia Has Several Defining Signs

Distinctive signs of language impairment distinguish several types of aphasia. The most prominent sign of aphasia is the substitution of a word by a sound, an incorrect word, or an unintended word. This characteristic is called **paraphasia**. At times an entirely novel word—called a **neologism**—may be generated by the substitution of a phoneme. Paraphasic speech in aphasic patients is evident both in spontaneous conversation and in attempts to read aloud from a text.

Conversational speech reveals another important aspect of aphasic speech: its fluency or ease of production. **Nonfluent speech** refers to talking with considerable effort, short sentences, and the absence of the usual melodic character of conversational speech. In contrast, fluent speech is normal in terms of the rate of production, melodic character, and overall ease of presentation. In some cases of aphasia, fluent speech is more abundant than normal. Many patients with aphasic syndromes also show disturbances in the ability to repeat words or sentences. This effect is evident in simple tasks such as the repetition of numbers or words presented orally by an examiner. Language comprehension is impaired to varying degrees.

Almost all aphasic patients show some impairment in writing (**agraphia**) and disturbances in reading (**alexia**). Finally, the brain impairments or disorders that produce aphasia also produce a distinctive motor impairment called **apraxia** (see Chapter 11). Apraxia is characterized by an impairment in the execution of learned movements that is unrelated to paralysis, coordination problems, sensory impairments, or the comprehension of instructions. The patient is unable to imitate some common gestures, such as sticking out the tongue or waving goodbye, although these acts

Box 19.1

The Wada Test

In the process of making clinical assessments and decisions, neurologists must know which hemisphere is specialized for language processing. Although clinical observations of brain-injured humans indicate that 95% of us show left-hemisphere specialization for verbal activities, typical psychological tests would have led us to expect a smaller percentage. A technique able to produce effects similar to those of brain injury without inflicting damage to the brain would be very valuable

for neurosurgeons who seek to minimize language impairments from brain operations. Wada and Rasmussen (1960) provided such a tool: the injection of a short-acting anesthetic (sodium amytal) into a single carotid artery, first on one side and then, several minutes later, on the other. Recall from Chapter 2 that the circulation of the anterior two-thirds of the cerebral hemisphere comes from branches of the carotid artery. Most of the anesthetic in the first pass through the vascular

system remains on the side of the brain where it was injected. The patient shows arrest of speech for a brief period when injected on the side of hemispheric specialization for language processing. After a few minutes the effects wear off, so the injection is much like a reversible brain lesion. The sodium amytal test (sometimes called the Wada test, after its discoverer) confirms stroke data indicating that about 95% of humans have a left-hemisphere specialization for language.

might appear in the spontaneous behavior of the patient. In the following section, we describe several syndromes that are related to specific brain lesions.

Different Types of Aphasia Result from Injury to Particular Brain Regions

Among the neurologists and researchers who have sought to classify the many different types of aphasia, a prime concern has been the relation between the particular form of language disorder and the region of brain destruction or impairment. Figure 19.6 shows the main brain regions of the left hemisphere that are related to language abilities. Studies of brain-damaged people indicate that language abilities depend on the left hemisphere in virtually all right-handed and most left-handed individuals. Damage to the right hemisphere produces major language incapacity in some left-handed individuals. Table 19.2 summarizes the main features of various types of aphasia.

Broca's aphasia.   As we noted earlier, Paul Broca in 1861 submitted postmortem evidence that a large frontal lesion in the left hemisphere produced loss of speech in a patient. This presentation was significant because it clearly showed that damage restricted to a particular brain region could produce the loss of a discrete psychological function. This type of aphasia, initially described by Broca, has come to be known as **Broca's aphasia**; it is also described as a nonfluent aphasia. Patients with Broca's aphasia have consid-

erable difficulty with speech and talk only in a labored and hesitant manner. Frequently they have lost the ability of readily naming persons or objects—an impairment referred to as **anomia**. Both reading and writing are also impaired. The ability to utter auto-

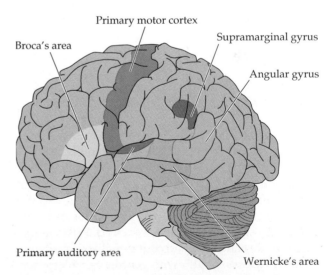

19.6 Cortical Speech and Language Areas in Humans Lesions in the anterior frontal region called Broca's area interfere with speech production; injury to an area of temporoparietal cortex called Wernicke's area interferes with language comprehension; injury to the supramarginal gyrus interferes with repetition of heard speech. For most individuals, these functional regions are found only on the left hemisphere.

Table 19.2

Language Symptomology in Aphasia

	TYPE OF APHASIA	SPONTANEOUS SPEECH	PARAPHASIA	COMPREHENSION	REPITITION	NAMING
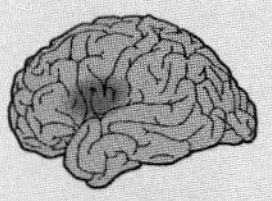	Broca's aphasia	Nonfluent	Uncommon	Good	Poor	Poor
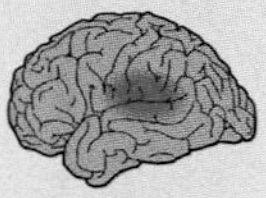	Wernicke's aphasia	Fluent	Common	Poor	Poor	Poor
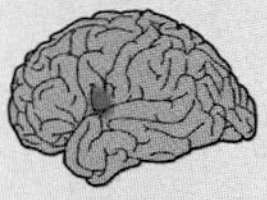	Conduction aphasia	Fluent	Common	Good	Poor	Poor
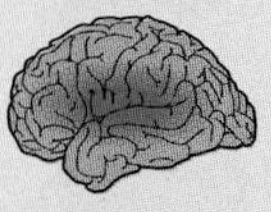	Global	Nonfluent	Variable	Poor	Poor	Poor
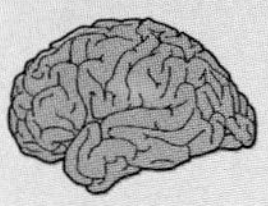	Subcortical aphasia	Fluent or nonfluent	Common	Variable	Good	Variable

matic speech is often preserved. Such speech includes greetings ("hello"); short, common expressions ("Oh, my God"); and swear words. Writing is also impaired, but *comprehension* remains relatively intact. Most patients with this disorder have apraxic difficulties and right hemiplegia—a partial paralysis involving the right side of the body. In addition to these deficits patients with Broca's aphasia may also show defects in grammar, although there is some controversy about whether this deficiency is a defining feature of this syndrome (Maratsos and Matheny, 1994).

Broca's aphasia is usually associated with lesions of the left frontal lobe, especially the third frontal gyrus and nearby regions of the lower end of the motor cortex (see Figure 19.6). CT scans of patients with Broca's aphasia are shown in Figure 19.7. Seven years after a stroke, one patient (Figure 19.7b) still spoke slowly, used nouns and very few verbs or function words, and spoke only with great effort. When asked to repeat "Go ahead and do it if possible," she could say only "Go to do it," with pauses between each word. Her CT scan revealed a large frontal lesion and destruction of subcortical areas, including the caudate nucleus and internal capsule. Broca's patients with brain lesions this extensive show little recovery of speech with the passing of time. Several investigators have argued that lesions restricted *solely* to the third frontal gyrus on the left side do not produce persis-

tent and severe Broca's aphasia and have suggested that the characteristic aphasic syndrome named after Broca invariably involves a more extended part of the frontal cortex (Friedland et al., 1993; Damasio, 1989), such as the frontal operculum and insula (see Figure 19.7f). In fact, the case presented by Broca in support of his view of localization of function actually extended well beyond the third frontal gyrus. A stronger critique of the relationship between the localization of a lesion in aphasia and the pattern of symptoms asserts that there is no unequivocal association between aphasic patterns and the anatomical distribution of lesions. This study involved more than 200 patients and careful reconstruction of the extent of damage based on CT and MRI scans.

Wernicke's aphasia. Carl Wernicke (1848–1905) was a neurologist who described several syndromes of aphasia resulting from brain lesions. The syndrome now known as **Wernicke's aphasia** includes a complex array of signs. Patients with this syndrome have very fluent verbal output, but what they say contains many paraphasias that often make their speech unintelligible. Sound substitutions (for example, "girl" becomes "curl") and word substitutions (e.g., "bread" becomes "cake") are common, as are neologisms. Word substitutions and speech errors are presented in a context that preserves syntactical structure, although sentences

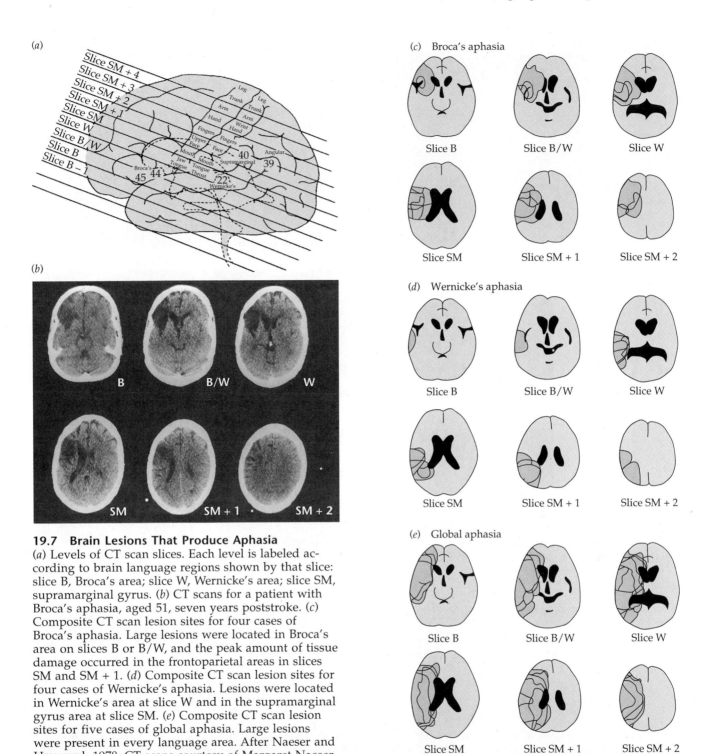

19.7 Brain Lesions That Produce Aphasia
(*a*) Levels of CT scan slices. Each level is labeled according to brain language regions shown by that slice: slice B, Broca's area; slice W, Wernicke's area; slice SM, supramarginal gyrus. (*b*) CT scans for a patient with Broca's aphasia, aged 51, seven years poststroke. (*c*) Composite CT scan lesion sites for four cases of Broca's aphasia. Large lesions were located in Broca's area on slices B or B/W, and the peak amount of tissue damage occurred in the frontoparietal areas in slices SM and SM + 1. (*d*) Composite CT scan lesion sites for four cases of Wernicke's aphasia. Lesions were located in Wernicke's area at slice W and in the supramarginal gyrus area at slice SM. (*e*) Composite CT scan lesion sites for five cases of global aphasia. Large lesions were present in every language area. After Naeser and Hayward, 1978. CT scans courtesy of Margaret Naeser.

seem empty of content. The ability to repeat words and sentences is impaired, and patients are unable to *understand* what they read or hear. In some cases, reading comprehension is more impaired than comprehension of spoken speech; in other cases the reverse is true. Unlike patients with Broca's aphasia, Wernicke's patients usually do not have other major neurological disabilities; that is, they do not display partial paralysis.

In Wernicke's aphasia the most prominent brain lesions are in posterior regions of the left superior temporal gyrus and extend partially into adjacent parietal cortex, including the supramarginal and the

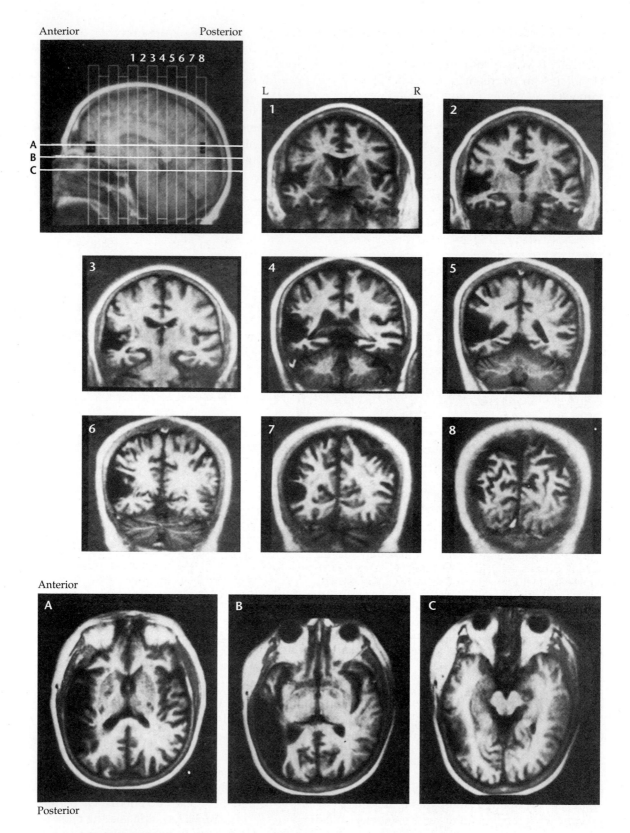

19.8 MRI Scans of a Wernicke's Patient's Brain
Numbers and letters in the sagittal view (*top left*) show locations of the coronal and horizontal scans, respectively. From Damasio and Damasio, 1989.

angular gyrus (Damasio, 1995). An MRI scan from a patient with Wernicke's syndrome is presented in Figure 19.8. When word deafness (inability to understand spoken words) is more evident than reading impairment, patients show greater involvement of the first temporal gyrus, especially fibers from auditory cortex. In contrast, when word blindness (inability to understand written words) predominates, greater destruction of the angular gyrus is evident.

Global aphasia. In some patients brain injury or disease results in total loss of the ability to understand language or to speak, read, or write. This syndrome is called **global aphasia**. These patients retain some ability for automatic speech, especially emotional exclamations. Very few words can be uttered, and no semblance of syntax is evident. The area of abnormality in the brain is broad, encompassing large realms of frontal, temporal, and parietal cortex, including Broca's area, Wernicke's area, and the supramarginal gyrus (Figure 19.9). The prognosis for language recovery in these patients is quite grave.

Conduction aphasia. Patients with **conduction aphasia** are characterized by fluent speech, minimal changes in comprehension of spoken words, but a major impairment in the repetition of words and sentences. When these patients attempt to repeat words, they offer phonemic paraphasias—words with incorrect phonemes substituting for correct sounds. The description of the brain lesion that underlies this form of aphasia is still controversial. Some researchers claim that the key ingredient is the destruction of the arcuate fasciculus, a bundle of fibers that connects Wernicke's area to Broca's area. Some cases involve the primary auditory cortex, as well as the insula and supramarginal gyrus.

Other forms of aphasia are less common and involve a different portrait of language impairments and involved brain regions (Benson, 1993). Aphasia with intact cortex and purely subcortical pathology has also been noted. Cognitive neuroscientists have approached these disorders as a way to understand the cognitive subsystems that form the ability to understand and use language (Kosslyn and Koenig, 1992) rather than defining syndromes from clusters of symptoms, which is the approach characteristic of clinical neurologists.

The Wernicke–Geschwind Model of Aphasia Is an Anatomical Representation of Some Features of Speech and Language

Aphasic disturbances span a wide range of language impairments, some quite general in character and others quite specialized, such as the inability to understand

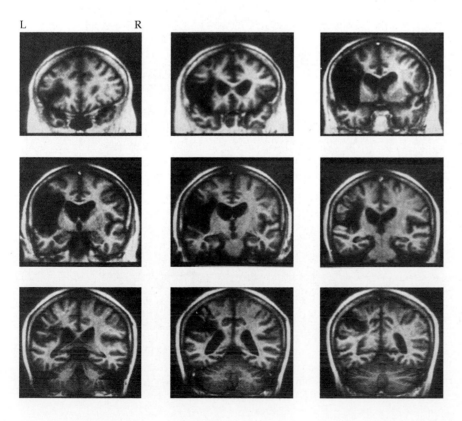

L   R

19.9 CT Scans of Patient with Global Aphasia
These sections begin at the anterior portion of the brain and proceed in a posterior direction. Note the widespread damage to the brain. From Damasio and Damasio, 1989.

Norman Geschwind
(1926–1984)

spoken language. One traditional approach to understanding apha- sic disturbances, bgun by Wernicke in the early twentieth century, uses a "connectionist" perspective to understand aphasia and related disorders. According to this view, deficits can be understood as a break in an interconnected network of components, each of which is involved with a particular feature of language analysis or production. The theory was developed in great detail by Norman Geschwind (1972). Geschwind's view is often referred to as disconnection theory to emphasize that symptoms of language impairment following brain injury may occur because regions lose their connections in a network. According to this perspective, when a word or sentence is heard, the results of analysis by the auditory cortex are transmitted to Wernicke's area. In order to say the word, outputs must be transmitted from Wernicke's area, to Broca's area where a speech plan is activated and then transmitted to adjacent motor cortex, which controls the relevant articulatory muscles. The angular gyrus (see Figure 19.6) links the auditory and visual regions. If a spoken word is to be spelled, the auditory pattern is transmitted to the angular gyrus, where the visual pattern is provoked.

According to the Wernicke–Geschwind model, saying the name of an observed object involves the transfer of visual information to the angular gyrus, which contains the rules for arousing the auditory pattern in Wernicke's area (Figure 19.10). From Wernicke's area

19.10 The Geschwind–Wernicke Connectionist Model
When a word is heard (*a*), the sensation from the ears is received by the primary auditory cortex, but the word cannot be understood until the signal has been processed in Wernicke's area nearby. If the word is to be spoken, some representation of it is transmitted from Wernicke's area to Broca's area through a bundle of nerve fibers called the arcuate fasciculus. In Broca's area the word evokes a detailed program for articulation, which is supplied to the face area of the motor cortex. The motor cortex in turn drives the muscles to produce speech. When a written word is read (*b*), the sensation is first registered by the visual cortex. It is then thought to be relayed to the angular gyrus, which associates the visual form of the word with the corresponding auditory pattern in Wernicke's area. Speaking the word then draws on the same systems of neurons as before. After Geschwind, 1979.

(*a*) Speaking a heard word

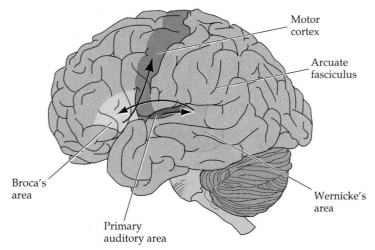

(*b*) Speaking a written word

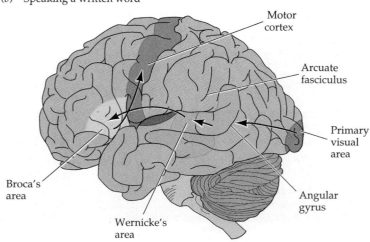

the auditory form is transmitted via the arcuate fasciculus to Broca's area. In this region the model for the spoken form is activated and transmitted to the face area of the motor cortex, and the word is then spoken. Thus, lesions involving the angular gyrus have the effect of disconnecting the systems involved in auditory and visual language. Patients with lesions in this region would be expected to have difficulty with written language, but they should be able to speak and understand speech. A lesion in Broca's area should disturb speech production but have little impact on comprehension. Many aspects of language disturbances following cortical lesions can be understood from this perspective, which has become the major model for the anatomical analysis of aphasias.

Users of Sign Language Show Aphasia Following Brain Injury

Human hands and arms have remarkable abilities to move in many different and elaborate ways. Some gestures of the hand convey meanings that seem almost universal; some have been used for centuries. Formal hand and arm gestures with specific rules of arrangement form the basis of nonvocal languages of the deaf such as American Sign Language (ASL). This language involves an elaborate code and grammar (Figure 19.11). An exhaustive analysis of ASL by two linguists (Klima and Bellugi, 1979) clearly establishes this gesture-based set of symbols as a language that is as elaborate as its vocal counterparts. In fact, sign languages show features as subtle as dialect. Adding to the complexity of ASL is its heavy reliance on visuospatial differences to convey differences in meaning

(Poizner, Bellugi, and Klimer, 1990). Given the unique features of sign language, investigators have been interested in finding out whether sign language is similar to spoken language in its neural organization. Is there hemispheric specialization for a language system based on hand signals, most of which are formed by the right hand, although some involve both hands?

Several case histories provide interesting data about aphasia in users of sign language. Meckler, Mack, and Bennett (1979) described a young man who was raised by deaf–mute parents and who became aphasic after an accident. Previously he had used both spoken and sign language for communication. Afterward, impairments in his spoken language, sign language, and writing were equally severe. He could copy complicated hand and finger movements when he was provided with the model of the experimenter's gestures, but he could not offer gestures in a spontaneous manner. Chiarello, Knight, and Mundel (1982) analyzed sign language deficits in an older deaf–mute. This person was deafened in infancy prior to the onset of speech and could not communicate vocally. She had well-developed sign language skills. Following a stroke at age 59, she showed a total inability to generate hand signals with either hand. CT scans indicated extensive damage in the left temporal cortex, including Wernicke's area. Months later, testing showed some return of sign language, although the recovery was restricted to simple phrases. Errors in these signals bore a striking resemblance to language mistakes in the speech and writing of people with comparable lesions who had used spoken language. Bellugi, Poizner, and Klima, (1983) have described aphasia in three

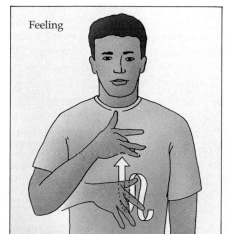

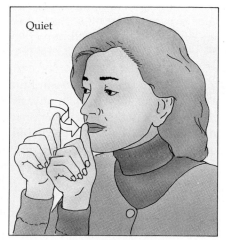

19.11 American Sign Language
Aphasia patients who are deaf show deficits in understanding and/or producing sign language that are analogous to language deficits in hearing patients.

deaf signers with damage to the left hemisphere. In these patients, differential damage in the left hemisphere impaired components of sign language. Damage in one region affected grammatical features, and damage elsewhere affected word production.

These cases indicate that the neural mechanisms of spoken and sign languages are similar. Cerebral injury in these cases affects a mechanism that controls rules for the ordering of symbolic information, whether conveyed by speech or by hand. Deaf patients with damage to the right hemisphere are like hearing patients with the same type of injury; they show impairments in various visuospatial tasks (described later in the chapter), but their signing is appropriate and includes all linguistic categories of expression.

Aphasic Bilinguals and Polyglots Usually Show Impairment in All Their Languages

People who can speak and write in more than one language have always been fascinating to researchers in aphasia. Do cerebral cortical injuries produce similar impairments in all languages? Do very different languages share common neural systems? The understanding of this issue is partly obscured by definitions of bilingualism. Few people acquire multiple languages at the same time in childhood; the age at which a second language is acquired is a critical factor in studies of aphasia. Another complicating factor is the frequency of use of each language. Furthermore, most studies have concerned a small group of Indo-European languages that have many similar characteristics. Few reports of aphasia in bilinguals involve Asian languages, most of which are very different from, for example, English, German, French, and Spanish.

Because most of the data on aphasia in bilinguals come from individual case histories, it is difficult to see the common or most characteristic findings. Par-adis and Goldblum (1989) have reviewed many published case histories and characterized the classes of symptoms and recovery from aphasia in bilinguals and polyglots. There are many different patterns of recovery, but in the most common form, shown by almost half of all case reports on bilinguals, both languages are similarly impaired and there is equal recovery in both. However, there are exceptions to this finding. Some patients after brain injury show alternate antagonism between the two languages they knew; in these cases, patients shift from one language to another following the injury.

Cases in which both languages are similarly affected by brain injury suggest that each language is similarly organized in the brain. Differential effects and different patterns of recovery, on the other hand, suggest that each language is subserved by different circuits. Some support for this conjecture comes from brain stimulation studies, which we describe shortly.

Brain Plasticity Related to Language Development Lasts Several Years

Both external and internal processes determine the acquisition of language. The internal aspect of language development is evidenced by the considerable regularity across all human languages in the timing of its stages. During the first year of life, the babbling of all children sounds similar, no matter in what culture they are reared (Stromswold, 1995). The highly specialized attributes of specific languages require learning during early development. Rare cases of children profoundly isolated during early development point to the importance of experience during critical periods early in language development. Restoration of hearing in an adult who had been deaf most of her life supports this critical-period hypothesis for the acquisition of language; she did not learn to speak (Curtiss, 1989). The notion of the special importance of childhood for language acquisition is also supported by the difficulty that postadolescents have in learning a second language.

The asymmetry of language areas of the brain that is characteristic of adults is also evident in human fetal brains (described later in the chapter). Synaptic development of language areas in the left hemisphere, such as Broca's area, is slower than that of the same region in the right hemisphere (Scheibel, 1982). The seeming intrinsic pattern of language development suggests a genetic basis. Some language disorders occur in many members of the same family. Studies of twins show higher concordance rates in monozygotic as opposed to dizygotic twins for certain types of language impairment (Lewis and Thompson, 1992).

One focus of studies is the development of lateralization in children, as seen in structures of the brain and functions such as dichotic listening. Newborn babies turn their heads far more often to the right than to the left (Turkewitz, 1988). Electrophysiological asymmetry of the infant cerebral hemispheres is evident in the response of babies to speech sounds. Thus, from quite early on, the human brain is structurally and functionally lateralized.

Language development takes time, and several features of recovery from language impairment following brain injury reflect this fact (see the final section of this chapter). What we can conclude is that the brain slowly loses the ability to compensate for injury. Language commonly develops after childhood aphasia resulting from brain injury. Language recovery is possible even after the removal of a hemisphere in childhood. These observations suggest that the right

Box 19.2
Childhood Loss of One Hemisphere

During early development the brain is a vulnerable organ, a fact that is especially apparent when looking at the effect of a prolonged, difficult birth involving a period of oxygen loss; some children sustain lateralized brain injury involving a single cerebral hemisphere. Early in development such a child may show paralysis on one side of the body and frequent seizures. These seizures can be difficult to control with medication, and they may occur so often that they endanger life. Major brain damage on one side is shown in radiological data, and the injured hemisphere can be quite shrunken.

Surgical removal of the malfunctioning hemisphere reduces seizures. Although at first some severe effects of the surgery are evident, over a long period of time the restoration of behavior is practically complete. This result is strikingly illustrated in a case presented by Smith and Sugar (1975). The boy in this study showed paralysis on his right side as an infant, and by five years of age he was experiencing 10 to 12 seizures a day. Although the boy's verbal comprehension was normal, his speech was hard to understand. To treat the problem, doctors removed all the cerebral cortex of the left hemisphere. Long-term

follow-up studies extended to age 26, when the patient had almost completed college. Tests revealed an above-normal IQ and superior language abilities; thus the early loss of most of the left hemisphere had not precluded language development. This patient also had remarkable development of nonverbal functions, including visuospatial tasks and manual tasks. Whereas adult hemispherectomy of the left side usually results in drastic impairment of language, affecting both speech and writing, this case provides an example of extensive functional recovery after childhood hemispherectomy.

hemisphere can take over the language functions of the left hemisphere if impairment occurs early in life.

Some People Have Trouble Reading Even Though They Can See and Act Intelligently

Some students never seem to learn to read. Their efforts are laden with frustration, and prolonged practice produces only small improvements. The inability to read is called **dyslexia** (from the Greek roots for "faulty reading"). Some dyslexic children show high IQ performance. The diagnosis of dyslexia includes many different groups of people who cannot read. It is more common in boys and left-handed people. There is some controversy about this syndrome, and its characteristics are probably broader than a reading disorder and encompass broader aspects of language dysfunction. Some regard dyslexia as a sensory processing problem, others as a memory disorder. Clearly, dyslexia is a fuzzy clinical category, but it has been connected to interesting anatomical and physiological findings. Many of these observations are reported in a monograph on this topic (Tallal et al., 1993). As we will see, there are many unsolved mysteries concerning dyslexia.

At least some dyslexic individuals have associated deficits in various tasks involving cerebral lateralization, especially those that involve the left hemi-

sphere. Such tasks include left/right discrimination and forms of verbal learning and memory. Some researchers have suggested that developmental impairments in reading may arise from the use of the right hemisphere in language (Coltheart, 1980).

Studies by Galaburda and collaborators (summarized in Galaburda, 1994) have shown various pathological features in the brains of dyslexic patients. An initial report discussed four cases with specific reading disabilities and other learning disabilities noted at an early age. These were postmortem observations of patients who had died from acute disease or trauma associated with injury that did not involve the brain. All four brains showed striking anomalies in the arrangements of cortical cells, especially in areas of the frontal and temporal cortical regions. These anomalies consisted of unusual groupings of cells in outer layers of the cerebral cortex that distorted the normal layered arrangements and columnar organization (Figure 19.12). Some cells were disoriented, and excessive cortical folding was observed. Nests of extra cells were seen. The researchers argue that these anomalies of cerebral cortical cell arrangements were developmental in character and probably arose quite early, perhaps during the middle of gestation, a period during which active cell migration is evident in cerebral cortex. The result of these deficits might be

(*a*)

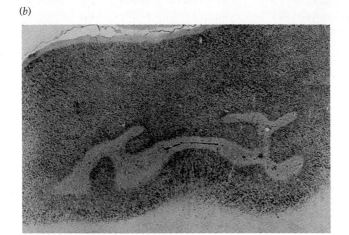

Planum temporale, viewed from above in isolation

Heschl's gyrus

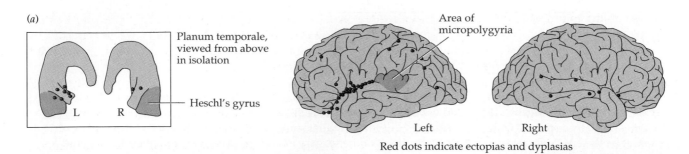

Area of micropolygyria

Left   Right

Red dots indicate ectopias and dyplasias

(*b*)

(*c*)

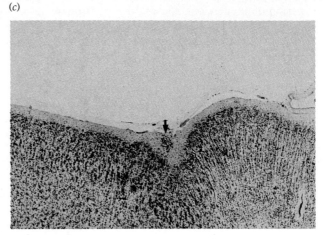

19.12 Neural Disorganization in A Dyslexic's Brain
(*a, left*) Drawings of the left and right planum temporale from the brain of a dyslexic show these regions as nearly symmetrical; in most people the left planum temporale is considerably larger. The dots and the shaded area represent regions where microscopic anomalies called ectopias, dysplasias, and micropolygyrias have been found in the brains of dyslexic individuals. (*a, right*) Note that anomalies are much more common in the left hemisphere, which is primarily responsible for language function. Micrographs of (*b*) micropolygyria (many tiny gyri") and (*c*) ectopias, clusters of neurons in unusual locations, such as this cluster in layer 1 (arrow), which is normally devoid of neuronal cell bodies. After Galaburda, 1994; micrographs courtesy of Albert Galaburda.

the production of unusual patterns of connectivity in language-related regions of the temporal cortex.

Galaburda, Sherman, and Galaburda also noted that the customary asymmetry in the overall extent of the planum temporale was much less noticeable in dyslexics (Rosen, Sherman, and Galaburda, 1993). Atypical asymmetries of a specific region around the sylvian sulcus within the temporal lobes has been described in boys with impairments of language skills (Plante et al., 1991). This anatomical finding is also found in family members of impaired boys, suggesting that it may be a transmissible factor (Plante, 1991). The presence or absence of asymmetry of the planum temporale in dyslexic brains is controversial. A study by Schultz and colleagues (1994) cautions that age and sex have a potent impact on these data. These researchers show that

differences found between dyslexics and nondyslexics might be accounted for by small age differences in various studies between control and patient populations. The investigators failed to see anatomical distinctions between dyslexics and controls when differences in overall brain size, age, and sex were controlled.

Another anatomical approach to dyslexia focuses on sensory processing and suggests that differences in sensory pathways of dyslexics might account for reading difficulties. Tallal and colleagues (1993), citing the anatomical work of Margaret Livingstone, have shown in postmortem examinations that dyslexics have smaller-than-normal neurons in both auditory and visual subcortical sites; this difference is especially evident in magnocellular areas of the lateral geniculate in dyslexics, where the neurons are both smaller and disorganized in arrangement. These deviations may result in impaired ability to process rapidly changing signals such as those involved in reading.

Some researchers have noted a relationship between dyslexia and disorders of the immune system. Several of the dyslexic patients and their relatives in Galaburda's study had disorders such as arthritis, food allergies, and migraine, which Galaburda and associates believe points to a common genetic mechanism—that is, a genetic factor that both determines cortical anomalies and prepares the way for immune-system defects. In some families with multigeneration dyslexics, a gene on chromosome 6 is associated with dyslexia. This gene is near regions associated with the human immune system. Experimental animals with immune-system defects have cortical anomalies akin to those observed in these patients. Perhaps a common basis for these disorders is an immunologically mediated impairment of cell aggregation and organization factors that operate during early cerebral cortical development.

An especially interesting type of dyslexia is called **deep dyslexia**. Deep dyslexia is characterized by errors in reading in which patients read a word as another word that is related in meaning; for example, the printed word "cow" is read as "horse." These patients are also unable to read aloud words that are abstract as opposed to concrete, and they make frequent errors in which they seem to fail to see small differences in words. Interest in this syndrome stems from the fact that it frequently results from injury to the left cerebral hemisphere. Some researchers believe that in these patients, reading is mediated by the right hemisphere; others argue that reading in deep dyslexics is mediated by residual left-hemisphere tissue.

Electrical Stimulation of the Brain Provides Information about Brain Organization of Language

Electrical stimulation of the brain is used to explore language functions of the human cerebral cortex. Subjects in these studies are patients undergoing surgery for the relief of seizures. Electrical stimulation helps neurosurgeons locate—and thus avoid—language-related cortical regions. By observing language interference produced by the electrical stimuli, the surgeon can identify these regions. Patients are given only local anesthesia, so that they can continue to communicate verbally.

Pioneering work by Penfield and Roberts (1959) provided a map of language-related zones of the left hemisphere (Figure 19.13). Pooled data from many patients showed that stimulation of a large anterior zone arrested speech. Speech simply stopped during the period of applied stimulation. Other forms of language interference, such as misnaming or impaired repetition of words, were evident from stimulation of both this region and more posterior temporoparietal cortex regions. More recent intensive studies of the effects of electrical stimulation of Broca's area add other features to the list of effects (Schaffler et al., 1993). In these studies, during stimulation patients were unable to comprehend auditory or visual semantic material; the impairment included the inability to follow oral commands, point to objects, or understand written questions. This difficulty might arise from an inability to understand syntactic information during the stimulation, so that the patients are unable to achieve a correct interpretation of questions or requests for action. The selectivity of verbal interference during electrical stimulation is shown by the fact that patients were able to copy from memory complex geometrical designs shown at the beginning of stimulation. Preservation of nonverbal activities was evident even at high intensities of the stimulus.

The investigation of language organization during neurosurgical procedures has been a special focus of George Ojemann and collaborators (summarized in Calvin and Ojemann, 1994). They examined the effects of electrical stimulation across a wide extent of cerebral cortex, focusing on the possible compartmentalization of linguistic systems such as naming, reading, speech production, and verbal memory. An interesting example of the effects of cortical stimulation on naming is shown in Figure 19.13*b*, which shows the different loci of naming errors in English and Spanish. Ojemann and Mateer (1979) present more detailed cortical maps (Figure 19.13*c*), which reveal several different systems. Stimulation of one system arrests speech and impairs all facial movements. This system, located in the inferior premotor frontal cortex, was regarded as the cortical, final motor pathway for speech. Stimulation of a second system alters sequential facial movements and impairs phoneme identification. This system included sites in the inferior frontal, temporal, and parietal cortex. A third system was defined by stimulation-induced memory errors; it surrounds the sites of the systems that impair phoneme identification. Reading errors are evident from stimulation of other cortical positions.

Ojemann (1983) described some interesting sex-related differences in observations of cortical electrical stimulation. In comparison to females, males show stimulation-induced naming changes from a wider area of lateral cortex, especially more sites in the frontal lobe. Individual differences in stimulation effects are also related to the patient's verbal abilities.

19.13   Electrical Stimulation of Some Brain Sites Can Interfere with Language

(*a*) Stimulation of these sites interfered with speech production; this is a summary of data obtained from many patients. (*b*) Map of stimulation sites that affected speech of a patient who was bilingual–fluent in Spanish and English. Note that different regions interfere with either one language or the other, but not both. (*c*) Detailed analysis of changes in language functions produced by electrical stimulation of the cerebral cortex: a summary of the cognitive effects of cortical electrical stimulation in four human subjects. Performance in naming (N), repeating movements (R), short-term memory (S), and language (L) was assessed during and after stimulation of the left hemisphere. A memory system (blue) is posterior to systems for language production and understanding. The final motor pathway for speech is shown by the green shaded region. *a* after Penfield and Roberts, 1959; *b* and *c* after Ojemann and Mateer, 1979.

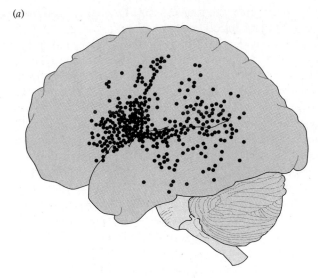

(*a*)

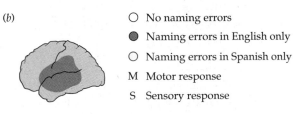

(*b*)

○ No naming errors
● Naming errors in English only
○ Naming errors in Spanish only
M Motor response
S Sensory response

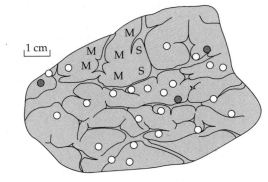

|1 cm|

Those with low verbal IQs show more frequent naming difficulties with stimulation of the parietal cortex.

Ojemann also noted that stimulation of the thalamus at the time of verbal input *increases* the accuracy of subsequent recall (as late as one week following stimulation). He suggests that there is a thalamic mechanism that specifically modulates the recall of verbal information. This conclusion fits with the description of patient N.A. in Chapter 17, in whom damage to the thalamus impaired verbal memory.

Many Patients Show Some Recovery from Aphasia

Many people with brain disorders that produce aphasia recover some language abilities. For some people language recovery depends on specific forms of speech therapy. The exact forms of speech therapy are mainly improvisations supported by some degree of clinical success rather than being generated by theories.

The relative extent of recovery from aphasia can be predicted from several factors. For example, recovery is better in survivors of brain damage due to trauma, such as a blow to the head, than in those whose brain damage is caused by stroke. Patients with more severe language loss recover less. Left-handed people show better recovery than those who are right-handed. In fact, right-handed individuals with near relatives who are left-handed recover from aphasia better than right-handed individuals without a family history of left-handedness.

Kertesz (1979) reports that the largest amount of recovery usually occurs during the initial three months following brain damage (Figure 19.14). In many instances, little further improvement is noted

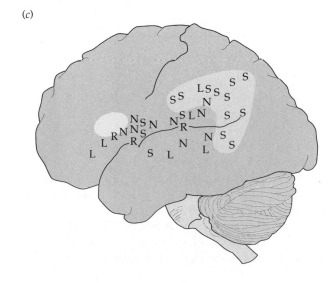

(*c*)

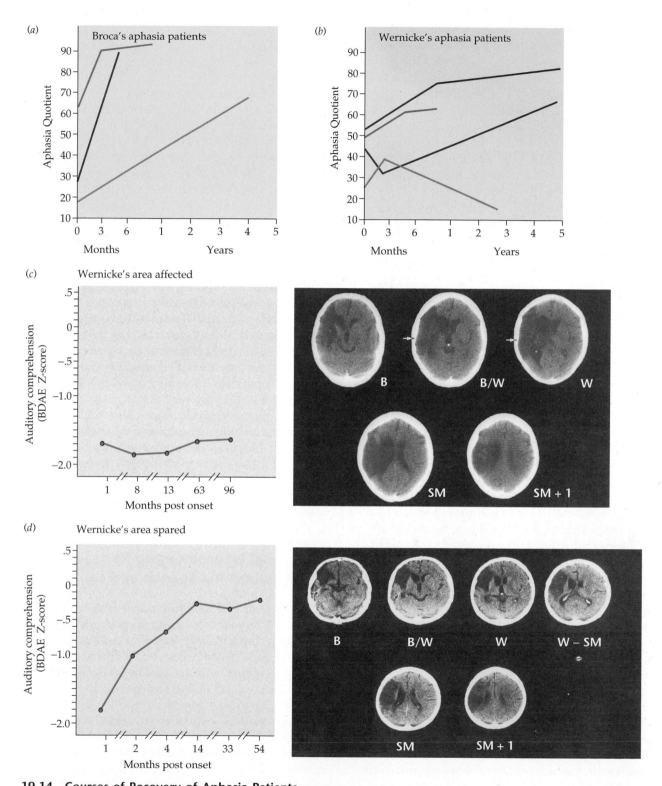

19.14 Courses of Recovery of Aphasia Patients
(*a*) The course of recovery from Broca's aphasia compared with that from
(*b*) Wernicke's aphasia. These graphs depict the Aphasia Quotient (AQ), a score
derived from a clinical test battery. Higher scores indicate better language performance. (*c*) The course of recovery of auditory comprehension of speech after a
stroke causing Wernicke's aphasia compared with (*d*) a Broca's aphasia patient. *a* and
b after Kertsz, 1979; *c* and *d* after Naeser, 1990. CT scans courtesy of Margaret Naeser.

after the lapse of one year, although this result may reflect impoverished therapeutic tools rather than a property of neural plasticity. In general, Broca's aphasics have the highest rate of recovery. The worse the initial severity, the worse the outcome. Kertesz suggests that there is a sequence of stages of recovery that are distinguished by linguistic properties and that patients show a transformation of type of aphasia. According to Kertesz, a common endpoint, no matter what the initial diagnosis, is anomic aphasia, a difficulty in "finding" words, although comprehension and ability to repeat words are normal. Anomic aphasia frequently stands as the residual symptom. Later in the chapter we describe the remarkable and virtually complete recovery from aphasia by children.

Improvement in language abilities following stroke might involve a shift to right-hemisphere control of language. Evidence for such hemispheric shifts in children is presented later in this chapter. A case presented by Cummings and colleagues (1979) lends some support to the hypothesis of a change from left- to right-hemisphere control of language in an adult. The case they described followed a massive stroke in the left hemisphere. CT scans showed total destruction of Wernicke's and Broca's areas in the left hemisphere. Immediately after the stroke, language was limited to small groups of words virtually bereft of meaning. Furthermore, verbal comprehension was severely impaired. Three years later the patient was able to produce comprehensible short phrases and correctly identify objects. Since his left-hemisphere language areas were totally destroyed, the investigators concluded that the elements of recovered language were mediated by right-hemisphere mechanisms. Recent studies on cerebral blood flow following stroke that results in aphasia offer some support for this view. One such study showed that patients with nearly complete recovery of language showed widespread right-hemisphere increases in cerebral blood flow. Those with incomplete recovery showed increases only in the right frontal region. Other studies indicate that blood flow in left inferior frontal regions is associated with recovery of fluent speech (Mlcoch et al., 1994). PET studies indicate that the metabolic activity of the left hemisphere is the best predictor of speech recovery (Heiss et al., 1993).

It is important to note that a concern for remediation following brain injury is relatively recent. For many years researchers regarded the nervous system as a rigidly organized organ without prospects of structural or functional plasticity. We are now in the midst of a major change toward more optimistic views about the prospects of a rational basis for rehabilitation following brain injury. Recovery of language is a top priority of these renewed efforts.

Therapy is a significant factor in the long-term recovery pattern of aphasia. As mentioned earlier, strategies employed by therapists tend to be improvised rather than based on knowledge of the brain mechanisms of speech. An emphasis on auditory stimulation and repetition characterizes many approaches (Sarno, 1981). An unusual innovation, called melodic intonation therapy, draws attention to the differences between song and speech. Aphasics can frequently sing words and phrases even though they show major handicaps with the ability to speak words. Melodic intonation therapy attempts to enhance communication by having patients sing sentences they would ordinarily attempt to deliver in conversational form. Therapists have experienced some success in slowly transforming the communication of such subjects from a song mode to a nonmelodic speech pattern. The rapid pace of developments in computers, including machines that speak, may be able to provide new dimensions in the rehabilitation of language disorders. Other behavioral interventions include instruction in the use of gestures or signing. Pharmacotherapy for aphasia holds some promise for the future (Small, 1994). Drugs that enhance catecholamine functioning have been used to hasten improvement or extend the time for behavioral intervention.

Functional Neuroimaging Portrays Brain Organization for Speech and Language

The advent of PET and functional-MRI techniques has allowed researchers to obtain portraits of the activity of the brain during periods of activation by various language tasks. A series of studies by Raichle and collaborators (summarized in Posner and Raichle, 1994) examined PET activation during different levels of the processing of words. These levels include (1) passive exposure to visually presented words, (2) passive exposure to spoken words, (3) oral repetition of the words, and (4) generation of a semantic association to a presented word. The successive levels of these experiments and the accompanying PET scans are presented in Figure 19.15. Passive viewing of words activates an area along the inner surface of the left hemisphere (Figure 19.15*a*). Hearing words in a passive condition shifts the focus of maximum brain activation to the temporal lobes (Fig-

Passively viewing words

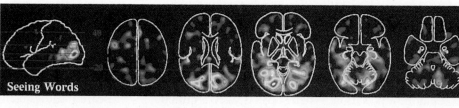

Listening to words

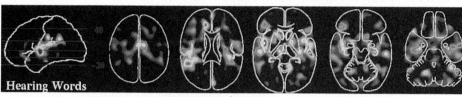

Speaking words

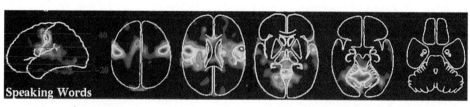

Generating a verb associated
with each noun shown

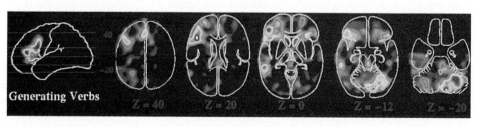

19.15 Subtractive PET Scans of Brain Activation in Progressively More Complex Language Tasks

(*Left*) For clarity concerning the tasks, we depict the subjects at a desk, but when the PET scans were made, the subjects reclined with their heads in a PET scanner and viewed a specially mounted display. (*Right*) PET scans corresponding to the tasks; see text for details on these results. After Posner and Raichle, 1994; PET scans courtesy of Marcus Raichle.

ure 19.15*b*). Repeating the words orally activates the motor cortex of both sides, the supplementary motor cortex, and a portion of the cerebellum and insular cortex (Figure 19.15*c*). During word repetition or reading aloud there was a peculiar absence of activity in Broca's area. This finding was clarified by examination of the data obtained under the condition of semantic association. When subjects were required to present a verb that was an appropriate semantic association for a presented noun, there was marked activation of language-related regions in the left hemisphere, including Broca's area (Figure 19.15*d*).

Another example of the use of imaging studies of language is the work of Mazoyer and colleagues with native French speakers (1993). Five different experimental conditions were studied, including blood responses in the brain to (1) listening to a story in a language unknown to the subjects—Tamil, (2) listening to a list of French words, (3) listening to "sentences" composed of French pseudowords, (4) listening to semantically unusual sentences, and (5) listening to a story in French. Asymmetry becomes particularly evident when meaning is added to the task. The results of this study, as well as those of Raichle's work, confirm the language zones revealed by the study of humans with aphasia.

The Left Brain Is Different from the Right Brain

By the early twentieth century, it was firmly established that the cerebral hemispheres were not equivalent in mediating language functions (Finger, 1994). The left hemisphere seemed to control this function and was commonly described as the dominant hemisphere. However, the right hemisphere does not just sit within the skull awaiting the call to duty when the left side of the brain is injured. In fact, many researchers have slowly drifted from notions of cerebral dominance to ideas of hemispheric specialization, or lateralization. This newer emphasis implies that some functional systems are connected more to one side of the brain than the other—that is, that functions become lateralized— and that each hemisphere is specialized for particular ways of working.

Lateralization of function is not a surprising idea; a broad look at the distribution of body organs shows considerable asymmetry between the right and left sides; for example, the heart is on the left and the liver is on the right. Virtually every species, even very simple ones, shows such lateral differences. Nevertheless, at the level of brain processing in normal individuals, the interconnections of the hemispheres or-

dinarily mask evidence of hemisphere specialization. But by studying patients whose interhemispheric pathways have been disconnected—split-brain patients—researchers have been able to see cerebral hemispheric specialization in cognitive, perceptual, emotional, and motor activities. Study of split-brain individuals has also provided the impetus for many research studies using normal subjects. In this section we consider some of the evidence that helps us understand the similarities and differences of functions of the two cerebral hemispheres.

Are There Two Minds in One Head?

The differential properties of the cerebral hemispheres are best illustrated in a series of studies by Roger Sperry and collaborators at the California Institute of Technology, which we mentioned briefly in Chapter 1. These experiments involved a small group of human patients who underwent a surgical procedure designed to provide relief from frequent, disabling epileptic seizures. In these patients epileptic activity that was initiated in one hemisphere spread to the other hemisphere via the corpus callosum, the large bundle of fibers that connect the two hemispheres. Surgically cutting the corpus callosum appreciably reduces the frequency and severity of such seizures.

Studies by other investigators in the 1930s had shown that this remedy for seizures was not accompanied by any apparent changes in brain function, as assessed by general behavioral tests such as IQ tests. But the human corpus callosum is a huge bundle of more than a million axons, and it seemed strange that the principal connection between the cerebral hemispheres could be cut without producing detectable changes in behavior. The eminent physiological psychologist Karl Lashley, with characteristic sardonic humor, suggested that perhaps the only function of the corpus callosum was to keep the two hemispheres from floating apart in the cerebrospinal fluid! Subsequent animal research has shown, however, that careful testing does reveal deficits in behavior as consequences of hemispheric disconnection. Results of hemispheric disconnection were first studied extensively in animals in the 1950s. For example, in one study on cats, both the corpus callosum and the optic chiasm were sectioned, so that each eye was connected only to the hemisphere on its own side. Such cats learned with their left eye that a particular symbol stood for reward but that the inverted symbol did not, while with the right eye they were able to learn the opposite—that the inverted symbol was rewarded rather than the upright symbol. Thus, each hemisphere was ignorant of what the other had learned (Sperry, Stamm, and Miner, 1956).

In 1960 neurosurgeon Joseph Bogen proposed splitting the brain of some patients in order to control the spread of epilepsy between hemispheres (Figure 19.16; Bogen et al., 1988). His operations helped these patients, and several of them were studied extensively both pre- and postoperatively through a series of psychological tests devised by Sperry and coworkers. In research on this group of patients, stimuli can be directed to either hemisphere by being presented to different places on the surface of the body. For example, objects the patient feels with the left hand result in activity in nerve cells of the sensory regions in the right hemisphere. Since the corpus callosum is cut in these patients, most of the information sent to one half of the brain cannot travel to the other half. By controlling stimuli in this fashion, the experimenter can present stimuli selectively to one hemisphere or the other and thus can test the capabilities of each hemisphere.

In some of Sperry's studies words were projected to either the left or the right hemisphere by presenting visual stimuli in either the right or the left side of the visual field. Split-brain subjects can easily read and verbally communicate words projected to their left hemisphere. No such linguistic capabilities were evident when the information was directed to the right hemisphere (Figure 19.17). Zaidel (1976) showed that the right hemisphere has a small amount of linguistic ability; for example, it can recognize simple words. In general, however, the vocabulary and grammatical capabilities of the right hemisphere are far less developed than they are in the left hemisphere.

Sperry's findings not only confirmed the earlier animal research but were more dramatic, since they showed that only the processes taking place in the left hemisphere could be described verbally by the patients. Thus, it is the left hemisphere that possesses language and speech mechanisms in most people. For our present concern, the important result is that each hemisphere by itself can process and store information without any participation by the other hemisphere. The ability of the "mute" right hemisphere was tested by nonverbal means. For example, a picture of a key might be projected to the left visual field and so reach only the right visual cortex. The subject would then be asked to touch a number of objects that she could not see and hold up the correct one. Such a task could be performed correctly by the left hand (controlled by the right hemisphere) but not by the right hand (controlled by the left hemisphere). In such a patient it is literally true that the left hemisphere does not know what the left hand is doing. While the left hemisphere controls speech, the

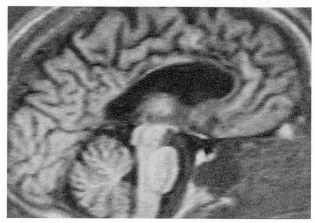

19.16   View of a Split Brain
This MRI shows the brain of a subject in which the corpus callosum was sectioned. In an intact brain, the large white band of corpus callosum occupies most of the dark region at the center; compare with figure 19.19*b*. Courtesy of Joseph Bogen.

right hemisphere seems to be somewhat better at processing spatial information, especially if the response is manual rather than simple recognition of a correct visual pattern.

Research with split-brain humans has sometimes been criticized because the results could be attributed to the fact that these patients have suffered from seizures for many years before surgery. Since prolonged seizure activity produces many changes in the brain, the apparent consequences of cutting the corpus callosum might have arisen from changes in epileptic brains. This argument has been weakened by the publication of observations of the effects of a partial callosal section in nonepileptics. For example, a posterior callosal section in a 16-year-old boy was reported by Damasio and colleagues (1980). The patient had a tumor just below the posterior part of the corpus callosum, and removing it required partial cutting of the corpus callosum. Following surgery the boy showed some of the classic signs of failure of interhemispheric transfer seen in epileptic split-brain patients. These signs included right visual field superiority in reading three-letter words and greater accuracy in naming objects presented in the right half of the visual field. Since the surgery severed most of the interhemispheric visual fibers, impairment of interhemispheric integration with visual input was predictable. On the other hand, since callosal fibers connecting somatosensory cortical regions remained intact, the subject understandably was able to name objects placed in either hand. The impairment of visual function and the integrity of somatosensory function in this patient provide strong

19.17 Testing of a Split-Brain Patient

Words or pictures projected to the left visual field activate the right visual cortex. In normals (*a*), right-visual-cortex activation excites corpus callosum fibers, which transmit verbal information to the left hemisphere where analysis and production of language takes place. In split-brain patients (*b*), the severing of callosal connections prevents language production in response to left-visual-field stimuli.

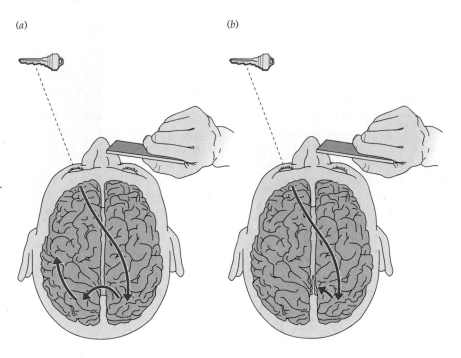

(a)   (b)

evidence of the necessity of callosal fibers for interhemispheric communication.

The Two Hemispheres Process Information Differently in Normal Humans

Virtually all the research concerning differences between the hemispheres in the processing of information has concentrated on two modalities: hearing and vision. In each modality, psychologists can detect differences in behavioral response that indicate that, in most people, the left cerebral hemisphere processes language.

The right-ear advantage. Are speech sounds presented to each ear perceived equally well? Using earphones, we can present different sounds to each ear at the same time; this process is called the **dichotic listening technique.** The subject hears a particular speech sound in one ear and, at the same time, a different vowel, consonant, or word in the other ear. The task for the subject is to identify or recall these sounds.

Although this technique may seem to be a program designed to produce confusion, in general, data from dichotic listening experiments indicate that right-handed persons identify verbal stimuli delivered to the right ear more accurately than simultaneously presented stimuli presented to the left ear. This result is described as a right-ear "advantage" for verbal information. In contrast, about 50% of left-handers reveal a reverse pattern, showing a left-ear advantage—more

accurate performance for verbal stimuli delivered to the left ear. Some data also show that the pattern of ear advantage in right-handers changes when the stimuli are nonverbal, such as musical sounds.

Doreen Kimura argues that auditory information exerts stronger neural effects on the opposite side than on the same side (Figure 19.18). That is, auditory stimuli presented to the right ear produce stronger effects on the left auditory cortex than on the right auditory cortex, and vice versa. Thus, whereas sounds presented to the right ear exert stronger control over language mechanisms in the left hemisphere, speech sounds presented to the left ear are less potent in activating language-processing regions in the left cerebral hemisphere (Kimura, 1973). Several studies have shown that right-handers' right- ear

Doreen Kimura

advantage for speech sounds is restricted to particular kinds of speech sounds (Tallal and Schwartz, 1980). The right-ear advantage is evident with simultaneously presented consonants such as "b," "d," "t," and "k," but not with vowel sounds.

Some investigators suggest that the right-ear advantage reflects a special feature of sound processing

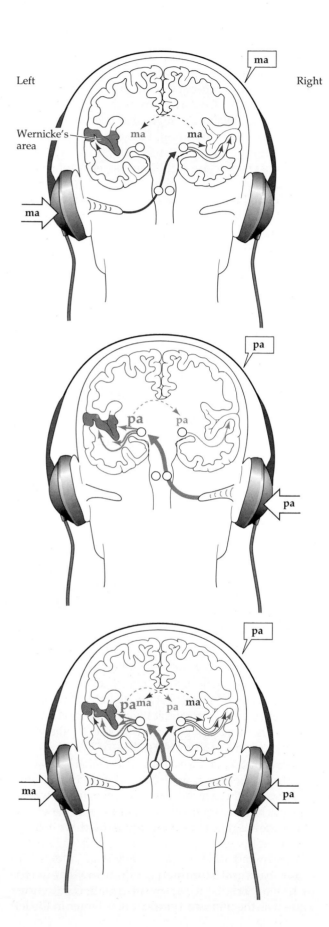

Left · Right

Wernicke's area

19.18 Kimura's Model of the Right-Ear Advantage
(*Top*) A word delivered to the left ear results in stronger stimulation of the right auditory cortex. (*Middle*) A word to the right ear results in stronger input to the left hemisphere. (*Bottom*) When words are delivered to both ears simultaneously, the one to the right ear is usually perceived because it has more direct connections to the left hemisphere After Kimura, 1973.

itself rather than of verbal features of the sounds being presented. Tallal and Schwartz have suggested that the right-ear/left-hemisphere advantage for processing speech sounds reflects a left-hemisphere specialization for processing any sounds with rapidly changing acoustic properties. Of course, rapid change characterizes some speech sounds, but not all. When the same speech sounds are artificially changed by extending them in time, the right-ear advantage for speech sounds is diminished. Hence in the dichotic listening experiment, the right-ear advantage reflects a specialization for processing not verbal sounds, but rapidly changing sounds. Tzeng and Wang (1984) suggest that the left hemisphere's ability to process rapidly changing acoustic features is the basis of the superiority of the left hemisphere for linguistic processing. This capacity enables a binding together of sound segments facilitating rapid transmission and analysis of speech.

Visual perception of linguistic stimuli. We can study hemispheric specialization in normal humans by briefly exposing visual half-fields to stimuli (see Figure 10.14). If the stimulus exposure is less than 100 to 150 milliseconds, input can be restricted to one hemisphere, because this amount of time is not sufficient for the eyes to shift their direction. Of course, in intact humans further processing may involve information transmitted through the corpus callosum to the other hemisphere.

Most studies show that verbal stimuli (words and letters) presented to the right visual field (going to the left hemisphere) are better recognized than the same input presented to the left visual field (going to the right hemisphere). On the other hand, nonverbal visual stimuli (such as faces) presented to the *left* visual field are better recognized than the same stimuli presented to the right visual field. Simpler visual processing, such as detection of light, hue, or simple patterns, is equivalent in the two hemispheres. But for more complex materials, in vision as well as audition, certain verbal stimuli are processed better in the left hemisphere of most individuals.

Are Left-Handed People Different?

Anthropologists speculate that the predominance of right-handedness goes back a long time into prehistory. People portrayed in cave paintings held things in their right hand, and Stone Age tools seem to be shaped for the right hand. Skull fractures of animals preyed upon by ancient humans are usually on the animal's left side, so anthropologists conclude that the attacker held an implement in the right hand. Throughout history many unusual attributes have been ascribed to the left-handed person—from an evil personality to a diffuse form of cerebral cortex organization. (Indeed, the term "sinistral" ["left-handed"] comes from the same Latin root as the word "sinister"!) Left-handed people make up a small percentage of human populations. A figure of around 10% is commonly reported, although this percentage may be lower in parts of the world where teachers actively discourage left-handedness. For example, there is a higher percentage of left-handed Chinese-Americans in more tolerant United States schools than among Chinese in China. Surveys of left-handed writing in American college populations reveal an incidence of 13.8% (Spiegler and Yeni-Komshian, 1983). This percentage is viewed as a dramatic increase over prior generations, perhaps reflecting a continuing decline in the social pressures toward right-handedness and an increase in the social acceptability of left-handedness.

Many studies have sought to show cognitive and emotional differences between left- and right-handed humans, the implication being that these groups differ in cerebral cortex organization. Some studies (using relatively small samples of subjects) have linked left-handedness to cognitive deficits. Such data tend to be contradictory, perhaps because some studies classify handedness with a single criterion (such as writing), whereas others employ many behaviors. Further, some individuals are ambidextrous—at least with regard to some tasks—or alternate their hand preference from task to task.

Hardyck, Petrinovich, and Goldman (1976) examined more than 7000 children in grades one through six for school achievement, intellectual ability, motivation, socioeconomic level, and the like. A detailed analysis of the data showed that left-handed children did not differ from right-handed children on any measure of cognitive performance. However, the idea that left-handed people are "damaged" humans has been common in the past and has even found occasional support. Silva and Satz (1979) note that several studies show a higher incidence of left-handedness in clinical populations than in the general population. They examined handedness in more than 1400 patients in a school for the mentally retarded and showed an incidence of 17.8% left-handers, about double the level in the general population. In this population more left-handers than right-handers had abnormal EEGs. Investigators have suggested that brain injury explains the high rate of left-handedness in this retarded population. Early brain injury, these investigators argue, can cause a shift in handedness. Since most people are right-handed, early one-sided brain injury is more likely to effect a change from right-handedness to left-handedness than the reverse.

Some left-handed persons write by using an inverted hand posture in which the hand is held curved, resting above the written line. Others have a writing posture that is a mirror image of the writing posture of most right-handers. The awkwardness of the inverted left-handed posture has been viewed as a product of either an attempt to model the characteristic slant of right-handers or a way to gain a better view of the written line. However, Levy and Reid (1976) offer a different perspective, arguing that these hand postures can be used to predict which hemisphere controls language functions. In their study they compared inverted and noninverted left-handers on visual-field tests. Both right-handers and *inverted* left-handers showed superiority of right-visual-field verbal tasks, implying left-hemisphere language control. In contrast, *noninverted* left-handers showed left-visual-field superiority for verbal tasks. A similar right-hemisphere language control was shown by one right-hander with an inverted writing posture—an extreme rarity. This work is controversial; the writing posture of left-handers is not related to other measures of hemispheric specialization, such as dichotic listening tasks (Springer and Deutsch, 1985).

The Human Brain Is Anatomically and Physiologically Asymmetrical

The search for the biological bases of functional lateralization includes both anatomical and neurophysiological studies. Comparing the left and right sides of the body, we note that they are not perfect mirror halves; the human brain, for example, is anatomically asymmetrical. (As Box 19.3 shows, such asymmetry is also found in other vertebrates.) Look in the mirror and smile—or if you are not up to that, grimace. Careful examination of facial folding and the edges of the lips shows decided asymmetry. The functional role of these facial asymmetries is unknown (although it has been claimed that expressions on the left side of the face are judged as more emotional, as we noted in Chapter 15).

Geschwind and Levitsky (1968) drew attention to brain structural asymmetry by finding that in 65% of human brains, a region of the cerebral cortex known as the **planum temporale** is larger in the left hemisphere than in the right (see Figure 19.12). In 11% the right side is larger. In some individuals, the magnitude of this left/right difference is almost 2 to 1. This region contains several auditory association cortices and part of Wernicke's speech area. Lesions of this approximate area usually produce Wernicke's aphasia. Thus, the region includes important components of language networks. Presumably the difference in the size of the area reflects the specialization (dominance) of one cerebral hemisphere for language. The larger left area implies more elaborate development of that side, which might include more nerve cells or greater elaboration of dendrites. This difference in cortical size is even more evident at birth; it appears in 86% of the infant brains examined. This evidence suggests an intrinsic basis for cerebral dominance in language, since the asymmetry appears before any environmental reinforcement of dominance can occur. An MRI study confirms the presence of this asymmetry and its relation to handedness (Steinmetz et al., 1991). In these observations, left-handers had less planum temporale asymmetry than did right-handers.

Direct anatomical observations and functional measures such as handedness and verbal abilities are not yet available from the same subjects. However, some indirect measures of temporal cortex size can be obtained from arteriograms (X-ray recordings) that reveal the size and course of the middle cerebral artery (Hochberg and LeMay, 1975; LeMay and Culebras, 1972). Of 44 right-handed patients, 86% showed a blood vessel pattern that implied greater left temporoparietal size, but this pattern was seen in only 17% of left-handers. Most left-handers showed no right/left differences.

CT scans reveal size differences in some large brain regions, and these differences can be related to overlying skull shape. Using this technique, LeMay (1977) showed that a majority of right-handers (61%) have wider frontal regions on the right, while only 40% of left-handers exhibit this pattern. In contrast, more left-handers had greater left frontal regions. The differences were more pronounced when only left-handers from left-handed families were compared with right-handers. Many gross measures of the cerebral hemispheres have revealed anatomic asymmetries, as Geschwind and Galaburda (1985) have summarized. Microscope comparisons of the left and right hemispheres reveal differences in fine structure between the two sides of the brain. The dendritic patterns of neurons in the right and left anterior speech areas are significantly different: cells on the left showed a more complex dendritic tree. This pattern was partially reversed in non-right-handed individuals (Scheibel et al., 1985).

Asymmetry in the distribution of transmitters has been noted in both human and animal studies. For example, regions of the human left thalamus contain more epinephrine than does the right thalamus (Geschwind and Galaburda, 1985). In rats, asymmetry in the concentration of dopamine in some regions of the basal ganglia is related to preferred turning direction (Glick et al., 1988). Hormonal relations to cerebral cortical asymmetry have been advanced by Diamond, Dowling, and Johnson (1981), who showed that the cerebral cortex is thicker in several areas on the left than on the right in female rats. In male rats the areas on the right are thicker. Removal of the testes at birth reversed this asymmetry.

Right/left asymmetry is also evident in vascular structures of the cerebral hemispheres and in measures of cerebral blood flow responses to verbal and nonverbal stimuli. Blood flow to any organ changes with tissue activity. This change is produced by varying the caliber of the blood vessels, producing dilation or constriction. Greater activation of left-hemisphere blood flow has been observed in response to verbal stimuli.

Many Theories Explain the Evolutionary Origins of Hemispheric Asymmetry and Specialization

To understand the workings of the brain it is useful to reflect on the advantages of certain biological states. Of course, the complete story of the rationale of some biological advantages is lost in the history of evolution.

Some see the origins of hemispheric specialization in the differential use of the limbs for many routine tasks. Picture early humans hunting. One hand holds the weapon and provides power, while the other is used in more delicate guidance or body balance. Archaeological studies of human skulls imply differential use of the limbs in attacking other humans. Proof offered for this idea is the greater frequency of left skull fracture in fossilized specimens of ancient people. In time the evolutionary successes offered by handedness might have been used in the emergence of language and speech.

Some theories about the emergence of speech and language focus on the motor aspects of speech, others on the cognitive properties of language. The speech motor apparatus involves many delicate muscle systems situated in the midline of the body, such as the tip of the tongue. Sensitivity and precision of stimulus analysis on the body surface are reduced in the exact midline. Perhaps this result reflects the mutual antagonism of right and left axon terminals in the skin. For speech this peculiarity of the midline would be catastrophic for precise control. Asymmetry of motor control of speech production might then

Box 19.3
Structural Asymmetry in the Vertebrate Nervous System

A quick glance in the mirror and an equally fleeting view of other vertebrates suggest that bilateral symmetry of the body is commonplace among animals. But a closer look reveals important exceptions. Among flatfishes—including such well-known edible fish as sole, flounder, and halibut—there are startling examples of bodily asymmetry that also include the brain (Rao and Finger, 1984). In adult flatfishes, both eyes are on the same side of the head (Figure A; Picasso wasn't the first to think of this arrangement). This structural oddity emerges during development. When the fish hatches from an egg, it has an ordinary fishlike symmetrical form, but as it develops, one eye migrates across the top of the head (Figure B). Some flatfishes are right-eyed, with both eyes on the right side of the head; others are left-eyed. Most flatfishes spend a large part of their time ly-

ing on the bottom of the sea, often covered with a light layer of sand, with only their eyes and nostrils exposed. When prey come near, the flatfish darts out to capture it. All flatfishes belong to the order Pleuronectiformes, and all fish in this order are asymmetrical as adults. Although both eyes are on one side of the head in these animals, the visual regions within the brain are symmetrical. However, the *olfactory* system in some flatfishes reveals a striking brain anatomical asymmetry (Figure C). The right nostril lies above the left, and the right olfactory receptor and pathways, including the olfactory regions of the brain, are distinctly larger than their counterparts on the left.

Structural asymmetry occurs in the brains of other nonhuman vertebrates, although it is not as pronounced as in flatfishes. Nonhuman primates show anatomical

asymmetries in the region of the temporal lobe analogous to those found in humans. Functional studies in nonhuman vertebrates reveal many examples of lateralization (one-sidedness), including the effects of lesions of the brain. Earlier in this chapter we saw that a surgical cut of the *left* hypoglossal cranial nerve in an adult male chaffinch results in the loss of the bird's song, whereas right-sided damage has little impact on the chaffinch's vocal behavior (Nottebohm, 1981).

Lateralization in human behavior is well-known. Most humans are right-handed in tasks involving finely coordinated activities, such as handwriting or tool use. Small differences in external appearance are also evident. Look in the mirror and smile; during such expressive gestures a slight facial asymmetry is observed. Some investigators believe this asymmetry is important

---

offer better unchallenged control of relevant parts of the speech apparatus. Such sidedness in the motor production of sound is seen even in the control of singing in birds, as we discussed earlier.

Arguments that propose a fundamental difference in cognitive style between the hemispheres suggest other connections to language and evolutionary advantages of cerebral specialization. According to this view, the left hemisphere provides processing that is analytic, and the right hemisphere offers a more holistic or general analysis of information. Some theorists suggest that hemisphere specialization allows for separate cognitive modes that are mutually incompatible. Any linguistic or cognitive response involves acting on elements differently, and hemisphere specialization, it is argued, is a good solution to this need.

The occasional errant flight of birds provides another clue to both the origins and advantages of bodily asymmetries. Some birds, while flying south during winter migration, end up in California instead of

the Southeast. Jared Diamond (1980) suggests that these animals confuse right and left; he suggests that a functional role of body asymmetries is to facilitate telling right from left. Hemispheric asymmetry thus can reduce the danger of spatial errors by providing a frame of reference.

We noted earlier that the French Academy of Sciences had once banned speculation on the origin of language, but no similar movement is afoot with respect to the topic of cerebral specialization. We have discussed only a small sample of current speculations. Further discussion might offer support for the wisdom of the French Academy in the late eighteenth century.

There Are Several Models of Cognitive Differences between the Human Cerebral Hemispheres

In the wake of research on human split-brain patients, considerable speculation developed about cognitive and emotional differences between the hemi-

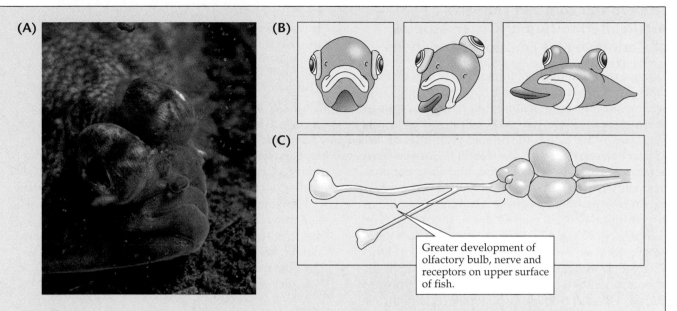

(A)

(B)

(C)

Greater development of olfactory bulb, nerve and receptors on upper surface of fish.

for emotional expression (see Chapter 15). But what about the human brain? Although anatomical differences between the human cerebral hemispheres went unnoticed by anatomists for a long time, recent research on functional differences between the cerebral hemispheres has refocused research on anatomical specializations in the human brain, including asymmetry of structure.

Morphological asymmetries are well documented in several parts of the human brain. Some regions of the temporal lobe relevant to verbal behavior are distinctly larger on the left side of the human brain (Galaburda, Sanides, and Geschwind, 1978). There is a gross asymmetry of the overall length and breadth of the right and left cerebral hemispheres. The frontal pole is larger on the right, while some parietal and occipital regions are wider on the left side of the brain (Chui and Damasio, 1980). Many other findings show that brain asymmetry is characteristic of humans. Relations between these anatomical findings and lateralized performance remain important topics for research.

spheres. This speculation has been further fueled by experimentation with normal humans. Some educators concerned about declining accomplishments in primary and secondary schools speak of educating "both halves of the brain." Increasing popularization of the themes of research in this area seems to lead to speculative leaps unbridled by facts.

Distinctions between left brain and right brain have been drawn ever since the dichotomy of verbal versus nonverbal grew from clinical observations of language disorders following left temporal and frontal injuries. Table 19.1 (p. 695) is a list proposed by various researchers of differences between the two hemispheres in cognitive processing. Leading this list is the distinction between verbal and nonverbal born from studies of aphasia. However, several experimental observations challenge this dichotomy. We have already noted that several studies using split-brain patients show language processing in the right hemisphere. This result is even more pronounced as researchers move away from using speech as the sole measure of linguistic abilities. For example, patients can point to objects whose name is flashed to the left visual field.

Although some experiments do show task differences between the cerebral hemispheres, the leap to the notion that we harbor two cognitive selves is beyond even inspired speculation. We must remember that many differences between the cerebral hemispheres are small and do not indicate that one side is more involved in the accomplishment of a particular function. It is usually very difficult to direct information exclusively to one hemisphere. Simultaneous processing by the two is the more likely story, and mutual interaction between the cerebral hemispheres is the typical state (Gazzaniga, LeDoux, and Wilson, 1977). Studying hemispheric specialization provides clues about information processing, and the clues indicate that mental unity is the customary human experience. Separate education of each hemisphere is not justified, at least from the vantage point of scientific inquiry to date.

The Frontal Lobes of Humans Are Related to Higher-Order Aspects of Cognitive and Emotional Functions

Because the complexity of human beings far exceeds that of other animals, researchers have sought characteristics of the brain that might account for human preeminence. Among the most striking differences is the comparative size of the human prefrontal cortex. In part because of its size, the frontal region has been regarded as the seat of intelligence and abstract thinking. Adding to the mystery of frontal lobe function is the unusual assortment of behavioral changes that follows surgical or accidental lesions of this region. The complexity of change following prefrontal damage is best epitomized by the last sentence of a report written by a physician describing the behavioral changes after accidental brain damage in the classic case of Phineas Gage. In 1848 Mr. Gage exploded gunpowder that sent an iron rod through his skull, producing a massive lesion of the prefrontal cortex. The last sentence of the physician's report reads, ". . . his mind was radically changed, so decidedly that his friends and acquaintances said that he was 'no longer Gage.'" Attempts to account for Gage's syndrome in neurological terms have undergone successive changes. In the latter part of the nineteenth century, neurologists began to realize that the bases of speech and motor behavior are localized in specific brain regions, but they were still reluctant to believe that moral reasoning and social behavior have localized neural mechanisms. We'll soon see, however, that Gage's symptoms are indeed related to damage to specific brain regions.

The Anatomy of the Frontal Lobe Forms a Basis for Understanding Its Complex Roles

The boundaries of the frontal lobes are not precisely defined, but the human frontal cortex is almost one-third of the entire cerebral cortical surface. At the posterior portion the frontal cortex includes motor and premotor regions (see Chapter 11). The anterior part is often referred to as **prefrontal cortex**, a critical component of a widespread neuronal network, with extensive linkages throughout the brain (Fuster, 1990). The prefrontal region is further subdivided into a dorsolateral area and an orbitofrontal region (Figure 19.19). In other animals the frontal cortex, especially prefrontal regions, is a smaller portion of the cerebral cortex (Figure 19.20).

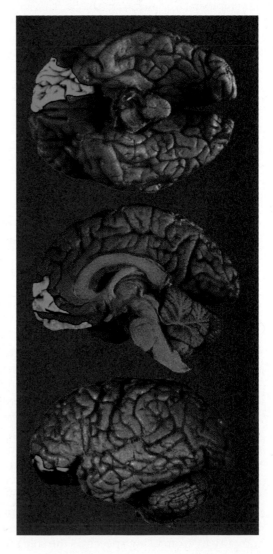

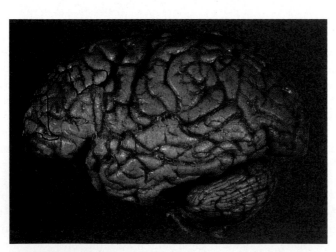

19.19 Prefrontal Cortex in Humans
Prefrontal cortex can be subdivided into a dorsolateral region (shown in blue above) and an orbitofrontal region (shown in green at right). Lesions in these different areas of prefrontal cortex have different effects upon behavior. Photographs courtesy of Michael Mega and Jeffrey Cummings.

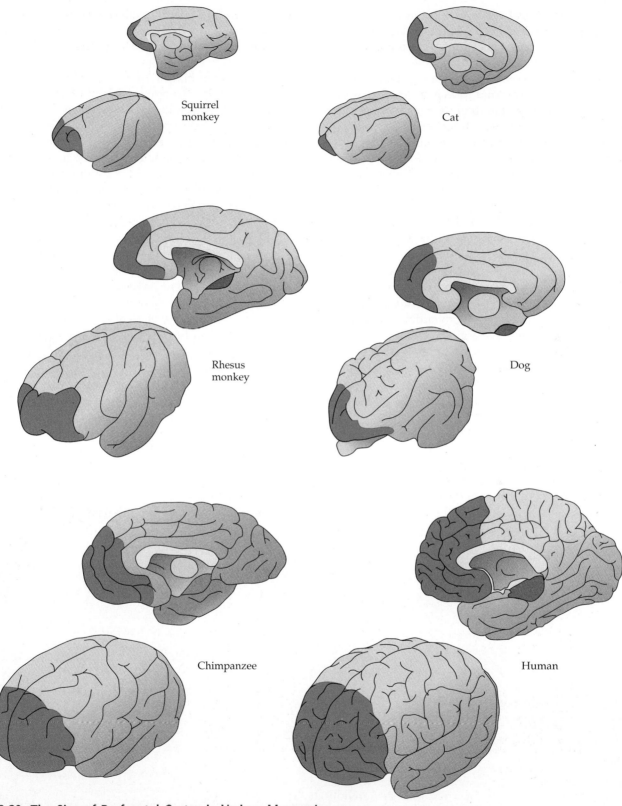

19.20 The Size of Prefrontal Cortex in Various Mammals
The relative percentage of prefrontal cortex is greatest in humans and decreases successively in other primates, carnivores, and rodents. The brains are drawn to different scales.

Now, a century and a half after Phineas Gage's accident, measurement of his skull and modern imaging techniques indicate that his injury was probably confined to the ventromedial region of both frontal lobes, sparing the dorsolateral region. Having made these measurements, Damasio and colleagues searched their extensive roster of neurological cases and found that Gage's syndrome matches that of several other patients with known brain damage in the region of Gage's probable injury (Damasio et al., 1994). Thus, the mysteries of frontal lobe function are gradually being resolved.

Frontal Lobe Injury in Humans Leads to Emotional, Motor, and Cognitive Changes

The clinical portrait of humans with frontal lesions reveals an unusual collection of emotional, motor, and cognitive changes. The emotional reactivity of these patients shows a persistent strange apathy, broken by bouts of euphoria (an exalted sense of well-being). Ordinary social conventions are readily cast aside by impulsive activity. Concern for the past or the future is rarely evident (Petrides and Milner, 1982; Duffy and Campbell, 1994). Frontal patients show shallow emotions, even including reduced responsiveness to pain. Frequently, though, there are episodes in which this apathy is replaced by boastfulness and silliness and, sometimes, unbridled sexual activities.

Cognitive changes in human frontal patients are very complicated and difficult to pinpoint, although one senses that something very different characterizes the frontal patient. Standard IQ test performance shows only slight changes after injury or stroke. Forgetfulness is shown in many tasks requiring sustained attention. In fact, some of these patients even forget their own warnings "to remember."

Clinical examination of frontal patients also reveals an array of strange impairments in motor activities, especially in the realm of "plans" for action. The patients seem to perseverate in any activity. For example, if the patient is asked to open and then close the fist, once the activity has begun—and it is difficult to initiate such acts in frontal patients—the patient continues a persistent sequence of fist opening and closing. The overall level of motor activity—especially ordinary, spontaneous movements—is quite diminished in frontal patients. For example, facial expression becomes blank, and there is a marked reduction in head and eye movements. Some reflexes evident only very early in life reappear in frontal cases, such as the infantile grasp reflex of the hand. Many clinical assessments of these patients have emphasized an impairment in goal-directed behavior, especially an inability to plan acts and use foresight. Daily activities of these patients seem disorganized and without a clear program for successive activities. Table 19.3 lists the main clinical features of patients with lesions of various portions of the frontal lobes.

Formal psychological tests are an important aspect of the assessment of the brain, but sometimes less formal behavioral assessments highlight a feature of brain impairment with striking clarity. At times, less formal behavioral observations reveal a behavioral

---

Table 19.3
Core Characteristics of the Regional Prefrontal Syndromes

DYSEXECUTIVE TYPE (DORSOLATERAL)	DISINHIBITED TYPE (ORBITOFRONTAL)	APATHETIC TYPE (MEDIOFRONTAL)
Diminished judgment, planning, insight, and temporal organization	Stimulus-driven behavior	Diminished spontaneity
Cognitive impersistence	Diminished social insight	Diminished verbal output (including mutism)
Motor programming deficits (may include aphasia and aproxia)	Distractibility	Diminished motor behavior (including akinesis)
Diminished self-care	Emotional lability	Urinary incontinence
		Lower extremity weakness and sensory loss
		Diminished spontaneous prosody
		Increased response latency

deficit that is not at all apparent from objective tests. This point was underscored by Lhermitte, Pillon, and Serdaru, (1986), who described an unusual phenomenon in patients with damaged frontal lobes—a syndrome characterized by spontaneous imitation of the gestures and behavior of the examiner. Lhermitte, Pillon, and Serdaru see this syndrome as related to one they identified as "utilization behavior," defined as an exaggerated dependence on the environment for behavioral cues.

The syndrome was observed during clinical exams in which the examiner made bodily gestures or engaged in writing or handling of objects. All patients with disease involving the frontal lobes spontaneously imitated the gestures of the examiner in detail. The slightest movement on the part of the examiner seemed to be an invitation to imitate. Patients were aware of their imitative behavior. Patient behavior in complex social situations also reflected the extraordinary environmental dependency of the behavior of frontal lobe patients. The social situations described by Lhermitte, Pillon, and Serdaru (1986) included observations of interactions in a home environment and in a doctor's office. In the latter situation, a patient saw a blood pressure gauge and immediately took the physician's blood pressure. After eyeing a tongue depressor, she placed it in front of the doctor's mouth. Upon walking into a bedroom, one patient proceeded to get undressed and go to bed. He hurried out of bed when the examiner picked up a piece of his clothing. In these acts there is a certain mechanical character; Lhermitte describes these patients as powerless in the face of influences from the outside world. The loss of self-criticism is another aspect of the behavior of these patients, as is evident in the act of urinating calmly against a public building.

Lhermitte suggests that some features of this deficit arise from the loss of frontal control over the activities of parietal cortex, which controls some aspects of sensorimotor activity. He suggests that the connection between the parietal and frontal cortex links the individual to the environment and subserves individual autonomy. Some of the features described by Lhermitte form part of a collection of characteristics that researchers now call "executive cognition"; the core characteristics of the frontal syndrome are referred to as the "dysexecutive type" (see Table 19.3). Executive cognition is said to include all the organizing principles that govern organized social behavior, such as those involved in producing context-sensitive goal-oriented behavior, self-monitoring, and planning activities.

Prefrontal Lesions in Nonhumans Produce Several Distinct Deficits

The study of prefrontal cortical function in animals began with the work of Carlyle Jacobsen in the 1930s. In his experiments with chimpanzees, Jacobsen employed delayed-response learning, as described in Chapter 17. This simple test situation revealed a remarkable impairment in chimpanzees with prefrontal lesions. These animals performed this task very poorly, in contrast with animals that sustained lesions in other brain regions. In interpreting this phenomenon, Jacobsen emphasized the memory function of the frontal cortex. Experimental and clinical observations of humans and other animals with frontal lesions have generated some hypotheses about the functions of the frontal lobes. Many types of symptoms become evident—almost an overabundance—and no immediately available generalizations can account for all these deficits. Some ideas fit more data than others and have thus become a strong focus for work in this area. These hypotheses include memory functions, planning controls, inhibitory control of behavior, and feedback control of behavior.

Spatial Perception Deficits Follow Some Types of Parietal Lobe Injury

Injury to the parietal lobe produces impairments such as these: Objects placed in the hand cannot be recognized by touch alone. One side of the body may be completely neglected, even to the point of being rejected as one's own. Faces cannot be recognized from photographs. Spatial orientation can become severely disturbed. The diversity of behavioral changes following injury to this region is related partly to its large expanse and its critical position adjacent to occipital, temporal, and frontal regions. The anterior end of the parietal region includes the postcentral gyrus, which is the primary cortical receiving area for somatic sensation. Brain injury in this area does not produce numbness; rather, it produces sensory deficits on the opposite side that seem to involve complex sensory processing. For example, objects placed in the hand opposite the injured somatosensory area can be felt but cannot be identified by touch and active manipulation. This deficit is called astereognosis (from the Greek *a-*, "lacking," *stereos*, "solid," and *gnosis*, "knowledge"). In some cases the deficit occurs on the same side as the brain injury (Corkin, Milner, and Rasmussen, 1970). More extensive injuries in the parietal cortex, not restricted to the somatosensory cortex, affect interactions between or among sensory modalities, such as visual/tactual matching tasks, which require the subject to identify visually an object that is touched, or the reverse.

When a Face Isn't a Face: Prosopagnosia

Suppose that one day you look in the mirror and you see someone who is not familiar to you! As incredible as this scenario might seem, a small group of people does suffer this fate after brain damage. This rare syndrome is called **prosopagnosia** (from the Greek *prosopon*, "face," and *gnosis*, "knowledge"). Such patients fail to recognize not only their own face but also the faces of relatives and friends. No amount of remedial training restores their ability to recognize anyone's face. In contrast, the ability to recognize *objects* is retained, and the patient readily identifies familiar people by the sounds of their voices. Faces simply lack meaning in the patient's life. No cognitive impairments, such as disorientation or confusion, accompany this condition. There is no evidence of diminished intellectual abilities. Visual acuity is maintained, although most patients have a small visual-field defect—that is, an area of the visual field where they are "blind."

The anatomical and neuropsychological features of this syndrome have been elegantly explored by Tranel and Damasio (1985). They noted that although earlier work focused on right-hemisphere lesions as the cause of the deficit, contemporary studies provide a more thorough anatomical picture of this disorder. Both postmortem examination and CT or MRI scans confirm that *bilateral* lesions are necessary for the syndrome to appear. The deficit involves inferior visual association regions of the occipitotemporal cortex. Lesions of the *superior* visual association areas that encompass occipitoparietal cortex, while producing some visual perceptual disorders, do not produce prosopagnosia.

Detailed neuropsychological analysis of patients with the syndrome provides insights into the underlying psychological mechanisms (Tranel and Damasio, 1985; Rizzo et al., 1986). The patients retain some complex perceptual abilities, including the ability to draw figures seen in photographs. Furthermore, prosopagnosia often involves other perceptual categories besides faces. Some prosopagnosic patients cannot recognize their own car and do not recognize common makes of cars, although they can distinguish between cars and trucks. Some are also unable to recognize types of clothes or distinctive foods. Birdwatchers are no longer able to recognize distinctive birds, and farmers can no longer recognize a particular animal, although they recognize animals as animals. Subfeatures of complex percepts can be pointed out, such as parts of a face. In addition, eye movements of patients recorded during their examination of a picture of a face are like those of controls, indicating that some basic perceptual processes proceed normally.

Tranel, Damasio, and Damasio (1988) asked patients to identify facial expressions, to estimate age and sex in photographs of strangers, and to identify the people in photographs of family members, friends, or other familiar faces. Patients could identify facial expressions and estimate age and sex but failed to recognize familiar faces. These findings suggest that visual input is analyzed in separate, parallel channels. The central feature of the deficit appears when the demand is to identify a specific stimulus configuration that depends on a memory trace. These patients have difficulty picking out a particular person from a group; the memory trace needed to activate context and familiarity appears not to be accessible. Damasio suggests that the basic impairment is not in the processes of complex visual analysis but more likely in the organization and use of pertinent memories.

Tranel and Damasio (1985) add some interesting data: They presented prosopagnosic patients with faces of familiar and unfamiliar people while recording electrodermal skin conductance, a response controlled by the autonomic nervous system. The familiar faces in the photos included the patient, family members, and close friends. Although patients could not *report* verbal recognition of the familiar faces, skin conductance changes were much more pronounced in response to familiar than to unfamiliar faces. These data indicate that recognition is taking place at some level, but overt identification and recognition are organized at a subsequent, perhaps more complex stage of visual information processing. This later stage might involve an integration of many different facets of memories pertinent to a particular face. Tranel and Damasio view the prosopagnosic deficit as a result of the "blocking of the activation that normally would be triggered by template matching"— the rich associative network of memories that enables someone to say, "I recognize Jane."

Neglect of One Side of the Body and Space Can Result from Parietal Lobe Injury

Brain damage involving the right inferior parietal cortex produces an unusual set of behavioral changes (Rafal, 1994). The key feature is the neglect of the left side of both the body and space. Patients may fail to dress the left side of their body and may even disclaim "ownership" of their left arm or leg. In some instances familiar people presented on the left side of the patient are completely neglected, although there may be no apparent visual-field defect. This phenomenon, called **hemispatial neglect,** can also be seen in simple test situations. A common test requires the patient to copy drawings of common objects. For example, when a patient is asked to draw the face of a clock, all the hour positions are crowded onto the right side (Figure 19.21; Schenkerberg, Bradford, and Ajax, 1980).

Associated with this dramatic change is a feature called extinction of simultaneous double stimulation. Most people can readily report the presence of two stimuli when stimulated simultaneously on both sides of the body. Patients with right inferior parietal lesions, however, are completely unable to note the double nature of the stimulation and usu-

ally report only the stimulus presented to the right side. This syndrome extends to visual imagery as well; for example, when dreaming, these patients scan only one side of dream scenes (Doricchi et al., 1991). Although many patients with injury to this region show recovery from unilateral neglect, the feature of extinction is quite persistent. Yet another dramatic feature of this syndrome is the frequent denial of illness. Patients may adamantly maintain that they are capable of engaging in their customary activities and do not recognize the impressive signs of unilateral neglect.

Many hypotheses have been offered to account for these symptoms. Table 19.4 lists mechanisms that might contribute to this syndrome. Some investigators have regarded the disorder as a consequence of the loss of the ability to analyze spatial patterns; this hypothesis is consistent with the fact that unilateral neglect occurs with lesions of the right hemisphere but not with lesions of the left hemisphere. Others regard the syndrome as an attentional deficit. The neurologist Mesulam (1985) notes that recordings of single cells from posterior parietal cortex in monkeys show firing patterns that are sensitive to manipulations of attention. For example, some nerve cells in this area increase their discharge rates when the animal's eyes follow or track a meaningful object, frequently one that has been associated with reward. Anatomical studies of the sources of inputs to the posterior parietal region show origins in several distinct cortical sectors, including polymodal cortical sensory areas, cingulate cortex, and frontal cortex, especially the frontal eye fields. In turn, posterior parietal cortex has outputs that extend to these regions. Mesulam proposes that each of these regions has a distinctive role in a network that governs attention. The posterior parietal component involves processes that yield an internal sensory map; frontal cortex governs relevant searching movements, and cingulate cortex processing provides motivational values.

Some Functions Show Recovery Following Brain Injury

The course of behavior following brain injury often reveals conspicuous changes. Striking examples of language recovery following stroke have been observed in many adults. Amazing examples of language recovery have been described in children following the removal of a diseased cerebral hemisphere. Many theories are offered to describe the mechanisms mediating the recov-

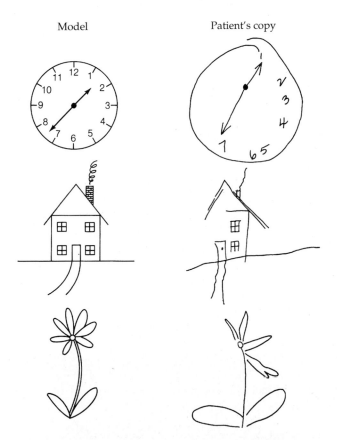

Model   Patient's copy

19.21 A Diagnostic Test for Hemispatial Neglect
When asked to duplicate drawings of common, symmetrical objects, patients suffering from neglect will ignore the left side of the model they are copying. From Kolb and Whishaw, 1990.

ery of function after lesions. Of course, recovery of function is characteristic of lesions involving many different organs. The surprise and puzzle of such effects following brain injury comes from the knowledge that, unlike other organs, the nervous system adds no significant amount of cells following birth. In addition, until recently the common view emphasized structural and functional fixedness of the brain—rigidity that seemed to provide little opportunity to compensate for a loss of elements. Current research on the recovery of brain functions has provided an exciting array of ideas and data that reveal several forms of brain plasticity. Studies in this area offer striking prospects for rehabilitation. Perhaps many different mechanisms together contribute to the patterns of recovery, so no single explanation can be offered as the sole basis.

In spite of these encouraging developments, prevention is clearly better than the cure. Motor vehicle accidents, horseback riding, diving, and contact sports are major causes of injuries to the brain and spinal cord. Box 19.4 describes the effects of boxing on the brain.

Some Recovery from Brain Injury Follows Relief from Generalized Physiological Abnormalities

Any brain injury destroys particular collections of nerve cells and produces more generalized disturbances that temporarily affect the responsiveness of other nerve cells. For example, in the region of a brain injury, frequently the properties of the blood–brain barrier change. Some researchers have suggested that the time course of functional deficits following structural damage to nerve cells might reflect the inhibitory impact of blood-borne substances, that are ordinarily prevented from reaching the environment of nerve cells (Seil, Leiman, and Kelly, 1976). In time, the changes in the blood vessels around a site of injury reestablish the blood–brain barrier and increase blood flow to transiently distressed but intact tissue. Many years ago the anatomist Monakow (1914) coined the term **diaschisis** to describe the distant inhibitory effects of brain lesions that seemed to be reversible. With time, usage of the this term has expanded to include a host of potentially reversible, nonspecific effects that

---

Table 19.4
Pathophysiological Mechanisms Contributing to the Neglect Syndrome

ABILITY AFFECTED	PUTATIVE NEURAL SUBSTRATE
Disengaging covert attention	Parietal lobe[a]
Voluntary shifts of attention	Superior parietal lobule
Hyper-engaging to local elements	Right temporoparietal junction
Arousal	Mesencephalic reticular formation; intralaminar thalamic nuclei
	Right-hemisphere activation of left hemisphere
Representation of space	Parietal or dorsolateral prefrontal cortex
Generating voluntary saccades	Frontal eye fields
Motor intention	Dorsolateral prefrontal cortex
Motivation for strategic orienting and sustained attention	Cingulate gyrus
Spatial working memory	Dorsolateral prefrontal cortex

[a]Right hemisphere parietal lesions affect disengagement of covert attention from locations; left hemisphere lesions affect disengagement from objects.
After Rafal, 1994.

Box 19.4
A Sport That Destroys the Mind

Men have used fists to settle arguments probably from the beginning of human history. Adding implements such as stones and knives to the fist increased the lethality of such aggressive encounters, but it was the addition of soft leather wound around the fist that signaled that fighting had become a sport. In ancient Greece and Rome, some boxers were admired for their courage and strength, while others, wearing leather wrappings studded with metal nuggets, bludgeoned each other to death for the entertainment of spectators. Boxing has a long history, much of it unpleasant. Although rules developed during the eighteenth century in England, including the use of padded gloves, the goal of prizefighting has always been not to display grace and agility, but to knock the opponent out. A bout usually ends when one fighter has sustained a brief loss of consciousness.

To achieve that goal, boxers aim relentlessly at the head, which sustains blow after blow—a history that comes to exact a price from the contestants. The result of so many blows to the head has been called dementia pugilistica, a fancy term used by neurologists to identify a state that is commonly known as punch-drunk. Punch-drunk boxers lead a life with markedly impaired cognitive abilities. In recent years several deaths have drawn atten-

tion once again to the dangers of boxing. Most boxing deaths are due to brain injuries, especially brain hemorrhage. Several professional societies, including the American Psychological Association and various medical and neurological societies, have urged the banning of this sport.

Although the neurological and psychological consequences of boxing have been noted before, CT scan data have indicated that very few boxers escape unscathed. Casson and collaborators (1982) studied ten active professional boxers who had been knocked out. These fighters ranged in age from 20 to 31 years, and the number of bouts per boxer ranged from 2 to 52. The group included those of championship caliber, as well as mediocre or poor boxers. None of the knockouts sustained by the fighters involved a loss of consciousness lasting more than ten seconds. This group is representative of the professional prizefighter.

At least five of the group had definitely abnormal CT scans. The abnormalities included mild generalized cortical atrophy, which in some cases included ventricular dilation. Only one boxer had a clearly normal brain picture. The age of the boxers was not related to the degree of cortical atrophy. The most successful boxers were

the ones with the most profound cortical atrophy. In fact, the total number of professional fights correlated directly with the magnitude of brain changes. During a career of boxing, a fighter accumulates many blows to the head; the most "successful" boxers thus frequently sustain the most punishment. The severity of neurological syndromes is also related to the duration of a boxer's career (Roberts, 1969). A Parkinson's-like consequence may result from boxing. A large-scale CT study of 338 active boxers showed that scans were abnormal in 7% (brain atrophy) and borderline in 12% (Jordan et al., 1992).

Amateur boxing presents a more optimistic portrait. Some studies report that amateur boxers show neither EEG abnormality nor brain structural changes as measured by MRI or CT (Haglund and Bergstrand, 1990; Haglund and Persson, 1990). Other studies have revealed a high incidence of abnormal EEGs after amateur boxing matches (Busse and Silverman, 1952). Since the cause of the neurological impairments is rapid acceleration of the brain, it is not surprising that significant neurological impairments are found in amateur boxers as well as in professionals: no small reason that many believe boxing is a sport whose time has passed.

make the immediate consequences of a brain lesion more intense than persistent deficits.

The Brain Regrows and Reorganizes Anatomically After Being Injured

Anatomical dogma for many years declared that changes in the adult central nervous system are sole-

ly destructive. The intricate structure and connections of nerve cells were considered to be structurally fixed once adulthood was reached. Injury, it was thought, could lead only to the shrinkage or death of nerve cells. Many impressive contemporary demonstrations to the contrary have now led us to emphasize the structural plasticity of nerve cells and their connections. Regeneration of the axons of the peripheral nervous system has always been accepted, but now comparable structural regrowth has been observed in the brain and spinal cord (Veraa and Grafstein, 1981). For example, injury to catecholamine-containing fibers in the medial forebrain bundle leads to regrowth of axonal portions connected to nerve cells. Dendrites in the brain may also grow back following injury. One form of regrowth following injury—**collateral sprouting**—is illustrated in Figure 19.22.

This change has been described in the peripheral nervous system, and the story goes like this: If a peripheral sensory or motor fiber is injured, the terminal portions degenerate and sensory or motor function in the affected region is immediately lost. Nerve fibers adjacent to the injured fibers recognize this injury (perhaps by a chemical signal delivered from the injured site), and they respond by developing sprouts or branches from intact axons. In time, usually weeks, these sprouts connect to denervated skin or muscle and acquire functional control of these regions on the periphery of the body (Diamond et al., 1976). This mechanism seems to result in functional compensation for a loss of neuronal connections. Incidentally, the injured nerve fiber (axon) slowly regrows, and as it approaches the skin or muscles it had been connected to, the sprouts retract. Again, chemical signals from the regrowing original fiber probably produce this change. Mark (1980) has suggested that a stage prior to the physical withdrawal of the fiber includes the cessation of synaptic effectiveness of the sprout-borne connections—a phenomenon he has labeled synaptic repression. This result implies that synapses can be turned off even though the structural connection is still present. This ability of synapses to be switched off is probably a significant feature of neural plasticity.

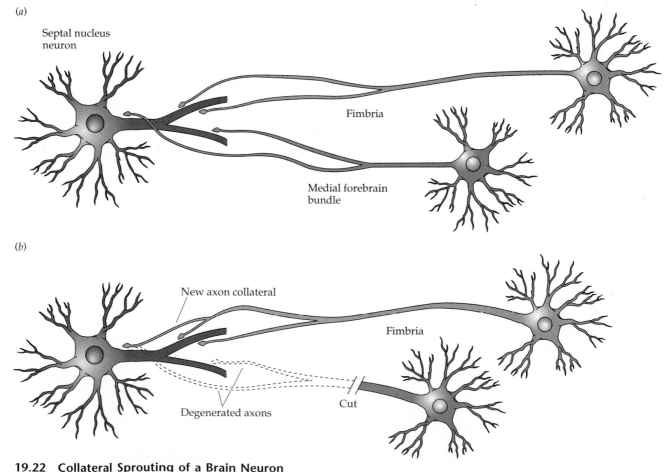

(a)

Septal nucleus neuron

Fimbria

Medial forebrain bundle

(b)

New axon collateral

Fimbria

Degenerated axons

Cut

19.22 Collateral Sprouting of a Brain Neuron
(a) Normal connections of fimbria and medial forebrain bundle to septal nucleus cell. (b) After severing of medial forebrain bundle, a fimbria axon develops a sprout that occupies a synaptic site formerly occupied by an axon terminal from the medial forebrain bundle. After Raisman, 1969.

Demonstrations of collateral sprouting in the brain and spinal cord, once rarely observed, are now reported with regularity. Some investigators suggest that collateral sprouting in the brain offers hope for functional repair following injury (Raisman, 1978). A growing view is that injury of the nervous system might release nerve growth factors. One group of researchers has reported that chemicals in the area of tissue surrounding brain injury contain a growth-promoting substance (Nieto-Sampedro and Cotman, 1985). The concentration of this yet unknown substance declines with distance from the injury site.

Observations of this sort indicate that brain connections are not as rigid anatomically as was once emphasized. The brain's response to injury does include structural modifications. However, are these anatomical changes relevant to the processes of functional repair? Around this question controversy swirls. Although structural repair in the brain in the form of collateral sprouting is now generally accepted, there is no evidence that links this change with functional recovery following injury to the brain or spinal cord. In fact, some investigators (Wall, 1980) suggest that collateral sprouting might generate behavioral ab-

normalities, since nerve cells come under the control of unusual inputs. This form of regeneration in the spinal cord has been linked to spasticity in reflexes elicited below the level of a spinal injury (Liu and Chambers, 1958). Intensive research currently in progress is aimed at evaluating the functional value of brain regrowth such as collateral sprouting.

Rehabilitation Can Facilitate Recovery from Brain Injury

For years hospitals and physicians have devoted considerable attention to providing rehabilitation for injuries that impair movement, especially if these defects developed from injury or disease of muscle or bone. For instance, teaching amputees to use prosthetic devices such as artificial limbs has been a common effort. Until recently, however, work with cognitive or perceptual handicaps that developed from brain impairments had received less intensive clinical and research interest. Several factors have provided the stimulus for a change of emphasis. Some recent studies have demonstrated that postinjury experience can affect recovery. It is important at this point to distinguish between the role of experience in *compensating* for brain injury and its role in *restoring* behavior lost after injury. It is well known that experiences significantly reduce the impact of brain injury by fostering compensatory behavior. For

example, vigorous eye movements can make up for large scotomas (blind spots in the visual field) that result from injury to the visual pathways. Behavior strategies can be changed after a brain injury to enable successful performance on a variety of tests.

The role of experience following a lesion in the possible reorganization of pathways was noted in Chapter 11, where we described how an individual whose arm afferents have been cut can recover control of the limbs. Berman and colleagues, (1978) described a striking phenomenon of recovery that involves a change in feedback signals governing behavior.

The importance of training and experience in promoting recovery has been suggested by clinical observations and has been studied in animal experiments. A well-known case of aphasia and slow but excellent recovery is that of the actress Patricia Neal (Neal, 1988). Before she had a stroke at the age of 39, Patricia Neal had won an Academy Award. She was the mother of three children, and at the time of her stroke she was pregnant. A series of strokes crippled one leg and left her aphasic, unable to speak, read, or write. Speech therapy was begun as soon as possible. Then her husband organized friends to come in on a schedule to talk with Pat and encourage her to speak and be active. Her baby was born normally. At this point Pat was still rather apathetic and was reluctant to continue to strive for further small gains: "I got fed up with working so hard. I felt certain that I was as good as I'd ever be. I was about eighty percent recovered. Still plenty of problems. But I was really ready to take a breather. And that's exactly what I would have done if Roald [Roald Dahl, her husband] hadn't made me go on. I had reached the danger point. The point where so many people stop work and just cruise along" (Griffith, 1970:89). Her husband then hired a gifted nurse, Valerie Eaton Griffith, who devised a program of motivation and training that helped Pat to make further gains. Four years after her stroke, Patricia Neal was able to star in another movie.

Recovery is probably never absolutely complete after a major brain lesion, but it can be full enough to permit an active life and even a resumption of professional activities, as the preceding example shows. Animal experiments have shown that both formal training and informal enriched experience can promote the recovery of function. Several studies performed with brain-lesioned rats have demonstrated that postlesion experience in a complex environment can improve subsequent problem-solving behavior (Will et al., 1977). Animals were placed in impoverished or enriched environments of the same kinds that had been shown to lead to changes in brain measures (see Chapter 18). Although the brain-injured animals still made more errors than did intact rats, those in the enriched environments made significantly fewer errors than those in the impoverished environments. Simply placing a group of animals together in a large cage had a measurable beneficial effect; giving the animals access to varied stimuli was even more helpful (Rosenzweig, 1980). Thus, even an injured brain can profit from experience. In the case of human patients, some rehabilitation experts have questioned the wisdom of placing certain patients in virtual sensory isolation (coma patients, or patients kept in fixed positions in isolated rooms for intravenous therapy). Such patients, even if they cannot respond, might be aided by visitors, music, and changing visual stimuli. Some current programs of rehabilitation are putting these insights into effect.

Brain Structures That Remain Intact after Injury Can Substitute for Damaged Structures

Recovery following brain injury demonstrates that remaining neural tissue can mediate required behaviors. One perspective suggests that there is appreciable redundancy of neural systems and that recovery involves the use of redundant pathways. However, what appears to be redundancy may arise from the complexity of the neural substrates of behavior and the simple ways in which recovery is assessed. Thus if the neural substrate for some behavior is broadly represented in the brain, behavior may be reinstated because of the extensiveness of neural controls rather than because of redundant or repeated systems. One type of unusual substitution has been described by Wall (1980), who studied the receptive field properties of dorsal column and thalamic cells following peripheral denervation. Wall noted that sizes of receptive fields of cells in this system change with denervation, especially in the direction of increasing size. Cells may also become responsive to bilateral inputs. Thus change occurs rapidly, and Wall suggests that denervation *unmasks* weakly excitable paths that come to control some neurons. Wall refers to this effect as a "homeostatic adjustment" of nerve cell excitability.

Switching of nerve cell responsiveness in sensory paths is also evident in the vestibular system. Cutting the vestibular nerve or removing the labyrinth on one side results in head tilting or deviation and other signs of postural asymmetry. In time, these effects abate, illustrating a phenomenon known as vestibular compensation. Some of this recovery depends on inputs from the spinal cord (Jensen, 1979). Another independent aspect of recovery is a change in the activity of brain stem vestibular neurons. The dynamic charac-

ter of cortical sensory systems is shown by Wall and Kaas (1986): cutting a peripheral nerve to one digit enlarged the receptive fields of some cortical neurons.

Functional imaging studies of stroke patients provide additional evidence about the role of substituted structures in mediating recovery. PET studies on hemiplegic patients show that whereas movement of the unaffected hand activates motor cortex only on the opposite side of the body, attempted movement of the affected hand activates motor cortex on *both* sides (Chollet and Weiller, 1994). These results suggest that motor cortex on the same side as the injury mediates recovered movements. Studies of activation in such patients have revealed that the cerebellum also plays a role in recovery.

Age Influences the Recovery of Function Following Brain Injury

Many clinical observations have led to the general proposition that brain lesions have less disastrous consequences when sustained early in life rather than later in life. The explanation offered for this phenomenon is that the younger brain possesses greater plasticity, although it is also acknowledged that the infant brain is more vulnerable to some destructive agents, such as viruses. A study of human language impairments and age provides an example of the relations between maturational state and recovery of function. In a survey of childhood aphasia, Woods and Teuber (1978) examined records of a large group of children who had lost language abilities following brain damage. The age of eight looms as a critical point in recovery from brain trauma. All children who became aphasic before the age of eight regained speech, no matter how great the impairment observed immediately following brain injury. (An example is given in Box 19.2.) The time for recovery of language ranged from one month to two years. Many children who became aphasic after age eight showed less complete recovery.

Differences in nerve cell regrowth processes have been related to age in several studies. Kalil and Reh (1979) note that cutting the pyramidal tract at the level of the medulla in infant hamsters results in massive regrowth. They also note that in contrast to adult hamsters treated in the same way, infant hamsters develop normal motor functions of the forepaw. According to Scheff, Bernardo, and Cotman (1978), regenerative capabilities seem to decline with age. Reactive regrowth in the aged rat brain, for example, is very sparse. The researchers argue that this result implies a reduction with aging in the ability to remodel circuitry. Studies in nonhumans that explore the factor of age in recovery yield both similarities with and differences from humans. Goldman (1976) studied the relation between maturation of the brain in monkeys and development of their behavior. One of her studies employed devices implanted in the brains of monkeys by means of which a local area of the cortex could be cooled and thus inactivated for a period of time in an awake monkey. This technique produces, in effect, a reversible brain lesion. Bilateral cooling of the prefrontal cortex in adult monkeys (three years old or older) impaired their performance on a delayed-response task, but it did not affect their general level of activity or motor coordination. In juvenile monkeys (18 months old or younger), however, the cooling had no effect on the test performance. This result is in line with other evidence that the frontal dorsolateral cortex in the monkey does not achieve its adult function until after the monkey is two years old.

Brain Lesions That Develop Slowly Have Different Effects from Those Produced by Similar but Rapidly Formed Lesions

The impairment caused by a brain lesion increases with the rate at which the lesion develops. Some investigators refer to this phenomenon as **lesion momentum,** or mass × velocity (Finger, 1978). Investigators experimenting with animals have studied lesion momentum by removing a given amount of tissue all at once or in stages separated by a few weeks. A lesion in the brain stem that incapacitates animals if made all at one time may have only slight effect if done in two successive stages. The partial lesion may stimulate regrowth or relearning or both, so that some compensation has already been achieved by the time the rest of the tissue is removed. Some experimenters have reported that sensory stimulation or retraining during the interval between successive lesions is necessary for the reduced impairment observed with staged destruction, but not all studies agree. Experimental findings suggest a mechanism for the staged-lesion effect: a lesion that causes loss of synaptic connections may result in the release of chemical signals that facilitate the sprouting of terminals. When a small lesion precedes a larger lesion by four days to two weeks, the response to the second lesion is significantly faster and more extensive than if the earlier lesion had not occurred. Thus the earlier lesion primes the system to respond to the subsequent lesion (Scheff, Bernardo, and Cotman, 1978).

Clinical cases also reveal effects of lesion momentum. For example, an adult patient with a brain tumor encroaching on the speech areas of his left hemisphere had several operations, spaced many months apart (Geschwind, 1976). Each time the tumor regrew, it was necessary to remove more of the cortical speech areas, and each time the patient recovered his speech. In the end he was still speaking, even though only a fragment of the speech areas remained. Aging can also be thought of as a slowly developing condition, which probably helps to mitigate its effects on the brain.

Lesion momentum is one of the reasons it is difficult to relate the effects of a disease-caused brain lesion to its size. This phenomenon can help us understand some cases that seem to contradict localization of function. That is, brain lesions in two patients may appear to be the same in size and location, yet one patient shows severe behavioral impairment while the second does not. Perhaps the lesion in the second patient developed slowly, allowing time both for growth in adjacent tissue and for elaboration of compensatory behavioral strategies. Thus, lesion momentum shows that the brain cannot be regarded as a fixed piece of machinery, but must be seen as a plastic structure that adapts to imposed conditions.

In this section we have noted several examples and mechanisms related to functional recovery following brain lesions. These various mechanisms are not mutually exclusive; all may contribute to the pattern of reinstating behavior, for regrowth may provide an opportunity for some forms of recovery but require the sustaining impact of experience. Therefore synaptic regrowth alone may not provide the substrate for recovery. Regrowth in conjunction with appropriately timed experience may be the formula for plasticity. As the field of neurological rehabilitation develops and efforts to aid the brain-injured become more extensive, we will gain more accurate knowledge of both the possibilities and the limits of recovery.

Summary

1. Humans are distinct in the animal kingdom for their language and associated cognitive abilities. Possible evolutionary origins of human speech may be seen in aspects of gestures.

2. Studies of communication among nonhumans provide analogies to human speech. For example, the control of birdsong is lateralized in the brains of some species of singing birds. Further, in some of these species early experience is essential for proper song development.

3. Limitations of the vocal tract in nonhumans are proposed as one reason that they do not have speech. But nonhuman primates like the chimpanzee can learn to use signs of the American Sign Language. However, controversy surrounds claims that these animals can arrange signs in novel orders to create new sentences.

4. Ninety-five percent of human language impairments involve injuries of the left hemisphere. Left anterior lesions produce an impairment in speech production called Broca's aphasia. More posterior lesions involving the temporoparietal cortex affect speech comprehension, as seen in Wernicke's aphasia.

5. Left-hemisphere lesions in users of sign language produce impairments in the use of sign language that are similar to impairments in spoken language shown by nondeaf aphasics.

6. Split-brain patients show striking examples of hemispheric specialization. Most words projected only to the right hemisphere cannot be read, while the same stimuli directed to the left hemisphere can be read. Verbal abilities of the right hemisphere are also reduced; however, spatial-relation tasks are performed better by the right hemisphere than by the left.

7. Normal humans also show many forms of cognitive specialization of the cerebral hemispheres, although these specializations are not as striking as those shown by split-brain patients. For example, most normal humans show a right-ear advantage and greater accuracy for verbal stimuli in the right visual field.

8. Anatomical asymmetry of the hemispheres is seen in some structures in the human brain. Especially striking is the large size difference in the planum temporale (which is larger in the left hemisphere of most right-handers).

9. Broad theoretical statements about different cognitive modes of the two hemispheres exceed confirmations from current experimental and clinical data. In most cases mental activity depends on interactions between the cerebral hemispheres.

10. The frontal lobes of humans are quite large compared with those of other animals. Injury in parts of this region produces an unusual syndrome of profound emotional changes, including reduced responsiveness to many stimuli. Tasks that require sustained attention show drastic impairment after frontal lesions.

11. In most patients, parietal cortex injuries on the right side produce many perceptual changes. A dramatic example is the inability to recognize familiar objects and the faces of familiar people. Some patients with right parietal injury neglect or ignore the left side of both the body and space.

12. Many functional losses following brain injury show at least partial recovery. Most recovery from aphasia occurs in the year following stroke, with fewer changes evident after that.

13. Mechanisms of functional recovery may involve structural regrowth of cell extensions—dendrites and axons—and the formation of new synapses.

14. Retraining is a significant part of functional recovery and may involve both compensation, by establishing new solutions to adaptive demands, and reorganization of surviving networks.

15. Greater recovery is evident in young individuals. Less impairment occurs when lesions are produced over a period of time—that is, when lesion momentum is reduced.

Recommended Readings

Corbalis, M. C. 1991. *The Lopsided Ape*. Oxford University Press, New York.

Gazzaniga, M. S. (ed.). 1995. *The Cognitive Neurosciences*. MIT Press, Cambridge, Mass.

Hellige, J. B. 1993. *Hemispheric Asymmetry*. Harvard University Press, Cambridge, Mass.

Kertesz, A. (ed.). 1994. *Localization and Neuroimaging in Neuropsychology*. Academic Press, San Diego.

Pinker, S. 1994. *The Language Instinct*. William Morrow, New York.

CHAPTER **A Final Word**

20

Orientation

As a student, you are of course relieved to read, at last, the final chapter of a textbook. As authors, we were relieved, too, to arrive here. But we feel moved to have a final word with you about why we took you through all the material and all the examples that make up this book. We want to highlight an overall theme that runs throughout the book and to discuss that theme explicitly before you go.

We have likened the brain to a machine and that analogy is accurate—the brain is a physical object whose parts must obey the laws of a material world. In the early chapters we described how the various parts of the brain communicate with each other through physical media such as neurotransmitters, hormones, and action potentials. When we described psychological phenomena such as learning, perception, and cognition, it was implicit that these aspects of the mind were a product of the machine called the brain.

However, we have also described a brain that is remarkably plastic, in a constant state of flux. But the brain is unlike any man-made machine because it is constantly remodeling itself—rearranging connections between its parts—in a manner that normally improves its function. As you know from bitter experience, all man-made machines reach their peak performance once they are assembled and simply tumble downhill after that. Computer scientists struggle and yearn to develop systems that can truly learn from experience, something accomplished quite easily when an egg and a sperm combine.

Because they study behavior, psychologists have a particular interest in changes in behavior, and, since the nineteenth century, they have assumed that the changes in behavior must reflect physical changes in the brain. The only alternative to such a view would have been a regression to the belief in spirits or demons as explanations of why people change. But the complexity of the brain was so overwhelming that few researchers even attempted to find how changes in behavior might be reflected in changes in brain structure or chemistry. However, over the past 30 years, increasingly powerful methods have been developed that have enabled psychologists and other neuroscientists to clearly demonstrate that the brain is indeed constantly changing and that experience alters neural structure.

Neural development. Of course the brains of developing individuals are even more plastic than those of adults—that's why infants learn new languages and recover from neural injuries so much more readily than adults. In Chapter 4 we reviewed the many processes that occur as the brain puts itself together and showed how cell–cell interactions play a crucial role in all of those processes. The notochord induces cells to become motoneurons, targets secrete neurotrophic factors to attract and sustain neurons, radial glial cells guide migrating cells to their final destination. Cells take on appropriate roles and make proper connections based on what neighboring cells are doing. Thus the cells of the developing nervous system are in constant communication with one another, and directly affect one another's fate. Because some of the neurons communicating these directions are sensory neurons, responding to stimuli in the environment, experience itself shapes the brain. The best studied example is in the visual system; as you have learned, early experience is crucial for forming the connections between the eye and brain that underlie normal adult vision.

Regulation of receptors. Even at the level of neurotransmitter receptors, plasticity and change are the norm. Remember from Chapter 6 that the number of neurotransmitter receptors in the postsynaptic region of a given synapse can increase or decrease depending on the amount of activity at that synapse. Usually this activity serves to regulate the activity of a particular pathway—basal ganglia cells receiving too little dopamine stimulation start making more

receptors until they become supersensitive. Overstimulation leads to "down-regulation" of the receptors so that the signal is attenuated. Since experience can clearly affect which of our brain cells are firing, it must affect the number and distribution of neurotransmitter receptors.

Hormones and behavior. The endocrine system (Chapter 7) also involves complicated feedback systems to maintain relatively steady hormone levels. But experience also modulates the pattern of hormone secretion—losing an aggressive encounter can lower testosterone secretion, stress can augment ACTH secretion and kill hippocampal cells, and exposure to pheromones can accelerate or delay puberty. While there are no data to implicate the role of pheromones in human pubertal development, the dramatic decline over the past century in the age at which individuals undergo puberty in our society indicates that some factors—better nutrition, greater exposure to sexual stimuli, or chemicals introduced into the environment by human activity—have affected our reproductive systems, too.

Sensory plasticity. As noted above, research with sensory systems is especially fruitful in demonstrating experiential effects. In Chapter 8 we learned that changes in tactile stimulation, even in adulthood, can alter the size and shape of brain regions that represent the body surface. This phenomenon was first demonstrated in response to several different types of experience in monkeys, and its existence in humans has recently been confirmed using noninvasive imaging techniques to examine people who had lost a hand in accidents. On the side of the brain receiving information from the remaining hand, stimulation to that hand excited a region of the somatosensory cortex sandwiched between brain regions responding to the face and upper arm; this is the normal pattern. But on the side of the brain that was no longer receiving information from the lost hand, the regions representing the face and upper arm were found to be immediately adjacent to each other: connections from the face and upper arm had shifted on that side of the brain to take over the region which had formerly been excited by stimuli from the hand. These data suggest that our senses are constantly competing not only for our attention, but for space in the brain—space to analyze and process that information which is most relevant to the business of surviving and reproducing.

Clinical issues.   Our bodies and brains constantly adjust to the time of day and time of year, as detailed in Chapter 14. In nonhuman animals, body weight and many other parameters are affected by whether the individual is exposed to summer-like long days or winter-like short days. Similarly, in humans the short days of winter seem to exacerbate some bouts of depression, so our nervous systems may also be carefully measuring the seasons. In Chapter 16 we saw that even severe psychopathologies such as schizophrenia are not entirely concordant in identical twins, so something other than genes can influence these disorders, and the best candidate for that other "something" is difference in experience. Hopes are blossoming that recovery from brain injuries may be accomplished with grafts of genetically manipulated cells. These procedures clearly work in some cases, and may be feasible one day in others. But to the extent that they work at all, it is because the rest of the brain is capable of changing, to integrate these new cells into an existing network.

Learning and memory.   In Chapters 17 and 18 we dealt with the processes that most explicitly depend upon structural alterations in the adult nervous system—learning and memory. If adult brains could not change, then we could not learn anything, and the college course for which you are reading this book would be a waste of time. (Please save opinions on this matter for course evaluation forms!) But we can learn, and scientists have made remarkable progress in finding structural changes that may underlie this ability. Again we find that even structures at the molecular level can be altered by experience, as illustrated by one of the foremost neurotransmitter receptors involved in learning, the NMDA receptor. At a particular kind of synapse, the NMDA receptor will allow ions to enter the postsynaptic cell and the presence of these ions changes the synapse so that it will transmit its signal more forcefully in the future. In other words, "neurons that fire together wire together." In 1949, psychologist Donald Hebb predicted the existence of such processes based on inferences from behavior and what was known of neuroscience at that time. As work with simple systems such as *Aplysia* proceeds, we find further evidence that both the strength of existing synapses and the number and pattern of synaptic connections can be altered by the learning experience. This work also emphasizes the reciprocal relationship of experience and the brain that we emphasized in Chapter 1: experience alters the brain, and the brain seeks out particular experiences.

These are only a few examples taken from the dozens of issues discussed in this book, but they nicely capsulize the "take-home message" we hope to have imparted to you concerning the neurosciences: the brain is dynamic—changing, malleable, adaptable. This emphasis reflects our biases, since we are psychologists as well as neuroscientists. But it also reflects a central problem in understanding the nervous system, the control of behavior. What is most impressive about the behavior of humans and other animals is the variety of behaviors individuals of a given species use to accomplish the same goals; the variety of behaviors each individual displays throughout life; and the variety of behaviors different species develop to solve life's basic problems of surviving and reproducing. We hope that you already had an appreciation for the diversity of behaviors within and across species, but few people who have not studied a book such as this one fully grasp that this diversity of behaviors requires a dynamic brain and that the changes it undergoes must be physical in nature: changes in receptors, neurotransmitters, numbers of cells, or neuronal connections. The remaining challenge—and it is a formidable one—is to try to understand exactly how experience changes the nervous system and exactly how those changes alter later behaviors. We and the other 22,000 or so other neuroscientists at work in the U.S., as well as our colleagues around the world, hope to keep you posted on our progress in this effort, and we hope our progess makes a concrete difference in your own life.

Molecular Biology: Basic Concepts and Important Techniques

APPENDIX

Genes Carry Information That Encodes the Synthesis of Proteins

The most important thing about **genes** is that they are *pieces of information*, inherited from parents, that affect the development and function of our cells. The information carried by the genes is a very specific sort: each gene codes for the construction of a specific string of amino acids to form a **protein** molecule. The various proteins, each encoded by its own gene, make up the physical structure and most of the constituents of cells, including enzymes. **Enzymes** are molecules that allow particular chemical reactions to occur in our cells. For example, only cells that have liver-typical proteins will look like a liver cell and be able to perform liver functions. Neurons are cells that make neuron-typical proteins so that they can look and act like neurons. The genetic information for making these sorts of proteins is crucial for an animal to live and for a nervous system to work properly.

One thing we will hope this book will help you understand is that everyday experience can affect whether and when particular genetic recipes for making various proteins are used. But first let's review how genetic information is stored and how proteins are made. Our discussion will be brief because we assume that you've been exposed to this material before in an introductory biology course.

Genetic Information Is Stored in Molecules of DNA

The information for making all of our proteins could, in theory, be stored in any sort of format—on sheets of paper, magnetic tape, a CD-ROM—but all living creatures on this planet store their genetic information in a chemical called **deoxyribonucleic acid**, or **DNA**. Each molecule of DNA consists of a long strand of chemicals called **nucleotides** strung one after the other. There are only four nucleotides: guanine, cytosine, thymine, and adenine (abbreviated "G," "C," "T," and "A"). The particular sequence of nucleotides (for example, GCTTACC or TGGTCC or TGA) holds the information that will eventually make a protein.

Because many millions of these nucleotides can be joined one after the other, a tremendous amount of information can be stored in very little space—on a single molecule of DNA.

A set of nucleotides that has been strung together can snuggle tightly against another string of nucleotides if it has the proper sequence: T nucleotides can fit across from A nucleotides, and Gs can fit across from Cs. Thus, T's are said to be complementary to As, while Cs are complementary to Gs. In fact, most of the time our DNA consists not of a single strand of nucleotides, but of two complementary strands of nucleotides wrapped around one another. The two strands of nucleotides are said to **hybridize** with one another, coiling slightly to form the famous double helix (Figure A.1). The double-stranded DNA twists and coils further, becoming visible in microscopes as **chromosomes**, which resemble twisted lengths of yarn. We and many other organisms are known as **eukaryotes** because we store our chromosomes in a membranous sphere called a **nucleus** inside each cell. You may remember that the ability of DNA to exist as two complementary strands of nucleotides is crucial for the duplication of the chromosomes, but that story will not concern us here. Just remember that, with very few exceptions, every cell in your body has a faithful copy of all the DNA you received from your parents.

DNA Is Transcribed to Produce Messenger RNA

The information from DNA is used to assemble another molecule—**ribonucleic acid**, or **RNA**—that serves as a template or guide for later steps. Like DNA, RNA is made up of a long string of four different nucleotides. For RNA, those nucleotides are G and C (which, you recall, are complementary to each other), and A and U (uracil), which are also complementary to each other. Note that the T nucleotide is found only in DNA and the U nucleotide is found only in RNA. When a particular gene becomes active, the double strand of DNA unwinds enough so that

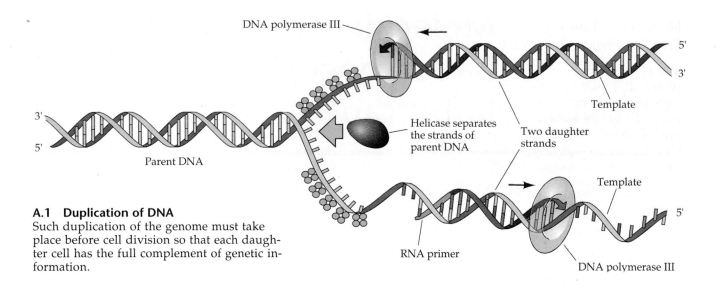

A.1 Duplication of DNA
Such duplication of the genome must take place before cell division so that each daughter cell has the full complement of genetic information.

one strand becomes free of the other and becomes available to special cellular machinery (including an enzyme called transcriptase) that begins **transcription**—the construction of a specific string of RNA nucleotides that are complementary to the exposed strand of DNA (Figure A.2). This length of RNA, sometimes called the message, or messenger RNA (mRNA), is also sometimes called a **transcript** because it contains a faithful transcript of the information in the DNA. Each DNA nucleotide has encoded for a specific RNA nucleotide (an RNA G for every DNA C, an RNA C for every DNA G, an RNA U for every DNA A, an RNA A for every DNA T). This transcript is made in the nucleus where the DNA resides; then the mRNA molecule moves to the cytoplasm, where protein molecules are assembled.

RNA Molecules Direct the Formation of Protein Molecules

In the cytoplasm are special organelles, called **ribosomes**, that attach themselves to a molecule of RNA, "read" the sequence of RNA nucleotides, and using that information, begin linking together amino acids to form a protein molecule. The structure and function of a protein molecule depend on which particular amino acids are put together and in what order. The decoding of an RNA transcript to manufacture a particular protein is called **translation** (see Figure A.2), as distinct from transcription, the construction of the mRNA molecule. Each trio (or "triplet") of RNA nucleotides encodes for one of about 20 different amino acids. Special molecules associated with the ribosome recognize the trio of RNA nucleotides and bring the appropriate amino acid so that the ribosome can fuse that amino acid to the previous one. If the resulting string of amino acids is short (say, 50

amino acids or so), it is called a **peptide**; if it is long, it is called a protein. Thus the ribosome assembles a very particular sequence of amino acids at the behest of a very particular sequence of RNA nucleotides, which were themselves encoded for in the DNA inherited from our parents. In short, the secret of life is: DNA makes RNA, and RNA makes protein.

There are fascinating amendments to this short story. Often the information from separate stretches of DNA is spliced together to make a single transcript; so-called "alternate splicing" can create different transcripts from the same gene. Sometimes a transcript is modified extensively before translation begins; special chemical processes can cleave long proteins to create one or several active peptides. But we will not consider those processes in this book. An important point to keep in mind is that each cell has the complete library of genetic information (collectively known as the **genome**), but makes only a fraction of all the proteins encoded for in that DNA. In modern biology we say that each cell **expresses** only some genes; that is, the cell transcribes certain genes and makes the corresponding gene products (protein molecules). Thus, each cell must come to express all the genes needed to perform its function. Modern biologists refer to the expression of a particular subset of the genome as cell differentiation: the process differentiates the appearance and function of different types of cells. During development, individual cells appear to become more and more specialized, expressing progressively fewer genes. Many molecular biologists are striving to understand what cellular and molecular mechanisms "turn on" or "turn off" gene expression in order to understand development and pathologies such as cancer.

Molecular Biologists Have Craftily Enslaved Microorganisms and Enzymes

Many basic methods of molecular biology are not explicitly discussed in the text, so we will not describe them in detail here. However, you should understand what some of the terms *mean*, even if you don't know exactly how the methods are performed. Molecular biologists have found ways to incorporate foreign DNA from other species into the DNA of microorganisms such as bacteria and viruses. After incorporating the foreign DNA, the microorganisms are allowed to reproduce rapidly, producing more and more copies of the (foreign) gene of interest. At this point the gene is said to be **cloned**, because the researcher can make as many copies as she likes. To ensure that the right gene is being cloned, the researcher generally clones many, many different genes, each into different bacteria, and then "screens" the bacteria rapidly to find the rare one that has incorporated the gene of interest.

When enough copies of the DNA have been made, the microorganisms are ground up and the DNA extracted. If sufficient DNA has been generated, chemical steps can then determine the exact sequence of nucleotides found in that stretch of DNA, a process known as **sequencing**. Once the sequence of nucleotides has been determined, the sequence of complementary nucleotides in the messenger RNA for that gene can be inferred. The sequence of mRNA nucleotides tells the investigator the sequence of amino acids that will be made from that transcript, because biologists know which amino acid is encoded for by each triplet of DNA nucleotides. In this manner scientists have discovered the amino acid sequence of neurotransmitter receptors, including the structure of photoreceptors that allows us to see.

In the past few years the business of obtaining many copies of DNA has been boosted by a technique called the **polymerase chain reaction**, or **PCR**. This technique exploits a special type of polymerase enzyme that, like other such enzymes, induces the formation of a DNA molecule that is complementary to an existing single strand of DNA. Because this particular polymerase enzyme evolved in bacteria that inhabit geothermal hot springs, it can function in a broad range of temperatures. By heating double-stranded DNA, we can cause the two strands to separate, making each strand available to polymerase enzymes which, when the temperature is cooled down enough, construct a new "mate" for each strand so that they are double-stranded again. The first PCR yields only double the number of DNA molecules you began with; repeating the process results in four times as many as at first. Repeatedly heating and cooling the DNA of interest in the presence of this heat-resistant polymerase enzyme soon yields millions of copies of the original DNA molecule.

Thus PCR amplifies even tiny amounts of DNA into amounts that are large enough for chemical analysis or other manipulations, such as introducing DNA into cells. For example, you might inject some of the DNA encoding a protein of interest into a fertilized mouse egg (a zygote) and then return the zygote to a pregnant mouse to grow. Occasionally the injected DNA becomes incorporated into the zygote's genome so the **transgenic** mouse that results carries and uses this foreign gene.

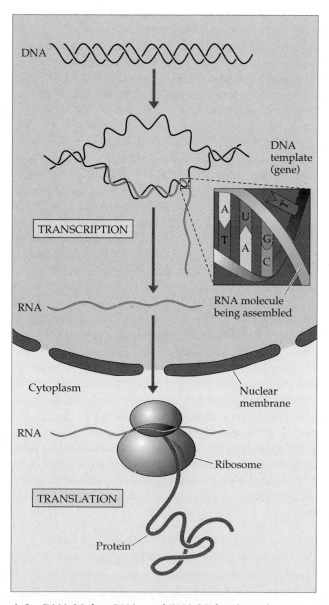

A.2 DNA Makes RNA, and RNA Makes Protein

Southern Blots Identify Particular Genes

Since all cells contain a complete copy of the genome, if we want to know whether a particular individual or a particular species carries a certain gene, we can gather DNA from just about any cell population (for humans, blood is drawn; for rodents, the tip of the tail may be used). Then we can grind up the cells and use chemical extraction procedures to isolate the DNA (discarding the RNA and protein). Finding a particular gene in that DNA really boils down to finding *a particular sequence of DNA nucleotides*. To do that, we can exploit the tendency of nucleic acids to hybridize with one another. If we were looking for the DNA sequence GCT, for example, we could manufacture the sequence CGA (there are machines to do that readily), which will then stick to (hybridize with) any DNA sequence of GCT. The manufactured sequence CGA is called a **probe** because it is made to include some radioactive molecules so that we can follow the radioactivity to find out where the sequence goes. Of course, such a short length of nucleotides will be found in many genes. In order for a probe to recognize one particular gene, it has to be at least 15 nucleotides long. When we extract DNA from an individual, it's convenient to let enzymes cut up the very long stretches of DNA into more manageable pieces of 1 to 20 thousand nucleotides each. A process called **gel electrophoresis** uses electrical current to separate those millions of pieces more or less by size. Large pieces move slowly through a tube of gelatinlike material, and small pieces move rapidly. The tube of gel is then sliced and placed on top of a sheet of paperlike material called nitrocellulose. When fluid is allowed to flow through the gel and nitrocellulose, DNA molecules are pulled out of the gel and deposited on the waiting nitrocellulose. This process of making a "sandwich" of gel and nitrocellulose and using fluid to move molecules from the former to the latter is called **blotting** (Figure A.3).

If the gene we are looking for is among those millions of DNA fragments sitting on the nitrocellulose, our radiolabeled probe should recognize and hybridize to the sequence. The nitrocellulose sheet is soaked in a solution containing our radiolabeled probe; we wait for the probe to find and hybridize with the gene of interest (if it is present), and rinse the sheet to remove probe molecules that did not find the gene. Then photographic film is placed next to the nitrocellulose. The particles emitted by the radioactive molecule will expose the film just as light does. If the radiolabeled probe found the gene, the film will be dark at one particular place, corresponding to the size of DNA fragment that contained the gene (see Figure A.3). This process of looking for a particular sequence of DNA is called **Southern blotting**, named after the man who developed the technique, Edward Southern, and the final film is often called a Southern blot. Southern blots are useful for determining whether related individuals share a particular gene or for assessing the evolutionary relatedness of different species.

Northern Blots Identify Particular RNA Transcripts

A more relevant method for our discussions is the **Northern blot** (whimsically named as the opposite of a Southern blot). A Northern blot can identify which tissues make use of a particular gene. If liver cells are making a particular protein, for example, then some transcripts for that gene should be present. So we can take the liver, grind it up, and use chemical processes to isolate most of the RNA (throwing the DNA and protein away). Unlike purified DNA, this mixture consists of RNA molecules of many different sizes—long, medium, and short transcripts. Gel electrophoresis will separate the transcripts by size, and we can blot the size-sorted mRNAs onto nitrocellulose sheets. To see whether the particular transcript we are looking for is among the mRNAs, we construct a radiolabeled probe (of either DNA nucleotides or RNA nucleotides) that is complementary to the transcript of interest and long enough that it will hybridize only to that particular transcript. We incubate the nitrocellulose in the probe, allow time for the probe to hybridize with the targeted transcript (if present), rinse off any unused probes, lay the nitrocellulose next to photographic film, and wait a day or so. If the transcript of interest is present, we should see a band on the film (see Figure A.3). Several bands indicates that our probe has hybridized to more than one transcript and we need to make a more specific probe or alter chemical conditions to make the probe less likely to bind similar transcripts. Because different gene transcripts are of different lengths, the transcript of interest should have reached a particular point in the gel electrophoresis; small transcripts should have moved far, large transcripts should have moved only a little. If our probe has found the right transcript, the single band of labeling should be at the point that is appropriate for a transcript of that length.

In Situ Hybridization Identifies Which Cells Possess a Particular Transcript

Northern blots can tell us whether a particular *organ* has transcripts for a particular gene product. For ex-

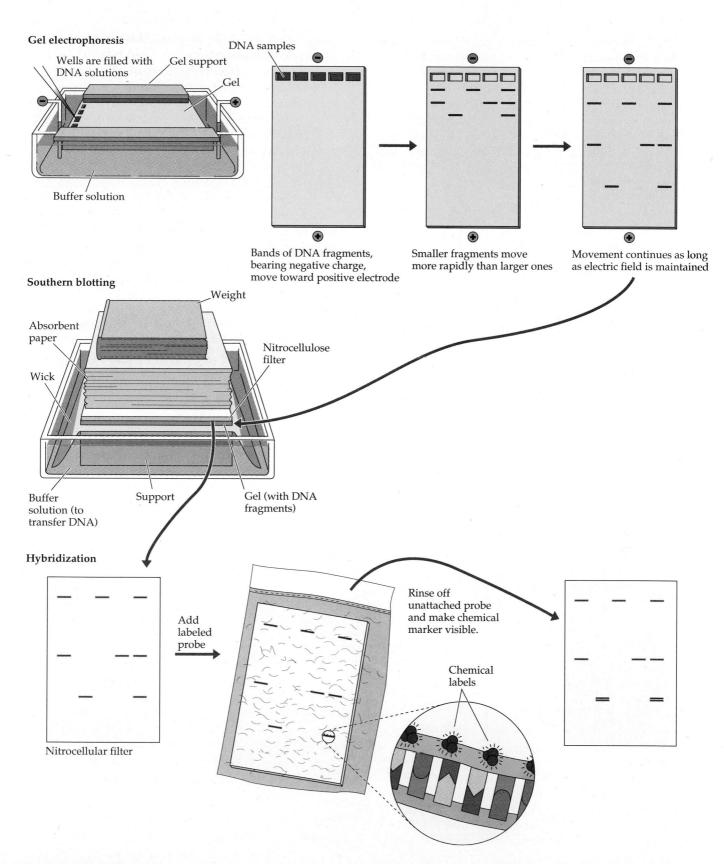

Gel electrophoresis

Wells are filled with DNA solutions

Gel support

Gel

DNA samples

Buffer solution

Bands of DNA fragments, bearing negative charge, move toward positive electrode

Smaller fragments move more rapidly than larger ones

Movement continues as long as electric field is maintained

Southern blotting

Weight

Absorbent paper

Wick

Nitrocellulose filter

Buffer solution (to transfer DNA)

Support

Gel (with DNA fragments)

Hybridization

Add labeled probe

Rinse off unattached probe and make chemical marker visible.

Chemical labels

Nitrocellular filter

A.3   Southern Blotting

ample, Northern blot analyses have indicated that there are thousands of genes that are transcribed only in the brain. Presumably the proteins encoded by these genes are used exclusively in the brain. But such results alone are not very informative because the brain consists of so many different kinds of glial and neuronal cells. We can refine Northern blot analyses somewhat by dissecting out a particular part of the brain, say the hippocampus, to isolate mRNAs. Sometimes, though, it is important to know *exactly*

which cells are making the transcript. In that case we use **in situ hybridization**.

With in situ hybridization we use the same sort of labeled probe, constructed of nucleotides that are complementary to (and will therefore hybridize with) the targeted transcript, as in Northern blots. Instead of using the probe to find and hybridize with the transcript on a sheet of nitrocellulose, however, we use the probe to find the transcripts "in place" (in situ)—that is, on a section of tissue. After rinsing off the probe molecules that didn't find a match, we can look for the probe in the tissue section. Any cells in the section that were transcribing the gene of interest will have transcripts in the cytoplasm and should have some of our labeled probe (Figure A.4). In situ hybridization can tell us exactly which cells are using a particular gene.

Western Blots Identify the Organ or Tissue Region Where a Particular Protein Is Made

Sometimes we may wish to identify a particular pro-

Bead of solution covering brain section, contains labelled probe

Labeled probe hybridyzing to RNA

RNA in cytoplasm of cell

Rinse off unattached probes and make chemical label visible

Chemical label identifies hippocampal regions which had been making targeted RNA.

A.4   In Situ Hybridization

tein rather than its transcript. In that case we can use antibodies. **Antibodies** are large, complicated molecules (proteins, in fact) that our immune system makes and releases into the bloodstream to fight invading microbes, thereby arresting and preventing disease (see Figure 15.19). By injecting a rabbit or mouse with the protein of interest, the animal can be induced to create antibodies that recognize and attach to that particular protein. Because there are ways to label such antibodies, they can be used to tell us whether the targeted protein is present. We can grind up an organ, isolate the proteins (throwing the DNA and RNA away), and separate them via gel electrophoresis. Then we can blot these proteins out of the gel and onto nitrocellulose. Next we use the antibodies to tell us whether the targeted protein is among those made by that organ. If our antibodies are identifying only the protein we care about, there should be a single band of labeling (if there are two then the antibodies recognize more than one protein). Because proteins come in different sizes, the single band of label should be at the position corresponding to the size of the protein we are studying. Such blots are called **Western blots**. (To review, Southern blots identify particular DNA pieces [genes], Northern blots identify particular RNA pieces [transcripts], and Western blots identify particular proteins [sometimes called products].)

Antibodies Can Also Tell Us Which Cells Possess a Particular Protein

If we need to know which particular cells within an organ such as the brain are making a particular protein, we can use the same sort of antibodies as we use in Western blots, but in this case directed at that protein in tissue sections. We slice up the brain, expose the sections to the antibodies, allow time for them to find and attach to the protein, rinse off unattached antibodies, and use chemical treatments to visualize the antibodies. Cells that were making the protein will be labeled from the chemical treatments (Figure A.5). Because antibodies from the *immune* system are used to identify *cells* with the aid of *chemical* treatment, this method is called **immunocytochemistry**, or **ICC**. This technique can even tell us where, within the cell, the protein is found. Such information can provide important clues about the function of the protein. For example, if the protein is found in axon terminals, it may be a neurotransmitter.

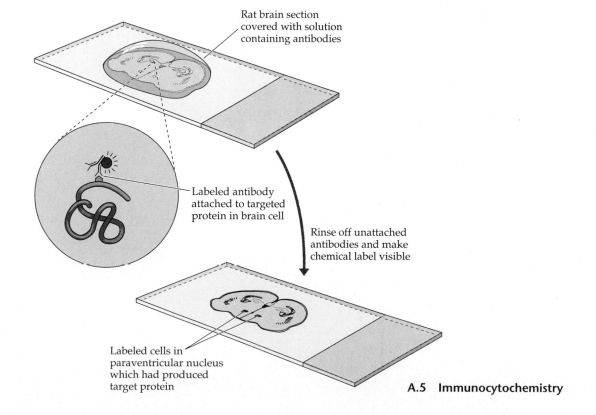

Rat brain section covered with solution containing antibodies

Labeled antibody attached to targeted protein in brain cell

Rinse off unattached antibodies and make chemical label visible

Labeled cells in paraventricular nucleus which had produced target protein

A.5   Immunocytochemistry

Glossary

2-DG 2-Deoxyglucose.

5HT Serotonin.

absolute refractory phase See *refractory phase*.

accommodation The process of focusing by the ciliary muscles and the lens to form a sharp image on the retina.

acetylcholine (ACh) One of the best known synaptic transmitters. Acetylcholine acts as an excitatory transmitter at synapses between motor nerves and skeletal muscles but as an inhibitory transmitter between the vagus nerve and the heart muscle.

acetylcholinesterase (AChE) An enzyme that inactivates the transmitter acetylcholine both at synaptic sites and elsewhere in the nervous system.

ACh Acetylcholine.

AChE Acetylcholinesterase.

Achromatopsia Lack of color (but not black-and-white) vision.

acquired immune deficiency syndrome (AIDS) A disease characterized by the loss of immune function that is spread by the human immunodeficiency virus (HIV).

act Complex behavior, as distinct from a simple movement. Also called action pattern.

ACTH Adrenocorticotropic hormone.

action pattern See *act*.

action potential The propagated electrical message of a neuron that travels along the axon to adjacent neurons. Also called the nerve impulse. See Figure 5.3.

activational effect A temporary change in behavior resulting from the administrationof a hormone to an adult animal. Contrast with *organizational effect*.

acupuncture The insertion of needles at designated points on the skin to alleviate pain.

adaptation The progressive loss of receptor sensitivity as stimulation is maintained. See Figure 8.7.

adenohypophysis See *anterior pituitary*.

adequate stimulus The type of stimulus for which a given sense organ is particularly adapted. Light energy is the adequate stimulus for photoreceptors.

ADH Antidiuretic hormone.

adipose tissue Tissue made up of fat cells.

adipsia A condition in which an individual refuses to drink.

adrenal cortex The outer covering of the adrenal gland. Each of the three cellular layers of the adrenal cortex produces different hormones. See Table 7.2.

adrenal gland An endocrine gland adjacent to the kidney. See Figure 7.14.

adrenal medulla The inner core of the adrenal gland. The adrenal medulla secretes epinephrine and norepinephrine. See Figure 7.14.

adrenaline See *epinephrine*.

Adrenocorticoids A class of steroid hormones that are secreted by the adrenal cortex.

adrenocorticotropic hormone (ACTH) A tropic hormone secreted by the anterior pituitary gland that controls the production and release of hormones of the adrenal cortex. See Figure 7.13.

adrenosteroids See *adrenocorticoids*.

afferent fiber An axon that carries nerve impulses from a sense organ to the central nervous system, or from one region into another region of interest. Contrast with *efferent fiber*.

afterpotential The positive or negative change in membrane potential that may follow a nerve impulse.

agnosia The inability to recognize objects, despite being able to describe them in terms of form and color; may occur after localized brain damage.

agonist A molecule, usually a drug, that binds a receptor and initiates a response like that of another molecule, usually a neurotransmitter. Contrast with *antagonist* (definition 1).

agraphia The inability to write.

AI Androgen insensitivity.

AIDS Acquired immune deficiency syndrome.

aldosterone A mineralocorticoid hormone, secreted by the adrenal cortex, that helps maintain homeostasis in the concentrations of ions in blood and extracellular fluid by inducing the kidneys to conserve sodium.

alexia The inability to read.

alkaloids A class of chemicals, found in plants, that includes many psychoactive agents, such as curare, the opium alkaloids (morphine and codeine), and lysergic acid (to which LSD is related).

all-or-none Referring to the fact that the amplitude of the nerve impulse is independent of the magnitude of the stimulus. Stimuli above a certain threshold produce nerve impulses of identical magnitude (although they may vary in frequency); stimuli below this threshold produce no nerve impulses. Contrast with *graded potential*. See Figure 5.3.

allomone A chemical signal that is released outside the body by one species and affects the behavior of other species. Contrast with *pheromone*. See Figure 7.4.

alpha motoneuron A motoneuron that controls the main contractile fibers (extrafusal fibers) of a muscle. See Figure 11.9.

alpha rhythm A brain potential that occurs during relaxed wakefulness, especially at the back of the head; its frequency is 8 to 12 Hz. See Figure 14.11.

alphafetoprotein A protein found in the plasma of fetuses. In rodents alphafetoprotein binds estrogens and prevents them from entering the brain.

ALS Amyotrophic lateral sclerosis.

altricial Referring to animals that are born in an undeveloped state and depend on maternal care, as human infants do. Contrast with *precocial*.

Alzheimer's disease A type of dementia that occurs in middle age or later.

amacrine cells Cells in the retina that contact both the bipolar cells and the ganglion cells, and are especially significant in inhibitory interactions within the retina. See Figure 10.8.

amblyopia Reduced visual acuity that is not caused by optical or retinal impairments.

amine hormones A class of compounds that are composed of a single amino acid that has been modified into a related molecule, such as melatonin or epinephrine. Also called monoamine hormones.

amnesia Severe impairment of memory.

amnestic An amnesia-causing agent.

AMPA receptor A glutamate receptor that also binds the glutamate agonist AMPA (alpha-amino-3-hydroxy-5-methyl-4-isoxazole-propionic acid). The AMPA receptor is responsible for most of the activity at glutaminergic synapses. See Box 5.3 and Figure 18.16.

amphetamine A molecule that resembles the structure of the catecholamine transmitters and that enhances their activity.

ampulla (pl. ampullae) An enlarged region of each semicircular canal that contains the receptor cells (hair cells) of the vestibular system. See Figure 9.18.

amygdala A group of nuclei in the medial anterior part of the temporal lobe. See Figure 2.18.

β-amyloid A protein that accumulates in senile plaques in Alzheimer's disease.

amyotrophic lateral sclerosis (ALS) A disease in which motoneurons and their target muscles waste away.

analogy A resemblance between two species that is due to convergence rather than to common ancestry.

androgen insensitivity (AI) The inability to respond to androgenic hormones; caused by a defect in the gene for the androgen receptor.

androgens A class of hormones that includes testosterone and other male hormones. See Table 7.2.

androstenedione The chief sex hormone secreted by the human adrenal cortex. Responsible for the adult pattern of body hair in men and women.

angiography A noninvasive technique for examining brain structure in humans by taking X-rays after special dyes are injected into cerebral blood vessels. Inferences about adjacent tissue can be made from examining the outline of the principal blood vessels.

angiotensin II A substance that is produced in the blood by the action of renin and that may be involved in control of thirst.

angular gyrus A brain region in which strokes can lead to word blindness.

anion A negatively charged ion, such as a protein or chloride ion. Contrast with *cation*.

anomia The inability to name persons or objects readily.

anomic aphasia Difficulty in recalling words, although comprehension and ability to repeat words are normal.

anorexia The absence of appetite.

anorexia nervosa A syndrome in which individuals severely deprive themselves of food.

antagonist 1. A molecule, usually a drug, that interferes with or prevents the action of a transmitter. Contrast with *agonist*. 2. A muscle which counteracts the effect of another muscle. Contrast with *synergist*.

anterior pituitary The front lobe of the pituitary gland; secretes tropic hormones. Also called adenohypophysis. See Figure 7.13.

anterograde amnesia The inability to form new memories beginning with the onset of the disorder.

anterograde degeneration The loss of the distal portion of an axon resulting from injury to the axon. Also called Wallerian degeneration. See Box 4.1.

antidiuretic hormone (ADH) A hormone from the posterior pituitary that controls the removal of water from blood by the kidneys. Also called vasopressin.

antigen A substance that stimulates the production of antibodies.

antipsychotic drug A drug that alleviates schizophrenia.

anxiety states A class of psychological disorders that include recurrent panic states, generalized persistent anxiety disorders, and posttraumatic stress disorders.

anxiolytics A class of substances that are used to combat anxiety; examples include alcohol, opiates, barbiturates, and the benzodiazepines.

aphagia The refusal to eat; often related to damage to the lateral hypothalamus.

aphasia An impairment in language understanding and/or production that is caused by brain injury.

apical dendrite The dendrite that extends from a pyramidal cell to the outermost surface of the cortex. Contrast with *basal dendrite*.

apoptosis See *cell death*.

appetitive behavior The second stage of mating behavior; helps establish or maintain sexual interaction. See Figure 12.2.

apraxia An impairment in the ability to begin and execute skilled voluntary movements, although there is no muscle paralysis.

arachnoid   The thin covering of the brain that lies between the dura mater and pia mater.

archicortex   Evolutionarily old cortex, such as the hippocampus in mammals. Thought to be more ancient than paleocortex.

arginine vasopressin   See *vasopressin*.

aromatase   An enzyme that converts many androgens into estrogens.

aromatization   The chemical reaction that converts testosterone to estradiol and other androgens to other estrogens.

aromatization hypothesis   The hypothesis that testicular androgens enter the brain and are there converted into estrogens to masculinize the developing nervous system of some rodents.

aspartic acid   Thought by many investigators to be a major excitatory synaptic transmitter in the central nervous system.

associative learning   A type of learning in which an association is formed between two stimuli or between a stimulus and a response; includes both classical and instrumental conditioning. Contrast with *nonassociative learning*.

astereognosis   The inability to recognize objects by touching and feeling them.

astrocyte   A star-shaped glial cell with numerous processes, or extensions, that run in all directions. The extensions of astrocytes provide structural support for the brain and may isolate receptive surfaces. See Figure 2.7.

ataxia   An impairment in the direction, extent, and rate of muscular movement; often caused by cerebellar pathology.

attribute model   Model in which different brain regions process different dimensions or attributes of a learning/memory situation—space, time, sensory dimensions, response, and emotional aspects.

auditory cortex   A region of the temporal lobe that receives input from the medial geniculate nucleus. See Figure 9.8.

auditory nerve   The VIII cranial nerve; it runs from the cochlea to the brain stem auditory nuclei. See Figure 9.1.

autocrine   Referring to a signal that is secreted by a cell into its environment and that feeds back to the same cell. See Figure 7.4.

autonomic ganglia   One of the three main divisions of the peripheral nervous system; includes the two chains of sympathetic ganglia and the more peripheral parasympathetic ganglia.

autonomic nervous system   The part of the peripheral nervous system that supplies neural connections to glands and to smooth muscles of internal organs. Composed of two divisions (sympathetic and parasympathetic) that act in opposite fashion. See Figure 2.14.

autonomic response specificity   Patterns of bodily response governed by the autonomic nervous system that are characteristic of an individual.

autoradiography   A histological technique that shows the distribution of radioactive chemicals in tissues.

autoreceptor   A receptor for a synaptic transmitter that is located in the presynaptic membrane. Autoreceptors tell the axon terminal how much transmitter has been released.

autosome   One of a pair of chromosomes that are identical. All chromosomes except the sex chromosomes are autosomes.

axon   A single extension from the cell that carries nerve impulses from the cell body to other neurons. See Figures 2.3, 2.4, 2.5.

axon collateral   A branch of an axon from a single neuron.

axon hillock   A cone-shaped area from which the axon originates out of the cell body. Depolarization must reach a critical threshold at the axon hillock for the neuron to transmit a nerve impulse. See Figure 2.5.

axon terminal   The end of an axon or collateral, which forms a synapse upon a neuron or other target.

axonal transport   The transportation of materials from the neuron cell body to distant regions in the dendrites and axons, and from the axon terminals back to the cell body.

axoplasmic streaming   The process that transports materials synthesized in the cell body to distant regions in the dendrites and axons.

B lymphocyte   An immune-system cell that mediates humoral immunity.

ballism   An uncontrollable violent tossing of the limbs. Lesions in the subthalamic nucleus can produce this syndrome in humans and monkeys.

ballistic movement   A rapid muscular movement that is thought to be organized or programmed by the cerebellum. Contrast with *ramp movement*.

baroreceptor   A pressure receptor in the heart or a major artery that detects a fall in blood pressure and communicates that information to the brain via the autonomic nervous system.

basal dendrite   One of several dendrites on a pyramidal cell that extend horizontally from the cell body. Contrast with *apical dendrite*.

basal ganglia   A group of forebrain nuclei found deep within the cerebral hemispheres. See Figures 2.10, 2.18, 11.17.

basal metabolism   The rate of metabolism when a body is at rest.

base   A component of a DNA or RNA molecule. DNA contains four bases (adenine, thymine, cytosine, and guanine), a pair of which forms each rung of the molecule. The order of these bases determines the genetic information of a DNA molecule.

basic neuroglial compartment   A level of brain organization that includes a single nerve cell with all its synaptic endings, associated glial cells, surrounding extracellular space, and vascular elements. See Figure 2.19.

basic rest–activity cycle   A cycle of repeating periods of rest and activity that occur both in waking hours and during sleep.

basilar artery   An artery formed by the fusion of the vertebral arteries; its branches supply blood to the brain stem and to posterior portions of the cerebral hemispheres. See Figure 2.21.

basilar membrane   A membrane in the cochlea that contains the principal structures involved in auditory transduction. See Figure 9.5.

BDNF   Brain-derived neurotropic factor.

behavioral intervention   An approach to finding relations between bodily variables and behavioral variables that involves intervening in the behavior of an organism and looking for resultant changes in bodily structure or function. See Figure 1.12.

behavioral toxicology   Study of effects of toxic substances on behavior and use of behavioral measures to assay toxicity of substances.

behavioral teratology   Study of impairments in behavior that are produced by embryonic or fetal exposure to toxic substances.

benzodiazepines   A class of anti-anxiety drugs that bind with high affinity to receptors in the central nervous system; one example is diazepam (Valium).

binaural interaction   The interaction of signals from two ears; especially important for localizing auditory stimuli.

binocular disparity   The slight difference between the views from the two eyes; important in depth perception.

biofeedback   A technique in which a bodily variable such as skin temperature or the gross electrical activity of the brain is monitored. The resulting information allows the subject to gain some control over the bodily variable and may be used in the treatment of various disorders.

bipolar cells   Interneurons of the retina that receive information from rods and cones and pass the information to retinal ganglion cells.

bipolar depression   A psychiatric disorder characterized by depressed periods that alternate with excessive, expansive moods. Also called manic-depressive psychosis. Contrast with *unipolar depression*.

bipolar neuron   A nerve cell that has a single dendrite at one end and a single axon at the other end; found in some vertebrate sensory systems. See Figures 2.4, 10.27.

blastocyst   An early developmental stage in which the organism is a hollow sphere whose wall is one cell thick.

blind spot   The place through which blood vessels enter the retina. Because there are no receptors in this region, light striking it cannot be seen. See Figure 10.2.

blood–brain barrier   The mechanisms that make the movement of substances from capillaries into brain cells more difficult than exchanges in other body organs, thus affording the brain greater protection from exposure to some substances found in the blood.

brain-derived neurotrophic factor (BDNF)   A protein purified from the brain of many animals that can keep some classes of neurons alive. Resembles nerve growth factor.

brain explant   A small piece of brain tissue isolated from the body.

brain stem   The region of the brain that consists of the midbrain, the pons, and the medulla.

Brattleboro rat   A rat that has a mutation in the gene for vasopressin that keeps the animal from producing functional hormone. Brattleboro rats show the symptoms of diabetes insipidus.

brightness   One of the basic dimensions of light perception; varies from dark to light. See Figure 10.5.

Broca's aphasia   An impairment in speech production; related to damage in Broca's area.

Broca's area   An area in the frontal region of the left hemisphere of the brain that is involved in the production of speech. See Figure 19.7.

brown adipose tissue   Tissue made up of fat cells that is found especially around vital organs in the trunk and around the cervical and thoracic levels of the spinal cord; is capable of intense metabolism and therefore can generate heat. Also called brown fat.

bulimia   A syndrome in which individuals believe themselves fatter than they are and periodically gorge themselves, usually with "junk food," and then either vomit or take laxatives to avoid weight gain. Also called bulimia nervosa.

caffeine   A stimulant compound found in coffee, cocoa, and other plants which may have evolved to protect plants against insect predators. Caffeine stimulates and causes uncoordinated behavior in insects and inhibits their growth and reproduction.

calcitonin   A hormone released by the thyroid gland.

calcium-dependent kinase   An enzyme that, in the presence of calcium, adds phosphate groups (PO_4) to protein molecules. Calcium-dependent kinase has been investigated in regard to memory.

calorie   The amount of energy required to raise the temperature of 1 milliliter of water by 1° C.

cAMP   Cyclic adenosine monophosphate.

carotid arteries   The major arteries that ascend the left and right sides of the neck to the brain. The branch that enters the brain is called the internal carotid artery. See Figure 2.21.

CAT   Computerized axial tomography.

cataplexy   The sudden loss of muscle tone, leading to collapse of the body without loss of consciousness.

cation   A positively charged ion, such as a potassium or sodium ion. Contrast with *anion*.

caudal   An anatomical term referring to structures toward the tail end of an organism. Contrast with *rostral*.

caudate nucleus One of the basal ganglia that has a long extension or tail. See Figure 2.18.

cell assembly A large group of cells that tend to be active at the same time because they have been activated simultaneously or in close succession in the past.

cell body The region of a neuron that is defined by the presence of the nucleus. See Figure 2.3.

cell death The final developmental process in shaping the nervous system, during which "surplus" nerve cells die. Also called apoptosis.

cell differentiation The developmental stage in which cells acquire distinctive characteristics, such as those of neurons, as the result of expressing particular genes. See Figure 4.3.

cell-mediated immunity An immunological response that involves T lymphocytes.

cell migration The movement of nerve cells from their site of origin to their final location. See Figures 4.3, 4.4.

cell proliferation The production of cells by mitotic division. See Figure 4.4.

cellular fluid See *intracellular fluid.*

central deafness A hearing impairment that is related to lesions in auditory pathways or centers, including sites in the brain stem, thalamus, or cortex.

central nervous system (CNS) The portion of the nervous system that includes the brain and the spinal cord. See Figure 2.14.

central pattern generator Neural circuitry that is responsible for generating a rhythmic pattern of behavior, such as walking.

central sulcus A major groove that divides the frontal lobe from the parietal lobe.

cephalic See *rostral.*

cerebellar cortex The outer surface of the cerebellum. See Figure 2.19.

cerebellum A structure located at the back of the brain, dorsal to the pons, which is involved in the central regulation of movement. See Figure 2.15.

cerebral cortex The outer covering of the cerebral hemispheres; consists largely of nerve cell bodies and their branches. See Figure 2.22.

cerebral hemispheres The right and left halves of the forebrain. See Figure 2.15.

cerebral ventricle A cavity in the brain that contains cerebrospinal fluid. See Figure 2.20.

cerebrospinal fluid (CSF) The fluid that fills the cerebral ventricles. See Figure 2.20.

cerveau isolé An animal in which the nervous system has been cut in the upper midbrain, dividing the brain from the brain stem. Contrast with *encéphale isolé.* See Figure 14.22.

cervical Referring to the neck region.

chemical transmitter See *synaptic transmitter.*

chemoaffinity hypothesis Notion that each cell has a chemical identity that directs it to synapse upon the proper target cell during development. See Box 4.2.

chlorpromazine An antipsychotic drug, one of the class of phenothiazines.

cholecystokinin (CCK) A hormone that is released from the lining of the duodenum and that may be involved in the satiation of hunger.

cholinergic Referring to cells that use acetylcholine as their synaptic transmitter.

choreic movement An uncontrollable, brief, and forceful muscular movement that is related to basal ganglia dysfunction.

choroid plexus A highly vascular portion of the lining of the ventricles that secretes cerebrospinal fluid.

chromosome A complex of condensed strands of DNA and associated protein molecules; found in the nucleus of cells.

ciliary muscle One of the muscles that controls the shape of the lens inside the eye, focusing an image on the retina.

cingulate cortex A region of medial cerebral cortex That lies dorsal to the corpus callosum. Also called the cingulum. See Figure 16.21.

circadian oscillator A theoretical circuit with an output that repeats about once per day.

circadian rhythms A pattern of behavioral, biochemical, and physiological fluctuations that have a 24-hour period.

circle of Willis A structure at the base of the brain that is formed by the joining of the carotid and basilar arteries. See Figure 2.21.

circuit A level of brain organization that includes an arrangement of neurons and their interconnections. These assemblages often perform a particular limited function. In a local circuit, all the neurons are contained within a particular region. Contrast with *system.*

circumventricular organ An organ that lies in the wall of a cerebral ventricle. Circumventricular organs contain receptor sites that can be affected by substances in the cerebrospinal fluid. See Figure 13.17.

classical conditioning A type of associative learning in which an originally neutral stimulus (the conditioned stimulus, or CS)—through pairing with another stimulus that elicits a particular response (the unconditioned stimulus, or US)—acquires the power to elicit that response when presented alone. A response elicited by the US is called an unconditioned response (UR); a response elicited by the CS alone is called a conditioned response (CR). Also called Pavlovian conditioning.

clitoris A small mound of tissue just anterior to the vaginal opening. Stimulation of the clitoris produces orgasm in most women.

cloaca (pl. cloacae) The sex organ in many birds, through which sperm are discharged (in the male) and eggs are laid (in the female). This is the same passage through which wastes are eliminated.

clones Asexually produced organisms that are genetically identical.

closed loop   Referring to a control mechanism that provides a flow of information from whatever is being controlled to the device that controls it. Contrast with *open loop*. See Figure 11.4.

CNS   Central nervous system.

CNV   Contingent negative variation.

coactivation   A central nervous system control program that activates or inhibits the skeletal motoneurons at the same time as it alters the sensitivity of the muscle spindles.

cochlea   A snail-shaped structure in the inner ear that contains the primary receptors for hearing. See Figure 9.3.

cochlear duct   One of three principal canals running along the length of the cochlea. See Figure 9.3.

cochlear microphonic potential   An electrical potential, produced by hair cells, that accurately copies the acoustic wave form of the stimulus.

cochlear nuclei   Brain stem nuclei that receive input from auditory hair cells and send output to the superior olivary complex. See Figure 9.8.

codon   A sequence of three bases on a DNA molecule. Each codon specifies a particular amino acid.

coitus   See *copulatory behavior*.

colliculus (pl. colliculi)   A small elevation. Two pairs of colliculi are found on the dorsal surface of the midbrain. The rostral pair (the superior colliculi) receive visual information (see Figure 10.14); the caudal pair (the inferior colliculi) receive auditory information (see Figure 9.8).

colloid   A large, gluelike molecule that cannot pass through the cell membrane. When injected into the peritoneum, colloids attract and retain water by osmotic pressure.

command neuron   A higher-level nerve cell that can selectively activate specific behaviors such as walking.

complex cortical cell   Neurons in the visual cortex that respond best to a bar of a particular size and orientation anywhere within a particular area of the visual field. See Figure 10.X.

computerized axial tomography (CAT)   A noninvasive technique for examining brain structure in humans through computer analysis of X-ray absorption at several positions around the head; affords a virtual direct view of the brain. The resulting images are referred to as CAT, or CT, scans. See Figure 2.24.

concordant   Referring to any trait that is seen in both individuals of identical twins. Contrast with *discordant*.

conditional learning   A type of learning that teaches that a particular response to a particular stimulus is appropriate in one setting but not in another.

conditioned response (CR)   See *classical conditioning*.

conditioned stimulus (CS)   See *classical conditioning*.

conditioned taste aversion   The behavior in which an animal refuses to eat a food if it previously became ill after eating that food.

condom   A rubber sheath that is fitted over the penis to trap semen during sexual intercourse in order to prevent pregnancy and the transmission of disease.

conduction aphasia   A language disorder in which comprehension remains intact but repetition of spoken language is impaired; related to damage of the pathways connecting Wernicke's area and Broca's area.

conductive deafness   A hearing impairment that is associated with pathology of the external-ear or middle-ear cavities.

cone   One of the receptor cells in the retina that are responsible for color vision. The three types of cones have somewhat different sensitivities to light of different wavelengths. See Figure 10.8.

congenital   Present at birth.

congenital adrenal hyperplasia (CAH)   Any of several genetic mutations that can result in exposure of a female fetus to androgen, which results in a clitoris that is larger than normal at birth.

consolidation   A stage of memory formation in which information in short-term or intermediate-term memory is transferred to long-term memory. See Figure 17.12.

consolidation hypothesis   See *perseveration/consolidation hypothesis*.

constraints on learning   Factors that restrict the ease of different kinds of learning in different species.

contingent negative variation (CNV)   A slow, event-related potential that is recorded from the scalp. A CNV arises in the interval between a warning signal and a signal that directs action.

convergence   The phenomenon of neural connections in which many cells send signals to a single cell. Contrast with *divergence*. See Figure 5.10.

convergent evolution   The evolutionary process by which responses to similar ecological features bring about similarities in behavior or structure among animals that are only distantly related (i.e., that differ in genetic heritage).

copulatory behavior   Coitus.

copulatory lock   Reproductive behavior in which the male's penis swells after ejaculation so that the male and female are forced to remain joined for five to ten minutes; occurs in dogs and some rodents, but not in humans.

cornea   The transparent outer layer of the eye, whose curvature is fixed, bends light rays, and is primarily responsible for forming the image on the retina.

coronal plane   The plane that divides the body or brain into front and back parts. Also called frontal plane or transverse plane. See Box 2.2.

corpus callosum   The band of axons that connects the two cerebral hemispheres. See Figure 2.20.

correlational approach   An approach to finding relations between bodily variables and behavioral variables that involves finding the extent to which a particular bodily measure covaries with a particular behavioral measure. See Figure 1.12.

cortex Outer layers. 1. The cerebral cortex consists of the outer layers (gray matter) of the cerebral hemispheres. See Figure 2.16. 2. The cerebellar cortex consists of the outer layers of the cerebellum. See Figure 2.16. 3. The adrenal cortex consists of the outer layers of the adrenal gland. See Figure 7.1.

cortical barrel A barrel-shaped portion of somatosensory cortex. Each barrel receives input from receptors from an individual whisker. See Figure 4.29.

cortical column One of the vertical columns that constitute the basic organization of the neocortex. See Figure 8.18.

cortical plate A structure arising from the early proliferation of cells at the rostral end of the neural tube; the beginnings of the cerebral cortex.

corticospinal system See *pyramidal system*.

corticosteroids A class of steroid hormones secreted from the adrenal cortex, including glucosteroids and mineralocorticoids.

corticotropin-releasing hormone (CRH) A releasing hormone, produced by the hypothalamus, that controls the daily rhythm of adrenocorticotropic hormone release.

cortisol A glucocorticoid hormone of the adrenal cortex.

CR Conditioned response

cranial Referring to the skull (cranium).

cranial nerves One of the three main subdivisions of the peripheral nervous system, composed of a set of pathways concerned mainly with sensory and motor systems associated with the head. See Figure 2.11.

cretinism Reduced stature and mental retardation caused by thyroid deficiency.

CRH Corticotropin-releasing hormone.

crib death See *sudden infant death syndrome*.

critical range The range within which a particular biological measure must remain to ensure good health.

cross-tolerance A condition in which the development of tolerance for an administered drug causes the individual to develop tolerance for another drug.

CS Conditioned stimulus.

CSF Cerebrospinal fluid.

CT scan See *computerized axial tomography*.

cupula (pl. cupulae) A small gelatinous column that forms part of the lateral-line system of aquatic animals and occurs within the vestibular system of mammals. See Figure 9.18.

Cushing's syndrome A condition in which levels of adrenal glucocorticoids are high, often arising from pituitary tumors, adrenal tumors, or deliberate therapy involving corticosteroids.

cyclic adenosine monophosphate A second messenger that is involved in the synaptic activities of dopamine, norepinephrine, and serotonin.

cyclic AMP Cyclic adenosine monophosphate.

cytoarchitectonics The study of anatomical divisions of the brain based on the kinds and spacing of cells and the distribution of axons.

cytokine A protein that induces the proliferation of other cells, as in the immune system. Examples include interleukins and interferons.

DA Dopamine.

deafferentation Removal of sensory (afferent) input.

death gene A gene that is expressed only when a cell becomes committed to natural cell death (apoptosis).

declarative memory A memory that can be stated or described. Contrast with *nondeclarative memory*.

deep dyslexia A form of dyslexia in which patients read a word as another word that is semantically related.

dehydration Excessive loss of water.

delta-sleep-inducing peptide (DSIP) A naturally occurring peptide that is reported to induce slow-wave sleep.

dementia Drastic failure of cognitive ability, including memory failure and loss of orientation.

dendrite One of the extensions of the cell body that are the receptive surfaces of the neuron. See Figures 2.3, 2.4.

dendritic branching The pattern and quantity of branching of dendrites. See Figure 18.5.

dendritic spine An outgrowth along the dendrite of a neuron. See Figures 2.3, 2.5. Also called dendrite thorn.

dendritic tree The full arrangement of dendrites of a single cell.

denervation supersensitivity Condition in which target cells, upon losing neural input, produce more than the normal number of receptors, resulting in an exaggerated response when synaptic transmitter is applied.

dentate gyrus A strip of grey matter in the hippocampal formation.

2-deoxyglucose (2-DG) A molecule that resembles glucose. When injected into an animal, 2-DG accumulates more readily in active neurons than in inactive neurons, so it can indicate which parts of the brain are active during a given task.

deoxyribonucleic acid (DNA) A nucleic acid that is present in the chromosomes of cells and codes hereditary information.

depolarization A reduction in membrane potential (the inner membrane surface becomes less negative in relation to the outer surface); caused by excitatory neural messages. Contrast with *hyperpolarization*. See Figure 5.2.

depression A psychiatric condition characterized by such symptoms as an unhappy mood; loss of interests, energy, and appetite; and difficulty in concentration. See bipolar depression, unipolar depression.

derepression The mechanism through which regions of the DNA molecule that are repressed from transcription become unblocked. This process allows for the selection of genetic information that will be used by a particular cell.

dermatome A strip of skin innervated by a particular spinal root. See Figure 8.16.

dexamethasone suppression test   A test of pituitary–adrenal function in which the subject is given dexamethasone, a synthetic glucocorticoid hormone, which should cause a decline in the production of adrenal corticosteroids.

diabetes insipidus   Excessive urination, caused by the failure of vasopressin to induce the kidneys to conserve water.

diabetes mellitus   Excessive glucose in urine, caused by the failure of insulin to induce glucose absorption by the body.

diaschisis   A temporary period of generalized impairment following brain injury.

dichotic listening technique   A test in which different sounds are presented to each ear at the same time; used to determine hemispheric differences in processing auditory information. See Figure 19.18.

diencephalon   The posterior part of the forebrain, including the thalamus and hypothalamus. See Figure 2.17.

differential classical conditioning   Classical conditioning in which two conditioned stimuli are used in the same animal; one (CS+) is *paired* with the unconditioned stimulus, and the other (CS−) is *unpaired* and has no consequence for the animal.

differentiation   See *cell differentiation*.

diffuse bipolar cell   A type of retinal bipolar neuron that receives input from several receptors. See Figure 10.11.

discordant   Referring to any trait that is seen in only one individual of identical twins. Contrast with *concordant*.

dishabituation   The restoration of response amplitude following habituation.

dissociative thinking   A condition, seen in schizophrenia, that is characterized by disturbances of thought and difficulty relating events properly.

distal   An anatomical term referring to structures toward the periphery or toward the end of a limb. Contrast with *proximal*. See Box 2.2.

diurnal   Active during the day.

divergence   The phenomenon of neural connections in which one cell sends signals to many other cells. Contrast with *convergence*. See Figure 5.15.

DNA   Deoxyribonucleic acid.

dopamine (DA)   A synaptic transmitter produced mainly in the basal forebrain and diencephalon that is active in the basal ganglia, the olfactory system, and limited parts of the cerebral cortex. See Figure 16.8.

dopaminergic   Referring to cells that use dopamine as their synaptic transmitter.

dorsal   An anatomical term referring to structures toward the back of the body or the top of the brain. Contrast with *ventral*. See Box 2.2.

dorsal root   See *roots*.

double dissociation   The phenomenon in which condition or treatment A causes impairment on behavioral test X but no impairment on test Y, whereas condition B causes impairment on test Y but not on X.

Down's syndrome   Mental retardation that is associated with an extra copy of chromosome 21.

DSIP   Delta-sleep-inducing peptide.

dual trace hypothesis   The hypothesis that formation of a memory involves first a relatively brief transient memory storage process followed by a stable change in the nervous system, which is a long-lasting memory trace.

duplex theory   A theory of pitch perception that combines place theory and volley theory.

dura mater   The outermost of the three coverings that embrace the brain and spinal cord.

dynamic phase of weight gain   The initial period following destruction of the ventromedial hypothalamus during which the animal's body weight increases rapidly. Contrast with *static phase of obesity*. See Figure 13.26.

dyscontrol syndrome   A condition consisting of temporal lobe disorders that may underlie some forms of human violence.

dyskinesia   See *tardive dyskinesia*.

dyslexia   A reading disorder attributed to brain impairment.

dyspareunia   Discomfort during intromission.

dysregulation hypothesis of depression   The hypothesis that depression reflects a failure in regulation of (dopamine) transmitter operations, resulting in erratic transmitter activities ungoverned by external stimuli.

dystrophin   A gene product that is needed for normal muscle function. Dystrophin is defective in some forms of muscular dystrophy.

eardrum   See *tympanic membrane*.

EC   Enriched condition.

ectoderm   The outer cellular layer of the developing fetus. The ectoderm gives rise to the skin and to the nervous system.

ectotherm   An animal whose body temperature is regulated by, and that gets most of its heat from, the environment. Contrast with *endotherm*.

edema   The swelling of tissue, especially in the brain, in response to injury.

EEG   Electroencephalography.

effective dose 50 (ED$_{50}$)   The dose of a drug that produces the desired effect in 50% of subjects. Contrast with lethal dose 50. See Figure 6.3

efferent fiber   An axon that carries information from the nervous system to the periphery. Contrast with *afferent fiber*.

ejaculation   The forceful expulsion of semen from the penis.

electrical synapse   The region between neurons where the presynaptic and postsynaptic membranes are so close that the nerve impulse can jump to the postsynaptic membrane without first being translated into a chemical message. See Figure 5.5.

electroencephalography (EEG) The recording and study of gross electrical activity of the brain recorded from large electrodes placed on the scalp. See Figure 14.11.

EMG Electromyography.

electromyography (EMG) The technique of recording electrical activity of muscles. See Figure 11.3.

ERG Electroretinography.

electroretinography (ERG) The electrical recording of responses of the retina to flashes of different stimuli.

embryo The earliest stage in a developing animal; humans are considered embryos until eight to ten weeks after conception.

EMG Electromyography.

encéphale isolé An experimental preparation in which an animal's brain stem has been separated from the spinal cord by a cut below the medulla. Contrast with *cerveau isolé*. See Figure 14.22.

encephalization factor A measure of brain size relative to body size.

encoding A process of memory formation in which the information entering sensory channels is passed into short-term memory. See Figure 17.12.

end-plate potential The action potential that is induced at the neuromuscular junction when the axon terminal releases its neurotransmitter, which in vertebrates is acetylcholine.

endocast A cast of the cranial cavity of a skull, especially useful for studying fossils of extinct species.

endocrine gland A gland that secretes products into the bloodstream to act on distant targets. Contrast with *exocrine gland*. See Figure 7.1.

endogenous opioids A family of peptide transmitters that have been called the body's own narcotics. See Table 5.4, under opioid peptides.

endogenous oscillator A circuit that generates regularly repeating sequences of neural activity or behavior.

endorphins One of three kinds of endogenous opioids. See Table 5.4, under opioid peptides.

endotherm An animal whose body temperature is regulated chiefly by internal metabolic processes. Examples include mammals and birds. Contrast with *ectotherm*.

enkephalins One of the three kinds of endogenous opioids. See Table 5.4, under opioid peptides.

enriched condition (EC) An experimental condition with a complex environment. See Figure 18.4.

entrainment The process of synchronizing a biological rhythm to an environmental stimulus. See Figure 14.1.

ependymal layer See *ventricular layer*.

epididymis A crescent-shaped structure next to the testis, in which sperm are stored.

epilepsy A brain disorder marked by major sudden changes in the electrophysiological state of the brain that are referred to as seizures. See Box 5.1.

epinephrine A compound that acts both as a hormone (secreted by the adrenal medulla) and as a synaptic transmitter. Also called adrenaline.

episodic memory Memory of a particular incident or a particular time and place.

EPSP Excitatory postsynaptic potential.

equilibrium potential The state in which the tendency of ions to flow from regions of high concentration is exactly balanced by the opposing potential difference across the membrane.

erectile dysfunction Failure to achieve a penile erection.

ERG Electroretinography

estradiol The primary type of estrogen that is secreted by the ovary.

estrogens A class of steroid hormones produced by female gonads. See Figure 7.13, Table 7.1.

estrus The period during which female animals are sexually receptive.

event-related potential A large change in electrical potential in the brain that is elicited by a discrete sensory or motor event. Also called evoked potential. See Box 5.2.

evoked otoacoustic emission A sound produced by the cochlea in response to acoustic stimulation. Contrast with *spontaneous otoacoustic emission*.

evoked potential See *event-related potential*.

evolution by natural selection The Darwinian theory that evolution proceeds by differential success in reproduction.

excitatory postsynaptic potential (EPSP) A depolarizing potential in the postsynaptic neuron that is caused by excitatory presynaptic impulses. Contrast with *inhibitory postsynaptic potential*.

excitotoxin A poison that overexcites neurons so much that it kills them.

exocrine gland A gland that secretes products through ducts to the site of action. Contrast with *endocrine gland*.

external capsule A light-colored band of fibers lateral to the putamen.

external ear The part of the ear that we readily see (called the pinna) and the canal that leads to the eardrum. See Figure 9.1.

external fertilization Reproductive fertilization that takes place outside the female's body, as in many fishes and amphibians. Contrast with *internal fertilization*.

extinction A feature of conditioning in which the learned response wanes when not reinforced.

extracellular fluid The fluid in the spaces between cells (interstitial fluid) and in the vascular system.

extracellular space The space between cells.

extrafusal fiber One of the ordinary muscle fibers that lie *outside* the spindles and provide most of the force for muscle contraction. Contrast with *intrafusal fiber*. See Figure 11.10.

extraocular muscle One of the muscles attached to the eyeball that control its position and movements. See Figure 10.7.

extrapyramidal system A motor system that includes the basal ganglia and some closely related brain stem structures.

facial nerve   A cranial nerve that innervates facial musculature and some sensory receptors. See Figure 2.11.

Factor S   Name given to a sleep-inducing substance extracted from the cerebrospinal fluid of sleep-deprived goats.

fallopian tube   The structure between the ovum and the uterus where fertilization takes place in humans. Also called the oviduct. See Figure 12.8.

fat   A large, complex carbohydrate that provides long-term energy storage. A lipid.

fatal familial insomnia   An inherited disorder in which humans sleep normally at the beginning of their life, but in midlife stop sleeping, and 7 to 24 months later die.

feature detector model   A model of visual pattern analysis in terms of linear and angular components of the stimulus array. Contrast with *spatial frequency filter model*.

feedback circuit   A circuit in which output information is used to modulate the input of that same circuit.

fertilization   The fusion of sperm and egg to produce a zygote.

fetal alcohol syndrome   A disorder, including mental retardation and characteristic facial anomalies, that affects children exposed to alcohol (through maternal ingestion) during fetal development.

fetus   A developing individual after the embryo stage. Humans are considered to be fetuses from ten weeks after fertilization until birth.

fictive locomotion   A walking pattern that is elicited by a treadmill from the hind limbs of cats with spinal cord section.

filial imprinting   A type of learning in which precocial animals in their first few days approach and follow the first relatively large moving object they see, usually their mother.

filopodium (pl. fillipodia)   A very fine, tubular outgrowth from the growth cone.

final common pathway   The motoneurons, because they direct all the activity of the spinal cord and brain to the muscles.

fission   The process of splitting in two. Some unicellular organisms reproduce by fisson; that is, they simply split into two daughter cells.

fixed action pattern   Complex preprogrammed species-specific behavior that is triggered by particular stimuli and carried out without sensory feedback. See also *modal action pattern*.

flaccid paralysis   A loss of reflexes below the level of transection of the spinal cord.

flexion reflex   The abrupt withdrawal of a limb in response to intense stimulation of the foot.

folia (s. folium)   The folds or convolutions of the cerebellar cortex.

follicle-stimulating hormone (FSH)   A tropic hormone, released by the anterior pituitary, that controls the production of estrogen and progesterone. See Figure 7.13.

forebrain   The frontal division of the neural tube that contains the cerebral hemispheres, the thalamus, and the hypothalamus. Also called the prosencephalon.

fornix   A fiber tract that extends from the hippocampus to the mammillary body. See Figure 2.18.

Fourier analysis   The analysis of a complex pattern into the sum of sine waves. See Box 9.1.

fourth ventricle   The passageway within the pons that receives cerebrospinal fluid from the third ventricle and releases it to surround the brain and spinal cord. See Figure 2.20.

fovea   A small depression in the center of the retina that has a dense concentration of cones and maximal visual acuity.

fragile X syndrome   A condition that is a frequent cause of inherited mental retardation; produced by a fragile site on the X chromosome that seems prone to breaking because the DNA there is unstable.

free-running period   The natural period of a behavior that is displayed if external stimuli do not provide entrainment.

frequency   The number of cycles per second in a sound wave; measured in hertz (Hz). See Box 9.1.

frontal lobe   The most anterior portion of the cerebral cortex.

frontal plane   See *coronal plane*.

FSH   Follicle-stimulating hormone.

GABA   Gamma-aminobutyric acid.

gamete   A sex cell, sperm or egg, which contains only unpaired chromosomes and therefore has only half the total number of autosomal chromosomes.

gamma-aminobutyric acid (GABA)   Probably the major inhibitory transmitter in the mammalian nervous system; widely distributed in both invertebrate and vertebrate nervous systems.

gamma efferent   A motor neuron that controls muscle spindle sensitivity. See Figure 11.10.

ganglion (pl. ganglia)   A collection of nerve cell bodies outside the central nervous system. See also *nucleus*.

ganglion cells   Cells in the retina whose axons form the optic nerve. See Figure 10.8.

gender identity   The way that one identifies oneself, and is identified by others, as a male or a female.

generalization   A feature of conditioning in which stimuli similar to the conditioned stimulus can elicit a conditioned response.

generalized seizure   An epileptic seizure that arises from pathology at brain sites and projects to widespread regions of the brain. Generalized seizures include loss of consciousness and symmetrical involvement of body musculature. See Figure 5.1.

generator potential   A local change in the resting potential of a receptor cell that mediates between the impact of stimuli and the initiation of nerve impulses. See Figure 5.4.

genetic constraints on learning   A concept, prominent from the 1960s to the early 1980s, that held that species-typical factors restrict the kinds of learning that a species can accomplish readily. Contrast with *specific abilities to learn and remember.*

genetic mosaic   An animal in which the cells of one part of the body have a different chromosomal makeup from the cells in another part. For example, the head of a male fruit fly can be induced to develop on the body of a female fruit fly.

GH   Growth hormone.

giant axon   A large-diameter axon; found in some invertebrates. The size of giant axons facilitates research on the properties of neural membrane structure and function. See Figure 5.3.

glia   See *glial cells.*

glial cells   Nonneural brain cells that provide structural, nutritional, and other supports to the brain. Also called glia or neuroglia. See Figure 2.7.

glioma   A brain tumor resulting from the aberrant production of glial cells.

global aphasia   The total loss of ability to understand language, or to speak, read, or write.

globus pallidus   One of the basal ganglia. See Figure 2.18.

glomerulus (pl. **glomeruli**)   A complex arbor of dendrites from a group of olfactory cells.

glossopharyngeal nerve   The ninth cranial nerve which serves taste receptors in the tongue. See Figure 2.11.

glucagon   A hormone, released by alpha cells in the islets of Langerhans, that increases blood glucose. See Figure 7.18.

glucocorticoids   A class of hormones, released by the adrenal cortex, that affect carbohydrate metabolism.

glucodetector   A cell that detects and informs the nervous system about levels of circulating glucose. Also called glucostat.

glucose   An important sugar molecule used by the body and brain for energy.

glucose transporter   A molecule that spans the external membrane of a cell and transports glucose molecules from outside the cell to the inside for use.

glucostat   See *glucodetector.*

glutamic acid   Thought by many investigators to be a major excitatory synaptic transmitter in the central nervous system.

glycogen   A complex carbohydrate made by the combining of glucose molecules for a short-term store of energy.

GnRH   Gonadotropin-releasing hormone.

Golgi tendon organ   One of the receptors located in tendons that send impulses to the central nervous system when a muscle contracts. See Figure 11.10.

Golgi type I cell   A type of large nerve cell.

gonadotropin-releasing hormone (GnRH)   A hypothalamic hormone that controls the release of luteinizing hormone and follicle-stimulating hormone from the pituitary. Also called luteinizing hormone–releasing hormone. See Figure 7.16.

gonads   The sexual organs (ovaries in females, testes in males), which produce gametes for reproduction.

graded potential   An electrical potential that is initiated at a postsynaptic site and can vary continuously in size. Also called local potential or postsynaptic potential. Contrast with *all-or-none.* See Figure 5.2.

grammar   The rules for usage of a particular language.

grand mal seizure   A type of generalized epileptic seizure in which nerve cells fire in high-frequency bursts. Grand mal seizures cause loss of consciousness and sudden muscle contraction. See Figure 5.1.

grandmother cell   An extrapolation of the feature detector model suggesting that if there were enough levels of analysis, a unit could be constructed that would enable a person to recognize his or her grandmother.

granule cell   A type of small nerve cell.

gray matter   Areas of the brain that are dominated by cell bodies and are devoid of myelin. Contrast with *white matter.*

growth cone   The growing tip of an axon or a dendrite. See Figure 4.11.

growth hormone (GH)   A tropic hormone, secreted by the anterior pituitary, that influences the growth of cells and tissues. Also called somatotropic hormone. See Figure 7.13.

gut hormone   A hormone that is released by the stomach or intestines, sometimes in response to food.

gyrus (pl. **gyri**)   A ridged or raised portion of a convoluted brain surface. Contrast with *sulcus.* See Figure 2.15.

habit   A stimulus–response bond that is acquired automatically, and often gradually, through occurrences of stimulus–response–reinforcement contingencies.

habituation   A form of nonassociative learning characterized by a reduction in response strength following repeated presentations of a stimulus. See Box 17.2.

hair cell   One of the receptor cells for hearing in the cochlea. Displacement of these cells by sound waves generates nerve impulses that travel to the brain. See Figure 9.3.

hallucinogens   A class of drugs that alter sensory perception and produce peculiar experiences.

Hebbian synapse   A synapse that is strengthened when it successfully drives the postsynaptic cell.

hemispatial neglect   A syndrome in which the patient ignores objects presented to one side and may even deny connection with that side of the body.

hermaphrodite   An individual that can reproduce as either a male or a female.

heterogametic   Referring to the sex that has two different sex chromosomes. Male mammals and female birds are heterogametic. Contrast with *homogametic.*

hindbrain   The rear division of the brain; in the mature vertebrate, the hindbrain contains the cerebellum, pons, and medulla. Also called the rhombencephalon. See Figure 2.17.

hippocampal gyrus   See *subiculum.*

hippocampus   A portion of the cerebral hemispheres found curled in the basal medial part of the temporal lobe that is thought to be important for learning and memory. See Figures 2.18, 17.2., 18.15.

histology   The study of tissue structure.

HIV   Human immunodeiciency virus.

homeostasis   The tendency for the internal environment to remain constant.

homeotherm   An animal that maintains a relatively constant body temperature. Examples include birds and mammals. Contrast with *poikilotherm*.

hominid   A primate of the family Hominidae, of which humans are the only living species.

homogametic   Referring to the sex that has two copies of the same sex chromosome. Female mammals and male birds are homogametic. Contrast with *heterogametic*.

homology   A structural or behavioral resemblance between two species that is based on common ancestry.

horizontal cells   Specialized retinal cells that contact both the receptor cells and the bipolar cells.

horizontal plane   The plane that divides the body or brain into upper and lower parts. See Box 2.2.

hormone   A chemical secreted by an endocrine gland that is conveyed by the bloodstream and regulates target organs or tissues. See Table 7.2.

horseradish peroxidase (HRP)   An enzyme found in horseradish and other plants that is used to determine the cells of origin of a particular set of axons. See Box 2.1.

HRP   Horseradish peroxidase.

hue   One of the basic dimensions of light perception. Hue varies around the color circle through blue, green, yellow, orange, and red. See Figure 10.5.

human immunodeficiency virus (HIV)   The virus that can be passed through genital, anal, or oral sex and causes acquired immune deficiency syndrome (AIDS).

humoral immunity   The type of immunity in which B lymphocytes produce antibodies that either directly destroy antigens, such as viruses or bacteria, or enhance their destruction by other cells.

hunger   The internal state of an animal seeking food. Contrast with *satiety*.

Huntington's chorea   A progressive genetic disorder characterized by choreic movements and profound changes in mental functioning. Also called Huntington's disease.

hypercomplex 1   Cells in the visual cortex that respond best to visual stimulation by bars of a given orientation and of limited length.

hypercomplex 2   Cells in the visual cortex that respond best to visual stimulation by two line segments meeting at a particular angle.

hyperphagia   A condition involving increasing food intake, often related to damage to the ventromedial hypothalamus.

hyperpolarization   An increase in membrane potential (the inner surface of the membrane becomes more negative in relation to the outer surface); caused by inhibitory neural messages. Contrast with *depolarization*. See Figure 5.2.

hypertonic   Referring to a solution with a higher concentration of salt than that found in interstitial fluid and blood plasma (more than about 0.9% salt). Contrast with *hypotonic*.

hypnogen   A sleep-producing substance that might accumulate in the brain and/or body.

hypofrontality hypothesis   The hypothesis that schizophrenia may reflect underactivation of the frontal lobes.

hypothalamic–pituitary portal system   System of capillaries that transport releasing hormones from the hypothalamus to the anterior pituitary.

hypothalamus   Part of the diencephalon, lying ventral to the thalamus. See Figures 2.15, 2.17.

hypotonic   A solution with a lower concentration of salt than that found in interstitial fluid and blood plasma (less than about 0.9% salt). Contrast with *hypertonic*.

hypovolemic thirst   The response to a reduced volume of extracellular fluid. Contrast with *osmotic thirst*.

hypoxia   A transient lack of oxygen.

IC   Impoverished condition.

iconic memory   A very brief type of memory that stores the sensory impression of a scene.

ideational apraxia   An impairment in the ability to carry out a *sequence* of actions even though each element or step can be done correctly.

identifiable neurons   Neurons that are large and similar from one individual to the next, enabling investigators to recognize and give code names to them.

ideomotor apraxia   The inability to carry out a simple motor activity in response to a verbal command even though this same activity is readily performed spontaneously.

IEG   Immediate early gene.

immediate early genes (IEGs)   A class of genes that show rapid but transient increases in response to extracellular signals such as neurotransmitters and growth factors. Examples include *fos* and *jun*.

immunocytochemistry   A method for detecting a particular protein in tissues in which an antibody recognizes and binds to the protein, and chemical methods are then used to leave a visible reaction product around each antibody. See Box 7.1, Figure A.5.

impermeable   Referring to a barrier that does not allow the substance of interest to pass through.

impoverished condition (IC)   An experimental condition with a drastically simplified environment. See Figure 18.4.

imprinting   A form of learning in which young animals learn to follow the first relatively large moving object they see, usually their mother.

in heat   Sexually receptive; in estrus.

in vitro   Literally "in glass," usually a laboratory dish; outside the body.

in vivo   Literally "in life"; within a living body.

incus   One of three tiny bones in the middle ear, between the malleus (attached to the tympanic membrane) and the stapes (attached to the cochlea).

induction The process by which one set of cells influences the fate of neighboring cells, usually by secreting a chemical factor that changes gene expression in the target cells.

inferior colliculi See *colliculus*.

infradian Referring to biological rhythms that have a frequency of less than once per day.

infundibulum The stalk of the pituitary gland.

inhibitory postsynaptic potential (IPSP) A hyperpolarizing potential in the postsynaptic neuron that is caused by inhibitory connections. IPSPs decrease the probability that the postsynaptic neuron will fire a nerve impulse. Contrast with *excitatory postsynaptic potential*. See Figure 5.4.

inner ear The cochlea and vestibular canals.

inner hair cell One of the receptor cells for hearing in the cochlea. See Figure 9.3.

innervate To provide neural input.

innervation The supply of neural input to an organ or a region of the nervous system.

innervation ratio The ratio expressing the number of muscle fibers innervated by a single motor axon. The fewer muscle fibers an axon innervates (that is, the lower the ratio), the finer the control of movements.

insomnia Lack of sleep or of sufficient sleep.

instrumental conditioning A form of associative learning in which the likelihood that an act (instrumental response) will be performed depends on the consequences (reinforcing stimuli) that follow it. Also called operant conditioning.

instrumental response See *instrumental conditioning*.

insulin A hormone, released by beta cells in the islets of Langerhans, that lowers blood glucose. See Figure 7.18.

intention tremor A tremor that occurs only during voluntary movement, such as reaching out to grasp an object.

intermediate-term memory (ITM) A form of memory that lasts longer than short-term memory and requires no rehearsal, but does not last as long as long-term memory.

internal capsule The fiber band that extends between the caudate nucleus on its medial side and the globus pallidus and putamen on its lateral side.

internal carotid artery See *carotid arteries*.

internal fertilization The process in which sperm fertilize eggs inside the female's body. All mammals, birds, and reptiles have internal fertilization. Contrast with *external fertilization*.

interneurons A neuron that is neither a sensory neuron nor a motoneuron.

interstitial cell-stimulating hormone (ICSH) See *luteinizing hormone*.

interstitial fluid See *extracellular fluid*.

intracellular fluid Water within cells. Also called cellular fluid.

intracellular signal A chemical signal that conveys information within a single cell.

intrafusal fibers One of the small muscle fibers *within* each muscle spindle. Contrast with *extrafusal fiber*.

intromission Insertion of the erect penis into the vagina during copulatory behavior.

inverted U-shaped curve A drug dose–response curve in which increasing doses first elicit increasing responses, but at higher doses, response declines with increasing dose.

ion An atom or molecule that has acquired an electrical charge by gaining or losing one or more electrons.

ion channel A pore in the cell membrane that permits the passage of certain ions through the membrane when the channels are open. See Figure 5.6.

IPSP Inhibitory postsynaptic potential.

iris The circular structure of the eye that provides an opening to form the pupil.

islets of Langerhans Clusters of cells in the pancreas that release two hormones (insulin and glucagon) with opposite effects on glucose utilization. See Figure 7.1.

isotonic Having the same concentration of salt as mammalian fluids have.

ITM Intermediate-term memory

kinase A class of enzymes that catalyze the addition of a phosphate group to certain proteins.

kindling A method of experimentally inducing an epileptic seizure by repeatedly stimulating a brain region.

Korsakoff's syndrome A memory disorder, related to a thiamine deficiency, that is generally associated with chronic alcoholism.

kuru A slow virus of the brain that produces trembling and eventually paralysis of the limbs.

labia (s. labium) The folds of skin that surround the opening of the human vagina. See Figure 12.16.

labile memory An early stage of memory formation during which the formation of a memory can be easily disrupted by conditions that influence brain activity.

laminar organization The horizontal layering of cells found in some brain regions. See Figures 2.22a, 8.18.

lateral An anatomical term meaning toward the side. Contrast with *medial*. See Box 2.2.

lateral geniculate nucleus (LGN) The part of the thalamus that receives information from the optic tract and sends it to visual areas in the occipital cortex. See Figure 10.15.

lateral hypothalamus (LH) A hypothalamic region that may be involved in eating. Lesions of the LH result in fasting and weight loss. See Figure 13.25.

lateral inhibition The phenomenon in which interconnected neurons inhibit their neighbors, producing contrast at the edges of regions. See Figure 8.8.

lateral-line system A sensory system, found in many kinds of fish and some amphibians, that informs the animal of water motion in relation to the body surface.

lateral ventricle   A complexly shaped lateral portion of the ventricular system within each hemisphere of the brain. See Figure 2.20.

learning set   The ability to solve a particular type of problem efficiently after prolonged experience with that type of problem.

lens   A structure in the eye that helps form an image on the retina. The shape of the lens is controlled by the ciliary muscles inside the eye. See Figure 10.3.

lentiform nucleus   The lens-shaped region in the basal ganglia that encompasses the globus pallidus and the putamen. Also called lenticular nucleus. See Figure 2.18.

leptin   A protein manufactured and secreted by fat cells, that may communicate to the brain the amount of body fat stored. Leptin is defective in *obese* mice.

lesion momentum   The phenomenon in which the brain is impaired more by a lesion that develops quickly than by a lesion that develops slowly.

lethal dose 50 (LD$_{50}$)   The dose of a drug that would be lethal for 50% of subjects. Contrast with *effective dose 50*. See Figure 6.3.

LGN   Lateral geniculate nucleus.

LH   Lateral hypothalamus or luteinizing hormone.

ligand   A substance that binds to receptor molecules, such as those at the surface of the cell.

limbic system   A loosely defined, widespread group of brain nuclei that innervate each other to form a network; involved in mechanisms of emotion and learning See Figure 2.18.

local circuit   See *circuit*.

local potential   See *graded potential*.

local potential change   A change in potential that is initiated at a postsynaptic site.

local potentiation   See *graded potential*.

localization of function   The concept that specific brain regions are responsible for various types of experience, behavior, and psychological processes.

locus coeruleus   A small nucleus in the brain stem whose neurons produce norepinephrine and modulate large areas of the forebrain. See Figure 14.24.

long-term depression (LTD)   A lasting *decrease* in the magnitude of responses of neurons after afferent cells have been stimulated with electrical stimuli of relatively *low* frequency. Contrast with *long-term potentiation*.

long-term memory (LTM)   An enduring form of memory that lasts for days, weeks, months, or years and has a very large capacity.

long-term potentiation (LTP)   A stable and enduring increase in the magnitude of the response of neurons after afferent cells to the region have been stimulated with bursts of electrical stimuli of moderately high frequency. Contrast with *long-term depression*. See Figures 18.15, 18.17.

lordosis   A female receptive posture in quadrupeds in which the hindquarters are raised and the tail is turned to one side, facilitating intromission by the male. See Figure 12.5.

LSD (lysergic acid diethylamide)   A hallucinogenic drug.

LTD   Long-term depression.

LTM   Long-term memory.

LTP   Long-term potentiation.

lumbar   Referring to the lower part of the spinal cord or back.

luteinizing hormone (LH)   A tropic hormone, released by the anterior pituitary, that influences the hormonal activities of the gonads.

luteinizing hormone–releasing hormone   See *gonadotropin-releasing hormone*.

lymphocytes   Immune-system cells. Two different classes of lymphocytes (B and T) mediate two types of immunological responses. See Figure 15.19.

lysergic acid diethylamide   LSD.

macrocolumn   A column of neurons that is thought to be the functional module of cortical operations. The human cerebral cortex is estimated to contain about a million macrocolumns.

magnetic resonance imaging (MRI)   A noninvasive technique that uses magnetic energy to generate images that reveal some of structural details in the living brain. See Figures 1.9. and 2.24.

magnocellular layers   The two ventral or inner layers of the lateral geniculate nucleus, so called because their cells are large. See Figure 10.15.

magnocellular nucleus of the basal forebrain   A region of the basal forebrain that modulates the activity of many areas of the neurocortex and is implicated in Alzheimer's disease. Also called Meynert's nucleus, basal nucleus of Meynert, or nucleus basalis of Meynert. See Figure 4.24.

magnocellular system   The division of primate visual pathways that appears to be mainly responsible for the perception of depth and movement. See Figure 10.15.

malleus   A middle-ear bone that is connected to the tympanic membrane; one of the chain of three ossicles that transmits sound across the middle ear. See Figure 9.1.

mammillary body   One of a pair of nuclei at the base of the brain that are slightly posterior to the pituitary stalk; a component of the limbic system. See Figure 2.15.

mammillothalamic tract   The fiber bundle that connects the mammillary bodies to the thalamus.

manic-depressive psychosis   See *bipolar depression*.

MAO   Monoamine oxidase. An enzyme that breaks down and thereby inactivates monoamine transmitters.

MAO inhibitor   An antidepressant drug that inhibits the enzyme monoamine oxidase, thus prolonging the action of catecholamine transmitters.

marsupial   An animal that is born at a very early developmental stage and that spends a period of its development in the maternal pouch.

medial   An anatomical term referring to structures toward the middle of an organ or organism. Contrast with *lateral*. See Box 2.2.

medial geniculate nucleus   A nucleus in the thalamus that receives input from the inferior colliculus and sends output to the auditory cortex. See Figure 9.8.

medulla   The caudal part of the hindbrain. Also called myelencephalon. See Figure 2.17.

meiosis   The process of forming gametes in which each new cell receives half the chromosomes, therefore not requiring duplication of DNA.

melatonin   An amine hormone that is released by the pineal gland.

membrane potential   A difference in electrical potential across the membrane of a nerve cell during an inactive period. Also called the resting potential. See Figure 5.1.

memory   A cognitive representation that is often acquired rapidly and that may last a long time.

memory trace   A persistent change in the brain that reflects the storage of memory.

meninges   The three protective sheets of tissue that surround the brain and spinal cord, called the dura mater, pia mater, and arachnoid.

menstruation   A visible flow of cells and blood that exits through the vagina between ovulations in some mammals, including humans and dogs.

mesencephalon   See *midbrain*.

messenger RNA (mRNA)   A strand of RNA that carries the code of a section of a strand of DNA to the cytoplasm. See the Appendix.

metabolic rate   The rate of the use of energy during a given period; measured in terms of kilocalories per day.

metencephalon   A subdivision of the hindbrain that includes the cerebellum and the pons. See Figure 2.17.

Meynert's nucleus   The collection of neurons in the basal forebrain which provides cholinergic innervation to much of the cortex. See Figure 4.24.

microfilament   A very small filament (7 nanometers in diameter) found within all cells. Microfilaments determine cell shape.

microglia   Extremely small glial cells that remove cellular debris from injured or dead cells.

microspectrophotometry   A technique for measuring the light absorption and therefore the chemical content of very small samples, such as the pigment in individual photoreceptors.

microtubule   A small hollow cylindrical structure (20 to 26 nanometers in diameter) in axons that is involved in axoplasmic transport. See Figure 2.6.

midbrain   The middle division of the brain. Also called the mesencephalon. See Figure 2.17.

middle ear   The cavity between the tympanic membrane and the cochlea. See Figure 9.1.

midget bipolar cells   Retinal bipolar cells that connect to just one cone. See Figure 10.11.

mineralocorticoids   A class of steroid hormone, released by the adrenal cortex, that affects ion concentrations in body tissues.

minicolumn   A narrow column of cerebral cortical cells; a subdivision of the macrocolumn.

minimal discriminable frequency difference   The smallest change in frequency that can be detected reliably between two tones.

mitosis   The process of division of somatic cells that involves duplication of DNA.

modal action pattern   A modification of the concept of a fixed action pattern that allows for some variability of the response between different individuals and within the same individual at different times.

modulation of memory formation   Facilitation or inhibition of memory formation by factors other than those directly involved in memory formation.

modulatory role   The role that some hormones play in maintaining the sensitivity of neural circuits and other structures to hormonal influences.

monoamine hormones   See *amine hormones*.

monoamine hypothesis of depression   The theory that depressive illness is associated with a decrease in the synaptic activity of connections that employ monoamine synaptic transmitters.

monoamine oxidase (MAO)   An enzyme that breaks down and thereby inactivates monoamine transmitters.

monoamines   A class of synaptic transmitters that contain a single amine group, NHs. Examples include the catecholamines and indoleamines. See Table 5.4.

monoclonal antibodies   Highly purified and specialized antibodies that enable investigators to identify a particular kind of cell.

monocular deprivation   The deprivation of light to one eye.

monogamy   A mating system in which a female and a male form a breeding pair that may last for one breeding period or for a lifetime. A durable and exclusive relation between a male and a female is called a pair bond.

monopolar neuron   A nerve cell with a single branch that leaves the cell body and then extends in two directions: one end is the receptive pole, the other end the output zone. See Figure 2.4.

monotreme   A mammal belonging to an order that contains only two species, the echidna and the platypus.

mossy fiber   One of the fibers that extend from the dentate gyrus to the hippocampus, where they synapse in area CA3. See Figure 18.15.

motoneuron   A nerve cell in the spinal cord that transmits motor messages from the spinal cord to muscles. Also called a motor neuron. See Figure 11.9.

motor cortex   A region of cerebral cortex that sends impulses to motoneurons. See Figures 11.14, 11.16.

motor plan   A plan for action in the nervous system.

motor unit   A single motor axon and all the muscle fibers that it innervates.

movement   A brief, unitary activity of a muscle or body part; less complex than an act.

MRH   Müllerian regression hormone.

MRI   Magnetic resonance imaging.

mRNA   Messenger RNA.

Müllerian duct system   A duct system in the embryo that will develop into female reproductive structures (fallopian tubes, uterus, and upper vagina) if testes are not present in the embryo. Contrast with *Wolffian duct system*. See Figure 12.16.

Müllerian regression hormone (MRH)   The hormone that causes shrinkage of the Müllerian ducts during development.

multipolar neuron   A nerve cell that has many dendrites and a single axon. See Figure 2.4.

muscarinic   Referring to cholinergic receptors that respond to the chemical muscarine as well as to acetylcholine. Muscarinic receptors mediate chiefly the inhibitory activities of acetylcholine. Contrast with *nicotinic*.

muscle fiber   See *extrafusal fiber*. See Figure 11.8.

muscle spindle   A muscle receptor that lies parallel to a muscle and sends impulses to the central nervous system when the muscle is stretched. See Figure 11.10.

muscular dystrophy   A disease that leads to degeneration and functional changes in muscles.

myasthenia gravis   A disorder characterized by a profound weakness of skeletal muscles; caused by a loss of acetylcholine receptors.

myelencephalon   See *medulla*. See Figures 2.15, 2.17.

myelin   The fatty insulation around an axon, formed by accessory cells. This myelin sheath improves the speed of conduction of nerve impulses. See Figures 2.7, 2.16.

myelination   The process of formation of myelin. See Figures 2.7, 4.15.

naloxone   A potent antagonist of opiates that is often administered to people who have taken drug overdoses. Naloxone binds to receptors for endogenous opioids.

narcolepsy   A disorder that involves frequent, intense episodes of sleep, which last from 5 to 30 minutes and can occur anytime during the usual waking hours.

natural selection   See *evolution by natural selection*.

NE   Norepinephrine.

negative feedback system   A control system in which some of the output is used to reduce the effect of input signals. See Figure 7.9.

negative symptom   In psychiatry, a symptom that reflects insufficient functioning. Examples include emotional and social withdrawal, blunted affect, slowness and impoverishment of thought and speech. Contrast with *positive symptom*.

nematocyst   A tiny but effective animal weapon to deliver poison. See Figure 6.7.

neocortex   The relatively recently evolved portions of the cerebral cortex. All of the cortex seen at the surface of the human brain is neocortex.

neologism   An entirely novel word, sometimes produced by aphasic patients.

neophobia   The avoidance of new things.

Nernst equation   An equation used to calculate the equilibrium potential at a membrane.

nerves   A collection of axons bundled together outside the central nervous system. Contrast with *tract*. See Figures 2.1, 2.13.

nerve cell   See *neuron*.

nerve growth factor (NGF)   A substance that markedly affects the growth of neurons in spinal ganglia and in the ganglia of the sympathetic nervous system. See Figure 4.18.

nerve impulse   The propagated electrical message of a neuron that travels along the axon to adjacent neurons. Also called the action potential. See Figure 5.3.

neural chain   A simple kind of neural circuit in which neurons are attached linearly, end to end. See Figure 5.15.

neural folds   In the developing embryo, ridges of ectoderm that form around the neural groove and come together to form the neural tube in the embryo. These neural folds will give rise to the entire nervous system. See Figure 4.2.

neural groove   In the developing embryo, the groove between the neural folds. See Figure 4.2.

neural tube   An embryonic structure with subdivisions that correspond to the future forebrain, midbrain, and hindbrain. The cavity of this tube will include the cerebral ventricles and the passages that connect them. See Figure 4.2.

neuroblast   An early form of a cell, during the stage of cell migration. See Figure 4.2.

neurocrine   Referring to synaptic transmitter function.

neuroendocrine cell   A neuron that releases hormones into local or systemic circulation.

neurofibrillary tangle   An abnormal whorl of neurofilaments within nerve cells. Neurofibrillary tangles are especially apparent in people suffering from dementia. See Figure 4.24.

neurofilament   A small rodlike structure found in axons. Neurofilaments are involved in the transport of materials. See Figure 2.6.

neurogenesis   The mitotic division of nonneuronal cells to produce neurons.

neuroglia   See *glial cells*.

neurohypophysis   See *posterior pituitary*.

neuromodulator   A substance that influences the activity of synaptic transmitters.

neuromuscular junction   The region where the motoneuron terminal and the adjoining muscle fiber meet; where the nerve transmits its message to the muscle fiber.

neuromuscular synapse elimination   In postnatal development, the withdrawal by motoneurons of some of their terminal branches until every muscle fiber is innervated by only a single motoneuron.

neuron   The basic unit of the nervous system. Each neuron is composed of a cell body, receptive extension(s) (dendrites), and a transmitting extension (axon). Also called a nerve cell. See Figures 2.2, 2.4.

neuron doctrine   The hypothesis that the brain is composed of separate cells that are distinct structurally, metabolically, and functionally.

neuronal cell death   The selective death (aptosis) of many nerve cells.

neuropathy   Peripheral nerve destruction.

neuropeptide   A peptide that is used by neurons for signaling.

neuropeptide Y   A peptide neurotransmitter that may carry some of the signals for feeding.

neurosecretory cell   See *neuroendocrine cell.*

neurospecificity   A theory of nervous system development which states that each axon grows to a particular site. See Box 4.2.

neurotoxicology   The study of the effects of toxins and poisons on the nervous system.

neurotransmitter   See *synaptic transmitter.*

neurotrophic factor   A target-derived chemical that acts as if it "feeds" certain neurons to help them survive.

NGF   Nerve growth factor.

nicotinic   Referring to cholinergic receptors that respond to nicotine. Nicotine receptors mediate chiefly the excitatory activities of acetylcholine, including at the neuromuscular junction. Contrast with *muscarinic.*

night terror   A sudden arousal from stage 3 or stage 4 slow-wave sleep that is marked by intense fear and autonomic activation.

nightmare   A long, frightening dream that awakens the sleeper from REM sleep.

nigrostriatal bundle (NSB)   A dopaminergic tract that extends from the substantia nigra of the midbrain to the lateral hypothalamus, the globus pallidus, and the caudate putamen.

Nissl stain   A histological stain that outlines all cell bodies because the dyes are attracted to RNA, which encircles the nucleus.

NMDA receptor   A glutamate receptor that also binds the glutamate agonist NMDA (*N*-methyl-D-aspartate). The NMDA receptor is both ligand-gated and voltage-sensitive, which enables it to participate in a wide variety of information processing. See Box 5.3 and Figure 18.16.

nociceptor   A receptor that responds to stimuli that produce tissue damage or pose the threat of damage.

nocturnal   Active during the dark periods of the daily cycle.

node of Ranvier   A gap between successive segments of the myelin sheath where the axon membrane is exposed. See Figure 2.7.

nonassociative learning   A type of learning in which presentation of a particular stimulus alters the strength or probability of a response according to the strength and temporal spacing of that stimulus; includes habituation and sensitization. Contrast with *associative learning.*

nondeclarative memory   A memory that is shown by performance rather than by conscious recollection. Also called procedural memory. Contrast with *declarative memory.*

nonequivalence of associations   A constraint on learning, stating that a given association is learned with differential ease by different species.

nonequivalence of responses   A constraint on learning, stating that the rapidity of learning a given instrumental behavior varies between species.

nonequivalence of stimuli   A constraint on learning, stating that the same stimulus has a differential ability to be learned by different species.

nonfluent speech   Talking with considerable effort, short sentences, and the absence of the usual melodic character of conversational speech.

nonprimary motor cortex   Frontal lobe regions adjacent to primary motor cortex that contribute to motor control and modulate the activity of the primary motor cortex. See Figure 11.16.

norepinephrine (NE)   A synaptic transmitter that is produced mainly in brain stem nuclei and in the adrenal medulla. Also called noradrenaline. See Table 5.4.

NSB   Nigrostriatal bundle.

nucleotide   A portion of a DNA or RNA molecule that is composed of a single base and the adjoining sugar/phosphate unit of the strand. See Figure A.2.

nucleus   An anatomical collection of neurons within the central nervous system (e.g., the caudate nucleus). See also *ganglion.*

nucleus basalis of Meynert   See *magnocellular nucleus of the basal forebrain.*

nucleus ruber   See *red nucleus.*

nutrient   A chemical that is needed for growth, maintenance, and repair of the body, but is not used as a source of energy.

nystagmus   An abnormal to-and-fro movement of the eye during attempts to fixate.

obsessive–compulsive disorder   A syndrome in which the affected individual engages in recurring, repetitive acts that are carried out without rhyme, reason, or the ability to stop.

occipital cortex   The cortex of the occipital lobe of the brain. Also called visual cortex. See Figures 2.15, 10.14.

occipital lobe   The posterior lobe of the brain.

ocular dominance column   An elongated band of cortical cells that respond preferentially to stimulation of one eye. See Figure 10.24.

ocular dominance histogram   A graph that portrays the strength of response of a brain neuron to stimuli presented to either the left eye or the right eye. Used to determine the effects of manipulating visual experience. See Figure 4.20.

olfactory bulb   An anterior projection of the brain that terminates in the upper nasal passages and, through small openings in the skull, provides receptors for smell.

olfactory epithelium   A sheet of cells, including olfactory receptors, that lines the dorsal portion of the nasal cavities and adjacent regions, including the septum that separates the left and right nasal cavities.

oligodendrocyte   A type of glial cell that is commonly associated with nerve cell bodies; some oligodendrocytes form myelin sheaths. See Figure 2.7.

ontogeny   The process in which an individual changes in the course of its lifetime—that is, grows up and grows old.

open loop   Referring to a control mechanism in which feedback from the output of the system is not provided to the input control. Contrast with *closed loop.*

operant conditioning   See *instrumental conditioning.*

opiates   A class of compounds that exert an effect like that of opium, including reduced pain sensitivity. See Table 5.4.

opioids   Peptides produced in various regions of the brain that bind to opiate receptors and act like opiates. See Table 5.4.

opium   A heterogenous extract of the juice of the seed pod of the opium poppy, *Papaver somniferum.* See Figure 6.5.

opponent-process hypothesis   The theory that color vision depends on systems that produce opposite responses to light of different wavelengths. See Figures 10.26, 10.27.

opsin   One of the two components of photopigments in the retina. The other component is RETINAL.

optic chiasm   The point at which the two optic nerves meet. See Figure 10.14.

optic nerve   The collection of ganglion cell axons that extend from the retina to the optic chiasm.

optic radiation   Axons from the lateral geniculate nucleus that terminate in the primary visual areas of the occipital cortex. See Figure 10.14.

optic tectum   The optical center of the midbrain. See Box 4.2.

optic tract   The axons of retinal ganglion cells after they have passed the optic chiasm; most terminate in the lateral geniculate nucleus. See Figure 10.14.

optokinetic system   A closed-loop system that controls eye movement and keeps the gaze on target.

organ of Corti   A structure in the inner ear that lies on the basilar membrane of the cochlea. It contains the hair cells and the terminations of the auditory nerve. See Figure 9.4.

organizational effect   The permanent alteration of the nervous system, and thus permanent change in behavior, resulting from the action of a steroid hormone on an animal early in its development. Contrast with *activational effect.*

organizational hypothesis   The hypothesis that early testicular steroids masculinize the developing brain to alter behavior permanently.

orgasm   The climax of sexual experience, marked by extremely pleasurable sensations.

oscillator circuit   A neural circuit that produces a recurring, repeating pattern of output. See Figure 5.17.

osmolality   The number of solute particles per unit volume of solvent.

osmoreceptor   One of the cells in the hypothalamus that are hypothesized to respond to changes in osmotic pressure.

osmosis   The passive movement of molecules from one place to another. The motive force behind osmosis is the constant vibration and movement of molecules.

osmotic pressure   The force produced by osmosis.

osmotic thirst   The response to increased osmotic pressure in brain cells. Contrast with hypovolemic thirst.

ossicles   One of three small bones that transmit sound across the middle ear, from the tympanic membrane to the oval window. See Figure 9.1.

otolith   A small bony crystal on the gelatinous membrane in the vestibular system.

outer hair cell   One of the receptor cells of the cochlea. See Figure 9.4.

oval window   The opening from the middle ear to the inner ear.

ovaries   The female gonads, which produce eggs for reproduction.

oviparity   Reproduction through egg laying. Contrast with *viviparity.*

ovulation   The production and release of an egg.

ovum (pl. ova)   An egg, the female gamete.

oxytocin   A hormone, released from the posterior pituitary, that triggers milk letdown in the nursing female. See Figure 7.12.

Pacinian corpuscle   A type of tactile receptor that is found especially in tissue overlying the abdominal cavity. See Figure 8.4.

pair bond   See *monogamy.*

paleocortex   Evolutionarily old cortex, such as the hippocampus. Thought to have evolved more recently than the archicortex.

pancreas   An endocrine gland, located near the posterior wall of the abdominal cavity, that secretes insulin and glucagon. See Figure 7.1.

papilla (pl. papillae)   A small bump that projects from the surface of the tongue. Papillae contain most of the taste receptor cells.

parabiotic   Referring to a surgical preparation that joins the peripheral circulation of two animals.

paracrine   Referring to cellular communication in which a chemical signal diffuses to nearby target cells through the intermediate extracellular space. See Figure 7.4.

paradoxical sleep   See *rapid-eye-movement sleep.*

parallel fibers   One of the axons of the granule cells that form the outermost layer of the cerebellar cortex. See Figure 2.19.

parallel processing   The use of several different circuits at the same time to process the same stimuli. A novelty in computers, but an ancient property of nervous systems.

paraphasia   A symptom of aphasia that is distinguished by the substitution of a word by a sound, an incorrect word, an unintended word, or a neologism (a meaningless word).

parasympathetic nervous system   One of the two systems that compose the autonomic nervous system. The parasympathetic division arises from both the cranial nerves and the sacral spinal cord. Contrast with *sympathetic nervous system*. See Figure 2.14. for the different functions of the two systems.

paraventricular nucleus   A nucleus of the hypothalamus. See Figure 7.11.

parietal lobe   A major sector of the cerebral hemispheres.

Parkinson's disease   A degenerative neurological disorder that involves dopaminergic neurons of the substantia nigra.

parthenogenesis   "Virgin birth"; the production of offspring without the contribution of a male or sperm.

partial seizure   An epileptic seizure that arises from pathological foci that are not widespread. Partial seizures include focal-repetitive motor spasms and do not involve loss of consciousness.

parvocellular system   The division of primate visual pathways that appears to be mainly responsible for analysis of color and form and for recognition of objects. See Figure 10.28.

parvocellular layer   One of the four dorsal or outer layers of the primate lateral geniculate nucleus, so called because their cells are relatively small.

passive avoidance response   A response that an organism has learned *not* to make, (e.g., learning not to enter a compartment where it has been given a shock).

patch-clamp technique   The use of very narrow pipette microelectrodes, clamped by suction onto tiny patches of the neural membrane, to record the electrical activity of a single square micron of membrane, including single ion channels.

Pavlovian conditioning   See *classical conditioning*.

penis   The male genital organ, which enters the female's vagina to deliver semen.

perforant path   The route of axons that "perforate" the subiculum to provide the main inputs to the hippocampal formation.

period   The interval of time between two similar points of successive cycles, such as sunset to sunset.

peripheral nervous system   The portion of the nervous system that includes all the nerves and neurons outside the brain and spinal cord.

permanent memory   A type of memory that lasts without decline for the life of an organism.

perseveration/consolidation hypothesis   The hypothesis that information passes through two stages in memory formation. During the first stage the memory is held by perseveration (repetition) of neural activity and is easily disrupted. During the second stage the memory becomes fixed, or consolidated, and is no longer easily disrupted.

PET   Positron emission tomography.

petit mal seizure   A type of generalized epileptic seizure that is characterized by a spike-and-wave electrical pattern. A person having a petit mal seizure is unaware of the environment and later cannot recall what happened.

phantom limb   The experience of sensory messages that are attributed to an amputated limb.

phase shift   A shift in the activity of a biological rhythm, typically provided by a synchronizing environmental stimulus.

phasic receptor   A receptor that shows a rapid fall in nerve impulse discharge as stimulation is maintained.

phencyclidine   An anesthetic agent that is also a psychedelic drug. Phencyclidine makes many people feel dissociated from themselves and their environment.

phenothiazines   A class of antipsychotic drugs which reduce the positive symptoms of schizophrenia.

phenylketonuria (PKU)   An inherited disorder of protein metabolism in which the absence of an enzyme leads to a toxic buildup of certain compounds, causing mental retardation.

pheromone   A chemical signal that is released outside the body of an animal and that affects other members of the same species. Contrast with *allomone*. See Figure 7.4.

phobic disorder   An intense, irrational fear that becomes centered on a specific object, activity, or situation that a person feels he or she must avoid.

phoneme   A sound that is produced for language.

phosphene   A perceived flash of light that is provoked by electrical or mechanical stimulation of the eyeball or visual cortex.

phosphorylation   The addition of phosphate groups (PO_4) to proteins.

photon   A quantum of light energy.

photopic system   A system in the retina that operates at high levels of light, shows sensitivity to color, and involves the cones. Contrast with *scotopic system*. See Table 10.1.

phrenology   The belief that bumps on the skull reflect enlargements of brain regions responsible for certain behavioral faculties. See Figure 1.15.

phylogeny   The evolutionary history of a particular group of organisms.

physical dependence   The state of an individual that has frequently taken high doses of a drug and will encounter unpleasant withdrawal symptoms if he or she stops.

physiological saline   A mixture of water and salt in which the concentration of salt is 0.9%, approximately equal in osmolarity to mammalian extracellular fluid.

pia mater   The innermost of the three coverings that embrace the brain and spinal cord.

pinna   See *external ear*.

pitch   A dimension of auditory experience in which sounds vary from low to high.

pituitary gland   A small, complex endocrine gland located in a socket at the base of the skull. The anterior pituitary and posterior pituitary are separate in function. See Figure 7.11.

PKU   Phenylketonuria.

place theory   A theory of frequency discrimination according to which pitch perception depends on the place of maximal displacement of the basilar membrane produced by a sound. Contrast with *volley theory*.

placebo effect   A response to an inert substance (a placebo) that mimics the effects of an actual drug. For example, people suffering pain frequently experience reflief from sugar tablets presented as medicine.

placenta   The specialized organ produced by the mammalian embryo that attaches to the walls of the uterus to provide nutrients, energy, and gas exchange to the fetus.

placental mammal   A mammal that produces a highly specialized placenta; includes all mammals except the marsupials and the monotremes.

planum temporale   A region of superior temporal cortex adjacent to the primary auditory area. See Figure 9.14.

pneumoencephalography   A technique for examining brain structure in humans by taking X rays after a gas is injected into the cerebral ventricles.

poikilotherm   An animal whose body temperature varies with the environment. Examples include reptiles. Contrast with *homeotherms*.

polyandry   A mating system in which one female mates with more than one male. Contrast with *polygyny*.

polygamy   A mating system in which an individual mates with more than one other animal.

polygraph   A device that measures several bodily responses, such as heart rate and blood pressure; popularly known as a "lie detector."

polygyny   A mating system in which one male mates with more than one female. Contrast with *polyandry*.

polymodal   Involving several sensory modalities.

pons   A portion of the metencephalon. See Figures 2.15, 9.8.

positive reward model   A model of addictive behavior that emphasizes the rewarding attributes of drug ingestion.

positive symptom   In psychiatry, an abnormal state. Examples include hallucinations, delusions, and excited motor behavior. Contrast with *negative symptom*.

positron emission tomography (PET)   A technique for examining brain function in intact humans by combining tomography with injections of radioactive substances used by the brain. Analysis of the metabolism of these substances reflects regional differences in brain activity. See Figure 2.24.

postcentral gyrus   The strip of parietal cortex, just behind the central sulcus, which receives somatosensory information from the entire body.

postcopulatory behavior   The final stage in mating behavior. Species-specific postcopulatory behaviors include rolling (in the cat) and grooming (in the rat).

posterior pituitary   The rear division of the pituitary gland. Also called neurohypophysis. See Figure 7.11.

postganglionic cell   A cell in the autonomic nervous system that resides in the peripheral ganglia and sends its axons to innervate target organs.

postsynaptic   Referring to the region of a synapse that receives and responds to neurotransmitter. Contrast with *presynaptic*.

postsynaptic potential   See *graded potential*.

posttetanic potentiation   A well-known example of neural plasticity in which a rapid series of action potentials (a tetanus) is induced in a nerve, with the result that subsequent single action potentials cause a stronger postsynaptic potential in the target.

postural tremor   A tremor that occurs when a person attempts to maintain a posture such as holding an arm or leg extended, often resulting from pathology of the basal ganglia or cerebellum.

potassium equilibrium potential   See *equilibrium potential*.

precentral gyrus   The strip of frontal cortex, just in front of the central sulcus, that is crucial for motor control.

precocial   Referring to animals that are born in a relatively developed state and who are able to survive without maternal care. Contrast with *altricial*.

preferred temperature   The environmental temperature at which an animal chooses to spend most of its time.

prefrontal cortex   The anteriormost region of the frontal lobe.

preganglionic cells   A cell of the autonomic nervous system that resides in the CNS and sends its axons to innervate autonomic ganglia. See Figure 2.14.

premature ejaculation   Ejaculation before the man and/or his partner have achieved the level of excitement desired.

premotor cortex   A region of nonprimary motor cortex, just anterior to the primary motor cortex. See Figure 11.16.

preoptic area   A region of the hypothalamus, just anterior to the level of the optic chiasm.

presynaptic   Referring to the region of a synapse that releases neurotransmitter. Contrast with *postsynaptic*.

primacy effect   The superior performance seen in a memory task for items at the start of a list. Contrast with *recency effect*.

primary motor cortex   The apparent executive region for initiation of movement; primarily the precentral gyrus.

primary visual cortex   The region of the occipital cortex where most visual information first arrives. Also called striate cortex, area 17, or Vl. See Figure 10.14.

procedural memory   See *nondeclarative memory*.

proceptive behavior A behavior displayed by an animal that prompts its partner to initiate mating behaviors.

progesterone The primary type of progestin secreted by the ovary.

progestins A major class of steroid hormones that are produced by the ovary, including progesterone. See Table 7.2.

projection neuron A large neuron that transmits messages between widely separated parts of the brain.

prolactin A protein hormone, produced by the anterior pituitary, that promotes mammary development for lactation in female mammals.

promiscuity A mating system in which animals mate with several members of the opposite sex and do not establish durable associations with sex partners.

proprioceptive Referring to information from the periphery about the body's position and movement.

prosencephalon See *forebrain*.

prosopagnosia A condition characterized by the inability to recognize faces.

prostate gland A male secondary sexual gland that contributes fluid to semen.

prosthetic device An artificial replacement of a body part lost by accident or disease.

protein hormone A class of hormones that consists of protein molecules.

protein kinase An enzyme that adds phosphate groups (PO_4) to protein molecules.

proximal An anatomical term referring to structures near the trunk or center of an organism. Contrast with *distal*. See Box 2.2.

psychedelic Referring to a mental state with intensified sensory perception and distortions or hallucinations. Psychedelic drugs produce such states.

psychoneuroimmunology The study of the immune system and its interaction with the nervous system and behavior.

psychopharmacology The study of the effects of drugs on the nervous system and behavior.

psychosocial dwarfism Reduced stature caused by stress early in life that inhibits deep sleep. See Box 7.2.

psychosomatic medicine A field of study that emphasizes the role of psychological factors in disease.

psychosurgery Surgery in which brain lesions are produced to modify severe psychiatric disorders.

psychotogen A substance that generates psychotic behavior.

pupil The aperture, formed by the iris, that allows light to enter the eye.

pure tone A tone with a single frequency of vibration. See Box 9.1.

Purkinje cell A type of large nerve cell in the cerebellar cortex.

pursuit movement A type of eye movement in which your gaze smoothly and continuously follows a moving object.

putamen One of the basal ganglia. See Figure 2.18.

pyramidal cell A type of large nerve cell that has a roughly pyramid-shaped cell body; found in the cerebral cortex. See Figure 2.22.

pyramidal system The motor system that includes neurons within the cerebral cortex and their axons, which form the pyramidal tract. Also called the corticospinal system. See Figure 11.13.

pyramidal tract The path of axons arising from the motor cortex and terminating in the spinal cord.

pyrogen A chemical, released by cells of the immune system, that elevates body temperature.

quantum (pl. quanta) A unit of radiant energy.

radial glia Glial cells that form early in development, spanning the width of the emerging cerebral hemispheres, and guide migrating neurons. See Figure 4.7.

radioimmunoassay (RIA) A technique that uses antibodies to measure the concentration of a substance, such as a hormone in blood.

ramp movement A slow, sustained motion that is thought to be generated in the basal ganglia. Also called smooth movement. Contrast with *ballistic*.

range fractionation A hypothesis of stimulus intensity perception stating that a wide range of intensity values can be encoded by a group of cells, each of which is a specialist for a particular range of stimulus intensities. See Figure 8.5.

raphe nucleus A group of neurons in the midline of the brain stem that contains serotonin and is involved in sleep mechanisms. See Figure 14.24.

rapid-eye-movement (REM) sleep A stage of sleep characterized by small-amplitude, fast-EEG waves, no postural tension, and rapid eye movements. Also called paradoxical sleep. Contrast with *slow-wave sleep*. See Figure 14.12, 14.13.

Raynaud's disease A circulatory disorder in which blood supply to the fingers may be shut off upon exposure to the cold and sometimes in response to emotional states.

recency effect The superior performance seen in a memory task for items at the end of a list; attributed to short-term memory. Contrast with *primacy effect*.

receptive field The stimulus region and features that cause the maximal response of a cell in a sensory system. See Figure 8.12, 10.16.

receptivity The state of readiness in the female to show responses that are necessary for the male to achieve intromission.

receptor The initial element in a sensory system, responsible for stimulus transduction. Examples include the hair cells in the cochlea or the rods and cones in the retina. See also *receptor molecule*.

receptor cell A specialized cell that responds to a particular energy or substance in the internal or external environment. The receptor cell converts this energy into a change in the electrical potential across its membrane.

receptor molecule   A protein that captures and reacts to molecules of the transmitter or hormone. Also called a receptor.

receptor site   A region of specialized membrane that contains receptor molecules located on the postsynaptic surface of a synapse. Receptor sites receive and react with chemical transmitters.

red nucleus   A brain stem structure related to the basal ganglia. Also called the nucleus ruber.

reflex   A simple, highly stereotyped, and unlearned response to a particular stimulus (e.g., an eyeblink in response to a puff of air). See Figure 11.11, 11.12.

reflex ovulation   Ovulation that in certain species is induced by copulation, thus not restricting successful mating to a regular ovulatory period of the female's cycle.

refraction   The bending of light rays by a change in the density of a medium, such as the cornea and the lens of our eyes.

refractory phase   1. A period during and after a nerve impulse in which the responsiveness of the axon membrane is reduced. A brief period of complete insensitivity to stimuli (absolute refractory phase) is followed by a longer period of reduced sensitivity (relative refractory phase) during which only strong stimulation produces a nerve impulse. 2. A period following copulation during which an individual cannot recommence copulation. The absolute refractory phase of the male sexual response is illustrated in Figure 12. 9.

regulation   An adaptive response to early injury, as when developing individuals compensate for missing or injured cells.

reinforcing stimulus   See *instrumental conditioning*.

relative refractory phase   See *refractory phase*.

releasing hormone   A hormone produced in the hypothalamus, that traverses the hypothalamic–pituitary portal system to control the pituitary's release of tropic hormones.

REM sleep   See *rapid-eye-movement sleep*.

renin   Hormone released by the kidneys when they detect reduced blood flow.

resting potential   A difference in electrical potential across the membrane of a nerve cell during an inactive period. Also called the membrane potential. See Figure 5.1.

rete mirabile   A network of fine blood vessels located at the base of the brain in which blood coming from the periphery reduces the temperature of arterial blood before it enters the brain.

reticular formation   An extensive region of the brain stem (extending from the medulla through the thalamus) that is involved in arousal. See Figure 14.23.

reticulospinal tract   A tract of axons arising from the brain stem reticular formation and descending to the spinal cord to modulate movement.

retina   The receptive surface inside the eye that contains the rods and cones. See Figure 10.8.

RETINAL   One of the two components of the photopigment found in the eye. The other component is called opsin.

retrieval   A process in memory during which a stored memory is used by an organism. See Figure 17.12.

retroactive amnesia   A type of memory loss in which events immediately preceding a head injury are not recalled.

retrograde amnesia   Difficulty in retrieving memories formed before the onset of amnesia.

retrograde degeneration   Destruction of the nerve cell body following injury to its axon. See Box 4.1.

retrograde signal   A signal that is thought to be released by the postsynaptic region that instructs the presynaptic neuron to increase subsequent transmitter release.

reuptake   The process by which released synaptic transmitter molecules are taken up and reused by the presynaptic neuron, thus stopping synaptic activity.

rhodopsin   The photopigment in rods that responds to light.

rhombencephalon   See *hindbrain*.

RIA   Radioimmunoassay.

ribonucleic acid (RNA)   A nucleic acid that implements information found in DNA. Two forms of RNA are transfer RNA and messenger RNA.

ribosomes   Structures in the cell body where the translation of genetic information (the production of proteins) takes place.

RNA   *Ribonucleic acid.*

rod   One of the light-sensitive receptor cells in the retina that are most active at low levels of light. See Figure 10.8.

roots   The two distinct branches of a spinal nerve, each of which serves a separate function. The dorsal root carries sensory information from the peripheral nervous system to the spinal cord. The ventral root carries motor messages from the spinal cord to the peripheral nervous system. See Figure 2.12.

rostral   An anatomical term referring to structures toward the head end of an organism. Also called cephalic. Contrast with *caudal*. See Box 2.2.

round window   A membrane separating the cochlear duct from the middle-ear cavity.

S-shaped curve   A common dose–response function. See Figure 6.3.

saccade   (saccadic movement) A series of rapid movements of the eyesthat occur regularly during normal viewing. Also called a saccadic movement.

saccule   A small, fluid-filled sac under the utricle that responds to static positions of the head. See Figure 9.18.

sacral   Referring to the lower part of the back or spinal cord.

sagittal plane   The plane that bisects the body or brain into right and left portions. See Box 2.2.

saltatory conduction   The form of conduction characteristic of myelinated axons, in which the nerve impulse jumps from one node of Ranvier to the next.

satiety   A feeling of fulfillment or satisfaction. Contrast with *hunger.*

saturation   One of the basic dimensions of light perception. Saturation varies from rich to pale (e.g., from red to pink to gray in the color solid of Figure 10.5).

schema   In terms of actions, a high-level program for movement.

schizophrenia   A severe psychopathology characterized by negative symptoms such as emotional withdrawal and impoverished thought, and by positive symptoms such as hallucinations and delusions.

schizotoxin   A hypothesized toxic substance that causes schizophrenia.

Schwann cell   The accessory cell that forms myelin in the peripheral nervous system.

SCN   Suprachiasmatic nucleus.

scotoma   A region of blindness caused by injury to the visual pathway or brain.

scotopic system   A system in the retina that operates at low levels of light and involves the rods. Contrast with *photopic system.* See Table 10.1.

second messenger   A slow-acting substance in the postsynaptic cell that amplifies the effects of nerve impulses and can initiate processes that lead to changes in electrical potential at the membrane.

secretin   A hormone that is released from the small intestine during digestion.

selective potentiation   The enhancement of the sensitivity or activity of certain neural circuits.

selectivity of reinforcement   The idea that across species, different reinforcements are differentially effective in strengthening associations.

semantic memory   Generalized memory—for instance, knowing the meaning of a word without knowing where or when you learned that word.

semen   A mixture of fluid, including sperm, that is released during ejaculation.

semicircular canal   One of the three fluid-filled tubes in the inner ear that are part of the vestibular system. Each of the tubes, which are at right angles to each other, detects angular acceleration. See Figure 9.18.

seminal vesicle   A gland that stores fluid to contribute to semen.

semipermeable membrane   A membrane that allows some but not all molecules to pass through.

senile dementia   A neurological disorder of the aged that is characterized by progressive behavioral deterioration, including personality change and profound intellectual decline.

senile plaques   A neuroanatomical change that correlates with senile dementia. Senile plaques are small areas of the brain that have abnormal cellular and chemical patterns. See Figure 4.24.

sensitive period   The period during development in which an organism can be permanently altered by a particular experience or treatment.

sensitization   1. A form of nonassociative learning in which an organism becomes more responsive to most stimuli after being exposed to unusually strong or painful stimulation. See Box 17.2. 2. A process in which the body shows an enhanced response to a given drug after repeated doses. Contrast with *tolerance.*

sensorineural deafness   A hearing impairment that originates from cochlear or auditory nerve lesions.

sensory neuron   A neuron that is directly affected by changes in the environment, such as light, an odor, or a touch.

sensory transduction   The process in which a receptor cell converts the energy in a stimulus into a change in the electrical potential across its membrane.

septal complex   A brain region that provides subcortical input to the hippocampal formation.

serotonergic   Referring to neurons that use serotonin as their synaptic transmitter.

serotonin (5-HT)   A synaptic transmitter that is produced in the raphe nuclei and is active in structures throughout the cerebral hemispheres. See Figure 14.23.

set point   The point of reference in a feedback system. An example is the setting of a thermostat.

set zone   The range of a variable that a feedback system tries to maintain.

sex chromosome   One of a pair of chromosomes that in female mammals are identical (XX) but in males are different (XY). Contrast with *autosomes.*

sex-determining region on the Y (*Sry*) gene   A gene on the Y chromosome that directs the developing gonads to become testes.

sexual attraction   The first step in the mating behavior of many animals, in which animals emit stimuli that attract members of the opposite sex.

sexual determination   The developmentally early event that normally decides whether the individual will become a male or a female.

sexual differentiation   The process by which individuals develop either malelike or femalelike bodies and behavior.

sexual dimorphism   A structural difference between the sexes.

sexual imprinting   A kind of imprinting in which early experience influences the choice of a mate later in life.

sexual receptivity   See *receptivity.*

sexual selection   Darwin's theoretical mechanism for the evolution of anatomical and behavioral differences between males and females.

Shaffer collateral   An axon branch from a neuron in area CA3 that projects to area CA1 in the hippocampus.

short-term memory (STM)   Memory that usually lasts only for seconds or as long as rehearsal continues.

SIDS   Sudden infant death syndrome.

simple cortical cell   A cell in the visual cortex that responds best to an edge or a bar of a particular width and with a particular direction and location in the visual field. See Figure 10.16*b.*

sinistral   Left-handed.

sleep apnea   A sleep disorder that involves the slowing or cessation of respiration during sleep, which wakens the patient. Excessive daytime somnolence results from the frequent nocturnal awakening.

sleep deprivation   The partial or total prevention of sleep.

sleep enuresis   Bed wetting.

sleep epoch   A period of one episode of short-wave sleep followed by an episode of REM sleep.

sleep-maintenance insomnia   Difficulty in staying asleep. Contrast with *sleep-onset insomnia*.

sleep-onset insomnia   Difficulty in getting to sleep. Contrast with *sleep-maintenance insomnia*.

sleep paralysis   A state in which the ability to move or talk is temporarily lost.

sleep recovery   The process of sleeping more than normally after a period of sleep deprivation, as though in compensation.

sleep spindle   A characteristic 14 to 18-Hz wave in the EEG of a person said to be in stage 2 sleep. See Figure 14.11.

slow-wave sleep (SWS)   Sleep, divided into stages 1 through 4, that is defined by the presence of slow-wave EEG activity. Contrast with *rapid-eye-movement sleep*. See Figure 14.13.

smooth movement   See *ramp movement*.

SOAE   Spontaneous otoacoustic emission.

sodium equilibrium potential   See *equilibrium potential*.

solute   The solid compound that is dissolved in a liquid. Contrast with *solvent*.

solvent   The liquid (often water) in which a compound is dissolved. Contrast with *solute*.

somatic intervention   An approach to finding relations between bodily variables and behavioral variables that involves manipulating bodily structure or function and looking for resultant changes in behavior. See Figure 1.12.

somatosensory cortex   The portion of parietal cortex that receives tactile stimuli from the body.

somatotropic hormone   See *growth hormone*.

somnambulism   Sleepwalking.

spatial frequency filter model   A model of pattern analysis that emphasizes Fourier analysis of visual stimuli. Contrast with *feature detector model*.

spatial summation   The summation at the axon hillock of postsynaptic potentials from across the cell body. If this summation reaches threshold a nerve impulse will be triggered. See Figure 5.4. Contrast with *temporal summation*.

specific abilities to learn and remember   The concept that specific abilities to learn and remember evolve where needed. Contrast with *genetic constraints on learning*.

specific hunger   The temporary, unlearned increase in preference for a particular food; related to a specific need.

specific nerve energies   The doctrine that the receptors and neural channels for the different senses are independent and operate in their own special ways, and can produce only one particular sensation.

spectrally opponent cell   A visual receptor cell that has opposite firing responses to different regions of the spectrum. See Figure 10.25, 10.26.

sperm   The gamete produced by males for fertilization of eggs (ova).

spinal animal   An animal whose spinal cord has been surgically disconnected from the brain to enable the study of behaviors that do not require brain control.

spinal nerve   A nerve that emerges from the spinal cord. There are 31 pairs of spinal nerves. See Figure 2.12.

spinal root   See *roots*.

spinal shock   A period of decreased synaptic excitability in the neurons of the spinal cord after it is isolated surgically from the brain.

spindle cell   A type of small, rod-shaped nerve cell.

split-brain individual   Referring to an individual whose corpus callosum has been severed, halting communication between the right and left hemispheres.

spontaneous otoacoustic emission (SOAE)   A sound that is produced by the ears of many normal people. Contrast with *evoked otoacoustic emissions*.

spontaneous recovery   A feature of classical conditioning in which, if there is no testing after extinction, the conditioned stimulus may again elicit a response.

stage 1 sleep   The initial stage of slow-wave sleep, which is characterized by small-amplitude EEG waves of irregular frequency, slow heart rate, and reduced muscle tension. See Figure 14.11.

stage 2 sleep   A stage of slow-wave sleep that is defined by bursts of regular 14 to 18-Hz EEG waves (called sleep spindles) that progressively increase and then decrease in amplitude. See Figure 14.11.

stage 3 sleep   A stage of slow-wave sleep that is defined by the spindles seen in stage 2 sleep mixed with larger-amplitude slow waves. See Figure 14.11.

stage 4 sleep   A stage of slow-wave sleep that is defined by the presence of high-amplitude slow waves of 1 to 4 Hz. See Figure 14.11.

stapedius   A middle-ear muscle that is attached to the stapes.

stapes   A middle-ear bone that is connected to the oval window. One of the three ossicles that conduct sounds across the middle ear.

static phase of obesity   A later period following destruction of the ventromedial hypothalamus during which an animal's weight stabilizes at an obese level and food intake is not much above normal. See Figure 13.26. Contrast with *dynamic phase of weight gain*.

stellate cell   A type of small nerve cell that has many branches.

stereocillium (pl. stereocilia)   A relatively stiff hair that protrudes from a hair cell in the auditory or vestibular system. See Figure 9.3.

stereopsis   The ability to perceive depth, using the slight difference in visual information from the two eyes. See Figure 10.28.

steroid hormones   A class of hormones that are composed of four interconnected rings of carbon atoms.

stimulation-elicited behavior   A motivational behavior, such as eating, drinking, or fearful escape, that is elicited by electrical stimulation of sites in the brain.

STM   Short-term memory.

stress   Any circumstance that upsets homeostatic balance. Examples include exposure to extreme cold or heat or an array of threatening psychological states.

stretch reflex   The contraction of a muscle in response to stretch of that muscle. See Figure 11.12.

striate cortex   See *primary visual cortex.*

striate region   The region of the brain that contains the basal ganglia, called striate because the external capsule and internal capsule appear as light-colored stripes across the gray matter.

striatum   The caudate nucleus and putamen together.

stroke   A disorder of blood vessels—either a block or a rupture of a vessel—that destroys or cripples particular brain regions.

subfornical organ   One of the circumventricular organs. See Figure 13.17.

subiculum   A region adjacent to the hippocampus that contributes to the hippocampal formation. Also called the hippocampal gyrus.

substantia nigra   A brain stem structure in humans that is related to the basal ganglia and named for its dark pigmentation. Depletion of dopaminergic cells in this region has been implicated in Parkinson's disease.

subventricular zone   A region around the brain ventricle that continues to manufacture the precursors of glial cells after birth.

sudden infant death syndrome (SIDS)   The sudden, unexpected death of an apparently healthy human infant who simply stops breathing, usually during sleep. SIDS is not well understood. Also called crib death.

sulcus (pl. sulci)   A furrow of convoluted brain surface. Contrast with *gyrus.* See Figure 2.15.

superior colliculi   See *colliculus.*

superior olivary complex   A brain stem structure that receives input from both right and left cochlear nuclei, and provides the first binaural analysis of auditory information. See Figure 9.8.

superordinate circuit   A neural circuit that is hierarchically superior to other, simple circuits.

supplementary motor cortex   A region of nonprimary motor cortex that receives input from the basal ganglia and modulates the activity of the primary motor cortex.

suprachiasmatic nucleus (SCN)   A small region of the hypothalamus above the optic chiasm that is the location of a circadian oscillator. See Figure 14.3.

supraoptic nucleus   A nucleus of the hypothalamus. See Figure 7.11.

SWS   Slow-wave sleep.

Sylvian sulcus   A deep fissure that demarcates the temporal lobe. See Figure 2.15.

sympathetic chain   A chain of ganglia that runs along each side of the spinal column; part of the sympathetic nervous system. See Figure 2.14.

sympathetic nervous system   One of two systems that compose the autonomic nervous system. The sympathetic nervous system arises from the thoracic and lumbar spinal cord. See Figure 2.14 for the different functions of the two systems. Contrast with *parasympathetic nervous system.*

synapse   An area composed of the presynaptic (axonal) terminal, the postsynaptic (usually dendritic) membrane, and the space (or cleft) between them. The synapse is the site at which neural messages travel from one neuron to another. Also called the synaptic region. See Figure 2.5.

synapse rearrangement   The loss of some synapses and development of others; a refinement of synaptic connections that is often seen in development.

synaptic assembly   A level of brain organization that includes the total collection of all synapses on a single cell. See Figure 5.15.

synaptic bouton   The presynaptic swelling of the axon terminal from which neural messages travel across the synaptic cleft to other neurons. See Figure 2.3, 2.5.

synaptic cleft   The space between the presynaptic and postsynaptic elements. This gap measures about 20 to 40 nanometers. See Figure 2.5, 5.12.

synaptic region   See *synapse.*

synaptic transmitter   The chemical in the presynaptic bouton that serves as the basis of communication between neurons. The transmitter travels across the synaptic cleft and reacts with the postsynaptic membrane when triggered by a nerve impulse. Also called neurotransmitter or chemical transmitter. See Figure 5.12, Table 5.4.

synaptic vesicle   A small, spherical structure that contains molecules of synaptic transmitter. See Figure 2.5.

synaptogenesis   The establishment of synaptic connections as axons and dendrites grow.

synergist   A muscle that acts together with another muscle. Contrast with *antagonist* (definition 2).

syrinx   The vocal organ in birds.

system   A high level of brain organization that includes specialized circuits (e.g., the visual system). Contrast with *circuit.*

T lymphocyte   An immune-system cell that attacks foreign microbes or tissue; "killer cell."

tardive dyskinesia   A disorder characterized by involuntary movements, especially involving the face, mouth, lips, and tongue. Related to prolonged use of antipsychotic drugs, such as chlorpromazine. See Box 16.2.

tastant   A substance that can be tasted.

taste aversion   See *conditioned taste aversion.*

taste bud   A cluster of 50 to150 cells that detects tastes. Taste buds are found in papillae on the tongue.

taxonomy   The classification of organisms.

tectorial membrane   A structure in the cochlear duct. See Figure 9.3.

tectum   The dorsal portion of the midbrain, including the inferior and superior colliculi.

telencephalon   The frontal subdivision of the forebrain which includes the cerebral hemispheres when fully developed. See Figure 2.17.

temporal lobe   A major sector of the cerebral hemispheres. See Figure 2.15.

temporal summation   The summation of postsynaptic potentials that reach the axon hillock at different times. The closer together the potentials are, the more complete the summation. Contrast with *spatial summation*.

tendon   Strong tissue that connects muscles to bone.

TENS   Transcutaneous electrical nerve stimulation.

tensor tympani   The muscle attached to the malleus and the tympanic membrane that modulates mechanical linkage to protect the delicate receptor cells of the inner ear from damaging sounds.

testes (s. **testis**)   The male gonads, which produce sperm and androgenic steroid hormones.

testosterone   A hormone, produced by male gonads, that controls a variety of bodily changes that become visible at puberty. See Figure 7.16, Table 7.2.

thalamus   The brain regions that surround the third ventricle. See Figure 2.18.

third ventricle   The midline ventricle that conducts cerebrospinal fluid from the lateral ventricles to the fourth ventricle. See Figure 2.20.

thirst   The internal state of an animal seeking water.

thoracic   Referring to the level of the chest, here the vertebrae that have ribs attached and the spinal cord segments originating from those vertebrae.

threshold   The stimulus intensity that is just adequate to trigger a nerve impulse at the axon hillock.

thyroid gland   An endocrine gland located below the vocal apparatus in the throat that regulates metabolic processes, especially carbohydrate use and body growth. See Figure 7.1.

thyroid-stimulating hormone (TSH)   A tropic hormone, released by the anterior pituitary gland, that increases the release of thyroxine and the uptake of iodide by the thyroid gland. See Figure 7.13.

thyrotropin-releasing hormone (TRH)   A hypothalamic hormone that regulates the release of thyroid-stimulating hormone. See Figure 7.10.

thyroxine   A hormone released by the thyroid gland.

tinnitus   A sensation of noises or ringing in the ears.

tip link   A fine, threadlike fiber that runs along and connects the tips of stereocilia. See Figure 9.6.

tolerance   A condition in which, with repeated exposure to a drug, the individual becomes less responsive to a constant dose. Contrast with *sensitization*.

tomography   A technique for revealing the detailed structure of a particular tissue using radiation. Examples include computerized axial tomography (CAT or CT), and positron emission tomography (PET).

tonic receptor   A receptor in which the frequency of nerve impulse discharge declines slowly or not at all as stimulation is maintained.

tonotopic organization   A major organizational feature in auditory systems in which neurons are arranged as an orderly map of stimulus frequency, with cells responsive to high frequencies located at a distance from those responsive to low frequencies.

torpor   The condition in which animals allow body temperature to fall drastically. During torpor, animals are unresponsive to most stimuli.

Tourette's syndrome   A heightened sensitivity to tactile, auditory, and visual stimuli that may be accompanied by the buildup of an urge to emit verbal or phonic tics.

toxin   A poisonous substance, especially one that is produced by living organisms.

tract   A bundle of axons found within the central nervous system. Contrast with *nerves*.

transcription   The process during which mRNA forms bases complementary to a strand of DNA. This message is then used to translate the DNA code into protein molecules.

transcutaneous electrical nerve stimulation (TENS)   The delivery of electrical pulses through electrodes attached to the skin, which excite nerves that supply the region to which pain is referred. TENS can relieve the pain in some instances.

transducer   A device that converts energy from one form to another (e.g., sensory receptor cells).

transduction   The process of converting one form of energy to another.

transfer RNA (tRNA)   A small molecule of RNA that conveys amino acids to ribosomes for translation.

translation   The process by which amino acids are linked together (directed by an mRNA molecule) to form protein molecules.

transmethylation hypothesis   A hypothesized explanation of schizophrenia suggesting that the addition of a methyl group to some naturally occurring brain compounds can convert them to hallucinogenic agents, or psychotogens.

transmitter   See *synaptic transmitter*.

transverse plane   See *coronal plane*.

tremor   A rhythmic, repetitive movement caused by brain pathology.

tremor-at-rest   A tremor that occurs when the affected region, such as a limb, is fully supported; a symptom of Parkinson's disease.

TSH   Thyroid-stimulating hormone.

trichromatic hypothesis   A theory of color perception that there are three different types of cones, each excited by a different region of the spectrum and each having a separate pathway to the brain.

tricyclic antidepressants   A class of compounds whose structure resembles that of chlorpromazine and of related antipsychotic drugs. Tricyclic antidepressants may relieve depression but only after two to three weeks of daily administration.

trigger feature A particular stimulus characteristic that is most effective in evoking responses from a particular cell.

trinucleotide repeat A repetition of the same three nucleotides within a gene, which can lead to dysfunction, as in the case of Huntington's disease and fragile X syndrome.

triplet code A code for an amino acid specified by three successive bases of a DNA molecule.

tRNA Transfer RNA.

tropic hormone An anterior pituitary hormone that affects the secretion of other endocrine glands. See Figure 7.13.

TRH Thyrotropin-releasing hormone.

TSH Thyroid-stimulating hormone.

tuning curve A graph of the responses of a single auditory nerve fiber or neuron to sounds that vary in frequency and intensity.

tympanic canal One of three principal canals running along the length of the cochlea. See Figure 9.3.

tympanic membrane The partition between the external ear and the middle ear. Also called the eardrum. See Figure 9.1.

ultradian Referring to a rhythmic biological event whose period is shorter than that of a circadian rhythm, usually from several minutes to several hours.

unconditioned response (UR) See *classical conditioning.*

unconditioned stimulus (US) See *classical conditioning.*

unipolar depression Depression that alternates with normal emotional states. Contrast with *bipolar depression.*

umyelinated axons Fine-diameter axons that lack a myelin sheath.

UR Unconditioned response.

urethra The duct that carries urine from the bladder to outside the body.

US Unconditioned stimulus.

uterus The organ in which the fertilized egg implants and develops in mammals. See Figure 12.8.

utricle A small, fluid-filled sac in the vestibular system that responds to static positions of the head. See Figure 9.18.

vagina The opening in female genitalia that permits entry of the penis during copulation and later releases the fetus or egg. See Figure 12.8.

vagus nerve The tenth cranial nerve. See Figure 2.11.

vas deferens A duct that connects the epididymis to the seminal vesicles. See Figure 12.8.

vasopressin A peptide hormone that promotes water conservation and increases blood pressure. Also called arginine vasopressin or antidiuretic hormone.

ventral An anatomical term referring to structures toward the belly or front of the body or the bottom of the brain. Contrast with *dorsal.* See Box 2.2.

ventral root See *roots.*

ventricles See *cerebral ventricles.*

ventricular layer A layer of homogeneous cells in the neural tube of a developing organism that is the source of all neural and glial cells in the mature organism. Also called the ependymal layer or ventricular zone. See Figure 4.4.

ventricular system A system of fluid-filled cavities inside the brain. See Figure 2.20.

ventromedial hypothalamus (VMH) A hypothalamic region involved in inhibiting eating, among other functions. See Figure 13.25.

vertebral arteries Arteries that ascend the vertebrae, enter the base of the skull, and join together to form the basilar artery. See Figure 2.21.

vestibular canal One of three principal canals running along the length of the cochlea. See Figure 9.18.

vestibular system A receptor system in the inner ear that responds to mechanical forces, such as gravity and acceleration. See Figure 9.18.

vestibuloocular reflex A rapid response that adjusts the eye to a change in head position.

visual agnosia A condition, following stroke, in which the ability to identify familiar objects visually is lost.

visual cortex See *occipital cortex.*

visual field The whole area that you can see without moving your head or eyes.

viviparity Reproduction in which the zygote develops extensively within the female until a well-formed individual emerges; "live birth." Contrast with *oviparity.*

VMH Ventromedial hypothalamus.

VNO Vomeronasal organ.

volley theory A theory of frequency discrimination that emphasizes the relation between sound frequency and the firing pattern of nerve cells. For example, a 500-Hz tone would produce 500 neural discharges per second by a nerve cell or group of nerve cells. Contrast with *place theory.*

voltametry A technique in which electrical current is monitored to measure biochemical levels in a brain region.

vomeronasal organ (VNO) A collection of specialized receptor cells near but separate from the olfactory epithelium. These sensory cells detect pheromones and send electrical signals to the accessory olfactory bulb in the brain.

vulva The region around the opening of the vagina.

W cells A retinal ganglion cell that has sluggish and variable responses to visual stimuli.

Wallerian degeneration See *anterograde degeneration.*

Wernicke's aphasia A language impairment that is characterized by fluent, meaningless speech and little language comprehension; related to damage to Wernicke's area.

Wernicke's area A region of the left hemisphere that is involved in language comprehension. See Figures 19.6, 19.8.

white matter A shiny layer underneath the cortex that consists largely of axons with white myelin sheaths. See Figure 2.16, 2.22. Contrast with *gray matter.*

Williams syndrome A disorder characterized by largely intact, even fluent linguistic function, but clear mental retardation on standard IQ tests. Individuals suffering from this syndrome have great difficulty in copying a pattern of blocks, or assembling a picture from its parts.

withdrawal symptom An uncomfortable symptom that arises when a person stops taking a drug that he or she has used frequently, especially at high doses.

Wolffian duct system A primitive duct system in the embryo that will develop into male structures (the epididymis, vas deferens, and seminal vesicles) if testes are present in the embryo. Contrast with *Müllerian duct system.* See Figure 12.16.

word blindness The inability to recognize written words.

X cell A retinal ganglion cell that continues to respond to maintained visual stimuli.

Y cell Retinal ganglion cell that responds strongly initially, but rapidly decreases its frequency of response as the visual stimulus is maintained.

zeitgeber Literally "time-giver"; the stimulus that entrains circadian rhythms, usually the light/dark cycle.

Zucker strain A strain of rats that display obesity.

zygote The fertilized egg.

References

Aarons, L. 1976. Sleep-assisted instruction. *Psychological Bulletin*, 83:1–40.

Aaronson, S. T., Rashed, S., Biber, M. P., and Hobson, J. A. 1982. Brain state and body position. A time-lapse video study of sleep. *Archives of General Psychiatry*, 39:330–335.

Abel, E. L. 1982. Consumption of alcohol during pregnancy: A review of effects on growth and development of offspring. *Human Biology*, 54:421–453.

Abel, E. L. 1984. Prenatal effects of alcohol. *Drug and Alcohol Dependence*, 14:1–10.

Abraham, S. F., Baker, R. M., Blaine, E. H., Denton, D. A., and McKinley, M. J. 1975. Water drinking induced in sheep by angiotensin—A physiological or pharmacological effect? *Journal of Comparative and Physiological Psychology*, 88:503–518.

Abraham, W. C., and Goddard, G. V. 1985. Multiple traces of neural activity in the hippocampus. In N. M. Weinberger, J. L. McGaugh, and G. Lynch (eds.), *Memory systems of the brain*, pp. 62–76. Guilford, New York.

Abraham, W. C., Dragunow, M., and Tate, W. P. 1991. The role of immediate early genes in the stabilization of long-term potentiation. *Molecular Neurobiology*, 5:297–314.

Ackerman, S. 1992. *Discovering the brain*. National Academy Press, Washington, D.C.

Ader, R. 1985. Conditioned immunopharmacological effects in animals: Implications for a conditioning model of pharmacotherapy. In L. White, B. Tursky, and G. E. Schwartz (eds.), *Placebo*, pp. 306–332. Guilford, New York.

Ader, R., and Cohen, N. 1993. Psychoneuroimmunology: Conditioning and stress. *Annual Review of Psychology*, 44:53–85.

Ader, R., Felten, D., and Cohen, N. 1990. Interactions between the brain and the immune system. *Annual Review of Pharmacology & Toxicology*, 30:561–602.

Adler, N., and Matthews, K. 1994. Health psychology: Why do some people get sick and some stay well? *Annual Review of Psychology*, 45:229–259.

Adolphs, R., Tranel, D., Damasio, H., and Damasio, A. 1994. Impaired recognition of emotion in facial expressions following bilateral damage to the human amygdala. *Nature*, 372:669–672.

Aggleton, J. P. 1993. The contribution of the amygdala to normal and abnormal emotional states. *Trends in Neurosciences*, 16:328–333.

Ahlgren, J. A., Cheng, C. C., Schrag, J. D., and DeVries, A. L. 1988. Freezing avoidance and the distribution of antifreeze glycopeptides in body fluids and tissues of Antarctic fish. *Journal of Experimental Biology*, 137:549–563.

Akbarian, S., Kim, J. J., Potkin, S. G., Hagman, J. O., Tafazzoli, A., Bunney, W. E., Jr., and Jones, E. G. 1995. Gene expression for glutamic acid decarboxylase is reduced without loss of neurons in prefrontal cortex of schizophrenics. *Archives of General Psychiatry*, 52:267–278.

Albers, J. 1975. *Interaction of color*. Yale University Press, New Haven.

Alberts, J. R. 1978. Huddling by rat pups: Multisensory control of contact behavior. *Journal of Comparative and Physiological Psychology*, 92:220–230.

Alberts, J. R. and Brunjes, P. C. 1978. Ontogeny of thermal and olfactory determinants of huddling in the rat. *Journal of Comparative and Physiological Psychology*, 92:897–906.

Albrecht, D. G., De Valois, R. L., and Thorell, L. G. 1980. Visual cortical neurons: Are bars or gratings the optimal stimuli? *Science*, 207:88–90.

Aldrich, M. A. 1993. The neurobiology of narcolepsy-cataplexy. *Progress in Neurobiology*, 41:533–541.

Alexander, B. K., and Hadaway, P. F. 1982. Opiate addiction: The case for an adaptive orientation. *Psychological Bulletin*, 92:367–381.

Alho, H., Varga, V., and Krueger, K. E. 1994. Expression of mitochondrial benzodiazepine receptor and its putative endogenous ligand diazepam binding inhibitor in cultured primary astrocytes and C-6 cells: Relation to cell growth. *Cell Growth and Differentiation*, 5:1005–1014.

Alkon, D. 1988. *Memory traces in the brain*. Cambridge University Press, New York.

Alkon, D. L. 1992. *Memory's voice: Deciphering the mind–brain code*. HarperCollins, New York.

Allendoerfer, K. L., and Shatz, C. J. 1994. The subplate, a transient neocortical structure: Its role in the development of connections between thalamus and cortex.

Annual Review of Neuroscience, 17:185–218.

Allison, T., and Cicchetti, D. V. 1975. Sleep in mammals: Ecological and constitutional correlates. *Science*, 194:732–734.

Almada, S. J., Zonderman, A. B., Shekelle, R. B., Dyer, A. R. et al. 1991. Neuroticism and cynicism and risk of death in middle-aged men: The Western Electric study. *Psychosomatic Medicine*, 53:165–175.

Alpert, M., and Friedhoff, A. J. 1980. An undopamine hypothesis of schizophrenia. *Schizophrenia Bulletin*, 6:387–390.

American Academy of Ophthalmology. 1994. Amblyopia: Etiology, diagnosis, and treatment. *Journal of Ophthalmic Nursing and Technology*, 13:273–275.

American Psychiatric Association. 1994. *Diagnostic and statistical manual of mental disorders: DSM–IV*, 4th ed. American Psychiatric Association, Washington, D.C.

Ames, B. N. 1983. Dietary carcinogens and anticarcinogens. Oxygen radicals and degenerative diseases. *Science*, 221:1256–1264.

Anand, B. K., and Brobeck, J. R. 1951. Localization of a 'feeding center' in the hypothalamus of the rat. *Proceedings of the Society for Experimental Biology and Medicine*, 77:323–324.

Andersen, P. M., Nilsson, P., Ala-Hurula, V., Keranen, M. L., Tarvainen, I., Haltia, T., Nilsson, L., Binzer, M., Forsgren, L., and Marklund, S. L. 1995. Amyotrophic lateral sclerosis associated with homozygosity for an Asp90Ala mutation in CuZn-superoxide dismutase. *Nature Genetics*, 10:61–66.

Andreasen, N. C. 1984. *The broken brain: The biological revolution in psychiatry*. Harper & Row, New York.

Andreasen, N. C. 1989. Neural mechanisms of negative symptoms. *British Journal of Psychiatry (Supplement)*, 93–99.

Andreasen, N. C. 1991. Assessment issues and the cost of schizophrenia. *Schizophrenia Bulletin*, 17:475–481.

Andreasen, N. C. 1994. Changing concepts of schizophrenia and the ahistorical fallacy. *American Journal of Psychiatry*, 151:1405–1407.

Andreasen, N. C., Flaum, M., Swayze, V. O., II, O'Leary, D. S., Alliger, R., Cohen, G., Ehrhardt, J., and Yuh, W. T. 1993. Intelligence and brain structure in normal individuals. *American Journal of Psychiatry*, 150:130–134.

Andreasen, N. C., Rezai, K., Alliger, R., Swayze, V. W., II, Flaum, M., Kirchner, P., Cohen, G., and O'Leary, D. S. 1992. Hypofrontality in neuroleptic-naive patients and in patients with chronic schizophrenia. Assessment with xenon 133 single-photon emission computed tomography and the Tower of London. *Archives of General Psychiatry*, 49:943–958.

Andreasen, N., Nassrallah, H. A., Dunn, V., Olson, S. C., Grove, W. M., Ehrhardt, J. C., Coffman, J. A., and Crossett, J. H. W. 1986. Structural abnormalities in the frontal system in schizophrenia. *Archives of General Psychiatry*, 43:136–144.

Angier, N. 1992. A potent peptide prompts an urge to cuddle. *New York Times*.

Angle, C. R. 1993. Childhood lead poisoning and its treatment. *Annual Review of Pharmacology and Toxicology*, 33:409–434.

Anholt, R. R. 1993. Molecular neurobiology of olfaction. *Critical Reviews in Neurobiology*, 7:1–22.

Arbas, E. A., Meinertzhagen, I. A., and Shaw, S. R. 1991. Evolution in nervous systems. *Annual Review of Neuroscience*, 14:9–38.

Arnold, A. P. 1980. Sexual differences in the brain. *American Scientist*, 68:165–173.

Arnold, A. P., and Schlinger, B. A. 1993. Sexual differentiation of brain and behavior: The zebra finch is not just a flying rat. *Brain, Behavior, and Evolution*, 42:231–241.

Arnsten, A. F., and Contant, T. A. 1992. Alpha-2 adrenergic agonists decrease distractibility in aged monkeys performing the delayed response task. *Psychopharmacology*, 108:159–169.

Arnsten, A. F., Cai, J. X., and Goldman-Rakic, P. S. 1988. The alpha-2 adrenergic agonist guanfacine improves memory in aged monkeys without sedative or hypotensive side effects: Evidence of alpha-2 receptor subtypes. *Journal of Neuroscience*, 8:4287–4298.

Aroniadou, V. A., Maillis, A., and Stefanis, C. C. 1993. Dihydropyridine-sensitive calcium channels are involved in the induction of N-methyl-D-aspartate receptor-independent long-term potentiation in visual cortex of adult rats. *Neuroscience Letters*, 151:77–80.

Asberg, M., Nordstrom, P., and Traskman-Bendz, L. 1986. Cerebrospinal fluid studies in suicide. An overview. *Annals of the New York Academy of Sciences*, 487:243–255.

Ashmore, J. F. 1994. The cellular machinery of the cochlea. *Experimental Physiology*, 79:113–134.

Ashmore, J. F., and Kolston, P. J. 1994. Hair cell based amplification in the cochlea. *Current Opinion in Neurobiology*, 4:503–508.

Atkinson, M. A., and Maclaren N. K. 1994. The pathogenesis of insulin-dependent diabetes mellitus. *New England Journal of Medicine*, 331:1428–1436.

Atkinson, M. A., Bowman, M. A., Campbell, L., Darrow, B. L., Kaufman, D. L., and Maclaren, N. K. 1994. Cellular immunity to a determinant common to glutamate decarboxylase and coxsackie virus in insulin-dependent diabetes. *Journal of Clinical Investigation*, 94:2125–2129.

Avan, P., Loth, D., Menguy, C., and Teyssou, M. 1992. Hypothetical roles of middle ear muscles in the guinea-pig. *Hearing Research*, 59:59–69.

Ax, A. F. 1953. The physiological differentiation between fear and anger in humans. *Psychosomatic Medicine*, 15:433–442.

Azar, B. 1995. NIAAA: 25 years of alcohol research. *American Psychological Association Monitor*, 26:5, 23.

Bachevalier, J., and Mishkin, M. 1984. An early and a late developing system for learning and retention in infant monkeys. *Behavioral Neuroscience*, 98:770–778.

Bachevalier, J., Hagger, C., and Bercu, B. B. 1989. Gender differences in visual habit formation in 3-month-old rhesus monkeys. *Developmental Psychobiology*, 22:585–599.

Bach-y-Rita, P. 1992. Recovery from brain damage. *Journal of Neurologic Rehabilitation*, 6:191–199.

Baddeley, A. 1990. *Human memory: Theory and practice*. Allyn and Bacon, Needham Heights, MA.

Baddeley, A. D., and Warrington, E. K. 1970. Amnesia and the distinction between long- and short-term memory. *Journal of Verbal Learning & Verbal Behavior*, 9:176–189.

Bailey, C. H., and Chen, M. 1984. Morphological basis of long-term habituation and sensitization in *Aplysia*. *Science*, 220:91–93.

Bailey, C. H., and Chen, M. 1984. Morphological basis of long-term habituation and sensitization in *Aplysia*. *Science*, 220:91–93.

Bailey, C. H., Castellucci, V. F., Koester, J., and Chen, M. 1983. Behavioral changes in aging *Aplysia*: A model system for studying the cellular basis of age-impaired learning, memory, and arousal. *Behavioral and Neural Biology*, 38:70–81.

Bailey, J. M., and Bell, A. P. 1993. Familiality of female and male homosexuality. *Behavior Genetics*, 23:313–322.

Bak, M., Girvin, J. P., Hambrecht, F. T., Kufta, C. V., Loeb, G. E., and Schmidt, E. M. 1990. Visual sensa-

tions produced by intracortical microstimulation of the human occipital cortex. *Medical and Biological Engineering and Computing*, 28:257–259.

Ballantine, H. T., Bouckoms, A. J., Thomas, E. K., and Giriunas, I. E. 1987. Treatment of psychiatric illness by stereotactic cingulotomy. *Biological Psychiatry*, 22:807–820.

Bancaud, J., Brunet-Bourgin, F., Chauvel, P., and Halgren, E. 1994. Anatomical origin of deja vu and vivid 'memories' in human temporal lobe. *Brain*, 117:71–90.

Barasa, A. 1960. Forma, grandezza e densita dei neuroni della corteccia cerebrale in mammiferi di gran-dezza corporea differente. *Zeitschrift für Zellforschung*, 53:69–89.

Barbour, H. G. 1912. Die Wirkung unmittelbarer Erwärmung und Abkühlung der Warmenzentren auf die Körpertemperatur. *Archiv für experimentalle Pathologie und Pharmakologie*, 70:1–26.

Barden, N., Reul, J. M., and Holsboer, F. 1995. Do antidepressants stabilize mood through actions on the hypothalamic–pituitary–adrenocortical system? *Trends in Neurosciences*, 18:6–11.

Bark, N. M. 1988. On the history of schizophrenia. Evidence of its existence before 1800. *New York State Journal of Medicine*, 88:374–383.

Barlow, H. B. 1953. Summation and inhibition in the frog's retina. *Journal of Physiology (London)*, 119:69–88.

Barlow, H. B., and Foldiak, P. F. 1989. Adaptation and decorrelation in the cortex. In R. Durbin, C. Miall, and G. Mitchison (eds.), *The computing neuron*. Addison-Wesley, Reading, MA.

Barlow, H. B., Fitzhugh, R., and Kuffler, S. W. 1957. Change of organization in the receptive fields of the cat's retina during dark adaptation. *Journal of Physiology*, 137:388–345.

Barnes, B. M. 1989. Freeze avoidance in a mammal: Body temperatures below 0 degree C in an Arctic hibernator. *Science*, 244:1593–1595.

Barnes, C. A. 1979. Memory deficits associated with senescence: A neurophysiological and behavioral study in the rat. *Journal of Physiological and Comparative Psychology*, 93:74–104.

Barnett, S. A. 1975. The rat: A study in behavior, Rev. ed. University of Chicago Press, Chicago.

Barnett, S. A. 1975. *The rat: A study in behavior*. University of Chicago Press, Chicago.

Barr, E., and Leiden, J. M. 1991. Systemic delivery of recombinant proteins by genetically modified myoblasts. *Science*, 254:1507–1509.

Barrionuevo, G., Schottler, F., and Lynch, G. 1980. The effects of repetitive low frequency stimulation on control and "potentiated" synaptic responses in the hippocampus. *Life Sciences*, 27:2385–2391.

Bartoshuk, L. M. 1993. Genetic and pathological taste variation: What can we learn from animal models and human disease? In D. Chadwick, J. Marsh, and J. Goode (eds.), *The molecular basis of smell and taste transduction*, pp. 251–267. Wiley, New York.

Bartoshuk, L. M., and Beauchamp, G. K. 1994. Chemical senses. *Annual Review of Psychology*, 45:419–449.

Bartoshuk, L. M., Fast, K., Karrer, T. A., Marino, S., Price, R. A., and Reed, D. A. 1992. PROP supertasters and the perception of sweetness and bitterness. *Chemical Senses*, 17:594.

Basbaum, A., and Fields, H. L. 1978. Endogenous pain control mechanisms: Review and hypothesis. *Annals of Neurology*, 4:451–462.

Basbaum, A., and Fields, H. L. 1984. Endogenous pain control systems: Brainstem spinal pathways and endorphin circuitry. *Annual Review of Neuroscience*, 7:309–339.

Baumgardner, T. L., Green, K. E., and Reiss, A. L. 1994. A behavioral neurogenetics approach to developmental disabilities: Gene–brain–behavior associations. *Current Opinion in Neurology*, 7:172–178.

Bayley, N. 1969. *Bayley scales of infant development*. The Psychological Corporation, New York.

Beach, F. A. 1971. Hormonal factors controlling the differentiation, development, and display of copulatory behavior in the ramstergig and related species. In E. Tobach, L. R. Aronson, and E. Shaw (eds.), *The biopsychology of development*, pp. 249–296. Academic Press, New York.

Beach, F. A. 1977. Human sexuality in four perspectives. In F. A. Beach (ed.), *Human sexuality in four perspectives*, pp. 1–21. Johns Hopkins University Press, Baltimore, MD.

Beach, F. A. 1977. *Human sexuality in four perspectives*. Johns Hopkins University Press, Baltimore.

Beach, F. A., and Holz, A. M. 1946. Mating behavior in male rats castrated at various ages and injected with androgen. *Journal of Experimental Zoology*, 101:91–142.

Bear, D. 1983. Hemispheric specialization and the neurology of emotion. *Archives of Neurology*, 40:195–202.

Bear, M. F., and Malenka, R. C. 1994. Synaptic plasticity. *Current Opinion in Neurobiology*, 4:389–399.

Beauchamp, G. K., Cowart, B. J., Mennella, J. A., and Marsh, R. R. 1994. Infant salt taste: Developmental, methodological, and contextual factors. *Developmental Psychobiology*, 27:353–365.

Becker, J. B., Breedlove, S. M., and Crews, D. 1992. *Behavioral endocrinology*. MIT Press, Cambridge, MA.

Beecher, H. K. 1959. *Measurement of subjective responses: Quantitative effects of drugs*. Oxford University Press, New York.

Beggs, W. D., and Foreman, D. L. 1980. Sound localization and early binaural experience in the deaf. *British Journal of Audiology*, 14:41–48.

Beitner-Johnson, D., Guitart, X., and Nestler, E. J. 1992. Common intracellular actions of chronic morphine and cocaine in dopaminergic brain reward regions. *Annals of the New York Academy of Sciences*, 654:70–87.

Bekkers, J. M., and Stevens, C. F. 1990. Presynaptic mechanism for long-term potentiation in the hippocampus. *Nature*, 346:724–729.

Bellinger, D. C., Stiles, K. M., and Needleman, H. L. 1992. Low-level lead exposure, intelligence and academic achievement: A long-term follow-up study. *Pediatrics*, 90:855–861.

Bellinger, D. L., Ackerman, K. D., Felten, S. Y., and Felten, D. L. 1992. A longitudinal study of age-related loss of noradrenergic nerves and lymphoid cells in the rat spleen. *Experimental Neurology*, 116:295–311.

Bellinger, D., Leviton, A., Waternaux, C., Needleman, H., and Rabinowitz, M. 1987. Longitudinal analyses of prenatal and postnatal lead exposure and early cognitive development. *New England Journal of Medicine*, 316:1037–1043.

Bellugi, U., Poizner, H., and Klima, E. S. 1983. Brain organization for language: Clues from sign aphasia. *Human Neurobiology*, 2:155–171.

Benke, T. 1993. Two forms of apraxia in Alzheimer's disease. *Cortex*, 29: 715–725.

Bennett, A. F., and Ruben, J. A. 1979. Endothermy and activity in vertebrates. *Science*, 206:649–654.

Bennett, E. L., Diamond, M. L., Krech, D., and Rosenzweig, M. R. 1964. Chemical and anatomical plasticity of brain. *Science*, 146:610–619.

Bennett, E. L., Orme, A. E., and Hebert, M. 1972. Cerebral protein synthesis inhibition and amnesia produced by scopolamine, cycloheximide, streptovitacin A, anisomycin, and emetine in rat. *Federation Proceedings*, 31:838.

Bennett, E. L., Rosenzweig, M. R., and Diamond, M. C. 1969. Rat brain: Effects of environmental enrichment on wet and dry weights. *Science*, 163:825–826.

Bennett, W. 1983. The nicotine fix. *Rhode Island Medical Journal*, 66:455–458.

Benson, A. J. 1990. Sensory functions and limitations of the vestibular system. In R. Warren, and A. H. Wertheim (eds.), *Perception and control of self–motion. Resources for ecological psychology*, pp. 145–170. Lawrence Erlbaum Associates, Hillsdale, NJ.

Benson, D. F. 1993. The history of behavioral neurology. *Neurologic Clinics*, 11:1–8.

Bentley, D. 1976. Genetic analysis of the nervous system. In J. C. Fentress (ed.), *Simpler networks and behavior*. Sinauer Associates, Sunderland, MA.

Berger, T. W. 1984. Long-term potentiation of hippocampal synaptic transmission affects rate of behavioral learning. *Science*, 224:627–630.

Berger, T. W., and Orr, W. B. 1983. Hippocampectomy selectively disrupts discrimination reversal conditioning of the rabbit nictitating membrane response. *Behavioural Brain Research*, 8:49–68.

Berger, T. W., and Thompson, R. F. 1978. Neuronal plasticity in the limbic system during classical conditioning of the rabbit nicitating membrane response, I. The hippocampus. *Brain Research*, 145:323–346.

Berlin, B., and Kay, P. 1969. *Basic color terms: Their universality and evolution*. University of California Press, Berkeley..

Berman, D., Derasmo, M. J., Marti, A., and Berman, A. J. 1978. Unilateral forelimb deafferentiation in the monkey: Purposive movement. *Journal of Medical Primatology*, 7:106–113.

Berman, K. F., and Weinberger, D. R. 1990. The prefrontal cortex in schizophrenia and other neuropsychiatric diseases: *In vivo* physiological correlates of cognitive deficits. *Progress in Brain Research*, 85:521–536.

Bern, H. 1990. The "new" endocrinology: Its scope and its impact. *American Zoologist*, 30:877–885.

Bernstein, I. S., and Gordon, T. P. 1974. The function of aggression in primate societies. *American Scientist*, 62:304–311.

Bernstein-Goral, H., and Bregman, B. S. 1993. Spinal cord transplants support the regeneration of axotomized neurons after spinal cord lesions at birth: a quantitative double-labeling study. *Experimental Neurology*, 123:118–132.

Berry, M., Rogers, A. W., and Eayrs, J. T. 1964. Pattern of cell migration during cortical histogenesis. *Nature*, 203:591–593.

Bert, J. 1971. Sleep in primates: A review of various results. *Medical Primatology*, 308–315.

Besedovsky, H. O., and del Rey, A. 1992. Immune-neuroendocrine circuits: Integrative role of cytokines. *Frontiers of Neuroendocrinology*, 13:61–94.

Besedovsky, H. O., del Rey, A. E., and Sorkin, E. 1985. Immune-neuroendocrine interactions. *Journal of Immunology*, 135:750s–754s.

Betancur, C., Neveu, P. J., Vitiello, S., and Le Moal, M. 1991. Natural killer cell activity is associated with brain asymmetry in male mice. *Brain, Behavior, and Immunity*, 5:162–169.

Bigelow, L., Nasrallah, H. A., and Rauscher, F. P. 1983. Corpus callosum thickness in chronic schizophrenia. *British Journal of Psychiatry*, 142:284–287.

Binder, J. R., Rao, S. M., Hammeke, T. A., Yetkin, F. Z., Jesmanowicz, A., Bandettini, P. A., Wong, E. C., Estkowski, L. D., Goldstein, M. D., Haughton, V. M. et al. 1994. Functional magnetic resonance imaging of human auditory cortex. *Annals of Neurology*, 35:662–672.

Bingman, V. P. 1993. Vision, cognition, and the avian hippocampus. In H. P. Zeigler, and J. J. Bischof (eds.), *Vision, brain, and behavior in birds*, pp. 391–408. MIT Press, Cambridge, MA.

Bini, G., Cruccu, G., Hagbarth, K., Schady, W., and Torebjork, E. 1984. Analgesic effect of vibration and cooling on pain induced by intraneural electrical stimulation. *Pain*, 18:239–248.

Birnbaumer, L., Abramowitz, J., and Brown, A. M. 1990. Receptor-effector coupling by G proteins. *Biochimica et Biophysica Acta*, 1031:163–224.

Birnholz, J. C. 1981. The development of human fetal eye movement patterns. *Science*, 213:679–681.

Bishop, D. V. 1986. Is there a link between handedness and hypersensitivity? *Cortex*, 22:289–296.

Björklund, A., and Stenevi, U. 1984. Intracerebral neural implants: Neuronal replacement and reconstruction of damaged circuitries. *Annual Review of Neuroscience*, 7:279–308.

Björklund, A., Hökfelt, T., and Kuhar, M. J. 1992. *Neuropeptide receptors in the CNS*. Elsevier, Amsterdam.

Björklund, A., Stenevi, U., Dunnett, S. B., and Iversen, S. D. 1981. Functional reactivation of the deafferented neostriatum by nigral transplants. *Nature*, 289:497–499.

Black, J. E., and Greenough, W. T. 1986. Developmental approaches to the memory process. In J. L. Martinez, and R. P. Kesner (eds.), *Learning and memory: A biological view*. Academic Press, New York.

Black, J. E., Sirevaag, A. M., Wallace, C. S., Savin, M. H., and Greenough, W. T. 1989. Effects of complex experience on somatic growth and organ development in rats. *Developmental Psychobiology*, 22:727–752.

Blakemore, C. 1976. The conditions required for the maintenance of binocularity in the kitten's visual cortex. *Journal of Physiology (London)*, 261:423–444.

Blakemore, C., and Campbell, F. W. 1969. On the existence of neurones in the human visual system selectively sensitive to the orientation and size

of retinal images. *Journal of Physiology (London)*, 203:237–260.

Blalock, J. E. 1984. The immune system as a sensory organ. *Journal of Immunology*, 132:1067–1070.

Blatteis, C. M., Hunger, W. S., Llanos, J., Ahokas, R. A., and Mashburn, T. A., Jr. 1984. Activation of acute-phase response by intrapreoptic injections of endogenous pyrogen in guinea pigs. *Brain Research Bulletin*, 12:689–695.

Blehar, M. C., and Rosenthal, N. E. 1989. Seasonal affective disorders and phototherapy. Report of a National Institute of Mental Health-sponsored workshop. *Archives of General Psychiatry*, 46:469–474.

Bleuler, E. 1911. *Dementia praecox; or, The group of schizophrenias*. Reprinted 1952. International Universities Press, New York.

Bliss, T. V. P., and Collingridge, G. L. 1993. A synaptic model of memory: Long-term potentiation in the hippocampus. *Nature*, 361:31–39.

Bliss, T. V. P., and Gardner-Medwin, A. R. 1973. Long-lasting potentiation of synaptic transmission in the dentate area of the unanaesthetized rabbit following stimulation of the perforant path. *Journal of Physiology*, 232:357–374.

Bliss, T. V. P., and Lømo, T. 1973. Long-lasting potentiation of synaptic transmission in the dentate area of the anaesthetized rabbit following stimulation of the perforant path. *Journal of Physiology (London)*, 202.001 056.

Bliwise, D. L. 1979. Neuropsychological function and sleep. *Clinics in Geriatric Medicine*, 5:381–394.

Bliwise, D. L. 1989. Neuropsychological function and sleep. *Clinics in Geriatric Medicine*, 5:381–394.

Bloch, V. 1970. Facts and hypotheses concerning memory consolidation processes. *Brain Research*, 24:561–575.

Bloch, V. 1976. Brain activation and memory consolidation. In M. R. Rosenzweig, and E. L. Bennett (eds.), *Neural mechanisms of learning and memory*. MIT Press, Cambridge, MA.

Bloch, V., and Laroche, S. 1984. Facts and hypotheses related to the search for the engram. In G. Lynch, J. L. McGaugh, and N. M. Weinberger (eds.), *Neurobiology of learning and memory*, pp. 249–260. Guilford, New York.

Bloom, F. E., and Kupfer, D. 1995. *Psychopharmacology: The fourth generation of progress*. Raven, New York.

Blue, M. E., and Parnavelas, J. G. 1983. The formation and maturation of synapses in the visual cortex of the rat. II. Quantitative analysis. *Journal of Neurocytology*, 12:697–712.

Bodnar, R. J., Kelly, D. D., Brutus, M., and Glusman, M. 1980. Stress-induced

analgesia: Neural and hormonal determinants. *Neuroscience and Biobehavioral Reviews*, 4:87–100.

Bogen, J. E., Schultz, D. H., and Vogel, P. J. 1988. Completeness of callostomy shown by magnetic resonance imaging in the long term. *Archives of Neurology*, 45:1203–1205.

Bohus, B., and Koolhaas, J. M. 1993. Stress and the cardiovascular system: Central and peripheral physiological mechanisms. In S. C. Stanford, and P. Salmon (eds.), *Stress: From synapse to syndrome*, pp. 75–117. Academic Press, London.

Bonese, K. F., Wainer, B. H., Fitch, F. W., Rothberg, R. M., and Schuster, C. R. 1974. Changes in heroin self-administration by a rhesus monkey after morphine immunisation. *Nature*, 252:708–710.

Bonhoeffer, F., and Huf, J. 1985. Position-dependent properties of retinal axons and their growth cones. *Nature*, 315:409–410.

Bonhoeffer, T., and Grinvald, A. 1991. Iso-orientation domains in cat visual cortex are arranged in pinwheel-like patterns. *Nature*, 353:429–431.

Borg, E., and Counter, S. A. 1989. The middle-ear muscles. *Scientific American*, 261:74–80.

Boswell, T., Richardson, R. D., Schwartz, M. W., D'Alessio, D. A., Woods, S. C., Sipols, A. J., Baskin, D. G., and Kenagy, G. J. 1993. NPY and galanin in a hibernator: Hypothalamic gene expression and effects on feeding. *Brain Research Bulletin*, 32:379–384.

Bothwell, M. 1995. Functional interactions of neurotrophins and neurotrophin receptors. *Annual Review of Neuroscience*, 18:223–253.

Bourguignon, E., and Greenbaum, L. S. 1973. *Diversity and homogeneity in world societies*. HRAF, New Haven, CT.

Bowmaker, J. K. 1984. Microspectrophotometry of vertebrate photoreceptors. A brief review. *Vision Research*, 24:1641–1650.

Bracewell, R. N. 1986. *The Hartley transform*. Oxford University Press, New York.

Brady, J. V., Porter, R. W., Conrad, D. G., and Mason, J. W. 1958. Avoidance behavior and the development of gastroduodenal ulcers. *Journal of the Experimental Analysis of Behavior*, 1:69–72.

Brain, P. F. 1994. Hormonal aspects of aggression and violence. In A. J. Reiss, Jr., K. A. Miczek, and J. A. Roth (eds.), *Understanding and preventing violence, Vol. 2: Biobehavioral influences*, pp. 173–244. National Academy Press, Washington, D.C.

Brasel, J. A., and Blizzard, R. M. 1974. The influence of the endocrine glands upon growth and development. In R. H. Williams (ed.), *Textbook of endocrinology*. Saunders, Philadelphia.

Bray, G. A. 1969. Effect of caloric restriction on energy expenditure in obese patients. *Lancet*, 2:397–398.

Bredberg, G. 1968. Cellular pattern and nerve supply of the human organ of Corti. *Acta Oto-Laryngologica*, 236:1.

Bredberg, G. 1968. Cellular pattern and nerve supply of the human organ of Corti. *Acta Otolaryngologica*, Supplement 236.

Bremner, J. D., Randall, P., Scott, T. M., Bronen, R. A., Seibyl, J. P., Southwick, S. M., Delaney, R. C., McCarthy, G., Charney, D. S., and Innis, R. B. 1995. MRI-based measurement of hippocampal volume in patients with combat-related posttraumatic stress disorder. *American Journal of Psychiatry*, 152:973–981.

Bremner, J. D., Scott, T. M., Delaney, R. C., Southwick, S. M., Mason, J. W., Johnson, D. R., Innis, R. B., McCarthy, G., and Charney, D. S. 1993. Deficits in short-term memory in posttraumatic stress disorder. *American Journal of Psychiatry*, 150:1015–1019.

Brennan, P., Kaba, H., and Keverne, E. B. 1990. Olfactory recognition: A simple memory system. *Science*, 250:1223–1226.

Brenowitz, E. A. 1991a. Altered perception of species-specific song by female birds after lesions of a forebrain nucleus. *Science*, 251:303–305.

Brenowitz, E. A. 1991b. Evolution of the vocal control system in the avian brain. *Seminars in the Neurosciences*, 3:399–407.

Brenowitz, E. A., and Arnold, A. 1986. Interspecific comparisons of the size of neural song control regions and song complexity in dueting birds: Evolutionary implications. *Journal of Neuroscience*, 6:2875–2879.

Brenowitz, E. A., Lent, K., and Kroodsma, D. E. 1995. Brain space for learned song in birds develops independently of song learning. *Journal of Neuroscience*, 15:6281–6286.

Brien, J. A. 1993. Ototoxicity associated with salicylates. A brief review. *Drug Safety*, 9:143–148.

Broberg, D. J., and Bernstein, I. L. 1989. Cephalic insulin release in anorexic women. *Physiology and Behavior*, 45:871–874.

Brodmann, K. 1909. *Vergleichende Lokisationslehre der Grosshirnrinde in ihren Prinzipien dargestellt auf Grund des Zellenbaues*. Barth, Leipzig.

Brook, J. S., Cohen, P., Whiteman, M., and Gordon, A. S. 1992. Psychosocial risk factors in the transition from moderate to heavy use or abuse of drugs. In M. D. Glantz, and R. W. Pickens (eds.), *Vulnerability to drug use*, pp. 359–388. American Psychological Association, Washington, D.C.

Brooks, V. B. 1984. Cerebellar function in motor control. *Human Neurobiology*, 2:251–260.

Brooks, V. B. 1986. *The neural basis of motor control*. Oxford University Press, New York.

Broughton, R. 1985. Slow-wave sleep awakenings in normal and in pathology: A brief review. In W. P. Koella, E. Ruther, and H. Schulz (eds.), *Sleep '84*, pp. 164–167. Fischer Verlag, Stuttgart.

Brown, G. L., Goodwin, F. K., Ballenger, J. C., Goyer, P. F., and Major, L. F. 1979. Aggression in humans correlates with cerebrospinal fluid amine metabolites. *Psychiatry Research*, 1:131–139.

Brown, J. 1958. Some tests of the decay theory of immediate memory. *Quarterly Journal of Experimental Psychology*, 10:12–21.

Brown, T. H., Zador, A. M., Mainen, Z. F., and Claiborne, B. J. 1992. Hebbian computations in hippocampal dendrites and spines. In T. M. McKenna, J. Davis, and S. F. Zornetzer (eds.), *Single neuron computation. Neural nets: Foundations to applications*, pp. 81–116. Academic Press, Boston.

Brown, W. A., and Heninger, G. 1975. Cortisol, growth hormone, free fatty acids and experimentally evoked affective arousal. *American Journal of Psychiatry*, 132:1172–1176.

Brown, W. L. 1968. An hypothesis concerning the function of the metapleural gland in ants. *American Naturalist*, 102:188–191.

Brownell, W. E., Bader, C. R., Bertrand, D., and de Ribaupierre, Y. 1985. Evoked mechanical responses of isolated cochlear outer hair cells. *Science*, 227:194–196.

Bryden, M. P. 1982. *Laterality: Functional asymmetry in the intact brain*. Academic Press, New York.

Buchsbaum, M., Mirsky, A., DeLisi, L. E., Morihisa, J., Karson, C., Mendelson, W., Johnson, J., King, A., and Kessler, R. 1984. The Genain quadruplets: Electrophysiological, positron emission and X-ray tomographic studies. *Psychiatry Research*, 13:95–108.

Buck, L. B. 1993. Receptor diversity and spatial patterning in the mammalian olfactory system. *Ciba Foundation Symposium*, 179:51–67, 88–96.

Buck, L., and Axel, R. 1991. A novel multigene family may encode odorant receptors: A molecular basis for odor recognition. *Cell*, 65:175–187.

Buhrich, N., Bailey, J. M., and Martin, N. G. 1991. Sexual orientation, sexual identity, and sex-dimorphic behaviors in male twins. *Behavior Genetics*, 21:75–96.

Bullock, T. H. 1984. Comparative neuroscience holds promise for quiet revolutions. *Science*, 225:473–478.

Busse, E. W., and Silverman, A. J. 1952. Electroencephalographic changes in professional boxers. *Journal of the American Medical Association*, 149:1522–1525.

Byrne, D. G., and Whyte, H. M. 1980. Life events and myocardial infarction revisited. *Psychosomatic Medicine*, 42:1–10.

Byrne, J. H., Castellucci, V. F., and Kandel, E. R. 1978. Contribution of individual mechanoreceptor sensory neurons to defensive gill-withdrawal reflex in *Aplysia*. *Journal of Neurophysiology*, 41:418–431.

Cacioppo, J. T., Klein, D. J., Berntson, G. G., and Hatfield, E. 1993. The psychophysiology of emotion. In M. Lewis, and J. M. Haviland (eds.), *Handbook of emotions*, pp. 119–142. Guilford, New York.

Cadoret, R. J., O'Gorman, T., Troughton, E., and Heywood, E. 1986. An adoption study of genetic and environmental factors in drug abuse. *Archives of General Psychiatry*, 43:1131–1136.

Cahill, L., and McGaugh, J. L. 1991. NMDA-induced lesions of the amygdaloid complex block the retention-enhancing effect of posttraining epinephrine. *Psychobiology*, 19:206–210.

Cahill, L., Babinsky, R., Markowitsch, H. J., and McGaugh, J. L. 1995. The amygdala and emotional memory. *Nature*, 377:295–296.

Cahill, L., Prins, B., Weber, M., and McGaugh, J. L. 1994. Beta-adrenergic activation and memory for emotional events. *Nature*, 371:702.

Calvin, W. H., and Ojemann, G. A. 1994. *Conversations with Neil's brain: The neural nature of thought and language*. Addison-Wesley, Reading, MA.

Campbell, F. W., and Robson, J. G. 1968. Application of Fourier analysis to the visibility of gratings. *Journal of Physiology (London)*, 197:551–566.

Campbell, R. 1982. The lateralisation of emotion: A critical review. *International Journal of Psychology*, 17:211–219.

Campbell, S. S., and Tobler, I. 1984. Animal sleep: A review of sleep duration across phylogeny. *Neuroscience and Biobehavioral Reviews*, 8:269–301.

Campfield, L. A., Smith, F. J., Guisez, Y., Devos, R., and Burn, P. 1995. Recombinant mouse OB protein: Evidence for a peripheral signal linking adiposity and central neural networks. *Science*, 269:546–549.

Campion, J., Latto, R., and Smith, Y. M. 1983. Is blindsight an effect of scattered light, spared cortex, and near-threshold vision? *Behavioral & Brain Sciences*, 6:423–486.

Cannon, W. B. 1929. *Bodily changes in pain, hunger, fear and rage*. Appleton, New York.

Capretta, P. J., Petersik, J. T., and Stewart, D. J. 1975. Acceptance of novel flavours is increased after early experience of diverse tastes. *Nature*, 254:689–691.

Carew, T. J. 1989. Development assembly of learning in *Aplysia*. *Trends in Neurosciences*, 12:389–394.

Carew, T. J., and Sahley, C. L. 1986. Invertebrate learning and memory: From behavior to molecule. *Annual Review of Neuroscience*, 9:435–487.

Carew, T. J., Hawkins, R. D., and Kandel, E. R. 1983. Differential classical conditioning of a defensive withdrawal reflex in *Aplysia californica*. *Science*, 219:397–400.

Carew, T. J., Walters, E. T., and Kandel, E. R. 1981a. Associative learning in *Aplysia*: Cellular correlates supporting a conditioned fear hypothesis. *Science*, 211:501–504.

Carew, T. J., Walters, E. T., and Kandel, E. R. 1981b. Classical conditioning in a simple withdrawal reflex in *Aplysia californica*. *Journal of Neuroscience*, 1:1426–1437.

Carlton, P. L., and Manowitz, P. 1984. Dopamine and schizophrenia: An analysis of the theory. *Neuroscience and Biobehavioral Reviews*, 8:137–153.

Carskadon, M. A. 1993. *Encyclopedia of sleep and dreaming*. Macmillan, New York.

Carter, C. S. 1992. Oxytocin and sexual behavior. *Neuroscience and Biobehavioral Reviews*, 16:131–144.

Cartwright, R. D. 1979. The nature and function of repetitive dreams: A survey and speculation. *Psychiatry*, 42:131–137.

Casey, D. E. 1989. Clozapine: Neuroleptic-induced EPS and tardive dyskinesia. *Psychopharmacology*, 99:S47–S53.

Casey, K. L. 1980. Reticular formation and pain: Toward a unifying concept. *Research Publications, Association for Research in Nervous and Mental Disease*, 58:93–105.

Cash, D., and Carew, T. J. 1989. A quantitative analysis of the development of the central nervous system in juvenile *Aplysia californica*. *Journal of Neurobiology*, 20:25–47.

Casseday, J. H., and Neff, W. D. 1975. Auditory localization: Role of auditory pathways in brain stem of the cat. *Journal of Neurophysiology*, 38:842–858.

Cassens, G., Wolfe, L., and Zola, M. 1990. The neuropsychology of depressions. *Journal of Neuropsychiatry and Clinical Neurosciences*, 2:202–213.

Casson, I. R., Sham, R., Campbell, E. A., Tarlau, M., and Didomenico, A. 1982. Neurological and CT evaluation of knocked-out boxers. *Journal of Neurology, Neurosurgery, and Psychiatry*, 45:170–174.

Castro, C. A., Silbert, L. H., McNaughton, B. L., and Barnes, C. A. 1989. Recovery of learning following decay of experimental saturation of LTE at perforant path synapses. *Nature*, 342:545–548.

Castro, C. A., Silbert, L. H., McNaughton, B. L., and Barnes, C. A. 1989. Recov-ery of learning following decay of experimental saturation of LTE at perforant path synapses. *Nature*, 342:545–548.

Caviness, V. S. 1980. The developmental consequences of abnormal cell position in the reeler mouse. *Trends in Neurosciences*, 3:31–33.

Caza, P. A., and Spear, N. E. 1984. Short-term exposure to an odor increases its subsequent preference in preweanling rats: A descriptive profile of the phenomenon. *Developmental Psychobiology*, 17:407–422.

Cespuglio, R., Faradji, H., Guidon, G., and Jouvet, M. 1984. Voltametric detection of brain 5-hydroxyindolamines: A new technology applied to sleep research. In A. Borbely, and J. L. Valatx (eds.), *Sleep mechanisms*, pp. 95–106. Springer-Verlag, Berlin.

Cha, K., Horch, K., and Normann, R. A. 1992. Simulation of a phosphene-based visual field: Visual acuity in a pixelized vision system. *Annals of Biomedical Engineering*, 20:439–449.

Challamel, M. J., Lahlou, S., and Jouvet, M. 1985. Sleep and smiling in neonate: A new approach. In W. P. Koella, E. Ruther, and H. Schulz (eds.), *Sleep '84*. Fischer Verlag, Stuttgart.

Chang, F. L., and Greenough, W. T. 1982. Lateralized effects of monocular training on dendritic branching in adult split-brain rats. *Brain Research*, 232:283–292.

Chang, F.-L., and Greenough, W. T. 1984. Transient and enduring morphological correlates of synaptic activity and efficacy change in the rat hippocampal slice. *Brain Research*, 309:35–46.

Chapman, C. R., Casey, K. L., Dubner, R., Foley, K. M., Gracely, R. H., and Reading, A. E. 1985. Pain measurement: An overview. *Pain*, 22:1–31.

Charney, D. S., Deutch, A. Y., Krystal, J. H., Southwick, S. M., and Davis, M. 1993. Psychobiologic mechanisms of posttraumatic stress disorder. *Archives of General Psychiatry*, 50:295–305.

Chen, D. Y., Deutsch, J. A., Gonzalez, M. F., and Gu, Y. 1993. The induction and suppression of c-fos expression in the rat brain by cholecystokinin and its antagonist L364,718. *Neuroscience Letters*, 149:91–94.

Cheng, M. F. 1977. Egg fertility and prolactin as determinants of reproductive recycling in doves. *Hormones and Behavior*, 9:85–98.

Chiarello, C., Knight, R., and Mandel, M. 1982. Aphasia in a prelingually deaf woman. *Brain*, 105:29–52.

Cho, Y. H., Berachochea, D., and Jaffard, R. 1993. Extended temporal gradient for the retrograde and anterograde amnesia produced by ibotenate en-torhinal cortex lesions in mice. *Journal of Neuroscience*, 13:1759–1766.

Cho, Y. H., Beracochea, D., and Jaffard, R. 1991. Temporally graded retrograde and anterograde amnesia following ibotenic entorhinal cortex lesion in mice. *Society for Neuroscience Abstracts*, 17:1045.

Choi, D. W. 1992. Exicitotoxic cell death. *Journal of Neurobiology*, 23:1261–1276.

Chollet, F., and Weiller, C. 1994. Imaging recovery of function following brain injury. *Current Opinion in Neurobiology*, 4:226–230.

Chow, K. L., and Stewart, D. L. 1972. Reversal of structural and functional effects of long-term visual deprivation in cats. *Experimental Neurology*, 34:409–433.

Chui, H. C., and Damasio, A. R. 1980. Human cerebral asymmetries evaluated by computerized tomography. *Journal of Neurology, Neurosurgery, and Psychiatry*, 43:873–878.

Chui, H. C., Bondareff, W., Zarow, C., and Slager, U. 1984. Stability of neuronal number in the human nucleus basalis of Meynert with age. *Neurobiology of Aging*, 5:83–88.

Clark, G. C., and Schuman, E. M. 1992. Snails' tales: Initial comparisons of synaptic plasticity underlying learning in *Hermissenda* and *Aplysia*. In L. R. Squire, and N. Butters (eds.), *Neuropsychology of memory*, 2nd ed., pp. 588–602. Guilford, New York.

Clark, W. W. 1991. Noise exposure from leisure activities: A review. *Journal of the Acoustical Society of America*, 90:175–181.

Clarkson, T. W. 1993. Molecular and ionic mimicry of toxic metals. *Annual Review of Pharmacology and Toxicology*, 33:545–571.

Clayton, N. S., and Krebs, J. R. 1994. Hippocampal growth and attrition in birds affected by experience. *Proceedings of the National Academy of Sciences, U.S.A.*, 91:7410–7414.

Clemens, L. G., Gladue, B. A., and Coniglio, L. P. 1978. Prenatal endogenous androgenic influences on masculine sexual behavior and genital morphology in male and female rats. *Hormones and Behavior*, 10:40–53.

Clutton-Brock, T. H., and Harvey, P. H. 1980. Primates, brains and ecology. *Journal of Zoology*, 190:309–323.

Coccaro, E. F., and Siever, L. J. 1995. Personalty disorders. In F. E. Bloom, D. J. Kupfer, B. S. Bunney, R. D. Ciaranello, K. L. Davis, G. F. Koob, H. Y. Meltzer, C. R. Schuster, R. I. Shater et al. (eds.), *Psychopharmacology: The fourth generation of progress*, pp. 1567–1679. Raven, New York.

Cohen, A. H., Baker, M. T., and Dobrov, T. A. 1989. Evidence for functional regeneration in the adult lamprey spinal cord following transection. *Brain Research*, 496:368–372.

Cohen, A. J., and Leckman, J. F. 1992. Sensory phenomena associated with Gilles de la Tourette's syndrome. *Journal of Clinical Psychiatry,* 53:319–323.

Cohen, D. B. 1979. *Sleep and dreaming: Origin, nature and functions.* Pergamon, Oxford.

Cohen, N. J., and Eichenbaum, H. 1993. *Memory, amnesia, and the hippocampal system.* MIT Press, Cambridge, MA.

Cohen, N. J., and Squire, L. R. 1980. Preserved learning and retention of pattern-analyzing skill in amnesia: Dissociation of knowing how and knowing what. *Science,* 210:207–210.

Cohen, S., Lichtenstein, E., Prochaska, J. O., Rossi, J. S., Gritz, E. R., Carr, C. R., Orleans, C. T., Schoenbach, V. J., Bierner, L., Abrams, D., DiClemente, C., Curry, S., Marlatt, G. A., Cummings, K. M., Emant, S. L., Giovino, G., and Ossip-Klein, D. 1989. Debunking myths about quitting: Evidence from 10 perspective studies of persons who attempt to quit smoking by themselves. *American Psychologist,* 44:1355–1365.

Cohen, T. E., Henzi, V., Kandel, E. R., and Hawkins, R. D. 1991. Further behavioral andcellular studies of dishabituation and sensitization in *Aplysia. Society for Neuroscience Abstracts,* 17:1302.

Colangelo, W., and Jones, D. G. 1982. The fetal alcohol syndrome: A review and assessment of the syndrome and its neurological sequelae. *Progress in Neurobiology,* 19:271–314.

Colebrook E., and Lukowiak, K. 1988. Learning by the *Aplysia* model system: Lack of correlation between gill and gill motor neurone responses. *Journal of Experimental Biology,* 135:411–429.

Colley, P. A., and Routtenberg, A. 1993. Long-term potentiation as synaptic dialogue. *Brain Research Review,* 18:115–122.

Collings, V. B. 1974. Human taste response as a function of locus of stimulation on the tongue and soft palate. *Perception and Psychophysics,* 16:169–174.

Coltheart, M. 1980. Deep dyslexia: A right hemisphere hypothesis. In M. Coltheart, K. Patterson, and J. C. Marshall (eds.), *Deep dyslexia.* Routledge & Kegan Paul, London.

Colwill, R. M., Absher, R. A., and Roberts, M. L. 1988. Conditional discrimination learning in *Aplysia californica. Journal of Neuroscience,* 8:4440–4444.

Condon, C. D., and Weinberger, N. M. 1991. Habituation produces frequency-specific plasticity of receptive fields in the auditory cortex. *Behavioral Neuroscience,* 105:416–430.

Conel, J. L. 1939. *The postnatal development of the human cerebral cortex.* 6 vols.

Harvard University Press, Cambridge, MA.

Conrad, A. J., Abebe, T., Austin, R., Forsythe, S., and Scheibel, A. B. 1991. Hippocampal pyramidal cell disarray in schizophrenia as a bilateral phenomenon. *Archives of General Psychiatry,* 48:413–417.

Constantine-Paton, M., Cline, H. T., and Debski, E. 1990. Patterned activity, synaptic convergence, and the NMDA receptor in developing visual pathways. *Annual Review of Neuroscience,* 13:129–154.

Convit, A., de Leon, M. J., Golomb, J., George, A. E., Tarshish, C. Y., Bobinski, M., Tsui, W., De Santi, S., Wegiel, J., and Wisniewski, H. 1993. Hippocampal atrophy in early Alzheimer's disease: anatomic specificity and validation. *Psychiatric Quarterly,* 64:371–387.

Cooper, J. R., Bloom, F. E., and Roth, R. H. 1982. *The biochemical basis of neuropharmacology,* 4th ed. Oxford, New York.

Cooper, R. 1994. *Sleep.* Chapman & Hall Medical, New York.

Corbett, S. W., and Keesey, R. E. 1982. Energy balance of rats with lateral hypothalamic lesions. *American Journal of Physiology,* 242:E273–E279.

Coren, S. 1992. *The left-hander syndrome: The causes and consequences of left-handedness.* Free Press, New York.

Corkin, S. 1984. Lasting consequences of bilateral medial temporal lobectomy: Clinical course and experimental findings in H.M. *Seminars in Neurology,* 4:249–259.

Corkin, S., Milner, B., and Rasmussen, T. 1970. Somatosensory thresholds: Contrasting effects of postcentral-gyrus and posterior parietal-lobe excisions. *Archives of Neurology,* 23:41–58.

Coryell, W., Noyes, R., Jr., and House, J. D. 1986. Mortality among outpatients with anxiety disorders. *American Journal of Psychiatry,* 143:508–510.

Cory-Slechta, D. A., Weiss, B., and Cox, C. 1985. Performance and exposure indices of rats exposed to low concentrations of lead. *Toxicology and Applied Pharmacology,* 78:291–299.

Costanzo, R. M. 1991. Regeneration of olfactory receptor cells. *Ciba Foundation Symposium,* 160:233–242.

Cotanche, D. A. 1987. Regeneration of hair cell stereociliary bundles in the chick cochlea following severe acoustic trauma. *Hearing Research,* 30:181–195.

Cotanche, D. A., and Lee, K. H. 1994. Regeneration of hair cells in the vestibulocochlear system of birds and mammals. *Current Opinion in Neurobiology,* 4:509–514.

Cowan, W. M. 1979. The development of the brain. *Scientific American,* 241(3):112–133.

Cowan, W. M., and Wenger, E. 1967. Cell loss in the trochlear nucleus of the chick during normal development and after radical extirpation of the optic vesicle. *Journal of Experimental Zoology,* 164:267–280.

Cowey, A. 1967. Perimetric study of field defects after cortical and retinal ablations. *Quarterly Journal of Experimental Psychology,* 19:232–245.

Coyle, J. T., Price, D. L., and DeLong, M. R. 1983. Alzheimer's disease: A disorder of cortical cholinergic innervation. *Science,* 219:1184–1190.

Cragg, B. G. 1975. The development of synapses in the visual system of the cat. *Journal of Comparative Neurology,* 160:147–166.

Craik, F. I. M. 1985. Paradigms in human memory research. In L. G. Nilsson, and T. Archer (eds.), *Perspectives on learning and memory,* pp. 197–221. Lawrence Erlbaum Associates, Hillsdale, NJ.

Craik, F. I. M. 1986. A functional account of age differences in memory. In F. Klix, and H. Hogendorf (eds.), *Human memory and cognitive capabilities,* Vol. A, pp. 409–422. North-Holland, Amsterdam.

Creasey, H., and Rapoport, S. I. 1985. The aging human brain. *Annals of Neurology,* 17:2–11.

Crews, D. 1994. Temperature, steroids and sex determination. *Journal of Endocrinology,* 142:1–8.

Crick, F., and Mitchison, G. 1983. The function of dream sleep. *Nature,* 304:111–114.

Crow, T. J. 1990. The continuum of psychosis and its genetic origins. The sixty-fifth Maudsley lecture. *British Journal of Psychiatry,* 156:788–797.

Cruce, J. A. F., Greenwood, M. R. C., Johnson, P. R., and Quartermain, D. 1974. Genetic versus hypothalamic obesity: Studies of intake and dietary manipulation in rats. *Journal of Comparative and Physiological Psychology,* 87:295–301.

Cummings, J. L. 1995. Dementia: The failing brain. *Lancet,* 345:1481–1484.

Cummings, J. L., Benson, D. F., Walsh, M. J., and Levine, H. L. 1979. Left-to-right transfer of language dominance: A case study. *Neurology,* 29:1547–1550.

Cunningham, K. A., Paris, J. M., and Goeders, N. E. 1992. Chronic cocaine enhances serotonin autoregulation and serotonin uptake binding. *Synapse,* 11:112–123.

Curcio, C. A., Sloan, K. R., Packer, O., Hendrickson, A. E., and Kalina, R. E. 1987. Distribution of cones in human and monkey retina: Individual variability and radial asymmetry. *Science,* 236:579–582.

Curran, H. V., Schifano, F., and Lader, M. 1991. Models of memory dysfunction? A comparison of the effects of scopolamine and lorazepam on memory, psychomotor performance and mood. *Psychopharmacology*, 103:83–90.

Curtis, S. 1977. *Genie. A psycholinguistic study of a modern day 'wild child.'* Academic Press, New York.

Curtiss, S. 1989. The independence and task-specificity of language. In M. H. Bornstein, and J. S. Bruner (eds.), *Interaction in human development. Crosscurrents in contemporary psychology*, pp. 105–137. Lawrence Erlbaum Associates, Hillsdale, NJ.

Czeisler, C. A., Zimmerman, J. C., Ronda, J. M., Moore-Ede, M. C., and Weitzman, E. D. 1980. Timing of REM sleep is coupled to the circadian rhythm of body temperature in man. *Sleep*, 2:329–346.

Dabbs, J. M., and Morris, R. 1990. Testosterone, social class, and antisocial behavior in a sample of 4,462 men. *Psychological Science*, 1:209–211.

Dabbs, J. M., Ruback, R. B., Frady, R. L., Hopper, C. H. et al. 1988. Saliva testosterone and criminal violence among women. *Personality & Individual Differences*, 9:269–275.

Daly, M., and Wilson, M. 1978. *Sex, evolution and behavior*. Duxbury Press, North Scituate, MA.

Damasio, A. R. 1989. The brain binds entities and events by multiregional activation from convergence zones. *Neural Computation*, 1:123–132.

Damasio, A. R., Chui, H. C., Corbett, J., and Kassell, N. 1980. Posterior callosal section in a non-epileptic patient. *Journal of Neurology, Neurosurgery, and Psychiatry*, 43:351–356.

Damasio, A. R., Eslinger, P. J., Damasio, H., Van Hoesen, G. W., and Cornell, S. 1985a. Multimodal amnesic syndrome following bilateral temporal and basal forebrain damage. *Archives of Neurology*, 42:252–259.

Damasio, A. R., Graff-Radford, N. R., Eslinger, P. J., Damasio, H., and Kassell, N. 1985b. Amnesia following basal forebrain lesions. *Archives of Neurology*, 42:263–271.

Damasio, A. R., Tranel, D., and Damasio, H. 1990. Face agnosia and the neural substrates of memory. *Annual Review of Neuroscience*, 13:89–109.

Damasio, H. 1995. *Human brain anatomy in computerized images*. Oxford University Press, New York.

Damasio, H., Grabowski, T., Frank, R., Galaburda, A. M., and Damasio, A. R. 1994. The return of Phineas Gage: Clues about the brain from the skull of a famous patient. *Science*, 264:1102–1105.

D'Amato, R. J., Alexander, G. M., Schwartzman, R. J., Kitt, C. A., Price, D. L., and Snyder, S. H. 1987. Evidence for neuromelanin involvement in MPTP-induced neurotoxicity. *Nature*, 327:324–326.

Dantz, B., Edgar, D. M., and Dement, W. C. 1994. Circadian rhythms in narcolepsy: Studies on a 90 minute day. *Electroencephalography and Clinical Neurophysiology*, 90:24–35.

Darian-Smith, I., Davidson, I., and Johnson, K. O. 1980. Peripheral neural representations of the two spatial dimensions of a textured surface moving over the monkey's finger pad. *Journal of Physiology*, 309:135–146.

Dark, J. 1984. Seasonal weight gain is attenuated in food-restricted ground squirrels with lesions of the suprachiasmatic nuclei. *Behavioral Neuroscience*, 98:830–835.

Dark, J., and Zucker, I. 1985. Seasonal cycles in energy balance: regulation by light. *Annals of the New York Academy of Sciences*, 453:170–181.

Dark, J., Forger, N. G., and Zucker, I. 1984. Rapid recovery of body mass after surgical removal of adipose tissue in ground squirrels. *Proceedings of the National Academy of Sciences, U.S.A.*, 81:2270–2272.

Dark, J., Miller, D. R., and Zucker, I. 1994. Reduced glucose availability induced torpor in Siberian hamsters. *American Journal of Physiology*, 267:R496–R501.

Darwin, C. 1872. *The expression of the emotions in man and animals*. J. Murray, London.

Darwin, F. 1888. *Life and letters of Charles Darwin. Vol 3*. John Murray, London.

Davenport, J. W. 1976. Environmental therapy in hypothyroid and other disadvantaged animal populations In R. N. Walsh, and W. T. Greenough (eds.), *Environments as therapy for brain dysfunction*. Plenum, New York.

Davidson, J. M., Camargo, C. A., and Smith, E. R. 1979. Effects of androgen on sexual behavior in hypogonadal men. *Journal of Clinical Endocrinology and Metabolism*, 48:955–958.

Davidson, R. J. 1994. Asymmetric brain function, affective style, and psychopathology: The role of early experience and plasticity. *Development & Psychopathology*, 6:741–758.

Davidson, R. J., Ekman, P., Saron, C. D., Senulis, J. A. et al. 1990. Approach-withdrawal and cerebral asymmetry: Emotional expression and brain physiology: I. *Journal of Personality & Social Psychology*, 58:330–341.

Davis, H. P., and Squire, L. R. 1984. Protein synthesis and memory: A review. *Psychological Bulletin*, 96:518–559.

Davis, J. M., Otto, D. A., Weil, D. E., and Grant, L. D. 1990. The comparative developmental neurotoxicity of lead in humans and animals. *Neurotoxicology and Teratology*, 12:215–229.

Davis, K. L., Kahn, R. S., Ko, G., and Davidson, M. 1991. Dopamine in schizophrenia: A review and reconceptualization. *American Journal of Psychiatry*, 148:1474–1486.

Daw, N. W., Brunken, W. J., and Parkinson, D. 1989. The function of synaptic transmitters in the retina. *Annual Review of Neuroscience*, 12:205–225.

Daw, N. W., Stein, P. S., and Fox, K. 1993. The role of NMDA receptors in information processing. *Annual Review of Neuroscience*, 16:207–222.

Dawson, D., and Encel, N. 1993. Melatonin and sleep in humans. *Journal of Pineal Research*, 15:1–12.

de Groot, C. M., Janus, M. D., and Bornstein, R. A. 1995. Clinical predictors of psychopathology in children and adolescents with Tourette Syndrome. *Journal of Psychiatric Research*, 29:59–70.

de Leon, M. J., Golomb, J., George, A. E., Convit, A., Tarshish, C. Y., McRae, T., De Santi, S., Smith, G., Ferris, S. H., Noz, M. et al. 1993. The radiologic prediction of Alzheimer disease:The atrophic hippocampal formation. *American Journal of Neuroradiology*, 14:897–906.

de Paiva, A., Poulain, B., Lawrence, G. W., Shone, C. C., Tauc, L., and Dolly, J. O. 1993. A role for the interchain disulfide or its participating thiols in the internalization of botulinum neurotoxin A revealed by a toxin derivative that binds to ecto-acceptors and inhibits transmitter release intracellularly. *Journal of Biological Chemistry*, 268:20838–20844.

De Valois, K. K., De Valois, R. L., and Yund, E. W. 1979. Responses of striate cortex cells to grating and checkerboard patterns. *Journal of Physiology*, 291:483–505.

De Valois, R. L., Albrecht, D. G., and Thorell, L. G. 1977. Spatial tuning of LGN and cortical cells in the monkey visual system. In H. Spekreijse, and H. van der Tweel (eds.), *Spatial contrast*, pp. 60–63. Elsevier, Amsterdam.

De Valois, R. L., and De Valois, K. K. 1975. Neural coding of color. In *Handbook of perception: Seeing. Vol. 5*. Academic Press, New York.

De Valois, R. L., and De Valois, K. K. 1980. Spatial vision. *Annual Review of Psychology*, 31:309–341.

De Valois, R. L., and De Valois, K. K. 1988. *Spatial vision*. Oxford University Press, New York.

De Valois, R. L., and De Valois, K. K. 1993. A multi-stage color model. *Vision Research*, 33:1053–1065.

Dekaban, A. S., and Sadowsky, D. 1978. Changes in brain weights during the span of human life: Relation of brain weights to body heights and body weights. *Annals of Neurology*, 4:345–356.

Delgado-Escueta, A. V., Mattson, R. H., King, L., Goldensohn, E. S., Spiegel, H., Madsen, J., Crandall, P., Dreifuss, F., and Porter, R. J. 1981. The nature of aggression during epileptic seizures. *New England Journal of Medicine*, 305:711–716.

DeLisi, L. E., Mirsky, A., Buchsbaum, M., van Kammen, D. P., Berman, K., Kafka, M., Ninan, P., Phelps, B., Karoum, F., Ko, G., Korpi, E., Linnoila, M., Sheinan, M., and Wyatt, R. 1984. The Genain quadruplets 25 years later: A diagnostic and biochemical followup. *Psychiatry Research*, 13:59–76.

DeLong, M. R., Georgopoulos, A. P., Crutcher, M. D., Mitchell, S. J., Richardson, R. T., and Alexander, G. E. 1984. Functional organization of the basal ganglia: contributions of single-cell recording studies. *Ciba Foundation Symposium*, 107:64–82.

Dement, W. C. 1974. *Some must watch while some must sleep*. W. H. Freeman, San Francisco.

Demmer, J., Dragunow, M., Lawlor, P. A., Mason, S. E., Leah, J. D., Abraham, W. C., and Tate, W. P. 1993. Differential expression of immediate early genes after hippocampal long-term potentiation in awake rats. *Brain Research*, 17:279–286.

Denk, W., Sugimore, M., and Llinas, R. 1995. Two types of calcium response limited to single spines in cerebellar Purkinje cells. *Proceedings of the National Academy of Sciences, U.S.A.*, 92:8279–8282.

Dennis, S. G., and Melzack, R. 1983. Perspectives on phylogenetic evolution of pain expression. In R. L. Kitchell, H. H. Erickson, E. Carstens, and L. E. Davis (eds.), *Animal pain*, pp. 151–161. American Physiological Society, Bethesda.

Denti, A., McGaugh, J. L., Landfield, P. W., and Shinkman, P. 1970. Effects of posttrial electrical stimulation of the mesencephalic reticular formation on avoidance learning in rats. *Physiology and Behavior*, 5:659–662.

Denton, D. 1982. *The hunger for salt*. Springer-Verlag, Berlin.

Deol, M. S., and Gluecksohn-Waelsch, S. 1979. The role of inner hair cells in hearing. *Nature*, 278:250–252.

Derrick, B. 1993. *Opioid receptor-dependent long-term potentiation*. Unpublished doctoral dissertation, University of California, Berkeley.

Derrick, B. E., and Martinez, J. L. 1994. Frequency-dependent associative long-term potentiation at the hippocampal mossy fiber-CA3 synapse. *Proceedings of the National Academy of Sciences, U.S.A.*, 91:10290–10294.

DeSalle, R., Gatesy, J., Wheeler, W., and Grimaldi, D. 1992. DNA sequences from a fossil termite in Oligo-Miocene amber and their phylogenetic implications. *Science*, 257:1933–1936.

Descartes, R. 1662. *De homine*. Petrum Leffen & Franciscum Moyardum, Paris.

Desimone, R., Albright, T. D., Gross, C. G., and Bruce, C. 1984. Stimulus-selective properties of inferior tempo-ral neurons in the macaque. *Journal of Neuroscience*, 4:2051–2062.

Desimone, R., and Duncan, J. 1995. Neural mechanisms of selective visual attention. *Annual Review of Neuroscience*, 18:193–222.

Devane, W. A., Dysarz, F. A., Johnson, M. R., Melvin, L. S., and Howlett, A. C. 1988. Determination and characterization of a cannabinoid receptor in rat brain. *Molecular Pharmacology*, 34:605–613.

Devane, W. A., Hanus, L., Breuer, A., Pertwee, R. G., Stevenson, L. A., Griffin, G., Gibsdon, D., Mandelbaum, A., Etinger, A., and Mechoulam, R. 1992. Isolation and structure of a brain constituent that binds the cannabinoid receptor. *Science*, 258:1946–1949.

Devinsky, O., and Bear, D. 1984. Varieties of aggressive behavior in temporal lobe epilepsy. *American Journal of Psychiatry*, 141: 651–656.

DeVoogd, T. J. 1994. Interactions between endocrinology and learning in the avian song system. *Annals of the New York Academy of Sciences*, 743:19–41.

Dewey, D. 1993. Error analysis of limb and orofacial praxis in children with developmental motor deficits. *Brain and Cognition*, 23:203–221.

Dewsbury, D. A. 1972. Patterns of copulatory behavior in male mammals. *Quarterly Review of Biology*, 47:1–33.

DeYoe, E. A., and Van Essen, D. C. 1988. Concurrent processing streams in monkey visual cortex. *Trends in Neurosciences*, 11:219–226.

Diamond, A. 1990a. The development and neural bases of memory functions as indexed by the AB and delayed response tasks in human infants and infant monkeys. *Annals of the New York Academy of Sciences*, 608:267–317.

Diamond, A. 1990b. Developmental time course in human infants and infant monkeys, and the neural bases of inhibitory control in reaching. *Annals of the New York Academy of Sciences*, 608:637–676.

Diamond, A. 1990c. Rate of maturation of the hippocampus and the developmental progression of children's performance on the delayed non-matching to sample and visual paired comparison tasks. *Annals of the New York Academy of Sciences*, 608:394–433.

Diamond, A., and Goldman-Rakic, P. S. 1989. Comparison of human infants and rhesus monkeys on Piaget's AB task: Evidence for dependence on dorsolateral prefrontal cortex. *Experimental Brain Research*, 74:24–40.

Diamond, J., Cooper, E., Turner, C., and Macintyre, L. 1976. Trophic regulation of nerve sprouting. *Science*, 193:371–377.

Diamond, M. C. 1967. Extensive cortical depth measurements and neuron size increases in the cortex of environmentally enriched rats. *Journal of Comparative Neurology*, 131:357–364.

Diamond, M. C., Dowling, G. A., and Johnson, R. E. 1981. Morphologic cerebral cortical asymmetry in male and female rats. *Experimental Neurology*, 71:261–268.

Diamond, M. C., Krech, D., and Rosenzweig, M. R. 1964. The effects of an enriched environment on the histology of the rat cerebral cortex. *Journal of Comparative Neurology*, 123:111–119.

Diamond, M. C., Lindner, B., Johnson, R., Bennett, E. L., and Rosenzweig, M. R. 1975. Differences in occipital cortical synapses from environmentally enriched, impoverished, and standard colony rats. *Journal of Neuroscience Research*, 1:109–119.

Dichgans, J. 1984. Clinical symptoms of cerebellar dysfunction and their topodiagnostical significance. *Human Neurobiology*, 2:269–279.

Dobbing, J. 1972. Undernutrition and the developing brain. The relevance of animal models to the human problem. *Bibliotheca Nutritio et Dieta*, 17:35–46.

Dobbing, J. 1976. Vulnerable periods in brain growth and somatic growth. In D. F. Roberts, and A. M. Thomson (eds.), *The biology of human fetal growth*, pp. 137–147. Taylor and Francis, London.

Dolphin, A. C., Errington, M. L., and Bliss, T. V. P. 1982. Long-term potentiation of the perforant path *in vivo* is associated with increased glutamate release. *Nature*, 297:496–498.

Donegan, N. H., Lowery, R. W., and Thompson, R. F. 1983. Effects of lesioning cerebellar nuclei on conditioned leg-flexion responses. *Society for Neuroscience Abstracts*, 9:331.

Doricchi, F., and Guariglia, C. P., Paolucci, S., Pizzamiglio, L. 1991. Disappearance of leftward rapid eye movements during sleep in left visual hemi-inattention. *Neuroreport*, 2:285–288.

Dorow, R., Horowski, R., Paschelke, G., and Amin, M. 1983. Severe anxiety induced by FG 7142, a beta-carboline ligand for benzodiazepine receptors. *Lancet*, 2:98–99.

Drachman, D. A., and Leavitt, J. 1972. Memory impairment in the aged: Storage versus retrieval deficit. *Journal of Experimental Psychology*, 93:302–308.

Drachman, D. B. 1983. Myasthenia gravis: Immunobiology of a receptor disorder. *Trends in Neurosciences*, 6:446–450.

Drevets, W. C., Videen, T. O., Price, J. L., Preskorn, S. H., Carmichael, S. T., and Raichle, M. E. 1992. A functional anatomical study of unipolar depression. *Journal of Neuroscience*, 12:3628–3641.

Drickamer, L. C. 1992. Behavioral selection of odor cues by young female mice affects age of puberty. *Developmental Psychobiology*, 25:461–470.

Druckman, D., and Bjork, R. A. 1994. *Learning, remembering, believing:Enhancing human performance.* National Academy Press, Washington, D.C.

Dudai, Y. 1988. Neurogenic dissection of learning and short term memory in *Drosophila. Annual Review of Neuroscience*, 11:537–563.

Dudai, Y., Jan, Y. N., Byers, D., Quinn, W. G., and Benzer, S. 1976. Dunce, a mutant of *Drosophila* deficient in learning. *Proceedings of the National Academy of Sciences, U.S.A.*, 73:1684–1688.

Duerr, J. S., and Quinn, W. G. 1982. Three *Drosophila* mutations that block associative learning also affect habituation and sensitization. *Proceedings of the National Academy of Sciences, U.S.A.*, 79:3646–3650.

Duffy, F. H., Burchfiel, J. L., and Lombroso, C. T. 1979. Brain electrical activity mapping (BEAM): A method for extending the clinical utility of EEG and evoked potential data. *Annals of Neurology*, 5:309–321.

Duffy, F. H., Jones, K., Bartels, P., McAnulty, G., and Albert, M. 1992. Unrestricted principal components analysis of brain electrical activity: Issues of data dimensionality, artifact, and utility. *Brain Tomography*, 4:291–307.

Duffy, J. D., and Campbell, J. J., III. 1994. The regional prefrontal syndromes: A theoretical and clinical overview. *Journal of Neuropsychiatry and Clinical Neurosciences*, 6:379–387.

Durup, G., and Fessard, A. 1935. L'electroencephalogramme de l'homme. *L'Anee Psychologique*, 36:1–32.

Eapen, V., Pauls, D. L., and Robertson, M. M. 1993. Evidence for autosomal dominant transmission in Tourette's syndrome. United Kingdom cohort study. *British Journal of Psychiatry*, 162:593–596.

Easton, R. D. 1992. Inherent problems of attempts to apply sonar and vibrotactile sensory aid technology to the perceptual needs of the blind. *Optometry and Vision Science*, 69:3–14.

Eccles, J. C. 1965. Possible ways in which synaptic mechanisms participate in learning, remembering and forgetting. In D. P. Kimble (ed.), *The anatomy of memory*, pp. 12–87. Science and Behavior Books, Palo Alto, CA.

Edwards, J. S., and Palka, J. 1991. Insect neural evolution—a fugue or an opera? *Seminars in the Neurosciences*, 3:391–398.

Egaas, B., Courchesne, E., and Saitoh, O. 1995. *Archives of Neurology*, 52:794–801.

Egeland, J. A., and Hostetter, A. M. 1983. Amish study, 1: Affective disorders among the Amish, 1976–1980. *American Journal of Psychiatry*, 140:56–71.

Egrise, D., Rubinstein, M., Schoutens, A., Cantraine, F., and Mendlewicz, J. 1986. Seasonal variation of platelet serotonin uptake and 3H–imipramine binding in normal and depressed subjects. *Biological Psychiatry*, 21:283–292.

Ehrenkranz, J., Bliss, E., and Sheard, M. H. 1974. Plasma testosterone: Correlation with aggressive behavior and social dominance in man. *Psychosomatic Medicine*, 36:469–475.

Eikelboom, R., and Stewart, J. 1981. Temporal and environmental cues in conditioned hypothermia and hyperthermia associated with morphine. *Psychopharmacology*, 72:147–153.

Eisenberg, J. F., and Wilson, D. E. 1978. Relative brain size and feeding strategies in *Chiroptera. Evolution*, 32:740–751.

Ekman, P. 1973. *Darwin and facial expression; a century of research in review.* Academic Press, New York.

Ekman, P. 1981. Methods for measuring facial action. In K. Scherer, and P. Ekman (eds.), *Handbook on methods of nonverbal communications research.* Cambridge University Press, New York.

Ekman, P., and Davidson, R. J. 1994. *The nature of emotion: Fundamental questions.* Oxford University Press, New York.

Ekman, P., Levenson, R. W., and Friesen, W. V. 1983. Autonomic nervous system activity distinguishes among emotions. *Science*, 221:1208–1210.

Ekstrand, B. R., Barrett, T. R., West, J. M., and Maier, W. G. 1977. The effect on human long-term memory. In R. Drucker-Colin, and J. L. McGaugh (eds.), *Neurobiology of sleep and memory.* Academic Press, New York.

Ellenhorn, M. J., and Barceloux, D. G. 1988. *Medical toxicology: Diagnosis and treatment of human poisoning.* Elsevier, New York.

Elmadjian, F., Hope, J. M., and Lamson, E. T. 1957. Excretion of epinephrine and norepinephrine in various emotional states. *Journal of Clinical Endocrinology*, 17:608–620.

Engel, A. G. 1984. Myasthenia gravis and myasthenic syndromes. *Annals of Neurology*, 16:519–535.

Engel, J. Jr., Babb, T. L., and Crandall, P. H. 1989. Surgical treatment of epilepsy: Opportunities for research into basic mechanisms of human brain function. *Acta Neurochirurgica, (Supplementum)*, 46:3–8.

Engel, J., Jr. 1992. Recent advances in surgical treatment of temporal lobe epilepsy. *Acta Neurologica Scandinavica (Supplementum)*, 140:71–80.

Epelbaum, M., Milleret, C., Buisseret, P., and Dufier, J. L. 1993. The sensitive period for strabismic amblyopia in humans. *Ophthalmology*, 100:323–327.

Epstein, A. N., Fitzsimons, J. T., and Rolls, B. J. 1970. Drinking induced by injection of angiotensin into the brain of the rat. *Journal of Physiology (London)*, 210:457–474.

Epstein, C. J. 1986. Developmental genetics. *Experientia*, 42:1117–1128.

Erhardt, V. R., and Goldman, M. B. 1992. Adverse endocrine effects. In M. S. Keshavan, and J. S. Kennedy (eds.), *Drug-induced dysfunction in psychiatry.* Hemisphere, New York.

Erickson, C. J. 1978. Sexual affiliation in animals: Pair bonds and reproductive strategies. In J. B. Hutchinson (ed.), *Biological determinants of sexual behaviour*, pp. 697–725. Wiley, New York.

Ericson, J., Thor, S., Edlund, T., Jessell, T. M., and Yamada, T. 1992. Early stages of motor neuron differentiation revealed by expression of homeobox gene Islet-1. *Science*, 256:1555–1560.

Evans, C. J., Keith, D. E., Morrison, H., Magendzo, K., and Edwards, R. H. 1992. Cloning of a delta opioid receptor by functional expression. *Science*, 258:1952–1955.

Evarts, E. V., Shinoda, Y., and Wise, S. P. 1984. *Neurophysiological approaches to higher brain functions.* Wiley, New York.

Everson, C. A. 1993. Sustained sleep deprivation impairs host defense. *American Journal of Physiology*, 265:R1148–R1154.

Everson, C. A., Bergmann, B. M., and Rechtschaffen, A. 1989. Sleep deprivation in the rat: III. Total sleep deprivation. *Sleep*, 12:13–21.

Eybalin, M. 1993. Neurotransmitters and neuromodulators of the mammalian cochlea. *Physiological Reviews*, 73:309–373.

Falk, D. 1993. Sex differences in visuospatial skills: Implications for hominid evolution. In K. R. Gibson, and T. Ingold (eds.), *Tools, language and cognition in human evolution*, pp. 216–229. Cambridge University Press, Cambridge, England.

Faraone, S. V., and Tsuang, M. T. 1985. Quantitative models of the genetic transmission of schizophrenia. *Psychological Bulletin*, 98:41–66.

Farbman, A. I. 1994. The cellular basis of olfaction. *Endeavour*, 18:2–8.

Farley, J., and Alkon, D. L. 1985. Cellular mechanisms of learning, memory, and information storage. *Annual Review of Psychology*, 36:419–494.

Fausto-Sterling, A. 1985. *Myths of gender.* Basic Books, New York.

Fazeli, M. S., Corbet, J., Dunn, M. J., Dolphin, A. C., and Bliss, T. V. 1993. Changes in protein synthesis accompanying long-term potentiation in the dentate gyrus *in vivo. Journal of Neuroscience*, 13:1346–1353.

Feder, H. H., and Whalen, R. E. 1965. Feminine behavior in neonatally castrated and estrogen-treated male rats. *Science*, 147:306–307.

Feinberg, I. 1982. Schizophrenia: Caused by a fault in programmed synaptic elimination during adolescence. *Journal of Psychiatry Research*, 17: 319–334.

Felten, D. L., Felten, S. Y., Bellinger, D. L., and Madden, K. S. 1993. Fundamental aspects of neural-immune signaling. *Psychotherapy and Psychosomatics*, 60:46–56.

Fendrich, R., Wessinger, C. M., and Gazzaniga, M. S. 1992. Residual vision in a scotoma: Implications for blindsight. *Science*, 258:1489–1491.

Fibiger, H. C., and Lloyd, K. G. 1984. The neurobiological substrates of tardive dyskinesia: The GABA hypothesis. *Trends in Neurosciences*, 8:462.

Fields, H. L. 1988. *Pain.* McGraw-Hill, New York.

Fields, S. 1990. Pheromone response in yeast. *Trends in Biochemical Sciences*, 15:270–273.

Fifkova, E., Anderson, C. L., Young, S. J., and Van Harreveld, A. 1982. Effect of anisomycin on stimulation-induced changes in dendritic spines of the dentate granule cells. *Journal of Neurocytology*, 11:183–210.

Finger, S. (ed.). 1978. *Recovery from brain damage: Research and theory.* Plenum, New York.

Finger, S. 1994. *Origins of neuroscience: A history of explorations into brain function.* Oxford University Press, New York.

Finlay, B. L., and Darlington, R. B. 1995. Linked regularities in the development and evolution of mammalian brains. *Science*, 268:1578–84.

Fiorino, D. F., Coury, A., Fibiger, H. C., and Phillips, A. G. 1993. Electrical stimulation of reward sites in the ventral tegmental area increases dopamine transmission in the nucleus accumbens of the rat. *Behavioural Brain Research*, 55:131–141.

Fishman, R. B., Chism, L., Firestone, G. L., and Breedlove, S. M. 1990. Evidence for androgen receptors in sexually dimorphic perineal muscles of neonatal male rats. Absence of androgen accumulation by the perineal motoneurons. *Journal of Neurobiology*, 21:694–704.

Fitts, P. M., and Posner, M. I. 1967. *Human performance.* Brooks/Cole, Belmont, CA.

Flood, J. F., Bennett, E. L., Orme, A. E., and Rosenzweig, M. R. 1975. Relation of memory formation to controlled amounts of brain protein synthesis. *Physiology and Behavior*, 15:97–102.

Flood, J. F., Bennett, E. L., Rosenzweig, M. R., and Orme, A. E. 1973. The influence of duration of protein synthesis inhibition on memory. *Physiology and Behavior*, 10:555–562.

Flood, J. F., Jarvik, M. E., Bennett, E. L., Orme, A. E., and Rosenzweig, M. R. 1977. The effect of stimulants, depressants and protein synthesis inhibition on retention. *Behavioral Biology*, 20:168–183.

Forger, N. G., and Breedlove, S. M. 1986. Sexual dimorphism in human and canine spinal cord: role of early androgen. *Proceedings of the National Academy of Sciences, U.S.A.*, 83: 7527–7531.

Forger, N. G., and Breedlove, S. M. 1987. Seasonal variation in mammalian striated muscle mass and motoneuron morphology. *Journal of Neurobiology*, 18:155–165.

Forger, N. G., Roberts, S. L., Wong, V., and Breedlove, S. M. 1993. Ciliary neurotrophic factor maintains motoneurons and their target muscles in developing rats. *Journal of Neuroscience*, 13: 4720–4726.

Forstl, H., Burns, A., Levy, R., Cairns, N., Luthert, P., and Lantos, P. 1993. Neuropathological correlates of behavioural disturbance in confirmed Alzheimer's disease. *British Journal of Psychiatry*, 163:364–368.

Foster, N. L., Cahse, T. N., Mansi, L., Brooks, R., Fedio, P., Patronas, H. J., and Di Chiro, G. 1984. Cortical abnormalities in Alzheimer's disease. *Annals of Neurology*, 16:649–654.

Francis, R. C. 1992. Sexual lability in teleosts developmental factors. *Quarterly Review of Biology*, 67:1–18.

Frank, E., and Fishbach, G. D. 1979. Early events in neuromuscular junction formation *in vitro*: Induction of acetylcholine receptor clusters in the postsynaptic membrane and morphology of newly formed synapses. *Journal of Cell Biology*, 83:143–158.

Frank, L. G., Glickman, S. E., and Licht, P. 1991. Fatal sibling aggression, precocial development, and androgens in neonatal spotted hyenas. *Science*, 252:702–704.

Frankenhaeuser, M. 1978. Psychoneuroendocrine approaches to the study of emotion as related to stress and coping. *Nebraska Symposium on Motivation*, 26:123–162.

Franz, S. I. 1902. On the functions of the cerebrum: I. The frontal lobes in relation to the production and retention of simple sensory-motor habits. *American Journal of Physiology*, 8:1–22.

Frazier, W. T., Kandel, E. R., Kupfermann, L., Waziri, R., and Coggeshall, R. E. 1967. Morphological and functional properties of identified neurons in the abdominal ganglion of *Aplysia californica. Journal of Neurophysiology*, 30:1288–1351.

Freud, S. 1915. *The interpretation of dreams.* Macmillan, New York.

Freud, S. 1974. *Cocaine papers.* New American Library, New York.

Freund, H. J. 1984. Premotor areas in man. *Trends in Neurosciences*, 7: 481–483.

Frey, U., Huang, Y. Y., and Kandel, E. R. 1993. Effects of cAMP simulate a late stage of LTP in hippocampal CA1 neurons. *Science*, 260:1661–1664.

Fridlund, A. 1988. What can asymmetry and laterality in EMG tell us about the face and brain? *International Journal of Neuroscience*, 39:53–69.

Fridlund, A. J. 1994. *Human facial expression: An evolutionary view.* Academic Press, San Diego.

Friedland, R. P., Koss, E., Lerner, A., Hedera, P., Ellis, W., Dronkers, N., Ober, B. A., and Jagust, W. J. 1993. Functional imaging, the frontal lobes, and dementia. *Dementia*, 4:192–203.

Friedman, L., and Jones, B. E. 1984. Study of sleep-wakefulness states by computer graphics and cluster analysis before and after lesions of the pontine tegmentum in the cat. *Electroencephalography and Clinical Neurophysiology*, 57:43–56.

Friedman, M. B. 1977. Interactions between visual and vocal courtship stimuli in the neuroendocrine response of female doves. *Journal of Comparative and Physiological Psychology*, 91:1408–1416.

Friedman, M. I. 1978. Hyperphagia in rats with experimental diabetes mellitus: A response to a decreased supply of utilizable fuels. *Journal of Comparative and Physiological Psychology*, 92:109–117.

Friedman, M., and Rosenman, R. H. 1974. *Type A behavior and your heart.* Knopf, New York.

Friedman, T. C., Garcia-Borreguero, D., Hardwick, D., Akuete, C. N., Stambuk, M. K., Dorn, L. D., Starkman, M. N., Loh, Y. P., and Chrousos, G. P. 1994. Diurnal rhythm of plasma delta-sleep-inducing peptide in humans: Evidence for positive correlation with body temperature and negative correlation with rapid eye movement and slow wave sleep. *Journal of Clinical Endocrinology and Metabolism*, 78:1085–1089.

Funahashi, S., Chafee, M. V., and Goldman-Rakic, P. S. 1993. Prefrontal neuronal activity in rhesus monkeys performing a delayed anti-saccade task. *Nature*, 365:753–756.

Fuster, J. M. 1985. The prefrontal cortex, mediator of cross-temporal contingencies. *Human Neurobiology*, 4:169–179.

Fuster, J. M. 1990. Prefrontal cortex and the bridging of temporal gaps in the perception-action cycle. *Annals of the New York Academy of Sciences*, 608:318–336.

Gage, F. H., and Björklund, A. 1984. Intracerebral grafting of neuronal cell suspensions into the adult brain. *Central Nervous System Trauma*, 1:47–56.

Gage, N. H., Dunnett, S. B., Stenevi, U., and Björklund, A. 1983. Aged rats: Recovery of motor impairments by intrastriatal nigral grafts. *Science*, 221:966–969.

Gaillard, J. M. 1985. Neurochemical regulation of the states of alertness. *Annals of Clinical Research*, 17:175–184.

Gaither, N. S., and Stein, B. E. 1979. Reptiles and mammals use similar sensory organizations in the midbrain. *Science*, 205:595–597.

Galaburda, A. M. 1994. Developmental dyslexia and animal studies: At the interface between cognition and neurology. *Cognition*, 56:833–839.

Galaburda, A. M., Sanides, F., and Geschwind, N. 1978. Human brain: Cytoarchitectonic left–right asymmetries in the temporal speech region. *Archives of Neurology*, 35: 812–817.

Gallagher, M., Nagahara, A. H., and Burwell, R. D. 1995. Cognition and hippocampal systems in aging: Animal models. In J. L. McGaugh, N. M. Weinberger, and G. Lynch (eds.), *Brain and memory: Modulation and mediation of neuroplasticity*, pp. 103–126. Oxford University Press, New York.

Gallant, J. L., Braun, J., and Van Essen, D. C. 1993. Selectivity for polar, hyperbolic, and Cartesian gratings in macaque visual cortex. *Science*, 259:100–103.

Galler, J. R., Ramsey, F. C., Morley, D. S., Archer, E., and Salt, P. 1990. The long-term effects of early kwashiorkor compared with marasmus. IV. Performance on the national high school entrance examination. *Pediatric Research*, 28:235–239.

Gallistel, C. R. 1990. *The organization of learning*. MIT Press, Cambridge, MA.

Gallistel, C. R. 1995. Is long-term potentiation a plausible basis for memory? In J. L. McGaugh, N. M. Weinberger, and G. Lynch (eds.), *Brain and memory: Modulation and mediation of neuroplasticity*, pp. 328–337. Oxford University Press, New York.

Gallistel, C. R., Gomita, Y., Yadin, E., and Campbell, K. A. 1985. Forebrain origins and terminations of the medial forebrain bundle metabolically activated by rewarding stimulation or by reward-blocking doses of pimozide. *Journal of Neuroscience*, 5: 1246–1261.

Gaoni, Y., and Mechoulam, R. 1964. *Journal of the American Chemical Society*, 86:1646.

Garcia, J., and Levine, M. S. 1974. Learning paradigms and the structure of the organism. In M. R. Rosenzweig, and E. L. Bennett (eds.), *Neural mechanisms of learning and memory*, pp. 193–205. The MIT Press, Cambridge, MA.

Garcia-Arraras, J. E., and Pappenheimer, J. R. 1983. Site of action of sleep–inducing muramyl peptide isolated from human urine: Microinjection studies in rabbit brains. *Journal of Neurophysiology*, 49:528–533.

Gardner, L. I. 1972. Deprivation dwarfism. *Scientific American*, 227(1):76–82.

Gardner, R. A., and Gardner, B. T. 1969. Teaching sign language to a chimpanzee. *Science*, 165:664–672.

Gardner, R. A., and Gardner, B. T. 1984. A vocabulary test for chimpanzees (*Pan troglodytes*). *Journal of Comparative Psychology*, 98:381–404.

Gazzaniga, M. S. 1992. *Nature's mind: The biological roots of thinking, emotions, sexuality, language, and intelligence*. Basic Books, New York.

Gazzaniga, M. S., LeDoux, J. E., and Wilson, D. H. 1977. Language, praxis, and the right hemisphere: Clues to some mechanisms of consciousness. *Neurology*, 27:1144–1147.

Geller, I., Backman, E., and Seifter, J. 1963. Effects of reserpine and morphine on behaviour suppressed by punishment. *Life Sciences*, 4:226–231.

Georgopoulos, A. P., Kalaska, J. F., Caminiti, R., and Massey, J. T. 1982. On the relations between the direction of two-dimensional arm movements and cell discharge in primate motor cortex. *Journal of Neuroscience*, 2:1527–1537.

Georgopoulos, A. P., Taira, M., and Lukashin, A. 1993. Cognitive neurophysiology of the motor cortex. *Science*, 260:47–52.

Gerall, A. A., Moltz, H., and Ward, I. L. 1992. *Handbook of behavioral neurobiology. Vol. 11: Sexual differentiation*. Plenum, New York.

Gerard, C. M., Mollereau, C., Vassart, G., and Parmentier, M. 1991. Molecular cloning of a human cannabinoid receptor which is also expressed in testis. *Biochemical Journal*, 279: 129–134.

Gerkema, M. P., and Daan, S. 1985. Ultradian rhythms in behavior: The case of the common vole (*Microtus arvalis*). In H. Schulz, and P. Lavie (eds.), *Ultradian rhythms in physiology and behavior*, pp. 11–32. Springer-Verlag, Berlin.

Gerstein, D. R., Luce, R. D., Smelser, N. J., and Sperlich, S. 1988. *The behavioral and social sciences: Achievements and opportunities*. National Academy Press, Washington, D.C.

Geschwind, N. 1972. Language and the brain. *Scientific American*, 226(4): 76–83.

Geschwind, N. 1976. Language and cerebral dominance. In T. N. Chase (ed.), *Nervous system. Vol. 2. The clinical neurosciences*, pp. 433–439. Raven, New York.

Geschwind, N. 1979. Specializations of the human brain. *Scientific American*, 241:180–199.

Geschwind, N., and Galaburda, A. M. 1985. Cerebral lateralization: Biological mechanisms, associations and pathology. *Archives of Neurology*, 42:428–459, 521–654.

Geschwind, N., and Levitsky, W. 1968. Human brain: Left-right asymmetries in temporal speech region. *Science*, 161:186–187.

Geyer, M. A., and Markou, A. 1995. Animal models of psychiatric disorders. In F. E. Bloom, and D. J. Kupfer (eds.), *Psychopharmacology, the fourth generation of progress*, pp. 787–798. Raven, New York.

Ghez, C., Hening, W., and Gordon, J. 1991. Organization of voluntary movement. *Current Opinion in Neurobiology*, 1:664–671.

Gibbs, J., and Smith, G. P. 1986. Satiety: The roles of peptides from the stomach and the intestine. *Federation Proceedings*, 45:1391–1395.

Gibbs, M. E., and Ng, K. T. 1977. Psychobiology of memory: Towards a model of memory formation. *Biobehavioral Reviews*, 1:113–136.

Gibbs, M. E., and Ng, K. T. 1979. Neuronal depolarization and the inhibition of short-term memory formation. *Physiology & Behavior*, 23: 369–375.

Gilbert, A. N., and Wysocki, C. J. 1987. The smell survey results. *National Geographic*, 172:514–525.

Gilbert, A. N., Yamazaki, K., Beauchamp, G. K., and Thomas, L. 1986. Olfactory discrimination of mouse strains (*Mus musculus*) and major histocompatibility types by humans (*Homo sapiens*). *Journal of Comparative Psychology*, 100:262–265.

Gillin, J. C., Sitaram, N., Janowsky, D., Risch, C., Huey, L., and Storch, F. 1985. Cholinergic mechanisms in REM sleep. In A. Wauquier, J. M. Gaillard, J. Monti, and M. Radulovacki (eds.), *Sleep: Neurotransmitters and neuromodulators*, pp. 153–165. Raven, New York.

Gillingham, J. C., and Clark, D. L. 1981. An analysis of prey-searching behavior in the western diamondback rattlesnake *Crotalus atrox*. *Behavioral & Neural Biology*, 32:235–240.

Gilman, S., Bloedel, J. R., and Lechtenberg, R. 1981. *Disorders of the cerebellum*. F. A. Davis, Philadelphia.

Glantz, M. D. 1992. A developmental psychopathology model of drug abuse vulnerability. In M. D. Glantz, and R. W. Pickens (eds.), *Vulnerability to drug abuse*, pp. 389–418. American Psychological Association, Washington, D.C.

Glantz, M., and Pickens, R. 1992. *Vulnerability to drug abuse*. American Psychological Association, Washington, D.C.

Glaser, R., Rice, J., Speicher, C. E., Stout, J. C., and Kiecolt-Glaser, J. K. 1986. Stress depresses interferon production by leukocytes concomitant with a decrease in natural killer cell activity. *Behavioral Neuroscience*, 100: 675–678.

Glavin, G. B. 1991. Dopamine and gastroprotection. The brain-gut axis. *Digestive Diseases and Sciences*, 36: 1670–1672.

Glick, S. D., and Hinds, P. A. 1984. Modulation of turning preferences by learning. *Behavioural Brain Research*, 12:335–337.

Glick, S. D., Carlson, J. N., Baird, J. L., Maisonneuve, I. M., and Bullock, A. E. 1988. Basal and amphetamine-induced asymmetries in striatal dopamine release and metabolism: Bilateral *in vivo* microdialysis in normal rats. *Brain Research*, 473:161–164.

Glick, S. D., Hinds, P. A., and Shapiro, R. M. 1981. Morphologic cerebral cortical asymmetry in male and female rats. *Experimental Neurology*, 71: 261–268.

Glickman, S. E. 1977. Comparative psychology. In P. Mussen, and M. R. Rosenzweig (eds.), *Psychology: An introduction*, 2nd ed. D. C. Heath, Lexington, MA.

Glickman, S. E., Frank, L. G., Davidson, J. M., Smith, E. R., and Siiteri, P. K. 1987. Androstenedione may organize or activate sex-reversed traits in female spotted hyenas. *Proceedings of the National Academy of Sciences, U.S.A.*, 84:344–347.

Globus, A., Rosenzweig, M. R., Bennett, E. L., and Diamond, M. C. 1973. Effects of differential experience on dendritic spine counts in rat cerebral cortex. *Journal of Comparative and Physiological Psychology*, 82:175–181.

Gloor, P., Olivier, A., Quesney, L. F., Andermann, F., and Horowitz, S. 1982. The role of the limbic system in experiential phenomena of temporal lobe epilepsy. *Annals of Neurology*, 12:129–144.

Goldberger, M. E., and Murray, M. 1985. Recovery of function and anatomical plasticity after damage to the adult and neonatal spinal cord. In C. Cotman (ed.), *Synaptic plasticity*, pp. 77–111. Guilford, New York.

Goldman, P. S. 1976. The role of experience in recovery of function following orbital prefrontal lesions in infant monkeys. *Neuropsychologia*, 14:401–412.

Goldman-Rakic, P. S. 1995a. Cellular basis of working memory. *Neuron*, 14: 477–485.

Goldman-Rakic, P. S. 1995b. Toward a circuit model of working memory and the guidance of voluntary motor action. In J. C. Houk, J. L. Davis, and D. G. Beiser (eds.), *Models of information processing in the basal ganglia*.

Computational neuroscience, pp. 131–148. MIT Press, Cambridge, MA.

Goldsmith, T. H. 1986. Interpreting transretinal recordings of spectral sensitivity. *Journal of Comparative Physiology. a. Sensory, Neural, and Behavioral Physiology*, 159:481–487.

Goldsmith, T. H. 1990. Optimization, constraint, and history in the evolution of eyes. *Quarterly Review of Biology*, 65:281–322.

Goldstein, G. W. 1990. Lead poisoning and brain cell function. *Environmental Health Perspectives*, 89:91–94.

Golomb, J., de Leon, M. J., George, A. E., Kluger, A., Convit, A., Rusinek, H., de Santi, S., Litt, A., Foo, S. H., and Ferris, S. H. 1994. Hippocampal atrophy correlates with severe cognitive impairment in elderly patients with suspected normal pressure hydrocephalus. *Journal of Neurology, Neurosurgery and Psychiatry*, 57: 590–593.

Goodman, C. 1979. Isogenic grasshoppers: Genetic variability and development of identified neurons. In X. O. Breakefeld (ed.), *Neurogenetics*. Elsevier, New York.

Goodman, M., Tagle, D. A., Fitch, D. H., Bailey, W., Czelusniak, J., Koop, B. F., Benson, P., and Slightom, J. L. 1990. Primate evolution at the DNA level and a classification of hominoids. *Journal of Molecular Evolution*, 30:260–266.

Gorelick, D. A., and Balster, R. L. 1995. Phencyclidine. In F. E. Bloom, and D. J. Kupfer (eds.), *Psychopharmacology, the fourth generation of progress*, pp. 1767–1776. Raven, New York.

Gorman, M. R. 1994. Male homosexual desire: Neurological investigations and scientific bias. *Perspectives in Biology and Medicine*, 38:61–81.

Gorski, R. A., Gordon, J. H., Shryne, J. E., and Southam, A. M. 1978. Evidence for a morphological sex difference within the medial preoptic area of the rat brain. *Brain Research*, 148: 333– 346.

Gorski, R. A., Gordon, J. H., Shryne, J. E., and Southam, A. M. 1978. Evidence for a morphological sex difference within the medial preoptic area of the rat brain. *Brain Research*, 148: 333–346.

Gorski, R. A., Harlan, R. E., Jacobson, C. D., Shryne, J. E., and Southam, A. M. 1980. Evidence for the existence of a sexually dimorphic nucleus in the preoptic area of the rat. *Journal of Comparative Neurology*, 193:529–539.

Gottesman, I. I. 1991. *Schizophrenia genesis*. W. H. Freeman, New York.

Gottlieb, G. 1976. The roles of experience in the development of behavior and the nervous system. In G. Gottlieb (ed.), *Studies on the development of behavior and the nervous system. Vol. 3. Neural and behavioral specificity*. Academic Press, New York.

Goulart, F. S. 1984. *The caffeine book*. Dodd, Mead, New York.

Gould, J. L. 1986. The biology of learning. *Annual Review of Psychology*, 37: 163–192.

Gould, S. J. 1981. *The mismeasure of man*. Norton, New York.

Grady, C. L., McIntosh, A. R., Horwitz, B., Maisog, J. M., Ungerleider, L. G., Mentis, M. J., Pietrini, P., Schapiro, M. B., and Haxby, J. V. 1995. Age-related reductions in human recognition memory due to impaired encoding. *Science*, 269:218–221.

Granstrom, E. 1983. Prostaglandin biochemistry, pharmacy and physiological function. The prostaglandins, thromboxanes and leukotrienes. *Acta Obstetricia et Gynecologica Scandinavica, Supplement*, 113:9–13.

Grant, S. G., O'Dell, T. J., Karl, K. A., Stein, P. L., Soriano, P., and Kandel, E. R. 1992. Impaired long-term potentiation, spatial learning, and hippocampal development in fyn mutant mice. *Science*, 256:1903–1910.

Gray, J. A. G. 1982. *The neurobiology of anxiety: An enquiry into the functions of the septo-hippocampal system*. Oxford, New York.

Graybiel, A. M. 1995. The basal ganglia. *Trends in Neurosciences*, 18:60–62.

Graybiel, A. M., Aosaki, T., Flaherty, A. W., and Kimura, M. 1994. The basal ganglia and adaptive motor control. *Science*, 265:1826–1831.

Green, S. 1991. Benzodiazepines, putative anxiolytics and animal models of anxiety. *Trends in Neurosciences*, 14:101–104.

Green, W. H., Campbell, M., and David, R. 1984. Psychosocial dwarfism: A critical review of the evidence. *Journal of the American Academy of Child Psychiatry*, 23:39–48.

Greenewalt, C. H. 1968. *Bird song: Acoustics and physiology*. Smithsonian Institution Press, Washington, D.C.

Greenough, W. T. 1976. Enduring brain effects of differential experience and training. In M. R. Rosenzweig, and E. L. Bennett (eds.), *Neural mechanisms of learning and memory*, pp. 255–278. MIT Press, Cambridge, MA.

Greenough, W. T. 1976. Enduring brain effects of differential experience and training. In M. R. Rosenzweig and E. L. Bennett (eds.), *Neural mechanisms of learning and memory*. MIT Press, Cambridge, MA.

Greenough, W. T., and Volkmar, F. R. 1973. Pattern of dendritic branching in occipital cortex of rats reared in complex environments. *Experimental Neurology*, 40:491–504.

Greenspan, R. J., Finn, J. A., Jr., and Hall, J. C. 1980. Acetylcholinesterase mutants in *Drosophila* and their effects on the structure and function of the central nervous system. *Journal of Comparative Neurology*, 189:741–774.

Greer, S. 1983. Cancer and the mind. *British Journal of Psychiatry*, 143: 535–543.

Greer, S., Morris, T., and Pettingale, K. W. 1979. Psychological response to breast cancer: Effect on outcome. *Lancet*, 2:785–787.

Grevert, P., Albert, L. H., and Goldstein, A. 1983. Partial antagonism of placebo analgesia by naloxone. *Pain*, 16: 129–143.

Grevert, P., and Goldstein, A. 1985. Placebo analgesia, naloxone, and the role of endogenous opioids. In L. White, B. Tursky, and G. E. Schwartz (eds.), *Placebo*, pp. 332–351. Guilford, New York.

Griffith, V. E. 1970. *A stroke in the family: A manual of home therapy.* Delacorte, New York.

Grillner, P., Hill, R., and Grillner, S. 1991. 7-Chlorokynurenic acid blocks NMDA receptor-induced fictive locomotion in lamprey—Evidence for a physiological role of the glycine site. *Acta Physiologica Scandinavica*, 141:131–132.

Grillner, S. 1985. Neurobiological bases of rhythmic motor acts in vertebrates. *Science*, 228:143–149.

Grillner, S. and Zangger, P. 1979. On the central generation of locomotion in the low spinal cat. *Experimental Brain Research*, 34:241–261.

Grillner, S., and Zangger, P. 1979. On the central generation of locomotion in the low spinal cat. *Experimental Brain Research*, 34:241–261.

Grinker, R. R. 1963. *Men under stress.* McGraw-Hill, New York.

Grinvald, A., Frostig, R. D., Siegel, R. M., and Bartfeld, E. 1991. High-resolution optical imaging of functional brain architecture in the awake monkey. *Proceedings of the National Academy of Sciences, U.S.A.*, 88: 11559–11563.

Grosof, D. H., Shapley, R. M., and Hawken, M. J. 1993. Macaque V1 neurons can signal 'illusory' contours. *Nature*, 365:550–552.

Grossman, A. 1992. *Endocrinology*, 3rd ed. Blackwell, London.

Grunt, J. A., and Young, W. C. 1953. Consistency of sexual behavior patterns in individual male guinea pigs following castration and androgen therapy. *Journal of Comparative and Physiological Psychology*, 46:138–144.

Grunt, J. A., and Young, W. C. 1953. Consistency of sexual behavior patterns in individual male guinea pigs following castration and androgen therapy. *Journal of Comparative and Physiological Psychology*, 46:138–144.

Guedry, F. E. Jr., Benson, A. J., and Moore, H. J. 1982. Influence of a visual display and frequency of whole-body angular oscillation on incidence of motion sickness. *Aviation Space and Environmental Medicine*, 53:564–569.

Gulevich, G., Dement, W., and Johnson, L. 1966. Psychiatric and EEG observations on a case of prolonged (264 hours) wakefulness. *Archives of General Psychiatry*, 15:29–35.

Gunston, G. D., Burkimsher, D., Malan, H., and Sive, A. A. 1992. Reversible cerebral shrinkage in kwashiorkor: An MRI study. *Archives of Disease in Childhood*, 67:1030–1032.

Gur, R. E. 1979. Cognitive concomitants of hemispheric dysfunction in schizophrenia. *Archives of General Psychiatry*, 36: 269–274.

Gur, R. E., Resnick, S. M., Alavi, A., Gur, R. C., Caroff, S., Dann, R., Silver, F. L., Saykin, A. J., Chawluk, J. B., Kushner, M. et al. 1987. Regional brain function in schizophrenia. I. A positron emission tomography study. *Archives of General Psychiatry*, 44:119–125.

Gurney, M. E., and Konishi, M. 1979. Hormone induced sexual differentiation of brain and behavior in zebra finches. *Science*, 208:1380–1382.

Gurney, M. E., Pu, H., Chiu, A. Y., Dal Canto, M. C., Polchow, C. Y., Alexander, D. D., Caliendo, J., Hentati, A., Kwon, Y. W., Deng, H. X. et al. 1994. Motor neuron degeneration in mice that express a human Cu,Zn superoxide dismutase mutation. *Science*, 264:1772–1775.

Gusella, J. F., and MacDonald, M. E. 1993. Hunting for Huntington's disease. *Molecular Genetic Medicine*, 3:139–158.

Hadley, M. E. 1992. *Endocrinology*, 3rd ed. Prentice-Hall, Englewood Cliffs, NJ.

Hager, J. 1982. Asymmetries in facial expression. In P. Ekman (ed.), *Emotion in the human face*, pp. 318–352. Cambridge University Press, New York.

Hagger, C., and Bachevalier, J. 1991. Visual habit formation in 3-month-old monkeys (*Macaca mulatta*): Reversal of sex difference following neonatal manipulations of androgens. *Behavioural Brain Research*, 45:57–63.

Haglund, Y., and Bergstrand, G. 1990. Does Swedish amateur boxing lead to chronic brain damage? 2. A retrospective study with CT and MRI. *Acta Neurologica Scandinavica*, 82:297–302.

Haglund, Y., and Persson, H. E. 1990. Does Swedish amateur boxing lead to chronic brain damage? 3. A retrospective clinical neurophysiological study. *Acta Neurologica Scandinavica*, 82:353–360.

Halaas, J. L., Gajiwala, K. S., Maffei, M., Cohen, S. L., Chait, B. T., Rabinowitz, D., Lallone, R. L., Burley, S. K., and Friedman, J. M. 1995. Weight-reducing effects of the plasma protein encoded by the obese gene. *Science*, 269:543–546.

Halgren, E., and Chauvel, P. 1993. Experiential phenomena evoked by human brain electrical stimulation. In O. Devinsky, A. Beric, and M. Dogali (eds.), *Electrical and magnetic stimulation of the brain and spinal cord*, pp. 123–140. Raven, New York.

Hall, J. C., and Greenspan, R. J. 1979. Genetic analysis of *Drosophila* neurobiology. *Annual Review of Genetics*, 13:127–195.

Hall, W. G., and Oppenheim, R. W. 1987. Developmental psychobiology: Prenatal, perinatal, and early postnatal aspects of behavioral development. *Annual Review of Psychology*, 38:91–128.

Hall, Z. 1992. *An introduction to molecular neurobiology.* Sinauer Associates, Sunderland, MA.

Halpern, D. F. 1986. A different answer to the question, "Do sex-related differences in spatial abilities exist?" *American Psychologist*, 41:1014–1015.

Hamburger, V. 1958. Regression versus peripheral control of differentiation in motor hypoplasia. *American Journal of Anatomy*, 102:365–410.

Hamburger, V. 1975. Cell death in the development of the lateral motor column of the chick embryo. *Journal of Comparative Neurology*, 160:535–546.

Hamer, D. H., Hu, S., Magnuson, V. L., Hu, N., and Pattatucci, A. M. 1993. A linkage between DNA markers on the X chromosome and male sexual orientation. *Science*, 261:321–327.

Hammond, P. 1974. Cat retinal ganglion cells: Size and shape of receptive field centres. *Journal of Physiology*, 242:99–118.

Haracz, J. L. 1984. A neural plasticity hypothesis of schizophrenia. *Neuroscience and Biobehavioral Reviews*, 8:55–73.

Hardyck C., Petrinovich, L., and Goldman R. 1976. Left-handedness and cognitive deficit. *Cortex*, 12:226–279.

Hare, E. 1988. Schizophrenia as a recent disease. *British Journal of Psychiatry*, 153:521–531.

Harris, E. W., and Cotman, C. W. 1986. Long-term potentiation of guinea pig mossy fiber responses is not blocked by N-methyl D-aspartate antagonists. *Neuroscience Letters*, 70:132–137.

Harris, R. M., and Woolsey, T. A. 1983. Computer-assisted analyses of barrel neuron axons and their putative synaptic contacts. *Journal of Comparative Neurology*, 220:63–79.

Hartmann, E. 1973. Sleep requirement: Long sleepers, short sleepers, variable sleepers, and insomniacs. *Psychosomatics*, 14:95–103.

Hartmann, E. 1978. *The sleeping pill.* Yale University Press, New Haven, CT.

Hartmann, E. 1984. *The nightmare: The psychology and biology of terrifying dreams.* Basic Books, New York.

Harvey, P. H., and Krebs, J. R. 1990. Comparing brains. *Science*, 249:140–146.

Hasher, L., and Zacks, R. T. 1979. Automatic and effortful processes in memory. *Journal of Experimental Psychology: General*, 108:356–388.

Haskett, R. F. 1985. Diagnostic categorization of psychiatric disturbance in Cushing's syndrome. *American Journal of Psychiatry*, 142:911–916.

Hatten, M. E. 1990. Riding the glial monorail: A common mechanism for glial-guided neuronal migration in different regions of the developing mammalian brain. *Trends in Neurosciences*, 13:179–184.

Hatten, M. E., and Heintz, N. 1995. Mechanisms of neural patterning and specification in the developing cerebellum. *Annual Review of Neuroscience*, 18:385–408.

Hauser, P., Zametkin, A. J., Martinez, P., Vitiello, B., Matochik, J. A., Mixson, A. J., and Weintraub, B. D. 1993. Attention deficit–hyperactivity disorder in people with generalized resistance to thyroid hormone. *New England Journal of Medicine*, 328:997–1001.

Hawkins, R. D., Abrams, T. W., Carew, T. J., and Kandel, E. R. 1983. A cellular mechanism of classical conditioning in *Aplysia*: Activity-dependent amplification of presynaptic facilitation. *Science*, 219:400–405.

Hawkins, R. D., Cohen, T. E., and Kandel, E. R. 1992. Motor neuron correlates of dishabituation and sensitization of the gill-withdrawal reflex in *Aplysia*. *Society for Neuroscience Abstracts*, 18:360.

Healy, S. D., and Krebs, J. R. 1993. Development of hippocampal specialisation in a food-storing bird. *Behavioural Brain Research*, 53:127–130.

Heath, R. G. 1972. Pleasure and brain activity in man. *Journal of Nervous and Mental Diseases*, 154:3–18.

Heath, R. G., Franklin, D. E., and Shraberg, D. 1979. Gross pathology of the cerebellum in patients diagnosed and treated as functional psychiatric disorders. *Journal of Nervous and Mental Disorders*, 167:585–592.

Hebb, D. O. 1949. *The organization of behavior*. Wiley, New York.

Heffner, H. E., and Heffner, R. S. 1986. Effect of unilateral and bilateral auditory cortex lesions on the discrimination of vocalizations by Japanese macaques. *Journal of Neurophysiology*, 56:683–701.

Heffner, H. E., and Heffner, R. S. 1989. Unilateral auditory cortex ablation in macaques results in a contralateral hearing loss. *Journal of Neurophysiology*, 62:789–801.

Hefti, F., and Mash, D. C. 1989. Localization of nerve growth factor receptors in the normal human brain and in Alzheimer's disease. *Neurobiology of Aging*, 10:75–87.

Hefti, F., and Weiner, W. J. 1986. Nerve growth factor and Alzheimer's disease. *Annals of Neurology*, 20:275–281.

Heilman, K. M., and Watson, R. T. 1983. Performance on hemispatial pointing task by patients with neglect syndrome. *Neurology*, 33:661–664.

Heinrich, B. 1981. The regulation of temperature in the honeybee swarm. *Scientific American*, 244:146–160.

Heisenberg, M., Heusipp, M., and Wanke, C. 1995. Structural plasticity in the *Drosophila* brain. *Journal of Neuroscience*, 15:1951–1960.

Heiss, W. D., Kessler, J., Karbe, H., Fink, G. R., and Pawlik, G. 1993. Cerebral glucose metabolism as a predictor of recovery from aphasia in ischemic stroke. *Archives of Neurology*, 50:958–964.

Heldmaier, G., and Ruf, T. 1992. Body temperature and metabolic rate during natural hypothermia in endotherms. *Journal of Comparative Physiology. B: Biochemical, Systemic and Environmental Physiology*, 162:696–706.

Helmholtz, H. L. F. von 1852. *Ueber die Theorie des zusammengesetzten Farben*. Berlin.

Helzer, J. E. 1987. Epidemiology of alcoholism. *Journal of Consulting and Clinical Psychology*, 55:284–292.

Hemmingsen, A. M. 1960. Energy metabolism as related to body size and respiratory surfaces, and its evolution. *Reports of Steno Memorial Hospital, Copenhagen*, 9:1–110.

Hendrickson, A. 1985. Dots, stripes and columns in monkey visual cortex. *Trends in Neurosciences*, 8:406–410.

Hennessy, M. B., Mendoza, S. P., Mason, W. A., Moberg, G. P. et al. 1995. Endocrine sensitivity to novelty in squirrel monkeys and titi monkeys: Species differences in characteristic modes of responding to the environment. *Physiology & Behavior*, 57:331–338.

Hetherington, A. W., and Ranson, S. W. 1940. Hypothalamic lesions and adiposity in the rat. *Anatomical Record*, 78:149–172.

Hewes, G. 1973. Primate communication and the gestural origin of language. *Current Anthropology*, 14:5–24.

Hietala, J., Syvalahti, E., Vuorio, K., Nagren, K., Lehikoinen, P., Ruotsalainen, U., Rakkolainen, V., Lehtinen, V., and Wegelius, U. 1994. Striatal D2 dopamine receptor characteristics in neuroleptic-naive schizophrenic patients studied with positron emission tomography. *Archives of General Psychiatry*, 51:116–123.

Higley, J. D., Mehlman, P. T., Taub, D. M., Higley, S. B., Suomi, S. J., Vickers, J. H., and Linnoila, M. 1992. Cerebrospinal fluid monoamine and adrenal correlates of aggression in free-ranging rhesus monkeys. *Archives of General Psychiatry*, 49:436–441.

Hille, B. 1992. *Ionic channels of excitable membranes*, 2nd ed. Sinauer Associates, Sunderland, MA.

Hillis, D. M., Moritz, C., and Mable, B. K. 1996. *Molecular systematics*, 2nd ed. Sinauer Associates, Sunderland, MA.

Hilts, P. J. 1995. *Memory's ghost: The strange tale of Mr. M. and the nature of memory*. Simon & Schuster, New York.

Hindler, C. G. 1989. Epilepsy and violence. *British Journal of Psychiatry*, 155:246–9.

Hingson, R., Alpert, J., Day, N., Dooling, E., Kayne, H., Morelock, S., Oppenheimer, E., and Zuckerman, B. 1982. Effects of maternal drinking and marijuana use on fetal growth and development. *Pediatrics*, 70:539–546.

Hirsch, H. V. B., and Spinelli, D. N. 1971. Modification of the distribution of receptive field orientation in cats by selective visual exposure during development. *Experimental Brain Research*, 12:509–527.

Hobson, J. A., and McCarley, R. W. 1977. The brain as a dream state generator: An activation-synthesis hypothesis of the dream process. *American Journal of Psychiatry*, 134:1335–1348.

Hochberg, F. H., and LeMay, M. 1975. Arteriographic correlates of handedness. *Neurology*, 25:218–222.

Hochstein, S., and Shapley, R. M. 1976. Quantitative analysis of retinal ganglion cell classifications. *Journal of Physiology*, 252:237–264.

Hodgkin, A. L., and Huxley, A. F. 1952. A quantitative description of membrane current and its application to conduction and excitation in nerve. *Journal of Physiology (London)*, 117:500–544.

Hodgkin, A. L., and Katz, B. 1949. The effect of sodium ions on the electrical activity of the giant axon of the squid. *Journal of Physiology (London)*, 108:37–77.

Hoffman, K. P., and Stone, J. 1971. Conduction velocity of afferents to cat visual cortex: A correlation with cortical receptive field properties. *Brain Research*, 32:460–466.

Hohman, G. W. 1966. Some effects of spinal cord lesions on experienced emotional feelings. *Psychophysiology*, 3:143–156.

Holcomb, H. H., Links, J., Smith, C., and Wong, D. 1989. Positron emission tomography: Measuring the metabolic and neurochemical characteristics of the living human nervous system. In N. C. Andreasen (ed.), *Brain imaging: Applications in psychiatry*, pp. 235–370. American Psychiatric Press, Washington, D.C.

Hollis, J. R., Connett, J. E., Stevens, V. J., and Greenlick, M. R. 1990. Stressful life events, Type A behavior, and the prediction of cardiovascular and total mortality over six years. MRFIT Group. *Journal of Behavioral Medicine*, 13:263–280.

Horai, S., Hayasaka, K., Kondo, R., Tsugane, K., and Takahata, N. 1995. Recent African origin of modern humans revealed by complete sequences of hominoid mitochondrial DNAs. *Proceedings of the National Academy of Sciences, U.S.A.*, 92:532–536.

Horne, J. A. 1981. The effects of exercise upon sleep: A critical review. *Biological Psychology*, 12:241–290.

Horne, J. A. 1986. Sleep function, with particular reference to sleep deprivation. *Annals of Clinical Research*, 17:199–208.

Huang, Y. Y., and Kandel, E. R. 1994. Recruitment of long-lasting and protein kinase A–dependent long-term potentiations in the CA1 region of the hippocampus requires repeated tetanization. *Learning and Memory*, 1:74–82.

Hubbard, A. 1993. A traveling-wave amplifier model of the cochlea. *Science*, 259:68–71.

Hubel, D. H., and Wiesel, T. N. 1959. Receptive fields of single neurones in the cat's striate cortex. *Journal of Physiology (London)*, 148:573–591.

Hubel, D. H., and Wiesel, T. N. 1965. Binocular interaction in striate cortex kittens reared with artificial squint. *Journal of Neurophysiology*, 28:1041–1059.

Hubel, D. H., and Wiesel, T. N. 1979. Brain mechanisms of vision. *Scientific American*, 241(3):150–168.

Hubel, D. H., Wiesel, T. N., and LeVay, S. 1977. Plasticity of ocular dominance in monkey striate cortex. *Philosophical Transactions of the Royal Society (London) Ser. B*, 278:377–409.

Huber, K. M., Mauk, M. D., and Kelly, P. T. 1995. Distinct LTP induction mechanisms: Contribution of NMDA receptors and voltage-dependent calcium channels. *Journal of Neurophysiology*, 73:270–279.

Hudspeth, A. J. 1989. How the ear's works work. *Nature*, 341:397–404.

Hudspeth, A. J. 1992. Hair-bundle mechanics and a model for mechano-electrical transduction by hair cells. *Society of General Physiologists Series*, 47:357–370.

Hughes, J., Smith, T. W., Kosterlitz, H. W., Fothergill, L. A., Morgan, B. A., and Morris, H. R. 1975. Identification of two related pentapeptides from the brain with potent opiate agonist activity. *Nature*, 258:577–579.

Humphrey, N. K. 1974. Vision in a monkey without striate cortex: A case study. *Perception*, 3:241–255.

Huntington, G. 1872. On chorea. *Medical and Surgical Reporter*, 26:317–321.

Huttenlocher, P. R., deCourten, C., Garey, L. J., and Van der Loos, H. 1982. Synaptogenesis in the human visual cortex—evidence for synapse elimination during normal development. *Neuroscience Letters*, 33:247–252.

Hyde, T. M., Aaronson, B. A., Randolph, C., Rickler, K. C., and Weinberger, D. R. 1992. Relationship of birth weight to the phenotypic expression of Gilles de la Tourette's syndrome in monozygotic twins. *Neurology*, 42:652–658.

Hyde, T. M., and Weinberger, D. R. 1990. The brain in schizophrenia. *Seminars in Neurology*, 10:276–286.

Idzikowski, C. 1984. Sleep and memory. *British Journal of Psychology*, 75:439–449.

Ignarro, L. J. 1991. Signal transduction mechanisms involving nitric oxide. *Biochemical Pharmacology*, 41:485–490.

Imperato-McGinley, J., Guerrero, L., Gautier, T., and Peterson, R. E. 1974. Steroid 5 α-reductase deficiency in man: An inherited form of male pseudohermaphroditism. *Science*, 86:1213–1215.

Ingram, D. K. 1985. Analysis of age-related impairments in learning and memory in rodent models. *Annals of the New York Academy of Sciences*, 444:312–331.

Insel, T. R. 1992. Toward a neuroanatomy of obsessive–compulsive disorder. *Archives of General Psychiatry*, 49:739–744.

Institute for Health Policy, Brandeis University. 1993. *Substance abuse: The nation's number one health problem*. Institute for Health Policy, Brandeis University, Waltham, MA.

Institute of Medicine, Committee on a National Neural Circuitry Database. 1991. *Mapping the brain and its functions: Integrating enabling technologies into neuroscience research*. National Academy Press, Washington, D.C.

Institute of Medicine. 1990. *Broadening the base of treatment for alcohol problems*. National Academy Press, Washington, D.C.

Isaacson, R. L. 1972. Hippocampal destruction in man and other animals. *Neuropsychologia*, 10:47–64.

Ito, J., Sakakibara, J., Iwasaki, Y., and Yonekura, Y. 1993. Positron emission tomography of auditory sensation in deaf patients and patients with cochlear implants. *Annals of Otology, Rhinology and Laryngology*, 102:797–801.

Ito, M. 1987. Cerebellar adaptive function in altered vestibular and visual environments. *Physiologist*, 30:S81.

Ivry, R. 1993. Cerebellar involvement in the explicit representation of temporal information. *Annals of the New York Academy of Sciences*, 682:214–230.

Iwamura, Y., and Tanaka, M. 1978. Postcentral neurons in hand region of area 2: Their possible role in the form discrimination of tactile objects. *Brain Research*, 150:662–666.

Jablensky, A., Sartorius, N., Ernberg, G., Anker, M., Korten, A., Cooper, J. E., Day, R., and Bertelsen, A. 1992. Schizophrenia: Manifestations, incidence and course in different cultures. A World Health Organization ten-country study. *Psychological Medicine (Monograph Supplement)*, 20:1–97.

Jackson, H., and Parks, T. N. 1982. Functional synapse elimination in the developing avian cochlear nucleus with simultaneous reduction in cochlear nerve axon branching. *Journal of Neuroscience*, 2:1736–1743.

Jacobs, G. H. 1984. Within-species variations in visual capacity among squirrel monkeys (*Saimiri sciureus*): Color vision. *Vision Research*, 24:1267–1277.

Jacobs, G. H. 1993. The distribution and nature of colour vision among the mammals. *Biological Reviews of the Cambridge Philosophical Society*, 68:413–471.

Jacobs, G. H., and Neitz, J. 1987. Inheritance of color vision in a New World monkey (*Saimiri sciureus*). *Proceedings of the National Academy of Sciences, U.S.A.*, 84:2545–2549.

Jacobs, G. H., Neitz, J., and Neitz, M. 1993. Genetic basis of polymorphism in the color vision of platyrrhine monkeys. *Vision Research*, 33:269–274.

Jacobs, L. F., and Spencer, W. D. 1994. Natural space-use patterns and hippocampal size in kangaroo rats. *Brain, Behavior & Evolution*, 44:125–132.

Jacobs, L. F., Gaulin, S. J., Sherry, D. F., and Hoffman, G. E. 1990. Evolution of spatial cognition: Sex-specific patterns of spatial behavior predict hippocampal size. *Proceedings of the National Academy of Sciences, U.S.A.*, 87:6349–6352.

Jacobson, M. 1991. *Developmental neurobiology*. Plenum Press, New York.

James, W. 1890. *Principles of psychology*. Holt, New York.

Jellies, J. A. 1981. *Associative olfactory conditioning in* Drosophila melanogaster *and memory retention through metamorphosis*. Unpublished master's thesis, Illinois State University, Normal, IL.

Jenike, M. A., Baer, L., Ballantine, T., Martuza, R. L., Tynes, S., Giriunas, I., Buttolph, M. L., and Cassem, N. H. 1991. Cingulotomy for refractory obsessive–compulsive disorder. A long-term follow-up of 33 patients.

Archives of General Psychiatry, 48: 548–555.

Jenkins, J., and Dallenbach, K. 1924. Oblivescence during sleep and waking. *American Journal of Psychology*, 35:605–612.

Jenkins, W. M., Merzenich, M. M., Ochs, M. T., Allard, T., and Guic-Robles, E. 1990. Functional reorganization of primary somatosensory cortex in adult owl monkeys after behaviorally controlled tactile stimulation. *Journal of Neurophysiology*, 63:82–104.

Jenkinson, D. H., and Nicholls, J. G. 1961. Contractures and permeability changes produced by acetylcholine in depolarized denervated muscle. *Journal of Physiology (London)*, 159:111–127.

Jensen, C. 1979. Learning performance in mice genetically selected for brain weight: Problems of generality. In M. E. Hahn, C. Jensen, and B. C. Dudek (eds.), *Development and evolution of brain size*. Academic Press, New York.

Jerison, H. J. 1985. Animal intelligence as encephalization. *Philosophical Transactions of the Royal Society (London)*, Series B, 308:21–35.

Jerison, H. J. 1991. *Brain size and the evolution of mind*. American Museum of Natural History, New York.

Jernigan, T. L., and Bellugi, U. 1990. Anomalous brain morphology on magnetic resonance images in Williams syndrome and Down syndrome. *Archives of Neurology*, 47:529–533.

Jernigan, T. L., Trauner, D. A., Hesselink, J. R., and Tallal, R. A. 1991. Maturation of human cerebrum observed *in vivo* during adolescence. *Brain*, 114:2037–1049.

Jessell, T. M., and Dodd, J. 1990. Floor plate-derived signals and the control of neural cell pattern in vertebrates. *Harvey Lectures*, 86:87–128.

Johannsen, L., Wecke, J., Obal, F., Jr., and Krueger, J. M. 1991. Macrophages produce somnogenic and pyrogenic muramyl peptides during digestion of *staphylococci*. *American Journal of Physiology*, 260:R126–R133.

Johanson, C. E., and Schuster, C. R. 1995. Cocaine. In F. E. Bloom, and D. J. Kupfer (eds.), *Psychopharmacology, the fourth generation of progress*, pp. 1685–1697. Raven, New York.

Johnson, E. M., Jr., and Deckwerth, T. L. 1993. Molecular mechanisms of developmental neuronal death. *Annual Review of Neuroscience*, 16:31–46.

Johnson, K. O., Hsiao, S. S., and Twombly, I. A. 1995. Neural mechanisms of tactile form recognition. In M. S. Gazzaniga (ed.), *The cognitive neurosciences*, pp. 253–267. MIT Press, Cambridge, MA.

Johnson, L. C. 1969. Psychological and physiological changes following total sleep deprivation. In A. Kales

(ed.), *Sleep: Physiology and pathology*. Lippincott, Philadelphia.

Johnson, P. L., and Stellar, J. R. 1994. Effects of accumbens DALA microinjections on brain stimulation reward and behavioral activation in intact and 6–OHDA treated rats. *Psychopharmacology*, 114:665–671.

Jones, K. E., Lyons, M., Bawa, P., and Lemon, R. N. 1994. Recruitment order of motoneurons during functional tasks. *Experimental Brain Research*, 100:503–508.

Jordan, B. D., Jahre, C., Hauser, W. A., Zimmerman, R. D., Zarrelli, M., Lipsitz, E. C., Johnson, V., Warren, R. F., Tsairis, P., and Folk, F. S. 1992. CT of 338 active professional boxers. *Radiology*, 185:509–512.

Jordan, C. L., Breedlove, S. M., and Arnold, A. P. 1991. Ontogeny of steroid accumulation in spinal lumbar motoneurons of the rat: Implications for androgen's site of action during synapse elimination. *Journal of Comparative Neurology*, 313: 441–448.

Jordan, C. L., Letinsky, M. S., and Arnold, A. P. 1988. Synapse elimination occurs late in the hormone-sensitive levator ani muscle of the rat. *Journal of Neurobiology*, 19:335–356.

Jouvet, M. 1967. Neurophysiology of the states of sleep. In G. C. Quarton, T. Melnechuk, and F. O. Schmitt (eds.), *The neurosciences*, pp. 529–544. Rockefeller University, New York.

Jouvet, M. 1972. *Neurophysiology and neurochemistry of sleep and wakefulness*. Springer, Berlin.

Julian, T., and McKenry, P. C. 1979. Relationship of testosterone to men's family functioning at mid-life: A research note. *Aggressive Behavior*, 15:281–289.

Julien, R. J. 1992. *A primer of drug action*, 6th ed. W. H. Freeman, New York.

Jurgens, U. 1990. Vocal communication in primates. In R. P. Kesner, and D. S. Olton (eds.), *Neurobiology of comparative cognition. Comparative cognition and neuroscience*, pp. 51–76. Lawrence Erlbaum Associates, Hillsdale, NJ.

Kaada, B. 1967. Brain mechanisms related to aggressive behavior. In C. D. Clemente, and D. B. Lindsley (eds.), *Aggression and defense*. University of California, Berkeley.

Kaas, J. H. 1991. Plasticity of sensory and motor maps in adult mammals. *Annual Review of Neuroscience*, 14: 137–167.

Kaas, J. H. 1995. The plasticity of sensory representations in adult primates. In J. L. McGaugh, N. M. Weinberger, and G. Lynch (eds.), *Brain and memory: Modulation and mediation of neuroplasticity*, pp. 206–221. Oxford University Press, New York.

Kaas, J. H., Nelson, R. J., Sur, M., Lin, C. S., and Merzenich, M. M. 1979. Multiple representations of the body within the primary somatosensory cortex of primates. *Science*, 204: 521–523.

Kaczmarek, K. A., Webster, J. G., Bach-y-Rita, P., and Tompkins, W. J. 1991. Electrotactile and vibrotactile displays for sensory substitution systems. *IEEE Transactions on Biomedical Engineering*, 38:1–16.

Kadekaro, M., Cohen, S., Terrell, M. L., Lekan, H., Gary, H., Jr., and Eisenberg, H. M. 1989. Independent activation of subfornical organ and hypothalamo–neurohypophysial system during administration of angiotensin II. *Peptides*, 10:423–429.

Kales, A. 1973. Treating sleep disorders. *American Family Physician*, 8:158–168.

Kales, A., and Kales, J. 1970. Evaluation, diagnosis and treatment of clinical conditions related to sleep. *Journal of the American Medical Association*, 213:2229–2235.

Kales, A., and Kales, J. D. 1974. Sleep disorders. Recent findings in the diagnosis and treatment of disturbed sleep. *New England Journal of Medicine*, 290:487–499.

Kalil, K., and Reh, T. 1979. Regrowth of severed axons in the neonatal central nervous system: Establishment of normal connections. *Science*, 205:1158–1161.

Kalin, N. H., Dawson, G., Tariot, P., Shelton, S., Barksdale, C., Weiler, S., and Thienemann, M. 1987. Function of the adrenal cortex in patients with major depression. *Psychiatry Research*, 22:117–125.

Kalivas, P. W., Sorg, B. A., and Hooks, M. S. 1993. The pharmacology and neural circuitry of sensitization to psychostimulants. *Behavioral Pharmacology*, 4:315–334.

Kamil, A. C. 1994. A synthetic approach to the study of animal intelligence. In L. A. Real (ed.), *Behavioral mechanisms in evolutionary ecology*, pp. 11–45. University of Chicago Press, Chicago.

Kamin, L. J. 1968. Attention-like processes in classical conditioning. In M. R. Jones (ed.), *Miami symposium on the prediction of behavior: Aversive stimulation*. University of Miami Press, Miami.

Kamin, L. J. 1969. Predictability, surprise, attention, and conditioning. In R. Church, and B. Campbell (eds.), *Punishment and aversive behavior*. Appleton Century Crofts, New York.

Kandel, E. R. 1976. *Cellular basis of behavior*. W. H. Freeman, San Francisco.

Kandel, E. R., Castellucci, V. F., Goelet, P., and Schacher, S. 1987. Cell-biological interrelationships between short-term and long-term memory. *Research Publications, Association for Re-*

search in Nervous and Mental Disease, 65:111–132.

Kandel, E. R., Schacher, S., Castellucci, V. F., and Goelet, P. 1986. The long and short of memory in *Aplysia*: A molecular perspective. *Fidia Research Foundation Neuroscience Award Lectures,* pp. 7–47.

Kandel, E. R., Schwartz, J. H., and Jessell, T. M. 1991. *Principles of neural science,* 3rd ed. Elsevier, New York.

Kanof, P., and Greengard, P. 1978. Brain histamine receptors as targets for antidepressant drugs. *Nature,* 272:329–333.

Karni, A., Tanne, D., Rubenstein, B. S., Askenasy, J. J., and Sagi, D. 1994. Dependence on REM sleep of overnight improvement of a perceptual skill. *Science,* 265:679–682.

Kauffman, G. L., Zhang, L., Xing, L. P., Seaton, J., and Colony, P., Demers, L. 1990. Central neurotensin protects the mucosa by a prostaglandin-mediated mechanism and inhibits gastric acid secretion in the rat. *Annals of the New York Academy of Sciences,* 597:175–190.

Kaufmann, C. A., Jeste, D. V., Shelton, R. C., Linnoila, M., Kafka, M. S., and Wyatt, R. J. 1986. Noradrenergic and neuroradiological abnormalities in tardive dyskinesia. *Biological Psychiatry,* 21:799–812.

Kaushall, P. I., Zetin, M., and Squire, L. R. 1981. A psychosocial study of chronic, circumscribed amnesia. *Journal of Nervous and Mental Disease,* 169(6):383–389.

Keele, S. W., and Summers, J. J. 1976. The structure of motor programs. In G. E. Stelmach (ed.), *Motor control: Issues and trends.* Academic Press, New York.

Keesey, R. E. 1980. A set-point analysis of the regulation of body weight. In A. J. Stunkard (ed.), *Obesity.* Saunders, Philadelphia.

Keesey, R. E., and Boyle, P. C. 1973. Effects of quinine adulteration upon body weight of LH-lesioned and intact male rats. *Journal of Comparative and Physiological Psychology,* 84: 38–46.

Keesey, R. E., and Corbett, S. W. 1984. Metabolic defense of the body weight set-point. *Research Publications, Association for Research in Nervous and Mental Disease,* 62:87–96.

Keesey, R. E., and Powley, T. L. 1986. The regulation of body weight. *Annual Review of Psychology,* 37:109–133.

Kelche, C., Dalrymple-Alford, J. C., and Will, B. 1988. Housing conditions modulate the effects of intracerebral grafts in rats with brain lesions. *Behavioural Brain Research,* 28:287–295.

Kelche, C., Roeser, C., Jeltsch, H., Cassel, J. C., and Will, B. 1995. The effects of intrahippocampal grafts, training, and postoperative housing on behavioral recovery after septohippocampal damage in the rat. *Neuro-*

biology of Learning and Memory, 63:155–166.

Kemali, D., Galderisi, M. S., Ariano, M. G., Cesarelli, M., Milici, N., Salvati, A., Valente, A., and Volpe, M. 1985. Clinical and neuropsychological correlates of cerebral ventricular enlargement in schizophrenia. *Journal of Psychiatric Research,* 19:587–596.

Kemp, D. T. 1978. Stimulated acoustic emissions from within the human auditory system. *Journal of the Acoustical Society of America,* 64:1386–1391.

Kemp, D. T. 1979. The evoked cochlear mechanical responses and the auditory microstructure—Evidence for a new element in cochlear mechanics. *Scandinavian Audiology Supplement,* 9:35–47.

Kendler, K. S. 1983. Overview: A current perspective on twin studies of schizophrenia. *American Journal of Psychiatry,* 140:1413–1425.

Kendler, K. S., and Robinette, C. D. 1983. Schizophrenia in the National Academy of Sciences-National Research Council Twin Registry: A 16 year update. *American Journal of Psychiatry,* 140:1551–1563.

Kendler, K. S., Ochs, A. L., Gorman, A. M., Hewitt, J. K., Ross, D. E., and Mirsky, A. F. 1991a. The structure of schizotypy: A pilot multitrait twin study. *Psychiatry Research,* 36:19–36.

Kendler, K. S., Silberg, J. L., Neale, M. C., Kessler, R. C., Heath, A. C., and Eaves, L. J. 1991b. The family history method: Whose psychiatric history is measured? *American Journal of Psychiatry,* 148:1501–1504.

Kennedy, T. E., Hawkins, R. D., and Kandel, E. R. 1992. Molecular interrelationships between short- and long-term memory. In L. R. Squire, and N. Butters (eds.), *Neuropsychology of memory* 2nd ed., pp. 557–574. Guilford Press, New York.

Kertesz, A. 1979. Recovery and treatment. In K. M. Heilman, and E. Valenstein (eds.), *Clinical neuropsychology.* Oxford, New York.

Kesner, R. P. 1980. An attribute analysis of memory: The role of the hippocampus. *Physiological Psychology,* 8:189–197.

Kesner, R. P. 1991. Neurobiological views of memory. In J. L. Martinez, and R. P. Kesner (eds.), *Learning and memory: A biological view,* 2nd ed., pp. 499–547. Academic Press, New York.

Kesner, R. P., and Novak, J. M. 1982. Serial position curve in rats: Role of the dorsal hippocampus. *Science,* 218:173–175.

Kesner, R. P., and Williams, J. M. Personal communication. Memory for magnitude of reinforcement: Dissociation between the amygdala and hippocampus.

Kesner, R. P., Bolland, B. L., and Dakis, M. 1993. Memory for spatial locations,

motor responses, and objects: Triple dissociation among the hippocampus, caudate nucleus, and extrastriate visual cortex. *Experimental Brain Research,* 93:462– 470.

Kesner, R. P., DiMattia B. V., and Crutcher, K. A. 1987. Evidence for neocortical involvement in reference memory. *Behavioral and Neural Biology,* 47:40–53.

Kessler, R. C., McGonagle, K. A., Zhao, S., Nelson, C. B., Hughes, M., Eshleman, S., Wittchen, H. U., and Kendler, K. S. 1994. Lifetime and 12-month prevalence of DSM-III-R psychiatric disorders in the United States. Results from the National Comorbidity Survey. *Archives of General Psychiatry,* 51:8–19.

Kety, S. 1976. Biological concomitants of affective states and their possible role in memory processes. In M. R. Rosenzweig, and E. L. Bennett (eds.), *Neural mechanisms of learning and memory,* pp. 321–326. MIT Press, Cambridge, MA.

Kety, S. 1983. Mental illness in the biological and adoptive families of schizophrenic adoptees: Findings relevant to genetic and environmental factors in etiology. *American Journal of Psychiatry,* 140:720–727.

Kety, S. S., Wender, P. H., Jacobsen, B., Ingraham, L. J., Jansson, L., Faber, B., and Kinney, D. K. 1994. Mental illness in the biological and adoptive relatives of schizophrenic adoptees. Replication of the Copenhagen Study in the rest of Denmark. *Archives of General Psychiatry,* 51:442–455.

Kety, S., Rosenthal, D., Wender, P. H., Schulsinger, F., and Jacobsen, B. 1975. Mental illness in the biological and adoptive families of adopted individuals who have become schizophrenic. A preliminary report based on psychiatric interviews. In R. R. Fieve, D. Rosenthal, and H. Brill (eds.), *Genetic research in psychiatry.* Johns Hopkins University, Baltimore.

Keynes, R. J., and Cook, G. M. 1992. Repellent cues in axon guidance. *Current Opinion in Neurobiology,* 2:55–59.

Keys, A., Brozek, J., Henschel, A., Mickelsen, O., and Taylor, H. L. 1950. *The biology of human starvation.* University of Minnesota, Minneapolis.

Kiang, N. Y. -S. 1965. *Discharge patterns of single fibers in the cat's auditory nerve.* MIT Press, Cambridge, MA.

Kiecolt-Glaser, J. K., and Glaser, R. 1995. Psychoneuroimmunology and health consequences: Data and shared mechanisms. *Psychosomatic Medicine,* 57:269–274.

Killiany, R. J., Moss, M. B., Albert, M. S., Sandor, T., Tieman, J., and Jolesz, F. 1993. Temporal lobe regions on magnetic resonance imaging identify patients with early Alzheimer's disease. *Archives of Neurology*, 50:949–954.

Kim, J. J., and Fanselow, M. S. 1992. Modality-specific retrograde amnesia of fear. *Science*, 256:675–677.

Kimelberg, H. K., and Norenberg, M. D. 1989. Astrocytes. *Scientific American*, 260:66–76.

Kimura, D. 1973. The asymmetry of the human brain. *Scientific American*, 360–368.

Kimura, M., Majde, J. A., Toth, L. A., Opp, M. R., and Krueger, J. M. 1994. Somnogenic effects of rabbit and recombinant human interferons in rabbits. *American Journal of Physiology*, 267:R53–R61.

Kinnamon, S. C., and Cummings, T. A. 1992. Chemosensory transduction mechanisms in taste. *Annual Review of Physiology*, 54:715–731.

Kinney, D. K., Woods, B. T., and Yurgelun-Todd, D. 1986. Neurologic abnormalities in schizophrenic patients and their families. II. Neurologic and psychiatric findings in relatives. *Archives of General Psychiatry*, 43:665–668.

Kinsey, A. C., Pomeroy, W. B., and Martin, C. E. 1948. *Sexual behavior in the human male*. Saunders, Philadelphia.

Kinsey, A. C., Pomeroy, W. B., Martin, C. E., and Gebbard, P. H. 1953. *Sexual behavior in the human female*. Saunders, Philadelphia.

Klaassen, C. D., Amdur, M. O., and Doull, J. 1986. *Casarett and Doull's toxicology*, 3rd ed. Macmillan, New York.

Kleiber, M. 1947. Body size and metabolic rate. *Physiological Reviews*, 15:511–541.

Klein, M., Shapiro, E., and Kandel, E. R. 1980. Synaptic plasticity and the modulation of the Ca^{++} current. *Journal of Experimental Biology*, 89:117–157.

Kleitman, N. 1969. Basic rest–activity cycle in relation to sleep and wakefulness. In A. Kales (ed.), *Sleep: Physiology and pathology*. Lippincott, Philadelphia.

Kleitman, N., and Engelmann, T. G. 1953. Sleep characteristics of infants. *Journal of Applied Physiology*, 6:269–282.

Kleitman, N., and Engelmann, T. G. 1953. Sleep characteristics of infants. *Journal of Applied Physiology*, 6:269–282.

Klima, E. S., and Bellugi, U. 1979. *The signs of language*. Harvard University Press, Cambridge, MA.

Kluckhohn, C. 1949. *Mirror for man*. Whittlesey House, New York.

Kluger, M. J. 1979. *Fever, its biology, evolution and function*. Princeton University Press, Princeton, NJ.

Kluger, M. J. 1986. Is fever beneficial? *Yale Journal of Biology and Medicine*, 59:89–95.

Klüver, H., and Bucy, P. C. 1938. An analysis of certain effects of bilateral temporal lobectomy in the rhesus monkey, with special reference to "psychic blindness." *Journal of Psychology*, 5:33–54

Knibestol, M., and Valbo, A. B. 1970. Single unit analysis of mechanoreceptor activity from the human glabrous skin. *Acta Physiologica Scandinavica*, 80:178–195.

Knobil, E., and Hotchkiss, J. 1985. The circhoral gonadotropic releasing hormone (GnRH) pulse generator of the hypothalamus and its physiological significance. In H. Schulz, and P. Lavie (eds.), *Ultradian rhythms in physiology and behavior*, pp. 32–41. Springer-Verlag, Berlin.

Knudsen, E. I. 1982. Auditory and visual maps of space in the optic tectum of the owl. *Journal of Neuroscience*, 2:1177–1194.

Knudsen, E. I. 1984a. Auditory properties of space-tuned units in owl's optic tectum. *Journal of Neurophysiology*, 52:709–723.

Knudsen, E. I. 1984b. The role of auditory experience in the development and maintenance of sound localization. *Trends in Neurosciences*, 7:326–330.

Knudsen, E. I. 1985. Experience alters the spatial tuning of auditory units in the optic tectum during a sensitive period in the barn owl. *Journal of Neuroscience*, 5:3094–3109.

Knudsen, E. I., and Knudsen, P. F. 1986. The sensitive period for auditory localization in barn owls is limited by age, not by experience. *Journal of Neuroscience*, 6:1918–1924.

Knudsen, E. I., and Konishi, M. 1978. A neural map of auditory space in the owl. *Science*, 200:795–797.

Knudsen, E. I., Knudsen, P. F., and Esterly, S. D. 1984. A critical period for the recovery of sound localization accuracy following monaural occlusion in the barn owl. *Journal of Neuroscience*, 4:1012–1020.

Knudsen, E., and Knudsen, P. 1985. Vision guides adjustment of auditory localization in young barn owls. *Science*, 230:545–548.

Kobatake, E., and Tanaka, K. 1994. Neuronal selectivities to complex object features in the ventral visual pathway of the macaque cerebral cortex. *Journal of Neurophysiology*, 71:856–867.

Kobilka, B. 1992. Adrenergic receptors as models for G protein-coupled receptors. *Annual Review of Neuroscience*, 15:87–114.

Koella, W. P. 1985. Serotonin and sleep. In W. P. Koella, E. Ruther, and H. Schulz (eds.), *Sleep '84*, pp. 6–10. Fischer Verlag, Stuttgart.

Kolb, B., and Whishaw, I. Q. 1990. *Fundamentals of human neuropsychology*. W. II. Freeman, San Francisco.

Koliatsos, V. E., Crawford, T. O., and Price, D. L. 1991. Axotomy induces nerve growth factor receptor immunoreactivity in spinal motor neurons. *Brain Research*, 549:297–304.

Kölmel, H. W. 1988. Pure homonymous hemiachromatopsia. Findings with neuro-ophthalmologic examination and imaging procedures. *European Archives of Psychiatry and Neurological Sciences*, 237: 237–243.

Kolodny, E. H., and Cable, W. J. L. 1982. Inborn errors of metabolism. *Annals of Neurology*, 11:221–232.

Kolodny, E. H., and Cable, W. J. L. 1982. Inborn errors of metabolism. *Annals of Neurology*, 11:221–232.

Konishi, M. 1985. Birdsong: From behavior to neuron. *Annual Review of Neuroscience*, 8:125–171.

Konopka, R. J., and Benzer, S. 1971. Clock mutants of *Drosophila melanogaster*. *Proceedings of the National Academy of Sciences, U.S.A.*, 68:2112–2116.

Koob, G. F. 1995. Animal models of drug addiction. In F. E. Bloom, and D. J. Kupfer (eds.), *Psychopharmacology, the fourth generation of progress*, pp. 759–772. Raven, New York.

Koob, G. F., Sandman, C. A., and Strand, F. L. 1990. *A decade of neuropeptides: Past, present, and future*. New York Academy of Sciences, New York.

Kopin, I. J., and Markey, S. P. 1988. MPTP toxicity: Implications for research in Parkinson's disease. *Annual Review of Neuroscience*, 11:81–96.

Korenman, S. G., and Barchas, J. D. 1993. *Biological basis of substance abuse*. Oxford University Press, New York.

Korol, D. L., Abel, T. W., Church, L. T., Barnes, C. A., and McNaughton, B. L. 1993. Hippocampal synaptic enhancement and spatial learning in the Morris swim task. *Hippocampus*, 3:127–132.

Kosslyn, S. M., and Koenig, O. 1992. *Wet mind: The new cognitive neuroscience*. Maxwell Macmillan International, New York.

Kosslyn, S. M., Chabris, C. F., Marsolek, C. J., and Koenig, O. 1992. Categorical versus coordinate spatial relations: Computational analyses and computer simulations. *Journal of Experimental Psychology: Human Perception and Performance*, 18:562–577.

Kovelman, J. A., and Scheibel, A. B. 1984. A neurohistological correlate of schizophrenia. *Biological Psychiatry*, 19:1601.

Kraepelin, E. 1919. *Dementia praecox and paraphrenia*. Livingstone, Edinburgh.

Krasne, F. B., and Glanzman, D. L. 1995. What we can learn from invertebrate learning. *Annual Review of Psychology*, 45:585–624.

Kraut, R. E., and Johnston, R. E. 1979. Social and emotional messages of smiling: An ethological approach. *Journal of Personality & Social Psychology*, 37:1539–1553.

Krebs, J. R., Sherry, D. F., Healy, S. D., Perry, V. H., and Vaccarino, A. L. 1989.

Hippocampal specialisation of food–storing birds. *Proceedings of the National Academy of Sciences, U.S.A,* 86:1388–1392.

Kreuz, L. E., and Rose, R. M. 1972. Assessment of aggressive behavior and plasma testosterone in a young criminal population. *Psychosomatic Medicine,* 34:321–332.

Krueger, J. M., and Majde, J. A. 1995. Cytokines and sleep. *International Archives of Allergy and Immunology,* 106:97–100.

Krueger, J. M., Walter, J., Dinarello, C. A., Wolff, S. M., and Chedid, L. 1984. Sleep-promoting effects of endogenous pyrogen (interleukin-1). *American Journal of Physiology,* 2246:R994–R999.

Kruesi, M. J. 1979. Cruelty to animals and CSF 5HIAA. *Psychiatry Research,* 28:115–116.

Krug, M., Lossner, B., and Ott, T. 1984. Anisomycin blocks the late phase of long-term potentiation in the dentate gyrus of freely moving rat. *Brain Research Bulletin,* 13:39–42.

Kruger, J. M., Walter, J., Dinarello, C. A., Wolff, S. M., and Chedid, L. 1984. Sleep–promoting effects of endogenous pyrogen (interleukin–1). *American Journal of Physiology,* 2246:R994–R999.

Krupa, D. J., Thompson, J. K., and Thompson, R. F. 1993. Localization of a memory trace in the mammalian brain. *Science,* 260:989–991.

Kruuk, H. 1975. *Hyaena.* Oxford University Press, London.

Kryger, M. H., Roth, T., and Dement, W. C. 1989. *Principles and practice of sleep medicine.* W. B. Saunders, New York.

Krystal, A., Krishnan, K. R., Raitiere, M., Poland, R., Ritchie, J. C., Dunnick, N. R., Hanada, K., and Nemeroff, C. B. 1990. Differential diagnosis and pathophysiology of Cushing's syndrome and primary affective disorder. *Journal of Neuropsychiatry and Clinical Neurosciences,* 2:34–43.

Kubanis, P., and Zornetzer, S. F. 1981. Age-related behavioral and neurobiological changes: a review with emphasis of memory. *Behavioral and Neural Biology,* 31:115–172.

Kuffler, S. W. 1953. Discharge patterns and functional organization of mammalian retina. *Journal of Neurophysiology,* 16:37–68.

Kuljis, R. O., and Rakic, P. 1990. Hypercolumns in primate visual cortex can develop in the absence of cues from photoreceptors. *Proceedings of the National Academy of Sciences, U.S.A.,* 87:5303–5306.

Kupfermann, I. T., Carew, T. J., and Kandel, E. R. 1974. Local, reflex, and central commands controlling gill and siphon movements in *Aplysia. Journal of Neurophysiology,* 37:996–1019.

Labbe, R., Firl, A., Mufson, E. J., and Stein, D. G. 1983. Fetal brain transplants: Reduction of cognitive deficits in rats with frontal cortex lesions. *Science,* 221:470–472.

LaCerra, M. M., and Ettenberg, A. 1984. A comparison of the rewarding properties of "free" versus "earned" amphetamine. *Society for Neuroscience Abstracts,* 10:1207.

Lacey, J. I., and Lacey, B. C. 1970. Some autonomic-central nervous system interrelationships. In P. Black (ed.), *Physiological correlates of emotion.* Academic Press, New York.

Lachman, H. M., Papolos, D. F., Boyle, A., Sheftel G., Juthani, M., Edwards, E., and Henn, F. A. 1993. Alterations in glucocorticoid inducible RNAs in the limbic system of learned helpless rats. *Brain Research,* 609:110–116.

Lack, D. 1968. *Ecological adaptations for breeding in birds.* Methuen, London.

Lack, D.1968. Ecological adaptations for breeding in birds. Methuen, London.

Lackner, J. R., and Shenker, B. 1985. Proprioceptive influences on auditory and visual spatial localization. *Journal of Neuroscience,* 5:579–584.

Lader, M. 1991. Animal models of anxiety: A clinical perspective. In P. Willner (ed.), *Behavioural models in psychopharmacology: Theoretical, industrial and clinical perspectives,* pp. 76–88. Cambridge University Press, Cambridge, England.

Land, M. F. 1984. Crustacea. In M. A. Ali (ed.), *Photoreception and vision in invertebrates,* pp. 401–438. Plenum, New York.

Land, M. F., and Fernald, R. D. 1992. The evolution of eyes. *Annual Review of Neuroscience,* 15:1–29.

Landau, B., and Levy, R. M. 1993. Neuromodulation techniques for medically refractory chronic pain. *Annual Review of Medicine,* 44:279–287.

Landmesser, L., and Pilar, G. 1974. Synaptic transmission and cell death during normal ganglionic development. *Journal of Physiology (London),* 241:737–749.

Landry, D. W., Zhao, K., Yang, G. X.-Q., Glickman, M., and Georgiadis, T. M. 1993. Antibody-catalyzed degradation of cocaine. *Science,* 259: 1899–1901.

Lange, C. S. 1887. Ueber Gemuthsbewegungen. Translated into English in W. James, and C. G. Lange (eds.), *The emotions,* pp. 33–90. Williams & Wilkins, Baltimore.

Lange, C. S. 1922. Ueber Gemüthsbewegungen. Translated into English in W. James, and C. G. Lange (eds.), *The emotions,* pp. 33–90. Williams & Wilkins, Baltimore.

Langlais, P. J., Mandel, R. J., and Mair, R. G. 1992. Diencephalic lesions, learning impairments, and intact retrograde memory following acute thi-

amine deficiency in the rat. *Behavioural Brain Research,* 48:177–185.

Langston, J. W. 1985. MPTP and Parkinson's disease. *Trends in Neurosciences,* 8:79–83.

Lanska, D. J., and Lanska, M. J. 1994. Kluver-Bucy syndrome in juvenile neuronal ceroid lipofuscinosis. *Journal of Child Neurology,* 9:67–69.

Larroche, J. C. 1966. The development of the central nervous system during intrauterine life. In F. Faulkner (ed.), *Human development.* Saunders, Philadelphia.

Lashley, K. S. 1950. In search of the engram. *Symposium for the Society of Experimental Biology,* 4:454–482.

Lashley, K. S., and Clark, G. 1946. The cytoarchitecture of the cerebral cortex of *Ateles:* A critical examination of architectonic studies. *Journal of Comparative Neurology,* 85:223–306.

Laufer, R., and Changeux, J. P. 1989. Activity-dependent regulation of gene expression in muscle and neuronal cells. *Molecular Neurobiology,* 3:1–53.

Lavie, P., and Kripke, D. F. 1981. Ultradian circa 1 1/2 hour rhythms: A multioscillatory system. *Life Sciences,* 29:2445–2450.

Lavond, D. G., Kim, J. J., and Thompson, R. F. 1993. Mammalian brain substrates of aversive classical conditioning. *Annual Review of Psychology,* 44:317–342.

Lawrence, G. W., Weller, U., and Dolly, J. O. 1994. Botulinum A and the light chain of tetanus toxins inhibit distinct stages of Mg.ATP-dependent catecholamine exocytosis from permeabilised chromaffin cells. *European Journal of Biochemistry,* 222:325–333.

Laxova, R. 1994. Fragile X syndrome. *Advances in Pediatrics,* 41: 305–342.

Le Magnen, P. 1991. *Neurobiology of feeding.* Academic Press, New York.

Leber, S. M., Breedlove, S. M., and Sanes, J. R. 1990. Lineage, arrangement, and death of clonally related motoneurons in chick spinal cord. *Journal of Neuroscience,* 10:2451–2462.

Lebrun, C. J., Blume, A., Herdegen, T., Seifert, K., Bravo, R., and Unger, T. 1995. Angiotensin II induces a complex activation of transcription factors in the rat brain: Expression of Fos, Jun and Krox proteins. *Neuroscience,* 65:93–99.

LeDoux, E. 1995. Emotion: Clues from the brain. *Annual Review of Psychology,* 46:209–235.

LeDoux, J. E. 1994. Emotion, memory, and the brain. *Scientific American,* 270:50–57.

Lee, K. S., Schottler, F., Oliver, M., and Lynch, G. 1980. Brief bursts of high-frequency stimulation produce two types of structural change in rat hippocampus. *Journal of Neurophysiology,* 44:247–258.

Lee, T. M., Carmichael, M. S., and Zucker, I. 1986. Circannual variations in circadian rhythms of ground squirrels. *American Journal of Physiology*, 250:831–836.

Lefebvre, P. P., Malgrange, B., Staecker, H., Moonen, G., and Van de Water, T. R. 1993. Retinoic acid stimulates regeneration of mammalian auditory hair cells. *Science*, 260:692–695.

Lehrman, D. S. 1964. The reproductive behavior of ring doves. *Scientific American*.

Leibel, R. L., and Hirsch, J. 1984. Diminished energy requirements in reduced-obese patients. *Metabolism*, 33:164–170.

Leibowitz, S. F. 1991. Brain neuropeptide Y: An integrator of endocrine, metabolic and behavioral processes. *Brain Research Bulletin*, 27:333–337.

LeMay, M. 1977. Asymmetries of the skull and handedness. *Journal of the Neurological Sciences*, 32:243–253.

LeMay, M., and Culebras, A. 1972. Human brain-morphologic differences in the hemispheres demonstrable by carotid angiography. *New England Journal of Medicine*, 287:168–170.

Lennartz, R. C., and Weinberger, N. M. 1992. Frequency selectivity is related to temporal processing in parallel thalamocortical auditory pathways. *Brain Research*, 583:81–92.

Lennie, P., Krauskopf, J., and Sclar, G. 1990. Chromatic mechanisms in striate cortex of macaque. *Journal of Neuroscience*, 10:649–669.

Leon, M., Croskerry, P. G., and Smith, G. K. 1978. Thermal control of mother–young contact in rats. *Physiology and Behavior*, 21:790–811.

Leonard, B. E. 1992. *Fundamentals of psychopharmacology*. Wiley, New York.

Leonard, J. L., Edstrom J., and Lukowiak, K. 1979. Reexamination of the gill withdrawal reflex of *Aplysia californica* Cooper (Gastropoda; Opisthobranchia). *Behavioral Neuroscience*, 103:585–604.

LeRoith, D., Shemer, J., and Roberts, C. T., Jr. 1992. Evolutionary origins of intercellular communication systems: Implications for mammalian biology. *Hormone Research*, 38:1–6.

LeRoith, D., Shiloach, J., and Roth, J. 1982. Is there an earlier phylogenetic precursor that is common to both the nervous and endocrine systems? *Peptides*, 3:211–215.

Lester, B. M., Anderson, L. T., Boukydis, C. F., Garcia-Coll, C. T., Vohr, B., and Peucker, M. 1989. Early detection of infants at risk for later handicap through acoustic cry analysis. *Birth Defects Original Article Series*, 25:99–118.

LeVay, S. 1991. A difference in hypothalamic structure between heterosexual and homosexual men. *Science*, 253:1034–1037.

LeVay, S. 1993. *The sexual brain*. MIT Press, Cambridge, MA.

Levenson, R. W., Ekman, P., and Friesen, W. V. 1990. Voluntary facial action generates emotion–specific autonomic nervous system activity. *Psychophysiology*, 27:363–384.

Leventhal, A. G. 1979. Evidence that the different classes of relay cells of the cat's lateral geniculate nucleus terminate in different layers of the striate cortex. *Experimental Brain Research*, 37:349–372.

Leventhal, A. G., Thompson, K. G., Liu, D., Zhou, Y., and Ault, S. J. 1995. Concomitant sensitivity to orientation, direction, and color of cells in layers 2, 3, and 4 of monkey striate cortex. *Journal of Neuroscience*, 15:1808–1818.

Leventhal, H., and Tomarken, A. J. 1986. Emotion: Today's problems. *Annual Review of Psychology*, 37:565–611.

Levi, L. 1965. The urinary output of adrenalin and noradrenalin during pleasant and unpleasant emotional states. *Psychosomatic Medicine*, 27:80.

Levi-Montalcini, R. 1963. In J. Allen (ed.), *The nature of biological diversity*. McGraw-Hill, New York.

Levi-Montalcini, R. 1964. Events in the developing nervous system. *Progress in Brain Research*, 4:1–29.

Levi-Montalcini, R. 1982. Developmental neurobiology and the natural history of nerve growth factor. *Annual Review of Neuroscience*, 5:341–362.

Levine, J. D., Gordon, N. C., and Fields, H. L. 1978. The mechanism of placebo analgesia. *Lancet*, 2:654–657.

Levine, J. S., and MacNichol, E. F. 1982. Color vision in fishes. *Scientific American*, 246:140–149.

Levine, S., and Ursin, H. 1980. *Coping and health*. Plenum, New York.

Levinthal, F., Macagno, E., and Levinthal, C. 1976. Anatomy and development of identified cells in isogenic organisms. *Cold Spring Harbor Symposium on Quantitative Biology*, 40:321–331.

Levit, P., Cooper, M. C., and Rakic, P. 1981. Coexistence of neural and glial precursor cells in the cerebral ventricular zone of the fetal monkey: An ultrastructural immunoperoxidase study. *Journal of Neuroscience*, 1:27–39.

Levitsky, W., and Geschwind, N. 1968. Asymmetries of the right and left hemisphere in man. *Transactions of the American Neurological Association*, 93:232–233.

Levy, D. L., Holzman, P. S., Matthysse, S., and Mendell, N. R. 1990. Eye tracking dysfunction and schizophrenia: A critical perspective. *Schizophrenia Bulletin*, 19:461–536.

Levy, J., and Reid, M. 1976. Variations in writing posture and cerebral organization. *Science*, 194:337–339.

Lewis, B. A., and Thompson, L. A. 1992. A study of developmental speech and language disorders in twins.

Journal of Speech and Hearing Research, 35:1086–1094.

Lewis, D. O. 1990. Neuropsychiatric and experiential correlates of violent juvenile delinquency. *Neuropsychology Review*, 1:125–136.

Lewis, D. O., Shankok, S. S., and Pincus, J. 1979. Juvenile male sexual assaulters. *American Journal of Psychiatry*, 136:1194–1195.

Lewis, M., and Haviland, J. M. 1993. *Handbook of emotions*. Guilford, New York.

Lewy, A. J., Ahmed, S., Jackson, J. M., and Sack, R. L. 1992. Melatonin shifts human circadian rhythms according to a phase-response curve. *Chronobiology International*, 9:380–392.

Ley, R. G., and Bryden, M. P. 1982. A dissociation of right and left hemispheric effects for recognizing emotional tone and verbal content. *Brain & Cognition*, 1:3–9.

Lhermitte, F., Chain, F., Escourolle, R., Ducarne, B., and Pillon, B. 1972. Anatomoclinical study of a case of prosopagnosia. *Revue Neurologique*, 126:329–346.

Lhermitte, F., Pillon, B., and Serdaru, M. 1986. Human autonomy and the frontal lobes. Part 1. Imitation and utilization behavior: A neuropsychological study of 75 patients. *Annals of Neurology*, 19:326–335.

Li, X. J., Li, S. H., Sharp, A. H., Nucifora, F. C. Jr., Schilling, G., Lanahan, A., Worley, P., Snyder, S. H., and Ross, C. A. 1995. A huntingtin-associated protein enriched in brain with implications for pathology. *Nature*, 378:398–406.

Licht, P., Frank, L. G., Pavgi, S., Yalcinkaya, T. M., Siiteri, P. K., and Glickman, S. E. 1992. Hormonal correlates of 'masculinization' in female spotted hyenas (*Crocuta crocuta*). 2. Maternal and fetal steroids. *Journal of Reproduction and Fertility*, 95:463–474.

Lichtman, J. W., and Purves, D. 1980. The elimination of redundant preganglionic innervation to hamster sympathetic ganglion cells in early postnatal life. *Journal of Physiology*, 301:213–228.

Lieberman, P. 1994. The origins and evolution of language. In T. Ingold (ed.), *Companion encyclopedia of anthropology*, pp. 108– 132. Routledge, London.

Liebowitz, M. R., Gorman, J. M., Fryer, A., Dillon, D., Levitt, M., and Klein, D. F. 1986. Possible mechanisms for lactate's induction of panic. *American Journal of Psychiatry*, 143:495–502.

Lieke, E. E., Frostig, R. D., Arieli, A., Ts'o, D. Y., Hildesheim, R., and Grinvald, A. 1989. Optical imaging of cortical activity: Real-time imaging using extrinsic dye-signals and high resolution imaging based on slow intrinsic-signals. *Annual Review of Physiology*, 51:543–559.

Lin, K. M., Poland, R. E., and Nakasaki, G. 1993. *Psychopharmacology and psychobiology of ethnicity*. American Psychiatric Press, Washington, D.C.

Lin, X. Y., and Glanzman, D. L. 1994. Long-term potentiation of *Aplysia* sensorimotor synapses in cell culture: Regulation by postsynaptic voltage. *Proceedings of the Royal Society (London), Series B*, 255:113–118.

Lindemann, B. 1995. Sweet and salty: Transduction in taste. *News in Physiological Sciences*, 10:166–170.

Linden, D. J. 1994. Long-term synaptic depression in the mammalian brain. *Neuron*, 12:457–472.

Linder, M. E., and Gilman, A. G. 1992. G proteins. *Scientific American*, 267(1):56–65.

Lindvall, O., Sawle, G., Widner, H., Rothwell, J. C., Bjorklund, A., Brooks, D., Brundin, P., Frackowiak, R., Marsden, C. D., Odin, P. et al. 1994. Evidence for long-term survival and function of dopaminergic grafts in progressive Parkinson's disease. *Annals of Neurology*, 35:172–180.

Lisman, J. 1989. A mechanism for the Hebb and the anti-Hebb processes underlying learning and memory. *Proceedings of the National Academy of Sciences, U.S.A.*, 86:9574–9578.

Liu, C. N., and Chambers, W. W. 1958. Intraspinal sprouting of dorsal root axons. *Archives of Neurology and Psychiatry*, 79:46–61.

Livingstone, M. S., and Hubel, D. 1984. Anatomy and physiology of a color system in the primate visual cortex. *Journal of Neuroscience*, 4:309–356.

Livingstone, M. S., and Hubel, D. 1988. Segregation of form, color, movement, and depth: Anatomy, physiology, and perception. *Science*, 240:740–749.

Lloyd, J. A. 1971. Weights of testes, thymi, and accessory reproductive glands in relation to rank in paired and grouped house mice (*Mus musculus*). *Proceedings of the Society for Experimental Biology and Medicine*, 137:19–22.

Lockhart, M., and Moore, J. W. 1975. Classical differential and operant conditioning in rabbits (*Orycytolagus cuniculus*) with septal lesions. *Journal of Comparative and Physiological Psychology*, 88:147–154.

Loeb, G. E. 1985. The functional replacement of the ear. *Scientific American*, 252:104–111.

Loeb, G. E. 1990. Cochlear prosthetics. *Annual Review of Neuroscience*, 13:357–371.

Loehlin, J. C., Willerman, L., and Horn, J. M. 1988. Human behavior genetics. *Annual Review of Psychology*, 39:101–133.

Loewenstein, W. R. 1971. Mechano-electric transduction in the Pacinian cor-

puscle. Initiation of sensory impulses in mechanoreception. In *Handbook of sensory physiology, Vol. 1*, pp. 269–290. Springer-Verlag, Berlin.

Logan, C. G., and Grafton, S. T. 1995. Functional anatomy of human eyeblink conditioning determined with regional cerebral glucose metabolism and positron emission tomography. *Proceedings of the National Academy of Sciences, U.S.A.*, 92:7500–7504.

Lowel, S., and Singer, W. 1992. Selection of intrinsic horizontal connections in the visual cortex by correlated neuronal activity. *Science*, 255:209–212.

Luchins, D. J., Cohen, D., Hanrahan, P., Eisdorfer, C., Paveza, G., Ashford, J. W., Gorelick, P., Hirschman, R., Freels, S., Levy, P. et al. 1992. Are there clinical differences between familial and nonfamilial Alzheimer's disease? *American Journal of Psychiatry*, 149:1023–1027.

Lundeberg, T. C. 1983. Vibratory stimulation for the alleviation of chronic pain. *Acta Physiologica Scandinavica (Supplementum)*, 523:1–51.

Luria, A. R. 1987. *The mind of a mnemonist*. Harvard University Press, Cambridge, MA.

Lush, I. E. 1989. The genetics of tasting in mice. VI. Saccharin, acesulfame, dulcin and sucrose. *Genetical Research*, 53:95–99.

Lynch, G., and Baudry, M. 1984. The biochemistry of memory: A new and specific hypothesis. *Science* 224: 1057–1063.

Lynch, G., Larson, J., Staubli, U., and Granger, R. 1991. Variants of synaptic potentiation and different types of memory operations in hippocampus and related structures. In L. R. Squire, N. M. Weinberger, G. Lynch, and J. L. McGaugh (eds.), *Memory: Organization and locus of change*, pp. 330–363. Oxford University Press, New York.

Lynch, M. A., Errington, M. L., and Bliss, T. V. 1989. Nordihydroguaiaretic acid blocks the synaptic component of long-term potentiation and the associated increases in release of glutamate and arachidonate: An *in vivo* study in the dentate gyrus of the rat. *Neuroscience*, 30:693–701.

Macagno, E., Lopresti, U., and Levinthal, C. 1973. Structural development of neuronal connections in isogenic organisms: Variations and similarities in the optic system of *Daphnia magna*. *Proceedings of the National Academy of Sciences, U.S.A.*, 70:57–61.

Macchi, G., Rustioni, A., and Spreafico, R. 1983. *Somatosensory integration in the thalamus: A reevaluation based on the new methodological approaches*. Elsevier, Amsterdam.

Mace, G. M., Harvey, P. H., and Clutton-Brock, T. H. 1981. Brain size and

ecology in small mammals. *Journal of Zoology*, 193:333–354.

MacLean, P. D. 1970. The triune brain, emotion, and scientific bias. In F. O. Schmitt (ed.), *The neurosciences*, pp. 336–348. Rockefeller University, New York.

MacLean, P. D. 1990. *The triune brain in evolution: role in paleocerebral functions*. Plenum Press, New York.

Macphail, E. 1985. Ecology and intelligence. In N. M. Weinberger, J. L. McGaugh, and G. Lynch (eds.), *Memory systems of the brain: Animal and human cognitive processes*, pp. 279–286. Guilford, New York.

Madrazo, I., Franco-Bourland, R., Ostrosky-Solis, F., Aguilera, M., Cuevas, C., Zamorano, C., Morelos, A., Magallon, E., and Guizar-Sahagun, G. 1990. Fetal homotransplants (ventral mesencephalon and adrenal tissue) to the striatum of parkinsonian subjects. *Archives of Neurology*, 47:1281–1285.

Maffei, L., and Fiorentini, A. 1973. The visual cortex as a spatial frequency analyser. *Vision Research*, 13: 1255–1267.

Magnusson, A., and Axelsson, J. 1993. The prevalence of seasonal affective disorder is low among descendants of Icelandic emigrants in Canada. *Archives of General Psychiatry*, 50:947–951.

Magnusson, A., and Stefansson, J. G. 1993. Prevalence of seasonal affective disorder in Iceland. *Archives of General Psychiatry*, 50:941–946.

Mair, W. G. P., Warrington, E. K., and Wieskrantz, L. 1979. Memory disorder in Korsakoff's psychosis. *Brain*, 102:749–783.

Malinow, R., and Tsien, R. W. 1990. Presynaptic enhancement shown by whole-cell recordings of long-term potentiation in hippocampal slices. *Nature*, 346:177–180.

Manetto, V., Medori, R., Cortelli, P., Montagna, P., Tinuper, P., Baruzzi, A., Rancurel, G., Hauw, J. J., Vanderhaeghen, J. J., Mailleux, P. et al. 1992. Fatal familial insomnia: Clinical and pathologic study of five new cases. *Neurology*, 42:312–319.

Manfredi, M., Bini, G., Cruccu, G., Accornero, N., Berardelli, A., and Medolago, L. 1981. Congenital absence of pain. *Archives of Neurology*, 38:507–511.

Maratsos, M., and Matheny, L. 1994. Language specificity and elasticity: Brain and clinical syndrome studies. *Annual Review of Psychology*, 45:487–516.

Margraf, J., and Roth, W. T. 1986. Sodium lactate infusions and panic attacks: A review and critique. *Psychosomatic Medicine*, 48:23–50.

Mariani, J., and Changeaux, J. P. 1981. Ontogenesis of olivocerebellar relationships. I. Studies by intracellular recordings of the multiple innervation of Purkinje cells by climbing fibers in the developing rat cerebellum. *Journal of Neuroscience*, 1:696–702.

Marin, R. S., and Tucker, G. J. 1981. Psychopathology and hemispheric dysfunction. *Journal of Nervous and Mental Disease*, 169:546–557.

Mark, R. F. 1980. Synaptic repression at neuromuscular junctions. *Physiological Reviews*, 60:355–395.

Mark, V. H., and Ervin, F. R. 1970. *Violence and the brain*. Harper & Row, New York.

Markin, V. S., and Hudspeth, A. J. 1995. Gating-spring models of mechano-electrical transduction by hair cells of the internal ear. *Annual Review of Biophysics and Biomolecular Structure*, 24:59–83.

Marlatt, G. A. 1992. Substance abuse: Implications of a biopsychological model for prevention, treatment, and relapse prevention. In J. Grabowski, and G. R. VandenBos (eds.), *Psychopharmacology: Basic mechanisms and applied interventions*, pp. 131–162. American Psychological Association, Washington, D.C.

Marler, P. 1991. Song-learning behavior: The interface with neuroethology. *Trends in Neurosciences*, 14:199–206.

Marler, P., and Peters, S. 1982. Developmental overproduction and selective attrition: New processes in the epigenesis of birdsong. *Developmental Psychobiology*, 15:369–378.

Marler, P., and Sherman, V. 1983. Song structure without auditory feedback: Emendations of the auditory template hypothesis. *Journal of Neuroscience*, 3:517–531.

Marler, P., and Sherman, V. 1985. Innate differences in singing behaviour of sparrows reared in isolation from adult conspecific song. *Animal Behavior*, 33:57–71.

Marler, P. 1970. Birdsong and speech development: Could there be parallels? *American Scientist*, 58:669–673.

Marsden, C. D., Rothwell, J. C., and Day, B. L. 1984. The use of peripheral feedback in the control of movement. *Trends in Neurosciences*, 7:253–257.

Marshall, J. F., Richardson, J. S., and Teitelbaum, P. 1974. Nigrostriatal bundle damage and the lateral hypothalamic syndrome. *Journal of Comparative and Physiological Psychology*, 87:800–830.

Martin, J. V., Wyatt, R. J., and Mendelson, W. B. 1985. Growth hormone secretion in sleep and waking. In W. P. Koella, E. Ruther, and H. Schulz (eds.), *Sleep '84*, pp. 185–188. Fischer Verlag, Stuttgart.

Martin, W. R., and Hayden, M. R. 1987. Cerebral glucose and dopa metabolism in movement disorders. *Canadi-*

an Journal of Neurological Sciences, 14:448–451.

Martinez, J. L., and Derrick, B. E. 1996. Long-term potentiation and learning. *Annual Review of Psychology*, 47:33.

Martinez, J. L., and Kesner, R. P. 1991. *Learning and memory: A biological view*, 2nd ed. Academic Press, New York.

Martuza, R. L., Chiocca, E. A., Jenike, M. A., Giriunas, I. E., and Ballantine, H. T. 1990. Stereotactic radiofrequency thermal cingulotomy for obsessive compulsive disorder. *Journal of Neuropsychiatry and Clinical Neurosciences*, 2:331–336.

Marx, J. 1992. Boring in on beta-amyloid's role in Alzheimer's. *Science*, 255: 688–689.

Marx, J. L. 1985. "Anxiety peptide" found in brain. *Science*, 227:934.

Masliah, E., Salmon, D. P., Butters, N., DeTeresa, R., Hill, R., Hansen, L. A., and Katzman, R. 1991. Physical basis of cognitive alterations in Alzheimer's disease: Synapse loss is the major correlate of cognitive impairment. *Annals of Neurology*, 30:572–580.

Mason, J. W. 1972. Organization of psychoendocrine mechanisms: A review and reconsideration of research. In N. S. Greenfield, and R. A. Sternbach (eds.), *Handbook of psychophysiology*. Holt, New York.

Masters, W. H., and Johnson, V. E. 1965. The sexual response cycles of the human male and female: Comparative anatomy and physiology. In F. A. Beach (ed.), *Sex and behavior*. Wiley, New York.

Masters, W. H., and Johnson, V. E. 1966. *Human sexual response*. Little, Brown, Boston.

Masters, W. H., and Johnson, V. E. 1970. *Human sexual inadequacy*. Little, Brown, Boston.

Masters, W. H., Johnson, V. E., and Kolodny, R. C. 1994. *Heterosexuality*. HarperCollins, New York.

Masterton, R. B. 1993. Central auditory system. *ORL: Journal of Oto-Rhino-Laryngology and Its Related Specialties*, 55:159–163.

Masterton, R. B., and Imig, T. J. 1984. Neural mechanisms for sound localization. *Annual Review of Physiology*, 46:275–287.

Mathias, R. 1994. NIDA, the FDA, and nicotine regulation. *NIDA Notes*, 9:5, 7.

Matsuda, L. A., Lolait, S. J., Brownstein, M. J., Young, A. C., and Bonner, T. I. 1990. Structure of a cannabinoid receptor and functional expression of the cloned cDNA. *Nature*, 346:561.

Matsumoto, A., and Ishii, S. 1992. *Atlas of endocrine organs*. Springer Verlag, Berlin.

Mazoyer, B. M., Tzourio, N., Frak, V., Syrota, A. et al. 1993. The cortical rep-

resentation of speech. *Journal of Cognitive Neuroscience*, 5:467–479.

McBurney, D. H., Smith, D. V., and Shick, T. R. 1972. Gustatory cross adaptation: Sourness and bitterness. *Perception & Psychophysics*, 11:2228–2232.

McCall, W. V., and Edinger, J. D. 1992. Subjective total insomnia: An example of sleep state misperception. *Sleep*, 15:71–73.

McClintock, M. K. 1971. Menstrual synchrony and suppression. *Nature*, 229:244–245.

McCormick, D. A., and Thompson, R. F. 1984. Cerebellum: Essential involvement in the classically conditioned eyelid response. *Science*, 223:296–299.

McDonald, R. J., and White, N. M. 1993. A triple dissociation of memory systems: Hippocampus, amygdala and dorsal striatum. *Behavioral Neuroscience*, 107:3–22.

McFadden, D. 1993a. A masculinizing effect on the auditory systems of human females having male co-twins. *Proceedings of the National Academy of Sciences, U.S.A.*, 90:11900–11904.

McFadden, D. 1993b. A speculation about the parallel ear asymmetries and sex differences in hearing sensitivity and otoacoustic emissions. *Hearing Research*, 68:143–151.

McFadden, D., and Champlin, C. A. 1990. Reductions in overshoot during aspirin use. *Journal of the Acoustical Society of America*, 87:2634–2642.

McFadden, D., and Mishra, R. 1993. On the relation between hearing sensitivity and otoacoustic emissions. *Hearing Research*, 71:208–213.

McFadden, D., and Pasanen, E. G. 1994. Otoacoustic emissions and quinine sulfate. *Journal of the Acoustical Society of America*, 96:3460–3474.

McGaugh, J. L. 1968. A multi-trace view of memory storage processes. In D. Bovet (ed.), *Attuali orientamenti della ricerca sull' apprendimento e la memoria*. Academia Nazionale dei Lincei, Rome.

McGaugh, J. L. 1983. Hormonal influences on memory. *Annual Review of Psychology*, 34:297–323.

McGaugh, J. L. 1992. Neuromodulatory systems and the regulation of memory storage. In L. R. Squire, and N. Butters (eds.), *Neuropsychology of memory*, 2nd ed., pp. 386–401. Guilford, New York.

McGaugh, J. L., and Herz, M. J. 1972. *Memory consolidation*. Albion, San Francisco.

McGaugh, J. L., Introini-Collison, I. B., Cahill, L. F., Castellano, C., Dalmaz, C., Parent, M. B., and Williams, C. L. 1993. Neuromodulatory systems and memory storage: Role of the amygdala. *Behavioural Brain Research*, 58:81–90.

McGaugh, J. L., Introini-Collison, E. B., Cahill, L., Kim, M., and Liang, K. C.

1992. Involvement of the amygdala in neuromodulatory influences on memory storage. In J. P. Aggleton (ed.), *The amygdala: Neurobiological aspects of emotion, memory, and mental dysfunction*, pp. 431–451. Wiley-Liss, New York.

McGaugh, J. L., Introini-Collison, I. B., Nagahara, A. H., Cahill, L. et al. 1990. Involvement of the amygdaloid complex in neuromodulatory influences on memory storage. *Neuroscience & Biobehavioral Reviews*, 14:425–431.

McGaugh, J. L., Weinberger, N. M., and Lynch, G. 1994. *Brain and memory: Modulation and mediation of neuroplasticity*. Oxford University Press, New York.

McGeer, P. L., McGeer, E. G., Suzuk, J., Dolman, C. E., and Nagai, T. 1984.Aging, Alzheimer's disease, and the cholinergic system of the basal forebrain. *Neurology*, 34:741–745.

McKim, W. A. 1991. *Drugs and behavior: An introduction to behavioral pharmacology*, 2nd ed. Prentice Hall, Englewood Cliffs, NJ.

McKinney, T. D., and Desjardins, C. 1973. Postnatal development of the testis, fighting behavior, and fertility in house mice. *Biology of Reproduction*, 9:279–294.

McKinney, W. T. 1988. *Models of mental disorders: A new comparative psychiatry*. Plenum, New York.

McLaughlin, S. K., McKinnon, P. J., Spickofsky, N., Danho, W., and Margolskee, R. F. 1994. Molecular cloning of G proteins and phosphodiesterases from rat taste cells. *Physiology and Behavior*, 56:1157–1164.

McMahon, H. T., Foran, P., Dolly, J. O., Verhage, M., Wiegant, V. M., and Nicholls, D. G. 1992. Tetanus toxin and botulinum toxins type A and B inhibit glutamate, gamma-aminobutyric acid, aspartate, and met-enkephalin release from synaptosomes. Clues to the locus of action. *Journal of Biological Chemistry*, 267:21338–21343.

McNamara, J. O. 1984. Role of neurotransmitters in seizure mechanisms in the kindling model of epilepsy. *Federation Proceedings*, 43:2516–2520.

McNaughton, B. L., and Morris, R. G. M. 1987. Hippocampal synaptic enhancement and information storage within a distributed memory system. *Trends in Neurosciences*, 10:408–415.

McNaughton, B. L., Barnes, C. A., Rao, G., Baldwin, J., and Rasmussen, M. 1986. Long-term enhancement of hippocampal synaptic transmission and the acquisition of spatial information. *Journal of Neuroscience*, 6:563–571.

Meckler, R. J., Mack, J. L., and Bennett, R. 1979. Sign language aphasia in a non-deaf mute. *Neurology*, 29:1037–1040.

Medawar, P. B. 1967. *The art of the soluble*. Methuen, London.

Meddis, R. 1975. On the function of sleep. *Animal Behavior*, 23:676–691.

Meddis, R. 1977. *The sleep instinct*. Routledge & Kegan Paul, London.

Meddis, R. 1979. The evolution and function of sleep. In D. A. Oakley, and H. C. Plotkin (eds.), *Brain, behavior and evolution*. Methuen, London.

Mednick, S. A., and Christiansen, K. D. 1977. *Biosocial bases of criminal behavior*. Gardner, New York.

Mednick, S. A., Huttunen, M. O., and Machon, R. A. 1994. Prenatal influenza infections and adult schizophrenia. *Schizophrenia Bulletin*, 20:263–267.

Medori, R., Montagna, P., Tritschler, H. J., LeBlanc, A., Cortelli, P., Tinuper, P., Lugaresi, E., and Gambetti, P. 1992. Fatal familial insomnia: A second kindred with mutation of prior protein gene at codon 178. *Neurology*, 42:669–670.

Mello, C. V., Vicario, D. S., and Clayton, D. F. 1992. Song presentation induces gene expression in the songbird forebrain. *Proceedings of the National Academy of Sciences, U.S.A.*, 89:6818–6822.

Melzack, R. 1984. Neuropsychological basis of pain measurement. *Advances in Pain Research*, 323–341.

Melzack, R. 1990. The tragedy of needless pain. *Scientific American*, 262:27–33.

Melzack, R., and Wall, P. D. 1965. Pain mechanisms: A new history. *Science*, 150:971–979.

Meredith, M. A., and Stein, B. E. 1983. Interactions among converging sensory inputs in the superior colliculus. *Science*, 221:389–391.

Merigan, W. H., and Maunsell, J. H. 1993. How parallel are the primate visual pathways? *Annual Review of Neuroscience*, 16:36–402.

Merrin, E. L. 1981. Schizophrenia and brain asymmetry. *Journal of Nervous and Mental Diseases*, 169:405–416.

Merzenich, M. M., and Jenkins, W. M. 1993. Reorganization of cortical representations of the hand following alterations of skin inputs induced by nerve injury, skin island transfers, and experience. *Journal of Hand Therapy*, 6:89–104.

Merzenich, M. M., and Kaas, J. H. 1980. Principles of organization of sensory-perceptual systems in mammals. In J. M. Sprague, and A. N. Epstein (eds.), *Progress in psychobiology and physiological psychology Vol. 9*. Academic Press, New York.

Merzenich, M. M., Schreiner, C., Jenkins, W., and Wang, X. 1993. Neural mechanisms underlying temporal integration, segmentation, and input sequence representation: some implications for the origin of learning disabilities. *Annals of the New York Academy of Sciences*, 682:1–22.

Mesulam, M. M. 1985. Attention, confusional states and neglect. In M. M. Mesulam (ed.), *Principles of behavioral neurology*. F. A. Davis, Philadelphia.

Mesulam, M. M. 1989. Behavioral neuroanatomy of cholinergic innervation in the primate cerebral cortex. *Exs*, 57:1–11.

Meyer-Bahlburg, H. F. L., and Ehrhardt, A. A. 1982. Prenatal sex hormones and human aggression: A review, and new data on progestogen effects. *Aggressive Behavior*, 8:39–62.

Miaskiewicz, S. L., Stricker, E. M., and Verbalis, J. G. 1989. Neurohypophyseal secretion in response to cholecystokinin but not meal-induced gastric distention in humans. *Journal of Clinical Endocrinology and Metabolism*, 68:837–843.

Middlebrooks, J. C., and Pettigrew, J. D. 1981. Functional classes of neurons in primary auditory cortex of the cat distinguished by sensitivity to sound location. *Journal of Neuroscience*, 1:107–120.

Mignot, E., Guilleminault, C., Bowersox, S., Frusthofer, B., Nishino, S., Maddaluno, J., Ciaranello, R., and Dement, W. C. 1989. Central alpha 1 adrenoceptor subtypes in narcolepsy-cataplexy: A disorder of REM sleep. *Brain Research*, 490:186–191.

Mignot, E., Nishino, S., Sharp, L. H., Arrigoni, J., Siegel, J. M., Reid, M. S., Edgar, D. M., Ciaranello, R. D., and Dement, W. C. 1993. Heterozygosity at the canarc-1 locus can confer susceptibility for narcolepsy: Induction of cataplexy in heterozygous asymptomatic dogs after administration of a combination of drugs acting on monoaminergic and cholinergic systems. *Journal of Neuroscience*, 13:1057–1064.

Mignot, E., Wang, C., Rattazzi, C., Gaiser, C., Lovett, M., Guilleminault, C., Dement, W. C., and Grumet, F. C. 1991. Genetic linkage of autosomal recessive canine narcolepsy with a *mu* immunoglobulin heavy-chain switch-like segment. *Proceedings of the National Academy of Sciences, U.S.A.*, 88:3475–3478.

Miles, L. E., and Dement, W. C. 1980. Sleep and aging. *Sleep*, 3:1–220.

Miller, I. J. Jr., and Reedy, F. E., Jr. 1990. Variations in human taste bud density and taste intensity perception. *Physiology and Behavior*, 47:1213–1219.

Miller, J. M., and Spelman, F. A. 1990. *Cochlear implants: Models of the electrically stimulated ear*. Springer-Verlag, New York.

Miller, N. E. 1979. Biomedical foundations for biofeedback. *Advances*, 6:30–36.

Milner, B. 1965. Memory disturbance after bilateral hippocampal lesions. In P. M. Milner, and S. E. Glickman (eds.), *Cognitive processes and the brain*. Van Nostrand, Princeton, NJ.

Milner, B. 1970. Memory and the medial temporal regions of the brain. In D. H. Pribram and D. E. Broadbent (eds.), *Biology of memory*. Academic Press, New York.

Milner, P. M. 1992. The functional nature of neuronal oscillations. *Trends in Neurosciences*, 15:387–388.

Milner, P. M. 1993. The mind and Donald O. Hebb. *Scientific American*, 268(1):124–129.

Mirmiran, M. 1986. The importance of fetal/neonatal REM sleep. *European Journal of Obstetrics Gynecology, and Reproductive Biology*, 21:283–291.

Mirsky, A. F., and Duncan, C. C. 1986. Etiology and expression of schizophrenia: Neurobiological and psychosocial factors. *Annual Review of Psychology*, 37:291–321.

Mirsky, A., DeLisi, L., Buchsbaum, M., Quinn, O., Schwerdt, P., Siever, L., Mann, L., Wingartner, H., Zec, R., Sostek, A., Alterman, I., Revere, V., Dawson, S., and Zahn, T. 1984. The Genain quadruplets: Psychological studies. *Psychiatry Research*, 13: 77–93.

Mishina, M., Kurosaki, T., Tobimatsu, T., Morimoto, Y., Noda, M., Yamamoto, T., Terao, M., Lindstrom, J., Takahashi, T., Kuno, M. et al. 1984. Expression of functional acetylcholine receptor from cloned cDNAs. *Nature*, 307:604–608.

Miyashita, Y. 1993. Inferior temporal cortex: Where visual perception meets memory. *Annual Review of Neuroscience*, 16:245–263.

Mizumori, S. J. Y., Rosenzweig, M. R., and Bennett, E. L. 1985. Long-term working memory in the rat: Effects of hippocampally applied anisomycin. *Behavioral Neuroscience*, 99:220–232.

Mlcoch, A. G., Bushnell, D. L., Gupta, S., and Milo, T. J. 1994. Speech fluency in aphasia. Regional cerebral blood flow correlates of recovery using single–photon emission computed tomography. *Journal of Neuroimaging*, 4:6–10.

Mohammed, A., Henriksson, B. G., Soderstrom, S., Ebendal, T., Olsson, T., and Sekl, J. R. 1993. Environmental influences on the central nervous system and their implications for the aging rat. *Behavioural Brain Research*, 23:182–191.

Mohler, C. W., and Wurtz, R. H. 1977. Role of striate cortex and superior colliculus is visual guidance of saccadic eye movements in monkeys. *Journal of Neurophysiology*, 40:74–94.

Moldin, S. O., Reich, T., and Rice, J. P. 1991. Current perspectives on the genetics of unipolar depression. *Behavior Genetics*, 21:211–242.

Monakow, C. 1914. *Die Lokalisation im Grosshirn und der Abbau der Funktion durch kortikale Herde.* J. F. Bergmann, Wiesbaden.

Moncada, S., Palmer, R. M., and Higgs, E. A. 1991. Nitric oxide: Physiology, pathophysiology, and pharmacology. *Pharmacological Reviews*, 43:109–142.

Money, J., and Ehrhardt, A. A. 1972. *Man and woman, boy and girl*. Johns Hopkins University, Baltimore.

Monti, J. M. 1987. Disturbances of sleep and wakefulness associated with the use of antihypertensive agents. *Life Sciences*, 41:1979–1988.

Monti-Bloch, L., Jennings-White, C., Dolberg, D. S., and Berliner, D. L. 1994. The human vomeronasal system. *Psychoneuroendocrinology*, 19:673–686.

Moore, C. L., Dou, H., and Juraska, J. M. 1992. Maternal stimulation affects the number of motor neurons in a sexually dimorphic nucleus of the lumbar spinal cord. *Brain Research*, 572:52–56.

Moore, R. Y. 1983. Organization and function of a central nervous system circadian oscillator: The suprachiasmatic nucleus. *Federation Proceedings*, 42:2783–2789.

Moore, R. Y., and Eichler, V. B. 1972. Loss of circadian adrenal corticosterone rhythm following suprachiasmatic lesions in the rat. *Brain Research*, 42:201–206.

Moore-Ede, M. C. 1982. *The clocks that time us: Physiology of the circadian timing system*. Harvard University Press, Cambridge, MA.

Moran, D. T., Jafek, B. W., and Rowley, J. C., III. 1991. The vomeronasal (Jacobson's) organ in man: Ultrastructure and frequency of occurrence. *Journal of Steroid Biochemistry and Molecular Biology*, 39:545–552.

Moran, E. F. 1981. Human adaptation to arctic zones. *Annual Review of Anthropology*, 10:1–25.

Morell, V. 1993. Enzyme may blunt cocaine's action. *Science*, 259:1928.

Morihisa, J., and McAnulty, G. B. 1985. Structure and function: Brain electrical activity mapping and computed tomography in schizophrenia. *Biological Psychiatry*, 20:3–19.

Morley, J. E. 1987. Neuropeptide regulation of appetite and weight. *Endocrine Reviews*, 8:256–287.

Morrell, F. 1991. The role of secondary epileptogenesis in human epilepsy. *Archives of Neurology*, 48:1221–1224.

Morris, R. G., Anderson, E., Lynch, G. S., and Baudry, M. 1986. Selective impairment of learning and blockage of long-term potentiation by an *N*-methyl-D-aspartate receptor antagonist, AP5. *Nature*, 319:774–776.

Morrison, A. R. 1983. A window on the sleeping brain. *Scientific American*, 248(4):94–102.

Moruzzi, G. 1972. The sleep–waking cycle. *Ergebnisse der Physiologie, Biologischen Chemie und Experimentellen Pharmakologie*, 64:1–165.

Moscovitch, M. 1985. Memory from infancy to old age: Implications for theories of normal and pathological memory. *Annals of the New York Academy of Sciences*, 444:78–96.

Moscovitch, M., and Olds, J. 1982. Asymmetries in spontaneous facial expressions and their possible relation to hemispheric specialization. *Neuropsychologia*, 20:71–81.

Moss, R. L., and Dudley, C. A. 1984. Molecular aspects of the interaction between estrogen and the membrane excitability of hypothalamic nerve cells. *Progress in Brain Research*, 61:3–22.

Mott, F. W. 1895. Experimental inquiry upon the afferent tracts of the central nervous system of the monkey. *Brain*, 18:1–20.

Mountcastle, V. B. 1979. An organizing principle for cerebral function: The unit module and the distributed system. In F. O. Schmitt, and F. G. Worden (eds.), *The neurosciences: Fourth study program*, pp. 21–42. MIT Press, Cambridge, MA.

Mountcastle, V. B. 1984. Central nervous mechanisms in mechanoreceptive sensibility. In I. Darian-Smith (ed.), *Handbook of physiology, Sec. 1, Vol. 3, Sensory Processes*, pp. 789–878. American Physiological Society, Bethesda, MD.

Mountcastle, V. B., Andersen, R. A., and Motter, B. C. 1981. The influence of attentive fixation upon the excitability of the light-sensitive neurons of the posterior parietal cortex. *Journal of Neuroscience*, 1:1218–1235.

Movshon, J. A., and van Sluyters, R. C. 1981. Visual neural development. *Annual Review of Psychology*, 32:477–522.

Moyer, J. R. Jr., Deyo, R. A., and Disterhoft, J. F. 1990. Hippocampectomy disrupts trace eye-blink conditioning in rabbits. *Behavioral Neuroscience*, 104:243–252.

Mpitsos, G. J., and Lukowiak, K. 1985. Learning in gastropod molluscs. In A. O. D. Willows (ed.), *The Molluscs. Vol. 8. Neurobiology and behavior*, pp 95–267. Academic Press, Orlando, Fla.

Mpitsos, G. J., Collins, S. D., and McClellan, A. D. 1978. Learning: A model system for physiological studies. *Science*, 199:497–506.

Mukhametov, L. M. 1984. Sleep in marine mammals. In A. Borbely, and J. L. Valatx (eds.), *Sleep mechanisms*. Springer-Verlag, Berlin.

Mulkey, R. M., Herron, C. E., and Malenka, R. C. 1993. An essential role for protein phosphatases in hippocampal long-term depression. *Science,* 261:1051–1055.

Murasugi, C. M., Salzman, C. D., and Newsome, W. T. 1993. Microstimulation in visual area MT: Effects of varying pulse amplitude and frequency. *Journal of Neuroscience,* 13:1719–1729.

Nadel, L., and Zola-Morgan, S. 1984. Infantile amnesia: a neurobiological perspective. In M. Moscovitch (ed.), *Infant memory,* pp. 145–172. Plenum Press, New York.

Naeser, M. A., and Hayward, R. W. 1978. Lesion localization in aphasia with cranial computed tomography and the Boston Diagnostic Aphasia Exam. *Neurology,* 28:545–551.

Natelson, B. H. 1985. Neurocardiology: An interdisciplinary area for the 80s. *Archives of Neurology,* 42:178–184.

Nathans, J. 1987. Molecular biology of visual pigments. *Annual Review of Neuroscience,* 10:163–194.

Nathans, J., and Hogness, D. S. 1984. Isolation and nucleotide sequence of the gene encoding human rhodopsin. *Proceedings of the National Academy of Sciences, U.S.A.,* 81:4852–4855.

Nathanson, J. A. 1984. Caffeine and related methylxanthines: Possible naturally occurring pesticides. *Science,* 226:184–187.

National Commission for the Protection of Human Subjects of Biomedical and Behavioral Research. 1978. *The Belmont report: Ethical principles and guidelines for the protection of human subjects of research.* U. S. Government Printing Office, Bethesda, MD.

National Research Council, Commission on Life Sciences. 1988. *Use of laboratory animals in biomedical and behavioral research.* National Academy Press, Washington, D.C.

National Research Council, Committee on Animals as Monitors of Environmental Hazards. 1991. *Animals as sentinels of environmental health hazards.* National Academy Press, Washington, D.C.

Neal, P. 1988. *As I am.* Simon and Schuster, New York.

Nee, L. E., Polinsky, R. J., Elbridge, R., Weingart, H., Smallber, S., and Ebert, M. 1983. A family with histologically confirmed Alzheimer's disease. *Archives of Neurology,* 40:203–208.

Needleman, H. L., Gunnoe, C., Leviton, A., Reed, M., Peresie, H., Maher, C., and Barrett, P. 1979. Deficits in psychological and classroom performance of children with elevated dentine lead levels. *New England Journal of Medicine,* 300:689–695.

Neff, W. D., and Casseday, J. H. 1977. Effects of unilateral ablation of auditory cortex on monaural cat's ability

to localize sound. *Journal of Neurophysiology,* 40:44–52.

Neher, E., and Sakmann, B. 1992. The patch clamp technique. *Scientific American,* 266(3):3, 44–51.

Neitz, J., and Jacobs, G. H. 1984. Electroretinogram measurements of cone spectral sensitivity in dichromatic monkeys. *Journal of the Optical Society of America. A. Optics and Image Science,* 1:1175–1180.

Neitz, J., Geist, T., and Jacobs, G. H. 1989. Color vision in the dog. *Visual Neuroscience,* 3:119–125.

Nelson, R. J. 1995. *Introduction to behavioral endocrinology.* Sinauer Associates, Sunderland, MA.

Nelson, R. J., Demas, G. E., Huang, P. L., Fishman, M. C., Dawson, V. L., Dawson, T. M., and Snyder, S. H. 1995. Behavioural abnormalities in male mice lacking neuronal nitric oxide synthase. *Nature,* 378:383–386.

Nestler, E. J., and Duman, R. S. 1995. Intracellular messenger pathways as mediators of neural plasticity. In F. E. Bloom, and D. J. Kupfer (eds.), *Psychopharmacology, the fourth generation of progress,* pp. 695–704. Raven, New York.

Neurobiology of Aging. 1992. Is beta-amyloid neurotoxic? 13:535–625.

Neveu, P. J. 1993. Brain lateralization and immunomodulation. *International Journal of Neuroscience,* 70:135–143.

Newsome, W. T., Wurtz, R. H., Dursteler, M. R., and Mikami, A. 1985. Deficits in visual motion processing following ibotenic acid lesions of the middle temporal visual area of the macaque monkey. *Journal of Neuroscience,* 5:825–840.

Nguyen, M. L., Meyer, K. K., and Winick, M. 1977. Early malnutrition and "late" adoption: A study of their effects on the development of Korean orphans adopted into American families. *American Journal of Clinical Nutrition,* 30:1734–1739.

Nicholls, J. G., Martin, A. R., and Wallace, B. G. 1992. *From neuron to brain,* 3rd ed. Sinauer Associates, Sunderland, MA.

Nieto-Sampedro, M., and Cotman, C. W. 1985. Growth factor induction and temporal order in central nervous system repair. In C. W. Cotman (ed.), *Synaptic plasticity,* pp. 407–457. Guilford, New York.

Nobler, M. S., Sackeim, H. A., Prohovnik, I., Moeller, J. R., Mukherjee, S., Schnur, D. B., Prudic, J., and Devanand, D. P. 1994. Regional cerebral blood flow in mood disorders. III. Treatment and clinical response. *Archives of General Psychiatry,* 51:884–897.

Nordberg, A. 1993. Clinical studies in Alzheimer patients with positron emission tomography. *Behavioural Brain Research,* 57:215–224.

Nordeen, E. J., Nordeen, K. W., Sengelaub, D. R., and Arnold, A. P. 1985.

Androgens prevent normally occurring cell death in a sexually dimorphic spinal nucleus. *Science,* 229:671–673.

Norman, A. W., and Litwack, G. 1987. *Hormones.* Academic Press, Orlando, Fla.

Norsell, U. 1980. Behavioral studies of the somatosensory system. *Physiological Reviews,* 60:327–354.

Northcutt, R. G. 1981. Evolution of the telencephalon in nonmammals. *Annual Review of Neuroscience,* 4:301–350.

Northcutt, R. G., and Davis, R. E. 1983. *Fish neurobiology.* University of Michigan Press, Ann Arbor.

Nottebohm, F. 1980. Brain pathways for vocal learning in birds: A review of the first 10 years. In J. M. Sprague, and A. N. Epstein (eds.), *Progress in psychobiology and physiological psychology, Vol. 9.* Academic Press, New York.

Nottebohm, F. 1981. A brain for all seasons: Cyclical anatomical changes in song control nuclei of the canary brain. *Science,* 214: 1368–1370.

Nottebohm, F. 1987. Plasticity in adult avian central nervous system: Possible relations between hormones, learning, and brain repair. In F. Plum (ed.), *Higher functions of the nervous system, Sec. 1, Vol. 5: Handbook of physiology.* American Physiological Society, Washington D.C.

Nottebohm, F. 1991. Reassessing the mechanisms and origins of vocal learning in birds. *Trends in Neurosciences,* 14:297–304.

Nottebohm, F., and Arnold, A. P. 1976. Sexual dimorphism in vocal control areas of the songbird brain. *Science,* 194:211–213.

Nottebohm, F., Stokes, T. M., and Leonard, C. M. 1976. Central control of song in the canary, *Serinus canarius. Journal of Comparative Neurology,* 165:457–486.

Novikov, S. N. 1993. The genetics of pheromonally mediated intermale aggression in mice: current status and prospects of the model. *Behavior Genetics,* 23:505–508.

Ojemann, G. A. 1983. The intrahemispheric organization of human language, derived with electrical stimulation techniques. *Trends in Neurosciences,* 6:184–189.

Ojemann, G., and Mateer, C. 1979. Human language cortex: Localization of memory, syntax, and sequential motor–phoneme identification systems. *Science,* 205:1401–1403.

Olds, J., and Milner, P. 1954. Positive reinforcement produced by electrical stimulation of septal area and other regions of the rat brain. *Journal of Comparative and Physiological Psychology,* 47:419–427.

Olsson, T., Mohammed, A. H., Donaldson, L. F., Henriksson, B. G., and Seckl, J. R. 1994. Glucocorticoid receptor and NGFI-A gene expression are induced in the hippocampus after environmental enrichment in adult rats. *Brain Research*, 23:349–353.

Ontiveros, A., Fontaine, R., Breton, G., Elie, R., Fontaine, S., and Dery, R. 1989. Correlation of severity of panic disorder and neuroanatomical changes on magnetic resonance imaging. *Journal of Neuropsychiatry and Clinical Neurosciences*, 1:404–408.

Oppenheim, R. W. 1991. Cell death during development of the nervous system. *Annual Review of Neuroscience*, 14:453–501.

Oster, H., and Rosenstein, D. *Baby FACS: Analyzing facial movements in infants and young children.* Unpublished coding manual.

Østerberg, G. 1935. Topography of the rods and cones in the human retina. *Acta ophthalmologica (Supplement 6)*,

Ottoboni, M. A. 1991. *The dose makes the poison: A plain language guide to toxicology, 2nd ed.* Vincente Books, Berkeley, CA.

Overstreet, D. H. 1993. The Flinders sensitive line rats: A genetic animal model of depression. *Neuroscience and Biobehavioral Reviews*, 17:51–68.

Panksepp, J. 1982. Toward a general psychobiological theory of emotions. *Behavioral & Brain Sciences*, 5:407–467.

Pantle, A., and Sekuler, R. 1968. Size detecting mechanisms in human vision. *Science*, 162:1146–1148.

Papez, J. W. 1937. A proposed mechanism of emotion. *Archives of Neurology and Psychiatry*, 38:725–745.

Papka, M., Ivry, R., and Woodruff-Pak, D. S. 1994. Eyeblink classical conditioning and time production in patients with cerebellar damage. *Society of Neuroscience Abstracts*, 20:360.

Papousek, H. 1992. Experimental studies of appetitional behavior in human newborns and infants. *Advances in Infancy Studies*, 7:xix–liii.

Pappenheimer, J. R., Koski, G., Fencl, V., Karnovsky, M. L., and Krueger, J. 1975. Extraction of sleep-promoting factor S from cerebrospinal fluid and from brains of sleep-deprived animals. *Journal of Neurophysiology*, 38:1299–1311.

Paradis, M., and Goldblum, M. C. 1989. Selective crossed aphasia in a trilingual aphasic patient followed by reciprocal antagonism. *Brain and Language*, 36:62–75.

Park, S., Como, P. G., Cui, L., and Kurlan, R. 1993. The early course of the Tourette's syndrome clinical spectrum. *Neurology*, 43:1712–1715.

Parkes, J. D. 1985. *Sleep and its disorders.* Saunders, Philadelphia.

Patterson, F. G. 1978. The gestures of a gorilla: Language acquisition in another pongid. *Brain and Language*, 5:72–97.

Patterson, T. A., Rosenzweig, M. R., and Bennett, E. L. 1987. Amnesia produced by anisomycin in an appetitive task is not due to conditioned aversion. *Behavioral and Neural Biology*, 47:17–26.

Pavlov, I. P. 1927. *Conditioned reflexes.* Oxford University Press, Oxford.

Pearson, K. G. 1993. Common principles of motor control in vertebrates and invertebrates. *Annual Review of Neuroscience*, 16:265–297.

Peele, S., and Brodsky, A. 1991. *The truth about addiction and recovery.* Simon & Schuster, New York.

Penfield, W., and Roberts, L. 1959. *Speech and brain-mechanisms.* Princeton University Press, Princeton, NJ.

Perl, E. R. 1980. Afferent basis of nociception and pain: evidence from the characteristics of sensory receptors and their projections to the spinal dorsal horn. *Research Publications, Association for Research in Nervous and Mental Disease*, 58:19–45.

Perlow, M. J., Freed, W. J., Hoffer, B. J., Seiger, A., Olson, L., and Wyatt, R. J. 1979. Brain grafts reduce motor abnormalities produced by destruction of nigrostriatal dopamine system. *Science*, 204:643–647.

Perrett, S. P., Ruiz, B. P., and Mauk, M. D. 1993. Cerebellar cortex lesions disrupt learning-dependent timing of conditioned eyelid responses. *Journal of Neuroscience*, 13:1708–1718.

Perry, V. H., Oehler, R., and Cowey, A. 1984. Retinal ganglion cells that project to the dorsal lateral geniculate nucleus in the macaque monkey. *Neuroscience*, 12:1101–1123.

Pert, A., Dionne, R., Ng, L., Bragin, E., Moody, T. W., and Pert, C. B. 1981. Alterations in rat central nervous system endorphins following transauricular electroacupuncture. *Brain Research*, 224:83–93.

Pert, C. B., and Snyder, S. H. 1973. Opiate receptor: Demonstration in nervous tissue. *Science*, 179:1011–1014.

Pert, C. B., and Snyder, S. H. 1993. Properties of opiate-receptor binding in rat brain. *Proceedings of the National Academy of Sciences, U.S.A.*, 70: 2243–2247.

Peschanski, M., Defer, G., N'Guyen, J. P., Ricolfi, F., Monfort, J. C., Remy, P., Geny, C., Samson, Y., Hantraye, P., Jeny, R. et al. 1994. Bilateral motor improvement and alteration of L-dopa effect in two patients with Parkinson's disease following intrastriatal transplantation of foetal ventral mesencephalon. *Brain*, 117:487–499.

Peterhans, E., and von der Heydt, R. 1989. Mechanisms of contour perception in monkey visual cortex. II. Contours bridging gaps. *Journal of Neuroscience*, 9:1749–1763.

Peters, A., Palay, S. L., and Webster, H. de F. 1991. *The fine structure of the nervous system: Neurons and their supporting cells.* 3rd ed. Oxford University Press, New York.

Petersen, O. H. 1992. Ion channels. Ten years of patch-clamp studies. *Biochemical Pharmacology*, 43:1–3.

Peterson, A. L., and Azrin, N. H. 1992. An evaluation of behavioral treatments for Tourette syndrome. *Behaviour Research and Therapy*, 30:167–174.

Peterson, B., Riddle, M. A., Cohen, D. J., Katz, L. D., Smith, J. C., Hardin, M. T., and Leckman, J. F. 1993. Reduced basal ganglia volumes in Tourette's syndrome using three-dimensional reconstruction techniques from magnetic resonance images. *Neurology*, 43:941–949.

Peterson, L. R., and Peterson, M. J. 1959. Short-term retention of individual verbal items. *J. Journal of Experimental Psychology*, 58:193–198.

Petre-Quadens, O. 1972. Sleep in mental retardation. In C. D. Clemente, D. R. Purpura, and F. E. Mayer (eds.), *Sleep and the maturing nervous system*, pp.1–2. Academic Press, New York.

Petrides, M., and Milner, B. 1982. Deficits on subject-ordered tasks after frontal-and temporal-lobe lesions in man. *Neuropsychologia*, 20:249–262.

Petrie, K., Dawson, A. G., Thompson, L., and Brook, R. 1993. A double-blind trial of melatonin as a treatment for jet lag in international cabin crew. *Biological Psychiatry*, 33:526–530.

Pettigrew, J. D., and Freeman, R. D. 1973. Visual experience without lines: Effect on developing cortical neurons. *Science*, 182:599–601.

Petty, F., Kramer, G., Wilson, L., and Jordan, S. 1994. In vivo serotonin release and learned helplessness. *Psychiatry Research*, 52:285–293.

Pfaffmann, C., Frank, M., and Norgren, R. 1979. Neural mechanisms and behavioral aspects of taste. *Annual Review of Psychology*, 30: 283–325.

Phoenix, C. H., Goy, R. W., Gerall, A. A., and Young, W. C. 1959. Organizing action of prenatally administered testosterone propionate on the tissues mediating mating behavior in the female guinea pig. *Endocrinology*, 65:369–382.

Pickens, R., and Thompson, T. 1968. Drug use by U.S. Army enlisted men in Vietnam: A followup on their return home. *Journal of Pharmacology and Experimental Therapeutics*, 161:122–129.

Piérón, H. 1913. *Le Problème physiologique du sommeil.* Masson, Paris.

Pines, M. (ed.). 1992. From Egg to Adult, pp. 30–38. Howard Hughes Medical Institute, Bethesda, MD.

Pinker, S. 1994. *The language instinct.* W. Morrow, New York.

Pitman, R. K., and Orr, S. P. 1995. Psychophysiology of emotional memory networks in posttraumatic stress disorder. In J. L. McGaugh, N. M. Weinberger, and G. Lynch (eds.), *Brain and memory: Modulation and mediation of neuroplasticity,* pp. 75–83. Oxford University Press, New York.

Pitts, J. W., and McClure, J. N. 1967. Lactate metabolism in anxiety neurosis. *New England Journal of Medicine,* 277:1329–1336.

Plante, E. 1991. MRI findings in the parents and siblings of specifically language-impaired boys. *Brain and Language,* 41:67–80.

Plante, E., Swisher, L., Vance, R., and Rapcsak, S. 1991. MRI findings in boys with specific language impairment. *Brain and Language,* 41:52–66.

Plomin, R., and Rende, R. 1991. Human behavioral genetics. *Annual Review of Psychology,* 42:161–190.

Plomin, R., Owen, M. H., and McGuffin, P. 1994. The genetic basis of complex human behaviors. *Science,* 264:1733–1739.

Ploog, D. W. 1992. Neuroethological perspectives on the human brain: From the expression of emotions to intentional signing and speech. In A. Harrington (ed.), *So human a brain: Knowledge and values in the neurosciences,* pp. 3–13. Birkhauser, Boston.

Plutchik, R. 1985. On emotion: The chicken-and-egg problem revisited. *Motivation and Emotion,* 9:197–200.

Plutchik, R. 1994. *The psychology and biology of emotion.* HarperCollins, New York.

Poggio, T., and Koch, C. 1987. Synapses that compute motion. *Scientific American,* 256(5):46–52.

Poinar, G. O. Jr. 1992. *Life in amber.* Stanford University Press, Stanford.

Poinar, G. O. Jr. 1994. The range of life in amber: Significance and implications in DNA studies. *Experientia,* 50:536–542.

Poizner, H., Bellugi, U., and Klima, E. S. 1990. Biological foundations of language: Clues from sign language. *Annual Review of Neuroscience,* 13:283–307.

Popock, S. J., Smith, M., and Baghurst, P. 1994. Environmental lead and children's intelligence: a systematic review of the epidemiological evidence. *BMJ,* 309:1189–1197.

Poritsky, R. 1969. Reconstruction from serial electron micrographs of a motoneuron. *Journal of Comparative Neurology,* 135:423–452.

Posner, M. I., and Petersen, S. E. 1990. The attention system of the human brain. *Annual Review of Neuroscience,* 13:25–42.

Posner, M. I., and Raichle, M. E. 1994. *Images of mind.* Scientific American Library, New York.

Post, R. M., and Weiss, S. R. R. 1995. Neurobiology of treatment-resistant mood disorders. In F. E. Bloom and D. J. Kupfer (eds.), *Psychopharmacology, the fourth generation,* pp. 1155–1170. Raven, New York.

Premack, D. 1971. Language in a chimpanzee? *Science,* 172:808–822.

Preti, G., Cutler, W. B., Garcia, C. R., Huggins, G. R., and Lawley, H. J. 1986. Human axillary secretions influence women's menstrual cycles: The role of donor extract of females. *Hormones and Behavior,* 20:474–482.

Price, D. L., Whitehouse, P. J., and Struble, R. G. 1985. Alzheimer's disease. *Annual Review of Medicine,* 36:349–356.

Price, M. A., and Vandenbergh, J. G. 1992. Analysis of puberty-accelerating pheromones. *Journal of Experimental Zoology,* 264:42–45.

Price, R. A., and Gottesman, I. I. 1991. Body fat in identical twins reared apart: Roles for genes and environment. *Behavior Genetics,* 21:1–7.

Price, R. A., Kidd, K. K., Cohen, D. J., Pauls, D. L., and Leckman, J. F. 1985. A twin study of Tourette syndrome. *Archives of General Psychiatry,* 42:815–820.

Probst, R., Lonsbury-Martin, B. L., and Martin, G. K. 1991. A review of otoacoustic emissions. *Journal of the Acoustical Society of America,* 89:2027–2067.

Pugh, E. N., Jr., and Lamb, T. D. 1990. Cyclic GMP and calcium: The internal messengers of excitation and adaptation in vertebrate photoreceptors. *Vision Research,* 30: 1923–1948.

Purdy, R. H., Moore, P. H., Jr., Morrow, A. L., and Paul, S. M. 1992. Neurosteroids and GABAA receptor function. *Advances in Biochemical Psychopharmacology,* 47:87–92.

Puri, S., Ray, A., Chakravarti, A. K., and Sen, P. 1994. Role of dopaminergic mechanisms in the regulation of stress responses in experimental animals. *Pharmacology, Biochemistry and Behavior,* 48:53–56.

Purves, D. 1988. *Body and brain: A trophic theory of neural connections.* Harvard University Press, Cambridge, MA.

Purves, D., and Lichtman, J. W. 1985. Geometrical differences among homologous neurons in mammals. *Science,* 228:298–302.

Purves, D., Orians, G. H., and Heller, H. C. 1995. *Life: The science of biology,* 4th ed. Sinauer Associates, Sunderland, MA.

Quinn, W. G., and Greenspan, R. J. 1984. Learning and courtship in *Drosophila:* Two stories with mutants. *Annual Review of Neuroscience,* 7:67–93.

Quinn, W. G., and Greenspan, R. J. 1984. Learning and courtship in *Drosophila:* Two stories with mutants. *Annual Review of Neuroscience,* 7:67–93.

Quinn, W. G., Harris, W. A., and Benzer, S. 1974. Conditioned behavior in *Drosophila melanogaster. Proceedings of the National Academy of Sciences, U.S.A.,* 71:708–712.

Rafal, R. D. 1994. Neglect. *Current Opinion in Neurobiology,* 4:231–236.

Rahe, R. H., Biersner, R. J., Ryman, D. H., and Arthur, R. J. 1972. Psychosocial predictors of illness behavior and failure in stressful training. *Journal of Health and Social Behavior,* 13: 393–397.

Raichle, M. E., Fiez, J. A., Videen, T. O., MacLeod, A. M., Pardo, J. V., Fox, P. T., and Petersen, S. E. 1994. Practice-related changes in human brain functional anatomy during nonmotor learning. *Cerebral Cortex,* 4:8–26.

Raisman, G. 1969. A comparison of the mode of termination of the hippocampal and hypothalamic afferents to the septal nuclei as revealed by electron microscopy of degeneration. *Experimental Brain Research,* 7:317–343.

Raisman, G. 1978. What hope for repair of the brain? *Annals of Neurology,* 3:101–106.

Raisman, G., and Field, P. M. 1971. Sexual dimorphism in the preoptic area of the rat. *Science,* 173:731–733.

Rakic, P. 1971. Guidance of neurons migrating to the fetal monkey neocortex. *Brain Research,* 33:471–476.

Rakic, P. 1985. Mechanisms of neuronal migration in developing cerebellar cortex. In G. M. Edelman, W. M. Cowan, and E. Gull (eds.), *Molecular basis of neural development.* Wiley, New York.

Rakic, P., Bourgeois, J. P., Eckenhoff, M. F., Zecevic, N., and Goldman-Rakic, P. S. 1986. Concurrent overproduction of synapses in diverse regions of the primate cerebral cortex. *Science,* 232:232–235.

Raleigh, M. J., Brammer, G. L., McGuire, M. T., Pollack, D. B., and Yuwiler, A. 1992. Individual differences in basal cisternal cerebrospinal fluid 5-HIAA and HVA in monkeys. The effects of gender, age, physical characteristics, and matrilineal influences. *Neuropsychopharmacology,* 7:295–304.

Ralph, M. R., and Lehman, M. N. 1991. Transplantation: A new tool in the analysis of the mammalian hypothalamic circadian pacemaker. *Trends in Neurosciences,* 14:362–366.

Ralph, M. R., and Menaker, M. 1988. A mutation of the circadian system in golden hamsters. *Science,* 241:1225–1227.

Ralph, M. R., Foster, R. G., Davis, F. C., and Menaker, M. 1990. Transplanted suprachiasmatic nucleus determines circadian period. *Science,* 247:975–978.

Ramón y Cájal, S. 1894. La Fine structure des centres nerveux. *Proceedings of the Royal Society of London,* 55:444–468.

Ranaldi, R., and Beninger, R. J. 1994. The effects of systemic and intracerebral injections of D1 and D2 agonists on brain stimulation reward. *Brain Research,* 651:283–292.

Rand, M. N., and Breedlove, S. M. 1987. Ontogeny of functional innervation of bulbocavernosus muscles in male and female rats. *Brain Research,* 430:150–152.

Randolph, M., and Semmes, J. 1974. Behavioral consequences of selective subtotal ablations in the postcentral gyrus of *Macaca mulatta. Brain Research,* 70:55–70.

Rao, P. D. P., and Finger, T. E. 1984. Asymmetry of the olfactory system in the brain of the winter flounder *Pseudopleuronectes americanus. Journal of Comparative Neurology,* 225:492–510.

Rapoport, J. L. 1989. The biology of obsessions and compulsions. *Scientific American,* 260(3):82–89.

Rauch, S. L., Jenike, M. A., Alpert, N. M., Baer, L., Breiter, H. C., Savage, C. R., and Fischman, A. J. 1994. Regional cerebral blood flow measured during symptom provocation in obsessive-compulsive disorder using oxygen 15-labeled carbon dioxide and positron emission tomography. *Archives of General·Psychiatry,* 51:62–70.

Rauch, S. L., Savage, C. R., Alpert, N. M., Miguel, E. C., Baer, L., Breiter, H. C., Fischman, A. J., Manzo, P. A., Moretti, C., and Jenike, M. A. 1995. A positron emission tomographic study of simple phobic symptom provocation. *Archives of General Psychiatry,* 52:20–28.

Recanzone, G. H., Schreiner, D. E., and Merzenich, M. M. 1993. Plasticity in the frequency representation of primary auditory cortex following discrimination training in adult owl monkeys. *Journal of Neuroscience,* 13:87–103.

Rechtschaffen, A., and Kales, A. 1968. *A manual of standardized terminology, techniques and scoring system for sleep stages of human subjects.* U.S. National Institute of Neurological Diseases and Blindness, Neurological Information Network, Bethesda, MD.

Redfern, P. A. 1970. Neuromuscular transmission in new-born rats. *Journal of Physiology,* 109:701–709.

Redican, W. K. 1982. An evolutionary perspective on human facial displays. In P. Ekman (ed.), *Emotion in the human face,* 2nd ed., pp. 212–280. Pergamon, Elmsford, New York.

Reed, D. M. 1990. The paradox of high risk of stroke in populations with low risk of coronary heart disease. *American Journal of Epidemiology,* 131:579–588.

Rehkamper, G., Haase, E., and Frahm, H. D. 1988. Allometric comparison of brain weight and brain structure volumes in different breeds of the domestic pigeon, *Columba livia* f. d. (fantails, homing pigeons, strassers). *Brain, Behavior & Evolution,* 31:141–149.

Reichardt, L. F., and Tomaselli, K. J. 1991. Extracellular matrix molecules and their receptors: Functions in neural development. *Annual Review of Neuroscience,* 14:531–570.

Reid, M. S., Tafti, M., Nishino, S., Siegel, J. M., Dement, W. C., and Mignot, E. 1994. Cholinergic regulation of cataplexy in canine narcolepsy in the pontine reticular formation is mediated by M2 muscarinic receptors. *Sleep,* 17:424–435.

Reiman, E. M., Raichle, M., Robins, E., Butler, F. K., Herscovitch, P., Fox, P., and Perlmutter, J. 1986. The application of positron emission tomography to the study of panic disorder. *American Journal of Psychiatry,* 143:469–477.

Reisberg, D., and Heuer, F. 1995. Emotion's multiple effects on memory. In J. L. McGaugh, N. M. Weinberger, and G. Lynch (eds.), *Brain and memory: Modulation and mediation of neuroplasticity,* pp. 84–92. Oxford University Press, New York.

Reisenzein, R. 1983. The Schachter theory of emotion: Two decades later. *Psychological Bulletin,* 94:239–264.

Rende, R., and Plomin, R. 1995. Nature, nurture, and the development of psychopathology. In D. Ciccheti, and D. J. Cohen (eds.), *Developmental psychopathology, Vol. 1: Theory and methods,* pp. 291–314. John Wiley & Sons, New York.

Renner, M. J., and Rosenzweig, M. R. 1987. *Enriched and impoverished environments: Effects on brain and behavior.* Springer-Verlag, New York.

Reppert, S. M. 1985. Maternal entrainment of the developing circadian system. *Annals of the New York Academy of Sciences,* 453:162–169.

Reppert, S. M., Perlow, M. J., Tamarkin, L., and Klein, D. C. 1979. A diurnal melatonin rhythm in primate cerebrospinal fluid. *Endocrinology,* 104:295–301.

Requin, J., and Stelmach, G. E. 1991. *Tutorials in neuroscience.* Kluwer, Dordrecht, Netherlands.

Rescorla, R. A. 1988. Behavioral studies of Pavlovian conditioning. *Annual Review of Neuroscience,* 11:329–352.

Ressler, K. J., Sullivan, S. L., and Buck, L. B. 1994. A molecular dissection of spatial patterning in the olfactory

system. *Current Opinion in Neurobiology,* 4:588–596.

Revusky, S., and Garcia, J. 1970. Learned associations over long delays. In G. H. Bower (ed.), *The psychology of learning and motivation: IV.* Academic Press, New York.

Reynolds, C. F., Kupfer, D. J., Taska, L. S., Hoch, C. H., and Sewitch, D. E. 1985. Sleep of healthy seniors: A revisit. *Sleep,* 8:20–29.

Rhode, W. S. 1984. Cochlear mechanics. *Annual Review of Physiology,* 46:231–246.

Ribeiro, R. C., Kushner, P. J., and Baxter, J. D. 1995. The nuclear hormone receptor gene superfamily. *Annual Review of Medicine,* 46:443–453.

Ribot, T. 1881. Les Maladies de la memoire (The diseases of memory). Translated by J. Fitzgerald. *Humboldt Library of Popular Scientific Literature,* 46:453–500.

Rice, D. C. 1990. The health effects of environmental lead exposure: Closing Pandora's box. In R. W. Russell, P. E. Flattau, and A. M. Pope (eds.), *Behavioral measures of neurotoxicity,* pp. 243–267. National Academy Press, Washington, D.C.

Rice, D. C., and Karpinski, K. F. 1988. Lifetime low-level lead exposure produces deficits in delayed alternation in adult monkeys. *Neurotoxicology and Teratology,* 10:207–214.

Rich, C. L., Young, D., and Fowler, R. C. 1986. San Diego suicide study. I. Young vs. old subjects. *Archives of General Psychiatry,* 43:577–582.

Richter, C. 1967. Sleep and activity: their relation to the 24-hour clock. *Proceedings of the Association for Research in Nervous and Mental Diseases,* 45:8–27.

Ridley, R. M., and Baker, H. F. 1991. Can fetal neural transplants restore function in monkeys with lesion-induced behavioural deficits? *Trends in Neurosciences,* 14:366–370.

Rieke, F. E. 1969. Lead intoxication in shipbuilding and shipscraping, 1941 to 1968. *Archives of Environmental Health,* 19:521–539.

Riley, V. 1981. Psychoneuroendocrine influences on immunocompetence and neoplasia. *Science,* 212:1100–1110.

Rinn, W. E. 1984. The neuropsychology of facial expression: A review of the neurological and psychological mechanisms for producing facial expressions. *Psychological Bulletin,* 95:52–77.

Rizzo, M., Corbett, J. J., Thompson, H. S., and Damasio, A. R. 1986. Spatial contrast sensitivity in facial recognition. *Neurology,* 36:1254–1256.

Rizzo, M., Hurtig, R., and Damasio, A. R. 1987. The role of scanpaths in facial recognition and learning. *Annals of Neurology,* 22:41–45.

Roberts, A. H. 1969. *Brain damage in boxers*. Pitman, London.

Roberts, D. F. 1973. *Climate and human variability.*Addison-Wesley, Reading, MA.

Roberts, W. W., and Mooney, R. D. 1974. Brain areas controlling thermoregulatory grooming, prone extension, locomotion, and tail vasodilation in rats. *Journal of Comparative and Physiological Psychology*, 86:470–480.

Robertson, D., and Irvine, D. R. 1989. Plasticity of frequency organization in auditory cortex of guinea pigs with partial unilateral deafness. *Journal of Comparative Neurology*, 282:456– 471.

Robins, L. N., and Regier, D. A. 1991. *Psychiatric disorders in America: the epidemiologic catchment area study*. Free Press, New York.

Rocca, W. A., Hofman, A., Brayne, C., Breteler, M. M., Clarke, M., Copeland, J. R., Dartigues, J. F., Engedal, K., Hagnell, O., Heeren, T. J., et al. 1991. The prevalence of vascular dementia in Europe: Facts and fragments from 1980–1990 studies. *Annals of Neurology*, 30:817–824.

Rockel, A. J., Hiorns, R. W., and Powell, T. P. 1974. Proceedings: Numbers of neurons through full depth of neocortex. *Journal of Anatomy*, 118:371.

Rodin, J., and Salovey, P. 1989. Health psychology. *Annual Review of Psychology*, 40:533–579.

Roelink, H., Augsburger, A., Heemskerk, J., Korzh, V., Norlin, S., Ruiz i Altaba, A., Tanabe, Y., Placzek, M., Edlund, T., Jessell, T. M. et al. 1994. Floor plate and motor neuron induction by vhh-1, a vertebrate homolog of hedgehog expressed by the notochord. *Cell*, 76:761–775.

Roland, E., and Larson, B. 1976. Focal increase of cerebral blood flow during stereognostic testing in man. *Archives of Neurology*, 33:551–558.

Roland, P. E. 1980. Quantitative assessment of cortical motor dysfunction by measurement of the regional cerebral blood flow. *Scandinavian Journal of Rehabilitation Medicine*, 7:27–41.

Roland, P. E. 1984. Metabolic measurements of the working frontal cortex in man. *Trends in Neurosciences*, 7:430–436.

Romero-Apis, D., Babayan-Mena, J. I., Fonte-Vazquez, A., Gutierrez-Perez, D., Martinez-Oropeza, S., and Murillo-Murillo, L. 1982. Perdida del ojo fijador en adulto con ambliopia estrabica. *Anales Sociedad Mexicana de Oftalmologia*, 56:445–452.

Rorabaugh, W. J. 1976. Estimated U.S. alcoholic beverage consumption, 1790–1860. *Journal of Studies on Alcohol*, 37:353–364.

Rose, S. P. 1992. *The making of memory: From molecules to mind*. Anchor Books–Doubleday, New York.

Rosen, G. D., Sherman, G. F., and Galaburda, A. M. 1993. Neuronal subtypes and anatomic asymmetry: Changes in neuronal number and cell-packing density. *Neuroscience*, 56:833–839.

Rosenbaum, D. A. 1991. *Human motor control*. Academic Press, San Diego.

Rosengren, A., Tibblin, G., and Wilhelmsen, L. 1991. Self-perceived psychological stress and incidence of coronary artery disease in middle-aged men. *American Journal of Cardiology*, 68:1171–1175.

Rosenman, R. H., Brand, R. J., Jenkins, C. D., Friedman, M., Straus, R., and Wurm, M. 1975. Coronary heart disease in the Western Collaborative Group Study: Final follow-up experience of 8 1/2 years. *Journal of the American Medical Association*, 233:872–877.

Rosenthal, D. 1963. *The Genain quadruplets*. Basic Books, New York.

Rosenthal, N. E., Sack, D. A., Carpenter, C. J., Parry, B. L., Mendelson, W. B., and Wehr, T. A. 1985. Antidepressant effects of light in seasonal affective disorder. *American Journal of Psychiatry*, 142:606–608.

Rosenzweig, M. R. 1946. Discrimination of auditory intensities in the cat. *American Journal of Psychology*, 59:127–136.

Rosenzweig, M. R. 1980. Animal models for effects of brain lesions and for rehabilitation. In P. Bach-y-Rita (ed.), *Recovery of function: Theoretical considerations for brain injury rehabilitation*, pp. 127–172. Hans Huber, Bern, Switzerland.

Rosenzweig, M. R. 1984. Experience, memory, and the brain. *American Psychologist*, 39:365–376.

Rosenzweig, M. R., and Bennett, E. L. 1977. Effects of environmental enrichment or impoverishment on learning and on brain values in rodents. In A. Oliveno (ed.), *Genetics, environment, and intelligence*, pp. 1–2. Elsevier/North-Holland, Amsterdam.

Rosenzweig, M. R., and Bennett, E. L. 1978. Experimental influences on brain anatomy and brain chemistry in rodents. In G. Gottlieb (ed.), *Studies on the development of behavior and the nervous system. Vol 4. Early influences*, pp. 289–327. Academic Press, New York.

Rosenzweig, M. R., and Glickman, S. E. 1985. Comparison of learning abilities among species. In N. M. Weinberger, J. G. McGaugh, and G. Lynch (eds.), *Memory systems of the brain*, pp. 296–307. Guilford, New York.

Rosenzweig, M. R., Bennett, E. L., Colombo, P. J., Lee, D. W., and Serrano, P. A. 1993. Short-term, intermediate-term, and long-term memory. *Behavioural Brain Research*, 57:193–198.

Rosenzweig, M. R., Bennett, E. L., Martinez, J. L., Colombo, P. J., Lee, D. W., and Serrano, P. A. 1992. Studying stages of memory formation with chicks. In L. R. Squire, and N. Butters (eds.), *Neuropsychology of memory*, 2nd ed., pp. 533–546. Guilford, New York.

Rosenzweig, M. R., Krech, D., and Bennett, E. L. 1961. Heredity, environment, brain biochemistry, and learning. In *Current trends in psychological theory*, pp. 87–110. University of Pittsburgh Press, Pittsburgh.

Rosenzweig, M., Krech, D., Bennett, E. L., and Diamond, M. 1962. Effects of environmental complexity and training on brain chemistry and anatomy: A replication and extension. *Journal of Comparative and Physiological Psychology*, 55:429–437.

Rossor, M. N., Emson, P. C., Mountjoy, C. Q., Roth, M., and Iversen, L. L. 1982. Neurotransmitters of the cerebral cortex in senile dementia of Alzheimer type. *Experimental Brain Research*, 5:135–157.

Rothschild, A. J. 1992. Disinhibition, amnestic reactions, and other adverse reactions secondary to triazolam: A review of the literature. *Journal of Clinical Psychiatry*, 53:69–79.

Rothwell, J. 1994. *Control of human voluntary movement*, 2nd ed. Chapman and Hall, London.

Rousseau, D. L. 1992. Case studies in pathological science. *American Scientist*, 80:54–63.

Rowland, L. P. 1987. Therapy in myasthenia gravis: Introduction. *Annals of the New York Academy of Sciences*, 505:566–567.

Roy, A. 1992. Hypothalamic-pituitary-adrenal axis function and suicidal behavior in depression. *Biological Psychiatry*, 32:812–816.

Rozin, P. 1976a. The evolution of intelligence and access to the cognitive unconscious. In J. M. Sprague, and A. Epstein (eds.), *Progress in Psychobiology and Physiological Psychology, VI*. Academic Press, New York.

Rozin, P. 1976b. The psychobiological approach to human memory. In M. R. Rosenzweig, and E. L. Bennett (eds.), *Neural mechanisms of learning and memory*. MIT Press, Cambridge, MA.

Ruben, R. J. 1993. Communication disorders in children: A challenge for health care. New York, 1992. *Preventive Medicine*, 22:585–588.

Ruberman, W., Weinblatt, E., Goldberg, J. D., and Chaudhary, B. S. 1984. Psychosocial influences on mortality after myocardial infarction. *New England Journal of Medicine*, 311:552–559.

Rumbaugh, D. M. 1977. *Language learning by a chimpanzee: The LANA project*. Academic Press, New York.

Rusak, B., and Boulos, Z. 1981. Pathways for photic entrainment of mammalian circadian rhythms. *Photochemistry and Photobiology*, 34:267–273.

Rusak, B., and Zucker, I. 1975. Biological rhythms and animal behavior. *Annual Review of Psychology*, 26: 137–171.

Rusak, B., and Zucker, I. 1979. Neural regulation of circadian rhythms. *Physiological Reviews*, 59:449–526.

Russell, R. W., Flattau, P. E., and Pope, A. M. 1990. *Behavioral measures of neurotoxicity*. National Academy Press, Washington, D.C.

Sack, R. L., Blood, M. L., and Lewy, A. J. 1992. Melatonin rhythms in night shift workers. *Sleep*, 15:434–441.

Sackett, G., and Korner, A. 1993. Organization of sleep-waking states in conjoined twin neonates. *Sleep*, 16: 414–427.

Sackheim, H., Gur, R. C., and Saucy, M. C. 1978. Emotions are expressed more intensely on the left side of the face. *Science*, 202:434–436.

Sacks, O., and Wasserman, R. 1987. The case of the colorblind painter. *New York Review of Books*, November 19:25–34.

Sahu, A., Kalra, P. S., and Kalra, S. P. 1988. Food deprivation and ingestion induce reciprocal changes in neuropeptide Y concentration in the paraventricular nucleus. *Peptides*, 9:83–86.

Salvini-Plawen, L. V. and Mayr, E. 1977. On the evolution of photoreceptors and eyes. *Evolutionary Biology*, 10:207–263.

Salvini-Plawen, L. von 1975. *Mollusca caudofoveata*. Universitetsforlaget, Oslo.

Salzman, C. D., Murasugi, C. M., Britten, K. H., and Newsome, W. T. 1992. Microstimulation in visual area MT: Effects on direction discrimination performance. *Journal of Neuroscience*, 12:2331–2355.

Samson, S., and Zatorre, R. J. 1991. Recognition memory for text and melody of songs after unilateral temporal lobe lesion: Evidence for dual encoding. *Journal of Experimental Psychology; Learning, Memory, and Cognition*, 17:793–804.

Samson, S., and Zatorre, R. J. 1994. Contribution of the right temporal lobe to musical timbre discrimination. *Neuropsychologia*, 32:231–240.

Sanacora, G., Kershaw, J., Finkelstein, J. A., and White, J. D. 1990. Increased hypothalamic content of preproneuropeptide Y messenger ribonucleic acid in genetically obese Zucker rats and its regulation by food deprivation. *Endocrinology*, 127:730–737.

Sanes, J. R., Marshall, L. M., and McMahan, U. J. 1978. Reinnervation of muscle fiber basal lamina after removal of myofibers. Differentiation of regenerating axons at original synaptic sites. *Journal of Cell Biology*, 78:176–198.

Sano, M., Stanley, M., Lawton, A., Cote, L., Williams, J., Stern, Y., Marder, K., and Mayeux, R. 1991. Tritiated imipramine binding. A peripheral marker for serotonin in Parkinson's disease. *Archives of Neurology*, 48:1052–1054.

Sano, M., Stern, Y., Cote, L., Williams, J. B., and Mayeux, R. 1990. Depression in Parkinson's disease: A biochemical model. *Journal of Neuropsychiatry and Clinical Neurosciences*, 2:88–92.

Sapolsky, R. M. 1992. *Stress, the aging brain, and the mechanisms of neuron death*. MIT Press, Cambridge, MA.

Sapolsky, R. M. 1993. Potential behavioral modification of glucocorticoid damage to the hippocampus. Special Issue: Alzheimer's disease: Animal models and clinical perspectives. *Behavioural Brain Research*, 57:175–182.

Sapolsky, R. M. 1994. *Why zebras don't get ulcers*. W. H. Freeman, New York.

Sapolsky, R. M., Uno, H., Rebert, C. S., and Finch, C. E. 1990. Hippocampal damage associated with prolonged glucocorticoid exposure in primates. *Journal of Neuroscience*, 10:2897–2902.

Sarno, M. T. 1981. Recovery and rehabilitation in aphasia. In M. T. Sarno (ed.), *Aphasia*. Academic Press, New York.

Sartorius, N., Jablensky, A., Korten, A., Ernberg, G., Anker, M., Cooper, J. E., and Day, R. 1986. Early manifestations and first– contact incidence of schizophrenia in different cultures. A preliminary report on the initial evaluation phase of the WHO Collaborative Study on determinants of outcome of severe mental disorders. *Psychological Medicine*, 16:909–928.

Satinoff, E. 1972. Salicylate: Action on normal body temperature in rats. *Science*, 176:532–533.

Satinoff, E. 1978. Neural organization and evolution of thermal regulation in mammals. *Science*, 201:16–22.

Satinoff, E. 1978. Neural Organization and evolution of thermal regulation in mammals. *Science*, 201:16–22.

Satinoff, E., and Rutstein, J. 1970. Behavioral thermoregulation in rats with anterior hypothalamic lesions. *Journal of Comparative and Physiological Psychology*, 71:77–82.

Satinoff, E., and Shan, S. Y. 1971. Loss of behavioral thermoregulation after lateral hypothalamic lesions in rats. *Journal of Comparative and Physiological Psychology*, 77:302–312.

Savage-Rumbaugh, E. S. 1990. Language acquisition in a nonhuman species: implications for the innateness debate. *Developmental Psychobiology*, 23:599–620.

Savage-Rumbaugh, E. S. 1993. *Language comprehension in ape and child*. University of Chicago Press, Chicago.

Savage-Rumbaugh, E. S., Murphy, J., Sevcik, R. A., Brakke, K. E., Williams, S. L., and Rumbaugh, D. M. 1993. Language comprehension in ape and child. *Monographs of the Society for Research in Child Development*, 58:1–222.

Savage-Rumbaugh, E. S., Rumbaugh, D. M., and Boysen, S. 1980. Do apes use language? *American Scientist*, 68:49–61.

Schacter, D. L., and Moscovitch, M. 1984. Infants, amnesics, and dissociable memory systems. In M. Moscovitch (ed.), *Infant memory*, pp. 173–216. Plenum Press, New York.

Schacter, S. 1975. Cognition and peripheralist-centralist controversies in motivation and emotion. In M. S. Gazzaniga, and C. Blakemore (eds.), *Handbook of psychobiology*. Academic Press, New York.

Schaffler, L., Luders, H. O., Dinner, D. S., Lesser, R. P., and Chelune, G. J. 1993. Comprehension deficits elicited by electrical stimulation of Broca's area. *Brain*, 116:695–715.

Schaie, K. W. 1994. The course of adult intellectual development. *American Psychologist*, 49:304–313.

Schatzberg, A. F., Rothschild, A. J., Stahl, J. B., Bond, T. C., Rosenbaum, A. H., Lofgren, S. B., MacLaughlin, R. A., Sullivan, A., and Cole, J. O. 1983. The dexamethasone suppression test: Identification of subtypes of depression. *American Journal of Psychiatry*, 140:88–91.

Scheff, S. W., Bernardo, L. S., and Cotman, C. W. 1978. Decrease in adrenergic axon sprouting in the senescent rat. *Science*, 202:775–778.

Scheibel, A. B. 1982. Age-related changes in the human forebrain. *Neurosciences Research Program Bulletin*, 20:577–583.

Scheibel, A. B., and Conrad, A. S. 1993. Hippocampal dysgenesis in mutant mouse and schizophrenic man: Is there a relationship? *Schizophrenia Bulletin*, 19:21–33.

Scheibel, A. B., Paul, L. A., Fried, I., Forsythe, A. B., Tomiyasu, U., Wechsler, A., Kao, A., and Slotnick, J. 1985. Dendritic organization of the anterior speech area. *Experimental Neurology*, 87:109–117.

Scheibel, M. E., Tomiyasu, U., and Scheibel, A. B. 1977. The aging human Betz cells. *Experimental Neurology*, 56:598–609.

Schenkerberg, T., Bradford, D. C., and Ajax, E. T. 1980. Line bisection and unilateral visual neglect in patients with neurologic impairment. *Neurology*, 30:509–518.

Scherer, K. R. 1993. Neuroscience projections to current debates in emotion psychology. *Cognition and Emotion*, 7:1–41.

Scheving, L. E., Vedral, D. F., and Pauley, J. E. 1968. Daily circadian rhythm in rats to d-amphetamine sulphate: Effect of blinding and continuous illumination on the rhythm. *Nature*, 219:621–622.

Schiff, B. B., and Lamon, M. 1989. Inducing emotion by unilateral contraction of facial muscles:A new look at hemispheric specialization and the experience of emotion. *Neuropsychologia*, 27:923–935.

Schiffman, S. S., Lockhead, E., and Maes, F. W. 1983. Amiloride reduces the taste intensity of Na^+ and Li^+ salts and sweeteners. *Proceedings of the National Academy of Sciences, U.S.A.*, 80: 6136–6140.

Schiffman, S. S., Simon, S. A., Gill, J. M., and Beeker, T. G. 1986. Bretylium tosylate enhances salt taste. *Physiology and Behavior*, 36:1129–1137.

Schildkraut, J. J., and Kety, S. S. 1967. Biogenic amines and emotion. *Science*, 156:21–30.

Schlaug, G., Jancke, L., Huang, Y., and Steinmetz, H. 1995. In vivo evidence of structural brain asymmetry in musicians. *Science*, 267:699–701.

Schliebs, R., Rose, S. P. R., and Stewart, M. G. 1985. Effect of passive-avoidance training on in vitro protein synthesis in forebrain slices of day-old chicks. *Journal of Neurochemistry*, 44: 1014–1028.

Schlupp, I., Marler, C., and Ryan, M. J. 1994. Benefit to male sailfin mollies of mating with heterospecific females. *Science*, 263:373–374.

Schmidt-Nielsen, K. 1960. *Animal physiology*. Prentice-Hall, Englewood Cliffs, NJ.

Schnapf, J. L., and Baylor, D. A. 1987. How photoreceptor cells respond to light. *Scientific American*, 256(4): 40–47.

Schneider, K. 1959. *Clinical psychopathology*. Grune & Stratton, New York.

Schneider-Helmert, D. 1985. Clinical evaluation of DSIP. In A. Wauquier, J. M. Gaillard, J. M. Monti, and M. Radulovacki (eds.), *Sleep: Neurotransmitters and neuromodulators*, pp. 279–291. Raven, New York.

Schreiber, S. S., Maren, S., Tocco, G., Shors, T. J., and Thompson, R. F. 1991. A negative correlation between the induction of long-term potentiation and activation of immediate early genes. *Brain Research*, 11:89–91.

Schulteis, G., and Martinez, J. L., Jr. 1992. Peripheral modulation of learning and memory: Enkephalins as a model system. *Psychopharmacology*, 109:347–364.

Schultz, R. T., Cho, N. K., Staib, L. H., Kier, L. E., Fletcher, J. M., Shaywitz, S. E., Shankweiler, D. P., Katz, L., Gore, J. C., Duncan, J. S. et al. 1994. Brain morphology in normal and dyslexic children:The influence of sex and age. *Annals of Neurology*, 35:732–742.

Schuman, E. M., and Madison, D. V. 1991. A requirement for the intercellular messenger nitric oxide in long-term potentiation. *Science*, 265:1503–1506.

Schuster, C. R. 1970. Psychological approaches to opiate dependence and self-administration by laboratory animals. *Federation Proceedings*, 29:1–5.

Schutz, F. 1965. Sexuelle Prägung bei Anatiden. *Zeitschrift für Tierpsychologie*, 22:50–103.

Schwartz, J. 1994. Low-level lead exposure and children's IQ: A meta-analysis and search for a threshold. *Environmental Research*, 65:42–55.

Schwartz, J. H., Castellucci, V. F., and Kandel, E. R. 1971. Functioning of identified neurons and synapses in abdominal ganglion of *Aplysia* in absence of protein synthesis. *Journal of Neurophysiology*, 34:939–963.

Schwartz, L. M. 1992. Insect muscle as a model for programmed cell death. *Journal of Neurobiology*, 23:1312–1326.

Schwartz, W. J., Smith, C. B., Davidsen, L., Savaki, H., Sokoloff, L., Mata, M., Fink, D. J., and Gainer, H. 1979. Metabolic mapping of functional activity in the hypothalamo- neurohypophysial system of the rat. *Science*, 205:723–725.

Schwartzkroin, P. A., and Wester, K. 1975. Long-lasting facilitation of a synaptic potential following tetanization in the *in vitro* hippocampal slice. *Brain Research*, 89:107–119.

Schwenk, K. 1994. Why snakes have forked tongues. *Science*, 263: 1573–1577.

Scientific American. 1992. Special Issue, September.

Sclafani, A., Springer, D., and Kluge, L. 1976. Effects of quinine adulteration on the food intake and body weight of obese and nonobese hypothalamic hyperphagic rats. *Physiology and Behavior*, 16:631–640.

Scoville, W. B., and Milner, B. 1957. Loss of recent memory after bilateral hippocampal lesions. *Journal of Neurology, Neurosurgery and Psychiatry*, 20:11–21.

Sedvall, C., Farde, L., Persson, A., and Wiesel, F. A. 1986. Imaging of neurotransmitter receptors in the living human brain. *Archives of General Psychiatry*, 43:995–1005.

Seeman, P., Guan, H. C., and Van Tol, H. H. 1993. Dopamine D4 receptors elevated in schizophrenia. *Nature*, 365:441–445.

Segal, N. L., Dysken, M. W., Bouchard, T. J., Jr., Pedersen, N. L., Eckert, E. D., and Heston, L. L. 1990. Tourette's disorder in a set of reared-apart triplets: Genetic and environmental influences. *American Journal of Psychiatry*, 147:196–199.

Sehgal, A., Price, J. L., Man, B., and Young, M. W. 1994. Loss of circadian behavioral rhythms and per RNA oscillations in the *Drosophila* mutant timeless. *Science*, 18:1603–1606.

Seidler, F. J., Bell, J. M., and Slotkin, T. A. 1990. Undernutrition and overnutrition in the neonatal rat: Long-term effects on noradrenergic pathways in brain regions. *Pediatric Research*, 27:191–197.

Seiger, A., Nordberg, A., von Holst, H., Backman, L., Ebendal, T., Alafuzoff, I. et al. 1993. Intracranial infusion of purified nerve growth factor to an Alzheimer patient: the first attempt of a possible future treatment strategy. *Behavioural Brain Research*, 57:255–261.

Seil, F. J., Drake-Baumann, R., and Johnson, M. L. 1994. Dystrophic dendrites induced in cultured Purkinje cells by exposure to vinblastine. *Brain Research*, 636:87–97.

Seil, F. J., Kelly, J. M., III, and Leiman, A. L. 1974. Anatomical organization of cerebral neocortex in tissue culture. *Experimental Neurology*, 45:435–450.

Seil, F. J., Leiman, A. L., and Kelly, J. 1976. Neuroelectric blocking factors in multiple sclerosis and normal human sera. *Archives of Neurology*, 33:418–422.

Selkoe, D. J. 1991. Amyloid protein and Alzheimer's disease. *Scientific American*, 165(5):68–71.

Selverston, A. I., and Moulins, M. 1985. Oscillatory neural networks. *Annual Review of Physiology*, 47:29–48.

Selye, H. 1956. *The stress of life*. McGraw-Hill, New York.

Serrano, P. A., Beniston, D. S., Oxonian, M. G., Rodriguez, W. A., Rosenzweig, M. R., and Bennett, E. L. 1994. Differential effects of protein kinase inhibitors and activators on memory formation in the 2-day-old chick. *Behavioral and Neural. Biology*, 61:60–72.

Serviere, J. Webster, W. R., and Calford, M. B. 1984. Isofrequency labelling revealed by a combined [14C]-2-deoxyglucose, electrophysiological, and horseradish peroxidase study of the inferior colliculus of the cat. *Journal of Comparative Neurology*, 228:463–478.

Serviere, J., Webster, W. R., and Calford, M. B. 1984. Isofrequency labelling revealed by a combined [14C]-2-deoxyglucose, electrophysiological, and horseradish peroxidase study of the inferior colliculus of the cat. *Journal of Comparative Neurology*, 228:463–477.

Seyfarth, R. M., and Cheney, D. L. 1984. The natural vocalizations of non-human primates. *Trends in Neurosciences*, 7:66–73.

Shapiro, C. M., Bortz, R., Mitchell, D., Bartel, P., and Jooste, P. 1981. Slow-wave sleep: A recovery period after exercise. *Science*, 214:1253–1254.

Shapiro, R. M. 1993. Regional neuropathology in schizophrenia:

Where are we? Where are we going? *Schizophrenia Research*, 10:187–239.

Sharp, P. E., McNaughton, B. L., and Barnes, C. A. 1983. Spontaneous synaptic enhancement in hippocampi of rats exposed to a spatially complex environment. *Society for Neuroscience Abstracts*, 9:647.

Shepherd, G. M. 1990. *The synaptic organization of the brain*, 3rd ed. Oxford, New York.

Sherrington, C. S. 1897. Part III. The central nervous system. In M. Foster (ed.), *A text-book of physiology*. Macmillan, London.

Sherrington, C. S. 1898. Experiments in examination of the peripheral distribution of the fibres of the posterior roots of some spinal nerves. *Philosophical Transactions of the Royal Society (London)*, 190:45–186.

Sherry, D. F. 1992. Memory, the hippocampus, and natural selection: Studies of food-storing birds. In L. R. Squire, and N. Butters (eds.), *Neuropsychology of memory*, 2nd ed., pp. 521–532. Guilford, New York.

Sherry, D. F., and Schacter, D. L. 1987. The evolution of multiple memory systems. *Psychological Review*, 94:439–454.

Sherry, D. F., and Vaccarino, A. L. 1989. Hippocampus and memory for food caches in black-capped chickadees. *Behavioral Neuroscience*, 103:308–318.

Sherry, D. F., Jacobs, L. F., and Gaulin, S. J. 1992. Spatial memory and adaptive specialization of the hippocampus. *Trends in Neurosciences*, 15:298–303.

Sherry, D. F., Jacobs, L. F., and Gaulin, S. J. 1993. "The hippocampus and spatial memory": Reply. *Trends in Neurosciences*, 16:57.

Sherry, D. F., Vaccarino, A. L., Buckenham, K., and Herz, R. S. 1989. The hippocampal complex of food-storing birds. *Brain, Behavior, and Evolution*, 34:308–317.

Shettleworth, S. J. 1993a. Varieties of learning and memory in animals. *Journal of Experimental Psychology: Animal Behavior Processes*, 19:5–14.

Shettleworth, S. J. 1993b. Where is the comparison in comparative cognition? Alternative research programs. *Psychological Science*, 4:179–184.

Shoulson, I. 1992. Neuroprotective clinical strategies for Parkinson's disease. *Annals of Neurology*, 32:S143–S145.

Sibley, C. G., and Ahlquist, J. E. 1987. DNA hybridization evidence of hominoid phylogeny: Results from an expanded data set. *Journal of Molecular Evolution*, 26:99–121.

Sibley, C. G., and Ahlquist, J. E. 1990. *Phylogeny and classification of birds: a study in molecular evolution*. Yale University Press, New Haven, CT.

Sibley, C. G., Comstock, J. A., and Ahlquist, J. E. 1990. DNA hybridization evidence of hominoid phylogeny: A reanalysis of the data. *Journal of Molecular Evolution*, 30:202–236.

Sidman, R. L., Green, M. C., and Appel, S. H. 1965. *Catalog of the neurological mutants of the mouse*. Harvard University Press, Cambridge, MA.

Siegel, R. K. 1989. *Intoxication: Life in pursuit of artificial paradise*. E. P. Dutton, New York.

Siever, L. J., and Davis, K. L. 1985. Overview: Toward a dysregulation hypothesis of depression. *American Journal of Psychiatry*, 142:1017–1031.

Sigman, M. 1995. Nutrition and child development: More food for thought. *Current Directions in Psychological Science*, 4:52–55.

Sigurdson, E., Staley, D., Matas, M., Hildahl, K., and Squair, K. 1994. A five year review of youth suicide in Manitoba. *Canadian Journal of Psychiatry*, 39:397–403.

Silberman, E. K., and Weingartner, H. 1986. Hemispheric lateralization of function related to emotion. *Brain and Cognition*, 5:322–353.

Silva, A. J., Paylor, R., Wehner, J. M., and Tonegawa, S. 1992. Impaired spatial learning in alpha-calcium-calmodulin kinase II mutant mice. *Science*, 257:206–211.

Silva, D. A., and Satz, P. 1979. Pathological left-handedness. Evaluation of a model. *Brain and Language*, 7:8–16.

Skagerberg, G., Bjartell, A., Vallet, P. G., and Charnay, Y. 1991. Immunocytochemical demonstration of DSIP-like immunoreactivity in the hypothalamus of the rat. *Peptides*, 12:1155–1159.

Skrede, K. K., and Malthe-Sorenssen, E. 1981. Increased resting and evoked release of transmitter following repetitive electrical tetanization in hippocampus: A biochemical correlate to long-lasting synaptic potentiation. *Brain Research*, 208:436–441.

Sladek, J. R., and Gash, D. M. 1984. Morphological and functional properties of transplanted vasopressin neurons. In J. R. Sladek, and D. M. Gash (eds.), *Neural transplants*, pp. 243–281. Plenum, New York.

Smale, L., Lee, T. M., Nelson, R. J., and Zucker, I. 1990. Prolactin counteracts effects of short day lengths on pelage growth in the meadow vole, *Microtus pennsylvanicus*. *Journal of Experimental Zoology*, 253:186–188.

Small, S. L. 1994. Pharmacotherapy of aphasia. A critical review. *Stroke*, 25:1282–1289.

Smith, A., and Sugar, O. 1975. Development of above normal language and intelligence 21 years after hemispherectomy. *Neurology*, 25:813–818.

Smith, C. 1985. Sleep states and learning. A review of the animal literature. *Neuroscience and Biobehavioral Reviews*, 9:157–169.

Smith, J. M., Kucharski, L., Oswald, W. T., and Waterman, L. J. 1979. A systematic investigation of tardive dyskinesia in inpatients. *American Journal of Psychiatry*, 136:918–922.

Smith, M. A., Grant, L. D., and Sors, A. I. 1989. *Lead exposure and child development: An international assessment*. Kluwer, Boston.

Smith, P. B., Compton, D. R., Welch, S. P., Razdan, R. K., Mechoulam, R., and Martin, B. R. 1994. The pharmacological activity of anandamide, a putative endogenous cannabinoid, in mice. *Journal of Pharmacology and Experimental Therapeutics*, 270:219–227.

Smolen, A. 1981. Postnatal development of ganglionic neurons in the absence of preganglionic input: Morphological synapse formation. *Developmental Brain Research*, 1:49–58.

Smythies, J. 1984. The transmethylation hypotheses of schizophrenia re-evaluated. *Trends in Neurosciences*, 7:48–53.

Snider, S. R. 1982. Cerebellar pathology in schizophrenia—Cause or consequence? *Neuroscience and Biobehavioral Reviews*, 6:47–53.

Snowdon, C. T. 1990. Mechanisms maintaining monogamy in monkeys. In D. A. Dewsbury (ed.), *Contemporary issues in comparative psychology*, pp. 225–251. Sinauer Associates, Sunderland, MA.

Snyder, F. 1969. Sleep and REM as biological enigmas. In A. Kales (ed.), *Sleep: Physiology and pathology*, pp. 266–280. Lippincott, Philadelphia.

Snyder, S. H. 1986. *Drugs and the brain*. W. H. Freeman, New York.

Snyder, S. H., and D'Amato, R. J. 1985. Predicting Parkinson's disease. *Nature*, 317:198–199.

Snyder, S. H., and D'Amato, R. J. 1986. MPTP: A neurotoxin relevant to the pathophysiology of Parkinson's disease. *Neurology*, 36:250–258.

Solomon, G. S. 1994. Anosmia in Alzheimer disease. *Perceptual and Motor Skills*, 79:1249–1250.

Sorensen, P. W., and Goetz, F. W. 1993. Pheromonal and reproductive function of F prostaglandins and their metabolites in teleost fish. *Journal of Lipid Mediators*, 6:385–393.

Sotelo, C. 1980. Mutant mice and the formation of cerebellar circuitry. *Trends in Neurosciences*, 3:33–36.

Spear, N. E. 1976. Retrieval of memories. A psychobiological approach. In W. K. Estes (ed.), *Handbook of learning and cognitive processes. Vol 4. Attention and memory*, pp. 17–90. Lawrence Erlbaum Associates, Hillsdale, NJ.

Spector, N. H. 1987. Old and new strategies in the conditioning of immune responses. *Annals of the New York Academy of Sciences*, 496:522–531.

Sperry, R. W. 1974. Lateral specialization in the surgically separated hemispheres. In F. O. Schmitt, and F. G. Worden (eds.), *Neuroscience 3rd study program*, pp. 5–20. MIT Press, Cambridge.

Sperry, R. W., Stamm, J., and Miner, N. 1956. Relearning tests for interocular transfer following division of optic chiasma and corpus callosum in cats. *Journal of Comparative and Physiological Psychology*, 49:529–533.

Sperry, R.W. 1984. Consciousness, personal identity and the divided brain. *Neuropsychologia*, 22:661–673.

Spiegler, B. J., and Yeni-Komshian, G. H. 1983. Incidence of left–handed writing in a college population with reference to family patterns of hand preference. *Neuropsychologia*, 21:651–659.

Springer, S. and Deutsch, G. 1985. *Left brain, right brain*. W. H. Freeman, New York.

Squire, L. R., Amaral, D. G., Zola-Morgan, S., Kritchevsky, M. P., and Press, G. 1989. Description of brain injury in the amnesic patient N.A. based on magnetic resonance imaging. *Experimental Neurology*, 105: 23–35.

Squire, L. R., and Butters, N. *Neuropsychology of memory*. Guilford, New York.

Squire, L. R., and Moore, R. Y. 1979. Dorsal thalamic lesion in a noted case of chronic memory dysfunction. *Annals of Neurology*, 6:503–506.

Squire, L. R., and Slater, P. C. 1975. Forgetting in very long-term memory as assessed by an improved questionnaire technique. *Journal of Experimental Psychology: Human Learning in Memory*, 104:50–54.

Squire, L. R., Knowlton, B., and Musen, G. 1993. The structure and organization of memory. *Annual Review of Psychology*, 44:453–495.

Standing, L. G. 1973. Learning 10,000 pictures. *Quarterly Journal of Experimental Psychology*, 25:207–222.

Stanford, S. C., and Gray, J. A. 1993. *Stress—From synapse to syndrome*. Academic Press, San Diego.

Stanley, B. G., Anderson, K. C., Grayson, M. H., and Leibowitz, S. F. 1989. Repeated hypothalamic stimulation with neuropeptide Y increases daily carbohydrate and fat intake and body weight gain in female rats. *Physiology and Behavior*, 46:173–177.

Starkman, M. N., Gebarski, S. S., Berent, S., and Schteingart, D. E. 1992. Hippocampal formation volume, memory dysfunction, and cortisol levels in patients with Cushing's syndrome. *Biological Psychiatry*, 32:756–765.

Starkstein, S. E., and Robinson, R. G. 1992. Neuropsychiatric aspects of stroke. In C. E. Coffey, J. L. Cummings, M. R. Lovell, and G. D. Pearlson (eds.), *The American Psychiatric Press textbook of geriatric neuropsychiatry*, pp. 457–477. American Psychiatric Press, Washington, D.C.

Starmer, G. A. 1994. *Drugs and traffic safety*. Federal Office of Road Safety, Canberra, Australia.

Staubli, U. V. 1995. Parallel properties of long-term potentiation and memory. In J. L. McGaugh, N. M. Weinberger, and G. Lynch (eds.), *Brain and memory: Modulation and mediation of neuroplasticity*, pp. 303–318. Oxford University Press, New York.

Staubli, U., Le, T. T., and Lynch, G. 1995. Variants of olfactory memory and their dependencies on the hippocampal formation. *Journal of Neuroscience*, 15:1162–1171.

Stein, B., and Meredith, M. A. 1993. *The merging of the senses*. MIT Press, Cambridge, MA.

Stein, M., and Miller, A. H. 1993. Stress, the hypothalamic-pituitary-adrenal axis, and immune function. *Advances in Experimental Medicine and Biology*, 335:1–5.

Stein, M., Keller, S., and Schleifer, S. 1981. The hypothalamus and the immune response. In H. Weiner, A. Hofer, and A. J. Stunkard (eds.), *Brain behavior and bodily disease*, pp. 45–63. Raven, New York.

Stein, M., Miller, A. H., and Trestman, R. L. 1991. Depression, the immune system, and health and illness. Findings in search of meaning. *Archives of General Psychiatry*, 48:171–177.

Steinmetz, H., Volkmann, J., Jancke, L., and Freund, H. J. 1991. Anatomical left-right asymmetry of language-related temporal cortex is different in left- and right-handers. *Annals of Neurology*, 29:315–319.

Stephan, F. K., and Zucker, I. 1972. Circadian rhythms in drinking behavior and locomotor activity of rats are eliminated by hypothalamic lesions. *Proceedings of the National Academy of Sciences, U.S.A.*, 69:1583–1586.

Stephan, H., Frahm, H., and Baron, G. 1981. New and revised data on volumes of brain structures in insectivores and primates. *Folia Primatologica*, 35:1–29.

Steptoe, A. 1993. Stress and the cardiovascular system: A psychosocial perspective. In S. C. Stanford, and P. Salmon (eds.), *Stress: From synapse to syndrome*, pp. 119–141. Academic Press, London.

Sternberg, D. E., VanKammen, D. P., Lerner, P., and Bunney, W. E. 1982. Schizophrenia: Dopamine beta-hydroxylase activity and treatment response. *Science*, 216:1423–1425.

Stitzer, M. L., and Higgins, S. T. 1995. Behavioral treatment of drug and alcohol abuse. In F. E. Bloom, and D. J. Kupfer (eds.), *Psychopharmacology, the fourth generation of progress*, pp. 1807–1819. Raven, New York.

Stoerig, P. 1993. Spatial summation in blindsight. *Visual Neuroscience*, 10:1141–1149.

Stone, J., Dreher, G., and Leventhal, A. 1979. Hierarchical and parallel mechanisms in the organization of visual cortex. *Brain Research*, 180:345–394.

Stone, R. 1994. Trail of toxins leads through conference rooms in Dallas. *Science*, 264:204.

Stricker, E. M. 1977. The renin-angiotensin system and thirst: a reevaluation. II. Drinking elicited in rats by caval ligation or isoproterenol. *Journal of Comparative and Physiological Psychology*, 91: 1220–1231.

Stricker, E. M. 1990. *Handbook of behavioral neurobiology, Vol. 10*. Plenum, New York.

Stromswold, K. 1995. The cognitive and neural bases of language acquisition. In M. S. Gazzaniga (ed.), *The cognitive neurosciences*, pp. 855–870. MIT Press, Cambridge, MA.

Stroud, R. M., and Finer-Moore, J. 1985. Acetylcholine receptor structure, function, and evolution. *Annual Review of Cell Biology*, 1:317–351.

Struhsaker, T. T. 1967. Social structure among vervet monkeys (*Cercopithecus aethiops*). *Behaviour*, 29:6–121.

Sullivan, R. M., and Leon, M. 1986. Early olfactory learning induces and enhanced olfactory bulb response in young rats. *Brain Research*, 392: 278–282.

Susser, E. S., and Lin, S. P. 1992. Schizophrenia after prenatal exposure to the Dutch Hunger Winter of 1944–1945. *Archives of General Psychiatry*, 49:983–988.

Sweet, W. H. 1973. Treatment of medically intractable mental disease by limited frontal leucotomy—Justifiable? *New England Journal of Medicine*, 289:1117–1125.

Swindale, N. V. 1990. Is the cerebral cortex modular? *Trends in Neurosciences*, 13:487–492.

Swindale, N. V. 1992. A model for the coordinated development of columnar systems in primate striate cortex. *Biological Cybernetics*, 66:217–230.

Syed, N. I., Bulloch, A. G., and Lukowiak, K. 1990. In vitro reconstruction of the respiratory central pattern generator of the mollusk Lymnaea. *Science*, 250:282–285.

Syed, N. I., Ridgway, R. L., Lukowiak, K., and Bulloch, A. G. 1992. Transplantation and functional integration of an identified respiratory interneuron in *Lymnaea stagnalis*. *Neuron*, 8:767–774.

Takagi, S. F. 1989. Standardized olfactometries in Japan—A review over ten years. *Chemical Senses*, 14:25–46.

Takahashi, J. S. 1995. Molecular neurobiology and genetics of circadian rhythms in mammals. *Annual Review of Neuroscience*, 18: 531–554.

Takahashi, Y. 1979. Growth hormone secretion related to the sleep and waking rhythm. In R. Drucker-Colin, M. Shkurovich, and M.B. Sterman (eds.), *The functions of sleep*. Academic Press, New York.

Takami, S., Getchell, T. V., McLaughlin, S. K., Margolskee, R. F., and Getchell, M. L. 1994. Human taste cells express the G protein alpha-gustducin and neuron-specific enolase. *Molecular Brain Research*, 22:193–203.

Tallal, P. et al. 1993. *Temporal information processing in the nervous system: Special reference to dyslexia and dysphasia*. New York Academy of Sciences, New York.

Tallal, P., and Schwartz, J. 1980. Temporal processing, speech perception and hemispheric asymmetry. *Trends in Neurosciences*, 3: 309–311.

Tamminga, C. A., and Schulz, S. C. 1991. *Schizophrenia research*. Raven, New York.

Tanaka, K. 1993. Neuronal mechanisms of object recognition. *Science*, 262:685–688.

Tanaka, Y., Kamo, T., Yoshida, M., and Yamadori, A. 1991. 'So-called' cortical deafness. Clinical, neurophysiological and radiological observations. *Brain*, 114:2385–2401.

Tandan, R., and Bradley, W. G. 1985. Amyotrophic lateral sclerosis: Part I. Clinical features, pathology, and ethical issues in management. *Annals of Neurology*, 18:271–281.

Tank, D. W., and Hopfield, J. J. 1987. Collective computation in neuronlike circuits. *Scientific American*, 257(6):104–114.

Taub, E. 1976. Movement in nonhuman primates deprived of somatosensory feedback. *Exercise and Sport Sciences Reviews*, 4:335–374.

Taylor, E. W. 1993. Molecular muscle. *Science*, 261:35–36.

Technau, G. M. 1984. Fiber number in the mushroom bodies of adult *Drosophila melanogaster* depends on age, sex and experience. *Journal of Neurogenetics*, 1:113–126.

Teitelbaum, P., and Stellar, E. 1954. Recovery from failure to eat produced by hypothalamic lesions. *Science*, 120:894–895.

Tempel, B. L., Bonini, N., Dawson, D. R., and Quinn, W. G. 1983. Reward learning in normal and mutant *Drosophila*. *Proceedings of the National Academy of Sciences, U.S.A.*, 80:1482–1486.

Tenn, W. 1968. *The seven sexes*. Ballantine Books, New York.

Teodoru, D. E., and Berman, A. J. 1980. The role of attempted movements in recovery from lateral dorsal rhizotomy. *Society for Neuroscience Abstracts*, G:25.

Terman, G. W., Shavit, Y., Lewis, J. W., Cannon, J. T., and Liebeskind, J. C. 1984. Intrinsic mechanisms of pain inhibition: Activation by stress. *Science*, 226:1270–1277.

Terrace, H. S. 1979. *Nim*. Knopf, New York.

Terry, R. D., Masliah, E., Salmon, D. P., Butters, N., DeTeresa, R., Hill, R., Hansen, L. A., and Katzman, R. 1991. Physical basis of cognitive alterations in Alzheimer's disease: Synapse loss is the major correlate of cognitive impairment. *Annals of Neurology*, 30:572–580.

Tessier-Lavigne, M., and Placzek, M. 1991. Target attraction: are developing axons guided by chemotropism? *Trends in Neurosciences*, 14:303–310.

Tessier-Lavigne, M., Placzek, M., Lumsden, A. G., Dodd, J., and Jessell, T. M. 1988. Chemotropic guidance of developing axons in the mammalian central nervous system. *Nature*, 336:775–778.

Tetrud, J. W., Langston, J. W., Irwin, I., and Snow, B. 1994. Parkinsonism caused by petroleum waste ingestion. *Neurology*, 44:1051–1054.

Teuber, H. L., Milner, B., and Vaughan, H. G. 1968. Persistent anterograde amnesia after stab wound of the basal brain. *Neuropsychologia*, 6:267–282.

Teyler, T. J., and DiScenna, P. 1986. Long-term potentiation. *Annual Review of Neuroscience*, 10:131–161.

Thibos, L. N., and Levick, W. R. 1985. Orientation bias of brisk-transient y-cells of the cat retina for drifting and alternating gratings. *Experimental Brain Research*, 58:1–10.

Thomas, C. B., Duszynski, K. R., and Shaffer, J. W. 1979. Family attitudes reported in youth as potential predictors of cancer. *Psychosomatic Medicine*, 41:287–302.

Thompson, G. N., and Halliday, D. 1990. Significant phenylalanine hydroxylation in vivo in patients with classical phenylketonuria. *Journal of Clinical Investigation*, 86:317–322.

Thompson, R. F. 1986. The neurobiology of learning and memory. *Science*, 233:941–947.

Thompson, R. F. 1990. Neural mechanisms of classical conditioning in mammals. *Philosophical Transactions of the Royal Society (London), Series B*, 329:161–170.

Thompson, R. F. 1992. Memory. *Current Opinion in Neurobiology*, 2: 203–208.

Thompson, T., and Schuster, C. R. 1964. Morphine self-administration, food reinforced and avoidance behaviour in rhesus monkeys. *Psychopharmacologia*, 5:87–94.

Thorndike, E. L. 1898. Animal intelligence: An experimental study of the associative processes in animals. *Psychological Review Monograph*.

Thorpy, M. J., and Yager, J. 1991. *The encyclopedia of sleep and sleep disorders*. Facts on File, New York.

Thurber, J., and White, E. B. 1929. *Is sex necessary? or, Why you feel the way you do*. Harper, New York.

Timberlake, W. 1993. Animal behavior: A continuing synthesis. *Annual Review of Psychology*, 44:675–708.

Tobias, P. V. 1980. L'Evolution du cerveau humain. *La Recherche*, 11:282–292.

Toenniessen, L. M., Casey, D. E., and McFarland, B. H. 1985. Tardive dyskinesia in the aged. Duration of treatment relationships. *Archives of General Psychiatry*, 42:278–284.

Tolman, E. C. 1949. There is more than one kind of learning. *Psychological Review*, 56:144–155.

Tolman, E. C., and Honzik, C. H. 1930. Introduction and removal of reward, and maze performance in rats. *University of California Publications in Psychology*, 4:257–275.

Tonkonogy, J. M. 1991. Violence and temporal lobe lesion: Head CT and MRI data. *Journal of Neuropsychiatry and Clinical Neurosciences*, 3:189–196.

Tootell, R. B., Silverman, M. S., Hamilton, S. L., De Valois, R. L., and Switkes, E. 1988a. Functional anatomy of macaque striate cortex. III. Color. *Journal of Neuroscience*, 8:1569–1593.

Tootell, R. B., Silverman, M. S., Switkes, E., and De Valois, R. L. 1982. De-oxyglucose analysis of retinotopic organization in primate striate cortex. *Science*, 218:902–904.

Tootell, R. B., Switkes, E., Silverman, M. S., and Hamilton, S. L. 1988b. Functional anatomy of macaque striate cortex. II. Retinotopic organization. *Journal of Neuroscience*, 8:1531–1568.

Torrey, E. F., Bowler, A. E., Taylor, E. H., and Gottesman, I. I. 1994. *Schizophrenia and manic depressive disorder*. Basic Books, New York.

Tranel, D., and Damasio, A. R. 1985. Knowledge without awareness: An autonomic index of facial recognition by prosopagnosics. *Science*, 228:1453–1454.

Tranel, D., Damasio, A. R., and Damasio, H. 1988. Intact recognition of facial expression, gender, and age in patients with impaired recognition of face identity. *Neurology*, 38:690–696.

Travis, J. 1992. Can 'hair cells' unlock deafness? *Science*, 257:1344–1345.

Treisman, M. 1977. Motion sickness—Evolutionary hypotheses. *Science*, 197:493–495.

Trimble, M. R. 1991. Interictal psychoses of epilepsy. *Advances in Neurology*, 55:143–152.

Trivers, R. L. 1972. Parental investment and sexual selection. In B. Campbell (ed.), *Sexual selection and the descent of man*. Aldine, Chicago.

True, W. R., Rice, J., Eisen, S. A., Heath, A. C., Goldberg, J., Lyons, M. J., and Nowak, J. 1993. A twin study of genetic and environmental contributions to liability for posttraumatic stress symptoms. *Archives of General Psychiatry,* 50:257–264.

Truman, J. W. 1983. Programmed cell death in the nervous system of an adult insect. *Journal of Comparative Neurology,* 216:445–452.

Ts'o, D. Y., Frostig, R. D., Lieke, E. E., and Grinvald, A. 1990. Functional organization of primate visual cortex revealed by high resolution optical imaging. *Science,* 249:417–420.

Tully, T. 1987. *Drosophila* learning and memory revisited. *Trends in Neurosciences,* 10:330–335.

Tulving, E. 1972. Episodic and semantic memory. In E. Tulving, and W. Donaldson (eds.), *Organization of memory,* pp. 381–403. Academic Press, New York.

Tulving, E. 1989. Memory: Performance, knowledge, and experience. *European Journal of Cognitive Psychology,* 1:3–26.

Tulving, E., Hayman, C. A., and Macdonald, C. A. 1991. Long-lasting perceptual priming and semantic learning in amnesia: A case experiment. *Journal of Experimental Psychology: Learning, Memory, and Cognition,* 17:595–617.

Turek, F. 1985. Circadian neural rhythms in mammals. *Annual Review of Physiology,* 47:49–64.

Turkewitz, G. 1988. A prenatal source for the development of hemispheric specialization. In D. L. Molfese, and S. J. Segalowitz (eds.), *Brain lateralization in children: Developmental implications,* pp. 73–81. Guilford, New York.

Turner, A. M., and Greenough, W. T. 1985. Differential rearing effects on rat visual cortex synapses. I. Synaptic and neuronal density and synapses per neuron. *Brain Research,* 329:195–203.

Tyrer, P., and Marsden, C. 1985. New antidepressant drugs: Is there anything new they tell us about depression? *Trends in Neurosciences,* 8:427–431.

Tzeng, O., and Wang, W. Y.–S. 1984. Search for a common neurocognitive mechanism for language and movements. *American Journal of Physiology,* 246:R904–R911.

U.S. Congress Joint Economic Committee. 1988. *The 1987 economic report of the president: Hearings before the Joint Economic Committee, Congress of the United States, 1987.* G.P.O., Washington, D.C.

U.S. Department of Health and Human Services. 1991. *Drug abuse and drug abuse research: The third triennial report to Congress.* National Institute on Drug Abuse, Rockville, MD.

U.S. Department of Health and Human Services. 1992. *National household survey on drug abuse: Population estimates 1991.* National Institute on Drug Abuse, Rockville, MD.

Udani, P. M. 1992. Protein energy malnutrition (PEM), brain and various

facets of child development. *Indian Journal of Pediatrics,* 59:165–186.

Uhl, G. R., Elmer, G. I., LaBuda, M. C., and Pickens, R. W. 1995. Genetic influences in drug abuse. In F. E. Bloom, and D. J. Kupfer (eds.), *Psychopharmacology, the fourth generation of progress,* pp. 1793–1806. Raven, New York.

Underwood, B. J. 1969. Attributes of memory. *Psychological Review,* 76:559–573.

Ursin, H., and Olff, M. 1993. The stress response. In S. C. Clanford, and P. Salmon (eds.), *Stress: From synapse to syndrome,* pp. 3–22. Academic Press, London.

Ursin, H., Baade, E., and Levine, S. 1978. *Psychobiology of stress: A study of coping men.* Academic Press, New York.

Vallbo, A. B. 1995. Single-afferent neurons and somatic sensation in humans. In M. S. Gazzaniga (ed.), *The cognitive neurosciences,* pp. 237–253. The MIT Press, Cambridge, MA.

Vallbo, A. B., and Johansson, R. S. 1984. Properties of cutaneous mechanoreceptors in the human hand related to touch sensation. *Human Neurobiology,* 3:3–15.

Valenstein, E. S. 1973. *Brain control.* Wiley-Interscience, New York.

Valenstein, E. S. 1980. *The psychosurgery debate: Scientific, legal, and ethical perspectives.* W. H. Freeman, San Francisco.

Valenstein, E. S. 1986. *Great and desperate cures: The rise and decline of psychosurgery and other radical treatments for mental illness.* Basic Books, New York.

Vallee, R. B., and Bloom, G. S. 1991. Mechanisms of fast and slow axonal transport. *Annual Review of Neuroscience,* 14:59–92.

van Bergeijk, W. A. 1967. The evolution of vertebrate hearing. In W. D. Neff (ed.), *Contributions to sensory physiology, Vol. 3.* Academic Press, New York.

Van de Castle, R. 1994. *Our dreaming mind.* Ballantine, New York.

Van Essen, D. C., Anderson, C. H., and Felleman, D. J. 1992. Information processing in the primate visual system: An integrated systems perspective. *Science,* 255:419–423.

Van Toller, S. 1979. *The nervous body: an introduction to the autonomic nervous system and behaviour.* Wiley, Chichester, England.

van Valen, L. 1974. Brain size and intelligence in man. *American Journal of Physical Anthropology,* 40:417–424.

van Zoeren, J. G., and Stricker, E. M. 1977. Effects of preoptic, lateral hypothalamic, or dopamine-depleting lesions on behavioral thermoregulation in rats exposed to the cold. *Journal of Comparative and Physiological Psychology,* 91:989–999.

Vander Wall, S. B. 1982. An experimental analysis of cache recovery in Clark's

nutcracker. *Animal Behaviour,* 30: 84–94.

Vassar, R., Ngai, J., and Axel, R. 1993. Spatial segregation of odorant receptor expression in the mammalian olfactory epithelium. *Cell,* 74:309–318.

Vaughan, W., and Greene, S. L. 1984. Pigeon visual memory capacity. *Journal of Experimental Psychology: Animal Behavior Processes,* 10:256–271.

Veraa, R. P., and Graftein, B. 1981. Cellular mechanisms for recovery from nervous system injury: A conference report. *Experimental Neurology,* 71:6–75.

Verma, I. M. 1990. Gene therapy. *Scientific American,* 263(5):68–72.

Virkkunen, M., and Linnoila, M. 1993. Brain serotonin, type II alcoholism and impulsive violence. *Journal of Studies on Alcohol (Supplement),* 11:163–169.

Vitaterna, M. H., King, D. P., Chang, A. M., Kornhauser, J. M., Lowrey, P. L., McDonald, J. D., Dove, W. F., Pinto, L. H., Turek, F. W., and Takahashi, J. S. 1994. Mutagenesis and mapping of a mouse gene, *Clock,* essential for circadian behavior. *Science,* 264: 719–725.

Vogel, G. W., Vogel, F., McAbee, R. S., and Thurmond, A. J. 1980. Improvement of depression by REM sleep deprivation: New findings and a theory. *Archives of General Psychiatry,* 37:247–253.

Volkmar, F. R., and Greenough, W. T. 1972. Rearing complexity affects branching of dendrites in the visual cortex of the rat. *Science,* 176: 1445–1447.

von Békésy, G. 1967. *Sensory inhibition.* Princeton University Press, Princeton, NJ.

von Bonin, G., and Bailey, P. 1947. *The neocortex of Macaca mulatta.* University of Illinois Press, Urbana.

von der Heydt, R., and Peterhans, E. 1989. Mechanisms of contour perception in monkey visual cortex. I. Lines of pattern discontinuity. *Journal of Neuroscience,* 9:1731–1748.

Voneida, T. J. 1990. The effect of rubrospinal tractotomy on a conditioned limb response in the cat. *Society for Neuroscience Abstracts,* 16:279.

Vonnegut, K. 1963. *Cat's cradle.* Delacorte, New York.

Vosshall, L. B., Price, J. L., Sehgal, A., Saez, L., and Young, M. W. 1994. Block in nuclear localization of period protein by a second clock mutation, timeless. *Science,* 263:1606–1609.

Wada, J. A., and Rasmussen, T. 1960. Intracarotid injection of sodium amytal for the lateralization of cerebral speech dominance: Experimental and clinical observations. *Journal of Neurosurgery,* 17:266–282.

Wagner, G. C., Beuving, L. J., and Hutchinson, R. R. 1980. The effects of gonadal hormone manipulations on aggressive target-biting in mice. *Aggressive Behavior*, 6:1–7.

Wahl, O. F. 1976. Monozygotic twins discordant for schizophrenia: A review. *Psychological Bulletin*, 83:91–106.

Wald, G. 1964. The receptors of human color vision. *Science*, 145:1007–1016.

Walker, E. F. 1991. *Schizophrenia: A life-course developmental perspective*. Academic Press, San Diego.

Wall, J. T., and Kaas, J. H. 1986. Long-term cortical consequences of reinnervation errors after nerve regeneration in monkeys. *Brain Research*, 372:400–404.

Wall, P. D. 1977. The presence of ineffective synapses and the circumstances which unmask them. *Philosophical Transactions of the Royal Society (London), Series B*, 221:361–372.

Wall, P. D. 1980. Mechanisms of plasticity of connection following damage of adult mammalian nervous systems. In P. Bach-y-Rita (ed.), *Recovery of function: Theoretical considerations for brain injury rehabilitation*, pp. 1–2. Hans Huber, Bern, Switzerland.

Wall, P. D., and Egger, M. D. 1971. Formation of new connexions in adult rat brains after partial deafferentation. *Nature*, 232:542–545.

Walls, G. L. 1942. *The vertebrate eye, Vol. 1*. Crankbrook Institute of Science, Bloomfield Hills, Mich.

Walters, E. T., and Byrne, J. H. 1983. Associative conditioning of single neurons suggests a cellular mechanism for learning. *Science*, 219:405–408.

Wang, J. B., Imai, Y., Eppler, C. M., Gregor, P., Spivak, C. E., and Uhl, G. R. 1993. Opiate receptor: cDNA cloning and expression. *Proceedings of the National Academy of Sciences, U.S.A.*, 90:10230–10234.

Wang, W. S.-Y. 1991. *The emergence of language: Development and evolution: Readings from "Scientific American" magazine*. W. H. Freeman, New York.

Ward, I. L. 1969. Differential effect of pre- and postnatal androgen on the sexual behavior of intact and spayed female rats. *Hormones and Behavior*, 1:25–36.

Warrington, E. K., and Silberstein, M. 1970. A questionnaire technique for investigating very long term memory. *Quarterly Journal of Experimental Psychology*, 22:508–512.

Watkins, J. C., and Collingridge, G. L. 1989. *The NMDA receptor*. IRL Press at Oxford University Press, Oxford.

Wauquier, A., Clincke, G. H. C., van den Broeck, A. E., and DePrins, E. 1985. Active and permissive roles of dopamine in sleep–wakefulness regulation. In A. Wauquier, J. M. Gaillard, J. M. Monti, and Radulovacki. M. (eds.), *Sleep: Neurotransmitters and neuromodulators*. Raven, New York.

Webb, W. B. 1978. The sleep of conjoined twins. *Sleep*, 1:205–211.

Webb, W. B. 1982. *Biological rhythms, sleep, and performance*. Wiley, Chichester, England.

Webb, W. B. 1992. *Sleep, the gentle tyrant*. Anker, Bolton, MA.

Weeks, J. C., and Levine, R. B. 1990. Postembryonic neuronal plasticity and its hormonal control during insect metamorphosis. *Annual Review of Neuroscience*, 13:183–194.

Wehr, T. A., Goodwin, F. K., Wirz-Justice, A., Breitmaier, J., and Craig, C. 1982. 48-hour sleep–wake cycles in manic-depressive illness: Naturalistic observations and sleep deprivation experiments. *Archives of General Psychiatry*, 39:559–565.

Wehr, T. A., Jacobsen, F. M., Sack, D. A., Arendt, J., Tamrkin, L., and Rosenthal, N. E. 1986. Phototherapy of seasonal affective disorder. *Archives of General Psychiatry*, 43:870–875.

Wehr, T. A., Sack, D. A., Duncan, W. C., Mendelson, W. B., Rosenthal, N. E., Gillina, J. C., and Goodwin, F. K. 1985. Sleep and circadian rhythms in affective patients isolated from external time cues. *Psychiatry Research*, 15:327–339.

Wehr, T., Sack, D., Rosenthal, N., Duncan, W., and Gillin, J. C. 1983. Circadian rhythm disturbances in manic-depressive illness. *Federation Proceedings*, 42:2809–2814.

Weil, A., and Rosen, W. 1993. *From chocolate to morphine: Everything you need to know about mind-altering drugs*. Houghton Mifflin, Boston.

Weinberger, D. R., Aloia, M. S., Goldberg, T. E., and Berman, K. F. 1994. The frontal lobes and schizophrenia. *Journal of Neuropsychiatry and Clinical Neurosciences*, 6:419–427.

Weinberger, D. R., Bigelow, L. B., Kleinman, J. E., Klein, S. T., Rosenblatt, J. E., and Wyatt, R. J. 1980. Cerebral ventricular enlargement in chronic schizophrenia. An association with poor response to treatment. *Archives of General Psychiatry*, 37:11–13.

Weinberger, D. R., Zigun, J. R., Bartley, A. J., Jones, D. W., and Torrey, E. F. 1992. Anatomical abnormalities in the brains of monozygotic twins discordant and concordant for schizophrenia. *Clinical Neuropharmacology*, 15:122A–123A.

Weinberger, N. M. 1995. Dynamic regulation of receptive fields and maps in the adult sensory cortex. *Annual Review of Neuroscience*, 18:129–159.

Weiner, H. 1992. *Perturbing the organism: The biology of stressful experience*. University of Chicago Press, Chicago.

Weiner, R. D. 1994. Treatment optimization with ECT. *Psychopharmacology Bulletin*, 30:313–320.

Weinshilboum, R. M. 1984. Human pharmacogenetics. *Federation Proceedings*, 43:2295–2297.

Weiskrantz, L. 1986. *Blindsight: A case study and implications*. Oxford University Press, New York.

Weiskrantz, L. 1993. Sources of blindsight. *Science*, 261:494–495.

Weisman, A. D., and Worden, J. W. 1976. The existential plight in cancer: Significance of the first 100 days. *International Journal of Psychiatry in Medicine*, 7:1–15.

Weiss, B. 1988. Neurobehavioral toxicity as a basis for risk assessment. *Trends in Pharmacological Sciences*, 9:59–62.

Weiss, B. 1992. Behavioral toxicology: A new agenda for assessing the risks of environmental pollution. In J. Grabowski, and G. R. VandenBos (eds.), *Psychopharmacology: Basic mechanisms and applied interventions*, pp. 167–207. American Psychological Association, Washington, D.C.

Weiss, J. M. 1977. Psychological and behavioral influences on gastrointestinal lesions in animal models. In J. D. Maser, and M. E. P. Seligman (eds.), *Psychopathology: Experimental methods*. W. H. Freeman, San Francisco.

Weitzman, E. D. 1981. Sleep and its disorders. *Annual Review of Neurosciences*, 4:381–417.

Weitzman, E. D. 1981. Sleep and its disorders. *Annual Review of Neurosciences*, 4:381–417.

Weitzman, E. D., Czeisler, C. A., Zimmerman, J. C., and Moore-Ede, M. C. 1981. Biological rhythms in man: Relationship of sleep-wake, cortisol, growth hormone, and temperature during temporal isolation. In J. B. Martin, S. Reichlin, and K. L. Bick (eds.), *Neurosecretion and brain peptides*. Raven, New York.

Weller, L., and Weller, A. 1993. Human menstrual synchrony: A critical assessment. *Neuroscience and Biobehavioral Reviews*, 17:427–439.

Wertheimer, M. 1925. *Drei Abhandlungen zur Gestalttheorie*. Philosophische Akademie, Neuhrsg., Erlangen.

West, R. W., and Greenough, W. T. 1972. Effect of environmental complexity on cortical synapses of rats: Preliminary results. *Behavioral Biology*, 7:279–284.

Westheimer, G. 1984. Spatial vision. *Annual Review of Psychology*, 35:201–226.

Wever, E. G. 1974. The evolution of vertebrate hearing. In *Handbook of sensory physiology Vol. 1. Audition*, Springer-Verlag, New York.

Wever, R. A. 1979. Influence of physical workload on freerunning circadian rhythms of man. *Pflugers Archiv. European Journal of Physiology*, 381:119–126.

Wexler, B. E., and Heninger, G. R. 1979. Alterations in cerebral laterality during acute psychotic illness. *Archives of General Psychiatry*, 36:278–284.

Wexler, N. S., Rose, E. A., and Housman, D. E. 1991. Molecular approaches to hereditary diseases of the nervous system: Huntington's disease as a paradigm. *Annual Review of Neuroscience*, 14:503–529.

White, L. E., and Hain, R. F. 1959. Anorexia in association with a destructive lesion of the hypothalamus. *Archives of Pathology*, 68:275–281.

White, N. M., and Milner, P. M. 1992. The psychobiology of reinforcers. *Annual Review of Psychology*, 43:443–471.

White, R. J. 1976. Medical and ethical problems of long-term profound unconsciousness. *Resuscitation*, 5:1–4.

Wible, C. G., Shenton, M. E., Hokama, H., Kikinis, R., Jolesz, F. A., Metcalf, D., and McCarley, R. W. 1995. Prefrontal cortex and schizophrenia. A quantitative magnetic resonance imaging study. *Archives of General Psychiatry*, 52:279–288.

Wiesel, T. N., and Hubel, D. H. 1963. Single-cell responses in striate cortex of kittens deprived of vision in one eye. *Journal of Neurophysiology*, 26:1003–1017.

Wiesel, T. N., and Hubel, D. H. 1965. Extent of recovery from the effects of visual deprivation in kittens. *Journal of Neurophysiology*, 28:1060–1072.

Wikler, K. C., and Rakic, P. 1990. Distribution of photoreceptor subtypes in the retina of diurnal and nocturnal primates. *Journal of Neuroscience*, 10:3390–3401.

Wiklund, C., and Sillén-Tullberg, B. 1985. Why distasteful butterflies have aposematic larvae and adults, but cryptic pupae: Evidence from predation experiments on the monarch and the European swallowtail. *Evolution*, 39:1155–1158.

Wilcox, S. 1979. Sex discrimination in *Gerris remigis*: Role of a surface wave signal. *Science*, 206:1325–1327.

Will, B. E., Rosenzweig, M. R., Bennett, E. L., Hebert, M., and Morimoto, H. 1977. Relatively brief environmental enrichment aids recovery of learning capacity and alters brain measures after postweaning brain lesions in rats. *Journal of Comparative and Physiological Psychology*, 91:33–50.

Williams, D. 1969. Neural factors related to habitual aggression. *Brain*, 92:503–520.

Willner, P. 1991. *Behavioural models in psychopharmacology*. Cambridge University Press, New York.

Wilson, D. L., and Berkman, L. F. 1983. Mortality risk associated with sleeping patterns among adults. *Sleep*, 6:102–107.

Wilson, J. D., and Foster, D. W. 1992. *Williams' textbook of endocrinology*, 8th ed. W. B. Saunders, Orlando, Fla.

Wilson, M. A., and McNaughton, B. L. 1994. Reactivation of hippocampal ensemble memories during sleep. *Science*, 165:676–679. Wilson, R. C., Kesner, J. S., Kaufman, J. M., Uemura, T., Akema, T., and Knobil, E. 1984. Central electrophysiologic correlates of pulsatile luteinizing hormone secretion in the rhesus monkey. *Neuroendocrinology*, 39:256–260.

Wimer, C. C., and Wimer, R. E. 1989. On the sources of strain and sex differences in granule cell number in the dentate area of house mice. *Developmental Brain Research*, 48:167–176.

Wimer, R. E., and Wimer, C. C. 1985. Animal behavior genetics: A search for the biological foundations of behavior. *Annual Review of Psychology*, 36:171–218.

Wimer, R. E., Wimer, C. C., Vaughn, J. E., Barber, R. P., Balvanz, B. A., and Chernow, C. R. 1976. The genetic organization of neuron number in Ammon's horns of house mice. *Brain Research*, 118:219–243.

Wingard, D. L., and Berkman, L. F. 1983. Mortality risk associated with sleeping patterns among adults. *Sleep*, 6:102–107.

Wingfield, J. C., Ball, G. F., Dufty, A. M., Hegner, R. E., and Ramenofsky, M. 1987. Testosterone and aggression in birds. *American Scientist*, 75:602–608.

Winick, M. 1976. *Malnutrition and brain development*. Oxford, New York.

Winick, M., Meyer, N. K., and Harris, R. C. 1975. Malnutrition and environmental enrichment by early adoption. *Science*, 190:1173–1175.

Winocur, G. 1990. Anterograde and retrograde amnesia in rats with dorsal hippocampal or dorsomedial thalamic lesions. *Behavioural Brain Research*, 38:145–154.

Wise, R. A. 1984. Neural mechanisms of the reinforcing action of cocaine. In J. Grabowski (ed.), *Cocaine: Pharmacology, effects and treatment of abuse*, pp. 15–33. National Institute on Drug Abuse, Washington, D.C.

Wise, R. A., Bauco, P., Carlezon, W. A., Jr., and Trojniar, W. 1992. Self-stimulation and drug reward mechanisms. *Annals of the New York Academy of Sciences*, 654:192–198.

Wise, S. P., and Strick, P. L. 1984. Anatomical and physiological organization of the non-primary motor cortex. *Trends in Neurosciences* 7:442–447.

Witelson, S. F., and Pallie, W. 1973. Left hemisphere specialization for language in the newborn. Neuroanatomical evidence of asymmetry. *Brain*, 96:641–646.

Wolf, S., and Wolff, H. G. 1947. *Human gastric function: An experimental study of a man and his stomach*. Oxford University Press, London.

Wolinsky, E., and Way, J. 1990. The behavioral genetics of *Caenorhabditis elegans*. *Behavior Genetics*, 20:169–189.

Wolske, M., Rompre, P. P., Wise, R. A., and West, M. O. 1993. Activation of single neurons in the rat nucleus accumbens during self-stimulation of the ventral tegmental area. *Journal of Neuroscience*, 13:1–12.

Woo, C. C., and Leon, M. 1987. Sensitive period for neural and behavioral response development to learned odors. *Developmental Brain Research*, 36:309–313.

Woo, C. C., Coopersmith, R., and Leon, M. 1987. Localized changes in olfactory bulb morphology associated with early olfactory learning. *Journal of Comparative Neurology*, 263:113–125.

Wood, J. M., Bootzin, R. R., Kihlstrom, J. F., and Schacter, D. L. 1992. Implicit and explicit memory for verbal information presented during sleep. *Psychological Science*, 3:236–239.

Woods, B. T., and Teuber, H. L. 1978. Changing patterns of childhood aphasia. *Annals of Neurology*, 3:273–280.

Woolsey, C. N. 1981a. *Cortical sensory organization: Multiple auditory areas*. Humana, Crescent Manor, NJ.

Woolsey, C. N. 1981b. *Cortical sensory organization: Multiple somatic areas*. Humana, Crescent Manor, NJ.

Woolsey, C. N. 1981c. *Cortical sensory organization: Multiple visual areas*. Humana, Crescent Manor, NJ.

Woolsey, T. A., and Wann, J. R. 1976. Areal changes in mouse cortical barrels following vibrissal damage at different postnatal ages. *Journal of Comparative Neurology*, 170:53–66.

Woolsey, T. A., Durham, D., Harris, R. M., Simous, D. T., and Valentino, K. 1981. Somatosensory development. In R. S. Aslin, J. R. Alberts, and M. R. Peterson (eds.), *Sensory and perceptual development: Influence of genetic and experiential factors*. Academic Press, New York.

Wright, A. A. et al. 1985. Memory processing of serial lists by pigeons, monkeys, and people. *Science*, 229:287–289.

Wu, J. Y., Cohen, L. B., and Falk, C. X. 1994. Neuronal activity during different behaviors in *Aplysia*: A distributed organization? *Science*, 263:820–823.

Yahr, P., and Gregory, J. E. 1993. The medial and lateral cell groups of the sexually dimorphic area of the gerbil hypothalamus are essential for male sex behavior and act via separate pathways. *Brain Research*, 631:287–296.

Yanagisawa, K., Bartoshuk, L. M., Karrer, T. A. et al. 1992. Anesthesia of the chorda tympani nerve: Insights into a source of dysgeusia. *Chemical Senses*, 17:724.

Yasuda, K., Raynor, K., Kong, H., Breder, C., Takeda, J., Reisine, T., and Bell, G. I. 1993. Cloning and functional comparison of kappa and opioid receptors from mouse brain. *Proceedings of the National Academy of Sciences, U.S.A.*, 90:6736–6740.

Yeo, C. H., Hardiman, M. J., and Glickstein, M. 1985. Classical conditioning of the nictitating membrane response of the rabbit. II. Lesions of the cerebellar cortex. *Experimental Brain Research*, 60:99–113.

Young, A. B. 1993. Role of excitotoxins in heredito-degenerative neurologic diseases. *Research Publications, Association for Research in Nervous and Mental Disease*, 71:175–189.

Yu, S., Pritchard, M., Kremer, E., Lynch, M., Nancarrow, J., Baker, E., Holman, K., Mulley, J. C., Warren, S. T., Schlessinger, D. et al. 1991. Fragile X genotype characterized by an unstable region of DNA. *Science*, 252:1179–1181.

Yudofsky, S. C., and Hales, R. E. 1992. *Textbook of neuropsychiatry*. American Psychiatric Press, Washington, D.C.

Zaidel, E. 1976. Auditory vocabulary of the right hemisphere following brain bisection or hemidecortication. *Cortex*, 12:191–211.

Zatorre, R. J., Evans, A. C., and Meyer, E. 1994. Neural mechanisms underlying melodic perception and memory for pitch. *Journal of Neuroscience*, 14:1908–1919.

Zecevic, D., Wu, J. Y., Cohen, L. B., London, J. A., Hopp, H. P., and Falk, C.

X. 1989. Hundreds of neurons in the *Aplysia* abdominal ganglion are active during the gill-withdrawal reflex. *Journal of Neuroscience*, 9:3681–3689.

Zecevic, N., and Rakic, P. 1976. Differentiation of Purkinje cells and their relationship to other components of developing cerebellar cortex in man. *Journal of Comparative Neurology*, 167:27–48.

Zeki, S. 1993. *A vision of the brain*. Blackwell, London.

Zeki, S., Watson, J. D., Lueck, C. J., Friston, K. J., Kennard, C., and Frackowiak, R. S. 1991. A direct demonstration of functional specialization in human visual cortex. *Journal of Neuroscience*, 11:641–649.

Zhang, Y., Proenca, R., Maffei, M., Barone, M., Leopold, L., and Friedman, J. M. 1994. Positional cloning of the mouse obese gene and its human homologue. *Nature*, 372:425–432.

Zihl, J., von Cramon, D., and Mai, N. 1983. Selective disturbance of movement vision after bilateral brain damage. *Brain*, 106:313–340.

Zohar, J., Insel, T. R., Zohar-Kadouch, R. C., Hill, J. L., and Murphy, D. L. 1988. Serotonergic responsivity in obsessive-compulsive disorder. Effects of chronic clomipramine treat-

ment. *Archives of General Psychiatry*, 45:167–172.

Zola-Morgan, S. M., and Squire, L. R. 1990. The primate hippocampal formation: Evidence for a time-limited role in memory storage. *Science*, 250:288–290.

Zola-Morgan, S., and Squire, L. R. 1993. Neuroanatomy of memory. *Annual Review of Neuroscience*, 16:547–563.

Zucker, I. 1976. Light, behavior, and biologic rhythms. *Hospital Practice*, 11:83–91.

Zucker, I. 1988. Seasonal affective disorders: Animal models *non fingo*. *Journal of Biological Rhythms*, 3:209–223.

Zucker, I., Boshes, M., and Dark, J. 1983. Suprachiasmatic nuclei influence circannual and circadian rhythms of ground squirrels. *American Journal of Physiology*, 244:R472–R480.

Zucker, L. M., and Zucker, T. F. 1961. "Fatty," a mutation in the rat. *Journal of Heredity*, 52:275–278.

Zuker, C. S. 1994. On the evolution of eyes: Would you like it simple or compound? *Science*, 265:742–743.

Zurek, P. M. 1981. Spontaneous narrowband acoustic signals emitted by human ears. *Journal of the Acoustical Society of America*, 69:514–523.

Illustration Credits

Chapter 1
1.1 "U.S. Is Losing War on Drugs, Analysts Say" © San Francisco Chronicle. Reprinted with permission. "Hormone Is Clue to Control of Weight"; "In Brain's Early Growth, Timetable May Be Crucial"; "In the Hope of Averting Learning Problems, an Early Test for Infant Ears"; "How Biology Affects Behavior and Vice Versa"; "Severe Trauma May Damage the Brain as Well as the Psyche"; "It's All in Our Heads"; all © 1995 by The New York Times Company. Reprinted with permission. *National Geographic* cover courtesy of the National Geographic Society. "The New Science of the Brain"; © 1995, Newsweek, Inc. All rights reserved. Reprinted with permission. Photograph by Douglas Levere.
1.13 Reproduced with gracious permission of Her Majesty Queen Elizabeth II, copyright reserved.
1.14 The Bettmann Archive.

Chapter 2
2.9 From *Gray's Anatomy*, 13th ed. Reprinted with permission of Churchill Livingstone, a division of Butler and Tanner, Ltd. (Dissection by M. C. E. Hutchinson, photograph by Kevin Fitzpatrick, Guy's Hospital Medical School, London.)
2.15 Brain sections courtesy of Michael Mega.
2.24 *Top*: CT scans © Dan McCoy/Rainbow. *Middle*: MRIs © Hank Morgan, Science Source/Photo Researchers, Inc.

Chapter 3
Box 3.1 Photographs © Art Wolfe.

Chapter 4
4.22 MRIs courtesy of James Golomb.
4.23 Courtesy of John Mazziotta.

Chapter 6
6.5 Biological Photo Service.
Box 6.1 (*a*) Biological Photo Service (*b*) © S. Lobban/Biological Photo Service (*c*) © G. I. Bernard/Earth Scenes (*d*) © Dan Guravich/Photo Researchers, Inc. (*e*) © S. W. Carter/Photo Researchers, Inc.
6.12 © 1986, M. H. English, Georgia Crime Lab/Photo Researchers, Inc.

Chapter 8
8.1 (*a*) © 1986 Scott Camazine/Photo Researchers, Inc. (*b*) © Art Wolfe (*c*) © Tom McHugh/Photo Researchers, Inc. (*d*) © Art Wolfe.

Chapter 11
11.1 David Madsen/© Tony Stone Images.
11.2 Courtesy of Peak Performance Technology.

Chapter 12
12.12 © David M. Phillips, Science Source/Photo Researchers, Inc.
Box 12.2 Female hyena courtesy of Stephen Glickman; © Lawrence Frank.
12.22 Courtesy of Roger Gorski.

Chapter 13
13.2 Arctic krill: Steinhart Aquarium, © Tom McHugh/Photo Researchers, Inc. Golden mantled ground squirrel: © Tim Davis/Photo Researchers, Inc.
13.5 (*a*) © Wm. Bacon III/Photo Researchers, Inc. (*b*) © 1989 G. J. James/Biological Photo Service
13.6 © Art Wolfe.
13.10 Courtesy of M. R. Rosenzweig.
13.19 Photograph by Mr. E. Slater, CSIRO Wildlife Division, Canberra.
13.28 Photograph by John Sholtis, the Rockefeller University.
13.29 (*a*) AP/Wide World Photos. Photographed by Monika Graff. (*b*) Kunsthistorisches Museum, Vienna.

Chapter 17
Box 17.2 Operant conditioning apparatus: © Richard Wood/The Picture Cube.
Pavlov and his staff: The Bettmann Archive.

Chapter 19
Box 19.3 Winter flounder: H. W. Pratt/Biological Photo Service.

Scientist photographs
p. 74 Charles Darwin, p. 74 Alfred Russel Wallace, p. 28 Karl Lashley: The Bettmann Archive; p. 551 Hans Selye, p. 540 James Olds, p. 370 Sir Charles Sherrington, p. 80 Theodore Bullock, p. 704 Norman Geschwind, p. 477 John Garcia: Neuroscience History Archives, Brain Research Institute, University of California, Los Angeles; p. 572 Elaine Walker: Annemarie Poyo, © Emory Univeristy Photography; p. 345 Torsten Wiesel, p. 694 Fernando Nottebohm: Robert Reichert; p. 624 Edward Tolman: Department of Psychology, University of California, Berkeley; p. 657 Eric Kandel: Rene Perez; p. 291 Georg von Békésy: courtesy of the Harvard University Archives.

Author Index

Subject Index

About the book

Editor: Peter Farley

Project Editors: Kathaleen Emerson, Kerry Falvey

Copy Editor: Stephanie Hiebert

Production Manager: Christopher Small

Book Production: Janice Holabird, Jefferson Johnson,
and Michele Ruschhaupt in QuarkXpress on the Macintosh

Art: J/B Woolsey Associates

Fine Art Consultant: Steven Diamond

Book and Cover Design: Jefferson Johnson and Christopher Small

Cover Manufacturer: Henry N. Sawyer Company

Book Manufacturer: Courier Companies, Inc.